NINTH EDITION

Understanding Psychology

Robert S. Feldman
University of Massachusetts, Amherst

Boston   Burr Ridge, IL   Dubuque, IA   Madison, WI   New York   San Francisco   St. Louis
Bangkok   Bogotá   Caracas   Kuala Lumpur   Lisbon   London   Madrid   Mexico City
Milan   Montreal   New Delhi   Santiago   Seoul   Singapore   Sydney   Taipei   Toronto

UNDERSTANDING PSYCHOLOGY
Published by McGraw-Hill, an imprint of The McGraw-Hill Companies, Inc., 1221 Avenue of the Americas, New York, NY 10020. Copyright © 2009, 2008, 2005, 2002, 1999, 1996, 1993, 1990, 1987 by the McGraw-Hill Companies, Inc. All rights reserved. No part of this publication may be reproduced or distributed in any form or by any means, or stored in a database or retrieval system, without the prior written consent of The McGraw-Hill Companies, Inc., including, but not limited to, in any network or other electronic storage or transmission, or broadcast for distance learning. Some ancillaries, including electronic and print components, may not be available to customers outside the United States.

This book is printed on acid-free paper.

3 4 5 6 7 8 9 0 DOW/DOW 0 9

ISBN: 978-0-07-337019-4
MHID: 0-07-337019-3

Vice President and
     Editor in Chief: Michael Ryan
Editorial Director: Beth Mejia
Publisher: Michael Sugarman
Director of Development: Dawn Groundwater
Development Editor: Barbara Conover
Supplements Editor: Emily Pecora
Editorial Coordinator: Jillian Allison
Executive Marketing Manager: James R.
     Headley
Production Editors: Melissa Williams and Scott
     Hitchcock, EPS Inc., NYC
Manuscript Editor: Laura Glenn
Cover Designer: Allister Fein
Interior Designer: Ellen Pettengell
Senior Production Supervisor: Rich DeVitto
Photo Researcher: Connie Mueller
Cover Photos: (c) Royalty-Free/Corbis

Psychology Advisory Board:
    Melissa Acevedo, Westchester Community
      College
    Jennifer Brooks, Collin County
      Community College
    Jeffrey Green, Virginia Commonwealth
      University
    Holly Haynes, Georgia Perimeter College
    Julie Bauer Morrison, Glendale
      Community College
    Phil Pegg, Western Kentucky University
    Tammy Rahhal, University of
      Massachusetts, Amherst
    Tanya Renner, University of Hawaii
    Carla Strassle, York College of
      Pennsylvania
    Jim Stringham, University of Georgia

This book was set in 9.5/12 Palatino by Electronic Publishing Services Inc. and printed on 45# Pub Influence Gloss by R.R. Donnelley and Sons.

Photo and text credits can be found following the References on page C-1, a continuation of the copyright page.

Library of Congress Cataloging-in-Publication Data
Feldman, Robert S. (Robert Stephen),
  Understanding psychology / Robert S. Feldman. -- 9th ed.
    p. cm.
  Includes bibliographical references and index.
  ISBN-13: 978-0-07-337019-4
  ISBN-10: 0-07-337019-3
  1. Psychology--Textbooks. I. Title.
  BF121.F34 2009
  150--dc22

                         2008039061

www.mhhe.com

To
Jonathan, Leigh, Alex, Joshua,
Julie, Sarah, and Kathy

About the Author

ROBERT S. FELDMAN is Professor of Psychology and Associate Dean of the College of Social and Behavioral Sciences at the University of Massachusetts at Amherst. Feldman, a winner of the College Distinguished Teacher award, has also taught courses at Mount Holyoke College, Wesleyan University, and Virginia Commonwealth University.

Feldman, who initiated the Minority Mentoring Program, teaches introductory psychology to classes ranging in size from 20 to nearly 500 students. He also has served as a Hewlett Teaching Fellow and Senior Online Teaching Fellow, and he frequently gives talks on the use of technology in teaching. He initiated distance learning courses in psychology at the University of Massachusetts.

Feldman also is actively involved in promoting the field of psychology. He is on the Board of Directors of the Federation of Behavioral, Psychological, and Cognitive Sciences, and also is on the Board of the Foundation for the Advancement of Behavioral and Brain Sciences.

A Fellow of the American Psychological Association and the Association for Psychological Science, Feldman received a B.A. with High Honors from Wesleyan University and an M.S. and Ph.D. from the University of Wisconsin–Madison. He is a winner of a Fulbright Senior Research Scholar and Lecturer award, and has written more than 100 books, book chapters, and scientific articles. His books include *Fundamentals of Nonverbal Behavior, Development of Nonverbal Behavior in Children, Social Psychology, Development Across the Life Span*, and *P.O.W.E.R. Learning: Strategies for Success in College and Life*, and they have been translated into a number of languages, including Spanish, French, Portuguese, Dutch, Chinese, and Japanese. His research interests include honesty and deception and the use of nonverbal behavior in impression management, and his research has been supported by grants from the National Institute of Mental Health and the National Institute on Disabilities and Rehabilitation Research.

Feldman's spare time is most often devoted to earnest, if not entirely expert, piano playing, and serious cooking. He also loves to travel. He has three children and lives with his wife, who is also a psychologist, overlooking the Holyoke mountain range in Amherst, Massachusetts.

Brief Contents

Contents

CHAPTER 3

Neuroscience and Behavior 58

CHAPTER 13

Personality 444

APPENDIX

Going by the Numbers: Statistics in Psychology A-2

Preface

Students first.

If I were to use only a few words to summarize my goal for this book, as well as my teaching philosophy, that's what I would say. I believe that an effective textbook must be oriented to students—informing them, engaging them, exciting them about the field, and expanding their intellectual capabilities. When students are engaged and challenged, they understand psychology at a deep and meaningful level. Only then are they able to learn and retain the material.

Luckily, psychology is a science that is inherently interesting to students. It is a discipline that speaks with many voices, offering a personal message to each student. To some, psychology provides a better understanding of others' behavior. Some view psychology as a pathway to self-understanding. Still others see the potential for a future career, and some are drawn to psychology by the opportunity for intellectual discovery that its study provides.

No matter what brings students into the introductory course and regardless of their initial motivation, *Understanding Psychology*, Ninth Edition, is designed to draw students into the field and stimulate their thinking. This revision integrates a variety of elements that foster students' understanding of psychology and its impact on our everyday lives. It also provides instructors with a fully integrated assessment package to objectively gauge their students' mastery of psychology's key principles and concepts.

A Framework for Learning and Assessment

Understanding Psychology, Ninth Edition, is the core of a learning-centered multimedia package that comprises a complete framework for learning and assessment. Conforming to recommendations of a 2002 APA task force report on undergraduate student competencies (Board of Educational Affairs, 2002), *every* component of the package is tied to specific psychological concepts and their application in everyday life. Though the book forms the core of this framework, its power to enrich and empirically demonstrate learning is expanded through a unique library of electronic activities with concept-based quizzes, all developed to accompany this text. Instructors can create a seamless, custom set of assignments from the available resources, or they can opt for a traditional, text-based approach, depending on their specific needs. A chart indicating how the features of the textbook directly address the APA student competencies is provided in Figure 1 on the following page. Equally important, every one of the thousands of test items in the Test Banks available to instructors is keyed to its corresponding APA competency in a document that is available on the text website.

PSYCHOLOGY AND EVERYDAY LIFE

Understanding Psychology, Ninth Edition, provides broad coverage of the field of psychology, including the theories, research, and applications that permeate the discipline. Along with the traditional areas of psychology (neuroscience, sensation and perception, states of consciousness, learning, memory, cognition, human

Book Feature	APA Learning Goals									
	Knowledge Base of Psychology	Research Methods in Psychology	Critical Thinking Skills in Psychology	Application of Psychology	Values in Psychology	Information and Technological Literacy	Communication Skills	Sociocultural and International Awareness	Personal Development	Career Planning and Development
Chapter Content	X	X	X	X	X	X	X	X	X	X
Prologue	X		X	X				X		
Looking Ahead	X	X	X		X					
Key Concepts	X		X	X				X		
Applying Psychology in the 21st Century	X	X		X				X	X	X
Exploring Diversity	X				X		X	X	X	
Neuroscience in Your Life	X	X	X	X						
Running Glossary	X			X		X				
Becoming an Informed Consumer of Psychology	X	X		X	X		X		X	X
Study Alerts	X	X		X						
Recap/Evaluate/Rethink	X		X	X						
Looking Back	X		X	X		X	X			
Epilogue	X		X	X				X		
Mastery Reviews	X	X	X	X		X		X		

FIGURE 1 This grid shows the relationship between the broad learning goals devised by the American Psychological Association and specific types of content in *Understanding Psychology*. In addition, each of the test items in the Test Bank for the book, consisting of nearly 4,000 individual, scorable items, is keyed to specific learning outcomes.

development, personality, abnormal behavior and treatment, and social psychology), the applied topics of gender, sexuality, and health psychology receive extensive attention.

Putting students first and teaching them the science of psychology by helping them make the connection between psychology and everyday life have been goals of this text from its first edition. The prologues that open each chapter, together with *Becoming an Informed Consumer of Psychology* sections, *Applying Psychology in the 21st Century* boxes, *Neuroscience in Your Life* features, and examples presented throughout the text, help students see the real benefits of psychological research. In addition, Psych 2.0 exercises and assessments in the Online Learning Center allow students to hone their ability to apply psychological concepts to everyday situations.

CHAPTER AND MODULAR FORMAT

The book contains 17 numbered chapters and an appendix covering the major areas of psychology. Each chapter is divided into 3 or more short modules, a format that has proven highly popular. Rather than facing a long and potentially daunting chapter, students can study material in smaller chunks, which psychological research long ago found to be the optimal way to learn.

Moreover, instructors can customize assignments for their students by asking them to read only those modules that fit their course outline and in the sequence that matches their syllabus. Alternatively, instructors who prefer to assign whole chapters can do so.

At the beginning of each module, one or more questions introduce the key concepts covered in the module. To reinforce key concepts, a series of online multimedia exercises and self-tests can be found on the Online Learning Center for the text (www.mhhe.com/feldmanup9). Additionally, the Online Learning Center provides review exercises and links to other Web sites that offer further information relevant to the key concepts and content for that section.

NEUROSCIENCE IN YOUR LIFE

This new feature, which appears in each chapter, emphasizes the importance of neuroscientific research within the various subfields of the discipline and in students' lives. Compelling brain scans, with both caption and textual explanation, illustrate significant neuroscientific findings that are increasingly influencing the field of psychology. In Chapter 2, Module 5, for example, a neurological study made clear the power of famous brand names. When a drink was labeled as Coke, several areas of the brain showed greater activation than when participants were unaware if the drink was Coke. The findings suggest that the Coca Cola brand image is so well imprinted in people's minds that information about the brand gets called up by the brain and influences their preferences—essentially overriding objective information about Coke's actual taste. In Chapter 8, Module 23, the feature compares the brain scans of people who actually practiced a piano finger exercise with the brain scans of those who only used mental rehearsal but did not touch the piano. The results were nearly identical and clearly show the value of mental imagery.

STUDY ALERT

Throughout the text, marginal notes point out especially important and difficult concepts and topics. These Study Alerts offer suggestions for learning the material effectively and for studying for tests. In Chapter 5, Module 14, for example, a Study Alert emphasizes the importance of differentiating the five stages of sleep; the feature in Module 15 makes clear the key issue about hypnosis – whether it represents a different state of consciousness or is similar to normal waking consciousness; and in Module 16 it highlights Figure 2 for its clear view of the different ways that drugs produce their effects at a neurological level.

PSYCH 2.0

An innovative combination of both print and online components, the Psych 2.0 Web site and accompanying guidebook combine the best of a *study guide* with the best of *online interactivity*. The Psych 2.0 Online Experience Guide, written by Tammy Rahhal of the University of Massachusetts–Amherst and Matthew Schulkind of Amherst College, provides a synopsis, pre-activity TIPS, and post-activity questions for each activity. The activities themselves offer experiential, observational, and visual learning opportunities in over ninety key concepts in introductory psychology. Psych 2.0 can be easily added to any syllabus or online or blended course. Available at one low price, Psych 2.0 is equally affordable with new or used texts. To view a demo of Psych 2.0, please visit http://www.mhhe.com/psych2demo.

VISUAL MASTERY REVIEWS

This edition provides reviews of five key concepts to help students master the difficult concepts in the course. These mastery sections follow the chapters in which the concepts are presented. Their format is more visual than verbal. They include self-assessment questions so that students can assess their understanding of these important topics, which were identified as challenging by classroom instructors, reviewers, survey respondents, and students:

- Mastering the difference between dependent and independent variables (p. 56)
- Mastering the action potential (p. 94)
- Mastering the difference between sensation and perception (p. 136)
- Mastering the distinction between reinforcement and punishment (p. 208)
- Mastering attitude change (p. 620)

Content Changes in the Ninth Edition

This edition incorporates a significant amount of new and updated information, reflecting the advances in the field and the suggestions of reviewers. Chapter 3 (Neuroscience and Behavior), Chapter 25, (Psychological Disorders), and Chapter 16 (Treatment of Psychological Disorders) have undergone especially heavy revisions. Well over 1,000 new citations have been added, and most of them refer to articles and books published after 2000. For instance, neuroscience and behavior, genetic foundations of language, traumatic memory, autism, and new treatment approaches to psychological disorders receive expanded coverage. Additionally, this edition incorporates a wide range of new topics. The following sample of new and revised topics provides a good indication of the book's currency.

Chapter 1—Introduction to Psychology
- Applications of psychology
- Women's early contributions to psychology

Chapter 2—Psychological Research
- Operational definitions
- Survey accuracy

Chapter 3—Neuroscience and Behavior
- Brain scan indicates brand preferences
- Neuroeconomics
- Neuroscience and brain injury treatment
- Brain specificity and music/language
- Hemispherectomy
- Hemimegalencephaly
- Locked-in syndrome
- Deep-brain stimulation
- Brain-computer interface
- Revised figures on limbic system, cerebral cortex, action potential, synapse, endocrine glands
- Added executive function to discussion of association areas
- Mirror neurons
- Sympathetic nervous system and voodoo death
- Neurogenesis

Chapter 4—Sensation and Perception
- Sensory interaction between visual, touch, and auditory stimuli
- Subliminal perception update
- Priming
- Face blindness
- Prosopagnosia
- Retinitis pigmentosa
- Artificial retina implantation
- Asymmetry of sound processing
- Subliminal perception

Chapter 5—States of Consciousness
- Meditation and brain activation
- College drinking
- Cultural differences in alcohol use
- Changes in drug and alcohol use
- New figure on meditation MRI scans
- Social norms and alcohol use
- Drinking problems among college students
- Sleep apnea

Chapter 6—Learning
- Motivating workers through operant conditioning
- Mirror neurons
- Updated discussion of Garcia and classical conditioning
- MRI scan during observation of different gestures

Chapter 7—Memory
- Memory and brain scans of taxi drivers
- Traumatic memory
- Propranolol
- Alzheimer's disease
- Amnesia
- Hippocampus and spatial memories
- New figure of chessboard/expertise

Chapter 8—Cognition and Language
- Creativity in the workplace
- Emotions and creativity
- Availability heuristic
- Genetic foundations of tonal languages
- Inventiveness and creativity

Chapter 9—Intelligence
- Brain activation during verbal and spatial problem-solving
- Cortical thickness and intelligence
- Incidence of mental retardation
- Gifted children
- Self-discipline and intelligence

Chapter 10—Motivation and Emotion
- Exercising to excess
- Ghrelin and hunger
- Exercise bulimia

- Food stimuli processing differences between anorexics and normals

Chapter 11—Sexuality and Gender
- Differential college success between men and women
- Differences in male/female processing of information doing spatial task
- Transsexualism
- Female ascendance in college

Chapter 12—Development
- Event-related potentials (ERPs) and emotions in infants
- Human Genome Project
- Alzheimer's disease
- Beta amyloid precursor protein
- Peer rejection
- Brain development and impulse control in adolescents
- Retirement
- Widowhood

Chapter 13—Personality
- Big 5 personality traits and brain processing
- National character
- Neo-Freudians
- Distinction between self-esteem and self-efficacy

Chapter 14—Health and Stress
- Social support and brain activation
- Link between stress and coronary heart disease
- Spirituality and coping
- Religious service attendance and mortality
- Positively and negatively framed messages

Chapter 15—Psychological Disorders
- Suicide bombers
- Depression and brain activation
- Dissociative identity disorder (DID)
- Posttraumatic stress disorder
- Autism
- Social phobias
- Biological causes of mood disorders
- Gender differences in depression

Chapter 16—Treatment of Psychological Disorders
- Work and family treatments
- Borderline personality disorder and brain activation
- Exposure therapy
- Evidence-based psychotherapy practice
- Behavior therapy efficacy
- Cognitive appraisal

- Atypical antipsychotics
- Rizperidone, olanzapine, paliperidone
- Antidepressant treatment for anorexia, anxiety disorders
- Beck's cognitive therapy
- Commonalities among therapies
- Interpersonal therapy
- Self-help therapy
- Bereavement groups
- Alcoholics Anonymous
- Neurological changes as a result of behavior therapy

Chapter 17—Social Psychology
- Interventions to reduce effects of negative stereotyping
- Importance of situational factors
- Ethnocentrism
- Implicit Associations Test (IAT)
- Stanford Prison Study
- Groups
- Sternberg love triangle
- Entrapment
- Social neuroscience
- Amygdala activation and racial stimuli
- Reducing damage to victims of stereotypes

STUDENTS FIRST: THE BOTTOM LINE

Based on extensive student feedback, systematic research involving a wide range of instructors, and endorsements received from reviewers at a variety of schools, I am confident that this edition reflects what instructors want and need: a book that motivates students to understand and apply psychology to their own lives. *Understanding Psychology*, Ninth Edition, is designed to expose readers to the content—and promise—of psychology, and to do so in a way that will nurture students' excitement about psychology and keep their enthusiasm alive for a lifetime.

State-of-the-Art Support Materials for Students and Instructors

Resources available for use with this text support both new and veteran instructors, whether they favor traditional text-based instruction or a blend of traditional and electronic media. The Ninth edition text and support materials provide complementary experiences for instructors and students. All of these components are built around the core concepts articulated in the text to promote a deeper understanding of psychology. This type of integration gives instructors the flexibility to use any of the text-specific electronic or print materials knowing they are completely compatible with one another.

FOR STUDENTS

Online Learning Center. The Student Center of the companion Web site for *Understanding Psychology*, Ninth Edition (www.mhhe.com/feldmanup9e), includes an array of module-by-module study aids, such as detailed outlines, flashcards, and self-quizzes (created by Dave Alfano of the Community College of Rhode Island). Additionally, ESL Pointers provide guidance to second-language learners. All material on the Student Center is accessible without a password.

Study Guide by Deb Briihl of Valdosta State University, with ESL component by Lisa Valentino of Seminole Community College. The printed Study Guide contains a comprehensive review of the text material. Features include text overviews plus multiple-choice, fill-in-the-blank, matching, and short-answer questions for each module. An answer key provides answers to all of the exercises in a chapter, along with feedback for all multiple-choice items. Also in the study guide is material created to help speakers of other languages understand and retain course content.

FOR INSTRUCTORS

McGraw-Hill *Connect Psychology*. McGraw-Hill *Connect Psychology* is a web-based assignment and assessment platform that gives students the means to better connect with their coursework, with their instructors, and with the important concepts that they will need to know for success now and in the future.

With *Connect Psychology* instructors can deliver assignments, quizzes and tests online. Nearly all the questions from the text are presented in an auto-gradable format and tied to the text's learning objectives. Instructors can edit existing questions and author entirely new problems. Track individual student performance–by question, assignment or in relation to the class overall–with detailed grade reports. Integrate grade reports easily with Learning Management Systems (LMS) such as WebCT and Blackboard. And much more.

By choosing *Connect Psychology* instructors are providing their students with a powerful tool for improving academic performance and truly mastering course material. *Connect Psychology* allows students to practice important skills at their own pace and on their own schedule. Importantly, students' assessment results and instructors' feedback are all saved online–so students can continually review their progress and plot their course to success.

Some instructors may also choose *Connect Psychology Plus* for their students. Like *Connect Psychology*, *Connect Psychology Plus* provides students with online assignments and assessments, plus 24/7 online access to an eBook–an online edition of the text–to aid them in successfully completing their work, wherever and whenever they choose.

Online Learning Center for Instructors. The password-protected instructor side of the Online Learning Center (www.mhhe.com/feldmanup9e) contains the Instructor's Manual, Test Bank files, PowerPoint slides, CPS Questions, Image Gallery, and other valuable material to help you design and enhance your course. See more information about specific assets below. Ask your local McGraw-Hill representative for password information.

Instructor's Manual by Susan Krauss Whitbourne, University of Massachusetts at Amherst. This comprehensive guide provides all the tools and resources instructors need to present and enhance their introductory psychology course. The Instructor's Manual contains detailed lecture launchers, learning objectives, interesting lecture and media presentation ideas, student assignments and handouts. The many tips and activities in this manual can be used with any class, regardless of size or teaching approach.

Test Banks. Test Bank I by Jamie McMinn of Westminster College; Test Bank II by Matthew Isaak of the University of Louisiana at Lafayette. Both test banks incorporate the new content in *Understanding Psychology*, Ninth Edition. Each test bank contains more than 2,000 multiple-choice items, classified by cognitive type and level of difficulty, and keyed to the appropriate key concept and page in the textbook. Fill-in-the-blank, matching, and short-answer questions are provided for all modules. Moreover, each of the thousands of test items is keyed to the APA core psychology competencies. All questions are compatible with EZ Test, McGraw-Hill's Computerized Test Bank program.

McGraw-Hill's EZ Test is a flexible and easy-to-use electronic testing program that allows instructors to create tests from book-specific items. It accommodates a wide range of question types, and allows instructors to edit existing questions, or create new ones. Multiple versions of the test can be created, and any test can be exported for use with course management systems such as WebCT or Blackboard. EZ Test Online is a new service that gives you a place to easily administer your EZ Test–created exams and quizzes online. The program is available for Windows and Macintosh environments.

Classroom Performance System Content. by Robert Moore of Iowa Valley Community College District. The Classroom Performance System (CPS) from eInstruction allows instructors to gauge immediately what students are learning during lectures. With CPS and student "clickers," available at a discount to adopters of *Understanding Psychology*, instructors can draw on the quiz and poll questions provided on the Instructor's Online Learning Center (or craft their own), and get instant feedback, even from students who are reluctant to speak out in class. In addition, CPS facilitates taking attendance, giving and grading pop quizzes, and giving formal, printed class tests with multiple versions of the test using CPS for immediate grading.

Image Gallery. More than 100 figures from the text can be downloaded from the Image Gallery on the Instructor's Online Learning Center.

PrepCenter. PrepCenter enables instructors to build classroom presentations whenever, wherever, and however they want. In one convenient online location, PrepCenter offers figures from the textbook, PowerPoint presentations for each key concept, dozens of video clips, and animations explaining biological and other difficult concepts. Each is ready to use or to drop into a PowerPoint slideshow or your course Web page. Individual resources can be researched by chapter, by concept, or by type of media. Access PrepCenter through the Instructor's Online Learning Center (www.mhhe. com/feldmanup9).

Optional Modules on Diversity and I/O Psychology. For instructors who like to incorporate lectures on diversity or industrial/organizational issues in their introductory psychology course, optional full-color modules on these topics can be packaged with students' copies of *Understanding Psychology*, Ninth Edition. The Diversity module, written by Mark H. Chae of William Paterson University, discusses the roots of diversity and addresses related issues, such as conflict and cooperation. The module on Industrial-Organizational Psychology, written by Carnot Nelson and Russell Johnson of the University of South Florida, broadly introduces this growing area of interest. Instructors may request these modules through their McGraw-Hill sales representative.

Additional Resources for Introductory Psychology

Please see your McGraw-Hill sales representative for information on policy, price, and availability of the following supplements.

Annual Editions: Psychology 08/09 (edited by Karen Duffy, State University College—Geneseo). This annually updated reader provides convenient, inexpensive access to current articles selected from the best of the public press. Organizational features include an annotated listing of selected World Wide Web sites; an annotated table of contents; a topic guide; a general introduction; brief overviews for each section; a topical index; and an instructor's resource guide with testing materials.

Classic Edition Sources: Psychology, 4e (edited by Terry Pettijohn of Ohio State University—Marion). This reader provides more than 40 selections of enduring intellectual value—classic articles, book excerpts, and research studies—that have shaped the study of psychology and our contemporary understanding of it.

Taking Sides: Clashing Views on Controversial Psychological Issues, 15e (edited by Brent Slife of Brigham Young University). This reader presents current controversial issues in a debate-style format designed to stimulate student interest and develop critical thinking skills. Each issue is thoughtfully framed with an issue summary, an issue introduction, and a postscript. An instructor's manual with testing material is available for each volume.

Acknowledgments

One of the central features of *Understanding Psychology* is the involvement of both professionals and students in the review process. The ninth edition of *Understanding Psychology* has relied heavily—and benefited substantially—from the advice of instructors and students from a wide range of backgrounds.

I am extraordinarily grateful to the following reviewers, who provided their time and expertise to help ensure that *Understanding Psychology*, Ninth Edition, reflects the best that psychology has to offer.

Melissa Acevedo
Valencia Community College

Jennifer Brooks
Collin County Community College

Jeffrey Green
Virginia Commonwealth University

Julie Bauer Morrison
Glendale Community College

Phil Pegg
Western Kentucky University

Tanya Renner
University of Hawaii

Carla Strassle
York College of Pennsylvania

Jim Stringham
University of Georgia

Bill Adler
Collin County Community College

Jacob Benfield
Colorado State University

Jerusha Detweiler-Bedell
Lewis and Clark College

Andrea Gere
Wabash Valley College

Elissa Koplik
Bloomfield College

Elizabeth Meadows
Central Michigan University

Brandon Randolph-Seng
Texas Tech University

Eric Stephens
University of the Cumberlands

Thomas Williams
Western Kentucky University

Also central to this revision of *Understanding Psychology* were the recommendations of the Psych 2.0 Advisory Board, listed on the copyright page. The Advisory Board members have provided valuable input during the development of Psych 2.0 that broadened the scope and effectiveness of these student activities:

I would also like to thank the many students who participated in focus groups to share ideas and suggestions for this revision:

Rina Balestri, Nassau Community College

Kevin Baver, County College of Morris

Casey Bell, County College of Morris

Evan Clementi, Nassau Community College

Lauren Dame, County College of Morris

Rhea Gabriela O. Duran, Nassau Community College

Rolando Edwards, Nassau Community College

Martino Fiducaro, Nassau Community College

Lisa Fleming, County College of Morris

Roxanne Gilbert, Nassau Community College

Isabelle F. Giles, Nassau Community College

Max Hahlbeck, University of Massachusetts Amherst

Angad Khurana, County College of Morris

Fay Maturan, County College of Morris

Joe W. Marve II, Nassau Community College

Susanne Neumann, County College of Morris

Chelsea Olivares, Nassau Community College

Forouzan Pooladi, Nassau Community College

Rahsan Samioglu, Nassau Community College

Stacey Samuelson, County College of Morris

Katherine Tiedemann, County College of Morris

Meghan Weber, County College of Morris

In addition, Jane W. Couperus of Hampshire College provided exceptional support in helping identify appropriate neuroscientific research to include in the Neuroscience in Your Life features. I thank her for her superb work.

Many teachers along my educational path have shaped my thinking. I was introduced to psychology at Wesleyan University, where several committed and inspiring teachers—and in particular Karl Scheibe—conveyed their sense of excitement about the field and made its relevance clear to me. Karl epitomizes the teacher-scholar combination to which I aspire, and I continue to marvel at my good fortune in having such a role model.

By the time I left Wesleyan I could envision no other career but that of psychologist. Although the nature of the University of Wisconsin, where I did my graduate work, could not have been more different from the much smaller Wesleyan, the excitement and inspiration were similar. Once again, a cadre of excellent teachers—led, especially, by the late Vernon Allen—molded my thinking and taught me to appreciate the beauty and science of the discipline of psychology.

My colleagues and students at the University of Massachusetts at Amherst provide ongoing intellectual stimulation, and I thank them for making the university a fine place to work. Several people also provided extraordinary research and editorial help. In particular, I am grateful to my superb students, past and present, including Jim Tyler, Chris Poirier, and Matt Zimbler. Finally, I am extremely grateful to John Graiff and Tolley Jones, whose hard work and dedication helped immeasurably with just about everything involving this book.

I also offer great thanks to the McGraw-Hill editorial team that participated in this edition of the book. Steve Debow's hands-on interest, as well as his friendship, helped support the book through the last decade. Editorial Director Beth Mejia created a creative, energetic, and supportive environment, and I am in awe of her enthusiasm, commitment, and never-ending good ideas. I also thank Barbara Conover, Developmental Editor on this edition. Barbara did a fine job of managing a myriad of details (as well as me). I'm also pleased that editor Suzanna Ellison worked on this edition of *Understanding Psychology*. She brought motivation, intelligence, and good ideas to the project. Finally, every reader of this book owes a debt to Rhona Robbin, developmental editor on the earliest editions of *Understanding Psychology*. Her relentless pursuit of excellence helped form the core of this book, and she taught me a great deal about the craft and art of writing. I would also like to thank marketing manager James Headley for his enthusiasm and commitment to this project. I am proud to be a part of this world-class team.

I am also grateful to the team that spent untold hours developing the teaching and learning tools that complement the book, including Art Kohn, Portland State University; Stephanie George, Media Producer; and my master-of-all-pedagogies colleague Susan Whitbourne, University of Massachusetts at Amherst. I am convinced their efforts have created an instructional framework that is boundary-breaking.

Finally, I remain completely indebted to my family. My parents, Leah Brochstein and the late Saul D. Feldman, provided a lifetime foundation of love and support, and I continue to see their influence in every corner of my life. I am grateful, too, to Harry Brochstein, who has enriched my life and thinking in many ways.

My extended family also plays a central role in my life. They include, more or less in order of age, my nieces and nephews, my terrific brother, and my brothers- and sisters-in-law, and the late Ethel Radler. Finally, my mother-in-law, the late Mary Evans Vorwerk, had an important influence on this book, and I remain ever grateful to her.

Ultimately, my children, Jonathan, Joshua, and Sarah; my daughters-in-law Leigh and Julie; my grandson Alex; and my wife, Katherine, remain the focal point of my life. I thank them, with immense love.

Robert S. Feldman
Amherst, Massachusetts

Using Understanding Psychology

If you're reading this page, you're probably taking an introductory psychology course. Maybe you're studying psychology because you've always been interested in what makes people tick. Or perhaps you've had a friend or family member who has sought assistance for a psychological disorder. Or maybe you have no idea what psychology is all about, but you know that taking introductory psychology would fulfill a degree requirement.

Whatever your motivation for taking the course and reading this book, here's my commitment to you: By the time you finish this text, you will have a better understanding of why people—including you—behave the way they do. You will know how, and why, psychologists conduct research and will have an understanding of the theories that guide their research. You will become acquainted with the breadth of the field and will obtain practical, useful information, as well as a wealth of knowledge that hopefully will excite your curiosity and increase your understanding of people's behavior.

To meet this commitment, *Understanding Psychology*, Ninth Edition, has been written with you, the reader, in mind. At every step in the development of the book, students and instructors have been consulted in an effort to identify the combination of learning tools that would maximize readers' ability to learn and retain the subject matter of psychology. The result is a book that contains features that will not only help you to understand psychology, but also make it a discipline that is part of your life.

Now it's your turn. You will need to take several steps to maximize the effectiveness of the learning tools in the book. These steps include familiarizing yourself with the scope and structure of the book, using the built-in learning aids, and employing a systematic study strategy.

Familiarize Yourself with the Scope and Organization of *Understanding Psychology*

Begin by reading the list of modules and skimming the detailed table of contents at the front of the book. From this exercise, you will get a sense of the topics covered and the logic behind the sequence of modules. Then take some time to flip through the book. Choose a section that looks particularly interesting to you, skim it, and see for yourself how the modules are laid out.

Each module provides logical starting and stopping points for reading and studying. You can plan your studying around the modules that cover a particular topic. For instance, if your instructor assigns a group of modules to read over the course of a week, you might plan to read and study one module each day, using later days in the week to review the material.

A Guide for Students

Use the Learning Aids
Built into the Book

Once you have acquired a broad overview of *Understanding Psychology*, you are ready to begin reading and learning about psychology. Each chapter contains learning aids that will help you master the material.

KEY CONCEPTS Each module begins with the key concepts discussed in that section. The key concepts, phrased as questions, provide a framework for understanding and organizing the material that follows. They will also help you to understand what the important content is.

Key Concepts for Chapter 8

What is thinking? ● What processes underlie reasoning and decision making?

MODULE 23

Thinking and Reasoning
Mental Images: Examining the Mind's Eye
Concepts: Categorizing the World
Reasoning: Making Up Your Mind
Computers and Problem Solving: Searching for Artificial Intelligence

How do people approach and solve problems? ● What are the major obstacles to problem solving? ● What is creativity?

MODULE 24

Problem Solving
Preparation: Understanding and Diagnosing Problems
Production: Generating Solutions
Judgment: Evaluating the Solutions
Impediments to Solutions: Why Is Problem Solving Such a Problem?
Creativity and Problem Solving
Applying Psychology in the 21ˢᵗ Century: Creativity in the Workplace
Becoming an Informed Consumer of Psychology: Thinking Critically and Creatively

How do people use language? ● How does language develop?

MODULE 25

Language
Grammar: Language's Language
Language Development: Developing a Way with Words
The Influence of Language on Thinking: Do Eskimos Have More Words for Snow Than Texans Do?
Do Animals Use Language?
Exploring Diversity: Teaching with Linguistic Variety: Bilingual Education

Prologue *Microbe-Busting Bandages*

What do jock itch, poison gas, and flesh-eating bacteria have in common? Gregory Schultz, 56, thinks he has the answer. The cancer researcher turned inventor has patented a technique for chemically bonding bacteria-fighting polymers to such fabrics as gauze bandages, cotton T shirts, and men's underpants. It's a technology with an unusually wide variety of uses, from underwear that doesn't stink to hospital dressings that thwart infections.

The bandages, coated with positively charged antimicrobial molecules, dramatically reduce the risk of infection, Schultz says, and as a bonus they can prevent outbreaks of the drug-resistant staph infections that have been racing through U.S. hospitals. "It basically punches holes in the bacteria," he says, "and they pop like balloons." (Morrissey, 2006)

Looking Ahead

Schultz's invention was a long time in coming. Two decades earlier, a student working in a burn unit mentioned that the way in which cells responded to cancer might be harnessed to help burn victims avoid infection. It took 20 years of puzzling over the problem before Schultz invented his antibacterial bandages.

It is clear that Schultz has the elusive quality that marks successful inventors: creativity. Where did his creativity come from? More generally, how do people use information to devise innovative solutions to problems? And how do people think about, understand, and, through language, describe the world?

Answers to these questions come from **cognitive psychology**, the branch of psychology that focuses on the study of higher mental processes, including thinking, language, memory, problem solving, knowing, reasoning, judging, and decision making. Clearly, the realm of cognitive psychology is broad.

Cognitive psychology centers on three major topics: thinking and reasoning, problem solving and creativity, and language. The first topic we consider in this chapter is thinking and reasoning. Then we examine different strategies for approaching problems, means of generating solutions, and ways of making judgments about the usefulness and accuracy of solutions. Finally, we discuss how language is developed and acquired, its basic characteristics, and the relationship between language and thought.

Cognitive psychology: The branch of psychology that focuses on the study of higher mental processes, including thinking, language, memory, problem solving, knowing, reasoning, judging, and decision making.

PROLOGUE Each chapter begins with a Prologue and ends with an Epilogue. The Prologue sets the stage for the chapter, providing a brief account of a real-life event that is relevant to the content of the modules, and demonstrating why the material in the chapter is important.

LOOKING AHEAD The Looking Ahead sections, which follow the prologues, identify the key themes and issues addressed in the chapter.

NEUROSCIENCE IN YOUR LIFE

This new feature, which appears in each chapter, emphasizes the importance of neuroscientific research within the various subfields of the discipline and in students' lives. Compelling brain scans, with both caption and textual explanation, illustrate significant neuroscientific findings that are increasingly influencing the field of psychology.

FIGURE 7 The brains of those with depression (left) show significantly less activation in response to photos of sad, angry, and fearful faces than those of people without the disorder (right). (Source: Ian Gotlib, Stanford Mood and Anxiety Disorders Laboratory, 2005.)

APPLYING PSYCHOLOGY IN THE 21ST CENTURY

A box in each chapter describing psychological research that is being applied to everyday problems. Read these boxes to understand how psychology promises to improve the human condition, in ways ranging from the development of ways to reduce violence to explaining the behavior of suicide bombers.

APPLYING PSYCHOLOGY IN THE 21ST CENTURY

The Sting and Stigma of Peer Rejection

Peer rejection can produce long-term psychological consequences.

Mari, our 7-year-old, burst into tears while getting ready for school. Turns out she was upset because two girls had been making fun of her clothes and she was worried they'd find fault with that day's outfit. Mari had complained about the teasing before, and we'd assured her that it didn't matter what those girls said or thought. They were just mean and jealous and should be ignored. But clearly, to Mari, their words couldn't be dismissed. They cut her like a knife, and we hadn't really taken it seriously because there was no blood. Her tears moved us to action. (Millner, 2007, p. 47)

Peer rejection in schools and on playgrounds is long thought to be just another normal part of growing up. But in more recent years, tragic instances of violence in school have made national headlines and inspired a rethinking of the importance of positive peer interactions. For example, Seung-Hui Cho, the shooter responsible for the Virginia Tech massacre, was reported to have been withdrawn and isolated and was the victim of peer rejection (Adams & Russakoff, 1999; Banerjee, 2007).

However, the everyday consequences of peer rejection in school aren't nearly as dramatic as what happened at Virginia Tech. Most of the time, victims bear the harm quietly and alone. Ultimately, though, being rejected by peers may lead students to become withdrawn and to disengage from school, eventually suffering declines in academic achievement.

A recent longitudinal study of schoolchildren from 5 to 11 years old revealed how peer rejection can lead to academic declines. The researchers found that children who are less well liked by their classmates started becoming victims of mistreatment, including rejection and abuse. Children who received rejection became less likely to participate in classroom activities (Buhs, Ladd, & Herald, 2006).

The study also found that peer rejection preceded and contributed to withdrawal, leading to further exclusion and abuse. Moreover, peer rejection seemed to perpetuate itself. For instance, children who were disliked in kindergarten experienced sustained peer rejection and mistreatment into later years. For whatever reason, some children were liked less than others early on and were targeted for rejection. This rejection, in turn, acted as a signal to other peers that these children should be disliked. Essentially, the rejection followed the child like a black cloud, signaling to new peers in subsequent years that this was an unlikable individual who should be avoided or mistreated. This stigmatizing effect of rejection, together with the disengagement from classroom activities that it precipitates, fed into a cycle of withdrawal and exclusion.

The researchers concluded that although peer rejection may not be as dramatic as verbal or physical abuse, it is nevertheless psychologically painful. Ultimately, it may have an even stronger effect than actual physical abuse on children's participation in school and their subsequent academic achievement (Buhs, Ladd, & Herald, 2006).

- Why do you think some children are more prone to be rejected by their peers than others are?
- What can a peer-rejected child (or his or her parents) do to break the cycle of rejection?

STUDY ALERT Throughout the text, marginal notes point out especially important and difficult concepts and topics. These new Study Alerts offer suggestions for learning the material effectively and for studying for tests.

 StudyALERT

It is important to understand the basic neuroscience of emotional experience.

EXPLORING DIVERSITY

Every chapter includes at least one section devoted to an aspect of racial, ethnic, gender, or cultural diversity. These features focus on the contributions of psychology to a fostering better understanding of multicultural issues that are so central to our global society.

Exploring DIVERSITY

Teaching with Linguistic Variety:
Bilingual Education

In New York City, 1 in 6 of the city's 1.1 million students is enrolled in some form of bilingual or English as a Second Language instruction. And New York City is far from the only school district with a significant population of nonnative English speakers. From the biggest cities to the most rural areas, the face—and voice—of education in the United States is changing. More and more schoolchildren today have last names like Kim, Valdez, and Karachnicoff. In seven states, including Texas and Colorado, more than one-quarter of the students are not native English speakers. For some 47 million Americans, English is their second language (Holloway, 2000; see Figure 1).

How to appropriately and effectively teach the increasing number of children who do not speak English is not always clear. Many educators maintain that *bilingual education* is best. With a bilingual approach, students learn some subjects in their native language while simultaneously learning English. Proponents of bilingualism believe that students must develop a sound footing in basic subject areas and that, initially at least, teaching those subjects in their native language is the only way to provide them with that foundation. During the same period, they learn English, with the eventual goal of shifting all instruction into English.

In contrast, other educators insist that all instruction ought to be in English from the moment students, including those who speak no English at all, enroll in school. In *immersion programs*, students are immediately plunged into English instruction in all subjects. The reasoning—endorsed by voters in California in a referendum designed to end bilingual education—is that teaching students in a language other than English simply hinders nonnative English speakers' integration into society and ultimately does them a disservice. Proponents of English immersion programs point as evidence to improvements in standardized test scores that followed the end of bilingual education programs (Wildavsky, 2000).

Are you one of the 50 million people in the United States who suffer from chronic pain? Psychologists and medical specialists have devised several strategies to fight pain. Among the most important approaches are the following:

BECOMING AN INFORMED CONSUMER

of Psychology

Managing Pain

- *Medication.* Painkilling drugs are the most popular treatment in fighting pain. Drugs range from those which directly treat the source of the pain—such as reducing swelling in painful joints—to those that work on the symptoms. Medication can be in the form of pills, patches, injections, or liquids. In a recent innovation, drugs are pumped directly into the spinal cord (Kalb, 2003; Pesmen, 2006).

- *Nerve and brain stimulation.* Pain can sometimes be relieved when a low-voltage electric current is passed through the specific part of the body that is in pain. In even more severe cases, electrodes can be implanted surgically directly into the brain, or a handheld battery pack can stimulate nerve cells to provide direct relief (Ross, 2000; Campbell & Ditto, 2002; Tugay et al., 2007)

- *Light therapy.* One of the newest forms of pain reduction involves exposure to specific wavelengths of red or infrared light. Certain kinds of light increase the production of enzymes that may promote healing (Underwood, 2003; Evcik et al., 2007).

- *Hypnosis.* For people who can be hypnotized, hypnosis can greatly relieve pain (Patterson, 2004; Neron & Stephenson, 2007).

- *Biofeedback and relaxation techniques.* Using *biofeedback*, people learn to control "involuntary" functions such as heartbeat and respiration. If the pain involves muscles, as in tension headaches or back pain, sufferers can be trained to relax their bodies systematically (Vitiello, Bonello, & Pollard, 2007).

- *Surgery.* In one of the most extreme methods, nerve fibers that carry pain messages to the brain can be cut surgically. Still, because of the danger that other bodily functions will be affected, surgery is a treatment of last resort, used most frequently with dying patients (Cullinane, Chu, & Mamelak, 2002).

- *Cognitive restructuring.* Cognitive treatments are effective for people who continually say to themselves, "This pain will never stop," "The pain is ruining my life," or "I can't take it anymore" and are thereby likely to make their pain even worse. By substituting more positive ways of thinking, people can increase their sense of control—and actually reduce the pain they experience (Spanos, Barber, & Lang, 2005; Bogart et al., 2007).

BECOMING AN INFORMED CONSUMER OF PSYCHOLOGY

One of the major goals of *Understanding Psychology* is to make readers more informed, critical consumers of information relating to psychological issues. These discussions give you the tools to evaluate information concerning human behavior that you may hear or read about in the media or on the Web.

RUNNING GLOSSARY When a key term or concept appears in the text, it appears either in **boldface** or in *italics*. Boldfaced words are of primary importance; italicized words are of secondary importance. Terms and concepts in bold are defined in the text where they are introduced and in the text margins, as well as in the glossary at the back of the book. In addition, boldfaced terms are included in the list of Key Terms at the end of every module, along with page references. You might want to highlight these terms.

RECAP/EVALUATE/RETHINK SEGMENTS

Every module ends with a *Recap/Evaluate/Rethink* segment. *Recap* sections review the key concepts found at the beginning of each module. *Evaluate* sections provide a series of questions on the module content that ask for concrete information, in a matching, multiple choice, fill-in, or true-false format. The questions in the *Rethink* sections are designed to encourage you to think critically about a topic or issue, and they often have more than one correct answer.

Answer *Evaluate* and *Rethink* questions! Your responses will indicate both your degree of mastery of the material and the depth of your knowledge. If you have no trouble with the questions, you can be confident that you are studying effectively. Use questions with which you have difficulty as a basis for further study.

LOOKING BACK, EPILOGUE, AND VISUAL MASTERY REVIEWS

Each chapter ends with a Looking Back section that extends the chapter content to the Web. The Epilogue refers back to the Prologue at the start of the set of modules, placing it in the context of the chapter's subject matter and asking questions designed to encourage you to think critically about what you've read.

In addition, several chapters conclude with a visual mastery review that revisits a key point from the chapter in a verbal and pictorial way. Studying these reviews and answering the questions that go with them will make recall and application of the material easier.

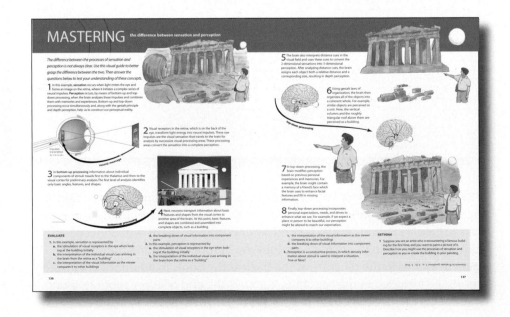

You'll find the same features in every chapter, providing familiar landmarks to help you chart your way through new material. This structure will help you organize, learn, and remember the content.

An additional note about this text: The reference citations follow the style endorsed by the American Psychological Association (APA). According to APA style, citations include a name and date, typically set off in parentheses at the end of a sentence and specifying the author of the work being cited and the year of publication, as in this example: (Angier & Chang, 2005). Each of these names and dates refers to a book or article included in the References section at the end of this book.

Making the Grade: A Practical Guide

No matter why you are taking introductory psychology, it's a safe bet you're interested in maximizing your understanding of the material and getting a good grade. And you want to accomplish these goals as quickly and efficiently as possible.

Good news: you're taking the right course, and you're learning the right material. Several subfields of psychology have identified a variety of guidelines and techniques that will help you learn and remember material not only related to psychology, but also relevant to every other discipline that you will study.

We'll consider a variety of guidelines relating to doing well in your psychology class—and every other class you'll take in your college career. Here's my guarantee to you: If you learn and follow the guidelines in each of these areas, you'll become a better student and get better grades. Always remember that *good students are made, not born,* and these suggestions will help you become an all-around better student.

Adopt a General Study Strategy

Let's begin with a brief consideration of a general study strategy, applicable to all of your courses, including introductory psychology. Psychologists have devised several excellent (and proven) techniques for improving study skills, two of which are described here: "P.O.W.E.R.," or *Prepare, Organize, Work, Evaluate,* and *Rethink;* and "SQ3R," or *Survey, Question, Read, Recite,* and *Review.* By employing one of these two procedures, you can increase your ability to learn and retain information and to think critically.

P.O.W.E.R. The *P.O.W.E.R.* learning strategy systematizes the acquisition of new material by providing a learning framework. It stresses the importance of learning objectives and appropriate preparation before you begin to study, as well as the significance of self-evaluation and the incorporation of critical thinking into the learning process. Specifically, use of the P.O.W.E.R. learning system entails the following steps:

- **Prepare.** Before starting any journey, we need to know where we are headed. Academic journeys are no different; we need to know what our goals are. The *Prepare* stage consists of thinking about what we hope to gain from reading a specific section of the text by identifying specific goals that we seek to accomplish. In *Understanding Psychology*, Ninth Edition, these goals are presented as broad questions at the start of each chapter and again at the beginning of each module.
- **Organize.** Once we know what our goals are, we can develop a route to accomplish those goals. The *Organize* stage involves developing a mental roadmap of where we are headed. *Understanding Psychology*

highlights the organization of each upcoming chapter. Read the outline at the beginning of each chapter to get an idea of what topics are covered and how they are organized.

- **Work.** The key to the P.O.W.E.R. learning system is actually reading and studying the material presented in the book. In some ways *Work* is the easy part, because, if you have carried out the steps in the preparation and organization stages, you'll know where you're headed and how you'll get there. Remember, the main text isn't the only material that you need to read and think about. It's also important to read the boxes and the material in the margins in order to gain a full understanding of the material.

- **Evaluate.** The fourth step, *Evaluate*, provides the opportunity to determine how effectively you have mastered the material. In *Understanding Psychology*, a series of questions at the end of each module permits a rapid check of your understanding of the material. Quizzes on the book's Web site, or Online Learning Center, provide additional opportunities to test yourself. Evaluating your progress is essential to assessing your degree of mastery of the material.

- **Rethink.** The final step in the *P.O.W.E.R.* learning system requires that you think critically about the content. Critical thinking entails re-analyzing, reviewing, questioning, and challenging assumptions. It affords you the opportunity to consider how the material fits with other information you have already learned. Every major section of *Understanding Psychology* ends with a *Rethink* section. Answering its thought provoking questions will help you understand the material more fully and at a deeper level.

SQ3R. Use of the SQ3R learning system entails the following specific steps:

- **Survey.** The first step of the SQ3R method is to *survey* the material by reading the outlines that open each module, the headings, figure captions, recaps, and Looking Ahead and Looking Back sections, providing yourself with an overview of the major points of the chapter.

- **Question.** The next step—the "Q"—is to *question*. Formulate questions about the material, either aloud or in writing, prior to actually reading a section of text. The questions posed at the beginning of each module and the *Evaluate* and *Rethink* questions that end each part of the chapter are examples.

- **Read.** Read carefully and, even more importantly, read actively and critically. While you are reading, answer the questions you have asked yourself. Critically evaluate material by considering the implications of what you are reading, thinking about possible exceptions and contradictions, and examining underlying assumptions.

- **Recite.** This step involves describing and explaining to yourself (or to a friend) the material you have just read and answering the questions you have posed earlier. Recite aloud; the recitation process helps to identify your degree of understanding of the material you have just read.

- **Review.** In this final step, review the material, looking it over, reading the Looking Back summaries, and answering the in-text review questions.

Manage Your Time

Without looking up from the page, answer this question: What time is it?

Most people are pretty accurate in their answer. And if you don't know for sure, it's very likely that you can find out. There may be a cell phone in your pocket; there may be a clock on the wall, desk, or computer screen; or maybe you're riding in a car that shows the time. Even if you don't have a timepiece of some sort nearby, your body keeps its own beat. Humans have an internal clock that regulates the beating of our heart, the pace of our breathing, the discharge of chemicals within our bloodstream, and myriad other bodily functions.

Managing your time as you study is a central aspect of academic success. But remember: The goal of time management is not to schedule every moment so we become pawns of a timetable that governs every waking moment of the day. Instead, the goal is to permit us to make informed choices as to how we use our time. Rather than letting the day slip by, largely without our awareness, the time management procedures we'll discuss can make us better able to harness time for our own ends.

We'll consider a number of steps to help you improve your time management skills.

Set your priorities. To figure out the best use of your time, you need to determine your priorities. *Priorities* are the tasks and activities you need and want to do, rank-ordered from most important to least important. There are no right or wrong priorities; maybe spending time on your studies is most important to you, or maybe your top priority is spending time with your family. Only you can decide. Furthermore, what's important to you now may be less of a priority to you next month, next year, or in five years.

The best procedure is to start off by identifying priorities for an entire term. What do you need to accomplish? Don't just choose obvious, general goals, such as "passing all my classes." Instead, think in terms of specific, measurable activities, such as "studying 10 hours before each chemistry exam."

Identify your prime time. Do you enthusiastically bound out of bed in the morning, ready to start the day and take on the world? Or is the alarm clock a hated and unwelcome sound that jars you out of pleasant slumber? Are you zombie-like by ten at night, or a person who is just beginning to rev up at midnight? Each of us has our own style based on some inborn body clock. Being aware of the time or times of day when you can do your best work will help you plan and schedule your time most effectively.

Master the Moment

Here's what you'll need to organize your time:

- A *master calendar* that shows all the weeks of the term on one page. It should include every week of the term and seven days per week. Using your class syllabi, write on the master calendar every assignment and test you will have, noting the date that it is due. Pencil in tentative assignments on the appropriate date. Also include on the master calendar important activities from your personal life, drawn from your list of priorities. And don't forget to schedule some free time for yourself.

- A *weekly timetable,* a master grid with the days of the week across the top and the hours, from 6:00 A.M. to midnight, along the side. Fill in the times of all your fixed, prescheduled activities—the times that your classes meet, when you have to be at work, the times you have to pick up your child at day care, and any other recurring appointments. Add assignment due dates, tests, and any other activities on the appropriate days of the week. Then pencil in blocks of time necessary to prepare for those events.

- A *daily to-do list.* Your daily to-do list can be written on a small, portable calendar that includes a separate page for each day of the week, or you can maintain a calendar electronically in a cell phone or a device such as a Treo, iPhone, or Blackberry. List all the things that you intend to do during the next day, and their priority. Start with the things you know you *must do* and which have fixed times, such as classes, work schedules, and appointments. Then add in the other things that you *should* accomplish, such as an hour of study for an upcoming test; work on research for an upcoming paper; or finishing up a lab report. Finally, list things that are a low priority but enjoyable, like a run or a walk.

Control your time. If you follow the schedules that you've prepared, you've taken the most important steps in time management. However, our lives are filled with surprises: Things always seem to take longer than we've planned. A crisis occurs; buses are late; computers break down; kids get sick.

The difference between effective time management and time management that doesn't work lies in how well you deal with the inevitable surprises. There are several ways to take control of your days and permit yourself to follow your intended schedule:

- **Just say no.** You don't have to agree to every request and every favor that others ask of you.

- **Get away from it all.** Go to the library. Lock yourself into your bedroom. Find an out-of-the-way unused classroom. Adopt a specific spot as your own, such as a corner desk in a secluded nook in the library. If you

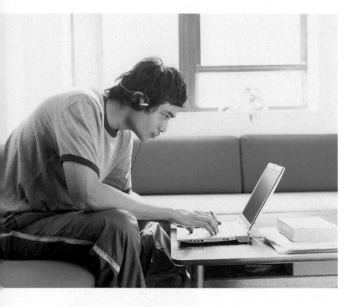

use it enough, your body and mind will automatically get into study mode as soon as you seat yourself at it.

- **Enjoy the sounds of silence.** Although many students insist they accomplish most while a television, radio, or CD is playing, scientific studies suggest otherwise—we are able to concentrate most when our environment is silent. Experiment and work in silence for a few days. You may find that you get more done in less time than you would in a more distracting environment.
- **Take an e-break.** We may not control when communications arrive, but we can make the message wait until we are ready to receive it. Take an e-break and shut down your communication sources for some period of time. Phone calls can be stored on voice-mail systems, and text messages, IMs, and e-mail can be saved on a phone or computer. They'll wait.
- **Expect the unexpected.** You'll never be able to escape from unexpected interruptions and surprises that require your attention. But by trying to anticipate them in advance, and thinking about how you'll react to them, you'll be positioning yourself to react more effectively when they do occur.

Read Your Textbook Effectively

Reading a textbook is different from reading for pleasure. With textbooks, you have specific goals: understanding, learning, and ultimately recalling the information. There are several steps you can take to achieve these goals:

- **Read the frontmatter.** If you'll be using a text extensively throughout the term, start by reading the preface and/or introduction and scanning the table of contents—what publishers call the *frontmatter*. It is there that the author has a chance to explain, often more personally than elsewhere in the text, what he or she considers important. Knowing this will give you a sense of what to expect as you read. (Note: You're reading part of the frontmatter at this very moment!)
- **Identify your personal objectives.** Before you begin an assignment, think about what your specific objectives are. Will you be reading a textbook on which you'll be thoroughly tested? Or, will your reading provide background information for future learning but it won't itself be tested? Is the material going to be useful to you personally? Your objectives for reading will help you determine which reading strategy to adopt and how much time you can devote to the reading assignment. You aren't expected to read everything with the same degree of intensity. Some material you may feel comfortable skimming; for other material you'll want to put in the maximum effort.
- **Identify and use the advance organizers.** The next step in reading a textbook is to become familiar with the *advance organizers*—outlines, overviews, section objectives, or other clues to the meaning and organization of new material—

provided in the material you are reading. Look at the start of every chapter in this book, which includes a chapter outline, plus a set of questions at the end of the "Looking Ahead" section. You can also create your own advance organizers by skimming material to be read and sketching out the general outline of the material you'll be reading. These steps can help you recall material better after you've read it.

- **Stay focused as you read.** There are a million and one possible distractions that can invade your thoughts as you read. Your job is to keep distracting thoughts at bay and focus on the material you are supposed to be reading. Here are some things you can do to help yourself stay focused:
  - **Read in small bites.** If you think it is going to take you 4 hours to read an entire chapter, break up the 4 hours into more manageable time periods. Promise yourself that you'll read for 1 hour in the afternoon, another hour in the evening, and the next 2 hours spaced out during the following day.
  - **Take a break.** Actually plan to take several short breaks to reward yourself while you're reading. During your break, do something enjoyable—eat a snack, watch a bit of a ball game on television, play a video game, or the like. Just try not to get drawn into your break activity to the point that it takes over your reading time.

- **Highlight and take notes as you read.** Highlighting and taking notes as you read a textbook are essential activities. Good annotations can help you learn and review the information prior to tests, as well as helping you to stay focused as you read. There are several things you can do to maximize the effectiveness of your notes:
  - **Rephrase key points.** Make notes to yourself, in your own words, about what the author is trying to get across. Don't just copy what's been said. Think about the material, and rewrite it in words that are your own. The very act of writing engages an additional type of perception—involving the physical sense of moving a pen or pressing a keyboard.

  - **Highlight or underline key points.** Often the first or last sentence in a paragraph, or the first or last paragraph in a section, will present a key point. Before you highlight anything, though, read the whole paragraph through. Then you'll be sure that what you highlight is, in fact, the key information. You should find yourself highlighting only one or two sentences or phrases per page. *In highlighting and underlining, less is more.* One guideline: No more than 10 percent of the material should be highlighted or underlined.
  - **Use arrows, diagrams, outlines, tables, timelines, charts, and other visuals to help you understand and later**

recall what you are reading. If three examples are given for a specific point, number them. If a sequence of steps is presented, number each step. If a paragraph discusses a situation in which an earlier point does not hold, link the original point to the exception by an arrow. Representing the material graphically will get you thinking about it in new and different ways. The act of creating visual annotations will not only help you to understand the material better but will also ease its later recall.

- **Look up unfamiliar words.** Even though you may be able to figure out the meaning of an unfamiliar word from its context, look up unfamiliar words in a dictionary or online. You'll also find out what the word sounds like, which will be important if your instructor uses the word in class.

Take Good Notes in Class

Perhaps you know students who manage to write down nearly everything their instructors say in class. And perhaps you have thought to yourself: "If only I took such painstaking notes, I'd do much better in my classes." Contrary to what many students think, however, good notetaking does not mean writing down every word that an instructor utters. With notetaking, less is often more. Let's consider some of the basic principles of notetaking:

- **Identify the instructor's—and your—goals for the course.** On the first day of class, most instructors talk about their objectives for the course. Most review the information on the class syllabus, the written document that explains the assignments for the semester. The information you get during that first session and through the syllabus is critical. In addition to the instructor's goals, you should have your own. What is it you want to learn from the course? How will the information from the course help you to enhance your knowledge, improve yourself as a person, achieve your goals?
- **Complete assignments before coming to class.** Your instructor enthusiastically describes the structure of the neuron, recounting excitedly how electrons flow across neurons, changing their electrical charge. One problem: You have only the vaguest idea what a neuron is. And the reason you don't know is that you haven't read the assignment.

    Chances are you have found yourself in this situation at least a few times, so you know firsthand that sinking feeling as you become more and more confused. The moral: Always go to class prepared. Instructors assume that their students have done what they've assigned, and their lectures are based upon that assumption.

- **Choose a notebook that assists in notetaking.** Loose-leaf notebooks are especially good for taking notes because they permit you to go back later and change the order of the pages or add additional material. Whatever kind of notebook you use, *use only one side of the page for writing; keep one side free of notes.* There may be times that you'll want to spread out your notes in front of you, and it's much easier if no material is written on the back of the pages.

  Walter Pauk devised what is sometimes called the Cornell Method of Notetaking. Using this method, draw a line down the left side of your notebook page, about 2 1/2 inches from the left-hand margin. Keep the notes you write in class to the right of the line. Indent major supporting details beneath each main idea, trying to use no more than one line for each item, and leave space between topics to add information. When it comes time to review your notes later, you'll be able to jot down a keyword, catch phrase, or major idea on the left side of the page (Pauk, 2007).

- **Listen for the key ideas.** Not every sentence in a lecture is equally important. One of the most useful skills you can develop is separating the key ideas from supporting information. Good lecturers strive to make just a few main points. The rest of what they say consists of explanation, examples, and other supportive material that expand upon the key ideas. To distinguish the key ideas from their support, you need to be alert and always searching for the *meta-message* of your instructor's words—that is, the underlying main ideas that a speaker is seeking to convey.

  How can you discern the meta-message? One way is to *listen for keywords.* Phrases like "you need to know …," "the most important thing that must be considered …," "there are four problems with this approach …," and—a big one—"this will be on the test …" should cause you to sit up and take notice. Also, if an instructor says the same thing in several ways, it's a clear sign that the material being discussed is important.

- **Use short, abbreviated phrases—not full sentences when taking notes.** Forget everything you've ever heard about always writing in full sentences. In fact, it's often useful to take notes in the form of an outline. An outline summarizes ideas in short phrases and indicates the relationship among concepts through the use of indentations.

- **Pay attention to what is written on the board or projected from overheads and PowerPoint slides. Remember these tips:**
  - **Listening is more important than seeing.** The information that your instructor projects on screen, while important, ultimately is less critical than what he or she is saying. Pay primary attention to the spoken word and secondary attention to the screen.
  - **Don't copy everything that is on every slide.** Instructors can present far more information on their slides than they would if they were writing on a blackboard. Oftentimes there is so much information that it's impossible to copy it all down. Don't even try. Instead, concentrate on taking down the key points.

- **Remember that key points on slides are ... key points.** The key points (often indicated by bullets) often relate to central concepts. Use these points to help organize your studying for tests, and don't be surprised if test questions directly assess the bulleted items on slides.
- **Check to see if the presentation slides are available online.** Some instructors make their class presentations available on the Web to their students, either before or after class time. If they do this before class, print them out and bring them to class. Then you can make notes on your copy, clarifying important points. If they are not available until after a class is over, you can still make good use of them when it comes time to study the material for tests.
- **Remember that presentation slides are not the same as good notes for a class.** If you miss a class, don't assume that getting a copy of the slides is sufficient. Studying the notes of a classmate who is a good note-taker will be far more beneficial than studying only the slides.

MEMORIZE EFFICIENTLY: USE PROVEN STRATEGIES TO MEMORIZE NEW MATERIAL

Here's a key principle of effective memorization: Memorize what you need to memorize. *Forget about the rest.*

The average textbook chapter has something like 20,000 words. But, within those 20,000 words, there may be only 30 to 40 specific concepts that you need to learn. And perhaps there are only 25 keywords. *Those* are the pieces of information on which you should focus in your efforts to memorize. By extracting what is important from what is less crucial, you'll be able to limit the amount of the material that you need to recall. You'll be able to focus on what you need to remember.

You have your choice of dozens of techniques of memorization. As we discuss the options, keep in mind that no one strategy works by itself. Also, feel free to devise your own strategies or add those that have worked for you in the past.

Rehearsal. Say it aloud: rehearsal. Think of this word in terms of its three syllables: re—hear—sal. If you're scratching your head as to why you should do this, it's to illustrate the point of *rehearsal:* to transfer material that you encounter into long-term memory.

To test if you've succeeded in transferring the word "rehearsal" into your memory, put down this book and go off for a few minutes. Do something entirely unrelated to reading this book. Have a snack, catch up on the latest sports scores on ESPN, or read the front page of a newspaper. If the word "rehearsal" popped into your head when you picked up this book again, you've passed your first memory test—the word "rehearsal" has been transferred into your memory.

Rehearsal is the key strategy in remembering information. If you don't rehearse material, it will never make it into your memory. Repeating the information, summarizing it, associating it with other memories, and above all thinking about it when you first come across it will ensure that rehearsal will be effective in placing the material into your memory.

Mnemonics. This odd word (pronounced with the "m" silent—"neh MON ix") describes formal techniques used to make material more readily remembered. *Mnemonics* are the tricks-of-the-trade that professional memory experts use, and you too can use them to nail down the information you will need to recall for tests.

Among the most common mnemonics are the following:

- **Acronyms.** *Acronyms* are words or phrases formed by the first letters of a series of terms. The word "laser" is an acronym for "light amplification by stimulated emissions of radiation," and "radar" is an acronym for "radio detection and ranging."

  Acronyms can be a big help in remembering things. For example, Roy G. Biv is a favorite of physics students who must remember the colors of the spectrum (red, orange, yellow, green, blue, indigo, and violet.) The benefit of acronyms is that they help us to recall a complete list of steps or items.
- **Acrostics.** *Acrostics* are sentences in which the first letters spell out something that needs to be recalled. The benefits—as well as the drawbacks—of acrostics are similar to those of acronyms.
- **Rhymes and jingles.** "Thirty days hath September, April, June, and November." If you know the rest of the rhyme, you're familiar with one of the most commonly used mnemonic jingles in the English language.

Use of multiple senses. The more senses you can involve when you're trying to learn new material, the better you'll be able to remember. Here's why: Every time we encounter new information, all of our senses are potentially at work. Each piece of sensory information is stored in a separate location in the brain, and yet all the pieces are linked together in extraordinarily intricate ways.

What this means is that when we seek to remember the details of a specific event, recalling a memory of one of the sensory experiences can trigger recall of the other types of memories. You can make use of the fact that memories are stored in multiple ways by applying the following techniques:

- **When you learn something, use your body.** Don't sit passively at your desk. Instead, move around. Stand up; sit down. Touch the page. Trace figures with your fingers. Talk to yourself. Think out loud. By involving every part of your body, you've increased the number of potential ways to trigger a relevant memory later, when you need to recall it. And when one memory is triggered, other related memories may come tumbling back.
- **Draw and diagram the material.** Structuring written material by graphically grouping and connecting key ideas and themes is a powerful technique. When we draw and diagram material, one of the things we're doing

is expanding the modalities in which information can be stored in our minds. Other types of drawing can be useful in aiding later recall. Creating drawings, sketches, and even cartoons can help us remember better.

- **Visualize.** You already know that memory requires three basic steps: the initial recording of information, the storage of that information, and, ultimately, the retrieval of the stored information. *Visualization* is a technique by which images are formed to ensure that material is recalled. Don't stop at visualizing images just in your mind's eye. Actually drawing what you visualize will help you to remember the material even better. Visualization is effective because it serves several purposes. It helps make abstract ideas concrete; it engages multiple senses; it permits us to link different bits of information together; and it provides us with a context for storing information.

- **Overlearning.** Lasting learning doesn't come until you have overlearned the material. *Overlearning* consists of studying and rehearsing material past the point of initial mastery. Through overlearning, recall becomes automatic. Rather than searching for a fact, going through mental contortions until perhaps the information surfaces, overlearning permits us to recall the information without even thinking about it.

TEST-TAKING STRATEGIES

Preparing for tests is a long-term proposition. It's not a matter of "giving your all" the night *before* the test. Instead, it's a matter of giving your all to every aspect of the course.

Here are some guidelines that can help you do your best on tests:

Know what you are preparing for. Determine as much as you can about the test *before* you begin to study for it. The more you know about a test beforehand, the more efficient your studying will be.

To find out about an upcoming test, ask this question:

- Is the test called a "test," an "exam," a "quiz," or something else? The names imply different things.
  - **Essay:** Requires a fairly extended, on-the-spot composition about some topic. Examples include questions that call on you to describe a person, process, or event, or those that ask you to compare or contrast two separate sets of material.
  - **Multiple-choice:** Usually contains a question or statement, followed by a number of possible answers (usually 4 or 5 of them). You are supposed to choose the best response from the choices offered.
  - **True–false:** Presents statements about a topic that are either accurate or inaccurate. You are to indicate whether each statement is accurate (true) or inaccurate (false).
  - **Matching:** Presents two lists of related information, arranged in column form. Typically, you are asked to pair up the items that go together (for example, a scientific term and its definition, or a writer and the title of a book he wrote).

- **Short-answer:** Requires brief responses (usually a few sentences at most) in a kind of mini-essay.
- **Fill-in:** Requires you to add one or more missing words to a sentence or series of sentences.

Match test preparation to question types. Each kind of test question requires a somewhat different style of preparation.

- **Essay questions.** Essay tests focus on the big picture—ways in which the various pieces of information being tested fit together. You'll need to know not just a series of facts, but also the connections between them, and you will have to be able to discuss these ideas in an organized and logical way.

  The best approach to studying for an essay test involves four steps:

  1. Carefully reread your class notes and any notes you've made on assigned readings that will be covered on the upcoming exam. Also go through the readings themselves, reviewing underlined or highlighted material and marginal notes.

  2. Think of likely exam questions. For example, use the key words, phrases, concepts, and questions that come up in your class notes or in your text. Some instructors give out lists of possible essay topics; if yours does, focus on this list, but don't ignore other possibilities.

  3. Without looking at your notes or your readings, answer each potential essay question—aloud. Don't feel embarrassed about doing this. Talking aloud is often more useful than answering the question in your head. You can also write down the main points that any answer should cover. (Don't write out *complete* answers to the questions unless your instructor tells you in advance exactly what is going to be on the test. Your time is probably better spent learning the material than rehearsing precisely formulated responses.)

  4. After you've answered the questions, check yourself by looking at the notes and readings once again. If you feel confident that you've answered specific questions adequately, check them off. You can go back later for a quick review. But if there are questions that you had trouble with, review that material immediately. Then repeat the third step above, answering the questions again.

- **Multiple-choice, true–false, and matching questions.** While the focus of review for essay questions should be on major issues and controversies, studying for multiple-choice, true–false, and matching questions requires more attention to the details. Almost anything is fair game for multiple choice, true–false, and matching questions, so you can't afford to overlook anything when studying. It's a good idea to write down important facts on index cards: They're portable and available all the time, and the act of creating them helps drive the material into your memory. Furthermore, you can shuffle them and test yourself repeatedly until you've mastered the material.

- **Short-answer and fill-in questions.** Short-answer and fill-in questions are similar to essays in that they require you to recall key pieces of information rather than, as is the case with multiple-choice, true–false, and matching questions, finding it on the page in front of you. However, short-answer and fill-in questions typically don't demand that you integrate or compare different types of information. Consequently, the focus of your study should be on the recall of specific, detailed information.

Test yourself. Once you feel you've mastered the material, test yourself on it. There are several ways to do this. Often textbooks are accompanied by web sites that offer automatically scored practice tests and quizzes. (*Understanding Psychology* does: go to www.mhhe.com/feldman/up9 to try one!) You can also create a test for yourself, in writing, making its form as close as possible to what you expect the actual test to be. For instance, if your instructor has told you the classroom test will be primarily made up of short-answer questions, your test should reflect that.

You might also construct a test and administer it to a classmate or a member of your study group. In turn, you could take a test that someone else has constructed. Constructing and taking practice tests are excellent ways of studying the material and cementing it into memory.

Deal with test anxiety. What does the anticipation of a test do to you? Do you feel shaky? Is there a knot in your stomach? Do you grit your teeth? *Test anxiety* is a temporary condition characterized by fears and concerns about test-taking. Almost everyone experiences it to some degree, although for some people it's more of a problem than for others. You'll never eliminate test anxiety completely, nor do you want to. A little bit of nervousness can energize us, making us more attentive and vigilant. Like any competitive event, testing can motivate us to do our best.

On the other hand, for some students, anxiety can spiral into the kind of paralyzing fear that makes their minds go blank. There are several ways to keep this from happening to you:

1. *Prepare thoroughly*. The more you prepare, the less test anxiety you'll feel. Good preparation can give you a sense of control and mastery, and it will prevent test anxiety from overwhelming you.
2. *Take a realistic view of the test*. Remember that your future success does not hinge on your performance on any single exam. Think of the big picture: put the task ahead in context, and remind yourself of all the hurdles you've passed so far.
3. *Learn relaxation techniques*. These techniques are covered in the text's chapter on health psychology, but the basic process is straightforward: Breathe evenly, gently inhaling and exhaling. Focus your mind on a pleas-ant, relaxing scene such as a beautiful forest or a peaceful farm, or on a restful sound such as that of ocean waves breaking on the beach.
4. *Visualize success*. Think of an image of your instructor handing back your test marked with a big "A." Or imagine your instructor congratulating you on your fine performance the day after the test. Positive visualizations that highlight your potential success can help replace images of failure that may fuel test anxiety.

What if these strategies don't work? If your test anxiety is so great that it's getting in the way of your success, make use of your college's resources. Most provide a learning resource center or a counseling center that can provide you with personalized help.

Form a study group. *Study groups* are small, informal groups of students who work together to learn course material and study for a test. Forming such a group can be an excellent way to prepare for any kind of test. Some study groups are formed for particular tests, while others meet consistently throughout the term. The typical study group meets a week or two before a test and plans a strategy for studying. Members share their understanding of what will be on the test, based on what an instructor has said in class and on their review of notes and text material. Together, they develop a list of review questions to guide their individual study. The group then breaks up, and the members study on their own.

A few days before the test, members of the study group meet again. They discuss answers to the review questions, go over the material, and share any new insights they may have about the upcoming test. They may also quiz one another about the material to identify any weaknesses or gaps in their knowledge.

Study groups can be extremely powerful tools because they help accomplish several things:

- They help members organize and structure the material to approach their studying in a systematic and logical way.
- They allow students to share different perspectives on the material.
- They make it more likely that students will not overlook any potentially important information.
- They force members to rethink the course material, explaining it in words that other group members will understand. As we will discuss in Chapter 14, this helps both understanding and recall of the information when it is needed on the test.
- Finally, they help motivate members to do their best. When you're part of a study group, you're no longer working just for yourself; your studying also benefits the other study group members. Not wanting to let down your classmates in a study group may encourage you to put in your best effort.

SOME FINAL COMMENTS

We have discussed numerous techniques for increasing your study, classroom, and test effectiveness. But you need not feel tied to a specific strategy. You might want to combine other elements to create your own study system. Additional learning tips and strategies for critical thinking are presented throughout *Understanding Psychology*.

Whatever learning strategies you use, you will maximize your understanding of the material in this book and master techniques that will help you learn and think critically in all of your academic endeavors. More importantly, you will optimize your understanding of the field of psychology. It is worth the effort: the excitement, challenges, and promise that psychology holds for you are significant.

CHAPTER 1

Introduction to Psychology

Key Concepts for Chapter 1

Prologue *A Rampage on Campus*

On a sunny spring day, Virginia Tech student Seung-Hui Cho walked into West Ambler Johnston Hall, a campus dormitory, and proceeded to shoot and kill student Emily Hilscher and resident assistant Ryan Clark. After stopping to mail a package containing a written and videotaped manifesto to a news agency, Cho proceeded to Norris Hall, a classroom building. He chained several doors shut and began to hunt down and shoot students and faculty members who were attending morning classes. Within minutes he had killed another 30 people and seriously wounded many more before finally taking his own life with a single gunshot to his head.

But in the midst of this senseless violence and tragic loss emerged acts of courage and selflessness. Amid the terror and chaos, several faculty members risked their own lives to ensure the safety of their students. For example, Professor Liviu Librescu restrained the shooter from entering his classroom, giving his students an opportunity to escape before Cho entered the room and ultimately shot and killed Librescu. With his sacrifice, Librescu saved the lives of scores of students (Banerjee, 2007).

Looking Ahead

The Virginia Tech massacre gave rise to a host of important psychological issues. For example, consider these questions asked by psychologists following the catastrophe:

- What physical changes occurred in the bodies of students fleeing for their lives from Cho?
- What memories did people have of the massacre afterward?
- Why were there so many contradictory eyewitness reports?
- What would be the long-term effects of the massacre on the health of the survivors and witnesses?
- What are the most effective ways to help people cope with the sudden and unexpected loss of young loved ones who were in the prime of their lives?

- Why did several people give up their own lives to save the lives of others?
- What could have motivated Cho's rampage?
- Was he psychologically disturbed?
- Could this tragedy have been prevented if Cho had received psychological therapy?

As we'll soon see, psychology addresses questions like these—and many, many more. In this chapter, we begin our examination of psychology, the different types of psychologists, and the various roles that psychologists play.

Psychologists at Work

Psychology is the scientific study of behavior and mental processes. The simplicity of this definition is in some ways deceiving, concealing ongoing debates about how broad the scope of psychology should be. Should psychologists limit themselves to the study of outward, observable behavior? Is it possible to study thinking scientifically? Should the field encompass the study of such diverse topics as physical and mental health, perception, dreaming, and motivation? Is it appropriate to focus solely on human behavior, or should the behavior of other species be included?

Most psychologists would argue that the field should be receptive to a variety of viewpoints and approaches. Consequently, the phrase *behavior and mental processes* in the definition of psychology must be understood to mean many things: It encompasses not just what people do but also their thoughts, emotions, perceptions, reasoning processes, memories, and even the biological activities that maintain bodily functioning.

Psychologists try to describe, predict, and explain human behavior and mental processes, as well as helping to change and improve the lives of people and the world in which they live. They use scientific methods to find answers that are far more valid and legitimate than those resulting from intuition and speculation, which are often inaccurate (see Figure 1).

Key Concepts

What is the science of psychology?

What are the major specialties in the field of psychology?

Where do psychologists work?

Psychology: The scientific study of behavior and mental processes.

Psychological Truths?

To test your knowledge of psychology, try answering the following questions:

1. Infants love their mothers primarily because their mothers fulfill their basic biological needs, such as providing food. True or false? _____
2. Geniuses generally have poor social adjustment. True or false? _____
3. The best way to ensure that a desired behavior will continue after training is completed is to reward that behavior every single time it occurs during training rather than rewarding it only periodically. True or false? _____
4. People with schizophrenia have at least two distinct personalities. True or false? _____
5. Parents should do everything they can to ensure their children have high self-esteem and a strong sense that they are highly competent. True or false? _____
6. Children's IQ scores have little to do with how well they do in school. True or false? _____
7. Frequent masturbation can lead to mental illness. True or false? _____
8. Once people reach old age, their leisure activities change radically. True or false? _____
9. Most people would refuse to give painful electric shocks to other people. True or false? _____
10. People who talk about suicide are unlikely to actually try to kill themselves. True or false? _____

Scoring: The truth about each of these items: They are all false. Based on psychological research, each of these "facts" has been proven untrue. You will learn the reasons why as we explore what psychologists have discovered about human behavior.

FIGURE 1 The scientific method is the basis of all psychological research and is used to find valid answers. Test your knowledge of psychology by answering these questions. (Source: Adapted from Lamal, 1979.)

The questions in Figure 1 provide just a hint of the topics that we will encounter in the study of psychology. Our discussions will take us through the range of what is known about behavior and mental processes.

The Subfields of Psychology: Psychology's Family Tree

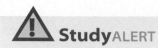

StudyALERT

The different subfields of psychology allow psychologists to explain the same behavior in multiple ways. Review Figure 2 for a summary of the subfields.

As the study of psychology has grown, it has given rise to a number of subfields (described in Figure 2). The subfields of psychology can be likened to an extended family, with assorted nieces and nephews, aunts and uncles, and cousins who, although they may not interact on a day-to-day basis, are related to one another because they share a common goal: understanding behavior. One way to identify the key subfields is to look at some of the basic questions about behavior that they address.

WHAT ARE THE BIOLOGICAL FOUNDATIONS OF BEHAVIOR?

In the most fundamental sense, people are biological organisms. *Behavioral neuroscience* is the subfield of psychology that mainly examines how the brain and the nervous system—but other biological processes as well—determine behavior. Thus, neuroscientists consider how our bodies influence our behavior. For example, they may examine the link between specific sites in the brain and the muscular tremors of people affected by Parkinson's disease or attempt to determine how our emotions are related to physical sensations. Behavioral neuroscientists might want to know what physiological changes occurred in students who fled from the killer during the Virginia Tech shootings.

HOW DO PEOPLE SENSE, PERCEIVE, LEARN, AND THINK ABOUT THE WORLD?

If you have ever wondered why you are susceptible to optical illusions, how your body registers pain, or how to make the most of your study time, an experimental psychologist can answer your questions. *Experimental psychology* is the branch of psychology that studies the processes of sensing, perceiving, learning, and thinking about the world. (The term *experimental psychologist* is somewhat misleading: Psychologists in every specialty area use experimental techniques.)

Several subspecialties of experimental psychology have become specialties in their own right. One is *cognitive psychology*, which focuses on higher mental processes, including thinking, memory, reasoning, problem solving, judging, decision making, and language. For example, a cognitive psychologist might be interested in what the survivors of the Virginia Tech massacre remembered about their experience.

WHAT ARE THE SOURCES OF CHANGE AND STABILITY IN BEHAVIOR ACROSS THE LIFE SPAN?

A baby producing her first smile . . . taking his first step . . . saying its first word. These universal milestones in development are also singularly special and unique for each person. *Developmental psychology* studies how people grow and change from the moment of conception through death. *Personality psychology* focuses on the consistency in people's behavior over time and the traits that differentiate one person from another.

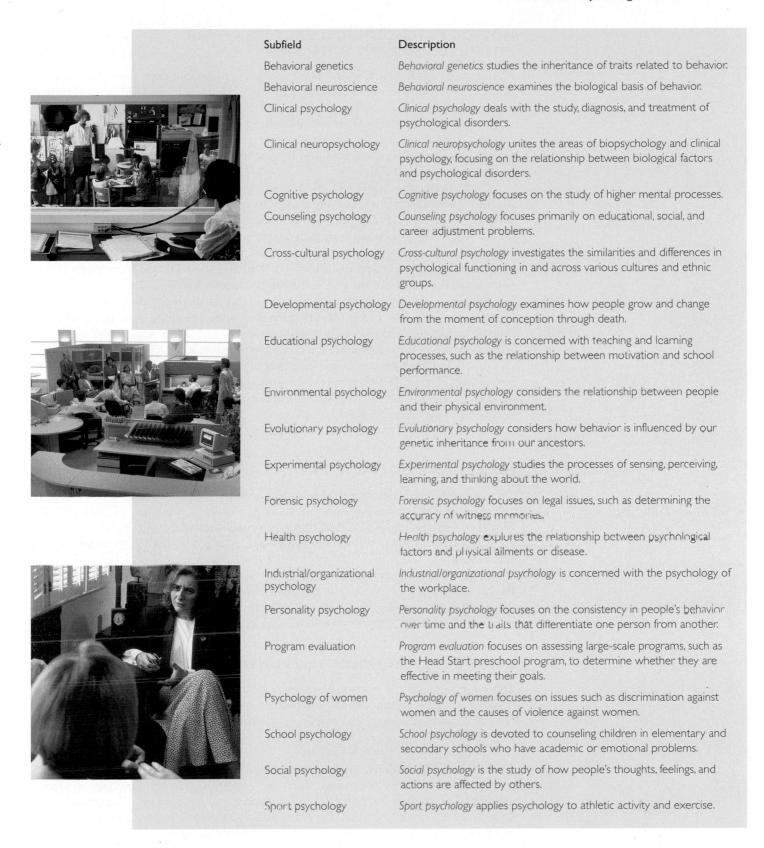

Subfield	Description
Behavioral genetics	*Behavioral genetics* studies the inheritance of traits related to behavior.
Behavioral neuroscience	*Behavioral neuroscience* examines the biological basis of behavior.
Clinical psychology	*Clinical psychology* deals with the study, diagnosis, and treatment of psychological disorders.
Clinical neuropsychology	*Clinical neuropsychology* unites the areas of biopsychology and clinical psychology, focusing on the relationship between biological factors and psychological disorders.
Cognitive psychology	*Cognitive psychology* focuses on the study of higher mental processes.
Counseling psychology	*Counseling psychology* focuses primarily on educational, social, and career adjustment problems.
Cross-cultural psychology	*Cross-cultural psychology* investigates the similarities and differences in psychological functioning in and across various cultures and ethnic groups.
Developmental psychology	*Developmental psychology* examines how people grow and change from the moment of conception through death.
Educational psychology	*Educational psychology* is concerned with teaching and learning processes, such as the relationship between motivation and school performance.
Environmental psychology	*Environmental psychology* considers the relationship between people and their physical environment.
Evolutionary psychology	*Evolutionary psychology* considers how behavior is influenced by our genetic inheritance from our ancestors.
Experimental psychology	*Experimental psychology* studies the processes of sensing, perceiving, learning, and thinking about the world.
Forensic psychology	*Forensic psychology* focuses on legal issues, such as determining the accuracy of witness memories.
Health psychology	*Health psychology* explores the relationship between psychological factors and physical ailments or disease.
Industrial/organizational psychology	*Industrial/organizational psychology* is concerned with the psychology of the workplace.
Personality psychology	*Personality psychology* focuses on the consistency in people's behavior over time and the traits that differentiate one person from another.
Program evaluation	*Program evaluation* focuses on assessing large-scale programs, such as the Head Start preschool program, to determine whether they are effective in meeting their goals.
Psychology of women	*Psychology of women* focuses on issues such as discrimination against women and the causes of violence against women.
School psychology	*School psychology* is devoted to counseling children in elementary and secondary schools who have academic or emotional problems.
Social psychology	*Social psychology* is the study of how people's thoughts, feelings, and actions are affected by others.
Sport psychology	*Sport psychology* applies psychology to athletic activity and exercise.

FIGURE 2 The major subfields of psychology.

HOW DO PSYCHOLOGICAL FACTORS AFFECT PHYSICAL AND MENTAL HEALTH?

Frequent depression, stress, and fears that prevent people from carrying out their normal activities are topics that would interest a health psychologist, a clinical psychologist, and a counseling psychologist. *Health psychology* explores the relationship between psychological factors and physical ailments or disease. For example, health psychologists are interested in assessing how long-term stress (a psychological factor) can affect physical health and in identifying ways to promote behavior that brings about good health.

Clinical psychology deals with the study, diagnosis, and treatment of psychological disorders. Clinical psychologists are trained to diagnose and treat problems that range from the crises of everyday life, such as unhappiness over the breakup of a relationship, to more extreme conditions, such as profound, lingering depression. Some clinical psychologists also research and investigate issues that vary from identifying the early signs of psychological disturbance to studying the relationship between family communication patterns and psychological disorders.

Like clinical psychologists, counseling psychologists deal with people's psychological problems, but the problems they deal with are more specific. *Counseling psychology* focuses primarily on educational, social, and career adjustment problems. Almost every college has a center staffed with counseling psychologists. This is where students can get advice on the kinds of jobs they might be best suited for, on methods of studying effectively, and on strategies for resolving everyday difficulties, such as problems with roommates and concerns about a specific professor's grading practices. Many large business organizations also employ counseling psychologists to help employees with work-related problems.

HOW DO OUR SOCIAL NETWORKS AFFECT BEHAVIOR?

Our complex networks of social interrelationships are the focus for a number of subfields of psychology. For example, *social psychology* is the study of how people's thoughts, feelings, and actions are affected by others. Social psychologists concentrate on such diverse topics as human aggression, liking and loving, persuasion, and conformity.

Cross-cultural psychology investigates the similarities and differences in psychological functioning in and across various cultures and ethnic groups. For example, cross-cultural psychologists examine how cultures differ in their use of punishment during child rearing.

EXPANDING PSYCHOLOGY'S FRONTIERS

The boundaries of the science of psychology are constantly growing. Three newer members of the field's family tree—evolutionary psychology, behavioral genetics, and clinical neuropsychology—have sparked particular excitement, and debate, within psychology.

Evolutionary Psychology. *Evolutionary psychology* considers how behavior is influenced by our genetic inheritance from our ancestors. The evolutionary approach suggests that the chemical coding of information in our cells not only determines traits such as hair color and race but also holds the key to understanding a broad variety of behaviors that helped our ancestors survive and reproduce.

Evolutionary psychology stems from Charles Darwin's arguments in his groundbreaking 1859 book, *On the Origin of Species*. Darwin suggested that a process of natural selection leads to the survival of the fittest and the development of traits that enable a species to adapt to its environment.

Evolutionary psychologists take Darwin's arguments a step further. They argue that our genetic inheritance determines not only physical traits such as skin and eye color, but certain personality traits and social behaviors as well. For example, evolutionary psychologists suggest that behavior such as shyness, jealousy, and cross-cultural similarities in qualities desired in potential mates are at least partially determined by genetics, presumably because such behavior helped increase the survival rate of humans' ancient relatives (Buss, 2003; Sefcek et al., 2007).

Although they are increasingly popular, evolutionary explanations of behavior have stirred controversy. By suggesting that many significant behaviors unfold automatically because they are wired into the human species, evolutionary approaches minimize the role of environmental and social forces. Still, the evolutionary approach has stimulated a significant amount of research on how our biological inheritance influences our traits and behaviors (Begley, 2005; Buss, 2004; Neher, 2006).

Behavioral Genetics. Another rapidly growing areas in psychology focuses on the biological mechanisms, such as genes and chromosomes, that enable inherited behavior to unfold. *Behavioral genetics* seeks to understand how we might inherit certain behavioral traits and how the environment influences whether we actually display such traits (Bjorklund, 2005; Rende, 2007; Moffitt & Caspi, 2007).

Clinical Neuropsychology. *Clinical neuropsychology* unites the areas of neuroscience and clinical psychology: It focuses on the origin of psychological disorders in biological factors. Building on advances in our understanding of the structure and chemistry of the brain, this specialty has already led to promising new treatments for psychological disorders as well as debates over the use of medication to control behavior.

Working at Psychology

Help Wanted: Assistant professor at a small liberal arts college. Teach undergraduate courses in introductory psychology and courses in specialty areas of cognitive psychology, perception, and learning. Strong commitment to quality teaching, as well as evidence of scholarship and research productivity, necessary.

* * *

Help Wanted: Industrial-organizational consulting psychologist. International firm seeks psychologists for full-time career positions as consultants to management. Candidates must have the ability to establish a rapport with senior business executives and help them find innovative and practical solutions to problems concerning people and organizations.

* * *

Help Wanted: Clinical psychologist. PhD, internship experience, and license required. Comprehensive clinic seeks psychologist to work with children and adults providing individual and group therapy, psychological evaluations, crisis intervention, and development of behavior treatment plans on multidisciplinary team.

FIGURE 3 The breakdown of where U.S. psychologists (who have a PhD or PsyD degree) work. Why do you think so many psychologists work in college and university settings? (Source: APA, 2007.)

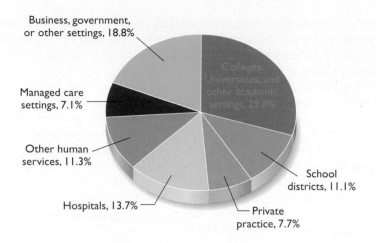

As these job ads suggest, psychologists are employed in a variety of settings. Many doctoral-level psychologists are employed by institutions of higher learning (universities and colleges) or are self-employed, usually working as private practitioners treating clients (see Figure 3). Other work sites include hospitals, clinics, mental health centers, counseling centers, government human-services organizations, and schools (APA, 2007).

Why do so many psychologists work in academic settings? Because these are effective settings for three major roles played by psychologists in society: teacher, scientist, and clinical practitioner. Many psychology professors are also actively involved in research or in serving clients. Whatever the particular job site, however, psychologists share a commitment to improving individual lives as well as society in general.

PSYCHOLOGISTS: A PORTRAIT

Although there is no "average" psychologist in terms of personal characteristics, we can draw a statistical portrait of the field. There are close to 300,000 psychologists working today in the United States, but they are outnumbered by psychologists in other countries. Europe has more than 290,000 psychologists, and there are 140,000 licensed psychologists in Brazil alone. Although most research is conducted in the United States, psychologists in other countries are increasingly influential in adding to the knowledge base and practices of psychology (Peiro & Lunt, 2003; Nelson, 2007; Stevens & Gielen, 2007).

In the United States, about half of all psychologists are men and half are women. But that's changing. Predictions are that by 2010 women will outnumber men in the field. Right now, almost three-fourths of new psychology doctorate degrees are earned by women (Frincke & Pate, 2004; Cynkar, 2007).

The vast majority of psychologists in the United States are white, limiting the diversity of the field. Only 6 percent of all psychologists are members of racial minority groups. Although the number of minority individuals entering the field is higher than a decade ago—around 20 percent of new master's degrees and 16 percent of new doctorate degrees are awarded to people of color—the numbers have not kept up with the dramatic growth of the minority population at large (Bailey, 2004; Hoffer et al., 2005; Maton et al., 2006).

The underrepresentation of racial and ethnic minorities among psychologists is significant for several reasons. First, the field of psychology is diminished by a lack of the diverse perspectives and talents that minority-group members can provide. Furthermore, minority-group psychologists serve as role models for members of minority communities, and their underrepresentation in the profession might deter other minority-group members from entering the field. Finally, because members of minority groups often prefer to receive psychological therapy from treatment providers of their own race or ethnic group, the rarity of minority psychologists can discourage some members of minority groups from seeking treatment (Bernal et al., 2002; Jenkins et al., 2003; Bryant et al., 2005).

THE EDUCATION OF A PSYCHOLOGIST

How do people become psychologists? The most common route is a long one. Most psychologists have a doctorate, either a *PhD* (doctor of philosophy) or, less frequently, a *PsyD* (doctor of psychology). The PhD is a research degree that requires a dissertation based on an original investigation. The PsyD is obtained by psychologists who wish to focus on the treatment of psychological disorders. (Psychologists are distinct from psychiatrists, who are physicians who specialize in the treatment of psychological disorders.)

Both the PhD and the PsyD typically take four or five years of work past the bachelor's level. Some fields of psychology involve education beyond the doctorate. For instance, doctoral-level clinical psychologists, who deal with people with psychological disorders, typically spend an additional year doing an internship.

About a third of people working in the field of psychology have a master's degree as their highest degree, which they earn after two or three years of graduate work. These psychologists teach, provide therapy, conduct research, or work in specialized programs dealing with drug abuse or crisis intervention. Some work in universities, government, and business, collecting and analyzing data.

StudyALERT

Be sure to be able to differentiate between a PhD (doctor of philosophy) and PsyD (doctor of psychology), as well as between psychologists and psychiatrists.

CAREERS FOR PSYCHOLOGY MAJORS

Although some psychology majors head for graduate school in psychology or an unrelated field, the majority join the workforce immediately after graduation. Most report that the jobs they take after graduation are related to their psychology background.

An undergraduate major in psychology provides excellent preparation for a variety of occupations. Because undergraduates who specialize in psychology develop good analytical skills, are trained to think critically, and are able to synthesize and evaluate information well, employers in business, industry, and the government value their preparation (Kuther, 2003).

The most common areas of employment for psychology majors are in the social services, including working as an administrator, serving as a counselor, and providing direct care. Some 20 percent of recipients of bachelor's degrees in psychology work in the social services or in some other form of public affairs. In addition, psychology majors often enter the fields of education or business or work for federal, state, and local governments (see Figure 4; APA, 2000; Murray, 2002).

FIGURE 4 Although many psychology majors pursue employment in social services, a background in psychology can prepare one for many professions outside the social services field. What is it about the science of psychology that makes it such a versatile field? (Source: From Tara L. Kuther, *The Psychology Major's Handbook*, 1st ed., p. 114. © 2003 Wadsworth, a part of Cengage Learning, Inc. Reproduced by permission. www.cengage.com/permissions)

Positions Obtained by Psychology Majors		
Business Field	**Education/Academic**	**Social Field**
Administrative assistant	Administration	Activities coordinator
Affirmative action officer	Child-care provider	Behavioral specialist
Advertising trainee	Child-care worker/	Career counselor
Benefits manager	supervisor	Case worker
Claims specialist	Data management	Child protection worker
Community relations officer	Laboratory assistant	Clinical coordinator
Customer relations	Parent/family education	Community outreach worker
Data management	Preschool teacher	Corrections officer
Employee recruitment	Public opinion surveyor	Counselor assistant
Employee counselor	Research assistant	Crisis intervention counselor
Human resources coordinator/	Teaching assistant	Employment counselor
manager/specialist		Group home attendant
Labor relations manager/specialist		Occupational therapist
Loan officer		Probation officer
Management trainee		Program manager
Marketing		Rehabilitation counselor
Personnel manager/officer		Residence counselor
Product and services research		Mental health assistant
Programs/events coordination		Social service assistant
Public relations		Social worker
Retail sales management		Substance abuse counselor
Sales representative		Youth counselor
Special features writing/reporting		
Staff training and development		
Trainer/training office		

RECAP/EVALUATE/RETHINK

RECAP

What is the science of psychology?

- Psychology is the scientific study of behavior and mental processes, encompassing not just what people do but their biological activities, feelings, perceptions, memory, reasoning, and thoughts. (p. 5)

What are the major specialties in the field of psychology?

- Behavioral neuroscientists focus on the biological basis of behavior, and experimental psychologists study the processes of sensing, perceiving, learning, and thinking about the world. (p. 6)

- Cognitive psychology, an outgrowth of experimental psychology, studies higher mental processes, including memory, knowing, thinking, reasoning, problem solving, judging, decision making, and language. (p. 6)

- Developmental psychologists study how people grow and change throughout the life span. (p. 6)

- Personality psychologists consider the consistency and change in an individual's behavior, as well as the individual differences that distinguish one person's behavior from another's. (p. 6)

- Health psychologists study psychological factors that affect physical disease, while clinical psychologists consider the study, diagnosis, and treatment of abnormal behavior. Counseling psychologists focus on educational, social, and career adjustment problems. (p. 8)

- Social psychology is the study of how people's thoughts, feelings, and actions are affected by others. (p. 8)

- Cross-cultural psychology examines the similarities and differences in psychological functioning among various cultures. (p. 8)

- Other increasingly important fields are evolutionary psychology, behavioral genetics, and clinical neuropsychology. (p. 8)

Where do psychologists work?

- Psychologists are employed in a variety of settings. Although the primary sites of employment are private practice and colleges, many psychologists are found in hospitals, clinics, community mental health centers, and counseling centers. (p. 10)

EVALUATE

Match each subfield of psychology with the issues or questions posed below.

a. Behavioral neuroscience
b. Experimental psychology
c. Cognitive psychology
d. Developmental psychology
e. Personality psychology
f. Health psychology
g. Clinical psychology
h. Counseling psychology
i. Educational psychology
j. School psychology
k. Social psychology
l. Industrial psychology

1. Joan, a college freshman, is worried about her grades. She needs to learn better organizational skills and study habits to cope with the demands of college.

2. At what age do children generally begin to acquire an emotional attachment to their fathers?

3. It is thought that pornographic films that depict violence against women may prompt aggressive behavior in some men.

4. What chemicals are released in the human body as a result of a stressful event? What are their effects on behavior?

5. Luis is unique in his manner of responding to crisis situations, with an even temperament and a positive outlook.

6. The teachers of 8-year-old Jack are concerned that he has recently begun to withdraw socially and to show little interest in schoolwork.

7. Janetta's job is demanding and stressful. She wonders if her lifestyle is making her more prone to certain illnesses, such as cancer and heart disease.

8. A psychologist is intrigued by the fact that some people are much more sensitive to painful stimuli than others are.

9. A strong fear of crowds leads a young man to seek treatment for his problem.

10. What mental strategies are involved in solving complex word problems?

11. What teaching methods most effectively motivate elementary school students to successfully accomplish academic tasks?

12. Jessica is asked to develop a management strategy that will encourage safer work practices in an assembly plant.

RETHINK

1. Do you think intuition and common sense are sufficient for understanding why people act the way they do? In what ways is a scientific approach appropriate for studying human behavior?
2. *From an educator's perspective:* Suppose you are a teacher who has a 7-year-old child in your class who is having unusual difficulty learning to read. Imagine that you could consult as many psychologists with different specialties that you wanted. What are the different types of psychologists that you might approach to address the problem?

Answers to Evaluate Question

1. a-4, b-8, c-10, d-2, e-5, f-7, g-9, h-1, i-11, j-6, k-3, l-12

KEY TERMS

psychology p. 5

A Science Evolves: The Past, the Present, and the Future

Seven thousand years ago, people assumed that psychological problems were caused by evil spirits. To allow those spirits to escape from a person's body, ancient healers chipped a hole in a patient's skull with crude instruments—a procedure called trephining.

* * *

According to the 17th-century philosopher Descartes, nerves were hollow tubes through which "animal spirits" conducted impulses in the same way that water is transmitted through a pipe. When a person put a finger too close to a fire, heat was transmitted to the brain through the tubes.

* * *

Franz Josef Gall, an 18th-century physician, argued that a trained observer could discern intelligence, moral character, and other basic personality characteristics from the shape and number of bumps on a person's skull. His theory gave rise to the field of phrenology, employed by hundreds of practitioners in the 19th century.

Although these explanations might sound far-fetched, in their own times they represented the most advanced thinking about what might be called the psychology of the era. Our understanding of behavior has progressed tremendously since the 18th century, but most of the advances have been recent. As sciences go, psychology is one of the new kids on the block. (For highlights in the development of the field, see Figure 1.)

The Roots of Psychology

We can trace psychology's roots back to the ancient Greeks, who considered the mind to be a suitable topic for scholarly contemplation. Later philosophers argued for hundreds of years about some of the questions psychologists grapple with today. For example, the 17th-century British philosopher John Locke believed that children were born into the world with minds like "blank slates" (*tabula rasa* in Latin) and that their experiences determined what kind of adults they would become. His views contrasted with those of Plato and the 15th-century French philosopher René Descartes, who argued that some knowledge was inborn in humans.

However, the formal beginning of psychology as a scientific discipline is generally considered to be in the late 19th century, when, in Leipzig, Germany, Wilhelm Wundt established the first experimental laboratory devoted to psychological phenomena. At about the same time, William James was setting up his laboratory in Cambridge, Massachusetts.

When Wundt set up his laboratory in 1879, his aim was to study the building blocks of the mind. He considered psychology to be the study of conscious experience. His perspective, which came to be known as **structuralism**, focused on uncovering the fundamental mental components of perception, consciousness, thinking, emotions, and other kinds of mental states and activities.

To determine how basic sensory processes shape our understanding of the world, Wundt and other structuralists used a procedure called **introspection**, in which they presented people with a stimulus—such as a bright green object or

Key Concepts

What are the origins of psychology?

What are the major approaches in contemporary psychology?

Wilhelm Wundt

Structuralism: Wundt's approach, which focuses on uncovering the fundamental mental components of consciousness, thinking, and other kinds of mental states and activities.

Introspection: A procedure used to study the structure of the mind in which subjects are asked to describe in detail what they are experiencing when they are exposed to a stimulus.

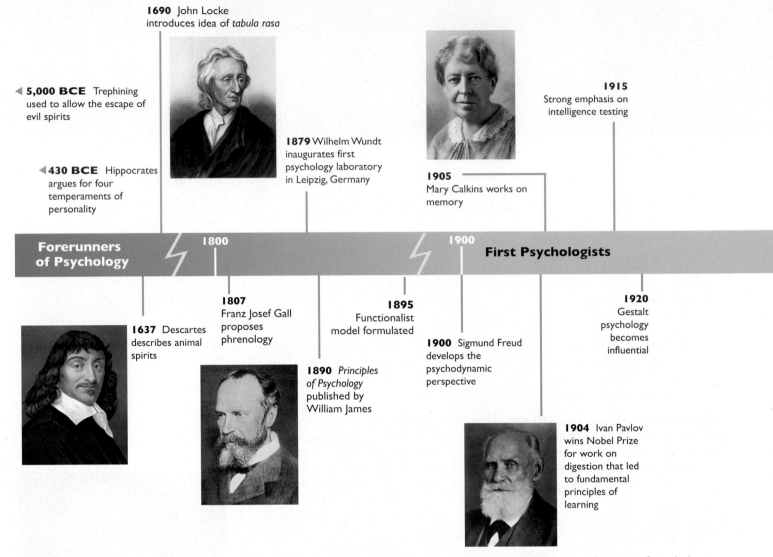

1690 John Locke introduces idea of *tabula rasa*

5,000 BCE Trephining used to allow the escape of evil spirits

430 BCE Hippocrates argues for four temperaments of personality

1879 Wilhelm Wundt inaugurates first psychology laboratory in Leipzig, Germany

1915 Strong emphasis on intelligence testing

1905 Mary Calkins works on memory

Forerunners of Psychology   **1800**

First Psychologists   **1900**

1807 Franz Josef Gall proposes phrenology

1637 Descartes describes animal spirits

1895 Functionalist model formulated

1920 Gestalt psychology becomes influential

1900 Sigmund Freud develops the psychodynamic perspective

1890 *Principles of Psychology* published by William James

1904 Ivan Pavlov wins Nobel Prize for work on digestion that led to fundamental principles of learning

FIGURE 1 This time line illustrates the major milestones in the development of psychology.

a sentence printed on a card—and asked them to describe, in their own words and in as much detail as they could, what they were experiencing. Wundt argued that by analyzing their reports, psychologists could come to a better understanding of the structure of the mind.

Over time, psychologists challenged Wundt's approach. They became increasingly dissatisfied with the assumption that introspection could reveal the structure of the mind. Introspection was not a truly scientific technique, because there were few ways an outside observer could confirm the accuracy of others' introspections. Moreover, people had difficulty describing some kinds of inner experiences, such as emotional responses. Those drawbacks led to the development of new approaches, which largely replaced structuralism.

The perspective that replaced structuralism is known as functionalism. Rather than focusing on the mind's structure, **functionalism** concentrated on what the mind *does* and how behavior *functions*. Functionalists, whose perspective became prominent in the early 1900s, asked what role behavior plays in allowing people to adapt to their environments. For example, a functionalist might examine the function of the emotion of fear in preparing us to deal with emergency situations.

Led by the American psychologist William James, the functionalists examined how behavior allows people to satisfy their needs and how our "stream of consciousness"

Functionalism: An early approach to psychology that concentrated on what the mind does—the functions of mental activity—and the role of behavior in allowing people to adapt to their environments.

1924
John B. Watson, an early behaviorist, publishes *Behaviorism*

1980
Jean Piaget, an influential developmental psychologist, dies

1957 Leon Festinger publishes *A Theory of Cognitive Dissonance*, producing a major impact on social psychology

2010
New subfields develop such as clinical neuropsychology and evolutionary psychology

1951
Carl Rogers publishes *Client-Centered Therapy*, helping to establish the humanistic perspective

1990 Greater emphasis on multiculturalism and diversity

2000

Modern Psychology

1953
B. F. Skinner publishes *Science and Human Behavior*, advocating the behavioral perspective

1969
Arguments regarding the genetic basis of IQ fuel lingering controversies

1985 Increasing emphasis on cognitive perspective

1928
Leta Stetter Hollingworth publishes work on adolescence

1981 David Hubel and Torsten Wiesel win Nobel Prize for work on vision cells in the brain

1954
Abraham Maslow publishes *Motivation and Personality*, developing the concept of self-actualization

2000
Elizabeth Loftus does pioneering work on false memory and eyewitness testimony

permits us to adopt to our environment. The American educator John Dewey drew on functionalism to develop the field of school psychology, proposing ways to best meet students' educational needs.

Another important reaction to structuralism was the development of gestalt psychology in the early 1900s. **Gestalt psychology** emphasizes how perception is organized. Instead of considering the individual parts that make up thinking, gestalt psychologists took the opposite tack, studying how people consider individual elements together as units or wholes. Led by German scientists such as Hermann Ebbinghaus and Max Wertheimer, gestalt psychologists proposed that "The whole is different from the sum of its parts," meaning that our perception, or understanding, of objects is greater and more meaningful than the individual elements that make up our perceptions. Gestalt psychologists have made substantial contributions to our understanding of perception.

Gestalt (geh SHTALLT) psychology: An approach to psychology that focuses on the organization of perception and thinking in a "whole" sense rather than on the individual elements of perception.

WOMEN IN PSYCHOLOGY: FOUNDING MOTHERS

As in many scientific fields, social prejudices hindered women's participation in the early development of psychology. For example, many universities would not even admit women to their graduate psychology programs in the early 1900s.

⚠️ **Study**ALERT

Knowing the basic outlines of the history of the field will help you understand how today's major perspectives have evolved.

Despite the hurdles they faced, women made notable contributions to psychology, although their impact on the field was largely overlooked until recently. For example, Margaret Floy Washburn (1871–1939) was the first woman to receive a doctorate in psychology, and she did important work on animal behavior. Leta Stetter Hollingworth (1886–1939) was one of the first psychologists to focus on child development and on women's issues. She collected data to refute the view, popular in the early 1900s, that women's abilities periodically declined during parts of the menstrual cycle (Hollingworth, 1943/1990; Denmark & Fernandez, 1993; Furumoto & Scarborough, 2002).

Mary Calkins (1863–1930), who studied memory in the early part of the 20th century, became the first female president of the American Psychological Association. Karen Horney (pronounced "HORN-eye") (1885–1952) focused on the social and cultural factors behind personality, and June Etta Downey (1875–1932) spearheaded the study of personality traits and became the first woman to head a psychology department at a state university. Anna Freud (1895–1982), the daughter of Sigmund Freud, also made notable contributions to the treatment of abnormal behavior, and Mamie Phipps Clark (1917–1983) carried out pioneering work on how children of color grew to recognize racial differences (Horney, 1937; Stevens & Gardner, 1982; Lal, 2002).

Today's Perspectives

The men and women who laid the foundations of psychology shared a common goal: to explain and understand behavior using scientific methods. Seeking to achieve the same goal, the tens of thousands of psychologists who followed those early pioneers embraced—and often rejected—a variety of broad perspectives.

The perspectives of psychology offer distinct outlooks and emphasize different factors. Just as we can use more than one map to find our way around a particular region—for instance, a map that shows roads and highways and another map that shows major landmarks—psychologists developed a variety of approaches to understanding behavior. When considered jointly, the different perspectives provide the means to explain behavior in its amazing variety.

Today, the field of psychology includes five major perspectives (summarized in Figure 2). These broad perspectives emphasize different aspects of behavior and mental processes, and each takes our understanding of behavior in a somewhat different direction.

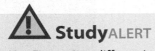

StudyALERT

Use Figure 2 to differentiate the five perspectives, which are important because they provide a foundation for every topic covered throughout the text.

Neuroscience

Views behavior from the perspective of biological functioning

Psychodynamic

Believes behavior is motivated by inner, unconscious forces over which a person has little control

Behavioral

Focuses on observable behavior

Cognitive

Examines how people understand and think about the world

Humanistic

Contends that people can control their behavior and that they naturally try to reach their full potential

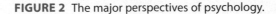

FIGURE 2 The major perspectives of psychology.

THE NEUROSCIENCE PERSPECTIVE: BLOOD, SWEAT, AND FEARS

When we get down to the basics, humans are animals made of skin and bones. The **neuroscience perspective** considers how people and nonhumans function biological-ly: how individual nerve cells are joined together, how the inheritance of certain char-acteristics from parents and other ancestors influences behavior, how the functioning of the body affects hopes and fears, which behaviors are instinctual, and so forth. Even more complex kinds of behaviors, such as a baby's response to strangers, are viewed as having critical biological components by psychologists who embrace the neurosci-ence perspective. This perspective includes the study of heredity and evolution, which considers how heredity may influence behavior; and behavioral neuroscience, which examines how the brain and the nervous system affect behavior.

Because every behavior ultimately can be broken down into its biological compo-nents, the neuroscience perspective has broad appeal. Psychologists who subscribe to this perspective have made major contributions to the understanding and betterment of human life, ranging from cures for certain types of deafness to drug treatments for people with severe mental disorders. Furthermore, advances in methods for examining the anatomy and functioning of the brain have permitted the neuroscientific perspec-tive to extend its influence across a broad range of subfields in psychology. (We'll see examples of these methods throughout this book in the *Neuroscience and Life* feature.)

Neuroscience perspective: The approach that views behavior from the perspective of the brain, the nervous system, and other biological functions.

THE PSYCHODYNAMIC PERSPECTIVE: UNDERSTANDING THE INNER PERSON

To many people who have never taken a psychology course, psychology begins and ends with the psychodynamic perspective. Proponents of the **psychodynamic perspective** argue that behavior is motivated by inner forces and conflicts about which we have little awareness or control. They view dreams and slips of the tongue as indi-cations of what a person is truly feeling within a seething cauldron of unconscious psychic activity.

The origins of the psychodynamic view are linked to one person: Sigmund Freud. Freud was a Viennese physician in the early 1900s whose ideas about unconscious determinants of behavior had a revolutionary effect on 20th-century thinking, not just in psychology but in related fields as well. Although some of the original Freudian principles have been roundly criticized, the contemporary psychodynamic perspec-tive has provided a means not only to understand and treat some kinds of psycho-logical disorders but also to understand everyday phenomena such as prejudice and aggression.

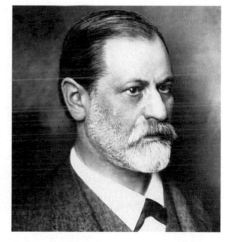

Sigmund Freud

THE BEHAVIORAL PERSPECTIVE: OBSERVING THE OUTER PERSON

Whereas the neuroscience and psychodynamic approaches look inside the organism to determine the causes of its behavior, the behavioral perspective takes a very differ-ent approach. The **behavioral perspective** grew out of a rejection of psychology's early emphasis on the inner workings of the mind. Instead, behaviorists suggested that the field should focus on observable behavior that can be measured objectively.

John B. Watson was the first major American psychologist to advocate a behav-ioral approach. Working in the 1920s, Watson was adamant in his view that one could gain a complete understanding of behavior by studying and modifying the environ-ment in which people operate.

In fact, Watson believed rather optimistically that it was possible to elicit any desired type of behavior by controlling a person's environment. This philosophy is clear in his own words: "Give me a dozen healthy infants, well-formed, and my own specified world to bring them up in and I'll guarantee to take any one at random and train him to become any type of specialist I might select—doctor, lawyer, artist, merchant-chief, and

Psychodynamic perspective: The approach based on the view that behavior is motivated by unconscious inner forces over which the individual has little control.

Behavioral perspective: The approach that suggests that observable, measur-able behavior should be the focus of study.

yes, even beggar-man and thief, regardless of his talents, penchants, tendencies, abilities, vocations and race of his ancestors" (Watson, 1924).

The behavioral perspective was championed by B. F. Skinner, a pioneer in the field. Much of our understanding of how people learn new behaviors is based on the behavioral perspective. As we will see, the behavioral perspective crops up along every byway of psychology. Along with its influence in the area of learning processes, this perspective has made contributions in such diverse areas as treating mental disorders, curbing aggression, resolving sexual problems, and ending drug addiction.

THE COGNITIVE PERSPECTIVE: IDENTIFYING THE ROOTS OF UNDERSTANDING

Cognitive perspective: The approach that focuses on how people think, understand, and know about the world.

Efforts to understand behavior lead some psychologists straight into the mind. Evolving in part from structuralism and in part as a reaction to behaviorism, which focused so heavily on observable behavior and the environment, the **cognitive perspective** focuses on how people think, understand, and know about the world. The emphasis is on learning how people comprehend and represent the outside world within themselves and how our ways of thinking about the world influence our behavior.

Many psychologists who adhere to the cognitive perspective compare human thinking to the workings of a computer, which takes in information and transforms, stores, and retrieves it. In their view, thinking is *information processing*.

Psychologists who rely on the cognitive perspective ask questions on subjects ranging from how people make decisions to whether a person can watch television and study at the same time. The common elements that link cognitive approaches are an emphasis on how people understand and think about the world and an interest in describing the patterns and irregularities in the operation of our minds.

THE HUMANISTIC PERSPECTIVE: THE UNIQUE QUALITIES OF THE HUMAN SPECIES

Humanistic perspective: The approach that suggests that all individuals naturally strive to grow, develop, and be in control of their lives and behavior.

Rejecting the view that behavior is determined largely by automatically unfolding biological forces, unconscious processes, or the environment, the **humanistic perspective** instead suggests that all individuals naturally strive to grow, develop, and be in control of their lives and behavior. Humanistic psychologists maintain that each of us has the capacity to seek and reach fulfillment.

According to Carl Rogers and Abraham Maslow, who were central figures in the development of the humanistic perspective, people will strive to reach their full potential if they are given the opportunity. The emphasis of the humanistic perspective is on *free will*, the ability to freely make decisions about one's own behavior and life. The notion of free will stands in contrast to *determinism*, which sees behavior as caused, or determined, by things beyond a person's control.

The humanistic perspective assumes that people have the ability to make their own choices about their behavior rather than relying on societal standards. More than any other approach, it stresses the role of psychology in enriching people's lives and helping them achieve self-fulfillment. By reminding psychologists of their commitment to the individual person in society, the humanistic perspective has been an important influence.

It is important not to let the abstract qualities of the broad approaches we have discussed lull you into thinking that they are purely theoretical: These perspectives underlie ongoing work of a practical nature, as we will discuss throughout this book. To start seeing how psychology can improve everyday life, read the *Applying Psychology in the 21st Century* box.

Psychology Matters

"Investigators search for clues at site of suicide bombing."

"Five students injured in high-school shooting."

"Eyewitness to killing proves unable to provide reliable clues."

"Cell phones blamed for rise in traffic fatalities."

"Childhood obesity linked to diabetes."

A quick review of any day's news headlines reminds us that the world is beset by a variety of stubborn problems that resist easy solutions. At the same time, a considerable number of psychologists are devoting their energies and expertise to addressing these problems and improving the human condition. Let's consider some of the ways in which psychology has addressed and helped work toward solutions of major societal problems (Zimbardo, 2004):

- **What are the causes of terrorism?** What motivates suicide bombers? Are they psychologically disordered, or can their behavior be seen as a rational response to a particular system of beliefs? As we'll see in Module 48 when we discuss abnormal behavior, psychologists are gaining an understanding of the factors that lead people to embrace suicide and to engage in terrorism to further a cause in which they deeply believe.

- **Why is aggression so prevalent, and how can more humane and peaceful alternatives be promoted?** Aggression, whether on the playground or the battlefield, is arguably the world's greatest problem. Psychologists have sought to understand how aggression begins in childhood and how it may be prevented. For example, Brad Bushman and Craig Anderson have been looking at the ways in which violent video games may result in heightened violence on the part of those who play them. They have found that people who play such games have an altered view of the world, seeing it as a more violent place. In addition, they are more apt to respond with aggression to others even when provoked only minimally (Bushman & Anderson, 2001, 2002; Crawford, 2002; Konijn, Bijvank, & Bushman, 2007).

Terrorism and its causes are among the world's most pressing issues. What can psychologists add to our understanding of the problem?

- **Why do eyewitnesses to crimes often remember the events inaccurately, and how can we increase the precision of eyewitness accounts?** Psychologists' research has come to an important conclusion: eyewitness testimony in criminal cases is often inaccurate and biased. Memories of crimes are often clouded by emotion, and the questions asked by police investigators often elicit inaccurate responses. Work by psychologists has been used to provide national guidelines for obtaining more accurate memories during criminal investigations (Loftus & Bernstein, 2005; Kassin, 2005; Busey & Loftus, 2007).

- **Does using a cell phone really impair people's driving ability?** Several states have enacted controversial laws banning cell phone usage while driving. Although many people feel that they are perfectly able to talk and drive at the same time, psychological research on attention tells a different story: merely talking on a cell phone—whether hands-free or not—impairs people's driving about as much as if they were legally drunk. The problem, of course, is that drivers' attention is taken away from the road and focused instead on the conversation (Strayer et al., 2005; Taggi et al., 2007).

- **What are the roots of obesity, and how can healthier eating and better physical fitness be encouraged?** Why are some people more predisposed to obesity than others are? What might be some social factors at play in the rising rate of obesity in childhood? As we'll discuss in Module 30, obesity is a complex problem with biological, psychological, and social underpinnings. Approaches to treating obesity therefore must take many factors into account in order to be successful. There is no magic bullet providing a quick fix, but psychologists recommend a number of strategies that help make weight-loss goals more achievable (Puhl & Latner, 2007).

These topics represent just a few of the issues that psychologists address on a daily basis. To further explore the many ways that psychology has an impact on everyday life, check out the Psychology Matters Web site of the American Psychological Association, which features psychological applications in everyday life, at www.psychologymatters.org.

RETHINK

What do *you* think are the major problems affecting society today? What are the psychological issues involved in these problems, and how might psychologists help find solutions to them?

RECAP/EVALUATE/RETHINK

RECAP

What are the origins of psychology?

- Wilhelm Wundt laid the foundation of psychology in 1879, when he opened his laboratory in Germany. (p. 15)
- Early perspectives that guided the work of psychologists were structuralism, functionalism, and gestalt theory. (p. 16)

What are the major approaches in contemporary psychology?

- The neuroscience approach focuses on the biological components of the behavior of people and animals. (p. 19)
- The psychodynamic perspective suggests that powerful, unconscious inner forces and conflicts about which people have little or no awareness are the primary determinants of behavior. (p. 19)
- The behavioral perspective deemphasizes internal processes and concentrates instead on observable, measurable behavior, suggesting that understanding and control of a person's environment are sufficient to fully explain and modify behavior. (p. 19)
- Cognitive approaches to behavior consider how people know, understand, and think about the world. (p. 20)
- The humanistic perspective emphasizes that people are uniquely inclined toward psychological growth and higher levels of functioning and that they will strive to reach their full potential. (p. 20)

EVALUATE

1. Wundt described psychology as the study of conscious experience, a perspective he called _____.
2. Early psychologists studied the mind by asking people to describe what they were experiencing when exposed to various stimuli. This procedure was known as _____.

3. The statement "In order to study human behavior, we must consider the whole of perception rather than its component parts" might be made by a person subscribing to which perspective of psychology?
4. Jeanne's therapist asks her to recount a violent dream she recently experienced in order to gain insight into the unconscious forces affecting her behavior. Jeanne's therapist is working from a _____ perspective.
5. "It is behavior that can be observed that should be studied, not the suspected inner workings of the mind." This statement was most likely made by someone with which perspective?
   a. cognitive perspective
   b. neuroscience perspective
   c. humanistic perspective
   d. behavioral perspective
6. "My therapist is wonderful! He always points out my positive traits. He dwells on my uniqueness and strength as an individual. I feel much more confident about myself—as if I'm really growing and reaching my potential." The therapist being described most likely follows a _____ perspective.

RETHINK

1. Focusing on one of the five major perspectives in use today (i.e., neuroscience, psychodynamic, behavioral, cognitive, and humanistic), can you describe the kinds of research questions and studies that researchers using that perspective might pursue?
2. *From a journalist's perspective:* Choose a current major political controversy. What psychological approaches or perspectives can be applied to that issue?

Answers to Evaluate Questions

1. structuralism; 2. introspection; 3. gestalt; 4. psychodynamic; 5. d; 6. humanistic

KEY TERMS

structuralism p. 15
introspection p. 15
functionalism p. 16

gestalt (geh SHTALLT)
   psychology p. 17
neuroscience perspective p. 19

psychodynamic perspective p. 19
behavioral perspective p. 19
cognitive perspective p. 20

humanistic perspective p. 20

Psychology's Key Issues and Controversies

As you consider the many topics and perspectives that make up psychology, ranging from a narrow focus on minute biochemical influences on behavior to a broad focus on social behaviors, you might find yourself thinking that the discipline lacks cohesion. However, the field is more unified than a first glimpse might suggest. For one thing, no matter what topical area a psychologist specializes in, he or she will rely primarily on one of the five major perspectives. For example, a developmental psychologist who specializes in the study of children could make use of the cognitive perspective or the psychodynamic perspective or any of the other major perspectives.

Psychologists also agree on what the key issues of the field are (see Figure 1). Although there are major arguments regarding how best to address and resolve the key issues, psychology is a unified science because psychologists of all perspectives agree that the issues must be addressed if the field is going to advance. As you contemplate these key issues, try not to think of them in "either/or" terms. Instead, consider the opposing viewpoints on each issue as the opposite ends of a continuum, with the positions of individual psychologists typically falling somewhere between the two ends.

Nature (heredity) versus nurture (environment) is one of the major issues that psychologists address. How much of people's behavior is due to their genetically determined nature (heredity), and how much is due to nurture, the influences of the physical and social environment in which a child is raised? Furthermore, what is

Key Concepts

What are psychology's key issues and controversies?

What is the future of psychology likely to hold?

⚠ StudyALERT

Use Figure 1 to learn the key issues that underlie every subfield of psychology.

Issue	Neuroscience	Psychodynamic	Behavioral	Cognitive	Humanistic
Nature (heredity) vs. nurture (environment)	Nature (heredity)	Nature (heredity)	Nurture (environment)	Both	Nurture (environment)
Conscious vs. unconscious determinants of behavior	Unconscious	Unconscious	Conscious	Both	Conscious
Observable behavior vs. internal mental processes	Internal emphasis	Internal emphasis	Observable emphasis	Internal emphasis	Internal emphasis
Free will vs. determinism	Determinism	Determinism	Determinism	Free will	Free will
Individual differences vs. universal principles	Universal emphasis	Universal emphasis	Both	Individual emphasis	Individual emphasis

FIGURE 1 Key issues in psychology and the positions taken by psychologists subscribing to the five major perspectives of psychology.

the interplay between heredity and environment? These questions have deep philosophical and historical roots, and they are involved in many topics in psychology.

A psychologist's take on this issue depends partly on which major perspective he or she subscribes to. For example, developmental psychologists whose focus is on how people grow and change throughout the course of their lives, may be most interested in learning more about hereditary influences if they follow a neuroscience perspective. In contrast, developmental psychologists who are proponents of the behavioral perspective would be more likely to focus on environment (Rutter, 2002, 2006).

However, every psychologist would agree that neither nature nor nurture alone is the sole determinant of behavior; rather, it is a combination of the two. In a sense, then, the real controversy involves how much of our behavior is caused by heredity and how much is caused by environmental influences.

A second major question addressed by psychologists concerns *conscious versus unconscious causes of behavior*. How much of our behavior is produced by forces of which we are fully aware, and how much is due to unconscious activity—mental processes that are not accessible to the conscious mind? This question represents one of the great controversies in the field of psychology. For example, clinical psychologists adopting a psychodynamic perspective argue that psychological disorders are brought about by unconscious factors, whereas psychologists employing the cognitive perspective suggest that psychological disorders largely are the result of faulty thinking processes.

The next issue is *observable behavior versus internal mental processes*. Should psychology concentrate solely on behavior that can be seen by outside observers, or should it focus on unseen thinking processes? Some psychologists, particularly those relying on the behavioral perspective, contend that the only legitimate source of information for psychologists is behavior that can be observed directly. Other psychologists, building on the cognitive perspective, argue that what goes on inside a person's mind is critical to understanding behavior, and so we must concern ourselves with mental processes.

Free will: The idea that behavior is caused primarily by choices that are made freely by the individual.

Determinism: The idea that people's behavior is produced primarily by factors outside of their willful control.

Free will versus determinism is another key issue. How much of our behavior is a matter of **free will** (choices made freely by an individual), and how much is subject to **determinism**, the notion that behavior is largely produced by factors beyond people's willful control? An issue long debated by philosophers, the free-will/determinism argument is also central to the field of psychology (Dennett, 2003; Cary, 2007).

For example, some psychologists who specialize in psychological disorders argue that people make intentional choices and that those who display so-called abnormal behavior should be considered responsible for their actions. Other psychologists disagree and contend that such individuals are the victims of forces beyond their control. The position psychologists take on this issue has important implications for the way they treat psychological disorders, especially in deciding whether treatment should be forced on people who don't want it.

The last of the key issues concerns *individual differences versus universal principles*. How much of our behavior is a consequence of our unique and special qualities, and how much reflects the culture and society in which we live? How much of our behavior is universally human? Psychologists who rely on the neuroscience perspective tend to look for universal principles of behavior, such as how the nervous system operates or the way certain hormones automatically prime us for sexual activity. Such psychologists concentrate on the similarities in our behavioral destinies despite vast differences in our upbringing. In contrast, psychologists who employ the humanistic perspective focus more on the uniqueness of every individual. They consider every person's behavior a reflection of distinct and special individual qualities.

The question of the degree to which psychologists can identify universal principles that apply to all people has taken on new significance in light of the tremendous demographic changes now occurring in the United States and around the world. As we discuss next, these changes raise new and critical issues for the discipline of psychology in the 21st century.

Exploring DIVERSITY

Understanding How Culture, Ethnicity, and Race Influence Behavior

A mother in Burr Ridge, Illinois, helps her son with his math assignment. After he complains that he is "terrible at math," she tries to cheer him up by saying, "Don't feel bad; some people are born to do well in math, and others have a lot of trouble with it. It's just the way things are." At the same time, on the other side of the world in Taipei, Taiwan, a mother is helping her daughter with her math homework. When the daughter complains that she's no good at math, the mother tells her to keep at it because everyone has pretty much the same ability in math, and it is hard work that guarantees success.

These two apparently simple parent-child exchanges reveal a deep difference in perspectives on the world. People in Europe and North America are far more likely to attribute success to unchanging causes, such as intelligence, than are people in Asia, who are more likely to attribute school performance to temporary, situational factors, such as the amount of expended effort.

These different perspectives may help explain the fact that Asian students often outperform U.S. students in international comparisons of student achievement. Asian students are taught that hard work and increased effort lead to academic success, and so they may be more willing to put in more effort to achieve success. In contrast, North American students tend to believe that their ability is fixed at birth and largely determines their success, and so they may be less willing to work hard (Chen & Stevenson, 1995; Leung, 2002; Pearce & Lin, 2007).

Our knowledge that people in different cultures can have very different views of the world underlines the importance of moving beyond North America and studying

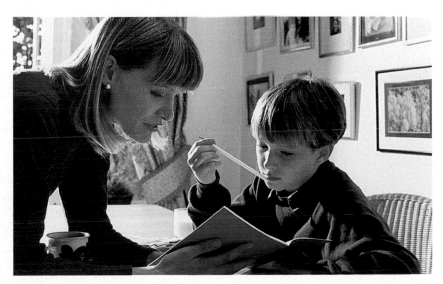

Members of different cultures attribute academic success to different factors. How might differing cultural perspectives affect the performance of Asian versus North American students?

other cultural groups in order to identify universal principles of behavior. Furthermore, broad cultural differences are not the only ones taken into account by psychologists in their attempts to identify general principles of behavior. Subcultural, ethnic, racial, and socioeconomic differences are increasingly important targets of study by psychologists (Tucker & Herman, 2002; Li, 2005; Cardemil, 2005).

Although the discipline is growing more aware of the importance of taking cultural and subcultural factors into account, progress has not been rapid in actual practice. For example, the amount of research conducted in the United States on groups other than white middle-class college students is woefully small.

There isn't even universal agreement on the use of terms such as *race* and *ethnic group*. Race, for instance, is a biological concept that, technically, should be used only to refer to classifications based on the physical characteristics of an organism or species. But in practice, the term has been used to denote anything from skin color to culture. In contrast, *ethnic group* and *ethnicity* are broader terms that refer to cultural background, nationality, religion, and language (Pääbo, 2001; Bonham, Warshauer-Baker, & Collins, 2005; Freeman, 2006).

To compound the difficulty, there are no universally acceptable names for races and ethnic groups. Psychologists—like other members of U.S. society—are divided on whether they should use the label *African American* (which focuses on geographical origins) or *black* (which focuses on skin color), just as they disagree about whether to use *Caucasian* or *white*, *Hispanic* or *Latino*, and *Native American* or *American Indian* (Phinney, 2003; CNPAAEMI, 2000; Wang & Sue, 2005).

Psychologists also know that the consequences of race cannot be understood without taking into account environmental and cultural factors. People's behavior is a joint product of their race and of the treatment they receive from others because of it. In sum, only by examining behavior across ethnic, cultural, and racial lines can psychologists differentiate principles that are universal from those that are culture-bound.

Psychology's Future

We have examined psychology's foundations, but what does the future hold for the discipline? Although the course of scientific development is notoriously difficult to predict, several trends seem likely:

- As its knowledge base grows, psychology will become increasingly specialized and new perspectives will evolve. For example, our growing understanding of the brain and the nervous system, combined with scientific advances in genetics and gene therapy, will allow psychologists to focus on *prevention* of psychological disorders rather than only on their treatment.

- The evolving sophistication of neuroscientific approaches is likely to have an increasing influence over other branches of psychology. For instance, social psychologists already are increasing their understanding of social behaviors such as persuasion by using brain scans as part of an evolving field known as *social neuroscience* (Harmon-Jones & Winkielman, 2007; Bunge & Wallis, 2008).

- Psychology's influence on issues of public interest also will grow. The major problems of our time—such as violence, terrorism, racial and ethnic prejudice, poverty, and environmental and technological disasters—have important psychological aspects (Zimbardo, 2004; Marshall et al., 2007; Hobfoll et al., 2007).

- Finally, as the population becomes more diverse, issues of diversity—embodied in the study of racial, ethnic, linguistic, and cultural factors—will become more important to psychologists providing services and doing research. The result will be a field that can provide an understanding of *human* behavior in its broadest sense (Leung & Blustein, 2000; Chang & Sue, 2005; Quintana et al., 2006).

"Expand Your Mind Beyond Virtual Reality . . . & Learn at the Speed of Light!" declares the sales pitch that arrives in the day's spam. "I have an astounding technology I'm going to share with you. Something so profound it will . . . transform your mind and soul forever."

From advertisements to television and radio talk shows to the Internet, we are subjected to a barrage of information about psychology. We are told that we can become better adjusted, smarter, more insightful, and happier individuals by learning the secrets that psychologists have revealed.

**BECOMING
AN INFORMED CONSUMER**
of Psychology
Thinking Critically About Psychology:
Distinguishing Legitimate
Psychology from Pseudo-Psychology

However, such promises are usually empty. So how can we separate accurate information, which is backed by science and objective research, from pseudo-psychology based on anecdotes, opinions, and even outright fraud? The best approach is to employ critical thinking techniques. Developed by psychologists who specialize in learning, memory, cognition, intelligence, and education, critical thinking procedures provide the tools to scrutinize assumptions, evaluate assertions, and think with greater precision (Halpern & Riggio, 2002; Lilienfeld, Lynn, & Lohr, 2003; Roediger & McCabe, 2007).

We'll be considering ways to boost critical thinking skills in *Becoming an Informed Consumer of Psychology* sections throughout the book. To get started, let's consider what you need in order to evaluate information of a psychological nature, whether the source is an advertisement, a television show, a magazine article, or even a book as seemingly reliable as a college textbook.

- For starters, know who is offering the information and advice. Are the providers of the information trained psychologists? What kinds of degrees do they have? Are they licensed? Are they affiliated with a particular institution? Before seriously relying on experts' advice, check out their credentials.

- Keep in mind that there is no free ride. If it is possible to solve major psychological ills by buying a $29.95 book, why do many people who suffer from such problems typically expend a considerable amount of time and money before they can be helped? If you could buy a computer program that would really "unlock the hidden truths" about others, wouldn't it be in widespread use? Be wary of simple, glib responses to major difficulties.

- Be aware that few universal cures exist for humankind's ills. No method or technique works for everyone. The range of difficulties attached to the human condition is so broad that any procedure that purports to resolve all problems is certain to disappoint.

- Finally, remember that no source of information or advice is definitive. The notion of infallibility is best left to the realm of religion, and you should approach psychological information and advice from a critical and thoughtful perspective.

RECAP/EVALUATE/RETHINK

RECAP

What are psychology's key issues and controversies?

- Psychology's key issues and controversies center on how much of human behavior is a product of nature or nurture, conscious or unconscious thoughts, observable actions or internal mental processes, free will or determinism, and individual differences or universal principles. (p. 23)

What is the future of psychology likely to hold?

- Psychology will become increasingly specialized, will pay greater attention to prevention instead of just treatment, will become more and more concerned with the public interest, and will take the growing diversity of the country's population into account more fully. (p. 26)

EVALUATE

1. The view that behavior is largely produced by factors beyond people's willful control is known as _____.

KEY TERMS

free will p. 24
determinism p. 24

2. In the nature-nurture issue, nature refers to heredity, and nurture refers to the _____.
3. Race is a biological concept, rather than a psychological one. True or false?

RETHINK

1. "The fact that some businesses now promote their ability to help people 'expand their minds beyond virtual reality' shows the great progress psychology has made lately." Criticize this statement in light of what you know about professional psychology and pseudo-psychology.
2. *From a social worker's perspective:* Imagine that you have a caseload of clients who come from diverse cultures, ethnicities, and races. How might you consider their diverse backgrounds when interacting with them and when assisting them with identifying and obtaining social services?

Answers to Evaluate Questions

1. determinism; 2. environment; 3. true

Psychology on the Web

1. Practice using several search strategies to find information on the Web about one of the key issues in psychology (e.g., free will versus determinism, nature versus nurture, or conscious versus unconscious determinants of behavior), using (a) a general-purpose search engine (such as Google at www.google.com) and (b) a more specialized search engine (such as Yahoo's Psychology section, under the "Social Science" heading, at www.yahoo.com). Summarize and then compare the kinds of information you have found through each strategy.

2. Search the Web for discussions of youth violence and try to find (a) an article in the general news media, (b) information from a psychological point of view (e.g., experimental information or recommendations for parents from a professional organization), and (c) political opinion or debate about how to address the issue of youth violence.

Epilogue

The field of psychology, as we have seen, is broad and diverse. It encompasses many different subfields and specialties practiced in a variety of settings, with new subfields continually arising. We have also seen that even within the various subfields of the field, it is possible to adopt several different approaches, including the neuroscience, psychodynamic, behavioral, cognitive, and humanistic perspectives.

For all its diversity, though, psychology focuses on certain key issues that serve to unify the field along common lines and shared findings. These issues will reappear as themes throughout this book as we discuss the work and accomplishments of psychologists in the many subfields of the discipline.

In light of what you've already learned about the field of psychology, reconsider the questions raised regarding the Virginia Tech massacre and answer the following questions:

1. If they were using the neuroscience perspective, on what kinds of factors might psychologists focus to explain people's fear responses to the shooter?
2. How would a psychologist using the psychodynamic perspective explain Cho's behavior differently from a psychologist using the cognitive perspective?
3. What aspects of the massacre would most interest a clinical psychologist? A social psychologist? A forensic psychologist?
4. What might be some ways in which both nature and nurture could have contributed to Cho's behavior?

CHAPTER 2

Psychological Research

Key Concepts for Chapter 2

A convenience store surveillance video shows each punch 91-year-old Leonard Sims took to the side of his face during a carjacking.

But the tape also caught a group of people standing only feet away.... "You can't really tell what they were focusing on," Maria Miller, a spokeswoman for the Wayne County prosecutor's office, said.

Miller said at least one bystander did report the May 4 attack outside the store in Detroit.

Sims was outside his car in the store parking lot about 8:30 p.m. when a man walked up and asked for a light for his cigarette, according to the prosecutor's office.

The man then punched Sims at least a half-dozen times in the side of his head while Sims held onto the car door. The video also shows the man using the door to knock Sims to the ground before taking the keys and driving off in the 2005 Chevy Malibu (Text from "Carjacker Beats 91-Year-Old Man as Bystanders Look On," The Associated Press, May 14, 2007. Used with permission of The Associated Press Copyright © 2007. All rights reserved. From *Grand Rapids Press*, May 15, 2007, p. B6.).

Looking Ahead

Why didn't the bystanders rush to help the 91-year-old Sims when he was attacked? Did they not notice it, even though they were only a few feet away? Or did they simply decide not to bother? Whatever the reason, they offered no help to him, and he sustained serious injuries.

If Sims's experience were an isolated incident, we might be able to attribute the bystanders' inaction to something particular about the situation or to the specific people involved. However, events such as this one are all too common.

In one infamous case, a woman named Kitty Genovese was attacked by a man near an apartment building in Queens, New York. At one point during the assault, which lasted 30 minutes, she managed to free herself and screamed, "Oh, my God, he stabbed me. Please help me!" In the stillness of the night, no fewer than 38 neighbors heard her screams. Windows opened, and lights went on. One couple pulled chairs up to the window and turned off the lights so that they could see better. Someone called out, "Let that girl alone." But shouts were not enough to scare off the killer. He chased Genovese, stabbing her eight more times, and sexually molested her before leaving her to die. And how many of those 38 witnesses came to her aid? As in Sims's case, not one person helped (Rogers & Eftimiades, 1995).

Such incidents remain dismaying—and perplexing. Why don't bystanders intervene in such situations, particularly when there are many of them who could potentially offer help? At the time of the Kitty Genovese murder, editorial writers suggested that the incidents could be attributed to the basic shortcomings

of "human nature," but such an assumption is woefully inadequate. Many people have risked their own lives to help others in dangerous situations, and so "human nature" encompasses a wide range of both negative and positive responses.

Psychologists puzzled over the problem for many years. After much research they reached an unexpected conclusion: Kitty Genovese probably would have been better off if only a few people, rather than many, had heard her cries for help. In fact, if only one bystander had been present, the chances that this person would have intervened might have been fairly high. It turns out that the fewer the witnesses to an assault, the better the victim's chances of getting help.

How did psychologists come to such a curious conclusion? After all, logic and common sense clearly suggest that more bystanders would produce a greater likelihood that someone would help a person in need. This seeming contradiction—and the way psychologists resolved it—illustrates a central challenge for the field of psychology: asking useful questions about the unknown, and getting valid answers.

Like professionals in any science, psychologists are vitally concerned with refining and expanding knowledge within their field. In the following modules we'll see how psychologists pose questions of interest and answer them through scientific research. We'll find that the answers psychologists obtain from their research not only advance our understanding of behavior, but also offer the potential to improve the human condition.

The Scientific Method

"Birds of a feather flock together" . . . or "Opposites attract"? "Two heads are better than one" . . . or "If you want a thing done well, do it yourself"? "The more the merrier" . . . or "Two's company, three's a crowd"?

If we were to rely on common sense to understand behavior, we'd have considerable difficulty—especially because commonsense views are often contradictory. In fact, one of the major undertakings for the field of psychology is to develop suppositions about behavior and to determine which of those suppositions are accurate.

Psychologists—as well as scientists in other disciplines—meet the challenge of posing appropriate questions and properly answering them by relying on the scientific method. The **scientific method** is the approach used by psychologists to systematically acquire knowledge and understanding about behavior and other phenomena of interest. As illustrated in Figure 1, it consists of four main steps: (1) identifying questions of interest, (2) formulating an explanation, (3) carrying out research designed to support or refute the explanation, and (4) communicating the findings.

Key Concepts

What is the scientific method?

What role do theories and hypotheses play in psychological research?

Scientific method: The approach through which psychologists systematically acquire knowledge and understanding about behavior and other phenomena of interest.

FIGURE 1 The scientific method, which encompasses the process of identifying, asking, and answering questions, is used by psychologists, and by researchers from every other scientific discipline, to come to an understanding about the world. What do you think are the advantages of this method?

 StudyALERT

Use Figure 1 to remember the four steps of the scientific method (identifying questions, formulating an explanation, carrying out research, and communicating the findings).

Theories:
Specifying Broad Explanations

In using the scientific method, psychologists start by identifying questions of interest. We have all been curious at some time about our observations of everyday behavior. If you have ever asked yourself why a particular teacher is so easily annoyed, why a friend is always late for appointments, or how your dog understands your commands, you have been formulating questions about behavior.

Psychologists, too, ask questions about the nature and causes of behavior. They may wish to explore explanations for everyday behaviors or for various phenomena. They may also pose questions that build on findings from their previous research or from research carried out by other psychologists. Or they may produce new questions that are based on curiosity, creativity, or insight.

Once a question has been identified, the next step in the scientific method is to develop a theory to explain the observed phenomenon. **Theories** are broad explanations and predictions concerning phenomena of interest. They provide a framework for understanding the relationships among a set of otherwise unorganized facts or principles.

All of us have developed our own informal theories of human behavior, such as "People are basically good" or "People's behavior is usually motivated by self-interest." However, psychologists' theories are more formal and focused. They are established on the basis of a careful study of the psychological literature to identify earlier relevant research and previously formulated theories, as well as psychologists' general knowledge of the field (Sternberg & Beall, 1991; McGuire, 1997).

Growing out of the diverse approaches employed by psychologists, theories vary both in their breadth and in their level of detail. For example, one theory might seek to explain and predict a phenomenon as broad as emotional experience. A narrower

Theories: Broad explanations and predictions concerning phenomena of interest.

theory might attempt to explain why people display the emotion of fear nonverbally after receiving a threat.

Psychologists Bibb Latané and John Darley, responding to the failure of bystanders to intervene when Kitty Genovese was murdered in New York, developed what they called a theory of *diffusion of responsibility* (Latané & Darley, 1970). According to their theory, the greater the number of bystanders or witnesses to an event that calls for helping behavior, the more the responsibility for helping is perceived to be shared by all the bystanders. Thus, the greater the number of bystanders in an emergency situation, the smaller the share of the responsibility each person feels—and the less likely it is that any single person will come forward to help.

Hypotheses:
Crafting Testable Predictions

Although the diffusion of responsibility theory seems to make sense, it represented only the beginning phase of Latané and Darley's investigative process. Their next step was to devise a way to test their theory. To do this, they needed to create a hypothesis. A **hypothesis** is a prediction stated in a way that allows it to be tested. Hypotheses stem from theories; they help test the underlying soundness of theories.

In the same way that we develop our own broad theories about the world, we also construct hypotheses about events and behavior. Those hypotheses can range from trivialities (such as why our English instructor wears those weird shirts) to more meaningful matters (such as what is the best way to study for a test). Although we rarely test these hypotheses systematically, we do try to determine whether they are right. Perhaps we try comparing two strategies: cramming the night before an exam versus spreading out our study over several nights. By assessing which approach yields better test performance, we have created a way to compare the two strategies.

A hypothesis must be restated in a way that will allow it to be tested, which involves creating an operational definition. An **operational definition** is the translation of a hypothesis into specific, testable procedures that can be measured and observed.

There is no single way to go about devising an operational definition for a hypothesis; it depends on logic, the equipment and facilities available, the psychological perspective being employed, and ultimately the creativity of the researcher. For example, one researcher might develop a hypothesis that uses as an operational definition of "fear" an increase in heart rate. In contrast, another psychologist might use as an operational definition of "fear" a written response to the question "How much fear are you experiencing at this moment?"

Latané and Darley's hypothesis was a straightforward prediction from their more general theory of diffusion of responsibility: The more people who witness an emergency situation, the less likely it is that help will be given to a victim. They could, of course, have chosen another hypothesis (try to think of one!), but their initial formulation seemed to offer the most direct test of the theory.

Psychologists rely on formal theories and hypotheses for many reasons. For one thing, theories and hypotheses allow them to make sense of unorganized, separate observations and bits of information by permitting them to place the pieces within a coherent framework. In addition, theories and hypotheses offer psychologists the opportunity to move beyond known facts and make deductions about unexplained phenomena and develop ideas for future investigation (Howitt & Cramer, 2000; Cohen, 2003; Gurin, 2006).

In short, the scientific method, with its emphasis on theories and hypotheses, helps psychologists pose appropriate questions. With properly stated questions in hand, psychologists then can choose from a variety of research methods to find answers.

Hypothesis: A prediction, stemming from a theory, stated in a way that allows it to be tested.

Operational definition: The translation of a hypothesis into specific, testable procedures that can be measured and observed.

 StudyALERT

Remember that a theory is a broad explanation, while a hypothesis is a more narrow prediction.

RECAP/EVALUATE/RETHINK

RECAP

What is the scientific method?

- The scientific method is the approach psychologists use to understand behavior. It consists of four steps: identifying questions of interest, formulating an explanation, carrying out research that is designed to support or refute the explanation, and communicating the findings. (p. 33)

What role do theories and hypotheses play in psychological research?

- Research in psychology is guided by theories (broad explanations and predictions regarding phenomena of interest) and hypotheses (theory-based predictions stated in a way that allows them to be tested). (p. 34)

- To test a hypothesis, researchers must formulate an operational definition, which translates the abstract concepts of the hypothesis into the actual procedures used in the study. (p. 35)

EVALUATE

1. An explanation for a phenomenon of interest is known as a _____.
2. To test this explanation, a researcher must state it in terms of a testable question known as a _____.

3. An experimenter is interested in studying the relationship between hunger and aggression. She decides that she will measure aggression by counting the number of times a participant will hit a punching bag. In this case, her _____ definition of aggression is the number of times the participant hits the bag.

RETHINK

1. Starting with the theory that diffusion of responsibility causes responsibility for helping to be shared among bystanders, Latané and Darley derived the hypothesis that the more people who witness an emergency situation, the less likely it is that help will be given to a victim. How many other hypotheses can you think of that are based on the same theory of diffusion of responsibility?

2. *From a lawyer's perspective:* Imagine that you are assigned to a case similar to the one of Kitty Genovese. Your supervisor, who is unfamiliar with psychological research, asks you to provide information about the eyewitnesses to explain why they did not help her. What would you include in your report?

Answers to Evaluate Questions

1. theory; 2. hypothesis; 3. operational

KEY TERMS

scientific method p. 33
theories p. 34
hypothesis p. 35
operational definition p. 35

Conducting Psychological Research

Research—systematic inquiry aimed at the discovery of new knowledge—is a central ingredient of the scientific method in psychology. It provides the key to understanding the degree to which hypotheses (and the theories behind them) are accurate.

Just as we can apply different theories and hypotheses to explain the same phenomena, we can use a number of alternative methods to conduct research. As we consider the major tools psychologist's use to conduct research, keep in mind that their relevance extends beyond testing and evaluating hypotheses in psychology. All of us carry out elementary forms of research on our own. For instance, a supervisor might evaluate an employee's performance; a physician might systematically test the effects of different doses of a drug on a patient; a salesperson might compare different persuasive strategies. Each of these situations draws on the research practices we are about to discuss.

Let's begin by considering several types of *descriptive research* designed to systematically investigate a person, group, or patterns of behavior. These methods include archival research, naturalistic observation, survey research, and case studies.

Key Concepts

What research methods do psychologists use?

How do psychologists establish cause-and-effect relationships in research studies?

Archival Research

Suppose that, like the psychologists Latané and Darley (1970), you were interested in finding out more about emergency situations in which bystanders did not provide help. One of the first places you might turn to would be historical accounts. By searching newspaper records, for example, you might find support for the notion that a decrease in helping behavior historically has accompanied an increase in the number of bystanders.

Using newspaper articles is an example of archival research. In **archival research**, existing data, such as census documents, college records, and newspaper clippings, are examined to test a hypothesis. For example, college records may be used to determine if there are gender differences in academic performance.

Archival research is a relatively inexpensive means of testing a hypothesis because someone else has already collected the basic data. Of course, the use of existing data has several drawbacks. For one thing, the data may not be in a form that allows the researcher to test a hypothesis fully. The information could be incomplete, or it could have been collected haphazardly (Simonton, 2000; Riniolo, Koledin, Drakulic, & Payne, 2003; Vega, 2006).

Most attempts at archival research are hampered by the simple fact that records with the necessary information often do not exist. In these instances, researchers often turn to another research method: naturalistic observation.

Archival research: Research in which existing data, such as census documents, college records, and newspaper clippings, are examined to test a hypothesis.

Naturalistic Observation

In **naturalistic observation**, the investigator observes some naturally occurring behavior and does not make a change in the situation. For example, a researcher investigating helping behavior might observe the kind of help given to victims in a high-crime

Naturalistic observation: Research in which an investigator simply observes some naturally occurring behavior and does not make a change in the situation.

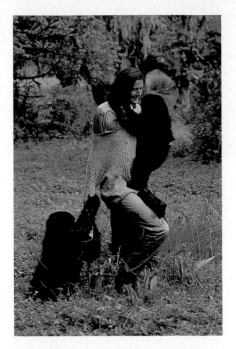

Dian Fossey, a pioneer in the study of endangered mountain gorillas in their native habitat, relied on naturalistic observation for her research. What are the advantages of this approach?

Survey research: Research in which people chosen to represent a larger population are asked a series of questions about their behavior, thoughts, or attitudes.

Case study: An in-depth, intensive investigation of an individual or small group of people.

area of a city. The important point to remember about naturalistic observation is that the researcher simply records what occurs, making no modification in the situation that is being observed (Schutt, 2001; Moore, 2002; Rustin, 2006).

Although the advantage of naturalistic observation is obvious—we get a sample of what people do in their "natural habitat"—there is also an important drawback: the inability to control any of the factors of interest. For example, we might find so few naturally occurring instances of helping behavior that we would be unable to draw any conclusions. Because naturalistic observation prevents researchers from making changes in a situation, they must wait until the appropriate conditions occur. Furthermore, if people know they are being watched, they may alter their reactions and produce behavior that is not truly representative.

Survey Research

There is no more straightforward way of finding out what people think, feel, and do than asking them directly. For this reason, surveys are an important research method. In **survey research**, a *sample* of people chosen to represent a larger group of interest (a *population*) is asked a series of questions about their behavior, thoughts, or attitudes. Survey methods have become so sophisticated that even with a very small sample researchers are able to infer with great accuracy how a larger group would respond. For instance, a sample of just a few thousand voters is sufficient to predict within one or two percentage points who will win a presidential election—if the representative sample is chosen with care (Sommer & Sommer, 2001; Groves et al., 2004; Igo, 2006).

Researchers investigating helping behavior might conduct a survey by asking people to complete a questionnaire in which they indicate their reluctance for giving aid to someone. Similarly, researchers interested in learning about sexual practices have carried out surveys to learn which practices are common and which are not and to chart changing notions of sexual morality over the last several decades.

However, survey research has several potential pitfalls. For one thing, if the sample of people who are surveyed is not representative of the broader population of interest, the results of the survey will have little meaning. For instance, if a sample of voters in a town only includes Republicans, it would hardly be useful for predicting the results of an election in which both Republicans and Democrats are voting (Daley, 2003; Dale, 2006).

In addition, survey respondents may not want to admit to holding socially undesirable attitudes. (Most racists know they are racists and might not want to admit it.) And in some cases, people may not even be consciously aware of what their true attitudes are, or why they hold them. To overcome such problems, researchers are developing alternative, and often ingenious, research techniques, as we consider in the *Applying Psychology in the 21st Century* box.

The Case Study

When a terrorist drove his car into a Scotland airport in 2007, many people wondered what it was about his personality or background that might have led to his behavior. To answer this question, psychologists might conduct a case study. In contrast to a survey, in which many people are studied, a **case study** is an in-depth, intensive investigation of a single individual or a small group. Case studies often include *psychological testing*, a procedure in which a carefully designed set of questions is used to gain some insight into the personality of the individual or group (Schaw, 2000; Gass et al., 2000; Addus, Chen, & Khan, 2007).

When case studies are used as a research technique, the goal is often not only to learn about the few individuals being examined but also to use

"This is the New York 'Times'
Business Poll again, Mr. Landau.
Do you feel better or worse about the economy
than you did twenty minutes ago?"

Taking the Pepsi Challenge: This Is Your Brain on Coca-Cola (and Pepsi)

Thirty years ago, Pepsi-Cola launched a revolutionary new marketing campaign that would become famous for its simplicity and persuasiveness. Called the "Pepsi Challenge," this campaign used basic principles of the scientific method to demonstrate that people preferred the taste of Pepsi to its rival, Coca-Cola. In a series of blind taste tests, people on the street were offered samples of both colas in unmarked cups and asked which they preferred. Viewers were then treated to the shocked reactions of Coke lovers when their preferred choice was revealed to be Pepsi.

Although the Pepsi Challenge has long been advertising history, neuroscientist Read Montague couldn't let go of a nagging unresolved question: If people prefer the taste of Pepsi, why has Coke remained so much more popular? Contrary to the logical prediction of a purely economical standpoint, people were making the irrational decision to buy the product they liked less. Was there something besides taste that was influencing their preference?

To answer this question, Montague replicated and extended the original Pepsi challenge in the laboratory. First, he gave people samples of Pepsi and Coke and asked which they liked better. When the cups were unlabeled, the tasters showed no particular preference for either cola (so much for Pepsi's original claim). But here's where the research got interesting: when one of the samples was labeled as Coke, most of the tasters said that sample tasted better—even though the other sample they tasted was also Coca-Cola. On the other hand, when one of the samples was labeled as Pepsi, the tasters again showed no particular preference. It seemed that brand

Neuroscience in Your Life

FIGURE 1 In a study showing the power of brand names, when a drink was labeled as Coke, several areas of the brain showed greater activation than when participants were unaware if the drink was Coke. Specifically, when participants knew they were tasting Coke, brain regions associated with memory and emotional influences on behavior became active, in addition to the appetite reward area. The specific areas that showed more activation included the hippocampus, the left parahippocampal cortex, midbrain, and dorsolateral prefrontal cortex. (Source: McClure et al., 2004, p. 384.)

name was more important than actual taste in determining people's cola preferences (McClure et al., 2004; Montague, 2006).

But Montague didn't stop there; he then recreated the Pepsi Challenge yet again—this time in a brain scanner. People took the same series of taste tests as before, but instead of asking their preference, the researchers used a functional magnetic resonance imaging (fMRI) scan to detect which areas of the tasters' brains were active at each moment. When the tasters did not know what cola they were tasting, only a region of the brain associated with appetite rewards became active. The same thing happened when they knowingly tasted Pepsi. But when the tasters were knowingly tasting Coca-Cola, their brains responded differently: in addition to the appetite reward area, other brain regions that are associated with memory and with emotional influences on behavior also became active (see Figure 1).

These findings suggest that the Coca-Cola brand image is so well imprinted in people's minds that information about the

brand gets called up by the brain and influences their preferences—essentially overriding objective information about Coca-Cola's actual taste. Montague stumbled onto neurological evidence that advertising can have a powerful influence on consumers' choices by changing the ways in which they think about products. Companies have since seized upon brain scanning as a technique for assessing and refining their advertising strategies—a practice that is part of the emerging science of *neuroeconomics* (Lehrer, 2006; McCabe, 2006; Oullier & Kelso, 2006).

- Why might people prefer a brand-name product over an unlabeled one, even when they are both exactly the same?
- Do you think there is anything inappropriate about companies using brain-scan research to develop advertisements that are better able to produce the desired reaction in people?

the insights gained from the study to improve our understanding of people in general. Sigmund Freud developed his theories through case studies of individual patients. Similarly, case studies of the London bombers might help identify others who are prone to violence.

The drawback to case studies? If the individuals examined are unique in certain ways, it is impossible to make valid generalizations to a larger population. Still, they sometimes lead the way to new theories and treatments for psychological disorders.

Correlational Research

Variables: Behaviors, events, or other characteristics that can change, or vary, in some way.

Correlational research: Research in which the relationship between two sets of variables is examined to determine whether they are associated, or "correlated."

In using the descriptive research methods we have discussed, researchers often wish to determine the relationship between two variables. **Variables** are behaviors, events, or other characteristics that can change, or vary, in some way. For example, in a study to determine whether the amount of studying makes a difference in test scores, the variables would be study time and test scores.

In **correlational research**, two sets of variables are examined to determine whether they are associated, or "correlated." The strength and direction of the relationship between the two variables are represented by a mathematical statistic known as a *correlation* (or, more formally, a *correlation coefficient*), which can range from +1.0 to −1.0.

A *positive correlation* indicates that as the value of one variable increases, we can predict that the value of the other variable will also increase. For example, if we predict that the more time students spend studying for a test, the higher their grades on the test will be, and that the less they study, the lower their test scores will be, we are expecting to find a positive correlation. (Higher values of the variable "amount of study time" would be associated with higher values of the variable "test score," and lower values of "amount of study time" would be associated with lower values of "test score.") The correlation, then, would be indicated by a positive number, and the stronger the association was between studying and test scores, the closer the number would be to +1.0. For example, we might find a correlation of +.85 between test scores and amount of study time, indicating a strong positive association.

In contrast, a *negative correlation* tells us that as the value of one variable increases, the value of the other decreases. For instance, we might predict that as the number of hours spent studying increases, the number of hours spent partying decreases. Here we are expecting a negative correlation, ranging between 0 and −1.0. More studying is associated with less partying, and less studying is associated with more partying. The stronger the association between studying and partying is, the closer the correlation will be to −1.0. For instance, a correlation of −.85 would indicate a strong negative association between partying and studying.

Of course, it's quite possible that little or no relationship exists between two variables. For instance, we would probably not expect to find a relationship between number of study hours and height. Lack of a relationship would be indicated by a correlation close to 0. For example, if we found a correlation of −.02 or +.03, it would indicate that there is virtually no association between the two variables; knowing how much someone studies does not tell us anything about how tall he or she is.

When two variables are strongly correlated with each other, it is tempting to assume that one variable causes the other. For example, if we find that more study time is associated with higher grades, we might guess that more studying *causes* higher grades. Although this is not a bad guess, it remains just a guess—because finding that two variables are correlated does not mean that there is a causal relationship between them. The strong correlation suggests that knowing how much a person studies can help us predict how that person will do on a test, but it does not mean that the studying causes the test performance. It might be, for instance, that people who are more interested in the subject matter tend to study more than do those who are less interested, and that the amount of interest, not the number of hours spent studying,

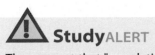

StudyALERT

The concept that "correlation does not imply causation" is a key principle.

predicts test performance. The mere fact that two variables occur together does not mean that one causes the other.

Another example illustrates the critical point that correlations tell us nothing about cause and effect but merely provide a measure of the strength of a relationship between two variables. We might find that children who watch a lot of television programs featuring high levels of aggression are likely to demonstrate a relatively high degree of aggressive behavior and that those who watch few television shows that portray aggression are apt to exhibit a relatively low degree of such behavior (see Figure 2). But we cannot say that the aggression is *caused* by the TV viewing, because many other explanations are possible.

For instance, it could be that children who have an unusually high level of energy seek out programs with aggressive content *and* are more aggressive. The children's energy level, then, could be the true cause of the children's higher incidence of aggression. It is also possible that people who are already highly aggressive choose to watch shows with a high aggressive content *because* they are aggressive. Clearly, then, any number of causal sequences are possible—none of which can be ruled out by correlational research.

The inability of correlational research to demonstrate cause-and-effect relationships is a crucial drawback to its use. There is, however, an alternative technique that does establish causality: the experiment.

Experimental Research

The *only* way psychologists can establish cause-and-effect relationships through research is by carrying out an experiment. In a formal **experiment**, the researcher investigates the relationship between two (or more) variables by deliberately changing one variable in a controlled situation and observing the effects of that change on other aspects of the situation. In an experiment, then, the conditions are created and controlled by the researcher, who deliberately makes a change in those conditions in order to observe the effects of that change.

Many studies show that the observation of violence in the media is associated with aggression in viewers. Can we conclude that the observation of violence causes aggression?

Experiment: The investigation of the relationship between two (or more) variables by deliberately producing a change in one variable in a situation and observing the effects of that change on other aspects of the situation

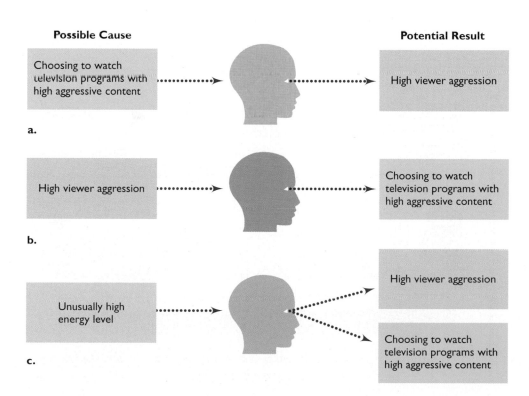

Possible Cause

a. Choosing to watch television programs with high aggressive content

Potential Result

High viewer aggression

b. High viewer aggression

Choosing to watch television programs with high aggressive content

c. Unusually high energy level

High viewer aggression

Choosing to watch television programs with high aggressive content

FIGURE 2 If we find that frequent viewing of television programs with aggressive content is associated with high levels of aggressive behavior, we might cite several plausible causes, as suggested in this figure. For example, choosing to watch shows with aggressive content could produce aggression (a); or being a highly aggressive person might cause one to choose to watch televised aggression (b); or having a high energy level might cause a person to both choose to watch aggressive shows and act aggressively (c). Correlational findings, then, do not permit us to determine causality. Can you think of a way to study the effects of televised aggression on aggressive behavior that is not correlational?

Experimental manipulation: The change that an experimenter deliberately produces in a situation.

The change that the researcher deliberately makes in an experiment is called the **experimental manipulation**. Experimental manipulations are used to detect relationships between different variables.

Several steps are involved in carrying out an experiment, but the process typically begins with the development of one or more hypotheses for the experiment to test. For example, Latané and Darley, in testing their theory of the diffusion of responsibility in bystander behavior, developed this hypothesis: The higher the number of people who witness an emergency situation is, the less likely it is that any of them will help the victim. They then designed an experiment to test this hypothesis.

Their first step was to formulate an operational definition of the hypothesis by conceptualizing it in a way that could be tested. Latané and Darley had to take into account the fundamental principle of experimental research mentioned earlier: Experimenters must manipulate at least one variable in order to observe the effects of the manipulation on another variable while keeping other factors in the situation constant. However, the manipulation cannot be viewed by itself, in isolation; if a cause-and-effect relationship is to be established, the effects of the manipulation must be compared with the effects of no manipulation or a different kind of manipulation.

Experimental Groups and Control Groups. Experimental research requires, then, that the responses of at least two groups be compared. One group will receive some special **treatment**—the manipulation implemented by the experimenter—and another group will receive either no treatment or a different treatment. Any group that receives a treatment is called an **experimental group**; a group that receives no treatment is called a **control group**. (In some experiments there are multiple experimental and control groups, each of which is compared with another group.)

Treatment: The manipulation implemented by the experimenter.
Experimental group: Any group participating in an experiment that receives a treatment.
Control group: A group participating in an experiment that receives no treatment.

By employing both experimental and control groups in an experiment, researchers are able to rule out the possibility that something other than the experimental manipulation produced the results observed in the experiment. Without a control group, we couldn't be sure that some other variable, such as the temperature at the time we were running the experiment, the color of the experimenter's hair, or even the mere passage of time, wasn't causing the changes observed.

For example, consider a medical researcher who thinks he has invented a medicine that cures the common cold. To test his claim, he gives the medicine one

"What if these guys in white coats who bring us food are, like, studying us and we're part of some kind of big experiment?"

day to a group of 20 people who have colds and finds that 10 days later all of them are cured.

Eureka? Not so fast. An observer viewing this flawed study might reasonably argue that the people would have gotten better even without the medicine. What the researcher obviously needed was a control group consisting of people with colds who *don't* get the medicine and whose health is also checked 10 days later. Only if there is a significant difference between experimental and control groups can the effectiveness of the medicine be assessed. Through the use of control groups, then, researchers can isolate specific causes for their findings—and draw cause-and-effect inferences.

Returning to Latané and Darley's experiment, we see that the researchers needed to translate their hypothesis into something testable. To do this, they decided to create a false emergency situation that would appear to require the aid of a bystander. As their experimental manipulation, they decided to vary the number of bystanders present. They could have

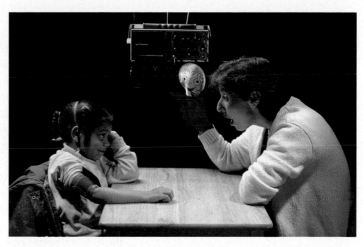

In this experiment, preschoolers' reactions to the puppet are monitored. Can you think of a hypothesis that might be tested in this way?

had just one experimental group with, say, two people present, and a control group for comparison purposes with just one person present. Instead, they settled on a more complex procedure involving the creation of groups of three sizes—consisting of two, three, and six people—that could be compared with one another.

Independent and Dependent Variables. Latané and Darley's experimental design now included an operational definition of what is called the **independent variable**. The independent variable is the condition that is manipulated by an experimenter. (You can think of the independent variable as being independent of the actions of those taking part in an experiment; it is controlled by the experimenter.) In the case of the Latané and Darley experiment, the independent variable was the number of people present, which was manipulated by the experimenters.

The next step was to decide how they were going to determine the effect that varying the number of bystanders had on behavior of those in the experiment. Crucial to every experiment is the **dependent variable**, the variable that is measured and is expected to change as a result of changes caused by the experimenter's manipulation of the independent variable. The dependent variable is dependent on the actions of the *participants* or *subjects*—the people taking part in the experiment.

Latané and Darley had several possible choices for their dependent measure. One might have been a simple yes/no measure of the participants' helping behavior. But the investigators also wanted a more precise analysis of helping behavior. Consequently, they also measured the amount of time it took for a participant to provide help.

Latané and Darley now had all the necessary components of an experiment. The independent variable, manipulated by them, was the number of bystanders present in an emergency situation. The dependent variable was the measure of whether bystanders in each of the groups provided help and the amount of time it took them to do so. Consequently, like all experiments, this one had both an independent variable and a dependent variable. *All* true experiments in psychology fit this straightforward model.

Random Assignment of Participants. To make the experiment a valid test of the hypothesis, Latané and Darley needed to add a final step to the design: properly assigning participants to a particular experimental group.

The significance of this step becomes clear when we examine various alternative procedures. For example, the experimenters might have assigned just males to the group with two bystanders, just females to the group with three bystanders, and both males and females to the group with six bystanders. If they had done this, however, any differences they found in helping behavior could not be attributed with any certainty solely to group size, because the differences might just as well have been due

Independent variable: The variable that is manipulated by an experimenter.

Dependent variable: The variable that is measured and is expected to change as a result of changes caused by the experimenter's manipulation of the independent variable.

 StudyALERT

To remember the difference between dependent and independent variables, recall that a hypothesis predicts how a dependent variable *depends* on the manipulation of the independent variable.

to the composition of the group. A more reasonable procedure would be to ensure that each group had the same composition in terms of gender; then the researchers would be able to make comparisons across groups with considerably more accuracy.

Participants in each of the experimental groups ought to be comparable, and it is easy enough to create groups that are similar in terms of gender. The problem becomes a bit more tricky, though, when we consider other participant characteristics. How can we ensure that participants in each experimental group will be equally intelligent, extroverted, cooperative, and so forth, when the list of characteristics—any one of which could be important—is potentially endless?

The solution is a simple but elegant procedure called **random assignment to condition:** Participants are assigned to different experimental groups or "conditions" on the basis of chance and chance alone. The experimenter might, for instance, flip a coin for each participant and assign a participant to one group when "heads" came up, and to the other group when "tails" came up. The advantage of this technique is that there is an equal chance that participant characteristics will be distributed across the various groups. When a researcher uses random assignment—which in practice is usually carried out using computer-generated random numbers—chances are that each of the groups will have approximately the same proportion of intelligent people, cooperative people, extroverted people, males and females, and so on.

Figure 3 provides another example of an experiment. Like all experiments, it includes the following set of key elements, which are important to keep in mind as you consider whether a research study is truly an experiment:

- An independent variable, the variable that is manipulated by the experimenter.
- A dependent variable, the variable that is measured by the experimenter and that is expected to change as a result of the manipulation of the independent variable.
- A procedure that randomly assigns participants to different experimental groups or "conditions" of the independent variable.
- A hypothesis that predicts the effect the independent variable will have on the dependent variable.

Only if each of these elements is present can a research study be considered a true experiment in which cause-and-effect relationships can be determined. (For a summary of the different types of research that we've discussed, see Figure 4 on page 46.)

Were Latané and Darley Right? To test their hypothesis that increasing the number of bystanders in an emergency situation would lower the degree of helping behavior, Latané and Darley placed the participants in a room and told them that the purpose of the experiment was to talk about personal problems associated with college. The discussion was to be held over an intercom, supposedly to avoid the potential embarrassment of face-to-face contact. Chatting about personal problems was not, of course, the true purpose of the experiment, but telling the participants that it was provided a way of keeping their expectations from biasing their behavior. (Consider how they would have been affected if they had been told that their helping behavior in emergencies was being tested. The experimenters could never have gotten an accurate assessment of what the participants would actually do in an emergency. By definition, emergencies are rarely announced in advance.)

The sizes of the discussion groups were two, three, and six people, which constituted the manipulation of the independent variable of group size. Participants were randomly assigned to these groups upon their arrival at the laboratory. Each group included a trained *confederate*, or employee, of the experimenters. In each two-person group, then, there was only one real "bystander."

As the participants in each group were holding their discussion, they suddenly heard through the intercom one of the other participants—the confederate—having what sounded like an epileptic seizure and calling for help.

Random assignment to condition: A procedure in which participants are assigned to different experimental groups or "conditions" on the basis of chance and chance alone.

a. Identify participants	b. Randomly assign participants to a condition	c. Manipulate the independent variable	d. Measure the dependent variable	e. Compare the results of the two groups

Group 1: Treatment group

Receive-drug condition

Group 2: Control group

No-drug condition

FIGURE 3 In this depiction of a study investigating the effects of the drug propranolol on stress, we can see the basic elements of all true experiments. The participants in the experiment were monkeys who were randomly assigned to one of two groups. Monkeys assigned to the treatment group were given propranolol, hypothesized to prevent heart disease, whereas those in the control group were not given the drug. Administration of the drugs, then, was the independent variable.

All the monkeys were given a high-fat diet that was the human equivalent of two eggs with bacon every morning, and they occasionally were reassigned to different cages to provide a source of stress. To determine the effects of the drug, the monkeys' heart rates and other measures of heart disease were assessed after 26 months. These measures constituted the dependent variable. (The results? As hypothesized, monkeys who received the drug showed lower heart rates and fewer symptoms of heart disease than those who did not.) (Source: Based on a study by Kaplan & Manuck, 1989.)

The participants' behavior was now what counted. The dependent variable was the time that elapsed from the start of the "seizure" to the time a participant began trying to help the "victim." If six minutes went by without a participant's offering help, the experiment was ended.

As predicted by the hypothesis, the size of the group had a significant effect on whether a participant provided help. The more people who were present, the less likely it was that someone would supply help, as you can see in Figure 5 on page 47 (Latané & Darley, 1970).

Because these results are so straightforward, it seems clear that the experiment confirmed the original hypothesis. However, Latané and Darley could not be sure that the results were truly meaningful until they determined whether the results represented a **significant outcome**. Using statistical analysis, researchers can determine whether a numeric difference is a real difference or is due merely to chance. Only when differences between groups are large enough that statistical tests show them to be significant is it possible for researchers to confirm a hypothesis (Cwikel, Behar, & Rabson-Hare, 2000; Cohen, 2002).

Significant outcome: Meaningful results that make it possible for researchers to feel confident that they have confirmed their hypotheses.

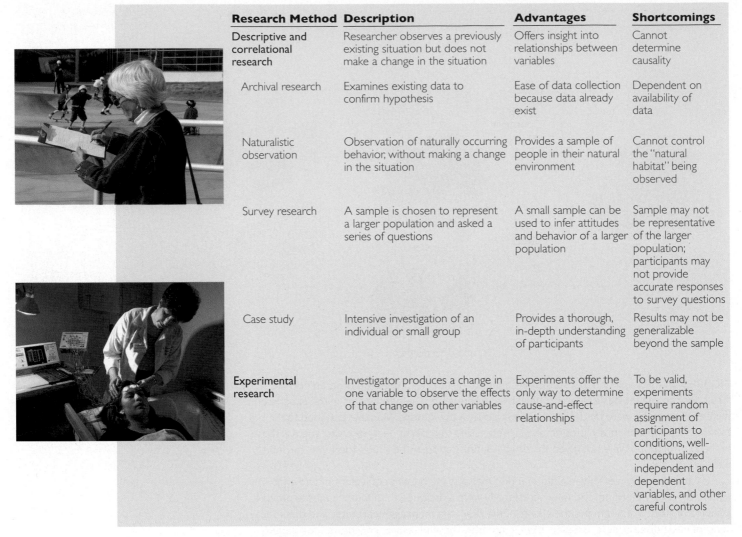

Research Method	Description	Advantages	Shortcomings
Descriptive and correlational research	Researcher observes a previously existing situation but does not make a change in the situation	Offers insight into relationships between variables	Cannot determine causality
Archival research	Examines existing data to confirm hypothesis	Ease of data collection because data already exist	Dependent on availability of data
Naturalistic observation	Observation of naturally occurring behavior, without making a change in the situation	Provides a sample of people in their natural environment	Cannot control the "natural habitat" being observed
Survey research	A sample is chosen to represent a larger population and asked a series of questions	A small sample can be used to infer attitudes and behavior of a larger population	Sample may not be representative of the larger population; participants may not provide accurate responses to survey questions
Case study	Intensive investigation of an individual or small group	Provides a thorough, in-depth understanding of participants	Results may not be generalizable beyond the sample
Experimental research	Investigator produces a change in one variable to observe the effects of that change on other variables	Experiments offer the only way to determine cause-and-effect relationships	To be valid, experiments require random assignment of participants to conditions, well-conceptualized independent and dependent variables, and other careful controls

FIGURE 4 Research strategies.

Moving Beyond the Study. The Latané and Darley study contains all the elements of an experiment: an independent variable, a dependent variable, random assignment to conditions, and multiple experimental groups. Consequently, we can say with some confidence that group size *caused* changes in the degree of helping behavior.

Of course, one experiment alone does not forever resolve the question of bystander intervention in emergencies. Psychologists require that findings be **replicated**, or repeated, sometimes using other procedures, in other settings, with other groups of participants, before full confidence can be placed in the results of any single experiment. A procedure called *meta-analysis* permits psychologists to combine the results of many separate studies into one overall conclusion (Peterson & Brown, 2005; Tenenbaum & Ruck, 2007).

In addition to replicating experimental results, psychologists need to test the limitations of their theories and hypotheses to determine under which specific circumstances they do and do not apply. It seems unlikely, for instance, that increasing the number of bystanders *always* results in less helping. Therefore, it is critical to continue carrying out experiments to understand the conditions in which exceptions to this general rule occur and other circumstances in which the rule holds (Aronson, 1994; Garcia et al., 2002).

Replicated research: Research that is repeated, sometimes using other procedures, settings, and groups of participants, to increase confidence in prior findings.

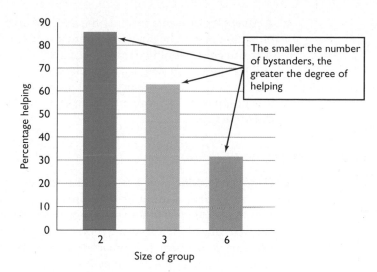

FIGURE 5 The Latané and Darley experiment showed that as the size of the group witnessing an emergency increased, helping behavior decreased. (Source: Latané & Darley, 1968.)

Before leaving the Latané and Darley study, it's important that we note that it represents a good illustration of the basic principles of the scientific method we considered earlier (as outlined in Figure 1 of Module 4 on page 33). The two psychologists began with a *question of interest*, in this case stemming from a real-world incident in which bystanders in an emergency did not offer help. They then *formulated an explanation* by specifying a theory of diffusion of responsibility, and from that formulated the specific hypothesis that increasing the number of bystanders in an emergency situation would lower the degree of helping behavior. Finally, they *carried out research* to confirm their hypothesis and they eventually *communicated their findings* by publishing their results. This four-step process embodied in the scientific method underlies all scientific inquiry, allowing us to develop a valid understanding of others'—and our own—behavior.

RECAP/EVALUATE/RETHINK

RECAP

What research methods do psychologists use?

- Archival research uses existing records, such as old newspapers or other documents, to test a hypothesis. In naturalistic observation, the investigator acts mainly as an observer, making no change in a naturally occurring situation. In survey research, people are asked a series of questions about their behavior, thoughts, or attitudes. The case study is an in-depth interview and examination of one person or group. (p. 37)

- These descriptive research methods rely on correlational techniques, which describe associations between variables but cannot determine cause-and-effect relationships. (p. 40)

How do psychologists establish cause-and-effect relationships in research studies?

- In a formal experiment, the relationship between variables is investigated by deliberately producing a change—called the experimental manipulation—in one variable and observing changes in the other variable. (p. 41)

- In an experiment, at least two groups must be compared to assess cause and effect relationships. The group receiving the treatment (the special procedure devised by the experimenter) is the experimental group; the second group (which receives no treatment) is the control group. There also may be multiple experimental groups, each of which is subjected to a different procedure and then compared with the others. (p. 42)

- The variable that experimenters manipulate is the independent variable. The variable that they measure and expect to change as a result of manipulation of the independent variable is called the dependent variable. (p. 43)

- In a formal experiment, participants must be assigned randomly to treatment conditions, so that participant characteristics are distributed evenly across the different conditions. (p. 44)

- Psychologists use statistical tests to determine whether research findings are significant. (p. 46)

EVALUATE

1. Match the following forms of research to their definitions:
   1. Archival research.
   2. Naturalistic observation.
   3. Survey research.
   4. Case study.
      a. Directly asking a sample of people questions about their behavior.
      b. Examining existing records to test a hypothesis.
      c. Looking at behavior in its true setting without intervening in the setting.
      d. Doing an in-depth investigation of a person or small group.

2. Match each of the following research methods with its primary disadvantage:
   1. Archival research.
   2. Naturalistic observation.
   3. Survey research.
   4. Case study.
      a. The researcher may not be able to generalize to the population at large.
      b. People's behavior can change if they know they are being watched.
      c. The data may not exist or may be unusable.
      d. People may lie in order to present a good image.

3. A friend tells you, "Anxiety about speaking in public and performance are negatively correlated. Therefore, high anxiety must cause low performance." Is this statement true or false, and why?

4. A psychologist wants to study the effect of attractiveness on willingness to help a person with a math problem. Attractiveness would be the _____ variable, and the amount of helping would be the _____ variable.

5. The group in an experiment that receives no treatment is called the _____ group.

RETHINK

1. Can you describe how a researcher might use naturalistic observation, case studies, and survey research to investigate gender differences in aggressive behavior at the workplace? First state a hypothesis and then describe your research approaches. What positive and negative features does each method have?

2. *From a healthcare worker's perspective*: Tobacco companies have asserted that no experiment has ever proved that tobacco use causes cancer. Can you explain this claim in terms of the research procedures and designs discussed in this module? What sort of research would establish a cause-and-effect relationship between tobacco use and cancer?

Answers to Evaluate Questions

1. 1-b, 2-c, 3-a, 4-d; 2. 1-c, 2-b, 3-d, 4-a; 3. False. Correlation does not imply causation. Just because two variables are related does not mean that one causes the other. Poor performance may cause people to become more anxious, or a third variable may cause both of these effects; 4. independent, dependent; 5. control

KEY TERMS

archival research p. 37
naturalistic observation p. 37
survey research p. 38
case study p. 38
variable p. 40

correlational research p. 40
experiment p. 41
experimental manipulation p. 42
treatment p. 42

experimental group p. 42
control group p. 42
independent variable p. 43
dependent variable p. 43

random assignment to condition p. 44
significant outcome p. 45
replicated research p. 46

Critical Research Issues

You probably realize by now that there are few simple formulas for psychological research. Psychologists must make choices about the type of study to conduct, the measures to take, and the most effective way to analyze the results. Even after they have made these essential decisions, they must still consider several critical issues. We turn first to the most fundamental of these issues: ethics.

The Ethics of Research

Put yourself in the place of one of the participants in the experiment conducted by Latané and Darley to examine the helping behavior of bystanders, in which another "bystander" simulating a seizure turned out to be a confederate of the experimenters (Latané & Darley, 1970). How would you feel when you learned that the supposed victim was in reality a paid accomplice?

Although you might at first experience relief that there had been no real emergency, you might also feel some resentment that you had been deceived by the experimenter. You might also experience concern that you had been placed in an embarrassing or compromising situation—one that might have dealt a blow to your self-esteem, depending on how you had behaved.

Most psychologists argue that deception is sometimes necessary to prevent participants from being influenced by what they think a study's true purpose is. (If you knew that Latané and Darley were actually studying your helping behavior, wouldn't you automatically have been tempted to intervene in the emergency?) To avoid such outcomes, a small proportion of research involves deception.

Nonetheless, because research has the potential to violate the rights of participants, psychologists are expected to adhere to a strict set of ethical guidelines aimed at protecting participants (American Psychological Association, 2002). Those guidelines involve the following safeguards:

- Protection of participants from physical and mental harm.
- The right of participants to privacy regarding their behavior.
- The assurance that participation in research is completely voluntary.
- The necessity of informing participants about the nature of procedures before their participation in the experiment.

All experiments must be reviewed by an independent panel before being conducted, including the minority of studies that involve deception (Smith, 2003; Fisher et al., 2002, 2003).

One of psychologists' key ethical principles is **informed consent**. Before participating in an experiment, the participants must sign a document affirming that they have been told the basic outlines of the study and are aware of what their participation will involve, what risks the experiment may hold, and the fact that their participation is purely voluntary and they may terminate it at any time. Furthermore, after participation in a study, they must be given a debriefing in which they receive an explanation of the study and the procedures that were involved. The only time informed consent

Key Concept

What major issues confront psychologists conducting research?

 StudyALERT

Because protection of participants is so essential, it is important to understand the key ethical guideline of informed consent.

Informed consent: A document signed by participants affirming that they have been told the basic outlines of the study and are aware of what their participation will involve.

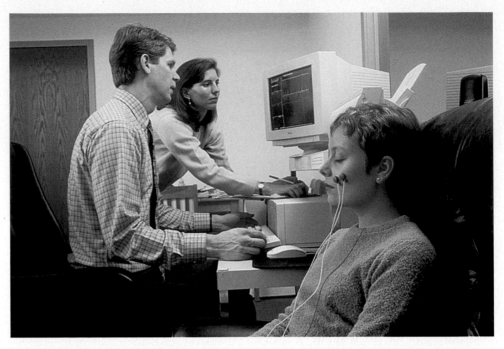

Although readily available and widely used as research subjects, college students may not represent the population at large. What are some advantages and drawbacks of using college students as subjects?

and a debriefing can be eliminated is in experiments in which the risks are minimal, as in a purely observational study in a public place (Koocher, Norcross, & Hill, 2005; Fallon, 2006; Barnett et al., 2007).

Exploring DIVERSITY

Choosing Participants Who Represent the Scope of Human Behavior

When Latané and Darley, both college professors, decided who would participate in their experiment, they turned to the most available people: college students. In fact, college students are used so frequently in experiments that psychology has been called—somewhat contemptuously—the "science of the behavior of the college sophomore" (Rubenstein, 1982).

Using college students as participants has both advantages and drawbacks. The big benefit is that because most research occurs in university settings, college students are readily available. Typically, they cost the researcher very little: They participate for either extra course credit or a relatively small payment.

The problem is that college students may not represent the general population adequately. They tend to be younger and better educated than a significant percentage of the rest of the population of the United States. Compared with older adults, their attitudes are likely to be less well formed, and they are more apt to be influenced by authority figures and peers (Sears, 1986).

College students are also disproportionately white and middle class. However, even in research that does not involve college students, participants tend to be white, middle-class participants; the use of African Americans, Latinos, Asians, and other minorities as participants is low (Graham, 1992; Guthrie, 1998). Because psychology is a science that purports to explain human behavior in general, something is therefore amiss. Consequently, psychological researchers have become increasingly sensitive to the importance of using participants who are fully representative of the general population. Furthermore, the National Institute of Mental Health and the National Science Foundation—the primary U.S. funding sources for psychological research—now require that experiments address issues of diverse populations (Carpenter, 2002; Lindley, 2006).

Research involving animals is controversial but, when conducted within ethical guidelines, yields significant benefits for humans.

Should Animals Be Used in Research?

Like those who work with humans, researchers who use nonhuman animals in experiments have their own set of exacting guidelines to ensure that the animals do not suffer. Specifically, researchers must make every effort to minimize discomfort, illness, and pain. Procedures that subject animals to distress are permitted only when an alternative procedure is unavailable and when the research is justified by its prospective value. Moreover, researchers strive to avoid causing physical discomfort, but they are also required to promote the *psychological* well-being of some species of research animals, such as primates (Rusche, 2003; Lutz & Novak, 2005; Auer et al., 2007).

But why should animals be used for research in the first place? Is it really possible to learn about human behavior from the results of research employing rats, gerbils, and pigeons?

The answer is that psychological research that does employ nonhumans is designed to answer questions different from those posed in research with humans. For example, the shorter life span of animals (rats live an average of two years) allows researchers to learn about the effects of aging in a relatively short time frame. It is also possible to provide greater experimental control over nonhumans and to carry out procedures that might not be possible with people. For example, some studies require large numbers of participants that share similar backgrounds or have been exposed to particular environments—conditions that could not practically be met with human beings.

Research with animals has provided psychologists with information that has profoundly benefited humans. For instance, it furnished the keys to detecting eye disorders in children early enough to prevent permanent damage, to communicating more effectively with severely retarded children, and to reducing chronic pain in people. Still, the use of research using nonhumans is controversial, involving complex moral and philosophical concerns. Consequently, all research involving nonhumans must be carefully reviewed beforehand to ensure that it is conducted ethically (Plous & Herzog, 2000; Herzog, 2005; Saucier & Cain, 2006; Hackam, 2007).

Threats to Experimental Validity: Avoiding Experimental Bias

Experimental bias: Factors that distort how the independent variable affects the dependent variable in an experiment.

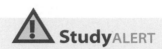

StudyALERT

It's important to know the main types of potential bias in experiments: experimenter expectations, participant expectations, and placebo effects.

Placebo: A false treatment, such as a pill, "drug," or other substance, without any significant chemical properties or active ingredient.

Even the best-laid experimental plans are susceptible to **experimental bias**—factors that distort the way the independent variable affects the dependent variable in an experiment. One of the most common forms of experimental bias is *experimenter expectations:* An experimenter unintentionally transmits cues to participants about the way they are expected to behave in a given experimental condition. The danger is that those expectations will bring about an "appropriate" behavior—one that otherwise might not have occurred (Rosenthal, 2002, 2003).

A related problem is *participant expectations* about appropriate behavior. If you have ever been a participant in an experiment, you know that you quickly develop guesses about what is expected of you. In fact, it is typical for people to develop their own hypotheses about what the experimenter hopes to learn from the study. If participants form their own hypotheses, it may the participant's expectations, rather than the experimental manipulation, that produce an effect.

To guard against participant expectations biasing the results of an experiment, the experimenter may try to disguise the true purpose of the experiment. Participants who do not know that helping behavior is being studied, for example, are more apt to act in a "natural" way than they would if they knew.

Sometimes it is impossible to hide the actual purpose of research; when that is the case, other techniques are available to prevent bias. Suppose you were interested in testing the ability of a new drug to alleviate the symptoms of severe depression. If you simply gave the drug to half your participants and not to the other half, the participants who were given the drug might report feeling less depressed merely because they knew they were getting a drug. Similarly, the participants who got nothing might report feeling no better because they knew that they were in a no-treatment control group.

To solve this problem, psychologists typically use a procedure in which all the participants receive a treatment, but those in the control group receive only a **placebo**, a false treatment, such as a pill, "drug," or other substance, that has no significant chemical properties or active ingredient. Because members of both groups are kept in the dark about whether they are getting a real or a false treatment, any differences in outcome can be attributed to the quality of the drug and not to the possible psychological effects of being administered a pill or other substance (Rajagopal, 2006; Crum & Langer, 2007).

However, there is one more safeguard that a careful researcher must apply in an experiment such as this one. To overcome the possibility that *experimenter* expectations will affect the participant, the person who administers the drug shouldn't know whether it is actually the true drug or the placebo. By keeping both the participant and the experimenter who interacts with the participant "blind" to the nature of the drug that is being administered, researchers can more accurately assess the effects of the drug. This method is known as the *double-blind procedure*.

BECOMING
AN INFORMED CONSUMER
of Psychology
Thinking Critically About Research

If you were about to purchase an automobile, it is unlikely that you would stop at the nearest car dealership and drive off with the first car a salesperson recommended. Instead, you would probably mull over the purchase, read about automobiles, consider the alternatives, talk to others about their experiences, and ultimately put in a fair amount of thought before you made such a major purchase.

In contrast, many of us are considerably less conscientious when we expend our intellectual, rather than financial, assets. People often jump to conclusions on the basis of incomplete and inaccurate information, and only rarely do they take the time to critically evaluate the research and data to which they are exposed.

Because the field of psychology is based on an accumulated body of research, it is crucial to scrutinize thoroughly the methods, results, and claims of researchers. Several basic questions can help us sort through what is valid and what is not. Among the most important questions to ask are the following:

- *What was the purpose of the research?* Research studies should evolve from a clearly specified theory. Furthermore, we must take into account the specific hypothesis that is being tested. Unless we know what hypothesis is being examined, it is not possible to judge how successful a study has been.

- *How well was the study conducted?* Consider who the participants were, how many were involved, what methods were employed, and what problems the researcher encountered in collecting the data. There are important differences, for example, between a case study that reports the anecdotes of a handful of respondents and a survey that collects data from several thousand people.

- *Are the results presented fairly?* It is necessary to assess statements on the basis of the actual data they reflect and their logic. For instance, when the manufacturer of car X boasts that "no other car has a better safety record than car X," this does not mean that car X is safer than every other car. It just means that no other car has been proved safer, though many other cars could be just as safe as car X. Expressed in the latter fashion, the finding doesn't seem worth bragging about.

These three basic questions can help you assess the validity of research findings you come across—both within and outside the field of psychology. The more you know how to evaluate research in general, the better you will be able to assess what the field of psychology has to offer.

RECAP/EVALUATE/RETHINK

RECAP

What major issues confront psychologists conducting research?

- One of the key ethical principles followed by psychologists is that of informed consent. Participants must be informed, before participation, about the basic outline of the experiment and the risks and potential benefits of their participation. (p. 49)

- Although the use of college students as participants has the advantage of easy availability, there are drawbacks too. For instance, students do not necessarily represent the population as a whole. The use of nonhuman animals as participants may also have costs in terms of the ability to generalize to humans, although the benefits of using animals in research have been profound. (p. 50)

- Experiments are subject to a number of biases, or threats. Experimenter expectations can produce bias when an experimenter unintentionally transmits cues to participants about her or his expectations regarding their behavior in a given experimental condition. Participant expectations can also bias an experiment. Among the tools experimenters use to help eliminate bias are placebos and double-blind procedures. (p. 52)

EVALUATE

1. Ethical research begins with the concept of informed consent. Before signing up to participate in an experiment, participants should be informed of
   a. The procedure of the study, stated generally.
   b. The risks that may be involved.
   c. Their right to withdraw at any time.
   d. All of the above.
2. List three benefits of using animals in psychological research.

3. Deception is one means experimenters can use to try to eliminate participants' expectations. True or false?
4. A false treatment, such as a pill, that has no significant chemical properties or active ingredient, is known as a _____.
5. According to a report, a study has shown that men differ from women in their preference for ice cream flavors. This study was based on a sample of two men and three women. What might be wrong with this study?

RETHINK

1. A researcher strongly believes that college professors tend to show female students less attention and respect in the classroom than they show male students. He sets up an experimental study involving observations of classrooms in different conditions. In explaining the study to the professors and students who will participate, what steps should the researcher take to eliminate experimental bias based on both experimenter expectations and participant expectations?
2. *From a research analyst's perspective*: You are hired to study people's attitudes toward welfare programs by developing and circulating a questionnaire via the Internet. Is this study likely to accurately reflect the views of the general population? Why or why not?

Answers to Evaluate Questions

1. d; 2. (1) We can study some phenomena in animals more easily than we can in people, because with animal subjects we have greater control over environmental and genetic factors. (2) Large numbers of similar participants can be easily obtained. (3) We can look at generational effects much more easily in animals, because of their shorter life span, than we can with people; 3. true; 4. placebo; 5. There are far too few participants. Without a larger sample, no valid conclusions can be drawn about ice cream preferences based on gender.

KEY TERMS

informed consent p. 49
experimental bias p. 52
placebo p. 52

Psychology on the Web

1. Identify a product or service that is advertised on the Internet using broad, unspecific claims, such as a weight-loss formula or a body-building method. Find at least two advertisements on the Internet for that product or service and evaluate the claims they make according to the principles discussed in this group of modules. Summarize the evidence that is presented for those claims, and describe a method by which you might confirm the claims by using actual research.

2. Find a Web site that focuses on an important social issue (e.g., urban violence, gender differences in hiring or promotion, poverty) and locate descriptions of a research study about the issue. Evaluate the study by identifying the hypotheses that were tested, the methods used to test them, and the validity of the results that were reported.

Epilogue

We have been discussing the ways in which psychologists seek to understand phenomena and answer questions of interest. We've examined the scientific method and its reliance on posing good questions, creating productive theories, and crafting testable hypotheses. We have also looked at the basic methods psychologists use to conduct research studies and compared correlational methods and experimental methods. Finally, we've explored some of the major challenges that psychologists have to deal with when conducting research, including ethical considerations, the use of animals in research, and potential bias.

Before leaving this topic, reconsider the lack of bystander help in the case of Leonard Sims, the 91-year-old who was carjacked and received no help from bystanders. Reflect on the following questions in light of what you now know about conducting psychological research.

1. Suppose you were interested in studying aggressive behavior among criminals such as the ones who beat Sims. Can you formulate a theory that might explain why criminals behave violently?
2. What hypotheses (testable predictions) can you construct to test your theory?
3. Design a correlational study to test one of your hypotheses. Which correlational method(s) (archival research, naturalistic observation, survey research, case study) would you use in your study?
4. Design an experimental study to test the same or another hypothesis. Describe the experiment, including the participants, the experimental manipulation, the treatment, and the independent and dependent variables.

MASTERING the difference between dependent and independent variables

Experiments are used to establish a cause-and-effect relationship between two variables. Use this visual guide to better understand how experiments can help researchers draw conclusions by using experimental and control groups and random assignment. Then answer the questions below to test your understanding of the concepts.

1 Researchers develop *theories* to explain behavior. As an example, they might theorize that children who are exposed to violence in the media behave more aggressively than other children. Based on this theory they develop a *hypothesis* to test the prediction that playing violent video games causes children to behave aggressively.

2 An experiment in a controlled setting is the most powerful method of establishing a cause-and-effect relationship. Participants in an experiment are randomly assigned to either the *experimental group* (the group that receives a treatment) or the *control group* (the group that receives no special treatment).

EVALUATE

1 In this example, the independent variable is _____ and the dependent variable is _____.
- **a** aggressive behavior; exposure to violent video games
- **b** the experimenter; who wins the card games
- **c** exposure to violent video games; aggression displayed by the children
- **d** the card games; the violent video games

2 In this example, the experimental group _____ and the control group _____.
- **a** plays cards; plays violent video games
- **b** plays violent video games; does not play violent video games
- **c** is randomly assigned to condition; is not randomly assigned
- **d** does not play violent video games; plays violent video games

3 In this example, the *independent variable,* the variable that researchers manipulate, is exposure to violent video games. The experimental group is given a violent video game to play, while the control group is not given the violent game.

4 Afterwards, the experimental group and control group are brought together to play card games. A researcher who doesn't know which children are in the experimental group or the control group watches through a two-way mirror and records signs of aggressive behavior (the *dependent variable*).

5 If the results show that the children in the experimental group (who had played the violent video games) were significantly more aggressive than the children in the control group (who hadn't played the game), the hypothesis is confirmed. The results would then support the researcher's theory that exposure to media violence *causes* aggression in children. Of course, no single experiment is sufficient to confirm a theory; additional research is needed.

3 Because the control group receives no treatment in this example, we cannot use it to draw conclusions about cause and effect. True or False?

RETHINK

1 Suppose you believe that listening to music while studying can improve test scores. Design an experiment that could be used to test your hypothesis. Be sure to include an experimental group and a control group.

Answers to Evaluate questions: 1. c; 2. b; 3. False

CHAPTER 3

Neuroscience and Behavior

Key Concepts for Chapter 3

Wendy Nissley carried her two-year-old daughter, Lacy, into O.R. 12 at Johns Hopkins Hospital to have half of her brain removed. Lacy suffers from a rare malformation of the brain, known as hemimegalencephaly, in which one hemisphere grows larger than the other. The condition causes seizures, and Lacy was having so many—up to forty in a day—that, at an age when other toddlers were trying out sentences, she could produce only a few language-like sounds. As long as Lacy's malformed right hemisphere was attached to the rest of her brain, it would prevent her left hemisphere from functioning normally. So Lacy's parents had brought her to Johns Hopkins for a hemispherectomy, which is probably the most radical procedure in neurosurgery (Kenneally, 2006, p. 36).

Looking Ahead

It took nearly a day, but the surgery to remove half of Lacy's brain was a success. Within a few months, Lacy was crawling and beginning to speak. Although the long-term effects of the radical operation are still unclear, it brought substantial improvement to Lacy's life.

The ability of surgeons to identify and remove damaged portions of the brain is little short of miraculous. The greater miracle, though, is the brain itself. An organ roughly half the size of a loaf of bread, the brain controls our behavior through every waking and sleeping moment. Our movements, thoughts, hopes, aspirations, dreams—our very awareness that we are human—all depend on the brain and the nerves that extend throughout the body, constituting the nervous system.

Because of the importance of the nervous system in controlling behavior, and because humans at their most basic level are biological beings, many researchers in psychology and other fields as diverse as computer science, zoology, and medicine have made the biological underpinnings of behavior their specialty. These experts collectively are called *neuroscientists* (Beatty, 2000; Posner & DiGiorlamo, 2000; Gazzaniga, Ivry, & Mangun, 2002; Cartwright, 2006).

Psychologists who specialize in considering the ways in which the biological structures and functions of the body affect behavior are known as **behavioral neuroscientists** (or *biopsychologists*). They seek to answer several key questions: How does the brain control the voluntary and involuntary functioning of the body? How does the brain communicate with other parts of the body? What is the physical structure of the brain, and how does this structure affect behavior? Are psychological disorders caused by biological factors, and how can such disorders be treated?

As you consider the biological processes that we'll discuss in this chapter, it is important to keep in mind why behavioral neuroscience is an essential part of psychology: Our understanding of human behavior requires knowledge of the brain and other parts of the nervous system. Biological factors are central to our sensory experiences, states of consciousness, motivation and emotion, development throughout the life span, and physical and psychological health. Furthermore, advances in behavioral neuroscience have led to the creation of drugs and other treatments for psychological and physical disorders. In short, we cannot understand behavior without understanding our biological makeup (Kosslyn et al., 2002; Plomin, 2003; Compagni & Manderscheid, 2006).

Behavioral neuroscientists (or biopsychologists): Psychologists who specialize in considering the ways in which the biological structures and functions of the body affect behavior.

Neurons: The Basic Elements of Behavior

Watching Serena Williams hit a stinging backhand, Dario Vaccaro carry out a complex ballet routine, or Derek Jeter swing at a baseball, you may have marveled at the complexity—and wondrous abilities—of the human body. But even the most everyday tasks, such as pouring a cup of coffee or humming a tune, depend on a sophisticated sequence of events in the body that is itself truly impressive.

The nervous system is the pathway for the instructions that permit our bodies to carry out such precise activities. Here we will look at the structure and function of neurons, the cells that make up the nervous system, including the brain.

The Structure of the Neuron

Playing the piano, driving a car, or hitting a tennis ball depends, at one level, on exact muscle coordination. But if we consider *how* the muscles can be activated so precisely, we see that more fundamental processes are involved. For the muscles to produce the complex movements that make up any meaningful physical activity, the brain has to provide the right messages to them and coordinate those messages.

Such messages—as well as those which enable us to think, remember, and experience emotion—are passed through specialized cells called neurons. **Neurons**, or nerve cells, are the basic elements of the nervous system. Their quantity is staggering—perhaps as many as 1 *trillion* neurons throughout the body are involved in the control of behavior (Boahen, 2005).

Although there are several types of neurons, they all have a similar structure, as illustrated in Figure 1. Like most cells in the body, neurons have a cell body that contains a nucleus. The nucleus incorporates the hereditary material that determines how a cell will function. Neurons are physically held in place by *glial cells*. Glial cells provide nourishment to neurons, insulate them, help repair damage, and generally support neural functioning (Fields, 2004; Kettenmann & Ransom, 2005; Bassotti et al., 2007).

In contrast to most other cells, however, neurons have a distinctive feature: the ability to communicate with other cells and transmit information across relatively long distances. Many of the body's neurons receive signals from the environment or relay the nervous system's messages to muscles and other target cells, but the vast majority of neurons communicate only with other neurons in the elaborate information system that regulates behavior.

As you can see in Figure 1, a neuron has a cell body with a cluster of fibers called **dendrites** at one end. Those fibers, which look like the twisted branches of a tree, receive messages from other neurons. On the opposite of the cell body is a long, slim, tubelike extension called an **axon**. The axon carries messages received by the dendrites to other neurons. The axon is considerably longer than the rest of the neuron. Although most axons are several millimeters in length, some are as long as three feet. Axons end in small bulges called **terminal buttons**, which send messages to other neurons.

The messages that travel through a neuron are electrical in nature. Although there are exceptions, those electrical messages, or *impulses*, generally move across neurons in one direction only, as if they were traveling on a one-way street. Impulses follow a

Key Concepts

Why do psychologists study the brain and nervous system?

What are the basic elements of the nervous system?

How does the nervous system communicate electrical and chemical messages from one part to another?

Neurons: Nerve cells, the basic elements of the nervous system.

Dendrite: A cluster of fibers at one end of a neuron that receives messages from other neurons.

Axon: The part of the neuron that carries messages destined for other neurons.

Terminal buttons: Small bulges at the end of axons that send messages to other neurons.

Dendrites

Axon (inside myelin sheath)

Cell body

Myelin sheath

Movement of electrical impulse

Terminal buttons

FIGURE 1 The primary components of the specialized cell called the neuron, the basic element of the nervous system. A neuron, like most types of cells in the body, has a cell body and a nucleus, but it also contains structures that carry messages: the dendrites, which receive messages from other neurons, and the axon, which carries messages to other neurons or body cells. In this neuron, as in most neurons, the axon is protected by the sausage-like myelin sheath. What advantages does the treelike structure of the neuron provide?

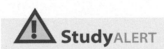

StudyALERT

Remember that *dendrites* *d*etect messages from other neurons; *a*xons carry signals *a*way from the cell body.

Myelin sheath: A protective coat of fat and protein that wraps around the axon.

route that begins with the dendrites, continues into the cell body, and leads ultimately along the tubelike extension, the axon, to adjacent neurons.

To prevent messages from short-circuiting one another, axons must be insulated in some fashion (just as electrical wires must be insulated). Most axons are insulated by a **myelin sheath**, a protective coating of fat and protein that wraps around the axon like links of sausage.

The myelin sheath also serves to increase the velocity with which electrical impulses travel through axons. Those axons that carry the most important and most urgently required information have the greatest concentrations of myelin. If your hand touches a painfully hot stove, for example, the information regarding the pain is passed through axons in the hand and arm that have a relatively thick coating of myelin, speeding the message of pain to the brain so that you can react instantly.

How Neurons Fire

All-or-none law: The rule that neurons are either on or off.

Resting state: The state in which there is a negative electrical charge of about –70 millivolts within a neuron.

Like a gun, neurons either fire—that is, transmit an electrical impulse along the axon—or don't fire. There is no in-between stage, just as pulling harder on a gun trigger doesn't make the bullet travel faster. Similarly, neurons follow an **all-or-none law**: They are either on or off, with nothing in between the on state and the off state. Once there is enough force to pull the trigger, a neuron fires.

Before a neuron is triggered—that is, when it is in a **resting state**—it has a negative electrical charge of about –70 millivolts (a millivolt is one one-thousandth of a volt). This charge is caused by the presence of more negatively charged ions within the neuron than outside it. (An ion is an atom that is electrically charged.) You might think of the neuron as a miniature battery in which the inside of the neuron represents the negative pole and the outside represents the positive pole.

When a message arrives at a neuron, gates along the cell membrane open briefly to allow positively charged ions to rush in at rates as high as 100 million ions per second. The sudden arrival of these positive ions causes the charge within the nearby part of the cell to change momentarily from negative to positive. When the positive charge reaches a critical level, the "trigger" is pulled, and an electrical impulse, known as an action potential, travels along the axon of the neuron (see Figure 2).

The **action potential** moves from one end of the axon to the other like a flame moving along a fuse. As the impulse travels along the axon, the movement of ions causes a change in charge from negative to positive in successive sections of the axon (see Figure 3). After the impulse has passed through a particular section of the axon, positive ions are pumped out of that section, and its charge returns to negative while the action potential continues to move along the axon.

Just after an action potential has passed through a section of the axon, the cell membrane in that region cannot admit positive ions again for a few milliseconds, and so a neuron cannot fire again immediately no matter how much stimulation it receives. It is as if the gun has to be reloaded after each shot. There then follows a period in which, though it is possible for the neuron to fire, a stronger stimulus is needed than would be if the neuron had reached its normal resting state. Eventually, though, the neuron is ready to fire once again.

These complex events can occur at dizzying speeds, although there is great variation among different neurons. The particular speed at which an action potential travels along an axon is determined by the axon's size and the thickness of its myelin sheath. Axons with small diameters carry impulses at about 2 miles per hour; longer and thicker ones can average speeds of more than 225 miles per hour.

Neurons differ not only in terms of how quickly an impulse moves along the axon but also in their potential rate of firing. Some neurons are capable of firing as many as a thousand times per second; others fire at much slower rates. The intensity of a stimulus determines how much of a neuron's potential firing rate is reached. A strong stimulus, such as a bright light or a loud sound, leads to a higher rate of firing than a less intense stimulus does. Thus, even though all impulses move at the same strength or speed through a particular axon—because of the all-or-none law—there is variation in the frequency of impulses, providing a mechanism by which we can distinguish the tickle of a feather from the weight of someone standing on our toes.

Mirror neurons. Although all neurons operate through the firing of action potentials, there is significant specialization among different types of neurons. For example,

Action potential: An electric nerve impulse that travels through a neuron's axon when it is set off by a "trigger," changing the neuron's charge from negative to positive.

FIGURE 2 Movement of an action potential across an axon. Just before Time 1, positively charged ions enter the cell membrane, changing the charge in the nearby part of the neuron from negative to positive and triggering an action potential. The action potential travels along the axon, as illustrated in the changes occurring from Time 1 to Time 3 (from top to bottom in this drawing). Immediately after the action potential has passed through a section of the axon, positive ions are pumped out, restoring the charge in that section to negative. The change in voltage illustrated at the top of the axon can be seen in greater detail in Figure 3 on page 64. (Source: Stevens, 1979.)

Time 1
Voltage

Time 2
Voltage

Time 3
Voltage

Positive charge

Negative charge

Direction of impulse

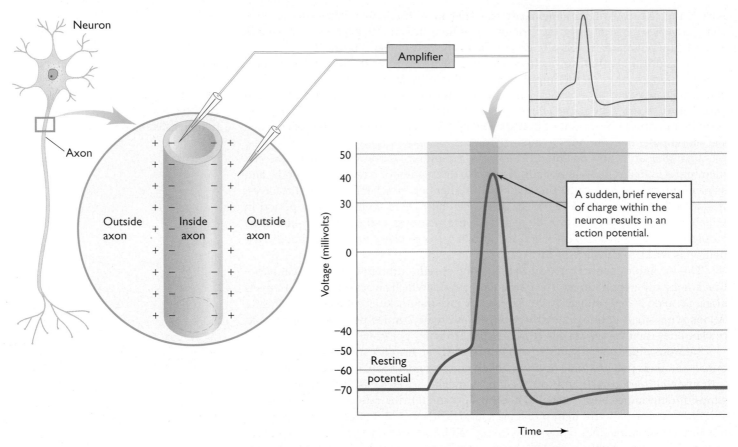

FIGURE 3 Changes in the electrical charge in a neuron during the passage of an action potential. In its normal resting state, a neuron has a negative charge. When an action potential is triggered, however, the charge becomes positive, increasing from around –70 millivolts to about +40 millivolts. Following the passage of the action potential, the charge becomes even more negative than it is in its typical state. It is not until the charge returns to its resting state that the neuron will be fully ready to be triggered once again.

Mirror neurons: Specialized neurons that fire not only when a person enacts a particular behavior, but also when a person simply observes *another* individual carrying out the same behavior.

in the last decade, neuroscientists have discovered the existence of **mirror neurons**, neurons that fire not only when a person enacts a particular behavior, but also when a person simply observes *another* individual carrying out the same behavior (Falck-Ytter, 2006; Lepage & Theoret, 2007; Schulte-Ruther et al., 2007).

Mirror neurons may help explain how (and why) humans have the capacity to understand others' intentions. Specifically, mirror neurons may fire when we view someone doing something, helping us to predict what their goals are and what they may do next.

The discovery of mirror neurons suggests that the capacity of even young children to imitate others may be an inborn behavior. Furthermore, mirror neurons may be at the root of empathy—those feelings of concern, compassion, and sympathy for others—and even the development of language in humans (Oberman, Pineda, & Ramachandran, 2007; Triesch, Jasso, & Deák, 2007).

Where Neurons Meet: Bridging the Gap

If you have looked inside a computer, you've seen that each part is physically connected to another part. In contrast, evolution has produced a neural transmission system that at some points has no need for a structural connection between its components. Instead, a chemical connection bridges the gap, known as a synapse, between two

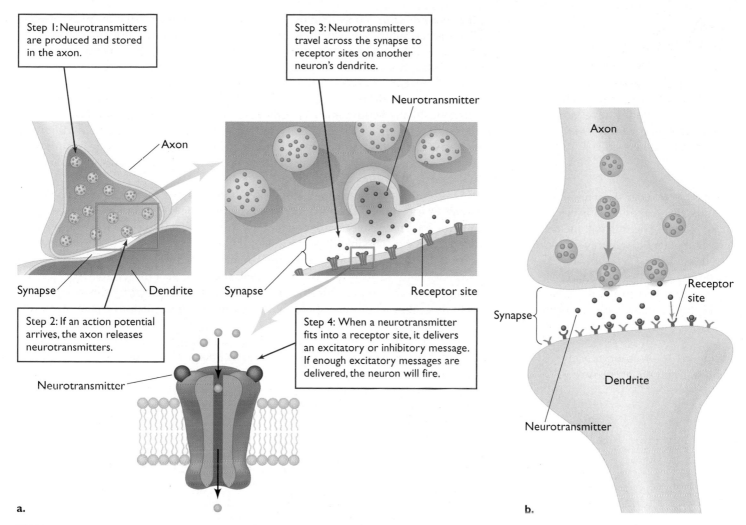

Step 1: Neurotransmitters are produced and stored in the axon.

Step 2: If an action potential arrives, the axon releases neurotransmitters.

Step 3: Neurotransmitters travel across the synapse to receptor sites on another neuron's dendrite.

Step 4: When a neurotransmitter fits into a receptor site, it delivers an excitatory or inhibitory message. If enough excitatory messages are delivered, the neuron will fire.

Axon

Synapse

Dendrite

Neurotransmitter

Synapse

Receptor site

Neurotransmitter

a.

Axon

Receptor site

Synapse

Dendrite

Neurotransmitter

b.

FIGURE 4 (a) A synapse is the junction between an axon and a dendrite. The gap between the axon and the dendrite is bridged by chemicals called neurotransmitters (Mader, 2000). (b) Just as the pieces of a jigsaw puzzle can fit in only one specific location in a puzzle, each kind of neurotransmitter has a distinctive configuration that allows it to fit into a specific type of receptor cell (Johnson, 2000). Why is it advantageous for axons and dendrites to be linked by temporary chemical bridges rather than by the hard wiring typical of a radio connection or telephone hookup?

neurons (see Figure 4). The **synapse** is the space between two neurons where the axon of a sending neuron communicates with the dendrites of a receiving neuron by using chemical messages (Fanselow & Poulos, 2005; Dean & Dresbach, 2006).

When a nerve impulse comes to the end of the axon and reaches a terminal button, the terminal button releases a chemical courier called a neurotransmitter. **Neurotransmitters** are chemicals that carry messages across the synapse to a dendrite (and sometimes the cell body) of a receiving neuron. Like a boat that ferries passengers across a river, these chemical messengers move toward the shorelines of other neurons. The chemical mode of message transmission that occurs between neurons is strikingly different from the means by which communication occurs inside neurons: Although messages travel in electrical form *within* a neuron, they move *between* neurons through a chemical transmission system.

There are several types of neurotransmitters, and not all neurons are capable of receiving the chemical message carried by a particular neurotransmitter. In the same way that a jigsaw puzzle piece can fit in only one specific location in a puzzle, each kind of neurotransmitter has a distinctive configuration that allows it to fit into a specific type of receptor site on the receiving neuron (see Figure 4b). It is only when a neurotransmitter fits precisely into a receptor site that successful chemical communication is possible.

Synapse: The space between two neurons where the axon of a sending neuron communicates with the dendrites of a receiving neuron by using chemical messages.

Neurotransmitters: Chemicals that carry messages across the synapse to the dendrite (and sometimes the cell body) of a receiver neuron.

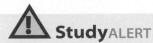

Excitatory message: A chemical message that makes it more likely that a receiving neuron will fire and an action potential will travel down its axon.

Inhibitory message: A chemical message that prevents or decreases the likelihood that a receiving neuron will fire.

Reuptake: The reabsorption of neurotransmitters by a terminal button.

If a neurotransmitter does fit into a site on the receiving neuron, the chemical message it delivers is basically one of two types: excitatory or inhibitory. **Excitatory messages** make it more likely that a receiving neuron will fire and an action potential will travel down its axon. **Inhibitory messages**, in contrast, do just the opposite; they provide chemical information that prevents or decreases the likelihood that the receiving neuron will fire.

Because the dendrites of a neuron receive both excitatory and inhibitory messages simultaneously, the neuron must integrate the messages by using a kind of chemical calculator. Put simply, if the excitatory messages ("Fire!") outnumber the inhibitory ones ("Don't fire!"), the neuron fires. In contrast, if the inhibitory messages outnumber the excitatory ones, nothing happens, and the neuron remains in its resting state (Mel, 2002; Rapport, 2005; Flavell et al., 2006).

If neurotransmitters remained at the site of the synapse, receiving neurons would be awash in a continual chemical bath, producing constant stimulation or constant inhibition of the receiving neurons—and effective communication across the synapse would no longer be possible. To solve this problem, neurotransmitters are either deactivated by enzymes or—more commonly—reabsorbed by the terminal button in an example of chemical recycling called **reuptake**. Like a vacuum cleaner sucking up dust, neurons reabsorb the neurotransmitters that are now clogging the synapse. All this activity occurs at lightning speed, with the process taking just several milliseconds (Helmuth, 2000; Holt & Jahn, 2004).

Our understanding of the process of reuptake has permitted the development of a number of drugs used in the treatment of psychological disorders. As we'll discuss later in the book, some antidepressant drugs, called *SSRIs* or *selective serotonin reuptake inhibitors*, permit certain neurotransmitters to remain active for a longer period at certain synapses in the brain, thereby reducing the symptoms of depression (Montgomery, 2006; Ramos, 2006).

Neurotransmitters: Multitalented Chemical Couriers

Neurotransmitters are a particularly important link between the nervous system and behavior. Not only are they important for maintaining vital brain and body functions, a deficiency or an excess of a neurotransmitter can produce severe behavior disorders. More than a hundred chemicals have been found to act as neurotransmitters, and neuroscientists believe that more may ultimately be identified (Penney, 2000; Schmidt, 2006).

Neurotransmitters vary significantly in terms of how strong their concentration must be to trigger a neuron to fire. Furthermore, the effects of a particular neurotransmitter vary, depending on the area of the nervous system in which it is produced. The same neurotransmitter, then, can act as an excitatory message to a neuron located in one part of the brain and can inhibit firing in neurons located in another part. (The major neurotransmitters and their effects are described in Figure 5.)

One of the most common neurotransmitters is *acetylcholine* (or *ACh*, its chemical symbol), which is found throughout the nervous system. ACh is involved in our every move, because—among other things—it transmits messages relating to our skeletal muscles. ACh is also involved in memory capabilities, and diminished production of ACh may be related to Alzheimer's disease (Mohapel et al., 2005; Bazalakova et al., 2007).

Another common excitatory neurotransmitter, *glutamate*, plays a role in memory. Memories appear to be produced by specific biochemical changes at particular synapses, and glutamate, along with other neurotransmitters, plays an important role in this process (Riedel, Platt, & Micheau, 2003; Winters & Bussey, 2005; Carvalho, 2006).

Gamma-amino butyric acid (GABA), which is found in both the brain and the spinal cord, appears to be the nervous system's primary inhibitory neurotransmitter. It moderates a variety of behaviors, ranging from eating to aggression. Several common substances, such as the tranquilizer Valium and alcohol, are effective because they permit GABA to operate more efficiently (Ball, 2004; Akirav, Raizel, & Maroun, 2006).

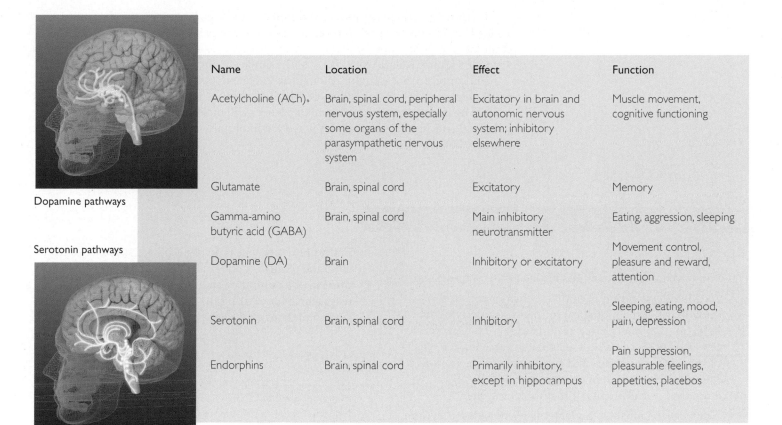

Dopamine pathways

Serotonin pathways

Name	Location	Effect	Function
Acetylcholine (ACh)	Brain, spinal cord, peripheral nervous system, especially some organs of the parasympathetic nervous system	Excitatory in brain and autonomic nervous system; inhibitory elsewhere	Muscle movement, cognitive functioning
Glutamate	Brain, spinal cord	Excitatory	Memory
Gamma-amino butyric acid (GABA)	Brain, spinal cord	Main inhibitory neurotransmitter	Eating, aggression, sleeping
Dopamine (DA)	Brain	Inhibitory or excitatory	Movement control, pleasure and reward, attention
Serotonin	Brain, spinal cord	Inhibitory	Sleeping, eating, mood, pain, depression
Endorphins	Brain, spinal cord	Primarily inhibitory, except in hippocampus	Pain suppression, pleasurable feelings, appetites, placebos

FIGURE 5 Major neurotransmitters.

Another major neurotransmitter is *dopamine (DA)*, which is involved in movement, attention, and learning. The discovery that certain drugs can have a significant effect on dopamine release has led to the development of effective treatments for a wide variety of physical and mental ailments. For instance, Parkinson's disease, from which actor Michael J. Fox suffers, is caused by a deficiency of dopamine in the brain. Techniques for increasing the production of dopamine in Parkinson's patients are proving effective (Kaasinen & Rinne, 2002; Willis, 2005; Iversen & Iversen, 2007).

In other instances, *over*production of dopamine produces negative consequences. For example, researchers have hypothesized that schizophrenia and some other severe mental disturbances are affected or perhaps even caused by the presence of unusually high levels of dopamine. Drugs that block the reception of dopamine reduce the symptoms displayed by some people diagnosed with schizophrenia (Baumeister & Francis, 2002; Bolonna, & Kerwin, 2005; Olijslagers et al., 2006).

Another neurotransmitter, *serotonin*, is associated with the regulation of sleep, eating, mood, and pain. A growing body of research points toward a broader role for serotonin, suggesting its involvement in such diverse behaviors as alcoholism, depression, suicide, impulsivity, aggression, and coping with stress (Zalsman & Apter, 2002; Addolorato et al., 2005; Montgomery, 2006).

Endorphins, another class of neurotransmitters, are a family of chemicals produced by the brain that are similar in structure to painkilling drugs such as morphine. The production of endorphins reflects the brain's effort to deal with pain as well as to elevate mood.

Michael J. Fox, who suffers from Parkinson's disease, has become a strong advocate for research into the disorder.

Endorphins also may produce the euphoric feelings that runners sometimes experience after long runs. The exertion and perhaps the pain involved in a long run may stimulate the production of endorphins, ultimately resulting in what has been called "runner's high" (Kolata, 2002; Pert, 2002; Stanojevic et al., 2007).

Endorphin release might also explain other phenomena that have long puzzled psychologists. For example, the act of taking placebos (pills or other substances that contain no actual drugs but that patients *believe* will make them better) may induce the release of endorphins, leading to the reduction of pain (Wager, 2005; Rajagopal, 2006; Crum & Langer, 2007).

RECAP/EVALUATE/RETHINK

RECAP

Why do psychologists study the brain and nervous system?

- A full understanding of human behavior requires knowledge of the biological influences underlying that behavior, especially those originating in the nervous system. Psychologists who specialize in studying the effects of biological structures and functions on behavior are known as behavioral neuroscientists. (p. 60)

What are the basic elements of the nervous system?

- Neurons, the most basic elements of the nervous system, carry nerve impulses from one part of the body to another. Information in a neuron generally follows a route that begins with the dendrites, continues into the cell body, and leads ultimately down the tubelike extension, the axon. (p. 61)

How does the nervous system communicate electrical and chemical messages from one part to another?

- Most axons are insulated by a coating called the myelin sheath. When a neuron receives a message to fire, it releases an action potential, an electric charge that travels through the axon. Neurons operate according to an all-or-none law: Either they are at rest, or an action potential is moving through them. There is no in-between state. (p. 62)

- Once a neuron fires, nerve impulses are carried to other neurons through the production of chemical substances, neurotransmitters, that actually bridge the gaps—known as synapses—between neurons. Neurotransmitters may be either excitatory, telling other neurons to fire, or inhibitory, preventing or decreasing the likelihood of other neurons firing. (p. 64)

- Endorphins, another type of neurotransmitter, are related to the reduction of pain. Endorphins aid in the production of a natural painkiller and are probably responsible for creating the kind of euphoria that joggers sometimes experience after running. (p. 67)

EVALUATE

1. The _____ is the fundamental element of the nervous system.
2. Neurons receive information through their _____ and send messages through their _____.
3. Just as electrical wires have an outer coating, axons are insulated by a coating called the _____ _____.
4. The gap between two neurons is bridged by a chemical connection called a _____.
5. Endorphins are one kind of _____, the chemical "messengers" between neurons.

RETHINK

1. How might psychologists use drugs that mimic the effects of neurotransmitters to treat psychological disorders?
2. *From the perspective of a health care provider:* How would you explain the placebo effect and the role of endorphins to patients who wish to try unproven treatment methods that they find on the Web?

Answers to Evaluate Questions

1. neuron; 2. dendrites, axons; 3. myelin sheath; 4. synapse; 5. neurotransmitter

KEY TERMS

behavioral neuroscientists (or biopsychologists) p. 60
neurons p. 61
dendrite p. 61

axon p. 61
terminal buttons p. 61
myelin sheath p. 62
all-or-none law p. 62

resting state p. 62
action potential p. 63
mirror neurons p. 64
synapse p. 65

neurotransmitters p. 65
excitatory message p. 66
inhibitory message p. 66
reuptake p. 66

The Nervous System and the Endocrine System: Communicating Within the Body

In light of the complexity of individual neurons and the neurotransmission process, it should come as no surprise that the connections and structures formed by the neurons are complicated. Because each neuron can be connected to 80,000 other neurons, the total number of possible connections is astonishing. For instance, estimates of the number of neural connections within the brain fall in the neighborhood of 10 quadrillion—a 1 followed by 16 zeros—and some experts put the number even higher. However, connections among neurons are not the only means of communication within the body; as we'll see, the endocrine system, which secretes chemical messages that circulate through the blood, also communicates messages that influence behavior and many aspects of biological functioning (Kandel, Schwartz, & Jessell, 2000; Boahen, 2005; Forlenza & Baum, 2004).

Key Concepts

How are the structures of the nervous system linked together?

How does the endocrine system affect behavior?

The Nervous System: Linking Neurons

Whatever the actual number of neural connections, the human nervous system has both logic and elegance. We turn now to a discussion of its basic structures.

CENTRAL AND PERIPHERAL NERVOUS SYSTEMS

As you can see from the schematic representation in Figure 1, the nervous system is divided into two main parts: the central nervous system and the peripheral nervous system. The **central nervous system (CNS)** is composed of the brain and spinal cord. The **spinal cord**, which is about the thickness of a pencil, contains a bundle of neurons that leaves the brain and runs down the length of the back (see Figure 2 on page 71). As you can see in Figure 1, the spinal cord is the primary means for transmitting messages between the brain and the rest of the body.

However, the spinal cord is not just a communication channel. It also controls some simple behaviors on its own, without any help from the brain. An example is the way the knee jerks forward when it is tapped with a rubber hammer. This behavior is a type of **reflex**, an automatic, involuntary response to an incoming stimulus. A reflex is also at work when you touch a hot stove and immediately withdraw your hand. Although the brain eventually analyzes and reacts to the situation ("Ouch—hot stove—pull away!"), the initial withdrawal is directed only by neurons in the spinal cord.

Three kinds of neurons are involved in reflexes. **Sensory (afferent) neurons** transmit information from the perimeter of the body to the central nervous system. **Motor (efferent) neurons** communicate information from the nervous system to muscles and glands. **Interneurons** connect sensory and motor neurons, carrying messages between the two.

The importance of the spinal cord and reflexes is illustrated by the outcome of accidents in which the cord is injured or severed. In some cases, injury results in *quadriplegia*, a condition in which voluntary muscle movement below the neck is lost. In a

Central nervous system (CNS): The part of the nervous system that includes the brain and spinal cord.
Spinal cord: A bundle of neurons that leaves the brain and runs down the length of the back and is the main means for transmitting messages between the brain and the body.
Reflex: An automatic, involuntary response to an incoming stimulus.
Sensory (afferent) neurons: Neurons that transmit information from the perimeter of the body to the central nervous system.
Motor (efferent) neurons: Neurons that communicate information from the nervous system to muscles and glands.
Interneurons: Neurons that connect sensory and motor neurons, carrying messages between the two.

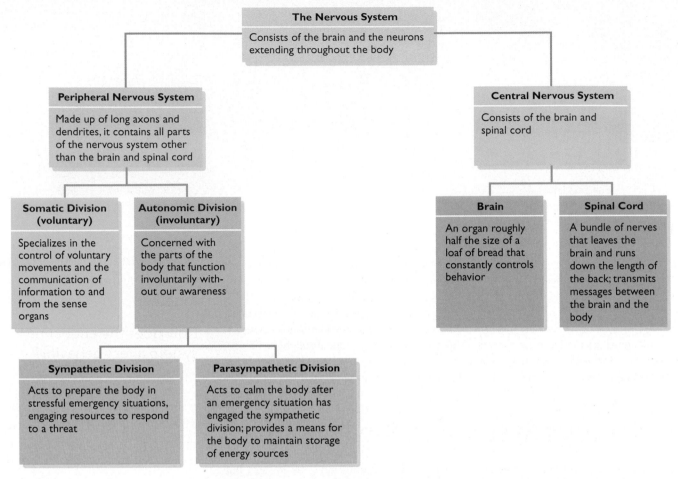

FIGURE 1 A schematic diagram of the relationship of the parts of the nervous system.

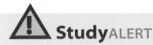
Peripheral nervous system: The part of the nervous system that includes the autonomic and somatic subdivisions; made up of neurons with long axons and dendrites, it branches out from the spinal cord and brain and reaches the extremities of the body.

Somatic division: The part of the peripheral nervous system that specializes in the control of voluntary movements and the communication of information to and from the sense organs.

Autonomic division: The part of the peripheral nervous system that controls involuntary movement of the heart, glands, lungs, and other organs.

less severe but still debilitating condition, *paraplegia*, people are unable to voluntarily move any muscles in the lower half of the body.

As suggested by its name, the **peripheral nervous system** branches out from the spinal cord and brain and reaches the extremities of the body. Made up of neurons with long axons and dendrites, the peripheral nervous system encompasses all the parts of the nervous system other than the brain and spinal cord. There are two major divisions—the somatic division and the autonomic division—both of which connect the central nervous system with the sense organs, muscles, glands, and other organs. The **somatic division** specializes in the control of voluntary movements—such as the motion of the eyes to read this sentence or those of the hand to turn this page—and the communication of information to and from the sense organs. On the other hand, the **autonomic division** controls the parts of the body that keep us alive—the heart, blood vessels, glands, lungs, and other organs that function involuntarily without our awareness. As you are reading at this moment, the autonomic division of the peripheral nervous system is pumping blood through your body, pushing your lungs in and out, and overseeing the digestion of your last meal.

Activating the Divisions of the Autonomic Nervous System. The autonomic division plays a particularly crucial role during emergencies. Suppose that as you are reading you suddenly sense that a stranger is watching you through the window. As you look up, you see the glint of something that might be a knife. As confusion clouds your mind and fear overcomes your attempts to think rationally, what happens to your body? If you are like most people, you react immediately on a physiological level.

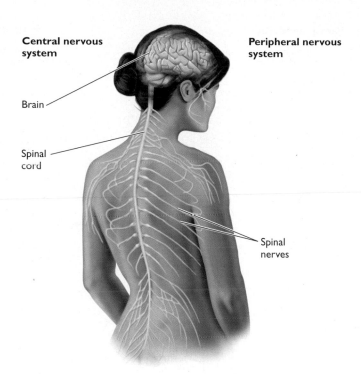

Central nervous system

Brain

Spinal cord

Peripheral nervous system

Spinal nerves

FIGURE 2 The central nervous system, consisting of the brain and spinal cord, and the peripheral nervous system.

Your heart rate increases, you begin to sweat, and you develop goose bumps all over your body.

The physiological changes that occur during a crisis result from the activation of one of the two parts of the autonomic nervous system: the **sympathetic division**. The sympathetic division acts to prepare the body for action in stressful situations by engaging all of the organism's resources to run away or confront the threat. This is often called the "fight or flight" response.

In contrast, the **parasympathetic division** acts to calm the body after the emergency has ended. When you find, for instance, that the stranger at the window is actually your roommate, who has lost his keys and is climbing in the window to avoid waking you, your parasympathetic division begins to predominate, lowering your heart rate, stopping your sweating, and returning your body to the state it was in before you became alarmed. The parasympathetic division also directs the body to store energy for use in emergencies.

The sympathetic and parasympathetic divisions work together to regulate many functions of the body (see Figure 3). For instance, sexual arousal is controlled by the parasympathetic division, but sexual orgasm is a function of the sympathetic division. The sympathetic and parasympathetic divisions also are involved in a number of disorders. For example, one explanation of documented examples of "voodoo death"—in which a person is literally scared to death resulting from a voodoo curse—may be produced by over-stimulation of the sympathetic division due to extreme fear (Sternberg, 2002).

Sympathetic division: The part of the autonomic division of the nervous system that acts to prepare the body for action in stressful situations, engaging all the organism's resources to respond to a threat.

Parasympathetic division: The part of the autonomic division of the nervous system that acts to calm the body after an emergency has ended.

The Evolutionary Foundations of the Nervous System

The complexities of the nervous system can be better understood if we take the course of evolution into consideration. The forerunner of the human nervous system is found in the earliest simple organisms to have a spinal cord. Basically, those organisms were simple input-output devices: When the upper side of the spinal cord was stimulated

FIGURE 3 The major functions of the autonomic nervous system. The sympathetic division acts to prepare certain organs of the body for stressful situations, and the parasympathetic division acts to calm the body after the emergency has been passed. Can you explain why each response of the sympathetic division might be useful in an emergency?

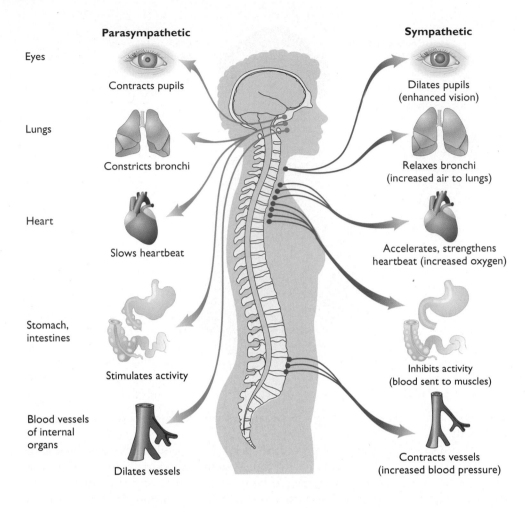

Parasympathetic

Eyes
Contracts pupils

Lungs
Constricts bronchi

Heart
Slows heartbeat

Stomach, intestines
Stimulates activity

Blood vessels of internal organs
Dilates vessels

Sympathetic

Dilates pupils (enhanced vision)

Relaxes bronchi (increased air to lungs)

Accelerates, strengthens heartbeat (increased oxygen)

Inhibits activity (blood sent to muscles)

Contracts vessels (increased blood pressure)

by, for instance, being touched, the organism reacted with a simple response, such as jerking away. Such responses were completely a consequence of the organism's genetic makeup.

Over millions of years, the spinal cord became more specialized, and organisms became capable of distinguishing between different kinds of stimuli and responding appropriately to them. Ultimately, a portion of the spinal cord evolved into what we would consider a primitive brain.

Today, the nervous system is *hierarchically organized*, meaning that relatively newer (from an evolutionary point of view) and more sophisticated regions of the brain regulate the older, and more primitive, parts of the nervous system. As we move up along the spinal cord and continue upward into the brain, then, the functions controlled by the various regions become progressively more advanced.

Why should we care about the evolutionary background of the human nervous system? The answer comes from researchers working in the area of **evolutionary psychology**, the branch of psychology that seeks to identify how behavior is influenced and produced by our genetic inheritance from our ancestors.

Evolutionary psychologists argue that the course of evolution is reflected in the structure and functioning of the nervous system and that evolutionary factors consequently have a significant influence on our everyday behavior. Their work, in conjunction with the research of scientists studying genetics, biochemistry, and medicine, has led to an understanding of how our behavior is affected by heredity, our genetically determined heritage. In fact, evolutionary psychologists have spawned a new and increasingly influential field: behavioral genetics.

Evolutionary psychology: The branch of psychology that seeks to identify behavior patterns that are a result of our genetic inheritance from our ancestors.

BEHAVIORAL GENETICS

Our evolutionary heritage manifests itself not only through the structure and functioning of the nervous system but through our behavior as well. In the view of a growing area of study, people's personality and behavioral habits are affected in part by their genetic heritage. **Behavioral genetics** studies the effects of heredity on behavior. Behavioral genetics researchers are finding increasing evidence that cognitive abilities, personality traits, sexual orientation, and psychological disorders are determined to some extent by genetic factors (Reif & Lesch, 2003; Viding et al., 2005; Ilies, Arvey, & Bouchard, 2006).

Behavioral genetics: The study of the effects of heredity on behavior.

Behavioral genetics lies at the heart of the nature-nurture question, one of the key issues in the study of psychology. Although no one would argue that our behavior is determined *solely* by inherited factors, evidence collected by behavioral geneticists does suggest that our genetic inheritance predisposes us to respond in particular ways to our environment, and even to seek out particular kinds of environments. For instance, research indicates that genetic factors may be related to such diverse behaviors as level of family conflict, schizophrenia, learning disabilities, and general sociability (Harlaar et al., 2005; Moffitt & Caspi, 2007).

Furthermore, important human characteristics and behaviors are related to the presence (or absence) of particular *genes*, the inherited material that controls the transmission of traits. For example, researchers have found evidence that novelty-seeking behavior is determined, at least in part, by a certain gene.

As we will consider later in the book when we discuss human development, researchers have identified some 25,000 individual genes, each of which appears in a specific sequence on a particular *chromosome*, a rod-shaped structure that transmits genetic information across generations. In 2003, after a decade of effort, researchers identified the sequence of the 3 billion chemical pairs that make up human *DNA*, the basic component of genes. Understanding the basic structure of the human *genome*—the "map" of humans' total genetic makeup—brings scientists a giant step closer to understanding the contributions of individual genes to specific human structures and functioning (Plomin & McGuffin, 2003; Andreasen, 2005; Dale & von Schantz, 2007).

Molecular Genetics and Psychological Disorders. Despite its relative infancy, the field of behavioral genetics has already made substantial contributions to our understanding of behavior. One branch of behavioral genetics, *molecular genetics*, seeks to identify specific genes that are associated with behavior and, in particular, psychological disorders. Genes that are physically close to one another on a particular chromosome tend to be linked and inherited together. By finding *genetic markers*—genes with a known location—that are linked to a disorder, scientists are beginning to learn how disorders such as schizophrenia and depression develop and can potentially be treated.

Molecular geneticists have already found that the risk of developing autism (a disorder that influences the development of language and effective social functioning) is increased in the presence of a gene related to early brain development. Children with this gene, a variation of the gene called *HOXA1*, are twice as likely to develop the disorder as children who do not have this variant (Hyman, 2003; Gregg et al., 2007).

Yet having the variant gene does not always lead to autism. More than 99.5 percent of people with the variant do not develop the disorder, and 60 percent of those with autism do not have the variant. It is probable that autism, like other disorders with a genetic basis, is not triggered by the presence or absence of a single, particular gene. More likely, it is produced by several genes in combination, as well as perhaps requiring the presence of certain environmental influences, such as infection or brain injury. The challenge for behavior geneticists, then, is not only to determine what genes are responsible for particular behaviors, but also to identify the environmental triggers that activate those genes (Sen et al., 2007).

In examining the genetic roots of various behaviors, the study of behavior genetics has stirred controversy. For instance, questions about the existence of genetic influences on criminality, intelligence, and homosexuality raise considerable emotion. Furthermore, it is unclear what the social and political consequences of discoveries in behavioral genetics would be. Would finding a strong genetic basis for criminal behavior lead to genetic screening and restricted civil rights for individuals having "criminal" genes? Clearly, behavioral genetic discoveries could have an impact on a number of important social issues.

Behavioral Genetics, Gene Therapy, and Genetic Counseling. Behavioral genetics also holds the promise of developing new diagnostic and treatment techniques for genetic deficiencies that can lead to physical and psychological difficulties. In *gene therapy*, scientists inject into a patient's bloodstream genes meant to cure a particular disease. When the genes arrive at the site of defective genes that are producing the illness, they trigger the production of chemicals that can treat the disease (Lymberis et al., 2004; Rattazzi, LaFuci, & Brown, 2004; Jaffé et al., 2006).

The number of diseases that can be treated through gene therapy is growing, as we will see when we discuss human development. For example, gene therapy is now being used in experimental trials involving people with certain forms of cancer and blindness (Nakamura, 2004; Wagner et al., 2004; Hirschler, 2007).

Advances in behavioral genetics also have led to the development of a profession that did not exist several decades ago: genetic counseling. Genetic counselors help people deal with issues related to inherited disorders. For example, genetic counselors provide advice to prospective parents about the potential risks in a future pregnancy, based on their family history of birth defects and hereditary illnesses. In addition, the counselor considers the parents' age and problems with children they already have. They also can take blood, skin, and urine samples to examine specific chromosomes.

Scientists have already developed genetic tests to determine whether someone is susceptible to certain types of cancer or heart disease, and it may not be long before analysis of a drop of blood can indicate whether a child—or potentially an unborn fetus—is susceptible to certain psychological disorders. How such knowledge will be used is a source of considerable speculation and controversy, controversy that is certain to grow as genetic testing becomes more common (Etchegary, 2004).

The Endocrine System: Of Chemicals and Glands

Endocrine system: A chemical communication network that sends messages throughout the body via the bloodstream.

Hormones: Chemicals that circulate through the blood and regulate the functioning or growth of the body.

Another of the body's communication systems, the **endocrine system** is a chemical communication network that sends messages throughout the body via the bloodstream. Its job is to secrete **hormones**, chemicals that circulate through the blood and regulate the functioning or growth of the body. It also influences—and is influenced by—the functioning of the nervous system. Although the endocrine system is not part of the brain, it is closely linked to the hypothalamus.

As chemical messengers, hormones are like neurotransmitters, although their speed and mode of transmission are quite different. Whereas neural messages are measured in thousandths of a second, hormonal communications may take minutes to reach their destination. Furthermore, neural messages move through neurons in specific lines (like a signal carried by wires strung along telephone poles), whereas hormones travel throughout the body, similar to the way radio waves are transmitted across the entire landscape. Just as radio waves evoke a response only when a radio is tuned to the correct station, hormones flowing through the bloodstream activate only those cells that are receptive and "tuned" to the appropriate hormonal message.

A key component of the endocrine system is the tiny **pituitary gland**, which is found near—and regulated by—the hypothalamus. The pituitary gland has sometimes been called the "master gland" because it controls the functioning of the rest of the endocrine system. But the pituitary gland is more than just the taskmaster of other

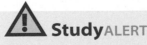

StudyALERT

The endocrine system produces hormones, chemicals that circulate through the body via the bloodstream.

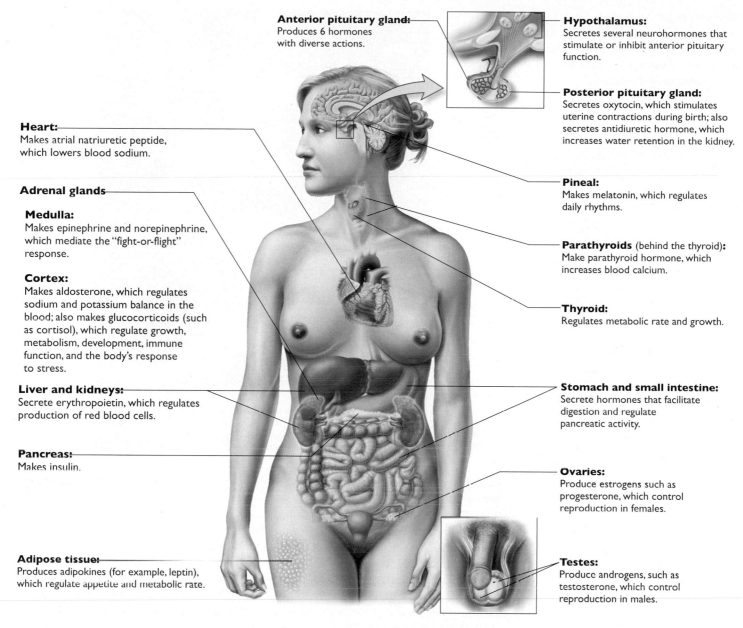

Anterior pituitary gland:
Produces 6 hormones
with diverse actions.

Hypothalamus:
Secretes several neurohormones that
stimulate or inhibit anterior pituitary
function.

Posterior pituitary gland:
Secretes oxytocin, which stimulates
uterine contractions during birth; also
secretes antidiuretic hormone, which
increases water retention in the kidney.

Heart:
Makes atrial natriuretic peptide,
which lowers blood sodium.

Pineal:
Makes melatonin, which regulates
daily rhythms.

Adrenal glands

Medulla:
Makes epinephrine and norepinephrine,
which mediate the "fight-or-flight"
response.

Parathyroids (behind the thyroid)**:**
Make parathyroid hormone, which
increases blood calcium.

Cortex:
Makes aldosterone, which regulates
sodium and potassium balance in the
blood; also makes glucocorticoids (such
as cortisol), which regulate growth,
metabolism, development, immune
function, and the body's response
to stress.

Thyroid:
Regulates metabolic rate and growth.

Stomach and small intestine:
Secrete hormones that facilitate
digestion and regulate
pancreatic activity.

Liver and kidneys:
Secrete erythropoietin, which regulates
production of red blood cells.

Pancreas:
Makes insulin.

Ovaries:
Produce estrogens such as
progesterone, which control
reproduction in females.

Adipose tissue:
Produces adipokines (for example, leptin),
which regulate appetite and metabolic rate.

Testes:
Produce androgens, such as
testosterone, which control
reproduction in males.

FIGURE 4 Location and function of the major endocrine glands. The pituitary gland controls
the functioning of the other endocrine glands and in turn is regulated by the hypothalamus.

glands; it has important functions in its own right. For instance, hormones secreted by
the pituitary gland control growth. Extremely short people and unusually tall ones
usually have pituitary gland abnormalities. Other endocrine glands, shown in
Figure 4, affect emotional reactions, sexual urges, and energy levels.

Despite its designation as the "master gland," the pituitary is actually a servant of the
brain, because the brain is ultimately responsible for the endocrine system's functioning.
The brain maintains the internal balance of the body through the hypothalamus.

Individual hormones can wear many hats, depending on circumstances. For
example, the hormone oxytocin is at the root of many of life's satisfactions and pleasures. In new mothers, oxytocin produces an urge to nurse newborn offspring. The
same hormone also seems to stimulate cuddling between species members. And—at
least in rats—it encourages sexually active males to seek out females more passion-
ately, and females to be more receptive to males' sexual advances. There's even

Pituitary gland: The major component
of the endocrine system, or "master
gland," which secretes hormones that
control growth and other parts of the
endocrine system.

Steroids can provide added muscle and strength, but they have dangerous side effects. A number of well-known athletes in a variety of sports have been accused of using the drugs illegally.

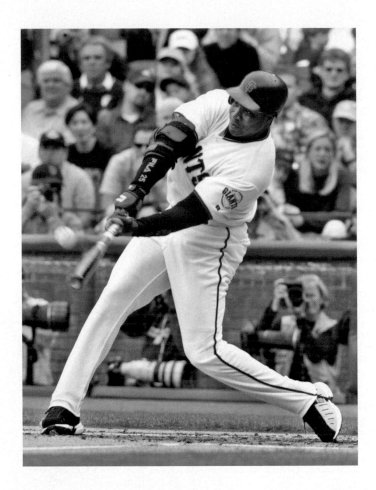

evidence that oxytocin is related to the development of trust in others, helping to grease the wheels of effective social interaction (Quadros et al., 2002; Kosfeld et al., 2005; Meinlschmidt & Heim, 2007).

Although hormones are produced naturally by the endocrine system, the ingestion of artificial hormones has proved to be both beneficial and potentially dangerous. For example, before the early 2000s, physicians frequently prescribed hormone replacement therapy (HRT) to treat symptoms of menopause in older women. However, because recent research suggests that the treatment has potentially dangerous side effects, health experts now warn that the dangers outweigh the benefits (Herrington & Howard, 2003).

The use of testosterone, a male hormone, and drugs known as *steroids*, which act like testosterone, is increasingly common. For athletes and others who want to bulk up their appearance, steroids provide a way to add muscle weight and increase strength. However, these drugs can lead to heart attacks, strokes, cancer, and even violent behavior, making them extremely dangerous. For example, in one infamous case, professional wrestler Chris Benoit strangled his wife, suffocated his son, and later hanged himself—acts that were attributed to his use of steroids (Klötz, 2006; Pagonis et al., 2006; Sandomir, 2007).

RECAP/EVALUATE/RETHINK

RECAP

How are the structures of the nervous system linked together?

- The nervous system is made up of the central nervous system (the brain and spinal cord) and the peripheral nervous system. The peripheral nervous system is made up of the somatic division, which controls voluntary movements and the communication of information to and from the sense organs, and the autonomic division, which controls involuntary functions such as those of the heart, blood vessels, and lungs. (p. 69)

- The autonomic division of the peripheral nervous system is further subdivided into the sympathetic and parasympathetic divisions. The sympathetic division prepares the body in emergency situations, and the parasympathetic division helps the body return to its typical resting state. (p. 70)

- Evolutionary psychology, the branch of psychology that seeks to identify behavior patterns that are a result of our genetic inheritance, has led to increased understanding of the evolutionary basis of the structure and organization of the human nervous system. Behavioral genetics extends this study to include the evolutionary and hereditary basis of human personality traits and behavior. (p. 72)

How does the endocrine system affect behavior?

- The endocrine system secretes hormones, chemicals that regulate the functioning of the body, via the bloodstream. The pituitary gland secretes growth hormones and influences the release of hormones by other endocrine glands, and in turn is regulated by the hypothalamus. (p. 74)

EVALUATE

1. If you put your hand on a red-hot piece of metal, the immediate response of pulling it away would be an example of a(n) _____.

2. The central nervous system is composed of the _____ and _____.

3. In the peripheral nervous system, the _____ division controls voluntary movements, whereas the _____ division controls organs that keep us alive and function without our awareness.

4. Maria saw a young boy run into the street and get hit by a car. When she got to the fallen child, she was in a state of panic. She was sweating, and her heart was racing. Her biological state resulted from the activation of what division of the nervous system?
   a. Parasympathetic
   b. Central
   c. Sympathetic

5. The emerging field of _____ studies ways in which our genetic inheritance predisposes us to behave in certain ways.

RETHINK

1. In what ways is the "fight-or-flight" response helpful to humans in emergency situations?

2. *From the perspective of a genetic counselor:* How would you explain the pros and cons of genetic counseling to someone who was interested in receiving genetic screening for various diseases and disorders?

Answers to Evaluate Questions

1. reflex; 2. brain, spinal cord; 3. somatic, autonomic; 4. c. sympathetic; 5. behavioral genetics

KEY TERMS

central nervous system
   (CNS) p. 69
spinal cord p. 69
reflex p. 69
sensory (afferent) neurons
   p. 69

motor (efferent) neurons
   p. 69
interneurons p. 69
peripheral nervous system
   p. 70
somatic division p. 70

autonomic division p. 70
sympathetic division p. 71
parasympathetic division
   p. 71
evolutionary psychology
   p. 72

behavioral genetics p. 73
endocrine system p. 74
hormones p. 74
pituitary gland p. 75

How Neuroscience Is Helping Patients with Brain Injuries

His skull crushed in a brutal mugging, the man had been left severely brain-damaged. For six years, he had lain in a stupor, eyes almost always closed, unable to communicate, fed through a tube. His mother visited him in the nursing home every day, she says, and every time she cried.

But now, she says, her 38-year-old son can eat, drink from a cup, laugh, watch a movie, and say, "I love you, Mommy." She still cries when she sees him, she says, "but it's tears of joy" (Goldberg, 2007, p. A1).

This patient was the first person in a minimally conscious state to benefit from a new procedure called *deep-brain stimulation*. Minimally conscious patients have damaged brains that keep them largely unresponsive and unaware of their surroundings, with only occasional moments of limited awareness. This particular patient was thought to be minimally conscious because his central thalamus, which is involved in arousal, was impaired.

Neuroscientist Nicholas Schiff and colleagues hoped that deep-brain stimulation, which consisted of surgically implanted electrodes in the brain that electrically stimulate a precise region, would trigger his thalamus into working better. To their great excitement, it did. The result was immediate, and the patient is likely to continue to improve (Hopkin, 2007; Schiff et al., 2007).

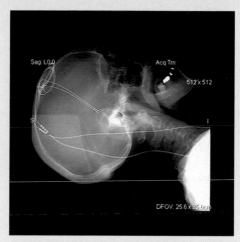

In deep brain stimulation, electrodes implanted in the brain stimulate precise areas.

This is just one example of how advances in neuroscience are returning quality of life to the most profoundly impaired patients—people who once had little or no hope of ever interacting with the world again. While Schiff is working on using technology to waken impaired brains through direct stimulation, other neuroscientists are developing techniques for reading brain signals from patients who are fully conscious and aware but, because of neurological disease or trauma, are unable to move or communicate in any way.

Such a condition, called *locked-in syndrome* because patients' alert minds are literally locked up inside an unresponsive body, produces poor quality of life unless patients can be given some means of communicating. Eye movements are sometimes used, but failing that, only the brain's

own activity remains as a potential link to the outside world. The trick, then, is to find a way to interface with the brain directly (Kubler, Winter, & Ludolph, 2005; Sledz, Oddy, & Beaumont, 2007).

To address cases of locked-in syndrome, researcher Jonathan Wolpaw has combined EEG scanning techniques with a powerful computer running specialized software that looks for changes in brain wave patterns associated with different brain states. With a great deal of training and practice, patients can learn to use brain signals to move a cursor on a computer screen, thereby controlling menus that can summon help, turn on lights, operate a television, and even type out messages and send e-mail (Heuser, 2006; Allison, Wolpaw, & Wolpaw, 2007; Wolpaw, 2007).

Other neuroscientists are developing technology to allow locked-in patients to operate a Web browser and use the Internet to communicate and to learn, and potentially even to shop or to run a business. While brain-computer interfaces are still too experimental to be practically useful, the day is not far off when they will deliver on their promise of regained autonomy for locked-in patients (Heuser, 2006; Karim et al., 2006).

- Why comp com nun loc'
- To br

this interruption on normal brain functioning. The procedure is sometimes called a "virtual lesion" because it produces effects analogous to what would occur if areas of the brain were physically cut. The enormous advantage of TMS, of course, is that the virtual cut is only temporary. In addition to identifying areas of the brain that are responsible for particular functions, TMS has the potential to treat certain kinds of psychological disorders, such as depression and schizophrenia, by shooting brief magnetic pulses through the brain (Simons, 2005; Fregni & Pascual-Leone, 2007; Sampson, Solvason, & Husain, 2007).

Advances in our understanding of the brain also are paving the way for the development of new methods for harnessing the brain's neural signals. We consider some of these intriguing findings in the *Applying Psychology in the 21st Century* box.

The Central Core: Our "Old Brain"

Central core: The "old brain," which controls basic functions such as eating and sleeping and is common to all vertebrates.

Although the capabilities of the human brain far exceed those of the brain of any other species, humans share some basic functions, such as breathing, eating, and sleeping, with more primitive animals. Not surprisingly, those activities are directed by a relatively primitive part of the brain. A portion of the brain known as the **central core** (see Figure 2) is quite similar in all vertebrates (species with backbones). The central core is sometimes referred to as the "old brain" because its evolution can be traced back some 500 million years to primitive structures found in nonhuman species.

If we were to move up the spinal cord from the base of the skull to locate the structures of the central core of the brain, the first part we would come to would be the *hindbrain*, which contains the medulla, pons, and cerebellum (see Figure 3). The *medulla* controls a number of critical body functions, the most important of which are breathing and heartbeat. The *pons* comes next, joining the two halves of the cerebellum, which lies adjacent to it. Containing large bundles of nerves, the pons acts as a transmitter of motor information, coordinating muscles and integrating movement between the right and left halves of the body. It is also involved in regulating sleep.

Cerebellum (ser uh BELL um): The part of the brain that controls bodily balance.

The **cerebellum** is found just above the medulla and behind the pons. Without the help of the cerebellum we would be unable to walk a straight line without staggering and lurching forward, for it is the job of the cerebellum to control bodily balance. It constantly monitors feedback from the muscles to coordinate their placement, movement, and tension. In fact, drinking too much alcohol seems to depress the activity of the cerebellum, leading to the unsteady gait and movement characteristic of drunkenness. The cerebellum is also involved in several intellectual functions, ranging from the analysis and coordination of sensory information to problem solving (Bower & Parsons, 2004; Paquier & Mariën, 2005; Vandervert, Schimpf, & Liu, 2007).

Reticular formation: The part of the brain extending from the medulla through the pons and made up of groups of nerve cells that can immediately activate other parts of the brain to produce general bodily arousal.

The **reticular formation** extends from the medulla through the pons, passing through the middle section of the brain—or *midbrain*—and into the front-most part of the brain, called the *forebrain*. Like an ever-vigilant guard, the reticular formation is made up of groups of nerve cells that can activate other parts of the brain immediately to produce general bodily arousal. If, for example, we are startled by a loud noise, the reticular formation can prompt a heightened state of awareness to determine whether a response is necessary. The reticular formation serves a different function when we are sleeping, seeming to filter out background stimuli to allow us to sleep undisturbed.

Thalamus: The part of the brain located in the middle of the central core that acts primarily to relay information about the senses.

Hidden within the forebrain, the **thalamus** acts primarily as a relay station for information about the senses. Messages from the eyes, ears, and skin travel to the

Cerebral cortex
(the "new brain")

Central core
(the "old brain")

FIGURE 2 The major divisions of the brain: the cerebral cortex and the central core. (Source: Seeley, Stephens, & Tate, 2000.)

Although the cerebellum is involved in several intellectual functions, its main duty is to control balance, constantly monitoring feedback from the muscles to coordinate their placement, movement, and tension.

Cerebral cortex

Corpus callosum
Bridge of fibers passing
information between the
two cerebral hemispheres

Hippocampus

Amygdala

Cerebellum
Controls bodily balance

Spinal cord
Responsible for communication
between brain and rest of body;
involved in simple reflexes

Thalamus
Relay center for cortex;
handles incoming and
outgoing signals

Midbrain

Hypothalamus
Responsible for regulating basic
biological needs: hunger, thirst,
temperature control

Olfactory bulb

Pituitary gland
"Master" gland that regulates
other endocrine glands

Pons
Involved in sleep and arousal

Medulla
Responsible for regulating largely
unconscious functions such as
breathing and circulation

FIGURE 3 The major structures in the brain. (Source: Brooker, Widmaier, Graham, & Stiling, 2008.)

thalamus to be communicated upward to higher parts of the brain. The thalamus also integrates information from higher parts of the brain, sorting it out so that it can be sent to the cerebellum and medulla.

The **hypothalamus** is located just below the thalamus. Although tiny—about the size of a fingertip—the hypothalamus plays an extremely important role. One of its major functions is to maintain *homeostasis*, a steady internal environment for the body. The hypothalamus helps provide a constant body temperature and monitors the amount of nutrients stored in the cells. A second major function is equally important: the hypothalamus produces and regulates behavior that is critical to the basic survival of the species, such as eating, self-protection, and sex.

Hypothalamus: A tiny part of the brain, located below the thalamus, that maintains homeostasis and produces and regulates vital behavior, such as eating, drinking, and sexual behavior.

In an eerie view of the future, science fiction writers have suggested that people someday will routinely have electrodes implanted in their brains. Those electrodes will permit them to receive tiny shocks that will produce the sensation of pleasure by stimulating certain centers of the brain. When they feel upset, people will simply activate their electrodes to achieve an immediate high.

Although far-fetched—and ultimately improbable—such a futuristic fantasy is based on fact. The brain does have pleasure centers in several areas, including some in the **limbic system**. Consisting of a series of doughnut-shaped structures that include the *amygdala* and *hippocampus*, the limbic system borders the top of the central core and has connections with the cerebral cortex (see Figure 4).

The structures of the limbic system jointly control a variety of basic functions relating to emotions and self-preservation, such as eating, aggression, and reproduction.

Limbic system: The part of the brain that controls eating, aggression, and reproduction.

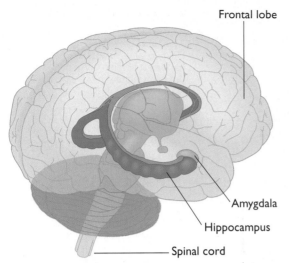

Frontal lobe

Amygdala

Hippocampus

Spinal cord

FIGURE 4 The limbic system consists of a series of doughnut-shaped structures that are involved in self-preservation, learning, memory, and the experience of pleasure.

Injury to the limbic system can produce striking changes in behavior. For example, injury to the amygdala, which is involved in fear and aggression, can turn animals that are usually docile and tame into belligerent savages. Conversely, animals that are usually wild and uncontrollable may become meek and obedient following injury to the amygdala (Bedard & Persinger, 1995; Gontkovsky, 2005).

Research examining the effects of mild electric shocks to parts of the limbic system and other parts of the brain has produced some thought-provoking findings. In one experiment, rats that pressed a bar received mild electric stimulation through an electrode implanted in their brains, which produced pleasurable feelings. Even starving rats on their way to food would stop to press the bar as many times as they could. Some rats would actually stimulate themselves literally thousands of times an hour—until they collapsed with fatigue (Olds & Fobes, 1981; Routtenberg & Lindy, 1965; Fountas & Smith, 2007).

The extraordinarily pleasurable quality of certain kinds of stimulation has also been experienced by humans, who, as part of the treatment for certain kinds of brain disorders, have received electrical stimulation to certain areas of the limbic system. Although at a loss to describe just what it feels like, these people report the experience to be intensely pleasurable, similar in some respects to sexual orgasm.

The limbic system and hippocampus in particular play an important role in learning and memory, a finding demonstrated in patients with epilepsy. In an attempt to stop their seizures, such patients have had portions of the limbic system removed. One unintended consequence of the surgery is that individuals sometimes have difficulty learning and remembering new information. In one case, a patient who had undergone surgery was unable to remember where he lived, although he had resided at the same address for eight years. Further, even though the patient was able to carry on animated conversations, he was unable, a few minutes later, to recall what had been discussed (Milner, 1966; Rich & Shapiro, 2007).

The limbic system, then, is involved in several important functions, including self-preservation, learning, memory, and the experience of pleasure. These functions are hardly unique to humans; in fact, the limbic system is sometimes referred to as the "animal brain" because its structures and functions are so similar to those of other mammals. To identify the part of the brain that provides the complex and subtle capabilities that are uniquely human, we need to turn to another structure—the cerebral cortex.

The Cerebral Cortex: Our "New Brain"

As we have proceeded up the spinal cord and into the brain, our discussion has centered on areas of the brain that control functions similar to those found in less sophisticated organisms. But where, you may be asking, are the portions of the brain that enable humans to do what they do best and that distinguish humans from all other animals? Those unique features of the human brain—indeed, the very capabilities that allow you to come up with such a question in the first place—are embodied in the ability to think, evaluate, and make complex judgments. The principal location of these abilities, along with many others, is the **cerebral cortex**.

The cerebral cortex is referred to as the "new brain" because of its relatively recent evolution. It consists of a mass of deeply folded, rippled, convoluted tissue. Although only about one-twelfth of an inch thick, it would, if flattened out, cover an area more than two feet square. This configuration allows the surface area of the cortex to be considerably greater than it would be if it were smoother and more uniformly packed into the skull. The uneven shape also permits a high level of integration of neurons, allowing sophisticated information processing.

The cortex has four major sections called **lobes**. If we take a side view of the brain, the *frontal lobes* lie at the front center of the cortex and the *parietal lobes* lie behind them. The *temporal lobes* are found in the lower-center portion of the cortex, with the *occipital*

Cerebral cortex: The "new brain," responsible for the most sophisticated information processing in the brain; contains four lobes.

Lobes: The four major sections of the cerebral cortex: frontal, parietal, temporal, and occipital.

lobes lying behind them. These four sets of lobes are physically separated by deep grooves called sulci. Figure 5 shows the four areas.

Another way to describe the brain is in terms of the functions associated with a particular area. Figure 5 also shows the specialized regions within the lobes related to specific functions and areas of the body. Three major areas are known: the motor areas, the sensory areas, and the association areas. Although we will discuss these areas as though they were separate and independent, keep in mind that this is an oversimplification. In most instances, behavior is influenced simultaneously by several structures and areas within the brain, operating interdependently. To give one example, as the scan in Figure 6 on the next page shows, people use a number of different areas of the brain when they were led to create sentences (a verbal task) compared with improvising musical tunes. Furthermore, when people suffer brain injury, uninjured portions of the brain can sometimes take over the functions that were previously handled by the damaged area. In short, the brain is extraordinarily adaptable (Sacks, 2003; Boller, 2004; Brown, Martinez, & Parsons, 2006).

THE MOTOR AREA OF THE CORTEX

If you look at the frontal lobe in Figure 5, you will see a shaded portion labeled **motor area.** This part of the cortex is largely responsible for the body's voluntary movement. Every portion of the motor area corresponds to a specific locale within the body. If we were to insert an electrode into a particular part of the motor area of the cortex and apply mild electrical stimulation, there would be involuntary movement in the corresponding part of the body. If we moved to another part of the motor area and stimulated it, a different part of the body would move.

The motor area is so well mapped that researchers have identified the amount and relative location of cortical tissue used to produce movement in specific parts of the human body. For example, the control of movements that are relatively large scale and require little precision, such as the movement of a knee or a hip, is centered in a very small space in the motor area. In contrast, movements that must be precise and delicate, such as facial expressions and finger movements, are controlled by a considerably larger portion of the motor area.

In short, the motor area of the cortex provides a guide to the degree of complexity and the importance of the motor capabilities of specific parts of the body. In fact, it may do even more: Increasing evidence shows that not only does the motor cortex

The part of the cortex that is largely responsible for the body's voluntary movement

Neuroscience in Your Life

FIGURE 6 Participants in an experiment improvised sentences or musical tunes during a PET scan. The results showed that while both activities use some of the same brain areas (cyan), there are also areas of the brain that were active only during one of the two activities (blue—sentences; red—melodies). The specific active areas are labeled according to Brodmann's areas (for example, BA6, BA22, etc.), a system used to map the brain (Brown et al., 2006).

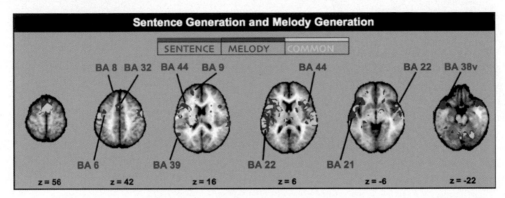

control different parts of the body, but it may also direct body parts into complex postures, such as the stance of a football center just before the ball is snapped to the quarterback or a swimmer standing at the edge of a diving board (Graziano, Tyler, & Moore, 2002; Dessing, Peper, Bullock, & Beek, 2005).

Ultimately, movement, like other behavior, is produced through the coordinated firing of a complex variety of neurons in the nervous system. The neurons that produce movement are linked in elaborate ways and work closely together.

THE SENSORY AREA OF THE CORTEX

Sensory area: The site in the brain of the tissue that corresponds to each of the senses, with the degree of sensitivity related to the amount of tissue.

Given the one-to-one correspondence between the motor area and body location, it is not surprising to find a similar relationship between specific portions of the cortex and the senses. The **sensory area** of the cortex includes three regions: one that corresponds primarily to body sensations (including touch and pressure), one relating to sight, and a third relating to sound. For instance, the *somatosensory area* in the parietal lobe encompasses specific locations associated with the ability to perceive touch and pressure in a particular area of the body. As with the motor area, the amount of brain tissue related to a particular location on the body determines the degree of sensitivity of that location: the greater the area devoted to a specific area of the body within the cortex, the more sensitive that area of the body. As you can see from the weird-looking individual in Figure 7, parts such as the fingers are related to a larger portion of the somatosensory area and are the most sensitive.

The senses of sound and sight are also represented in specific areas of the cerebral cortex. An *auditory area* located in the temporal lobe is responsible for the sense of hearing. If the auditory area is stimulated electrically, a person will hear sounds such as clicks or hums. It also appears that particular locations within the auditory area respond to specific pitches (Hudspeth, 2000; Brown & Martinez, 2007).

The visual area in the cortex, located in the occipital lobe, responds in the same way to electrical stimulation. Stimulation by electrodes produces the experience of flashes of light or colors, suggesting that the raw sensory input of images from the eyes is received in this area of the brain and transformed into meaningful stimuli. The visual area provides another example of how areas of the brain are intimately related to specific areas of the body: specific structures in the eye are related to a particular part of the cortex—with, as you might guess, more area of the brain given to the most sensitive portions of the retina (Wurtz & Kandel, 2000; Stenbacka & Vanni, 2007).

THE ASSOCIATION AREAS OF THE CORTEX

In a freak accident in 1848, an explosion drove a 3-foot-long iron bar completely through the skull of railroad worker Phineas Gage, where it remained after the accident. Amazingly, Gage survived, and, despite the rod lodged through his head, a few minutes later seemed to be fine.

But he wasn't. Before the accident, Gage was hard-working and cautious. Afterward, he became irresponsible, drank heavily, and drifted from one wild scheme to another. In the words of one of his physicians, "he was 'no longer Gage'" (Harlow, 1869, p. 14).

What had happened to the old Gage? Although there is no way of knowing for sure, we can speculate that the accident injured the region of Gage's cerebral cortex known as the **association areas**, which generally are considered to be the site of higher mental processes such as thinking, language, memory, and speech (Rowe et al., 2000).

FIGURE 7 The greater the amount of tissue in the somatosensory area of the brain that is related to a specific body part, the more sensitive is that body part. If the size of our body parts reflected the corresponding amount of brain tissue, we would look like this strange creature.

The association areas make up a large portion of the cerebral cortex and consist of the sections that are not directly involved in either sensory processing or directing movement. The association areas control *executive functions*, which are abilities relating to planning, goal setting, judgment, and impulse control.

Much of our understanding of the association areas comes from patients who, like Phineas Gage, have suffered some type of brain injury. For example, when parts of the association areas are damaged, people undergo personality changes that affect their ability to make moral judgments and process emotions. At the same time, people with damage in those areas can still be capable of reasoning logically, performing calculations, and recalling information (Damasio et al., 1994).

Injuries to the association areas of the brain can produce *aphasia*, problems with language. In *Broca's aphasia*, speech becomes halting, laborious, and often ungrammatical, and a speaker is unable to find the right words. In contrast, *Wernicke's aphasia* produces difficulties both in understanding others' speech and in the production of language. The disorder is characterized by speech that sounds fluent but makes no sense, as in this example from a Wernick's patient: "Boy, I'm sweating, I'm awful nervous, you know, once in a while I get caught up, I can't mention the tarripoi, a month ago, quite a little . . . ." (Gardner, 1975, p. 68; Kearns, 2005; Caplan et al., 2007).

Association areas: One of the major regions of the cerebral cortex; the site of the higher mental processes, such as thought, language, memory, and speech.

Shortly after he was born, Jacob Stark's arms and legs started jerking every 20 minutes. Weeks later he could not focus his eyes on his mother's face. The diagnosis: uncontrollable epileptic seizures involving his entire brain.

His mother, Sally Stark, recalled: "When Jacob was two and a half months old, they said he would never learn to sit up, would never be able to feed himself. . . . They told us to take him home, love him and find an institution. (Blakeslee, 1992, p. C3)

Instead, Jacob had brain surgery when he was 5 months old in which physicians removed 20 percent of his brain. The operation was a complete success. Three years later Jacob seemed normal in every way, with no sign of seizures.

The surgery that helped Jacob was based on the premise that the diseased part of his brain was producing seizures throughout the brain. Surgeons reasoned that if they removed the misfiring portion, the remaining parts of the brain, which appeared intact in PET scans, would take over. They correctly bet that Jacob could still lead a normal life after surgery, particularly because the surgery was being done at so young an age.

Neuroplasticity: Changes in the brain that occur throughout the life span relating to the addition of new neurons, new interconnections between neurons, and the reorganization of information-processing areas.
Neurogenesis: The creation of new neurons.

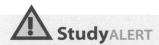

StudyALERT

Remember that *neuroplasticity* is the reorganization of existing neuronal connections, while *neurogenesis* is the creation of new neurons.

The success of Jacob's surgery illustrates that the brain has the ability to shift functions to different locations after injury to a specific area or in cases of surgery. But equally encouraging are some new findings about the *regenerative* powers of the brain and nervous system.

Scientists have learned in recent years that the brain continually reorganizes itself in a process termed **neuroplasticity**. Although for many years conventional wisdom held that no new brain cells are created after childhood, new research finds otherwise. Not only do the interconnections between neurons become more complex throughout life, but it now appears that new neurons are also created in certain areas of the brain during adulthood—a process called **neurogenesis**. In fact, new neurons may become integrated with existing neural connections after some kinds of brain injury during adulthood (Bhardwaj et al., 2006; Jang, You, & Ahn, 2007; Poo & Isaacson, 2007).

The ability of neurons to renew themselves during adulthood has significant implications for the potential treatment of disorders of the nervous system. For example, drugs that trigger the development of new neurons might be used to counter diseases like Alzheimer's that are produced when neurons die (Steiner, Wolf, & Kempermann, 2006; Tsai, Tsai, & Shen, 2007).

Furthermore, specific experiences can modify the way in which information is processed. For example, if you learn to read Braille, the amount of tissue in your cortex related to sensation in the fingertips will expand. Similarly, if you take up the violin, the area of the brain that receives messages from your fingers will grow—but only relating to the fingers that actually move across the violin's strings (Schwartz & Begley, 2002; Kolb, Gibb, & Robinson, 2003).

The future also holds promise for people who suffer from the tremors and loss of motor control produced by Parkinson's disease, although the research is mired in controversy. Because Parkinson's disease is caused by a gradual loss of cells that stimulate the production of dopamine in the brain, many investigators have reasoned that a procedure that would increase the supply of dopamine might be effective. They seem to be on the right track. When stem cells—immature cells from human fetuses that have the potential to develop into a variety of specialized cell types, depending on where they are implanted—are injected directly into the brains of Parkinson's sufferers, they take root and stimulate dopamine production. Preliminary results have been promising, with some patients showing great improvement (Levy et al., 2004; Korecka, Verhaagen, & Hol, 2007; Parish & Arenas, 2007).

Stem cells thus hold great promise. When a stem cell divides, each newly created cell has the potential to be transformed into more specialized cells that have the potential to repair damaged cells. Because many of the most disabling diseases, ranging from cancer to stroke, result from cell damage, the potential of stem cells to revolutionize medicine is significant.

However, because the source of implanted stem cells typically is aborted fetuses, their use is controversial. Some critics have argued that the use of stem cells in research and treatment should be prohibited, while supporters argue that the potential benefits of the research are so great that stem cell research should be unrestricted. The issue has been politicized, and the question of whether and how stem cell research should be regulated is not clear (Rosen, 2005; Giacomini, Baylis, & Robert, 2007; Holden, 2007).

The Specialization of the Hemispheres: Two Brains or One?

The most recent development, at least in evolutionary terms, in the organization and operation of the human brain probably occurred in the last million years: a specialization of the functions controlled by the left and right sides of the brain (McManus, 2004; Sun et al., 2005).

The brain is divided into two roughly mirror-image halves. Just as we have two arms, two legs, and two lungs, we have a left brain and a right brain. Because of the way nerves in the brain are connected to the rest of the body, these symmetrical left and right halves, called **hemispheres**, control motion in—and receive sensation from—the side of the body opposite their location. The left hemisphere of the brain, then, generally controls the right side of the body, and the right hemisphere controls the left side of the body. Thus, damage to the right side of the brain is typically indicated by functional difficulties in the left side of the body.

Despite the appearance of similarity between the two hemispheres of the brain, they are somewhat different in the functions they control and in the ways they control them. Certain behaviors are more likely to reflect activity in one hemisphere than in the other, or are **lateralized**.

For example, for most people, language processing occurs more in the left side of the brain. In general, the left hemisphere concentrates more on tasks that require verbal competence, such as speaking, reading, thinking, and reasoning. In addition, the left hemisphere tends to process information sequentially, one bit at a time (Turkewitz, 1993; Banich & Heller, 1998; Hines, 2004).

The right hemisphere has its own strengths, particularly in nonverbal areas such as the understanding of spatial relationships, recognition of patterns and drawings, music, and emotional expression. The right hemisphere tends to process information globally, considering it as a whole (Ansaldo, Arguin, & Roch-Locours, 2002; Holowka & Petitto, 2002).

Keep in mind that the differences in specialization between the hemispheres are not great, and the degree and nature of lateralization vary from one person to another. If, like most people, you are right-handed, the control of language is probably concentrated more in your left hemisphere. By contrast, if you are among the 10 percent of people who are left-handed or are ambidextrous (you use both hands interchangeably), it is much more likely that the language centers of your brain are located more in the right hemisphere or are divided equally between the left and right hemispheres.

Furthermore, the two hemispheres of the brain function in tandem. It is a mistake to think of particular kinds of information as being processed solely in the right or the left hemisphere. The hemispheres work interdependently in deciphering, interpreting, and reacting to the world.

In addition, people who suffer injury to the left side of the brain and lose linguistic capabilities often recover the ability to speak: The right side of the brain often takes over some of the functions of the left side, especially in young children; the extent of recovery increases the earlier the injury occurs (Gould et al., 1999; Kempermann & Gage, 1999; Johnston, 2004).

Researchers also have unearthed evidence that there may be subtle differences in brain lateralization patterns between males and females and members of different cultures, as we see next.

Hemispheres: Symmetrical left and right halves of the brain that control the side of the body opposite to their location.

Lateralization: The dominance of one hemisphere of the brain in specific functions, such as language.

 StudyALERT

Although the hemispheres of the brain specialize in particular kinds of functions, the degree of specialization is not great, and the two hemispheres work interdependently.

The interplay of biology and environment in behavior is especially clear when we consider evidence suggesting that even in brain structure and function there are both sex and cultural differences. Let's consider sex differences first. Accumulating evidence seems to show intriguing differences in males' and females' brain lateralization and weight (Hugdahl & Davidson, 2002; Boles, 2005; Clements et al., 2006).

Human Diversity and the Brain

For instance, most males tend to show greater lateralization of language in the left hemisphere. For them, language is clearly relegated largely to the left side of the brain. In contrast, women display less lateralization, with language abilities apt to be more evenly divided between the two hemispheres. Such differences in brain lateralization may account, in part, for the superiority often displayed by females on certain measures of verbal skills, such as the onset and fluency of speech (Frings et al., 2006; Petersson et al., 2007).

Other research suggests that men's brains are somewhat bigger than women's brains even after taking differences in body size into account. In contrast, part of the *corpus callosum*, a bundle of fibers that connects the hemispheres of the brain, is proportionally larger in women than in men (Cahill, 2005; Luders et al., 2006; Smith et al., 2007).

Men and women also may process information differently. For example, in one study, fMRI brain scans of men making judgments discriminating real from false words showed activation of the left hemisphere of the brain, whereas women used areas on both sides of the brain (Rossell et al., 2002).

The meaning of such sex differences is far from clear. Consider one possibility related to differences in the proportional size of the corpus callosum. Its greater size in women may permit stronger connections to develop between the parts of the brain that control speech. In turn, this would explain why speech tends to emerge slightly earlier in girls than in boys.

Before we rush to such a conclusion, though, it is important to consider an alternative hypothesis: The reason verbal abilities emerge earlier in girls may be that infant girls receive greater encouragement to talk than do infant boys. In turn, this greater early experience may foster the growth of certain parts of the brain. Hence, physical brain differences may be a *reflection* of social and environmental influences rather than a *cause* of the differences in men's and women's behavior. At this point, it is impossible to know which of these alternative hypotheses is correct.

Culture also gives rise to differences in brain lateralization. Native speakers of Japanese seem to process information regarding vowel sounds primarily in the brain's left hemisphere. In contrast, North and South Americans, Europeans, and individuals of Japanese ancestry who learn Japanese later in life handle vowel sounds principally in the right hemisphere. One explanation for this difference is that certain characteristics of the Japanese language, such as the ability to express complex ideas by using only vowel sounds, result in the development of a specific type of brain lateralization in native speakers (Tsunoda, 1985; Kess & Miyamoto, 1994; Lin et al., 2005).

The Split Brain: Exploring the Two Hemispheres

The patient, V.J., had suffered severe seizures. By cutting her corpus callosum, the fibrous portion of the brain that carries messages between the hemispheres, surgeons hoped to create a firebreak to prevent the seizures from spreading. The operation did decrease the frequency and severity of V.J.'s attacks. But V.J. developed an unexpected side effect: She lost the ability to write at will, although she could read and spell words aloud. (Strauss, 1998, p. 287)

People like V.J., whose corpus callosum has been surgically cut to stop seizures and who are called *split-brain patients*, offer a rare opportunity for researchers investigating the independent functioning of the two hemispheres of the brain. For example, psychologist Roger Sperry—who won the Nobel Prize for his work—developed a number of ingenious techniques for studying how each hemisphere operates (Sperry, 1982; Gazzaniga, 1998; Savazzi et al., 2007).

In one experimental procedure, blindfolded patients touched an object with their right hand and were asked to name it (see Figure 8). Because the right side of the body corresponds to the language-oriented left side of the brain, split-brain patients were able to name it. However, if blindfolded patients touched the object with their left hand, they were unable to name it aloud, even though the information had registered in their brains: When the blindfold was removed, patients could identify the object they had touched. Information can be learned and remembered, then, using only the right side of the brain. (By the

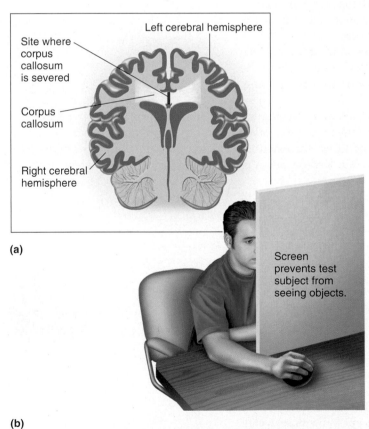

(a)

(b)

Screen prevents test subject from seeing objects.

Left cerebral hemisphere

Site where corpus callosum is severed

Corpus callosum

Right cerebral hemisphere

FIGURE 8 The hemispheres of the brain. (a) The corpus callosum connects the cerebral hemispheres of the brain. (b) A split-brain patient is tested by touching objects behind a screen. Patients could name objects when they touched it with their right hand, but couldn't if they touched with their left hand. If a split-brain patient with her eyes closed was given a pencil to hold and called it a pencil, what hand was the pencil in? (Source: Brooker et al. 2008, p. 943.)

way, unless you've had split-brain surgery, this experiment won't work with you, because the bundle of fibers connecting the two hemispheres of a normal brain immediately transfers the information from one hemisphere to the other.)

It is clear from experiments like this one that the right and left hemispheres of the brain specialize in handling different sorts of information. At the same time, it is important to realize that both hemispheres are capable of understanding, knowing, and being aware of the world, in somewhat different ways. The two hemispheres, then, should be regarded as different in terms of the efficiency with which they process certain kinds of information, rather than as two entirely separate brains. The hemispheres work interdependently to allow the full range and richness of thought of which humans are capable.

BECOMING AN INFORMED CONSUMER of Psychology

Learning to Control Your Heart—and Mind—Through Biofeedback

When Tammy DeMichael was involved in a horrific car accident that broke her neck and crushed her spinal cord, experts told her that she was doomed to be a quadriplegic for the rest of her life, unable to move from the neck down. But they were wrong. Not only did she regain the use of her arms, but she was able to walk 60 feet with a cane (Morrow & Wolf, 1991; Hess et al., 2007).

The key to DeMichael's astounding recovery: biofeedback. **Biofeedback** is a procedure in which a person learns to control through conscious thought internal physiological processes such as blood pressure, heart and respiration rate, skin temperature, sweating, and the constriction of particular muscles. Although it traditionally had been thought that the heart rate, respiration rate, blood pressure, and other bodily functions are under the control of parts of the brain over which we have no influence, psychologists have discovered that these responses are actually susceptible to voluntary control (Nagai et al., 2004; Cho et al., 2007).

In biofeedback, a person is hooked up to electronic devices that provide continuous feedback relating to the physiological response in question. For instance, a person interested in controlling headaches through biofeedback might have electronic sensors placed on certain muscles on her head and learn to control the constriction and relaxation of those muscles. Later, when she felt a headache starting, she could relax the relevant muscles and abort the pain (Andrasik, 2007).

In DeMichael's case, biofeedback was effective because not all of the nervous system's connections between the brain and her legs were severed. Through biofeedback, she learned how to send messages to specific muscles, "ordering" them to move. Although it took more than a year, DeMichael was successful in restoring a large degree of her mobility.

Although the control of physiological processes through the use of biofeedback is not easy to learn, it has been employed with success in a variety of ailments, including emotional problems (such as anxiety, depression, phobias, tension headaches, insomnia, and hyperactivity), physical illnesses with a psychological component (such as asthma, high blood pressure, ulcers, muscle spasms, and migraine headaches), and physical problems (such as DeMichael's injuries, strokes, cerebral palsy, and curvature of the spine) (Cho et al., 2007; Morone & Greco, 2007).

Biofeedback: A procedure in which a person learns to control through conscious thought internal physiological processes such as blood pressure, heart and respiration rate, skin temperature, sweating, and the constriction of particular muscles.

RECAP

How do researchers identify the major parts and functions of the brain?

- Brain scans take a "snapshot" of the internal workings of the brain without having to cut surgically into a person's skull. Major brain-scanning techniques include the electroencephalogram (EEG), positron emission tomography (PET), functional magnetic resonance imaging (fMRI), and transcranial magnetic stimulation imaging (TMS). (p. 79)

What are the major parts of the brain, and for what behaviors is each part responsible?

- The central core of the brain is made up of the medulla (which controls functions such as breathing and the heartbeat), the pons (which coordinates the muscles and the two sides of the body), the cerebellum (which controls balance), the reticular formation (which acts to heighten awareness in emergencies), the thalamus (which communicates sensory messages to and from the brain), and the hypothalamus (which maintains homeostasis, or body equilibrium, and regulates behavior related to basic survival). The functions of the central core structures are similar to those found in other vertebrates. This central core is sometimes referred to as the "old brain." (p. 82)

- The cerebral cortex—the "new brain"—has areas that control voluntary movement (the motor area); the senses (the sensory area); and thinking, reasoning, speech, and memory (the association areas). The limbic system, found on the border of the "old" and "new" brains, is associated with eating, aggression, reproduction, and the experiences of pleasure and pain. (p. 84)

How do the two halves of the brain operate interdependently?

- The brain is divided into left and right halves, or hemispheres, each of which generally controls the opposite side of the body. Each hemisphere can be thought of as being specialized in the functions it carries out: The left specializes in verbal tasks, such as logical reasoning, speaking, and reading; the right specializes in nonverbal tasks, such as spatial perception, pattern recognition, and emotional expression. (p. 88)

How can an understanding of the nervous system help us find ways to alleviate disease and pain?

- Biofeedback is a procedure by which a person learns to control internal physiological processes. By controlling involuntary responses, people are able to relieve anxiety, tension, migraine headaches, and a wide range of other psychological and physical problems. (p. 91)

EVALUATE

1. Match the name of each brain scan with the appropriate description:
   a. EEG
   b. fMRI
   c. PET
   1. By locating radiation within the brain, a computer can provide a striking picture of brain activity.
   2. Electrodes placed around the skull record the electrical signals transmitted through the brain.

3. This technique provides a three-dimensional view of the brain by aiming a magnetic field at the body.
2. Match the portion of the brain with its function:
   a. medulla
   b. pons
   c. cerebellum
   d. reticular formation
   1. Maintains breathing and heartbeat.
   2. Controls bodily balance.
   3. Coordinates and integrates muscle movements.
   4. Activates other parts of the brain to produce general bodily arousal.
3. A surgeon places an electrode on a portion of your brain and stimulates it. Immediately, your right wrist involuntarily twitches. The doctor has most likely stimulated a portion of the _____ area of your brain.
4. Each hemisphere controls the _____ side of the body.
5. Nonverbal realms, such as emotions and music, are controlled primarily by the _____ hemisphere of the brain, whereas the _____ hemisphere is more responsible for speaking and reading.

RETHINK

1. Before sophisticated brain-scanning techniques were developed, behavioral neuroscientists' understanding of the brain was based largely on the brains of people who had died. What limitations would this pose, and in what areas would you expect the most significant advances once brain-scanning techniques became possible?
2. Could personal differences in people's specialization of right and left hemispheres be related to occupational success? For example, might an architect who relies on spatial skills have a pattern of hemispheric specialization different from that of a writer?
3. *From the perspective of an educator:* How might you use different techniques to teach reading to boys and girls based on the brain evidence?

Answers to Evaluate Questions

1. a-2, b-3, c-1; 2. a-1, b-3, c-2, d-4; 3. motor; 4. opposite; 5. right, left

KEY TERMS

central core p. 82
cerebellum (ser uh BELL um) p. 82
reticular formation p. 82
thalamus p. 83

hypothalamus p. 83
limbic system p. 83
cerebral cortex p. 84
lobes p. 84
motor area p. 85

sensory area p. 86
association areas p. 87
neuroplasticity p. 88
neurogenesis p. 88
hemispheres p. 89

lateralization p. 89
biofeedback p. 91

Psychology on the Web

1. Biofeedback research is continuously changing and being applied to new areas of human functioning. Find at least two Web sites that discuss recent research on biofeedback, and summarize the research and any findings it has produced. Include in your summary your best estimate of future applications of this technique.
2. Find one or more Web sites on Parkinson's disease and learn more about this topic. Specifically, find reports of new treatments for Parkinson's disease that do not involve the use of fetal tissue. Write a summary of your findings.

Epilogue

In our examination of neuroscience, we've traced the ways in which biological structures and functions of the body affect behavior. Starting with neurons, we considered each of the components of the nervous system, culminating in an examination of how the brain permits us to think, reason, speak, recall, and experience emotions—the hallmarks of being human.

Before proceeding, turn back for a moment to the chapter prologue about Lacy Nissley, whose brain malformation was relieved by a daring medical procedure in which half of her brain was removed. Consider the following questions.

1. Since a substantial portion of Lacy's brain was removed during the surgery, has she necessarily lost forever the functions of those brain regions? Why or why not?
2. Because of the specialization of the hemispheres of the brain, which functions would be most affected had her left hemisphere been removed? Her right hemisphere? Why do you think so?
3. Do you think biofeedback techniques could be used to control epileptic seizures, such as those that were affecting Lacy? Why or why not?

MASTERING the action potential

The action potential is an electrical impulse that travels along the axon of a neuron. Use this visual guide to understand the process by which the impulse travels through a neuron and on to other neurons. Then answer the questions below to test your understanding of the concepts.

Axon (inside myelin sheath)

Myelin sheath

Movement of electrical impulse

1 The nervous system communicates by means of electrical signals or impulses that travel from one neuron to another. These impulses regulate our behavior, instructing our muscles, for example, how to respond to a ball moving toward us through the air.

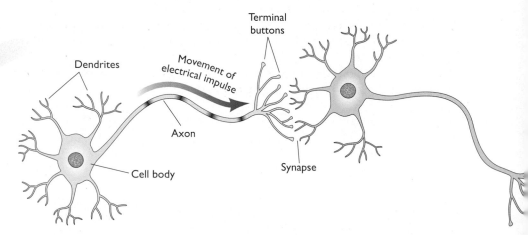

Terminal buttons

Dendrites

Movement of electrical impulse

Axon

Cell body

Synapse

2 Impulses travel from the neuron's dendrites, through the cell body and the axon to the terminal buttons. The terminal buttons release chemicals called neurotransmitters into the synapse, where they are sent to the dendrites of the adjacent neuron to transmit the impulse to the next neuron.

EVALUATE

1 An action potential travels across an axon
   a in a chemical form
   b as an electrical impulse
   c as a sound wave
   d in a corkscrew pattern

2 The _____ is the space between neurons that is bridged by chemicals released from the terminal buttons.

Movement of electrical impulse

Axon

3 In its normal, resting state, a neuron has a negative internal electrical charge. When the neuron is activated, its internal charge briefly becomes positive as an electrical impulse, called an *action potential*, moves through the neuron. An action potential travels through the neuron like a flame along a fuse. After it has passed, the negative charge is restored.

Time 1

Voltage

Time 2

Voltage

Time 3

Voltage

Positive charge

Negative charge

Direction of impulse

A sudden, brief reversal of charge results in an action potential.

50

30

0   Threshold

Voltage

−40
−50
−60   Resting
−70   potential

Time

4 An action potential is generated only if the charge of the incoming impulse is sufficiently strong to cross the neuron's cell membrane and raise the neuron's charge to a level of +40 millivolts. Equally important, the impulse does not travel faster, nor is it stronger, if the voltage exceeds the threshold. Neurons operate according to an *all-or-none law:* Either a neuron is at rest, or an action potential is moving through it. There is no in-between state.

5 Most impulses move in one direction, either away from or toward the brain or spinal cord. When we catch a ball, neurons in the hand send a signal to the brain for interpretation; the brain, in turn, sends a signal telling the hand what to do next. Due to the speed at which nerve impulses travel—some move as quickly as 225 miles per hour—the whole process occurs with amazing rapidity and coordination.

3 The all-or-none law says that all neurons must fire at the same time for an impulse to be transmitted. True or False?

RETHINK

1 What is the process by which one neuron sends a message to another neuron?

Answers to Evaluate questions: 1. b; 2. synapse; 3. false

CHAPTER 4

Sensation and Perception

Key Concepts for Chapter 4

Prologue *Only Blank Faces*

Several years ago, when Margaret Mitchell picked up her son Duncan from his Seattle school, he looked at her curiously and asked, "Are you my mommy?"

Ms. Mitchell, an attorney by training, was taken aback. When she answered, "'Yes, I'm your mommy,'" he recognized her voice and was reassured.

A short while later, Duncan, then 4 years old, was diagnosed with prosopagnosia, a selective developmental condition often referred to as "faceblindness." Although his eyesight is perfectly fine, he can't always identify people by their faces. In school, for instance, Duncan has trouble matching the faces and names of teachers and pupils.

Like many other prosopagnosics, Duncan, now 8, has a memory that functions normally in other ways. He can visually distinguish between cars and houses and toys. He knows his dog and cat and other neighborhood pets. He's a sociable child and likes being around people. But the frustration of not being able to discern faces has made everyday life from attending school to making friends unbearably difficult. His parents engineer much of his social life around one-on-one play dates so he can try to remember classmates. (Tesoriero, 2007, p. A1)

Looking Ahead

People with faceblindness such as Duncan Mitchell can see faces, of course. They see the parts that make up a facial configuration—an oval shape with two eyes, a nose, and a mouth. But they lack the specialized processing ability most of us take for granted that allows us to detect the subtle differences that make each individual face unique. Although they can readily detect face-related information, prosopagnosics have difficulty with finding that information meaningful—with seeing that face as a friend or foe.

Disorders such as faceblindness illustrate how much we depend on our senses to function normally. Our senses offer a window to the world, not only providing us with an awareness, understanding, and appreciation of the world's beauty, but alerting us to its dangers. Our senses enable us to feel the gentlest of breezes, see flickering lights miles away, and hear the soft murmuring of distant songbirds.

In the next four modules, we focus on the field of psychology that is concerned with the ways our bodies take in information through the senses and the ways we interpret that information. We will explore both sensation and perception. Sensation encompasses the processes by which our sense organs receive information from the environment. Perception is the brain's and the sense organs' sorting out, interpretation, analysis, and integration of stimuli.

Although perception clearly represents a step beyond sensation, in practice it is sometimes difficult to find the precise boundary between the two. Indeed, psychologists—and philosophers as well—have argued for years over the distinction. The primary difference is that sensation can be thought of as an organism's first encounter with a raw sensory stimulus, whereas perception is the process by which it interprets, analyzes, and integrates that stimulus with other sensory information.

For example, if we were considering sensation, we might ask about the loudness of a ringing fire alarm. If we were considering perception, we might ask whether someone recognizes the ringing sound as an alarm and identifies its meaning.

To a psychologist interested in understanding the causes of behavior, sensation and perception are fundamental topics because so much of our behavior is a reflection of how we react to and interpret stimuli from the world around us. The areas of sensation and perception deal with a wide range of questions—among them, how we respond to the characteristics of physical stimuli; what processes enable us to see, hear, and experience pain; why visual illusions fool us; and how we distinguish one person from another. As we explore these issues, we'll see how the senses work together to provide us with an integrated view and understanding of the world.

Sensing the World Around Us

As Isabel sat down to Thanksgiving dinner, her father carried the turkey in on a tray and placed it squarely in the center of the table. The noise level, already high from the talking and laughter of family members, grew louder still. As Isabel picked up her fork, the smell of the turkey reached her and she felt her stomach growl hungrily. The sight and sound of her family around the table, along with the smells and tastes of the holiday meal, made Isabel feel more relaxed than she had since starting school in the fall.

Put yourself in this setting and consider how different it might be if any one of your senses were not functioning. What if you were blind and unable to see the faces of your family members or the welcome shape of the golden-brown turkey? What if you had no sense of hearing and could not listen to the conversations of family members or were unable to feel your stomach growl, smell the dinner, or taste the food? Clearly, you would experience the dinner very differently from someone whose sensory apparatus was intact.

Moreover, the sensations mentioned above barely scratch the surface of sensory experience. Although perhaps you were taught, as I was, that there are just five senses—sight, sound, taste, smell, and touch—that enumeration is too modest. Human sensory capabilities go well beyond the basic five senses. For example, we are sensitive not merely to touch but to a considerably wider set of stimuli—pain, pressure, temperature, and vibration, to name a few. In addition, vision has two subsystems—relating to day and night vision—and the ear is responsive to information that allows us not only to hear but also to keep our balance.

To consider how psychologists understand the senses and, more broadly, sensation and perception, we first need a basic working vocabulary. In formal terms, **sensation** is the activation of the sense organs by a source of physical energy. **Perception** is the sorting out, interpretation, analysis, and integration of stimuli carried out by the sense organs and brain. A **stimulus** is any passing source of physical energy that produces a response in a sense organ.

Stimuli vary in both type and intensity. Different types of stimuli activate different sense organs. For instance, we can differentiate light stimuli (which activate the sense of sight and allow us to see the colors of a tree in autumn) from sound stimuli (which, through the sense of hearing, permit us to hear the sounds of an orchestra). In addition, stimuli differ in intensity, relating to how strong a stimulus needs to be before it can be detected.

Questions of stimulus type and intensity are considered in a branch of psychology known as psychophysics. **Psychophysics** is the study of the relationship between the physical aspects of stimuli and our psychological experience of them. Psychophysics played a central role in the development of the field of psychology, and many of the first psychologists studied issues related to psychophysics (Chechile, 2003; Gardner, 2005; Hock & Ploeger, 2006).

Key Concepts

What is sensation, and how do psychologists study it?

What is the relationship between a physical stimulus and the kinds of sensory responses that result from it?

 StudyALERT

Remember that sensation refers to the activation of the sense organs (a physical response), whereas perception refers to how stimuli are interpreted (a psychological response).

The activation of the sense organs by a source of physical energy.

The sorting out, interpretation, analysis, and integration of stimuli by the sense organs and brain.

Energy that produces a response in a sense organ.

The study of the relationship between the physical aspects of stimuli and our psychological experience of them.

Absolute threshold: The smallest intensity of a stimulus that must be present for the stimulus to be detected.

Absolute Thresholds: Detecting What's Out There

Just when does a stimulus become strong enough to be detected by our sense organs? The answer to this question requires an understanding of the concept of absolute threshold. An **absolute threshold** is the smallest intensity of a stimulus that must be present for it to be detected (Aazh & Moore, 2007).

Our senses are extremely responsive to stimuli. For example, the sense of touch is so sensitive that we can feel a bee's wing falling on our cheeks when it is dropped from a distance of 1 centimeter. Test your knowledge of the absolute thresholds of other senses by completing the questionnaire in Figure 1.

In fact, our senses are so fine-tuned that we might have problems if they were any more sensitive. For instance, if our ears were slightly more acute, we would be able to hear the sound of air molecules in our ears knocking into the eardrum—a phenomenon that would surely prove distracting and might even prevent us from hearing sounds outside our bodies.

Of course, the absolute thresholds we have been discussing are measured under ideal conditions. Normally our senses cannot detect stimulation quite as well because of the presence of noise. *Noise*, as defined by psychophysicists, is background stimulation that interferes with the perception of other stimuli. Hence, noise refers not just to auditory stimuli, as the word suggests, but also to unwanted stimuli that interfere with other senses.

For example, picture a talkative group of people crammed into a small, crowded, smoke-filled room at a party. The din of the crowd makes it hard to hear individual voices, and the smoke makes it difficult to see, or even taste, the food. In this case, the smoke and the crowded conditions would both be considered "noise" because they are preventing sensation at more discriminating levels.

Crowded conditions, sounds, and sights can all be considered as noise that interferes with sensation. Can you think of other examples of noise that is not auditory in nature?

FIGURE 1 This test can shed some light on how sensitive the human senses are. (Source: Galanter, 1962.)

How Sensitive Are You?

To test your awareness of the capabilities of your senses, answer the following questions:

1. How far can a candle flame be seen on a clear, dark night:
   a. From a distance of 10 miles _____
   b. From a distance of 30 miles _____
2. How far can the ticking of a watch be heard under quiet conditions?
   a. From 5 feet away _____
   b. From 20 feet away _____
3. How much sugar is needed to allow it to be detected when dissolved in 2 gallons of water?
   a. 2 tablespoons _____
   b. 1 teaspoon _____
4. Over what area can a drop of perfume be detected?
   a. A 5-foot by 5-foot area _____
   b. A 3-room apartment _____

Scoring: In each case, the answer is b, illustrating the tremendous sensitivity of our senses.

Difference Thresholds: Noticing Distinctions Between Stimuli

Suppose you wanted to choose the six best apples from a supermarket display—the biggest, reddest, and sweetest apples. One approach would be to compare one apple with another systematically until you were left with a few so similar that you could not tell the difference between them. At that point, it wouldn't matter which ones you chose.

Psychologists have discussed this comparison problem in terms of the **difference threshold**, the smallest level of added (or reduced) stimulation required to sense that a *change* in stimulation has occurred. Thus, the difference threshold is the minimum change in stimulation required to detect the difference between two stimuli, and so it also is called a **just noticeable difference** (Nittrouer & Lowenstein, 2007).

The stimulus value that constitutes a just noticeable difference depends on the initial intensity of the stimulus. The relationship between changes in the original value of a stimulus and the degree to which a change will be noticed forms one of the basic laws of psychophysics: Weber's law. **Weber's law** (with *Weber* pronounced "vay-ber") states that a just noticeable difference is a *constant proportion* of the intensity of an initial stimulus.

For example, Weber found that the just noticeable difference for weight is 1:50. Consequently, it takes a 1-ounce increase in a 50-ounce weight to produce a noticeable difference, and it would take a 10-ounce increase to produce a noticeable difference if the initial weight were 500 ounces. In both cases, the same proportional increase is necessary to produce a just noticeable difference—1:5 = 10:500. Similarly, the just noticeable difference distinguishing changes in loudness between sounds is larger for sounds that are initially loud than it is for sounds that are initially soft, but the *proportional* increase remains the same.

Weber's law helps explain why a person in a quiet room is more startled by the ringing of a telephone than is a person in an already noisy room. To produce the same amount of reaction in a noisy room, a telephone ring might have to approximate the loudness of cathedral bells. Similarly, when the moon is visible during the late afternoon, it appears relatively dim—yet against a dark night sky, it seems quite bright.

Difference threshold (just noticeable difference): The smallest level of added or reduced stimulation required to sense that a change in stimulation has occurred.

Weber's law: A basic law of psychophysics stating that a just noticeable difference is in constant proportion to the intensity of an initial stimulus.

 StudyALERT

Remember that Weber's law holds for every type of sensory stimuli: vision, sound, taste, and so on.

Sensory Adaptation: Turning Down

You enter a movie theater, and the smell of popcorn is everywhere. A few minutes later, though, you barely notice the smell. The reason you acclimate to the odor is sensory adaptation. **Adaptation** is an adjustment in sensory capacity after prolonged exposure to unchanging stimuli. Adaptation occurs as people become accustomed to a stimulus and change their frame of reference. In a sense, our brain mentally turns down the volume of the stimulation it's experiencing (Calin-Jageman & Fischer, 2007).

One example of adaptation is the decrease in sensitivity that occurs after repeated exposure to a strong stimulus. If you were to hear a loud tone over and over again, eventually it would begin to sound softer. Similarly, although jumping into a cold lake may be temporarily unpleasant, eventually you probably will get used to the temperature.

This apparent decline in sensitivity to sensory stimuli is due to the inability of the sensory nerve receptors to fire off messages to the brain indefinitely. Because these receptor cells are most responsive to *changes* in stimulation, constant stimulation is not effective in producing a sustained reaction.

An adjustment in sensory capacity after prolonged exposure to unchanging stimuli.

Judgments of sensory stimuli are also affected by the context in which the judgments are made. This is the case because judgments are made not in isolation from other stimuli but in terms of preceding sensory experience. You can demonstrate this for yourself by trying a simple experiment:

Take two envelopes, one large and one small, and put fifteen nickels in each one. Now lift the large envelope, put it down, and lift the small one. Which seems to weigh more? Most people report that the small one is heavier, although, as you know, the weights are nearly identical. The reason for this misconception is that the visual context of the envelope interferes with the sensory experience of weight. Adaptation to the context of one stimulus (the size of the envelope) alters responses to another stimulus (the weight of the envelope) (Coren & Ward, 2004).

RECAP/EVALUATE/RETHINK

RECAP

What is sensation, and how do psychologists study it?

- Sensation is the activation of the sense organs by any source of physical energy. In contrast, perception is the process by which we sort out, interpret, analyze, and integrate stimuli to which our senses are exposed. (p. 99)

What is the relationship between a physical stimulus and the kinds of sensory responses that result from it?

- Psychophysics studies the relationship between the physical nature of stimuli and the sensory responses they evoke. (p. 99)

- The absolute threshold is the smallest amount of physical intensity at which a stimulus can be detected. Under ideal conditions absolute thresholds are extraordinarily sensitive, but the presence of noise (background stimuli that interfere with other stimuli) reduces detection capabilities. (p. 100)

- The difference threshold, or just noticeable difference, is the smallest change in the level of stimulation required to sense that a change has occurred. According to Weber's law, a just noticeable difference is a constant proportion of the intensity of an initial stimulus. (p. 101)

- Sensory adaptation occurs when we become accustomed to a constant stimulus and change our evaluation of it. Repeated exposure to a stimulus results in an apparent decline in sensitivity to it. (p. 101)

EVALUATE

1. _____ is the stimulation of the sense organs; _____ is the sorting out, interpretation, analysis, and integration of stimuli by the sense organs and the brain.
2. The term *absolute threshold* refers to the _____ intensity of a stimulus that must be present for the stimulus to be detected.
3. Weber discovered that for a difference between two stimuli to be perceptible, the stimuli must differ by at least a _____ proportion.
4. After completing a very difficult rock climb in the morning, Carmella found the afternoon climb unexpectedly easy. This case illustrates the phenomenon of _____.

RETHINK

1. Do you think it is possible to have sensation without perception? Is it possible to have perception without sensation?
2. *From the perspective of a manufacturer:* How might you need to take psychophysics into account when developing new products or modifying existing ones?

Answers to Evaluate Questions

1. sensation; perception; 2. smallest; 3. constant; 4. adaptation

KEY TERMS

sensation p. 99
perception p. 99
stimulus p. 99
psychophysics p. 99

absolute threshold p. 100
difference threshold (just
   noticeable difference) p. 101
Weber's law p. 101

adaptation p. 101

Vision: Shedding Light on the Eye

If, as poets say, the eyes provide a window to the soul, they also provide us with a window to the world. Our visual capabilities permit us to admire and react to scenes ranging from the beauty of a sunset, to the configuration of a lover's face, to the words written on the pages of a book.

Vision starts with light, the physical energy that stimulates the eye. Light is a form of electromagnetic radiation waves, which, as shown in Figure 1, are measured in wavelengths. The sizes of wavelengths correspond to different types of energy. The range of wavelengths that humans are sensitive to—called the *visual spectrum*—is relatively small. Many nonhuman species have different capabilities. For instance, some reptiles and fish sense energies of longer wavelengths than humans do, and certain insects sense energies of shorter wavelengths than humans do.

Light waves coming from some object outside the body (such as the tree in Figure 2) are sensed by the only organ that is capable of responding to the visible spectrum: the eye. Our eyes convert light to a form that can be used by the neurons that serve as messengers to the brain. The neurons themselves take up a relatively small percentage of the total eye. Most of the eye is a mechanical device that is similar in many respects to a nonelectronic camera that uses film, as you can see in Figure 2.

Despite the similarities between the eye and a camera, vision involves processes that are far more complex and sophisticated than those of any camera. Furthermore, once an image reaches the neuronal receptors of the eye, the eye/camera analogy ends, for the processing of the visual image in the brain is more reflective of a computer than it is of a camera.

Key Concepts

What basic processes underlie the sense of vision?

How do we see colors?

FIGURE 1 The visible spectrum—the range of wavelengths to which people are sensitive—is only a small part of the kinds of wavelengths present in our environment. Is it a benefit or disadvantage to our everyday lives that we aren't more sensitive to a broader range of visual stimuli? Why?

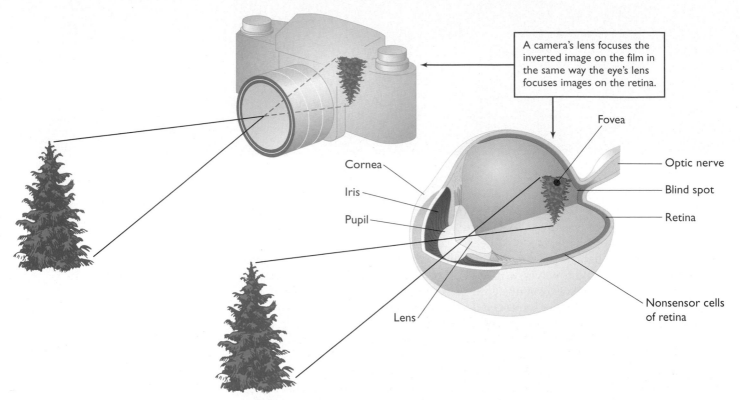

A camera's lens focuses the inverted image on the film in the same way the eye's lens focuses images on the retina.

FIGURE 2 Although human vision is far more complicated than the most sophisticated camera, in some ways basic visual processes are analogous to those used in photography. Like the automatic lighting system on a traditional, nondigital camera, the human eye dilates to let in more light and contracts to block out light.

Illuminating the Structure of the Eye

The ray of light being reflected off the tree in Figure 2 first travels through the *cornea*, a transparent, protective window. The cornea, because of its curvature, bends (or *refracts*) light as it passes through to focus it more sharply. After moving through the cornea, the light traverses the pupil. The *pupil* is a dark hole in the center of the *iris*, the colored part of the eye, which in humans ranges from a light blue to a dark brown. The size of the pupil opening depends on the amount of light in the environment. The dimmer the surroundings are, the more the pupil opens to allow more light to enter.

Why shouldn't the pupil be open completely all the time, allowing the greatest amount of light into the eye? The answer relates to the basic physics of light. A small pupil greatly increases the range of distances at which objects are in focus. With a wide-open pupil, the range is relatively small, and details are harder to discern. The eye takes advantage of bright light by decreasing the size of the pupil and thereby becoming more

Like the automatic lighting system on a camera, the pupil in the human eye expands to let in more light (left) and contracts to block out light (right). Can humans adjust their ears to let in more or less sound in similar manner?

discerning. In dim light the pupil expands to enable us to view the situation better—but at the expense of visual detail. (Perhaps one reason candlelight dinners are thought of as romantic is that the dim light prevents one from seeing a partner's physical flaws.)

Once light passes through the pupil, it enters the *lens*, which is directly behind the pupil. The lens acts to bend the rays of light so that they are properly focused on the rear of the eye. The lens focuses light by changing its own thickness, a process called *accommodation*: It becomes flatter when viewing distant objects and rounder when looking at closer objects.

REACHING THE RETINA

Having traveled through the pupil and lens, the image of the tree finally reaches its ultimate destination in the eye—the **retina**. Here the electromagnetic energy of light is converted to electrical impulses for transmission to the brain. It is important to note that because of the physical properties of light, the image has reversed itself in traveling through the lens, and it reaches the retina upside down (relative to its original position). Although it might seem that this reversal would cause difficulties in understanding and moving about the world, this is not the case. The brain interprets the image in terms of its original position.

The retina consists of a thin layer of nerve cells at the back of the eyeball (see Figure 3). There are two kinds of light-sensitive receptor cells in the retina. The names they have been given describe their shapes: rods and cones. **Rods** are thin, cylindrical receptor cells that are highly sensitive to light. **Cones** are cone-shaped, light-sensitive receptor cells that are responsible for sharp focus and color perception, particularly in bright light. The rods and cones are distributed unevenly throughout the retina. Cones are concentrated on the part of the retina called the *fovea*. The fovea is a particularly sensitive region of the retina. If you want to focus on something of particular interest, you will automatically try to center the image on the fovea to see it more sharply.

The rods and cones not only are structurally dissimilar but they also play distinctly different roles in vision. Cones are primarily responsible for the sharply focused perception of color, particularly in brightly lit situations; rods are related to vision in dimly lit situations and are largely insensitive to color and to details as sharp as those the cones are capable of recognizing. The rods play a key role in *peripheral vision*—seeing objects that are outside the main center of focus—and in night vision.

Rods and cones also are involved in *dark adaptation*, the phenomenon of adjusting to dim light after being in brighter light. (Think of the experience of walking into a dark movie theater and groping your way to a seat but a few minutes later seeing the seats quite clearly.) The speed at which dark adaptation occurs is a result of the rate of change in the chemical composition of the rods and cones. Although the cones reach their greatest level of adaptation in just a few minutes, the rods take 20 to 30 minutes to reach the maximum level. The opposite phenomenon—*light adaptation*, or the process of adjusting to bright light after exposure to dim light—occurs much faster, taking only a minute or so.

SENDING THE MESSAGE FROM THE EYE TO THE BRAIN

When light energy strikes the rods and cones, it starts a chain of events that transforms light into neural impulses that can be communicated to the brain. Even before the neural message reaches the brain, however, some initial coding of the visual information takes place.

What happens when light energy strikes the retina depends in part on whether it encounters a rod or a cone. Rods contain *rhodopsin*, a complex reddish-purple substance whose composition changes chemically when energized by light. The substance in cone receptors is different, but the principles are similar. Stimulation of the nerve cells in the eye triggers a neural response that is transmitted to other nerve cells in the retina called *bipolar cells* and *ganglion cells*.

Retina: The part of the eye that converts the electromagnetic energy of light to electrical impulses for transmission to the brain.

Rods: Thin, cylindrical receptor cells in the retina that are highly sensitive to light.

Cones: Cone-shaped, light-sensitive receptor cells in the retina that are responsible for sharp focus and color perception, particularly in bright light.

 Study

Remember that *cones* relate to *color* vision.

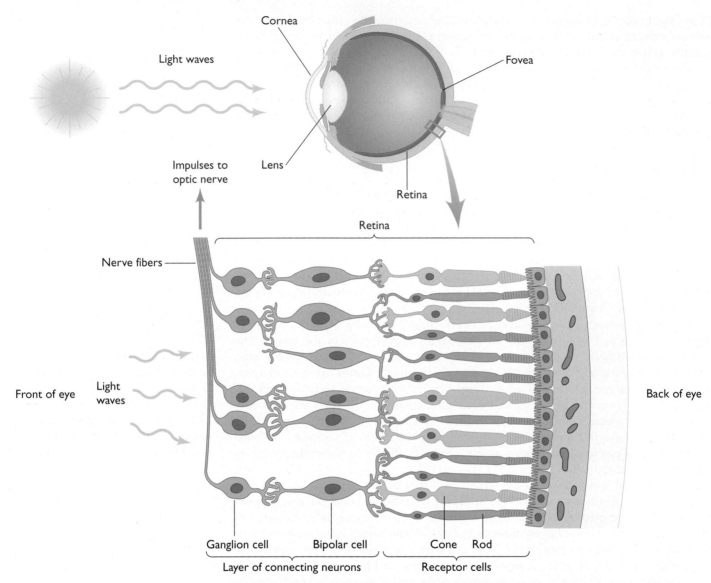

Cornea

Light waves

Fovea

Impulses to
optic nerve

Lens

Retina

Retina

Nerve fibers

Front of eye

Light
waves

Back of eye

Ganglion cell   Bipolar cell   Cone   Rod

Layer of connecting neurons   Receptor cells

FIGURE 3 The basic cells of the eye. Light entering the eye travels through the ganglion and bipolar cells and strikes the light-sensitive rods and cones located at the back of the eye. The rods and cones then transmit nerve impulses to the brain via the bipolar and ganglion cells. (Source: Shier, Butler, & Lewis, 2000.)

Bipolar cells receive information directly from the rods and cones and communicate that information to the ganglion cells. The ganglion cells collect and summarize visual information, which is then moved out the back of the eyeball and sent to the brain through a bundle of ganglion axons called the **optic nerve**.

Optic nerve: A bundle of ganglion axons that carry visual information to the brain.

Because the opening for the optic nerve passes through the retina, there are no rods or cones in the area, and that creates a blind spot. Normally, however, this absence of nerve cells does not interfere with vision because you automatically compensate for the missing part of your field of vision. (To find your blind spot, see Figure 4.)

Once beyond the eye itself, the neural impulses relating to the image move through the optic nerve. As the optic nerve leaves the eyeball, its path does not take the most direct route to the part of the brain right behind the eye. Instead, the optic nerves from each eye meet at a point roughly between the two eyes—called the *optic chiasm* (pronounced ki-asm)—where each optic nerve then splits.

When the optic nerves split, the nerve impulses coming from the right half of each retina are sent to the right side of the brain, and the impulses arriving from the left half

FIGURE 4 To find your blind spot, close your right eye and look at the haunted house with your left eye. You will see the ghost on the periphery of your vision. Now, while staring at the house, move the page toward you. When the book is about a foot from your eye, the ghost will disappear. At this moment, the image of the ghost is falling on your blind spot.

But also notice how, when the page is at that distance, not only does the ghost seem to disappear, but the line seems to run continuously through the area where the ghost used to be. This simple experiment shows how we automatically compensate for missing information by using nearby material to complete what is unseen. That's the reason you never notice the blind spot. What is missing is replaced by what is seen next to the blind spot. Can you think of any advantages that this tendency to provide missing information gives humans as a species?

of each retina are sent to the left side of the brain. Because the image on the retinas is reversed and upside down, however, those images coming from the right half of each retina actually originated in the field of vision to the person's left, and the images coming from the left half of each retina originated in the field of vision to the person's right (see Figure 5).

PROCESSING THE VISUAL MESSAGE

By the time a visual message reaches the brain, it has passed through several stages of processing. One of the initial sites is the ganglion cells. Each ganglion cell gathers information from a group of rods and cones in a particular area of the eye and compares the amount of light entering the center of that area with the amount of light in the area around it. Some ganglion cells are activated by light in the center (and darkness in the surrounding area). Other ganglion cells are activated when there is darkness in the center and light in the surrounding areas. The outcome of this process is to maximize the detection of variations in light and darkness. The image that is passed on to the brain, then, is an enhanced version of the actual visual stimulus outside the body (Kubovy, Epstein, & Gepshtein, 2003; Pearson & Clifford, 2005; Lascaratos et al., 2007).

The ultimate processing of visual images takes place in the visual cortex of the brain, and it is here that the most complex kinds of processing occur. Psychologists David Hubel and Torsten Wiesel won the Nobel Prize in 1981 for their discovery that many neurons in the cortex are extraordinarily specialized, being activated only by visual stimuli of a particular shape or pattern—a process known as **feature detection**. They found that some cells are activated only by lines of a particular width, shape, or orientation. Other cells are activated only by moving, as opposed to stationary, stimuli (Hubel & Wiesel, 2004; Pelli et al., 2006).

The activation of neurons in the cortex by visual stimuli of specific shapes or patterns.

More recent work has added to our knowledge of the complex ways in which visual information coming from individual neurons is combined and processed. Different parts of the brain process nerve impulses in several individual systems simultaneously. For instance, one system relates to shapes, one to colors, and others to movement, location, and depth. Furthermore, different parts of the brain are involved in the perception of specific *kinds* of stimuli, showing distinctions, for example, between the perception of human faces, animals, and inanimate stimuli (Nuala, Campbell, & Flaherty, 2005; Werblin & Roska, 2007; Winston et al., 2007).

If separate neural systems exist for processing information about specific aspects of the visual world, how are all these data integrated by the brain? The brain makes use of information regarding the frequency, rhythm, and timing of the firing of

FIGURE 5 Because the optic nerve coming from each eye splits at the optic chiasm, the image to a person's right is sent to the left side of the brain and the image to the person's left is transmitted to the right side of the brain.
(Source: Mader, 2000.)

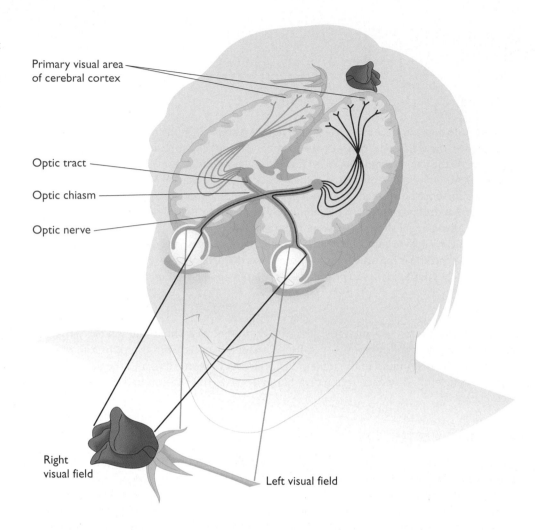

Primary visual area of cerebral cortex

Optic tract

Optic chiasm

Optic nerve

Right visual field

Left visual field

particular sets of neural cells. Furthermore, the brain's integration of visual information does not occur in any single step or location in the brain but rather is a process that occurs on several levels simultaneously. The ultimate outcome, though, is indisputable: a vision of the world around us (De Gelder, 2000; Macaluso, Frith, & Driver, 2000; Werner, Pinna, & Spillmann, 2007).

Color Vision and Color Blindness: The 7-Million-Color Spectrum

Although the range of wavelengths to which humans are sensitive is relatively narrow, at least in comparison with the entire electromagnetic spectrum, the portion to which we are capable of responding allows us great flexibility in sensing the world. Nowhere is this clearer than in terms of the number of colors we can discern. A person with normal color vision is capable of distinguishing no less than 7 million different colors (Bruce, Green, & Georgeson, 1997; Rabin, 2004).

Although the variety of colors that people are generally able to distinguish is vast, there are certain individuals whose ability to perceive color is quite limited—the color-blind. Interestingly, the condition of these individuals has provided some of the most important clues to understanding how color vision operates (Neitz, Neitz, & Kainz, 1996; Bonnardel, 2006).

Approximately 7 percent of men and .4 percent of women are color-blind. For most people with color-blindness, the world looks quite dull (see Figure 6). Red fire engines

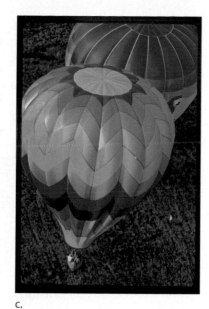

a.   b.   c.

FIGURE 6 (a) To someone with normal vision, the hot-air balloon in the foreground appears with regions of very pure red, orange, yellow, green, blue, and violet, as well as off-white; and the balloon in the rear is a bright shade of red-orange. (b) A person with red-green color blindness would see the scene in part (a) like this, in hues of blue and yellow. (c) A person who is blue-yellow blind, conversely, would see it in hues of red and green.

appear yellow, green grass seems yellow, and the three colors of a traffic light all look yellow. In fact, in the most common form of color-blindness, all red and green objects are seen as yellow. There are other forms of color-blindness as well, but they are quite rare. In yellow-blue blindness, people are unable to tell the difference between yellow and blue, and in the most extreme case an individual perceives no color at all. To such a person the world looks something like the picture on a black-and-white television set.

EXPLAINING COLOR VISION

To understand why some people are color-blind, we need to consider the basics of color vision. Two processes are involved. The first process is explained by the **trichromatic theory of color vision.** This theory suggests that there are three kinds of cones in the retina, each of which responds primarily to a specific range of wavelengths. One is most responsive to blue-violet colors, one to green, and the third to yellow-red (Brown & Wald, 1964). According to trichromatic theory, perception of color is influenced by the relative strength with which each of the three kinds of cones is activated. If we see a blue sky, the blue-violet cones are primarily triggered, and the others show less activity.

The theory that there are three kinds of cones in the retina, each of which responds primarily to a specific range of wavelengths.

However, there are aspects of color vision that the trichromatic theory is less successful at explaining. For example, the theory does not explain what happens after you stare at something like the flag shown in Figure 7 for about a minute. Try this yourself and then look at a blank white page: You'll see an image of the traditional red, white, and blue U.S. flag. Where there was yellow, you'll see blue, and where there were green and black, you'll see red and white.

The phenomenon you have just experienced is called an *afterimage*. It occurs because activity in the retina continues even when you are no longer staring at the original picture. However, it also demonstrates that the trichromatic theory does not explain color vision completely. Why should the colors in the afterimage be different from those in the original?

FIGURE 7 Stare at the dot in this flag for about a minute and then look at a piece of plain white paper. What do you see? Most people see an afterimage that converts the colors in the figure into the traditional red, white, and blue U.S. flag. If you have trouble seeing it the first time, blink once and try again.

Opponent-process theory of color vision: The theory that receptor cells for color are linked in pairs, working in opposition to each other.

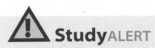 **Study**ALERT

Keep in mind that there are two explanations for color vision: trichromatic and opponent-process theories.

Because trichromatic processes do not provide a full explanation of color vision, alternative explanations have been proposed. According to the **opponent-process theory of color vision**, receptor cells are linked in pairs, working in opposition to each other. Specifically, there are a blue-yellow pairing, a red-green pairing, and a black-white pairing. If an object reflects light that contains more blue than yellow, it will stimulate the firing of the cells sensitive to blue, simultaneously discouraging or inhibiting the firing of receptor cells sensitive to yellow—and the object will appear blue. If, in contrast, a light contains more yellow than blue, the cells that respond to yellow will be stimulated to fire while the blue ones are inhibited, and the object will appear yellow (Robinson, 2007).

The opponent-process theory provides a good explanation for afterimages. When we stare at the yellow in the figure, for instance, our receptor cells for the yellow component of the yellow-blue pairing become fatigued and are less able to respond to yellow stimuli. In contrast, the receptor cells for the blue part of the pair are not tired, because they are not being stimulated. When we look at a white surface, the light reflected off it would normally stimulate both the yellow and the blue receptors equally. But the fatigue of the yellow receptors prevents this from happening. They temporarily do not respond to the yellow, which makes the white light appear to be blue. Because the other colors in the figure do the same thing relative to their specific opponents, the afterimage produces the opponent colors—for a while. The afterimage lasts only a short time, because the fatigue of the yellow receptors is soon overcome, and the white light begins to be perceived more accurately.

Both opponent processes and trichromatic mechanisms are at work, but in different parts of the visual sensing system. Trichromatic processes work within the retina itself, whereas opponent mechanisms operate both in the retina and at later stages of neuronal processing (Chen, Zhou, & Gong, 2004; Gegenfurtner, 2003; Baraas et al., 2006).

As our understanding of the processes that permit us to see has increased, some psychologists have begun to develop new techniques to help those with serious vision problems—visually impaired and people with total blindness—to overcome their deficiencies. One of the most promising devices is discussed in the *Applying Psychology in the 21st Century* box.

Vision Revision: Giving Sight Back to the Blind

Linda M. first realized that something was wrong with her vision when she couldn't find things she dropped. Linda was exhibiting the early signs of retinitis pigmentosa (RP), an incurable disease that attacks cells in the retina and ultimately would destroy her vision, possibly within 10 years. She was only 21 at the time. (Casey, 2006, p.1)

Linda's vision progressively worsened until she went completely blind by age 50. Ten years after that, a seemingly miraculous event occurred: Linda began seeing patterns of light that corresponded to objects in the physical world around her. This was no miracle; her RP had not gone away spontaneously. Although it sounds like science fiction, researchers had surgically implanted an experimental electronic device called an artificial retina in one of Linda's eyes.

Even though the rods and cones in the retinas of people with diseases such as Linda's degrade to the point of blindness, some photoreceptors continue to function—when they are artificially stimulated with an electrode, the patient can see flashes of light. Moreover, since patients such as Linda had once experienced normal vision, they can accurately localize the flash to the corresponding location on the retina that was stimulated.

The discovery of this ability in the mid 1990s gave researchers the first tantalizing hope of one day developing a prosthetic device that could return some form of vision to the blind. Development of the technology took some time to get off the ground, but a number of experimental devices have entered the human testing

FIGURE 8 This light-sensitive chip is implanted into the eye's retina and is able to convey visual information into ganglion cells and ultimately to the brain. (Source: Adapted, with permission, of *IEEE Engineering and Medicine and Biology* 25:15 (2005).)

stage in recent years, including the one that was implanted in Linda (Humayun et al., 1996; Weiland & Humayun, 2006; Yanai et al., 2007).

Artificial retinas like the one Linda has are complex electronic devices that rely on an external, eyeglass-mounted video camera to "see" the patient's environment. Signals from the camera are sent to a video-processing unit that the patient wears; this unit electronically simplifies the picture that the camera sees to put it in a form that the prosthetic device can relay to the patient's retina. This greatly simplified visual information is wirelessly transmitted to an electronic receptor behind the patient's ear, from which wires run to an array of tiny electrodes that are implanted directly on the patient's retina. The electrodes stimulate photoreceptor cells on the retina to reproduce the simplified visual information patterns that the camera picked up.

Other designs are also being tried. One of these omits the external camera altogether by implanting light-sensitive chips

directly under the retina (see Figure 8). Such chips detect light entering the eye and striking them; they then send electrical impulses to the ganglion cells that normally convey visual information from the retina to the nervous system. They therefore function in much the same way as natural photoreceptors would, although the visual information that they can capture and relay to the brain is still limited to simple patterns formed by dots of light (Wickelgren, 2006).

These devices and others like them do not yet come close to enabling the blind to again see like normal-sighted people. The subtleties of texture, color, and intensity that we take for granted are, for now, too complex for any artificial vision device to capture. They do not even capture enough detail for patients to recognize faces or to read printed text—not yet, anyway. But with training and practice, patients can interpret the rough patterns of light flashes that these devices produce to locate and count objects, to differentiate simple shapes, to make out the form and orientation of printed letters, and to tell that an object is moving (and in which direction). Although these may seem to us like disappointingly rudimentary visual feats, they open up new worlds of possibility for people who could previously see absolutely nothing (Yanai et al., 2007).

- Although recipients of artificial retinas can see the patterns of light flashes immediately after they recover from surgery, it takes months and even years of experience for them to be able to use this visual information to its fullest. Why would this be?

- Artificial retinas can only help those blind people who once had normal vision that deteriorated because of degenerative disease. Why do you think artificial retinas cannot help people who were blind from birth?

RECAP/EVALUATE/RETHINK

RECAP

What basic processes underlie the sense of vision?

- Vision depends on sensitivity to light, electromagnetic waves in the visible part of the spectrum that are either reflected off objects or produced by an energy source. The eye shapes the light into an image that is transformed into nerve impulses and interpreted by the brain. (p. 103)
- As light enters the eye, it passes through the cornea, pupil, and lens and ultimately reaches the retina, where the electromagnetic energy of light is converted to nerve impulses for transmission to the brain. These impulses leave the eye via the optic nerve. (p. 104)
- The visual information gathered by the rods and cones is transferred via bipolar and ganglion cells through the optic nerve, which leads to the optic chiasm—the point where the optic nerve splits. (p. 107)

How do we see colors?

- Color vision seems to be based on two processes described by the trichromatic theory and the opponent-process theory. (p. 109)
- The trichromatic theory suggests that there are three kinds of cones in the retina, each of which is responsive to a certain range of colors. The opponent-process theory presumes pairs of different types of cells in the eye that work in opposition to each other. (p. 110)

EVALUATE

1. Light entering the eye first passes through the _____, a protective window.

2. The structure that converts light into usable neural messages is called the _____.
3. A woman with blue eyes could be described as having blue pigment in her _____.
4. What is the process by which the thickness of the lens is changed in order to focus light properly?
5. The proper sequence of structures that light passes through in the eye is the _____, _____, _____, and _____.
6. Match each type of visual receptor with its function.
   - a. Rods
   - b. Cones
   - 1. Used for dim light, largely insensitive to color.
   - 2. Detect color, good in bright light.
7. _____ theory states that there are three types of cones in the retina, each of which responds primarily to a different color.

RETHINK

1. If the eye had a second lens that "unreversed" the image hitting the retina, do you think there would be changes in the way people perceive the world?
2. *From the perspective of an advertising specialist:* How might you market your products similarly or differently to those who are color-blind versus those who have normal color vision?

Answers to Evaluate Questions

1. cornea; 2. retina; 3. iris; 4. accommodation; 5. cornea, pupil, lens, retina; 6. a-1, b-2; 7. trichromatic

KEY TERMS

retina p. 105
rods p. 105
cones p. 105

optic nerve p. 106
feature detection p. 107

trichromatic theory of color vision p. 109

opponent-process theory of color vision p. 110

Hearing and the Other Senses

The blast-off was easy compared with what the astronaut was experiencing now: space sickness. The constant nausea and vomiting were enough to make him wonder why he had worked so hard to become an astronaut. Even though he had been warned that there was a two-thirds chance that his first experience in space would cause these symptoms, he wasn't prepared for how terribly sick he really felt.

Whether or not the astronaut wishes he could head right back to earth, his experience, a major problem for space travelers, is related to a basic sensory process: the sense of motion and balance. This sense allows people to navigate their bodies through the world and keep themselves upright without falling. Along with hearing—the process by which sound waves are translated into understandable and meaningful forms—the sense of motion and balance resides in the ear.

Sensing Sound

Although many of us think primarily of the outer ear when we speak of the ear, that structure is only one simple part of the whole. The outer ear acts as a reverse megaphone, designed to collect and bring sounds into the internal portions of the ear (see Figure 1). The location of the outer ears on different sides of the head helps with *sound localization*, the process by which we identify the direction from which a sound is coming. Wave patterns in the air enter each ear at a slightly different time, and the brain uses the discrepancy as a clue to the sound's point of origin. In addition, the two outer ears delay or amplify sounds of particular frequencies to different degrees.

Sound is the movement of air molecules brought about by a source of vibration. Sounds travel through the air in wave patterns similar in shape to those made in water when a stone is thrown into a still pond. Sounds, arriving at the outer ear in the form of wavelike vibrations, are funneled into the *auditory canal*, a tubelike passage that leads to the eardrum. The eardrum is aptly named because it operates like a miniature drum, vibrating when sound waves hit it. The more intense the sound, the more the eardrum vibrates. These vibrations are then transferred into the *middle ear*, a tiny chamber containing three bones (the *hammer*, the *anvil*, and the *stirrup*) that transmit vibrations to the *oval window*, a thin membrane leading to the inner ear. Because the hammer, anvil, and stirrup act as a set of levers, they not only transmit vibrations but increase their strength. Moreover, because the opening into the middle ear (the eardrum) is considerably larger than the opening out of it (the *oval window*), the force of sound waves on the oval window becomes amplified. The middle ear, then, acts as a tiny mechanical amplifier.

The *inner ear* is the portion of the ear that changes the sound vibrations into a form in which they can be transmitted to the brain. (As you will see, it also contains the organs that allow us to locate our position and determine how we are moving through space.) When sound enters the inner ear through the oval window, it moves into the **cochlea**, a coiled tube that looks something like a snail and is filled with fluid that vibrates in response to sound. Inside the cochlea is the **basilar membrane**, a structure that runs through the center of the cochlea, dividing it into an upper chamber and

The movement of air molecules brought about by a source of vibration.

The part of the ear that vibrates when sound waves hit it.

Cochlea (KOKE lee uh): A coiled tube in the ear filled with fluid that vibrates in response to sound.

Basilar membrane: A vibrating structure that runs through the center of the cochlea, dividing it into an upper chamber and a lower chamber and containing sense receptors for sound.

113

FIGURE 1 The major parts of the ear. (Source: Brooker et al., 2008, Fig. 45.6).

Hair cells: Tiny cells covering the basilar membrane that, when bent by vibrations entering the cochlea, transmit neural messages to the brain.

a lower chamber. The basilar membrane is covered with **hair cells**. When the hair cells are bent by the vibrations entering the cochlea, the cells send a neural message to the brain (Cho, 2000; Zhou, Liu, & Davis, 2005).

THE PHYSICAL ASPECTS OF SOUND

As we mentioned earlier, what we refer to as sound is actually the physical movement of air molecules in regular, wavelike patterns caused by a vibrating source. Sometimes it is even possible to see these vibrations: If you have ever seen an audio speaker that has no enclosure, you know that, at least when the lowest notes are playing, you can see the speaker moving in and out. Less obvious is what happens next: The speaker pushes air molecules into waves with the same pattern as its movement. Those wave patterns soon reach your ear, although their strength has been weakened considerably during their travels. All other sources that produce sound work in essentially the same fashion, setting off wave patterns that move through the air to the ear. Air—or some other medium, such as water—is necessary to make the vibrations of objects reach us. This explains why there can be no sound in a vacuum.

We are able to see the audio speaker moving when low notes are played because of a primary characteristic of sound called frequency. *Frequency* is the number of wave cycles that occur in a second. At very low frequencies there are relatively few wave cycles per second (see Figure 2). These cycles are visible to the naked eye as vibrations in the speaker. Low frequencies are translated into a sound that is very low in pitch. (*Pitch* is the characteristic that makes sound seem "high" or "low.") For example, the lowest frequency that humans are capable of hearing is 20 cycles per second. Higher

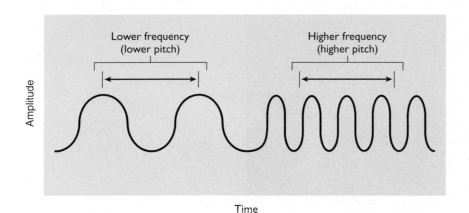

Time

FIGURE 2 The sound waves produced by different stimuli are transmitted— usually through the air—in different patterns, with lower frequencies indicated by fewer peaks and valleys per second. (Source: Seeley, Stephens, & Tate, 2000.)

frequencies are heard as sounds of higher pitch. At the upper end of the sound spectrum, people can detect sounds with frequencies as high as 20,000 cycles per second.

Amplitude is a feature of wave patterns that allows us to distinguish between loud and soft sounds. Amplitude is the spread between the up-and-down peaks and valleys of air pressure in a sound wave as it travels through the air. Waves with small peaks and valleys produce soft sounds; those with relatively large peaks and valleys produce loud sounds (see Figure 2).

We are sensitive to broad variations in sound amplitudes. The strongest sounds we are capable of hearing are over a trillion times as intense as the very weakest sound we can hear. This range is measured in *decibels*. When sounds get higher than 120 decibels, they become painful to the human ear.

Sorting Out Theories of Sound. How are our brains able to sort out wavelengths of different frequencies and intensities? One clue comes from studies of the basilar membrane, the area in the cochlea that translates physical vibrations into neural impulses. It turns out that sounds affect different areas of the basilar membrane, depending on the frequency of the sound wave. The part of the basilar membrane nearest to the oval window is most sensitive to high-frequency sounds, and the part nearest to the cochlea's inner end is most sensitive to low-frequency sounds. This finding has led to the **place theory of hearing**, which states that different areas of the basilar membrane respond to different frequencies.

However, place theory does not tell the full story of hearing, because very low frequency sounds trigger neurons across such a wide area of the basilar membrane that no single site is involved. Consequently, an additional explanation for hearing has been proposed: frequency theory. The **frequency theory of hearing** suggests that the entire basilar membrane acts like a microphone, vibrating as a whole in response to a sound. According to this explanation, the nerve receptors send out signals that are tied directly to the frequency (the number of wave crests per second) of the sounds to which we are exposed, with the number of nerve impulses being a direct function of a sound's frequency. Thus, the higher the pitch of a sound (and therefore the greater the frequency of its wave crests), the greater the number of nerve impulses that are transmitted up the auditory nerve to the brain.

Neither place theory nor frequency theory provides the full explanation for hearing. Place theory provides a better explanation for the sensing of high-frequency sounds, whereas frequency theory explains what happens when low-frequency sounds are encountered. Medium-frequency sounds incorporate both processes (Hirsh & Watson, 1996; Hudspeth, 2000).

After an auditory message leaves the ear, it is transmitted to the auditory cortex of the brain through a complex series of neural interconnections. As the message is transmitted, it is communicated through neurons that respond to specific types of sounds. Within the auditory cortex itself, there are neurons that respond selectively to very specific sorts of sound features, such as clicks and whistles. Some neurons

Place theory of hearing: The theory that different areas of the basilar membrane respond to different frequencies.

Frequency theory of hearing: The theory that the entire basilar membrane acts like a microphone, vibrating as a whole in response to a sound.

Study ALERT

Be sure to understand the differences between the place and frequency theories of hearing.

The weightlessness of the ear's otoliths produces space sickness in most astronauts.

respond only to a specific pattern of sounds, such as a steady tone but not an intermittent one. Furthermore, specific neurons transfer information about a sound's location through their particular pattern of firing (Middlebrooks et al., 2005; Wang, Lu, Snider, Liang, 2005; Tervaniemi et al., 2006).

If we were to analyze the configuration of the cells in the auditory cortex, we would find that neighboring cells are responsive to similar frequencies. The auditory cortex, then, provides us with a "map" of sound frequencies, just as the visual cortex furnishes a representation of the visual field. In addition, because of the asymmetry in the two hemispheres of the brain (which we discussed in the last chapter), the left and right ears process sound differently. The right ear reacts more to speech, while the left ear responds more to music (Sininger & Cone-Wesson, 2004, 2006).

Balance: The Ups and Downs of Life. Several structures of the ear are related more to our sense of balance than to our hearing. The **semicircular canals** of the inner ear (refer to Figure 1) consist of three tubes containing fluid that sloshes through them when the head moves, signaling rotational or angular movement to the brain. The pull on our bodies caused by the acceleration of forward, backward, or up-and-down motion, as well as the constant pull of gravity, is sensed by the **otoliths**, tiny, motion-sensitive crystals in the semicircular canals. When we move, these crystals shift like sands on a windy beach. The brain's inexperience in interpreting messages from the weightless otoliths is the cause of the space sickness commonly experienced by two-thirds of all space travelers, mentioned at the start of this module (Flam, 1991; Stern & Koch, 1996).

Semicircular canals: Three tubelike structures of the inner ear containing fluid that sloshes through them when the head moves, signaling rotational or angular movement to the brain.

Otoliths: Tiny, motion-sensitive crystals within the semicircular canals that sense body acceleration.

Smell and Taste

Until he bit into a piece of raw cabbage on that February evening . . . , Raymond Fowler had not thought much about the sense of taste. The cabbage, part of a pasta dish he was preparing for his family's dinner, had an odd, burning taste, but he did not pay it much attention. Then a few minutes later, his daughter handed him a glass of cola, and he took a swallow. "It was like sulfuric acid," he said. "It was like the hottest thing you could imagine boring into your mouth." (Goode, 1999b, pp. D1–D2)

It was evident that something was very wrong with Fowler's sense of taste. After extensive testing, it became clear that he had damaged the nerves involved in his sense of taste, probably because of a viral infection or a medicine he was taking. (Luckily for him, a few months later his sense of taste returned to normal.)

Even without disruptions in our ability to perceive the world such as those experienced by Fowler, we all know the important roles that taste and smell play. We'll consider these two senses next.

SMELL

Although many animals have keener abilities to detect odors than we do, the human sense of smell (*olfaction*) permits us to detect more than 10,000 separate smells. We also have a good memory for smells, and long-forgotten events and memories—good and bad—can be brought back with the mere whiff of an odor associated with a memory (DiLorenzo & Youngentob, 2003; Stevenson & Case, 2005; Willander & Larsson, 2006).

Results of "sniff tests" have shown that women generally have a better sense of smell than men do (Engen, 1987). People also have the ability to distinguish males from females on the basis of smell alone. In one experiment, blindfolded students who were asked to sniff the breath of a female or male volunteer who was hidden from view were able to distinguish the sex of the donor at better than chance levels. People can also distinguish happy from sad emotions by sniffing underarm smells, and women are able to identify their babies solely on the basis of smell just a few hours after birth (Doty et al., 1982; Haviland-Jones & Chen, 1999).

The sense of smell is sparked when the molecules of a substance enter the nasal passages and meet *olfactory cells*, the receptor neurons of the nose, which are spread across the nasal cavity. More than 1,000 separate types of receptors have been identified on those cells so far. Each of these receptors is so specialized that it responds only to a small band of different odors. The responses of the separate olfactory cells are then transmitted to the brain, where they are combined into recognition of a particular smell (Murphy et al., 2004; Zhou & Buck, 2006; Marshall et al., 2006).

Smell may also act as a hidden means of communication for humans. It has long been known that nonhumans release *pheromones*, chemicals they secrete into the environment that produce a reaction in other members of the same species, permitting the transmission of messages such as sexual availability. For instance, the vaginal secretions of female monkeys contain pheromones that stimulate the sexual interest of male monkeys (Holy, Dulac, & Meister, 2000; Touhara, 2007).

More than 1,000 receptor cells, known as olfactory cells, are spread across the nasal cavity. The cells are specialized to react to particular odors. Do you think it is possible to "train" the nose to pick up a greater number of odors?

TASTE

The sense of taste (*gustation*) involves receptor cells that respond to four basic stimulus qualities: sweet, sour, salty, and bitter. A fifth category also exists, a flavor called *umami*, although there is controversy about whether it qualifies as a fundamental taste. Umami is a hard-to-translate Japanese word, although the English "meaty" or "savory" comes close. Chemically, umami involves food stimuli that contain amino acids (the substances that make up proteins) (Shi, Huang, & Zhang, 2005; McCabe & Rolls, 2007).

Although the specialization of the receptor cells leads them to respond most strongly to a particular type of taste, they also are capable of responding to other tastes as well. Ultimately, every taste is simply a combination of the basic flavor qualities, in the same way that the primary colors blend into a vast variety of shades and hues (Dilorenzo & Youngentob, 2003; Yeomans et al., 2007).

The receptor cells for taste are located in roughly 10,000 *taste buds*, which are distributed across the tongue and other parts of the mouth and throat. The taste buds wear out and are replaced every ten days or so.

There are 10,000 taste buds on the tongue and other parts of the mouth. Taste buds wear out and are replaced every ten days. What would happen if taste buds were not regenerated?

That's a good thing, because if our taste buds weren't constantly reproducing, we'd lose the ability to taste after we'd accidentally burned our tongues.

The sense of taste differs significantly from one person to another, largely as a result of genetic factors. Some people, dubbed "supertasters," are highly sensitive to taste; they have twice as many taste receptors as "nontasters," who are relatively insensitive to taste. Supertasters (who, for unknown reasons, are more likely to be female than male) find sweets sweeter, cream creamier, and spicy dishes spicier, and weaker concentrations of flavor are enough to satisfy any cravings they may have. In contrast, because they aren't so sensitive to taste, nontasters may seek out relatively sweeter and fattier foods in order to maximize the taste. As a consequence, they may be prone to obesity (Bartoshuk, 2000; Snyder, Fast, & Bartoshuk, 2004; Pickering & Gordon, 2006).

Are you a supertaster? To find out, complete the questionnaire in Figure 3.

FIGURE 3 All tongues are not created equal, according to taste researchers Linda Bartoshuk and Laurie Lucchina. Instead, they suggest that the intensity of a flavor experienced by a given person is determined by that person's genetic background. This taste test can help determine if you are a nontaster, average taster, or supertaster. (Source: Bartoshuk & Lucchina, 1997.)

Take a Taste Test

1. Taste Bud Count
   Punch a hole with a standard hole punch in a square of wax paper. Paint the front of your tongue with a cotton swab dipped in blue food coloring. Put wax paper on the tip of your tongue, just to the right of center. With a flashlight and magnifying glass, count the number of pink, unstained circles. They contain taste buds.
2. Sweet Taste
   Rinse your mouth with water before tasting each sample. Put 1/2 cup sugar in a measuring cup, and then add enough water to make 1 cup. Mix. Coat front half of your tongue, including the tip, with a cotton swab dipped in the solution. Wait a few moments. Rate the sweetness according to the scale shown below.
3. Salt Taste
   Put 2 teaspoons of salt in a measuring cup and add enough water to make 1 cup. Repeat the steps listed above, rating how salty the solution is.
4. Spicy Taste
   Add 1 teaspoon of Tabasco sauce to 1 cup of water. Apply with a cotton swab to first half inch of the tongue, including the tip. Keep your tongue out of your mouth until the burn reaches a peak, then rate the burn according to the scale.

TASTE SCALE

	SUPERTASTERS	NONTASTERS
No. of taste buds	25 on Average	10
Sweet rating	56 on Average	32
Tabasco	64 on Average	31

Average tasters lie in between supertasters and nontasters. Bartoshuk and Lucchina lack the data at this time to rate salt reliably, but you can compare your results with others taking the test.

The Skin Senses: Touch, Pressure, Temperature, and Pain

It started innocently when Jennifer Darling hurt her right wrist during gym class. At first it seemed like a simple sprain. But even though the initial injury healed, the excruciating, burning pain accompanying it did not go away. Instead, it spread to her other arm and then to her legs. The pain, which Jennifer described as similar to "a hot iron on your arm," was unbearable—and never stopped.

The source of Darling's pain turned out to be a rare condition known as "reflex sympathetic dystrophy syndrome," or RSDS for short. For a victim of RSDS, a stimulus as mild as a gentle breeze or the touch of a feather can produce agony. Even bright sunlight or a loud noise can trigger intense pain.

Pain like Darling's can be devastating, yet a lack of pain can be equally bad. If you never experienced pain, for instance, you might not notice that your arm had brushed against a hot pan, and you would suffer a severe burn. Similarly, without the warning sign of abdominal pain that typically accompanies an inflamed appendix, your appendix might eventually rupture, spreading a fatal infection throughout your body.

In fact, all our **skin senses**—touch, pressure, temperature, and pain—play a critical role in survival, making us aware of potential danger to our bodies. Most of these senses operate through nerve receptor cells located at various depths throughout the skin, distributed unevenly throughout the body. For example, some areas, such as the fingertips, have many more receptor cells sensitive to touch and as a consequence are notably more sensitive than other areas of the body (Gardner & Kandel, 2000; see Figure 4).

Probably the most extensively researched skin sense is pain, and with good reason: People consult physicians and take medication for pain more than any other symptom or condition. Pain costs $100 billion a year in the United States alone (Kalb, 2003; Pesmen, 2006).

Pain is a response to a great variety of different kinds of stimuli. A light that is too bright can produce pain, and sound that is too loud can be painful. One explanation is that pain is an outcome of cell injury; when a cell is damaged, regardless of the source of damage, it releases a chemical called *substance P* that transmits pain messages to the brain.

Some people are more susceptible to pain than others. For example, women experience painful stimuli more intensely than men. These gender differences are associated with the production of hormones related to menstrual cycles. In addition, certain genes are linked to the experience of pain, so that we may inherit our sensitivity to pain (Apkarian et al., 2005; Edwards & Fillingim, 2007).

But the experience of pain is not determined by biological factors alone. For example, women report that the pain experienced in childbirth is moderated to some degree by the joyful nature of the situation. In contrast, even a minor stimulus can produce the perception of strong pain if it is accompanied by anxiety (like a visit to the dentist). Clearly, then, pain is a perceptual response that depends heavily on our emotions and thoughts (Hadjistavropoulos, Craig, & Fuchs-Lacelle, 2004; Rollman, 2004; Lang et al., 2006).

According to the **gate-control theory of pain**, particular nerve receptors in the spinal cord lead to specific areas of the brain related to pain. When these receptors are activated because of an injury or problem with a part of the body, a "gate" to the brain is opened, allowing us to experience the sensation of pain (Melzack & Katz, 2004).

Skin senses: The senses of touch, pressure, temperature, and pain.

 StudyALERT

Remember that there are multiple skin senses, including touch, pressure, temperature, and pain.

Gate-control theory of pain: The theory that particular nerve receptors in the spinal cord lead to specific areas of the brain related to pain.

FIGURE 4 Skin sensitivity in various areas of the body. The lower the average threshold is, the more sensitive a body part is. The fingers and thumb, lips, nose, cheeks, and big toe are the most sensitive. Why do you think certain areas are more sensitive than others? (Source: Kenshalo, *The Skin Senses.* 1968. Courtesy of Charles C. Thomas, Publisher, Ltd., Springfield, Illinois.)

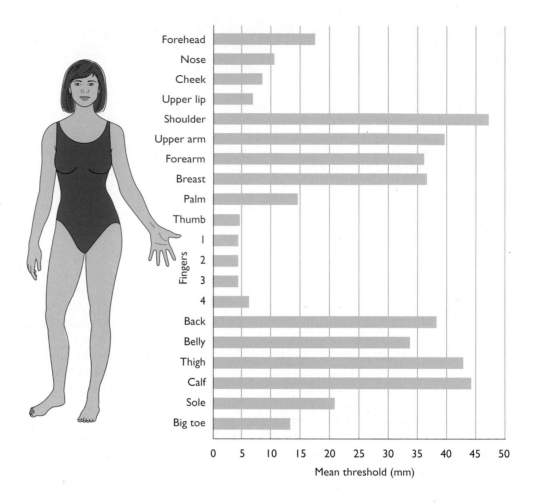

However, another set of neural receptors can, when stimulated, close the "gate" to the brain, thereby reducing the experience of pain. The gate can be shut in two different ways. First, other impulses can overwhelm the nerve pathways relating to pain, which are spread throughout the brain. In this case, nonpainful stimuli compete with and sometimes displace the neural message of pain, thereby shutting off the painful stimulus. This explains why rubbing the skin around an injury (or even listening to distracting music) helps reduce pain. The competing stimuli can overpower the painful ones (Villemure, Slotnick, & Bushnell, 2003).

Psychological factors account for the second way a gate can be shut. Depending on an individual's current emotions, interpretation of events, and previous experience, the brain can close a gate by sending a message down the spinal cord to an injured area, producing a reduction in or relief from pain. Thus, soldiers who are injured in battle may experience no pain—the surprising situation in more than half of all combat injuries. The lack of pain probably occurs because a soldier experiences such relief at still being alive that the brain sends a signal to the injury site to shut down the pain gate (Turk, 1994; Gatchel & Weisberg, 2000; Pincus & Morley, 2001).

The ancient practice of acupuncture is still used in the twenty-first century. How does the gate-control theory of pain explain how acupuncture works?

Gate-control theory also may explain cultural differences in the experience of pain. Some of these variations are astounding. For example, in India people who participate in the "hook-swinging" ritual to celebrate the power of the gods have steel hooks embedded under the skin and muscles of their backs. During the ritual, they swing from a pole, suspended by the hooks. What would seem likely to induce excruciating pain instead produces a state of celebration and near euphoria. In fact, when the hooks are later removed, the wounds heal quickly, and after two weeks almost no visible marks remain (Kosambi, 1967; Melzack & Wall, 2001).

Gate-control theory suggests that the lack of pain is due to a message from the participant's brain, which shuts down the pain pathways. Gate-control theory also may explain the effectiveness of *acupuncture*, an ancient Chinese technique in which sharp needles are inserted into various parts of the body. The sensation from the needles may close the gateway to the brain, reducing the experience of pain. It is also possible that the body's own painkillers—called endorphins—as well as positive and negative emotions, play a role in opening and closing the gate (Daitz, 2002; Fee et al., 2002; Witt et al., 2006).

Are you one of the 50 million people in the United States who suffer from chronic pain? Psychologists and medical specialists have devised several strategies to fight pain. Among the most important approaches are the following:

BECOMING
AN INFORMED CONSUMER
of Psychology

Managing Pain

- *Medication.* Painkilling drugs are the most popular treatment in fighting pain. Drugs range from those which directly treat the source of the pain—such as reducing swelling in painful joints—to those that work on the symptoms. Medication can be in the form of pills, patches, injections, or liquids. In a recent innovation, drugs are pumped directly into the spinal cord (Kalb, 2003; Pesmen, 2006).

- *Nerve and brain stimulation.* Pain can sometimes be relieved when a low-voltage electric current is passed through the specific part of the body that is in pain. In even more severe cases, electrodes can be implanted surgically directly into the brain, or a handheld battery pack can stimulate nerve cells to provide direct relief (Ross, 2000; Campbell & Ditto, 2002; Tugay et al., 2007).

- *Light therapy.* One of the newest forms of pain reduction involves exposure to specific wavelengths of red or infrared light. Certain kinds of light increase the production of enzymes that may promote healing (Underwood, 2003; Evçik et al., 2007).

- *Hypnosis.* For people who can be hypnotized, hypnosis can greatly relieve pain (Patterson, 2004; Neron & Stephenson, 2007).

- *Biofeedback and relaxation techniques.* Using *biofeedback*, people learn to control "involuntary" functions such as heartbeat and respiration. If the pain involves muscles, as in tension headaches or back pain, sufferers can be trained to relax their bodies systematically (Vitiello, Bonello, & Pollard, 2007).

- *Surgery.* In one of the most extreme methods, nerve fibers that carry pain messages to the brain can be cut surgically. Still, because of the danger that other bodily functions will be affected, surgery is a treatment of last resort, used most frequently with dying patients (Cullinane, Chu, & Mamelak, 2002).

- *Cognitive restructuring.* Cognitive treatments are effective for people who continually say to themselves, "This pain will never stop," "The pain is ruining my life," or "I can't take it anymore" and are thereby likely to make their pain even worse. By substituting more positive ways of thinking, people can increase their sense of control—and actually reduce the pain they experience (Spanos, Barber, & Lang, 2005; Bogart et al., 2007).

How Our Senses Interact

When Matthew Blakeslee shapes hamburger patties with his hands, he experiences a vivid bitter taste in his mouth. Esmerelda Jones (a pseudonym) sees blue when she listens to the note C sharp played on the piano; other notes evoke different hues—so much so that the piano keys are actually color-coded, making it easier for her to remember and play musical scales. (Ramachandran & Hubbard, 2004, p. 53)

The explanation? Both of these people have an unusual condition known as *synesthesia*, in which exposure to one sensation (such as sound) evokes an additional one (such as vision).

The origins of synesthesia are a mystery. It is possible that people with synesthesia have unusually dense neural linkages between the different sensory areas of the brain. Another hypothesis is that they lack neural controls that usually inhibit connections between sensory areas (Ramachandran & Hubbard, 2001; Shannon, 2003; Ramachandran, 2004; Pearce, 2007).

Whatever the reason for synesthesia, it is a rare condition. (If you'd like to check out this phenomenon, see Figure 5.) Even so, the senses of all of us do interact and integrate in a variety of ways. For example, the taste of food is influenced by its texture and temperature. We perceive food that is warmer as sweeter (think of the sweetness of steamy hot chocolate compared with cold chocolate milk). Spicy foods stimulate some of the same pain receptors that are also stimulated by heat—making the use of "hot" as a synonym for "spicy" quite accurate (Cruz & Green, 2000; Green & George, 2004; Balaban, McBurney, & Affeltranger, 2005).

It's important, then, to think of our senses as interacting with one another. For instance, increasing evidence from brain imaging studies show that the senses work in tandem to build our understanding of the world around us (see Figure 6; Macaluso & Driver, 2005).

Moreover, despite the fact that very different sorts of stimuli activate our individual senses, they all react according to the same basic principles that we discussed at the start of this chapter. For example, our responses to visual, auditory, and taste stimuli all follow Weber's law involving our sensitivity to changes in the strength of stimuli.

In short, in some ways our senses are more similar to one another than different. Each of them is designed to pick up information from the environment and translate it into useable information. Furthermore, individually and collectively, our senses help us to understand the complexities of the world around us, allowing us to navigate through the world effectively and intelligently.

FIGURE 5 Try to pick out the 2s in the display in (a). Most people take several seconds to find them buried among the 5s and to see that the 2s form a triangle. For people with certain forms of synesthesia, however, it's easy, because they perceive the different numbers in contrasting colors, as in (b). (Source: From "Hearing Colors, Tasting Shapes" by Vilayanur S. Ramachandran and Edward M. Hubbard. Copyright © 2003 by Scientific American, Inc. All rights reserved.)

a.

b.

Neuroscience in Your Life

FIGURE 6 Participants in a study examining sensory processing were exposed to visual, touch, and auditory stimuli. Some parts of the brain responded to only one type of stimuli (a). For example, different areas were activated by visual stimuli (green), auditory stimuli (pink), or touch stimuli (blue). However, other parts of the brain responded only when combinations of different types of stimuli were presented (b). In contrast, when a stimulus was presented both visually and by touch (red/orange), areas of the brain were activated that were not activated when each type of stimulus was presented alone. Additionally, some areas of the brain (white) were preferentially activated when stimuli were presented in all three modalities (visual, auditory, and touch), a result suggesting that these areas might be involved in sensory integration. (Source: Macaluso & Driver, Figure 1(a).)

RECAP/EVALUATE/RETHINK

RECAP

What role does the ear play in the senses of sound, motion, and balance?

- Sound, motion, and balance are centered in the ear. Sounds, in the form of vibrating air waves, enter through the outer ear and travel through the auditory canal until they reach the eardrum. (p. 113)

- The vibrations of the eardrum are transmitted into the middle ear, which consists of three bones: the hammer, the anvil, and the stirrup. These bones transmit vibrations to the oval window. (p. 113)

- In the inner ear, vibrations move into the cochlea, which encloses the basilar membrane. Hair cells on the basilar membrane change the mechanical energy of sound waves into nerve impulses that are transmitted to the brain. The ear is also involved in the sense of balance and motion. (p. 114)

- Sound has a number of physical characteristics, including frequency and amplitude. The place theory of hearing and the frequency theory of hearing explain the processes by which we distinguish sounds of varying frequency and intensity. (p. 115)

How do smell and taste function?

- Smell depends on olfactory cells (the receptor cells of the nose), and taste is centered in the tongue's taste buds. (p. 117)

What are the skin senses, and how do they relate to the experience of pain?

- The skin senses are responsible for the experiences of touch, pressure, temperature, and pain. Gate-control theory suggests that particular nerve receptors, when activated, open a "gate" to specific areas of the brain related to pain, and that another set of receptors closes the gate when stimulated. (p. 119)

- Among the techniques used frequently to alleviate pain are medication, hypnosis, biofeedback, relaxation techniques, surgery, nerve and brain stimulation, and cognitive therapy. (p. 121)

EVALUATE

1. The tubelike passage leading from the outer ear to the eardrum is known as the _____ _____.

2. The purpose of the eardrum is to protect the sensitive nerves underneath it. It serves no purpose in actual hearing. True or false?

3. The three middle ear bones transmit their sound to the _____.

4. The _____ theory of hearing states that the entire basilar membrane responds to a sound, vibrating more or less, depending on the nature of the sound.

5. The three fluid-filled tubes in the inner ear that are responsible for our sense of balance are known as the _____ _____.

6. The _____ _____ theory states that when certain skin receptors are activated as a result of an injury, a "pathway" to the brain is opened, allowing pain to be experienced.

RETHINK

1. Much research is being conducted on repairing faulty sensory organs through devices such as personal guidance systems and eyeglasses, among others. Do you think that researchers should attempt to improve normal sensory capabilities beyond their "natural" range (for example, make human visual or audio capabilities more sensitive than normal)? What benefits might this ability bring? What problems might it cause?

2. *From the perspective of a social worker:* How would you handle the case of a deaf child whose hearing could be restored with a cochlear implant, but different family members had conflicting views on whether the procedure should be done?

Answers to Evaluate Questions

1. auditory canal; 2. false—it vibrates when sound waves hit it, and transmits the sound; 3. oval window; 4. frequency; 5. semicircular canals; 6. gate-control.

KEY TERMS

sound p. 113
eardrum p. 113
cochlea (KOKE lee uh)
    p. 113

basilar membrane p. 113
hair cells p. 114
place theory of hearing
    p. 115

frequency theory of
    hearing p. 115
semicircular canals p. 116
otoliths p. 116

skin senses p. 119
gate-control theory of pain
    p. 119

Perceptual Organization: Constructing Our View of the World

Consider the vase shown in Figure 1a for a moment. Or is it a vase? Take another look, and instead you may see the profiles of two people.

Now that an alternative interpretation has been pointed out, you will probably shift back and forth between the two interpretations. Similarly, if you examine the shapes in Figure 1b long enough, you will probably experience a shift in what you're seeing. The reason for these reversals is this: Because each figure is two-dimensional, the usual means we employ for distinguishing the figure (the object being perceived) from the *ground* (the background or spaces within the object) do not work.

The fact that we can look at the same figure in more than one way illustrates an important point. We do not just passively respond to visual stimuli that happen to fall on our retinas. Rather, we actively try to organize and make sense of what we see.

We turn now from a focus on the initial response to a stimulus (sensation) to what our minds make of that stimulus—perception. Perception is a constructive process by which we go beyond the stimuli that are presented to us and attempt to construct a meaningful situation.

The Gestalt Laws of Organization

Some of the most basic perceptual processes can be described by a series of principles that focus on the ways we organize bits and pieces of information into meaningful wholes. Known as **gestalt laws of organization**, these principles were set forth in the

Key Concepts

What principles underlie our organization of the visual world and allow us to make sense of our environment?

How are we able to perceive the world in three dimensions when our retinas are capable of sensing only two-dimensional images?

What clues do visual illusions give us about our understanding of general perceptual mechanisms?

Gestalt laws of organization: A series of principles that describe how we organize bits and pieces of information into meaningful wholes.

a. b.

FIGURE 1 When the usual cues we use to distinguish figure from ground are absent, we may shift back and forth between different views of the same figure. If you look at each of these objects long enough, you'll probably experience a shift in what you're seeing. In (a), you can see either a vase or the profiles of two people. In (b), the shaded portion of the figure, called a Necker cube, can appear to be either the front or the back of the cube.

"I'm turning into my mother."

Understanding this cartoon involves the separation of the figure and ground. If you're having trouble appreciating the humor, stare at the woman on the right, who eventually will be transformed.

StudyALERT

The gestalt laws of organization are classic principles in the field of psychology. Figure 2 can help you remember them.

early 1900s by a group of German psychologists who studied patterns, or *gestalts* (Wertheimer, 1923). Those psychologists discovered a number of important principles that are valid for visual (as well as auditory) stimuli, illustrated in Figure 2: closure, proximity, similarity, and simplicity.

Figure 2a illustrates *closure*: We usually group elements to form enclosed or complete figures rather than open ones. We tend to ignore the breaks in Figure 2a and concentrate on the overall form. Figure 2b demonstrates the principle of *proximity*: We perceive elements that are closer together as grouped together. As a result, we tend to see pairs of dots rather than a row of single dots in Figure 2b.

Elements that are *similar* in appearance we perceive as grouped together. We see, then, horizontal rows of circles and squares in Figure 2c rather than vertical mixed columns. Finally, in a general sense, the overriding gestalt principle is *simplicity*: When we observe a pattern, we perceive it in the most basic, straightforward manner that we can. For example, most of us see Figure 2d as a square with lines on two sides, rather than as the block letter *W* on top of the letter *M*. If we have a choice of interpretations, we generally opt for the simpler one.

Although gestalt psychology no longer plays a prominent role in contemporary psychology, its legacy endures. One fundamental gestalt principle that remains influential is that two objects considered together form a whole that is different from the simple combination of the objects. Gestalt psychologists argued that the perception of stimuli in our environment goes well beyond the individual elements that we sense. Instead, it represents an active, constructive process carried out within the brain (Humphreys & Muller, 2000; Lehar, 2003; van der Helm, 2006; see Figure 3).

Top-Down and Bottom-Up Processing

Ca- yo- re-d t-is -en-en-e, w-ic- ha- ev-ry -hi-d l-tt-r m-ss-ng? It probably won't take you too long to figure out that it says, "Can you read this sentence, which has every third letter missing?"

If perception were based primarily on breaking down a stimulus into its most basic elements, understanding the sentence, as well as other ambiguous stimuli, would not be possible. The fact that you were probably able to recognize such an imprecise stimulus illustrates that perception proceeds along two different avenues, called top-down processing and bottom-up processing.

a. Closure **b.** Proximity   **c.** Similarity **d.** Simplicity

FIGURE 2 Organizing these various bits and pieces of information into meaningful wholes constitutes some of the most basic processes of perception, which are summed up in the gestalt laws of organization. Do you think any other species share this organizational tendency? How might we find out?

FIGURE 3 Although at first it is difficult to distinguish anything in this drawing, keep looking, and eventually you'll probably be able to see the figure of a dog (James, 1966). The dog represents a gestalt, or perceptual whole, which is something greater than the sum of the individual elements.

In **top-down processing**, perception is guided by higher-level knowledge, experience, expectations, and motivations. You were able to figure out the meaning of the sentence with the missing letters because of your prior reading experience, and because written English contains redundancies. Not every letter of each word is necessary to decode its meaning. Moreover, your expectations played a role in your being able to read the sentence. You were probably expecting a statement that had *something* to do with psychology, not the lyrics to a Fergie song.

Top-down processing is illustrated by the importance of context in determining how we perceive objects. Look, for example, at Figure 4. Most of us perceive that the first row consists of the letters *A* through *F*, while the second contains the numbers 10 through 14. But take a more careful look and you'll see that the "B" and the "13" are identical. Clearly, our perception is affected by our expectations about the two sequences—even though the two stimuli are exactly the same.

However, top-down processing cannot occur on its own. Even though top-down processing allows us to fill in the gaps in ambiguous and out-of-context stimuli, we would be unable to perceive the meaning of such stimuli without bottom-up processing. Bottom-up processing consists of the progression of recognizing and processing information from individual components of a stimuli and moving to the perception of the whole. We would make no headway in our recognition of the sentence without being able to perceive the individual shapes that make up the letters. Some perception, then, occurs at the level of the patterns and features of each of the separate letters.

Top-down and bottom-up processing occur simultaneously, and interact with each other, in our perception of the world around us. Bottom-up processing permits us to process the fundamental characteristics of stimuli, whereas top-down processing

Top-down processing: Perception that is guided by higher-level knowledge, experience, expectations, and motivations.

Perception that consists of the progression of recognizing and processing information from individual components of a stimuli and moving to the perception of the whole.

ABCDEF

10 11 12 13 14

FIGURE 4 The power of context is shown in this figure. Note how the B and the 13 are identical. (Source: Coren & Ward, 1989.)

allows us to bring our experience to bear on perception. As we learn more about the complex processes involved in perception, we are developing a better understanding of how the brain continually interprets information from the senses and permits us to make responses appropriate to the environment (Buschman & Miller, 2007).

Perceptual Constancy

Consider what happens as you finish a conversation with a friend and he begins to walk away from you. As you watch him walk down the street, the image on your retina becomes smaller and smaller. Do you wonder why he is shrinking?

Of course not. Despite the very real change in the size of the retinal image, you factor into your thinking the knowledge that your friend is moving farther away from you because of perceptual constancy. *Perceptual constancy* is a phenomenon in which physical objects are perceived as unvarying and consistent despite changes in their appearance or in the physical environment.

In some cases, though, our application of perceptual constancy can mislead us. One good example of this involves the rising moon. When the moon first appears at night, close to the horizon, it seems to be huge—much larger than when it is high in the sky later in the evening. You may have thought that the apparent change in the size of the moon was caused by the moon's being physically closer to the earth when it first appears. In fact, though, this is not the case at all: the actual image of the moon on our retina is the same, whether it is low or high in the sky.

Instead, the moon appears to be larger when it is close to the horizon primarily because of the phenomenon of perceptual constancy. When the moon is near the horizon, the perceptual cues of intervening terrain and objects such as trees on the horizon produce a misleading sense of distance. The phenomenon of perceptual constancy leads us to take that assumed distance into account when we view the moon, and it leads us to misperceive the moon as relatively large.

In contrast, when the moon is high in the sky, we see it by itself, and we don't try to compensate for its distance from us. In this case, then, perceptual constancy leads us to perceive it as relatively small. To experience perceptual constancy, try looking at

When the moon is near the horizon, we do not see it by itself and perceptual constancy leads us to take into account a misleading sense of distance.

the moon when it is relatively low on the horizon through a paper-towel tube; the moon suddenly will appear to "shrink" back to normal size (Coren, 1992b; Ross & Plug, 2002; Imamura & Nakamizo, 2006).

Perceptual constancy applies not just to size (as with the moon illusion) but to shape and color as well. For example, despite the varying images on the retina as an airplane approaches, flies overhead, and disappears, we do not perceive the airplane as changing shape (Redding, 2002; Wickelgren, 2004).

Depth Perception: Translating 2-D to 3-D

As sophisticated as the retina is, the images projected onto it are flat and two-dimensional. Yet the world around us is three-dimensional, and we perceive it that way. How do we make the transformation from 2-D to 3-D?

The ability to view the world in three dimensions and to perceive distance—a skill known as **depth perception**—is due largely to the fact that we have two eyes. Because there is a certain distance between the eyes, a slightly different image reaches each retina. The brain integrates the two images into one composite view, but it also recognizes the difference in images and uses it to estimate the distance of an object from us. The difference in the images seen by the left eye and the right eye is known as *binocular disparity*.

To get a sense of binocular disparity for yourself, hold a pencil at arm's length and look at it first with one eye and then with the other. There is little difference between the two views relative to the background. Now bring the pencil just six inches away from your face, and try the same thing. This time you will perceive a greater difference between the two views.

The fact that the discrepancy between the images in the two eyes varies according to the distance of objects that we view provides us with a means of determining distance. If we view two objects and one is considerably closer to us than the other is, the retinal disparity will be relatively large and we will have a greater sense of depth between the two. However, if the two objects are a similar distance from us, the retinal disparity will be minor, and we will perceive them as being a similar distance from us.

In some cases, certain cues permit us to obtain a sense of depth and distance with just one eye. These cues are known as *monocular cues*. One monocular cue—*motion parallax*—is the change in position of an object on the retina caused by movement of your body relative to the object. For example, suppose you are a passenger in a moving car, and you focus your eye on a stable object such as a tree. Objects that are closer than the tree will appear to move backward, and the nearer the object is, the more quickly it will appear to move. In contrast, objects beyond the tree will seem to move at a slower speed, but in the same direction as you are. Your brain is able to use these cues to calculate the relative distances of the tree and other objects.

Similarly, experience has taught us that if two objects are the same size, the one that makes a smaller image on the retina is farther away than is the one that provides a larger image—an example of the monocular cue of *relative size*. But it's not just size of an object that provides information about distance; the quality of the image on the retina helps us judge distance. The monocular cue of *texture gradient* provides information about distance because the details of things that are far away are less distinct (Proffitt, 2006).

Finally, anyone who has ever seen railroad tracks that seem to join together in the distance knows that distant objects appear to be closer together than are nearer ones, a phenomenon called linear perspective. People use *linear perspective* as a monocular cue in estimating distance, allowing the two-dimensional image on the retina to record the three-dimensional world (Bruce, Green, & Georgeson, 1997; Dobbins et al., 1998; Shimono & Wade, 2002; Bruggeman, Yonas, & Konczak, 2007).

Depth perception: The ability to view the world in three dimensions and to perceive distance.

Railroad tracks that seem to join together in the distance are an example of linear perspective.

Motion Perception: As the World Turns

When a batter tries to hit a pitched ball, the most important factor is the motion of the ball. How is a batter able to judge the speed and location of a target that is moving at some 90 miles per hour?

The answer rests in part on several cues that provide us with relevant information about the perception of motion. For one thing, the movement of an object across the retina is typically perceived relative to some stable, unmoving background. Moreover, if the stimulus is heading toward us, the image on the retina will expand in size, filling more and more of the visual field. In such cases, we assume that the stimulus is approaching—not that it is an expanding stimulus viewed at a constant distance.

It is not, however, just the movement of images across the retina that brings about the perception of motion. If it were, we would perceive the world as moving every time we moved our heads. Instead, one of the critical things we learn about perception is to factor information about our own head and eye movements along with information about changes in the retinal image.

Perceptual Illusions: The Deceptions of Perceptions

If you look carefully at the Parthenon, one of the most famous buildings of ancient Greece, still standing at the top of an Athens hill, you'll see that it was built with a bulge on one side. If it didn't have that bulge—and quite a few other architectural "tricks" like it, such as columns that incline inward—it would look as if it were crooked and about to fall down. Instead, it appears to stand completely straight, at right angles to the ground.

b.

c.

a.

FIGURE 5 In building the Parthenon, the Greeks constructed an architectural wonder that looks perfectly straight, with right angles at every corner, as in (a). However, if it had been built with completely true right angles, it would have looked as it does in (b). To compensate for this illusion, the Parthenon was designed to have a slight upward curvature, as shown in (c). (Source: Coren & Ward, 1989, p. 5.)

The fact that the Parthenon appears to be completely upright is the result of a series of visual illusions. **Visual illusions** are physical stimuli that consistently produce errors in perception. In the case of the Parthenon, the building appears to be completely square, as illustrated in Figure 5a. However, if it had been built that way, it would look to us as it does in Figure 5b. The reason for this is an illusion that makes right angles placed above a line appear as if they were bent. To offset the illusion, the Parthenon was constructed as in Figure 5c, with a slight upward curvature.

The *Müller-Lyer illusion* (illustrated in Figure 6) has fascinated psychologists for decades. Although the two lines are the same length, the one with the arrow tips pointing inward (Figure 6a, left) appears to be longer than the one with the arrow tips pointing outward (Figure 6a, right).

Although all kinds of explanations for visual illusions have been suggested, most concentrate either on the physical operation of the eye or on our misinterpretation of the visual stimulus. For example, one explanation for the Müller-Lyer illusion is that eye movements are greater when the arrow tips point inward, making us perceive the line as longer than it is when the arrow tips face outward. In contrast, a different explanation for the illusion suggests that we unconsciously attribute particular significance to each of the lines (Gregory, 1978; Redding & Hawley, 1993). When we see the left line in Figure 6a we tend to perceive it as if it were the inside corner of a room extending away from us, as illustrated in Figure 6b. In contrast, when we view the right line in Figure 6a we perceive it as the relatively close outside corner of a rectangular object such as the building corner in Figure 6c. Because previous experience leads us to assume that the outside corner is closer than the inside corner, we make the further assumption that the inside corner must therefore be larger.

Despite the complexity of the latter explanation, a good deal of evidence supports it. For instance, cross-cultural studies show that people raised in areas where there are few right angles—such as the Zulu in Africa—are much less susceptible to the illusion than are people who grow up where most structures are built using right angles and rectangles (Segall, Campbell, & Herskovits, 1966).

Visual illusions: Physical stimuli that consistently produce errors in perception.

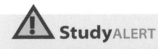 **Study**ALERT

The explanation for the Müller-Lyer illusion is complicated. Figure 6 will help you master it.

a. **b.** **c.**

FIGURE 6 In the Müller-Lyer illusion (a), the horizontal line appears longer than the lower one. One explanation for the Müller-Lyer illusion suggests that the line with arrow points directed inward is interpreted as the inside corner of a rectangular room extending away from us (b), and the line with arrow points directed outward is viewed as the relatively close corner of a rectangular object, such as the building corner in (c). Our previous experience with distance cues leads us to assume that the outside corner is closer than the inside corner and that the inside corner must therefore be longer.

Exploring DIVERSITY
Culture and Perception

As the example of the Zulu indicates, the culture in which we are raised has clear consequences for how we perceive the world. Consider the drawing in Figure 7. Sometimes called the "devil's tuning fork," it is likely to produce a mind-boggling effect, as the center tine of the fork alternates between appearing and disappearing.

Now try to reproduce the drawing on a piece of paper. Chances are that the task is nearly impossible for you—unless you are a member of an African tribe with little exposure to Western cultures. For such individuals, the task is simple; they have no trouble reproducing the figure. The reason is that Westerners automatically interpret the drawing as something that cannot exist in three dimensions, and they therefore are inhibited from reproducing it. The African tribal members, in contrast, do not make the assumption that the figure is "impossible" and instead view it in two dimensions, a perception that enables them to copy the figure with ease (Deregowski, 1973).

Cultural differences are also reflected in depth perception. A Western viewer of Figure 8 would interpret the hunter in the drawing as aiming for the antelope in the foreground, while an elephant stands under the tree in the background. A member of an

FIGURE 7 The "devil's tuning fork" has three prongs . . . or does it have two?

FIGURE 8 Is the man aiming for the elephant or the antelope? Westerners assume that the differences in size between the two animals indicate that the elephant is farther away, and therefore the man is aiming for the antelope. In contrast, members of some African tribes, not used to depth cues in two-dimensional drawings, assume that the man is aiming for the elephant. (The drawing is based on Deregowski, 1973.) Do you think Westerners, who view the picture in three dimensions, could explain what they see to someone who views the scene in two dimensions and eventually get that person to view it in three dimensions?

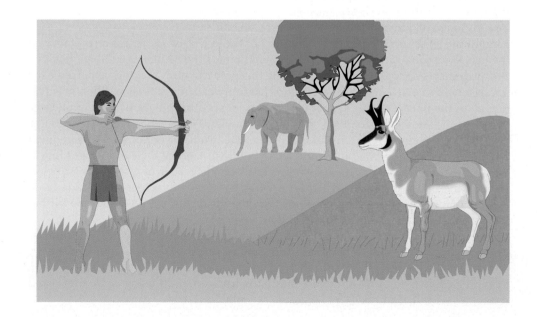

isolated African tribe, however, interprets the scene very differently by assuming that the hunter is aiming at the elephant. Westerners use the difference in sizes between the two animals as a cue that the elephant is farther away than the antelope (Hudson, 1960).

The misinterpretations created by visual illusions are ultimately due, then, to errors in both fundamental visual processing and the way the brain interprets the information it receives. But visual illusions, by illustrating something fundamental about perception, become more than mere psychological curiosities. There is a basic connection between our prior knowledge, needs, motivations, and expectations about how the world is put together and the way we perceive it. Our view of the world is very much an outcome, then, of fundamental psychological factors. Furthermore, each person perceives the environment in a way that is unique and special (Knoblich & Sebanz, 2006; Repp & Knoblich, 2007).

SUBLIMINAL PERCEPTION

Can stimuli that we're not consciously aware of change our behavior? In some ways, yes.

Subliminal perception refers to the perception of messages about which we have no awareness. The stimulus could be a written word, a sound, or even a smell that activates the sensory system but that is not intense enough for a person to report having experienced it. For example, in some studies people are exposed to a descriptive label—called a *prime*—about a person (such as the word *smart* or *happy*) so briefly that they cannot report seeing the label. Later, however, they form impressions that are influenced by the content of the prime. Somehow, they have been influenced by the prime that they say they couldn't see, providing some evidence for subliminal perception (Greenwald, Draine, & Abrams, 1996; Key, 2003).

Although subliminal messages (which social psychologists refer to as *priming*) can influence behavior in subtle ways, there's little evidence that it can lead to major changes in attitudes or behavior. Most research suggests that they cannot. Although we are able to perceive at least some kinds of information of which we are unaware, there's little evidence that subliminal messages can change our attitudes or behavior in any substantial way (Greenwald, 2002; Dijksterhuis, Chartrand, & Aarts, 2007; Pratkanis et al., 2007).

Extrasensory Perception (ESP). Given the lack of evidence that subliminal perception can affect our behavior in substantial ways, psychologists are particularly skeptical of reports of *extrasensory perception*, or ESP—perception that does not involve our known senses. Although half of the general population of the United States believes it exists, most psychologists reject the existence of ESP, asserting that there is no sound documentation of the phenomenon (Swets & Bjork, 1990; Hyman, 1994; Gallup Poll, 2001).

However, a debate in one of the most prestigious psychology journals, *Psychological Bulletin*, heightened interest in ESP. According to proponents of ESP, reliable evidence exists for an "anomalous process of information transfer," or psi. These researchers, who painstakingly reviewed considerable evidence, argue that a cumulative body of research shows reliable support for the existence of psi (Bem & Honorton, 1994; Storm & Ertel, 2001; Parra & Argibay, 2007).

Their conclusion has been challenged on several counts. For example, critics suggest that the research methodology was inadequate and that the experiments supporting psi are flawed (Hyman, 1994; Milton & Wiseman, 1999; Kennedy, 2004).

Because of questions about the quality of the research, as well as a lack of any credible theoretical explanation for how extrasensory perception might take place, most psychologists continue to believe that there is no reliable scientific support for ESP (Rose & Blackmore, 2002; Wiseman & Greening, 2002). Still, the exchanges in *Psychological Bulletin* are likely to heighten the debate. More important, the renewed interest in ESP among psychologists is likely to inspire more research, which is the only way the issue can be resolved.

RECAP/EVALUATE/RETHINK

RECAP

What principles underlie our organization of the visual world and allow us to make sense of our environment?

- Perception is a constructive process in which people go beyond the stimuli that are physically present and try to construct a meaningful interpretation. (p. 125)

- The gestalt laws of organization are used to describe the way in which we organize bits and pieces of information into meaningful wholes, known as gestalts, through closure, proximity, similarity, and simplicity. (p. 126)

- In top-down processing, perception is guided by higher-level knowledge, experience, expectations, and motivations. In bottom-up processing, perception consists of the progression of recognizing and processing information from individual components of a stimuli and moving to the perception of the whole. (p. 127)

- Perceptual constancy permits us to perceive stimuli as unvarying in size, shape, and color despite changes in the environment or the appearance of the objects being perceived. (p. 128)

How are we able to perceive the world in three dimensions when our retinas are capable of sensing only two-dimensional images?

- Depth perception is the ability to perceive distance and view the world in three dimensions even though the images projected on our retinas are two-dimensional. We are able to judge depth and distance as a result of binocular disparity and monocular cues, such as motion parallax, the relative size of images on the retina, and linear perspective. (p. 129)

- Motion perception depends on cues such as the perceived movement of an object across the retina and information about how the head and eyes are moving. (p. 130)

What clues do visual illusions give us about our understanding of general perceptual mechanisms?

- Visual illusions are physical stimuli that consistently produce errors in perception, causing judgments that do not reflect the physical reality of a stimulus accurately. One of the best-known illusions is the Müller-Lyer illusion. (p. 131)

- Visual illusions are usually the result of errors in the brain's interpretation of visual stimuli. Furthermore, culture clearly affects how we perceive the world. (p. 132)

- Subliminal perception refers to the perception of messages about which we have no awareness. The reality of the phenomenon, as well as of ESP, is open to question and debate. (p. 133)

EVALUATE

1. Match each of the following organizational laws with its meaning:

    a. Closure   **1.** Elements close together are grouped together.

    b. Proximity   **2.** Patterns are perceived in the most basic, direct manner possible.

    c. Similarity   **3.** Groupings are made in terms of complete figures.

    d. Simplicity   **4.** Elements similar in appearance are grouped together.

2. _____ analysis deals with the way in which we break an object down into its component pieces in order to understand it.

3. Processing that involves higher functions such as expectations and motivations is known as _____ , whereas processing that recognizes the individual components of a stimulus is known as _____.

4. When a car passes you on the road and appears to shrink as it gets farther away, the phenomenon of _____ _____ permits you to realize that the car is not in fact getting smaller.

5. _____ is the ability to view the world in three dimensions instead of two.

6. The brain makes use of a phenomenon known as _____ _____, or the difference in the images the two eyes see, to give three dimensions to sight.

RETHINK

1. In what ways do painters represent three-dimensional scenes in two dimensions on a canvas? Do you think artists in non-Western cultures use the same or different principles to represent three-dimensionality? Why?

2. *From the perspective of a corporate executive:* What arguments might you make if a member of your staff proposed a subliminal advertising campaign? Do you think your explanation would be enough to convince them? Why?

Answers to Evaluate Questions

1. a-3, b-1, c-4, d-2; 2. feature; 3. top-down, bottom-up; 4. perceptual constancy; 5. depth perception; 6. binocular disparity

KEY TERMS

gestalt laws of
   organization p. 125

top-down processing p. 127
bottom-up processing p. 127

depth perception p. 129
visual illusions p. 131

Psychology on the Web

1. Select one topic of personal interest to you that was mentioned in this set of modules (for instance, cochlear implants, visual illusions, psi). Find one "serious" or scientific Web site and one "popular" or commercial Web site with information about the chosen topic. Compare the type, level, and reliability of the information that you find on each site. Write a summary of your findings.
2. Are there more gestalt laws of organization than the four we've considered (closure, proximity, similarity, and simplicity)? Find the answer to this question on the Web and write a summary of any additional gestalt laws you find.

Epilogue

We have noted the important distinction between sensation and perception, and we have examined the processes that underlie both of them. We've seen how external stimuli evoke sensory responses and how our different senses process the information contained in those responses. We also have focused on the physical structure and internal workings of the individual senses, including vision, hearing, balance, smell, taste, and the skin senses, and we've explored how our brains organize and process sensory information to construct a consistent, integrated picture of the world around us.

To complete our investigation of sensation and perception, let's reconsider the story of Duncan Mitchell, the boy who couldn't recognize faces. Using your knowledge of sensation and perception, answer the following questions:

1. What part of the visual system seems to be damaged in prosopagnosia? Is this a disease of the eye at all?
2. What strategies could a person with prosopagnosia employ to compensate for the inability to recognize faces?
3. Does prosopagnosia seem to be more a failure of bottom-up processing or of top-down processing—or is it both? Why do you think so?

The difference between the processes of sensation and perception is not always clear. Use this visual guide to better grasp the difference between the two. Then answer the questions below to test your understanding of these concepts.

1 In this example, **sensation** occurs when light enters the eye and forms an image on the retina, where it initiates a complex series of neural impulses. **Perception** occurs, by means of bottom-up and top-down processing, when the brain analyzes these impulses and combines them with memories and experiences. Bottom-up and top-down processing occur simultaneously and, along with the gestalt principle and depth perception, help us to construct our perceptual reality.

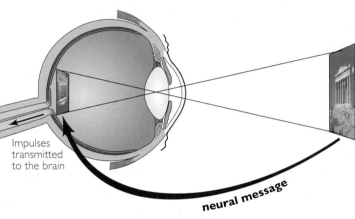

Impulses transmitted to the brain

neural message

2 Visual receptors in the retina, which is on the back of the eye, transform light energy into neural impulses. These raw impulses are the visual sensation that travels to the brain for analysis by successive visual processing areas. These processing areas convert the sensation into a complete perception.

3 In **bottom-up processing** information about individual components of stimuli travels first to the thalamus and then to the visual cortex for preliminary analysis. The first level of analysis identifies only basic angles, features, and shapes.

bottom-up processing

4 Next, neurons transport information about basic features and shapes from the visual cortex to another area of the brain. At this point, basic features and shapes are combined and assembled into complete objects, such as a building.

EVALUATE

1. In this example, sensation is represented by
  a. the stimulation of visual receptors in the eye when looking at the building initially
  b. the interpretation of the individual visual cues arriving in the brain from the retina as a "building"
  c. the interpretation of the visual information as the viewer compares it to other buildings

  d. the breaking down of visual information into component parts
2. In this example, perception is represented by
  a. the stimulation of visual receptors in the eye when looking at the building initially
  b. the interpretation of the individual visual cues arriving in the brain from the retina as a "building"

5 The brain also interprets distance cues in the visual field and uses these cues to convert the 2-dimensional sensations into 3-dimensional perception. After analyzing distance cues, the brain assigns each object both a relative distance and a corresponding size, resulting in depth perception.

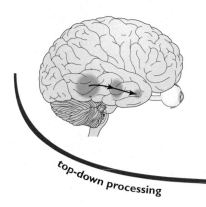

6 Using gestalt laws of organization, the brain then organizes all of the objects into a coherent whole. For example, similar objects are perceived as a unit. Here, the vertical columns and the roughly triangular roof above them are perceived as a building.

top-down processing

7 In top-down processing, the brain modifies perception based on previous personal experiences and memories. For example, the brain might contain a memory of a friend's face which the brain uses to enhance facial features and fill in missing information.

8 Finally, top-down processing incorporates personal expectations, needs, and drives to enhance what we see. For example, if we expect a place or person to be beautiful, our perception might be altered to match our expectation.

c. the interpretation of the visual information as the viewer compares it to other buildings

d. the breaking down of visual information into component parts

3. Perception is a constructive process, in which sensory information about stimuli is used to interpret a situation. True or false?

RETHINK

1 Suppose you are an artist who is encountering a famous building for the first time, and you want to paint a picture of it. Describe how you might use the processes of sensation and perception as you re-create the building in your painting.

Answers to Evaluate questions: 1. a; 2. b; 3. True

CHAPTER 5

States of Consciousness

Key Concepts for Chapter 5

Martha Yasso was tired all the time—so tired that whenever her 3-year-old son went down for a nap, she grabbed the chance to rest as well. But even with those precious extra minutes of sleep, she was still so exhausted by late afternoon that she could barely keep her eyes open. One day last fall, as her son played in the den of their New York home, Yasso's eyelids got heavier and heavier. Just before she nodded off completely, she felt her son's hands on her face. He was shouting, "Mama, Mama! Wake up!" That was the turning point. . . . She called her doctor, who referred her to the New York University Sleep Disorders Center. After a night in the sleep lab, with electrodes monitoring her brain waves, breathing, and movements, Yasso finally understood what was behind her overwhelming fatigue. NYU pulmonologist Ana Krieger told Yasso that during the eight hours she thought she was asleep, she had actually awakened 245 times. "That number shocked me," Yasso says. "But it also explained a lot." (Kantrowitz, 2006, p. 51)

Looking Ahead

Martha Yasso was suffering from a sleep disorder known as *sleep apnea*, which is characterized by constricted breathing during sleep that forces the sleeper to wake up momentarily—sometimes as many as hundreds of times each night. Fortunately, after her diagnosis, Martha was able to find rest with an electronic device that helps to keep her airway open while she sleeps.

For most of us, sleep occurs naturally. In this and the following modules we'll consider a range of topics about sleep and, more broadly, states of consciousness. **Consciousness** is the awareness of the sensations, thoughts, and feelings we experience at a given moment. Consciousness is our subjective understanding of both the environment around us and our private internal world, unobservable to outsiders.

In *waking consciousness*, we are awake and aware of our thoughts, emotions, and perceptions. All other states of consciousness are considered *altered states of consciousness*. Among these, sleeping and dreaming occur naturally; drug use and hypnosis, in contrast, are methods of deliberately altering one's state of consciousness.

In the past, because consciousness is so personal a phenomenon, psychologists were sometimes reluctant to study it. After all, who can say that your consciousness is similar to or, for that matter, different from anyone else's? Although the earliest psychologists, including William James (1890), saw the study of consciousness as central to the field, later psychologists suggested that it was out of bounds for the discipline. They argued that consciousness could be understood only by relying "unscientifically" on what experimental participants said they were experiencing. In this view, it was philosophers—not psychologists—who should speculate on such knotty issues as whether consciousness is separate from the physical body, how people know they exist, and how the body and mind are related to each other (Rychlak, 1997; Gennaro, 2004; Barresi, 2007).

Contemporary psychologists reject the view that the study of consciousness is unsuitable for the field of psychology. Instead, they argue that several approaches permit the scientific study of consciousness. For example, behavioral neuroscientists can measure brain-wave patterns under conditions of consciousness ranging from sleep to waking to hypnotic trances. And new understanding of the chemistry of drugs such as marijuana and alcohol has provided insights into the way they produce their pleasurable—as well as adverse—effects (Damasio, 2003; Mosher & Akins, 2007).

Whatever state of consciousness we are in—be it waking, sleeping, hypnotic, or drug-induced—the complexities of consciousness are profound.

Consciousness: The awareness of the sensations, thoughts, and feelings being experienced at a given moment.

Sleep and Dreams

Mike Trevino, 29, slept nine hours in nine days in his quest to win a 3,000-mile, cross-country bike race. For the first 38 hrs. and 646 miles, he skipped sleep entirely. Later he napped—with no dreams he can remember—for no more than 90 minutes a night. Soon he began to imagine that his support crew was part of a bomb plot. "It was almost like riding in a movie. I thought it was a complex dream, even though I was conscious," says Trevino, who finished second. (Springen, 2004, p. 47)

Trevino's case is unusual—in part because he was able to function with so little sleep for so long—and it raises a host of questions about sleep and dreams. Can we live without sleep? What is the meaning of dreams? More generally, what is sleep?

Although sleeping is a state that we all experience, there are still many unanswered questions about sleep that remain, along with a considerable number of myths. Test your knowledge of sleep and dreams by answering the questionnaire in Figure 1.

Key Concepts

What are the different states of consciousness?

What happens when we sleep, and what are the meaning and function of dreams?

What are the major sleep disorders, and how can they be treated?

How much do we daydream?

FIGURE 1 There are many unanswered questions about sleep. Taking this quiz can help you clear up some of the myths.

Sleep Quiz

Although sleeping is something we all do for a significant part of our lives, myths and misconceptions about the topic abound. To test your own knowledge of sleep and dreams, try answering the following questions before reading further.

_____ 1. Some people never dream *True or false?*	_____ 6. If we lose some sleep we will eventually make up all the lost sleep the next night or another night. *True or false?*
_____ 2. Most dreams are caused by bodily sensations such as an upset stomach. *True or false?*	_____ 7. No one has been able to go for more than 48 hours without sleep. *True or false?*
_____ 3. It has been proved that people need eight hours of sleep to maintain mental health. *True or false?*	_____ 8. Our muscles are the most relaxed of the night when we are dreaming. *True or false?*
_____ 4. When people do not recall their dreams, it is probably because they are secretly trying to forget them. *True or false?*	_____ 9. Sleep enables the brain to rest because little brain activity takes place during sleep. *True or false?*
_____ 5. Depriving someone of sleep will invariably cause the individual to become mentally imbalanced. *True or false?*	_____ 10. Drugs have been proved to provide a long term cure for sleeplessness. *True or false?*

Scoring: This is an easy set of questions to score for every item is false. But don't lose any sleep if you missed them; they were chosen to represent the most common myths regarding sleep.

The Stages of Sleep

Most of us consider sleep a time of tranquility when we set aside the tensions of the day and spend the night in uneventful slumber. However, a closer look at sleep shows that a good deal of activity occurs throughout the night.

Measures of electrical activity in the brain show that the brain is quite active during the night. It produces electrical discharges with systematic, wavelike patterns that change in height (or amplitude) and speed (or frequency) in regular sequences. There is also significant physical activity in muscle and eye movements.

People progress through a series of distinct stages of sleep during a night's rest—known as *stage 1* through *stage 4* and *REM sleep*—moving through the stages in cycles lasting about 90 minutes. Each of these sleep stages is associated with a unique pattern of brain waves, which you can see in Figure 2.

When people first go to sleep, they move from a waking state in which they are relaxed with their eyes closed into **stage 1 sleep**, which is characterized by relatively rapid, low-amplitude brain waves. This is actually a stage of transition between wakefulness and sleep and lasts only a few minutes. During stage 1, images sometimes appear, as if we were viewing still photos, although this is not true dreaming, which occurs later in the night.

As sleep becomes deeper, people enter **stage 2 sleep**, which makes up about half of the total sleep of those in their early 20s and is characterized by a slower, more regular wave pattern. However, there are also momentary interruptions of sharply pointed, spiky waves that are called, because of their configuration, *sleep spindles*. It becomes increasingly difficult to awaken a person from sleep as stage 2 progresses.

As people drift into **stage 3 sleep**, the brain waves become slower, with higher peaks and lower valleys in the wave pattern. By the time sleepers arrive at **stage 4 sleep**, the pattern is even slower and more regular, and people are least responsive to outside stimulation.

Stage 1 sleep: The state of transition between wakefulness and sleep, characterized by relatively rapid, low-amplitude brain waves.

Stage 2 sleep: A sleep deeper than that of stage 1, characterized by a slower, more regular wave pattern, along with momentary interruptions of "sleep spindles."

Stage 3 sleep: A sleep characterized by slow brain waves, with greater peaks and valleys in the wave pattern than in stage 2 sleep.

Stage 4 sleep: The deepest stage of sleep, during which we are least responsive to outside stimulation.

FIGURE 2 Brain-wave patterns (measured by an EEG apparatus) vary significantly during the different stages of sleep (Hobson, 1989). As sleep moves from stage 1 through stage 4, brain waves become slower.

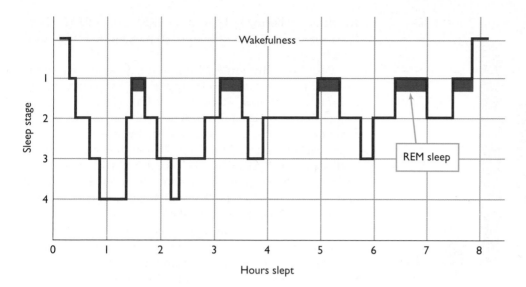

Wakefulness

Sleep stage

REM sleep

Hours slept

FIGURE 3 During the night, the typical sleeper passes through all four stages of sleep and several REM periods.
(Source: From Ernest Hartmann, *The Biology of Dreaming* (1967), p. 6. Courtesy of Charles C Thomas Publisher, Ltd., Springfield, Illinois.)

As you can see in Figure 3, stage 4 sleep is most likely to occur during the early part of the night. In the first half of the night, sleep is dominated by stages 3 and 4. The second half is characterized by stages 1 and 2—as well as a fifth stage during which dreams occur.

REM Sleep: The Paradox of Sleep

Several times a night, when sleepers have cycled back to a shallower state of sleep, something curious happens. Their heart rate increases and becomes irregular, their blood pressure rises, their breathing rate increases, and males—even male infants— have erections. Most characteristic of this period is the back-and-forth movement of their eyes, as if they were watching an action-filled movie. This period of sleep is called **rapid eye movement**, or **REM sleep**, and it contrasts with stages 1 through 4,

Rapid eye movement (REM) sleep: Sleep occupying 20 percent of an adult's sleeping time, characterized by increased heart rate, blood pressure, and breathing rate; erections; eye movements; and the experience of dreaming.

People progress through four distinct stages of sleep during a night's rest spread over cycles lasting about 90 minutes. REM sleep, which occupies only 20 percent of adults' sleeping time, occurs in stage 1 sleep. These photos, taken at different times of night, show the synchronized patterns of a couple accustomed to sleeping in the same bed.

FIGURE 4 Although most people report sleeping between eight and nine hours per night, the amount varies a great deal (Borbely, 1996). Where would you place yourself on this graph, and why do you think you need more or less sleep than others?

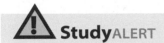

StudyALERT

It is important to differentiate the five stages of sleep (stage 1, stage 2, stage 3, stage 4, and REM sleep), which produce different brain-wave patterns.

which are collectively labeled *non-REM* (or *NREM*) sleep. REM sleep occupies a little over 20 percent of adults' total sleeping time.

Paradoxically, while all this activity is occurring, the major muscles of the body appear to be paralyzed. In addition, and most important, REM sleep is usually accompanied by dreams, which—whether or not people remember them—are experienced by *everyone* during some part of their night's sleep. Although some dreaming occurs in non-REM stages of sleep, dreams are most likely to occur in the REM period, where they are the most vivid and easily remembered (Titone, 2002; Conduit, Crewther, & Coleman, 2004; Jun et al., 2006).

There is good reason to believe that REM sleep plays a critical role in everyday human functioning. People deprived of REM sleep—by being awakened every time they begin to display the physiological signs of that stage—show a *rebound effect* when allowed to rest undisturbed. With this rebound effect, REM-deprived sleepers spend significantly more time in REM sleep than they normally would.

Why Do We Sleep, and How Much Sleep Is Necessary?

Sleep is a requirement for normal human functioning, although, surprisingly, we don't know exactly why. It is reasonable to expect that our bodies would require a tranquil "rest and relaxation" period to revitalize themselves, and experiments with rats show that total sleep deprivation results in death. But why?

Some researchers, using an evolutionary perspective, suggest that sleep permitted our ancestors to conserve energy at night, a time when food was relatively hard to come by. Others suggest that the reduced activity of the brain during non-REM sleep may give neurons in the brain a chance to repair themselves. Another hypothesis suggests that the onset of REM sleep stops the release of neurotransmitters called *monoamines*, and so permits receptor cells to get some necessary rest and to increase their sensitivity during periods of wakefulness. Still, these explanations remain speculative (Siegel, 2003; McNamara, 2004; Steiger, 2007).

Scientists have also been unable to establish just how much sleep is absolutely required. Most people today sleep between seven and eight hours each night, which is three hours a night *less* than people slept a hundred years ago. In addition, there is wide variability among individuals, with some people needing as little as three hours of sleep (see Figure 4). Sleep requirements also vary over the course of a lifetime: As they age, people generally need less and less sleep.

People who participate in sleep deprivation experiments, in which they are kept awake for stretches as long as 200 hours, show no lasting effects. It's no fun—they feel weary and irritable, can't concentrate, and show a loss of creativity, even after only minor deprivation. They also show a decline in logical reasoning ability. However, after being allowed to sleep normally, they bounce back quickly and are able to perform at predeprivation levels after just a few days (Veasey et al., 2002; McClelland & Pilcher, 2007).

In short, as far as we know, most people suffer no permanent consequences of such temporary sleep deprivation. But—and this is an important but—a lack of sleep can make us feel edgy, slow our reaction time, and lower our performance on academic and physical tasks. In addition, we put ourselves, and others, at risk when we

Thematic Event	Percentage of Dreams Reporting at Least One Event	
	Males	Females
Aggression	47%	44%
Friendliness	38	42
Sexuality	12	04
Misfortune	36	33
Success	15	08
Failure	15	10

FIGURE 5 Although dreams tend to be subjective to the person having them, there are common elements that frequently occur in everyone's dreams. Why do you think so many common dreams are unpleasant and so few are pleasant? Do you think this tells us anything about the function of dreams? (Source: Schneiger & Domhoff, (2002).)

carry out routine activities, such as driving, when we're very sleepy (Stickgold, Winkelman, & Wehrwein, 2004; Philip et al., 2005; Anderson & Home, 2006).

The Function and Meaning of Dreaming

I was sitting at my desk when I remembered that this was the day of my chemistry final! I was terrified, because I hadn't studied a bit for it. In fact, I had missed every lecture all semester. In a panic, I began running across campus desperately searching for the classroom, to which I'd never been. It was hopeless; I knew I was going to fail and flunk out of college.

If you have had a similar dream—a surprisingly common dream among people involved in academic pursuits—you know how utterly convincing are the panic and fear that the events in the dream can bring about. *Nightmares*, unusually frightening dreams, occur fairly often. In one survey, almost half of a group of college students who kept records of their dreams over a two-week period reported having at least one nightmare. This works out to some 24 nightmares per person each year, on average (Blagrove, Farmer, & Williams, 2004; Schredl, Barthold, & Zimmer, 2006; Neilson, Stenstrom, & Lein, 2006).

However, most of the 150,000 dreams the average person experiences by the age of 70 are much less dramatic. They typically encompass everyday events such as going to the supermarket, working at the office, and preparing a meal. Students dream about going to class; professors dream about lecturing. Dental patients dream of getting their teeth drilled; dentists dream of drilling the wrong tooth. The English have tea with the queen in their dreams; in the United States, people go to a bar with the president (Domhoff, 1996; Schredl, & Piel, 2005; Taylor & Bryant, 2007). Figure 5 shows the most common themes found in people's dreams.

THE FAR SIDE®   **BY GARY LARSON**

"I've got it again, Larry ... an eerie feeling like there's something on top of the bed."

Theory	Basic Explanation	Meaning of Dreams	Is Meaning of Dream Disguised?
Unconscious wish fulfillment theory (Freud)	Dreams represent unconscious wishes the dreamer wants to fulfill	Latent content reveals unconscious wishes	Yes, by manifest content of dreams
Dreams-for-survival theory	Information relevant to daily survival is reconsidered and reprocessed	Clues to everyday concerns about survival	Not necessarily
Activation-synthesis theory	Dreams are the result of random activation of various memories, which are tied together in a logical story line	Dream scenario that is constructed is related to dreamer's concerns	Not necessarily

FIGURE 6 Three theories of dreams. As researchers have yet to agree on the fundamental meaning of dreams, several theories about dreaming have emerged.

But what, if anything, do all these dreams mean? Whether dreams have a specific significance and function is a question that scientists have considered for many years, and they have developed the three alternative theories we discuss below (and summarized in Figure 6).

DO DREAMS REPRESENT UNCONSCIOUS WISH FULFILLMENT?

Unconscious wish fulfillment theory: Sigmund Freud's theory that dreams represent unconscious wishes that dreamers desire to see fulfilled.

Latent content of dreams: According to Freud, the "disguised" meanings of dreams, hidden by more obvious subjects.

Manifest content of dreams: According to Freud, the apparent story line of dreams.

Sigmund Freud viewed dreams as a guide to the unconscious (Freud, 1900). In his **unconscious wish fulfillment theory**, he proposed that dreams represent unconscious wishes that dreamers desire to see fulfilled. However, because these wishes are threatening to the dreamer's conscious awareness, the actual wishes—called the **latent content of dreams**—are disguised. The true subject and meaning of a dream, then, may have little to do with its apparent story line, which Freud called the **manifest content of dreams**.

To Freud, it was important to pierce the armor of a dream's manifest content to understand its true meaning. To do this, Freud tried to get people to discuss their dreams, associating symbols in the dreams with events in the past. He also suggested that certain common symbols with universal meanings appear in dreams. For example, to Freud, dreams in which a person is flying symbolize a wish for sexual intercourse. (See Figure 7 for other common symbols.)

Many psychologists reject Freud's view that dreams typically represent unconscious wishes and that particular objects and events in a dream are symbolic. Rather, they believe that the direct, overt action of a dream is the focal point of its meaning. For example, a dream in which we are walking down a long hallway to take an exam for which we haven't studied does not relate to unconscious, unacceptable wishes. Instead, it simply may mean that we are concerned about an impending test. Even more complex dreams can often be interpreted in terms of everyday concerns and stress (Picchioni et al., 2002; Cartwright et al., 2006).

Symbol (Manifest Content of Dream)	Interpretation (Latent Content)
Climbing up a stairway, crossing a bridge, riding an elevator, flying in an airplane, walking down a long hallway, entering a room, train traveling through a tunnel	Sexual intercourse
Apples, peaches, grapefruits	Breasts
Bullets, fire, snakes, sticks, umbrellas, guns, hoses, knives	Male sex organs
Ovens, boxes, tunnels, closets, caves, bottles, ships	Female sex organs

FIGURE 7 According to Freud, dreams contain common symbols with universal meanings.

Moreover, some dreams reflect events occurring in the dreamer's environment as he or she is sleeping. For example, sleeping participants in one experiment were sprayed with water while they were dreaming. Those unlucky volunteers reported more dreams involving water than did a comparison group of participants who were left to sleep undisturbed (Dement & Wolpert, 1958). Similarly, it is not unusual to wake up to find that the doorbell that was heard ringing in a dream is actually an alarm clock telling us it is time to get up.

On the other hand, brain PET scan research lends support for the wish fulfillment view. For instance, the limbic and paralimbic regions of the brain, which are associated with emotion and motivation, are particularly active during REM sleep. At the same time, the association areas of the prefrontal cortex, which control logical analysis and attention, are inactive during REM sleep. The high activation of emotional and motivational centers of the brain during dreaming makes it more plausible that dreams may reflect unconscious wishes and instinctual needs, just as Freud suggested (Braun et al., 1998; Occhionero, 2004; Wehrle et al., 2007).

DREAMS-FOR-SURVIVAL THEORY

According to the **dreams-for-survival theory**, dreams permit us to reconsider and reprocess during sleep information that is critical for our daily survival. Dreaming is considered an inheritance from our animal ancestors, whose small brains were unable to sift sufficient information during waking hours. Consequently, dreaming provided a mechanism that permitted the processing of information 24 hours a day.

> **Dreams-for-survival theory:** The theory suggesting that dreams permit information that is critical for our daily survival to be reconsidered and reprocessed during sleep.

According to this theory, dreams represent concerns about our daily lives, illustrating our uncertainties, indecisions, ideas, and desires. Dreams are seen, then, as consistent with everyday living. Rather than being disguised wishes, as Freud suggested, they represent key concerns growing out of our daily experiences (Winson, 1990; Ross, 2006).

Research supports the dreams-for-survival theory, suggesting that certain dreams permit people to focus on and consolidate memories, particularly dreams that pertain to "how-to-do-it" memories related to motor skills. For example, rats seem to dream about mazes that they learned to run through during the day, at least according to the patterns of brain activity that appear while they are sleeping (Kenway & Wilson, 2001; Stickgold, Hobson, Fosse, & Fosse, 2001; Kuriyama, Stickgold, & Walker, 2004; Smith, 2006).

A similar phenomenon appears to work in humans. For instance, in one experiment, participants learned a visual memory task late in the day. They were then sent to bed, but awakened at certain times during the night. When they were awakened at times that did not interrupt dreaming, their performance on the memory task typically improved the next day. But when they were awakened during rapid eye movement (REM) sleep—the stage of sleep when people dream—their performance declined. The implication is that dreaming, at least when it is uninterrupted, can play a role in helping us remember material to which we have been previously exposed (Karni et al., 1992, 1994).

ACTIVATION-SYNTHESIS THEORY

According to psychiatrist J. Allan Hobson, who proposed **activation-synthesis theory**, the brain produces random electrical energy during REM sleep, possibly as a result of changes in the production of particular neurotransmitters. This electrical energy randomly stimulates memories lodged in various portions of the brain. Because we have a need to make sense of our world even while asleep, the brain takes these chaotic memories and weaves them into a logical story line, filling in the gaps to produce a rational scenario (Porte & Hobson, 1996; Hobson, 2005).

> Hobson's theory that the brain produces random electrical energy during REM sleep that stimulates memories lodged in various portions of the brain.

However, Hobson does not entirely reject the view that dreams reflect unconscious wishes. He suggests that the particular scenario a dreamer produces is not random but instead is a clue to the dreamer's fears, emotions, and concerns. Hence, what starts out as a random process culminates in something meaningful.

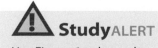 **Study**ALERT

Use Figure 6 to learn the differences between the three main explanations of dreaming.

Sleep Disturbances: Slumbering Problems

At one time or another, almost all of us have difficulty sleeping—a condition known as insomnia. It could be due to a particular situation, such as the breakup of a relationship, concern about a test score, or the loss of a job. Some cases of insomnia, however, have no obvious cause. Some people are simply unable to fall asleep easily, or they go to sleep readily but wake up frequently during the night. Insomnia is a problem that afflicts as many as one-third of all people (American Insomnia Association, 2005; Bains, 2006; Cooke & Ancoli-Israel, 2006).

Some people who *think* they have sleeping problems actually are mistaken. For example, researchers in sleep laboratories have found that some people who report being up all night actually fall asleep in 30 minutes and stay asleep all night. Furthermore, some people with insomnia accurately recall sounds that they heard while they were asleep, which gives them the impression that they were awake during the night (Semler & Harvey, 2005; Yapko, 2006).

Other sleep problems are less common than insomnia, although they are still widespread. For instance, some 20 million people suffer from sleep apnea, the disorder from which the mother in the chapter Prologue suffered. *Sleep apnea* is a condition in which a person has difficulty breathing while sleeping. The result is disturbed, fitful sleep, as the person is constantly reawakened when the lack of oxygen becomes great enough to trigger a waking response. Some people with apnea wake as many as 500 times during the course of a night, although they may not even be aware that they have wakened. Not surprisingly, such disturbed sleep results in extreme fatigue the next day. Sleep apnea also may play a role in *sudden infant death syndrome (SIDS)*, a mysterious killer of seemingly normal infants who die while sleeping (Rambaud & Guilleminault, 2004; Gami et al., 2005; Aloia et al., 2007).

Night terrors are sudden awakenings from non-REM sleep that are accompanied by extreme fear, panic, and strong physiological arousal. Usually occurring in stage 4 sleep, night terrors may be so frightening that a sleeper awakens with a shriek. Although night terrors initially produce great agitation, victims usually can get back to sleep fairly quickly. They occur most frequently in children between the ages of 3 and 8 (Lowe, Humphreys, & Williams, 2007).

Narcolepsy is uncontrollable sleeping that occurs for short periods while a person is awake. No matter what the activity—holding a heated conversation, exercising, or driving—a narcoleptic will suddenly fall asleep. People with narcolepsy go directly from wakefulness to REM sleep, skipping the other stages. The causes of narcolepsy are not known, although there could be a genetic component because narcolepsy runs in families (Mahmood, 2005; Ervik et al., 2006).

We know relatively little about sleeptalking and sleepwalking, two sleep disturbances that are usually harmless. Both occur during stage 4 sleep and are more common in children than in adults. Sleeptalkers and sleepwalkers usually have a vague consciousness of the world around them, and a sleepwalker may be able to walk with agility around obstructions in a crowded room. Unless a sleepwalker wanders into a dangerous environment, sleepwalking typically poses little risk (Baruss, 2003; Guilleminault et al., 2005; Lee-Chiong, 2006).

Circadian Rhythms: Life Cycles

Circadian rhythms: Biological processes that occur regularly on approximately a 24-hour cycle.

The fact that we cycle back and forth between wakefulness and sleep is one example of the body's circadian rhythms. **Circadian rhythms** (from the Latin *circa diem*, or "around the day") are biological processes that occur regularly on approximately a 24-hour cycle. Sleeping and waking, for instance, occur naturally to the beat of an internal

8:00 A.M.
• Risk for heart attack and stroke is highest
• Symptoms of rheumatoid arthritis are worst
• Helper T lymphocytes are at their lowest daytime level

7:00 A.M.
• Hay fever symptoms are worst

6:00 A.M.
• Onset of menstruation is most likely
• Insulin levels in the bloodstream are lowest
• Blood pressure and heart rate begin to rise
• Levels of the stress hormone cortisol increase
• Melatonin levels begin to fall

Noon
• Level of hemoglobin in the blood is at its peak

4:00 A.M.
• Asthma attacks are most likely to occur

3:00 P.M.
• Grip strength, respiratory rate, and reflex sensitivity are highest

2:00 A.M.
• Levels of growth hormone are highest

4:00 P.M.
• Body temperature, pulse rate, and blood pressure peak

1:00 A.M.
• Pregnant women are most likely to go into labor
• Immune cells called helper T lymphocytes are at their peak

6:00 P.M.
• Urinary flow is highest

9:00 P.M.
• Pain threshold is lowest

11:00 P.M.
• Allergic responses are most likely

FIGURE 8 Day times, night times: regular body changes over every 24-hour period. Over the course of the day, our circadian rhythms produce a wide variety of effects. (Source: Young, 2000.)

pacemaker that works on a cycle of about 24 hours. Several other bodily functions, such as body temperature, hormone production, and blood pressure, also follow circadian rhythms (Saper et al., 2005; Beersma & Gordijn, 2007; Blatter & Cajochen, 2007).

Circadian cycles are complex, and they involve a variety of behaviors (see Figure 8). For instance, sleepiness occurs not just in the evening but throughout the day in regular patterns, with most of us getting drowsy in midafternoon—regardless of whether we have eaten a heavy lunch. By making an afternoon siesta part of their everyday habit, people in several cultures take advantage of the body's natural inclination to sleep at this time (Wright, 2002; Takahashi et al., 2004; Reilly & Waterhouse, 2007).

The brain's *suprachiasmatic nucleus (SCN)* controls circadian rhythms. However, the relative amount of light and darkness, which varies with the seasons of the year, also plays a role in regulating circadian rhythms. In fact, some people experience *seasonal affective disorder*, a form of severe depression in which feelings of despair and hopelessness increase during the winter and lift during the rest of the year. The disorder appears to be a result of the brevity and gloom of winter days. Daily exposure to bright lights is sometimes sufficient to improve the mood of those with this disorder (Roush, 1995; Oren & Terman, 1998; Young, 2000; Eagles, 2001; Golden et al., 2005; Rohan et al., 2007).

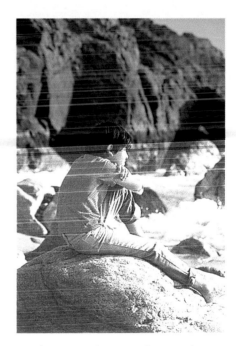

Daydreams are fantasies that people construct while they are awake. What are the similarities and differences between daydreams and night dreams?

Without Sleep

It is the stuff of magic: Our past mistakes can be wiped out and the future filled with noteworthy accomplishments. Fame, happiness, and wealth can be ours. In the next moment, though, the most horrible tragedies can occur, leaving us devastated, alone, and penniless.

The source of these scenarios is **daydreams**, fantasies that people construct while awake. Unlike dreaming that occurs during sleep, daydreams are more under people's

Daydreams: Fantasies that people construct while awake.

control. Therefore, their content is often more closely related to immediate events in the environment than is the content of the dreams that occur during sleep. Although they may include sexual content, daydreams also pertain to other activities or events that are relevant to a person's life.

Daydreams are a typical part of waking consciousness, even though our awareness of the environment around us declines while we are daydreaming. People vary considerably in the amount of daydreaming they do. For example, around 2 to 4 percent of the population spend at least half their free time fantasizing. Although most people daydream much less frequently, almost everyone fantasizes to some degree. Studies that ask people to identify what they are doing at random times during the day have shown that they are daydreaming about 10 percent of the time (Lynn et al., 1996; Holler, 2006; Singer, 2006).

**BECOMING
AN INFORMED CONSUMER
of Psychology**
Sleeping Better

Do you have trouble sleeping? You're not alone—70 million people in the United States have sleep problems. For those of us who spend hours tossing and turning in bed, psychologists studying sleep disturbances have a number of suggestions for overcoming insomnia (Edinger et al., 2001; Finley & Cowley, 2005; Benca, 2005). Here are some ideas.

- *Exercise during the day (at least six hours before bedtime) and avoid naps.* Not surprisingly, it helps to be tired before going to sleep! Moreover, learning systematic relaxation techniques and biofeedback can help you unwind from the day's stresses and tensions.

- *Choose a regular bedtime and stick to it.* Adhering to a habitual schedule helps your internal timing mechanisms regulate your body more effectively.

- *Avoid drinks with caffeine after lunch.* The effects of beverages such as coffee, tea, and some soft drinks can linger for as long as 8 to 12 hours after they are consumed.

- *Drink a glass of warm milk at bedtime.* Your grandparents were right when they dispensed this advice: Milk contains the chemical tryptophan, which helps people fall asleep.

- *Avoid sleeping pills.* Even though 25 percent of U.S. adults report having taken medication for sleep in the previous year, in the long run sleep medications can do more harm than good because they disrupt the normal sleep cycle.

- *Try not to sleep.* This approach works because people often have difficulty falling asleep because they are trying so hard. A better strategy is to go to bed only when you feel tired. If you don't get to sleep within 10 minutes, leave the bedroom and do something else, returning to bed only when you feel sleepy. Continue this process all night if necessary. But get up at your usual hour in the morning, and don't take any naps during the day. After three or four weeks, most people become conditioned to associate their beds with sleep—and fall asleep rapidly at night (Sloan et al., 1993; Ubell, 1993; Smith, 2001).

For long-term problems with sleep, you might consider visiting a sleep disorders center. For information on accredited clinics, consult the American Academy of Sleep Medicine at www.aasmnet.org.

RECAP/EVALUATE/RETHINK

RECAP

What are the different states of consciousness?

- Consciousness is a person's awareness of the sensations, thoughts, and feelings at a given moment. Waking consciousness can vary from more active to more passive states. (p. 140)

- Altered states of consciousness include naturally occurring sleep and dreaming, as well as hypnotic and drug-induced states. (p. 140)

What happens when we sleep, and what are the meaning and function of dreams?

- The brain is active throughout the night, and sleep proceeds through a series of stages identified by unique patterns of brain waves. (p. 142)

- REM (rapid eye movement) sleep is characterized by an increase in heart rate, a rise in blood pressure, an increase in the rate of breathing, and, in males, erections. Dreams occur during this stage. (p. 143)

- According to Freud, dreams have both a manifest content (an apparent story line) and a latent content (a true meaning). He suggested that the latent content provides a guide to a dreamer's unconscious, revealing unfulfilled wishes or desires. (p. 146)

- The dreams-for-survival theory suggests that information relevant to daily survival is reconsidered and reprocessed in dreams. The activation-synthesis theory proposes that dreams are a result of random electrical energy that stimulates different memories, which then are woven into a coherent story line. (p. 147)

What are the major sleep disorders, and how can they be treated?

- Insomnia is a sleep disorder characterized by difficulty sleeping. Sleep apnea is a condition in which people have difficulty sleeping and breathing at the same time. People with narcolepsy have an uncontrollable urge to sleep. Sleepwalking and sleeptalking are relatively harmless. (p. 148)

How much do we daydream?

- Wide individual differences exist in the amount of time devoted to daydreaming. Almost everyone daydreams or fantasizes to some degree. (p. 149)

EVALUATE

1. _____ is the term used to describe our understanding of the world external to us, as well as our own internal world.
2. A great deal of neural activity goes on during sleep. True or false?
3. Dreams occur in _____ sleep.
4. _____ _____ are internal bodily processes that occur on a daily cycle.
5. Freud's theory of unconscious _____ _____ states that the actual wishes an individual expresses in dreams are disguised because they are threatening to the person's conscious awareness.
6. Match the theory of dreaming with its definition.

   1. Activation-synthesis theory
   2. Dreams-for-survival theory
   3. Dreams as wish fulfillment

   a. Dreams permit important information to be reprocessed during sleep.
   b. The manifest content of dreams disguises the latent content of the dreams.
   c. Electrical energy stimulates random memories, which are woven together to produce dreams.

RETHINK

1. Suppose that a new "miracle pill" will allow a person to function with only one hour of sleep per night. However, because a night's sleep is so short, a person who takes the pill will never dream again. Knowing what you do about the functions of sleep and dreaming, what would be some advantages and drawbacks of such a pill from a personal standpoint? Would you take such a pill?

2. *From the perspective of an educator:* How might you use the findings in sleep research to maximize student learning?

Answers to Evaluate Questions

1. consciousness; 2. true; 3. REM; 4. circadian rhythms; 5. wish fulfillment; 6. 1-c, 2-a, 3-b

KEY TERMS

consciousness p. 140
stage 1 sleep p. 142
stage 2 sleep p. 142
stage 3 sleep p. 142
stage 4 sleep p. 142
rapid eye movement (REM)
  sleep p. 143

unconscious wish
  fulfillment theory p. 146
latent content of dreams
  p. 146
manifest content of dreams
  p. 146

dreams-for-survival theory
  p. 147
activation-synthesis theory
  p. 147
circadian rhythms p. 148
daydreams p. 149

Hypnosis and Meditation

You are feeling relaxed and drowsy. You are getting sleepier. Your body is becoming limp. Your eyelids are feeling heavier. Your eyes are closing; you can't keep them open anymore. You are totally relaxed. Now, place your hands above your head. But you will find they are getting heavier and heavier—so heavy you can barely keep them up. In fact, although you are straining as hard as you can, you will be unable to hold them up any longer.

An observer watching the above scene would notice a curious phenomenon. Many of the people listening to the voice are dropping their arms to their sides. The reason for this strange behavior? Those people have been hypnotized.

Hypnosis: A Trance-Forming Experience?

People under **hypnosis** are in a trancelike state of heightened susceptibility to the suggestions of others. In some respects, it appears that they are asleep. Yet other aspects of their behavior contradict this notion, for people are attentive to the hypnotist's suggestions and may carry out bizarre or silly suggestions.

Despite their compliance when hypnotized, people do not lose all will of their own. They will not perform antisocial behaviors, and they will not carry out self-destructive acts. People will not reveal hidden truths about themselves, and they are capable of lying. Moreover, people cannot be hypnotized against their will—despite popular misconceptions (Gwynn & Spanos, 1996; Raz, 2007).

There are wide variations in people's susceptibility to hypnosis. About 5 to 20 percent of the population cannot be hypnotized at all, and some 15 percent are very easily hypnotized. Most people fall somewhere in between. Moreover, the ease with which a person is hypnotized is related to a number of other characteristics. People who are readily hypnotized are also easily absorbed while reading books or listening to music, becoming unaware of what is happening around them, and they often spend an unusual amount of time daydreaming. In sum, then, they show a high ability to concentrate and to become completely absorbed in what they are doing (Kirsch & Braffman, 2001; Rubichi et al., 2005; Benham et al., 2006).

A DIFFERENT STATE OF CONSCIOUSNESS?

The question of whether hypnosis is a state of consciousness that is qualitatively different from normal waking consciousness is controversial. Some psychologists believe that hypnosis represents a state of consciousness that differs significantly from other states. In this view, the high suggestibility, increased ability to recall and construct images, and acceptance of suggestions that clearly contradict reality suggest it is a different state. Moreover, changes in electrical activity in the brain are associated

Key Concepts

What is hypnosis, and are hypnotized people in a different state of consciousness?

What are the effects of meditation?

Hypnosis: A trancelike state of heightened susceptibility to the suggestions of others.

Despite common misconceptions, people cannot be hypnotized against their will, nor do they lose all will of their own. Why, then, do people sometimes behave so unusually when asked to by a hypnotist?

with hypnosis, supporting the position that hypnosis is a state of consciousness different from normal waking (Hilgard, 1992; Kallio & Revonsuo, 2003; Fingelkurts & Kallio, 2007).

On the other side of the controversy are psychologists who reject the notion that hypnosis is a state significantly different from normal waking consciousness. They argue that altered brain-wave patterns are not sufficient to demonstrate a qualitative difference because no other specific physiological changes occur when people are in trances. Furthermore, little support exists for the contention that adults can recall memories of childhood events accurately while hypnotized. That lack of evidence suggests that there is nothing qualitatively special about the hypnotic trance (Lynn et al., 2003; Lynn, Fassler, & Knox, 2005; Hongchun & Ming, 2006).

There is increasing agreement that the controversy over the nature of hypnosis has led to extreme positions on both sides of the issue. More recent approaches suggest that the hypnotic state may best be viewed as lying along a continuum in which hypnosis is neither a totally different state of consciousness nor totally similar to normal waking consciousness (Lynn et al., 2000; Kihlstrom, 2005; Jamieson, 2007).

As arguments about the true nature of hypnosis continue, though, one thing is clear: Hypnosis has been used successfully to solve practical human problems. In fact, psychologists working in many different areas have found hypnosis to be a reliable, effective tool. It has been applied to a number of areas, including the following:

- *Controlling pain*. Patients suffering from chronic pain may be given the suggestion, while hypnotized, that their pain is gone or reduced. They also may be taught to hypnotize themselves to relieve pain or gain a sense of control over their symptoms. Hypnosis has proved to be particularly useful during childbirth and dental procedures (Mehl-Madrona, 2004; Hammond, 2007).

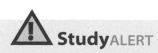

StudyALERT

The question of whether hypnosis represents a different state of consciousness or is similar to normal waking consciousness is a key issue.

- *Reducing smoking.* Although it hasn't been successful in stopping drug and alcohol abuse, hypnosis sometimes helps people stop smoking through hypnotic suggestions that the taste and smell of cigarettes are unpleasant (Elkins et al., 2006; Fuller, 2006).

- *Treating psychological disorders.* Hypnosis sometimes is used during treatment for psychological disorders. For example, it may be employed to heighten relaxation, reduce anxiety, increase expectations of success, or modify self-defeating thoughts (Zarren & Eimer, 2002; Iglesias, 2005; Golden, 2006).

- *Assisting in law enforcement.* Witnesses and victims are sometimes better able to recall the details of a crime when hypnotized. In one often-cited case, a witness to the kidnapping of a group of California schoolchildren was placed under hypnosis and was able to recall all but one digit of the license number on the kidnapper's vehicle. However, hypnotic recollections may also be inaccurate, just as other recollections are often inaccurate. Consequently, the legal status of hypnosis is unresolved (Whitehouse et al., 2005; Kazar, 2006; Knight & Meyer, 2007).

- *Improving athletic performance.* Athletes sometimes turn to hypnosis to improve their performance. For example, some baseball players have used hypnotism to increase their concentration when batting, with considerable success (Lindsay, Maynard, & Thomas, 2005; Grindstaff & Fisher, 2006).

Meditation: Regulating Our Own State of Consciousness

When traditional practitioners of the ancient Eastern religion of Zen Buddhism want to achieve greater spiritual insight, they turn to a technique that has been used for centuries to alter their state of consciousness. This technique is called meditation.

Meditation is a learned technique for refocusing attention that brings about an altered state of consciousness. Meditation typically consists of the repetition of a *mantra*—a sound, word, or syllable—over and over. In other forms of meditation, the focus is on a picture, flame, or specific part of the body. Regardless of the nature of the particular initial stimulus, the key to the procedure is concentrating on it so thoroughly that the meditator becomes unaware of any outside stimulation and reaches a different state of consciousness.

After meditation, people report feeling thoroughly relaxed. They sometimes relate that they have gained new insights into themselves and the problems they are facing. The long-term practice of meditation may even improve health because of the biological changes it produces. For example, during meditation, oxygen usage decreases, heart rate and blood pressure decline, and brain-wave patterns change (Arambula et al., 2001; Barnes et al., 2004; Lee et al., 2007; see Figure 1).

Anyone can meditate by following a few simple procedures. The fundamentals include sitting in a quiet room with the eyes closed, breathing deeply and rhythmically, and repeating a word or sound—such as the word *one*—over and over. Practiced twice a day for 20 minutes, the technique is effective in bringing about relaxation (Benson et al., 1994; Aftanas & Golosheykin, 2005).

Meditation is a means of altering consciousness that is practiced in many different cultures, though it can take different forms and serve different purposes across cultures. In fact, one impetus for the study of consciousness is the realization that people in many different cultures routinely seek ways to alter their states of consciousness (Walsh & Shapiro, 2006).

Meditation: A learned technique for refocusing attention that brings about an altered state of consciousness.

 StudyALERT

Remember that although there are several alternate techniques used in meditation, they are all designed to bring about an altered state of consciousness in which attention is refocused.

Neuroscience in Your Life

FIGURE 1 To understand the long-term effects of meditation, researchers compared the brain activation of novice and experienced meditators. These fMRI brain scans show the regions of brain activation during meditation as compared to when at rest in (A) expert meditators who had between 10,000 and 54,000 hours of practice in meditating and (B) novice meditators who had no experience mediating. The colors reflect positive activation as compared to rest (strongest is yellow) and negative activation as compared to rest (strongest is light blue). Finally, experts and novices were compared (C). In (C), red hues show greater activation in the experts and blue hues show greater activation for the novices. The findings suggest that long-term meditation produces significant changes in regions of the brain related to concentration and attention.

(A) 12 Expert Meditators

(B) 12 Age-Matched Novices

(C) Experts vs. Novices

Left Hemisphere   Right Hemisphere   Axial

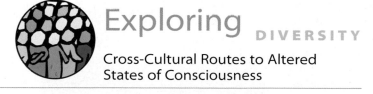

Exploring DIVERSITY

Cross-Cultural Routes to Altered States of Consciousness

A group of Native American Sioux men sit naked in a steaming sweat lodge as a medicine man throws water on sizzling rocks to send billows of scalding steam into the air.

Aztec priests smear themselves with a mixture of crushed poisonous herbs, hairy black worms, scorpions, and lizards. Sometimes they drink the potion.

During the sixteenth century, a devout Hasidic Jew lies across the tombstone of a celebrated scholar. As he murmurs the name of God repeatedly, he seeks to be possessed by the soul of the dead wise man's spirit. If successful, he will attain a mystical state, and the deceased's words will flow out of his mouth.

Each of these rituals has a common goal: suspension from the bonds of everyday awareness and access to an altered state of consciousness. Although they may seem exotic from the vantage point of many Western cultures, these rituals represent an apparently universal effort to alter consciousness (Fine, 1994; Bartocci, 2004; Irwin, 2006).

Some scholars suggest that the quest to alter consciousness represents a basic human desire (Siegel, 1989). Whether or not we accept such an extreme view, it is clear that variations in states of consciousness share some basic characteristics across a variety of cultures. One is an alteration in thinking, which may become shallow, illogical, or otherwise different from normal. In addition, people's sense of time can become disturbed, and their perceptions of the physical world and of themselves may change. They may lose self-control, doing things that they would never otherwise do. Finally, they may feel a sense of *ineffability*—the inability to understand an experience rationally or describe it in words (Martindale, 1981; Finkler, 2004; Travis, 2006).

Of course, realizing that efforts to produce altered states of consciousness are widespread throughout the world's societies does not answer a fundamental question: Is the experience of unaltered states of consciousness similar across different cultures?

Because humans share basic biological commonalties in the ways their brains and bodies are wired, we might assume that the fundamental experience of consciousness is similar across cultures. As a result, we could suppose that consciousness shows some basic similarities across cultures. However, the ways in which certain aspects of consciousness are interpreted and viewed show substantial differences from culture to culture. For example, people in disparate cultures view the experience of the passage of time in varying ways. For instance, Arabs appear to perceive the passage of time more slowly than North Americans (Alon & Brett, 2007).

RECAP/EVALUATE/RETHINK

RECAP

What is hypnosis, and are hypnotized people in a different state of consciousness?

- Hypnosis produces a state of heightened susceptibility to the suggestions of the hypnotist. Under hypnosis, significant behavioral changes occur, including increased concentration and suggestibility, heightened ability to recall and construct images, lack of initiative, and acceptance of suggestions that clearly contradict reality. (p. 153)

What are the effects of meditation?

- Meditation is a learned technique for refocusing attention that brings about an altered state of consciousness. (p. 155)

- Different cultures have developed their own unique ways to alter states of consciousness. (p. 156)

EVALUATE

1. _____ is a state of heightened susceptibility to the suggestions of others.

2. A friend tells you, "I once heard of a person who was murdered by being hypnotized and then told to jump from the Golden Gate Bridge!" Could such a thing have happened? Why or why not?

3. _____ is a learned technique for refocusing attention to bring about an altered state of consciousness.

4. Leslie repeats a unique sound, known as a _____, when she engages in meditation.

1. Why do you think people in almost every culture seek ways of altering their states of consciousness?

2. *From the perspective of a human resources specialist:* Would you allow (or even encourage) employees to engage in meditation during the workday? Why or why not?

Answers to Evaluate Questions

1. hypnosis; 2. no; people who are hypnotized cannot be made to perform self-destructive acts; 3. meditation; 4. mantra

KEY TERMS

hypnosis p. 153
meditation p. 155

Drug Use: The Highs and Lows of Consciousness

John Brodhead's bio reads like a script for an episode of VH1's Behind the Music. A young rebel from the New Jersey suburbs falls in with a fast crowd, gets hooked on parties and booze and, with intensive counseling and a bit of tough love, manages to get his life back together. What makes his story different? Just one thing: his age. John is 13. (Rogers, 2002)

John Brodhead was lucky. Now in recovery, John had begun to drink when he was in the sixth grade. He is not alone: The number of kids who start drinking by the eighth grade has increased by almost a third since the 1970s, even though alcohol consumption overall has stayed fairly steady among the general population.

Drugs of one sort or another are a part of almost everyone's life. From infancy on, most people take vitamins, aspirin, cold-relief medicine, and the like, and surveys find that 80 percent of adults in the United States have taken an over-the-counter pain reliever in the last six months. However, these drugs rarely produce an altered state of consciousness (Dortch, 1996).

In contrast, some substances, known as psychoactive drugs, lead to an altered state of consciousness. **Psychoactive drugs** influence a person's emotions, perceptions, and behavior. Yet even this category of drugs is common in most of our lives. If you have ever had a cup of coffee or sipped a beer, you have taken a psychoactive drug. A large number of individuals have used more potent—and more dangerous—psychoactive drugs than coffee and beer (see Figure 1); for instance, surveys find that 41 percent of high school seniors have used an illegal drug in the last year. In addition, 30 percent report having been drunk on alcohol. The figures for the adult population are even higher (Johnston, O'Malley, & Bachman, 2007).

Of course, drugs vary widely in the effects they have on users, in part because they affect the nervous system in very different ways. Some drugs alter the limbic system, and others affect the operation of specific neurotransmitters across the synapses of neurons. For example, some drugs block or enhance the release of neurotransmitters, others block the receipt or the removal of a neurotransmitter, and still others mimic the effects of a particular neurotransmitter (see Figure 2).

The most dangerous drugs are addictive. **Addictive drugs** produce a biological or psychological dependence in the user, and withdrawal from them leads to a craving for the drug that, in some cases, may be nearly irresistible. In *biologically based* addictions, the body becomes so accustomed to functioning in the presence of a drug that it cannot function without it. *Psychologically based* addictions are those in which people believe that they need the drug to respond to the stresses of daily living. Although we generally associate addiction with drugs such as heroin, everyday sorts of drugs, such as caffeine (found in coffee) and nicotine (found in cigarettes), have addictive aspects as well (Li et al., 2007).

We know surprisingly little about the underlying causes of addiction. One of the problems in identifying those causes is that different drugs (such as alcohol and cocaine) affect the brain in very different ways—yet they may be equally addicting. Furthermore, it takes longer to become addicted to some drugs than to others, even though the ultimate consequences of addiction may be equally grave (Nestler & Malenka, 2004; Crombag & Robinson, 2004; Smart, 2006).

Key Concept

What are the major classifications of drugs, and what are their effects?

John Brodhead began to drink heavily when he was in the sixth grade.

Drugs that influence a person's emotions, perceptions, and behavior.

Drugs that produce a biological or psychological dependence in the user so that withdrawal from them leads to a craving for the drug that, in some cases, may be nearly irresistible.

 StudyALERT

Use Figure 2 to learn the different ways that drugs produce their effects on a neurological level.

FIGURE 1 How many teenagers use drugs? The results of the most recent comprehensive survey of 14,000 high school seniors across the United States show the percentage of respondents who have used various substances for nonmedical purposes at least once (Johnston, O'Malley, & Bachman, 2007). Can you think of any reasons why teenagers—as opposed to older people—might be particularly likely to use drugs? (Source: Johnston, L. D., O'Malley, P. M., Bachman, J. G., & Schulenberg, J. E. (2007). *Monitoring the Future: National results on adolescent drug use: Overview of key findings, 2006*. (NIH Publication No. 07-6202). Bethesda, MD: National Institute on Drug Abuse.)

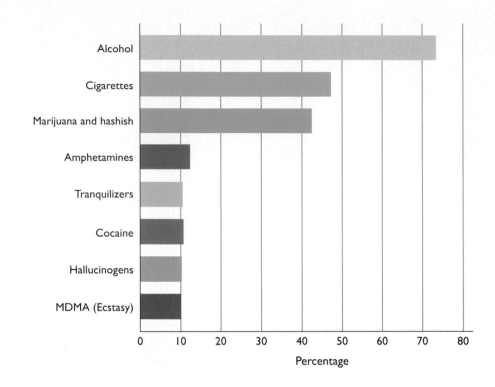

Why do people take drugs in the first place? There are many reasons, ranging from the perceived pleasure of the experience itself, to the escape that a drug-induced high affords from the everyday pressures of life, to an attempt to achieve a religious or spiritual state. However, other factors having little to do with the nature of the experience itself, also lead people to try drugs (McDowell & Spitz, 1999).

For instance, the highly publicized drug use of role models such as movie stars and professional athletes, the easy availability of some illegal drugs, and peer pressure all play a role in the decision to use drugs. In some cases, the motive is simply the thrill of trying something new. Finally, genetic factors may predispose some people to be more susceptible to drugs and to become addicted to them. Regardless of the forces that lead a person to begin using drugs, drug addiction is among the most difficult of

FIGURE 2 Different drugs affect different parts of the nervous system and brain and each drug functions in one of these specific ways.

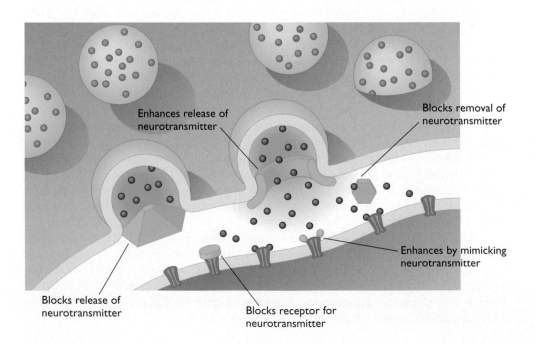

all behaviors to modify, even with extensive treatment (Lemonick, 2000; Mosher & Akins, 2007; Ray & Hutchison, 2007).

Because of the difficulty in treating drug problems, there is little disagreement that the best hope for dealing with the overall societal problem of substance abuse is to prevent people from becoming involved with drugs in the first place. However, there is little accord on how to accomplish this goal.

Even drug reduction programs widely publicized for their effectiveness—such as DARE (Drug Abuse Resistance Education)—are of questionable effectiveness. Used in more than 80 percent of school districts in the United States, DARE consists of a series of 17 lessons on the dangers of drugs, alcohol, and gangs taught to fifth- and sixth-graders by a police officer. The program is highly popular with school officials, parents, and politicians. The problem? Repeated careful evaluations have been unable to demonstrate that the DARE program is effective in reducing drug use over the long term. In fact, one study even showed that DARE graduates were more likely to use marijuana than was a comparison group of nongraduates (Kalb, 2001b; West & O'Neal, 2006; Des Jarlais, 2006).

Stimulants: Drug Highs

It's 1:00 a.m., and you still haven't finished reading the last chapter of the text on which you will be tested later in the morning. Feeling exhausted, you turn to the one thing that may help you stay awake for the next two hours: a cup of strong black coffee.

If you have ever found yourself in such a position, you have resorted to a major *stimulant*, caffeine, to stay awake. *Caffeine* is one of a number of **stimulants**, drugs whose effect on the central nervous system causes a rise in heart rate, blood pressure, and muscular tension. Caffeine is present not only in coffee; it is an important ingredient in tea, soft drinks, and chocolate as well (see Figure 3).

Caffeine produces several reactions. The major behavioral effects are an increase in attentiveness and a decrease in reaction time. Caffeine can also bring about an improvement in mood, most likely by mimicking the effects of a natural brain chemical, adenosine. Too much caffeine, however, can result in nervousness and insomnia. People can build up a biological dependence on the drug. Regular users who suddenly stop drinking coffee may experience headaches or depression. Many people who drink large amounts of coffee on weekdays have headaches on weekends because

Stimulants: Drugs that have an arousal effect on the central nervous system, causing a rise in heart rate, blood pressure, and muscular tension.

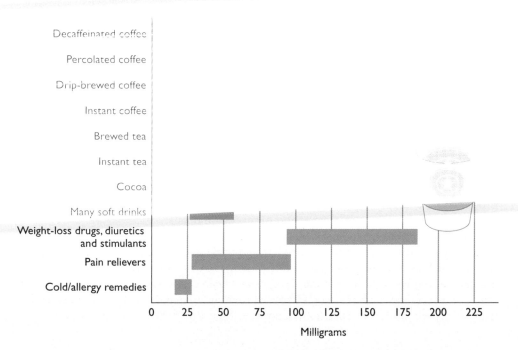

FIGURE 3 How much caffeine do you consume? This chart shows the range of caffeine found in common foods and drinks. The average coffee drinker in the United States consumes about 200 milligrams of caffeine each day, or around three cups of coffee. (Source: New York Times Graphics)

of the sudden drop in the amount of caffeine they are consuming (Juliano & Griffiths, 2004; Satel, 2006; Kendler, Myers, & Gardner, 2006).

Nicotine, found in cigarettes, is another common stimulant. The soothing effects of nicotine help explain why cigarette smoking is addictive. Smokers develop a dependence on nicotine, and those who suddenly stop smoking develop a strong craving for the drug. This is not surprising: Nicotine activates neural mechanisms similar to those activated by cocaine, which, as we see next, is also highly addictive (Collins & Izenwasser, 2004; Haberstick et al., 2007).

AMPHETAMINES

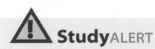

StudyALERT

Figure 4, which summarizes the different categories of drugs (stimulants, depressants, narcotics, and hallucinogens), will help you learn the effects of particular drugs.

Amphetamines such as Dexedrine and Benzedrine, popularly known as speed, are strong stimulants. In small quantities, amphetamines—which stimulate the central nervous system—bring about a sense of energy and alertness, talkativeness, heightened confidence, and a mood "high." They increase concentration and reduce fatigue. Amphetamines also cause a loss of appetite, increased anxiety, and irritability. When taken over long periods of time, amphetamines can cause feelings of being persecuted by others, as well as a general sense of suspiciousness. People taking amphetamines may lose interest in sex. If taken in too large a quantity, amphetamines overstimulate the central nervous system to such an extent that convulsions and death can occur (Carhart-Harris, 2007).

Methamphetamine is a white, crystalline drug that U.S. police now say is the most dangerous street drug. "Meth" is highly addictive and relatively cheap, and it produces a strong, lingering high. It has made addicts of people across the social spectrum, ranging from soccer moms to urban professionals to poverty-stricken inner-city residents. After becoming addicted, users take it more and more frequently and in increasing doses. Long-term use of the drug can lead to brain damage (Thompson et al., 2004; Sharma, Sjoquist, & Ali, 2007).

More than 1.5 million people in the United States are regular methamphetamine users. Because it can be made from nonprescription cold pills, retailers such as Wal-Mart and Target have removed these medications from their shelves. Illicit labs devoted to the manufacture of methamphetamine have sprung up in many locations around the United States (Jefferson, 2005).

COCAINE

Although its use has declined over the last decade, the stimulant cocaine and its derivative, crack, still represent a serious concern. Cocaine is inhaled or "snorted" through the nose, smoked, or injected directly into the bloodstream. It is rapidly absorbed into the body and takes effect almost immediately.

When used in relatively small quantities, cocaine produces feelings of profound psychological well-being, increased confidence, and alertness. Cocaine produces this "high" through the neurotransmitter dopamine. Dopamine is one of the chemicals that transmit between neurons messages that are related to ordinary feelings of pleasure. Normally when dopamine is released, excess amounts of the neurotransmitter are reabsorbed by the releasing neuron. However, when cocaine enters the brain, it blocks reabsorption of leftover dopamine. As a result, the brain is flooded with dopamine-produced pleasurable sensations (Redish, 2004; Jarlais et al., 2007). Figure 4 provides a summary of the effects of cocaine and other illegal drugs.

However, there is a steep price to be paid for the pleasurable effects of cocaine. The brain may become permanently rewired, triggering a psychological and physical addiction in which users grow obsessed with obtaining the drug. Over time, users deteriorate mentally and physically. In extreme cases, cocaine can cause hallucinations—a common one is of insects crawling over one's body. Ultimately, an overdose of cocaine can lead to death (Carpenter, 2001; Nestler, 2001; George & Moselhy, 2005; Paulozzi, 2006).

Drugs	Street Name	Effects	Withdrawal Symptoms	Adverse/Overdose Reactions
Stimulants				
Cocaine	Coke, blow, snow, lady, crack	Increased confidence, mood elevation, sense of energy and alertness, decreased appetite, anxiety, irritability, insomnia, transient drowsiness, delayed orgasm	Apathy, general fatigue, prolonged sleep, depression, disorientation, suicidal thoughts, agitated motor activity, irritability, bizarre dreams	Elevated blood pressure, increase in body temperature, face picking, suspiciousness, bizarre and repetitious behavior, vivid hallucinations, convulsions, possible death
Amphetamines				
Benzedrine	Speed			
Dexedrine	Speed			
Depressants				
Alcohol	Booze	Anxiety reduction, impulsiveness, dramatic mood swings, bizarre thoughts, suicidal behavior, slurred speech, disorientation, slowed mental and physical functioning, limited attention span	Weakness, restlessness, nausea and vomiting, headaches, nightmares, irritability, depression, acute anxiety, hallucinations, seizures, possible death	Confusion, decreased response to pain, shallow respiration, dilated pupils, weak and rapid pulse, coma, possible death
Barbiturates				
Nembutal	Yellowjackets, yellows			
Seconal				
Phenobarbital	Reds			
Rohypnol	Roofies, rope, "date-rape drug"	Muscle relaxation, amnesia, sleep	Seizures	Seizures, coma, incapacitation, inability to resist sexual assault
Narcotics				
Heroin	H, hombre, junk, smack, dope, crap, horse	Anxiety and pain reduction, apathy, difficulty in concentration, slowed speech, decreased physical activity, drooling, itching, euphoria, nausea	Anxiety, vomiting, sneezing, diarrhea, lower back pain, watery eyes, runny nose, yawning, irritability, tremors, panic, chills and sweating, cramps	Depressed levels of consciousness, low blood pressure, rapid heart rate, shallow breathing, convulsions, coma, possible death
Morphine	Drugstore dope, cube, first line, mud			
Hallucinogens				
Cannabis	Bhang, kif, ganja, dope, grass, pot, hemp, joint, weed, bone, Mary Jane, reefer	Euphoria, relaxed inhibitions, increased appetite, disoriented behavior	Hyperactivity, insomnia, decreased appetite, anxiety	Severe reactions rare but include panic, paranoia, fatigue, bizarre and dangerous behavior, decreased testosterone over long-term; immune-system effects
Marijuana				
Hashish				
Hash oil				
MDMA	Ecstasy	Heightened sense of oneself and insight, feelings of peace, empathy, energy	Depression, anxiety, sleeplessness	Increase in body temperature, memory difficulties
LSD	Acid, quasey, microdot, white lightning	Heightened aesthetic responses; vision and depth distortion; heightened sensitivity to faces and gestures; magnified feelings; paranoia, panic, euphoria	Not reported	Nausea and chills, increased pulse, temperature, and blood pressure; slow, deep breathing; loss of appetite; insomnia; bizarre, dangerous behavior

FIGURE 4 Drugs and their effects. A comprehensive breakdown of effects of the most commonly used drugs.

Almost 2.5 million people in the United States are occasional cocaine users, and as many as 1.8 million people use the drug regularly. Given the strength of cocaine, withdrawal from the drug is difficult. Although the use of cocaine among high school students has declined in recent years, the drug still represents a major problem (Johnston, O'Malley, & Bachman, 2004).

Depressants: Drug Lows

Depressants: Drugs that slow down the nervous system.

In contrast to the initial effect of stimulants, which is an increase in arousal of the central nervous system, the effect of **depressants** is to impede the nervous system by causing neurons to fire more slowly. Small doses result in at least temporary feelings of *intoxication*—drunkenness—along with a sense of euphoria and joy. When large amounts are taken, however, speech becomes slurred and muscle control becomes disjointed, making motion difficult. Ultimately, heavy users may lose consciousness entirely.

ALCOHOL

The most common depressant is alcohol, which is used by more people than is any other drug. Based on liquor sales, the average person over the age of 14 drinks 2½ gallons of pure alcohol over the course of a year. This works out to more than 200 drinks per person. Although alcohol consumption has declined steadily over the last decade, surveys show that more than three-fourths of college students indicate that they have had a drink within the last 30 days (Jung, 2002; Midanik, Tam, & Weisner, 2007).

One of the more disturbing trends is the high frequency of binge drinking among college students. For men, *binge drinking* is defined as having five or more drinks in one sitting; for women, who generally weigh less than men and whose bodies absorb alcohol less efficiently, binge drinking is defined as having four or more drinks at one sitting (Mokdad et al., 2007).

Around 50 percent of male college students and 40 percent of female college students say they engaged in binge drinking at least once within the prior two weeks (see Figure 5). Some 17 percent of female students and 31 percent of male students

Although most alcohol consumers are casual users, there are more than 14 million alcoholics in the United States. The effects of alcohol vary significantly, depending on who is drinking it and the setting in which people drink. If alcohol were a newly discovered drug, do you think its sale would be legal?

Men

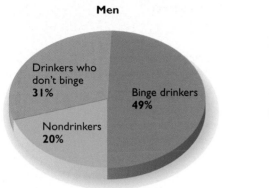

Drinkers who don't binge
31%

Binge drinkers
49%

Nondrinkers
20%

Women

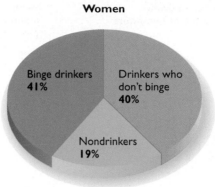

Binge drinkers
41%

Drinkers who don't binge
40%

Nondrinkers
19%

FIGURE 5 Drinking habits of college students (Wechsler et al., 2003). For men, binge drinking was defined as consuming five or more drinks in one sitting; for women, the total was four or more.

admitted drinking on 10 or more occasions during the last 30 days. Furthermore, even light drinkers were affected by the high rate of alcohol use: Two-thirds of lighter drinkers said that they had had their studying or sleep disturbed by drunk students, and a quarter of the women said they had been the target of an unwanted sexual advance by a drunk classmate (Wechsler et al., 1994, 2000, 2002; Park & Grant, 2005).

Generally, women are typically somewhat lighter drinkers than men—although the gap between the sexes is narrowing for older women and has closed completely for teenagers. Women are more susceptible to the effects of alcohol, and alcohol abuse may harm the brains of women more than men (Wuethrich, 2001; Mann et al., 2005; Mancinelli, Binetti, & Ceccanti, 2007).

There are also cultural and ethnic differences in alcohol consumption. For example, teenagers in Europe drink more than teenagers in the United States. Furthermore, people of East Asian backgrounds who live in the United States tend to drink significantly less than do Caucasians and African Americans, and their incidence of alcohol-related problems is lower. It may be that physical reactions to drinking, which may include sweating, a quickened heartbeat, and flushing, are more unpleasant for East Asians than for other groups (Garcia-Andrade, Wall, & Ehlers, 1997; Garlow, Purselle, & Heninger, 2007; Kantrowitz & Underwood, 2007).

Although alcohol is a depressant, most people claim that it increases their sense of sociability and well-being. The discrepancy between the actual and the perceived effects of alcohol lies in the initial effects it produces in the majority of individuals who use it: release of tension and stress, feelings of happiness, and loss of inhibitions (Steele & Josephs, 1990; Sayette, 1993).

As the dose of alcohol increases, however, the depressive effects become more pronounced (see Figure 6). People may feel emotionally and physically unstable. They also show poor judgment and may act aggressively. Moreover, memory is impaired, brain processing of spatial information is diminished, and speech becomes slurred and incoherent. Eventually they may fall into a stupor and pass out. If they drink enough alcohol in a short time, they may die of alcohol poisoning (Murphy et al., 1998; Zeigler et al., 2005; Thatcher & Clark, 2006).

Although most people fall into the category of casual users, 14 million people in the United States—1 in every 13 adults—have a drinking problem. *Alcoholics*, people with alcohol-abuse problems, come to rely on alcohol and continue to drink even though it causes serious difficulties. In addition, they become increasingly immune to the effects of alcohol. Consequently, alcoholics must drink progressively more to experience the initial positive feelings that alcohol produces.

In some cases of alcoholism, people must drink constantly in order to feel well enough to function in their daily lives. In other cases, though, people drink inconsistently, but occasionally go on binges in which they consume large quantities of alcohol.

It is not clear why certain people become alcoholics and develop a tolerance for alcohol, whereas others do not. There may be a genetic cause, although the question of whether there is a specific inherited gene that produces alcoholism is controversial.

Number of drinks consumed in two hours		Alcohol in blood (percentage)	Typical effects
	2	0.05	Judgment, thought, and restraint weakened; tension released, giving carefree sensation
	3	0.08	Tensions and inhibitions of everyday life lessened; cheerfulness
	4	0.10	Voluntary motor action affected, making hand and arm movements, walk, and speech clumsy
	7	0.20	Severe impairment—staggering, loud, incoherent, emotionally unstable, 100 times greater traffic risk; exuberance and aggressive inclinations magnified
	9	0.30	Deeper areas of brain affected, with stimulus-response and understanding confused; stuporous; blurred vision
	12	0.40	Incapable of voluntary action; sleepy, difficult to arouse; equivalent of surgical anesthesia
	15	0.50	Comatose; centers controlling breathing and heartbeat anesthetized; death increasingly probable

Note: A drink refers to a typical 12-ounce bottle of beer, a 1.5-ounce shot of hard liquor, or a 5-ounce glass of wine.

FIGURE 6 The effects of alcohol. The quantities represent only rough benchmarks; the effects vary significantly depending on an individual's weight, height, recent food intake, genetic factors, and even psychological state.

What is clear is that the chances of becoming an alcoholic are considerably higher if alcoholics are present in earlier generations of a person's family. However, not all alcoholics have close relatives who are alcoholics. In these cases, environmental stressors are suspected of playing a larger role (Whitfield et al., 2004; Nurnberger & Bierut, 2007; Zimmermann et al., 2007). (For more on alcohol use in college, see the *Applying Psychology in the 21st Century* box.)

BARBITURATES

Barbiturates, which include drugs such as Nembutal, Seconal, and phenobarbital, are another form of depressant. Frequently prescribed by physicians to induce sleep or

Time in a Bottle

Throwing up in the men's room might not seem like much of a birthday celebration. But for Gregg Rock, and a lot of newly legal drinkers, it's the price of turning 21. For Rock, it started with "pre-drinking" a bottle of Bacardi rum with college buddies last Wednesday before walking into a University of Minnesota tavern. It was midnight, the magic hour he became legal. On the bar rail there were soon "The Three Wise Men" (Jim Beam, Johnny Walker, Jack Daniels). The sound system played the Ramones' "I Wanna Be Sedated." Rock pounded. Then his body rebelled. "Yes, I puked," said a visibly relieved Rock, a senior. "But I know my limit." (Gegax, 2005, p. 28)

Greg Rock's midnight drinking binge during the first hour of his 21st birthday is a ritual known as "power hour" on some college campuses. For many students, drinking alcohol has become as much a part of the college experience as long lines at the campus bookstore. According to one study, 40 percent of American college students would be classified as heavy drinkers;

moreover, there seems to be something peculiar to the college environment that encourages this high rate of alcohol use. College students were actually less inclined to drink than their non-college-bound peers when they were in high school—but once they hit college, the students ramped up their drinking considerably until they had surpassed their non-student peers (O'Malley & Johnston, 2002).

To examine drinking in college, researcher Clayton Neighbors and his colleagues investigated several factors that might encourage drinking among college students. They found that social norms were among the best predictors of drinking; students who drank more tended to perceive other students as being frequent drinkers and they also tended to think that their friends—and to a lesser extent, even their parents—would approve of their drinking behavior. In addition, men, and members of fraternities or sororities, tended to drink more. By contrast, students whose motivation to drink was more of a response to peer pressure tended to drink less (Neighbors et al., 2007).

Students were more likely to have alcohol-related problems if they used drinking to try to forget their problems.

Drinking problems were also associated with believing that drinking would produce cognitive and behavioral impairment, aggression, or negative self-perceptions, primarily because those students with drinking problems were likely to see these negative consequences as positives.

What this study suggests is that while there might be some special factors contributing to the development of alcohol-related problems among college students, the biggest problem is excessive drinking. Students drink more when they think that it's fun, that everyone's doing it, and that it's what other people want or expect them to do. One approach to stemming the tide of college drinking, then, might center on changing students' perceptions: getting out the message that plenty of students actually don't drink and don't think highly of those who do (Neighbors et al., 2007).

- Why do you think students who drink because of peer pressure actually tend to drink less than others?
- Why might students who drink a lot tend to think that other students drink a lot also?
- How might students' perceptions of their peers' drinking behaviors and attitudes toward drinking be modified?

reduce stress, barbiturates produce a sense of relaxation. Yet they too are psychologically and physically addictive and, when combined with alcohol, can be deadly, since such a combination relaxes the muscles of the diaphragm to such an extent that the user stops breathing.

ROHYPNOL

Rohypnol is sometimes called the "date rape drug," because when it is mixed with alcohol, it can prevent victims from resisting sexual assault. Sometimes people who are unknowingly given the drug are so incapacitated that they have no memory of the assault.

Even legal drugs, when used improperly, lead to addiction.

Narcotics: Drugs that increase relaxation and relieve pain and anxiety.

Narcotics are drugs that increase relaxation and relieve pain and anxiety. Two of the most powerful narcotics, *morphine* and *heroin*, are derived from the poppy seed pod. Although morphine is used medically to control severe pain, heroin is illegal in the United States. This status has not prevented its widespread use.

Heroin users usually inject the drug directly into their veins with a hypodermic needle. The immediate effect has been described as a "rush" of positive feeling, similar in some respects to a sexual orgasm—and just as difficult to describe. After the rush, a heroin user experiences a sense of well-being and peacefulness that lasts three to five hours. When the effects of the drug wear off, however, the user feels extreme anxiety and a desperate desire to repeat the experience. Moreover, larger amounts of heroin are needed each time to produce the same pleasurable effect. These last two properties are all the ingredients necessary for biological and psychological addiction: The user is constantly either shooting up or attempting to obtain ever-increasing amounts of the drug. Eventually, the life of the addict revolves around heroin.

Because of the powerful positive feelings the drug produces, heroin addiction is particularly difficult to cure. One treatment that has shown some success is the use of methadone. *Methadone* is a synthetic chemical that satisfies a heroin user's physiological cravings for the drug without providing the "high" that accompanies heroin. When heroin users are placed on regular doses of methadone, they may be able to function relatively normally. The use of methadone has one substantial drawback, however: Although it removes the psychological dependence on heroin, it replaces the biological addiction to heroin with a biological addiction to methadone. Researchers are attempting to identify nonaddictive chemical substitutes for heroin as well as substitutes for other addictive drugs that do not replace one addiction with another (Amato et al., 2005; Verdejo, Toribio, & Orozco, 2005; Joe et al., 2007).

HALLUCINOGENS: PSYCHEDELIC DRUGS

What do mushrooms, jimsonweed, and morning glories have in common? Besides being fairly common plants, each can be a source of a powerful hallucinogen, a drug that is capable of producing **hallucinations**, or changes in the perceptual process.

Hallucinogen: A drug that is capable of producing hallucinations, or changes in the perceptual process.

The most common hallucinogen in widespread use today is *marijuana*, whose active ingredient—tetrahydrocannabinol (THC)—is found in a common weed, cannabis. Marijuana is typically smoked in cigarettes or pipes, although it can be cooked and eaten. Just over 31 percent of high school seniors and 12 percent of eighth-graders report having used marijuana in the last year (Johnston, O'Malley, & Bachman, 2007; see Figure 7).

The effects of marijuana vary from person to person, but they typically consist of feelings of euphoria and general well-being. Sensory experiences seem more vivid and intense, and a person's sense of self-importance seems to grow. Memory may be impaired, causing users to feel pleasantly "spaced out." However, the

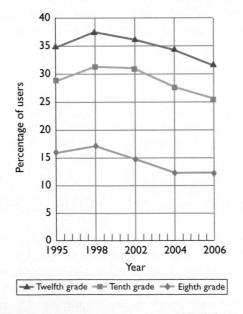

FIGURE 7 Although the level of marijuana use has declined slightly in recent years, overall the absolute number of teenagers who have used the drug in the last year remains relatively high. (Source: Johnston, O'Malley, & Bachman, 2007.)

effects are not universally positive. Individuals who use marijuana when they feel depressed can end up even more depressed, because the drug tends to magnify both good and bad feelings.

There are clear risks associated with long-term, heavy marijuana use. Although marijuana does not seem to produce addiction by itself, some evidence suggests that there are similarities in the way marijuana and drugs such as cocaine and heroin affect the brain. Furthermore, there is some evidence that heavy use at least temporarily decreases the production of the male sex hormone testosterone, potentially affecting sexual activity and sperm count (Block, 2000; Iverson, 2000; Lane et al., 2007).

In addition, marijuana smoked during pregnancy may have lasting effects on children who are exposed prenatally, although the results are inconsistent. Heavy use also affects the ability of the immune system to fight off germs and increases stress on the heart, although it is unclear how strong these effects are. There is one unquestionably negative consequence of smoking marijuana: The smoke damages the lungs much the way cigarette smoke does, producing an increased likelihood of developing cancer and other lung diseases (Cornelius et al., 1995; Julien, 2001).

Despite the possible dangers of marijuana use, there is little scientific evidence for the popular belief that users "graduate" from marijuana to more dangerous drugs. Furthermore, the use of marijuana is routine in certain cultures. For instance, some people in Jamaica habitually drink a marijuana-based tea related to religious practices. In addition, marijuana has several medical uses; it can be used to prevent nausea from chemotherapy, treat some AIDS symptoms, and relieve muscle spasms for people with spinal cord injuries. In a controversial move, several states have made the use of the drug legal if it is prescribed by a physician—although it remains illegal under U.S. federal law (Iverson, 2000; Seamon et al., 2007).

MDMA (ECSTASY) AND LSD

MDMA ("Ecstasy") and *lysergic acid diethylamide (LSD, or "acid")* fall into the category of hallucinogens. Both drugs affect the operation of the neurotransmitter serotonin in the brain, causing an alteration in brain-cell activity and perception (Cloud, 2000; Buchert et al., 2004).

Ecstasy users report a sense of peacefulness and calm. People on the drug report experiencing increased empathy and connection with others, as well as feeling more relaxed, yet energetic. Although the data are not conclusive, some researchers have found declines in memory and performance on intellectual tasks, and such findings suggest that there may be long-term changes in serotonin receptors in the brain (Parrott, 2002; Montgomery et al., 2005; El-Mallakh & Abraham, 2007).

LSD, which is structurally similar to serotonin, produces vivid hallucinations. Perceptions of colors, sounds, and shapes are altered so much that even the most mundane experience—such as looking at the knots in a wooden table—can seem moving and exciting. Time perception is distorted, and objects and people may be viewed in a new way, with some users reporting that LSD increases their understanding of the world. For others, however, the experience brought on by LSD can be terrifying, particularly if users have had emotional difficulties in the past. Furthermore, people occasionally experience flashbacks, in which they hallucinate long after they initially used the drug (Baruss, 2003; Wu, Schlenger, & Galvin, 2006).

This drawing, made by someone taking LSD, suggests the effects of hallucinogens on thinking.

In a society bombarded with commercials for drugs that are guaranteed to do everything from curing the common cold to giving new life to "tired blood," it is no wonder that drug-related problems are a major social issue. Yet many people with drug and alcohol problems deny that they have them, and even close friends and family members may fail to realize when occasional social use of drugs or alcohol has turned into abuse.

BECOMING
AN INFORMED CONSUMER
of Psychology
Identifying Drug and Alcohol Problems

Certain signs, however, indicate when use becomes abuse (Archambault, 1992; National Institute on Drug Abuse, 2000). Among them are the following:

- Always getting high to have a good time.
- Being high more often than not.
- Getting high to get oneself going.
- Going to work or class while high.
- Missing or being unprepared for class or work because you were high.
- Feeling badly later about something you said or did while high.
- Driving a car while high.
- Coming in conflict with the law because of drugs.
- Doing something while high that you wouldn't do otherwise.
- Being high in nonsocial, solitary situations.
- Being unable to stop getting high.
- Feeling a need for a drink or a drug to get through the day.
- Becoming physically unhealthy.
- Failing at school or on the job.
- Thinking about liquor or drugs all the time.
- Avoiding family or friends while using liquor or drugs.

Any combination of these symptoms should be sufficient to alert you to the potential of a serious drug problem. Because drug and alcohol dependence are almost impossible to cure on one's own, people who suspect that they have a problem should seek immediate attention from a psychologist, physician, or counselor.

You can also get help from national hotlines. For alcohol difficulties, call the National Council on Alcoholism at (800) 622-2255. For drug problems, call the National Institute on Drug Abuse at (800) 662-4357. You can also check your telephone book for a local listing of Alcoholics Anonymous or Narcotics Anonymous. Finally, check out the Web sites of the National Institute on Alcohol Abuse and Alcoholism (www.niaaa.nih.gov) and the National Institute on Drug Abuse (www.nida.nih.gov).

RECAP/EVALUATE/RETHINK

RECAP

What are the major classifications of drugs, and what are their effects?

- Drugs can produce an altered state of consciousness. However, they vary in how dangerous they are and in whether they are addictive. (p. 159)

- Stimulants cause arousal in the central nervous system. Two common stimulants are caffeine and nicotine. More dangerous are cocaine and amphetamines, which in large quantities can lead to convulsions and death. (p. 161)

- Depressants decrease arousal in the central nervous system. They can cause intoxication along with feelings of euphoria. The most common depressants are alcohol and barbiturates. (p. 164)

- Alcohol is the most frequently used depressant. Its initial effects of released tension and positive feelings yield to depressive effects as the dose of alcohol increases. Both heredity and environmental stressors can lead to alcoholism. (p. 164)

- Morphine and heroin are narcotics, drugs that produce relaxation and relieve pain and anxiety. Because of their addictive qualities, morphine and heroin are particularly dangerous. (p. 167)

- Hallucinogens are drugs that produce hallucinations or other changes in perception. The most frequently used hallucinogen is marijuana, which has several long-term risks. Two other hallucinogens are LSD and Ecstasy. (p. 168)

- A number of signals indicate when drug use becomes drug abuse. A person who suspects that he or she has a drug problem should get professional help. People are almost never capable of solving drug problems on their own. (p. 169)

EVALUATE

1. Drugs that affect a person's consciousness are referred to as _____.
2. Match the type of drug to an example of that type.
   1. Narcotic—a pain reliever
   2. Amphetamine—a strong stimulant
   3. Hallucinogen—capable of producing hallucinations
   a. LSD
   b. Heroin
   c. Dexedrine or speed
3. Classify each drug listed as a stimulant (S), depressant (D), hallucinogen (H), or narcotic (N).
   1. Nicotine
   2. Cocaine
   3. Alcohol
   4. Morphine
   5. Marijuana
4. The effects of LSD can recur long after the drug has been taken. True or false?
5. _____ is a drug that has been used to treat people with heroin addiction.

RETHINK

1. Why have drug education campaigns largely been ineffective in stemming the use of illegal drugs? Should the use of certain now-illegal drugs be made legal? Would it be more effective to stress reduction of drug use rather than a complete prohibition of drug use?
2. *From the perspective of a substance abuse counselor:* How would you explain why people start using drugs to the family members of someone who was addicted? What types of drug prevention programs would you advocate?

Answers to Evaluate Questions

1. psychoactive; 2. 1-b, 2-c, 3-a; 3. 1-S, 2-S, 3-D, 4-N, 5-H; 4. true; 5. methadone

KEY TERMS

psychoactive drugs p. 159   stimulants p. 161   narcotics p. 167
addictive drugs p. 159   depressants p. 164   hallucinogen p. 168

Psychology on the Web

1. Find a resource on the Web that interprets dreams and another that reports the results of scientific dream research. Compare the nature and content of the two sites in terms of the topics covered, the reliability of information provided, and the promises made about the use of the site and its information. Write a summary of what you found.
2. There is considerable debate about the effectiveness of DARE, the Drug Abuse Resistance Education program. Find a discussion of both sides of the issue on the Web, and summarize the arguments on each side. State your own preliminary conclusions about the DARE program.

Epilogue

Our examination of states of consciousness has ranged widely. It focuses both on natural factors such as sleep, dreaming, and daydreaming and on more intentional modes of altering consciousness, including hypnosis, meditation, and drugs. As we consider why people seek to alter their consciousness, we need to reflect on the uses and abuses of the various consciousness-altering strategies in which people engage.

Return briefly to the case of Martha Yasso, who was nodding off during the day because sleep apnea had made her nights so restless. Consider the following questions in light of your understanding of sleep and dreams:

1. Why do you think that Yasso's frequent sleep interruptions—which were so momentary she was unaware of them—could result in such fatigue?
2. How might Yasso's sleep interruptions affect her progress through the different stages of sleep?
3. What might be some other consequences of Yasso's chronic sleep deficit besides her extreme fatigue?
4. Why might Yasso's sleep disorder have become more dangerous when her son became a toddler?

Learning

Key Concepts for Chapter 6

Declan lies on his back wanting his belly scratched. The eight-year-old black Labrador cross swings his legs in the air for a few minutes before resigning himself to chewing on someone's shoe.

In the office he behaves like any pet dog, but in the field he is like a tornado—focused on finding illegal drugs being smuggled. Declan is a drug-detector dog for the Customs Service and has been busting drug smugglers with his handler, Kevin Hattrill, for eight years.

Airport passengers look on with curiosity as Declan darts around people and their luggage. Within minutes he sniffs out a person of interest, who is taken away and questioned by airport authorities.

Dogs like Declan are trained to detect illegal drugs, such as cannabis, methamphetamine, and cocaine, or explosives. Hattrill said the dogs were dual response-trained when they detected something. "If the odor is around a passenger, they are trained to sit beside them. If it's around cargo, they are trained to scratch. When they detect something, their whole temperament will change.

"The dogs can screen up to 300 people within 10 to 15 minutes at the airport. Nothing else can do that." (McKenzie-McLean, 2006, p. 7)

Looking Ahead

Declan's expertise did not just happen, of course. It is the result of painstaking training procedures—the same ones that are at work in each of our lives, illustrated by our ability to read a book, drive a car, play poker, study for a test, or perform any of the numerous activities that make up our daily routine. Like Declan, each of us must acquire and then refine our skills and abilities through learning.

Learning is a fundamental topic for psychologists and plays a central role in almost every specialty area of psychology. For example, a psychologist studying perception might ask, "How do we learn that people who look small from a distance are far away and not simply tiny?" A developmental psychologist might inquire, "How do babies learn to distinguish their mothers from other people?" A clinical psychologist might wonder, "Why do some people learn to be afraid when they see a spider?" A social

psychologist might ask, "How do we learn to believe that we've fallen in love?"

Each of these questions, although drawn from very different branches of psychology, can be answered only through an understanding of basic learning processes. In each case, a skill or a behavior is acquired, altered, or refined through experience.

Psychologists have approached the study of learning from several angles. Among the most fundamental are studies of the type of learning that is illustrated in responses ranging from a dog salivating when it hears its owner opening a can of dog food to the emotions we feel when our national anthem is played. Other theories consider how learning is a consequence of rewarding circumstances. Finally, several other approaches focus on the cognitive aspects of learning, or the thought processes that underlie learning.

Psychology on the Web

1. B. F. Skinner had an impact on society and on thought that is only hinted at in our discussion of learning. Find additional information on the Web about Skinner's life and influence. See what you can find out about his ideas for an ideal, utopian society based on the principles of conditioning and behaviorism. Write a summary of your findings.

2. Select a topic discussed in this set of modules that is of interest to you—for example, reinforcement versus punishment, teaching complex behaviors by shaping, violence in video games, relational versus analytical learning styles, behavior modification, and so on. Find at least two sources of information on the Web about your topic and summarize the results of your quest. It may be most helpful to find two different approaches to your topic and compare them.

Epilogue

Here we have discussed several kinds of learning, ranging from classical conditioning, which depends on the existence of natural stimulus–response pairings, to operant conditioning, in which reinforcement is used to increase desired behavior. These approaches to learning focus on outward, behavioral learning processes. Cognitive approaches to learning focus on mental processes that enable learning.

We have also noted that learning is affected by culture and individual differences, with individual learning styles potentially affecting the ways in which people learn most effectively. And we saw some ways in which our learning about learning can be put to practical use, through such means as behavior-modification programs designed to decrease negative behaviors and increase positive ones.

Return to the prologue of this set of modules and consider the following questions in relation to Declan, the drug-and-bomb-sniffing airport security dog:

1. Is Declan's learning primarily an example of classical conditioning, operant conditioning, or cognitive learning? Why?
2. Do you think punishment would be an effective teaching strategy for Declan? Why?
3. How might different schedules of reinforcement be used to train Declan? Which schedule would likely have been most effective?
4. How can Declan tell whether to scratch or sit when he smells an illegal drug? How would shaping have been used to train him to make this distinction?
5. Do you think that any Labrador can be trained to do Declan's job, or would it likely require a Labrador with special qualities?

MASTERING the distinction between reinforcement and punishment

The distinction between reinforcement and punishment is not always clear, but the two processes have very different consequences for behavior. Reinforcement increases a behavior, while punishment decreases it. Use this visual guide to better grasp the difference, and then answer the questions below to test your understanding of the concepts.

1 Alex's sloppiness bothers his roommate, Eddy, who says he can't study in a messy room. How might Eddy use reinforcement and punishment to change Alex's untidy behavior?

2 Using *positive reinforcement* to encourage Alex to keep their dorm room clean, Eddy could reward Alex after he cleans up his side of the room by helping him with calculus, something that has value to Alex. Eddy adds the tutoring to increase Alex's neat behavior.

3 Another approach would involve *negative reinforcement*, removing something Alex finds unpleasant as a reward for neat behavior. For example, Eddy could turn off his stereo when Alex is in the room so that he wouldn't have to listen to Eddy's hip-hop music, music Alex dislikes. Eddy *removes* (takes away) the hip-hop music to increase Alex's neat behavior.

EVALUATE

1 In this example, positive reinforcement is represented by _____ and negative reinforcement is represented by _____.
a tutoring in calculus; refusing to lend Eddy's MP3 player to Alex
b playing loud music; turning off the stereo
c tutoring in calculus; turning off the stereo
d playing loud music; refusing to lend Eddy's MP3 player to Alex

2 In this example, the negative punishment is _____ and the positive punishment is _____.
a playing loud music; turning off the stereo
b playing loud music; refusing to lend Eddy's MP3 player to Alex
c refusing to lend Eddy's MP3 player to Alex; playing loud music
d refusing to lend Eddy's MP3 player to Alex; tutoring in calculus

4 Of course, Eddy could discourage Alex's undesirable behavior by using *positive punishment*. In this case, he could play his hip-hop music loudly when Alex leaves the room in a messy condition. That is, Eddy *adds* the loud music to *decrease* Alex's messy behavior.

5 Or Eddy could resort to *negative punishment* and take away something Alex values when his side of the room is messy. Refusing to lend Alex his MP3 player until he cleans up the room is an example of negative punishment. Eddy *removes* (takes away) his MP3 player to *decrease* Alex's messy behavior.

3 Reinforcement leads to an increase in a previous response, while punishment leads to a decrease in the previous response. True or false?

RETHINK

How could the principles of reinforcement and punishment be used to explain how Alex learned to be such a sloppy person in the first place?

Answers to Evaluate questions: 1. c; 2. c; 3. True

CHAPTER 7
Memory

Key Concepts for Chapter 7

Prologue *Who Am I, Where Am I, and How Did I Get Here?*

A former stockbroker named Doug Bruce walked into a police station in Coney Island and told the cops that he didn't know his name. Without a wallet or identification, he'd awoken a few minutes earlier on a subway train, befuddled but unharmed, with a case of what doctors call total retrograde amnesia. He could form sentences without a problem, but remembered nothing of his past and only patchy facts about the world.

He was checked into a nearby hospital, and a call was made to the only number that Bruce, then 35, had with him. It was scrawled on a slip of pink paper found in his knapsack. He was retrieved by a friend and chaperoned home, which turned out to be a gorgeous loft in downtown Manhattan with cockatoos and a dog. He has yet to regain his memory and is still basically a blank slate, learning pop culture, sports, science, arts—everything—one day at a time. (Segal, 2006, p. C01)

Looking Ahead

Doug Bruce's story raises several questions regarding the nature of memory loss: What was the nature of the physical trauma that devastated Doug's memories? Why couldn't he remember anything about his past or his identity, yet he remembered how to speak and write and dress himself? Will his lost memories ever return?

Stories like Doug Bruce's illustrate not only the important role memory plays in our lives, but also its fragility. Memory allows us to retrieve a vast amount of information. We are able to remember the name of a friend we haven't talked with for years and recall the details of a picture that hung in our bedroom as a child. At the same time, though, memory failures are common. We forget where we left the keys to the car and fail to answer an exam question about material we studied only a few hours earlier. Why?

We turn now to the nature of memory, considering the ways in which information is stored and retrieved. We examine the problems of retrieving information from memory, the accuracy of memories, and the reasons information is sometimes forgotten. We also consider the biological foundations of memory and discuss some practical means of increasing memory capacity.

The Foundations of Memory

You are playing a game of Trivial Pursuit, and winning the game comes down to one question: On what body of water is Mumbai located? As you rack your brain for the answer, several fundamental processes relating to memory come into play. You may never, for instance, have been exposed to information regarding Mumbai's location. Or if you have been exposed to it, it may simply not have registered in a meaningful way. In other words, the information might not have been recorded properly in your memory. The initial process of recording information in a form usable to memory, a process called *encoding*, is the first stage in remembering something.

Even if you had been exposed to the information and originally knew the name of the body of water, you may still be unable to recall it during the game because of a failure to retain it. Memory specialists speak of *storage*, the maintenance of material saved in memory. If the material is not stored adequately, it cannot be recalled later.

Memory also depends on one last process—*retrieval*: Material in memory storage has to be located and brought into awareness to be useful. Your failure to recall Mumbai's location, then, may rest on your inability to retrieve information that you learned earlier.

In sum, psychologists consider **memory** to be the process by which we encode, store, and retrieve information (see Figure 1). Each of the three parts of this definition—encoding, storage, and retrieval—represents a different process. You can think of these processes as being analogous to a computer's keyboard (encoding), hard drive (storage), and software that accesses the information for display on the screen (retrieval). Only if all three processes have operated will you experience success and be able to recall the body of water on which Mumbai is located: the Arabian Sea.

Recognizing that memory involves encoding, storage, and retrieval gives us a start in understanding the concept. But how does memory actually function? How do we explain what information is initially encoded, what gets stored, and how it is retrieved?

According to the *three-system approach to memory* that dominated memory research for several decades, there are different memory storage systems or stages through which information must travel if it is to be remembered (Atkinson & Shiffrin, 1968, 1971). Historically, the approach has been extremely influential in the development of our understanding of memory, and—although new theories have augmented it—it still provides a useful framework for understanding how information is recalled.

Key Concepts

What is memory?

Are there different kinds of memory?

What are the biological bases of memory?

Memory: The process by which we encode, store, and retrieve information.

Encoding
(Initial recording
of information)

Storage
(Information saved
for future use)

Retrieval
(Recovery of
stored information)

FIGURE 1 Memory is built on three basic processes—encoding, storage, and retrieval—that are analogous to a computer's keyboard, hard drive, and software to access the information for display on the screen. The analogy is not perfect, however, because human memory is less precise than a computer. How might you modify the analogy to make it more accurate?

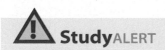

FIGURE 2 In this three-stage model of memory, information initially recorded by the person's sensory system enters sensory memory, which momentarily holds the information. The information then moves to short-term memory, which stores it for 15 to 25 seconds. Finally, the information can move into long-term memory, which is relatively permanent. Whether the information moves from short-term to long-term memory depends on the kind and amount of rehearsal of the material that is carried out. (Source: Atkinson & Shifrin, 1968.)

Sensory memory: The initial, momentary storage of information, lasting only an instant.

Short-term memory: Memory that holds information for 15 to 25 seconds.

Long-term memory: Memory that stores information on a relatively permanent basis, although it may be difficult to retrieve.

⚠️ **Study**ALERT

Although the three types of memory are discussed as separate memory stores, these are not mini-warehouses located in specific areas of the brain. Instead, they represent three different types of memory systems with different characteristics.

The three-system memory theory proposes the existence of the three separate memory stores shown in Figure 2. **Sensory memory** refers to the initial, momentary storage of information that lasts only an instant. Here an exact replica of the stimulus recorded by a person's sensory system is stored very briefly. In a second stage, **short-term memory** holds information for 15 to 25 seconds and stores it according to its meaning rather than as mere sensory stimulation. The third type of storage system is **long-term memory**. Information is stored in long-term memory on a relatively permanent basis, although it may be difficult to retrieve.

Sensory Memory

A momentary flash of lightning, the sound of a twig snapping, and the sting of a pinprick all represent stimulation of exceedingly brief duration, but they may nonetheless provide important information that can require a response. Such stimuli are initially—and fleetingly—stored in sensory memory, the first repository of the information the world presents to us. Actually, there are several types of sensory memories, each related to a different source of sensory information. For instance, *iconic memory* reflects information from the visual system. *Echoic memory* stores auditory information coming from the ears. In addition, there are corresponding memories for each of the other senses.

Sensory memory can store information for only a very short time. If information does not pass into short-term memory, it is lost for good. For instance, iconic memory seems to last less than a second and echoic memory typically fades within two or three seconds. However, despite the brief duration of sensory memory, its precision is high: Sensory memory can store an almost exact replica of each stimulus to which it is exposed (Darwin, Turvey, & Crowder, 1972; Long & Beaton, 1982; Sams et al., 1993; Deouell et al., 2006).

Psychologist George Sperling (1960) demonstrated the existence of sensory memory in a series of clever and now-classic studies. He briefly exposed people to a series of 12 letters arranged in the following pattern:

F   T   Y   C
K   D   N   L
Y   W   B   M

When exposed to this pattern of letters for just $1/20$th of a second, most people could recall only four or five of the letters accurately. Although they knew that they had seen more, the memory of those letters had faded by the time they reported the first few letters. It was possible, then, that the information had initially been accurately stored in sensory memory, but during the time it took to verbalize the first four or five letters the memory of the other letters faded.

To test that possibility, Sperling conducted an experiment in which a high, medium, or low tone sounded just after a person had been exposed to the full pattern of letters. People were told to report the letters in the highest line if a high tone was sounded, the middle line if the medium tone occurred, or the lowest line at the sound of the low tone. Because the tone occurred after the exposure, people had to rely on their memories to report the correct row.

A momentary flash of lightning leaves a sensory visual memory, a fleeting but exact replica of the stimulus that fades away.

The results of the study clearly showed that people had been storing the complete pattern in memory. They accurately recalled the letters in the line that had been indicated by the tone regardless of whether it was the top, middle, or bottom line. Obviously, *all* the lines they had seen had been stored in sensory memory. Despite its rapid loss, then, the information in sensory memory was an accurate representation of what people had seen.

By gradually lengthening the time between the presentation of the visual pattern and the tone, Sperling was able to determine with some accuracy the length of time that information was stored in sensory memory. The ability to recall a particular row of the pattern when a tone was sounded declined progressively as the period between the visual exposure and the tone increased. This decline continued until the period reached about one second in duration, at which point the row could not be recalled accurately at all. Sperling concluded that the entire visual image was stored in sensory memory for less than a second.

In sum, sensory memory operates as a kind of snapshot that stores information—which may be of a visual, auditory, or other sensory nature—for a brief moment in time. But it is as if each snapshot, immediately after being taken, is destroyed and replaced with a new one. Unless the information in the snapshot is transferred to some other type of memory, it is lost.

Short-Term Memory

Because the information that is stored briefly in sensory memory consists of representations of raw sensory stimuli, it is not meaningful to us. If we are to make sense of it and possibly retain it, the information must be transferred to the next stage of memory: short-term memory. Short-term memory is the memory store in which information first has meaning, although the maximum length of retention there is relatively short (Hamilton & Martin, 2007).

The specific process by which sensory memories are transformed into short-term memories is not clear. Some theorists suggest that the information is first translated into graphical representations or images, and others hypothesize that the transfer occurs when the sensory stimuli are changed to words (Baddeley & Wilson, 1985). What is clear, however, is that unlike sensory memory, which holds a relatively full and detailed—if short-lived—representation of the world, short-term memory has incomplete representational capabilities.

In fact, the specific amount of information that can be held in short-term memory has been identified as seven items, or "chunks," of information, with variations up to plus or minus two chunks. A **chunk** is a meaningful grouping of stimuli that can be stored as a unit in short-term memory. According to George Miller (1956), a chunk can be individual letters or numbers, permitting us to hold a seven-digit phone number (like 226-4610) in short-term memory.

Chunk: A meaningful grouping of stimuli that can be stored as a unit in short-term memory.

But a chunk also may consist of larger categories, such as words or other meaningful units. For example, consider the following list of 21 letters:

P B S F O X C N N A B C C B S M T V N B C

FIGURE 3 Examine the chessboard containing the chess pieces for about five seconds, and then, after covering up the board, try to draw the position of the pieces on the blank chessboard. (You could also use a chessboard of your own and place the pieces in the same positions.) Unless you are an experienced chess player, you are likely to have great difficulty carrying out such a task. Yet chess masters—those who win tournaments—do this quite well (deGroot, 1966). They are able to reproduce correctly 90 percent of the pieces on the board. In comparison, inexperienced chess players are typically able to reproduce only 40 percent of the board properly. The chess masters do not have superior memories in other respects; they generally test normally on other measures of memory. What they can do better than others is see the board in terms of chunks or meaningful units and reproduce the position of the chess pieces by using those units.

Because the list exceeds seven chunks, it is difficult to recall the letters after one exposure. But suppose they were presented as follows:

PBS FOX CNN ABC CBS MTV NBC

In this case, even though there are still 21 letters, you'd be able to store them in short-term memory, since they represent only seven chunks.

Chunks can vary in size from single letters or numbers to categories that are far more complicated. The specific nature of what constitutes a chunk varies according to one's past experience. You can see this for yourself by trying an experiment that was first carried out as a comparison between expert and inexperienced chess players and is illustrated in Figure 3 (deGroot, 1978; Ross, 2006; Oberauer, 2007).

Although it is possible to remember seven or so relatively complicated sets of information entering short-term memory, the information cannot be held there very long. Just how brief is short-term memory? If you've ever looked up a telephone number in a phone directory, repeated the number to yourself, put away the directory, and then forgotten the number after you've tapped the first three numbers into your phone, you know that information does not remain in short-term memory very long. Most psychologists believe that information in short-term memory is lost after 15 to 25 seconds—unless it is transferred to long-term memory.

REHEARSAL

The transfer of material from short- to long-term memory proceeds largely on the basis of **rehearsal**, the repetition of information that has entered short-term memory. Rehearsal accomplishes two things. First, as long as the information is repeated, it is maintained in short-term memory. More important, however, rehearsal allows us to transfer the information into long-term memory (Kvavilashvili & Fisher, 2007).

Whether the transfer is made from short- to long-term memory seems to depend largely on the kind of rehearsal that is carried out. If the information is simply repeated over and over again—as we might do with a telephone number while we rush from the phone book to the phone—it is kept current in short-term memory, but it will not necessarily be placed in long-term memory. Instead, as soon as we stop punching in the phone numbers, the number is likely to be replaced by other information and will be completely forgotten.

In contrast, if the information in short-term memory is rehearsed using a process called elaborative rehearsal, it is much more likely to be transferred into long-term memory. *Elaborative rehearsal* occurs when the information is considered and organized in some fashion. The organization might include expanding the information to make it fit into a logical framework, linking it to another memory, turning it into an image, or transforming it in some other way. For example, a list of vegetables to be purchased at a store could be woven together in memory as items being used to prepare an elaborate salad, could be linked to the items bought on an earlier shopping trip, or could be thought of in terms of the image of a farm with rows of each item.

By using organizational strategies such as these—called *mnemonics*—we can vastly improve our retention of information. Mnemonics (pronounced "neh MON ix") are formal techniques for organizing information in a way that makes it more likely to be remembered. For instance, when a beginning musician learns that the spaces on the music staff spell the word *FACE*, or when we learn the rhyme "Thirty days hath September, April, June, and November . . .," we are using mnemonics (Bellezza, 2000; Carney & Levin, 2003; Sprenger, 2007).

WORKING MEMORY

Rather than seeing short-term memory as an independent way station into which memories arrive, either to fade or to be passed on to long-term memory, many contemporary memory theorists conceive of short-term memory as far more active. In this view, short-term memory is like an information processing system that manages both new material gathered from sensory memory and older material that has been pulled from long-term storage. In this increasingly influential view, short-term memory is referred to as **working memory** and defined as a set of temporary memory stores that actively manipulate and rehearse information (Bayliss et al., 2005a, 2005b; Unsworth & Engle, 2005).

Working memory is thought to contain a *central executive* processor that is involved in reasoning and decision making. The central executive coordinates three distinct storage-and-rehearsal systems: the *visual store*, the *verbal store*, and the *episodic buffer*. The visual store specializes in visual and spatial information, whereas the verbal store holds and manipulates material relating to speech, words, and numbers. The episodic buffer contains information that represents episodes or events (Baddeley, 2001; Martin, 2005; Bröder & Schiffer, 2006; see Figure 4).

Working memory permits us to keep information in an active state briefly so that we can do something with the information. For instance, we use working memory

Rehearsal: The repetition of information that has entered short-term memory.

Working memory: A set of active, temporary memory stores that actively manipulate and rehearse information.

FIGURE 4 Working memory is an active "workspace" in which information is retrieved and manipulated, and in which information is held through rehearsal (Gathercole & Baddeley, 1993). It consists of a "central executive" that coordinates the visual store (which concentrates on visual and spatial information), the verbal store (which concentrates on speech, words, and numbers), and the episodic buffer (which represents episodes or occurrences that are encountered). (Source: Adapted from Baddeley, Chincotta, & Adlam, 2001.)

when we're doing a multistep arithmetic problem in our heads, storing the result of one calculation while getting ready to move to the next stage. (I make use of my working memory when I figure a 20 percent tip in a restaurant by first calculating 10 percent of the total bill and then doubling it.)

Although working memory aids in the recall of information, it uses a significant amount of cognitive resources during its operation. In turn, this can make us less aware of our surroundings—something that has implications for the debate about the use of cell telephones in automobiles. If a phone conversation requires thinking, it will burden working memory and leave drivers less aware of their surroundings, an obviously dangerous state of affairs (Sifrit, 2006; Strayer & Drews, 2007).

Furthermore, stress can reduce the effectiveness of working memory by reducing its capacity. In fact, one study found that students with the highest working memory capacity and greatest math ability were the ones who were most vulnerable to pressure to perform well. Those who should have performed best, then, were the ones most apt to choke on the test because their working memory capacities were reduced by the stress (Beilock & Carr, 2005; Carey, 2005).

Long-Term Memory

Material that makes its way from short-term memory to long-term memory enters a storehouse of almost unlimited capacity. Like a new file we save on a hard drive, the information in long-term memory is filed and coded so that we can retrieve it when we need it.

Evidence of the existence of long-term memory, as distinct from short-term memory, comes from a number of sources. For example, people with certain kinds of brain damage have no lasting recall of new information received after the damage occurred, although people and events stored in memory before the injury remain intact (Milner, 1966). Because information that was encoded and stored before the injury can be recalled and because short-term memory after the injury appears to be operational—new material can be recalled for a very brief period—we can infer that there are two distinct types of memory: one for short-term and one for long-term storage.

Results from laboratory experiments are also consistent with the notion of separate short-term and long-term memory. For example, in one set of studies people were asked to recall a relatively small amount of information (such as a set of three letters). Then, to prevent practice of the initial information, participants were required to recite some extraneous material aloud, such as counting backward by threes (Brown, 1958; Peterson & Peterson, 1959). By varying the amount of time between the presentation of the initial material and the need for its recall, investigators found that recall was quite good when the interval was very short but declined rapidly thereafter. After 15 seconds had gone by, recall hovered at around 10 percent of the material initially presented.

Apparently, the distraction of counting backward prevented almost all the initial material from reaching long-term memory. Initial recall was good because it was coming from short-term memory, but those memories were lost at a rapid rate. Eventually, all that could be recalled was the small amount of material that had made its way into long-term storage despite the distraction of counting backward.

The ability to remember specific skills and the order in which they are used is known as procedural memory. If driving a car involves procedural memory, is it safe to use a cell phone while driving?

The distinction between short- and long-term memory is also supported by the *serial position effect*, in which the ability to recall information in a list depends on where in the list an item appears. For instance, often a *primacy effect* occurs, in which items presented early in a list are remembered better. There is also a *recency effect*, in which items presented late in a list are remembered best.

LONG-TERM MEMORY MODULES

Just as short-term memory is often conceptualized in terms of working memory, many contemporary researchers now regard long-term memory as having several different components, or *memory modules*. Each of these modules represents a separate memory system in the brain.

One major distinction within long-term memory is that between declarative memory and procedural memory. **Declarative memory** is memory for factual information: names, faces, dates, and facts, such as "a bike has two wheels." In contrast, **procedural memory** (or *nondeclarative memory*) refers to memory for skills and habits, such as how to ride a bike or hit a baseball. Information about *things* is stored in declarative memory; information about *how to do things* is stored in procedural memory (Schacter, Wagner, & Buckner, 2000; Eichenbaum, 2004; Feldhusen, 2006).

Declarative memory can be subdivided into semantic memory and episodic memory. **Semantic memory** is memory for general knowledge and facts about the world, as well as memory for the rules of logic that are used to deduce other facts. Because of semantic memory, we remember that the ZIP code for Beverly Hills is 90210, that Mumbai is on the Arabian Sea, and that *memoree* is the incorrect spelling of *memory*. Thus, semantic memory is somewhat like a mental almanac of facts (Nyberg & Tulving, 1996; Tulving, 2002).

In contrast, **episodic memory** is memory for events that occur in a particular time, place, or context. For example, recall of learning to ride a bike, our first kiss, or arranging a surprise 21st birthday party for our brother is based on episodic memories. Episodic memories relate to particular contexts. For example, remembering *when* and *how* we learned that $2 \times 2 = 4$ would be an episodic memory; the fact itself (that $2 \times 2 = 4$) is a semantic memory. (Also see Figure 5.)

Episodic memories can be surprisingly detailed. Consider, for instance, how you'd respond if you were asked to identify what you were doing on a specific day two years

Declarative memory: Memory for factual information: names, faces, dates, and the like.

Procedural memory: Memory for skills and habits, such as riding a bike or hitting a baseball, sometimes referred to as *nondeclarative memory*.

Semantic memory: Memory for general knowledge and facts about the world, as well as memory for the rules of logic that are used to deduce other facts.

Episodic memory: Memory for events that occur in a particular time, place, or context.

FIGURE 5 Long-term memory can be subdivided into several different types. What type of long-term memory is involved in your recollection of the moment you first arrived on your campus at the start of college? What type of long-term memory is involved in remembering the lyrics to a song, compared with the tune of a song?

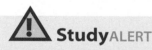 **Study**ALERT

Use Figure 5 to help clarify the distinctions between the different types of long-term memory.

ago. Impossible? You may think otherwise as you read the following exchange between a researcher and a participant in a study who was asked, in a memory experiment, what he was doing "on Monday afternoon in the third week of September two years ago."

PARTICIPANT: Come on. How should I know?

EXPERIMENTER: Just try it anyhow.

PARTICIPANT: OK. Let's see: Two years ago . . . I would be in high school in Pittsburgh . . . That would be my senior year. Third week in September—that's just after summer—that would be the fall term . . . Let me see. I think I had chemistry lab on Mondays. I don't know. I was probably in chemistry lab. Wait a minute—that would be the second week of school. I remember he started off with the atomic table—a big fancy chart. I thought he was crazy trying to make us memorize that thing. You know, I think I can remember sitting . . . (Lindsay & Norman, 1977).

Episodic memory, then, can provide information about events that happened long in the past (Reynolds & Takooshian, 1988). But semantic memory is no less impressive, permitting us to dredge up tens of thousands of facts ranging from the date of our birthday to the knowledge that $1 is less than $5.

SEMANTIC NETWORKS

Try to recall, for a moment, as many things as you can think of that are the color red.

Now pull from your memory the names of as many fruits as you can recall.

Did the same item appear on both tasks? For many people, an apple comes to mind in both cases, since it fits equally well in each category. And the fact that you might have thought of an apple on the first task makes it even more likely that you'll think of it when doing the second task.

It's actually quite amazing that we're able to retrieve specific material from the vast store of information in our long-term memories. According to some memory researchers, one key organizational tool that allows us to recall detailed information from long-term memory is the associations that we build between different pieces of information. In this view, knowledge is stored in **semantic networks**, mental representations of clusters of interconnected information (Collins & Quillian, 1969; Collins & Loftus, 1975; Cummings et al., 2006).

Semantic networks: Mental representations of clusters of interconnected information.

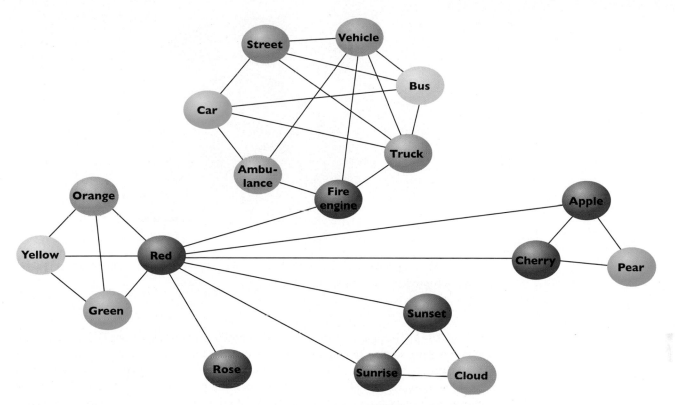

FIGURE 6 Semantic networks in memory consist of relationships between pieces of information, such as those relating to the concept of a fire engine. The lines suggest the connections that indicate how the information is organized within memory. The closer together two concepts are, the greater the strength of the association. (Source: Collins & Loftus, 1975.)

Consider, for example, Figure 6, which shows some of the relationships in memory relating to fire engines, the color red, and a variety of other semantic concepts. Thinking about a particular concept leads to recall of related concepts. For example, seeing a fire engine may activate our recollections of other kinds of emergency vehicles, such as an ambulance, which in turn may activate recall of the related concept of a vehicle. And thinking of a vehicle may lead us to think about a bus that we've seen in the past. Activating one memory triggers the activation of related memories in a process known as *spreading activation*.

THE NEUROSCIENCE OF MEMORY

Can we pinpoint a location in the brain where long-term memories reside? Is there a single site that corresponds to a particular memory, or is memory distributed in different regions across the brain? Do memories leave an actual physical trace that scientists can view?

The search for the *engram*, the term for the physical memory trace that corresponds to a memory, has proved to be a major puzzle to psychologists and other neuroscientists interested in memory. Using advanced brain scanning procedures in their efforts to determine the neuroscientific basis of memory formation, investigators have learned that certain areas and structures of the brain specialize in different types of memory-related

"The matters about which I'm being questioned, Your Honor, are all things I should have included in my long-term memory but which I mistakenly inserted in my short-term memory."

Amygdala

Hippocampus

FIGURE 7 The hippocampus and amygdala, parts of the brain's limbic system, play a central role in the consolidation of memories. (Source: Van De Graff, 2000.)

activities. The *hippocampus*, a part of the brain's limbic system (see Figure 7), plays a central role in the consolidation of memories. Located within the brain's *medial temporal lobes*, just behind the eyes, the hippocampus aids in the initial encoding of information, acting as a kind of neurological e-mail system. That information is subsequently passed along to the cerebral cortex of the brain, where it is actually stored (Wilson, 2002; Govindarajan, Kelleher, & Tonegawa, 2006; Peters et al., 2007).

The significance of the hippocampus is exemplified by studies of individuals who have particularly good, yet specialized, types of memories. For instance, taxi drivers in London, England, must have accurate, complete recall of the location of the maze of streets and alleys within a six-mile radius of the center of the city. It takes years of study to memorize the material. MRI brain scans of taxi drivers show that, relative to non–taxi drivers with fewer navigational skills, the back of the hippocampus is larger while the front is smaller. The findings are consistent with the idea that particular areas of the hippocampus are involved in the consolidation of spatial memories (see Figure 8; Maguire et al., 2000; McGuire, Woollett, & Spiers, 2006; Spiers & Maguire, 2007).

The *amygdala*, another part of the limbic system, also plays an important role in memory. The amygdala is especially involved with memories involving emotion (Hamann, 2001; Buchanan & Adolphs, 2004). For example, if you are frightened by a large Doberman, you're likely to remember the event vividly—an outcome related to the functioning of the amygdala. Encountering the Doberman, or any large dog, in the future is likely to reactivate the amygdala and bring back the unpleasant memory.

Memory at the Level of Neurons. Although it is clear that the hippocampus and amygdala play a central role in memory formation, how is the transformation of information into a memory reflected at the level of neurons?

One answer is *long-term potentiation*, which shows that certain neural pathways become easily excited while a new response is being learned. At the same time, the number of synapses between neurons increase as the dendrites branch out to receive messages. These changes reflect a process called *consolidation*, in which memories become fixed and stable in long-term memory. Long-term memories take some time to

Neuroscience in Your Life

FIGURE 8 In a novel experiment, researchers used MRI scans to examine the size of the hippo-campus (an area of the brain related to memory) in London taxi drivers who need to have accu-rate recall of the maze of streets and alleys in the city. The MRI scans illustrated that the posterior (back) part of the hippocampus (A) was larger in taxi drivers whose spatial and navigational memories were highly developed as compared to non-taxi drivers (represented in yellow). In contrast, the size of the anterior (front) hippocampus (B) in taxi drivers was smaller than that of non-taxi drivers (seen in red). (Source: Maguire et al., 2000, Figure 1b, c.)

(A)

(B)

stabilize; this explains why events and other stimuli are not suddenly fixed in memory. Instead, consolidation may continue for days and even years (McGaugh, 2003; Meeter & Murre, 2004; Kawashima et al., 2006).

Because a stimulus may contain different sensory aspects, visual, auditory, and other areas of the brain may be simultaneously processing information about that stimulus. Information storage appears to be linked to the sites where this processing occurs, and is therefore located in the particular areas that initially processed the infor-mation in terms of its visual, auditory, and other sensory stimuli. For this reason, memory traces are distributed throughout the brain. For example, when you recall a beautiful beach sunset, your recollection draws on memory stores located in visual areas of the brain (the view of the sunset), auditory areas (the sounds of the ocean), and tactile areas (the feel of the wind) (Desimone, 1992; Brewer et al., 1998; Squire et al., 2004).

In short, the physical stuff of memory—the engram—is produced by a complex of biochemical and neural processes. Although memory researchers have made consider-able strides in understanding the neuroscience behind memory, more remains to be learned—and remembered. (For more on the biological basis of memory, see the *Applying Psychology in the 21st Century* box.)

Dulling the Edges of Painful Memories

Marjorie Lindholm, 24, had just returned from getting her mom's car fixed in Littleton, Colorado, when she heard the news: Twenty-two students had died, maybe more, shot by another student at a college in Virginia. Immediately, she was swept back to Columbine High School on April 20, 1999, reliving the moments, minute by breathless minute, when two students went on a shooting rampage, killing 12 of her classmates and a teacher before committing suicide.

"I started crying, then shaking," she said. "I remembered everything I saw at Columbine. I got physically ill. There is no way I'm going to forget that day." (Stepp, 2007, p. HE01)

Marjorie Lindholm, like the many other people who are plagued by disturbing memories of traumatic events, would probably have welcomed the possibility of taking a pill to make those disturbing memories disappear. And as improbable as it may seem, that possibility may soon be a reality.

Researcher Roger Pitman has been taking advantage of the way in which the brain stores and retrieves long-term memories to develop a drug treatment that can temporarily block intense memories from forming—and it might even help to selectively reduce the intensity of long-held traumatic memories. When a new memory

Could certain drugs reduce the sting of painful memories?

is stored, it takes some time for memory consolidation, the neural changes in the brain that hold the memory in long-term storage, to occur. Certain conditions, such as being in a highly emotional state at the time, can intensify the memories that are being consolidated. This is one reason why traumatic memories can sometimes be so powerful and even intrusive for many years after the event.

But if certain conditions can intensify memories that are being stored, can other conditions weaken them? Pitman's research shows that they can. For example, the blood-pressure drug propranolol was known to have an effect on areas of the brain that are responsible for memory storage. Pitman gave a small group of hospital patients who had just suffered an accident or a rape either a course of treatment with propranolol or a placebo. Three months later, when the patients were exposed to reminders of their

traumatic experiences, those who had taken the propranolol had a less stressful reaction than those who had taken the placebo (Jha, 2006; Brunet et al., 2007).

But reducing the intensity of a traumatic memory as it is being consolidated is quite different from helping people to overcome intense memories of traumatic events that happened long ago. However, an intriguing aspect of the way in which memory works actually makes the same treatment possible even for memories that are decades old. Reawakening the memory by talking about the event in depth is akin to taking it out of deep storage and un-consolidating it; afterward, the memory needs to be reconsolidated and re-stored, in much the same way as a new memory would be (Debiec, Doyère, & Nader, 2006; Duvarci, ben Mamou, & Nader, 2006).

Pitman's goal is to use propranolol to interfere with the reconsolidation of traumatic memories that have been reawakened in this way. The idea is not to block the memory entirely, but to reduce its intensity upon reconsolidation so that the victim will remember what happened but not be tortured by the memory. If that happens, victims may be treated more successfully (Pitman & Delahanty, 2005).

- Why would researchers want only to reduce the intensity of a traumatic memory rather than erase it altogether?
- What might be some of the practical or ethical issues involved with erasing unwanted memories?

RECAP/EVALUATE/RETHINK

RECAP

What is memory?

- Memory is the process by which we encode, store, and retrieve information. (p. 213)

Are there different kinds of memory?

- Sensory memory, corresponding to each of the sensory systems, is the first place where information is saved. Sensory memories are very brief, but they are precise, storing a nearly exact replica of a stimulus. (p. 214)

- Roughly seven (plus or minus two) chunks of information can be transferred and held in short-term memory. Information in short-term memory is held from 15 to 25 seconds and, if not transferred to long-term memory, is lost. (p. 215)

- Some theorists view short-term memory as a working memory, in which information is retrieved and manipulated, and held through rehearsal. In this view, it is a central executive processor involved in reasoning and decision making; it coordinates a visual store, a verbal store, and an episodic buffer. (p. 217)

- Memories are transferred into long-term storage through rehearsal. If memories are transferred into long-term memory, they become relatively permanent. (p. 218)

- Long-term memory can be viewed in terms of memory modules, each of which is related to separate memory systems in the brain. For instance, we can distinguish between declarative memory and procedural memory. Declarative memory is further divided into episodic memory and semantic memory. (p. 219)

- Semantic networks suggest that knowledge is stored in long-term memory as mental representations of clusters of interconnected information. (p. 220)

What are the biological bases of memory?

- The hippocampus and amygdala are especially important in the establishment of memory. (p. 222)

- Memories are distributed across the brain, relating to the different sensory information-processing systems involved during the initial exposure to a stimulus. (p. 223)

EVALUATE

1. Match the type of memory with its definition:
   1. Long-term memory
   2. Short-term memory
   3. Sensory memory
   a. Holds information 15 to 25 seconds.
   b. Stores information on a relatively permanent basis.
   c. Direct representation of a stimulus.
2. A(n) _____ is a meaningful group of stimuli that can be stored together in short-term memory.
3. There appear to be two types of declarative memory: _____ memory, for knowledge and facts, and _____ memory, for personal experiences.
4. Some memory researchers believe that long-term memory is stored as associations between pieces of information in _____ networks.

RETHINK

1. It is a truism that "you never forget how to ride a bicycle." Why might this be so? In what type of memory is information about bicycle riding stored?
2. *From a marketing specialist's perspective*: How might ways of enhancing memory be used by advertisers and others to promote their products? What ethical principles are involved? Can you think of a way to protect yourself from unethical advertising?

Answers to Evaluate Questions

1. 1-b, 2-a, 3-c; 2. chunk; 3. semantic, episodic; 4. semantic

KEY TERMS

memory p. 213

sensory memory p. 214

short-term memory p. 214

long-term memory p. 214

chunk p. 215

rehearsal p. 217

working memory p. 217

declarative memory p. 219

procedural memory p. 219

semantic memory p. 219

episodic memory p. 219

semantic networks p. 220

Recalling Long-Term Memories

An hour after his job interview, Ricardo was sitting in a coffee shop, telling his friend Laura how well it had gone, when the woman who had interviewed him walked in. "Well, hello, Ricardo. How are you doing?" Trying to make a good impression, Ricardo began to make introductions, but suddenly realized he could not remember the name of the interviewer. Stammering, he desperately searched his memory, but to no avail. "I *know* her name," he thought to himself, "but here I am, looking like a fool. I can kiss this job good-bye."

Have you ever tried to remember someone's name, convinced that you knew it but unable to recall it no matter how hard you tried? This common occurrence—known as the **tip-of-the-tongue phenomenon**—exemplifies how difficult it can be to retrieve information stored in long-term memory (Schwartz, 2001, 2002; Cleary, 2006).

Retrieval Cues

Perhaps recall of names and other memories is not perfect because there is so much information stored in long-term memory. Because the material that makes its way to long-term memory is relatively permanent, the capacity of long-term memory is vast. For instance, if you are like the average college student, your vocabulary includes some 50,000 words, you know hundreds of mathematical "facts," and you are able to conjure up images—such as the way your childhood home looked—with no trouble at all. In fact, simply cataloging all your memories would probably take years of work.

How do we sort through this vast array of material and retrieve specific information at the appropriate time? One way is through retrieval cues. A *retrieval cue* is a stimulus that allows us to recall more easily information that is in long-term memory. It may be a word, an emotion, or a sound; whatever the specific cue, a memory will suddenly come to mind when the retrieval cue is present. For example, the smell of roasting turkey may evoke memories of Thanksgiving or family gatherings.

Retrieval cues guide people through the information stored in long-term memory in much the same way that a search engine such as Google guides people through the World Wide Web. They are particularly important when we are making an effort to *recall* information, as opposed to being asked to *recognize* material stored in memory. In **recall**, a specific piece of information must be retrieved—such as that needed to answer a fill-in-the-blank question or to write an essay on a test. In contrast, **recognition** occurs when people are presented with a stimulus and asked whether they have been exposed to it previously, or are asked to identify it from a list of alternatives.

As you might guess, recognition is generally a much easier task than recall (see Figures 1 and 2). Recall is more difficult because it consists of a series of processes: a search through memory, retrieval of potentially relevant information, and then

Key Concept

What causes difficulties and failures in remembering?

Tip-of-the-tongue phenomenon: The inability to recall information that one realizes one knows—a result of the difficulty of retrieving information from long-term memory.

Recall: Memory task in which specific information must be retrieved.
Recognition: Memory task in which individuals are presented with a stimulus and asked whether they have been exposed to it in the past or to identify it from a list of alternatives.

FIGURE 1 Try to recall the names of these characters. Because this is a recall task, it is relatively difficult.

FIGURE 2 Naming the characters in Figure 1 (a recall task) is more difficult than solving the recognition problem posed in this list.

Answer this recognition question:	
Which of the following are the names of the seven dwarfs in the Disney movie _Snow White and the Seven Dwarfs?_	
Goofy	Bashful
Sleepy	Meanie
Smarty	Doc
Scaredy	Happy
Dopey	Angry
Grumpy	Sneezy
Wheezy	Crazy

(The correct answers are Bashful, Doc, Dopey, Grumpy, Happy, Sleepy, and Sneezy.)

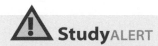 **Study**ALERT

Remember the distinction between recall (in which specific information must be retrieved) and recognition (in which information is presented and must be identified or distinguished from other material).

Levels-of-processing theory: The theory of memory that emphasizes the degree to which new material is mentally analyzed.

a decision regarding whether the information you have found is accurate. If the information appears to be correct, the search is over, but if it does not, the search must continue. In contrast, recognition is simpler because it involves fewer steps (Miserando, 1991; Leigh, Zinkhan, & Swaminathan, 2006).

Levels of Processing

One determinant of how well memories are recalled is the way in which material is first perceived, processed, and understood. The **levels-of-processing theory** emphasizes the degree to which new material is mentally analyzed. It suggests that the amount of information processing that occurs when material is initially encountered is central in determining how much of the information is ultimately remembered. According to this approach, the depth of information processing during exposure to material—meaning the degree to which it is analyzed and considered—is critical; the greater the intensity of its initial processing is, the more likely we are to remember it (Craik, 1990; Troyer et al., 2006).

Because we do not pay close attention to much of the information to which we are exposed, very little mental processing typically takes place, and we forget new material almost immediately. However, information to which we pay greater attention is processed more thoroughly. Therefore, it enters memory at a deeper level—and is less apt to be forgotten than is information processed at shallower levels.

The theory goes on to suggest that there are considerable differences in the ways in which information is processed at various levels of memory. At shallow levels, information is processed merely in terms of its physical and sensory aspects. For example, we may pay attention only to the shapes that make up the letters in the word _dog_. At an intermediate level of processing, the shapes are translated into meaningful units—in this case, letters of the alphabet. Those letters are considered in the context of words, and specific phonetic sounds may be attached to the letters.

At the deepest level of processing, information is analyzed in terms of its meaning. We may see it in a wider context and draw associations between the meaning of the information and broader networks of knowledge. For instance, we may think of dogs not merely as animals with four legs and a tail, but also in terms of their relationship to cats and other mammals. We may form an image of our own dog, thereby relating the concept to our own lives. According to the levels-of-processing approach, the deeper the initial level of processing of specific information is, the longer the information will be retained.

There are considerable practical implications to the notion that recall depends on the degree to which information is initially processed. For example, the depth of information processing is critical when learning and studying course material. Rote memorization of a list of key terms for a test is unlikely to produce long-term recollection of information, because processing occurs at a shallow level. In contrast, thinking about the meaning of the terms and reflecting on how they relate to information that one currently knows results in far more effective long-term retention (Conway, 2002; Wenzel, Zetocha, & Ferraro, 2007).

Explicit and Implicit Memory

If you've ever had surgery, you probably hoped that the surgeons were focused completely on the surgery and gave you their undivided attention while slicing into your body. The reality in most operating rooms is quite different, though. Surgeons may be chatting with nurses about a new restaurant as soon as they sew you up.

If you are like most patients, you are left with no recollection of the conversation that occurred while you were under anesthesia. However, it is very possible that although you had no conscious memories of the discussions on the merits of the restaurant, on some level you probably did recall at least some information. In fact, careful studies have found that people who are anesthetized during surgery can sometimes recall snippets of conversations they heard during surgery—even though they have no conscious recollection of the information (Kihlstrom et al., 1990; Sebel, Bonke, & Winogard, 1993).

The discovery that people have memories about which they are unaware has been an important one. It has led to speculation that two forms of memory, explicit and implicit, may exist side by side. **Explicit memory** refers to intentional or conscious recollection of information. When we try to remember a name or date we have encountered or learned about previously, we are searching our explicit memory.

In contrast, **implicit memory** refers to memories of which people are not consciously aware, but which can affect subsequent performance and behavior. Skills that operate automatically and without thinking, such as jumping out of the path of an automobile coming toward us as we walk down the side of a road, are stored in implicit memory. Similarly, a feeling of vague dislike for an acquaintance, without knowing why we have that feeling, may be a reflection of implicit memories. Perhaps the person reminds us of someone else in our past that we didn't like, even though we are not aware of the memory of that other individual (Tulving, 2000; Uttl, Graf & Consentino, 2003; Coates, Butler, & Berry, 2006).

Implicit memory is closely related to the prejudice and discrimination people exhibit toward members of minority groups. As we first discussed in the module on conducting psychological research, even though people may say and even believe they harbor no prejudice, assessment of their implicit memories may reveal that they have negative associations about members of minority groups. Such associations can influence people's behavior without their being aware of their underlying beliefs (Greenwald, Nosek, & Banaji, 2003; Greenwald, Nosek, & Sriram, 2006).

One way that memory specialists study implicit memory is through experiments that use priming. **Priming** is a phenomenon in which exposure to a word or concept (called a *prime*) later makes it easier to recall related information. Priming effects occur even when people have no conscious memory of the original word or concept (Schacter & Badgaiyan, 2001; Toth & Daniels, 2002; Shacter et al., 2004).

The typical experiment designed to illustrate priming helps clarify the phenomenon. In priming experiments, participants are rapidly exposed to a stimulus such as a word, an object, or perhaps a drawing of a face. The second phase of the experiment is done after an interval ranging from several seconds to several months. At that point, participants are exposed to incomplete perceptual information that is related to the first stimulus, and they are asked whether they recognize it. For example, the new material may consist of the first letter of a word that had been presented earlier, or a part of a face that had been shown earlier. If participants are able to identify the stimulus more readily than they identify stimuli that have not been presented earlier, priming has taken place. Clearly, the earlier stimulus has been remembered—although the material resides in implicit memory, not explicit memory.

Explicit memory: Intentional or conscious recollection of information.

Implicit memory: Memories of which people are not consciously aware, but which can affect subsequent performance and behavior.

Priming: A phenomenon in which exposure to a word or concept (called a prime) later makes it easier to recall related information, even when there is no conscious memory of the word or concept.

The same thing happens to us in our everyday lives. Suppose several months ago you watched a documentary on the planets, and the narrator described the moons of Mars, focusing on its moon named Phobos. You promptly forget the name of the moon, at least consciously. Then, several months later, you're completing a crossword puzzle that you have partially filled in, and it includes the letters *obos*. As soon as you look at the set of letters, you think of Phobos, and suddenly recall for the first time since your initial exposure to the information that it is one of the moons of Mars. The sudden recollection occurred because your memory was primed by the letters *obos*.

In short, when information that we are unable to consciously recall affects our behavior, implicit memory is at work. Our behavior may be influenced by experiences of which we are unaware—an example of what has been called "retention without remembering" (Horton et al., 2005).

Flashbulb Memories

Where were you on February 1, 2003? You will most likely draw a blank until this piece of information is added: February 1, 2003, was the date the Space Shuttle *Columbia* broke up in space and fell to Earth.

You probably have little trouble recalling your exact location and a variety of other trivial details that occurred when you heard about the shuttle disaster, even though the incident happened a few years ago. Your ability to remember details about this fatal event illustrates a phenomenon known as flashbulb memory. **Flashbulb memories** are memories related to a specific, important, or surprising event that are so vivid they represent a virtual snapshot of the event.

Several types of flashbulb memories are common among college students. For example, involvement in a car accident, meeting one's roommate for the first time, and the night of high school graduation are all typical flashbulb memories (Davidson & Glisky, 2002; Romeu, 2006; Bohn & Berntsen, 2007; see Figure 3).

Of course, flashbulb memories do not contain every detail of an original scene. I remember vividly that some four decades ago I was sitting in Mr. Sharp's tenth-grade geometry class when I heard that President John Kennedy had been shot. However, although I recall where I was sitting and how my classmates reacted to the news, I do not recollect what I was wearing or what I had for lunch that day.

Furthermore, the details recalled in flashbulb memories are often inaccurate. For example, think back to the tragic day when the World Trade Center in New York was attacked by suicidal terrorists. Do you remember watching television that morning and seeing images of the first plane, and then the second plane, striking the towers?

If you do, you are among the 73 percent of Americans who recall viewing the initial television images of both planes on September 11. However, that recollection is wrong: In fact, television broadcasts showed images only of the second plane on September 11. No video of the first plane was available until early the following morning, September 12, when it was shown on television (Begley, 2002).

Flashbulb memories illustrate a more general phenomenon about memory: Memories that are exceptional are more easily retrieved (although not necessarily accurately) than are those relating to events that are commonplace. The more distinctive a stimulus is, and the more personal relevance the event has, the more likely we are to recall it later (Berntsen & Thomsen, 2005; Shapiro, 2006).

Even with a distinctive stimulus, however, we may not remember where the information came from. *Source amnesia* occurs when an individual has a memory for some material but cannot recall where he or she encountered it before. For example, you may have experienced source amnesia when you met someone you knew and you just couldn't remember where you'd met that person initially.

Flashbulb memories: Memories centered on a specific, important, or surprising event that are so vivid it is as if they represented a snapshot of the event.

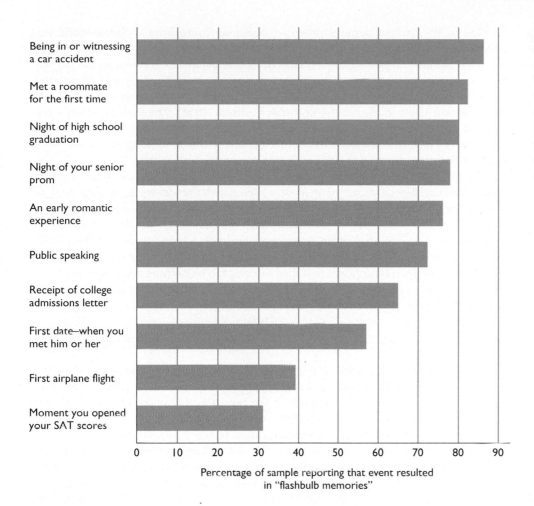

FIGURE 3 These are the most common flashbulb memory events, based on a survey of college students. What are some of your flashbulb memories? (Source: From David C. Rubin, "The Subtle Deceiver: Recalling Our Past," *Psychology Today*, September 1985, pp. 39–46. Reprinted with permission from *Psychology Today* magazine, (Copyright © 1985 Sussex Publishers, LLC.))

The bar chart shows categories with the x-axis labeled "Percentage of sample reporting that event resulted in 'flashbulb memories'" ranging from 0 to 90:

- Being in or witnessing a car accident
- Met a roommate for the first time
- Night of high school graduation
- Night of your senior prom
- An early romantic experience
- Public speaking
- Receipt of college admissions letter
- First date—when you met him or her
- First airplane flight
- Moment you opened your SAT scores

Constructive Processes in Memory: Rebuilding the Past

As we have seen, although it is clear that we can have detailed recollections of significant and distinctive events, it is difficult to gauge the accuracy of such memories. In fact, it is apparent that our memories reflect, at least in part, **constructive processes**, processes in which memories are influenced by the meaning we give to events. When we retrieve information, then, the memory that is produced is affected not just by the direct prior experience we have had with the stimulus, but also by our guesses and inferences about its meaning.

The notion that memory is based on constructive processes was first put forward by Frederic Bartlett, a British psychologist. He suggested that people tend to remember information in terms of **schemas**, organized bodies of information stored in memory that bias the way new information is interpreted, stored, and recalled (Bartlett, 1932). Our reliance on schemas means that memories often consist of a general reconstruction of previous experience. Bartlett argued that schemas are based not only on the specific material to which people are exposed, but also on their understanding of the situation, their expectations about the situation, and their awareness of the motivations underlying the behavior of others.

Constructive processes: Processes in which memories are influenced by the meaning we give to events.

Schemas: Organized bodies of information stored in memory that bias the way new information is interpreted, stored, and recalled.

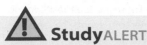

One of the earliest demonstrations of schemas came from a classic study that involved a procedure similar to the children's game of "telephone," in which information from memory is passed sequentially from one person to another. In the study, a participant viewed a drawing in which there were a variety of people of differing racial and ethnic backgrounds on a subway car, one of whom—a white person—was shown with a razor in his hand (Allport & Postman, 1958). The first participant was asked to describe the drawing to someone else without looking back at it. Then that person was asked to describe it to another person (without looking at the drawing), and then the process was repeated with still one more participant.

The report of the last person differed in significant, yet systematic, ways from the initial drawing. Specifically, many people described the drawing as depicting an African American with a knife—an incorrect recollection, given that the drawing showed a razor in the hand of a Caucasian person. The transformation of the Caucasian's razor into an African American's knife clearly indicates that the participants held a schema that included the unwarranted prejudice that African Americans are more violent than Caucasians and thus more apt to be holding a knife. In short, our expectations and knowledge—and prejudices—affect the reliability of our memories (McDonald & Hirt, 1997; Newby-Clark & Ross, 2003).

MEMORY IN THE COURTROOM: THE EYEWITNESS ON TRIAL

For Calvin Willis, the inadequate memories of two people cost him more than two decades of his life. Willis was the victim of mistaken identity when a young rape victim picked out his photo as the perpetrator of the rape. On that basis, he was tried, convicted, and sentenced to life in prison. Twenty-one years later, DNA testing showed that Willis was innocent, and the victim's identification wrong (Corsello, 2005).

Unfortunately, Willis is not the only victim to whom apologies have had to be made; many cases of mistaken identity have led to unjustified legal actions. Research on eyewitness identification of suspects, as well as on memory for other details of crimes, has shown that eyewitnesses are apt to make significant errors when they try to recall details of criminal activity—even if they are highly confident about their recollections (Miller, 2000; Thompson, 2000; Wells, Olson, & Charman, 2002; Zaragoza, Belli, & Payment, 2007).

One reason is the impact of the weapons used in crimes. When a criminal perpetrator displays a gun or knife, it acts like a perceptual magnet, attracting the eyes of the witnesses. As a consequence, witnesses pay less attention to other details of the crime and are less able to recall what actually occurred (Belli & Loftus, 1996; Steblay et al., 2003; Zaitsu, 2007).

One reason eyewitnesses are prone to memory-related errors is that the specific wording of questions posed to them by police officers or attorneys can affect the way they recall information, as a number of experiments illustrate. For example, in one experiment the participants were shown a film of two cars crashing into each other. Some were then asked the question, "About how fast were the cars going when they *smashed* into each other?" On average, they estimated the speed to be 40.8 miles per hour. In contrast, when another group of participants was asked, "About how fast were the cars going when they *contacted* each other?" the average estimated speed was only 31.8 miles per hour (Loftus & Palmer, 1974; see Figure 4).

The problem of memory reliability becomes even more acute when children are witnesses, because increasing evidence suggests that children's memories are highly vulnerable to the influence of others (Loftus, 1993; Douglas, Goldstein, & Bjorklund, 2000). For instance, in one experiment, 5- to 7-year-old girls who had just had a routine physical examination were shown an anatomically explicit doll. The girls were shown the doll's genital area and asked, "Did the doctor touch you here?" Three of the girls who did not have a vaginal or anal exam said that the doctor had in fact touched them in the genital area, and one of those three made up the detail "The doctor did it with a stick" (Saywitz & Goodman, 1990).

About how fast were the cars going when they_____ each other?

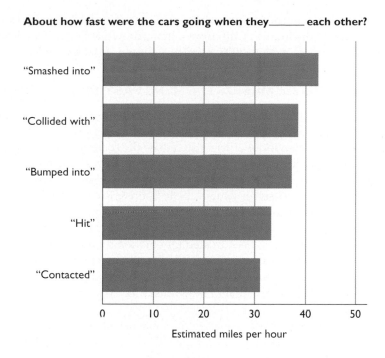

Estimated miles per hour

FIGURE 4 After viewing an accident involving two cars, the participants in a study were asked to estimate the speed of the two cars involved in the collision. Estimates varied substantially, depending on the way the question was worded. (Source: Loftus & Palmer, 1974.)

Children's memories are especially susceptible to influence when the situation is highly emotional or stressful. For example, in trials in which there is significant pretrial publicity or in which alleged victims are questioned repeatedly, often by untrained interviewers, the memories of the alleged victims may be influenced by the types of questions they are asked (Scullin, Kanaya, & Ceci, 2002; Lamb & Garretson, 2003; Quas et al., 2007).

Repressed and False Memories: Separating Truth from Fiction. Consider the case of George Franklin Sr., a man charged with murdering his daughter's playmate. The entire case was based on memories of Franklin's daughter, who claimed that she had repressed them until she began to have flashbacks of the event two decades later. Gradually, the memories became clearer, until she recalled her father lifting a rock over his head and then seeing her friend covered with blood. On the basis of her memories, her father was convicted—but later was cleared of the crime after an appeal of the conviction.

There is good reason to question the validity of *repressed memories*, recollections of events that are initially so shocking that the mind responds by pushing them into the unconscious. Supporters of the notion of repressed memory (based on Freud's psychoanalytic theory) suggest that such memories may remain hidden, possibly throughout a person's lifetime, unless they are triggered by some current circumstance, such as the probing that occurs during psychological therapy.

However, memory researcher Elizabeth Loftus maintains that so-called repressed memories may well be inaccurate or even wholly false—representing *false memory*. For example, false memories develop when people are unable to recall the source of a memory of a particular event about which they have only vague recollections. When the source of the memory becomes unclear or ambiguous, people may become confused about whether they actually experienced the event or whether it was imagined. Ultimately, people come to believe that the event actually occurred (Loftus, 2004; Lewandowsky, Werner, & Oberauer, 2005; Wade et al., 2007).

There is great controversy regarding the legitimacy of repressed memories. Many therapists give great weight to authenticity of repressed memories, and their views are supported by research showing that there are specific regions of the brain that help keep unwanted memories out of awareness. On the other side of the issue are researchers who maintain that there is insufficient scientific support for the existence of such memories. There is also a middle ground: memory researchers who suggest that false

Six years after being convicted of murder based on a so-called repressed memory of his daughter, George Franklin Sr.'s conviction was overturned.

memories are a result of normal information processing. The challenge for those on all sides of the issue is to distinguish truth from fiction (Brown & Pope, 1996; Roediger & McDermott, 2000; Anderson et al, 2004; Strange, Clifasefi, & Garry, 2007).

AUTOBIOGRAPHICAL MEMORY: WHERE PAST MEETS PRESENT

Your memory of experiences in your own past may well be a fiction—or at least a distortion of what actually occurred. The same constructive processes that make us inaccurately recall the behavior of others also reduce the accuracy of autobiographical memories. **Autobiographical memories** are our recollections of circumstances and episodes from our own lives. Autobiographical memories encompass the episodic memories we hold about ourselves (Rubin, 1999; Sutin & Robins, 2007).

For example, we tend to forget information about our past that is incompatible with the way in which we currently see ourselves. One study found that adults who were well adjusted but who had been treated for emotional problems during the early years of their lives tended to forget important but troubling childhood events, such as being in foster care. College students misremember their bad grades—but remember their good ones (see Figure 5; Walker, Skowronski, & Whompson, 2003; Kemps & Tiggemann, 2007).

Similarly, when a group of 48-year-olds were asked to recall how they had responded on a questionnaire they had completed when they were high school freshman, their accuracy was no better than chance. For example, although 61 percent of the questionnaire respondents said that playing sports and other physical activities was their favorite pastime, only 23 percent of the adults recalled it accurately (Offer et al., 2000).

It is not just certain kinds of events that are distorted; particular periods of life are remembered more easily than others are. For example, when people reach late adulthood, they remember periods of life in which they experienced major transitions, such as attending college and working at their first job, better than they remember their middle-age years. Similarly, although most adults' earliest memories of their own lives are of events that occurred when they were toddlers, toddlers show evidence of recall of events that occurred when they were as young as 6 months old (Simcock & Hayne, 2002; Wang, 2003; Cordnoldi, De Beni, & Helstrup, 2007).

Autobiographical memories: Our recollections of circumstances and episodes from our own lives.

FIGURE 5 We tend to distort memories of unpleasant events. For example, college students are much more likely to accurately recall their good grades, while inaccurately recalling their poor ones (Bahrick, et al., 1996). Now that you know this, how well do you think you can recall your high school grades?

Exploring DIVERSITY
Are There Cross-Cultural Differences in Memory?

Travelers who have visited areas of the world in which there is no written language often have returned with tales of people with phenomenal memories. For instance, storytellers in some preliterate cultures can recount long chronicles that recall the names and activities of people over many generations. Those feats led experts to argue initially that people in preliterate societies develop a different, and perhaps better, type of memory than do those in cultures that employ a written language. They suggested that in a society that lacks writing, people are motivated to recall information with accuracy, especially information relating to tribal histories and traditions that would be lost if they were not passed down orally from one generation to another (Daftary & Meri, 2002; Berntsen & Rubin, 2004).

Today, memory researchers dismiss that view. For one thing, preliterate peoples don't have an exclusive claim to amazing memory feats. Some Hebrew scholars memorize thousands of pages of text and can recall the locations of particular words on the page. Similarly, poetry singers in the Balkans can recall thousands of lines of poetry. Even in cultures in which written language exists, then, astounding feats of memory are possible (Strathern & Stewart, 2003; Rubin et al., 2007).

Memory researchers now suggest that there are both similarities and differences in memory across cultures. Basic memory processes such as short-term memory capacity and the structure of long-term memory—the "hardware" of memory—are universal and operate similarly in people in all cultures. In contrast, cultural differences can be

Storytellers in many cultures can recount hundreds of years of history in vivid detail. Research has found that this amazing ability is due less to basic memory processes than to the ways in which they acquire and retain information.

seen in the way information is acquired and rehearsed—the "software" of memory. Culture determines how people frame information initially, how much they practice learning and recalling it, and the strategies they use to try to recall it (Mack, 2003; Wang & Conway, 2006).

RECAP/EVALUATE/RETHINK

RECAP

What causes difficulties and failures in remembering?

- The tip-of-the-tongue phenomenon is the temporary inability to remember information that one is certain one knows. Retrieval cues are a major strategy for recalling information successfully. (p. 227)

- The levels-of-processing approach to memory suggests that the way in which information is initially perceived and analyzed determines the success with which it is recalled. The deeper the initial processing, the greater the recall. (p. 228)

- Explicit memory refers to intentional or conscious recollection of information. In contrast, implicit memory refers to memories of which people are not consciously aware, but which can affect subsequent performance and behavior. (p. 229)

- Flashbulb memories are memories centered on a specific, important event. The more distinctive a memory is, the more easily it can be retrieved. (p. 230)

- Memory is a constructive process: We relate memories to the meaning, guesses, and expectations we give to

events. Specific information is recalled in terms of schemas, organized bodies of information stored in memory that bias the way new information is interpreted, stored, and recalled. (p. 231)

- Eyewitnesses are apt to make substantial errors when they try to recall the details of crimes. The problem of memory reliability becomes even more acute when the witnesses are children. (p. 232)

- Autobiographical memory is influenced by constructive processes. (p. 234)

EVALUATE

1. While with a group of friends at a dance, Eva bumps into a man she dated last month, but when she tries to introduce him to her friends, she cannot remember his name. What is the term for this occurrence?

2. _____ is the process of retrieving a specific item from memory.

3. A friend tells you, "I know exactly where I was and what I was doing when I heard that Heath Ledger died." What is this type of memory phenomenon called?

4. _____ _____ _____ theory states that the more a person analyzes a statement, the more likely he or she is to remember it later.

RETHINK

1. Research shows that an eyewitness's memory for details of crimes can contain significant errors. How might a lawyer use this information when evaluating an eyewitness's testimony? Should eyewitness accounts be permissible in a court of law?

2. *From a social worker's perspective*: Should a child victim of sexual abuse be allowed to testify in court, based on what you've learned about children's memories under stress?

Answers to Evaluate Questions

1. tip-of-the-tongue phenomenon; 2. recall; 3. flashbulb memory; 4. levels-of-processing

KEY TERMS

tip-of-the-tongue phenomenon p. 227
recall p. 227
recognition p. 227

levels-of-processing theory p. 228
explicit memory p. 229
implicit memory p. 229

priming p. 229
flashbulb memories p. 230
constructive processes p. 231
schemas p. 231

autobiographical memories p. 234

Forgetting: When Memory Fails

Known in the scientific literature by the alias of H.M., he could remember, quite literally, nothing—nothing, that is, that had happened since the loss of his brain's temporal lobes and hippocampus during experimental surgery to reduce epileptic seizures. Until that time, H.M.'s memory had been quite normal. But after the operation he was unable to recall anything for more than a few minutes, and then the memory was seemingly lost forever. He did not remember his address, or the name of the person to whom he was talking. H.M. would read the same magazine over and over again. According to his own description, his life was like waking from a dream and being unable to know where he was or how he got there. (Milner, 1966, 2005)

As the case of H.M. illustrates, a person without a normal memory faces severe difficulties. All of us who have experienced even routine instances of forgetting—such as not remembering an acquaintance's name or a fact on a test—understand the very real consequences of memory failure.

Of course, memory failure is also essential to remembering important information. The ability to forget inconsequential details about experiences, people, and objects helps us avoid being burdened and distracted by trivial stores of meaningless data. Forgetting permits us to form general impressions and recollections. For example, the reason our friends consistently look familiar to us is because we're able to forget their clothing, facial blemishes, and other transient features that change from one occasion to the next. Instead, our memories are based on a summary of various critical features—a far more economical use of our memory capabilities.

The first attempts to study forgetting were made by German psychologist Hermann Ebbinghaus about a hundred years ago. Using himself as the only participant in his study, Ebbinghaus memorized lists of three-letter nonsense syllables— meaningless sets of two consonants with a vowel in between, such as FIW and BOZ. By measuring how easy it was to relearn a given list of words after varying periods of time had passed since the initial learning, he found that forgetting occurred systematically, as shown in Figure 1. As the figure indicates, the most rapid forgetting occurs in the first nine hours, particularly in the first hour. After nine hours, the rate of forgetting slows and declines little, even after the passage of many days.

Despite his primitive methods, Ebbinghaus's study had an important influence on subsequent research, and his basic conclusions have been upheld. There is almost always a strong initial decline in memory, followed by a more gradual drop over time. Furthermore, relearning of previously mastered material is almost always faster than starting from scratch, whether the material is academic information or a motor skill such as serving a tennis ball (Wixted & Carpenter, 2007).

Key Concepts

Why do we forget information?

What are the major memory impairments?

FIGURE 1 In his classic work, Ebbinghaus found that the most rapid forgetting occurs in the first nine hours after exposure to new material. However, the rate of forgetting then slows down and declines very little even after many days have passed (Ebbinghaus, 1885, 1913). Check your own memory: What were you doing exactly two hours ago? What were you doing last Tuesday at 5 p.m.? Which information is easier to retrieve?

Why We Forget

Why do we forget? One reason is that we may not have paid attention to the material in the first place—a failure of *encoding*. For example, if you live in the United States, you probably have been exposed to thousands of pennies during your life. Despite this experience, you probably don't have a clear sense of the details of the coin. (See this for yourself by looking at Figure 2.) Consequently, the reason for your memory failure is that you probably never encoded the information into long-term memory initially. Obviously, if information was not placed in memory to start with, there is no way the information can be recalled.

FIGURE 2 One of these pennies is the real thing. Can you find it? Why is this task harder than it seems at first?
(Source: Nickerson & Adams, 1979.)
If you don't have a penny handy, the correct answer is "A."

But what about material that has been encoded into memory and that can't later be remembered? Several processes account for memory failures, including decay, interference, and cue-dependent forgetting.

Decay is the loss of information through nonuse. This explanation for forgetting assumes that *memory traces*, the physical changes that take place in the brain when new material is learned, simply fade away over time (Grann, 2007).

Although there is evidence that decay does occur, this does not seem to be the complete explanation for forgetting. Often there is no relationship between how long ago a person was exposed to information and how well that information is recalled. If decay explained all forgetting, we would expect that the more time that has elapsed between the initial learning of information and our attempt to recall it, the harder it would be to remember it, because there would be more time for the memory trace to decay. Yet people who take several consecutive tests on the same material often recall more of the initial information when taking later tests than they did on earlier tests. If decay were operating, we would expect the opposite to occur (Payne, 1986).

Because decay does not fully account for forgetting, memory specialists have proposed an additional mechanism: **interference**. In interference, information in memory disrupts the recall of other information (Naveh-Benjamin, Guez, & Sorek, 2007).

To distinguish between decay and interference, think of the two processes in terms of a row of books on a library shelf. In decay, the old books are constantly crumbling and rotting away, leaving room for new arrivals. Interference processes suggest that new books knock the old ones off the shelf, where they become inaccessible.

Finally, forgetting may occur because of **cue-dependent forgetting**, forgetting that occurs when there are insufficient retrieval cues to rekindle information that is in memory (Tulving & Thompson, 1983). For example, you may not be able to remember where you lost a set of keys until you mentally walk through your day, thinking of each place you visited. When you think of the place where you lost the keys—say, the library—the retrieval cue of the library may be sufficient to help you recall that you left them on the desk in the library. Without that retrieval cue, you may be unable to recall the location of the keys.

Most research suggests that interference and cue-dependent forgetting are key processes in forgetting (Mel'nikov, 1993; Bower, Thompson, & Tulving, 1994). We forget things mainly because new memories interfere with the retrieval of old ones or because appropriate retrieval cues are unavailable, not because the memory trace has decayed.

"He must have forgotten something."

Decay: The loss of information in memory through its nonuse.

Interference: The phenomenon by which information in memory disrupts the recall of other information.

Cue-dependent forgetting: Forgetting that occurs when there are insufficient retrieval cues to rekindle information that is in memory.

 StudyALERT

Memory loss through decay comes from nonuse of the memory; memory loss through interference is due to the presence of other information in memory.

Proactive and Retroactive Interference: The Before and After of Forgetting

There are actually two sorts of interference that influence forgetting: proactive and retroactive. In **proactive interference**, information learned earlier disrupts the recall of newer material. Suppose, as a student of foreign languages, you first learned French in the 10th grade, and then in the 11th grade you took Spanish. When in the 12th grade you take a college achievement test in Spanish, you may find you have difficulty recalling the Spanish translation of a word because all you can think of is its French equivalent (Bunting, 2006).

In contrast, **retroactive interference** refers to difficulty in the recall of information because of later exposure to different material. If, for example, you have difficulty on a French achievement test because of your more recent exposure to Spanish, retroactive

Proactive interference: Interference in which information learned earlier disrupts the recall of newer material.

Retroactive interference: Interference in which there is difficulty in the recall of information learned earlier because of later exposure to different material.

FIGURE 3 Proactive interference occurs when material learned earlier interferes with the recall of newer material. In this example, studying French before studying Spanish interferes with performance on a Spanish test. In contrast, retroactive interference exists when material learned after initial exposure to other material interferes with the recall of the first material. In this case, retroactive interference occurs when recall of French is impaired because of later exposure to Spanish.

interference is the culprit (see Figure 3). One way to remember the difference between proactive and retroactive interference is to keep in mind that *proactive* interference progresses in time—the past interferes with the present—whereas *retro*active interference retrogresses in time, working backward as the present interferes with the past (Jacoby et al., 2007).

Although the concepts of proactive and retroactive interference illustrate how material may be forgotten, they still do not explain whether forgetting is caused by the actual loss or modification of information or by problems in the retrieval of information. Most research suggests that material that has apparently been lost because of interference can eventually be recalled if appropriate stimuli are presented (Tulving & Psotka, 1971; Anderson, 1981), but the question has not been fully answered.

Memory Dysfunctions: Afflictions of Forgetting

First you notice that you're always misplacing things, or that common nouns are evading you as stubbornly as the names of new acquaintances. Pretty soon you're forgetting appointments and getting flustered when you drive in traffic. On bad days you find you can't hold numbers in your mind long enough to dial the phone. You try valiantly to conceal your lapses, but they become ever more glaring. You crash your car. You spend whole mornings struggling to dress yourself properly. And even as you lose the ability to read or play the piano, you're painfully aware of what's happening to you. (Cowley, 2000b, p. 46)

Alzheimer's disease: An illness characterized in part by severe memory problems.

These memory problems are symptomatic of **Alzheimer's disease**, an illness characterized in part by severe memory problems. Alzheimer's is the fourth leading cause of death among adults in the United States, affecting an estimated 5 million people.

In the beginning, Alzheimer's symptoms appear as simple forgetfulness of things such as appointments and birthdays. As the disease progresses, memory loss becomes more profound, and even the simplest tasks—such as using a telephone—are forgotten. Ultimately, victims may lose their ability to speak or comprehend language, and physical deterioration sets in, leading to death.

The causes of Alzheimer's disease are not fully understood. Increasing evidence suggests that Alzheimer's results from an inherited susceptibility to a defect in the production of the protein beta amyloid, which is necessary for the maintenance of nerve cell connections. When the synthesis of beta amyloid goes awry, large clumps of cells form, triggering inflammation and the deterioration of nerve cells in the brain (Selkoe, 2002; Detoledo-Morrell, Stoub, & Wang, 2007; Horínek, Varjassyová, & Hort, 2007; see Figure 4).

Neuroscience in Your Life

FIGURE 4 This series of brain images clearly shows the changes caused by the spread of Alzheimer's disease over 18 months, with the normal tissue (signified by the purple color) retreating substantially after 18 months.

Initially   6 months later   12 months later   18 months later

Alzheimer's disease is one of a number of memory dysfunctions. Another is **amnesia**, memory loss that occurs without other mental difficulties. The type of amnesia immortalized in countless Hollywood films involves a victim who receives a blow to the head and is unable to remember anything from his or her past. In reality, amnesia of this type, known as retrograde amnesia, is quite rare. In **retrograde amnesia**, memory is lost for occurrences prior to a certain event. Usually, lost memories gradually reappear, although full restoration may take as long as several years. In certain cases, some memories are lost forever. But even in cases of severe memory loss, the loss is generally selective. For example, although people suffering from retrograde amnesia may be unable to recall friends and family members, they still may be able to play complicated card games or knit a sweater quite well (Verfaellie & Keane, 2002; Bright et al., 2006).

A second type of amnesia is exemplified by people who remember nothing of their current activities. In **anterograde amnesia** loss of memory occurs for events that follow an injury. Information cannot be transferred from short-term to long-term memory, resulting in the inability to remember anything other than what was in long-term storage before the accident (Gilboa et al., 2006).

Amnesia is also a result of **Korsakoff's syndrome**, a disease that afflicts long-term alcoholics. Although many of their intellectual abilities may be intact, Korsakoff's sufferers display a strange array of symptoms, including hallucinations and a tendency to repeat the same story over and over.

Fortunately, most of us have intact memory, and the occasional failures we suffer may actually be preferable to having a perfect memory. Consider, for instance, the case of a man who had total recall. After reading passages of Dante's *The Divine Comedy* in Italian—a language he did not speak—he was able to repeat them from memory some 15 years later. He could memorize lists of 50 unrelated words and recall them at will more than a decade later. He could even repeat the same list of words backward, if asked (Luria, 1968; Cole & Levtin, 2006).

Such a skill at first may seem to be enviable, but it actually presented quite a problem. The man's memory became a jumble of lists of words, numbers, and names, and when he tried to relax, his mind was filled with images. Even reading was difficult, since every word evoked a flood of thoughts from the past that interfered with his ability to understand the meaning of what he was reading. Partially as a consequence of the man's unusual memory, psychologist A. R. Luria, who studied his case, found him to be a "disorganized and rather dull-witted person" (Luria, 1968, p. 65). We might be grateful, then, that forgetfulness plays a role in our lives.

Amnesia: Memory loss that occurs without other mental difficulties.

Retrograde amnesia: Amnesia in which memory is lost for occurrences prior to a certain event.

Anterograde amnesia: Amnesia in which memory is lost for events that follow an injury.

Korsakoff's syndrome: A disease that afflicts long-term alcoholics, leaving some abilities intact but including hallucinations and a tendency to repeat the same story.

StudyALERT

Except for Alzheimer's disease, memory disorders are relatively rare.

# of Psychology

Improving Your Memory

Apart from the advantages of forgetting, say, a bad date, most of us would like to find ways to improve our memories. Among the effective strategies for studying and remembering course material:

- *Use the keyword technique.* If you are studying a foreign language, try the *keyword technique* of pairing a foreign word with a common English word that has a similar sound. This English word is known as the *keyword*. For example, to learn the Spanish word for duck (*pato*, pronounced *pot-o*), you might choose the keyword *pot*; for the Spanish word for horse (*caballo*, pronounced *cob-eye-yo*), the keyword might be *eye*. Once you have thought of a keyword, imagine the Spanish word "interacting" with the English keyword. You might envision a duck taking a bath in a pot to remember the word *pato*, or a horse with a large, bulging eye in the center of its head to recall *caballo* (Carney & Levin, 1998; Wyra, Lawon, & Hungi, 2007).

- *Rely on organization cues.* Recall material you read in textbooks by organizing the material in memory the first time you read it. Organize your reading on the basis of any advance information you have about the content and about its arrangement. You will then be able to make connections and see relationships among the various facts and process the material at a deeper level, which in turn will later aid recall.

- *Take effective notes.* "Less is more" is perhaps the best advice for taking lecture notes that facilitate recall. Rather than trying to jot down every detail of a lecture, it is better to listen and think about the material, and take down the main points. In effective note taking, thinking about the material when you first hear it is more important than writing it down. This is one reason that borrowing someone else's notes is a bad idea; you will have no framework in memory that you can use to understand them (Feldman, 2005).

- *Practice and rehearse.* Although practice does not necessarily make perfect, it helps. By studying and rehearsing material past initial mastery—a process called *overlearning*—people are able to show better long-term recall than they show if they stop practicing after their initial learning of the material.

- *Don't believe claims about drugs that improve memory.* Advertisements for One-a-Day vitamins with ginkgo biloba or Quanterra Mental Sharpness Product would have you believe that taking a drug or supplement can improve your memory. Not so, according to the results of numerous studies. No research has shown that commercial memory enhancers are effective (Gold, Cahill, & Wenk, 2002; McDaniel, Maier, & Einstein, 2002; Burns, Bryan, & Nettelbeck, 2006).

RECAP/EVALUATE/RETHINK

RECAP

Why do we forget information?

- Several processes account for memory failure, including decay, interference (both proactive and retroactive), and cue-dependent forgetting. (p. 239)

What are the major memory impairments?

- Among the memory dysfunctions are Alzheimer's disease, which leads to a progressive loss of memory; and amnesia, a memory loss that occurs without other mental difficulties and that can take two forms: retrograde amnesia and anterograde amnesia. Korsakoff's syndrome is a disease that afflicts long-term alcoholics, resulting in memory impairment. (p. 240)

- Among the techniques for improving memory are the keyword technique to memorize foreign language vocabulary; using the encoding specificity phenomenon; organizing text material and lecture notes; and practice and rehearsal, leading to overlearning. (p. 242)

EVALUATE

1. If, after learning the history of the Middle East for a class two years ago, you now find yourself unable to recall what you learned, you are experiencing memory _____, caused by nonuse.
2. Difficulty in accessing a memory because of the presence of other information is known as _____.
3. _____ interference occurs when material is difficult to retrieve because of subsequent exposure to other material; _____ interference refers to difficulty in retrieving material as a result of the interference of previously learned material.
4. Match the following memory disorders with the correct information:
   1. Affects alcoholics; may result in hallucinations.
   2. Memory loss occurring without other mental problems.
   3. Beta amyloid defect; progressive forgetting and physical deterioration.
   a. Alzheimer's disease
   b. Korsakoff's syndrome
   c. Amnesia

RETHINK

1. What are the implications of proactive and retroactive interference for learning multiple foreign languages? Would earlier language training in a different language help or hinder learning a new language?
2. *From a healthcare provider's perspective*: Alzheimer's disease and amnesia are two of the most pervasive memory dysfunctions that threaten many individuals. What sorts of activities might health care providers offer their patients to help them combat their memory loss?

Answers to Evaluate Questions

1. decay; 2. interference; 3. retroactive, proactive; 4. 1-b, 2-c, 3-a

KEY TERMS

Psychology on the Web

1. The study of repressed memories can lead down unusual pathways—even more unusual than the criminal investigation pathway. Two other areas in which repressed memories play a large part are alien abduction and reincarnation. Find two sources on the Web that deal with one of these issues—one supportive and one skeptical. Read what they say and relate it to your knowledge of memory. Summarize your findings and indicate which side of the controversy your study of memory leads you to favor.
2. Memory is a topic of serious interest to psychologists, but it is also a source of amusement. Find a Web site that focuses on the amusing side of memory (such as memory games, tests of recall, or lists of mnemonics; hint: there's even a mnemonics generator out there!). Write down the addresses of any interesting sites that you encounter and summarize what you found.

Epilogue

Our examination of memory has highlighted the processes of encoding, storage, and retrieval and theories about how these processes occur. We also encountered several phenomena relating to memory, including the tip-of-the-tongue phenomenon and flash-bulb memories. Above all, we observed that memory is a constructive process by which interpretations, expectations, and guesses contribute to the nature of our memories.

Before moving on to the next chapter, return to the prologue on Doug Bruce's lost memories. Consider the following questions in light of what you now know about memory.

1. Does Doug Bruce seem to have retrograde or anterograde amnesia? How can you tell?
2. Why do you think Doug Bruce could selectively lose all memory of his past and his identity, yet still remember how to walk, talk, and dress himself?
3. Do you think that Doug Bruce's lack of memories from his past would affect his ability to form new memories? Why do you think so?
4. Some experts believe that Doug Bruce's "amnesia" is really just a hoax. What evidence in his story might suggest that?
5. Is there any way for researchers to tell whether an amnesia patient such as Doug Bruce has truly forgotten information or is merely pretending?

CHAPTER 8

Cognition and Language

Key Concepts for Chapter 8

Prologue *Microbe-Busting Bandages*

What do jock itch, poison gas, and flesh-eating bacteria have in common? Gregory Schultz, 56, thinks he has the answer. The cancer researcher turned inventor has patented a technique for chemically bonding bacteria-fighting polymers to such fabrics as gauze bandages, cotton T shirts, and men's underpants. It's a technology with an unusually wide variety of uses, from underwear that doesn't stink to hospital dressings that thwart infections.

The bandages, coated with positively charged antimicrobial molecules, dramatically reduce the risk of infection, Schultz says, and as a bonus they can prevent outbreaks of the drug-resistant staph infections that have been racing through U.S. hospitals. "It basically punches holes in the bacteria," he says, "and they pop like balloons." (Morrissey, 2006)

Looking Ahead

Schultz's invention was a long time in coming. Two decades earlier, a student working in a burn unit mentioned that the way in which cells responded to cancer might be harnessed to help burn victims avoid infection. It took 20 years of puzzling over the problem before Schultz invented his antibacterial bandages.

It is clear that Schultz has the elusive quality that marks successful inventors: creativity. Where did his creativity come from? More generally, how do people use information to devise innovative solutions to problems? And how do people think about, understand, and, through language, describe the world?

Answers to these questions come from **cognitive psychology**, the branch of psychology that focuses on the study of higher mental processes, including thinking, language, memory, problem solving, knowing, reasoning, judging, and decision making. Clearly, the realm of cognitive psychology is broad.

Cognitive psychology centers on three major topics: thinking and reasoning, problem solving and creativity, and language. The first topic we consider in this chapter is thinking and reasoning. Then we examine different strategies for approaching problems, means of generating solutions, and ways of making judgments about the usefulness and accuracy of solutions. Finally, we discuss how language is developed and acquired, its basic characteristics, and the relationship between language and thought.

Cognitive psychology: The branch of psychology that focuses on the study of higher mental processes, including thinking, language, memory, problem solving, knowing, reasoning, judging, and decision making.

Thinking and Reasoning

What are you thinking about at this moment?

The mere ability to pose such a question underscores the distinctive nature of the human ability to think. No other species contemplates, analyzes, recollects, or plans the way humans do. Understanding what thinking is, however, goes beyond knowing that we think. Philosophers, for example, have argued for generations about the meaning of thinking, with some placing it at the core of human beings' understanding of their own existence.

Psychologists define **thinking** as the manipulation of mental representations of information. A representation may take the form of a word, a visual image, a sound, or data in any other sensory modality stored in memory. Thinking transforms a particular representation of information into new and different forms, allowing us to answer questions, solve problems, or reach goals.

Although a clear sense of what specifically occurs when we think remains elusive, our understanding of the nature of the fundamental elements involved in thinking is growing. We begin by considering our use of mental images and concepts, the building blocks of thought.

Mental Images: Examining the Mind's Eye

Think of your best friend.

Chances are that you "see" some kind of visual image when asked to think of her or him, or any other person or object, for that matter. To some cognitive psychologists, such mental images constitute a major part of thinking.

Mental images are representations in the mind of an object or event. They are not just visual representations; our ability to "hear" a tune in our heads also relies on a mental image. In fact, every sensory modality may produce corresponding mental images (Kosslyn, 2005; De Beni, Pazzaglia, & Gardini, 2007).

Research has found that our mental images have many of the properties of the actual stimuli they represent. For example, it takes the mind longer to scan mental images of large objects than of small ones, just as the eye takes longer to scan an actual large object than an actual small one. Similarly, we are able to manipulate and rotate mental images of objects, just as we are able to manipulate and rotate them in the real world (Shepard et al., 2000; Mast & Kosslyn, 2002; Iachini & Giusberti, 2004; see Figure 1).

Some experts see the production of mental images as a way to improve various skills. For instance, many athletes use mental imagery in their training. Basketball players may try to produce vivid and detailed images of the court, the basket, the ball,

Key Concepts

What is thinking?

What processes underlie reasoning and decision making?

Thinking: The manipulation of mental representations of information.

"What do you think I think about what you think I think you've been thinking about?"

Mental images: Representations in the mind that resemble the object or event being represented.

FIGURE 1 Try to mentally rotate one of each pair of patterns to see if it is the same as the other member of that pair. It's likely that the farther you have to mentally rotate a pattern, the longer it will take to decide if the patterns match one another. Does this mean that it will take you longer to visualize a map of the world than a map of the United States? Why or why not? (Source: From Shepard, R. N., & Metzler, J. (1971). Mental rotation of three-dimensional objects. *Science, 171*, no. 3972, 701-703 (Figure. 1, p. 702). Reprinted with permission from AAAS.)

a.

b.

c.

Many athletes use mental imagery to focus on a task, a process they call "getting in the zone." What are some other occupations that require the use of strong mental imagery?

Concepts: Categorizations of objects, events, or people that share common properties.

and the noisy crowd. They may visualize themselves taking a foul shot, watching the ball, and hearing the swish as it goes through the net. And it works: The use of mental imagery can lead to improved performance in sports (MacIntyre, Moran, & Jennings, 2002; Mamassis & Doganis, 2004).

Mental imagery may improve other types of skills as well. For example, piano players who simply mentally rehearse an exercise show brain activity that is virtually identical to that of the people who actually practice the exercise manually (see Figure 2). Apparently, carrying out the task involved the same network of brain cells as the network used in mentally rehearsing it (Pascual-Leone et al., 1995; Cisek & Kalaska, 2004; Kensinger & Schacter, 2006).

Concepts: Categorizing the World

If someone asks you what is in your kitchen cabinet, you might answer with a detailed list of items ("a jar of peanut butter, three boxes of macaroni and cheese, six unmatched dinner plates," and so forth). More likely, though, you would respond by naming some broader categories, such as "food" and "dishes."

Using such categories reflects the operation of concepts. **Concepts** are categorizations of objects, events, or people that share common properties. Concepts enable us to organize complex phenomena into simpler, and therefore more easily usable, cognitive categories (Goldstone & Kersten, 2003; Murphy, 2005; Connolly, 2007).

Concepts help us classify newly encountered objects on the basis of our past experience. For example, we can surmise that someone tapping a handheld screen is probably using some kind of computer or PDA, even if we have never encountered that specific model before. Ultimately, concepts influence behavior; we would assume, for

Neuroscience in Your Life

FIGURE 2 Compared with the brain scans of people who actually practiced a piano finger exercise, the brain scans of those who only used mental rehearsal but did not touch the piano were nearly identical. The results of the experiment clearly show the value of mental imagery. (Source: Pascual-Leone et al., 1995.)

instance, that it might be appropriate to pet an animal after determining that it is a dog, whereas we would behave differently after classifying the animal as a wolf.

When cognitive psychologists first studied concepts, they focused on those which were clearly defined by a unique set of properties or features. For example, an equilateral triangle is a closed shape that has three sides of equal length. If an object has these characteristics, it is an equilateral triangle; if it does not, it is not an equilateral triangle.

Other concepts—often those with the most relevance to our everyday lives—are more ambiguous and difficult to define. For instance, broader concepts such as "table" and "bird" have a set of general, relatively loose characteristic features, rather than unique, clearly defined properties that distinguish an example of the concept from a nonexample. When we consider these more ambiguous concepts, we usually think in terms of examples called **prototypes**. Prototypes are typical, highly representative examples of a concept that correspond to our mental image or best example of the concept. For instance, although a robin and an ostrich are both examples of birds, the robin is an example that comes to most people's minds far more readily. Consequently, robin is a prototype of the concept "bird." Similarly, when we think of the concept of a table, we're likely to think of a coffee table before we think of a drafting table, making a coffee table closer to our prototype of a table.

Relatively high agreement exists among people in a particular culture about which examples of a concept are prototypes, as well as which examples are not. For instance, most people in Western cultures consider cars and trucks good examples of vehicles, whereas elevators and wheelbarrows are not considered very good examples. Consequently, cars and trucks are prototypes of the concept of a vehicle (see Figure 3).

Concepts enable us to think about and understand more readily the complex world in which we live. For example, the suppositions we make about the reasons for other people's behavior are based on the ways in which we classify behavior. Hence, our conclusion that a person who washes her hands 20 times a day could vary, depending on whether we place her behavior within the conceptual framework of a health-care worker or a mental patient. Similarly, physicians make diagnoses by drawing on concepts and prototypes of symptoms that they learned about in medical school. Finally, concepts and prototypes facilitate our efforts to draw suitable conclusions through the cognitive process we turn to next: reasoning.

Prototypes: Typical, highly representative examples of a concept.

FIGURE 3 Prototypes are typical, highly representative examples of a concept. For instance, a highly typical prototype of the concept "furniture" is a chair, whereas a stove is not a good prototype. High agreement exists within a culture about which examples of a concept are prototypes. (Source: Adapted from Rosch & Mervis, 1975.)

Ranking of Prototype from Most to Least Typical	Concept Category			
	Furniture	Vehicle	Weapon	Vegetable
1—Most Typical	Chair	Car	Gun	Peas
2	Sofa	Truck	Knife	Carrots
3	Table	Bus	Sword	String beans
4	Dresser	Motorcycle	Bomb	Spinach
5	Desk	Train	Hand grenade	Broccoli
6	Bed	Trolley car	Spear	Asparagus
7	Bookcase	Bicycle	Cannon	Corn
8	Footstool	Airplane	Bow and arrow	Cauliflower
9	Lamp	Boat	Club	Brussels sprouts
10	Piano	Tractor	Tank	Lettuce
11	Cushion	Cart	Tear gas	Beets
12	Mirror	Wheelchair	Whip	Tomato
13	Rug	Tank	Ice pick	Lima beans
14	Radio	Raft	Fists	Eggplant
15—Least Typical	Stove	Sled	Rocket	Onion

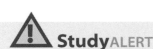

StudyALERT

Figure 3 will help you remember that prototypes represent "best" or most common examples of a particular concept. For example, a Prius might be a prototype of the concept of "hybrid car."

Reasoning: Making Up Your Mind

> Professors deciding when students' assignments are due.
> An employer determining who to hire out of a pool of job applicants.
> The president concluding that it is necessary to send troops to a foreign nation.

What do these three situations have in common? Each requires *reasoning*, the process by which information is used to draw conclusions and make decisions.

Although philosophers and logicians have considered the foundations of reasoning for centuries, it is only relatively recently that cognitive psychologists have begun to investigate how people reason and make decisions. Their efforts have contributed to our understanding of formal reasoning processes as well as the cognitive shortcuts we routinely use—shortcuts that sometimes may lead our reasoning capabilities astray (Johnson-Laird, 2006).

How do you view these structures? Whether you categorize them as two houses of worship (left & middle), as two similar examples of architecture (middle & right), or simply as three buildings, you are using concepts.

SYLLOGISTIC REASONING: THE FORMAL RULES OF LOGIC

If you've ever played a card game like poker and tried to figure out what cards your opponent was holding, you probably used **syllogistic reasoning**, a kind of formal reasoning in which a person draws a conclusion from a set of assumptions. In using syllogistic reasoning, we begin with a general assumption that we believe is true and then derive specific implications from that assumption. If the assumption is true, the conclusions must also be true (Fisk & Sharp, 2002; Marrero & Gamez, 2004; Shynkaruk & Thompson, 2006).

A major technique for studying syllogistic reasoning involves asking people to evaluate a series of statements that present two assumptions, or premises, that are used to derive a conclusion. For example, consider the following syllogism:

Premise 1   All professors are mortal.
Premise 2   Dr. Rivera is a professor.
Conclusion   Therefore, Dr. Rivera is mortal.

Because both premises are true, by applying logic appropriately we come to an accurate conclusion. More abstractly, we can state the syllogism as the following:

Premise 1   All A's are B.
Premise 2   C is an A.
Conclusion   Therefore, C is a B.

However, even if the premises are correct, people may apply logic incorrectly. For example, consider the following syllogism:

Premise 1   All A's are B.
Premise 2   C is an A.
Conclusion   Therefore, all A's are C.

Although it may not be immediately apparent, the conclusion is illogical—something we will see more readily if we make the syllogism more concrete:

Premise 1   All professors are mortal.
Premise 2   Professor Rivera is a professor.
Conclusion   Therefore, all professors are Dr. Rivera.

In short, syllogistic reasoning is only as accurate as the premises and the validity of the logic applied to the premises.

ALGORITHMS AND HEURISTICS

When faced with making a decision, we often turn to various kinds of cognitive shortcuts, known as algorithms and heuristics, to help us. An **algorithm** is a rule that, if applied appropriately, guarantees a solution to a problem. We can use an algorithm even if we cannot understand why it works. For example, you may know that you can find the length of the third side of a right triangle by using the formula $a^2 + b^2 = c^2$, although you may not have the foggiest notion of the mathematical principles behind the formula.

For many problems and decisions, however, no algorithm is available. In those instances, we may be able to use heuristics to help us. A **heuristic** is a cognitive shortcut that may lead to a solution. Heuristics enhance the likelihood of success in coming to a solution, but, unlike algorithms, they cannot ensure it. For example, when I play tic-tac-toe, I follow the heuristic of placing an X in the center square when I start the game. This tactic doesn't guarantee that I will win, but experience has taught me that it will increase my chances of success. Similarly, some students follow the heuristic of preparing for a test by ignoring the assigned textbook reading and only studying their lecture notes—a strategy that may or may not pay off.

Syllogistic reasoning: Formal reasoning in which people draw a conclusion from a set of assumptions.

Algorithm: A rule that, if applied appropriately, guarantees a solution to a problem.

Heuristic: A cognitive shortcut that may lead to a solution.

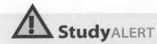 **Study**ALERT

Remember that algorithms are rules that *always* provide a solution, while heuristics are shortcuts that *may* provide a solution.

Although heuristics often help people solve problems and make decisions, certain kinds of heuristics may lead to inaccurate conclusions. For example, we sometimes use the *representativeness heuristic*, a rule we apply when we judge people by the degree to which they represent a certain category or group of people. Suppose, for instance, you are the owner of a fast-food store that has been robbed many times by teenagers. The representativeness heuristic would lead you to raise your guard each time someone of this age group enters your store (even though, statistically, it is unlikely that any given teenager will rob the store) (Fisk, Bury, & Holden, 2006).

The *availability heuristic* involves judging the probability of an event on the basis of how easily the event can be recalled from memory. According to this heuristic, we assume that events we remember easily are likely to have occurred more frequently in the past—and are more likely to occur in the future—than events that are harder to remember.

For instance, the availability heuristic makes us more afraid of dying in a plane crash than in an auto accident, despite statistics clearly showing that airplane travel is much safer than auto travel. Similarly, although 10 times as many people die from falling out of bed than from lightning strikes, we're more afraid of being hit by lightning. The reason is that plane crashes and lightning strikes receive far more publicity, and they are therefore more easily remembered (Vaughn & Weary, 2002; Oppenheimer, 2004; Fox, 2006; Kluger, 2006).

Are algorithms and heuristics confined to human thinking, or can we program computers to mimic human thinking and problem solving? As we discuss next, scientists are certainly trying.

Computers and Problem Solving: Searching for Artificial Intelligence

To the music experts, there was no mistaking who had written the piano piece: Johann Sebastian Bach, the prolific German composer who was born in the 15th century.

But the experts were wrong. The piece they all thought was a Bach composition was actually created by a computer named "EMI" by David Cope of the University of California. After a variety of actual Bach pieces had been scanned into its memory, EMI was able to produce music that was so similar to Bach's actual music that it fooled knowledgeable listeners (Johnson, 1997; Cope, 2001).

Such computer mimicry is possible because composers have a particular "signature" that reflects patterns, sequences, and combinations of notes. By employing those "signatures," computers can create compositions that have the full scope and emotional appeal of actual works—and show just as much creativity as those written by the actual composer (Cope, 2001, 2003).

Computers are making significant inroads in terms of the ability to solve problems and carry out some forms of intellectual activities. According to experts who study *artificial intelligence*, the field that examines how to use technology to imitate the outcome of human thinking, problem solving, and creative activities, computers can show rudiments of humanlike thinking because of their knowledge of where to look—and where not to look—for an answer to a problem. They suggest that the capacity of computer programs (such as those that play chess) to evaluate potential moves and to ignore unimportant possibilities gives them thinking ability (Sabater & Sierra, 2005; Prasad, 2006; Copeland & Proudfoot, 2007).

Many of the questions surrounding the ability of computers to think and behave creatively have not been answered. Still, it is clear that computers are becoming increasingly sophisticated, ever more closely approximating human thought processes.

A computer using artificial intelligence software was able to mimic compositions by Johann Sebastian Bach so successfully it fooled expert musicologists.

RECAP/EVALUATE/RETHINK

RECAP

What is thinking?

- Cognitive psychology encompasses the higher mental processes, including the way people know and understand the world, process information, make decisions and judgments, and describe their knowledge and understanding to others. (p. 248)

- Thinking is the manipulation of mental representations of information. Thinking transforms such representations into novel and different forms, permitting people to answer questions, solve problems, and reach goals. (p. 249)

- Mental images are representations in the mind of an object or event. (p. 249)

- Concepts are categorizations of objects, events, or people that share common properties. Prototypes are representative examples of concepts. (p. 250)

What processes underlie reasoning and decision making?

- In syllogistic reasoning, people derive implications from a set of assumptions that they know to be true. (p.253)

- Decisions sometimes (but not always) may be improved through the use of algorithms and heuristics. An algorithm is a rule that, if applied appropriately, guarantees a solution; a heuristic is a cognitive shortcut that may lead to a solution but is not guaranteed to do so. (p. 253)

EVALUATE

1. _____ _____ are representations in the mind of an object or event.
2. _____ are categorizations of objects that share common properties.
3. When you think of the concept "chair," you immediately think of a comfortable easy chair. A chair of this type could be thought of as a _____ of the category "chair."
4. When you ask your friend how best to study for your psychology final, he tells you, "I've always found it best to skim over the notes once, then read the book, then go over the notes again." What decision-making tool might this be an example of?

RETHINK

1. How might the availability heuristic contribute to prejudices based on race, age, and gender? Can awareness of this heuristic prevent this from happening?
2. *From the perspective of a human resources specialist:* How might you use the research on mental imagery to improve employees' performance?

Answers to Evaluate Questions

1. mental images; 2. concepts; 3. prototype; 4. heuristic

KEY TERMS

cognitive psychology p. 248   mental images p. 249   prototypes p. 251   algorithm p. 253
thinking p. 249   concepts p. 250   syllogistic reasoning p. 253   heuristic p. 253

Problem Solving

According to an old legend, a group of Vietnamese monks guard three towers on which sit 64 golden rings. The monks believe that if they succeed in moving the rings from the first tower to the third according to a series of rigid rules, the world as we know it will come to an end. (Should you prefer that the world remain in its present state, there's no need for immediate concern: The puzzle is so complex that it will take the monks about a trillion years to solve it.)

In the Tower of Hanoi puzzle, a simpler version of the task facing the monks, three disks are placed on three posts in the order shown in Figure 1. The goal of the puzzle is to move all three disks to the third post, arranged in the same order, by using as few moves as possible. There are two restrictions: Only one disk can be moved at a time, and no disk can ever cover a smaller one during a move.

Why are cognitive psychologists interested in the Tower of Hanoi problem? Because the way people go about solving such puzzles helps illuminate how people solve complex, real-life problems. Psychologists have found that problem solving typically involves the three steps illustrated in Figure 2: preparing to create solutions, producing solutions, and evaluating the solutions that have been generated.

Preparation: Understanding and Diagnosing Problems

When approaching a problem like the Tower of Hanoi, most people begin by trying to understand the problem thoroughly. If the problem is a novel one, they probably will pay particular attention to any restrictions placed on coming up with a solution—such as the rule for moving only one disk at a time in the Tower of Hanoi problem. If, by contrast, the problem is a familiar one, they are apt to spend considerably less time in this preparation stage.

Problems vary from well defined to ill defined (Reitman, 1965; Arlin, 1989; Evans, 2004). In a *well-defined problem*—such as a mathematical equation or the solution to a jigsaw puzzle—both the nature of the problem itself and the information needed to

Key Concepts

How do people approach and solve problems?

What are the major obstacles to problem solving?

What is creativity?

 StudyALERT

Use the three steps of problem solving to organize your studying: Preparation, Production, and Judgment (PPJ)

FIGURE 1 The goal of the Tower of Hanoi puzzle is to move all three disks from the first post to the third and still preserve the original order of the disks, using the fewest number of moves possible while following the rules that only one disk at a time can be moved and no disk can cover a smaller one during a move. Try it yourself before you look at the solution, which is listed according to the sequence of moves. (Solution: Move C to 3, B to 2, C to 2, A to 3, C to 1, B to 3, C to 3, and C to 3.)

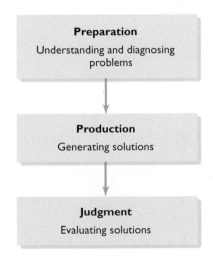

Preparation
Understanding and diagnosing problems

Production
Generating solutions

Judgment
Evaluating solutions

FIGURE 2 Steps in problem solving.

solve it are available and clear. Thus, we can make straightforward judgments about whether a potential solution is appropriate. With an *ill-defined problem*, such as how to increase morale on an assembly line or to bring peace to the Middle East, not only may the specific nature of the problem be unclear, the information required to solve the problem may be even less obvious.

KINDS OF PROBLEMS

Typically, a problem falls into one of the three categories shown in Figure 3: arrangement, inducing structure, and transformation. Solving each type requires somewhat different kinds of psychological skills and knowledge (Spitz, 1987; Chronicle, MacGregor, & Ormerod, 2004).

Arrangement problems require the problem solver to rearrange or recombine elements in a way that will satisfy a certain criterion. Usually, several different arrangements can be made, but only one or a few of the arrangements will produce a solution. Anagram problems and jigsaw puzzles are examples of arrangement problems (Coventry, Venn, Smith, & Morley, 2003).

In *problems of inducing structure*, a person must identify the existing relationships among the elements presented and then construct a new relationship among them. In such a problem, the problem solver must determine not only the relationships among the elements but also the structure and size of the elements involved. In the example shown in Figure 3, a person must first determine that the solution requires the numbers to be considered in pairs (14-24-34-44-54-64). Only after identifying that part of the problem can a person determine the solution rule (the first number of each pair increases by one, while the second number remains the same).

The Tower of Hanoi puzzle represents the third kind of problem—*transformation problems*—which consist of an initial state, a goal state, and a method for changing the initial state into the goal state. In the Tower of Hanoi problem, the initial state is the original configuration, the goal state is to have the three disks on the third peg, and the method is the rules for moving the disks (Mataix-Cols & Bartres-Faz, 2002; Emick & Welsh, 2005; Majeres, 2007).

Whether the problem is one of arrangement, inducing structure, or transformation, the preparation stage of understanding and diagnosing is critical in problem solving because it allows us to develop our own cognitive representation of the problem and to place it within a personal framework. We may divide the problem into subparts or ignore some information as we try to simplify the task. Winnowing out nonessential information is often a critical step in the preparation stage of problem solving.

REPRESENTING AND ORGANIZING THE PROBLEM

A crucial aspect of the initial encounter with a problem is the way in which we represent it to ourselves and organize the information presented to us (Brown & Walter, 1993; Davidson, Deuser, & Sternberg, 1994). Consider the following problem:

A man climbs a mountain on Saturday, leaving at daybreak and arriving at the top near sundown. He spends the night at the top. The next day, Sunday, he leaves at daybreak and heads down the mountain, following the same path that he climbed the day before. The question is this: Will there be any time during the second day when he will be at exactly the same point on the mountain as he was at exactly that time on the first day?

"I don't know about hair care, Rapunzel, but I'm thinking a good cream rinse plus protein conditioner might just solve both our problems."

a. Arrangement problems

1. Anagrams: Rearrange the letters in each set to make an English word:

2. Two strings hang from a ceiling but are too far apart to allow a person to hold one and walk to the other. On the floor are a book of matches, a screwdriver, and a few pieces of cotton. How could the strings be tied together?

b. Problems of inducing structure

1. What number comes next in the series?

   1 4 2 4 3 4 4 4 5 4 6 4

2. Complete these analogies:

   baseball is to bat as tennis is to _____

   merchant is to sell as customer is to _____

c. Transformation problems

1. Water jars: A person has three jars with the following capacities:

   Jar A:
28 ounces

   Jar B:
7 ounces

   Jar C:
5 ounces

   How can the person measure exactly 11 ounces of water?

2. Ten coins are arranged in the following way. By moving only *two* of the coins, make two rows that each contains six coins.

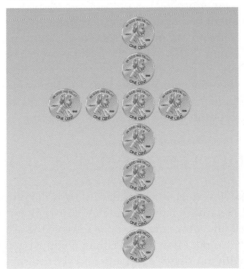

FIGURE 3 The three major categories of problems: (a) arrangement, (b) inducing structure, and (c) transformation. Solutions appear in Figure 4 on p. 260. (Sources: Bourne & Dominowski, *Cognitive Processes*, 1st ed., © 1979. Reproduced in print and electronic formats by permission of Pearson Education, Inc., Upper Saddle River, New Jersey; Aschcraft, 1994.)

FIGURE 4 Solutions to the problems in Figure 3 on the previous page. (Source: Bourne & Dominowski, *Cognitive Processes*, 1st ed., © 1979. Reproduced in print and electronic formats by permission of Pearson Education, Inc., Upper Saddle River, New Jersey.)

a. Arrangement problems

1. FACET, DOUBT, THICK, NAIVE, ANVIL

2. The screwdriver is tied to one of the strings. This makes a pendulum that can be swung to reach the other string.

b. Problems of inducing structure

1. 7

2. racket; buy

c. Transformation problems

1. Fill jar A; empty into jar B once and into jar C twice. What remains in jar A is 11 ounces

2.

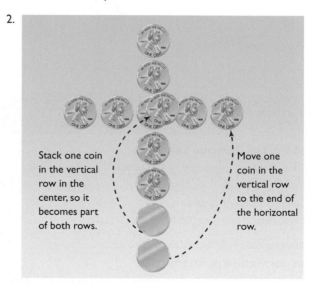

If you try to solve this problem by using algebraic or verbal representations, you will have a good deal of trouble. However, if you represent the problem with the kind of simple diagram shown in Figure 5, the solution will become apparent.

Our ability to represent a problem—and the kind of solution we eventually come to—depends on the way a problem is phrased, or framed. Consider, for example, if you were a cancer patient having to choose between surgery and radiation and were given the two sets of treatment options shown in Figure 6 (Tversky & Kahneman, 1987; Chandran & Menon, 2004). When the options are framed in terms of the likelihood of survival, only 18 percent of participants in a study chose radiation over surgery. However, when the choice was framed in terms of the likelihood of dying, 44 percent chose radiation over surgery—even though the outcomes are identical in both sets of framing conditions.

Production: Generating Solutions

After preparation, the next stage in problem solving is the production of possible solutions. If a problem is relatively simple, we may already have a direct solution stored in long-term memory, and all we need to do is retrieve the appropriate information. If we cannot retrieve or do not know the solution, we must generate possible solutions and compare them with information in long- and short-term memory.

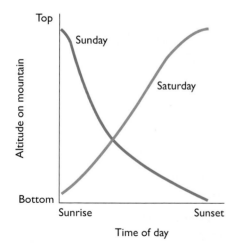

FIGURE 5 You can solve the mountain-climbing problem by using a graph. Keep in mind that the goal is not to determine the time, but just to indicate whether an exact time exists. Consequently, the speed at which the traveler is moving is unimportant (Anderson, 1980). Can you think of other approaches that might lead to a solution?

Problem: Surgery or radiation?	
Survival Frame	**Mortality Frame**
Surgery: Of 100 people having surgery, 90 live through the post-operative period, 68 are alive at the end of the first year, and 34 are alive at the end of five years.	**Surgery:** Of 100 people having surgery, 10 die during surgery, 32 die by the end of the first year, and 66 die by the end of five years.
Radiation: Of 100 people having radiation therapy, all live through the treatment, 77 are alive at the end of one year, and 22 are alive at the end of five years.	**Radiation:** Of 100 people having radiation therapy, none die during the treatment, 23 die by the end of one year, and 78 die by the end of five years.
Far more patients choose surgery	Far more patients choose radiation

 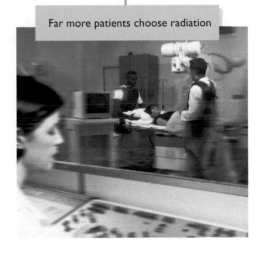

FIGURE 6 A decision often is affected by the way a problem is framed. In this case, most would choose radiation over surgery, despite similar results.

At the most basic level, we can solve problems through trial and error. Thomas Edison invented the lightbulb only because he tried thousands of different kinds of materials for a filament before he found one that worked (carbon). The difficulty with trial and error, of course, is that some problems are so complicated that it would take a lifetime to try out every possibility. For example, according to some estimates, there are some 10^{120} possible sequences of chess moves (Fine & Fine, 2003).

In place of trial and error, complex problem solving often involves the use of heuristics, cognitive shortcuts that can generate solutions. Probably the most frequently applied heuristic in problem solving is a **means-ends analysis**, which involves repeated tests for differences between the desired outcome and what currently exists. Consider this simple example (Newell & Simon, 1972; Huber, Beckmann, & Herrmann, 2004; Chrysikou, 2006):

> I want to take my son to preschool. What's the difference between what I have and what I want? One of distance. What changes distance? My automobile. My automobile won't work. What is needed to make it work? A new battery. What has new batteries? An auto repair shop . . .

In a means-end analysis, each step brings the problem solver closer to a resolution. Although this approach is often effective, if the problem requires indirect steps that temporarily *increase* the discrepancy between a current state and the solution, means-ends analysis can be counterproductive. For example, sometimes the fastest

Means-ends analysis: Repeated testing for differences between the desired outcome and what currently exists.

route to the summit of a mountain requires a mountain climber to backtrack temporarily; a means-end approach—which implies that the mountain climber should always forge ahead and upward—will be ineffective in such instances.

For other problems, the best approach is to work backward by focusing on the goal, rather than the starting point, of the problem. Consider, for example, the water lily problem:

> Water lilies are growing on Blue Lake. The water lilies grow rapidly, so that the amount of water surface covered by lilies doubles every 24 hours.

> On the first day of summer, there was just one water lily. On the 90th day of the summer, the lake was entirely covered. On what day was the lake half covered? (Reisberg, 1997)

If you start searching for a solution to the problem by thinking about the initial state on day 1 (one water lily) and move forward from there, you're facing a daunting task of trial-and-error estimation. But try taking a different approach: Start with day 90, when the entire lake was covered with lilies. Given that the lilies double their coverage daily, on the prior day only half the lake was covered. The answer, then, is day 89, a solution found by working backward (Bourne et al., 1986; Hunt, 1994).

FORMING SUBGOALS: DIVIDING PROBLEMS INTO THEIR PARTS

Another heuristic commonly used to generate solutions is to divide a problem into intermediate steps, or *subgoals*, and solve each of those steps. For instance, in our modified Tower of Hanoi problem, we could choose several obvious subgoals, such as moving the largest disk to the third post.

If solving a subgoal is a step toward the ultimate solution to a problem, identifying subgoals is an appropriate strategy. In some cases, however, forming subgoals is not all that helpful and may actually increase the time needed to find a solution. For example, some problems cannot be subdivided. Others—like some complicated mathematical problems—are so complex that it takes longer to identify the appropriate subdivisions than to solve the problem by other means (Reed, 1996; Kaller et al., 2004; Fishbach, Dhar, & Zhang, 2006).

INSIGHT: SUDDEN AWARENESS

Some approaches to generating possible solutions focus less on step-by-step heuristics than on the sudden bursts of comprehension that one may experience during efforts to solve a problem. Just after World War I, the German psychologist Wolfgang Köhler examined learning and problem-solving processes in chimpanzees (Köhler, 1927). In his studies, Köhler exposed chimps to challenging situations in which the elements of the solution were all present; all the chimps needed to do was put them together.

In one of Köhler's studies, chimps were kept in a cage in which boxes and sticks were strewn about, and a bunch of tantalizing bananas hung from the ceiling, out of reach. Initially, the chimps made trial-and-error attempts to get to the bananas: They would throw the sticks at the bananas, jump from one of the boxes, or leap wildly from the ground. Frequently, they would seem to give up in frustration, leaving the bananas dangling temptingly overhead. But then, in what

THE FAR SIDE® BY GARY LARSON

© 1981 FarWorks, Inc. All Rights Reserved/Dist. by Creators Syndicate

PRIMATE RESEARCH LAB

The Far Side® by Gary Larson © 1981 FarWorks, Inc. All Rights Reserved. The Far Side® and the Larson® signature are registered trademarks of FarWorks, Inc. Used with permission.

(a)

(b)

(c)

In an impressive display of insight, Sultan, one of the chimpanzees in Köhler's experiments in problem solving, sees a bunch of bananas that is out of reach (a). He then carries over several crates (b), stacks them, and stands on them to reach the bananas (c).

seemed like a sudden revelation, they would stop whatever they were doing and stand on a box to reach the bananas with a stick. Köhler called the cognitive process underlying the chimps' new behavior **insight**, a sudden awareness of the relationships among various elements that had previously appeared to be unrelated.

Insight: A sudden awareness of the relationships among various elements that had previously appeared to be independent of one another.

Although Köhler emphasized the apparent suddenness of insightful solutions, subsequent research has shown that prior experience and trial-and-error practice in problem solving must precede "insight." Consequently, the chimps' behavior may simply represent the chaining together of previously learned responses, no different from the way a pigeon learns, by trial and error, to peck a key (Epstein, 1996; Windholz & Lamal, 2002).

Judgment: Evaluating the Solutions

The final stage in problem solving is judging the adequacy of a solution. Often this is a simple matter: If the solution is clear—as in the Tower of Hanoi problem—we will know immediately whether we have been successful (Varma, 2007).

If the solution is less concrete or if there is no single correct solution, evaluating solutions becomes more difficult. In such instances, we must decide which alternative solution is best. Unfortunately, we often quite inaccurately estimate the quality of our own ideas. For instance, a team of drug researchers working for a particular company may consider their remedy for an illness to be superior to all others, overestimating the likelihood of their success and downplaying the approaches of competing drug companies (Eizenberg & Zaslavsky, 2004).

Theoretically, if we rely on appropriate heuristics and valid information to make decisions, we can make accurate choices among alternative solutions. However, as we see next, several kinds of obstacles to and biases in problem solving affect the quality of the decisions and judgments we make.

Impediments to Solutions: Why Is Problem Solving Such a Problem?

Consider the following problem-solving test (Duncker, 1945):

> You are given a set of tacks, candles, and matches, each in a small box, and told your goal is to place three candles at eye level on a nearby door, so that wax will not drip on the floor as the candles burn (see Figure 7). How would you approach this challenge?

If you have difficulty solving the problem, you are not alone. Most people cannot solve it when it is presented in the manner illustrated in the figure, in which the objects are *inside* the boxes. However, if the objects were presented *beside* the boxes, just resting on the table, chances are that you would solve the problem much more readily—which, in case you are wondering, requires tacking the boxes to the door and then placing the candles inside them (see Figure 9 on page 266).

The difficulty you probably encountered in solving this problem stems from its presentation, which misled you at the initial preparation stage. Actually, significant obstacles to problem solving can exist at each of the three major stages. Although cognitive approaches to problem solving suggest that thinking proceeds along fairly rational, logical lines as a person confronts a problem and considers various solutions, several factors can hinder the development of creative, appropriate, and accurate solutions.

FUNCTIONAL FIXEDNESS AND MENTAL SET

Functional fixedness: The tendency to think of an object only in terms of its typical use.

The difficulty most people experience with the candle problem is caused by **functional fixedness**, the tendency to think of an object only in terms of its typical use. For instance, functional fixedness probably leads you to think of this book as something to read, instead of its potential use as a doorstop or as kindling for a fire. In the candle problem, because the objects are first presented inside the boxes, functional fixedness leads most people to see the boxes simply as containers for the objects they hold rather than as a potential part of the solution. They cannot envision another function for the boxes.

Mental set: The tendency for old patterns of problem solving to persist.

Functional fixedness is an example of a broader phenomenon known as **mental set**, the tendency for old patterns of problem solving to persist. A classic experiment (Luchins, 1946) demonstrated this phenomenon. As you can see in Figure 8 on page 265, the object of the task is to use the jars in each row to measure out the designated amount of liquid. (Try it yourself to get a sense of the power of mental set before moving on.)

If you have tried to solve the problem, you know that the first five rows are all solved in the same way: First fill the largest jar (B) and then from it fill the middle-size jar (A) once and the smallest jar (C) two times. What is left in B is the designated amount. (Stated as a formula, the designated amount is B–A–2C.)

FIGURE 7 The problem here is to place three candles at eye level on a nearby door so that the wax will not drip on the floor as the candles burn—using only material in the figure. For a solution turn to Figure 9 on p. 266.

Given jars with these capacities (in ounces):

	A	B	C	Obtain:
1.	21	127	3	100
2.	14	163	25	99
3.	18	43	10	5
4.	9	42	6	21
5.	20	59	4	31
6.	28	76	3	25

FIGURE 8 Try this classic demonstration, which illustrates the importance of mental set in problem solving. The object is to use the jars in each row to measure out the designated amount of liquid. After you figure out the solution for the first five rows, you'll probably have trouble with the sixth row—even though the solution is actually easier. In fact, if you had tried to solve the problem in the sixth row first, you probably would have had no difficulty at all.

The demonstration of mental set comes in the sixth row of the problem, a point at which you probably encountered some difficulty. If you are like most people, you tried the formula and were perplexed when it failed. Chances are, in fact, that you missed the simple (but different) solution to the problem, which involves merely subtracting C from A. Interestingly, people who were given the problem in row 6 *first* had no difficulty with it at all.

Mental set can affect perceptions, as well as patterns of problem solving. It can prevent you from seeing beyond the apparent constraints of a problem. For example, try to draw four straight lines so that they pass through all nine dots in the grid below—without lifting your pencil from the page.

```
•  •  •
•  •  •
•  •  •
```

If you had difficulty with the problem, it was probably because you felt compelled to keep your lines within the grid. If you had gone outside the boundaries, however, you would have succeeded by using the solution shown in Figure 10. (The phrase "thinking outside the box"—a term commonly used in business today to encourage creativity—stems from research on overcoming the constraining effects of mental set.)

INACCURATE EVALUATION OF SOLUTIONS

When a nuclear power plant in Pennsylvania suffered a malfunction in 1979, the plant operators immediately had to solve a problem of the most serious kind. Several monitors gave contradictory information about the source of the problem: One suggested pressure that was too high, leading to the danger of an explosion; others indicated pressure that was too low, which could lead to a meltdown. Although the pressure was, in fact, too low, the supervisors on duty relied on the one monitor—which turned out to be faulty—that suggested that the pressure was too high. Once they had made their decision and acted on it, they ignored the contradictory evidence from the other monitors (Wickens, 1984).

The operators' mistake exemplifies **confirmation bias**, in which problem solvers favor initial hypotheses and ignore contradictory information that supports alternative

Confirmation bias: The tendency to favor information that supports one's initial hypotheses and ignore contradictory information that supports alternative hypotheses or solutions.

FIGURE 9 A solution to the problem in Figure 7 involves tacking the boxes to the door and placing the candles in the boxes.

hypotheses or solutions. Even when we find evidence that contradicts a solution we have chosen, we are apt to stick with our original hypothesis.

Confirmation bias occurs for several reasons. For one thing, because rethinking a problem that appears to be solved already takes extra cognitive effort, we are apt to stick with our first solution. For another, we give greater weight to subsequent information that supports our initial position than to information that is not supportive of it (Gilovich, Griffin, & Kahneman, 2002; Evans & Feeney, 2004; Parmley, 2007).

Creativity and Problem Solving

Despite obstacles to problem solving, many people adeptly discover creative solutions to problems. One enduring question that cognitive psychologists have sought to answer is what factors underlie **creativity**, the ability to generate original ideas or solve problems in novel ways.

Although identifying the stages of problem solving helps us understand how people approach and solve problems, it does little to explain why some people come up with better solutions than others do. For instance, even the possible solutions to a simple problem often show wide discrepancies. Consider, for example, how you might respond to the question "How many uses can you think of for a newspaper?"

Now compare your solution with this one proposed by a 10-year-old boy:

> You can read it, write on it, lay it down and paint a picture on it . . . You could put it in your door for decoration, put it in the garbage can, put it on a chair if the chair is messy. If you have a puppy, you put newspaper in its box or put it in your backyard for the dog to play with. When you build something and you don't want anyone to see it, put newspaper around it. Put newspaper on the floor if you have no mattress, use it to pick up something hot, use it to stop bleeding, or to catch the drips from drying clothes. You can use a newspaper for curtains, put it in your shoe to cover what is hurting your foot, make a kite out of it, shade a light that is too bright. You can wrap fish in it, wipe windows, or wrap money in it . . . You put washed shoes in newspaper, wipe eyeglasses with it, put it under

Creativity: The ability to generate original ideas or solve problems in novel ways.

FIGURE 10 A solution to the nine-dot problem requires the use of lines drawn beyond the boundaries of the figure—something that our mental set may prevent us from seeing easily.

a dripping sink, put a plant on it, make a paper bowl out of it, use it for a hat if it is raining, tie it on your feet for slippers. You can put it on the sand if you had no towel, use it for bases in baseball, make paper airplanes with it, use it as a dustpan when you sweep, ball it up for the cat to play with, wrap your hands in it if it is cold. (Ward, Kogan, & Pankove, 1972)

This list shows extraordinary creativity. Unfortunately, it is much easier to identify *examples* of creativity than to determine its causes. Several factors, however, seem to be associated with creativity (Simonton, 2003; Kaufman & Baer, 2005; Schepers, van den Berg, 2007).

One of these factors is **divergent thinking**, the ability to generate unusual, yet appropriate, responses to problems or questions. This type of thinking contrasts with **convergent thinking**, which produces responses that are based primarily on knowledge and logic. For instance, someone relying on convergent thinking would answer "You read it" to the query "What can you do with a newspaper?" In contrast, "You use it as a dustpan" is a more divergent—and creative—response (Baer, 1993; Runco & Sakamoto, 1993; Finke, 1995; Sternberg, 2001; Ho, 2004; Runco, 2006; Cropley, 2006).

Another aspect of creativity is its *cognitive complexity*, or preference for elaborate, intricate, and complex stimuli and thinking patterns. For instance, creative people often have a wider range of interests and are more independent and more interested in philosophical or abstract problems than are less creative individuals (Barron, 1990). In addition, there may be differences in how the brain processes information in more creative people, as we discuss in the *Applying Psychology in the 21st Century* box.

One factor that is *not* closely related to creativity is intelligence. Traditional intelligence tests, which ask focused questions that have only one acceptable answer, tap convergent thinking skills. Highly creative people may therefore find that such tests penalize their divergent thinking. This may explain why researchers consistently find that creativity is only slightly related to school grades and intelligence when intelligence is measured using traditional intelligence tests (Hong, Milgram, & Gorsky, 1995; Sternberg & O'Hara, 2000).

"I'll be happy to give you innovative thinking. What are the guidelines?"

Divergent thinking: The ability to generate unusual, yet nonetheless appropriate, responses to problems or questions.

Convergent thinking: The ability to produce responses that are based primarily on knowledge and logic.

 StudyALERT

Remember *d*ivergent thinking produces *d*ifferent and *d*iverse kinds of responses, while *c*onvergent thinking produces more *c*ommonsense kinds of responses.

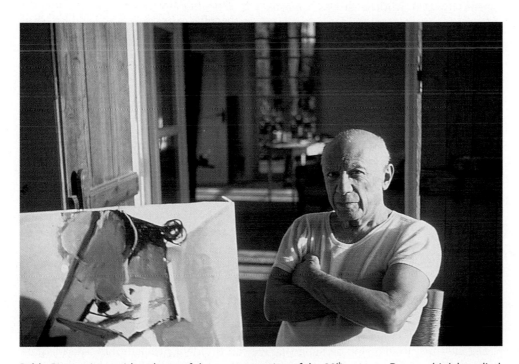

Pablo Picasso is considered one of the greatest artists of the 20th century. Do you think he relied more on convergent or divergent thinking in his art?

Creativity in the Workplace

Working for a progressive company helped Orkut Buyukkokten make his dream come true. "My dream is to connect all Internet users so they can all relate to each other," Buyukkokten once said. This young software engineer may have been dreaming big, but so did his employer, Google. In a mutually beneficial arrangement, Google gave Buyukkokten and all its other engineers one workday per week on paid time to develop their own creative projects. Being paid to work on his dream helped Buyukkokten to produce a creative masterpiece: he developed Orkut, the . . . social networking service that would quickly grow to include millions of users worldwide. (Levy, 2004, p. 40)

Orkut—the man and the service—is far from being the only success story at Google. Many of the company's original, creative service offerings came from employees who were given the time, the tools, and the right atmosphere to nurture their creativity. The success of this initiative underscores that almost anyone can be creative if given the proper support and resources (Nebenzahl, 2007).

Industrial-organizational psychologists are exploring ways of nurturing creativity in the workplace. For instance, researcher Teresa Amabile and colleagues studied the

Orkut Buyukkokten, a Google software engineer, developed an innovative social networking service.

interplay between creativity and emotion in project teams. Teams of professionals who were working together on a creative project (such as developing a new product or solving a very complex problem) kept individual diaries in which they logged their daily work experiences, including their emotions and their perceptions regarding what went on with the project team that day and their own efforts in it. Examining the diaries, the researchers found that creativity was associated with a positive mood. When people were in a good mood on a given day, they were more likely to have creative ideas on that day or within the next couple of days (Amabile et al., 2005).

The relationship between emotion and creativity also worked in the opposite direction. Having a creative idea was associated with a subsequent change in emotion. Most often the resulting emotion was positive one—such as elation or satis-

faction at having solved a problem. But sometimes it was a negative one, such as frustration when a creative idea could not be readily implemented for lack of resources. In either case, though, the emotional consequence of a creative moment tended not to be very long lasting—it almost never carried over to the next day.

Amabile also found that positive feedback, support, and recognition are crucial to making creative endeavors rewarding. People felt good when their ideas were taken seriously and they were given the support they needed to do a good job. But there was also evidence that the creative act was itself intrinsically pleasurable. Workers reported a sense of involvement, enjoyment, and even passion for their work when it was creative. As one respondent wrote in his diary, "Then I tried something that had not been done before, to my knowledge, and it is working wonderfully at this moment. Ain't science wonderful? God, I love it when a plan comes together" (Amabile, Barsade, Mueller, & Staw, 2005, p. 387).

- Why do you think it sometimes takes a day or two for a positive mood to produce creative ideas?
- What might be some direct and indirect benefits to businesses and employees of creating an environment that fosters creativity, as Google has done?

BECOMING AN INFORMED CONSUMER of Psychology

Thinking Critically and Creatively

Can we learn to be better thinkers?

Cognitive researchers have found that people can learn the abstract rules of logic and reasoning and that such knowledge can improve our reasoning about the underlying causes of everyday events in our lives. Research suggests that critical and creative thinkers are made, not born. Consider, for instance, these suggestions for increasing critical thinking and creativity (Burbach, Matkin, & Fritz, 2004; Kaufman & Baer, 2006):

- *Redefine problems.* We can modify boundaries and assumptions by rephrasing a problem at either a more abstract or a more concrete level.
- *Use subgoals.* By developing subgoals, we can divide a problem into intermediate steps. This process, known as *fractionation*, allows us to examine each part for new

possibilities and approaches, leading to a novel solution for the problem as a whole.

- *Adopt a critical perspective.* Rather than passively accepting assumptions or arguments, we can evaluate material critically, consider its implications, and think about possible exceptions and contradictions.
- *Consider the opposite.* By considering the opposite of a concept we're seeking to understand, we can sometimes make progress. For example, to define "good mental health," it may be useful to consider what "bad mental health" means.
- *Use analogies.* Analogies provide alternative frameworks for the interpretation of facts and help us uncover new understanding. One particularly effective means of coming up with analogies is to look for examples in the animal world. For instance, architects discovered how to construct the earliest skyscrapers by noting how lily pads on a pond could support the weight of a person (Getner & Holyoak, 1997; Bearman, Ball, & Omerod, 2007; Cho, Holyoak, & Cannon, 2007).
- *Think divergently.* Instead of the most logical or common use for an object, consider how you might use the object if you were forbidden to use it in the usual way.
- *Use heuristics.* Heuristics are cognitive shortcuts that can help bring about a solution to a problem. If the problem has a single correct answer and you can use or construct a heuristic, you can often find the solution more rapidly and effectively.
- *Experiment with various solutions.* Don't be afraid to use different routes to find solutions for problems (verbal, mathematical, graphic, even dramatic). For instance, try to come up with every conceivable idea you can, no matter how wild or bizarre it may seem at first. After you've come up with a list of solutions, review each one and try to think of ways to make what at first appeared impractical seem more feasible.

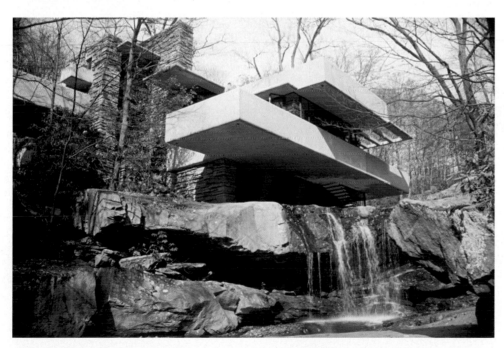

Falling water, designed by legendary architect Frank Lloyd Wright, is known as a masterpiece of visionary architecture. What processes might account for Wright's creativity?

RECAP/EVALUATE/RETHINK

RECAP

How do people approach and solve problems?

- Problem solving typically involves three major stages: preparation, production of solutions, and evaluation of solutions that have been generated. (p. 257)

- Preparation involves placing the problem in one of three categories. In arrangement problems, a group of elements must be rearranged or recombined in a way that will satisfy a certain criterion. In problems of inducing structure, a person first must identify the existing relationships among the elements presented and then construct a new relationship among them. Finally, transformation problems consist of an initial state, a goal state, and a method for changing the initial state into the goal state. (p. 258)

- A crucial aspect of the preparation stage is the representation and organization of the problem. (p. 258)

- In the production stage, people try to generate solutions. They may find solutions to some problems in long-term memory. Alternatively, they may solve some problems through simple trial and error and use algorithms and heuristics to solve more complex problems. (p. 260)

- Using the heuristic of a means-ends analysis, a person will repeatedly test for differences between the desired outcome and what currently exists, trying each time to come closer to the goal. (p. 261)

- Köhler's research with chimpanzees illustrates insight, a sudden awareness of the relationships among elements that had previously seemed unrelated. (p. 262)

What are the major obstacles to problem solving?

- Several factors hinder effective problem solving. Mental set, of which functional fixedness is an example, is the tendency for old patterns of problem solving to persist. Inappropriate use of algorithms and heuristics can also act as an obstacle to the production of solutions. Confirmation bias, in which initial hypotheses are favored, can hinder the accurate evaluation of solutions to problems. (p. 264)

What is creativity?

- Creativity is the ability to combine responses or ideas in novel ways. Creativity is related to divergent thinking (the ability to generate unusual, but still appropriate, responses to problems or questions) and cognitive complexity. (p. 266)

EVALUATE

1. Solving a problem by trying to reduce the difference between the current state and the goal state is known as a _____.

2. _____ is the term used to describe the sudden "flash" of revelation that often accompanies the solution to a problem.

3. Thinking of an object only in terms of its typical use is known as _____ _____. A broader, related tendency for old problem-solving patterns to persist is known as a _____ _____.

4. _____ _____ describes the phenomenon of favoring an initial hypothesis and ignoring subsequent competing hypotheses.

5. Generating unusual but appropriate approaches to a question is known as _____ _____.

RETHINK

1. Is the reasoning in the following syllogism correct or incorrect? Why?
   Creative people often have trouble with traditional intelligence tests.
   I have trouble with traditional intelligence tests.
   Therefore, I am a creative person.

2. *From the perspective of a manufacturer*: How might you encourage your employees to develop creative ways to improve the products that you produce?

Answers to Evaluate Questions

1. transformation; 2. insight; 3. functional fixedness, mental set; 4. confirmation bias; 5. divergent thinking.

KEY TERMS

means-ends analysis p. 261
insight p. 263
functional fixedness p. 264
mental set p. 264
confirmation bias p. 266
creativity p. 266
divergent thinking p. 267
convergent thinking p. 267

Language

'Twas brillig, and the slithy toves

Did gyre and gimble in the wabe:

All mimsy were the borogoves,

And the mome raths outgrabe.

Although few of us have ever come face to face with a tove, we have little difficulty in discerning that in Lewis Carroll's (1872) poem "Jabberwocky," the expression *slithy toves* contains an adjective, *slithy*, and the noun it modifies, *toves*.

Our ability to make sense out of nonsense, if the nonsense follows typical rules of language, illustrates the complexity of both human language and the cognitive processes that underlie its development and use. The use of **language**—the communication of information through symbols arranged according to systematic rules—is an important cognitive ability, one that is indispensable for us to communicate with one another. Not only is language central to communication, it is also closely tied to the very way in which we think about and understand the world. No wonder psychologists have devoted considerable attention to studying language (Fitch & Sanders, 2005; Stapel & Semin, 2007; Hoff, 2008).

Grammar: Language's Language

To understand how language develops and relates to thought, we first need to review some of the formal elements of language. The basic structure of language rests on **grammar**, the system of rules that determine how our thoughts can be expressed.

Grammar deals with three major components of language: phonology, syntax, and semantics. **Phonology** is the study of the smallest basic units of speech, called **phonemes**, that affect meaning, and of the way we use those sounds to form words and produce meaning. For instance, the *a* sound in *fat* and the *a* sound in *fate* represent two different phonemes in English (Hardison, 2006).

Linguists have identified more than 800 different phonemes among all the world's languages. Although English speakers use just 52 phonemes to produce words, other languages use from as few as 15 to as many as 141. Differences in phonemes are one reason people have difficulty learning other languages. For example, to a Japanese speaker, whose native language does not have an *r* phoneme, pronouncing such English words as *roar* present some difficulty (Gibbs, 2002; Iverson et al., 2003).

Syntax refers to the rules that indicate how words and phrases can be combined to form sentences. Every language has intricate rules that guide the order in which words may be strung together to communicate meaning. English speakers have no difficulty recognizing that "TV down the turn" is not a meaningful sequence, whereas "Turn down the TV" is. To understand the effect of syntax in English, consider the changes in meaning caused by the different word orders in the following three utterances: "John kidnapped the boy," "John, the kidnapped boy," and "The boy kidnapped John" (Eberhard, Cutting, & Bock, 2005; Robert, 2006).

Key Concepts

How do people use language?

How does language develop?

Language: The communication of information through symbols arranged according to systematic rules.

Grammar: The system of rules that determine how our thoughts can be expressed.
Phonology: The study of the smallest units of speech, called phonemes.
Phonemes: The smallest units of speech.

Syntax: Ways in which words and phrases can be combined to form sentences.

271

Semantics: The rules governing the meaning of words and sentences.

The third major component of language is **semantics**, the meanings of words and sentences. Semantic rules allow us to use words to convey the subtlest nuances. For instance, we are able to make the distinction between "The truck hit Laura" (which we would be likely to say if we had just seen the vehicle hitting Laura) and "Laura was hit by a truck" (which we would probably say if someone asked why Laura was missing class while she recuperated) (Richgels, 2004; Pietarinen, 2006).

Despite the complexities of language, most of us acquire the basics of grammar without even being aware that we have learned its rules. Moreover, even though we may have difficulty explicitly stating the rules of grammar, our linguistic abilities are so sophisticated that we can utter an infinite number of different statements. How do we acquire such abilities?

Language Development: Developing a Way with Words

To parents, the sounds of their infant babbling and cooing are music to their ears (except, perhaps, at three o'clock in the morning). These sounds also serve an important function. They mark the first step on the road to the development of language.

BABBLING

Babble: Meaningless speechlike sounds made by children from around the age of 3 months through 1 year.

Children **babble**—make speechlike but meaningless sounds—from around the age of 3 months through 1 year. While babbling, they may produce, at one time or another, any of the sounds found in all languages, not just the one to which they are exposed. Even deaf children display their own form of babbling, for infants who are unable to hear yet who are exposed to sign language from birth "babble" with their hands (Pettito, 1993; Locke, 2006).

An infant's babbling increasingly reflects the specific language being spoken in the infant's environment, initially in terms of pitch and tone and eventually in terms of specific sounds. Young infants can distinguish among all 869 phonemes that have been identified across the world's languages. However, after the age of 6 to 8 months, that ability begins to decline. Infants begin to "specialize" in the language to which they are exposed as neurons in their brains reorganize to respond to the particular phonemes infants routinely hear.

Some theorists argue that a *critical period* exists for language development early in life, in which a child is particularly sensitive to language cues and most easily acquires language. In fact, if children are not exposed to language during this critical period, later they will have great difficulty overcoming this deficit (Bates, 2005; Shafer & Garrido-Nag, 2007).

Cases in which abused children have been isolated from contact with others support the theory of such critical periods. In one case, for example, a girl named Genie was exposed to virtually no language from the age of 20 months until she was rescued at age 13 years. She was unable to speak at all. Despite intensive instruction, she learned only some words and was never able to master the complexities of language (Rymer, 1994; Veltman & Browne, 2001).

PRODUCTION OF LANGUAGE

By the time children are approximately 1 year old, they stop producing sounds that are not in the language to which they have been exposed. It is then a short step to the production of actual words. In English, these are typically short words that start with a consonant sound such as *b, d, m, p,* and *t*—this helps explain why *mama* and *dada* are so often among babies' first words. Of course, even before they produce their first words, children can understand a fair amount of the language they hear. Language comprehension precedes language production.

A syllable in signed language, similar to the ones seen in the manual babbling of deaf infants and in the spoken babbling of hearing infants. The similarities in language structure suggest that language has biological roots.

After the age of 1 year, children begin to learn more complicated forms of language. They produce two-word combinations, the building blocks of sentences, and sharply increase the number of different words they are able to use. By age 2, the average child has a vocabulary of more than 50 words. Just six months later, that vocabulary has grown to several hundred words. At that time, children can produce short sentences, although they use **telegraphic speech**—sentences that sound as if they were part of a telegram, in which words not critical to the message are left out. Rather than saying, "I showed you the book," a child using telegraphic speech may say, "I show book," and "I am drawing a dog" may become "Drawing dog." As children get older, of course, they use less telegraphic speech and produce increasingly complex sentences (Volterra et al., 2003).

By age 3, children learn to make plurals by adding *s* to nouns and to form the past tense by adding *-ed* to verbs. This skill also leads to errors, since children tend to apply rules inflexibly. In such **overgeneralization**, children employ rules even when doing so results in an error. Thus, although it is correct to say "he walked" for the past tense of *walk*, the *-ed* rule doesn't work quite so well when children say "he runned" for the past tense of *run* (Howe, 2002; Rice et al., 2004; Gershkoff-Stowe, Connell, & Smith, 2006).

By age 5, children have acquired the basic rules of language. However, they do not attain a full vocabulary and the ability to comprehend and use subtle grammatical rules until later. For example, a 5-year-old boy who sees a blindfolded doll and is asked, "Is the doll easy or hard to see?" would have great trouble answering the question. In fact, if he were asked to make the doll easier to see, he would probably try to remove the doll's blindfold. By the time they are 8 years old, however, children have little difficulty understanding this question, because they realize that the doll's blindfold has nothing to do with an observer's ability to see the doll (Chomsky, 1969; Hoff, 2003).

UNDERSTANDING LANGUAGE ACQUISITION: IDENTIFYING THE ROOTS OF LANGUAGE

Anyone who spends even a little time with children will notice the enormous strides that they make in language development throughout childhood. However, the reasons for this rapid growth are far from obvious. Psychologists have offered two major explanations, one based on learning theory and the other based on innate processes.

Learning Theory Approaches: Language as a Learned Skill. The **learning-theory approach** suggests that language acquisition follows the principles of reinforcement and conditioning discovered by psychologists who study learning. For example, a child who says "mama" receives hugs and praise from her mother, which reinforce the behavior of saying "mama" and make its repetition more likely. This view suggests that children first learn to speak by being rewarded for making sounds that approximate speech. Ultimately, through a process of shaping, language becomes more and more like adult speech (Skinner, 1957; Ornat & Gallo, 2004).

In support of the learning-theory approach to language acquisition, the more that parents speak to their young children, the more proficient the children become in language use. In addition, by the time they are 3 years old, children who hear higher levels of linguistic sophistication in their parents' speech show a greater rate of vocabulary growth, vocabulary use, and even general intellectual achievement than do children whose parents' speech is more simple (Hart & Risley, 1997).

The learning-theory approach is less successful in explaining how children acquire language rules. Children are reinforced not only when they use language correctly, but also when they use it incorrectly. For example, parents answer a child's "Why the dog won't eat?" as readily as they do the correctly phrased question, "Why won't the dog eat?" Listeners understand both sentences equally well. Learning theory, then, has difficulty fully explaining language acquisition.

Telegraphic speech: Sentences in which words not critical to the message are left out.

Overgeneralization: The phenomenon by which children apply language rules even when the application results in an error.

Learning-theory approach (to language development): The theory suggesting that language acquisition follows the principles of reinforcement and conditioning.

Noam Chomsky argues that all languages share a universal grammar.

Nativist approach (to language development): The theory that a genetically determined, innate mechanism directs language development.

Universal grammar: Noam Chomsky's theory that all the world's languages share a common underlying structure.

Language-acquisition device: A neural system of the brain hypothesized by Noam Chomsky to permit understanding of language.

Nativist Approaches: Language as an Innate Skill. Pointing to such problems with learning-theory approaches to language acquisition, linguist Noam Chomsky (1968, 1978, 1991) provided a groundbreaking alternative. Chomsky argued that humans are born with an innate linguistic capability that emerges primarily as a function of maturation. According to his **nativist approach** to language, all the world's languages share a common underlying structure called a **universal grammar**. Chomsky suggested that the human brain has a neural system, the **language-acquisition device**, that not only lets us understand the structure language provides but also gives us strategies and techniques for learning the unique characteristics of our native language (McGilvray, 2004; Lidz & Gleitman, 2004; White, 2007).

Chomsky used the concept of the language-acquisition device as a metaphor, and he did not identify a specific area of the brain in which it resides. However, evidence collected by neuroscientists suggests that the ability to use language, which was a significant evolutionary advance in human beings, is tied to specific neurological developments (Sakai, 2005; Sahin, Pinker, & Halgren, 2007; Willems & Hagoort, 2007).

For example, scientists have discovered a gene related to the development of language abilities that may have emerged as recently—in evolutionary terms—as 100,000 years ago. Furthermore, it is clear that there are specific sites within the brain that are closely tied to language, and that the shape of the human mouth and throat are tailored to the production of speech. And there is evidence that features of specific types of languages are tied to particular genes, such as in "tonal" languages in which pitch is used to convey meaning (Hauser, Chomsky, & Fitch, 2002; Chandra, 2007; Dediu & Ladd, 2007).

Still, Chomsky's view has its critics. For instance, learning theorists contend that the apparent ability of certain animals, such as chimpanzees, to learn the fundamentals of human language (as we discuss later in this module) contradicts the innate linguistic capability view.

Interactionist approach (to language development): The view that language development is produced through a combination of genetically determined predispositions and environmental circumstances that help teach language.

Interactionist Approaches. To reconcile the differing views, many theorists take an **interactionist approach** to language development. The interactionist approach suggests that language development is produced through a combination of genetically determined predispositions and environmental circumstances that help teach language.

Specifically, proponents of the interactionist approach suggest that the brain's hardwired language-acquisition device that Chomsky and geneticists point to provides the hardware for our acquisition of language, whereas the exposure to language in our environment that learning theorists observe allows us to develop the appropriate software. But the issue of how language is acquired remains hotly contested (Lana, 2002; Pinker & Jackendoff, 2005; Hoff, 2008).

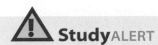

StudyALERT

It's important to be able to compare and contrast the major approaches to language development: learning theory, nativist, and interactionist approaches.

The Influence of Language on Thinking: Do Eskimos Have More Words for Snow Than Texans Do?

Do Eskimos living in the frigid Arctic have a more expansive vocabulary for discussing snow than people living in warmer climates?

It makes sense, and arguments that the Eskimo language has many more words than English for snow have been made since the early 1900s. At that time, linguist Benjamin Lee Whorf contended that because snow is so relevant to Eskimos' lives, their language provides a particularly rich vocabulary to describe it—considerably larger than what we find in other languages, such as English (Martin & Pullum, 1991; Pinker, 1994).

The contention that the Eskimo language is especially abundant in snow-related terms led to the **linguistic-relativity hypothesis**, the notion that language shapes and, in fact, may determine the way people in a specific culture perceive and understand the world. According to this view, language provides us with categories that we use to construct our view of people and events in the world around us. Consequently, language shapes and produces thought (Whorf, 1956; Kay & Regier, 2007; Zhang, He, & Zhang, 2007).

Let's consider another possibility, however. Suppose that instead of language's being the *cause* of certain ways of thinking, thought *produces* language. The only reason to expect that Eskimo language might have more words for snow than English does is that snow is considerably more relevant to Eskimos than it is to people in other cultures.

Which view is correct? Most recent research refutes the linguistic-relativity hypothesis and suggests, instead, that thinking produces language. In fact, new analyses of the Eskimo language suggest that Eskimos have no more words for snow than English speakers, for if one examines the English language closely, one sees that it is hardly impoverished when it comes to describing snow (consider, for example, *sleet*, *slush*, *blizzard*, *dusting*, and *avalanche*).

Still, the linguistic-relativity hypothesis has not been entirely discarded. A newer version of the hypothesis suggests that speech patterns may influence certain aspects of thinking. For example, in some languages, such as English, speakers distinguish between nouns that can be counted (such as "five chairs") and nouns that require a measurement unit to be quantified (such as "a liter of water"). In some other languages, such as the Mayan language called Yucatec, however, all nouns require a measurement unit. In such cultures, people appear to think more closely about what things are made of than do people in cultures in which languages such as English are spoken. In contrast, English speakers focus more on the shape of objects (Gentner, Goldin, & Goldin-Meadow, 2003; Tsukasaki & Ishii, 2004).

In short, although research does not support the linguistic-relativity hypothesis that language *causes* thought, it is clear that language influences how we think. And, of course, it certainly is the case that thought influences language, suggesting that language and thinking interact in complex ways (Kim, 2002; Ross, 2004; Thorkildsen, 2006).

Linguistic-relativity hypothesis: The notion that language shapes and may determine the way people in a particular culture perceive and understand the world.

StudyALERT

The linguistic-relativity hypothesis suggests *language* leads to thought.

He's pretty good at rote categorization and single-object relational tasks, but he's not so hot at differentiating between representational and associational signs, and he's very weak on syntax.

Do Animals Use Language?

One question that has long puzzled psychologists is whether language is uniquely human or if other animals are able to acquire it as well. Many animals communicate with one another in rudimentary forms. For instance, fiddler crabs wave their claws to signal, bees dance to indicate the direction in which food will be found, and certain birds call "*zick, zick*" during courtship and "*kia*" when they are about to fly away. However, researchers have yet to demonstrate conclusively that these animals use true language, which is characterized in part by the ability to produce and communicate new and unique meanings by following a formal grammar.

Psychologists have, however, been able to teach chimps to communicate at surprisingly high levels. For instance, after four years of training, a chimp named Washoe learned to make signs for 132 words and combine those signs into simple sentences. Even more impressively, Kanzi, a pygmy chimpanzee, has linguistic skills that some psychologists claim are close to those of a 2-year-old human being. Kanzi's trainers suggest that he can create grammatically sophisticated sentences and can even invent new rules of syntax (Raffaele, 2006; Savage-Rumbaugh, Toth, & Schick, 2007).

Despite the skills displayed by primates such as Kanzi, critics contend that the language such animals use still lacks the grammar and the complex and novel constructions of human language. Instead, they maintain that the chimps are displaying a skill no different from that of a dog that learns to lie down on command to get a reward. Furthermore, we lack firm evidence that animals can recognize and respond to the mental states of others of their species, an important aspect of human communication. Consequently, the issue of whether other animals can be

Sue Savage-Rumbaugh with a primate friend, Panbanisha. Does the use of sign language by primates indicate true mastery of language?

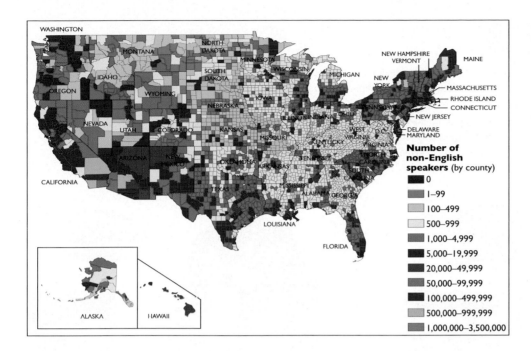

WASHINGTON

MONTANA

NORTH DAKOTA

OREGON

IDAHO

WYOMING

SOUTH DAKOTA

MINNESOTA

WISCONSIN

MICHIGAN

NEW HAMPSHIRE
VERMONT

MAINE

NEW YORK

MASSACHUSETTS

RHODE ISLAND

CONNECTICUT

NEVADA

UTAH

COLORADO

NEBRASKA

IOWA

ILLINOIS INDIANA OHIO

PENNSYLVANIA

NEW JERSEY

DELAWARE
MARYLAND

CALIFORNIA

ARIZONA

NEW MEXICO

KANSAS

MISSOURI

KENTUCKY

WEST VIRGINIA

VIRGINIA

D.C.

OKLAHOMA

ARKANSAS

TENNESSEE

NORTH CAROLINA

SOUTH CAROLINA

TEXAS

MISSISSIPPI

ALABAMA GEORGIA

LOUISIANA

FLORIDA

ALASKA

HAWAII

**Number of
non-English
speakers** (by county)

- 0
- 1–99
- 100–499
- 500–999
- 1,000–4,999
- 5,000–19,999
- 20,000–49,999
- 50,000–99,999
- 100,000–499,999
- 500,000–999,999
- 1,000,000–3,500,000

FIGURE 1 The language of diversity. Some 22 percent of the people in the United States speak a language other than English at home. Most of them speak Spanish; the rest speak an astounding variety of different languages. Where are the largest clusters of non-English speakers in the United States, and what do you think explains these concentrations? (Source: MLA Language Map, 2005, based on 2000 Census).

taught to communicate in a way that resembles human language remains controversial (Povinelli & Vonk, 2004; Aboitiz et al., 2006; Hillix, 2007).

In New York City, 1 in 6 of the city's 1.1 million students is enrolled in some form of bilingual or English as a Second Language instruction. And New York City is far from the only school district with a significant population of nonnative English speakers. From the biggest cities to the most rural areas, the face—and voice—of education in the United States is changing. More and more schoolchildren today have last names like Kim, Valdez, and Karachnicoff. In seven states, including Texas and Colorado, more than one-quarter of the students are not native English speakers. For some 47 million Americans, English is their second language (Holloway, 2000; see Figure 1).

Exploring DIVERSITY

Teaching with Linguistic Variety: Bilingual Education

How to appropriately and effectively teach the increasing number of children who do not speak English is not always clear. Many educators maintain that *bilingual education* is best. With a bilingual approach, students learn some subjects in their native language while simultaneously learning English. Proponents of bilingualism believe that students must develop a sound footing in basic subject areas and that, initially at least, teaching those subjects in their native language is the only way to provide them with that foundation. During the same period, they learn English, with the eventual goal of shifting all instruction into English.

In contrast, other educators insist that all instruction ought to be in English from the moment students, including those who speak no English at all, enroll in school. In *immersion programs*, students are immediately plunged into English instruction in all subjects. The reasoning—endorsed by voters in California in a referendum designed to end bilingual education—is that teaching students in a language other than English simply hinders nonnative English speakers' integration into society and ultimately does them a disservice. Proponents of English immersion programs point as evidence to improvements in standardized test scores that followed the end of bilingual education programs (Wildavsky, 2000).

Although the controversial issue of bilingual education versus immersion has strong political undercurrents, evidence shows that the ability to speak two languages provides significant cognitive benefits over speaking only one language. For example,

Neuroscience in Your Life

FIGURE 2 Brain functioning in bilingual speakers. When bilingual speakers carried out language tasks in their native and second languages, brain activity differed depending on when in life each speaker learned the second language. For example, the brain scan in (a), which shows two separate areas of the brain activated, is from a native English speaker who learned French in adulthood. In contrast, the brain scan in (b) is from a speaker who learned both English and Turkish in infancy. For that person, substantial overlap exists between the areas of the brain that are activated. (Source: Kim, Relkin, Lee, & Hirsch, 1997).

(a)

■ Native (English)
□ Second (French)
+ Center-of-mass

(b)

■ Native 1 (Turkish)
□ Native 2 (English)
■ Common
+ Center-of-mass

bilingual speakers show more cognitive flexibility and may understand concepts more easily than those who speak only one language. They have more linguistic tools for thinking because of their multiple-language abilities. In turn, this makes them more creative and flexible in solving problems (Heyman & Diesendruck, 2002; Bialystok & Martin, 2004; Kuo, 2007).

Research also suggests that speaking several languages changes the organization of the brain, as does the timing of the acquisition of a second language. For example, one study compared bilingual speakers on linguistic tasks in their native and second languages. The study found that those who had learned their second language as adults showed different areas of brain activation compared with those who had learned their second language in childhood (Kim et al., 1997; see Figure 2).

Related to questions about bilingual education is the matter of *biculturalism*, that is, being a member of two cultures and its psychological impact. Some psychologists argue that society should promote an *alternation model* of bicultural competence. Such a model supports members of a culture in their efforts to maintain their original cultural identity, as well as in their integration into the adopted culture. In this view, a person can belong to two cultures and have two cultural identities without having to choose between them. Whether society will adopt the alternation model remains to be seen (Carter, 2003; Benet-Martínez, Lee, & Leu, 2006; Tadmor, 2007).

RECAP/EVALUATE/RETHINK

RECAP

How do people use language?

- Language is the communication of information through symbols arranged according to systematic rules. All languages have a grammar—a system of rules that determines how thoughts can be expressed—that encompasses the three major components of language: phonology, syntax, and semantics. (p. 271)

How does language develop?

- Language production, which follows language comprehension, develops out of babbling, which then leads to the production of actual words. After 1 year of age, children use two-word combinations, increase their vocabulary, and use telegraphic speech, which drops words not critical to the message. By age 5, acquisition of language rules is relatively complete. (p. 272)

- Learning theorists suggest that language is acquired through reinforcement and conditioning. In contrast, the nativist approach suggests that an innate language-acquisition device guides the development of language. The interactionist approach argues that language development is produced through a combination of genetically determined predispositions and environmental circumstances that help teach language. (p. 273)

- The linguistic-relativity hypothesis suggests that language shapes and may determine the way people think about the world. Most evidence suggests that although language does not determine thought, it does affect the way people store information in memory and how well they can retrieve it. (p. 275)

- The degree to which language is a uniquely human skill remains an open question. Some psychologists contend that even though certain primates communicate at a high level, those animals do not use language; other psychologists suggest that those primates truly understand and produce language in much the same way as humans. (p. 276)

- People who speak more than one language may have a cognitive advantage over those who speak only one. (p. 277)

EVALUATE

1. Match the component of grammar with its definition:
   1. Syntax
   2. Phonology
   3. Semantics
   a. Rules showing how words can be combined into sentences.
   b. Rules governing the meaning of words and sentences.
   c. The study of the sound units that affect speech.
2. Language production and language comprehension develop in infants about the same time. True or false?
3. _____ _____ refers to the phenomenon in which young children omit nonessential portions of sentences.
4. A child knows that adding -ed to certain words puts them in the past tense. As a result, instead of saying "He came," the child says "He comed." This is an example of _____.
5. _____ theory assumes that language acquisition is based on principles of operant conditioning and shaping.
6. In his theory of language acquisition, Chomsky argues that language acquisition is an innate ability tied to the structure of the brain. True or false?

RETHINK

1. Do people who use two languages, one at home and one at school, automatically have two cultures? Why might people who speak two languages have cognitive advantages over those who speak only one?
2. *From the perspective of a childcare provider*: How would you encourage children's language abilities at the different stages of development?

Answers to Evaluate Questions

1. 1-a, 2-c, 3-b; 2. false; language comprehension precedes language production; 3. telegraphic speech; 4. overgeneralization; 5. learning; 6. true

KEY TERMS

language p. 271
grammar p. 271
phonology p. 271
phonemes p. 271
syntax p. 271
semantics p. 272

babble p. 272
telegraphic speech p. 273
overgeneralization p. 273
learning-theory approach
(to language development)
p. 273

nativist approach
(to language development)
p. 274
universal grammar p. 274
language-acquisition
device p. 274

interactionist approach
(to language development)
p. 274
linguistic-relativity
hypothesis p. 275

Psychology on the Web

1. In addition to mental images of sights and sounds, are there mental representations that correspond to the other senses? See whether you can answer this question by searching the Web. Summarize your findings in writing.
2. Do animals think? What evidence is there on either side of this question? Search the Web for at least one example of research and/or argument on each side of this question. Summarize your findings and use your knowledge of cognitive psychology to state your own position on this question.

Epilogue

The study of cognition occupies a central place in the field of psychology, encompassing a variety of areas—including thinking, problem solving, decision making, creativity, language, memory, and intelligence. Specialists in cognitive psychology have made significant advances in the last decade that have influenced the entire field of psychology.

Before proceeding, turn back to the prologue about Gregory Schultz's invention of a new kind of infection-reducing bandage. Answer the following questions in light of what you have learned about reasoning, problem solving, and creativity:

1. What factors led up to Schultz's development of his bandage?
2. How do the concepts of functional fixedness and mental set relate to Schultz's inventiveness? Are they related to the notion of prototypes?
3. How do you think insight is involved in Schultz's inventiveness?
4. In what ways do you think divergent and convergent thinking are involved in the processes of invention? Do they play different roles in the various stages of the act of invention, including identifying the need for an invention, devising possible solutions, and creating a practical invention?

Intelligence

Key Concepts for Chapter 9

When Chris Burke was born, physicians suggested to his parents that he immediately be institutionalized. He had Down syndrome, a common birth defect that produces mental retardation, and the physicians predicted that the chances of his leading anything like a normal life were slim. Chris's parents ignored the advice, and raised Chris like their other children.

It was a decision that led to an extraordinary life, in which Chris has made significant contributions to society. He speaks regularly on behalf of people with developmental disabilities, has co-authored book chapters, and has appeared regularly in a variety of television shows. (Hassold & Patterson, 1999; McDaniel & Burke, 2001)

Most aspiring college students wait until they are in high school to take the SAT test, but when Vino Vasudevan took them, she was only 13. . . . Vino, who had come to the United States as an infant when her parents immigrated from India, achieved perfect 800 math and 800 verbal scores, a rarity even among high school students.

Her performance was not totally surprising, though. Vino had read 100 books by the time she was 5. At the age of 7 she had mastered seventh-grade math. When she was 8, she took a college algebra class. She scored 80 on her first test, and 100 on her second. (Fields-Meyer, 1999, p. 63)

Looking Ahead

Two very different people, with widely different intellectual capabilities and strengths—and yet, at their core, Chris Burke and Vino Vasudevan share basic aspects of humanity and even, one could argue, intelligence that ultimately make them more similar than different.

In the following modules, we consider intelligence in all its many varieties. Intelligence represents a focal point for psychologists intent on understanding how people are able to adapt their behavior to the environment in which they live. It also represents a key aspect of how individuals differ from one another in the way in which they learn about and understand the world.

We begin by considering the challenges involved in defining and measuring intelligence. If you are like most people,

you have probably wondered how smart you are compared with others. Psychologists, too, have pondered the nature of intelligence. We examine some of their conceptions of intelligence as well as efforts to develop and use standardized tests as a means of measuring intelligence. We also consider the two extremes of individual differences in intelligence: mental retardation and giftedness. Finally, we explore what are probably the two most controversial issues surrounding intelligence: the degree to which intelligence is influenced by heredity and by the environment, and whether traditional tests of intelligence are biased toward the dominant cultural groups in society—difficult issues that have both psychological and social significance.

What Is Intelligence?

Members of the of the Trukese tribe in the South Pacific often sail a hundred miles in open ocean waters. Although their destination may be just a small dot of land less than a mile wide, the Trukese are able to navigate precisely toward it without the aid of a compass, chronometer, sextant, or any of the other sailing tools that are used by Western navigators. They are able to sail accurately, even when the winds do not allow a direct approach to the island and they must take a zigzag course. (Gladwin, 1964; Mytinger, 2001)

How are the Trukese able to navigate so effectively? If you asked them, they could not explain it. They might tell you that they use a process that takes into account the rising and setting of the stars and the appearance, sound, and feel of the waves against the side of the boat. But at any given moment as they are sailing along, they could not identify their position or say why they are doing what they are doing. Nor could they explain the navigational theory underlying their sailing technique.

Some people might say that the inability of the Trukese to explain in Western terms how their sailing technique works is a sign of primitive or even unintelligent behavior. In fact, if we gave Trukese sailors a Western standardized test of navigational knowledge and theory or, for that matter, a traditional test of intelligence, they might do poorly on it. Yet, as a practical matter, it is not possible to accuse the Trukese of being unintelligent: Despite their inability to explain how they do it, they are able to navigate successfully through the open ocean waters.

Trukese navigation points out the difficulty in coming to grips with what is meant by intelligence. To a Westerner, traveling in a straight line along the most direct and quickest route by using a sextant and other navigational tools is likely to represent the most "intelligent" kind of behavior; in contrast, a zigzag course, based on the "feel" of the waves, would not seem very reasonable. To the Trukese, who are used to their own system of navigation, however, the use of complicated navigational tools might seem so overly complex and unnecessary that they might think of Western navigators as lacking in intelligence.

It is clear from this example that the term *intelligence* can take on many different meanings. If, for instance, you lived in a remote part of the Australian outback, the way you would differentiate between more intelligent and less intelligent people might have to do with successfully mastering hunting skills, whereas to someone living in the heart of urban Miami, intelligence might be exemplified by being "streetwise" or by achieving success in business.

Each of these conceptions of intelligence is reasonable. Each represents an instance in which more intelligent people are better able to use the resources of their environment than are less intelligent people, a distinction that is presumably basic to any definition of intelligence. Yet it is also clear that these conceptions represent very different views of intelligence.

That two such different sets of behavior can exemplify the same psychological concept has long posed a challenge to

Key Concepts

What are the different definitions and conceptions of intelligence?

What are the major approaches to measuring intelligence, and what do intelligence tests measure?

What does the Trukese people's method of navigation—which is done without maps or instruments—tell us about the nature of intelligence?

psychologists. For years they have grappled with the issue of devising a general definition of intelligence. Ironically, laypersons have fairly clear ideas of what intelligence is, although the nature of their ideas is related to their culture. Westerners view intelligence as the ability to form categories and debate rationally. In contrast, people in Eastern cultures and some African communities view intelligence more in terms of understanding and relating to one another (Nisbett, 2003; Sternberg, 2005; Brislin, Worthley, & MacNab, 2006).

The definition of intelligence that psychologists employ contains some of the same elements found in the layperson's conception. To psychologists, **intelligence** is the capacity to understand the world, think rationally, and use resources effectively when faced with challenges.

This definition does not lay to rest a key question asked by psychologists: Is intelligence a unitary attribute, or are there different kinds of intelligence? We turn now to various theories of intelligence that address the issue.

Theories of Intelligence: Are There Different Kinds of Intelligence?

Perhaps you see yourself as a good writer but as someone who lacks ability in math. Or maybe you view yourself as a "science" person who easily masters physics but has few strengths in interpreting literature. Perhaps you view yourself as generally fairly smart, with intelligence that permits you to excel across domains.

The different ways in which people view their own talents mirrors a question that psychologists have grappled with: Is intelligence a single, general ability, or is it multifaceted and related to specific abilities? Early psychologists interested in intelligence assumed that there was a single, general factor for mental ability, which they called g, or the **g-factor**. This general intelligence factor was thought to underlie performance in every aspect of intelligence, and it was the g-factor that was presumably being measured on tests of intelligence (Spearman, 1927; Gottfredson, 2004; Colom, Jung, & Haier, 2006).

More recent theories see intelligence in a different light. Rather than viewing intelligence as a unitary entity, they consider it to be a multidimensional concept that includes different types of intelligence (Tenopyr, 2002; Stankov, 2003; Sternberg & Pretz, 2005).

FLUID AND CRYSTALLIZED INTELLIGENCE

Some psychologists suggest that there are two different kinds of intelligence: fluid intelligence and crystallized intelligence. **Fluid intelligence** reflects information-processing capabilities, reasoning, and memory. If we were asked to solve an analogy, group a series of letters according to some criterion, or remember a set of numbers, we would be using fluid intelligence. We use fluid intelligence when we're trying to rapidly solve a puzzle (Cattell, 1998; Kane & Engle, 2002; Saggino et al., 2006).

In contrast, **crystallized intelligence** is the accumulation of information, skills, and strategies that people have learned through experience and that they can apply in problem-solving situations. It reflects our ability to call up information from long-term memory. We would be likely to rely on crystallized intelligence, for instance, if we were asked to participate in a discussion about the solution to the causes of poverty, a task that allows us to draw on our own past experiences and knowledge of the world. In contrast to fluid intelligence, which reflects a more general kind of intelligence, crystallized intelligence is more a reflection of the culture in

Intelligence: The capacity to understand the world, think rationally, and use resources effectively when faced with challenges.

g or *g*-factor: The single, general factor for mental ability assumed to underlie intelligence in some early theories of intelligence.

Fluid intelligence: Intelligence that reflects information-processing capabilities, reasoning, and memory.

Crystallized intelligence: The accumulation of information, skills, and strategies that are learned through experience and can be applied in problem-solving situations.

Piloting a helicopter requires the use of both fluid intelligence and crystallized intelligence. Which of the two kinds of intelligence do you believe is more important for such a task?

which a person is raised. The differences between fluid intelligence and crystallized intelligence become especially evident in the elderly, who show declines in fluid, but not crystallized, intelligence (Schretlen et al., 2000; Aartsen, Martin, & Zimprich, 2002; Buehner et al., 2006).

GARDNER'S MULTIPLE INTELLIGENCES: THE MANY WAYS OF SHOWING INTELLIGENCE

Psychologist Howard Gardner has taken an approach very different from traditional thinking about intelligence. Gardner argues that rather than asking "How smart are you?" we should be asking a different question: "How are you smart?" In answering the latter question, Gardner has developed a **theory of multiple intelligences** that has become quite influential (Gardner, 2000).

"*To be perfectly frank, I'm not nearly as smart as you seem to think I am.*"

Gardner argues that we have at a minimum eight different forms of intelligence, each relatively independent of the others: musical, bodily kinesthetic, logical-mathematical, linguistic, spatial, interpersonal, intrapersonal, and naturalist. (Figure 1 describes the eight types of intelligence, with some of Gardner's examples of people who excel in each type.) In Gardner's view, each of the multiple intelligences is linked to an independent system in the brain. Furthermore, he suggests that there may be even more types of intelligence, such as *existential intelligence,* which involves identifying and thinking about the fundamental questions of human existence. For example, the Dalai Lama might exemplify this type of intelligence (Gardner, 1999, 2000).

Although Gardner illustrates his conception of the specific types of intelligence with descriptions of well-known people, each person has the same eight kinds of intelligence—in different degrees. Moreover, although the eight basic types of intelligence are presented individually, Gardner suggests that these separate intelligences do not operate in isolation. Normally, any activity encompasses several kinds of intelligence working together.

The concept of multiple intelligences has led to the development of intelligence tests that include questions in which more than one answer can be correct; these provide an opportunity for test takers to demonstrate creative thinking. In addition, many educators, embracing the concept of multiple intelligences, have designed classroom curricula that are meant to draw on different aspects of intelligence (Armstrong, 2000, 2003; Kelly & Tangney, 2006).

Theory of multiple intelligences: Gardner's intelligence theory that proposes that there are eight distinct spheres of intelligence.

 StudyALERT

Remember that Gardner's theory suggests that each individual has every kind of intelligence, but in different degrees.

IS INFORMATION PROCESSING INTELLIGENCE?

One of the newer contributions to understanding intelligence comes from the work of cognitive psychologists who take an *information-processing approach.* They assert that the way people store material in memory and use that material to solve intellectual tasks provides the most accurate measure of intelligence. Consequently, rather than focusing on the structure of intelligence or its underlying content or dimensions, information-processing approaches examine the *processes* involved in producing intelligent behavior (Hunt, 2005; Neubauer & Fink, 2005; Pressley & Harris, 2006).

For example, research shows that people with high scores on tests of intelligence spend more time on the initial encoding stages of problems, identifying the parts of a problem and retrieving relevant information from long-term memory, than do people with lower scores. This initial emphasis on recalling relevant information pays off in the end; those who use this approach are more successful in finding solutions than are those who spend relatively less time on the initial stages (Sternberg, 1990; Deary & Der, 2005; Hunt, 2005).

Other information-processing approaches examine the sheer speed of processing. For example, research shows that the speed with which people are able to retrieve

1. Musical intelligence (skills in tasks involving music). Case example:

When he was 3, Yehudi Menuhin was smuggled into San Francisco Orchestra concerts by his parents. By the time he was 10 years old, Menuhin was an international performer.

2. Bodily kinesthetic intelligence (skills in using the whole body or various portions of it in the solution of problems or in the construction of products or displays, exemplified by dancers, athletes, actors, and surgeons). Case example:

Fifteen-year-old Babe Ruth played third base. During one game, his team's pitcher was doing very poorly and Babe loudly criticized him from third base. Brother Matthias, the coach, called out, "Ruth, if you know so much about it, *you* pitch!" Ruth said later that at the very moment he took the pitcher's mound, he *knew* he was supposed to be a pitcher.

3. Logical-mathematical intelligence (skills in problem solving and scientific thinking). Case example:

Barbara McClintock, who won the Nobel Prize in medicine, describes one of her breakthroughs, which came after thinking about a problem for half an hour . . . : "Suddenly I jumped and ran back to the (corn) field. At the top of the field (the others were still at the bottom) I shouted, 'Eureka, I have it!'"

4. Linguistic intelligence (skills involved in the production and use of language). Case example:

At the age of 10, T. S. Eliot created a magazine called *Fireside*, to which he was the sole contributor.

5. Spatial intelligence (skills involving spatial configurations, such as those used by artists and architects). Case example:

Natives of the Truk Islands navigate at sea without instruments. During the actual trip, the navigator must envision mentally a reference island as it passes under a particular star and from that he computes the number of segments completed, the proportion of the trip remaining, and any corrections in heading.

6. Interpersonal intelligence (skills in interacting with others, such as sensitivity to the moods, temperaments, motivations, and intentions of others). Case example:

When Anne Sullivan began instructing the deaf and blind Helen Keller, her task was one that had eluded others for years. Yet, just two weeks after beginning her work with Keller, Sullivan achieved great success.

7. Intrapersonal intelligence (knowledge of the internal aspects of oneself; access to one's own feelings and emotions). Case example:

In her essay "A Sketch of the Past," Virginia Woolf displays deep insight into her own inner life through these lines, describing her reaction to several specific memories from her childhood that still, in adulthood, shock her: "Though I still have the peculiarity that I receive these sudden shocks, they are now always welcome; after the first surprise, I always feel instantly that they are particularly valuable. And so I go on to suppose that the shock-receiving capacity is what makes me a writer."

8. Naturalist intelligence (ability to identify and classify patterns in nature). Case example:

During prehistoric times, hunter/gatherers would rely on naturalist intelligence to identify what flora and fauna were edible. People who are adept at distinguishing nuances between large numbers of similar objects may be expressing naturalist intelligence abilities.

FIGURE 1 Howard Gardner believes that there are eight major kinds of intelligence, corresponding to abilities in different domains. In what area does your greatest intelligence reside, and why do you think you have particular strengths in that area? (Source: Adapted from Gardner, 2000.)

information from memory is related to verbal intelligence. In general, people with high scores on measures of intelligence react more quickly on a variety of information-processing tasks, ranging from reactions to flashing lights to distinguishing between letters. The speed of information processing, then, may underlie differences in intelligence (Deary & Der, 2005; Jenson, 2005; Gontkovsky & Beatty, 2006).

The Biological Basis of Intelligence

Using brain-scanning methods, researchers have identified several areas of the brain that relate to intelligence. For example, the brains of people completing intelligence test questions in both verbal and spatial domains show activation in a similar location: the lateral prefrontal cortex (see Figure 2). That area is above the outer edge of the eyebrow, about where people rest their heads in the palms of their hands if they are thinking hard about a problem. This area of the brain is critical to juggling many pieces of information simultaneously and solving new problems. In addition, higher intelligence is related to the thickness of the cerebral cortex (Duncan , 2005; Saggino et al., 2006; Schaer & Eliez, 2007).

These findings suggest that there is a global "workspace" in the brain that organizes and coordinates information, helping to transfer material to other parts of the brain. In this view, the activity in the workspace represents general intelligence (Gray, Chabris, & Braver, 2003).

Research using nonhumans has also begun to help us better understand the biological underpinnings of intelligence. For example, rats raised in enriched environments (meaning an environment containing more toys, tunnels, and so on) develop more complex connections between neurons, along with more rapid learning and better memory. Other studies show differences in metabolism (the rate at which food is converted to energy and expended by the body) that seem to be related to intelligence (Rampon et al., 2000; Haier, 2003).

Ultimately, the search for the biological underpinnings of intelligence will not lead in a single direction. Rather, the most plausible scenario is that multiple areas of the brain, as well as multiple kinds of functioning, are related to intelligent behavior.

Neuroscience in Your Life

FIGURE 2 The areas in red represent areas activated during spatial and verbal problems. This study showed that the lateral prefrontal cortex (see arrows) is activated when the brain is confronted with problems in both of these domains. The findings suggest that the lateral prefrontal cortex might be involved in more general functions related to intelligence. (Source: Duncan et al., 2000.)

Spatial domains

Verbal domains

Practical and Emotional Intelligence: Toward a More Intelligent View of Intelligence

Consider the following situation:

> An employee who reports to one of your subordinates has asked to talk with you about waste, poor management practices, and possible violations of both company policy and the law on the part of your subordinate. You have been in your present position only a year, but in that time you have had no indications of trouble about the subordinate in question. Neither you nor your company has an "open door" policy, so it is expected that employees should take their concerns to their immediate supervisors before bringing a matter to the attention of anyone else. The employee who wishes to meet with you has not discussed this matter with her supervisors because of its delicate nature. (Sternberg, 1998, p. 17)

Your response to this situation has a lot to do with your future success in a business career, according to psychologist Robert Sternberg. The question is one of a series designed to help give an indication of your intelligence. However, it is not traditional intelligence that the question is designed to tap, but rather intelligence of a specific kind: practical intelligence. **Practical intelligence** is intelligence related to overall success in living (Sternberg, 2000, 2002; Sternberg & Hedlund, 2002; Wagner, 2002; Muammar, 2007).

Noting that traditional tests were designed to relate to academic success, Sternberg points to evidence showing that most traditional measures of intelligence do not relate especially well to *career* success (McClelland, 1993). Specifically, although successful business executives usually score at least moderately well on intelligence tests, the rate at which they advance and their ultimate business achievements are only minimally associated with traditional measures of their intelligence.

Sternberg argues that career success requires a very different type of intelligence from that required for academic success. Whereas academic success is based on knowledge of a specific information base obtained from reading and listening, practical intelligence is learned mainly through observation of others' behavior. People who are high in practical intelligence are able to learn general norms and principles and apply them appropriately. Consequently, practical intelligence tests, like the one shown in Figure 3, measure the ability to employ broad principles in solving everyday problems (Polk, 1997; Sternberg & Pretz, 2005; Stemler & Sternberg, 2006).

In addition to practical intelligence, Sternberg argues there are other two other basic, interrelated types of successful intelligence: analytical and creative. Analytical intelligence focuses on abstract but traditional types of problems measured on IQ tests, while creative intelligence involves the generation of novel ideas and products (Benderly, 2004; Sternberg et al., 2004; Sternberg et al., 2005).

Some psychologists broaden the concept of intelligence even further beyond the intellectual realm to include emotions. **Emotional intelligence** is the set of skills that underlie the accurate assessment, evaluation, expression, and regulation of emotions (Zeidner, Matthews, & Roberts, 2004; Mayer, Salovey, & Caruso, 2004; Humphrey et al., 2007).

Emotional intelligence underlies the ability to get along well with others. It provides us with an understanding of what other people are feeling and experiencing and permits us to respond appropriately to others' needs. Emotional intelligence is the basis of empathy for others, self-awareness, and social skills.

Abilities in emotional intelligence may help explain why people with only modest scores on traditional intelligence tests can be quite successful, despite their lack of traditional intelligence. High emotional intelligence may enable an individual to tune into others' feelings, permitting a high degree of responsiveness to others.

Although the notion of emotional intelligence makes sense, it has yet to be quantified in a rigorous manner. Furthermore, the view that emotional intelligence is so

Practical intelligence: According to Sternberg, intelligence related to overall success in living.

Emotional intelligence: The set of skills that underlie the accurate assessment, evaluation, expression, and regulation of emotions.

StudyALERT

Traditional intelligence relates to academic performance; practical intelligence relates to success in life; and emotional intelligence relates to emotional skills.

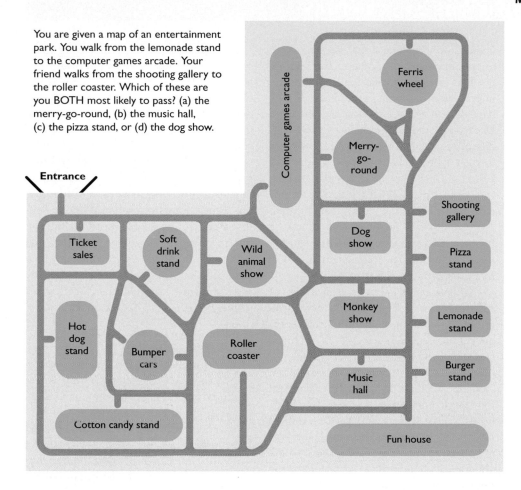

You are given a map of an entertainment park. You walk from the lemonade stand to the computer games arcade. Your friend walks from the shooting gallery to the roller coaster. Which of these are you BOTH most likely to pass? (a) the merry-go-round, (b) the music hall, (c) the pizza stand, or (d) the dog show.

FIGURE 3 Most standard tests of intelligence primarily measure analytical skills; more comprehensive tests measure creative and practical abilities as well. (Source: "Test your intelligence" from Sternberg, R. J. (2000). The Holey Grail of general intelligence. *Science, 289*, no. 5478, 399–401. Reprinted with permission from AAAS.)

important that skills related to it should be taught in school has raised concerns among some educators. They suggest that the nurturance of emotional intelligence is best left to students' families, especially because there is no well-specified set of criteria for what constitutes emotional intelligence (Sleek, 1997; Becker, 2003).

Still, the notion of emotional intelligence reminds us that there are many ways to demonstrate intelligent behavior—just as there are multiple views of the nature of intelligence (Fox & Spector, 2000; Barrett & Salovey, 2002). Figure 4 presents a summary of the different approaches used by psychologists, and the *Applying Psychology in the 21st Century* box illustrates how our own views of intelligence affect our test performance.

Major Approaches to Intelligence	
Approach	**Characteristics**
Fluid and crystallized intelligence	Fluid intelligence relates to reasoning, memory, and information-processing capabilities; crystallized intelligence relates to information, skills, and strategies learned through experience
Gardner's multiple intelligences	Eight independent forms of intelligence
Information-processing approaches	Intelligence is reflected in the ways people store and use material to solve intellectual tasks
Practical intelligence	Intelligence in terms of nonacademic, career, and personal success
Emotional intelligence	Intelligence that provides an understanding of what other people are feeling and experiencing and permits us to respond appropriately to others' needs

FIGURE 4 Just as there are many views of the nature of intelligence, there are also numerous ways to demonstrate intelligent behavior. This summary provides an overview of the various approaches used by psychologists.

Is Discipline More Important Than Intelligence for Academic Success?

Zoe Bellars, an eighth-grader at Swanson Middle School in Arlington, Virginia, is taking intensified algebra and second-year Spanish, has a voice scholarship at a music school, and plays first flute in Swanson's symphonic band. Zoe always does her homework the minute she gets home from school. (Mathews, 2006, p. A10)

Zoe Bellars is clearly a talented, accomplished student. She hopes to attend a highly selective college and is preparing herself to be a strong competitor for admission, even though she has yet to enter high school. Zoe's talent and intelligence suggest that she will do well when she gets to college, but she also has another attribute going for her: her unusual level of self-discipline.

To understand the role of self-discipline in academic success, psychologists Angela Duckworth and Martin Seligman conducted an extensive investigation. They noted that intelligence has long been studied as an important determinant of academic success, but that other nonintellectual strengths are important contributors, too, although they haven't received nearly as much attention. Duckworth and Seligman focused on self-discipline as one of these strengths because, in their words, "We believe that many of America's children have trouble making choices that require them to sacrifice short-term pleasure for long-term gain, and that programs that build self-discipline may be the royal road to building academic achievement" (Duckworth & Seligman, 2005; Mathews, 2006, p. A10).

The researchers obtained measures of self-discipline from hundreds of eighth-grade students; these included self-report questionnaires, parent and teacher ratings, and direct measures of self-discipline. For example, the experiments gave students an envelope containing a single dollar, but they were offered a choice: keep the dollar now, or give it back and get two dollars next week. Academic achievement was measured using report card grades, school attendance, standardized test scores, time doing homework, and selection into competitive high schools.

The results of their study were clear: self-discipline was a more important factor than IQ scores for almost all measures of academic success. Why should students who are willing to wait a week to make an extra dollar be more likely to succeed academically? The key is in their willingness to delay gratification in order to achieve a more desirable long-term outcome. Studying is work, and the payoff comes sometime later. Without self-discipline, students are more inclined to forego studying for other activities that are more immediately rewarding. Raw intellect alone may provide the capacity to learn, but even geniuses can't learn a lesson if they rarely open a book.

- Why do you think self-discipline is a better predictor than IQ of many real-world indicators of academic performance (such as grades or time spent studying) but not achievement tests?
- What might be some other nonintellectual personal characteristics that predict academic performance? Why aren't explicit measures of these nonintellectual strengths used to determine college admissions?

Assessing Intelligence

Intelligence tests: Tests devised to quantify a person's level of intelligence.

Given the variety of approaches to the components of intelligence, it is not surprising that measuring intelligence has proved challenging. Psychologists who study intelligence have focused much of their attention on the development of **intelligence tests** and have relied on such tests to quantify a person's level of intelligence. These tests have proved to be of great benefit in identifying students in need of special attention in school, diagnosing cognitive difficulties, and helping people make optimal educational and vocational choices. At the same time, their use has proved controversial, raising important social and educational issues.

Historically, the first effort at intelligence testing was based on an uncomplicated, but completely wrong, assumption: that the size and shape of a person's head could be used as an objective measure of intelligence. The idea was put forward by Sir Francis Galton (1822–1911), an eminent English scientist whose ideas in other domains proved to be considerably better than his notions about intelligence.

Galton's motivation to identify people of high intelligence stemmed from personal prejudices. He sought to demonstrate the natural superiority of people of high social class (including himself) by showing that intelligence is inherited. He hypothesized that head configuration, being genetically determined, is related to brain size, and therefore is related to intelligence.

Galton's theories were proved wrong on virtually every count. Head size and shape are not related to intellectual performance, and subsequent research has found little relationship between brain size and intelligence. However, Galton's work did have at least one desirable result: He was the first person to suggest that intelligence could be quantified and measured in an objective manner (Jensen, 2002).

BINET AND THE DEVELOPMENT OF IQ TESTS

The first real intelligence tests were developed by the French psychologist Alfred Binet (1857–1911). His tests followed from a simple premise: If performance on certain tasks or test items improved with *chronological*, or physical, age, performance could be used to distinguish more intelligent people from less intelligent ones within a particular age group. On the basis of this principle, Binet devised the first formal intelligence test, which was designed to identify the "dullest" students in the Paris school system in order to provide them with remedial aid.

Alfred Binet

Binet began by presenting tasks to same-age students who had been labeled "bright" or "dull" by their teachers. If a task could be completed by the bright students but not by the dull ones, he retained that task as a proper test item; otherwise it was discarded. In the end he came up with a test that distinguished between the bright and dull groups, and   with further work—one that distinguished among children in different age groups (Binet & Simon, 1916; Sternberg & Jarvin, 2003).

On the basis of the Binet test, children were assigned a score relating to their **mental age**, the average age of individuals who achieve a particular level of performance on a test. For example, if the average 8-year-old answered, say, 45 items correctly on a test, anyone who answered 45 items correctly would be assigned a mental age of 8 years. Consequently, whether the person taking the test was 20 years old or 5 years old, he or she would have the same mental age of 8 years (Cornell, 2006).

Mental age: The average age of individuals who achieve a particular level of performance on a test.

Assigning a mental age to students provided an indication of their general level of performance. However, it did not allow for adequate comparisons among people of different chronological ages. By using mental age alone, for instance, we might assume that a 20 year old responding at a 18 year old's level would be as bright as a 5 year old answering at a 3 year old's level, when actually the 5 year old would be displaying a much greater *relative* degree of slowness.

Intelligence quotient (IQ): A score that takes into account an individual's mental and chronological ages.

A solution to the problem came in the form of the **intelligence quotient**, or **IQ**, a score that takes into account an individual's mental *and* chronological ages. Historically, the first IQ scores employed the following formula, in which *MA* stands for mental age and *CA* for chronological age:

$$\text{IQ score} = \frac{\text{MA}}{\text{CA}} \times 100$$

Using this formula, we can return to the earlier example of a 20 year old performing at a mental age of 18 and calculate an IQ score of $(18/20) \times 100 = 90$. In contrast, the 5 year old performing at a mental age of 3 comes out with a considerably lower IQ score: $(3/5) \times 100 = 60$.

As a bit of trial and error with the formula will show you, anyone who has a mental age equal to his or her chronological age will have an IQ equal to 100. Moreover, people with a mental age that is greater than their chronological age will have IQs that exceed 100.

Although the basic principles behind the calculation of an IQ score still hold, today IQ scores are figured out in a different manner and are known as *deviation IQ scores*. First, the average test score for everyone of the same age who takes the test is determined, and that average score is assigned an IQ of 100. Then, with the aid of statistical techniques that calculate the differences (or "deviations") between each score and the average, IQ scores are assigned.

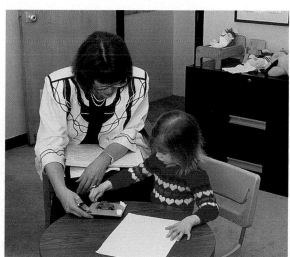

Now in its fifth edition, the Stanford-Binet test consists of a series of items that vary in nature according to the age of the person being tested. What can we learn about a person from a test of this type?

FIGURE 5 The average and most common IQ score is 100, and 68 percent of all people are within a 30-point range centered on 100. Some 95 percent of the population have scores that are within 30 points above or below 100, and 99.8 percent have scores that are between 55 and 145.

The average IQ score is 100, and 68% of people score between 85 and 115.

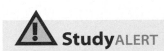

Study ALERT

It's important to know the traditional formula for IQ scores in which IQ is the ratio of mental age divided by chronological age, multiplied by 100. Remember, though, that the actual calculation of IQ scores today is done in a more sophisticated manner.

As you can see in Figure 5, when IQ scores from large numbers of people are plotted on a graph, they form a *bell-shaped distribution* (called "bell-shaped" because it looks like a bell when plotted). Approximately two-thirds of all individuals fall within 15 IQ points of the average score of 100. As scores increase or fall beyond that range, the percentage of people in a category falls considerably.

CONTEMPORARY IQ TESTS: GAUGING INTELLIGENCE

Remnants of Binet's original intelligence test are still with us, although the test has been revised in significant ways. Now in its fifth edition and called the *Stanford-Binet Intelligence Scale,* the test consists of a series of items that vary in nature according to the age of the person being tested (Roid, 2003). For example, young children are asked to copy figures or answer questions about everyday activities. Older people are asked to solve analogies, explain proverbs, and describe similarities that underlie sets of words.

The test is administered orally. An examiner begins by finding a mental age level at which a person is able to answer all the questions correctly, and then moves on to successively more difficult problems. When a mental age level is reached at which no items can be answered, the test is over. By studying the pattern of correct and incorrect responses, the examiner is able to compute an IQ score for the person being tested. In addition, the Stanford-Binet test yields separate subscores that provide clues to a test-taker's particular strengths and weaknesses.

The IQ test most frequently used in the United States was devised by psychologist David Wechsler and is known as the *Wechsler Adult Intelligence Scale–III,* or, more commonly, the *WAIS-III.* There is also a children's version, the *Wechsler Intelligence Scale for Children–IV,* or *WISC-IV.* Both the WAIS-III and the WISC-IV have two major parts: a verbal scale and a performance (or nonverbal) scale.

As you can see from the sample questions in Figure 6, the verbal and performance scales include questions of very different types. Verbal tasks consist of more traditional kinds of problems, including vocabulary definition and comprehension of various concepts. In contrast, the performance (nonverbal) part involves the timed assembly of small objects and the arrangement of pictures in a logical order. Although an individual's scores on the verbal and performance sections of the test are generally within close range of each other, the scores of a person with a language deficiency or a background of severe environmental deprivation may show a relatively large discrepancy between the two sections. By providing separate scores, the WAIS-III and WISC-IV give a more precise picture of a person's specific abilities compared with other IQ tests (Kaufman & Lichtenberger, 1999, 2000).

WAIS-III (Adult)

NAME	GOAL OF ITEM	EXAMPLE
VERBAL SCALE		
Information	Assess general information	Who wrote *Tom Sawyer*?
Comprehension	Assess understanding and evaluation of social norms and past experience	Why is copper often used for electrical wires?
Arithmetic	Assess math reasoning through verbal problems	Three women divided 18 golf balls equally among themselves. How many golf balls did each person receive?
Similarities	Test understanding of how objects or concepts are alike, tapping abstract reasoning	In what way are a circle and a triangle alike?
PERFORMANCE SCALE		
Digit symbol	Assess speed of learning	Test-taker must learn what symbols correspond to what digits, and then must replace a multidigit number with the appropriate symbols.
Matrix reasoning	Test spatial reasoning	Test-taker must decide which of the five possibilities replaces the question mark and completes the sequence.
Block design item	Test understanding of relationship of parts to whole	Problems require test-takers to reproduce a design in fixed amount of time

FIGURE 6 Typical kinds of items found on the verbal and performance (nonverbal) scales of the Wechsler Adult Intelligence Scale (WAIS-III) and the Wechsler Intelligence Scale for Children (WISC-IV). (Source: Simulated items similar to those in the *Wechsler Adult Intelligence Scale – Third Edition*. Copyright © 1997 by NCS Pearson, Inc. Reproduced with permission. All rights reserved.)

(continues)

Because the Stanford-Binet, WAIS-III, and WISC-IV all require individualized, one-on-one administration, it is relatively difficult and time-consuming to administer and score them on a large-scale basis. Consequently, there are now a number of IQ tests that allow group administration. Rather than having one examiner ask one person at a time to respond to individual items, group IQ tests are strictly paper-and-pencil tests. The primary advantage of group tests is their ease of administration (Anastasi & Urbina, 1997).

However, sacrifices are made in group testing that in some cases may outweigh the benefits. For instance, group tests generally offer fewer kinds of questions than do

WISC-IV (Child)		
NAME	**GOAL OF ITEM**	**EXAMPLE**
VERBAL SCALE		
Information	Assess general information	How many nickels make a dime?
Comprehension	Assess understanding and evaluation of social norms and past experience	What is the advantage of keeping money in the bank?
Arithmetic	Assess math reasoning through verbal problems	If two buttons cost 15 cents, what will be the cost of a dozen buttons?
Similarities	Test understanding of how objects or concepts are alike, tapping abstract reasoning	In what way are an hour and a week alike?
PERFORMANCE SCALE		
Digit symbol	Assess speed of learning	Match symbols to numbers using key.
Picture completion	Visual memory and attention	Identify what is missing.
Object assembly	Test understanding of relationship of parts to wholes	Put pieces together to form a whole.

FIGURE 6, CONTINUED

tests administered individually. Furthermore, people may be more motivated to perform at their highest ability level when working on a one-to-one basis with a test administrator than they are in a group. Finally, in some cases, it is simply impossible to employ group tests, particularly with young children or people with unusually low IQs (Aiken, 1996).

ACHIEVEMENT AND APTITUDE TESTS

Achievement test: A test designed to determine a person's level of knowledge in a given subject area.

IQ tests are not the only kind of tests that you might have taken during the course of your schooling. Two other kinds of tests, related to intelligence but intended to measure somewhat different phenomena, are achievement tests and aptitude tests. An **achievement test** is a test designed to determine a person's level of knowledge in a specific subject area. Rather than measuring general ability, as an intelligence test does, an achievement test concentrates on the specific material a person has learned. High school students sometimes take specialized achievement tests in specific areas such as world history and chemistry as a college entrance requirement; lawyers must pass an achievement test (in the form of the bar exam) in order to practice law.

An **aptitude test** is designed to predict a person's ability in a particular area or line of work. Most of us take one or the other of the best-known aptitude tests in the process of pursuing admission to college: the SAT and the ACT. The SAT and ACT are meant to predict how well people will do in college, and the scores have proved over the years to be moderately correlated with college grades (Hoffman, 2001).

Although in theory the distinction between aptitude tests and achievement tests is precise, it is difficult to develop an aptitude test that does not rely at least in part on past achievement. For example, the SAT has been strongly criticized for being less an aptitude test (predicting college success) than an achievement test (assessing prior performance).

Aptitude test: A test designed to predict a person's ability in a particular area or line of work.

RELIABILITY AND VALIDITY: TAKING THE MEASURE OF TESTS

When we use a ruler, we expect to find that it measures an inch in the same way it did the last time we used it. When we weigh ourselves on the bathroom scale, we hope that the variations we see on the scale are due to changes in our weight and not to errors on the part of the scale (unless the change in weight is in an unwanted direction!).

In the same way, we hope that psychological tests have **reliability**—that they measure consistently what they are trying to measure. We need to be sure that each time we administer the test, a test-taker will achieve the same results—assuming that nothing about the person has changed relevant to what is being measured.

Suppose, for instance, that when you first took the SAT exams, you scored 400 on the verbal section of the test. Then, after taking the test again a few months later, you scored 700. Upon receiving your new score, you might well stop celebrating for a moment to question whether the test is reliable, for it is unlikely that your abilities could have changed enough to raise your score by 300 points (Coyle, 2006).

But suppose your score changed hardly at all, and both times you received a score of about 400. You couldn't complain about a lack of reliability. However, if you knew your verbal skills were above average, you might be concerned that the test did not adequately measure what it was supposed to measure. In sum, the question has now become one of validity rather than reliability. A test has **validity** when it actually measures what it is supposed to measure.

Reliability: The property by which tests measure consistently what they are trying to measure.

Validity: The property by which tests actually measure what they are supposed to measure.

Knowing that a test is reliable is no guarantee that it is also valid. For instance, Sir Francis Galton assumed that skull size is related to intelligence, and he was able to measure skull size with great reliability. However, the measure of skull size was not valid—it had nothing to do with intelligence. In this case, then, we have reliability without validity.

However, if a test is unreliable, it cannot be valid. Assuming that all other factors—motivation to score well, knowledge of the material, health, and so forth—are similar, if a person scores high the first time he or she takes a specific test and low the second time, the test cannot be measuring what it is supposed to measure. Therefore, the test is both unreliable and not valid.

Test validity and reliability are prerequisites for accurate assessment of intelligence—as well as for any other measurement task carried out by psychologists. Consequently, the measures of personality carried out by personality psychologists, clinical psychologists' assessments of psychological disorders, and social psychologists' measures of attitudes must meet the tests of validity and reliability for the results to be meaningful (Feldt, 2005; Phelps, 2005; Yao et al., 2006).

Norms: Standards of test performance that permit the comparison of one person's score on a test with the scores of other individuals who have taken the same test.

Assuming that a test is both valid and reliable, one further step is necessary in order to interpret the meaning of a particular test-taker's score: the establishment of norms. **Norms** are standards of test performance that permit the comparison of one person's score on a test to the scores of others who have taken the same test. For example, a norm permits test-takers to know that they have scored, say, in the top 15 percent of those who have taken the test previously. Tests for which norms have been developed are known as *standardized tests.*

Test designers develop norms by calculating the average score achieved by a specific group of people for whom the test has been designed. Then the test designers can determine the extent to which each person's score differs from the scores of the other individuals who have taken the test in the past and provide future test-takers with a qualitative sense of their performance.

Obviously, the samples of test-takers who are employed in the establishment of norms are critical to the norming process. The people used to determine norms must be representative of the individuals to whom the test is directed.

Adaptive Testing: Using Computers to Assess Performance

Ensuring that tests are reliable and valid, and are based on appropriate norms, has become more critical with the introduction of computers to administer standardized tests. The Educational Testing Service (ETS)—the company that devises the SAT and the Graduate Record Examination (GRE), used for college and graduate school admission—is moving to computer administration of all its standardized tests.

In computerized versions, not only are test questions viewed and answered on a computer, the test itself is individualized. Under *adaptive testing,* students do not necessarily receive identical sets of test questions. Instead, the computer first presents a randomly selected question of moderate difficulty. If the test-taker answers it correctly, the computer will then present a randomly chosen item of slightly greater difficulty. If the answer is wrong, the computer will present a slightly easier item. Each question becomes slightly harder or easier than the question preceding it, depending on whether the previous response is correct. Ultimately, the greater the number of difficult questions answered correctly, the higher the score (Wainer et al., 2000; Chang & Ansley, 2003; Marszalek, 2007; see Figure 7).

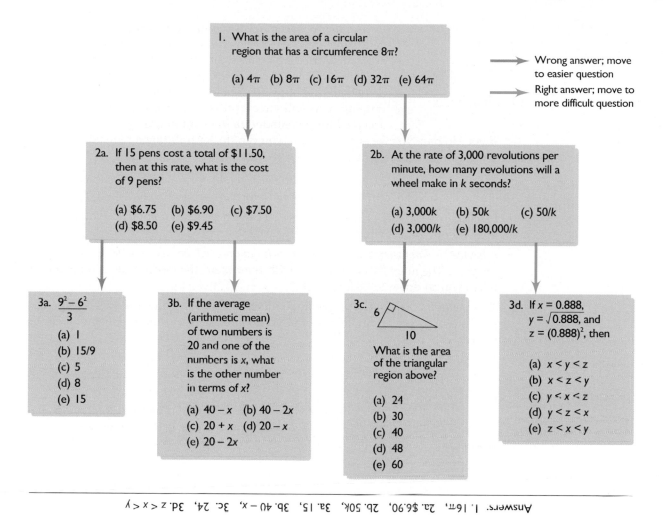

1. What is the area of a circular region that has a circumference 8π?

   (a) 4π   (b) 8π   (c) 16π   (d) 32π   (e) 64π

→ Wrong answer; move to easier question

→ Right answer; move to more difficult question

2a. If 15 pens cost a total of $11.50, then at this rate, what is the cost of 9 pens?

   (a) $6.75   (b) $6.90   (c) $7.50
   (d) $8.50   (e) $9.45

2b. At the rate of 3,000 revolutions per minute, how many revolutions will a wheel make in k seconds?

   (a) 3,000k (b) 50k (c) 50/k
   (d) 3,000/k (e) 180,000/k

3a. $\dfrac{9^2 - 6^2}{3}$

   (a) 1
   (b) 15/9
   (c) 5
   (d) 8
   (e) 15

3b. If the average (arithmetic mean) of two numbers is 20 and one of the numbers is x, what is the other number in terms of x?

   (a) $40 - x$ (b) $40 - 2x$
   (c) $20 + x$ (d) $20 - x$
   (e) $20 - 2x$

3c.

   What is the area of the triangular region above?

   (a) 24
   (b) 30
   (c) 40
   (d) 48
   (e) 60

3d. If $x = 0.888$, $y = \sqrt{0.888}$, and $z = (0.888)^2$, then

   (a) $x < y < z$
   (b) $x < z < y$
   (c) $y < x < z$
   (d) $y < z < x$
   (e) $z < x < y$

Answers: 1. 16π,   2a. $6.90,   2b. 50k,   3a. 15,   3b. 40 − x,   3c. 24,   3d. z < x < y

FIGURE 7 Adaptive testing. In the Graduate Record Examination, the computer randomly selects a first question of medium difficulty. If the test-taker answers the question correctly, the computer poses a more difficult question. Once the test-taker gives an incorrect answer, he or she is given a question at the next easiest level, as illustrated in this example. Test-takers are graded based on the level of difficulty of the questions they answer correctly, meaning that two test-takers who answer the same number of questions correctly can end up with very different scores. What do you think are the drawbacks of adaptive testing of this sort? Do you think such tests may discriminate against test-takers who are less familiar with computers compared with those who have easy access to them? (Source: New York Times Graphics.)

Because computerized adaptive testing pinpoints a test-taker's level of proficiency fairly quickly, the total time spent taking the exam is shorter than it is with a traditional exam. Test-takers are not forced to spend a great deal of time answering questions that are either much easier or much harder than they can handle.

Critics of computerized adaptive testing suggest that it may discriminate against test-takers who have limited access to computers and thus may have less practice with them or may be more intimidated by the testing medium. ETS disputes this claim, although some of its own research shows that women and older test-takers display greater anxiety at the beginning of the test. Despite this anxiety, however, their performance ultimately is not affected, and most research suggests that computerized adaptive testing provides scores equivalent to those of traditional paper-and-pencil measures for most types of testing (Tonidandel, Quinones, & Adams, 2002; Passo, Berger, & Tan, 2007).

Even though psychologists disagree about the nature of intelligence, intelligence tests—as well as many other kinds of tests—are widely used in a variety of situations. For example, if you are thinking about becoming a physician, a lawyer, or almost any other kind of professional in a field that requires advanced training, you will have to take a formal exam in order to be accepted for post-undergraduate training.

If you do have to take such an exam, you can do several things to maximize your score, including the following (Lurie, 2005; Feldman, 2006):

- *Learn as much as you can about the test before you take it.* Know what sections will be on the test and how much each section is worth.

- *Practice.* Try as many practice tests as you can find. The more practice you have, the easier it will be when you actually take the test.

- *If the test is administered on a computer, as it probably will be, take practice tests on a computer.* The more familiar you are with computers, the more at ease you will feel when you sit down to take the test.

- *Time yourself carefully.* Don't spend too much time on early items at the expense of later ones. Your goal should be not perfection, but maximization of the number of correct responses you get.

- *Be aware of the scoring policy.* If you are not penalized for wrong answers, guess. If there are penalties, be more conservative about guessing.

- *If it is a paper-and-pencil test, complete answer sheets accurately.* Check and check again. If the test is on a computer, check your answer thoroughly before going on to the next question, because you won't be able to go back and change your answer once you've submitted it.

RECAP/EVALUATE/RETHINK

RECAP

What are the different definitions and conceptions of intelligence?

- Because intelligence can take many forms, defining it is challenging. One commonly accepted view is that intelligence is the capacity to understand the world, think rationally, and use resources effectively when faced with challenges. (p. 286)

- The earliest psychologists assumed that there is a general factor for mental ability called *g*. However, later psychologists disputed the view that intelligence is unidimensional. (p. 286)

- Some researchers suggest that intelligence can be broken down into fluid intelligence and crystallized intelligence. Gardner's theory of multiple intelligences proposes that there are eight spheres of intelligence. (p. 286)

- Information-processing approaches examine the processes underlying intelligent behavior rather than focusing on the structure of intelligence. (p. 287)

- Practical intelligence is intelligence related to overall success in living; emotional intelligence is the set of skills that underlie the accurate assessment, evaluation, expression, and regulation of emotions. (p. 290)

What are the major approaches to measuring intelligence, and what do intelligence tests measure?

- Intelligence tests have traditionally compared a person's mental age and chronological age to yield an IQ, or intelligence quotient, score. (p. 292)

- Specific tests of intelligence include the Stanford-Binet test, the Wechsler Adult Intelligence Scale–III (WAIS-III), and the Wechsler Intelligence Scale for Children–IV (WISC-IV). Achievement tests and aptitude tests are other types of standardized tests. (p. 294)

- Tests are expected to be both reliable and valid. Reliability refers to the consistency with which a test measures what it is trying to measure. A test has validity when it actually measures what it is supposed to measure. (p. 297)

- Norms are standards of test performance that permit the comparison of one person's score on a test to the scores of others who have taken the same test. (p. 298)

EVALUATE

1. _____ is a measure of intelligence that takes into account a person's chronological and mental ages.

2. _____ tests predict a person's ability in a specific area; _____ tests determine the specific level of knowledge in an area.

3. Some psychologists make the distinction between _____ intelligence, which reflects reasoning, memory, and information-processing capabilities, and _____ intelligence, which is the information, skills, and strategies that people have learned through experience.

4. Cognitive psychologists use a(n) _____-_____ approach to measure intelligence.

RETHINK

1. What is the role of emotional intelligence in the classroom? How might emotional intelligence be tested? Should emotional intelligence be a factor in determining academic promotion to the next grade?

2. *From the human resource specialist's perspective:* Job interviews are really a kind of test. In what ways does a job interview resemble an aptitude test? An achievement test? Do you think job interviews can be made to have validity and reliability?

Answers to Evaluate Questions

1. IQ; 2. aptitude, achievement; 3. fluid, crystallized; 4. information-processing

KEY TERMS

intelligence p. 286
g or g-factor p. 286
fluid intelligence p. 286
crystallized intelligence
    p. 286

theory of multiple
    intelligences p. 287
practical intelligence p. 290
emotional intelligence
    p. 290

intelligence tests p. 292
mental age p. 293
intelligence quotient (IQ)
    p. 293
achievement test p. 296

aptitude test p. 297
reliability p. 297
validity p. 297
norms p. 298

Variations in Intellectual Ability

"Hey, hey, hey, Fact Track!" The 11-year-old speaker chose one of his favorite programs. . .

"What is your name?" appeared on the monitor.

"Daniel Skandera," he typed. A menu scrolled up listing the program's possibilities. Daniel chose multiplication facts, Level 1. . . .

Randomly generated multiplication facts flashed on the screen: "4 × 6," "2 × 9," "3 × 3," "7 × 6." Daniel responded, deftly punching in his answers on the computer's numeric key-pad . . .

The computer tallied the results. "You completed 20 problems in 66 seconds. You beat your goal. Problems correct = 20. Congratulations Daniel!" And with that the 11-year-old retreated hastily to the TV room. The Lakers and 76ers were about to tip off for an NBA championship game. (Heward & Orlansky, 1988, p. 100)

If you consider people with mental retardation as inept and dull, it is time to revise your view. As in the case of Daniel Skandera, individuals with deficits of intellectual abilities can lead full, rounded lives and in some cases perform well in certain kinds of academic endeavors.

More than 7 million people in the United States, including around 11 per 1,000 children, have been identified as far enough below average in intelligence that they can be regarded as having a serious deficit. Individuals with low IQs (people with mental retardation or intellectual disabilities) as well as those with unusually high IQs (the intellectually gifted) require special attention if they are to reach their full potential.

Mental Retardation (Intellectual Disabilities)

Although sometimes thought of as a rare phenomenon, mental retardation (or, as it is increasingly being called, intellectual disabilities) occurs in 1 to 3 percent of the population. There is wide variation among those labeled as mentally retarded, in large part because of the inclusiveness of the definition developed by the American Association on Intellectual and Developmental Disabilities. The association suggests that **mental retardation (or intellectual disability)** is a disability characterized by significant limitations both in intellectual functioning and in conceptual, social, and practical adaptive skills (AAMR, 2002). (Although experts are increasingly using the term "intellectual disability" instead of "mental retardation," our discussion will use the original term because it continues to be more widespread.)

Although below-average intellectual functioning can be measured in a relatively straightforward manner—using standard IQ tests—it is more difficult to determine how to gauge limitations in adaptive behavior. Ultimately, this imprecision leads to a lack of uniformity in how experts apply the labels *mental retardation* and *intellectual disabilities*. Furthermore, it has resulted in significant variation in the abilities of people

Key Concepts

How can the extremes of intelligence be characterized?

How can we help people reach their full potential?

Daniel Skandera playing the xylophone, one of his many talents.

Mental retardation (or intellectual disability): A condition characterized by significant limitations both in intellectual functioning and in conceptual, social, and practical adaptive skills.

who are categorized as mentally retarded, ranging from those who can be taught to work and function with little special attention to those who virtually cannot be trained and must receive institutional treatment throughout their lives (Detterman, Gabriel, & Ruthsatz, 2000; Greenspan, 2006).

Most people with mental retardation have relatively minor deficits and are classified as having *mild retardation*. These individuals, who have IQ scores ranging from 55 to 69, constitute some 90 percent of all people with mental retardation. Although their development is typically slower than that of their peers, they can function quite independently by adulthood and are able to hold jobs and have families of their own (Bates, Cuvo, Miner, & Korabeck, 2001; Smith, 2006).

At greater levels of retardation—*moderate retardation* (IQs of 40 to 54), *severe retardation* (IQs of 25 to 39), and *profound retardation* (IQs below 25)—the difficulties are more pronounced. For people with moderate retardation, deficits are obvious early, with language and motor skills lagging behind those of peers. Although these individuals can hold simple jobs, they need to have a moderate degree of supervision throughout their lives. Individuals with severe and profound mental retardation are generally unable to function independently and typically require care for their entire lives (Garwick, 2007).

IDENTIFYING THE ROOTS OF MENTAL RETARDATION

Fetal alcohol syndrome: The most common cause of mental retardation in newborns, occurring when the mother uses alcohol during pregnancy.

What are the causes of mental retardation? In nearly one-third of the cases there is an identifiable biological reason. The most common biological cause is **fetal alcohol syndrome**, caused by a mother's use of alcohol while pregnant. Increasing evidence shows that even small amounts of alcohol intake can produce intellectual deficits (West & Blake, 2005; Manning & Hoyme, 2007).

Down syndrome, the type of mental retardation experienced by actor Chris Burke, represents another major biological cause of mental retardation. *Down syndrome* results from the presence of an extra chromosome. In other cases of mental retardation, an abnormality occurs in the structure of a chromosome. Birth complications, such as a temporary lack of oxygen, may also cause retardation. In some cases, mental retardation occurs after birth, following a head injury, a stroke, or infections such as meningitis (Plomin, 2005; Bittles et al., 2007).

Familial retardation: Mental retardation in which no apparent biological defect exists but there is a history of retardation in the family.

However, the majority of cases of mental retardation are classified as **familial retardation**, in which no apparent biological defect exists but there is a history of retardation in the family. Whether the family background of retardation is caused by environmental factors, such as extreme continuous poverty leading to malnutrition, or by some underlying genetic factor is usually impossible to determine (Zigler et al., 2002).

INTEGRATING INDIVIDUALS WITH MENTAL RETARDATION

Important advances in the care and treatment of those with retardation have been made in the last three decades. Much of this change was instigated by the Education for All Handicapped Children Act of 1975 (Public Law 94-142). In this federal law, Congress stipulated that people with retardation are entitled to a full education and that they must be educated and trained in the *least restrictive environment*. The law increased the educational opportunities for individuals with mental retardation, facilitating their integration into regular classrooms as much as possible—a process known as *mainstreaming* (Katsiyannis et al., 2005; Aussilloux & Baghdadli, 2006; Gibb et al., 2007).

The philosophy behind mainstreaming suggests that the interaction of students with and without mental retardation in regular classrooms will improve educational opportunities for those with retardation, increase their social acceptance, and facilitate their integration into society as a whole. Of course, special education classes still exist; some individuals with retardation function at too low a level to benefit from placement

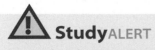

StudyALERT

Remember that in most cases of mental retardation, there is no biological deficiency, but a history of mental retardation exists in the family.

in regular classrooms. Moreover, children with mental retardation who are mainstreamed into regular classes typically attend special classes for at least part of the day (Hastings & Oakford, 2003; Williamson et al., 2006).

Some educators argue that an alternative to mainstreaming, called *full inclusion,* might be more effective. Full inclusion is the integration of all students, even those with the most severe educational disabilities, into regular classes and an avoidance of special, segregated special education classes. Teacher aides are assigned to help the children with special needs progress. Schools with full inclusion have no separate special education classes. However, full inclusion is a controversial practice, and it is not widely applied (Praisner, 2003; Spence-Cochran & Pearl, 2006).

The Intellectually Gifted

Another group of people—the intellectually gifted—differ from those with average intelligence as much as do individuals with mental retardation, although in a different manner. Accounting for 2 to 4 percent of the population, the **intellectually gifted** have IQ scores greater than 130. Vino Vasudevan, the 13 year old described in the chapter prologue who was studying college algebra, exemplifies a case of someone who is particularly intellectually gifted.

Intellectually gifted: The 2 to 4 percent of the population who have IQ scores greater than 130.

Although the stereotype associated with the gifted suggests that they are awkward, shy social misfits who are unable to get along well with peers, most research indicates that just the opposite is true. The intellectually gifted are most often outgoing, well adjusted, healthy, popular people who are able to do most things better than the average person can (Winner, 2003; Gottfredson & Deary, 2004; Lubinski et al., 2006).

For example, in a famous study by psychologist Lewis Terman that started in the early 1920s, 1,500 children who had IQ scores above 140 were followed for the rest of their lives. From the start, the members of this group were more physically, academically, and socially capable than their nongifted peers. In addition to doing better in school, they also showed better social adjustment than average. All these advantages paid off in terms of career success: As a group, the gifted received more awards and distinctions, earned higher incomes, and made more contributions in art and literature than typical individuals. Perhaps most important, they reported greater satisfaction in life than the nongifted (Hegarty, 2007).

Of course, not every member of the group Terman studied was successful. Furthermore, high intelligence is not a homogeneous quality; a person with a high overall IQ is not necessarily gifted in every academic subject, but may excel in just one or two. A high IQ is not a universal guarantee of success (Shurkin, 1992; Winner, 2003; Clemons, 2006).

Although special programs attempting to overcome the deficits of people with mental retardation abound, programs targeted at the intellectually gifted are more rare. One reason for this lack of attention is that although there are as many gifted individuals as there are those with mental retardation, the definition of *gifted* is vague, especially compared with definitions of mental retardation. Furthermore, there is a persistent view that the gifted ought to be able to "make it on their own"; if they can't, they really weren't gifted in the first place (Robinson, 2003; Parke, 2003; Sparks, 2007).

More enlightened approaches, however, have acknowledged that without some form of special attention, the gifted become bored and frustrated with the pace of their schooling and may never reach their potential. Consequently, programs for the gifted are designed to provide enrichment that allows participants' talents to flourish (Adams-Byers, Squilkr, & Swift, 2004; Delcourt, Comell, & Goldberg, 2007).

RECAP/EVALUATE/RETHINK

RECAP

How are extremes of intelligence characterized?

- The levels of mental retardation (or intellectual disability) include mild, moderate, severe, and profound retardation. (p. 304)

- About one-third of the cases of retardation have a known biological cause; fetal alcohol syndrome is the most common. Most cases, however, are classified as familial retardation, for which there is no known biological cause. (p. 304)

- The intellectually gifted are people with IQ scores greater than 130. Intellectually gifted people tend to be healthier and more successful than are the nongifted. (p. 305)

How can we help people reach their full potential?

- Advances in the treatment of people with mental retardation include mainstreaming, or the integration of individuals with mental retardation into regular education classrooms as much as possible (along with some participation in segregated special education classes); and full inclusion, in which all students, even those with the most severe educational disabilities, are fully integrated into regular classes (and separate classes are avoided). (p. 305)

EVALUATE

1. The term *mental retardation* is applied specifically to people with an IQ below 60. True or false?

2. _____ is a disorder caused by an extra chromosome that is responsible for some cases of mental retardation.

3. _____ is the process by which students with mental retardation are placed in normal classrooms to facilitate learning and reduce isolation.

4. Most forms of retardation have no identifiable biological cause. True or false?

5. People with high intelligence are generally shy and socially withdrawn. True or false?

RETHINK

1. Why do you think negative stereotypes of gifted individuals and people with mental retardation persist, even in the face of contrary evidence? How can these stereotypes be changed?

2. *From a school administrator's perspective:* What advantages and disadvantages do you think full inclusion programs would present for students with mental retardation? For students without mental retardation?

Answers to Evaluate Questions

1. false; the term is used to describe a wide range of people with various degrees of mental impairment; 2. Down syndrome; 3. mainstreaming; 4. true; 5. false; the gifted are generally more socially adept than those with a lower IQ

KEY TERMS

mental retardation (or intellectual disability) p. 303

fetal alcohol syndrome p. 304

familial retardation p. 304

intellectually gifted p. 305

Group Differences in Intelligence: Genetic and Environmental Determinants

Kwang is often washed with a pleck tied to a:
  (a) rundel
  (b) flink
  (c) pove
  (d) quirj

Are traditional IQ tests culturally biased?

Are there racial differences in intelligence?

To what degree is intelligence influenced by the environment, and to what degree by heredity?

If you found this kind of item on an intelligence test, you would probably complain that the test was totally absurd and had nothing to do with your intelligence or anyone else's—and rightly so. How could anyone be expected to respond to items presented in a language that was so unfamiliar?

Yet to some people, even more reasonable questions may appear just as nonsensical. Consider the example of a child raised in a city who is asked about procedures for milking cows, or someone raised in a rural area who is asked about subway ticketing procedures. Obviously, the previous experience of the test-takers would affect their ability to answer correctly. And if such types of questions were included on an IQ test, a critic could rightly contend that the test had more to do with prior experience than with intelligence.

Although IQ tests do not include questions that are so clearly dependent on prior knowledge as questions about cows and subways, the background and experiences of test-takers do have the potential to affect results. In fact, the issue of devising fair intelligence tests that measure knowledge unrelated to culture and family background and experience is central to explaining an important and persistent finding: Members of certain racial and cultural groups consistently score lower on traditional intelligence tests than do members of other groups. For example, as a group, blacks tend to average 10 to 15 IQ points lower than whites. Does this variation reflect a true difference in intelligence, or are the questions biased in regard to the kinds of knowledge they test? Clearly, if whites perform better because of their greater familiarity with the kind of information that is being tested, their higher IQ scores are not necessarily an indication that they are more intelligent than members of other groups (Jensen, 2003; Templer & Arikawa, 2006; Fagan & Holland, 2007).

There is good reason to believe that some standardized IQ tests contain elements that discriminate against minority-group members whose experiences differ from those of the white majority. Consider the question "What should you do if another child grabbed your hat and ran off with it?" Most white middle-class children answer that they would tell an adult, and this response is scored as correct. However, a reasonable response might be to chase the person and fight to get the hat back, the answer that is chosen by many urban black children—but one that is scored as incorrect (Miller-Jones, 1991; Aiken, 1997; Reynolds & Ramsay, 2003).

Furthermore, tests may include even subtler forms of bias against minority groups. For example, assessments of cognitive ability developed in the United States may favor responses that implicitly reflect North American or European values, customs, or traditions. At the same time, such tests are biased against African and other cultural value systems (Helms, 1992; Byrne & Watkins, 2003).

For example, the traditional Western value of "rugged individualism" means that correct answers to test items may require a test-taker to reason independently of a particular social context. In contrast, the African cultural value of communalism, in which one's group is valued more than individuals are, may leave test-takers from that tradition unable to answer a question that provides no information about the social context (Greenfield, 1997; Kwate, 2001).

Exploring DIVERSITY

The Relative Influence of Genetics and Environment: Nature, Nurture, and IQ

In an attempt to produce a **culture-fair IQ test**, one that does not discriminate against the members of any minority group, psychologists have tried to devise test items that assess experiences common to all cultures or emphasize questions that do not require language usage. However, test makers have found this difficult to do, because past experiences, attitudes, and values almost always have an impact on respondents' answers.

Culture-fair IQ test: A test that does not discriminate against the members of any minority group.

For example, children raised in Western cultures group things on the basis of what they are (such as putting *dog* and *fish* into the category of *animal*). In contrast, members of the Kpelle tribe in Africa see intelligence demonstrated by grouping things according to what they *do* (grouping *fish* with *swim*). Similarly, children in the United States asked to memorize the position of objects on a chessboard perform better than do African children living in remote villages if household objects familiar to the U.S. children are used. But if rocks are used instead of household objects, the African children do better. In short, it is difficult to produce a test that is truly culture-fair (Sandoval et al., 1998; Serpell, 2000; Valencia & Suzuki, 2003).

The efforts of psychologists to produce culture-fair measures of intelligence relate to a lingering controversy over differences in intelligence between members of minority and majority groups. In attempting to identify whether there are differences between such groups, psychologists have had to confront the broader issue of determining the relative contribution to intelligence of genetic factors (heredity) and experience (environment)—the nature-nurture issue that is one of the basic issues of psychology.

Richard Herrnstein, a psychologist, and Charles Murray, a sociologist, fanned the flames of the debate with the publication of their book *The Bell Curve* in the mid-1990s (Herrnstein & Murray, 1994). They argued that an analysis of IQ differences between whites and blacks demonstrated that although environmental factors played a role, there were also basic genetic differences between the two races. They based their argument on a number of findings. For instance, on average, whites score 15 points higher than do blacks on traditional IQ tests even when socioeconomic status (SES) is taken into account. According to Herrnstein and Murray, middle- and upper-SES blacks score lower than do middle- and upper-SES whites, just as lower-SES blacks score lower on average than do lower-SES whites. Intelligence differences between blacks and whites, they concluded, could not be attributed to environmental differences alone.

Heritability: A measure of the degree to which a characteristic is related to genetic, inherited factors.

Moreover, intelligence in general shows a high degree of **heritability**, a measure of the degree to which a characteristic can be attributed to genetic, inherited factors (e.g., Grigorenko, 2000; Plomin, 2003; Petrill, 2005; Miller & Penke, 2007). As can be seen in Figure 1, the closer the genetic link between two related people, the greater the correspondence of IQ scores. Using data such as these, Herrnstein and Murray argued that differences between races in IQ scores were largely caused by genetically based differences in intelligence.

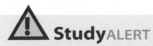

StudyALERT

Remember that the differences in IQ scores are much greater when comparing individuals than when comparing groups.

However, many psychologists reacted strongly to the arguments laid out in *The Bell Curve*, refuting several of the book's basic arguments. One criticism is that even when attempts are made to hold socioeconomic conditions constant, wide variations remain among individual households. Furthermore, no one can convincingly assert that the living conditions of blacks and whites are identical even when their

Relationship	Genetic overlap	Rearing	Correlation
Monozygotic (identical) twins	100%	Together	.86
Dizygotic (fraternal) twins	50%	Together	.62
Siblings	50%	Together	.41
Siblings	50%	Apart	.24
Parent-child	50%	Together	.35
Parent-child	50%	Apart	.31
Adoptive parent-child	0%	Together	.16
Unrelated children	0%	Together	.25
Spouses	0%	Apart	.29

The difference between these two correlations shows the impact of the environment

The relatively low correlation for unrelated children raised together shows the importance of genetic factors

FIGURE 1 The relationship between IQ and closeness of genetic relationship. In general, the more similar the genetic and environmental background of two people, the greater the correlation. Note, for example, that the correlation for spouses, who are genetically unrelated and have been reared apart, is relatively low, whereas the correlation for identical twins reared together is substantial. (Source: Adapted from Henderson, 1982.)

socioeconomic status is similar. In addition, as we discussed earlier, there is reason to believe that traditional IQ tests may discriminate against lower-SES urban blacks by asking for information pertaining to experiences they are unlikely to have had (American Psychological Association Task Force on Intelligence, 1996; Hall, 2002; Horn, 2002; Nisbett, 2007).

Moreover, blacks who are raised in economically enriched environments have similar IQ scores to whites in comparable environments. For example, a study by Sandra Scarr and Richard Weinberg (1976) examined black children who had been adopted at an early age by white middle-class families of above-average intelligence. The IQ scores of those children averaged 106—about 15 points above the average IQ scores of unadopted black children in the study. Other research shows that the racial gap in IQ narrows considerably after a college education, and cross-cultural data demonstrate that when racial gaps exist in other cultures, it is the economically disadvantaged groups that typically have lower scores. In short, the evidence that genetic factors play the major role in determining racial differences in IQ is not compelling (Winston, 2004; Sternberg, Grigorenko, & Kidd, 2005; Fagan & Holland, 2007).

Furthermore, drawing comparisons between different races on any dimension, including IQ scores, is an imprecise, potentially misleading, and often fruitless venture. By far, the greatest discrepancies in IQ scores occur when comparing *individuals*, not when comparing mean IQ scores of different *groups*. There are blacks who score high on IQ tests and whites who score low, just as there are whites who score high and blacks who score low. For the concept of intelligence to aid in the betterment of society, we must examine how *individuals* perform, not the groups to which they belong (Angoff, 1988; Fagan & Holland, 2002, 2007).

The more critical question to ask, then, is not whether hereditary or environmental factors primarily underlie intelligence, but whether there is anything we can do to maximize the intellectual development of each individual. If we can find ways to do this, we will be able to make changes in the environment—which may take the form of enriched home and school environments—that can lead each person to reach his or her potential.

Social and economic inequality, as well as heredity and other environmental factors, are associated with differences in intelligence. People who have greater educational opportunities and who suffer fewer economic constraints are able to maximize their intelligence.

RECAP/EVALUATE/RETHINK

RECAP

Are traditional IQ tests culturally biased?

- Traditional intelligence tests have frequently been criticized for being biased in favor of the white middle-class population. This controversy has led to attempts to devise culture-fair tests, IQ measures that avoid questions that depend on a particular cultural background. (p. 307)

Are there racial differences in intelligence?

- Issues of racial differences in intelligence are very controversial, in part because of the difficulty of defining the concept of race scientifically and disagreement over what constitutes an unbiased measure of race. (p. 308)

To what degree is intelligence influenced by the environment, and to what degree by heredity?

- Attempting to distinguish environmental from hereditary factors in intelligence is probably futile and certainly misguided. Because individual IQ scores vary far more than do group IQ scores, it is more critical to ask what can be done to maximize the intellectual development of each individual. (p. 308)

EVALUATE

1. Intelligence tests may be biased toward the prevailing culture in such a way that minorities are put at a disadvantage when taking these tests. True or false?
2. A(n) _____ - _____ test tries to use only questions appropriate to all the people taking the test.

3. IQ tests can accurately determine the intelligence of entire groups of people. True or false?
4. Intelligence can be seen as a combination of _____ and _____ factors.

RETHINK

1. There's been a steady rise in average IQ scores in the United States over the last several decades. Why might this be the case? Do you think it represents an actual increase in intelligence?
2. *From a college admissions officer's perspective:* Imagine that you notice that students who are members of minority groups systematically receive lower scores on standardized college entrance exams. What suggestions do you have for helping these students improve their scores? What advice about their college applications would you give these students to help them be competitive applicants?

Answers to Evaluate Questions

1. true; 2. culture-fair; 3. false; IQ tests are used to measure individual intelligence; within any group there are wide variations in individual intelligence; 4. hereditary, environmental

KEY TERMS

culture-fair IQ test p. 308   heritability p. 308

Psychology on the Web

1. Many sites on the Web permit you to assess your IQ. Take at least two such tests and (a) compare your results, (b) indicate what mental qualities seemed to be tested on the tests, and (c) discuss your impression of the reliability and validity of the tests. Write up your conclusions.
2. Find a way to assess at least one other of your multiple intelligences (that is, one not tested by the IQ tests you took) on the Web. What sort of intelligence was the test supposed to be testing? What sorts of items were included? How valid and reliable do you think it was, both in and of itself and compared with the IQ tests you took?

Epilogue

We've just examined one of the most controversial areas of psychology—intelligence. Some of the most heated discussions in all of psychology focus on this topic, engaging educators, policy makers, politicians, and psychologists. The issues include the very meaning of intelligence, its measurement, individual extremes of intelligence, and, finally, the heredity–environment question. We saw that the quest to partition intelligence into hereditary factors versus environmental factors is generally pointless. In the area of intelligence, the focus of our efforts should be on making sure that every individual has the opportunity to achieve his or her potential.

Before we leave the topic of intelligence, return to the stories of the two persons of widely different intellectual capabilities discussed in the prologue, Chris Burke and Vino Vasudevan. Consider the following questions on the basis of what you have learned about intelligence.

1. Chris Burke's physicians concluded in his infancy that he would never be able to function effectively in society and should be immediately institutionalized. How do you think the physicians came to their conclusions, and why do you think they were proven wrong?
2. In what ways would placing Burke in a separate educational program have helped or hurt his chances of reaching his full potential?
3. How might the educational acceleration of Vino Vasudevan help and hinder her later development? Do you think slowing down her educational progress might be beneficial? How?
4. Based on research relating to individuals who have unusually high IQ scores, what do you think Vino's emotional intelligence is like?

CHAPTER 10

Motivation and Emotion

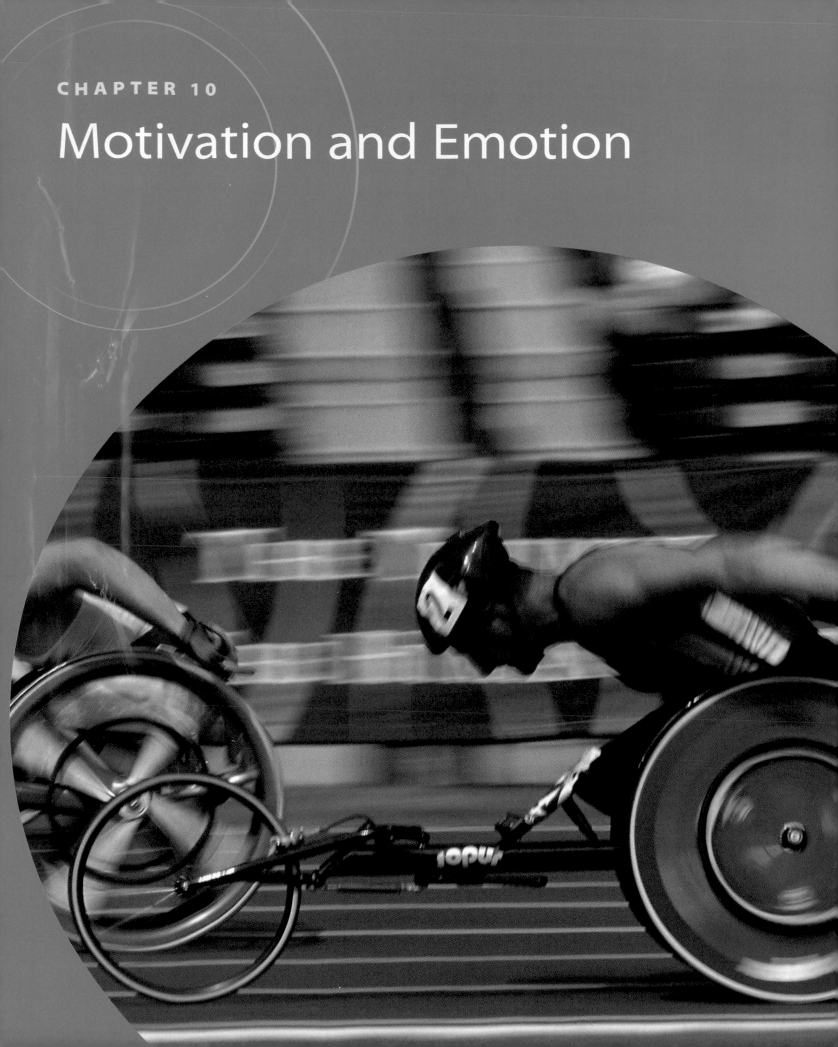

Key Concepts for Chapter 10

Prologue *Armed with Bravery*

In just a moment, 27-year-old Aron Ralston's life changed. An 800-pound boulder dislodged in a narrow canyon where Ralston was hiking in an isolated Utah canyon, pinning his lower arm to the ground.

For the next five days, Ralston lay in the dense, lonely forest, unable to escape. An experienced climber who had search-and-rescue training, he had ample time to consider his options. He tried unsuccessfully to chip away at the rock, and he rigged up ropes and pulleys around the boulder in a vain effort to move it.

Finally, out of water and nearly dehydrated, Ralston reasoned there was only one option left short of dying. In acts of incredible bravery, Ralston broke two bones in his wrist, applied a tourniquet, and used a dull pen knife to amputate his arm beneath the elbow.

Freed from his entrapment, Ralston climbed down from where he had been pinned, and then hiked five miles to safety. (Ralston, 2004; Martin, 2006)

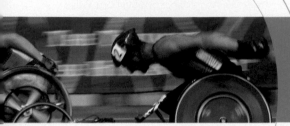

Looking Ahead

Ralston, who now has a prosthetic arm, recovered from his ordeal. He remains an active outdoorsman and hiker.

The topics of motivation and emotion are central in attempting to explain Ralston's extraordinary courage and will to live. Psychologists who study motivation seek to discover the particular desired goals—the motives—that underlie behavior. Behaviors as basic as drinking to satisfy thirst and as inconsequential as taking a stroll to get exercise exemplify motives. Psychologists specializing in the study of motivation assume that such underlying motives steer our choices of activities.

While motivation concerns the forces that direct future behavior, emotion pertains to the feelings we experience throughout our lives. The study of emotions focuses on our internal experiences at any given moment. All of us feel a variety of emotions: happiness at succeeding at a difficult task, sadness over the death of a loved one, anger at being treated unfairly. Because emotions not only play a role in motivating our behavior but also act as a reflection of our underlying motivation, they play an important role in our lives.

We begin this set of modules by focusing on the major conceptions of motivation, discussing how different motives and needs jointly affect behavior. We consider motives that are biologically based and universal in the animal kingdom, such as hunger, as well as motives that are unique to humans, such as the need for achievement.

We then turn to emotions. We consider the roles and functions that emotions play in people's lives and discuss several approaches that explain how people understand their emotions. Finally, we look at how nonverbal behavior communicates emotions.

MODULE 29

Explaining Motivation

When Lance Armstrong completed the final leg of the Tour de France before a cheering crowd of a half million people, it meant more than winning the world's most prestigious cycling race. The moment represented a triumph of human motivation and spirit—with a dash of miracle.

Only 33 months earlier, no one would have thought that Armstrong would be the winner of the Tour de France. In fact, the odds were against his ever cycling again. At that time, he learned he had testicular cancer that had spread to his lungs and brain and contained 12 tumors and two lesions. Doctors gave him a 50-50 chance of surviving.

His treatment was grueling. He suffered through surgery and four rounds of intense chemotherapy, separated by a month each. But he never gave up. Pushing himself, he would ride 20 to 50 miles a day following each of the one-week chemotherapy sessions.

Then the unexpected happened: The cancer disappeared, surprising everyone. And Armstrong picked up where he had left off, training hours each day and entering cycling competitions. (Abt, 1999, p. D4)

Several years later, Armstrong was not only healthy, but crossing the finish line first at the Tour de France—a testament to his enormous will to succeed.

What motivation lay behind Armstrong's resolve? Was it anticipating the emotional thrill of winning the Tour de France? The potential rewards that would follow if he succeeded? The excitement of participating? The satisfaction of achieving a long-sought goal?

To answer such questions, psychologists employ the concept of **motivation**, the factors that direct and energize the behavior of humans and other organisms. Motivation has biological, cognitive, and social aspects, and the complexity of the concept has led psychologists to develop a variety of approaches. All seek to explain the energy that guides people's behavior in specific directions.

Key Concept

How does motivation direct and energize behavior?

Motivation: The factors that direct and energize the behavior of humans and other organisms.

Instincts: Inborn patterns of behavior that are biologically determined rather than learned.

Instinct Approaches: Born to Be Motivated

When psychologists first tried to explain motivation, they turned to **instincts**, inborn patterns of behavior that are biologically determined rather than learned. According to instinct approaches to motivation, people and animals are born preprogrammed with sets of behaviors essential to their survival. Those instincts provide the energy that channels behavior in appropriate directions. Hence, sexual behavior may be a response to an instinct to reproduce, and exploratory behavior may be motivated by an instinct to examine one's territory.

This conception presents several difficulties, however. For one thing, psychologists do not agree on what, or even how many, primary instincts exist. One early psychologist, William McDougall (1908), suggested that there are 18 instincts. Other theorists came up with even more—with one sociologist (Bernard, 1924) claiming that there are exactly 5,759 distinct instincts!

What motivated Lance Armstrong to stick with his rigorous training regime?

Furthermore, explanations based on the concept of instincts do not go very far toward explaining why one specific pattern of behavior, and not others, has appeared in a given species. In addition, although it is clear that much animal behavior is based on instincts, because much of the variety and complexity of human behavior is learned, that behavior cannot be seen as instinctual.

As a result of these shortcomings, newer explanations have replaced conceptions of motivation based on instincts. However, instinct approaches still play a role in certain theories, especially those based on evolutionary approaches that focus on our genetic inheritance. Furthermore, Freud's work suggests that instinctual drives of sex and aggression motivate behavior (Katz, 2001).

Drive-Reduction Approaches: Satisfying Our Needs

After rejecting instinct theory, psychologists first proposed simple drive-reduction theories of motivation to take its place (Hull, 1943). **Drive-reduction approaches** suggest that a lack of some basic biological requirement such as water produces a drive to obtain that requirement (in this case, the thirst drive).

To understand this approach, we begin with the concept of drive. A **drive** is motivational tension, or arousal, that energizes behavior to fulfill a need. Many basic drives, such as hunger, thirst, sleep, and sex, are related to biological needs of the body or of the species as a whole. These are called *primary drives*. Primary drives contrast with secondary drives, in which behavior fulfills no obvious biological need. In *secondary drives*, prior experience and learning bring about needs. For instance, some people have strong needs to achieve academically and professionally. We can say that their achievement need is reflected in a secondary drive that motivates their behavior (McKinley et al., 2004; Seli, 2007).

We usually try to satisfy a primary drive by reducing the need underlying it. For example, we become hungry after not eating for a few hours and may raid the refrigerator, especially if the next scheduled meal is not imminent. If the weather turns cold, we put on extra clothing or raise the setting on the thermostat to keep warm. If our bodies need liquids to function properly, we experience thirst and seek out water.

HOMEOSTASIS

Homeostasis, the body's tendency to maintain a steady internal state, underlies primary drives. Using feedback loops, homeostasis brings deviations in body functioning back to an optimal state, similar to the way a thermostat and a furnace work in a home heating system to maintain a steady temperature (see Figure 1). Receptor cells throughout the body constantly monitor factors such as temperature and nutrient levels. When deviations from the ideal state occur, the body adjusts in an effort to return to an optimal state. Many fundamental needs, including the needs for food, water, stable body temperature, and sleep, operate via homeostasis (Canteras, 2002; Machado, Suchecki, & Tufik, 2005; Black, 2006).

Although drive-reduction theories provide a good explanation of how primary drives motivate behavior, they cannot fully explain a behavior in which the goal is not to reduce a drive, but rather to maintain or even increase the level of excitement or arousal. For instance, some behaviors seem to be motivated by nothing more than curiosity, such as rushing to check e-mail messages. Similarly, many people pursue thrilling activities such as riding a roller coaster or steering a raft down the rapids of a river. Such behaviors certainly don't suggest that people seek to reduce all drives, as drive-reduction approaches would indicate (Begg & Langley, 2001; Rosenbloom & Wolf, 2002).

Both curiosity and thrill-seeking behavior, then, shed doubt on drive-reduction approaches as a complete explanation for motivation. In both cases, rather than

Drive-reduction approaches to motivation: Theories suggesting that a lack of a basic biological requirement such as water produces a drive to obtain that requirement (in this case, the thirst drive).

Drive: Motivational tension, or arousal, that energizes behavior to fulfill a need.

Homeostasis: The body's tendency to maintain a steady internal state.

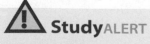 **Study**ALERT

To remember the concept of homeostasis, keep in mind the analogy of a thermostat that regulates the temperature in a house.

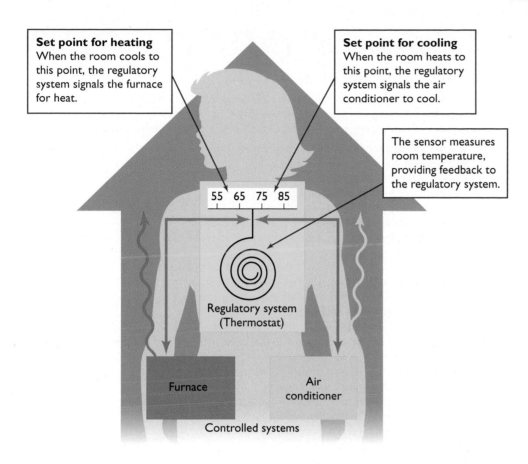

Set point for heating
When the room cools to this point, the regulatory system signals the furnace for heat.

Set point for cooling
When the room heats to this point, the regulatory system signals the air conditioner to cool.

The sensor measures room temperature, providing feedback to the regulatory system.

55 65 75 85

Regulatory system (Thermostat)

Furnace

Air conditioner

Controlled systems

FIGURE 1 With homeostasis, a series of feedback loops is used to regulate body functions, similar to the way a thermostat turns on the furnace when a room's air temperature becomes too cool and turns it off when the air temperature becomes too warm. Similarly, when body temperature becomes too low, the blood vessels constrict, and we shiver and seek warmth. When body temperature becomes too high, the blood vessels expand, and we sweat as our bodies try to lower the temperature. Can you think of other internal systems that operate via homeostasis?

seeking to reduce an underlying drive, people and animals appear to be motivated to increase their overall level of stimulation and activity. To explain this phenomenon, psychologists have devised an alternative: arousal approaches to motivation.

Arousal Approaches: Beyond Drive Reduction

Arousal approaches seek to explain behavior in which the goal is to maintain or increase excitement. According to **arousal approaches to motivation**, each person tries to maintain a certain level of stimulation and activity. As with the drive-reduction model, this model suggests that if our stimulation and activity levels become too high, we try to reduce them. But, in contrast to the drive-reduction model, the arousal model also suggests that if levels of stimulation and activity are too low, we will try to increase them by seeking stimulation.

People vary widely in the optimal level of arousal they seek out, with some people looking for especially high levels of arousal. For example, people who participate in daredevil sports, high-stakes gamblers, and criminals who pull off high-risk robberies may be exhibiting a particularly high need for arousal (see Figure 2; Zuckerman & Kuhlman, 2000; Zuckerman, 2002; Cavenett & Nixon, 2006).

Arousal approaches to motivation: The belief that we try to maintain certain levels of stimulation and activity, increasing or reducing them as necessary.

Incentive Approaches: Motivation's Pull

When a luscious dessert appears on the table after a filling meal, its appeal has little or nothing to do with internal drives or the maintenance of arousal. Rather, if we choose to eat the dessert, such behavior is motivated by the external stimulus of the

FIGURE 2 Some people seek high levels of arousal, while others are more easygoing. You can get a sense of your own preferred level of stimulation by completing this questionnaire. (Source: "Do You Seek Out Sensation?" questionnaire from Marvin Zuckerman, "The Search for High Sensation," *Psychology Today*, February 1978, pp. 30-46. Reprinted with permission from *Psychology Today* magazine, (Copyright © 1978 Sussex Publishers, LLC.).)

Do You Seek Out Sensation?

How much stimulation do you crave in your everyday life? You will have an idea after you complete the following questionnaire, which lists some items from a scale designed to assess your sensation-seeking tendencies. Circle either A or B in each pair or statements.

1. A I would like a job that requires a lot of travelling.
   B I would prefer a job in one location.
2. A I am invigorated by a brisk, cold day.
   B I can't wait to get indoors on a cold day.
3. A I get bored seeing the same old faces.
   B I like the comfortable familiarity of everyday friends.
4. A I would prefer living in an ideal society in which everyone was safe, secure, and happy.
   B I would have preferred living in the unsettled days of our history.
5. A I sometimes like to do things that are a little frightening.
   B A sensible person avoids activities that are dangerous.
6. A I would not like to be hypnotized.
   B I would like to have the experience of being hypnotized.
7. A The most important goal of life is to live it to the fullest and to experience as much as possible.
   B The most important goal of life is to find peace and happiness.
8. A I would like to try parachute jumping.
   B I would never want to try jumping out of a plane, with or without a parachute.
9. A I enter cold water gradually, giving myself time to get used to it.
   B I like to dive or jump right into the ocean or a cold pool.
10. A When I go on a vacation, I prefer the comfort of a good room and bed.
    B When I go on a vacation, I prefer the change of camping out.
11. A I prefer people who are emotionally expressive, even if they are a bit unstable.
    B I prefer people who are calm and even-tempered.
12. A A good painting should shock or jolt the senses.
    B A good painting should give one a feeling of peace and security.
13. A People who ride motorcycles must have some kind of unconscious need to hurt themselves.
    B I would like to drive or ride a motorcycle.

Scoring: Give yourself one point for each of the following responses: 1*A*, 2*A*, 3*A*, 4*B*, 5*A*, 6*B*, 7*A*, 8*A*, 9*B*, 10*B*, 11*A*, 12*A*, 13*B*. Find your total score by adding up the number of points and then use the following scoring key.

0–3 very low sensation seeking

4–5 low

6–9 average

10–11 high

12–13 very high

Keep in mind, of course, that this short questionnaire, for which the scoring is based on the results of college students who have taken it, provides only a rough estimate of your sensation-seeking tendencies. Moreover, as people get older, their sensation-seeking scores tend to decrease. Still, the questionnaire will at least give you an indication of how your sensation-seeking tendencies compare with those of others.

dessert itself, which acts as an anticipated reward. This reward, in motivational terms, is an *incentive*.

Incentive approaches: Theories suggesting that motivation stems from the desire to obtain valued external goals, or incentives.

Incentive approaches to motivation suggest that motivation stems from the desire to obtain valued external goals, or incentives. In this view, the desirable properties of external stimuli—whether grades, money, affection, food, or sex—account for a person's motivation.

Although the theory explains why we may succumb to an incentive (such as a mouthwatering dessert) even though we lack internal cues (such as hunger), it does not provide a complete explanation of motivation, because organisms sometimes seek to fulfill needs even when incentives are not apparent. Consequently, many psychologists believe that the internal drives proposed by drive-reduction theory work in tandem with the external incentives of incentive theory to "push" and "pull" behavior, respectively. Thus, at the same time that we seek to satisfy our underlying hunger needs (the push of drive-reduction theory), we are drawn to food that appears very appetizing (the pull of incentive theory). Rather than contradicting each other, then, drives and incentives may work together in motivating behavior (Pinel, Assanand, & Lehman, 2000; Lowery, Fillingim, & Wright, 2003; Berridge, 2004).

Cognitive Approaches: The Thoughts Behind Motivation

Cognitive approaches to motivation suggest that motivation is a product of people's thoughts, expectations, and goals—their cognitions. For instance, the degree to which people are motivated to study for a test is based on their expectation of how well studying will pay off in terms of a good grade.

Cognitive theories of motivation draw a key distinction between intrinsic and extrinsic motivation. *Intrinsic motivation* causes us to participate in an activity for our own enjoyment rather than for any concrete, tangible reward that it will bring us. In contrast, *extrinsic motivation* causes us to do something for money, a grade, or some other concrete, tangible reward. For example, when a physician works long hours because she loves medicine, intrinsic motivation is prompting her; if she works hard to make a lot of money, extrinsic motivation underlies her efforts (Pedersen, 2002; Lepper, Corpus, & Iyengar, 2005; Shaikholeslami & Khayyer, 2006).

We are more apt to persevere, work harder, and produce work of higher quality when motivation for a task is intrinsic rather than extrinsic. In fact, in some cases providing rewards for desirable behavior (thereby increasing extrinsic motivation) actually may decrease intrinsic motivation (Deci, Koestner, & Ryan, 2001; Henderlong & Lepper, 2002; James, 2005).

Cognitive approaches to motivation: Theories suggesting that motivation is a product of people's thoughts and expectations—their cognitions.

Maslow's Hierarchy: Ordering Motivational Needs

What do Eleanor Roosevelt, Abraham Lincoln, and Albert Einstein have in common? The common thread, according to a model of motivation devised by psychologist Abraham Maslow, is that each of them fulfilled the highest levels of motivational needs underlying human behavior.

Maslow's model places motivational needs in a hierarchy and suggests that before more sophisticated, higher-order needs can be met, certain primary needs must be satisfied (Maslow, 1970, 1987). A pyramid can represent the model, with the more basic needs at the bottom and the higher-level needs at the top (see Figure 3). To activate a specific higher-order need, thereby guiding behavior, a person must first fulfill the more basic needs in the hierarchy.

The basic needs are primary drives: needs for water, food, sleep, sex, and the like. To move up the hierarchy, a person must first meet these basic physiological needs. Safety needs come next in the hierarchy; Maslow suggests that people need a safe, secure environment in order to function effectively. Physiological and safety needs compose the lower-order needs.

FIGURE 3 Maslow's hierarchy shows how our motivation progresses up the pyramid from the broadest, most fundamental biological needs to higher-order ones. (After Maslow, 1970.) Do you agree that lower-order needs must be satisfied before higher-order needs? Do hermits and monks who attempt to fulfill spiritual needs while denying basic physical needs contradict Maslow's hierarchy?

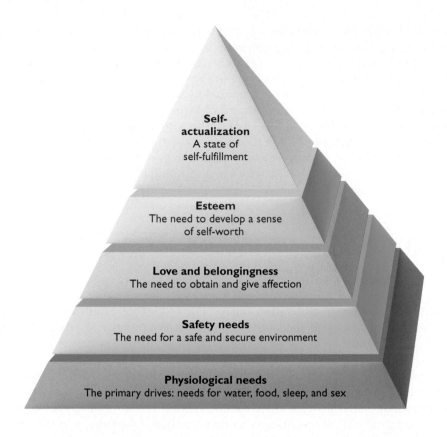

Self-actualization: A state of self-fulfillment in which people realize their highest potential, each in his or her own unique way.

Only after meeting the basic lower-order needs can a person consider fulfilling higher-order needs, such as the needs for love and a sense of belonging, esteem, and self-actualization. Love and belongingness needs include the needs to obtain and give affection and to be a contributing member of some group or society. After fulfilling these needs, a person strives for esteem. In Maslow's thinking, esteem relates to the need to develop a sense of self-worth by recognizing that others know and value one's competence.

Once these four sets of needs are fulfilled—no easy task—a person is able to strive for the highest-level need, self-actualization. **Self-actualization** is a state of self-fulfillment in which people realize their highest potentials, each in his or her own unique way. Although Maslow first suggested that self-actualization occurred in only a few, famous individuals, he later expanded the concept to encompass everyday people. For example, a parent with excellent nurturing skills who raises a family, a teacher who year after year creates an environment that maximizes students' opportunities for success, and an artist who realizes his creative potential all may be self-actualized. The important thing is that people feel at ease with themselves and satisfied that they are using their talents to the fullest. In a sense, achieving self-actualization reduces the striving and yearning for greater fulfillment that mark most people's lives and instead provides a sense of satisfaction with the current state of affairs (Piechowski, 2003; Reiss & Havercamp, 2005; Laas, 2006).

Although research has been unable to validate the specific ordering of Maslow's stages, and although it is difficult to measure self-actualization objectively, Maslow's model is important for two reasons: It highlights the complexity of human needs, and it emphasizes the idea that until more basic biological needs are met, people will be relatively unconcerned with higher-order needs. For example, if people are hungry, their first interest will be in obtaining food; they will not be concerned with needs such as love and self-esteem (Hanley & Abell, 2002; Samantaray, Srivastava, & Misbra, 2002).

Applying the Different Approaches to Motivation

The various theories of motivation (summarized in Figure 4) give several different perspectives on motivation. Which provides the fullest account of motivation? Actually, many of the approaches are complementary, rather than contradictory. In fact, employing more than one approach can help us understand motivation in a particular instance.

Consider, for example, Aron Ralston's accident while hiking (described in the prologue). His interest in climbing in an isolated and potentially dangerous area may be explained by arousal approaches to motivation. From the perspective of instinct approaches, we realize that Aron had an overwhelming instinct to preserve his life at all costs. From a cognitive perspective, we see his careful consideration of various strategies to extricate himself from the boulder.

In short, applying multiple approaches to motivation in a given situation provides a broader understanding than we might obtain by employing only a single approach. We'll see this again when we consider specific motives—such as the needs for food, achievement, affiliation, and power—and draw on several of the theories for the fullest account of what motivates our behavior.

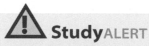 **Study**ALERT

Use Figure 4 to learn the distinctions among the different explanations for motivation (instinct, drive reduction, arousal, incentive, cognitive, and Maslow's hierarchy of needs).

Instinct

People and animals are born with preprogrammed sets of behaviors essential to their survival.

Drive reduction

When some basic biological requirement is lacking, a drive is produced.

Arousal

People seek an optimal level of stimulation. If the level of stimulation is too high, they act to reduce it; if it is too low, they act to increase it.

Incentive

External stimuli direct and energize behavior.

Cognitive

Thoughts, expectations, and understanding of the world direct motivation.

Hierarchy of needs

Needs form a hierarchy; before higher-order needs are met, lower-order needs must be fulfilled.

FIGURE 4 The major approaches to motivation.

RECAP/EVALUATE/RETHINK

RECAP

How does motivation direct and energize behavior?

- Motivation relates to the factors that direct and energize behavior. (p. 315)
- Drive is the motivational tension that energizes behavior to fulfill a need. (p. 316)
- Homeostasis, the maintenance of a steady internal state, often underlies motivational drives. (p. 316)
- Arousal approaches suggest that we try to maintain a particular level of stimulation and activity. (p. 317)
- Incentive approaches focus on the positive aspects of the environment that direct and energize behavior. (p. 318)
- Cognitive approaches focus on the role of thoughts, expectations, and understanding of the world in producing motivation. (p. 319)
- Maslow's hierarchy suggests that there are five basic needs: physiological, safety, love and belongingness, esteem, and self-actualization. Only after the more basic needs are fulfilled can a person move toward meeting higher-order needs. (p. 320)

EVALUATE

1. _____ are forces that guide a person's behavior in a certain direction.
2. Biologically determined, inborn patterns of behavior are known as _____.

3. Your psychology professor tells you, "Explaining behavior is easy! When we lack something, we are motivated to get it." Which approach to motivation does your professor subscribe to?
4. By drinking water after running a marathon, a runner tries to keep his or her body at an optimal level of functioning. This process is called _____.
5. I help an elderly person cross the street because doing a good deed makes me feel good. What type of motivation is at work here? What type of motivation would be at work if I were to help an elderly man across the street because he paid me $20?
6. According to Maslow, a person with no job, no home, and no friends can become self-actualized. True or false?

RETHINK

1. Which approaches to motivation are more commonly used in the workplace? How might each approach be used to design employment policies that can sustain or increase motivation?
2. *From the perspective of an educator:* Do you think that giving students grades serves as an external reward that would decrease intrinsic motivation for the subject matter? Why or why not?

Answers to Evaluate Questions

1. motives; 2. instincts; 3. drive reduction; 4. homeostasis; 5. intrinsic, extrinsic; 6. false; lower-order needs must be fulfilled before self-actualization can occur

KEY TERMS

motivation p. 315
instincts p. 315
drive-reduction approaches to motivation p. 316
drive p. 316

homeostasis p. 316
arousal approaches to motivation p. 317
incentive approaches to motivation p. 318

cognitive approaches to motivation p. 319
self-actualization p. 320

Human Needs and Motivation: Eat, Drink, and Be Daring

As a sophomore at the University of California, Santa Cruz, Lisa Arndt followed a menu of her own making: For breakfast she ate cereal or fruit, with 10 diet pills and 50 chocolate-flavored laxatives. Lunch was a salad or sandwich; dinner: chicken and rice. But it was the feast that followed that Arndt relished most. Almost every night at about 9 p.m., she would retreat to her room and eat an entire small pizza and a whole batch of cookies. Then she'd wait for the day's laxatives to take effect. "It was extremely painful," says Arndt of those days . . . "But I was that desperate to make up for my bingeing. I was terrified of fat the way other people are afraid of lions or guns." (Hubbard, O'Neill, & Cheakalos, 1999, p. 59)

Lisa was one of the 10 million women (and 1 million men) who are estimated to suffer from an eating disorder. These disorders, which usually appear during adolescence, can bring about extraordinary weight loss and other forms of physical deterioration. Extremely dangerous, they sometimes result in death.

Why are Lisa and others like her subject to such disordered eating, which revolves around the motivation to avoid weight gain at all costs? And why do so many other people engage in overeating, which leads to obesity?

To answer these questions, we must consider some of the specific needs that underlie behavior. In this module, we examine several of the most important human needs. We begin with hunger, the primary drive that has received the most attention from researchers, and then turn to secondary drives—those uniquely human endeavors, based on learned needs and past experience, that help explain why people strive to achieve, to affiliate with others, and to seek power over others.

Key Concepts

What biological and social factors underlie hunger?

How are needs relating to achievement, affiliation, and power motivation exhibited?

The Motivation Behind Hunger and Eating

Two-thirds of the people in the United States are overweight, and almost a quarter are so heavy that they have **obesity**, body weight that is more than 20 percent above the average weight for a person of a particular height. And the rest of the world is not far behind: A billion people around the globe are overweight or obese. The World Health Organization has said that worldwide obesity has reached epidemic proportions, producing increases in heart disease, diabetes, cancer, and premature deaths (Hill, Catenacci, & Wyatt, 2005; Stephenson & Banet-Weiser, 2007).

The most widely used measure of obesity is *body mass index (BMI)*, which is based on a ratio of weight to height. People with a BMI greater than 30 are considered obese, whereas those with a BMI between 25 and 30 are overweight. (Use the formulas in Figure 1 to determine your own BMI.)

Although the definition of obesity is clear from a scientific point of view, people's perceptions of what an ideal body looks like vary significantly across different cultures and, within Western cultures, from one time period to another. For instance, many contemporary Western cultures stress the importance of slimness in women—a relatively recent view. In 19th century Hawaii, the most attractive women were those who were the heaviest. Furthermore, for most of the 20th century—except for periods in the

Obesity: Body weight that is more than 20 percent above the average weight for a person of a particular height.

FIGURE 1 Use this procedure to find your body mass index.

To calculate your body mass index, follow these steps:

1. Indicate your weight in pounds: _____ pounds
2. Indicate your height in inches: _____ inches
3. Divide your weight (item 1) by your height (item 2), and write the outcome here: _____
4. Divide the result above (item 3) by your height (item 2), and write the outcome here: _____
5. Multiply the number above by 703, and write the product here: _____. This is your body mass index.

Example:
For a person who weights 210 pounds and who is 6 feet tall, divide 210 pounds by 72 inches, which equals 2.917. Then divide 2.917 by 72 inches (item 3), which yields .041. Multiplying .041 (from item 4) by 703 yields a BMI of 28.5.

Interpretation:
• Underweight = less than 18.5
• Normal weight = 18.5–24.9
• Overweight = 25–29.9
• Obesity = BMI of 30 or greater

Keep in mind that a BMI greater than 25 may or may not be due to excess body fat. For example, professional athletes may have little fat but weigh more than the average person because they have greater muscle mass.

1920s and the most recent decades—the ideal female figure was relatively full. Even today, weight standards differ among different cultural groups. For instance, in some traditional Arab cultures, obese women are so prized as wives that parents force-feed their female children to make them more desirable (Naik, 2004; Blixen et al., 2006; Marsh et al., 2007).

Regardless of cultural standards for appearance and weight, no one doubts that being overweight represents a major health risk. However, controlling weight is complicated, because eating behavior involves a variety of mechanisms. In our discussion of what motivates people to eat, we'll start with the biological aspects of eating.

BIOLOGICAL FACTORS IN THE REGULATION OF HUNGER

In contrast to human beings, other species are unlikely to become obese. Internal mechanisms regulate not only the quantity of food they take in but also the kind of food they desire. For example, rats that have been deprived of particular foods seek out alternatives that contain the specific nutrients their diet is lacking, and many species, given the choice of a wide variety of foods, select a well-balanced diet (Bouchard & Bray, 1996; Woods et al., 2000; Jones & Corp, 2003).

Complex mechanisms tell organisms whether they require food or should stop eating. It's not just a matter of an empty stomach causing hunger pangs and a full one alleviating those pangs. (Even individuals who have had their stomachs removed still experience the sensation of hunger.) One important factor is changes in the chemical composition of the blood. For instance, changes in levels of glucose, a kind of sugar, regulate feelings of

"Gee, I had no idea you were married to a supermodel."

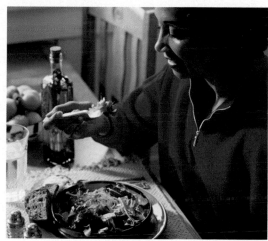

FIGURE 2 The hypothalamus acts as the brain's "feeding center," being primarily responsible for the monitoring of food intake.

hunger. In addition, the hormone *ghrelin* communicates to the brain feelings of hunger (Chapelot et al., 2004; Teff, 2007; Wren & Bloom, 2007).

The brain's *hypothalamus* (see Figure 2) monitors glucose levels. Increasing evidence suggests that the hypothalamus carries the primary responsibility for monitoring food intake. Injury to the hypothalamus has radical consequences for eating behavior, depending on the site of the injury. For example, rats whose *lateral hypothalamus* is damaged may literally starve to death. They refuse food when it is offered, and unless they are force-fed, they eventually die. Rats with an injury to the *ventromedial hypothalamus* display the opposite problem: extreme overeating. Rats with this injury can increase in weight by as much as 400 percent. Similar phenomena occur in humans who have tumors of the hypothalamus (Woods, Seeley, Porte, & Schwartz, 1998; Woods & Seeley, 2002; Seymour, 2006).

Although the important role the hypothalamus plays in regulating food intake is clear, the exact way this organ operates is still unclear. One hypothesis suggests that injury to the hypothalamus affects the **weight set point**, or the particular level of weight that the body strives to maintain, which in turn regulates food intake. Acting as a kind of internal weight thermostat, the hypothalamus calls for either greater or less food intake (Capaldi, 1996; Woods et al., 2000; Berthoud, 2002).

In most cases, the hypothalamus does a good job. Even people who are not deliberately monitoring their weight show only minor weight fluctuations in spite of substantial day-to-day variations in how much they eat and exercise. However, injury to the hypothalamus can alter the weight set point, and a person then struggles to meet the internal goal by increasing or decreasing food consumption. Even temporary exposure to certain drugs can alter the weight set point (Cabanac & Frankhan, 2002; Hallschmid et al., 2004).

Genetic factors determine the weight set point, at least in part. People seem destined, through heredity, to have a particular **metabolism**, the rate at which food is converted to energy and expended by the body. People with a high metabolic rate can eat virtually as much as they want without gaining weight, whereas others, with low metabolism, may eat literally half as much yet gain weight readily (Jequier, 2002; Westerterp, 2006).

Weight set point: The particular level of weight that the body strives to maintain.

Metabolism: The rate at which food is converted to energy and expended by the body.

SOCIAL FACTORS IN EATING

You've just finished a full meal and feel completely stuffed. Suddenly your host announces with great fanfare that he will be serving his "house specialty" dessert, bananas flambé, and that he has spent the better part of the afternoon preparing it.

Even though you are full and don't even like bananas, you accept a serving of his dessert and eat it all.

Clearly, internal biological factors do not fully explain our eating behavior. External social factors, based on societal rules and on what we have learned about appropriate eating behavior, also play an important role. Take, for example, the simple fact that people customarily eat breakfast, lunch, and dinner at approximately the same times every day. Because we tend to eat on schedule every day, we feel hungry as the usual hour approaches, sometimes quite independently of what our internal cues are telling us.

Similarly, we put roughly the same amount of food on our plates every day, even though the amount of exercise we may have had, and consequently our need for energy replenishment, varies from day to day. We also tend to prefer particular foods over others. Rats and dogs may be a delicacy in certain Asian cultures, but few people in Western cultures find them appealing despite their potentially high nutritional value. Even the amount of food we eat varies according to cultural norms. For instance, people in the United States eat bigger portions than people in France. In sum, cultural influences and our individual habits play important roles in determining when, what, and how much we eat (Miller & Pumariega, 2001; Rozin et al., 2003).

Other social factors relate to our eating behavior as well. Some of us head toward the refrigerator after a difficult day, seeking solace in a pint of Heath Bar Crunch ice cream. Why? Perhaps when we were children, our parents gave us food when we were upset. Eventually, we may have learned, through the basic mechanisms of classical and operant conditioning, to associate food with comfort and consolation. Similarly, we may learn that eating, which focuses our attention on immediate pleasures, provides an escape from unpleasant thoughts. Consequently, we may eat when we feel distressed (Bulik et al., 2003; O'Connor & O'Connor, 2004; Elfhag, Tynelius, & Rasmussen, 2007).

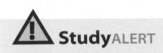

StudyALERT

A key point: Eating and hunger are influenced both by biological and social factors.

THE ROOTS OF OBESITY

Given that both biological and social factors influence eating behavior, determining the causes of obesity has proved to be a challenging task. Researchers have followed several paths.

Some psychologists suggest that oversensitivity to external eating cues based on social factors, coupled with insensitivity to internal hunger cues, produces obesity. Others argue that overweight people have higher weight set points than other people do. Because their set points are unusually high, their attempts to lose weight by eating less may make them especially sensitive to external, food-related cues and therefore more apt to overeat, perpetuating their obesity (Tremblay, 2004; West, Harvey-Berino, & Raczynski, 2004).

But why may some people's weight set points be higher than those of others? One biological explanation is that obese individuals have a higher level of the hormone *leptin*, which appears to be designed, from an evolutionary standpoint, to "protect" the body against weight loss. The body's weight-regulation system thus appears to be designed more to protect against losing weight than to protect against gaining it. Therefore, it's easier to gain weight than to lose it (Ahiima & Osei, 2004; Zhang et al., 2005; Levin, 2006).

Another biologically based explanation for obesity relates to fat cells in the body. Starting at birth, the body stores fat either by increasing the number of fat cells or by increasing the size of existing fat cells. Furthermore, any loss of weight past infancy does not decrease the number of fat cells; it only affects their size. Consequently, people are stuck with the number of fat cells they inherit from an early age, and the rate of weight gain during the first 4 months of life is related to being overweight during later childhood (Stettler et al, 2002).

According to the weight-set-point hypothesis, the presence of too many fat cells from earlier weight gain may result in the set point's becoming "stuck" at a higher

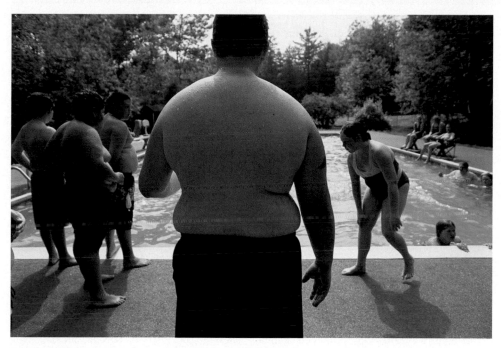

Although obesity is reaching epidemic proportions in the United States, its exact causes remain unclear.

level than is desirable. In such circumstances, losing weight becomes a difficult proposition, because one is constantly at odds with one's own internal set point when dieting (Freedman, 1995; Leibel, Rosenbaum & Hirsch, 1995).

Not everyone agrees with the set-point explanation for obesity. Pointing to the rapid rise in obesity over the last several decades in the United States, some researchers suggest that the body does not try to maintain a fixed weight set point. Instead, they suggest, the body has a *settling point*, determined by a combination of our genetic heritage and the nature of the environment in which we live. If high-fat foods are prevalent in our environment and we are genetically predisposed to obesity, we settle into an equilibrium that maintains relatively high weight. In contrast, if our environment is nutritionally healthier, a genetic predisposition to obesity will not be triggered, and we will settle into an equilibrium in which our weight is lower (Comuzzie & Allison, 1998; Pi-Sunyer, 2003).

Eating Disorders

Eating disorders are among the 10 most frequent causes of disability in young women. One devastating weight-related disorder is **anorexia nervosa**. In this severe eating disorder, people may refuse to eat while denying that their behavior and appearance—which can become skeleton-like—are unusual. Some 10 percent of people with anorexia literally starve themselves to death (Striegel-Moore & Bulik, 2007).

Anorexia nervosa mainly afflicts females between the ages of 12 and 40, although both men and women of any age may develop it. People with the disorder typically come from stable homes, and they are often successful, attractive, and relatively affluent. The disorder often occurs after serious dieting, which somehow gets out of control. Life begins to revolve around food: Although people with the disorder eat little, they may cook for others, go shopping for food frequently, or collect cookbooks (Reijonen et al., 2003; Polivy, Herman, & Boivin, 2005; Myers, 2007).

Anorexia nervosa: A severe eating disorder in which people may refuse to eat while denying that their behavior and appearance—which can become skeleton-like—are unusual.

Despite looking skeleton-like to others, people with the weight disorder anorexia nervosa see themselves as overweight.

Exercising to Excess

It certainly was a while before anyone recognized that 26-year-old Peach Friedman had a problem. Although she went from a fit 145 lbs. to a skeletal 100 lbs. in only three months, Friedman—who would start every day with a 10-mile run and end it with dance classes or swimming or more running, while limiting herself to as few as 800 calories—recalls that her peers responded positively to her ever-shrinking frame. She refused to let a morsel of food pass her lips without a punishing workout to cancel it out. . . . By that time Friedman had stopped menstruating, suffered from bouts of nausea, and was at risk for heart failure. (Souter & Wong, 2006, p. 166)

If you're like most people, you probably recognize a refusal to eat or the practice of binging and purging as eating disorders while frequent exercise, on the other hand, probably strikes you as a good thing. Most of the time you would be right, given that more than half of Americans aren't getting enough exercise—and young people in particular are more sedentary than they should be. For a growing number of people like Peach Friedman, however, exercising has gone beyond being a routine component of a balanced and healthy lifestyle to become an all-out obsession (Centers for Disease Control and Prevention, 2007).

Exercising to excess in an attempt to become thinner is an eating disorder known as *exercise bulimia*. Unlike anorexia, people with exercise bulimia don't control their weight by refusing to eat. Instead, they focus on purging the calories that they do consume; but whereas individuals with bulimia purge by vomiting or using laxatives, those with exercise bulimia purge by monitoring and working off every calorie they eat. As with other eating disorders, people with exercise bulimia can acquire a frail, sickly, and even skeletal appearance while still seeing themselves as overweight and being preoccupied with the fear of eating more calories than they are burning off (Heywood & McCabe, 2006; Abraham et al., 2007).

Since exercise is usually beneficial to health and many people such as competitive athletes exercise very frequently or for long periods of time, when does exercising become a disorder? One indicator is exercise that goes beyond the point of benefit to where the excessive activity starts doing more harm than good. For example, a person with exercise bulimia may sustain sports injuries such as muscle sprains or joint injuries, yet nevertheless continue working out despite the pain (Hrabosky et al., 2007).

Another indicator is a compulsion to exercise—people with exercise dependency tend to feel anxious and guilty about missing a workout and to let their exercise activities interfere with their work and with their social lives. One study suggests that it is this compulsion rather than the actual quantity of exercise that indicates the presence of a disorder (Hausen Blas & Downs, 2002; Adkins & Keel, 2005).

- When does getting enough exercise become an unhealthy preoccupation?
- Why do you think exercise bulimia is considered an eating disorder when it doesn't involve eating behavior?

Bulimia: A disorder in which a person binges on large quantities of food, followed by efforts to purge the food through vomiting or other means.

A related problem, **bulimia**, from which Lisa Arndt (described earlier) suffered, is a disorder in which people binge on large quantities of food. For instance, they may consume an entire gallon of ice cream and a whole pie in a single sitting. After such a binge, sufferers feel guilt and depression and often induce vomiting or take laxatives to rid themselves of the food—behavior known as purging. Constant bingeing-and-purging cycles and the use of drugs to induce vomiting or diarrhea can lead to heart failure. Often, though, the weight of a person with bulimia remains normal (Mora-Giral et al., 2004; Couturier & Lock, 2006; also see the *Applying Psychology in the 21st Century* box).

Eating disorders represent a growing problem: Estimates show that between 1 and 4 percent of high school–age and college-age women have either anorexia nervosa or bulimia. As many as 10 percent of women suffer from bulimia at some point in their lives. Furthermore, an increasing number of men are diagnosed with eating disorders; an estimated 10 to 13 percent of all cases occur in males (Kaminski et al,, 2005; Swain, 2006; Park, 2007).

What are the causes of anorexia nervosa and bulimia? Some researchers suspect a biological cause such as a chemical imbalance in the hypothalamus or pituitary gland, perhaps brought on by genetic factors. Furthermore, scans of the brains of people with eating disorders show that they process information about food differently from healthy individuals (see Figure 3; Polivy & Herman, 2002; Santel et al., 2006).

Others believe that the cause has roots in society's valuation of slenderness and the parallel notion that obesity is undesirable. These researchers maintain that people with anorexia nervosa and bulimia become preoccupied with their weight and take to heart the cliché that one can never be too thin. This may explain why, as countries

Neuroscience in Your Life

FIGURE 3 In this study, participants—either patients with anorexia or healthy individuals—viewed images of different foods when hungry or full to examine their cognitive processing. Comparison of fMRI scans of patients with anorexia (left column) and healthy participants (right column) showed significant differences in their reactions to the food stimuli. The figures show that anorexics generate little additional brain activity when hungry (green) as compared to when full (red), whereas those without anorexia show additional (green) activity when hungry as compared to when full (red). The differences suggest that patients with anorexia differ from non-anorexics in terms of their attention to food stimuli, which in turn may be related to restrictions in the eating behavior of the anorexics. (Source: Santel et al., 2006, Figure 4.)

become more developed and Westernized, and dieting becomes more popular, eating disorders increase. Finally, some psychologists suggest that the disorders result from overly demanding parents or other family problems (Grilo et al., 2003; Couturier & Lock, 2006).

The complete explanations for anorexia nervosa and bulimia remain elusive. These disorders most likely stem from both biological and social causes, and successful treatment probably encompasses several strategies, including therapy and dietary changes (Richard, 2005; Wilson, Grilo, & Vitousek, 2007; O'Brien & LeBow, 2007).

If you or a family member needs advice or help with an eating problem, contact the American Anorexia Bulimia Association at www.aabainc.org or call 212-575-6200. You can get more information at www.nlm.nih.gov/medlineplus/eatingdisorders.html.

BECOMING
AN INFORMED CONSUMER
of Psychology
Dieting and Losing Weight Successfully

Although 60 percent of the people in the United States say they want to lose weight, it's a losing battle for most of them. Most people who diet eventually regain the weight they have lost, and so they try again and get caught in a seemingly endless cycle of weight loss and gain (Newport & Carroll, 2002; Parker-Pope, 2003; Cachelin & Regan, 2006).

You should keep several things in mind when trying to lose weight (Gatchel & Oordt, 2003; Heshka et al., 2003):

- *There is no easy route to weight control.* You will have to make permanent changes in your life to lose weight without gaining it back. The most obvious strategy—cutting down on the amount of food you eat—is just the first step toward a lifetime commitment to changing your eating habits.
- *Keep track of what you eat and what you weigh.* Unless you keep careful records, you won't really know how much you are eating and whether any diet is working.

- *Eat "big" foods.* Eat foods that are bulky and heavy but low in calories, such as grapes and soup. Such foods trick your body into thinking you've eaten more and thus decrease hunger.

- *Cut out television.* One reason for the epidemic of obesity is the number of hours spent viewing television by people in the United States. Not only does watching television preclude other activities that burn calories (even walking around the house is helpful), people often gorge on junk food while watching (Hu et al., 2003).

- *Exercise.* Exercise at least 30 consecutive minutes three times each week. When you exercise, you use up fat stored in your body as fuel for muscles, which is measured in calories. As you use up this fat, you will probably lose weight. Almost any activity helps burn calories (see Figure 4).

- *Decrease the influence of external, social stimuli on your eating behavior.* Serve yourself smaller portions of food, and leave the table before you see what is being served for dessert. Don't even buy snack foods such as nachos and potato chips; if they're not readily available in the kitchen cupboard, you're not apt to eat them. Wrap refrigerated foods in aluminum foil so that you cannot see the contents and be tempted every time you open the refrigerator.

- *Avoid fad diets.* No matter how popular they are at a particular time, extreme diets, including liquid diets, usually don't work in the long run and can be dangerous to your health.

- *Avoid taking any of the numerous diet pills advertised on television that promise quick and easy results.*

- *Maintain good eating habits.* When you have reached your desired weight, maintain the new habits you learned while dieting to avoid gaining back the weight you have lost.

- *Set reasonable goals.* Know how much weight you want to lose before you start to diet. Don't try to lose too much weight too quickly or you may doom yourself to failure. Even small changes in behavior—such as walking 15 minutes a day or eating a few less bites at each meal—can prevent weight gain (Hill et al., 2003).

FIGURE 4 Ways to burn 150 calories: People can expend 150 calories by spending more time at a less vigorous activity or spending less time at a more vigorous activity. (Source: "Less pain, more gain," *Time*, July 22, 1996. Copyright TIME INC. Reprinted by permission. TIME is a registered trademark of Time Inc. All rights reserved.)

More vigorous/ less time

Stair walking for 15 minutes
Shoveling snow for 15 minutes
Running 1½ miles in 15 minutes (10 min./mile)
Jumping rope for 15 minutes
Bicycling 4 miles in 15 minutes
Basketball (playing a game) for 15–20 minutes
Wheelchair basketball for 20 minutes
Swimming laps for 20 minutes
Water aerobics for 30 minutes
Walking 2 miles in 30 minutes (15 min./mile)
Raking leaves for 30 minutes
Pushing a stroller 1½ miles in 30 minutes
Dancing fast (social) for 30 minutes
Bicycling 5 miles in 30 minutes
Basketball (shooting baskets) for 30 minutes
Walking 1¾ miles in 35 minutes (20 min./mile)
Wheeling self in wheelchair for 30–45 minutes
Gardening for 35–45 minutes
Playing touch football for 30–45 minutes
Playing volleyball for 45 minutes
Washing windows or floors for 45–60 minutes
Washing and waxing a car for 45–60 minutes

Less vigorous/ more time

The Need for Achievement: Striving for Success

Although hunger may be one of the more potent primary drives in our day-to-day lives, powerful secondary drives that have no clear biological basis also motivate us. Among the more prominent of these is the need for achievement.

The **need for achievement** is a stable, learned characteristic in which a person obtains satisfaction by striving for and attaining a level of excellence (McClelland et al., 1953). People with a high need for achievement seek out situations in which they can compete against some standard—be it grades, money, or winning at a game—and prove themselves successful. But they are not indiscriminate when it comes to picking their challenges: They tend to avoid situations in which success will come too easily (which would be unchallenging) and situations in which success is unlikely. Instead, people high in achievement motivation generally choose tasks that are of intermediate difficulty (Speirs & Finch, 2006).

In contrast, people with low achievement motivation tend to be motivated primarily by a desire to avoid failure. As a result, they seek out easy tasks, being sure to avoid failure, or seek out very difficult tasks for which failure has no negative implications, because almost anyone would fail at them. People with a high fear of failure will stay away from tasks of intermediate difficulty, because they may fail where others have been successful (Martin & Marsh, 2002; Puca, 2005; Morrone & Pintrich, 2006).

A high need for achievement generally produces positive outcomes, at least in a success-oriented culture such as Western society. For instance, people motivated by a high need for achievement are more likely to attend college than are their low-achievement counterparts; and once they are in college, they tend to receive higher grades in classes that are related to their future careers. Furthermore, high achievement motivation indicates future economic and occupational success (McClelland, 1985; Thrash & Elliot, 2002).

MEASURING ACHIEVEMENT MOTIVATION

How can we measure a person's need for achievement? The measuring instrument used most frequently is the *Thematic Apperception Test (TAT)* (Spangler, 1992). In the TAT, an examiner shows a series of ambiguous pictures, such as the one in Figure 5. The examiner tells participants to write a story that describes what is happening, who the people are, what led to the situation, what the people are thinking or wanting, and what will happen next. Researchers then use a standard scoring system to determine the amount of achievement imagery in people's stories. For example, someone who writes a story in which the main character strives to beat an opponent, studies in order to do well at some task, or works hard in order to get a promotion shows clear signs of an achievement orientation. The inclusion of such achievement-related imagery in the participants' stories is assumed to indicate an unusually high degree of concern with—and therefore a relatively strong need for—achievement (Tuerlinckx, DeBoeck, & Lens, 2002).

The Need for Affiliation: Striving for Friendship

Few of us choose to lead our lives as hermits. Why?

One main reason is that most people have a **need for affiliation**, an interest in establishing and maintaining relationships with other people. Individuals with a high need for affiliation write TAT stories that emphasize the desire to maintain or reinstate friendships and show concern over being rejected by friends.

Need for achievement: A stable, learned characteristic in which a person obtains satisfaction by striving for and attaining a level of excellence.

 StudyALERT

A key feature of people with a high need for achievement is that they prefer tasks of *moderate* difficulty.

FIGURE 5 This ambiguous picture is similar to those used in the Thematic Apperception Test to determine people's underlying motivation (© 1943 by the President and Fellows of Harvard College; 1971 by Henry A. Murray.) What do you see? Do you think your response is related to your motivation?

Need for affiliation: An interest in establishing and maintaining relationships with other people.

People who have higher affiliation needs are particularly sensitive to relationships with others. They desire to be with their friends more of the time, and alone less often, compared with people who are lower in the need for affiliation. However, gender is a greater determinant of how much time is actually spent with friends: Regardless of their affiliative orientation, female students spend significantly more time with their friends and less time alone than male students do (Cantwell & Andrews, 2002; Johnson, 2004; Semykina & Linz, 2007).

The Need for Power: Striving for Impact on Others

Need for power: A tendency to seek impact, control, or influence over others, and to be seen as a powerful individual.

If your fantasies include becoming president of the United States or running Microsoft, your dreams may reflect a high need for power. The **need for power**, a tendency to seek impact, control, or influence over others and to be seen as a powerful individual, is an additional type of motivation (Lee-Chai & Bargh, 2001; Winter, 2007; Zians, 2007).

As you might expect, people with strong needs for power are more apt to belong to organizations and seek office than are those low in the need for power. They also tend to work in professions in which their power needs may be fulfilled, such as business management and—you may or may not be surprised—teaching (Jenkins, 1994). In addition, they seek to display the trappings of power. Even in college, they are more likely to collect prestigious possessions, such as electronic equipment and sports cars.

Some significant gender differences exist in the display of need for power. Men with high power needs tend to show unusually high levels of aggression, drink heavily, act in a sexually exploitative manner, and participate more frequently in competitive sports—behaviors that collectively represent somewhat extravagant, flamboyant behavior. In contrast, women display their power needs with more restraint; this is congruent with traditional societal constraints on women's behavior. Women with high power needs are more apt than men are to channel those needs in a socially responsible manner, such as by showing concern for others or displaying highly nurturing behavior (Maroda, 2004; Winter, 1988, 1995, 2007).

RECAP/EVALUATE/RETHINK

RECAP

What biological and social factors underlie hunger?

- Eating behavior is subject to homeostasis, as most people's weight stays within a relatively stable range. The hypothalamus in the brain is central to the regulation of food intake. (p. 325)

- Social factors, such as mealtimes, cultural food preferences, and other learned habits, also play a role in the regulation of eating, determining when, what, and how much one eats. An oversensitivity to social cues and an insensitivity to internal cues may also be related to obesity. In addition, obesity may be caused by an unusually high weight set point—the weight the body attempts to maintain—and genetic factors. (p. 325)

How are needs relating to achievement, affiliation, and power motivation exhibited?

- Need for achievement refers to the stable, learned characteristic in which a person strives to attain a level of excellence. Need for achievement is usually measured through the Thematic Apperception Test (TAT), a series of pictures about which a person writes a story. (p. 331)

- The need for affiliation is a concern with establishing and maintaining relationships with others, whereas the need for power is a tendency to seek to exert an impact on others. (p. 331)

EVALUATE

1. Match the following terms with their definitions:
   1. Hypothalamus
   2. Lateral hypothalamic damage
   3. Ventromedial hypothalamic damage
   a. Leads to refusal of food and starvation
   b. Responsible for monitoring food intake
   c. Causes extreme overeating

2. The _____ _____ _____ is the specific level of weight the body strives to maintain.
3. _____ is the rate at which energy is produced and expended by the body.
4. Julio is the type of person who constantly strives for excellence. He feels intense satisfaction when he is able to master a new task. Julio most likely has a high need for _____.
5. Debbie's Thematic Apperception Test (TAT) story depicts a young girl who is rejected by one of her peers and seeks to regain her friendship. What major type of motivation is Debbie displaying in her story?
   a. Need for achievement
   b. Need for motivation
   c. Need for affiliation
   d. Need for power

RETHINK

1. In what ways do societal expectations, expressed by television shows and commercials, contribute to both obesity and excessive concern about weight loss? How could television contribute to better eating habits and attitudes toward weight? Should it be required to do so?
2. *From the perspective of a human resources specialist:* How might you use characteristics such as need for achievement, need for power, and need for affiliation to select workers for jobs? What additional criteria would you have to consider?

Answers to Evaluate Questions

1. 1-b, 2-a, 3 c; 2. weight set point; 3. metabolism; 4. achievement; 5. c.

KEY TERMS

obesity p. 323

weight set point p. 325

metabolism p. 325

anorexia nervosa p. 327

bulimia p. 328

need for achievement p. 331

need for affiliation p. 331

need for power p. 332

Understanding Emotional Experiences

Karl Andrews held in his hands the envelope he had been waiting for. It could be the ticket to his future: an offer of admission to his first-choice college. But what was it going to say? He knew it could go either way; his grades were pretty good and he had been involved in some extracurricular activities, but his SAT scores had been not so terrific. He felt so nervous that his hands shook as he opened the thin envelope (not a good sign, he thought). Here it comes. "Dear Mr. Andrews," it read. "The Trustees of the University are pleased to admit you. . . ." That was all he needed to see. With a whoop of excitement, Karl found himself jumping up and down gleefully. A rush of emotion overcame him as it sank in that he had, in fact, been accepted. He was on his way.

At one time or another, all of us have experienced the strong feelings that accompany both very pleasant and very negative experiences. Perhaps we have felt the thrill of getting a sought-after job, the joy of being in love, the sorrow over someone's death, or the anguish of inadvertently hurting someone. Moreover, we experience such reactions on a less intense level throughout our daily lives: the pleasure of a friendship, the enjoyment of a movie, and the embarrassment of breaking a borrowed item.

Despite the varied nature of these feelings, they all represent emotions. Although everyone has an idea of what an emotion is, formally defining the concept has proved to be an elusive task. Here, we'll use a general definition: **Emotions** are feelings that generally have both physiological and cognitive elements and that influence behavior.

Think, for example, about how it feels to be happy. First, we obviously experience a feeling that we can differentiate from other emotions. It is likely that we also experience some identifiable physical changes in our bodies: Perhaps the heart rate increases, or—as in the example of Karl Andrews—we find ourselves "jumping for joy." Finally, the emotion probably encompasses cognitive elements: Our understanding and evaluation of the meaning of what is happening prompts our feelings of happiness.

It is also possible, however, to experience an emotion without the presence of cognitive elements. For instance, we may react with fear to an unusual or novel situation (such as coming into contact with an erratic, unpredictable individual), or we may experience pleasure over sexual excitation without having cognitive awareness or understanding of just what it is about the situation that is exciting.

Some psychologists argue that entirely separate systems govern cognitive responses and emotional responses. A current controversy focuses on whether the emotional response predominates over the cognitive response or vice versa. Some theorists suggest that we first respond to a situation with an emotional reaction and later try to understand it. For example, we may enjoy a complex modern symphony without at first understanding it or knowing why we like it. In contrast, other theorists propose that people first develop cognitions about a situation and then react emotionally. This school of thought suggests that we must think about and understand a stimulus or situation, relating it to what we already know, before we can react on an emotional level (Murphy & Zajonc, 1993; Lazarus, 1995; Oatley, Keltner, & Jenkins, 2006).

Because proponents of both sides of this debate can cite research to support their viewpoints, the question is far from resolved. Perhaps the sequence varies from situation to situation, with emotions predominating in some instances and

Key Concepts

What are emotions, and how do we experience them?

What are the functions of emotions?

What are the explanations for emotions?

How does nonverbal behavior relate to the expression of emotions?

Emotions: Feelings that generally have both physiological and cognitive elements and that influence behavior.

cognitive processes occurring first in others. Both sides agree that we can experience emotions that involve little or no conscious thought. We may not know why we're afraid of mice, understanding objectively that they represent no danger, but we may still be frightened when we see them. Neuroimaging studies of the brain may help resolve this debate, as well as others, about the nature of emotions (Lewis & Haviland-Jones, 2000; Barrett & Wager, 2006; Niedenthal, 2007).

The Functions of Emotions

Imagine what it would be like if we didn't experience emotion—no depths of despair, no depression, no remorse, but at the same time no happiness, joy, or love. Obviously, life would be considerably less satisfying, and even dull, if we lacked the capacity to sense and express emotion.

But do emotions serve any purpose beyond making life interesting? Indeed they do. Psychologists have identified several important functions that emotions play in our daily lives (Frederickson & Branigan, 2005; Frijda, 2005; Gross, 2006; Siemer, Mauss, & Gross, 2007). Among the most important of those functions are the following:

- *Preparing us for action.* Emotions act as a link between events in our environment and our responses. For example, if you saw an angry dog charging toward you, your emotional reaction (fear) would be associated with physiological arousal of the sympathetic division of the autonomic nervous system, the activation of the "fight-or-flight" response.

- *Shaping our future behavior.* Emotions promote learning that will help us make appropriate responses in the future. For instance, your emotional response to unpleasant events teaches you to avoid similar circumstances in the future.

- *Helping us interact more effectively with others.* We often communicate the emotions we experience through our verbal and nonverbal behaviors, making our emotions obvious to observers. These behaviors can act as a signal to observers, allowing them to understand better what we are experiencing and to help them predict our future behavior.

Determining the Range of Emotions: Labeling Our Feelings

If we were to list the words in the English language that have been used to describe emotions, we would end up with at least 500 examples (Averill, 1975). The list would range from such obvious emotions as *happiness* and *fear* to less common ones, such as *adventurousness* and *pensiveness*.

One challenge for psychologists has been to sort through this list to identify the most important, fundamental emotions. Theorists have hotly contested the issue of cataloging emotions and have come up with different lists, depending on how they define the concept of emotion. In fact, some reject the question entirely, saying that *no* set of emotions should be singled out as most basic, and that emotions are best understood by breaking them down into their component parts. Other researchers argue for looking at emotions in terms of a hierarchy, dividing them into positive and negative categories, and then organizing them into increasingly narrower subcategories (see Figure 1; Manstead, Frijda, & Fischer, 2003; Dillard & Shen, 2007).

Still, most researchers suggest that a list of basic emotions would include, at a minimum, happiness, anger, fear, sadness, and disgust. Other lists are broader, including emotions such as surprise, contempt, guilt, and joy (Ekman, 1994a; Shweder, 1994; Tracy & Robins, 2004).

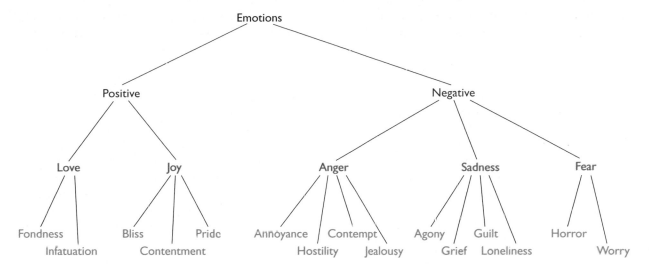

FIGURE 1 One approach to organizing emotions is to use a hierarchy, which divides emotions into increasingly narrow subcategories. (Source: Adapted from Fischer, Shaver, & Carnochan, 1990.)

One difficulty in defining a basic set of emotions is that substantial differences exist in descriptions of emotions among various cultures. For instance, Germans report experiencing *schadenfreude*, a feeling of pleasure over another person's difficulties, and the Japanese experience *hagaii*, a mood of vulnerable heartache colored by frustration. In Tahiti, people experience *musu*, a feeling of reluctance to yield to unreasonable demands made by one's parents.

Finding *schadenfreude*, *hagaii*, or *musu* in a particular culture doesn't mean that the members of other cultures are incapable of experiencing such emotions, of course. It does suggest, though, that fitting a particular emotion into a linguistic category to describe that emotion may make it easier to discuss, contemplate, and perhaps experience (Russell & Sato, 1995; Li, Wang, & Fischer, 2004; Kuppens et al., 2006).

The Roots of Emotions

I've never been so angry before; I feel my heart pounding, and I'm trembling all over. . . . I don't know how I'll get through the performance. I feel like my stomach is filled with butterflies. . . . That was quite a mistake I made! My face must be incredibly red. . . . When I heard the footsteps in the night, I was so frightened that I couldn't catch my breath.

If you examine our language, you will find that there are literally dozens of ways to describe how we feel when we experience an emotion, and that the language we use to describe emotions is, for the most part, based on the physical symptoms that are associated with a particular emotional experience (Kobayashi, Schallert, & Ogren, 2003; Manstead & Wagner, 2004; Spackman, Fujiki, & Brinton, 2006).

Consider, for instance, the experience of fear. Pretend that it is late on New Year's Eve. You are walking down a dark road, and you hear a stranger approaching behind you. It is clear that he is not trying to hurry by but is coming directly toward you. You think about what you will do if the stranger attempts to rob you or, worse, hurt you in some way.

While these thoughts are running through your head, something dramatic will be happening to your body. The most likely reactions, which are associated with activation of the autonomic nervous system, include an increase in your rate of breathing, an acceleration of your heart rate, a widening of your pupils (to increase visual sensitivity), and a dryness in your mouth as the functioning of your salivary glands, and in fact of your entire digestive system, ceases. At the same time, though, your sweat glands probably will increase their activity, because increased sweating will help you rid yourself of the excess heat developed by any emergency activity in which you engage.

Of course, all these physiological changes are likely to occur without your awareness. At the same time, though, the emotional experience accompanying them will be obvious to you: You most surely would report being fearful.

Although it is easy to describe the general physical reactions that accompany emotions, defining the specific role that those physiological responses play in the experience of emotions has proved to be a major puzzle for psychologists. As we shall see, some theorists suggest that specific bodily reactions *cause* us to experience a particular emotion—we experience fear, for instance, *because* the heart is pounding and we are breathing deeply. In contrast, other theorists suggest that the physiological reaction results from the experience of an emotion. In this view, we experience fear, and as a result the heart pounds and our breathing deepens.

THE JAMES-LANGE THEORY: DO GUT REACTIONS EQUAL EMOTIONS?

To William James and Carl Lange, who were among the first researchers to explore the nature of emotions, emotional experience is, very simply, a reaction to instinctive bodily events that occur as a response to some situation or event in the environment. This view is summarized in James's statement, "We feel sorry because we cry, angry because we strike, afraid because we tremble" (James, 1890).

James and Lange took the view that the instinctive response of crying at a loss leads us to feel sorrow, that striking out at someone who frustrates us results in our feeling anger, that trembling at a menacing threat causes us to feel fear. They suggested that for every major emotion there is an accompanying physiological or "gut" reaction of internal organs—called a *visceral experience*. It is this specific pattern of visceral response that leads us to label the emotional experience.

In sum, James and Lange proposed that we experience emotions as a result of physiological changes that produce specific sensations. The brain interprets these sensations as specific kinds of emotional experiences (see the first part of Figure 2). This view has come to be called the **James-Lange theory of emotion** (Laird & Bresler, 1990; Cobo et al., 2002).

James-Lange theory of emotion: The belief that emotional experience is a reaction to bodily events occurring as a result of an external situation ("I feel sad because I am crying").

The James-Lange theory has some serious drawbacks, however. For the theory to be valid, visceral changes would have to occur relatively quickly, because we experience some emotions—such as fear upon hearing a stranger rapidly approaching on a dark night—almost instantaneously. Yet emotional experiences frequently occur even before there is time for certain physiological changes to be set into motion. Because of the slowness with which some visceral changes take place, it is hard to see how they could be the source of immediate emotional experience.

The James-Lange theory poses another difficulty: Physiological arousal does not invariably produce emotional experience. For example, a person who is jogging has an increased heartbeat and respiration rate, as well as many of the other physiological changes associated with certain emotions. Yet joggers typically do not think of such changes in terms of emotions. There cannot be a one-to-one correspondence, then, between visceral changes and emotional experience. Visceral changes by themselves may not be sufficient to produce emotion.

Finally, our internal organs produce a relatively limited range of sensations. Although some types of physiological changes are associated with specific emotional experiences, it is difficult to imagine how each of the myriad emotions that people are capable of experiencing could be the result of a unique visceral change. Many emotions actually are associated with relatively similar sorts of visceral changes, a fact that contradicts the James-Lange theory (Davidson et al., 1994; Cameron, 2002).

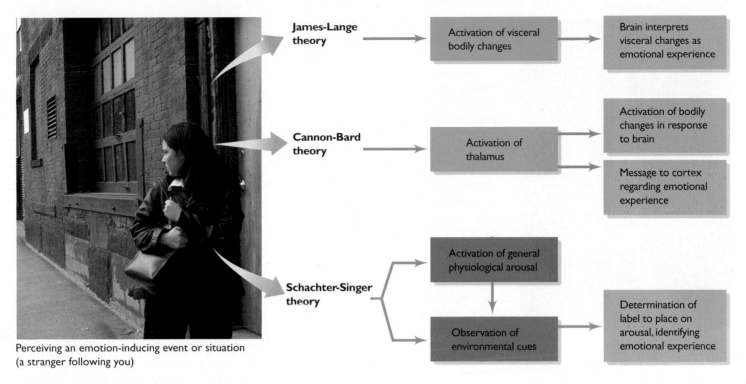

Perceiving an emotion-inducing event or situation
(a stranger following you)

FIGURE 2 A comparison of three models of emotion.

THE CANNON-BARD THEORY: PHYSIOLOGICAL REACTIONS AS THE RESULT OF EMOTIONS

In response to the difficulties inherent in the James-Lange theory, Walter Cannon, and later Philip Bard, suggested an alternative view. In what has come to be known as the **Cannon-Bard theory of emotion**, they proposed the model illustrated in the second part of Figure 2 (Cannon, 1929). This theory rejects the view that physiological arousal alone leads to the perception of emotion. Instead, the theory assumes that both physiological arousal *and* the emotional experience are produced simultaneously by the same nerve stimulus, which Cannon and Bard suggested emanates from the thalamus in the brain.

The theory states that after we perceive an emotion-producing stimulus, the thalamus is the initial site of the emotional response. Next, the thalamus sends a signal to the autonomic nervous system, thereby producing a visceral response. At the same time, the thalamus also communicates a message to the cerebral cortex regarding the nature of the emotion being experienced. Hence, it is not necessary for different emotions to have unique physiological patterns associated with them—as long as the message sent to the cerebral cortex differs according to the specific emotion.

The Cannon-Bard theory seems to have been accurate in rejecting the view that physiological arousal alone accounts for emotions. However, more recent research has led to some important modifications of the theory. For one thing, we now understand that the hypothalamus and the limbic system, not the thalamus, play a major role in emotional experience. In addition, the simultaneous occurrence of the physiological and emotional responses, which is a fundamental assumption of the Cannon-Bard theory, has yet to be demonstrated conclusively. This ambiguity has allowed room for yet another theory of emotions: the Schachter-Singer theory.

Cannon-Bard theory of emotion: The belief that both physiological arousal and emotional experience are produced simultaneously by the same nerve stimulus.

 StudyALERT

Use Figure 2 to distinguish the three classic theories of emotion (James-Lange, Cannon-Bard, and Schachter-Singer).

THE SCHACHTER-SINGER THEORY: EMOTIONS AS LABELS

Suppose that, as you are being followed down that dark street on New Year's Eve, you notice a man being followed by another shady figure on the other side of the street. Now assume that instead of reacting with fear, the man begins to laugh and act gleeful.

This is the high, swaying suspension bridge that was used to increase the physiological arousal of male subjects. What other types of behavior can be explained by the Schachter-Singer theory of emotion?

Schachter-Singer theory of emotion: The belief that emotions are determined jointly by a nonspecific kind of physiological arousal and its interpretation, based on environmental cues.

Would the reactions of this other individual be sufficient to lay your fears to rest? Might you, in fact, decide there is nothing to fear, and get into the spirit of the evening by beginning to feel happiness and glee yourself?

According to an explanation that focuses on the role of cognition, the **Schachter-Singer theory of emotion**, this might very well happen. This approach to explaining emotions emphasizes that we identify the emotion we are experiencing by observing our environment and comparing ourselves with others (Schachter & Singer, 1962).

Schachter and Singer's classic experiment found evidence for this hypothesis. In the study, participants were told that they would receive an injection of a vitamin. In reality, they were given epinephrine, a drug that causes an increase in physiological arousal, including higher heart and respiration rates and a reddening of the face, responses that typically occur during strong emotional reactions. The members of both groups were then placed individually in a situation where a confederate of the experimenter acted in one of two ways. In one condition he acted angry and hostile, and in the other condition he behaved as if he were exuberantly happy.

The purpose of the experiment was to determine how the participants would react emotionally to the confederate's behavior. When they were asked to describe their own emotional state at the end of the experiment, the participants exposed to the angry confederate reported that they felt angry, while those exposed to the happy confederate reported feeling happy. In sum, the results suggest that participants turned to the environment and the behavior of others for an explanation of the physiological arousal they were experiencing.

The results of the Schachter-Singer experiment, then, supported a cognitive view of emotions, in which emotions are determined jointly by a relatively nonspecific kind of physiological arousal *and* the labeling of that arousal on the basis of cues from the environment (refer to the third part of Figure 2). Later research has found that arousal is not as nonspecific as Schachter and Singer assumed. When the source of physiological arousal is unclear, however, we may look to our surroundings to determine just what we are experiencing.

CONTEMPORARY PERSPECTIVES ON THE NEUROSCIENCE OF EMOTIONS

When Schachter and Singer carried out their groundbreaking experiment in the early 1960s, the ways in which they could evaluate the physiology that accompanies emotion were relatively limited. However, advances in the measurement of the nervous system and other parts of the body have allowed researchers to examine more closely the biological responses involved in emotion. As a result, contemporary research on emotion points to a revision of earlier views that physiological responses associated with emotions are undifferentiated. Instead, evidence is growing that specific patterns of biological arousal are associated with individual emotions (Levenson, 1994; Franks & Smith, 2000; Vaitl, Schienle, & Stark, 2005; Woodson, 2006).

For instance, researchers have found that specific emotions produce activation of very different portions of the brain. In one study, participants undergoing positron emission tomography (PET) brain scans were asked to recall events, such as deaths and funerals, that made them feel sad, or events that made them feel happy, such as weddings and births. They also looked at photos of faces that appeared to be happy or sad. The results of the PET scans were clear: Happiness was related to a decrease in activity in certain areas of the cerebral cortex, whereas sadness was associated with increases in activity in particular portions of the cortex (George et al., 1995; Hamann, Ely, Hoffman, & Kilts, 2002; Prohovnik, Skudlarski, Fulbright, Gore, & Wexler, 2004).

In addition, the *amygdala*, in the brain's temporal lobe, is important in the experience of emotions, for it provides a link between the perception of an emotion-producing stimulus and the recall of that stimulus later. For example, if we've once been attacked by a vicious pit bull, the amygdala processes that information and

FIGURE 3 Connections from the amygdala, seen here in red, allow it to mediate many of the autonomic expressions of emotional states through the hippocampus (blue) and visual cortex (orange). (Source: Line art from Dolan, R. J. (2002). Emotion, cognition, and behavior. *Science, 298,* no. 5596, 1191-1194 (Figure 1, p. 1192). Drawing of brain reprinted with permission from AAAS.)

leads us to react with fear when we see a pit bull later—an example of a classically conditioned fear response (Adolphs, 2002; Miller et al., 2005; Berntson et al., 2007).

Because neural pathways connect the amygdala, the visual cortex, and the *hippocampus* (which plays an important role in the consolidation of memories), some scientists speculate that emotion-related stimuli can be processed and responded to almost instantaneously (see Figure 3). This immediate response occurs so rapidly that higher-order, more rational thinking, which takes more time, seems not to be involved initially. In a slower, but more thoughtful, response to emotion-evoking stimuli, emotion-related sensory information is first evaluated and then sent on to the amygdala. It appears that the quicker system offers an immediate response to emotion-evoking stimuli, whereas the slower system helps confirm a threat and prepare a more thoughtful response (Dolan, 2002).

MAKING SENSE OF THE MULTIPLE PERSPECTIVES ON EMOTION

As new approaches to emotion continue to develop, it is reasonable to ask why so many theories of emotion exist and, perhaps more important, which one provides the most complete explanation. Actually, we have only scratched the surface. There are almost as many explanatory theories of emotion as there are individual emotions (e.g., DeCoster, 2003; Manstead, Frijda, & Fischer, 2003; Frijda, 2005; Prinz, 2007).

Why are theories of emotion so plentiful? For one thing, emotions are not a simple phenomenon but are intertwined closely with motivation, cognition, neuroscience, and a host of related branches of psychology. For example, evidence from brain imaging studies shows that even when people come to supposedly rational, nonemotional decisions—such as making moral, philosophical judgments—emotions come into play (Greene et al., 2001).

In short, emotions are such complex phenomena, encompassing both biological and cognitive aspects, that no single theory has been able to explain fully all the facets of emotional experience. Furthermore, contradictory evidence of one sort or another challenges each approach, and therefore no theory has proved invariably accurate in its predictions.

This abundance of perspectives on emotion is not a cause for despair—or unhappiness, fear, or any other negative emotion. It simply reflects the fact that psychology is an evolving, developing science. As we gather more evidence, the specific answers to questions about the nature of emotions will become clearer.

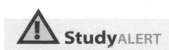

StudyALERT

It is important to understand the basic neuroscience of emotional experience.

Exploring DIVERSITY

Do People in All Cultures Express Emotion Similarly?

Consider, for a moment, the six photos displayed in Figure 4. Can you identify the emotions being expressed by the person in each of the photos?

If you are a good judge of facial expressions, you will conclude that these expressions display six of the basic emotions: happiness, anger, sadness, surprise, disgust, and fear. Hundreds of studies of nonverbal behavior show that these emotions are consistently distinct and identifiable, even by untrained observers (Ekman & O'Sullivan, 1991).

Interestingly, these six emotions are not unique to members of Western cultures; rather, they constitute the basic emotions expressed universally by members of the human race, regardless of where individuals have been raised and what learning experiences they have had. Psychologist Paul Ekman convincingly demonstrated this point when he studied the members of an isolated New Guinea jungle tribe who had had almost no contact with Westerners (Ekman, 1972). The people of the tribe did not speak or understand English, had never seen a movie, and had had very limited experience with Caucasians before Ekman's arrival. Yet their nonverbal responses to emotion-evoking stories, as well as their ability to identify basic emotions, were quite similar to those of Westerners.

FIGURE 4 These photos demonstrate six of the primary emotions: happiness, anger, sadness, surprise, disgust, and fear.

Being so isolated, the New Guineans could not have learned from Westerners to recognize or produce similar facial expressions. Instead, their similar abilities and manner of responding emotionally appear to have been present innately. Although one could argue that similar experiences in both cultures led the members of each one to learn similar types of nonverbal behavior, this appears unlikely, because the two cultures are so very different. The expression of basic emotions, then, seems to be universal (Ekman, 1994b; Izard, 1994; Matsumoto, 2002).

Why do people across cultures express emotions similarly? A hypothesis known as the **facial-affect program** gives one explanation. The facial-affect program—which is assumed to be universally present at birth—is analogous to a computer program that is turned on when a particular emotion is experienced. When set in motion, the "program" activates a set of nerve impulses that make the face display an appropriate expression. Each primary emotion produces a unique set of muscular movements, forming the kinds of expressions shown in Figure 4. For example, the emotion of happiness is universally displayed by movement of the zygomatic major, a muscle that raises the corners of the mouth—forming what we would call a smile (Ekman, Davidson, & Friesen, 1990; Ekman, 2003; Kohler et al., 2004; Kim et al., 2007).

"And just exactly what is that expression intended to convey?"

The importance of facial expressions is illustrated by an intriguing notion known as the **facial-feedback hypothesis**. According to this hypothesis, facial expressions not only *reflect* emotional experience, they also help *determine* how people experience and label emotions (Izard, 1990). Basically put, "wearing" an emotional expression provides muscular feedback to the brain that helps produce an emotion congruent with that expression. For instance, the muscles activated when we smile may send a message to the brain indicating the experience of happiness—even if there is nothing in the environment that would produce that particular emotion. Some theoreticians have gone further, suggesting that facial expressions are *necessary* for an emotion to be experienced (Rinn, 1984, 1991). According to this view, if no facial expression is present, the emotion cannot be felt.

Facial-affect program: Activation of a set of nerve impulses that make the face display the appropriate expression.

Facial-feedback hypothesis: The hypothesis that facial expressions not only reflect emotional experience but also help determine how people experience and label emotions.

Support for the facial-feedback hypothesis comes from a classic experiment carried out by psychologist Paul Ekman and colleagues (Ekman, Levenson, & Friesen, 1983). In the study, professional actors were asked to follow very explicit instructions regarding the movements of muscles in their faces. You might try this example yourself:

- Raise your brows and pull them together.
- Raise your upper eyelids.
- Now stretch your lips horizontally back toward your ears.

After carrying out these directions—which, as you may have guessed, are meant to produce an expression of fear—the actors' heart rates rose and their body temperatures declined, physiological reactions that characterize fear. Overall, facial expressions representing the primary emotions produced physiological effects similar to those accompanying the genuine emotions in other circumstances (Keillor et al., 2002; Soussignan, 2002).

RECAP/EVALUATE/RETHINK

RECAP

What are emotions, and how do we experience them?

- Emotions are broadly defined as feelings that may affect behavior and generally have both a physiological component and a cognitive component. Debate continues over whether separate systems govern cognitive and emotional responses and whether one has primacy over the other. (p. 335)

What are the functions of emotions?

- Emotions prepare us for action, shape future behavior through learning, and help us interact more effectively with others. (p. 336)

What are the explanations for emotions?

- Several theories explain emotions. The James-Lange theory suggests that emotional experience is a reaction to bodily, or visceral, changes that occur as a response to an environmental event and are interpreted as an emotional response. (p. 338)

- In contrast, the Cannon-Bard theory contends that both physiological arousal and an emotional experience are produced simultaneously by the same nerve stimulus and that the visceral experience does not necessarily differ among differing emotions. (p. 339)

- The Schachter-Singer theory suggests that emotions are determined jointly by a relatively nonspecific physiological arousal and the subsequent labeling of that arousal, using cues from the environment to determine how others are behaving in the same situation. (p. 339)

- The most recent approaches to emotions focus on their biological origins. For instance, it now seems that specific patterns of biological arousal are associated with individual emotions. Furthermore, new scanning techniques have identified the specific parts of the brain that are activated during the experience of particular emotions. (p. 340)

How does nonverbal behavior relate to the expression of emotions?

- A person's facial expressions can reveal emotions. In fact, members of different cultures understand the emotional expressions of others in similar ways. One explanation for this similarity is that an innate facial-affect

program activates a set of muscle movements representing the emotion being experienced. (p. 342)

- The facial-feedback hypothesis suggests that facial expressions not only reflect, but also produce, emotional experiences. (p. 343)

EVALUATE

1. Emotions are always accompanied by a cognitive response. True or false?
2. The _____ - _____ theory of emotion states that emotions are a response to instinctive bodily events.
3. According to the _____ - _____ theory of emotion, both an emotional response and physiological arousal are produced simultaneously by the same nerve stimulus.
4. Your friend—a psychology major—tells you, "I was at a party last night. During the course of the evening, my general level of arousal increased. Since I was at a party where people were enjoying themselves, I assume I must have felt happy." What theory of emotion does your friend subscribe to?
5. What are the six primary emotions that can be identified from facial expressions?

RETHINK

1. If researchers learned how to control emotional responses so that targeted emotions could be caused or prevented, what ethical concerns might arise? Under what circumstances, if any, should such techniques be used?
2. *From the perspective of an advertising executive:* How might you use the findings by Schachter and Singer on the labeling of arousal to create interest in a product? Can you think of other examples whereby people's arousal could be manipulated, which would lead to different emotional responses?

Answers to Evaluate Questions

1. false; emotions may occur without a cognitive response; 2. James-Lange; 3. Cannon-Bard; 4. Schachter-Singer; 5. surprise, sadness, happiness, anger, disgust, and fear

KEY TERMS

emotions p. 335
James-Lange theory of emotion p. 338

Cannon-Bard theory of emotion p. 339

Schachter-Singer theory of emotion p. 340
facial-affect program p. 343

facial-feedback hypothesis p. 343

Psychology on the Web

1. Find two different Web sites that deal with nonverbal behavior. One site should present a fairly "academic" discussion of the topic, and the other should be more informal. (Hint: The terms *nonverbal behavior* and *nonverbal communication* may lead you to more formal discussions of the topic, whereas *body language* may lead you to less formal discussions.) Compare and contrast your findings from the two sites.

2. Find one or more Web sites that offer information on polygraphs (lie detectors). The sites should be intended either to advertise (i.e., to sell) lie detectors or lie detection services or to debunk lie detector tests (e.g., by showing how to cheat on them). Evaluate the information on the Web site(s), using your understanding of the lie detection techniques discussed earlier. Summarize your findings and conclusions.

Epilogue

Motivation and emotions are two interrelated aspects of psychology. In these modules, we first considered the topic of motivation, which has spawned a great deal of theory and research examining primary and secondary drives. We then turned to a discussion of emotions, beginning with their functions and proceeding to a review of three major theories that seek to explain what emotions are and how they, and their associated physiological symptoms, emerge in the individual. Finally, we looked at cultural differences in the expression and display of emotions and discussed the facial-affect program, which seems to be innate and to regulate the nonverbal expression of the basic emotions.

Return to the opening scenario of this group of modules, which describes how hiker Aron Ralston amputated his own arm in order to free himself from being trapped by a boulder. Using your knowledge of motivation and emotion, consider the following questions:

1. Which approach or approaches to motivation—instinctual, drive reduction, arousal, incentive, or cognitive—most effectively explains Ralston's decision to amputate his arm to free himself?

2. Many observers commented on Ralston's "will to live" as they sought to explain his decision to amputate his arm. How could you translate the concept of "will to live" into motivational terms?

3. What function might Ralston's emotions have served in helping or impeding his decision-making processes when he found his arm trapped under the boulder?

4. After he was rescued, Ralston said that once he had made the decision to sever his arm, "all the desires and joys and euphorias of a future life came rushing into me, and maybe this is how I handled the pain." How would you interpret this comment in terms of your understanding of motivation and emotion?

CHAPTER 11

Sexuality and Gender

Key Concepts for Chapter 11

What are the major differences between male and female gender roles?

Why, and under what circumstances, do we become sexually aroused?

What is "normal" sexual behavior? ● How do most people behave sexually? ● How prevalent are rape and other forms of non-consenting sex, and what are their causes? ● What are the major sexually transmitted infections? ● What sexual difficulties do people most frequently encounter?

Prologue *Trapped in a Girl's Body*

From almost the time she could talk, Tye Clark, a curly-haired girl with big brown eyes, would constantly tell her parents, "I'm a boy." Although Tye wanted to look like one—she insisted on short hair and boy's jeans—her parents, Rory Cohen and Matt Clark, would gently remind her that she was, in fact, a little girl. As she got older, Tye was often mistaken for a boy and was even occasionally refused entry into girls' restrooms. At school and at home, she wrestled with an unease about who she was. Says Tye, now 16: "I knew I had a girl's body, but that would only connect when I looked down at it. . . ."

Two and a half years ago, Tye's therapist delivered a shocking explanation for the confusion that had plagued the family for years. Tye, said the therapist, was transgendered: a boy trapped in a girl's body. "It was like a punch in the stomach," said Tye's mother Rory. "You don't want to hear it, but it sounds real." Yet there was one person in the room who wasn't surprised. "I was never a girl," said Tye. (Meadows, 2006, p. 94)

Looking Ahead

Tye Clark's discomfort with her own body, her exploration of gender boundaries, and, eventually, the transition from female to male were difficult for her and her family to grapple with. But after publically adopting a male identity—being reclassified as a male by his middle school—Tye felt a degree of contentment and self-acceptance that had previously been elusive.

Tye's story illustrates the emotion and confusion that often characterizes one of the most universal of behaviors: sexuality. Exemplifying major personal as well as societal concerns, sex and the interrelated topic of gender are also key topics for psychologists in a variety of specialties. For instance, psychologists interested in motivation view sexuality in terms of sexual needs, drives, and gratification. Neuroscientists consider sexuality from the perspective of the relationship of the brain and nervous system to the functioning of the sexual organs. Social psychologists and psychologists who specialize in the study of women focus on society's rules of sexual conduct and the role sexual behavior plays in interpersonal behavior.

In this set of modules, we consider human sexuality from several of these vantage points. We begin by examining gender, discussing differences in societal expectations about how men and women should behave and the impact of those expectations on behavior and attitudes. Next we turn to sexual behavior. We describe the biological aspects of sexual excitement and arousal and then examine the variety of sexual activities in which people engage. We conclude with a discussion of nonconsenting sex, sexually transmitted infections, and the psychological aspects of sexual difficulties.

Gender and Sex

"It's a girl!" "It's a boy!"

One of these exclamations, or some variant, is typically the first sentence uttered upon the birth of a child. However, the consequences of whether we are born with male or female sex organs extend well beyond the moment of birth. Throughout our lives, the ways that others think of us, and even the ways in which we view ourselves, are based to a large extent on whether we are labeled as a woman or a man by society—our gender.

Gender is the perception of being male or female. Although there is a good deal of overlap between the concepts of sex and gender, they are not the same: *Sex* typically refers to sexual anatomy and sexual behavior, whereas *gender* refers to the sense of maleness or femaleness related to our membership in a given society.

Gender Roles: Society's Expectations for Women and Men

Our conclusions about what is or is not "appropriate" behavior for others and ourselves are based on **gender roles**. Gender roles are the set of expectations, defined by a particular society, that indicate what is appropriate behavior for men and women.

If men's and women's gender roles were equivalent, they would have only a minor impact on our lives. However, expectations about men and women differ significantly, and these beliefs may result in favoritism toward members of one of the sexes. Gender roles also may produce *stereotyping*, judgments about individual members of a group on the basis of their membership in that group. Stereotypes about

Key Concept

What are the major differences between male and female gender roles?

Gender: The perception of being male or female.

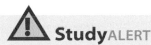 **Study**ALERT

The distinction between gender and sex is subtle. Keep in mind that sex relates to anatomy, and gender relates to perception.

Gender roles: The set of expectations, defined by a particular society, that indicate what is appropriate behavior for men and women.

From the moment of birth, gender differences are defined by outside influences. Is it possible for a family to block these influences completely? Would it be desirable to do so?

349

FIGURE 1 In spite of numerous differences among cultures, research has found strong similarities in the content of gender stereotypes. (Source: Williams & Best, 1990.)

Words Used to Describe Males		Words Used to Describe Females
Active	Initiative	Affected
Adventurous	Inventive	Affectionate
Aggressive	Lazy	Attractive
Ambitious	Logical	Charming
Arrogant	Loud	Curious
Assertive	Masculine	Dependent
Autocratic	Opportunistic	Dreamy
Clear-thinking	Progressive	Emotional
Coarse	Rational	Fearful
Courageous	Realistic	Feminine
Cruel	Reckless	Gentle
Daring	Robust	Mild
Determined	Rude	Sensitive
Disorderly	Self-confident	Sentimental
Dominant	Serious	Sexy
Egotistical	Severe	Softhearted
Energetic	Stern	Submissive
Enterprising	Stolid	Superstitious
Forceful	Strong	Talkative
Hardheaded	Unemotional	Weak
Hardhearted	Wise	
Independent		

Sexism: Negative attitudes and behavior toward a person based on that person's gender.

gender roles are reflected in **sexism**, negative attitudes and behavior toward a person that are based on that person's gender.

People in Western societies like ours generally hold well-defined stereotypes about men and women, which prevail regardless of age, economic status, and social and educational background. Men are more apt to be viewed as having traits involving competence, such as independence, objectivity, and competitiveness. In contrast, women tend to be seen as having traits involving warmth and expressiveness, such as gentleness and awareness of others' feelings. Because Western society traditionally values competence more than warmth and expressiveness, the perceived differences between men and women are biased in favor of men (Eagly, Beall, & Sternberg, 2005; Hyde, 2008; Kiefer, 2006).

In addition, cross-cultural research finds remarkable similarity in the content of gender stereotypes in different societies. For example, a 25-nation study identified a core set of descriptors that were consistently used to describe men and women (Williams & Best, 1990). Women were seen as sentimental, submissive, and superstitious, whereas men were seen as adventurous, forceful, and independent (see Figure 1). These stereotypical similarities across cultures may be due to similarities in status between men and women across the cultures; in most, men receive somewhat higher status than women (Lips, 2003; Durik et al., 2006).

Such stereotypes matter. By shaping beliefs about how men and women should behave, they potentially keep inequalities between the genders alive. Stereotypes put pressure on people to fulfill the stereotypes, and they may lead people to perform in accordance with the stereotypes rather than in accordance with their own abilities (Lips, 2003).

SEXISM ON THE JOB

Differences still exist regarding which occupations are deemed appropriate for men and for women. Women continue to be viewed as best suited for traditionally female jobs: "pink-collar" jobs such as secretary, nurse, cashier, and other female-dominated

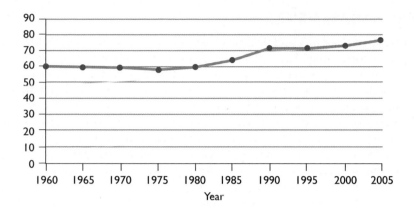

FIGURE 2 Although men's wages have stagnated since 2001, women still earn an average of 80 cents for every dollar that men earn. The disparity is even worse for women who are members of minority groups. What factors account for the continuing gap between men and women's wages? (Source: U.S. Bureau of Labor Statistics, 2005.)

professions that often feature low pay and low status. Men and women alike still report that they expect greater success when they enter a profession viewed as appropriate for their gender. Furthermore, women hold lower expectations than do men about their entering and peak salaries (Crawford & Unger, 2004; MacPherson, 2002; Casad, 2007).

Those expectations reflect the reality that women, on average, earn less than men. Although the gap has been decreasing, women overall earn an average of 80 cents for every dollar that men earn. Women who are members of minority groups are even worse off: Black women earn 71 cents for every dollar men make, and Hispanic women earn just 58 cents for every dollar men earn. Furthermore, even when they are in the same professions as men, women generally earn less than men do in comparable positions (Crosby, Williams, & Biernat, 2004; U.S. Bureau of Labor Statistics, 2005; see Figure 2).

Despite these inequities, attitudes are shifting. Most people endorse gender equality in the workplace, and they believe that women should be given the same opportunities as men. For example, just about as many men as women endorse the idea that jobs should be family-friendly by offering flexible work schedules. In addition, polls today find that most men no longer believe that a woman's most appropriate role is to care for her home and children while men should be earning money—a shift from the 1970s, when the majority of men did endorse that traditional view (Bond et al., 2003; Barnett, 2004).

Still, even when women are successful on the job and are promoted into upper-level, high-status positions, they may face significant hurdles in their efforts to move up the corporate ladder. Such obstacles are especially true for professional women who become mothers, who tend to be newly perceived as warm, but less competent than they were prior to motherhood. The same thing doesn't happen to men who become fathers; they are most likely to be viewed as warm *and* competent (Cuddy, Fiske, & Glick, 2004).

Because of such stereotypic views, many women eventually hit what has come to be called the glass ceiling. The *glass ceiling* is an invisible barrier within an organization that, because of gender discrimination, may prevent women from being promoted beyond a certain level. The glass ceiling is even found in colleges and universities. For example, although women fill 29 percent of science and engineering jobs at U.S. educational institutions, they occupy only 15 percent of those positions at the top 50 research universities (Whisenant, Pedersen, & Obenour, 2002; Ripley, 2005; Lyness & Heilman, 2006).

As phenomena such as the glass ceiling make clear, male gender stereotypes are typically more positive than female stereotypes. Although such stereotypes reflect people's perceptions and not necessarily the reality of the world, people often act as if they were real and modify their behavior to conform to the stereotypes. As a result, gender stereotypes limit both women's and men's behavior and ultimately lead to the unfortunate consequence of preferential treatment of men.

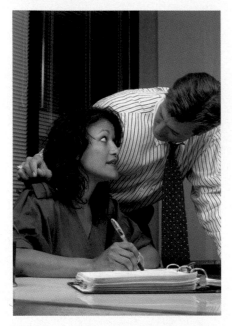

Sexual harassment consists of unwanted sexual attention. How is it possible for men and women to perceive this issue so differently?

SEXUAL HARASSMENT

In addition to pay inequity and limited job advancement, women—even those in high-status professions—may face workplace sexism in the form of *sexual harassment*, defined as unwanted sexual attention, the creation of a hostile or abusive environment, or explicit coercion to engage in unwanted sexual activity. Sexual harassment is not a minor problem. One-fifth of women surveyed in polls say that they have been sexually harassed at work. And it is not just women who encounter harassment: Some 10 percent of men report experiencing sexual harassment on the job (Matchen & DeSouza & Fansler, 2003; Fineran, 2002; Willness, Steel, & Lee, 2007).

Sexual harassment is not just a workplace issue. Thirty percent of the female graduates of one large California university reported being the recipients of some form of harassment. Such harassment begins earlier in life: In one survey, 81 percent of middle and high school students reported receiving some form of sexual harassment in school, and 6 in 10 experienced physical sexual harassment at some point in their school lives (see Figure 3). One third of students are afraid of being sexually harassed, with girls more than twice as likely as boys to report concern. Overall, estimates suggest that one of every two women will be harassed at some point during her academic or working life (Fitzgerald, 2003; AAUW, 2001).

Sexual harassment often has less to do with sex than with power (similar to the motivation behind many cases of rape, as we'll discuss in a later module). In this view, higher-status persons who engage in harassment may be less interested in receiving sexual favors than in demonstrating their power over the victim (O'Donohue, 1997; Huerta et al., 2006).

FIGURE 3 Sexual harassment in school. The number of students who report experiencing unwelcomed sexual attention often or occasionally at school is significant. (Source: American Association of University Women, 2001.)

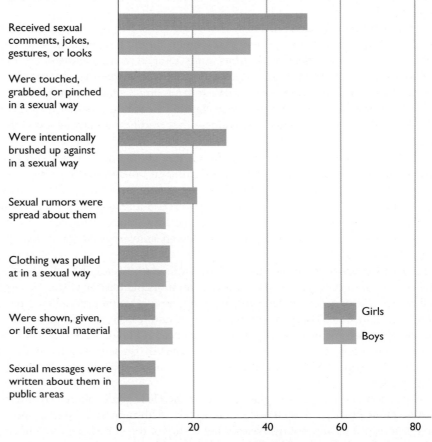

In some cases, harassment stems from *benevolent sexism,* stereotyped and restrictive attitudes that appear, on the surface, to be beneficial to women. For example, a male employer may compliment a woman on her attractiveness or offer her an easy job so that she won't have to "work so hard." The reality, however, is that such comments or "favors" may undermine the employee's sense of competence, and she may feel that she is not being taken seriously (Glick & Fiske, 2001; Glick et al., 2004; Forbes, Jung, & Haas, 2006).

Regardless of the motivation that lies behind sexual harassment, the consequences for the victim are clear. Feelings of shame and embarrassment are standard. Because targets of harassment are typically in lower-status positions, such feelings may be compounded by a sense of helplessness and powerlessness. People in these situations often suffer emotional and physical consequences, and the quality of their work may decline. Furthermore, they are less likely to believe they can attain higher positions (Jorgenson & Wauhl, 2000; Magley, 2002; Miner-Rubino & Cortina, 2007).

Gender Differences: More Similar Than Dissimilar

Not surprisingly, gender stereotyping, combined with other factors, results in actual behavior differences between men and women. Before we consider the nature of gender differences, however, it is important to keep in mind that in most respects men and women are more similar to one another than they are different. Furthermore, the differences that have been found reflect *average* male and female differences, and this finding tells us little or nothing about any *individual* male or female.

For example, even if we find that males, on the whole, generally tend to be more talkative than females—as research shows they do, despite the stereotype that women talk more—an individual man can be less talkative than most women. Similarly, an individual woman may be more talkative than most men. When we consider any single person, our focus should be on the individual rather than on his or her gender group. It is important to take this into account as we examine the findings on gender differences (Mehl et al., 2007).

PERSONALITY FACTORS

One of the most pronounced differences between men and women lies in their degree of aggressive behavior. By the time they are 2 years old, boys tend to display more aggression than girls do, and this higher level of aggression persists throughout the life span. Furthermore, compared with men, women experience greater anxiety and guilt about their aggressiveness and are more concerned about its effects on their victims (Feingold, 1994; Munroe et al., 2000; Hyde, 2008).

Men generally seem to have higher self-esteem than women do, although the size of the difference is not great and is based on different factors. Women's self-esteem is influenced to a large extent by their perception of their sense of interdependence and connection with others. In contrast, men's self-esteem stems from their assessment of their unique characteristics and abilities, traits that help them distinguish themselves from other people (Kling et al., 2003; Lawrence, Ashford, & Dent, 2006).

Men and women differ in how positively they view their own abilities and how they estimate the probability of their future success. In general, women evaluate themselves more harshly than do men. For example, a survey of first-year college students compared men's and women's views of whether they were above or below average. As you can see in Figure 4, more men than women considered themselves above average in overall academic and mathematical ability, competitiveness, and emotional

FIGURE 4 Male first-year college students are much more likely than female first-year college students to rate themselves as above average in academic ability, mathematical ability, and emotional health. (Source: *The American Freshman: National Norms for Fall 2004.* Astin, Korn, & Berz. Higher Education Research Council, UCLA.)

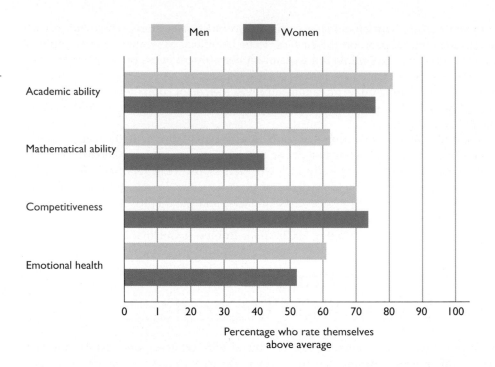

health. Such self-perceptions matter, because they influence motivation, as well as academic and career choices. They even influence performance. For example, when women experience *stereotype threat*—the perception that a performance measure is sensitive to gender differences—their performance declines (Steele, Spencer, & Aronson, 2002; Keller, 2007).

The content of men's and women's speech also differs, with women's speech being more precise. However, women's speech patterns lead others to view them as more tentative and less assertive. Women more often raise their pitch at the end of a sentence, and add "tags" at the end of an opinion, rather than stating the opinion outright. For example, instead of saying "It's awfully warm today," a female speaker might say instead "It's awfully warm today, *isn't it?*" thereby appearing less certain of her opinion. When females use such tentative language, they are judged to be less

Research has shown that boys from age 2 tend to be more aggressive than girls, a pattern that continues throughout the life span.

competent and knowledgeable than they are when they speak assertively (Matlin, 1996; Carli & Bukatko, 2000; Popp, Donovan, & Crawford, 2003).

Women's and men's nonverbal behavior differs as well in several significant respects. In conversations with people of the other sex, women look at their partner significantly more while listening than while speaking, whereas men's levels of looking while speaking and listening are about the same. The effect of the male's pattern is to communicate power and dominance, whereas the woman's pattern is associated more with cooperation. Women, however, are generally better than men at decoding the facial expressions of others (Coats & Feldman, 1996; Burgoon & Bacue, 2003; LaFrance & Harris, 2004).

COGNITIVE ABILITIES

No general differences exist between men and women in overall IQ scores, learning, memory, problem solving, and concept-formation tasks. A few differences in more specific cognitive areas have been identified, although the true nature of those differences—and even their existence—has been called into question by more recent research (Halpern, 2000).

When Eleanor Maccoby and Carol Jacklin carried out a pioneering study of sex differences in 1974, they concluded that girls outperformed boys in verbal abilities and that boys had superior quantitative and spatial abilities. That conclusion was accepted widely as one of the truisms of the psychological literature.

However, recent and more sophisticated analyses have questioned the specific nature and magnitude of those differences. Psychologist Janet Hyde and colleagues, for instance, examined the mathematical performance of males and females in 100 studies encompassing some 4 million subjects. Contrary to traditional wisdom, females slightly outperformed males in math in elementary and middle school. The finding was reversed in high school, where males scored higher in mathematical problem solving. This difference is reflected in SAT scores, where girls score about 7 percent lower than boys (Hyde, Fennema, & Lamon, 1990; Ripley, 2005; Jackson & Rushton, 2006).

Yet the apparent male superiority in math is not universal. In some parts of the world, the sexes are on a par. For example, Japanese boys and girls perform quite similarly on math tests except for the single math area of probability—and Japanese girls routinely outperform both boys and girls in the United States on comparable tests of mathematical ability. Furthermore, in some places, girls outshine boys in math. In Iceland, for instance, female high school students score significantly better on standardized math tests than boys. Overall, the differences between males and females in math are inconsistent, and generally those differences are insignificant and, if anything, appear to be declining (Benbow, Lubinski, & Hyde, 1997; Angier & Chang, 2005; Walt, 2005; Lubinski & Benbow, 2006).

Psychologists have drawn a similar conclusion about the extent of gender differences in verbal skills. Despite the earlier view that women show greater verbal abilities than men, a more careful analysis of 165 studies of gender differences in verbal ability, representing the testing of close to 1.5 million subjects, has led to the conclusion that verbal gender differences are insignificant. Furthermore, verbal SAT scores are quite similar for boys and girls (Angier & Chang, 2005; Hyde, 2005).

Current evidence suggests, then, that gender differences in cognitive skills are minimal. On the other hand, particular tests of mathematical and verbal skills do elicit differences in performance, as in the example of the mathematics part of the SAT, where very high scorers are predominantly male. In addition, as we discuss in the *Applying Psychology in the 21st Century* box, there are differences between men and

Who Goes to College, and Who Does Well? Explaining the Gender-Reversal on College Campuses

Higher education classes are increasingly populated by females.

"She does all her readings for classes, and I don't always," said Ben Turner, who graduated from American University this spring, about his girlfriend. "She's more organized than me, so if there's a paper due a week from Monday, she's already started, and I know I'll be doing it the weekend before. She studies more than I do because she doesn't like cramming and being stressed. She just has a better work ethic than I do." (Lewin, 2006, p. 18)

The disparity between Ben Turner's approach to academic work and that of his girlfriend is being played out at colleges and universities across America. Although higher education was once dominated by men, women have closed the academic gender gap and are rapidly surpassing their male classmates on many measures of academic achievement.

U.S. Department of Education statistics paint a picture in which women succeed in higher education more than men. Greater proportions of female high school students than their male counterparts report plans to graduate from college, and a greater proportion of the females have further plans to attend graduate or professional school afterward. And they follow through with these plans: women are more likely to go directly to college after high school, where they are increasingly finding themselves to be in the majority. Whereas the proportion of male and female college undergraduates was roughly 60/40 respectively in 1970, that proportion is reversed today. Women are more likely than men to finish their bachelor's degrees and less likely to drop out, such that more women than men in the general population aged 25–29 have college degrees. Women now outnumber men in graduate school attendance, including the field of psychology (as we discussed in the first chapter of the book). Female enrollment in professional degree programs such as dentistry, medicine, and law has grown at a particularly astounding rate, rising from less than 10 percent in 1970 to nearly half by 2000 (Freeman, 2004).

The explanation for the gender difference is not clear. It's not the case that men are abandoning academia—they are attending and graduating from college in greater numbers than before, too. Rather, it's the case that women are more motivated to succeed in higher education, which may be the result of changing roles and increased career opportunities for women. Women may see higher education as a way to achieve greater independence and a better life. In fact, the disparity between male and female college enrollment is greatest among low-income families. Men, on the other hand, may feel that their options are less dependent on having a college degree. For example, the immediate reward of a decent-paying job in blue-collar jobs, for instance, may be more attractive to many men than spending several years in college (Lewin, 2006).

There is also discrepancy between the effort that men and women put forward while in college. Men often don't work as hard in college as women do. One large survey found that women spend more hours than men preparing for class, while men spend more hours than women relaxing, socializing, and participating in physical fitness activities, and they are more likely to come to class unprepared (National Survey of Student Engagement, 2006). Why this is so is less clear, but some researchers feel that men simply have less to worry about because they face fewer career barriers than women do, while others point to a difference in maturity level between male and female college students. Whatever the reason, it is clear that men and women have different views of what it takes to succeed in college (Lewin, 2006).

- What factors might account for the surpassing of men by women in college enrollment and graduation?
- Some experts see the gender difference in higher education achievement as an emerging crisis for men. Do you agree with that assessment?

women in regard to motivation to excel academically (Hyde, 2005; Lippa, 2005; Ripley, 2005).

Furthermore, even when no differences are found in men's and women's performance on specific tasks, there may be underlying differences in how the brain processes information. For example, one study that found no differences in accuracy and reaction time between men and women in identifying similarities between three-dimensional shapes also found that men and women differed in what parts of their

Neuroscience in Your Life

FIGURE 5 Although males and females performed similarly in terms of accuracy and reaction time on a task involving comparisons of three-dimensional objects, different parts of their brains were activated while carrying out the task. The top row shows areas of the brain that male participants use more than females during this task, and the bottom row shows areas of the brain that female participants use more than males during this task. (Source: Hugdahl et al., 2006.)

brains were being activated while they were carrying out the task (see Figure 5). In short, gender differences are complex, and we still do not have the full story on differences between men and women in cognitive abilities (Hugdahl et al., 2006).

Sources of Gender Differences: Where Biology and Society Meet

If the identification of gender differences has presented a difficult challenge for researchers, the search for their causes has proved even more daunting. Given the indisputable fact that sex is a biological variable, it would seem reasonable to look at factors involving biological differences between men and women. It is also true that, from the time they are born, people are treated differently on the basis of their sex. Consequently, we must take into account both biological and social factors when we try to understand the source of gender differences.

Although we'll consider biological and environmental variables separately, neither alone can provide a full explanation for gender differences. Some combination of the two, interacting with each other, will ultimately provide us with an understanding of why men and women may behave differently.

BIOLOGICAL AND EVOLUTIONARY FACTORS

Do differences between male and female brains underlie sex and gender differences? This intriguing hypothesis has been put forward by some psychologists studying brain structure and functioning. For instance, girls who were exposed before birth to unusually high levels of *androgen,* a male hormone, because their mothers accidentally took a drug containing that hormone while pregnant, preferred different toys from those preferred by girls not exposed to androgens. Specifically, they were more likely to play with toys that are stereotypically preferred by boys (such as cars) and less likely to play with toys stereotypically associated with girls (such as dolls). Although you can probably think of several alternative explanations for these results, one possibility is that exposure to the male hormone may have affected the development of the girls' brains, making them favor toys that involve certain kinds of skills, such as those related to spatial abilities (Mealey, 2000; Hines et al., 2002, Fink et al., 2007).

Similarly, some evidence suggests that women perform better on tasks involving verbal skill and muscular coordination during periods when their production of the female sex hormone *estrogen* is relatively high, compared with periods when it is low. In contrast, they perform better on tasks involving spatial relationships when the estrogen level is relatively low (Kimura, 1999; Rosenberg & Park, 2002).

Some psychologists argue that evolutionary forces lead to certain differences between men's and women's behavior. For example, David Buss and colleagues point to differences in the nature of jealousy between men and women. Men are more jealous in cases of sexual infidelity than in cases of emotional infidelity; women are more jealous in cases of emotional infidelity than in cases of sexual infidelity (Buss et al., 1992; Buss, 2003).

According to Buss's controversial explanation, the root cause for the differences in jealousy lies in the evolutionary implications of sexual, versus emotional, infidelity for men and women. He argues that for males, sexual infidelity represents a threat to their ability to ensure that their children are actually their own (and are the ones who have inherited their genes). In contrast, females have no doubt that a child that they carry through pregnancy is their own. However, their major concern is ensuring the male's protection and support during child rearing. Thus, to females, maintaining males' emotional attachment is crucial.

Psychologists relying on the evolutionary approach also argue that similarities in the division of labor between men and women across different cultures suggest that sex differences are due to evolutionary factors. Their argument is that even in very different types of cultures, men tend to be more aggressive, competitive, and prone to taking risks than women are—traits that had an evolutionary advantage (Mealey, 2000; Buss, 2003; Chang & Geary, 2007).

However, many critics question the assumptions of the evolutionary approach. Rather than assuming that the differences are due to evolutionary forces, some psychologists suggest that differences in males' and females' beliefs about the meaning of infidelity are the actual cause of their jealousy differences. For instance, men may believe that women have sex only when they are in love. Consequently, sexual infidelity may be seen as a sign that a woman is in love with another man, and may produce more jealousy than emotional infidelity alone would. In contrast, women may believe that men are capable of having sex without being in love, and consequently they may find a man's sexual infidelity less bothersome because it does not necessarily mean that he is in love with someone else (DeSteno et al., 2002; Fernandez et al., 2007).

Psychologists Alice Eagly and Wendy Wood criticize evolutionary explanations for gender differences on different grounds. They argue, in their *biosocial approach,* that one important source of gender differences is the difference in the physical capabilities of men and women. Consistently across cultures, the division of labor between men and women is based largely on men's size, strength, and speed and women's capacity for pregnancy and caring for children. However, the specific nature of activities in which men and women specialize varies from one culture to another, depending on the specifics of a culture (Wood & Eagly, 2002).

The extent to which biological and evolutionary factors may underlie gender differences is an unanswered, and highly controversial, question. One thing is clear, however: Biological factors and evolutionary factors alone do not explain the complete range of differences between male and female behavior. To fully understand the source of gender differences, we also must consider the social environment, as we do next.

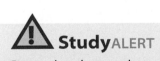

StudyALERT

Remember that gender differences are caused by a combination of biological, evolutionary, and social factors.

THE SOCIAL ENVIRONMENT

Starting from the moment of birth, with blue blankets for boys and pink ones for girls, most parents and other adults provide environments that differ in important respects according to gender. For example, boys and girls are given different kinds of toys, and—until protests recently brought the practice to an end—items in the largest toy

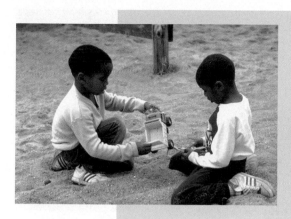

Boy's World	Girl's World
• Action figures	• Barbie
• Sports collectibles	• Baby dolls
• Radio remote-control cars	• Doll houses
• Tonka trucks	• Collectible horses
• Boy's role play	• Play kitchens
• Walkie-talkies	• Housekeeping toys
	• Girl's dress-up
	• Jewelry
	• Cosmetics
	• Bath and body

FIGURE 6 The placement of toys according to gender was commonplace until protests forced a nationwide chain to discontinue the practice.

store chain in the United States were laid out according to the gender appropriateness of particular toys (see Figure 6; Bannon, 2000; Wood, Desmarais, & Gugula, 2002).

Parents interact with their children differently, depending on their sex. Fathers play more roughly with their infant sons than with their infant daughters. Middle-class mothers tend to talk more to their daughters than to their sons. It is clear that adults frequently treat children differently on the basis of gender (McHale, Crouter, & Tucker, 1999; Tenenbaum & Leaper, 2002).

Such differences in behavior, and there are many more, produce different social-ization experiences for men and women. *Socialization* is the process by which an indi-vidual learns the rules and norms of appropriate behavior. In this case, it refers to learning what society considers appropriate behavior for men and women. According to the processes of social learning theory, boys and girls are taught, and rewarded for performing, the socially perceived appropriate behaviors for men and for women, respectively (Archer & Lloyd, 2002; Liben & Bigler, 2002; Leaper & Friedman, 2007).

It is not just parents, of course, who provide socialization experiences for children. Society as a whole communicates clear messages to children as they are growing up. Children's reading books traditionally have portrayed girls in stereotypically nurtur-ing roles, whereas boys have been given more physical and action-oriented roles. Television, too, acts as a particularly influential source of socialization. Men outnum-ber women on television, and women are often cast in such stereotypical roles as housewife, secretary, and mother. The potency of television as an agent of socialization is underscored by data indicating that the more television children watch, the more sexist they become (Furnham, Pallangyo, & Gunter, 2001; Turkel, 2002; Ogletree et al., 2004; Abelman, 2006).

Our educational system also treats boys and girls differently. For example, in elementary school, boys are five times more likely to receive attention from classroom teachers than girls. Boys receive significantly more praise, criticism, and remedial help than girls do. They are also more likely to be praised for the intelligence shown in their work, whereas girls are more apt to be commended for their neatness. Even in college classes, male students receive more eye contact from their professors than female stu-dents, men are called upon more frequently in class, and men are more apt to receive extra help from their professors (AAUW, 1992; Sadker & Sadker, 1994; Einarsson & Granstroem, 2002; Koch, 2003).

Socialization produces a **gender schema**, a mental framework that organizes and guides a child's understanding of information relevant to gender. On the basis of their schemas for appropriate and inappropriate behavior for males and females, children begin to behave in ways that reflect society's gender roles. Hence, children who are

Gender schema: A mental framework that organizes and guides a child's understanding of information relevant to gender.

Androgynous people tend to defy stereotypes by combining the psychological and behavioral characteristics thought typical of both sexes.

offered the opportunity to sew a costume for a school play may evaluate the activity not in terms of the intrinsic components of the process (such as the mechanics of using a needle and thread), but in terms of whether the activity is compatible with their gender schema. Such evaluation may potentially limit the range of experiences to which children are exposed (Bem, 1998; Martin, Ruble, & Szkrybalo, 2002; Le Maner-Idrissi & Renault, 2006).

"Sometimes it would be helpful if you were a bit more androgynous."

RECAP/EVALUATE/RETHINK

RECAP

What are the major differences between male and female gender roles?

- Gender is the perception of being male or female. Gender roles are the expectations, defined by society, of what is appropriate behavior for men and women. When gender roles reflect favoritism toward one sex, they lead to stereotyping and produce sexism. (p. 349)

- The gender-role stereotype for men suggests that they are endowed with competence-related traits, whereas women are seen in terms of their capacity for warmth and expressiveness. Actual sex differences are much less clear, and of smaller magnitude, than the stereotypes would suggest. The differences that do exist are produced by a combination of biological and environmental factors. (p. 350)

- Biological causes of sex difference are reflected by evidence suggesting a possible difference in brain structure and functioning between men and women and may be associated with differential exposure to hormones before birth. (p. 357)

- An evolutionary approach explains gender differences in terms of different male-female concerns regarding the inheritance of genes and the need for child rearing, but this approach is highly controversial. (p. 358)

- Socialization experiences produce gender schemas, mental frameworks that organize and guide a child's understanding of information relevant to gender. (p. 359)

EVALUATE

1. _____ are sets of societal expectations about what is appropriate behavior for men and women.
2. Gender stereotypes seem to be much less prevalent today than they were several decades ago. True or false?
3. Which of the following statements about male-female differences in aggression is true?
   a. Males are physically more aggressive than females only during childhood.
   b. Male-female differences in aggression first become evident during adolescence.
   c. Males are more aggressive than females throughout the life span.
   d. Females and males feel equally anxious about their aggressive acts.
4. _____ are frameworks that organize understanding of gender-specific information.

RETHINK

1. The U.S. Congress has enacted laws prohibiting women in the armed forces from participating directly in combat in the interest of keeping them safe. Do you think such laws are protective or sexist? How might this be an example of "benevolent sexism"?
2. *From the perspective of a business executive:* Evidence shows that sexism in the workplace is widespread. If you wanted to end sexism in organizational settings, can you think of ways to narrow the gap between men and women in terms of occupations and salary?

Answers to Evaluate Questions

1. gender roles; 2. false; they are still prevalent; 3. c; 4. gender schemas

KEY TERMS

gender p. 349
gender roles p. 349
sexism p. 350
gender schema p. 359

Understanding Human Sexual Response: The Facts of Life

When I started "tuning out," teachers thought I was sick—physically sick that is. They kept sending me to the school nurse to have my temperature taken. If I'd told them I was carrying on with Jennifer Lopez in their classes, while supposedly learning my Caesar and my Latin vocabulary, they'd have thought I was—well, delirious. I was! (based on Coles & Stokes, 1985, pp. 18–19)

Not everyone's sexual fantasies are as consuming as those reported by this teenage boy. Yet sex is an important consideration in most people's lives, for although the physical aspects of human sex are not all that different from those of other species, the meaning, values, and feelings that humans place on sexual behavior elevate it to a special plane. To fully appreciate this difference, however, it is necessary to understand the basic biology underlying sexual responses.

Key Concept

Why, and under what circumstances, do we become sexually aroused?

The Basic Biology of Sexual Behavior

Anyone who has seen two dogs mating knows that sexual behavior has a biological basis. Their sexual behavior appears to occur naturally, without much prompting on the part of others. A number of genetically controlled factors influence the sexual behavior of nonhuman animals. For instance, animal behavior is affected by the presence of certain hormones in the blood. Moreover, female animals are receptive to sexual advances only during certain relatively limited periods of the year.

Human sexual behavior, by comparison, is more complicated, although the underlying biology is not all that different from that of related species. In males, for example, the *testes* begin to secrete **androgens**, male sex hormones, at puberty. (See Figure 1 for the basic anatomy of the male and female **genitals**, or sex organs.) Not only do androgens produce secondary sex characteristics, such as the growth of body hair and a deepening of the voice, they also increase the sex drive. Because the level of androgen production by the testes is fairly constant, men are capable of (and interested in) sexual activities without any regard to biological cycles. Given the proper stimuli leading to arousal, male sexual behavior can occur at any time (Goldstein, 2000).

Women show a different pattern. When they reach maturity at puberty, the two *ovaries* begin to produce **estrogens** and **progesterone**, female sex hormones. However, those hormones are not produced consistently; instead, their production follows a cyclical pattern. The greatest output occurs during **ovulation**, when an egg is released from the ovaries, making the chances of fertilization by a sperm cell highest. While in nonhumans the period around ovulation is the only time the female is receptive to sex, people are different. Although there are variations in reported sex drive, women are receptive to sex throughout their cycles (Leiblum & Chivers, 2007).

In addition, some evidence suggests that males have a stronger sex drive than females, although the difference may be the result of society's discouragement of female sexuality rather than of innate differences between men and women. It is clear that men think about sex more than women: while 54 percent of men report thinking about sex every day, only 19 percent of women report thinking about it on a daily basis (Mendelsohn, 2003; Gangestad et al., 2004; Baumeister & Stillman, 2006).

Androgens: Male sex hormones secreted by the testes.
Genitals: The male and female sex organs.

Estrogens: Class of female sex hormones.
Progesterone: A female sex hormone secreted by the ovaries.
Ovulation: The point at which an egg is released from the ovaries.

FIGURE 1 Cutaway side views of the female and male sex organs.

Female

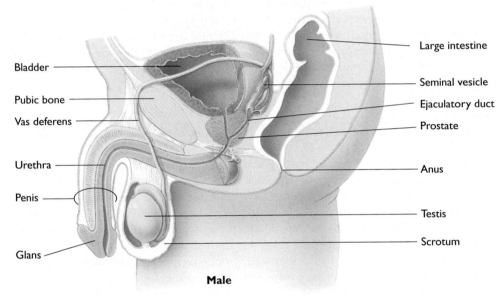

Male

Though biological factors "prime" people for sex, it takes more than hormones to motivate and produce sexual behavior. In animals the presence of a partner who provides arousing stimuli leads to sexual activity. Humans are considerably more versatile; not only other people but nearly any object, sight, smell, sound, or other stimulus can lead to sexual excitement. Because of prior associations, then, people may be turned on sexually by the smell of perfume or the sound of a favorite song hummed softly in their ears. The reaction to a specific, potentially arousing stimulus, as we shall see, is highly individual—what turns one person on may do just the opposite for another (Benson, 2003).

Psychological Aspects of Sexual Excitement: What Turns People On?

If you were to argue that the major human sex organ is the brain, in a sense you would be right. Much of what is considered sexually arousing in our society has little or nothing to do with our genitals; instead, it is related to external stimuli that, through a process of learning, have come to be labeled as erotic, or sexually stimulating.

For example, there are no areas of the body that *automatically* produce sexual arousal when touched. Areas of the body, called **erogenous zones**, that have an unusually rich array of nerve receptors are particularly sensitive not just to sexual touch but to any kind of touch. When a physician touches a breast or a penis, the information sent to the brain by the nerve cells is essentially the same as that sent when a sexual partner touches that spot. What differs is the interpretation given to the touch. Sexual arousal is likely only when a certain part of the body is touched in what people define as a sexual manner and when a person is receptive to sexual activity (Gagnon, 1977; Goldstein, 2000).

Although people can learn to respond sexually to almost any stimulus, there is a good deal of agreement within a society or culture about what usually represents an erotic stimulus. In many Western societies breast size is often the standard by which female appeal is measured, but in many other cultures breast size is irrelevant (Rothblum, 1990; Furnham & Swami, 2007).

Sexual fantasies also play an important role in producing sexual arousal. Not only do people have fantasies of a sexual nature during their everyday activities, about 60 percent of all people have fantasies during sexual intercourse. In fact, such fantasies often include having sex with someone other than one's partner of the moment (Hicks & Leitenberg, 2001; Trudel, 2002).

Men's and women's fantasies differ little from each other in terms of content or quantity, although men seem to fantasize about sex more than women do (Jones & Barlow, 1990; Hsu et al., 1994). As you can see in Figure 2, thoughts of being sexually irresistible and of engaging in oral-genital sex are most common for both sexes. It is important to note that fantasies do not represent an actual desire for their fulfillment in the real world. Thus, we should not assume from data about female fantasies that women want to be sexually overpowered or assume from data about male fantasies that every male is desirous of forcing sexual overtures on a submissive victim (Shulman & Horne, 2006).

Erogenous zones: Areas of the body that are particularly sensitive because of the presence of an unusually rich array of nerve receptors.

The Phases of Sexual Response: The Ups and Downs of Sex

Although the kinds of stimuli that produce sexual arousal are to some degree unique to each individual, we all share some basic aspects of sexual responsiveness. According to pioneering work done by William Masters and Virginia Johnson (1966), who studied sexual behavior in carefully controlled laboratory settings, sexual responses follow a regular pattern consisting of four phases: excitement, plateau, orgasm, and resolution. Although other researchers argue that sexual responses proceed somewhat differently (e.g., Kaplan, 1974; Zilbergeld & Ellison, 1980), Masters and Johnson's research is the most widely accepted account of what happens when people become sexually excited (Masters & Johnson, 1994).

In the *excitement phase,* which can last from just a few minutes to over an hour, an arousing stimulus begins a sequence that prepares the genitals for sexual intercourse. In the male, the *penis* becomes erect when blood flows into it; in the female, the *clitoris* swells because of an increase in the blood supply to that area, and the *vagina* becomes lubricated. Women may also experience a "sex flush," a red rash that typically spreads over the chest and throat.

Next comes the **plateau phase**, the body's preparation for orgasm. During this stage, the maximum level of sexual arousal is attained as the penis and clitoris swell with blood. Women's breasts and vaginas expand, heartbeat and blood pressure rise, and breathing rate increases. Muscle tension becomes greater as the body prepares itself for the next stage, orgasm. Although it is difficult to explain the sensation of **orgasm** beyond saying that it is an intense, highly pleasurable experience, the biological events that accompany the feeling are fairly straightforward. When the orgasm

Plateau phase: The period in which the maximum level of arousal is attained, the penis and clitoris swell with blood, and the body prepares for orgasm.

Orgasm: The peak of sexual excitement, during which rhythmic muscular contractions occur in the genitals.

FIGURE 2 The kinds of fantasies that men and women have during sexual intercourse are fairly similar (Sue, 1979). Why do you think this is true? Do you think the fantasies are similar in non-Western cultures?

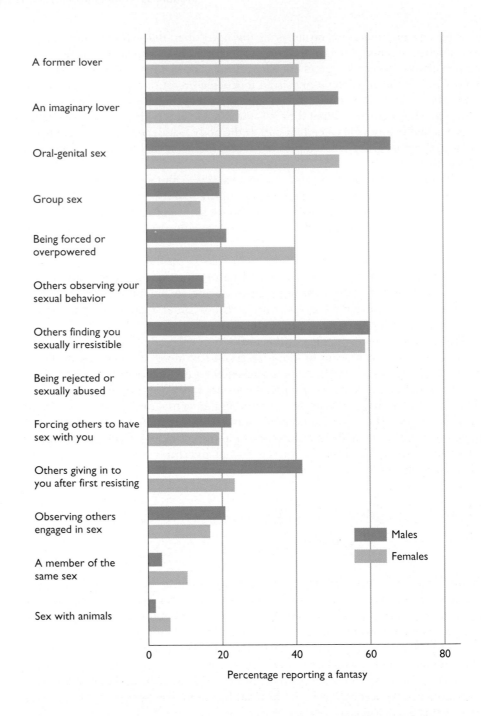

stage is reached, rhythmic muscular contractions occur in the genitals every eight-tenths of a second. In the male, the contractions expel *semen*, a fluid containing sperm, from the penis—a process known as *ejaculation*. For women and men, breathing and heart rates reach their maximum.

After orgasm, people move into the last stage of sexual arousal, the **resolution stage**. The body returns to its resting state, reversing the changes brought about by arousal. The genitals resume their unaroused size and shape, and blood pressure, breathing, and heart rate return to normal.

Male and female responses differ significantly during the resolution stage; these differences are depicted in Figure 3. Women are able to cycle back to the orgasm phase and experience repeated orgasms. Ultimately, of course, females enter the final resolution stage, and then they return to their prestimulation state. In contrast, it generally is thought that men enter a refractory period during the resolution stage.

Resolution stage: The interval after orgasm in which the body returns to its unaroused state, reversing the changes brought about by arousal.

a. Male pattern

b. Female patterns

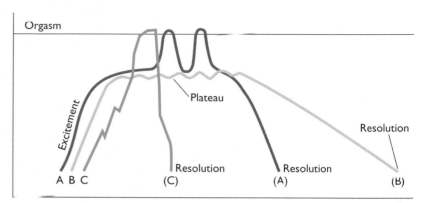

FIGURE 3 A four-stage model of the sexual response cycle for males and females based on the findings of Masters and Johnson (1966). Note how the male pattern (a) includes a refractory period. Part (b) shows three possible female patterns. In A, the pattern is closest to the male cycle, except that the woman has two orgasms in a row. In B, there is no orgasm, whereas in C orgasm is reached quickly and the woman rapidly returns to an unaroused state. (Source: After Masters & Johnson, 1966.)

During the **refractory period**, men are unable to develop an erection and therefore are unable to have another orgasm and ejaculate. The refractory period may last from a few minutes to several hours, although in the elderly it may continue for several days (Goldstein, 2000).

Refractory period: A temporary period that follows the resolution stage and during which the male cannot develop an erection again.

Waris Dirie was just an innocent, unknowing child of 5 when she begged her mother to let her be circumcised like virtually all females in Somalia. "When you've been told over and over that, until this happens, you're filthy and no man would ever marry you, you believe what everybody says," Dirie explains. "I just wanted to be like the other girls."

Exploring DIVERSITY

Female Circumcision: A Celebration of Culture—or Genital Mutilation?

Months later her awful wish came true. As her mother held down the crying, blindfolded Diri, a gypsy performed the circumcision using a dirty, dull razor and no anesthetic. She sewed the ragged wound with thorns and thread. "It's not a pain you forget," says Dirie, in a whisper. She was left with only a tiny opening, and urinating became torture. Later, menstruation was so unbearable that Dirie routinely fainted. (Cheakalos & Heyn, 1998, p. 149)

The operation in question—female circumcision—represents one of the most controversial procedures relating to sex throughout the world. In such an operation, the clitoris is removed, resulting in permanent inability to experience sexual pleasure.

Some 80 million women, living mostly in Africa and Asia, have undergone female circumcision. More than 90 percent of Nigerian women have been circumcised during childhood, and more than 90 percent intend to circumcise their daughters. Furthermore, in some cases, more extensive surgery is carried out, in which additional parts of the female genitals are removed or are sewn together with catgut or thorns (Obermeyer, 2001; Lacey, 2002; Renshaw, 2006).

Those who practice female circumcision say it upholds an ancient societal tradition and is no different from other cultural customs. Its purpose, they say, is to preserve virginity before marriage, keep women faithful to their husbands after marriage, and enhance a woman's beauty. Furthermore, proponents believe that it differs little

StudyALERT

Use Figure 3 to help remember the different patterns of sexual response and how they differ between men and women.

from the common Western practice of male circumcision, in which the foreskin of the penis is surgically removed soon after birth.

Critics, in contrast, argue that female circumcision is nothing less than female mutilation. Not only does the practice permanently eliminate sexual pleasure, it can also lead to constant pain and infection and, in some cases, death. Furthermore, because the procedure is traditionally conducted in a ritualistic fashion without an anesthetic, using a razor blade, sawtooth knife, or glass, the circumcision itself can be physically traumatic (Dugger, 1996; Renshaw, 2006).

The procedure raises some difficult issues, which have been brought to light in various court cases. For instance, a Nigerian immigrant, living temporarily in the United States, went to court to argue that she should be allowed to remain permanently. Her plea: If she and her young daughters were sent back to Nigeria, her daughters would face circumcision upon their return. The court agreed and permitted her to stay indefinitely (Gregory, 1994; Dugger, 1996).

In reaction to the controversy about female circumcision, Congress made the practice illegal in the United States. Still, some critics argue that female circumcision is a valued cultural custom, and that no one, particularly someone judging from the perspective of another culture, should prevent people from carrying out the customs they think are important. In addition, they point out that the practice of *male* circumcision, in which the foreskin of the penis is surgically removed, is an accepted practice in the United States, based largely on religious, social, and cultural traditions (Boyle et al. 2002; Johnsdotter & Essén, 2005; Renshaw, 2006).

RECAP/EVALUATE/RETHINK

RECAP

Why, and under what circumstances, do we become sexually aroused?

- Although biological factors, such as the presence of androgens (male sex hormones) and estrogens and progesterone (female sex hormones), prime people for sex, almost any kind of stimulus can produce sexual arousal, depending on a person's prior experience. (p. 363)

- People's sexual responses follow a regular pattern consisting of four phases: excitement, plateau, orgasm, and resolution. (p. 365)

EVALUATE

1. Match the phase of sexual arousal with its characteristics
   1. Excitement phase
   2. Plateau phase
   3. Orgasm phase
   4. Resolution phase
      a. Maximum level of sexual arousal
      b. Erection and lubrication
      c. Rhythmic muscular contractions and ejaculation
      d. Return of body to resting state

2. Men are generally thought to enter a _____ period after sex, in which orgasm is impossible for a varying period of time.
3. Whereas men are interested in sexual activity regardless of their biological cycles, women are truly receptive to sex only during ovulation, when the production of their sex hormones is greatest. True or false?
4. Men's and women's sexual fantasies are essentially similar to each other. True or false?

RETHINK

1. Why do you think humans differ from other species in their year-round receptivity to sex and in the number and variety of stimuli they perceive as sexual? What evolutionary purpose might this difference serve in humans?
2. *From the perspective of a sex counselor:* How do people learn to be aroused by the stimuli that their society considers erotic? When do they learn this, and where does the message come from?

Answers to Evaluate Questions

1. 1-b, 2-a, 3-c, 4-d; 2. refractory; 3. false; women are receptive throughout their cycle; 4. true

KEY TERMS

androgens p. 363

genitals p. 363

estrogens p. 363

progesterone p. 363

ovulation p. 363

erogenous zones p. 365

plateau phase p. 365

orgasm p. 365

resolution stage p. 366

refractory period p. 367

The Diversity of Sexual Behavior

A boy who practices this habit can never be the best that Nature intended him to be. His wits are not so sharp. His memory is not so good. His power of fixing his attention on whatever he is doing is lessened. . . . A boy like this is a poor thing to look at. . . . [He is] untrustworthy, unreliable, untruthful, and probably even dishonest. (Schofield & Vaughan-Jackson, 1913, pp. 30–42)

The cause of this condition: masturbation—at least according to the authors of the early 1900s sex manual *What Every Boy Should Know*. The consequences of masturbation for women were considered no less severe. In the words of one 19th-century physician, "There is hardly an end to the diseases caused by masturbation: dyspepsia, spinal disease, headache, epilepsy, various kinds of fits . . . impaired eyesight, palpitation of the heart, pain in the side and bleeding at the lungs, spasm of the heart, and sometimes sudden death" (Gregory, 1856).

Such views may seem bizarre and far-fetched to you, as they do to contemporary experts on human sexual behavior. However, at one time they were considered perfectly sound by quite reasonable people. Indeed, trivia buffs might be interested to learn that cornflakes owe their invention to a 19th-century physician, J. W. Kellogg, who believed that because the enjoyment of tasty food provoked sexual excitation, an alternative of "unstimulating" grains was needed.

Clearly, sex and sex-related behavior are influenced by expectations, attitudes, beliefs, and the state of medical and biological knowledge in a given period. Today we know that sexual behavior may take diverse forms, and much of what was once seen as "unnatural" and "lewd" is often more likely to be accepted in contemporary society. Similarly, sexual behavior that is commonplace in one culture is seen as appalling in others. For instance, seven societies are known in which kissing never occurs (Ford & Beach, 1951; Mason, 1995). In sum, distinctions between normal and abnormal sexual behavior are not easy to draw. This reality certainly hasn't prevented people from trying to draw them, however.

Key Concepts

What is "normal" sexual behavior?

How do most people behave sexually?

How prevalent are rape and other forms of nonconsenting sex, and what are their causes?

What are the major sexually transmitted infections?

What sexual difficulties do people most frequently encounter?

Times change: The veiled sexuality of Victorian-era paintings has given way to a more frank acknowledgment of sexual behavior.

Approaches to Sexual Normality

One approach is to define abnormal sexual behavior in terms of deviation from the average, or typical, behavior. To determine abnormality, we simply observe what behaviors are rare and uncommon in a society and label those deviations from the norm as abnormal.

The difficulty with such an approach, however, is that some behaviors that are statistically unusual hardly seem worthy of concern. Even though most people have sexual intercourse in the bedroom, does the fact that someone prefers sex in the dining room imply abnormality? If some people prefer portly sexual partners, are they abnormal in a society that holds slimness in high regard? As the answer to both of these questions is clearly no, an approach that defines sexual abnormality in terms of deviation from the average is inappropriate. (The same difficulties are encountered in considering definitions of psychological abnormality.)

An alternative approach would be to compare sexual behavior against some standard or ideal. But here, again, there is a problem: What standard should we use? Some of us might suggest philosophy, some might turn to the Bible, and some might even consider psychology the ultimate determinant. The trouble is that none of these potential sources of standards is universally acceptable. Furthermore, since standards change radically with shifts in societal attitudes and new knowledge, such an approach is undesirable. For instance, 40 years ago, the American Psychiatric Association labeled homosexuality a mental illness. However, as evidence to the contrary accumulated, in 1973 the organization determined that homosexuality should no longer be considered a mental disorder. Obviously the behavior had not changed. Only the label placed on it by the psychiatric profession had been modified.

In light of the difficulties with other approaches, probably the most reasonable definition of sexual normality is one that considers the psychological consequences of the behavior. In this approach, sexual behavior is considered abnormal if it produces a sense of distress, anxiety, or guilt—or if it is harmful to some other person. According to this view, then, sexual behaviors can be viewed as abnormal only when they have a negative impact on a person's sense of well-being or if they hurt someone else.

It is important to recognize that what is seen as normal and what is seen as abnormal sexual behavior are dictated primarily by societal values, and that there have been

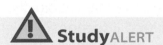

StudyALERT

Remember the different approaches to sexual normality (deviation from the average, comparison to a standard, and psychological consequences).

Same-sex marriages, already legal in Massachusetts and California, represent a significant social issue dividing people in the United States.

dramatic shifts from one generation to another in definitions of what constitutes appropriate sexual behavior. People can and should make their own personal value judgments about what is appropriate in their own sex lives, but there are few universally accepted absolute rights and wrongs.

Surveying Sexual Behavior: What's Happening Behind Closed Doors?

For most of recorded history, the vast variety of sexual practices remained shrouded in ignorance. However, in the late 1930s, biologist Alfred Kinsey launched a series of surveys on the sexual behavior of people in the United States. The result was the first comprehensive attempt to see what people were actually doing sexually, highlighted by the publication of Kinsey's landmark volumes *Sexual Behavior in the Human Male* (Kinsey et al., 1948) and *Sexual Behavior in the Human Female* (Kinsey et al., 1953).

Kinsey's efforts represented the first major systematic approach to learning about human sexual behavior. Kinsey and his colleagues interviewed tens of thousands of individuals, and the interview techniques they devised are still regarded as exemplary because of their ability to elicit sensitive information without causing embarrassment.

On the other hand, Kinsey's samples reflected an overrepresentation of college students, young people, well-educated individuals, urban dwellers, and people living in Indiana and the northeast (Kirby, 1977). Furthermore, as with all surveys involving volunteer participants, it is unclear how representative his data are of people who refused to participate in the study. Similarly, because no survey observes behavior directly, it is difficult to assess how accurately people's descriptions of what they do in private match their actual sexual practices.

Kinsey's work set the stage for later surveys, although because of political reasons (the use of government funding for sex surveys is controversial), surprisingly few comprehensive large-scale, representative surveys—either in the United States or in other countries—have been carried out since Kinsey did his initial work (Pinkerton et al., 2003). However, by examining the common results gleaned from different samples of subjects, we now have a reasonably complete picture of contemporary sexual practices—to which we turn next.

MASTURBATION: SOLITARY SEX

If you listened to physicians 75 years ago, you would have been told that **masturbation**, sexual self-stimulation, often using the hand to rub the genitals, would lead to a wide variety of physical and mental disorders, ranging from hairy palms to insanity. If those physicians had been correct, however, most of us would be wearing gloves to hide the sight of our hair-covered palms—for masturbation is one of the most frequently practiced sexual activities. Some 94 percent of all males and 63 percent of all females have masturbated at least once, and among college students, the frequency ranges from "never" to "several times a day" (Hunt, 1974; Michael et al., 1994; Laqueur, 2003, Polonsky, 2006).

Men and women typically begin to masturbate for the first time at different ages, as you can see in Figure 1. Furthermore, men masturbate considerably more often than women, although there are differences in frequency according to age. Male masturbation is most common in the early teens and then declines, whereas females both begin and reach a maximum frequency later. There are also some racial differences: African American men and women masturbate less than whites do (Oliver & Hyde, 1993; Pinkerton, Bogart, Cecil, & Abramson, 2002).

Although masturbation is often considered an activity to engage in only if no other sexual outlets are available, this view bears little relationship to reality. Close to three-quarters of married men (age 20 to 40) report masturbating an average

Masturbation: Sexual self-stimulation.

FIGURE 1 The age at which a sample of college students first masturbated. The percentages are based on only those people who had experience with masturbation. (Source: Arafat & Cotton, 1974.)

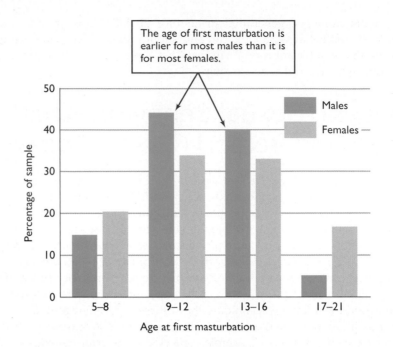

The age of first masturbation is earlier for most males than it is for most females.

of 24 times a year, and 68 percent of the married women in the same age group masturbate an average of 10 times a year (Hunt, 1974; Michael et al., 1994; Das, 2007).

Despite the high incidence of masturbation, attitudes toward it still reflect some of the negative views of yesteryear. For instance, one survey found that around 10 percent of people who masturbated experienced feelings of guilt, and 5 percent of the males and 1 percent of the females considered their behavior perverted (Arafat & Cotton, 1974). Despite these negative attitudes, however, most experts on sex view masturbation as a healthy and legitimate—and harmless—sexual activity. In addition, masturbation is seen as providing a means of learning about one's own sexuality and a way of discovering changes in one's body such as the emergence of precancerous lumps (Coleman, 2002; Levin, 2007).

Heterosexuality

Heterosexuality: Sexual attraction and behavior directed to the other sex.

People often believe that the first time they have sexual intercourse they have achieved one of life's major milestones. However, **heterosexuality**, sexual attraction and behavior directed to the other sex, consists of far more than male-female intercourse. Kissing, petting, caressing, massaging, and other forms of sex play are all components of heterosexual behavior. Still, the focus of sex researchers has been on the act of intercourse, especially in terms of its first occurrence and its frequency.

PREMARITAL SEX

Double standard: The view that premarital sex is permissible for males but not for females.

Until fairly recently, premarital sexual intercourse, at least for women, was considered one of the major taboos in our society. Traditionally, women have been warned by society that "nice girls don't do it"; men have been told that although premarital sex is okay for them, they should make sure they marry virgins. This view that premarital sex is permissible for males but not for females is called the **double standard** (Liang, 2007).

Although as recently as the 1960s the majority of adult Americans believed that premarital sex was always wrong, since that time there has been a dramatic change in public opinion. For example, as you can see in Figure 2, the percentage of middle-age people who say sex before marriage is "not wrong at all" has increased considerably,

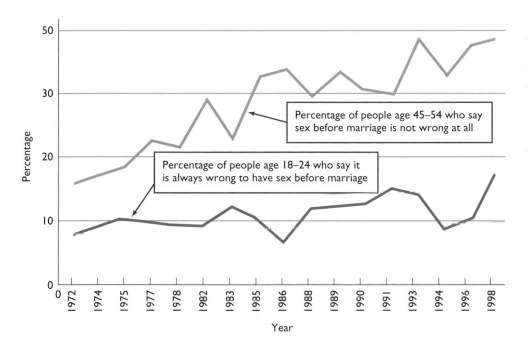

Percentage of people age 45–54 who say sex before marriage is not wrong at all

Percentage of people age 18–24 who say it is always wrong to have sex before marriage

FIGURE 2 The percentage of adults who find premarital sex is not wrong at all has risen dramatically over the last 25 years, whereas the percentage of adults who think premarital sex is always wrong has increased only slightly. (Source: Gallup Poll News Service, 1998.) What changes in society account for this shift in attitudes toward intercourse?

and overall 60 percent of Americans say premarital sex is okay. More than half say that living together before marriage is morally acceptable (C&F Report, 2001; Thornton & Young-DeMarco, 2001).

Changes in attitudes toward premarital sex were matched by changes in actual rates of premarital sexual activity. For instance, the most recent figures show that just over one-half of women between the ages of 15 and 19 have had premarital sexual intercourse. These figures are close to double the number of women in the same age range who reported having intercourse in 1970. Clearly, the trend over the last several decades has been toward more women engaging in premarital sexual activity (Jones, Darroch, & Singh, 2005).

Males, too, have shown an increase in the incidence of premarital sexual intercourse, although the increase has not been as dramatic as it has been for females—probably because the rates for males were higher to begin with. For instance, the first surveys of premarital intercourse carried out in the 1940s showed an incidence of 84 percent across males of all ages; recent figures put the figure at closer to 95 percent. Moreover, the average age of males' first sexual experience has been declining steadily. Almost half of males have had sexual intercourse by the age of 18, and by the time they reach age 20, 88 percent have had intercourse. There also are race and ethnicity differences: African Americans tend to have sex for the first time earlier than do Puerto Ricans, who have sex earlier than whites do. Racial and ethnic differences probably reflect differences in socioeconomic opportunities and family structure (Arena, 1984; Singh et al., 2000; Hyde, 2008).

What may be most interesting about the patterns of premarital sex is that they show a convergence of male and female attitudes and behavior. But is the change sufficient to signal an end to the double standard?

Probably. For many people, particularly younger individuals, the double standard has been succeeded by a new view: *permissiveness with affection*. According to those holding this view, premarital intercourse is permissible for both men and women if it occurs within a long-term, committed, or loving relationship (DeGaton, Weed, & Jensen, 1996; Hyde, 2008).

Still, the double standard has not disappeared completely. Where differing standards remain, the attitudes are almost always more lenient toward the male than toward the female (Sprecher & Hatfield, 1996).

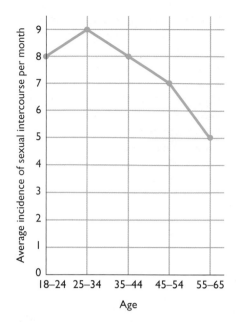

FIGURE 3 Once a couple is past their mid-thirties, the average number of times per month they have sexual intercourse declines (Clements, 1994). Why do older couples have intercourse less frequently than do younger ones?

Extramarital sex: Sexual activity between a married person and someone who is not his or her spouse.

Homosexuals: Persons who are sexually attracted to members of their own sex.

Bisexuals: Persons who are sexually attracted to people of the same sex and the other sex.

Furthermore, there are substantial cultural differences regarding the incidence and acceptability of premarital intercourse. For instance, the proportions of male teenagers who have intercourse before their 17th birthdays in Jamaica, the United States, and Brazil are about 10 times the level reported in the Philippines. And in some cultures, such as those in sub-Saharan Africa, women become sexually active at an earlier age than do men—although this may be due to the fact that they marry at a younger age than men do (Singh et al., 2000).

MARITAL SEX

To judge by the number of articles about sex in heterosexual marriages, one would think that sexual behavior was the number one standard by which marital bliss is measured. Married couples are often concerned that they are having too little sex, too much sex, or the wrong kind of sex (Harvey, Wenzel, & Sprecher, 2005).

Although there are many different dimensions along which sex in marriage is measured, one is certainly the frequency of sexual intercourse. What is typical? As with most other types of sexual activities, there is no easy answer to the question, because there are such wide variations in patterns between individuals. We do know that 43 percent of married couples have sexual intercourse a few times a month and 36 percent of couples have it two or three times a week. With increasing age and length of marriage, the frequency of intercourse declines. Still, sex continues into late adulthood, with almost half of people reporting that they engage in sexual activity at least once a month and that its quality is high (Michael et al., 1994; Powell, 2006; see Figure 3).

Although early research found **extramarital sex** to be widespread, the current reality appears to be otherwise. According to surveys, 85 percent of married women and more than 75 percent of married men are faithful to their spouses. Furthermore, the median number of sex partners, inside and outside of marriage, since the age of 18 for men was six, and for women, two. Accompanying these numbers is a high, consistent degree of disapproval of extramarital sex, with 9 of 10 people saying that it is "always" or "almost always" wrong (Michael et al., 1994; Allan et al., 2004; Daines, 2006).

Homosexuality and Bisexuality

Homosexuals are sexually attracted to members of their own sex, whereas **bisexuals** are sexually attracted to people of the same sex and the other sex. Many male homosexuals prefer the term *gay* and female homosexuals, the label *lesbian*, because they refer to a broader array of attitudes and lifestyles than the term *homosexual*, which focuses on the sexual act.

The number of people who choose same-sex sexual partners at one time or another is considerable. Estimates suggest that around 20 to 25 percent of males and about 15 percent of females have had at least one gay or lesbian experience during adulthood. The exact number of people who identify themselves as exclusively homosexual has proved difficult to gauge, with some estimates as low as 1.1 percent and some as high as 10 percent. Most experts suggest that between 5 and 10 percent of both men and women are exclusively gay or lesbian during extended periods of their lives (Hunt, 1974; Sells, 1994; Firestein, 1996).

Although people often view homosexuality and heterosexuality as two completely distinct sexual orientations, the issue is not that simple. Pioneering sex researcher Alfred Kinsey acknowledged this when he considered sexual orientation along a scale or continuum, with "exclusively homosexual" at one end and "exclusively heterosexual" at the other. In the middle were people who showed both homosexual and heterosexual behavior (see Figure 4). Kinsey's approach suggests that sexual orientation is dependent on a person's sexual feelings and behaviors and romantic feelings (Weinberg, Williams, & Pryor, 1991).

0	1	2	3	4	5	6
Exclusive heterosexual behavior	Primarily heterosexual, but incidents of homosexual behavior	Primarily heterosexual, but more than incidental homosexual behavior	Equal amounts of heterosexual and homo-sexual behavior	Primarily homosexual, but more than incidental heterosexual behavior	Primarily homosexual, but incidents of heterosexual behavior	Exclusively homosexual behavior

FIGURE 4 The Kinsey scale is designed to define the degree to which sexual orientation is heterosexual, homosexual, or bisexual. Although Kinsey saw people as falling along a continuum, most people believe that they belong to a specific category. (Source: From Kinsey, A. C., Pomeroy, W. B., & Martin, C. E. (1948). *Sexual behavior in the human male*, p. 638. Indiana University Press; originally published by W. B. Saunders Company, 1948. Reprinted by permission of The Kinsey Institute for Research in Sex, Gender, and Reproduction, Inc.)

What determines whether people become homosexual or heterosexual? Although there are a number of theories, none has proved completely satisfactory.

Some explanations for sexual orientation are biological in nature, suggesting that there are genetic causes. Evidence for a genetic origin of sexual orientation comes from studies of identical twins, which have found that when one twin identified him- or herself as homosexual, the occurrence of homosexuality in the other twin was higher than it was in the general population. Such results occur even for twins who have been separated early in life and who therefore are not necessarily raised in similar social environments (Hamer et al., 1993; Turner, 1995; Kirk, Bailey, & Martin, 2000; Gooren, 2006).

Hormones also may play a role in determining sexual orientation. For example, research shows that women exposed to DES, or diethylstilbestrol, before birth (their mothers took the drug to avoid miscarriage) were more likely to be homosexual or bisexual (Meyer-Bahlburg, 1997).

Some evidence suggests that differences in brain structures may be related to sexual orientation. For instance, the structure of the anterior hypothalamus, an area of the brain that governs sexual behavior, differs in male homosexuals and heterosexuals. Similarly, other research shows that, compared with heterosexual men or women, gay men have a larger anterior commissure, which is a bundle of neurons connecting the right and left hemispheres of the brain (LeVay, 1993; Byne, 1996).

However, research suggesting that biological causes are at the root of homosexuality is not conclusive because most findings are based on only small samples of individuals. Still, the possibility is real that some inherited or biological factor exists that predisposes people toward homosexuality, if certain environmental conditions are met (Veniegas, 2000; Teodorov et al., 2002; Rahman, Kumari, & Wilson, 2003).

Extensive research has found that bisexuals and homosexuals enjoy the same overall degree of mental and physical health as heterosexuals.

*"Frankly, I've repressed my sexuality so long I've
actually forgotten what my orientation is."*

Little evidence suggests that sexual orientation is brought about by child-rearing practices or family dynamics. Although proponents of psychoanalytic theories once argued that the nature of the parent-child relationship can produce homosexuality (e.g., Freud, 1922/1959), research evidence does not support such explanations (Isay, 1994; Roughton, 2002).

Another explanation for sexual orientation rests on learning theory (Masters & Johnson, 1979). According to this view, sexual orientation is learned through rewards and punishments in much the same way that we may learn to prefer swimming over tennis. For example, a young adolescent who had an unpleasant heterosexual experience might develop disagreeable associations with the other sex. If the same person had a rewarding, pleasant gay or lesbian experience, homosexuality might be incorporated into his or her sexual fantasies. If such fantasies are used during later sexual activities—such as masturbation—they may be positively reinforced through orgasm, and the association of homosexual behavior and sexual pleasure eventually may cause homosexuality to become the preferred form of sexual behavior.

Although the learning-theory explanation is plausible, several difficulties rule it out as a definitive explanation. Because our society has traditionally held homosexuality in low esteem, one ought to expect that the negative treatment of homosexual behavior would outweigh the rewards attached to it. Furthermore, children growing up with a gay or lesbian parent are statistically unlikely to become homosexual, thus contradicting the notion that homosexual behavior may be learned from others (Golombok, 1995; Victor & Fish, 1995; Tasker, 2005).

Because of the difficulty in finding a consistent explanation, we can't answer the question of what determines sexual orientation. It does seem unlikely that that any single factor orients a person toward homosexuality or heterosexuality. Instead, it seems reasonable to assume that a combination of biological and environmental factors is involved (Bem, 1996; Hyde, 2008).

Although we don't know at this point exactly why people develop a certain sexual orientation, one thing is clear: There is no relationship between sexual orientation and psychological adjustment. Gays, lesbians, and bisexuals generally enjoy the same quality of mental and physical health that heterosexuals do, although the discrimination they experience may produce higher rates of some disorders, such as depression (Poteat & Espelage, 2007). Bisexuals and homosexuals also hold equivalent ranges and types of attitudes about themselves, independent of sexual orientation. For such reasons, the American Psychological Association and most other mental health organizations have endorsed efforts to eliminate discrimination against gays and lesbians, such as revoking the ban against homosexuals in the military (Cochran, 2000; Perez, DeBord, & Bieschke, 2000; Morris, Waldo, & Rothblum, 2001).

Transsexualism

Transsexuals are people who believe they were born with the body of the other gender. In fundamental ways, transsexualism represents less a sexual difficulty than a gender issue involving one's sexual identity (Meyerowitz, 2004; Heath, 2006).

Transsexuals (like Tye Clark, whose story was discussed at the beginning of the chapter) sometimes seek sex-change operations in which their existing genitals are surgically removed and the genitals of the desired sex are fashioned. Several steps, including intensive counseling and hormone injections, along with living as a member of the desired sex for several years, precede surgery, which is, not surprisingly, highly

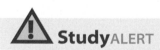

StudyALERT

The determinants of sexual orientation have proven difficult to pinpoint. It is important to know the variety of explanations that have been put forward.

Transsexual: Persons who believe they were born with the body of the other gender.

complicated. The outcome, though, can be quite positive (O'Keefe & Fox, 2003; Stegerwald & Janson, 2003; Lobato et al., 2006).

Transsexualism is part of a broader category known as transgenderism. The term *transgenderism* encompasses not only transsexuals but also people who view themselves as a third gender, transvestites (who dress in the clothes of the other gender), or others who believe that traditional male-female gender classifications inadequately characterize themselves (Prince, 2005; Hyde, 2008).

Sexual Difficulties

When sex—an activity that should be pleasurable, joyful, and intimate—is forced on someone, it becomes one of the ultimate acts of aggression and brutality, and few crimes produce such profound and long-lasting consequences. But sexual crimes are not the only category of serious problems related to sex. Few personal difficulties produce as much anxiety, embarrassment, and even shame as do sexually transmitted infections and sexual dysfunctions. We now turn to the major types of problems related to sex.

RAPE

Rape occurs when one person forces another person to submit to sexual activity such as intercourse or oral-genital sex. Although it usually applies to a male forcing a female, rape can be said to occur when members of either sex are forced into sexual activities without their consent.

Rape: The act by which one person forces another person to submit to sexual activity.

Most people think of rape as a rare crime committed by strangers. Unfortunately, they are wrong on both counts. In fact, rape occurs far more frequently than is commonly thought, and rapists are typically acquaintances of their victims. Although it is hard to obtain reliable estimates, most research suggests that there is a 14 to 25 percent chance that a woman will be the victim of a rape during her lifetime. Furthermore, more than 200,000 sexual assaults directed against women are reported to police in the United States each year. However, only about a third of rapes and sexual assaults are reported to police, so the actual figure is much higher (Wiehe & Richards, 1995; Catalano, 2006).

Furthermore, a national survey conducted at 35 universities revealed the startling finding that one out of eight female college students reported having been raped. Among the women who had been raped, about half said the rapists were first dates, casual dates, or romantic acquaintances—a phenomenon called **date rape**. Girls in high school also suffer both sexual and physical abuse: In one survey, 9 percent of 14- to 18-year-old girls said they had been forced into sexual activity by a date, and in more than half of those cases the incident had been accompanied by hitting, slapping, or shoving (Koss, 1993; Ackard & Neumark-Sztainer, 2002; Aiello, 2006).

Date rape: Rape in which the rapist is either a date or a romantic acquaintance.

Women in some segments of society are more at risk for rape than are others. Although the likelihood of sexual assault is considerably lower among Latino women in comparison to non-Latino white women, the rate for black women is slightly higher in comparison to white women. Such racial differences may stem from differing cultural views of women and male dominance (Koss, 1993; Black & Weisz, 2004).

Although on the surface it might appear that rape is primarily a crime of sex, other types of motivation also underlie the behavior. In many cases, the rapist uses sex as a means of demonstrating power and control over the victim. In such cases, there is little that is sexually satisfying about rape to the rapist; instead, the pleasure comes from forcing someone else to be submissive (Gowaty, 2003; Yamawaki, Darby, & Queiroz, 2007).

In other cases of rape, the primary motivation is anger. Sexual behavior is used to show the male rapist's rage at women in general, usually because of some perceived rejection or hurt that he has suffered in the past. Such rapes are likely to include physical violence and degrading acts against the victim.

Some rapes are based on a desire for sexual gratification. Some men hold the attitude that it is appropriate and desirable for them to actively seek out sex. To them, sexual encounters represent a form of "war" between the sexes—with winners and losers—and violence is sometimes considered an appropriate way to obtain what they want. According to their reasoning, using force to obtain sexual gratification is permissible (Malamuth et al., 1995; Hall, 1996; Mann & Hollin, 2007).

Finally, there is a common, although unfounded, societal belief that many women offer token resistance to sex, saying no to sex when they mean yes. If a man holds such a view, he may ignore a woman's protestations that she doesn't want sex (Anderson, Cooper, & Okamura, 1997; Yost & Zurbriggen, 2006).

The repercussions of rape are devastating for the victims. During a rape, women experience fear, terror, and physical pain. Later, victims report shock, disbelief, panic, extreme anxiety, and suspiciousness—reactions that are sometimes intensified by implications that somehow the victim was to blame because of her style of dress or her presence in the wrong neighborhood.

The psychological reactions to rape are no different whether it is date rape or rape by a stranger. These feelings may continue for years, even though the victim outwardly appears to have recovered. However, immediate psychological intervention, such as that provided by rape crisis centers, may be helpful in diminishing the long-term reactions to rape (Monnier et al., 2002; Zaslow, 2003; Ullman & Townsend, 2007).

CHILDHOOD SEXUAL ABUSE

One form of sexual behavior that is surprisingly common, yet little understood, is the sexual abuse of children. Although it is difficult to make accurate estimates of the true incidence of child sexual abuse, since most cases go unreported, experts estimate that each year a half million children are sexually abused. Between 5 and 10 percent of boys and 20 percent of girls will be abused at some point (Villarosa, 2002; Finkelor & Jones, 2004; see Figure 5).

Who commits child sexual abuse? In most cases it is a relative or acquaintance; in only about one-quarter of the cases is the abuse carried out by a stranger. The most vulnerable age for being molested is between 7 and 13 years old, and the abusers tend to be about 20 years older than their victims. In most instances, the abuser is a male heterosexual. Furthermore, there are increasing cases of child predators using the Web to make contact with potential victims (Wolfe, 1999; Finkelhor et al., 2005).

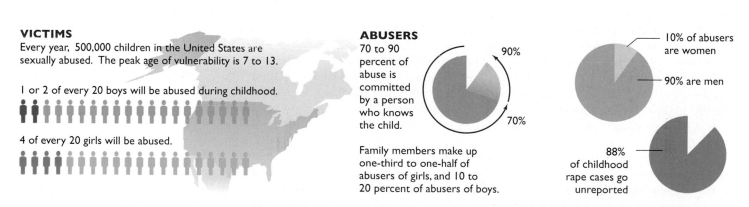

VICTIMS
Every year, 500,000 children in the United States are sexually abused. The peak age of vulnerability is 7 to 13.

1 or 2 of every 20 boys will be abused during childhood.

4 of every 20 girls will be abused.

ABUSERS
70 to 90 percent of abuse is committed by a person who knows the child.

90%
70%

Family members make up one-third to one-half of abusers of girls, and 10 to 20 percent of abusers of boys.

10% of abusers are women

90% are men

88% of childhood rape cases go unreported

FIGURE 5 Studies have found that the sexual abuse of children often is committed by a person who knows the child, with almost a third of the abusers being family members. (Source: Dr. David Finkelhor, University of New Hampshire.)

The short- and longer-term consequences of childhood sexual abuse can be extremely damaging. In terms of initial effects, victims report fear, anxiety, depression, anger, and hostility. Long-term effects may include depression, self-destructive behavior, feelings of isolation, poor self-esteem, and substance abuse. Although they may experience sexual difficulties later in life, the victims are not more likely to become sexual abusers themselves. Ultimately, the consequences of childhood sexual abuse are related to the specific nature of the abuse. Experiences involving fathers, genital contact, and the use of force are the most damaging (Hawke, Jainchill, & De Leon, 2000; Berliner & Elliott, 2002; Penza, Heim, & Nemeroff, 2006).

SEXUALLY TRANSMITTED INFECTIONS (STIs)

Millions of people suffer the discomfort—not to mention the psychological distress—of a **sexually transmitted infection (STI)**, a medical condition acquired through sexual contact. Estimates suggest that one in five people in the United States is infected with some form of STI, and at least one in four will probably contract an STI during their lifetimes. The United States has the highest rate of sexually transmitted infections of all the economically developed countries in the world, in part because people in the United States don't talk about sex as frankly or provide as much sex education as people in other developed nations do (see Figure 6; Centers for Disease Control and Prevention, 2000).

Sexually transmitted infection (STI): A disease acquired through sexual contact.

These are the major STIs:

- *Chlamydia.* The most widespread STI is *chlamydia*, a disease that in women initially produces no symptoms and in men causes a burning sensation during urination and a discharge from the penis. If it is left untreated, chlamydia can lead to pelvic inflammation, urethral damage, arthritis, and even sterility. There are almost 3 million new cases each year in the United States. Because it usually produces no symptoms in females, the Center for Disease Control recommends that sexually active women under age 26 be tested for the disease every year. Once diagnosed, chlamydia can be cured with antibiotics, most often azithromycin or doxycycline (Ku et al., 2002; CDC, 2004).

- *Genital herpes. Genital herpes* is a virus related to the cold sores that sometimes appear around the mouth. Herpes first appears as small blisters or sores around the genitals that later break open, causing severe pain. These sores heal after a few weeks, but the disease usually reappears, typically four or five times in the year following infection. Later outbreaks are less frequent, but the infection, which cannot be cured, often causes psychological distress for those who know they are infected. During the active phases of the disease it can be transmitted to sexual partners. Genital herpes is common among college-age students: around 17 percent of 20- to 29-year-olds have the infection (Farrell, 2005).

- *Trichomoniasis. Trichomoniasis* is an infection occurring in the vagina or penis. Caused by a parasite, it is often without symptoms, especially in men. Eventually, it can cause painful urination and intercourse, a discharge from the vagina, itching, and an unpleasant odor. The 5 million cases reported each year can be treated with antibiotics.

- *Gonorrhea. Gonorrhea* is one of the STIs that has been recognized the longest by scientists. Gonorrhea often has no symptoms but can produce a burning sensation during urination or a discharge from the penis or vagina. The infection can lead to fertility problems and, in women, pelvic inflammatory disease. Although antibiotics usually can cure gonorrhea, a number of drug-resistant strains of the disease are growing, making treatment more difficult.

- *Syphilis.* If untreated, *syphilis* may affect the brain, the heart, and a developing fetus, and can even be fatal. Syphilis first reveals itself through a small sore at

FIGURE 6 Estimates of the numbers of new cases annually of sexually transmitted infections in the United States. There are many more new cases of chlamydia each year than any other sexually transmitted infection. (Source: Centers for Disease Control and Prevention, 2003.)

the point of sexual contact. In its secondary stage, it may include a rash. Syphilis can be treated successfully with antibiotics if it is diagnosed early enough.

- *Genital warts.* Another common STI is *genital warts* (caused by the *human papilloma virus*). Genital warts are small, lumpy warts that form on or near the penis or vagina. The warts are easy to diagnose because of their distinctive appearance: They look like small cauliflower bulbs. They usually form about two months after exposure and can be treated with a drug called metronidazole.

- *AIDS.* In the last two decades, no sexually transmitted infection has had a greater impact on sexual behavior—and society as a whole—than **acquired immune deficiency syndrome (AIDS)**. Although in the United States AIDS at first was found primarily in gay men, it has spread to other populations, such as intravenous drug users and heterosexuals. In the United States, AIDS is the leading cause of death among men 25 to 44 years of age and the third leading cause of death among women in that age range. The worldwide figures are even more daunting: Already, 25 million people have died from AIDS, and people living with the disease number 33 million worldwide (Quinn & Overbaugh, 2005; UNAIDS, 2007).

> **Acquired immune deficiency syndrome (AIDS):** A sexually transmitted infection caused by a virus that destroys the body's immune system.

The spread of AIDS is particularly pronounced among women, who now comprise almost half the cases worldwide. The annual number of AIDS cases increased 15 percent among women, compared with 1 percent among men, between 1999 and 2003. Younger women and women of color are particularly vulnerable. For instance, the rate of AIDS diagnosis was around 25 times higher for African-American women than for white women, and four times higher for Hispanic women (Quinn & Overbaugh, 2005).

The extent of the AIDS epidemic has led to significant changes in sexual behavior. People are less likely to engage in "casual" sex with new acquaintances, and the use of condoms during sexual intercourse has increased. Nonetheless, the only foolproof method of avoiding AIDS is total abstinence—an alternative that many people find unrealistic. However, there are several ways to reduce the risk of contracting AIDS, as well as other sexually transmitted infections; these methods have come to be called "safer sex" practices (Carr, 2002):

- *Know your sexual partner—well.* Before having sex with someone, learn about his or her sexual history.

- *Use condoms.* For those in sexual relationships, condoms are the most reliable means of preventing transmission of the AIDS virus.

- *Avoid the exchange of bodily fluids, particularly semen.* In particular, avoid anal intercourse. The AIDS virus can spread through small tears in the rectum, making anal intercourse without condoms particularly dangerous. Oral sex, once thought relatively safe, is now viewed as potentially dangerous.

- *Stay sober.* Using alcohol and drugs impairs judgment and can lead to poor decisions—and it makes using a condom correctly more difficult.

- *Consider the benefits of monogamy.* People in long-term, monogamous relationships with partners who have been faithful are at a lower risk of contracting AIDS.

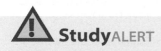

StudyALERT

Use Figure 6 to learn the major types of sexually transmitted infections and their prevalence.

SEXUAL PROBLEMS

Few people would feel embarrassed by a sprained ankle or broken arm. In contrast, sexual difficulties are often a source of concern and self-consciousness because of the importance that society places on "desirable" sexual conduct. And such difficulties are surprisingly common, with 43 percent of women and 31 percent of men experiencing problems associated with sexual performance. Among the most widespread are the disorders we discuss below (Laumann et al., 1999; Goldstein, 2000; Rosner, 2001).

Erectile dysfunction is the inability of a male to achieve or maintain an erection. The rare case is a male who has never been able to have an erection, and the more

> **Erectile dysfunction:** The inability of a male to achieve or maintain an erection.

common case is a male who, though now unable to have an erection, has had one at least once in the past. Erectile dysfunction is not an uncommon problem, even among younger men—about 5 to 10 percent of men under 50 have erection problems. It is the rare man who has never experienced it at least once during his lifetime. This is hardly surprising, because the ability to achieve and hold an erection is sensitive to alcohol, drugs, performance fears, anxiety, and a host of other factors. Erectile dysfunction becomes a more serious problem when it occurs more than occasionally (Mendelssohn, 2003; Peterson & Fuerst, 2007).

Drugs such as Viagra have brought about significant advances in the treatment of erectile dysfunction, as well as bringing the disorder into the open through a constant barrage of advertisements on television and in magazines. Viagra treats erectile dysfunction by increasing the flow of blood through a man's penis and producing an erection relatively quickly.

In **premature ejaculation**, a male is unable to delay orgasm as long as he wishes. Because "as long as he wishes" is dependent on a man's—and his partner's—attitudes and opinions about how long is appropriate, this is a difficult disorder to diagnose. Sometimes the problem can be resolved simply by having a male redefine how long he wants to delay ejaculation. Premature ejaculation is most often a psychological problem, as there are rarely physical reasons for it. One cause may be early sexual learning: Because sexual experiences during adolescence are often accompanied by a fear of being caught, some men learn early in their lives to reach orgasm as quickly as possible (Astbury-Ward, 2002; Barnes & Eardley, 2007).

Premature ejaculation: The inability of a male to delay orgasm as long as he wishes.

Inhibited ejaculation is the opposite problem. In this case, the male is unable to ejaculate when he wants to, if at all. Sometimes learning general relaxation techniques is sufficient to allow men to overcome the difficulty.

Inhibited ejaculation: The inability of a male to ejaculate when he wants to, if at all.

Some women experience **anorgasmia**, or a lack of orgasm. In *primary orgasmic dysfunction*, a woman has never experienced orgasm. In *secondary orgasmic dysfunction*, a woman has had an orgasm at some point but no longer does, or does so only under certain conditions—such as during masturbation but not during sexual intercourse. Because the lack of orgasm during sexual intercourse is so common (some one-third of women report they do not receive sufficient stimulation to reach orgasm during sexual intercourse), this state of affairs is not dysfunctional at all but is merely a normal variation of female sexuality.

Anorgasmia (an-or-GAZ-mee-uh): A female's lack of orgasm.

Finally, **inhibited sexual desire** occurs when the motivation for sexual activity is restrained or lacking entirely. When people with inhibited sexual desire find themselves in circumstances that typically would evoke sexual feelings, they begin to turn off sexually and may even experience a kind of "sexual anesthesia." Ultimately they may begin to avoid situations of a sexual nature, thereby forgoing intimacy with others (Meston, 2003; Hertlein, Weeks, & Gambescia, 2007).

Inhibited sexual desire: A sexual dysfunction in which the motivation for sexual activity is restrained or lacking entirely.

It is important to realize that many of the problems we have discussed turn up at one time or another in most people's sex lives. It is only when these problems persist, cause undue anxiety, and turn sex from play into work that they are cause for concern. Furthermore, treatments for common sexual problems have a good rate of success (Masters & Johnson, 1994; Rosner, 2001).

As we have seen, surveys of college women make clear that the greatest danger of rape comes not from some unknown assailant but from a fellow student. There are ways, however, to reduce the likelihood of date rape. The following suggestions provide some guidance for women and men (Shultz, Scherman, & Marshall, 2000; American College Health Association, 2006; Watkins, 2007):

BECOMING AN INFORMED CONSUMER

# of Psychology

Lowering the Risks of Date Rape

- Women should believe in their rights to set limits and communicate those limits clearly, firmly, and early on. They should say no when they mean no.

- Women should be assertive when someone is pressuring them to engage in an activity in which they don't want to engage. They should keep in mind that men may interpret passivity as permission.

- Women should be aware of situations in which they are at risk.

- Women should keep in mind the fact that some men interpret certain kinds of dress as sexually provocative, and that not all men subscribe to the same standards of sex as they do.

- Women should keep close tabs on what they are given to drink in social situations; victims of date rape have sometimes been given mind-altering— "date-rape"—drugs.

- Men should be aware of their dates' views on sexual behavior.

- Men should not hold the view that the goal of dating is to "score."

- The word *No* should be understood to mean no and not be interpreted as an invitation to continue.

- Men should not assume that certain kinds of dress or flirtatious behavior are an invitation to sex.

- Both men and women should understand that alcohol and drugs cloud judgment and hinder communication between them.

RECAP/EVALUATE/RETHINK

RECAP

What is "normal" sexual behavior?

- There are a number of approaches to determining normality: deviation from the average, comparison of sexual behavior with some standard or ideal, and consideration of the psychological and physical consequences of the behavior to the person and to others. (p. 372)

How do most people behave sexually?

- The frequency of masturbation is high, particularly for males. Although increasingly liberal, attitudes toward masturbation have traditionally been negative even though no negative consequences have been detected. (p. 373)

- Heterosexuality, or sexual attraction to members of the other sex, is the most common sexual orientation. (p. 374)

- The double standard by which premarital sex is thought to be more permissible for men than for women has declined, particularly among young people. For many people, the double standard has been replaced by endorsement of "permissiveness with affection," the view that premarital intercourse is permissible if it occurs in the context of a loving and committed relationship. (p. 374)

- The frequency of marital sex varies widely. However, younger couples tend to have sexual intercourse more frequently than older ones. In addition, most men and women do not engage in extramarital sex. (p. 376)

- Homosexuals are sexually attracted to members of their own sex; bisexuals are sexually attracted to people of the same sex and the other sex. No explanation for why people become homosexual has been confirmed; among the possibilities are genetic or biological factors, childhood and family influences, and prior learning experiences and conditioning. However, no relationship exists between sexual orientation and psychological adjustment. (p. 376)

How prevalent are rape and other forms of nonconsenting sex, and what are their causes?

- Rape occurs when one person forces another person to submit to sexual activity. Often the victim is acquainted with the rapist. The motivation for rape is only sometimes sexual gratification. More frequently it is power, aggression, or anger. (p. 379)

- Childhood sexual abuse is surprisingly widespread. Most often the perpetrator is an acquaintance or a family member. (p. 380)

What are the major sexually transmitted infections?

- Acquired immune deficiency syndrome, or AIDS, is bringing about profound changes in people's sexual practices. Other sexually transmitted infections include chlamydia, genital herpes, trichomoniasis, gonorrhea, syphilis, and genital warts. (p. 381)

What sexual difficulties do people most frequently encounter?

- Among the major sexual problems reported by males are erectile dysfunction, premature ejaculation, and inhibited ejaculation. For females, the major problem is anorgasmia, or a lack of orgasm. Both men and women may suffer from inhibited sexual desire. (p. 382)

EVALUATE

1. The work carried out by _____ in the 1930s was the first systematic study of sexual behavior ever undertaken.
2. Although the incidence of masturbation among young adults is high, once men and women become involved in intimate relationships, they typically cease masturbating. True or false?
3. The increase in premarital sex in recent years has been greater for women than for men. True or false?

4. _____ _____ _____ refers to the view that premarital sex is acceptable within a loving, long-term relationship.
5. Research comparing homosexuals and heterosexuals clearly demonstrates that there is no difference in the level of adjustment or psychological functioning between the two groups. True or false?
6. Which of the following is unlikely to be a motivation for the act of rape?
   a. Need for power
   b. Desire for sexual intimacy
   c. Desire for sexual gratification
   d. Anger against women in general
7. Which of the following STIs is the most widespread?
   a. Genital herpes
   b. Gonorrhea
   c. Chlamydia
   d. Syphilis

RETHINK

1. What societal factors have led to a reduction in the double standard by which sexuality in men and women is regarded differently? Do you think the double standard has completely vanished?
2. *From the perspective of a politician:* What responsibilities do people who learn they have a sexually transmitted infection have to their sexual partners, and what responsibilities do public health officials have? Should legislation be designed to restrict sexual behavior for those who have sexually transmitted infections?

Answers to Evaluate Questions

1. Kinsey; 2. false; even people in married relationships show a continued incidence of masturbation; 3. true; 4. permissiveness with affection; 5. true 6. b; 7. c

KEY TERMS

masturbation p. 373
heterosexuality p. 374
double standard p. 374
extramarital sex p. 376
homosexuals p. 376
bisexuals p. 376

transsexual p. 378
rape p. 379
date rape p. 379
sexually transmitted
   infection (STI) p. 381

acquired immune deficiency
   syndrome (AIDS) p. 382
erectile dysfunction p. 382
premature ejaculation p. 383
inhibited ejaculation p. 383

anorgasmia (an-or-GAZ-
   mee-uh) p. 383
inhibited sexual desire p. 383

Psychology on the Web

1. Find at least two recent news articles or discussions on the Web dealing with the issue of gender equality in school or the workplace, especially unequal treatment of individuals because of their gender. Summarize in writing what you found, and discuss your own attitudes toward this issue.
2. Find information on the Web about date rape, including guidelines or suggestions published by other colleges, for preventing rape among students. Summarize your findings, including recommendations for behavioral or policy changes that might be effective at your college. If your college's policies toward or publications about this topic could benefit from your findings, bring them to the attention of the appropriate office at your institution and suggest specific changes.

Epilogue

We have seen how the topics of gender and sex are dealt with by psychologists, first with regard to gender roles, gender stereotyping, gender schemas, and sexism. The expectations of society regarding male and female characteristics and behaviors lead to inequities in the treatment of men and women in school, the workplace, and the rest of society—inequities that largely favor men.

With regard to sexuality, we discussed the nature of the physical processes that surround sexuality and addressed the controversial issue of "normality" in sexual behavior. We saw the broad diversity of sexual behavior, and we discussed premarital sex and marital sex, as well as heterosexuality, homosexuality, and bisexuality. We also examined rape and other forms of nonconsenting sex, including childhood sexual abuse.

Finally, we looked at the sexual problems that people may have, including sexually transmitted infections and sexual dysfunctions. We explored the nature of these problems and discussed ways to treat and deal with them.

Before we turn to the subject of human development in the next few modules, return to the prologue of this chapter, concerning Tye Clark's sense that she is a boy trapped in a girl's body. Using your knowledge of gender and sex, consider the following questions:

1. Why might Tye's family, friends, and peers at school react negatively to her desire to become male?
2. Is Tye's tomboyish appearance and her taste for male activities sufficient to conclude that she is transgendered?
3. How is Tye's transgenderism different from lesbianism?
4. Might Tye simply grow out of her gender confusion and decide to remain female?
5. If Tye does decide to live out her life as a lesbian woman, what challenges and difficulties can she expect along the way?

Development

Key Concepts for Chapter 12

After meeting randomly through an Internet dating site, Danielle Link's and Glen Zilly's first date didn't go all that well. They felt that the chemistry just wasn't there.

But despite their initial lack of enthusiasm, they continued dating, and their relationship began to grow. They eventually fell in love.

But what they didn't know was that their first date was not their first encounter. They'd met initially as toddlers, being cared for by the same babysitter, Louise Hughes. They'd been together five days a week for years.

It was six months before Link and Zilly found out that they'd actually known each other as toddlers. Zilly's mother figured out the connection during a phone call with her daughter. "I was in love before this happened, but after finding this out, I realized our relationship was meant to be," said Link. (*People*, 2007, p. 18)

Looking Ahead

Although it's far from clear that Link's and Zilly's relationship was "meant to be," it does raise questions of whether and how their early experiences affected their relationship decades later. Their story also serves as an introduction to one of the broadest and most important areas of psychology, developmental psychology. Developmental psychology is the branch of psychology that studies the patterns of growth and change that occur throughout life. It deals with issues ranging from new ways of conceiving children to learning how to raise children most sensibly to understanding the milestones of life that we all face.

Developmental psychologists study the interaction between the unfolding of biologically predetermined patterns of behavior and a constantly changing, dynamic environment. They ask how our genetic background affects our behavior throughout our lives and whether our potential is limited by heredity. Similarly, they seek to understand the way in which the environment works with—or against—our genetic capabilities, how the world we live in affects our development, and how we can be encouraged to reach our full potential.

We begin by examining the approaches developmental psychologists use to study the environmental and genetic factors: the nature–nurture issue. Then we consider the very start of development, beginning with conception and the nine months of life before birth. We look at both genetic and environmental influences on the unborn individual and the way they can affect behavior throughout the remainder of the life cycle.

Next, we examine development that occurs after birth, witnessing the enormous and rapid growth that takes place during the early stages of life, and focusing on physical, social, and cognitive change throughout infancy, toddlerhood, and middle childhood. We then move on to development from adolescence through adulthood. We end with a discussion of the ways in which people prepare themselves for death.

Nature and Nurture: The Enduring Developmental Issue

How many bald, six-foot-six, 250-pound volunteer firefighters in New Jersey wear droopy mustaches, aviator-style eyeglasses, and a key ring on the right side of the belt? The answer is two: Gerald Levey and Mark Newman. They are twins who were separated at birth. Each twin did not even know the other existed until they were reunited—in a fire station—by a fellow firefighter who knew Newman and was startled to see his double, Levey, at a firefighters' convention.

The lives of the twins, although separate, took remarkably similar paths. Levey went to college, studying forestry; Newman planned to study forestry in college but instead took a job trimming trees. Both had jobs in supermarkets. One had a job installing sprinkler systems; the other installed fire alarms.

Both men are unmarried and find the same kind of woman attractive: "tall, slender, long hair." They share similar hobbies, enjoying hunting, fishing, going to the beach, and watching old John Wayne movies and professional wrestling. Both like Chinese food and drink the same brand of beer. Their mannerisms are also similar—for example, each one throws his head back when he laughs. And, of course, there is one more thing: They share a passion for fighting fires.

The similarities we see in twins Gerald Levey and Mark Newman vividly raise one of the fundamental questions posed by **developmental psychology**, the study of the patterns of growth and change that occur throughout life. The question is this: How can we distinguish between the *environmental* causes of behavior (the influence of parents, siblings, family, friends, schooling, nutrition, and all the other experiences to which a child is exposed) and *hereditary* causes (those based on the genetic makeup of an individual that influence growth and development throughout life)? This question embodies the **nature–nurture issue**. In this context, nature refers to hereditary factors, and nurture to environmental influences.

Although the question was first posed as a nature-*versus*-nurture issue, developmental psychologists today agree that *both* nature and nurture interact to produce specific developmental patterns and outcomes. Consequently, the question has evolved into *How and to what degree* do environment and heredity both produce their effects? No one grows up free of environmental influences, nor does anyone develop without being affected by his or her inherited *genetic makeup*. However, the debate over the comparative influence of the two factors remains active, with different approaches and different theories of development emphasizing the environment or heredity to a greater or lesser degree (Pinker, 2002; Gottesman & Hanson, 2005; Rutter, 2006).

For example, some developmental theories rely on basic psychological principles of learning and stress the role learning plays in producing changes in behavior in a developing child. Such theories emphasize the role of the environment in

Key Concept

How do psychologists study the degree to which development is an interaction of hereditary and environmental factors?

Developmental psychology: The branch of psychology that studies the patterns of growth and change that occur throughout life.

Nature–nurture issue: The issue of the degree to which environment and heredity influence behavior.

Gerald Levey and Mark Newman

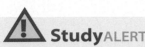

StudyALERT

The nature-nurture issue is a key question that is pervasive throughout the field of psychology, asking how and to what degree do environment and heredity produce their joint effects.

development. In contrast, other developmental theories emphasize the influence of one's physiological makeup and functioning on development. Such theories stress the role of heredity and *maturation*—the unfolding of biologically predetermined patterns of behavior—in producing developmental change. Maturation can be seen, for instance, in the development of sex characteristics (such as breasts and body hair) that occurs at the start of adolescence. Furthermore, the work of behavioral geneticists, who study the effects of heredity on behavior, and the theories of evolutionary psychologists, who identify behavior patterns that result from our genetic inheritance, have influenced developmental psychologists. Both behavioral geneticists and evolutionary psychologists have highlighted the importance of heredity in influencing human behavior (Buss, 2003; Reif & Lesch, 2003; Ilies, Arvey, & Bouchard, 2006).

Despite their differences over theory, developmental psychologists concur on some points. They agree that genetic factors not only provide the potential for specific behaviors or traits to emerge, but also place limitations on the emergence of such behavior or traits. For instance, heredity defines people's general level of intelligence, setting an upper limit that—regardless of the quality of the environment—people cannot exceed. Heredity also places limits on physical abilities; humans simply cannot run at a speed of 60 miles an hour, nor will they grow as tall as 10 feet, no matter what the quality of their environment (Pinker, 2004; Dodge, 2004).

Figure 1 lists some of the characteristics most affected by heredity. As you consider these items, it is important to keep in mind that these characteristics are not *entirely* determined by heredity, for environmental factors also play a role.

Developmental psychologists also agree that in most instances environmental factors play a critical role in enabling people to reach the potential capabilities that their genetic background makes possible. If Albert Einstein had received no intellectual stimulation as a child and had not been sent to school, it is unlikely that he would have reached his genetic potential. Similarly, a great athlete such as baseball star Derek Jeter would have been unlikely to display much physical skill if he had not been raised in an environment that nurtured his innate talent and gave him the opportunity to train and perfect his natural abilities.

Clearly, the relationship between heredity and environment is far from simple. As a consequence, developmental psychologists typically take an *interactionist* position on the nature–nurture issue, suggesting that a combination of hereditary and environmental factors influences development. Developmental psychologists face the challenge of identifying the relative strength of each of these influences on the individual, as well as that of identifying the specific changes that occur over the course of development (McGregor & Capone, 2004; Moffitt, Caspi, & Rutter, 2006).

FIGURE 1 Characteristics influenced significantly by genetic factors. Although these characteristics have strong genetic components, they are also affected by environmental factors.

Physical Characteristics	Intellectual Characteristics	Emotional Characteristics and Disorders
Height	Memory	Shyness
Weight	Intelligence	Extraversion
Obesity	Age of language acquisition	Emotionality
Tone of voice	Reading disability	Neuroticism
Blood pressure	Mental retardation	Schizophrenia
Tooth decay		Anxiety
Athletic ability		Alcoholism
Firmness of handshake		
Age of death		
Activity level		

Determining the Relative Influence of Nature and Nurture

Developmental psychologists use several approaches to determine the relative influence of genetic and environmental factors on behavior. In one approach, researchers can experimentally control the genetic makeup of laboratory animals by carefully breeding them for specific traits. For instance, by observing animals with identical genetic backgrounds placed in varied environments, researchers can learn the effects of specific kinds of environmental stimulation. Although researchers must be careful when generalizing the findings of non-human research to a human population, findings from animal research provide important information that cannot be obtained, for ethical reasons, by using human participants.

Human twins serve as another important source of information about the relative effects of genetic and environmental factors. If **identical twins** (those who are genetically identical) display different patterns of development, those differences have to be attributed to variations in the environment in which the twins were raised. The most useful data come from identical twins (such as Gerald Levey and Mark Newman) who are adopted at birth by different sets of adoptive parents and raised apart in differing environments. Studies of nontwin siblings who are raised in totally different environments also shed some light on the issue. Because they have relatively similar genetic backgrounds, siblings who show similarities as adults provide strong evidence for the importance of heredity (Gottesman, 1997; Sternberg, 2002a).

Researchers can also take the opposite tack. Instead of concentrating on people with similar genetic backgrounds who are raised in different environments, they may consider people raised in similar environments who have totally dissimilar genetic backgrounds. If they find, for example, similar courses of development in two adopted children who have different genetic backgrounds and have been raised in the same family, they have evidence for the importance of environmental influences on development. Moreover, psychologists can carry out research involving animals with dissimilar genetic backgrounds; by experimentally varying the environment in which they are raised, they can determine the influence of environmental factors (independent of heredity) on development (Petrill & Deater-Deckard, 2004).

Identical twins: Twins who are genetically identical.

Developmental Research Techniques

Because of the demands of measuring behavioral change across different ages, developmental researchers use several unique methods. The most frequently used, **cross-sectional research**, compares people of different ages at the same point in time. Cross-sectional studies provide information about differences in development between different age groups (Creasey, 2005; Huijie, 2006).

Suppose, for instance, we were interested in the development of intellectual ability in adulthood. To carry out a cross-sectional study, we might compare a sample of 25, 45, and 65 year olds who all take the same IQ test. We then can determine whether average IQ test scores differ in each age group.

Cross-sectional research has limitations, however. For instance, we cannot be sure that the differences in IQ scores we might find in our example are due to age differences alone. Instead, the scores may reflect differences in the educational attainment of the cohorts represented. A *cohort* is a group of people who grow up at similar times, in similar places, and in similar conditions. In the case of IQ differences, any age differences we find in a cross-sectional study may reflect educational differences among the cohorts studied: People in the older age group may belong to a cohort that was less likely to attend college than were the people in the younger groups.

A longitudinal study, the second major research strategy used by developmental psychologists, provides one way around this problem. **Longitudinal research** traces

Cross-sectional research: A research method that compares people of different ages at the same point in time.

 StudyALERT

Be sure to be able to distinguish the three different types of developmental research—cross-sectional (comparing people of different ages at the same time); longitudinal (studying participants as they age); and sequential (a combination of cross-sectional and longitudinal).

Longitudinal research: A research method that investigates behavior as participants age.

the behavior of one or more participants as the participants age. Longitudinal studies assess *change* in behavior over time, whereas cross-sectional studies assess *differences* among groups of people.

For instance, consider how we might investigate intellectual development during adulthood by using a longitudinal research strategy. First, we might give an IQ test to a group of 25 year olds. We'd then come back to the same people 20 years later and retest them at age 45. Finally, we'd return to them once more when they were 65 years old and test them again.

By examining changes at several points in time, we can clearly see how individuals develop. Unfortunately, longitudinal research requires an enormous expenditure of time (as the researcher waits for the participants to get older), and participants who begin a study at an early age may drop out, move away, or even die as the research continues. Moreover, participants who take the same test at several points in time may become "test-wise" and perform better each time they take it, having become more familiar with the test.

Sequential research: A research method that combines cross-sectional and longitudinal research by considering a number of different age groups and examining them at several points in time.

To make up for the limitations in both cross-sectional and longitudinal research, investigators have devised an alternative strategy. Known as **sequential research**, it combines cross-sectional and longitudinal approaches by taking a number of different age groups and examining them at several points in time. For example, investigators might use a group of 3, 5, and 7 year olds, examining them every six months for a period of several years. This technique allows a developmental psychologist to tease out the specific effects of age changes from other possibly influential factors.

RECAP/EVALUATE/RETHINK

RECAP

How do psychologists study the degree to which development is an interaction of hereditary and environmental factors?

- Developmental psychology studies growth and change throughout life. One fundamental question is how much developmental change is due to heredity and how much is due to environment—the nature–nurture issue. Heredity seems to define the upper limits of our growth and change, whereas the environment affects the degree to which the upper limits are reached. (p. 391)

- Cross-sectional research compares people of different ages with one another at the same point in time. In contrast, longitudinal research traces the behavior of one or more participants as the participants become older. Finally, sequential research combines the two methods by taking several different age groups and examining them at several points in time. (p. 393)

EVALUATE

1. Developmental psychologists are interested in the effects of both _____ and _____ on development.

2. Environment and heredity both influence development, with genetic potentials generally establishing limits on environmental influences. True or false?

3. By observing genetically similar animals in differing environments, we can increase our understanding of the influences of hereditary and environmental factors in humans. True or false?

4. _____ research studies the same individuals over a period of time, whereas _____ - _____ research studies people of different ages at the same time.

RETHINK

1. When researchers find similarities in development between very different cultures, what implications might such findings have for the nature–nurture issue?

2. *From the perspective of a childcare provider:* Consider what factors might determine why a child is not learning to walk at the same pace as his peers. What kinds of environmental influences might be involved? What kinds of genetic influences might be involved? What recommendations might you make to the child's parents about the situation?

Answers to Evaluate Questions

1. heredity (or nature), environment (or nurture); 2. true; 3. true; 4. longitudinal, cross-sectional

KEY TERMS

Developmental psychology p. 391

Nature–nurture issue p. 391
Identical twins p. 393

Cross-sectional research p. 393

Longitudinal research p. 393
Sequential research p. 394

Prenatal Development: Conception to Birth

When Jennifer and Brian Buchkovich learned the results of a routine test carried out on their unborn infant, they were shocked and frightened. Their son, Ethan, had spina bifida, a birth defect involving an incompletely formed spinal cord. It's a disorder that typically leads to physical malformations, a lack of muscular control, and sometimes mental retardation. But there was one slim ray of hope: an experimental operation that could reduce the probability of the damage. The drawback, though, was that the risky surgery would have to be performed prior to birth, while Ethan was still in the womb. (*People Weekly*, 2000)

The Buchkoviches took the risk, and it appears to have paid off: Although Ethan has shown some developmental delays, he's just a bit behind schedule.

Our increasing understanding of the first stirrings of life spent inside a mother's womb has permitted significant medical advances like those that helped Ethan Buchkovich. Yet our knowledge of the biology of *conception*—when a male's sperm cell penetrates a female's egg cell—and its aftermath makes the start of life no less of a miracle. Let's consider how an individual is created by looking first at the genetic endowment that a child receives at the moment of conception.

Key Concepts

What is the nature of development before birth?

What factors affect a child during the mother's pregnancy?

The Basics of Genetics

The one-cell entity established at conception contains 23 pairs of **chromosomes**, rod-shaped structures that contain all basic hereditary information. One member of each pair is from the mother, and the other is from the father.

Each chromosome contains thousands of **genes**—smaller units through which genetic information is transmitted. Either individually or in combination, genes produce the particular characteristics of each person. Composed of sequences of *DNA (deoxyribonucleic acid)* molecules, genes are the biological equivalent of "software" that programs the future development of all parts of the body's hardware. Humans have some 25,000 different genes (see Figure 1).

Some genes control the development of systems common to all members of the human species—the heart, circulatory system, brain, lungs, and so forth; others shape the characteristics that make each human unique, such as facial configuration, height, and eye color. The child's sex is also determined by a particular combination of genes. Specifically, a child inherits an X chromosome from its mother and either an X or a Y chromosome from its father. When it receives an XX combination, it is a female; with an XY combination, it develops as a male. Male development is triggered by a single gene on the Y chromosome, and without the presence of that specific gene, the individual will develop as a female (see Figure 2).

As behavioral geneticists have discovered, genes are also at least partially responsible for a wide variety of personal characteristics, including cognitive abilities, personality traits, and psychological disorders. Of course, few of these characteristics are determined by a single gene. Instead, most traits result from a combination of multiple genes, which operate together with environmental influences (Plomin & McGuffin, 2003; Haberstick et al., 2005; Ramus, 2006).

Chromosomes: Rod-shaped structures that contain all basic hereditary information.

Genes: The parts of the chromosomes through which genetic information is transmitted.

StudyALERT

It's important to understand the basic building-blocks of genetics: chromosomes, which contain genes, which in turn are composed of sequences of DNA.

a. Conception

b. 23 pairs of chromosomes

c. DNA sequence

d. Genes

FIGURE 1 Every individual's characteristics are determined by the individual's specific genetic information. At the moment of conception (a), humans receive 23 pairs of chromosomes (b), half from the mother and half from the father. These chromosomes are made up of coils of DNA (c). Each chromosome contains thousands of genes (d) that "program" the future development of the body.

THE HUMAN GENOME PROJECT

Our understanding of genetics took a giant leap forward in 2001, when scientists were able to map the specific location and sequence of every human gene as part of the massive *Human Genome Project*. The accomplishment was one of the most important in the history of biology (International Human Genome Sequencing Consortium, 2001).

The success of the Human Genome Project is likely to produce a revolution in health care, as scientists identify the particular genes responsible for genetically caused disorders. It is already leading not only to the identification of risk factors in children, but also to the development of new treatments for physical and psychological disorders.

FIGURE 2 When an egg and a sperm meet at the moment of fertilization, the egg provides an X chromosome, and the sperm provides either an X or a Y chromosome. If the sperm contributes an X chromosome, the child will have an XX pairing on the 23rd chromosome and will be a girl. If the sperm contributes a Y chromosome, the result will be an XY pairing—a boy.

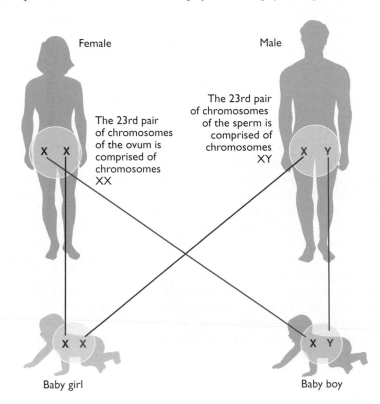

Female

Male

The 23rd pair of chromosomes of the ovum is comprised of chromosomes XX

The 23rd pair of chromosomes of the sperm is comprised of chromosomes XY

X X

X Y

X X

X Y

Baby girl

Baby boy

For example, in *gene therapy*, health-care providers inject genes to correct particular diseases directly into a patient's bloodstream. When the gene arrives at the location of a problem (or potential problem), it leads the body to produce chemicals that can alleviate the danger. In other cases, additional genes are inserted that replace missing or defective cells. Eventually, it also may be possible to "harvest" defective cells from a child prior to birth. These cells could be treated by gene therapy and reintroduced into the unborn child, thereby repairing the defect (Lymberis et al., 2004; Sato et al., 2007).

Although the promise of gene therapy is real, the number of diseases that can be treated today is actually fairly limited. Furthermore, the long-term success of gene therapy remains unknown. In fact, after they initially seem to be cured, some recipients of gene therapy have relapsed, and some have suffered from unpleasant side effects. Still, the potential uses of gene therapy are growing rapidly. For example, such disorders as AIDS, cancer, rheumatoid arthritis, and macular degeneration are strong candidates for the procedure (Chisholm et al., 2007; Feret et al., 2007; Rossi, June, & Kohn, 2007).

The complex sequence of genes can be harnessed in gene therapy, in which genes are used to correct health problems.

The Earliest Development

When an egg becomes fertilized by the sperm, the resulting one-celled entity, called a **zygote**, immediately begins to develop. The zygote starts out as a microscopic speck. Three days after fertilization, though, the zygote increases to around 32 cells, and within a week it has grown to 100–150 cells. These first two weeks are known as the *germinal period*.

Zygote: The new cell formed by the union of an egg and sperm.

Two weeks after conception, the developing individual enters the *embryonic period*, which lasts from week 2 through week 8, and he or she is now called an **embryo**. As an embryo develops through an intricate, preprogrammed process of cell division, it grows 10,000 times larger by 4 weeks of age, attaining a length of about one-fifth of an inch. At this point it has developed a rudimentary beating heart, a brain, an intestinal tract, and a number of other organs. Although all these organs are at a primitive stage of development, they are clearly recognizable. Moreover, by week 8, the embryo is about an inch long, and has discernible arms and legs and a face.

Embryo: A developed zygote that has a heart, a brain, and other organs.

From week 8 and continuing until birth, the developing individual enters the *fetal period* and is called a **fetus**. At the start of this period, it begins to be responsive to touch; it bends its fingers when touched on the hand. At 16 to 18 weeks, its movements become strong enough for the mother to sense them. At the same time, hair may begin to grow on the fetus's head, and the facial features become similar to those the child will display

Fetus: A developing individual, from eight weeks after conception until birth.

These remarkable photos of live fetuses display the degree of physical development at prenatal ages 4 and 15 weeks.

at birth. The major organs begin functioning, although the fetus could not be kept alive outside the mother. In addition, a lifetime's worth of brain neurons are produced—although it is unclear whether the brain is capable of thinking at this early stage.

By week 24, a fetus has many of the characteristics it will display as a newborn. In fact, when an infant is born prematurely at this age, it can open and close its eyes; suck; cry; look up, down, and around; and even grasp objects placed in its hands, although it is still unable to survive for long outside the mother.

The fetus continues to develop before birth. It begins to grow fatty deposits under the skin, and it gains weight. The fetus reaches the **age of viability**, the point at which it can survive if born prematurely, at about prenatal age 22 weeks, although through advances in medical technology this crucial age is getting earlier. At prenatal age 28 weeks, the fetus weighs less than 3 pounds and is about 16 inches long. It may be capable of learning: One study found that the infants of mothers who had repeatedly read aloud the Dr. Seuss story *The Cat in the Hat* before the infants' birth preferred the sound of that particular story to other stories after they were born (Spence & DeCasper, 1982).

Before birth, a fetus passes through several *sensitive periods* (also referred to as *critical periods*). A sensitive period is the time when organisms are particularly susceptible to certain kinds of stimuli. For example, fetuses are especially affected by their mothers' use of drugs during certain sensitive periods before birth. If they are exposed to a particular drug before or after the sensitive period, it may have relatively little impact, but if exposure comes during a critical period, the impact will be significant (Konig, 2005; Werker & Tees, 2005; Uylings, 2006).

Sensitive periods can also occur after birth. Some language specialists suggest, for instance, that there is a period in which children are particularly receptive to developing language. If children are not exposed to appropriate linguistic stimuli, their language development may be impaired (Innocenti, 2007; Sohr-Preston & Scaramella, 2007).

In the final weeks of pregnancy, the fetus continues to gain weight and grow. At the end of the normal 38 weeks of pregnancy, the fetus typically weighs 7 pounds and is about 20 inches in length. However, the story is different for *preterm infants*, who are born before week 38. Because they have not been able to develop fully, they are at higher risk for illness, future problems, and even death. For infants who have been in the womb for more than 30 weeks, the prospects are relatively good. However, for those born before week 30, the story is often less positive. Such newborns, who may weigh as little as 2 pounds at birth, are in grave danger because they have immature organs; they have less than a 50-50 chance of survival. If they do survive—and it takes extraordinarily heroic (and expensive) medical intervention to assure this—they may later experience significant developmental delays.

GENETIC INFLUENCES ON THE FETUS

The process of fetal growth that we have just described reflects normal development, which occurs in 95 to 98 percent of all pregnancies. Some individuals are less fortunate, for in the remaining 2 to 5 percent of cases, children are born with serious birth defects. A major cause of such defects is faulty genes or chromosomes. Here are some of the more common genetic and chromosomal difficulties.

- *Phenylketonuria (PKU).* A child born with the inherited disease phenylketonuria cannot produce an enzyme that is required for normal development. This deficiency results in an accumulation of poisons that eventually cause profound mental retardation. The disease is treatable, however, if it is caught early. Most infants today are routinely tested for PKU, and children with the disorder can be placed on a special diet that allows them to develop normally (Ievers-Landis et al., 2005; Christ et al., 2006).

- *Sickle-cell anemia.* About 10 percent of the African-American population has the possibility of passing on sickle-cell anemia, a disease that gets its name from

Age of viability: The point at which a fetus can survive if born prematurely.

StudyALERT

Critical (or sensitive) periods, which can occur before or after birth, are important because they indicate the time that organisms are particularly susceptible to damage that may affect them for the rest of their lives.

the abnormally shaped red blood cells it causes. Children with the disease may have episodes of pain, yellowish eyes, stunted growth, and vision problems (Taras & Potts-Datema, 2005; Selove, 2007).

- *Tay-Sachs disease*. Children born with Tay-Sachs disease, a disorder most often found in Jews of Eastern European ancestry, usually die by age 3 or 4 because of the body's inability to break down fat. If both parents carry the genetic defect that produces the fatal illness, their child has a one in four chance of being born with the disease (Leib et al., 2005).

- *Down syndrome*. Down syndrome, one of the causes of mental retardation, occurs when the zygote receives an extra chromosome at the moment of conception. Down syndrome is often related to the mother's age; mothers over 35 and younger than 18 stand a higher risk than other women of having a child with the syndrome (Roizen & Patterson, 2003).

PRENATAL ENVIRONMENTAL INFLUENCES

Genetic factors are not the only causes of difficulties in fetal development. Environmental influences—the *nurture* part of the nature–nurture equation—also affect the fetus. Some of the more profound consequences are brought about by **teratogens**, environmental agents such as a drug, chemical, virus, or other factor that produce a birth defect. Among the major prenatal environmental influences on the fetus are the following:

Teratogens: Environmental agents such as a drug, chemical, virus, or other factor that produce a birth defect.

- *Mother's nutrition*. What a mother eats during her pregnancy can have important implications for the health of her baby. Seriously undernourished mothers cannot provide adequate nutrition to a growing fetus, and they are likely to give birth to underweight babies. Poorly nourished babies are also more susceptible to disease, and a lack of nourishment may have an adverse impact on their mental development (Adams & Parker, 1990; Ricciuti, 1993; Sigman, 1995; Zigler, Finn-Stevenson, & Hall, 2002; Najman et al., 2004).

- *Mother's illness*. Several diseases that have a relatively minor effect on the health of a mother can have devastating consequences for a developing fetus if they are contracted during the early part of a pregnancy. For example, rubella (German measles), syphilis, diabetes, and high blood pressure may each produce a permanent effect on the fetus. The virus that causes AIDS can also be passed from mother to child before birth, as well as through breast-feeding after birth (Nesheim et al., 2004; Magoni et al., 2005).

- *Mother's emotional state*. A mother's emotional state affects her baby. Mothers who are anxious and tense during the last months of their pregnancies are more apt to have irritable infants who sleep and eat poorly. The reason? The autonomic nervous system of the fetus becomes especially sensitive as a result of chemical changes produced by the mother's emotional state (Relier, 2001; Hollins, 2007).

- *Mother's use of drugs*. Mothers who take illegal, physically addictive drugs such as cocaine run the risk of giving birth to babies who are similarly addicted. Their newborns suffer painful withdrawal symptoms and sometimes show permanent physical and mental impairment as well. Even legal drugs taken by a pregnant woman (who may not know that she has become pregnant) can have a tragic effect (Ikonomidou et al, 2000; Schecter, Finkelstein, & Koren, 2005).

- *Alcohol*. Alcohol is extremely dangerous to fetal development. For example, 1 out of every 750 infants is born with *fetal alcohol syndrome* (*FAS*), a condition resulting in below-average intelligence, growth delays, and facial deformities. FAS is now the primary preventable cause of mental retardation. Even mothers who use small amounts of alcohol during pregnancy place their child at risk. *Fetal alcohol effects* (*FAE*) is a condition in which children display some, although not all, of the problems of FAS due to their mother's consumption of alcohol during pregnancy (Wass, Mattson, & Riley, 2004; Henderson, Kesmodel, & Gray, 2007; Niccools, 2007).

- *Nicotine use*. Pregnant mothers who smoke put their children at considerable risk. Smoking by pregnant women leads to more than 100,000 miscarriages and the deaths of over 5,000 babies in the United States alone each year (Haslam & Lawrence, 2004).

Several other environmental factors have an impact on the child before and during birth (see Figure 3). Keep in mind, however, that although we have been discussing the influences of genetics and environment separately, neither factor works alone. Furthermore, despite the emphasis here on some of the ways in which development can go wrong, the vast majority of births occur without difficulty. And in most instances, subsequent development also proceeds normally.

ALTERNATIVE PATHS TO CONCEPTION

For most couples, conception is routine, and pregnancy unfolds without incident. In other cases, though, conception represents a major challenge. Sometimes it results because the male produces too few sperm. In other cases, the inability to become pregnant, known as infertility, is due to the advanced age of the parents, use of drugs, or previous cases of sexually transmitted disease.

Scientists have devised several remedies to overcome infertility. One option is *in vitro fertilization (IVF)*. In vitro fertilization is a procedure in which a woman's eggs are removed from her ovaries, and a man's sperm is used to fertilize the eggs in a laboratory. A fertilized egg is then implanted in a woman's uterus. Similarly, *gamete intrafallopian transfer (GIFT)* and *zygote intrafallopian transfer (ZIFT)* are procedures in which an egg and sperm or fertilized egg are implanted in a woman's fallopian tubes. In IVF, GIFT, and ZIFT, the fertilized egg typically is implanted in the woman who provided the eggs. In some cases, eggs are implanted in a *surrogate mother*, a woman who agrees to carry the child to term.

FIGURE 3 A variety of environmental factors can play a role in prenatal development.

Environmental Factor	Possible Effect on Prenatal Development
Rubella (German measles)	Blindness, deafness, heart abnormalities, stillbirth
Syphilis	Mental retardation, physical deformities, maternal miscarriage
Addictive drugs	Low birth weight, addiction of infant to drug, with possible death after birth from withdrawal
Nicotine	Premature birth, low birth weight and length
Alcohol	Mental retardation, lower-than-average birth weight, small head, limb deformities
Radiation from X rays	Physical deformities, mental retardation
Inadequate diet	Reduction in growth of brain, smaller-than-average weight and length at birth
Mother's age—younger than 18 at birth of child	Premature birth, increased incidence of Down syndrome
Mother's age—older than 35 at birth of child	Increased incidence of Down syndrome
DES (diethylstilbestrol)	Reproductive difficulties and increased incidence of genital cancer in children of mothers who were given DES during pregnancy to prevent miscarriage
AIDS	Possible spread of AIDS virus to infant; facial deformities; growth failure
Accutane	Mental retardation and physical deformities

RECAP/EVALUATE/RETHINK

RECAP

What is the nature of development before birth?

- Each chromosome contains genes, through which genetic information is transmitted. Genes, which are composed of DNA sequences, are the "software" that programs the future development of the body's hardware. (p. 395)

- Genes affect not only physical attributes but also a wide array of personal characteristics such as cognitive abilities, personality traits, and psychological disorders. (p. 395)

- At the moment of conception, a male's sperm cell and a female's egg cell unite, with each contributing to the new individual's genetic makeup. The union of sperm and egg produces a zygote, which contains 23 pairs of chromosomes—with one member of each pair coming from the father and the other coming from the mother. (p. 397)

- After two weeks the zygote becomes an embryo. By week 8, the embryo is called a fetus and is responsive to touch and other stimulation. At about week 22 it reaches the age of viability, which means it may survive if born prematurely. A fetus is normally born after 38 weeks of pregnancy, weighing around 7 pounds and measuring about 20 inches. (p. 397)

What factors can affect a child during the mother's pregnancy?

- Genetic abnormalities produce birth defects such as phenylketonuria (PKU), sickle-cell anemia, Tay-Sachs disease, and Down syndrome. (p. 398)

- Among the environmental influences on fetal growth are the mother's nutrition, illnesses, and drug intake. (p. 399)

EVALUATE

1. Match each of the following terms with its definition:
   1. Zygote
   2. Gene
   3. Chromosome
   a. Smallest unit through which genetic information is passed
   b. Fertilized egg
   c. Rod-shaped structure containing genetic information
2. Specific kinds of growth must take place during a _____ period if the embryo is to develop normally.
3. A _____ is an environmental agent such as a drug, chemical, virus, or other factor that produces a birth defect.

RETHINK

1. Given the possible effects of the environment on a developing fetus, do you think pregnant women should be prosecuted for the use of alcohol and other drugs that may do serious harm to their unborn children? Defend your position.
2. *From the perspective of an educator:* How would you utilize your knowledge of sensitive periods in language development to improve students' learning? Would you want to teach children more than one language during this time?

Answers to Evaluate Questions

1. 1-b, 2-a, 3-c; 2. critical; 3. teratogen

KEY TERMS

chromosomes p. 395   zygote p. 397   fetus p. 397   teratogens p. 399
genes p. 395   embryo p. 397   age of viability p. 398

Infancy and Childhood

His head was molded into a long melon shape and came to a point at the back , . . . He was covered with a thick greasy white material known as "vernix," which made him slippery to hold, and also allowed him to slip easily through the birth canal. In addition to a shock of black hair on his head, his body was covered with dark, fine hair known as "lanugo." His ears, his back, his shoulders, and even his cheeks were furry . . . . His skin was wrinkled and quite loose, ready to scale in creased places such as his feet and hands . . . . His ears were pressed to his head in unusual positions—one ear was matted firmly forward on his cheek. His nose was flattened and pushed to one side by the squeeze as he came through the pelvis. (Brazelton, 1969, p. 3)

What kind of creature is this? Although the description hardly fits that of the adorable babies seen in advertisements for baby food, we are in fact talking about a normal, completely developed child just after the moment of birth. Called a **neonate**, a newborn arrives in the world in a form that hardly meets the standards of beauty against which we typically measure babies. Yet ask any parents: Nothing is more beautiful or exciting than the first glimpse of their newborn.

The Extraordinary Newborn

Several factors cause a neonate's strange appearance. The trip through the mother's birth canal may have squeezed the incompletely formed bones of the skull together and squashed the nose into the head. The skin secretes *vernix*, a white, greasy covering, for protection before birth, and the baby may have *lanugo*, a soft fuzz, over the entire body for a similar purpose. The infant's eyelids may be puffy with an accumulation of fluids because of the upside-down position during birth.

All these features change during the first two weeks of life as the neonate takes on a more familiar appearance. Even more impressive are the capabilities a neonate begins to display from the moment of birth—capabilities that grow at an astounding rate over the ensuing months.

REFLEXES

A neonate is born with a number of **reflexes**—unlearned, involuntary responses that occur automatically in the presence of certain stimuli. Critical for survival, many of those reflexes unfold naturally as part of an infant's ongoing maturation. The *rooting reflex*, for instance, causes neonates to turn their heads toward things that touch their cheeks—such as the mother's nipple or a bottle. Similarly, a *sucking reflex* prompts infants to suck at things that touch their lips. Among other reflexes are a *gag reflex* (to clear the throat), the startle reflex (a series of movements in which an infant flings out the arms, fans the fingers, and arches the back in response to a sudden noise),

Key Concepts

What are the major competencies of newborns?

What are the milestones of physical and social development during childhood?

How does cognitive development proceed during childhood?

Neonate: A newborn child.

Reflexes: Unlearned, involuntary responses that occur automatically in the presence of certain stimuli.

Many of the reflexes that a neonate is born with are critical for survival and unfold naturally as a part of an infant's ongoing maturation. Do you think humans have more or fewer reflexes than other animals?

StudyALERT

The basic reflexes—unlearned, involuntary responses—include the rooting reflex, the sucking reflex, the gag reflex, the startle reflex, and the Babinski reflex.

Habituation: The decrease in the response to a stimulus that occurs after repeated presentations of the same stimulus.

and the *Babinski reflex* (a baby's toes fan out when the outer edge of the sole of the foot is stroked).

Infants lose these primitive reflexes after the first few months of life, replacing them with more complex and organized behaviors. Although at birth a neonate is capable of only jerky, limited voluntary movements, during the first year of life the ability to move independently grows enormously. The typical baby rolls over by the age of about 3 months, sits without support at about 6 months, stands alone at about 11 months, and walks at just over a year old. Not only does the ability to make large-scale movements improve during this time, fine-muscle movements become increasingly sophisticated (see Figure 1).

DEVELOPMENT OF THE SENSES: TAKING IN THE WORLD

When proud parents peer into the eyes of their neonate, is the child able to return their gaze? Although it was thought for some time that newborns can see only a hazy blur, most current findings indicate that the capabilities of neonates are far more impressive. Although their eyes have a limited capacity to focus on objects that are not within a seven- to eight-inch distance from the face, neonates can follow objects moving within their field of vision. They also show the rudiments of depth perception, as they react by raising their hands when an object appears to be moving rapidly toward the face (Gelman & Kit-Fong Au, 1996; Maurer et al., 1999).

You might think that it would be hard to figure out just how well neonates can see, because their lack of both language and reading ability clearly prevents them from saying what direction the E on a vision chart is facing. However, researchers have devised a number of ingenious methods, relying on the newborn's biological responses and innate reflexes, to test perceptual skills.

For instance, infants who see a novel stimulus typically pay close attention to it, and, as a consequence, their heart rates increase. But if they repeatedly see the same stimulus, their attention to it decreases, as indicated by a return to a slower heart rate. This phenomenon is known as **habituation**, the decrease in the response to a stimulus

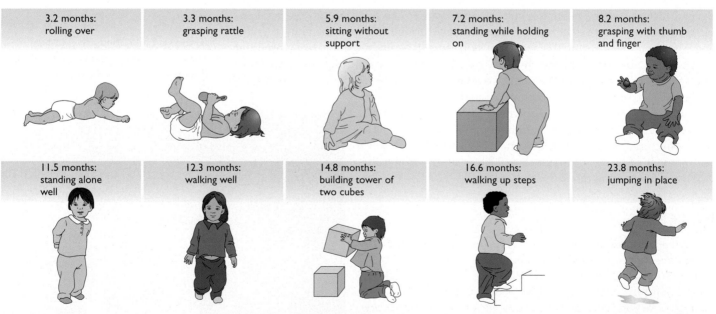

FIGURE 1 Although at birth a neonate can make only jerky, limited voluntary movements, during the first year of life the ability to move independently grows enormously. The ages indicate the time when 50 percent of children are able to perform each skill (Frankenburg et al., 1992). Remember, however, that the time when each skill appears can vary considerably. For example, 25 percent of children are able to walk well at age 11 months, and by 15 months 90 percent of children are walking well.

that occurs after repeated presentations of the same stimulus. By studying habituation, developmental psychologists can tell when a child who is too young to speak can detect and discriminate a stimulus (Gurnwald et al., 2003; Hannon & Johnson, 2005; del Rosal et al., 2006).

Researchers have developed many other methods for measuring neonate and infant perception. One technique, for instance, involves babies sucking on a nipple attached to a computer. A change in the rate and vigor with which the babies suck helps researchers infer that babies can perceive variations in stimuli. Other approaches include examining babies' eye movements and observing which way babies move their heads in response to a visual stimulus (George, 1999; Franklin, Pilling, & Davies, 2005).

Through the use of such research techniques, we now know that infants' visual perception is remarkably sophisticated from the start of life. At birth, babies prefer patterns with contours and edges over less distinct patterns, indicating that they can respond to the configuration of stimuli. Furthermore, even newborns are aware of size constancy, because they are apparently sensitive to the phenomenon by which objects stay the same size even though the image on the retina may change size as the distance between the object and the retina varies (Norcia et al., 2005; Moore et al., 2007).

In fact, neonates can discriminate facial expressions—and even imitate them. As you can see in Figure 2, newborns who see an adult with a happy, sad, or surprised facial expression can produce a good imitation of the adult's expression. Even very young infants, then, can respond to the emotions and moods that their caregivers' facial expressions reveal. This capability provides the foundation for social interaction skills in children (Meltzoff, 1996; Lavelli & Fogel, 2005; Grossman, Striano, & Friederici, 2007).

Other visual abilities grow rapidly after birth. By the end of their first month, babies can distinguish some colors from others, and after four months they can focus on near or far objects. By age 4 or 5 months they are able to recognize two- and three-dimensional objects, and they can perceive the gestalt organizing principles discovered by psychologists who study perception. By the age of 7 months, neural systems related to the processing of information about facial expressions are highly sophisticated,

FIGURE 2 This newborn infant is clearly imitating the expressions of the adult model in these amazing photos. How does this ability contribute to social development? (Courtesy of Dr. Tiffany Field.)

Neuroscience in Your Life

FIGURE 3 Using a procedure that measures event-related potentials (ERPs), the electrophysiological responses in the brain, researchers found that 7-month-old infants show distinct responses to happy, fearful, and neutral facial expressions in different regions of the brain. For example, approximately 400 milliseconds after seeing a fearful face (see arrow) infants show greater brain activity than when seeing either a neutral or happy face. (Source: Leppanen et al., 2007, Fig. 2.)

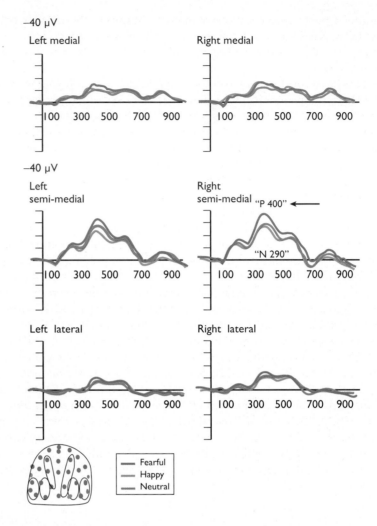

causing babies to respond differently to specific facial expressions (see Figure 3). Overall, their perceptual abilities rapidly improve: Sensitivity to visual stimuli, for instance, becomes three to four times greater at 1 year of age than it was at birth (Johnson, 2004; Striano & Vaish, 2006; Leppanen et al., 2007).

In addition to vision, infants display other impressive sensory capabilities. Newborns can distinguish different sounds to the point of being able to recognize their own mothers' voices at the age of 3 days. They can also make the subtle perceptual distinctions that underlie language abilities. For example, at 2 days of age, infants can distinguish between their native tongue and foreign languages, and they can discriminate between such closely related sounds as *ba* and *pa* when they are 4 days old. By 6 months of age, they can discriminate virtually any difference in sound that is relevant to the production of language. Moreover, they can recognize different tastes and smells at a very early age. There even seems to be something of a built-in sweet tooth: Neonates prefer liquids that have been sweetened with sugar over their unsweetened counterparts (Cohen & Cashon, 2003; Rivera-Gaxiola et al., 2005).

The Growing Child: Infancy Through Middle Childhood

It was during the windy days of March that the problem in the day care center first arose. Its source: 10-month-old Russell Ruud. Otherwise a model of decorum, Russell had somehow learned how to unzip the Velcro chin strap to his winter hat. He would remove the hat whenever he got the urge, seemingly oblivious to the potential health problems that might follow.

But that was just the start of the real difficulty. To the chagrin of the teachers in the day care center, not to speak of the children's parents, soon other children were following his lead, removing their own caps at will. Russell's mother, made aware of the anarchy at the day care center—and the other parents' distress over Russell's behavior—pleaded innocent. "I never showed Russell how to unzip the Velcro," claimed his mother, Judith Ruud, an economist with the Congressional Budget Office in Washington, D.C. "He learned by trial and error, and the other kids saw him do it one day when they were getting dressed for an outing." (Goleman, 1993a, C10)

At the age of 10 months, Russell asserted his personality, illustrating the tremendous growth that occurs in a variety of domains during the first year of life. Throughout the remainder of childhood, moving from infancy into middle childhood and the start of adolescence around age 11 or 12, children develop physically, socially, and cognitively in extraordinary ways. In the remainder of this module, we'll consider this development.

PHYSICAL DEVELOPMENT

Children's physical growth provides the most obvious sign of development. During the first year of life, children typically triple their birthweight, and their height increases by about half. This rapid growth slows down as the child gets older—think how gigantic adults would be if that rate of growth were constant—and from age 3 to the beginning of adolescence at around age 13, growth averages a gain of about 5 pounds and 3 inches a year (see Figure 4).

The physical changes that occur as children develop are not just a matter of increasing growth; the relationship of the size of the various body parts to one another changes dramatically as children age. As you can see in Figure 5 on page 409, the head of a fetus (and a newborn) is disproportionately large. However, the head soon becomes more proportional in size to the rest of the body as growth occurs mainly in the trunk and legs.

DEVELOPMENT OF SOCIAL BEHAVIOR: TAKING ON THE WORLD

As anyone who has seen an infant smiling at the sight of his or her mother can guess, at the same time that infants grow physically and hone their perceptual abilities, they also develop socially. The nature of a child's early social development provides the foundation for social relationships that will last a lifetime.

Attachment, the positive emotional bond that develops between a child and a particular individual, is the most important form of social development that occurs during infancy. The earliest studies of attachment were carried out by animal ethologist Konrad Lorenz (1966). Lorenz focused on newborn goslings, which under normal circumstances instinctively follow their mother, the first moving object they perceive after birth. Lorenz found that goslings whose eggs were raised in an incubator and which viewed him immediately after hatching would follow his every movement, as if he were their mother. He labeled this process *imprinting*, behavior that takes place during a critical period and involves attachment to the first moving object that is observed.

Our understanding of attachment progressed when psychologist Harry Harlow, in a classic study, gave infant monkeys the choice of cuddling a wire "monkey" that provided milk or a soft, terry-cloth "monkey" that was warm but did not provide milk. Their choice was clear: They spent most of their time clinging to the warm cloth "monkey," although they made occasional forays to the wire monkey to nurse. Obviously, the cloth monkey provided greater comfort to the infants; milk alone was insufficient to create attachment (Harlow & Zimmerman, 1959; Blum, 2002; see Figure 6 on page 409).

Building on this pioneering work with nonhumans, developmental psychologists have suggested that human attachment grows through the responsiveness of infants' caregivers to the signals the babies provide, such as crying, smiling, reaching, and

Attachment: The positive emotional bond that develops between a child and a particular individual.

 StudyALERT

Attachment—the positive emotional bond that develops between a child and a particular individual—is a key concept in understanding the social development of children.

FIGURE 4 The average heights and weights of males and females in the United States from birth through age 20. At what ages are girls typically heavier and taller than boys? (Source: National Center for Health Statistics, 2000.)

clinging. The greater the responsiveness of the caregiver to the child's signals, the more likely it is that the child will become securely attached. Full attachment eventually develops as a result of the complex series of interactions between caregiver and child. In the course of these interactions, the infant plays as critical and active a role as the caregiver in the formation of the bond. Infants who respond positively to a caregiver produce more positive behavior on the part of the caregiver, which in turn produces an even stronger degree of attachment in the child.

Assessing Attachment. Developmental psychologists have devised a quick and direct way to measure attachment. Developed by Mary Ainsworth, the *Ainsworth strange situation* consists of a sequence of events involving a child and (typically) his or her mother. Initially, the mother and baby enter an unfamiliar room, and the mother permits the baby to explore while she sits down. An adult stranger then enters the room, after which the mother leaves. The mother returns, and the stranger leaves. The mother once again leaves the baby alone, and the stranger returns. Finally, the stranger leaves, and the mother returns (Ainsworth et al., 1978; Izard & Abe, 2004; Combrink-Graham & McKenna, 2006).

Babies' reactions to the experimental situation vary drastically, depending, according to Ainsworth, on their degree of attachment to the mother. One-year-old children who are *securely attached* employ the mother as a kind of home base, exploring independently but returning to her occasionally. When she leaves, they exhibit distress, and they go to her when she returns. *Avoidant* children do not cry when the

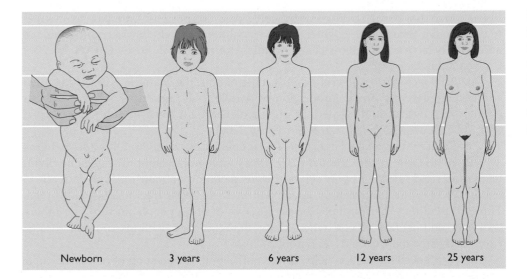

FIGURE 5 As development progresses, the size of the head relative to the rest of the body decreases until the individual reaches adulthood. Why do you think the head starts out so large? (Source: Adapted from W. J. Robbins, *Growth*, Fig. 5. Copyright © 1928 Yale University Press. Used by permission of Yale University Press.)

| Newborn | 3 years | 6 years | 12 years | 25 years |

mother leaves, and they seem to avoid her when she returns, as if they were indifferent to her. *Ambivalent* children display anxiety before they are separated and are upset when the mother leaves, but they may show ambivalent reactions to her return, such as seeking close contact but simultaneously hitting and kicking her. A fourth reaction is *disorganized-disoriented;* these children show inconsistent, often contradictory behavior.

The nature of attachment between children and their mothers has far-reaching consequences for later development. For example, children who are securely attached to their mothers tend to be more socially and emotionally competent than are their less securely attached peers, and others find them more cooperative, capable, and playful. Furthermore, children who are securely attached at age 1 show fewer psychological difficulties when they grow older compared with avoidant and ambivalent youngsters. As adults, children who are securely attached tend to have more successful romantic relationships. On the other hand, being securely attached at an early age does not guarantee good adjustment later, and, conversely, children who lack secure attachment do not always have difficulties later in life (Mikulincer & Shaver, 2005; Roisman et al., 2005; Hardy, 2007).

The Father's Role. Although early developmental research focused largely on the mother-child relationship, more recent research has highlighted the father's role in parenting, and with good reason: The number of fathers who are primary caregivers for their children has grown significantly, and fathers play an increasingly important role in their children's lives. For example, in almost 13 percent of families with children, the father is the parent who stays at home to care for preschoolers (Parke, 2004; Day & Lamb, 2004; Halford, 2006).

When fathers interact with their children, their play often differs from that of mothers. Fathers engage in more physical, rough-and-tumble sorts of activities, whereas mothers play more verbal and traditional games, such as peekaboo. Despite such behavioral differences, the nature of attachment between fathers and children compared with that between mothers and children can be similar. In fact, children can form multiple attachments simultaneously (Paquette, Carbonneau, & Dubeau, 2003; Borisenko, 2007; Pellis & Pellis, 2007).

Social Relationships with Peers. By the time they are 2 years old, children become less dependent on their parents and more self-reliant, increasingly preferring to play with friends. Initially, play is relatively independent:

FIGURE 6 Although the wire "mother" dispensed milk to the hungry infant monkey, the infant preferred the soft, terry-cloth "mother." Do you think human babies would react the same way? What does this experiment tell us about attachment? (Source: Harry Harlow Primate Laboratory/University of Wisconsin.)

Even though they may be sitting side by side, 2 year olds pay more attention to toys than to one another when playing. Later, however, children actively interact, modifying one another's behavior and later exchanging roles during play (Lindsey & Colwell, 2003; Colwell & Lindsey, 2005).

Cultural factors also affect children's styles of play. For example, Korean American children engage in a higher proportion of parallel play than their Anglo-American counterparts, while Anglo-American preschoolers are involved in more pretend play (Bai, 2005; Drewes, 2005; Suizzo & Bornstein, 2006).

As children reach school age, their social interactions begin to follow set patterns, as well as becoming more frequent. They may engage in elaborate games involving teams and rigid rules. This play serves purposes other than mere enjoyment. It allows children to become increasingly competent in their social interactions with others. Through play they learn to take the perspective of other people and to infer others' thoughts and feelings, even when those thoughts and feelings are not directly expressed (Royzman, Cassidy, & Baron, 2003).

In short, social interaction helps children interpret the meaning of others' behavior and develop the capacity to respond appropriately. Furthermore, children learn physical and emotional self-control: They learn to avoid hitting a playmate who beats them at a game, be polite, and control their emotional displays and facial expressions (e.g., smiling even when receiving a disappointing gift). Situations that provide children with opportunities for social interaction, then, may enhance their social development (Feldman, 1993; Lengua & Long, 2002; Talukdar & Shastri, 2006).

The Consequences of Child Care Outside the Home. Research on the importance of social interaction is corroborated by work that examines the benefits of child care out of the home, which is an important part of an increasing number of children's lives. For instance, almost 30 percent of preschool children whose mothers work outside the home spend their days in child-care centers. By the age of 6 months, almost two-thirds of infants are cared for by people other than their mothers for part of the day. Most of these infants begin child care before the age of 4 months and are cared for by people other than their mothers for almost 30 hours per week (NICHD Early Child Care Research Network, 2006; National Research Council, 2000; see Figure 7).

Do out-of-the-home child-care arrangements benefit children's development? If the programs are of high quality, they can. According to the results of a large study supported by the U.S. National Institute of Child Health and Development, children

FIGURE 7 According to a recent study by the National Institute of Child Health and Human Development, children were more likely to spend time in some kind of child care outside the home or family as they got older. (NICHD, 2006).

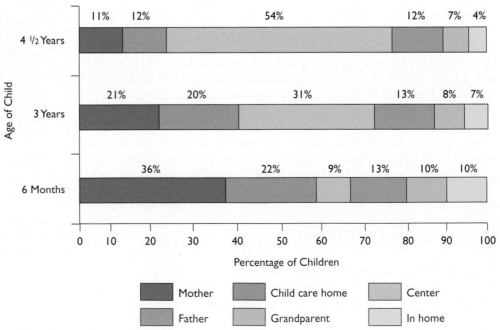

who attend high-quality child-care centers may not only do as well as children who stay at home with their parents, but in some respects may actually do better. Children in child care are generally more considerate and sociable than other children are, and they interact more positively with teachers. They may also be more compliant and regulate their own behavior more effectively, and their mothers show increased sensitivity to their children (NICHD Early Child Care Research Network, 1999, 2001).

In addition, especially for children from poor or disadvantaged homes, child care in specially enriched environments—those with many toys, books, a variety of children, and high-quality care providers—often proves to be more intellectually stimulating than the home environment. Such child care can lead to increased intellectual achievement, demonstrated in higher IQ scores, and better language development. In fact, children in care centers sometimes are found to score higher on tests of cognitive abilities than those who are cared for by their mothers or by sitters or home day-care providers—effects lasting into adulthood (Wilgoren, 1999; Burchinal et al., 2000).

However, outside-the-home child care does not have universally positive outcomes. Children may feel insecure after placement in low-quality child care or in multiple child-care settings. Furthermore, some research suggests that infants who are involved in outside care more than 20 hours a week in the first year show less secure attachment to their mothers than do those who have not been in outside-the-home child care. Finally, children who spent long hours in child care as infants and preschoolers may have a reduced ability to work independently and to manage their time effectively when they reach elementary school (NICHD Early Child Care Research Network, 1998, 2001; Vandellet et al., 2005; Belsky et al., 2007).

The key to the success of nonparental child care is its quality. High-quality child care produces benefits; low-quality child care provides little or no gain, and may even hinder children's development. In short, significant benefits result from the social interaction and intellectual stimulation provided by high-quality child-care centers—especially for children from impoverished environments (NICHD Early Child Care Research Network, 2000, 2002; National Association for the Education of Young Children, 2005; Zaslow et al., 2006).

Parenting Styles and Social Development. Parents' child-rearing practices are critical in shaping their children's social competence, and—according to classic research by developmental psychologist Diana Baumrind—four main categories describe different parenting styles (Figure 8). Rigid and punitive, **authoritarian parents** value

Authoritarian parents: Parents who are rigid and punitive and value unquestioning obedience from their children.

Parenting Style	Parent Behavior	Type of Behavior Produced in Child
Authoritarian	Rigid, punitive, strict standards (example: "If you don't clean your room, I'm going to take away your iPod for good and ground you.")	Unsociable, unfriendly, withdrawn
Permissive	Lax, inconsistent, undemanding (example: "It might be good to clean your room, but I guess it can wait.")	Immature, moody, dependent, low self-control
Authoritative	Firm, sets limits and goals, uses reasoning, encourages independence (example: "You'll need to clean your room before we can go out to the restaurant. As soon as you finish, we'll leave.")	Good social skills, likable, self-reliant, independent
Uninvolved	Detached emotionally, sees role only as providing food, clothing, and shelter (example: "I couldn't care less if your room is a pigsty.")	Indifferent, rejecting behavior

FIGURE 8 According to developmental psychologist Diana Baumrind (1971), four main parenting styles characterize child rearing.

Permissive parents: Parents who give their children relaxed or inconsistent direction and, although they are warm, require little of them.

Authoritative parents: Parents who are firm, set clear limits, reason with their children, and explain things to them.

Uninvolved parents: Parents who show little interest in their children and are emotionally detached.

StudyALERT

Know the four major types of child-rearing practices—authoritarian, permissive, authoritative, and uninvolved—and their effects.

Temperament: Basic, innate disposition.

unquestioning obedience from their children. They have strict standards and discourage expressions of disagreement. **Permissive parents** give their children relaxed or inconsistent direction and, although warm, require little of them. In contrast, **authoritative parents** are firm, setting limits for their children. As the children get older, these parents try to reason and explain things to them. They also set clear goals and encourage their children's independence. Finally, **uninvolved parents** show little interest in their children. Emotionally detached, they view parenting as nothing more than providing food, clothing, and shelter for children. At their most extreme, uninvolved parents are guilty of neglect, a form of child abuse (Baumrind, 2005; Winsler, Madigan, & Aquilino, 2005; Lagacé-Séguin & d'Entremont, 2006).

As you might expect, the four kinds of child-rearing styles seem to produce very different kinds of behavior in children (with many exceptions, of course). Children of authoritarian parents tend to be unsociable, unfriendly, and relatively withdrawn. In contrast, permissive parents' children show immaturity, moodiness, dependence, and low self-control. The children of authoritative parents fare best: With high social skills, they are likable, self-reliant, independent, and cooperative. Worst off are the children of uninvolved parents; they feel unloved and emotionally detached, and their physical and cognitive development is impeded. As we discuss in the *Applying Psychology in the 21st Century* box, children with low social skills face peer rejection that can have lasting results (Saarni, 1999; Snyder et al., 2005; Berk, 2005).

Before we rush to congratulate authoritative parents and condemn authoritarian, permissive, and uninvolved ones, it is important to note that in many cases nonauthoritative parents also produce perfectly well-adjusted children. Moreover, children are born with a particular **temperament**—a basic, innate disposition. Some children are naturally easygoing and cheerful, whereas others are irritable and fussy, or pensive and quiet. The kind of temperament a baby is born with may in part bring about specific kinds of parental child-rearing styles (Porter & Hsu, 2003; Lengua & Kovacs, 2005; Majdandzic & van den Boom, 2007).

In addition, children vary considerably in their degree of *resilience*, the ability to overcome circumstances that place them at high risk for psychological or even physical harm. Highly resilient children have temperaments that evoke positive responses from caregivers. Such children display unusual social skills: outgoingness, intelligence, and a feeling that they have control over their lives. In a sense, resilient children try to shape their own environment, rather than being victimized by it (Luthar, Cicchetti, & Becker, 2000; Deater-Deckard, Ivy, & Smith, 2005; Vellacot, 2007).

We also need to keep in mind that these findings regarding child-rearing styles apply primarily to U.S. society, which highly values children's growing independence and diminishing reliance on their parents. In contrast, Japanese parents encourage dependence to promote the values of cooperation and community life. These differences in cultural values result in very different philosophies of child rearing. For example, Japanese mothers believe it is a punishment to make a young child sleep alone; thus, many children sleep next to their mothers throughout infancy and toddlerhood (Kawasaki et al., 1994; Dennis et al., 2002; Jones, 2007).

In sum, a child's upbringing results from the child-rearing philosophy parents hold, the specific practices they use, and the nature of their own and their child's personalities. As is the case with other aspects of development, then, behavior is a function of a complex interaction of environmental and genetic factors.

Erikson's Theory of Psychosocial Development. In tracing the course of social development, some theorists have considered how the challenges of society and culture change as an individual matures. Following this path, psychoanalyst Erik Erikson developed one of the more comprehensive theories of social development. Erikson (1963) viewed the developmental changes occurring throughout life as a series of eight stages of psychosocial development, of

"Please, Jason. Don't you want to grow up to be an autonomous peson?"

The Sting and Stigma of Peer Rejection

Peer rejection can produce long-term psychological consequences.

> Mari, our 7-year-old, burst into tears while getting ready for school. Turns out she was upset because two girls had been making fun of her clothes and she was worried they'd find fault with that day's outfit. Mari had complained about the teasing before, and we'd assured her that it didn't matter what those girls said or thought. They were just mean and jealous and should be ignored. But clearly, to Mari, their words couldn't be dismissed. They cut her like a knife, and we hadn't really taken it seriously because there was no blood. Her tears moved us to action. (Millner, 2007, p. 47)

Peer rejection in schools and on playgrounds is long thought to be just another normal part of growing up. But in more recent years, tragic instances of violence in school have made national headlines and inspired a rethinking of the importance of positive peer interactions. For example, Seung-Hui Cho, the shooter responsible for the Virginia Tech massacre, was reported to have been withdrawn and isolated and was the victim of peer rejection (Adams & Russakoff, 1999; Banerjee, 2007).

However, the everyday consequences of peer rejection in school aren't nearly as dramatic as what happened at Virginia Tech. Most of the time, victims bear the harm quietly and alone. Ultimately, though, being rejected by peers may lead students to become withdrawn and to disengage from school, eventually suffering declines in academic achievement.

A recent longitudinal study of schoolchildren from 5 to 11 years old revealed how peer rejection can lead to academic declines. The researchers found that children who are less well liked by their classmates started becoming victims of mistreatment, including rejection and abuse. Children who received rejection became less likely to participate in classroom activities (Buhs, Ladd, & Herald, 2006).

The study also found that peer rejection preceded and contributed to withdrawal, leading to further exclusion and abuse. Moreover, peer rejection seemed to perpetuate itself. For instance, children who were disliked in kindergarten experienced sustained peer rejection and mistreatment into later years. For whatever reason, some children were liked less than others early on and were targeted for rejection. This rejection, in turn, acted as a signal to other peers that these children should be disliked. Essentially, the rejection followed the child like a black cloud, signaling to new peers in subsequent years that this was an unlikable individual who should be avoided or mistreated. This stigmatizing effect of rejection, together with the disengagement from classroom activities that it precipitates, fed into a cycle of withdrawal and exclusion.

The researchers concluded that although peer rejection may not be as dramatic as verbal or physical abuse, it is nevertheless psychologically painful. Ultimately, it may have an even stronger effect than actual physical abuse on children's participation in school and their subsequent academic achievement (Buhs, Ladd, & Herald, 2006).

- Why do you think some children are more prone to be rejected by their peers than others are?
- What can a peer-rejected child (or his or her parents) do to break the cycle of rejection?

which four occur during childhood. **Psychosocial development** involves changes in our interactions and understanding of one another as well as in our knowledge and understanding of ourselves as members of society.

Erikson suggests that passage through each of the stages necessitates the resolution of a crisis or conflict. Accordingly, Erikson represents each stage as a pairing of the most positive and most negative aspects of the crisis of that period. Although each crisis is never resolved entirely—life becomes increasingly complicated as we grow older—it has to be resolved sufficiently to equip us to deal with demands made during the following stage of development.

In the first stage of psychosocial development, the **trust-versus-mistrust stage** (ages birth to 1½ years), infants develop feelings of trust if their physical requirements and psychological needs for attachment are consistently met and their interactions with the world are generally positive. In contrast, inconsistent care and unpleasant interactions with others can lead to mistrust and leave an infant unable to meet the challenges required in the next stage of development.

Psychosocial development: Development of individuals' interactions and understanding of each other and of their knowledge and understanding of themselves as members of society.

Trust-versus-mistrust stage: According to Erikson, the first stage of psychosocial development, occurring from birth to age 1½ years, during which time infants develop feelings of trust or lack of trust.

Autonomy-versus-shame-and-doubt stage: The period during which, according to Erikson, toddlers (ages 1½ to 3 years) develop independence and autonomy if exploration and freedom are encouraged, or shame and self-doubt if they are restricted and overprotected.

Initiative-versus-guilt stage: According to Erikson, the period during which children ages 3 to 6 years experience conflict between independence of action and the sometimes negative results of that action.

Industry-versus-inferiority stage: According to Erikson, the last stage of childhood, during which children age 6 to 12 years may develop positive social interactions with others or may feel inadequate and become less sociable.

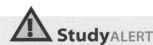 **Study**ALERT

Four of Erikson's stages of psychosocial development occur during childhood: trust-versus-mistrust, autonomy-versus-shame-and-doubt, initiative-versus-guilt, and industry-versus-inferiority.

Cognitive development: The process by which a child's understanding of the world changes as a function of age and experience.

In the second stage, the **autonomy-versus-shame-and-doubt stage** (ages 1½ to 3 years), toddlers develop independence and autonomy if exploration and freedom are encouraged, or they experience shame, self-doubt, and unhappiness if they are overly restricted and protected. According to Erikson, the key to the development of autonomy during this period is that the child's caregivers provide the appropriate amount of control. If parents provide too much control, children cannot assert themselves and develop their own sense of control over their environment; if parents provide too little control, the children become overly demanding and controlling.

Next, children face the crises of the **initiative-versus-guilt stage** (ages 3 to 6). In this stage, children's desire to act independently conflicts with the guilt that comes from the unintended and unexpected consequences of such behavior. Children in this period come to understand that they are persons in their own right, and they begin to make decisions about their behavior. If parents react positively to children's attempts at independence, they will help their children resolve the initiative-versus-guilt crisis positively.

The fourth and last stage of childhood is the **industry-versus-inferiority stage** (ages 6 to 12). During this period, increasing competency in all areas, whether social interactions or academic skills, characterizes successful psychosocial development. In contrast, difficulties in this stage lead to feelings of failure and inadequacy.

Erikson's theory suggests that psychosocial development continues throughout life, and he proposes four more crises that are faced after childhood (described in the next module). Although his theory has been criticized on several grounds—such as the imprecision of the concepts he employs and his greater emphasis on male development than female development—it remains influential and is one of the few theories that encompass the entire life span.

COGNITIVE DEVELOPMENT: CHILDREN'S THINKING ABOUT THE WORLD

Suppose you had two drinking glasses of different shapes—one short and broad and one tall and thin. Now imagine that you filled the short, broad one with soda about halfway and then poured the liquid from that glass into the tall one. The soda would appear to fill about three-quarters of the second glass. If someone asked you whether there was more soda in the second glass than there had been in the first, what would you say?

You might think that such a simple question hardly deserves an answer; of course there is no difference in the amount of soda in the two glasses. However, most 4 year olds would be likely to say that there is more soda in the second glass. If you then poured the soda back into the short glass, they would say there is now less soda than there was in the taller glass.

Why are young children confused by this problem? The reason is not immediately obvious. Anyone who has observed preschoolers must be impressed by how far they have progressed from the early stages of development. They speak with ease, know the alphabet, count, play complex games, use computers, tell stories, and communicate ably. Yet despite this seeming sophistication, there are deep gaps in children's understanding of the world. Some theorists have suggested that children cannot understand certain ideas and concepts until they reach a particular stage of **cognitive development**—the process by which a child's understanding of the world changes as a function of age and experience. In contrast to the theories of physical and social development discussed earlier (such as those of Erikson), theories of cognitive development seek to explain the quantitative and qualitative intellectual advances that occur during development.

Piaget's Theory of Cognitive Development. No theory of cognitive development has had more impact than that of Swiss psychologist Jean Piaget. Piaget (1970) suggested that children around the world proceed through a series of four stages in a fixed order. He maintained that these stages differ not only in the *quantity* of information acquired at each stage but in the *quality* of knowledge and understanding as well. Taking an interactionist point of view, he suggested that movement from one stage to the next occurs when a child reaches an appropriate level of maturation *and* is exposed to relevant types of experiences. Piaget assumed that, without having such experiences, children cannot reach their highest level of cognitive growth.

Piaget proposed four stages: the sensorimotor, preoperational, concrete operational, and formal operational (see Figure 9). Let's examine each of them and the approximate ages that they span.

Sensorimotor Stage: Birth to 2 Years. During the **sensorimotor stage**, children base their understanding of the world primarily on touching, sucking, chewing, shaking, and manipulating objects. In the initial part of the stage, children have relatively little competence in representing the environment by using images, language, or other kinds of symbols. Consequently, infants lack what Piaget calls **object permanence**, the awareness that objects—and people—continue to exist even if they are out of sight.

How can we know that children lack object permanence? Although we cannot ask infants, we can observe their reactions when a toy they are playing with is hidden under a blanket. Until the age of about 9 months, children will make no attempt to locate the hidden toy. However, soon after that age they will begin an active search for the missing object, indicating that they have developed a mental representation of the toy. Object permanence, then, is a critical development during the sensorimotor stage.

Preoperational Stage: 2 to 7 Years. The most important development during the **preoperational stage** is the use of language. Children develop internal representational systems that allow them to describe people, events, and feelings. They even use symbols in play, pretending, for example, that a book pushed across the floor is a car.

Although children use more advanced thinking in this stage than they did in the earlier sensorimotor stage, their thinking is still qualitatively inferior to that of adults. We see this when we observe a preoperational child using **egocentric thought**, a way of thinking in which the child views the world entirely from his or her own perspective. Preoperational children think that everyone shares their perspective and knowledge. Thus, children's stories and explanations to adults can be maddeningly uninformative, as they are delivered without any context. For example, a preoperational child may start a story with "He wouldn't let me go," neglecting to mention who "he" is or where the storyteller wanted to go. We also see egocentric thinking when children at the preoperational stage play hiding games. For instance, 3 year olds frequently hide with their faces against a wall, covering their eyes—although they are still in plain view. It seems to them that if *they* cannot see, then no one else will be able to see them, because they assume that others share their view.

In addition, preoperational children have not yet developed the ability to understand the **principle of conservation**, which is the knowledge that quantity is unrelated

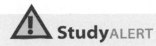

StudyALERT

Use Figure 9 to help remember Piaget's stages of cognitive development.

Sensorimotor stage: According to Piaget, the stage from birth to 2 years, during which a child has little competence in representing the environment by using images, language, or other symbols.

Object permanence: The awareness that objects—and people—continue to exist even if they are out of sight.

Preoperational stage: According to Piaget, the period from 2 to 7 years of age that is characterized by language development.

Egocentric thought: A way of thinking in which a child views the world entirely from his or her own perspective.

Principle of conservation: The knowledge that quantity is unrelated to the arrangement and physical appearance of objects.

Cognitive Stage	Approximate Age Range	Major Characteristics
Sensorimotor	Birth–2 years	Development of object permanence, development of motor skills, little or no capacity for symbolic representation
Preoperational	2–7 years	Development of language and symbolic thinking, egocentric thinking
Concrete operational	7–12 years	Development of conservation, mastery of concept of reversibility
Formal operational	12 years–adulthood	Development of logical and abstract thinking

FIGURE 9 According to Piaget, all children pass through four stages of cognitive development.

FIGURE 10 These tests are frequently used to assess whether children have learned the principle of conservation across a variety of dimensions. Do you think children in the preoperational stage can be taught to avoid conservation mistakes before the typical age of mastery?

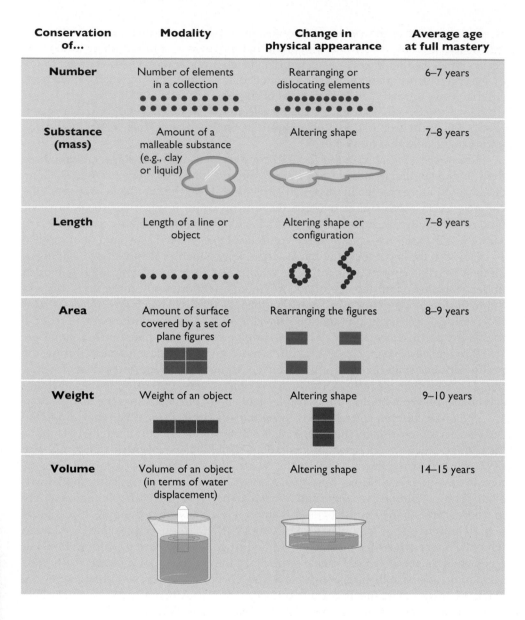

Conservation of...	Modality	Change in physical appearance	Average age at full mastery
Number	Number of elements in a collection	Rearranging or dislocating elements	6–7 years
Substance (mass)	Amount of a malleable substance (e.g., clay or liquid)	Altering shape	7–8 years
Length	Length of a line or object	Altering shape or configuration	7–8 years
Area	Amount of surface covered by a set of plane figures	Rearranging the figures	8–9 years
Weight	Weight of an object	Altering shape	9–10 years
Volume	Volume of an object (in terms of water displacement)	Altering shape	14–15 years

Children who have not mastered the principle of conservation assume that the volume of a liquid increases when it is poured from a short, wide container to a tall, thin one. What other tasks might a child under age 7 have difficulty comprehending?

to the arrangement and physical appearance of objects. Children who have not mastered this concept do not know that the amount, volume, or length of an object does not change when its shape or configuration changes. The question about the two glasses—one short and broad and the other tall and thin—with which we began our discussion of cognitive development illustrates this point clearly. Children who do not understand the principle of conservation invariably state that the amount of liquid changes as it is poured back and forth. They cannot comprehend that a transformation in appearance does not imply a transformation in amount. Instead, it seems as reasonable to the child that there is a change in quantity as it does to the adult that there is no change.

In a number of other ways, some quite startling, the failure to understand the principle of conservation affects children's responses. Research demonstrates that principles that are obvious to and unquestioned by adults may be completely misunderstood by children during the preoperational period, and that it is not until the next stage of cognitive development that children grasp the concept of conservation (See Figure 10).

Concrete Operational Stage: 7 to 12 Years. Mastery of the principle of conservation marks the beginning of the **concrete operational stage**. However, children do not fully understand some aspects of conservation—such as conservation of weight and volume—for a number of years.

During the concrete operational stage, children develop the ability to think in a more logical manner, and begin to overcome some of the egocentrism characteristic of the preoperational period. One of the major principles children learn during this stage is reversibility, the idea that some changes can be undone by reversing an earlier action. For example, they can understand that when someone rolls a ball of clay into a long sausage shape, that person can re-create the original ball by reversing the action. Children can even conceptualize this principle in their heads, without having to see the action performed before them.

Although children make important advances in their logical capabilities during the concrete operational stage, their thinking still displays one major limitation: They are largely bound to the concrete, physical reality of the world. For the most part, they have difficulty understanding questions of an abstract or hypothetical nature.

Formal Operational Stage: 12 Years to Adulthood. The **formal operational stage** produces a new kind of thinking that is abstract, formal, and logical. Thinking is no longer tied to events that individuals observe in the environment but makes use of logical techniques to resolve problems.

The way in which children approach the "pendulum problem" devised by Piaget (Piaget & Inhelder, 1958) illustrates the emergence of formal operational thinking. The problem solver is asked to figure out what determines how fast a pendulum swings. Is it the length of the string, the weight of the pendulum, or the force with which the pendulum is pushed? (For the record, the answer is the length of the string.)

Children in the concrete operational stage approach the problem haphazardly, without a logical or rational plan of action. For example, they may simultaneously change the length of the string and the weight on the string and the force with which they push the pendulum. Because they are varying all the factors at once, they cannot tell which factor is the critical one. In contrast, people in the formal operational stage approach the problem systematically. Acting as if they were scientists conducting an experiment, they examine the effects of changes in one variable at a time. This ability to rule out competing possibilities characterizes formal operational thought.

Although formal operational thought emerges during the teenage years, some individuals use this type of thinking only infrequently. Moreover, it appears that many individuals never reach this stage at all; most studies show that only 40 to 60 percent of college students and adults fully reach it, with some estimates running as low as 25 percent of the general population. In addition, in certain cultures—particularly those that are less technologically oriented than Western societies—almost no one reaches the formal operational stage (Keating & Clark, 1980; Super, 1980; Genovese, 2006).

Stages versus Continuous Development: Is Piaget Right? No other theorist has given us as comprehensive a theory of cognitive development as that of Piaget. Still, many contemporary theorists suggest that a better explanation of how children develop cognitively can be provided by theories that do not involve a stage approach. For instance, children are not always consistent in their performance of tasks that—if Piaget's theory is accurate—ought to be performed equally well at a particular stage (Feldman, 2003, 2004).

Furthermore, some developmental psychologists suggest that cognitive development proceeds in a more continuous fashion than Piaget's stage theory implies. They propose that cognitive development is primarily quantitative in nature, rather than qualitative. They argue that although there are differences in when, how, and to what

Concrete operational stage: According to Piaget, the period from 7 to 12 years of age that is characterized by logical thought and a loss of egocentrism.

Formal operational stage: According to Piaget, the period from age 12 to adulthood that is characterized by abstract thought.

extent a child can use specific cognitive abilities—reflecting quantitative changes—the underlying cognitive processes change relatively little with age (Gelman & Baillargeon, 1983; Case & Okamoto, 1996).

Piaget also underestimated the age at which infants and children can understand specific concepts and principles; in fact, they seem to be more sophisticated in their cognitive abilities than Piaget believed. For instance, some evidence suggests that infants as young as 5 months have rudimentary mathematical skills (Wynn, 1995, 2000; Wynn, Bloom, & Chiang, 2002).

Despite such criticisms, most developmental psychologists agree that although the processes that underlie changes in cognitive abilities may not unfold in the manner suggested by his theory, Piaget has generally provided us with an accurate account of age-related changes in cognitive development. Moreover, his theory has had an enormous influence in education. For example, Piaget suggests that individuals cannot increase their cognitive performance unless both cognitive readiness brought about by maturation and appropriate environmental stimulation are present. This view has inspired the nature and structure of educational curricula and teaching methods. Researchers have also used Piaget's theory and methods to investigate issues surrounding animal cognition, such as whether primates show object permanence (they seem to; Hauser, 2000; Egan, 2005; Cunningham, 2006).

INFORMATION-PROCESSING APPROACHES: CHARTING CHILDREN'S MENTAL PROGRAMS

If cognitive development does not proceed as a series of stages, as Piaget suggested, what does underlie the enormous growth in children's cognitive abilities that even the most untutored eye can observe? To many developmental psychologists, changes in **information processing**, the way in which people take in, use, and store information, account for cognitive development (Lacerda, von Hofsten, & Heimann, 2001; Cashon & Cohen, 2004; Munakata, 2006).

According to this approach, quantitative changes occur in children's ability to organize and manipulate information. From this perspective, children become increasingly adept at information processing, much as a computer program may become more sophisticated as a programmer modifies it on the basis of experience. Information-processing approaches consider the kinds of "mental programs" that children invoke when approaching problems.

Several significant changes occur in children's information-processing capabilities. For one thing, speed of processing increases with age, as some abilities become more automatic. The speed at which children can scan, recognize, and compare stimuli increases with age. As they grow older, children can pay attention to stimuli longer and discriminate between different stimuli more readily, and they are less easily distracted (Myerson et al., 2003; Van den Wildenberg & Van der Molen, 2004).

Memory also improves dramatically with age. Preschoolers can hold only two or three chunks of information in short-term memory, 5 year olds can hold four, and 7 year olds can hold five. (Adults are able to keep seven, plus or minus two, chunks in short-term memory.) The size of chunks also grows with age, as does the sophistication and organization of knowledge stored in memory (see Figure 11). Still, memory capabilities are impressive at a very early age: Even before they can speak, infants can remember for months events in which they actively participated (Cowan et al., 2003; Bayliss et al., 2005).

Information processing: The way in which people take in, use, and store information.

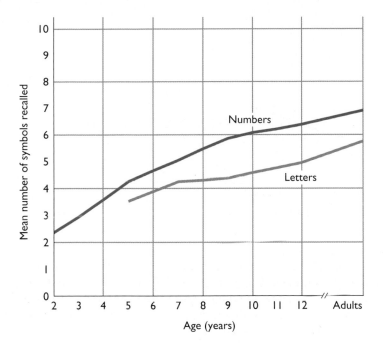

Finally, improvement in information processing relates to advances in **metacognition**, an awareness and understanding of one's own cognitive processes. Metacognition involves the planning, monitoring, and revising of cognitive strategies. Younger children, who lack an awareness of their own cognitive processes, often do not realize their incapabilities. Thus, when they misunderstand others, they may fail to recognize their own errors. It is only later, when metacognitive abilities become more sophisticated, that children are able to know when they *don't* understand. Such increasing sophistication reflects a change in children's *theory of mind*, their knowledge and beliefs about the way the mind operates (McCormick, 2003; Bernstein, Loftus, & Meltzoff, 2005; Matthews & Funke, 2006).

Vygotsky's View of Cognitive Development: Considering Culture.   According to Russian developmental psychologist Lev Vygotsky, the culture in which we are raised significantly affects our cognitive development. In an increasingly influential view, Vygotsky suggests that the focus on individual performance of both Piagetian and information-processing approaches is misplaced. Instead, he holds that we cannot understand cognitive development without taking into account the social aspects of learning (Vygotsky, 1926/1997; Maynard & Martini, 2005; Rieber & Robinson, 2006).

Vygotsky argues that cognitive development occurs as a consequence of social interactions in which children work with others to jointly solve problems. Through such interactions, children's cognitive skills increase, and they gain the ability to function intellectually on their own. More specifically, he suggests that children's cognitive abilities increase when they encounter information that falls within their zone of proximal development. The **zone of proximal development, or ZPD**, is the level at which a child can almost, but not fully, comprehend or perform a task on his or her own. When children receive information that falls within the ZPD, they can increase their understanding or master a new task. In contrast, if the information lies outside children's ZPD, they will not be able to master it (see Figure 12).

Metacognition: An awareness and understanding of one's own cognitive processes.

Zone of proximal development (ZPD): According to Vygotsky, the level at which a child can almost, but not fully, comprehend or perform a task on his or her own.

FIGURE 12 Although the performances of the two children working at a task without aid are similar, the second child benefits more from aid and thus has a larger zone of proximal development (ZPD).

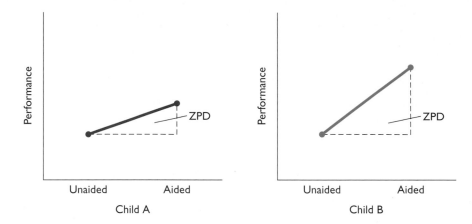

In short, cognitive development occurs when parents, teachers, or skilled peers assist a child by presenting information that is both new and within the ZPD. This type of assistance, called *scaffolding*, provides support for learning and problem solving that encourages independence and growth. Vygotsky claims that scaffolding not only promotes the solution of specific problems, but also aids in the development of overall cognitive abilities (Schaller & Crandall, 2004).

More than other approaches to cognitive development, Vygotsky's theory considers how an individual's specific cultural and social context affects intellectual growth. The way in which children understand the world grows out of interactions with parents, peers, and other members of a specific culture (John-Steiner & Mahn, 2003; Kozulin et al., 2003).

RECAP/EVALUATE/RETHINK

RECAP

What are the major competencies of newborns?

- Newborns, or neonates, have reflexes, unlearned, involuntary responses that occur automatically in the presence of certain stimuli. (p. 403)

- Sensory abilities also develop rapidly; infants can distinguish color, depth, sound, tastes, and smells relatively soon after birth. (p. 404)

- After birth, physical development is rapid; children typically triple their birthweight in a year. (p. 407)

What are the milestones of physical and social development during childhood?

- Attachment—the positive emotional bond between a child and a particular individual—marks social development in infancy. Measured in the laboratory by means of the Ainsworth strange situation, attachment relates to later social and emotional adjustment. (p. 407)

- As children become older, the nature of their social interactions with peers changes. Initially play occurs relatively independently, but it becomes increasingly cooperative. (p. 409)

- The different child-rearing styles include authoritarian, permissive, authoritative, and uninvolved. (p. 411)

- According to Erikson, eight stages of psychosocial development involve people's changing interactions and understanding of themselves and others. During childhood, the four stages are trust-versus-mistrust (birth to 1½ years), autonomy-versus-shame-and-doubt (1½ to 3 years), initiative-versus-guilt (3 to 6 years), and industry-versus-inferiority (6 to 12 years). (p. 412)

How does cognitive development proceed during childhood?

- Piaget's theory suggests that cognitive development proceeds through four stages in which qualitative changes occur in thinking: the sensorimotor stage (birth to 2 years), the preoperational stage (2 to 7 years), the concrete operational stage (7 to 12 years), and the formal operational stage (12 years to adulthood). (p. 414)

- Information-processing approaches suggest that quantitative changes occur in children's ability to organize and manipulate information about the world, such as significant increases in speed of processing, attention span, and memory. In addition, children advance in metacognition, the awareness and understanding of one's own cognitive processes. (p. 418)

- Vygotsky argued that children's cognitive development occurs as a consequence of social interactions in which children and others work together to solve problems. (p. 419)

EVALUATE

1. Researchers studying newborns use _____, or the decrease in the response to a stimulus that occurs after repeated presentations of the same stimulus, as an indicator of a baby's interest.
2. The emotional bond that develops between a child and its caregiver is known as _____.
3. Match the parenting style with its definition:
   1. Permissive
   2. Authoritative
   3. Authoritarian
   4. Uninvolved
   a. Rigid; highly punitive; demanding obedience
   b. Gives little direction; lax on obedience
   c. Firm but fair; tries to explain parental decisions
   d. Emotionally detached and unloving
4. Erikson's theory of _____ development involves a series of eight stages, each of which must be resolved for a person to develop optimally.
5. Match the stage of development with the thinking style characteristic of that stage:
   1. Egocentric thought
   2. Object permanence
   3. Abstract reasoning
   4. Conservation; reversibility
   a. Sensorimotor
   b. Formal operational
   c. Preoperational
   d. Concrete operational
6. _____ - _____ theories of development suggest that the way in which a child handles information is critical to his or her development.
7. According to Vygotsky, information that is within a child's _____ ____ _____ _____ is most likely to result in cognitive development.

RETHINK

1. Do you think the widespread use of IQ testing in the United States contributes to parents' views that their children's academic success is due largely to the children's innate intelligence? Why? Would it be possible (or desirable) to change this view?
2. *From the perspective of a childcare provider:* If a parent were not sure whether to enroll his or her child in your program, what advice would you give about the possible positive and negative consequences about day care?

Answers to Evaluate Questions

1. habituation; 2. attachment; 3. 1-b, 2-c, 3-a, 4-d; 4. psychosocial; 5. 1-c, 2-a, 3-b, 4-d; 6. information-processing; 7. zone of proximal development

KEY TERMS

neonate p. 403
reflexes p. 403
habituation p. 405
attachment p. 407
authoritarian parents p. 411
permissive parents p. 412
authoritative parents p. 412
uninvolved parents p. 412
temperament p. 412

psychosocial development
    p. 413
trust-versus-mistrust stage
    p. 413
autonomy-versus-shame-
    and-doubt stage p. 414
initiative-versus-guilt
    stage p. 414

industry-versus-inferiority
    stage p. 414
cognitive development p. 414
sensorimotor stage p. 415
object permanence p. 415
preoperational stage p. 415
egocentric thought p. 415
principle of
    conservation p. 415

concrete operational stage
    p. 417
formal operational stage
    p. 417
information processing
    p. 418
metacognition p. 419
zone of proximal
    development (ZPD) p. 419

Adolescence: Becoming an Adult

Joseph Charles, Age 13: Being 13 is very hard at school. I have to be bad in order to be considered cool. I sometimes do things that aren't good. I have talked back to my teachers and been disrespectful to them. I do want to be good, but it's just too hard. (Gibbs, 2005, p. 51)

*****

Trevor Kelson, Age 15: "Keep the Hell Out of my Room!" says a sign on Trevor's bedroom wall, just above an unmade bed, a desk littered with dirty T-shirts and candy wrappers, and a floor covered with clothes. Is there a carpet? "Somewhere," he says with a grin. "I think it's gold." (Fields-Meyer, 1995, p. 53)

*****

Lauren Barry, Age 18: "I went to a National Honor Society induction. The parents were just staring at me. I think they couldn't believe someone with pink hair could be smart. I want to be a high-school teacher, but I'm afraid that, based on my appearance, they won't hire me." (Gordon et al., 1999, p. 47)

Key Concept

What major physical, social, and cognitive transitions characterize adolescence?

Although Joseph, Trevor, and Lauren have never met, they share anxieties that are common to adolescence—concerns about friends, parents, appearance, independence, and their futures. **Adolescence**, the developmental stage between childhood and adulthood, is a crucial period. It is a time of profound changes and, occasionally, turmoil. Considerable biological change occurs as adolescents attain sexual and physical maturity. At the same time, and rivaling these physiological changes, important social, emotional, and cognitive changes occur as adolescents strive for independence and move toward adulthood.

Because many years of schooling precede most people's entry into the workforce in Western societies, the stage of adolescence is fairly long, beginning just before the teenage years and ending just after them. No longer children but considered by society to be not quite adults, adolescents face a period of rapid physical, cognitive, and social change that affects them for the rest of their lives.

Dramatic changes in society also affect adolescents' development. More than half of all children in the United States will spend all or some of their childhood and adolescence in single-parent families. Furthermore, adolescents spend considerably less time with their parents, and more with their peers, than they did several decades ago. Finally, the ethnic and cultural diversity of adolescents as a group is increasing dramatically. A third of all adolescents today are of non-European descent, and by the year 2050 the number of adolescents of Hispanic, African American, Native American, and Asian origin collectively will surpass that of whites (National Adolescent Health Information Center, 2003).

Adolescence: The developmental stage between childhood and adulthood.

Physical Development: The Changing Adolescent

If you think back to the start of your own adolescence, the most dramatic changes you probably remember are physical ones. A spurt in height, the growth of breasts in girls,

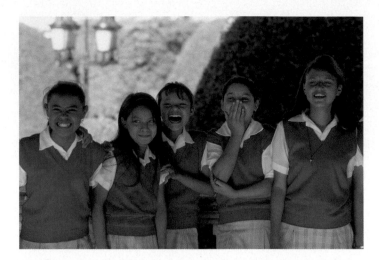

Although puberty begins around age 11 or 12 for girls and 13 or 14 for boys, there are wide variations. What are some advantages and disadvantages of early puberty?

Puberty: The period at which maturation of the sexual organs occurs, beginning at about age 11 or 12 for girls and 13 or 14 for boys.

FIGURE 1 The range of ages during which major sexual changes occur during adolescence is shown by the colored bars. (Source: Based on Tanner, 1978.)

deepening voices in boys, the development of body hair, and intense sexual feelings cause curiosity, interest, and sometimes embarrassment for individuals entering adolescence.

The physical changes that occur at the start of adolescence result largely from the secretion of various hormones, and they affect virtually every aspect of an adolescent's life. Not since infancy has development been so dramatic. Weight and height increase rapidly because of a growth spurt that typically begins around age 10 for girls and age 12 for boys. Adolescents may grow as much as 5 inches in one year.

Puberty, the period at which maturation of the sexual organs occurs, begins at about age 11 or 12 for girls, when menstruation starts. However, there are wide variations (see Figure 1). For example, some girls begin to menstruate as early as age 8 or 9 or as late as age 16. Furthermore, in Western cultures, the average age at which adolescents reach sexual maturity has been steadily decreasing over the last century, most likely as a result of improved nutrition and medical care. Sexual *attraction* to others begins even before the maturation of the sexual organs, at around age 10 (see Figure 1; Tanner, 1990; Finlay, Jones, & Coleman, 2002).

For boys, the onset of puberty is marked by their first ejaculation, known as *spermarche*. Spermarche usually occurs around the age of 13 (see Figure 1). At first, relatively few sperm are produced during an ejaculation, but the amount increases significantly within a few years.

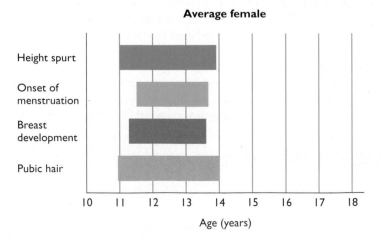

The age at which puberty begins has implications for the way adolescents feel about themselves—as well as the way others treat them. Early-maturing boys have a distinct advantage over later-maturing boys. They do better in athletics, are generally more popular with peers, and have more positive self-concepts (Ge et al., 2003; Becker & Luthar, 2007).

The picture differs for girls. Although early-maturing girls are more sought after as dates and have better self-esteem than do later-maturing girls, some consequences of early physical maturation may be less positive. For example, early breast development may set them apart from their peers and be a source of ridicule (Franko & Striegel-Moore, 2002; Olivardia & Pope, 2002; Nadeem & Graham, 2005).

Late physical maturation may produce certain psychological difficulties for both boys and girls. Boys who are smaller and less coordinated than their more mature peers tend to feel ridiculed and less attractive. Similarly, late-maturing girls are at a disadvantage in middle school and early high school. They hold relatively low social status and may be overlooked in dating (Lanza & Collins, 2002).

Clearly, the rate at which physical changes occur during adolescence can affect the way in which people are viewed by others and the way they view themselves. Just as important as physical changes, however, are the psychological and social changes that unfold during adolescence.

Moral and Cognitive Development: Distinguishing Right from Wrong

In a European country, a woman is near death from a special kind of cancer. The one drug that the doctors think might save her is a medicine that a medical researcher has recently discovered. The drug is expensive to make, and the researcher is charging ten times the cost, or $5,000, for a small dose. The sick woman's husband, Henry, approaches everyone he knows in hopes of borrowing money, but he can get together only about $2,500. He tells the researcher that his wife is dying and asks him to lower the price of the drug or let him pay later. The researcher says, "No, I discovered the drug, and I'm going to make money from it." Henry is desperate and considers stealing the drug for his wife.

What would you tell Henry to do?

KOHLBERG'S THEORY OF MORAL DEVELOPMENT

In the view of psychologist Lawrence Kohlberg, the advice you give Henry reflects your level of moral development. According to Kohlberg, people pass through a series of stages in the evolution of their sense of justice and in the kind of reasoning they use to make moral judgments (Kohlberg, 1984). Largely because of the various cognitive limitations that Piaget described, preadolescent children tend to think either in terms of concrete, unvarying rules ("It is always wrong to steal" or "I'll be punished if I steal") or in terms of the rules of society ("Good people don't steal" or "What if everyone stole?").

Adolescents, however, can reason on a higher plane, having typically reached Piaget's formal operational stage of cognitive development. Because they are able to comprehend broad moral principles, they can understand that morality is not always black and white and that conflict can exist between two sets of socially accepted standards.

Kohlberg (1984) suggests that the changes in moral reasoning can be understood best as a three-level sequence (see Figure 2). His theory assumes that people move through the levels in a fixed order, and that they cannot reach the highest level until about age 13—primarily because of limitations in cognitive development before that age. However, many people never reach the highest level of moral reasoning. In fact,

| | Sample Moral Reasoning of Subjects | |
Level	In Favor of Stealing the Drug	Against Stealing the Drug
Level 1 Preconventional morality: At this level, the concrete interests of the individual are considered in terms of rewards and punishments.	"If you let your wife die, you will get in trouble. You'll be blamed for not spending the money to save her, and there'll be an investigation of you and the druggist for your wife's death."	"You shouldn't steal the drug because you'll be caught and sent to jail if you do. If you do get away, your conscience will bother you thinking how the police will catch up with you at any minute."
Level 2 Conventional morality: At this level, people approach moral problems as members of society. They are interested in pleasing others by acting as good members of society.	"If you let your wife die, you'll never be able to look anybody in the face again."	"After you steal the drug, you'll feel bad thinking how you've brought dishonor on your family and yourself; you won't be able to face anyone again."
Level 3 Postconventional morality: At this level, people use moral principles which are seen as broader than those of any particular society.	"If you don't steal the drug, and if you let your wife die, you'll always condemn yourself for it afterward. You won't be blamed and you'll have lived up to the outside rule of the law, but you won't have lived up to your own conscience and standards of honesty."	"If you steal the drug, you won't be blamed by other people, but you'll condemn yourself because you won't have lived up to your own conscience and standards of honesty."

FIGURE 2 Developmental psychologist Lawrence Kohlberg theorized that people move through a three-level sequence of moral reasoning in a fixed order. However, he contended that few people ever reach the highest level of moral reasoning.

Kohlberg found that only a relatively small percentage of adults rise above the second level of his model (Kohlberg & Ryncarz, 1990; Hedgepeth, 2005; Powers, 2006).

Although Kohlberg's theory has had a substantial influence on our understanding of moral development, the research support is mixed. One difficulty with the theory is that it pertains to moral *judgments*, not moral *behavior*. Knowing right from wrong does not mean that we will always act in accordance with our judgments. In addition, the theory applies primarily to Western society and its moral code; cross-cultural research conducted in cultures with different moral systems suggests that Kohlberg's theory is not necessarily applicable (Coles, 1997; Damon, 1999; Nucci, 2002; Barandiaran, Pascual, & Samaniego, 2006).

MORAL DEVELOPMENT IN WOMEN

One glaring shortcoming of Kohlberg's research is that he primarily used male participants. Furthermore, psychologist Carol Gilligan (1996) argues that because of men's and women's distinctive socialization experiences, a fundamental difference exists in the way each gender views moral behavior. According to Gilligan, men view morality primarily in terms of broad principles, such as justice and fairness. In contrast, women see it in terms of responsibility toward individuals and willingness to make sacrifices to help a specific individual within the context of a particular relationship. Compassion for individuals is a more salient factor in moral behavior for women than it is for men.

Because Kohlberg's model defines moral behavior largely in terms of abstract principles such as justice, Gilligan finds that it inadequately describes the moral development of females. She suggests that women's morality centers on individual well-being and social relationships—a morality of *caring*. In her view, compassionate concern for the welfare of others represents the highest level of morality.

The fact that Gilligan's conception of morality differs greatly from Kohlberg's suggests that gender plays an important role in determining what a person sees as moral.

Although the research evidence is not definitive, it seems plausible that their differing conceptions of what constitutes moral behavior may lead men and women to regard the morality of a specific behavior in different ways (Weisz & Black, 2002; Lippa, 2005; Jorgensen, 2006).

Social Development: Finding Oneself in a Social World

"Who am I?" "How do I fit into the world?" "What is life all about?"

Questions such as these assume special significance during the teenage years, as adolescents seek to find their place in the broader social world. As we will see, this quest takes adolescents along several routes.

ERIKSON'S THEORY OF PSYCHOSOCIAL DEVELOPMENT: THE SEARCH FOR IDENTITY

Erikson's theory of psychosocial development emphasizes the search for identity during the adolescent years. As was noted earlier, psychosocial development encompasses the way people's understanding of themselves, one another, and the world around them changes during the course of development (Erikson, 1963).

The fifth stage of Erikson's theory (summarized, with the other stages, in Figure 3), the **identity-versus-role-confusion stage**, encompasses adolescence. During this stage, a time of major testing, people try to determine what is unique about themselves. They attempt to discover who they are, what their strengths are, and what kinds of roles they are best suited to play for the rest of their lives—in short, their **identity**. A person confused about the most appropriate role to play in life may lack a stable identity, adopt an unacceptable role such as that of a social deviant, or have difficulty maintaining close personal relationships later in life (Updegraff et al., 2004; Vleioras & Bosma, 2005; Goldstein, 2006).

Identity-versus-role-confusion stage: According to Erikson, a time in adolescence of major testing to determine one's unique qualities.

Identity: The distinguishing character of the individual: who each of us is, what our roles are, and what we are capable of.

Stage	Approximate Age	Positive Outcomes	Negative Outcomes
1. Trust-vs.-mistrust	Birth–1½ years	Feelings of trust from environmental support	Fear and concern regarding others
2. Autonomy-vs.-shame-and-doubt	1½–3 years	Self-sufficiency if exploration is encouraged	Doubts about self, lack of independence
3. Initiative-vs.-guilt	3–6 years	Discovery of ways to initiate actions	Guilt from actions and thoughts
4. Industry-vs.-inferiority	6–12 years	Development of sense of competence	Feelings of inferiority, no sense of mastery
5. Identity-vs.-role-confusion	Adolescence	Awareness of uniqueness of self, knowledge of role to be followed	Inability to identify appropriate roles in life
6. Intimacy-vs.-isolation	Early adulthood	Development of loving, sexual relationships and close friendships	Fear of relationships with others
7. Generativity-vs.-stagnation	Middle adulthood	Sense of contribution to continuity of life	Trivialization of one's activities
8. Ego-integrity-vs.-despair	Late adulthood	Sense of unity in life's accomplishments	Regret over lost opportunities of life

FIGURE 3 Erikson's stages of psychosocial development. According to Erikson, people proceed through eight stages of psychosocial development across their lives. He suggested that each stage requires the resolution of a crisis or conflict and may produce both positive and negative outcomes.

During the identity-versus-role-confusion period, an adolescent feels pressure to identify what to do with his or her life. Because these pressures come at a time of major physical changes as well as important changes in what society expects of them, adolescents can find the period an especially difficult one. The identity-versus-role-confusion stage has another important characteristic: declining reliance on adults for information, with a shift toward using the peer group as a source of social judgments. The peer group becomes increasingly important, enabling adolescents to form close, adultlike relationships and helping them clarify their personal identities. According to Erikson, the identity-versus-role-confusion stage marks a pivotal point in psychosocial development, paving the way for continued growth and the future development of personal relationships.

During early adulthood, people enter the **intimacy-versus-isolation stage**. Spanning the period of early adulthood (from post-adolescence to the early 30s), this stage focuses on developing close relationships with others. Difficulties during this stage result in feelings of loneliness and a fear of such relationships, whereas successful resolution of the crises of the stage results in the possibility of forming relationships that are intimate on a physical, intellectual, and emotional level.

Intimacy-versus-isolation stage: According to Erikson, a period during early adulthood that focuses on developing close relationships.

Generativity-versus-stagnation stage: According to Erikson, a period in middle adulthood during which we take stock of our contributions to family and society.

Ego-integrity-versus-despair stage: According to Erikson, a period from late adulthood until death during which we review life's accomplishments and failures.

Development continues during middle adulthood as people enter the **generativity-versus-stagnation stage**. Generativity is the ability to contribute to one's family, community, work, and society, and to assist the development of the younger generation. Success in this stage results in a person's feeling positive about the continuity of life, whereas difficulties lead a person to feel that his or her activities are trivial or stagnant and have done nothing for upcoming generations. In fact, if a person has not successfully resolved the identity crisis of adolescence, he or she may still be foundering in identifying an appropriate career, for example.

Finally, the last stage of psychosocial development, the **ego-integrity-versus-despair** stage, spans later adulthood and continues until death. Now a sense of accomplishment signifies success in resolving the difficulties presented by this stage of life; failure to resolve the difficulties results in regret over what might have been achieved but was not.

Notably, Erikson's theory suggests that development does not stop at adolescence but continues throughout adulthood, a view that a substantial amount of research now confirms. For instance, a 22-year study by psychologist Susan Whitbourne found considerable support for the fundamentals of Erikson's theory, determining that psychosocial development continues through adolescence and adulthood. In sum, adolescence is not an end point but rather a way station on the path of psychosocial development (Whitbourne et al., 1992; McAdams et al., 1997).

Although Erikson's theory provides a broad outline of identity development, critics have pointed out that his approach is anchored in male-oriented concepts of individuality and competitiveness. In an alternative conception, psychologist Carol Gilligan suggests that women may develop identity through the establishment of relationships. In her view, a primary component of women's identity is the construction of caring networks among themselves and others (Gilligan, 2004).

Stormy Adolescence: Myth or Reality? Does puberty invariably foreshadow a stormy, rebellious period of adolescence?

At one time, psychologists thought that most children entering adolescence were beginning a period fraught with stress and unhappiness. However, research now shows that this characterization is largely a myth, that most young people pass through adolescence without appreciable turmoil in their lives, and that parents speak easily—and fairly often—with their children about a variety of topics (van Wel, Linssen, & Abma, 2000; Granic, Hollenstein, & Dishion, 2003).

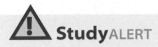

StudyALERT

The characterization of a stormy adolescence is a myth for most adolescents.

Not that adolescence is completely calm! In most families with adolescents, the amount of arguing and bickering clearly rises. Most young teenagers, as part of their search for identity, experience tension between their attempts to become independent from their parents and their actual dependence on them. They may experiment with a range of behaviors, flirting with a variety of activities that their parents, and even society as a whole, find objectionable. Happily, though, for most families such tensions stabilize during middle adolescence—around age 15 or 16—and eventually decline around age 18 (Smetana, Daddis, & Chuang, 2003; Smetana, 2005).

One reason for the increase in discord during adolescence appears to be the protracted period in which children stay at home with their parents. In prior historical periods—and in some non-Western cultures today—children leave home immediately after puberty and are considered adults. Today, however, sexually mature adolescents may spend as many as seven or eight years with their parents. Current social trends even hint at an extension of the conflicts of adolescence beyond the teenage years, because a significant number of young adults—known as *boomerang children*—return to live with their parents after leaving home for some period, typically for economic reasons. Although some parents welcome the return of their children, others are less sympathetic, opening the way to conflict (Bianchi & Casper, 2000; Lewin, 2003).

Another source of strife with parents lies in the way adolescents think. Adolescence fosters *adolescent egocentrism*, a state of self-absorption in which a teenager views the world from his or her own point of view. Egocentrism leads adolescents to be highly critical of authority figures, unwilling to accept criticism, and quick to fault others. It also makes them believe that they are the center of everyone else's attention, leading to self-consciousness. Furthermore, they develop *personal fables*, the belief that their experience is unique, exceptional, and shared by no one else. Such personal fables may make adolescents feel invulnerable to the risks that threaten others (Elkind, 1998; Frankenberger, 2004; Tucker Blackwell, 2006).

Finally, parent-adolescent discord occurs because adolescents are much more apt to engage in risky behavior than later in life. In large part, their riskiness is due to the immaturity of brain systems that regulate impulse control, some of which do not fully develop until people are in their 20s (Steinberg, 2007).

ADOLESCENT SUICIDE

Although the vast majority of teenagers pass through adolescence without major psychological difficulties, some experience unusually severe psychological problems. Sometimes those problems become so extreme that adolescents take their own lives. Suicide is the third leading cause of death for adolescents (after accidents and homicide) in the United States. More teenagers and young adults die from suicide than from cancer, heart disease, AIDS, birth defects, stroke, pneumonia and influenza, and chronic lung disease combined (CDC, 2004).

A teenager commits suicide every 90 minutes. Furthermore, the reported rate of suicide may actually be understated, because medical personnel hesitate to report suicide as a cause of death. Instead, they frequently label a death as an accident in an effort to protect the survivors. Overall, as many as 200 adolescents may attempt suicide for every one who actually takes his or her own life (CDC, 2000).

Male adolescents are five times more likely to commit suicide than are females, although females *attempt* suicide more often than males do. The rate of adolescent suicide is significantly greater among whites than among nonwhites.

These students are mourning the deaths of two classmates who committed suicide. The rate of suicide among teenagers has risen significantly over the last few decades. Can you think of any reasons for this phenomenon?

However, the suicide rate of African-American males has increased much more rapidly than has that of white males over the last two decades. Native Americans have the highest suicide rate of any ethnic group in the United States, and Asian Americans have the lowest rate (CDC, 2004; Gutierrez et al., 2005; Boden, Fergusson, & Horwood, 2007).

Although the rate of suicide has slowly declined, the rates are still higher for adolescents than any other age group except for the elderly. Some psychologists suggest that the sharp rise in stress that teenagers experience—in terms of academic and social pressure, alcoholism, drug abuse, and family difficulties—provokes the most troubled adolescents to take their own lives. However, that is not the whole story, for the suicide rate for other age groups has remained fairly stable in the last few decades. It is unlikely that stress has increased only for adolescents and not for the rest of the population (Lubell et al., 2004).

Although the question of why adolescent suicide rates are so high remains unanswered, several factors put adolescents at risk. One factor is depression, characterized by unhappiness, extreme fatigue, and—a variable that seems especially important—a profound sense of hopelessness. In other cases, adolescents who commit suicide are perfectionists, inhibited socially and prone to extreme anxiety when they face any social or academic challenge (see Figure 4; CDC, 2004; Richardson et al., 2005; Caelian, 2006).

Family background and adjustment difficulties are also related to suicide. A long-standing history of conflicts between parents and children may lead to adolescent behavior problems, such as delinquency, dropping out of school, and aggressive tendencies. In addition, teenage alcoholics and abusers of other drugs have a relatively high rate of suicide (Stronski et al., 2000; Winstead & Sanchez, 2005).

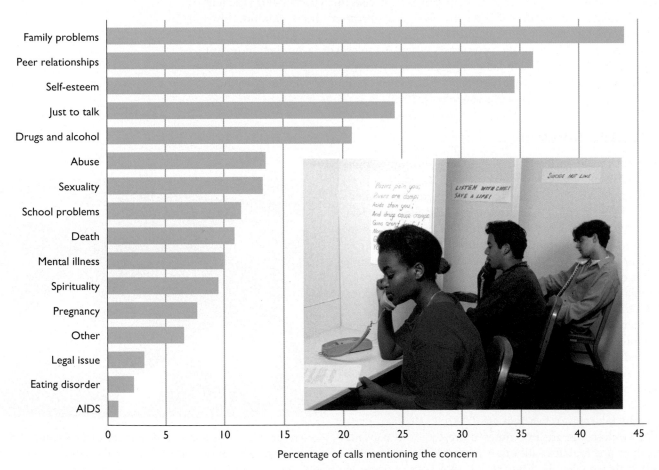

FIGURE 4 According to a review of phone calls to one telephone help line, adolescents who were considering suicide most often mentioned family, peer relationships, and self-esteem problems. (Source: Boehm & Campbell, 1995.)

Several warning signs indicate when a teenager's problems may be severe enough to warrant concern about the possibility of a suicide attempt. They include the following:

- School problems, such as missing classes, truancy, and a sudden change in grades

- Frequent incidents of self-destructive behavior, such as careless accidents

- Loss of appetite or excessive eating

- Withdrawal from friends and peers

- Sleeping problems

- Signs of depression, tearfulness, or overt indications of psychological difficulties, such as hallucinations

- A preoccupation with death, an afterlife, or what would happen "if I died"

- Putting affairs in order, such as giving away prized possessions or making arrangements for the care of a pet

- An explicit announcement of thoughts of suicide

If you know someone who shows signs that he or she is suicidal, urge that person to seek professional help. You may need to take assertive action, such as enlisting the assistance of family members or friends. Talk of suicide is a serious signal for help, not a confidence to be kept.

For immediate help with a suicide-related problem, call 1-800-273-8255, a national hotline staffed with trained counselors, or visit the Web at www. suicidepreventionlifeline.org.

Exploring DIVERSITY

Rites of Passage: Coming of Age Around the World

It is not easy for male members of the Awa tribe in New Guinea to make the transition from childhood to adulthood. First come whippings with sticks and prickly branches, both for the boys' own past misdeeds and in honor of those tribesmen who were killed in warfare. In the next phase of the ritual, adults jab sharpened sticks into the boys' nostrils. Then they force a five-foot length of vine into the boys' throats, until they gag and vomit. Finally, tribesmen cut the boys' genitals, causing severe bleeding.

Although the rites that mark the coming of age of boys in the Awa tribe sound horrifying to Westerners, they are comparable to those in other cultures. In some, youths must kneel on hot coals without displaying pain. In others, girls must toss wads of burning cotton from hand to hand and allow themselves to be bitten by hundreds of ants (Selsky, 1997).

Other cultures have less fearsome, although no less important, ceremonies that mark the passage from childhood to adulthood. For instance, when a girl first menstruates in traditional Apache tribes, the event is marked by dawn-to-dusk chanting. Western religions, too, have several types of celebrations, including bar and bat mitzvahs at age 13 for Jewish boys and girls and confirmation ceremonies for children in many Christian denominations (Magida, 2006).

In most societies, males, but not females, are the focus of coming-of-age ceremonies. The renowned anthropologist Margaret Mead remarked, only partly in jest, that the preponderance of male ceremonies might reflect the fact that "the worry that boys will not grow up to be men is much more widespread than that girls will not grow up to be women" (1949, p. 195). Said another way, it may be that in most cultures men traditionally have higher status than women, and therefore those cultures regard boys' transition into adulthood as more important.

However, another fact may explain why most cultures place greater emphasis on male rites than on female ones. For females, the transition from childhood is marked by a definite, biological event: menstruation. For males, in contrast, no single event can be used to pinpoint entry into adulthood. Thus, men are forced to rely on culturally determined rituals to acknowledge their arrival into adulthood.

RECAP/EVALUATE/RETHINK

RECAP

What major physical, social, and cognitive transitions characterize adolescence?

- Adolescence, the developmental stage between childhood and adulthood, is marked by the onset of puberty, the point at which sexual maturity occurs. The age at which puberty begins has implications for the way people view themselves and the way others see them. (p. 423)

- Moral judgments during adolescence increase in sophistication, according to Kohlberg's three-level model. Although Kohlberg's levels provide an adequate description of males' moral judgments, Gilligan suggests that women view morality in terms of caring for individuals rather than in terms of broad, general principles of justice. (p. 425)

- According to Erikson's model of psychosocial development, adolescence may be accompanied by an identity crisis. Adolescence is followed by three more stages of psychosocial development that cover the remainder of the life span. (p. 427)

- Suicide is the third leading cause of death in adolescents. (p. 429)

EVALUATE

1. _____ is the period during which the sexual organs begin to mature.
2. Delayed maturation typically provides both males and females with a social advantage. True or false?

3. _____ proposed a set of three levels of moral development ranging from reasoning based on rewards and punishments to abstract thinking involving concepts of justice.
4. Erikson believed that during adolescence, people must search for _____, whereas during the early adulthood, the major task is _____.

RETHINK

1. In what ways do school cultures help or hurt teenage students who are going through adolescence? What school policies might benefit early-maturing girls and late-maturing boys? Explain how same-sex schools could help, as some have argued.
2. *From the perspective of a social worker:* How might you determine if an adolescent is at risk for suicide? What strategies would you use to prevent the teen from committing suicide? Would you use different strategies depending on the teenager's gender?

Answers to Evaluate Questions

1. puberty; 2. false; both male and female adolescents suffer if they mature late; 3. Kohlberg; 4. identity, intimacy

KEY TERMS

adolescence p. 423
puberty p. 424
identity-versus-role-
 confusion stage p. 427

identity p. 427
intimacy-versus-isolation
 stage p. 428

generativity-versus-
 stagnation stage p. 428
ego-integrity-versus-despair
 stage p. 428

Adulthood

I thought I got better as I got older. I found out that wasn't the case in a real hurry last year. After going twelve years in professional football and twelve years before that in amateur football without ever having surgery performed on me, the last two seasons of my career I went under the knife three times. It happened very quickly and without warning, and I began to ask myself, "Is this age? Is this what's happening?" Because up until that moment, I'd never realized that I was getting older. (Kotre & Hall, 1990, pp. 257, 259–260)

As a former professional football player, Brian Sipes intensely felt the changes in his body brought about by aging. But the challenges he experienced are part of a normal process that affects all people as they move through adulthood.

Psychologists generally agree that early adulthood begins around age 20 and lasts until about age 40 to 45, with middle adulthood beginning then and continuing until around age 65. Despite the enormous importance of these periods of life in terms of both the accomplishments that occur in them and their overall length (together they span some 44 years), they have been studied less than has any other stage. For one reason, the physical changes that occur during these periods are less apparent and more gradual than are those at other times during the life span. In addition, the diverse social changes that arise during this period defy simple categorization. However, developmental psychologists have recently begun to focus on the period, particularly on the social changes in the family and women's careers.

Physical Development: The Peak of Health

For most people, early adulthood marks the peak of physical health. From about 18 to 25 years of age, people's strength is greatest, their reflexes are quickest, and their chances of dying from disease are quite slim. Moreover, reproductive capabilities are at their highest level.

Around age 25, the body becomes slightly less efficient and more susceptible to disease. Overall, however, ill health remains the exception; most people stay remarkably healthy during early adulthood. (Can you think of any machine other than the body that can operate without pause for so long a period?)

During middle adulthood people gradually become aware of changes in their bodies. People often experience weight gain (although they can avoid such increases through diet and exercise). Furthermore, the sense organs gradually become less sensitive, and reactions to stimuli are slower. But generally, the physical declines that occur during middle adulthood are minor and often unnoticeable (DiGiovanna, 1994; Forzanna et al., 1994).

The major biological change that does occur during middle adulthood pertains to reproductive capabilities. On average, during their late 40s or early 50s, women begin **menopause**, during which they stop menstruating and are no longer fertile. Because menopause is accompanied by a significant reduction in the production of estrogen, a female hormone, women sometimes experience symptoms such as hot flashes, sudden

Key Concepts

What are the principal kinds of physical, social, and intellectual changes that occur in early and middle adulthood, and what are their causes?

How does the reality of late adulthood differ from the stereotypes about that period?

How can we adjust to death?

Menopause: The period during which women stop menstruating and are no longer fertile.

433

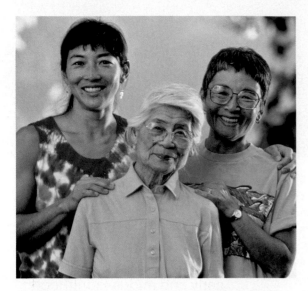

Women's reactions to menopause vary significantly across cultures, and according to one study, the more a society values old age, the less difficulty its women have during menopause. Why do you think this would be the case?

sensations of heat. Many symptoms can be treated through *hormone therapy (HT)*, in which menopausal women take the hormones estrogen and progesterone.

However, hormone therapy poses several dangers, such as an increase in the risk of breast cancer, blood clots, and coronary heart disease. These uncertainties make the routine use of HT controversial. Currently, the medical consensus seems to be that younger women with severe menopausal symptoms ought to consider HT on a short-term basis. On the other hand, HT is less appropriate for older women after menopause (Plonczynski & Plonczynski, 2007; Rossouw et al., 2007; Lindh-Åstrand et al., 2007).

Menopause was once blamed for a variety of psychological symptoms, including depression and memory loss. However, such difficulties, if they do occur, may be caused by women's expectations about reaching an "old" age in a society that highly values youth. For example, women's reactions to menopause vary significantly across cultures. The more a society values old age, the less difficulty its women have during menopause (Elliot, Berman, & Kim, 2002; Beyene, Gilliss, & Lee, 2007).

For men, the aging process during middle adulthood is somewhat subtler. There are no physiological signals of increasing age equivalent to the end of menstruation in women; that is, no male menopause exists. In fact, men remain fertile and are capable of fathering children until well into late adulthood. However, some gradual physical decline occurs: Sperm production decreases, and the frequency of orgasm tends to decline. Once again, though, any psychological difficulties associated with these changes are usually brought about not so much by physical deterioration as by the inability of an aging individual to meet the exaggerated standards of youthfulness.

Social Development: Working at Life

Whereas physical changes during adulthood reflect development of a quantitative nature, social developmental transitions are qualitative and more profound. During this period, people typically launch themselves into careers, marriage, and families.

The entry into early adulthood is usually marked by leaving one's childhood home and entering the world of work. People envision life goals and make career choices. Their lives often center on their careers, which form an important part of their identity (Vaillant & Vaillant, 1990; Levinson, 1990, 1992).

In their early 40s, however, people may begin to question their lives as they enter a period called the *midlife transition*. The idea that life will end at some point becomes increasingly influential in their thinking, and they may question their past accomplishments (Gould, 1978). Facing signs of physical aging and feeling dissatisfaction with their lives, some individuals experience what has been popularly labeled a *midlife crisis*.

In most cases, though, the passage into middle age is relatively calm. Most 40 year olds view their lives and accomplishments positively enough to proceed relatively smoothly through midlife, and the 40s and 50s are often a particularly rewarding period. Rather than looking to the future, people concentrate on the present, and their involvement with their families, friends, and other social groups takes on new importance. A major developmental thrust of this period is coming to terms with one's circumstances (Whitbourne, 2000).

Finally, during the last stages of adulthood people become more accepting of others and of their own lives and are less concerned about issues or problems that once bothered them. People come to accept the fact that death is inevitable, and they try to understand their accomplishments in terms of the broader meaning of life. Although people may begin, for the first time, to label themselves as "old," many also develop a sense of wisdom and feel freer to enjoy life (Baltes & Kunzmann, 2003; Miner-Rubino, Winter, & Stewart, 2004; Ward-Baker, 2007).

Marriage, Children, and Divorce: Family Ties

In the typical fairy tale, a dashing young man and a beautiful young woman marry, have children, and live happily ever after. However, that scenario does not match the realities of love and marriage in the 21st century. Today, it is just as likely that the man and woman would first live together, then get married and have children, but ultimately get divorced.

The percentage of U.S. households made up of unmarried couples has increased dramatically over the last two decades. At the same time, the average age at which marriage takes place is higher than at any time since the turn of the last century. These changes have been dramatic, and they suggest that the institution of marriage has changed considerably from earlier historical periods.

When people do marry, the probability of divorce is high, especially for younger couples. Even though divorce rates have been declining since they peaked in 1981, about half of all first marriages end in divorce. Before they are 18 years old, two-fifths of children will experience the breakup of their parents' marriages. Moreover, the rise in divorce is not just a U.S. phenomenon: The divorce rate has accelerated over the last several decades in most industrialized countries. In some countries, the increase has been enormous. In South Korea, for example, the divorce rate quadrupled from 11 percent to 47 percent in the 12-year period ending in 2002 (Schaefer, 2000; Lankov, 2004; Olson & DeFrain, 2005).

Changes in marriage and divorce trends have doubled the number of single-parent households in the United States over the last two decades. Almost 25 percent of all family households are now headed by one parent, compared with 13 percent in 1970. If present trends continue, almost three-fourths of American children will spend some portion of their lives in a single-parent family before they turn 18. For children in minority households, the numbers are even higher. Almost 60 percent of all black children and more than a third of Hispanic children live in homes with only one parent. Furthermore, in most single-parent families, it is the mother, rather than the father, with whom the children reside—a phenomenon that is consistent across racial and ethnic groups throughout the industrialized world (U.S. Bureau of the Census, 2000).

What are the economic and emotional consequences for children living in homes with only one parent? Single-parent families are often economically less well off, and this economic disadvantage has an impact on children's opportunities. Over a third of single-mother families with children have incomes below the poverty line. In addition, good child care at an affordable price is often hard to find. Furthermore, for children of divorce, the parents' separation is often a painful experience that may result in obstacles to their establishing close relationships later in life. Children may blame themselves for the breakup or feel pressure to take sides (U.S. Bureau of the Census, 2000; Wallerstein et al., 2000; Liu, He, & Wu, 2007).

Most evidence, however, suggests that children from single-parent families are no less well adjusted than are those from two-parent families. In fact, children may be more successful growing up in a harmonious single-parent family than in a two-parent family that engages in continuous conflict (Harold et al., 1997; Clarke-Stewart et al., 2000; Kelly, 2000; Olson & DeFrain, 2006).

Changing Roles of Men and Women: The Time of Their Lives

One of the major changes in family life in the last two decades has been the evolution of men's and women's roles. More women than ever before act simultaneously as wives, mothers, and wage earners—in contrast to women in traditional marriages, in which the husband is the sole wage earner and the wife assumes primary responsibility for care of the home and children.

Close to 75 percent of all married women with school-age children are now employed outside the home, and 55 percent of mothers with children under age 6 are working. In the mid-1960s, only 17 percent of mothers of 1 year olds worked full-time; now, more than half are in the labor force (U.S, Bureau of the Census, 2001; Halpern, 2005).

Most married working women are not free of household responsibilities. Even in marriages in which the spouses hold jobs that have similar status and require similar hours, the distribution of household tasks between husbands and wives has not changed substantially. Working wives are still more likely than husbands to feel responsible for traditional homemaking tasks such as cooking and cleaning. In contrast, husbands still view themselves as responsible primarily for household tasks such as repairing broken appliances and doing yard work (Ganong & Coleman, 1999; Juster, Ono, & Stafford, 2002).

Women's "Second Shift." The number of hours put in by working mothers can be staggering. One survey, for instance, found that if we add the number of hours worked on the job and in the home, employed mothers of children under 3 years of age put in an average of 90 hours per week! The additional work performed by women is sometimes called the "second shift." National surveys show women who are both employed and mothers put in an extra month of 24-hour days during the course of a year. Researchers see similar patterns in many developing societies throughout the world, with women working at full-time jobs and also having primary responsibilities for child care (Hochschild, 2001; Jacobs & Gerson, 2004; Bureau of Labor Statistics, 2007).

Consequently, rather than careers being a substitute for what women do at home, they often exist in addition to the role of homemaker. It is not surprising that some wives feel resentment toward husbands who spend less time on child care and housework than the wives had expected before the birth of their children (Stier & Lewin-Epstein, 2000; Kiecolt, 2003; Gerstel, 2005).

The Later Years of Life: Growing Old

> I've always enjoyed doing things in the mountains—hiking or, more recently, active cliff-climbing. The more difficult the climb, the more absorbing it is. The climbs I really remember are the ones I had to work on. Maybe a particular section where it took two or three tries before I found the right combination of moves that got me up easily—and, preferably, elegantly. It's a wonderful exhilaration to get to the top and sit down and perhaps have lunch and look out over the landscape and be so grateful that it's still possible for me to do that sort of thing. (Lyman Spitzer, age 74, quoted in Kotre & Hall, 1990, pp. 358–359)

If you can't quite picture a 74 year old rock-climbing, some rethinking of your view of late adulthood may be in order. In spite of the societal stereotype of "old age" as a time of inactivity and physical and mental decline, gerontologists, specialists who study aging, are beginning to paint a very different portrait of late adulthood.

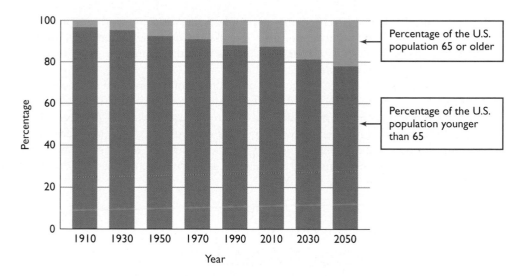

FIGURE 1 Projections suggest that by the year 2050, 20 percent of the U.S. population will be over age 65. What implications does this statistic have for U.S. society?

By focusing on the period of life that starts at around age 65, gerontologists are making important contributions to clarifying the capabilities of older adults. Their work is demonstrating that significant developmental processes continue even during old age. And as life expectancy increases, the number of people who reach older adulthood will continue to grow substantially (see Figure 1). Consequently, developing an understanding of late adulthood has become a critical priority for psychologists (Birren, 1996; Moody, 2000; Schaie, 2005).

Physical Changes in Late Adulthood: The Aging Body

Napping, eating, walking, conversing. It probably doesn't surprise you that these relatively nonstrenuous activities represent the typical pastimes of late adulthood. But it is striking that these activities are identical to the most common leisure activities reported in a survey of college students (Harper, 1978). Although the students cited more active pursuits—such as sailing and playing basketball—as their favorite activities, in actuality they engaged in such sports relatively infrequently, spending most of their free time napping, eating, walking, and conversing.

Although the leisure activities in which older adults engage may not differ all that much from the ones that younger people pursue, many physical changes are, of course, brought about by the aging process. The most obvious are those of appearance—hair thinning and turning gray, skin wrinkling and folding, and sometimes a slight loss of height as the thickness of the disks between vertebrae in the spine decreases—but subtler changes also occur in the body's biological functioning. For example, sensory capabilities decrease as a result of aging: Vision, hearing, smell, and taste become less sensitive. Reaction time slows, and physical stamina changes (Stenklev & Laukli, 2004; Schieber, 2006; Madden, 2007).

What are the reasons for these physical declines? **Genetic preprogramming theories of aging** suggest that human cells have a built-in time limit to their reproduction. These theories suggest that after a certain time cells stop dividing or become harmful to the body—as if a kind of automatic self-destruct button had been pushed. In contrast, **wear-and-tear theories of aging** suggest that the mechanical functions of

Genetic preprogramming theories of aging: Theories that suggest that human cells have a built-in time limit to their reproduction, and that after a certain time they are no longer able to divide.

Wear-and-tear theories of aging: Theories that suggest that the mechanical functions of the body simply stop working efficiently.

the body simply work less efficiently as people age. Waste by-products of energy production eventually accumulate, and mistakes are made when cells divide. Eventually the body, in effect, wears out, just as an old automobile does (Ly et al., 2000; Miquel, 2006; Hayflick, 2007).

Evidence supports both the genetic preprogramming and the wear-and-tear views, and it may be that both processes contribute to natural aging. It is clear, however, that physical aging is not a disease, but a natural biological process. Many physical functions do not decline with age. For example, sex remains pleasurable well into old age (although the frequency of sexual activity decreases), and some people report that the pleasure they derive from sex increases during late adulthood (Gelfand, 2000; DeLamater & Sill, 2005).

Cognitive Changes: Thinking About—and During—Late Adulthood

At one time, many gerontologists would have agreed with the popular view that older adults are forgetful and confused. Today, however, most research indicates that this assessment is far from an accurate one of older people's capabilities.

One reason for the change in view is that more sophisticated research techniques exist for studying the cognitive changes that occur in late adulthood. For example, if we were to give a group of older adults an IQ test, we might find that the average score was lower than the score achieved by a group of younger people. We might conclude that this signifies a decline in intelligence. Yet if we looked a little more closely at the specific test, we might find that that conclusion was unwarranted. For instance, many IQ tests include portions based on physical performance (such as arranging a group of blocks) or on speed. In such cases, poorer performance on the IQ test may be due to gradual decreases in reaction time—a physical decline that accompanies late adulthood and has little or nothing to do with the intellectual capabilities of older adults.

Other difficulties hamper research into cognitive functioning during late adulthood. For example, older people are often less healthy than younger ones; when only *healthy* older adults are compared to healthy younger adults, intellectual differences are far less evident. Furthermore, the average number of years in school is often lower in older adults (for historical reasons) than in younger ones, and older adults may be less motivated to perform well on intelligence tests than younger people. Finally, traditional IQ tests may be inappropriate measures of intelligence in late adulthood. Older adults sometimes perform better on tests of practical intelligence than do younger individuals (Willis & Schaie, 1994; Dixon & Cohen, 2003).

Still, some declines in intellectual functioning during late adulthood do occur, although the pattern of age differences is not uniform for different types of cognitive abilities (see Figure 2). In general, skills relating to *fluid intelligence* (which involves information-processing skills such as memory, calculations, and analogy solving) show declines in late adulthood. In contrast, skills relating to *crystallized intelligence* (intelligence based on the accumulation of information, skills, and strategies learned through experience) remain steady and in some cases actually improve (Stankov, 2003; Rozencwajg et al., 2005; van Hooren et al., 2007).

Even when changes in intellectual functioning occur during late adulthood, people often are able to compensate for any decline. They can still learn what they want to; it may just take more time. Furthermore, teaching older adults strategies for dealing with new problems can prevent declines in performance (Saczynski, Willis, & Schaie, 2002; Cavallini, Pagnin, & Vecchi, 2003; Peters et al., 2007).

Although there are declines in fluid intelligence in late adulthood, skills relating to crystallized intelligence remain steady and may actually improve.

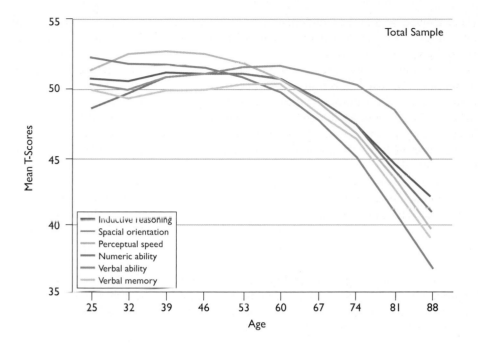

FIGURE 2 Age-related changes in intellectual skills vary according to the specific cognitive ability in question.
(Source: Schaie, K. W. (2005). Longitudinal studies. In *Developmental influences on adult intelligence: The Seattle Longitudinal Study*, Figure 5.7a (p. 127). Copyright © 2005 by Oxford University Press, Inc. By permission of Oxford University Press, Inc. www.oup.co.uk)

MEMORY CHANGES IN LATE ADULTHOOD: ARE OLDER ADULTS FORGETFUL?

One of the characteristics most frequently attributed to late adulthood is forgetfulness. How accurate is this assumption?

Most evidence suggests that memory change is not an inevitable part of the aging process. For instance, research shows that older people in cultures in which older adults are held in high esteem, such as mainland China, are less likely to show memory losses than are those living in cultures in which the expectation is that memory will decline. Similarly, when older people in Western societies are reminded of the advantages of age (for example, "age brings wisdom"), they tend to do better on tests of memory (Levy, 1996; Hess, Hinson, & Statham, 2004; Dixon et al., 2007).

Even when people show memory declines during late adulthood, their deficits are limited to certain types of memory. For instance, losses tend to be limited to episodic memories, which relate to specific experiences in people's lives. Other types of memories, such as semantic memories (which refer to general knowledge and facts) and implicit memories (memories of which we are not consciously aware), are largely unaffected by age (Fleischman et al., 2004; Mitchell & Schmitt, 2006; St. Jacques & Levine, 2007).

Declines in episodic memories can often be traced to changes in the lives of older adults. For instance, it is not surprising that a retired person, who may no longer face the same kind of consistent intellectual challenges encountered on the job, may have less practice in using memory or even be less motivated to remember things, leading to an apparent decline in memory. Even in cases in which long-term memory declines, older adults can profit from training that targets memory skills (Fritsch et al., 2007; West, Bagwell, & Dark-Freudeman, 2007).

In the past, older adults with severe cases of memory decline, accompanied by other cognitive difficulties, were said to suffer from senility. *Senility* is a broad, imprecise term typically applied to older adults who experience progressive deterioration of mental abilities, including memory loss, disorientation to time and place, and general confusion. Once thought to be an inevitable state that accompanies aging, senility

Alzheimer's disease: A progressive brain disorder that leads to a gradual and irreversible decline in cognitive abilities.

is now viewed by most gerontologists as a label that has outlived its usefulness. Rather than senility being the cause of certain symptoms, the symptoms are deemed to be caused by some other factor.

Some cases of memory loss, however, are produced by actual disease. For instance, **Alzheimer's disease** is a progressive brain disorder that leads to a gradual and irreversible decline in cognitive abilities. Nineteen percent of people age 75 to 84 have Alzheimer's, and almost 50 percent of people over age 85 are affected by the disease. Unless a cure is found, some 14 million people will experience Alzheimer's by 2050—more than three times the current number (Cowley, 2000b; Feinberg, 2002; Lovestone, 2005; Rogers, 2007).

Alzheimer's occurs when production of the *beta amyloid precursor protein* goes awry, producing large clumps of cells that trigger inflammation and deterioration of nerve cells. The brain shrinks, neurons die, and several areas of the hippocampus and frontal and temporal lobes deteriorate. So far, there is no effective treatment (Lanctot, Herrmann, & Mazzotta, 2001; Blennow & Vanmechelen, 2003; Wolfe, 2006; Medeiros et al., 2007).

In other cases, cognitive declines may be caused by temporary anxiety and depression, which can be treated successfully, or may even be due to overmedication. The danger is that people with such symptoms may be left untreated, thereby continuing their decline (Selkoe, 1997; Sachs-Ericsson et al., 2005).

In sum, declines in cognitive functioning in late adulthood are, for the most part, not inevitable. The key to maintaining cognitive skills may lie in intellectual stimulation. Like the rest of us, older adults need a stimulating environment in order to hone and maintain their skills (Bosma et al., 2003; Glisky, 2007).

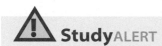 **Study**ALERT

It's important to be able to describe the nature of intellectual changes during late adulthood.

THE SOCIAL WORLD OF LATE ADULTHOOD: OLD BUT NOT ALONE

Just as the view that old age predictably means mental decline has proved to be wrong, so has the view that late adulthood inevitably brings loneliness. People in late adulthood most often see themselves as functioning members of society, with only a small number of them reporting that loneliness is a serious problem (Binstock & George, 1996; Jylha, 2004).

Certainly, late adulthood brings significant challenges. People who have spent their adult lives working enter retirement, bringing about a major shift in the role they play. Moreover, many people must face the death of their spouse. Especially if the marriage has been a long and good one, the death of a partner means the loss of a companion, confidante, and lover. It can also bring about changes in economic well-being.

Disengagement theory of aging: A theory that suggests that aging produces a gradual withdrawal from the world on physical, psychological, and social levels.

There is no single way to age successfully. According to the **disengagement theory of aging**, aging produces a gradual withdrawal from the world on physical, psychological, and social levels. However, such disengagement serves an important purpose, providing an opportunity for increased reflectiveness and decreased emotional investment in others at a time of life when social relationships will inevitably be ended by death (Adams, 2004; Wrosch, Bauer, & Scheier, 2005).

Activity theory of aging: A theory that suggests that the elderly who are most successful while aging are those who maintain the interests and activities they had during middle age.

The **activity theory of aging** presents an alternative view of aging, holding that the people who age most successfully are those who maintain the interests, activities, and level of social interaction they experienced during middle adulthood. According to activity theory, late adulthood should reflect a continuation, as much as possible, of the activities in which people participated during the earlier part of their lives (Crosnoe & Elder, 2002; Nimrod & Kleiber, 2007).

Both disengagement and activity can lead to successful aging. Not all people in late adulthood need a life filled with activities and social interaction to be happy; as in every stage of life, some older adults are just as satisfied leading a relatively inactive, solitary existence. What may be more important is how people view the aging process: Evidence shows that positive self-perceptions of aging are associated with increased longevity (Levy et al., 2002; Levy & Myers, 2004).

Regardless of whether people become disengaged or maintain their activities from earlier stages of life, most engage in a process of **life review**, in which they examine and evaluate their lives. Remembering and reconsidering what has occurred in the past, people in late adulthood often come to a better understanding of themselves, sometimes resolving lingering problems and conflicts, and facing their lives with greater wisdom and serenity.

Clearly, people in late adulthood are not just marking time until death. Rather, old age is a time of continued growth and development, as important as any other period of life.

Life review: The process by which people examine and evaluate their lives.

BECOMING AN INFORMED CONSUMER of Psychology

Adjusting to Death

At some time in our lives, we all face death—certainly our own, as well as the deaths of friends, loved ones, and even strangers. Although there is nothing more inevitable in life, death remains a frightening, emotion-laden topic. Certainly, little is more stressful than the death of a loved one or the contemplation of our own imminent death, and preparing for death is one of our most crucial developmental tasks (Aiken, 2000).

A generation ago, talk of death was taboo. The topic was never mentioned to dying people, and gerontologists had little to say about it. That changed, however, with the pioneering work of Elisabeth Kübler-Ross (1969), who brought the subject of death into the open with her observation that those facing impending death tend to move through five broad stages:

- *Denial.* In this stage, people resist the idea that they are dying. Even if told that their chances for survival are small, they refuse to admit that they are facing death.

- *Anger.* After moving beyond the denial stage, dying people become angry—angry at people around them who are in good health, angry at medical professionals for being ineffective, angry at God.

- *Bargaining.* Anger leads to bargaining, in which the dying try to think of ways to postpone death. They may decide to dedicate their lives to religion if God saves them; they may say, "If only I can live to see my son married, I will accept death then."

- *Depression.* When dying people come to feel that bargaining is of no use, they move to the next stage: depression. They realize that their lives really are coming to an end, leading to what Kübler-Ross calls "preparatory grief" for their own deaths.

- *Acceptance.* In this stage, people accept impending death. Usually they are unemotional and uncommunicative; it is as if they have made peace with themselves and are expecting death with no bitterness.

It is important to keep in mind that not everyone experiences each of these stages in the same way. In fact, Kübler-Ross's stages pertain only to people who are fully aware that they are dying and have the time to evaluate their impending death. Furthermore, vast differences occur in the way individuals react to impending death. The specific cause and duration of dying, as well as the person's sex, age, and personality and the type of support received from family and friends, all have an impact on how people respond to death (Carver & Scheier, 2002; Coyle, 2006).

Few of us enjoy the contemplation of death. Yet awareness of its psychological aspects and consequences can make its inevitable arrival less anxiety-producing and perhaps more understandable.

RECAP/EVALUATE/RETHINK

RECAP

What are the principal kinds of physical, social, and intellectual changes that occur in early and middle adulthood, and what are their causes?

- Early adulthood marks the peak of physical health. Physical changes occur relatively gradually in men and women during adulthood. (p. 433)
- One major physical change occurs at the end of middle adulthood for women: They begin menopause, after which they are no longer fertile. (p. 433)
- During middle adulthood, people typically experience a midlife transition in which the notion that life is not unending becomes more important. In some cases this may lead to a midlife crisis, although the passage into middle age is typically relatively calm. (p. 434)
- As aging continues during middle adulthood, people realize in their 50s that their lives and accomplishments are fairly well set, and they try to come to terms with them. (p. 434)
- Among the important developmental milestones during adulthood are marriage, family changes, and divorce. Another important determinant of adult development is work. (p. 435)

How does the reality of late adulthood differ from the stereotypes about that period?

- Old age may bring marked physical declines caused by genetic preprogramming or physical wear and tear. Although the activities of people in late adulthood are not all that different from those of younger people, older adults experience declines in reaction time, sensory abilities, and physical stamina. (p. 437)
- Intellectual declines are not an inevitable part of aging. Fluid intelligence does decline with age, and long-term memory abilities are sometimes impaired. In contrast, crystallized intelligence shows slight increases with age, and short-term memory remains at about the same level. (p. 438)
- Disengagement theory sees successful aging as a process of gradual withdrawal from the physical, psychological, and social worlds. In contrast, activity theory suggests that the maintenance of interests and activities from earlier years leads to successful aging. (p. 440)

How can we adjust to death?

- According to Kübler-Ross, dying people move through five stages as they face death: denial, anger, bargaining, depression, and acceptance. (p. xx)

EVALUATE

1. Rob recently turned 40 and surveyed his goals and accomplishments to date. Although he has accomplished a lot, he realized that many of his goals will not be met in his lifetime. This stage is called a _____ _____.
2. In households where both partners have similar jobs, the division of labor that generally occurs is the same as in "traditional" households where the husband works and the wife stays at home. True or false?
3. _____ _____ theories suggest that there is a maximum time span in which cells are able to reproduce. This time limit explains the eventual breakdown of the body.
4. Lower IQ test scores during late adulthood do not necessarily mean a decrease in intelligence. True or false?
5. During old age, a person's _____ intelligence continues to increase, whereas _____ intelligence may decline.
6. In Kübler-Ross's _____ stage, people resist the idea of death. In the _____ stage, they attempt to make deals to avoid death, and in the _____ stage, they passively await death.

RETHINK

1. Is the possibility that life may be extended for several decades a mixed blessing? What societal consequences might an extended life span bring about?
2. *From the perspective of a health care provider:* What sorts of recommendations would you make to your older patients about how to deal with aging? How would you handle someone who believed that getting older had only negative consequences?

Answers to Evaluate Questions

1. midlife transition; 2. true; 3. genetic preprogramming; 4. true; 5. crystallized, fluid; 6. denial, bargaining, acceptance

KEY TERMS

menopause p. 433
genetic preprogramming theories of aging p. 437

wear-and-tear theories of aging p. 437
Alzheimer's disease p. 440

disengagement theory of aging p. 440
activity theory of aging p. 440

life review p. 441

Psychology on the Web

1. Find information on the Web about gene therapy. What recent advances in gene therapy have been made by researchers? What developments appear to be on the horizon? What ethical issues have been raised regarding the use of gene therapy to produce children with characteristics specified by their parents?
2. Find different answers to the question "Why do people die?" Search the Web for scientific, philosophical, and spiritual/religious answers. Write a summary in which you compare the different approaches to this question. How does the thinking in any one realm influence the thinking in the others?

Epilogue

We have traced major events in the development of physical, social, and cognitive growth throughout the life span. Clearly, people change throughout their lives.

As we explored each area of development, we encountered anew the nature–nurture issue, concluding in every significant instance that both nature and nurture contribute to a person's development of skills, personality, and interactions. Specifically, our genetic inheritance—nature—lays down general boundaries within which we can advance and grow, and our environment—nurture—helps determine the extent to which we take advantage of our potential.

Before proceeding to the next set of modules, turn once again to the prologue that introduced this one, on Danielle Link and Glen Zilly, the married couple who originally met as toddlers in day care. Using your knowledge of human development, consider the following questions.

1. Do you think that Danielle and Glen's early shared experiences may have had some influence on their later attraction to one another?
2. How might Danielle and Glen's development been affected by the experience of receiving child care outside the home?
3. Describe how Danielle and Glen might have related to each other as toddlers.
4. At which of Erikson's stages of psychosocial development were Danielle and Glen when they played together as toddlers? At which stage were they when they reunited as young adults?

Personality

Key Concepts for Chapter 13

Prologue *Wanted: Software engineer. Must be a messy, extroverted dog owner.*

Last summer, Google asked every employee who had been working at the company for at least five months to fill out a 300-question survey.

Some questions were factual: What programming languages are you familiar with? What Internet mailing lists do you subscribe to?

Some looked for behavior: Is your work space messy or neat?

And some looked at personality: Are you an extrovert or an introvert?

And some fell into no traditional category in the human resources world: What magazines do you subscribe to? What pets do you have?

"We wanted to cast a very wide net," said Laszlo Bock, Google's vice president for people operations. "It is not unusual to walk the halls here and bump into dogs. Maybe people who own dogs have some personality trait that is useful." (Hansell, 2007, p. A1)

Looking Ahead

Why is Google concerned about the personal habits and quirks of its thousands of employees? Analysts are seeking to determine if various measures of employees' personality traits and behavior consistently predict who will perform well at a given job. Google executives hope to find enough useful predictors so that they can eventually automate the process of sifting through the hundreds of job applications they receive each week and identify the most promising job candidates.

Although we don't yet know if Google will be successful in identifying the traits that distinguish its most successful employees, it is clear that personality is a central area for psychologists in understanding human behavior. **Personality** is the pattern of enduring characteristics that produce consistency and individuality in a given person. Personality encompasses the behaviors that make each of us unique and that differentiate us from others. It is also personality that leads us to act consistently in different situations and over extended periods of time.

We will consider a number of approaches to personality. For historical reasons, we begin with psychodynamic theories of personality, which emphasize the importance of the unconscious. Next, we consider approaches that concentrate on identifying the most fundamental personality traits; theories that view personality as a set of learned behaviors; biological and evolutionary perspectives on personality; and approaches, known as humanistic theories, that highlight the uniquely human aspects of personality. We end our discussion by focusing on how personality is measured and how personality tests can be used.

Personality: The pattern of enduring characteristics that produce consistency and individuality in a given person.

Psychodynamic Approaches to Personality

The college student was intent on making a good first impression on an attractive woman he had spotted across a crowded room at a party. As he walked toward her, he mulled over a line he had heard in an old movie the night before: "I don't believe we've been properly introduced yet." To his horror, what came out was a bit different. After threading his way through the crowded room, he finally reached the woman and blurted out, "I don't believe we've been properly seduced yet."

Although this student's error may seem to be merely an embarrassing slip of the tongue, according to some personality theorists such a mistake is not an error at all (Motley, 1987). Instead, *psychodynamic personality theorists* might argue that the error illustrates one way in which behavior is triggered by inner forces that are beyond our awareness. These hidden drives, shaped by childhood experiences, play an important role in energizing and directing everyday behavior.

Psychodynamic approaches to personality are based on the idea that personality is motivated by inner forces and conflicts about which people have little awareness and over which they have no control. The most important pioneer of the psychodynamic approach was Sigmund Freud. A number of Freud's followers, including Carl Jung, Karen Horney, and Alfred Adler, refined Freud's theory and developed their own psychodynamic approaches.

Key Concepts

How do psychologists define and use the concept of personality?

What do the theories of Freud and his successors tell us about the structure and development of personality?

Psychodynamic approaches to personality: Approaches that assume that personality is motivated by inner forces and conflicts about which people have little awareness and over which they have no control.

Freud's Psychoanalytic Theory: Mapping the Unconscious Mind

Sigmund Freud, an Austrian physician, developed **psychoanalytic theory** in the early 1900s. According to Freud's theory, conscious experience is only a small part of our psychological makeup and experience. He argued that much of our behavior is motivated by the **unconscious**, a part of the personality that contains the memories, knowledge, beliefs, feelings urges, drives, and instincts of which the individual is not aware.

Like the unseen mass of a floating iceberg, the contents of the unconscious far surpass in quantity the information in our conscious awareness. Freud maintained that to understand personality, it is necessary to expose what is in the unconscious. But because the unconscious disguises the meaning of the material it holds, the content of the unconscious cannot be observed directly. It is therefore necessary to interpret clues to the unconscious—slips of the tongue, fantasies, and dreams—to understand the unconscious processes that direct behavior. A slip of the tongue such as the one quoted earlier (sometimes termed a *Freudian slip*) may be interpreted as revealing the speaker's unconscious sexual desires.

To Freud, much of our personality is determined by our unconscious. Some of the unconscious is made up of the *preconscious*, which contains material that is not threatening and is easily brought to mind, such as the knowledge that 2 + 2 = 4. But deeper in the unconscious are instinctual drives, the wishes, desires, demands, and needs that

Psychoanalytic theory: Freud's theory that unconscious forces act as determinants of personality.

Unconscious: A part of the personality that contains the memories, knowledge, beliefs, feelings, urges, drives, and instincts of which the individual is not aware.

447

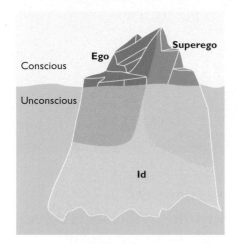

FIGURE 1 In Freud's model of personality, there are three major components: the id, the ego, and the superego. As the iceberg analogy shows, only a small portion of personality is conscious. Why do you think that only the ego and superego have conscious components?

 StudyALERT

Remember that the three parts of personality in Freud's theory—the id, the ego, and the superego—are abstract conceptions that don't exist as physical structures in the brain.

Id: The raw, unorganized, inborn part of personality whose sole purpose is to reduce tension created by primitive drives related to hunger, sex, aggression, and irrational impulses.

Ego: The part of the personality that provides a buffer between the id and the outside world.

Superego: According to Freud, the final personality structure to develop; it represents the rights and wrongs of society as handed down by a person's parents, teachers, and other important figures.

Psychosexual stages: Developmental periods that children pass through during which they encounter conflicts between the demands of society and their own sexual urges.

Fixations: Conflicts or concerns that persist beyond the developmental period in which they first occur.

are hidden from conscious awareness because of the conflicts and pain they would cause if they were part of our everyday lives. The unconscious provides a "safe haven" for our recollections of threatening events.

STRUCTURING PERSONALITY: ID, EGO, AND SUPEREGO

To describe the structure of personality, Freud developed a comprehensive theory that held that personality consists of three separate but interacting components: the id, the ego, and the superego. Freud suggested that the three structures can be diagrammed to show how they relate to the conscious and the unconscious (see Figure 1).

Although the three components of personality described by Freud may appear to be actual physical structures in the nervous system, they are not. Instead, they represent abstract conceptions of a general *model* of personality that describes the interaction of forces that motivate behavior.

If personality consisted only of primitive, instinctual cravings and longings, it would have just one component: the id. The **id** is the raw, unorganized, inborn part of personality. From the time of birth, the id attempts to reduce tension created by primitive drives related to hunger, sex, aggression, and irrational impulses. Those drives are fueled by "psychic energy," which we can think of as a limitless energy source constantly putting pressure on the various parts of the personality.

The id operates according to the *pleasure principle*, in which the goal is the immediate reduction of tension and the maximization of satisfaction. However, in most cases reality prevents the fulfillment of the demands of the pleasure principle: We cannot always eat when we are hungry, and we can discharge our sexual drives only when the time and place are appropriate. To account for this fact of life, Freud suggested a second component of personality, which he called the ego.

The **ego**, which begins to develop soon after birth, strives to balance the desires of the id and the realities of the objective, outside world. In contrast to the pleasure-seeking id, the ego operates according to the *reality principle*, in which instinctual energy is restrained to maintain the safety of the individual and to help integrate the person into society. In a sense, then, the ego is the "executive" of personality: It makes decisions, controls actions, and allows thinking and problem solving of a higher order than the id's capabilities permit.

The **superego**, the final personality structure to develop in childhood, represents the rights and wrongs of society as taught and modeled by a person's parents, teachers, and other significant individuals. The superego includes the *conscience*, which prevents us from behaving in a morally improper way by making us feel guilty if we do wrong. The superego helps us control impulses coming from the id, making our behavior less selfish and more virtuous.

Both the superego and the id are unrealistic in that they do not consider the practical realities imposed by society. The superego, if left to operate without restraint, would create perfectionists unable to make the compromises that life requires. An unrestrained id would create a primitive, pleasure-seeking, thoughtless individual seeking to fulfill every desire without delay. As a result, the ego must mediate between the demands of the superego and the demands of the id.

DEVELOPING PERSONALITY: PSYCHOSEXUAL STAGES

Freud also provided us with a view of how personality develops through a series of five **psychosexual stages**, during which individuals encounter conflicts between the demands of society and their own sexual urges (in which sexuality is more about experiencing pleasure and less about lust). According to Freud, failure to resolve the conflicts at a particular stage can result in **fixations**, conflicts or concerns that persist beyond the developmental period in which they first occur. Such conflicts may be due to having needs ignored or (conversely) being overindulged during the earlier period.

Freud suggests that the superego, the part of personality that represents the rights and wrongs of society, develops from direct teaching from parents, teachers, and other significant individuals.

The sequence Freud proposed is noteworthy because it explains how experiences and difficulties during a particular childhood stage may predict specific characteristics in the adult personality. This theory is also unique in associating each stage with a major biological function, which Freud assumed to be the focus of pleasure in a given period.

In the first psychosexual stage of development, called the **oral stage**, the baby's mouth is the focal point of pleasure (see Figure 2 for a summary of the stages). During the first 12 to 18 months of life, children suck, eat, mouth, and bite anything they can put into their mouths. To Freud, this behavior suggested that the mouth is the primary site of a kind of sexual pleasure, and that weaning (withdrawing the breast or bottle) represents the main conflict during the oral stage. If infants are either overindulged (perhaps by being fed every time they cry) or frustrated in their search for oral gratification, they may become fixated at this stage. For example, fixation might occur if an infant's oral needs were constantly gratified immediately at the first sign of hunger, rather than if the infant learned that feeding takes place on a schedule because eating

StudyALERT

The five psychosexual stages of personality development in Freud's theory—oral, anal, phallic, latency, and genital—indicate how personality develops as people age.

Oral stage: According to Freud, a stage from birth to age 12 to 18 months, in which an infant's center of pleasure is the mouth.

Stage	Age	Major Characteristics
Oral	Birth to 12–18 months	Interest in oral gratification from sucking, eating, mouthing, biting
Anal	12–18 months to 3 years	Gratification from expelling and withholding feces; coming to terms with society's controls relating to toilet training
Phallic	3 to 5–6 years	Interest in the genitals, coming to terms with Oedipal conflict leading to identification with same-sex parent
Latency	5–6 years to adolescence	Sexual concerns largely unimportant
Genital	Adolescence to adulthood	Reemergence of sexual interests and establishment of mature sexual relationships

FIGURE 2 Freud's theory of personality development suggests that there are several distinct stages.

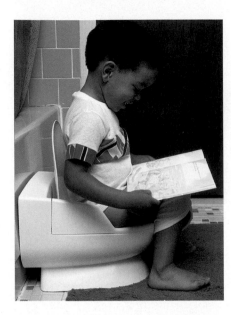

According to Freud, a child goes through the anal stage from age 12 to 18 months until 3 years of age. Toilet training is a crucial event at this stage, one that psychoanalytic theory claims directly influences the formation of an individual's personality.

Anal stage: According to Freud, a stage from age 12 to 18 months to 3 years of age, in which a child's pleasure is centered on the anus.
Phallic stage: According to Freud, a period beginning around age 3 during which a child's pleasure focuses on the genitals.
Oedipal conflict: A child's sexual interest in his or her opposite-sex parent, typically resolved through identification with the same-sex parent.
Identification: The process of wanting to be like another person as much as possible, imitating that person's behavior and adopting similar beliefs and values.
Latency period: According to Freud, the period between the phallic stage and puberty during which children's sexual concerns are temporarily put aside.
Genital stage: According to Freud, the period from puberty until death, marked by mature sexual behavior (that is, sexual intercourse).

whenever an infant wants to eat is not always realistic. Fixation at the oral stage might produce an adult who was unusually interested in oral activities—eating, talking, smoking—or who showed symbolic sorts of oral interests: being either "bitingly" sarcastic or very gullible ("swallowing" anything).

From around age 12 to 18 months until 3 years of age—a period when the emphasis in Western cultures is on toilet training—a child enters the **anal stage**. At this point, the major source of pleasure changes from the mouth to the anal region, and children obtain considerable pleasure from both retention and expulsion of feces. If toilet training is particularly demanding, fixation might occur. Fixation during the anal stage might result in unusual rigidity, orderliness, punctuality—or extreme disorderliness or sloppiness—in adulthood.

At about age 3, the **phallic stage** begins. At this point there is another major shift in the primary source of pleasure for the child. Now interest focuses on the genitals and the pleasures derived from fondling them. During this stage the child must also negotiate one of the most important hurdles of personality development: the **Oedipal conflict**. According to Freudian theory, as children focus attention on their genitals, the differences between male and female anatomy become more salient. Furthermore, according to Freud, at this time the male unconsciously begins to develop a sexual interest in his mother, starts to see his father as a rival, and harbors a wish to kill his father—as Oedipus did in the ancient Greek tragedy. But because he views his father as too powerful, he develops a fear that his father may retaliate drastically by removing the source of the threat: the son's penis. The fear of losing one's penis leads to *castration anxiety*, which ultimately becomes so powerful that the child represses his desires for his mother and identifies with his father. **Identification** is the process of wanting to be like another person as much as possible, imitating that person's behavior and adopting similar beliefs and values. By identifying with his father, a son seeks to obtain a woman like his unattainable mother.

For girls, the process is different. Freud reasoned that girls begin to experience sexual arousal toward their fathers and begin to experience penis envy. They wish they had the anatomical part that, at least to Freud, seemed most clearly "missing" in girls. Blaming their mothers for their lack of a penis, girls come to believe that their mothers are responsible for their "castration." (This aspect of Freud's theory later provoked accusations that he considered women to be inferior to men.) Like males, though, they find that they can resolve such unacceptable feelings by identifying with the same-sex parent, behaving like her and adopting her attitudes and values. In this way, a girl's identification with her mother is completed.

At this point, the Oedipal conflict is said to be resolved, and Freudian theory assumes that both males and females move on to the next stage of development. If difficulties arise during this period, however, all sorts of problems are thought to occur, including improper sex-role behavior and the failure to develop a conscience.

After the resolution of the Oedipal conflict, typically at around age 5 or 6, children move into the **latency period**, which lasts until puberty. During this period, sexual interests become dormant, even in the unconscious. Then, during adolescence, sexual feelings reemerge, marking the start of the final period, the **genital stage**, which extends until death. The focus during the genital stage is on mature, adult sexuality, which Freud defined as sexual intercourse.

DEFENSE MECHANISMS

Freud's efforts to describe and theorize about the underlying dynamics of personality and its development were motivated by very practical problems that his patients faced in dealing with *anxiety*, an intense, negative emotional experience. According to Freud, anxiety is a danger signal to the ego. Although anxiety can arise from realistic fears—such as seeing a poisonous snake about to strike—it can also occur in the form of *neurotic anxiety*, in which irrational impulses emanating from the id threaten to burst through and become uncontrollable.

Because anxiety, obviously, is unpleasant, Freud believed that people develop a range of defense mechanisms to deal with it. **Defense mechanisms** are unconscious strategies that people use to reduce anxiety by concealing its source from themselves and others.

The primary defense mechanism is **repression**, in which unacceptable or unpleasant id impulses are pushed back into the unconscious. Repression is the most direct method of dealing with anxiety; instead of handling an anxiety-producing impulse on a conscious level, we simply ignore it. For example, a college student who feels hatred for his mother may repress those personally and socially unacceptable feelings. The feelings remain lodged within the unconscious, because acknowledging them would provoke anxiety. Similarly, memories of childhood abuse may be repressed. Although such memories may not be consciously recalled, according to Freud they can affect later behavior, and they may be revealed through dreams or slips of the tongue or symbolically in some other fashion.

If repression is ineffective in keeping anxiety at bay, we might use other defense mechanisms. Freud, and later his daughter Anna Freud (who became a well-known psychoanalyst), formulated an extensive list of potential defense mechanisms. The major defense mechanisms are summarized in Figure 3 (Conte & Plutchik, 2004; Hentschel et al., 2004; Cramer, 2007).

All of us employ defense mechanisms to some degree, according to Freudian theory, and they can serve a useful purpose by protecting us from unpleasant information. Yet some people fall prey to them to such an extent that they must constantly direct a large amount of psychic energy toward hiding and rechanneling unacceptable impulses. When this occurs, everyday living becomes difficult. In such cases, the result is a mental disorder produced by anxiety—what Freud called "neurosis" (a term rarely used by psychologists today, although it endures in everyday conversation).

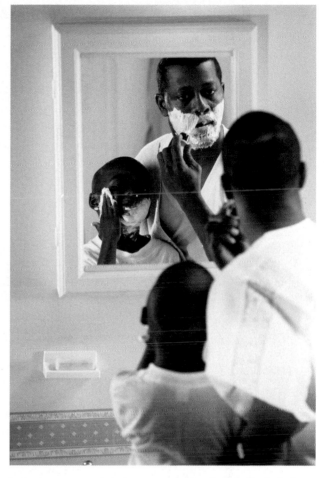

Imitating a person's behavior and adopting similar beliefs and values is part of Freud's concept of identification. How can this concept be applied to the definition of gender roles? Is identification similar in all cultures?

EVALUATING FREUD'S LEGACY

Freud's theory has had a significant impact on the field of psychology—and even more broadly on Western philosophy and literature. The ideas of the unconscious, defense mechanisms, and childhood roots of adult psychological difficulties have been accepted by many people.

However, many contemporary personality psychologists have leveled significant criticisms against psychoanalytic theory. Among the most important is the lack of compelling scientific data to support it. Although individual case studies *seem* supportive, we lack conclusive evidence showing that the personality is structured and operates along the lines Freud laid out. The lack of evidence is due, in part, to the fact that Freud's conception of personality is built on unobservable abstract concepts. Moreover, it is not clear that the stages of personality that Freud laid out provide an accurate description of personality development. We also know now that important changes in personality can occur in adolescence and adulthood—something that Freud did not believe happened. Instead, he argued that personality largely is set by adolescence.

The vague nature of Freud's theory also makes it difficult to predict how certain developmental difficulties will be displayed in an adult. For instance, if a person is fixated at the anal stage, according to Freud, he or she may be unusually messy—or unusually neat. Freud's theory offers no way to predict how the difficulty will be exhibited (Macmillan, 1996; Crews, 1996). Furthermore, Freud can be faulted for seeming to view women as inferior to men, because he argued that women have weaker superegos than men do and in some ways unconsciously yearn to be men (the concept of penis envy).

Defense mechanisms: In Freudian theory, unconscious strategies that people use to reduce anxiety by concealing the source of the anxiety from themselves and others.

Repression: The primary defense mechanism in which unacceptable or unpleasant id impulses are pushed back into the unconscious.

Freud's Defense Mechanisms		
Defense Mechanism	**Explanation**	**Example**
Repression	Unacceptable or unpleasant impulses are pushed back into the unconscious.	A woman is unable to recall that she was raped.
Regression	People behave as if they were at an earlier stage of development.	A boss has a temper tantrum when an employee makes a mistake.
Displacement	The expression of an unwanted feeling or thought is redirected from a more threatening powerful person to a weaker one.	A brother yells at his younger sister after a teacher gives him a bad grade.
Rationalization	People provide self-justifying explanations in place of the actual, but threatening, reason for their behavior.	A student who goes out drinking the night before a big test rationalizes his behavior by saying the test isn't all that important.
Denial	People refuse to accept or acknowledge an anxiety-producing piece of information.	A student refuses to believe that he has flunked a course.
Projection	People attribute unwanted impulses and feelings to someone else.	A man who is unfaithful to his wife and feels guilty suspects that his wife is unfaithful.
Sublimation	People divert unwanted impulses into socially approved thoughts, feelings, or behaviors.	A person with strong feelings of aggression becomes a soldier.
Reaction formation	Unconscious impulses are expressed as their opposite in consciousness.	A mother who unconsciously resents her child acts in an overly loving way toward the child.

FIGURE 3 According to Freud, people are able to use a wide range of defense mechanisms to cope with anxieties.

StudyALERT

Use Figure 3 to remember the most common defense mechanisms (unconscious strategies used to reduce anxiety by concealing its source from ourselves and others).

Finally, Freud made his observations and derived his theory from a limited population. His theory was based almost entirely on upper-class Austrian women living in the strict, puritanical era of the early 1900s, who had come to him seeking treatment for psychological and physical problems. How far one can generalize beyond this population is a matter of considerable debate. For instance, in some Pacific Island societies, the role of disciplinarian is played by the mother's oldest brother, not the father. In such a culture, it is unreasonable to argue that the Oedipal conflict will progress in the same way that it did in Austrian society, where the father typically was the major disciplinarian. In short, a cross-cultural perspective raises questions about the universality of Freud's view of personality development (Doi, 1990; Altman, 1996; Spielberger, 2007).

Still, Freud generated an important method of treating psychological disturbances called *psychoanalysis*. As we will see when we discuss treatment approaches to psychological disorders, psychoanalysis remains in use today (Messer & McWilliams, 2003; Heller, 2005; Riolo, 2007).

Moreover, Freud's emphasis on the unconscious has been partially supported by current research on dreams and implicit memory. As we first noted when we discussed dreaming, advances in neuroscience are consistent with some of Freud's arguments. For example, the fact that some behavior is motivated by occurrences that apparently have been forgotten, as well as the discovery of neural pathways relating to emotional memories, supports the notion of repression. Furthermore, cognitive and social psychologists have found increasing evidence that unconscious processes help us think about and evaluate our world, set goals, and choose a course of action.

It remains to be seen the degree to which future neuroscientific advances will support the criticisms leveled against Freud's psychoanalytic theory (Derryberry, 2006; Litowitz, 2007).

The Neo-Freudian Psychoanalysts: Building on Freud

Freud laid the foundation for important work done by a series of successors who were trained in traditional Freudian theory but later rejected some of its major points. These theorists are known as **neo-Freudian psychoanalysts**.

The neo-Freudians placed greater emphasis than Freud had on the functions of the ego, suggesting that it has more control than does the id over day-to-day activities. They focused more on the social environment and minimized the importance of sex as a driving force in people's lives. They also paid greater attention to the effects of society and culture on personality development.

Neo-Freudian psychoanalysts: Psychoanalysts who were trained in traditional Freudian theory but who later rejected some of its major points.

JUNG'S COLLECTIVE UNCONSCIOUS

One of the most influential neo-Freudians, Carl Jung (pronounced "yoong"), rejected Freud's view of the primary importance of unconscious sexual urges. Instead, he looked at the primitive urges of the unconscious more positively, arguing that they represented a more general, and positive, life force that encompasses an inborn drive motivating creativity and more positive resolution of conflict (Lothane, 2005; Cassells, 2007).

Jung suggested that we have a universal **collective unconscious**, a common set of ideas, feelings, images, and symbols that we inherit from our relatives, the whole human race, and even nonhuman animal ancestors from the distant past. This collective unconscious is shared by everyone and is displayed in behavior that is common across diverse cultures—such as love of mother, belief in a supreme being, and even behavior as specific as fear of snakes (Oehman & Mineka, 2003; Drob, 2005; Hauke, 2006).

Jung went on to propose that the collective unconscious contains **archetypes**, universal symbolic representations of a particular person, object, or experience. For instance, a mother archetype, which contains reflections of our ancestors' relationships with mother figures, is suggested by the prevalence of mothers in art, religion, literature, and mythology. (Think of the Virgin Mary, Earth Mother, wicked stepmothers in fairy tales, Mother's Day, and so forth!) Jung also suggested that men possess an unconscious feminine archetype affecting how they behave, whereas women have an unconscious male archetype that colors their behavior (Jung, 1961; Bair, 2003; Smetana, 2007).

To Jung, archetypes play an important role in determining our day-to-day reactions, attitudes, and values. For example, Jung might explain the popularity of the *Star Wars* movies as being due to their use of broad archetypes of good (Luke Skywalker) and evil (Darth Vader).

Although no reliable research evidence confirms the existence of the collective unconscious—and even Jung acknowledged that such evidence would be difficult to produce—Jung's theory has had significant influence in areas beyond psychology. For example, personality types derived from Jung's personality approach form the basis for the Myers-Briggs personality test, which is widely used in business and industry (Gladwell, 2004; Bayne, 2005; Furnham & Cump, 2005).

Collective unconscious: According to Jung, a common set of ideas, feelings, images, and symbols that we inherit from our ancestors, the whole human race, and even animal ancestors from the distant past.

Archetypes: According to Jung, universal symbolic representations of a particular person, object, or experience (such as good and evil).

HORNEY'S NEO-FREUDIAN PERSPECTIVE

Karen Horney (pronounced "HORN-eye") was one of the earliest psychologists to champion women's issues and is sometimes called the first feminist psychologist. Horney suggested that personality develops in the context of social relationships and depends

In terms of Jung's theory, Batman and the Joker represent the archetypes, or universally recognizable symbols, of good and evil, respectively.

particularly on the relationship between parents and child and how well the child's needs are met. She rejected Freud's suggestion that women have penis envy, asserting that what women envy most in men is not their anatomy but the independence, success, and freedom that women often are denied (Horney, 1937; Miletic, 2002; Smith, 2007).

Horney was also one of the first to stress the importance of cultural factors in the determination of personality. For example, she suggested that society's rigid gender roles for women lead them to experience ambivalence about success, fearing that they will make enemies if they are too successful. Her conceptualizations, developed in the 1930s and 1940s, laid the groundwork for many of the central ideas of feminism that emerged decades later (Eckardt, 2005; Jones, 2006).

ADLER AND THE OTHER NEO-FREUDIANS

Inferiority complex: According to Adler, a problem affecting adults who have not been able to overcome the feelings of inferiority that they developed as children, when they were small and limited in their knowledge about the world.

Alfred Adler, another important neo-Freudian psychoanalyst, also considered Freudian theory's emphasis on sexual needs misplaced. Instead, Adler proposed that the primary human motivation is a striving for superiority, not in terms of superiority over others but in a quest for self-improvement and perfection.

Adler used the term **inferiority complex** to describe situations in which adults have not been able to overcome the feelings of inferiority they developed as children, when they were small and limited in their knowledge about the world. Early social

Karen Horney was one of the earliest proponents of women's issues.

relationships with parents have an important effect on children's ability to outgrow feelings of personal inferiority and instead to orient themselves toward attaining more socially useful goals, such as improving society.

Other neo-Freudians included such figures as Erik Erikson, whose theory of psychosocial development we discussed in earlier modules, and Freud's daughter, Anna Freud. Like Adler and Horney, they focused less than Freud on inborn sexual and aggressive drives and more on the social and cultural factors behind personality.

RECAP/EVALUATE/RETHINK

RECAP

How do psychologists define and use the concept of personality?

- Personality is the pattern of enduring characteristics that produce consistency and individuality in a given person. (p. 446)

What do the theories of Freud and his successors tell us about the structure and development of personality?

- According to psychodynamic approaches to personality, much behavior is caused by parts of personality that are found in the unconscious and of which we are unaware. (p. 447)

- Freud's psychoanalytic theory, one of the psychodynamic approaches, suggests that personality is composed of the id, the ego, and the superego. The id is the unorganized,

inborn part of personality whose purpose is to immediately reduce tensions relating to hunger, sex, aggression, and other primitive impulses. The ego restrains instinctual energy to maintain the safety of the individual and to help the person be a member of society. The superego represents the rights and wrongs of society and includes the conscience. (p. 448)

- Freud's psychoanalytic theory suggests that personality develops through a series of psychosexual stages (oral, anal, phallic, latency, and genital), each of which is associated with a primary biological function. (p. 448)

- Defense mechanisms, according to Freudian theory, are unconscious strategies with which people reduce anxieties relating to impulses from the id. (p. 451)

- Freud's psychoanalytic theory has provoked a number of criticisms, including a lack of supportive scientific data, the theory's inadequacy in making predictions, and its reliance on a highly restricted population. On the other hand, recent neuroscience research has offered some support for the concept of the unconscious. (p. 451)

- Neo-Freudian psychoanalytic theorists built on Freud's work, although they placed greater emphasis on the role of the ego and paid more attention to the role of social factors in determining behavior. (p. 453)

EVALUATE

1. _____ approaches state that behavior is motivated primarily by unconscious forces.
2. Match each section of the personality (according to Freud) with its description:
   1. Ego
   2. Id
   3. Superego
   a. Determines right from wrong on the basis of cultural standards.
   b. Operates according to the "reality principle"; energy is redirected to integrate the person into society.
   c. Seeks to reduce tension brought on by primitive drives.

3. Which of the following represents the proper order of personality development, according to Freud?
   a. Oral, phallic, latency, anal, genital
   b. Anal, oral, phallic, genital, latency
   c. Oral, anal, phallic, latency, genital
   d. Latency, phallic, anal, genital, oral
4. _____ _____ is the term Freud used to describe unconscious strategies used to reduce anxiety.

RETHINK

1. Can you think of ways in which Freud's theories of unconscious motivations are commonly used in popular culture? How accurately do you think such popular uses of Freudian theories reflect Freud's ideas?
2. *From the perspective of an advertising executive:* How might you use Jung's concept of archetypes in designing your advertisements? Which of the archetypes would you use?

Answers to Evaluate Questions

1. psychodynamic; 2. 1-b, 2-c, 3-a; 3. c; 4. defense mechanisms

KEY TERMS

personality p. 446
psychodynamic approaches
   to personality p. 447
psychoanalytic theory p. 447
unconscious p. 447
id p. 448

ego p. 448
superego p. 448
psychosexual stages p. 448
fixations p. 448
oral stage p. 449
anal stage p. 450

phallic stage p. 450
Oedipal conflict p. 450
identification p. 450
latency period p. 450
genital stage p. 450
defense mechanisms p. 451

repression p. 451
neo-Freudian
   psychoanalysts p. 453
collective unconscious p. 453
archetypes p. 453
inferiority complex p. 454

Trait, Learning, Biological and Evolutionary, and Humanistic Approaches to Personality

"Tell me about Nelson," said Johnetta.

"Oh, he's just terrific. He's the friendliest guy I know—goes out of his way to be nice to everyone. He hardly ever gets mad. He's just so even-tempered, no matter what's happening. And he's really smart, too. About the only thing I don't like is that he's always in such a hurry to get things done. He seems to have boundless energy, much more than I have."

"He sounds great to me, especially in comparison to Rico," replied Johnetta. "He is so self-centered and arrogant that it drives me crazy. I sometimes wonder why I ever started going out with him."

Friendly. Even-tempered. Smart. Energetic. Self-centered. Arrogant.

The above exchange is made up of a series of trait characterizations of speakers' friends. In fact, much of our own understanding of others' behavior is based on the premise that people possess certain traits that are consistent across different situations. For example, we generally assume that if someone is outgoing and sociable in one situation, he or she is outgoing and sociable in other situations (Gilbert et al., 1992; Gilbert, Miller, & Ross, 1998; Mischel, 2004).

Dissatisfaction with the emphasis in psychoanalytic theory on unconscious—and difficult to demonstrate—processes in explaining a person's behavior led to the development of alternative approaches to personality, including a number of trait-based approaches. Other theories reflect established psychological perspectives, such as learning theory, biological and evolutionary approaches, and the humanistic approach.

Trait Approaches: Placing Labels on Personality

If someone asked you to characterize another person, it is probable that—like Johnetta and her friend—you would come up with a list of that individual's personal qualities, as you see them. But how would you know which of those qualities are most important to an understanding of that person's behavior?

Personality psychologists have asked similar questions. To answer them, they have developed a model of personality known as trait theory. **Trait theory** seeks to explain, in a straightforward way, the consistencies in individuals' behavior. **Traits** are consistent personality characteristics and behaviors displayed in different situations.

Trait theorists do not assume that some people have a trait and others do not; rather, they propose that all people possess certain traits, but that the degree to which a particular trait applies to a specific person varies and can be quantified. For instance, you may be relatively friendly, whereas I may be relatively unfriendly. But we both have a "friendliness" trait, although your degree of "friendliness" is higher than mine. The major challenge for trait theorists taking this approach has been to identify the

Key Concept

What are the major aspects of trait, learning, biological and evolutionary, and humanistic approaches to personality?

Trait theory: A model of personality that seeks to identify the basic traits necessary to describe personality.

Traits: Consistent personality characteristics and behaviors displayed in different situations.

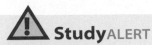

Extraversion
• Sociable
• Lively
• Active
• Assertive
• Sensation-seeking

Neuroticism
• Anxious
• Depressed
• Guilt feelings
• Low self-esteem
• Tense

Psychoticism
• Aggressive
• Cold
• Egocentric
• Impersonal
• Impulsive

FIGURE 1 According to Eysenck, personality could best be described in terms of just three major dimensions: extraversion, neuroticism, and psychoticism. Eysenck was able to predict behavior accurately in a variety of types of situations by evaluating people along these three dimensions (Eysenck, 1990). How do you think an airline pilot would score on Eysenck's scale?

specific primary traits necessary to describe personality. As we shall see, different theorists have come up with surprisingly different sets of traits.

ALLPORT'S TRAIT THEORY: IDENTIFYING BASIC CHARACTERISTICS

When personality psychologist Gordon Allport systematically pored over an unabridged dictionary in the 1930s, he came up with some 18,000 separate terms that could be used to describe personality. Although he was able to pare down the list to a mere 4,500 descriptors after eliminating words with the same meaning, he was left with a problem crucial to all trait approaches: Which of those traits were the most basic?

Allport eventually answered this question by suggesting that there are three fundamental categories of traits: cardinal, central, and secondary (Allport, 1961, 1966). A *cardinal trait* is a single characteristic that directs most of a person's activities. For example, a totally selfless woman may direct all her energy toward humanitarian activities; an intensely power-hungry person may be driven by an all-consuming need for control.

Most people, however, do not develop a single, comprehensive cardinal trait. Instead, they possess a handful of central traits that make up the core of personality. *Central traits*, such as honesty and sociability, are the major characteristics of an individual; they usually number from five to ten in any one person. Finally, *secondary traits* are characteristics that affect behavior in fewer situations and are less influential than central or cardinal traits. For instance, a reluctance to eat meat and a love of modern art would be considered secondary traits (Nicholson, 2003; Glicksohn & Nahari, 2007).

CATTELL AND EYSENCK: FACTORING OUT PERSONALITY

Later attempts to identify primary personality traits have centered on a statistical technique known as factor analysis. *Factor analysis* is a statistical method of identifying associations among a large number of variables to reveal more general patterns. For example, a personality researcher might administer a questionnaire to many participants, asking them to describe themselves by referring to an extensive list of traits. By statistically combining responses and computing which traits are associated with one another in the same person, a researcher can identify the most fundamental patterns or combinations of traits—called *factors*—that underlie participants' responses.

Using factor analysis, personality psychologist Raymond Cattell (1965) suggested that 16 pairs of *source traits* represent the basic dimensions of personality. Using those source traits, he developed the Sixteen Personality Factor Questionnaire, or 16 PF, a measure that provides scores for each of the source traits (Cattell, Cattell, & Cattell, 1993; 2000).

Another trait theorist, psychologist Hans Eysenck (1995), also used factor analysis to identify patterns of traits, but he came to a very different conclusion about the nature of personality. He found that personality could best be described in terms of just three major dimensions: *extraversion*, *neuroticism*, and *psychoticism*. The extraversion dimension relates to the degree of sociability, whereas the neurotic dimension encompasses emotional stability. Finally, psychoticism refers to the degree to which reality is distorted. By evaluating people along these three dimensions, Eysenck was able to predict behavior accurately in a variety of situations. Figure 1 lists specific traits associated with each of the dimensions.

THE BIG FIVE PERSONALITY TRAITS

For the last two decades, the most influential trait approach contends that five traits or factors—called the "Big Five"—lie at the core of personality. Using modern factor analytic statistical techniques, a host of researchers have identified a similar set of five factors that underlie personality. The five factors, described in

The Big Five Personality Factors and Dimensions of Sample Traits

Openness to experience

Independent—Conforming

Imaginative—Practical

Preference for variety—Preference for routine

Conscientiousness

Careful—Careless

Disciplined—Impulsive

Organized—Disorganized

Extraversion

Talkative—Quiet

Fun-loving—Sober

Sociable—Retiring

Agreeableness

Sympathetic—Fault-finding

Kind—Cold

Appreciative—Unfriendly

Neuroticism (Emotional Stability)

Stable—Tense

Calm—Anxious

Secure—Insecure

FIGURE 2 Five broad trait factors, referred to as the "Big Five," are considered to be the core of personality. You can memorize these traits by using the mnemonic OCEAN, representing the first letter of each trait. (Source: Adapted from Pervin, 1990, Chapter 3, and McCrae & Costa, 1986, p. 1002.)

Figure 2, are *openness to experience, conscientiousness, extraversion, agreeableness,* and *neuroticism* (emotional stability).

The Big Five emerge consistently across a number of domains. For example, factor analyses of major personality inventories, self-report measures made by observers of others' personality traits, and checklists of self-descriptions yield similar factors. In addition, the Big Five emerge consistently in different populations of individuals, including children, college students, older adults, and speakers of different languages. Cross-cultural research conducted in areas ranging from Europe to the Middle East to Africa also has been supportive. Finally, studies of brain functioning show that Big Five personality traits are related to the way the brain processes information (see Neuroscience in Your Life Figure 3; Rossier, Dahourou, & McCrae, 2005; McCrae et al., 2005; Schmitt et al., 2007).

In short, a growing consensus exists that the Big Five represent the best description of personality traits we have today. Still, the debate over the specific number and kinds of traits—and even the usefulness of trait approaches in general—remains a lively one.

EVALUATING TRAIT APPROACHES TO PERSONALITY

Trait approaches have several virtues. They provide a clear, straightforward explanation of people's behavioral consistencies. Furthermore, traits allow us to readily compare one person with another. Because of these advantages, trait approaches to personality have had an important influence on the development of several useful personality measures (Funder, 1991; Wiggins, 2003; Larsen & Buss, 2006).

 StudyALERT

You can remember the "Big Five" set of personality traits by using the acronym OCEAN (*o*penness to experience, *c*onscientiousness, *e*xtraversion, *a*greeableness, and *n*euroticism).

Neuroscience in Your Life

FIGURE 3 In a study examining participants' Big 5 trait scores, areas of the left orbitofrontal cortex (A) and right orbitofrontal cortex (B) were found to be related to extraversion scores. (Source: Deckersbach et al., 2006, Figure 2)

However, trait approaches also have some drawbacks. For example, we have seen that various trait theories describing personality come to very different conclusions about which traits are the most fundamental and descriptive. The difficulty in determining which of the theories is the most accurate has led some personality psychologists to question the validity of trait conceptions of personality in general.

Actually, there is an even more fundamental difficulty with trait approaches. Even if we are able to identify a set of primary traits, we are left with little more than a label or description of personality—rather than an explanation of behavior. If we say that someone who donates money to charity has the trait of generosity, we still do not know *why* that person became generous in the first place or the reasons for displaying generosity in a specific situation. In the view of some critics, then, traits do not provide explanations for behavior; they merely describe it.

Learning Approaches: We Are What We've Learned

The psychodynamic and trait approaches we've discussed concentrate on the "inner" person—the fury of an unobservable but powerful id or a hypothetical but critical set of traits. In contrast, learning approaches to personality focus on the "outer" person. To a strict learning theorist, personality is simply the sum of learned responses to the external environment. Internal events such as thoughts, feelings, and motivations are ignored. Although the existence of personality is not denied, learning theorists say that it is best understood by looking at features of a person's environment.

SKINNER'S BEHAVIORIST APPROACH

According to the most influential learning theorist, B. F. Skinner (who carried out pioneering work on operant conditioning), personality is a collection of learned behavior patterns (Skinner, 1975). Similarities in responses across different situations are caused by similar patterns of reinforcement that have been received in such situations in the past. If I am sociable both at parties and at meetings, it is because I have been reinforced for displaying social behaviors—not because I am fulfilling an unconscious wish based on experiences during my childhood or because I have an internal trait of sociability.

Strict learning theorists such as Skinner are less interested in the consistencies in behavior across situations than in ways of modifying behavior. Their view is that humans are infinitely changeable through the process of learning new behavior patterns. If we are able to control and modify the patterns of reinforcers in a situation, behavior that other theorists would view as stable and unyielding can be changed and ultimately improved. Learning theorists are optimistic in their attitudes about the potential for resolving personal and societal problems through treatment strategies based on learning theory.

SOCIAL COGNITIVE APPROACHES TO PERSONALITY

Not all learning theories of personality take such a strict view in rejecting the importance of what is "inside" a person by focusing solely on the "outside." Unlike other learning approaches to personality, **social cognitive approaches** emphasize the influence of cognition—thoughts, feelings, expectations, and values—as well as observation of other's behavior, on personality. According to Albert Bandura, one of the main proponents of this point of view, people can foresee the possible outcomes of certain behaviors in a specific setting without actually having to carry them out. This understanding comes primarily through *observational learning*—viewing the actions of others and observing the consequences (Bandura, 1986, 1999).

For instance, children who view a model behaving in, say, an aggressive manner tend to copy the behavior if the consequences of the model's behavior are seen to be positive. If, in contrast, the model's aggressive behavior has resulted in no consequences or negative consequences, children are considerably less likely to act aggressively. According to social cognitive approaches, then, personality develops through repeated observation of the behavior of others.

Social cognitive approaches to personality: Theories that emphasize the influence of a person's cognitions—thoughts, feelings, expectations, and values—as well as observation of others' behavior, in determining personality.

Self-efficacy: Belief in one's personal capabilities. Self-efficacy underlies people's faith in their ability to carry out a particular behavior or produce a desired outcome.

Self-esteem: The component of personality that encompasses our positive and negative self-evaluations.

SELF-EFFICACY

Bandura places particular emphasis on the role played by **self-efficacy**, belief in one's personal capabilities. Self-efficacy underlies people's faith in their ability to carry out a specific task or produce a desired outcome. People with high self-efficacy have higher aspirations and greater persistence in working to attain goals and ultimately achieve greater success than do those with lower self-efficacy (Bandura, 2001; Bandura & Locke, 2003; Glickler, 2006).

How do we develop self-efficacy? One way is by paying close attention to our prior successes and failures. If we try snowboarding and experience little success, we'll be less likely to try it again. However, if our initial efforts appear promising, we'll be more likely to attempt it again. Direct reinforcement and encouragement from others also play a role in developing self-efficacy (Devonport & Lane, 2006).

Compared with other learning theories of personality, social cognitive approaches are distinctive in their emphasis on the reciprocity between individuals and their environment. Not only is the environment assumed to affect personality, but people's behavior and personalities are also assumed to "feed back" and modify the environment (Bandura, 1999, 2000).

SELF-ESTEEM

Our behavior also reflects the view we have of ourselves and the way we value the various parts of our personalities. **Self-esteem** is the component of personality that encompasses our positive and negative self-evaluations. Unlike self-efficacy, which focuses on our views of whether we are able to carry out a task, self-esteem relates to how we feel about ourselves.

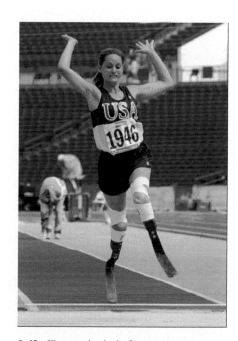

Self-efficacy, the belief in one's own capabilities, leads to higher aspirations and greater persistence.

FIGURE 4 The cycle of low self-esteem begins with an individual's already having low self-esteem. As a consequence, the person will have low performance expectations and expect to fail a test, thereby producing anxiety and reduced effort. As a result, the person will actually fail, and failure in turn reinforces low self-esteem.

Although people have a general level of self-esteem, it is not unidimensional. We may see ourselves positively in one domain but negatively in others. For example, a good student may have high self-esteem in academic domains but lower self-esteem in sports (Crocker & Park, 2004; Swann, Chang-Schneider, & Larsen McClarty, 2007; Salmela-Aro & Nurmi, 2007).

Self-esteem has strong cultural components. For example, having high *relationship harmony*—a sense of success in forming close bonds with other people—is more important to self-esteem in Asian cultures than it is in more individualistic Western societies (Spencer-Rodgers et al., 2004; Lun & Bond, 2006).

Although almost everyone goes through periods of low self-esteem (after, for instance, an undeniable failure), some people are chronically low in self-esteem. For them, failure seems to be an inevitable part of life. In fact, low self-esteem may lead to a cycle of failure in which past failure breeds future failure.

Consider, for example, students with low self-esteem who are studying for a test. Because of their low self-esteem, they expect to do poorly on the test. In turn, this belief raises their anxiety level, making it increasingly difficult to study and perhaps even leading them not to work as hard. Because of these attitudes, the ultimate outcome is that they do, in fact, perform badly on the test. Ultimately, the failure reinforces their low self-esteem, and the cycle is perpetuated, as illustrated in Figure 4. In short, low self-esteem can lead to a cycle of failure that is self-destructive.

EVALUATING LEARNING APPROACHES TO PERSONALITY

Because they ignore the internal processes that are uniquely human, traditional learning theorists such as Skinner have been accused of oversimplifying personality to such an extent that the concept becomes meaningless. In the eyes of their critics, reducing behavior to a series of stimuli and responses, and excluding thoughts and feelings from the realm of personality, leaves behaviorists practicing an unrealistic and inadequate form of science.

Of course, some of these criticisms are blunted by social cognitive approaches, which explicitly consider the role of cognitive processes in personality. Still, learning approaches tend to share a highly *deterministic* view of human behavior, maintaining that behavior is shaped primarily by forces beyond the control of the individual. As in psychoanalytic theory (which suggests that personality is determined by the unconscious forces) and trait approaches (which views personality in part as a mixture of genetically determined traits), learning theory's reliance on deterministic principles deemphasizes the ability of people to pilot their own course through life.

Nonetheless, learning approaches have had a major impact on the study of personality. For one thing, they have helped make personality psychology an objective, scientific venture by focusing on observable behavior and their environment. In addition, they have produced important, successful means of treating a variety of psychological disorders. The degree of success of these treatments is a testimony to the merits of learning theory approaches to personality.

Biological and Evolutionary Approaches: Are We Born with Personality?

Approaching the question of what determines personality from a different direction, **biological and evolutionary approaches** to personality suggest that important components of personality are inherited. Building on the work of behavioral geneticists, researchers using biological and evolutionary approaches argue that personality is determined at least in part by our genes, in much the same way that our height is largely a result of genetic contributions from our ancestors. The evolutionary perspective assumes that personality traits that led to survival and reproductive success of our ancestors are more likely to be preserved and passed on to subsequent generations (Buss, 2001).

The importance of genetic factors in personality is illustrated by studies of twins. For instance, personality psychologists Auke Tellegen and colleagues at the University of Minnesota examined the personality traits of pairs of twins who were genetically identical but were raised apart from each other (Tellegen et al., 1988, 2004). In the study, each twin was given a battery of personality tests, including one that measured 11 key personality characteristics.

The results of the personality tests indicated that in major respects the twins were quite similar in personality, despite having separated at an early age. Moreover, certain traits were more heavily influenced by heredity than were others. For example, social potency (the degree to which a person assumes mastery and leadership roles in social situations) and traditionalism (the tendency to follow authority) had particularly strong genetic components, whereas achievement and social closeness had relatively weak genetic components (see Figure 5).

Biological and evolutionary approaches to personality: Theories that suggest that important components of personality are inherited.

Remember that biological and evolutionary approaches focus on the way in which people's genetic heritage affects personality.

Biological and evolutionary approaches to personality seek to explain the consistencies in personality that are found in some families.

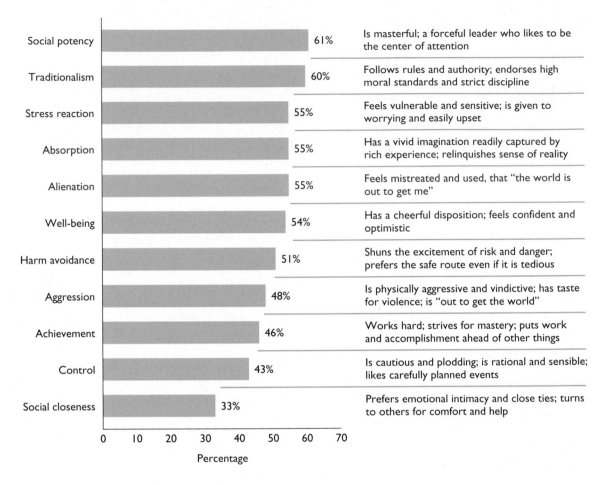

Social potency	61%	Is masterful; a forceful leader who likes to be the center of attention
Traditionalism	60%	Follows rules and authority; endorses high moral standards and strict discipline
Stress reaction	55%	Feels vulnerable and sensitive; is given to worrying and easily upset
Absorption	55%	Has a vivid imagination readily captured by rich experience; relinquishes sense of reality
Alienation	55%	Feels mistreated and used, that "the world is out to get me"
Well-being	54%	Has a cheerful disposition; feels confident and optimistic
Harm avoidance	51%	Shuns the excitement of risk and danger; prefers the safe route even if it is tedious
Aggression	48%	Is physically aggressive and vindictive; has taste for violence; is "out to get the world"
Achievement	46%	Works hard; strives for mastery; puts work and accomplishment ahead of other things
Control	43%	Is cautious and plodding; is rational and sensible; likes carefully planned events
Social closeness	33%	Prefers emotional intimacy and close ties; turns to others for comfort and help

Percentage

FIGURE 5 The inherited roots of personality. The percentages indicate the degree to which 11 personality characteristics reflect the influence of heredity. (Source: Tellegen et al., 1988.)

Temperament: The innate disposition that emerges early in life.

Furthermore, it is increasingly clear that the roots of adult personality emerge in the earliest periods of life. Infants are born with a specific **temperament**, an innate disposition. Temperament encompasses several dimensions, including general activity level and mood. For instance, some individuals are quite active, while others are relatively calm. Similarly, some are relatively easygoing, while others are irritable, easily upset, and difficult to soothe. Temperament is quite consistent, with significant stability from infancy well into adolescence (Caspi et al., 2003; Wachs et al., 2004; Evans & Rothbart, 2007).

Some researchers contend that specific genes are related to personality. For example, people with a longer dopamine-4 receptor gene are more likely to be thrill seekers than are those without such a gene. These thrill seekers tend to be extroverted, impulsive, quick-tempered, and always in search of excitement and novel situations (Zuckerman & Kuhlman, 2000; Robins, 2005; Golimbet et al., 2007).

Does the identification of specific genes linked to personality, coupled with the existence of temperaments from the time of birth, mean that we are destined to have certain types of personalities? Hardly. First, it is unlikely that any single gene is linked to a specific trait. For instance, the dopamine-4 receptor accounts for only around 10 percent of the variation in novelty seeking between different individuals. The rest of the variation is attributable to other genes and environmental factors (Keltikangas-Järvinen et al., 2004; Lahti et al., 2005).

More importantly, genes interact with the environment. As we see in discussions of the heritability of intelligence and the nature–nurture issue, it is impossible to completely divorce genetic factors from environmental factors. Although studies of identical twins raised in different environments are helpful, they are not definitive, because it is impossible to assess and control environmental factors fully. Furthermore, estimates of the influence of genetics are just that—estimates—and apply to groups, not individuals. Consequently, findings such as those shown in Figure 5 must be regarded as approximations.

Finally, even if more genes are found to be linked to specific personality characteristics, genes still cannot be viewed as the sole cause of personality. For one thing, genetically determined characteristics may not be expressed if they are not "turned on" by particular environmental experiences. Furthermore, behaviors produced by genes may help to create a specific environment. For instance, a cheerful, smiley baby may lead her parents to smile more and be more responsive, thereby creating an environment that is supportive and pleasant. In contrast, the parents of a cranky, fussy baby may be less inclined to smile at the child; in turn, the environment in which that child is raised will be a less supportive and pleasant one. In a sense, then, genes not only influence a person's behavior—they also help produce the environment in which a person develops (Scarr, 1993, 1998; Plomin & Caspi, 1999; Kim-Cohen et al., 2003, 2005).

Although an increasing number of personality theorists are taking biological and evolutionary factors into account, no comprehensive, unified theory that considers biological and evolutionary factors is widely accepted. Still, it is clear that certain personality traits have substantial genetic components, and that heredity and environment interact to determine personality (Plomin et al., 2003; Ebstein, Benjamin, & Belmaker, 2003; Bouchard, 2004).

Infants are born with particular temperaments, dispositions that are consistent throughout childhood.

Humanistic Approaches: The Uniqueness of You

Where, in all the approaches to personality that we have discussed, is an explanation for the saintliness of a Mother Teresa, the creativity of a Michelangelo, and the brilliance and perseverance of an Einstein? An understanding of such unique individuals—as well as more ordinary sorts of people who have some of the same attributes—comes from humanistic theory.

According to humanistic theorists, all the approaches to personality we have discussed share a fundamental misperception in their views of human nature. Instead of seeing people as controlled by unconscious, unseen forces (as do psychodynamic approaches), a set of stable traits (trait approaches), situational reinforcements and punishments (learning theory), or inherited factors (biological and evolutionary approaches), **humanistic approaches** emphasize people's inherent goodness and their tendency to move toward higher levels of functioning. It is this conscious, self-motivated ability to change and improve, along with people's unique creative impulses, that humanistic theorists argue make up the core of personality.

Humanistic approaches to personality: Theories that emphasize people's innate goodness and desire to achieve higher levels of functioning.

ROGERS AND THE NEED FOR SELF-ACTUALIZATION

The major proponent of the humanistic point of view is Carl Rogers (1971). Along with other humanistic theorists, such as Abraham Maslow, Rogers maintains that all people have a fundamental need for **self-actualization**, a state of self-fulfillment in which people realize their highest potential, each in a unique way. He further suggests that people develop a need for positive regard that reflects the desire to be loved and respected. Because others provide this positive regard, we grow dependent on them. We begin to see and judge ourselves through the eyes of other people, relying on their values and being preoccupied with what they think of us.

According to Rogers, one outgrowth of placing importance on the opinions of others is that a conflict may grow between people's experiences and their *self-concepts*, the set of beliefs they hold about what they are like as individuals. If the

Self-actualization: A state of self-fulfillment in which people realize their highest potential, each in a unique way.

"So, while extortion, racketeering, and murder may be bad acts, they don't make you a bad person."

Unconditional positive regard:
An attitude of acceptance and respect on the part of an observer, no matter what a person says or does.

discrepancies are minor, so are the consequences. But if the discrepancies are great, they will lead to psychological disturbances in daily functioning, such as the experience of frequent anxiety.

Rogers suggests that one way of overcoming the discrepancy between experience and self-concept is through the receipt of unconditional positive regard from another person—a friend, a spouse, or a therapist. **Unconditional positive regard** refers to an attitude of acceptance and respect on the part of an observer, no matter what a person says or does. This acceptance, says Rogers, gives people the opportunity to evolve and grow both cognitively and emotionally and to develop more realistic self-concepts. You may have experienced the power of unconditional positive regard when you confided in someone, revealing embarrassing secrets because you knew the listener would still love and respect you, even after hearing the worst about you (Snyder, 2002; Marshall, 2007).

In contrast, *conditional positive regard* depends on your behavior. In such cases, others withdraw their love and acceptance if you do something of which they don't approve. The result is a discrepancy between your true self and what others wish you would be, leading to anxiety and frustration (see Figure 6).

EVALUATING HUMANISTIC APPROACHES

Although humanistic theories suggest the value of providing unconditional positive regard toward people, unconditional positive regard toward humanistic theories has been less forthcoming. The criticisms have centered on the difficulty of verifying the basic assumptions of the approach, as well as on the question of whether unconditional positive regard does, in fact, lead to greater personality adjustment.

Humanistic approaches have also been criticized for making the assumption that people are basically "good"—a notion that is unverifiable—and, equally important, for using nonscientific values to build supposedly scientific theories. Still, humanistic theories have been important in highlighting the uniqueness of human beings and guiding the development of a significant form of therapy designed to alleviate psychological difficulties (Cain, 2002; Bauman & Kopp, 2006).

FIGURE 6 According to the humanistic view of Carl Rogers, people have a basic need to be loved and respected. If you receive unconditional positive regard from others, you will develop a more realistic self-concept; but if the response is conditional, it may lead to anxiety and frustration.

Comparing Approaches to Personality

In light of the multiple approaches we have discussed, you may be wondering which of the theories provides the most accurate description of personality. That is a question that cannot be answered precisely. Each theory is built on different assumptions and focuses on somewhat different aspects of personality (see Figure 7). Furthermore, there is no clear way to scientifically test the various approaches and their assumptions against one another. Given the complexity of every individual, it seems reasonable that personality can be viewed from a number of perspectives simultaneously (Pervin, 2003).

Theoretical Approach and Major Theorists	Conscious Versus Unconscious Determinants of Personality	Nature (Hereditary Factors) Versus Nurture (Environmental Factors)	Free Will Versus Determinism	Stability Versus Modifiability
Psychodynamic (Freud, Jung, Horney, Adler)	Emphasizes the unconscious	Stresses innate, inherited structure of personality while emphasizing importance of childhood experience	Stresses determinism, the view that behavior is directed and caused by factors outside one's control	Emphasizes the stability of characteristics throughout a person's life
Trait (Allport, Cattell, Eysenck)	Disregards both conscious and unconscious	Approaches vary	Stresses determinism, the view that behavior is directed and caused by factors outside one's control	Emphasizes the stability of characteristics throughout a person's life
Learning (Skinner, Bandura)	Disregards both conscious and unconscious	Focuses on the environment	Stresses determinism, the view that behavior is directed and caused by factors outside one's control	Stresses that personality remains flexible and resilient throughout one's life
Biological and Evolutionary (Tellegen)	Disregards both conscious and unconscious	Stresses the innate, inherited determinants of personality	Stresses determinism, the view that behavior is directed and caused by factors outside one's control	Emphasizes the stability of characteristics throughout a person's life
Humanistic (Rogers, Maslow)	Stresses the conscious more than unconscious	Stresses the interaction between both nature and nurture	Stresses the freedom of individuals to make their own choices	Stresses that personality remains flexible and resilient throughout one's life

FIGURE 7 The multiple perspectives of personality.

RECAP/EVALUATE/RETHINK

RECAP

What are the major aspects of trait, learning, biological and evolutionary, and humanistic approaches to personality?

- Trait approaches have been used to identify relatively enduring dimensions along which people differ from one another—dimensions known as traits. (p. 457)

- Learning approaches to personality concentrate on observable behavior. To a strict learning theorist, personality is the sum of learned responses to the external environment. (p. 458)

- Social cognitive approaches concentrate on the role of cognition in determining personality. Those approaches pay particular attention to self-efficacy and self-esteem in determining behavior. (p. 461)

- Biological and evolutionary approaches to personality focus on the way in which personality characteristics are inherited. (p. 463)

- Humanistic approaches emphasize the inherent goodness of people. They consider the core of personality in terms of a person's ability to change and improve. (p. 465)

- The major personality approaches differ substantially from one another; the differences may reflect both their focus on different aspects of personality and the overall complexity of personality. (p. 467)

EVALUATE

1. Carl's determination to succeed is the dominant force in all his activities and relationships. According to Gordon Allport's theory, this is an example of a _____ trait. In contrast, Cindy's fondness for old western movies is an example of a _____ trait.
2. A person who enjoys activities such as parties and hang gliding might be described by Eysenck as high on what trait?
3. Proponents of which approach to personality would be most likely to agree with the statement "Personality can be thought of as learned responses to a person's upbringing and environment"?
   a. Humanistic
   b. Biological and evolutionary
   c. Learning
   d. Trait

4. A person who would make the statement "I know I can't do it" would be rated by Bandura as low on _____ - _____.
5. Which approach to personality emphasizes the innate goodness of people and their desire to grow?
   a. Humanistic
   b. Psychodynamic
   c. Learning
   d. Biological and evolutionary

RETHINK

1. If personality traits are merely descriptive and not explanatory, of what use are they? Can assigning a trait to a person be harmful—or helpful? Why or why not?
2. *From the perspective of an educator:* How might you encourage your students' development of self-esteem and self-efficacy? What steps would you take to ensure that their self-esteem did not become over-inflated?

Answers to Evaluate Questions

1. cardinal, secondary; 2. extraversion; 3. c; 4. self-efficacy; 5. a

KEY TERMS

trait theory p. 457
traits p. 457
social cognitive approaches
  to personality p. 461
self-efficacy p. 461

self-esteem p. 461
biological and evolutionary
  approaches to personality
  p. 463
temperament p. 464

humanistic approaches to
  personality p. 465
self-actualization p. 465
unconditional positive
  regard p. 466

Assessing Personality: Determining What Makes Us Distinctive

You have a need for other people to like and admire you.

You have a tendency to be critical of yourself.

You have a great deal of unused potential that you have not turned to your advantage.

Although you have some personality weaknesses, you generally are able to compensate for them.

Relating to members of the opposite sex has presented problems to you.

Although you appear to be disciplined and self-controlled to others, you tend to be anxious and insecure inside.

At times you have serious doubts about whether you have made the right decision or done the right thing.

You prefer a certain amount of change and variety and become dissatisfied when hemmed in by restrictions and limitations.

You do not accept others' statements without satisfactory proof.

You have found it unwise to be too frank in revealing yourself to others.

If you think these statements provide a surprisingly accurate account of your personality, you are not alone: Most college students think that these descriptions are tailored just to them. In fact, the statements were designed intentionally to be so vague that they apply to just about anyone (Forer, 1949; Russo, 1981).

The ease with which we can agree with such imprecise statements underscores the difficulty in coming up with accurate and meaningful assessments of people's personalities. Psychologists interested in assessing personality must be able to define the most meaningful ways of discriminating between one person's personality and another's. To do this, they use **psychological tests**, standard measures devised to assess behavior objectively. With the results of such tests, psychologists can help people better understand themselves and make decisions about their lives. Psychological tests are also employed by researchers interested in the causes and consequences of personality (Aiken, 2000; Kaplan & Saccuzzo, 2001; Hambleton, 2006).

Like the assessments that seek to measure intelligence, all psychological tests must have reliability and validity. *Reliability* refers to the measurement consistency of a test. If a test is reliable, it yields the same result each time it is administered to a specific person or group. In contrast, unreliable tests give different results each time they are administered.

For meaningful conclusions to be drawn, tests also must be valid. Tests have *validity* when they actually measure what they are designed to measure. If a test is constructed to measure sociability, for instance, we need to know that it actually measures sociability, not some other trait.

Key Concepts

How can we most accurately assess personality?

What are the major types of personality measures?

Psychological tests: Standard measures devised to assess behavior objectively; used by psychologists to help people make decisions about their lives and understand more about themselves.

 StudyALERT

The distinction between reliability and validity is important. For instance, a test that measures trustfulness is reliable if it yields the same results each time it is administered, while it would be valid if it measures trustfulness accurately.

Finally, psychological tests are based on *norms*, standards of test performance that permit the comparison of one person's score on a test with the scores of others who have taken the same test. For example, a norm permits test takers who have received a certain score on a test to know that they have scored in the top 10 percent of all those who have taken the test.

Norms are established by administering a specific test to a large number of people and determining the typical scores. It is then possible to compare a single person's score with the scores of the group, providing a comparative measure of test performance against the performance of others who have taken the test.

The establishment of appropriate norms is not a simple endeavor. For instance, the specific group that is employed to determine norms for a test has a profound effect on the way an individual's performance is evaluated. In fact, as we discuss next, the process of establishing norms can take on political overtones.

Exploring DIVERSITY

Should Race and Ethnicity Be Used to Establish Norms?

The passions of politics may confront the objectivity of science when test norms are established, at least in the realm of standardized tests that are meant to predict future job performance. In fact, a national controversy has developed around the question of whether different norms should be established for members of various racial and ethnic groups (Brown, 1994; Babrina & Bondi, 2003; Manly, 2005, 2006).

At issue is the U.S. government's 50-year-old General Aptitude Test Battery, a test that measures a broad range of abilities from eye-hand coordination to reading proficiency. The problem that sparked the controversy is that African Americans and Hispanics tend to score lower on the test, on average, than do members of other groups. The lower scores often are due to a lack of prior relevant experience and job opportunities, which in turn has been due to prejudice and discrimination.

To promote the employment of minority racial groups, the government developed a separate set of norms for African Americans and Hispanics. Rather than using the pool of all people who took the test, the scores of African American and Hispanic applicants were compared only with the scores of other African Americans and Hispanics. Consequently, a Hispanic who scored in the top 20 percent of the Hispanics taking the test was considered to have performed equivalently to a white job applicant who scored in the top 20 percent of the whites who took the test, even though the absolute score of the Hispanic might be lower than that of the white.

Critics of the adjusted norming system suggest that such a procedure discriminates in favor of certain racial and ethnic groups at the expense of others, thereby fanning the flames of racial bigotry. The practice was challenged legally, and with the passage of the Civil Rights Act in 1991, race norming on the General Aptitude Test Battery was discontinued (Galef, 2001).

However, proponents of race norming continue to argue that norming procedures that take race into account are an affirmative action tool that simply permits minority job seekers to be placed on an equal footing with white job seekers. Furthermore, a panel of the National Academy of Sciences concurred with the practice of adjusting test norms. It suggested that the unadjusted test norms are not very useful in predicting job performance, and that they would tend to screen out otherwise qualified minority-group members. And a U.S. federal court opinion ruled in 2001 that using "bands" of score ranges was not necessarily discriminatory, unless the bands were designed on the basis of race (Fleming, 2000; Seventh U.S. Circuit Court of Appeals, 2001).

Job testing is not the only area in which issues arise regarding norms and the meaning of test scores. The issue of how to treat racial differences in IQ scores is also controversial and divisive. Clearly, race norming raises profound and intense feelings that may come into conflict with scientific objectivity (American Psychological Association, 1993; Leiter & Leiter, 2003; Rushton & Jensen, 2006).

The issue of establishing norms for tests is further complicated by the existence of a wide array of personality measures and approaches to assessment. We consider some of these measures, which have a variety of characteristics and purposes, next.

Self-Report Measures of Personality

If someone wanted to assess your personality, one possible approach would be to carry out an extensive interview with you to determine the most important events in your childhood, your social relationships, and your successes and failures. Obviously, though, such a technique would take extraordinary time and effort.

It is also unnecessary. Just as physicians draw only a small sample of your blood to test it, psychologists can utilize **self-report measures** that ask people about a relatively small sample of their behavior. This sampling of self-report data is then used to infer the presence of particular personality characteristics. For example, a researcher who was interested in assessing a person's orientation to life might administer the questionnaire shown in Figure 1. Although the questionnaire consists of only a few questions, the answers can be used to generalize about personality characteristics. (Try it yourself!)

One of the best examples of a self-report measure, and one of the most frequently used personality tests, is the **Minnesota Multiphasic Personality Inventory-2 (MMPI-2)**. Although the original purpose of this measure was to identify people with specific sorts of psychological difficulties, it has been found to predict a variety of other behaviors. For instance, MMPI scores have been shown to be good predictors of whether college students will marry within 10 years and whether they will get an advanced degree. Police departments use the test to measure whether police

Self-report measures: A method of gathering data about people by asking them questions about a sample of their behavior.

Minnesota Multiphasic Personality Inventory-2 (MMPI-2): A widely used self-report test that identifies people with psychological difficulties and is employed to predict some everyday behaviors.

The Life Orientation Test–Revised

Use the following scale to answer the items below:

0	1	2	3	4
Strongly disagree	Disagree	Neutral	Agree	Strongly agree

1. In uncertain times, I usually expect the best.
2. It's easy for me to relax.
3. If something can go wrong for me, it will.
4. I'm always optimistic about my future.
5. I enjoy my friends a lot.
6. It's important for me to keep busy.
7. I hardly ever expect things to go my way.
8. I don't get upset too easily.
9. I rarely count on good things happening to me.
10. Overall, I expect more good things to happen to me than bad.

Scoring. First, reverse your answers to questions 3, 7, and 9. Do this by changing a 0 to a 4, a 1 to a 3, a 3 to a 1, and a 4 to a 0 (answers of 2 stay as 2). Then sum the reversed scores, and add them to the scores you gave to questions 1, 4, and 10. (Ignore questions 2, 5, 6, and 8, which are filler items.)

The total score you get is a measure of a particular orientation to life: your degree of optimism. The higher your scores, the more positive and hopeful you generally are about life. For comparison purposes the average score for college students is 14.3, according to the results of a study by Scheier, Carver, and Bridges (1994). People with a higher degree of optimism generally deal with stress better than do those with lower scores.

FIGURE 1 The Life Orientation Test–Revised. Complete this test by indicating the degree to which you agree with each of the ten statements, using the scale from 0 to 4 for each item. Try to be as accurate as possible. There are no right or wrong answers. (Source: Copyright © 1994 by The American Psychological Association. Adapted with permission from Table 6 (p. 1073) from Scheier, M. F., Carver, C. S., & Bridges, M. W. (1994). Distinguishing optimism from neuroticism (and trait anxiety, self-mastery, and self-esteem): A reevaluation of the Life Orientation Test. *Journal of Personality and Social Psychology, 67,* 1063-1078.)

officers are likely to use their weapons. Psychologists in Russia administer a modified form of the MMPI to their astronauts and Olympic athletes (Weis, Crockett, & Vieth, 2004; Butcher, 2005; Sellborn & Ben-Porath, 2006).

The test consists of a series of 567 items to which a person responds "true," "false," or "cannot say." The questions cover a variety of issues, ranging from mood ("I feel useless at times") to opinions ("People should try to understand their dreams") to physical and psychological health ("I am bothered by an upset stomach several times a week" and "I have strange and peculiar thoughts").

There are no right or wrong answers. Instead, interpretation of the results rests on the pattern of responses. The test yields scores on 10 separate scales, plus three scales meant to measure the validity of the respondent's answers. For example, there is a "lie scale" that indicates when people are falsifying their responses in order to present themselves more favorably (through items such as "I can't remember ever having a bad night's sleep") (Butcher, 2005; Stein & Graham, 2005; Bacchiochi, 2006).

How did the authors of the MMPI determine what specific patterns of responses indicate? The procedure they used is typical of personality test construction—a process known as **test standardization**. To create the test, the test authors asked groups of psychiatric patients with a specific diagnosis, such as depression or schizophrenia, to complete a large number of items. They then determined which items best differentiated members of those groups from a comparison group of normal participants, and included those specific items in the final version of the test. By systematically carrying out this procedure on groups with different diagnoses, the test authors were able to devise a number of subscales that identified different forms of abnormal behavior (see Figure 2).

When the MMPI is used for the purpose for which it was devised—identification of personality disorders—it does a good job. However, like other personality tests, it presents an opportunity for abuse. For instance, employers who use it as a screening

Test standardization: A technique used to validate questions in personality tests by studying the responses of people with known diagnoses.

Clinical scales

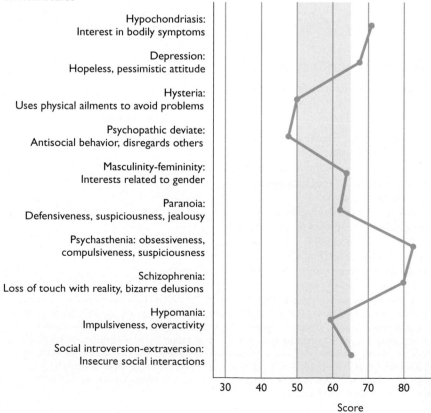

FIGURE 2 A profile on the MMPI-2 of a person who suffers from obsessional anxiety, social withdrawal, and delusional thinking.

(Source: Based on data from Halgin & Whitbourne, 1994, p. 72, and Minnesota Multiphasic Personality Inventory-2. Copyright © by the Regents of the University of Minnesota, 1942, 1943 (renewed 1970, 1989).)

Giving Entire Cultures a Personality Test

If you think about personality differences in the people you know, you will likely bring to mind examples of those who seem to be especially high or low on certain personality dimensions. Perhaps you can easily distinguish who among your friends is extraverted and who is introverted. And if you're like most people, you also think of personality traits in terms of group differences. Perhaps you believe that Texans are rugged and independent or that New Englanders tend to be independent and unfriendly. Furthermore, most of us are aware of stereotypes of people from our own and other cultures—Americans are extraverted, British people are reserved and unemotional, Japanese and German people are organized and conscientious, and so forth.

Do these stereotypes reflect genuine cross-cultural differences in the personalities of people who are typical of these cultures – that is, do they have a grain of truth to them, if perhaps exaggerated—or are they merely baseless stereotypes? To answer that question, a large group of researchers from around the globe administered the Revised NEO Personality Inventory (NEO-PI-R), a personality test that can be used cross-culturally, on people living in 50 different cultures. In addition, they administered a measure of perceptions of *national character*— common beliefs about people from those cultures. The measure of national character was a short questionnaire on which respondents could indicate the characteristics of a typical member of their own culture. A comparison of these averaged personality profiles allowed researchers to address whether the actual personalities of people within a given culture matched beliefs about the national character of people from those cultures (McCrae et al., 2005; Terracciano et al., 2005).

The results of the study, which involved thousands of participants, found several things. First, members of a given culture were able to produce consistent summaries of their national character. For example, Canadians see themselves as highly agreeable, Australians see themselves as extraverted, and Americans see themselves as extraverted but not particularly agreeable.

More importantly, though, the profiles of national character did not match the *actual* personality profiles of individuals within those cultures. The researchers concluded that whatever national character is, it is not a generalization about the actual personality characteristics of a culture's members. Instead, it may represent assessments that were once historically accurate but are presently outdated, exaggerations of ingroup-outgroup differences, or reflections of more specific and subtle kinds of traits rather than the broad traits captured by these measures. In short, national character is an indicator of how people within a culture see themselves rather than of how they actually are (Robins, 2005; Terracciano et al., 2005).

- How would you describe the American national character? Do you think your description is based more on your impressions of actual people, or on a cultural myth regarding the American personality?
- Why do you think people's impressions of their national characters are so inaccurate?

---

tool for job applicants may interpret the results improperly, relying too heavily on the results of individual scales instead of taking into account the overall patterns of results, which require skilled interpretation. Furthermore, critics point out that the individual scales overlap, making their interpretation difficult. In sum, although the MMPI remains the most widely used personality test and has been translated into more than 100 different languages, it must be used with caution (Greene & Clopton, 2004; Valsiner, Diriwächter, & Sauck, 2005; also see the *Applying Psychology in the 21st Century* box).

Projective Methods

If you were shown the shape presented in Figure 3 and asked what it represented to you, you might not think that your impressions would mean very much. But to a psychodynamic theoretician, your responses to such an ambiguous figure would provide valuable clues to the state of your unconscious, and ultimately to your general personality characteristics.

The shape in the figure is representative of inkblots used in **projective personality tests**, in which a person is shown an ambiguous stimulus and asked to describe it or tell a story about it. The responses are considered to be "projections" of the individual's personality.

The best-known projective test is the **Rorschach test**. Devised by Swiss psychiatrist Hermann Rorschach (1924), the test involves showing a series of symmetrical

Projective personality test: A test in which a person is shown an ambiguous stimulus and asked to describe it or tell a story about it.

Rorschach test: A test that involves showing a series of symmetrical visual stimuli to people who then are asked what the figures represent to them.

 StudyALERT

In projective tests such as the Rorschach, researchers present an ambiguous stimulus and ask a person to describe or tell a story about it, and use the responses to make inferences about personality.

FIGURE 3 This inkblot is similar to the type used in the Rorschach personality test. What do you see in it? (Source: Alloy, Jacobson, & Acocella, 1999.)

Thematic Apperception Test (TAT): A test consisting of a series of pictures about which a person is asked to write a story.

Behavioral assessment: Direct measures of an individual's behavior used to describe personality characteristics.

"Rorschach! What's to become of you?"

stimuli, similar to the one in Figure 3, to people who are then asked what the figures represent to them. Their responses are recorded, and through a complex set of clinical judgments on the part of the examiner, people are classified by their personality type. For instance, respondents who see a bear in one inkblot are thought to have a strong degree of emotional control, according to the scoring guidelines developed by Rorschach (Weiner, 2004; Silverstein, 2007).

The **Thematic Apperception Test (TAT)** is another well-known projective test. The TAT consists of a series of pictures about which a person is asked to write a story. The stories are then used to draw inferences about the writer's personality characteristics (Weiner, 2004; Langan-Fox & Grant, 2006).

Tests with stimuli as ambiguous as those used in the Rorschach and TAT require particular skill and care in their interpretation—too much, in many critics' estimation. The Rorschach in particular has been criticized for requiring too much inference on the part of the examiner, and attempts to standardize scoring have frequently failed. Furthermore, many critics complain that the Rorschach does not provide much valid information about underlying personality traits. Despite such problems, both the Rorschach and the TAT are widely used, especially in clinical settings, and their proponents suggest that their reliability and validity are great enough to provide useful inferences about personality (Wood et al., 2003; Garb et al., 2005; Society for Personality Assessment, 2005).

Behavioral Assessment

If you were a psychologist subscribing to a learning approach to personality, you would be likely to object to the indirect nature of projective tests. Instead, you would be more apt to use **behavioral assessment**—direct measures of an individual's behavior designed to describe characteristics indicative of personality. As with observational research, behavioral assessment may be carried out naturalistically by observing people in their own settings: in the workplace, at home, or in school. In other cases, behavioral assessment occurs in the laboratory, under controlled conditions in which a psychologist sets up a situation and observes an individual's behavior (Ramsay, Reynolds, & Kamphaus, 2002; Gladwell, 2004; Miller & Leffard, 2007).

Regardless of the setting in which behavior is observed, an effort is made to ensure that behavioral assessment is carried out objectively, quantifying behavior as much as possible. For example, an observer may record the number of social contacts a person initiates, the number of questions asked, or the number of aggressive acts. Another method is to measure the duration of events: the duration of a temper tantrum in a child, the length of a conversation, the amount of time spent working, or the time spent in cooperative behavior.

Behavioral assessment is particularly appropriate for observing—and eventually remedying—specific behavioral difficulties, such as shyness in children. It provides a means of assessing the specific nature and incidence of a problem and subsequently allows psychologists to determine whether intervention techniques have been successful.

Behavioral assessment techniques based on learning theories of personality have also made important contributions to the treatment of certain kinds of psychological difficulties. Indeed, the knowledge of normal personality provided by the various personality theories has led to significant advances in our understanding and treatment of both physical and psychological disorders.

BECOMING
AN INFORMED CONSUMER

of Psychology

Assessing Personality Assessments

Like the personality tests being developed by Google (which we discussed in the chapter prologue), assessments of personality are routinely used to help with hiring decisions. However, before relying too heavily on the results of personality testing, keep several points in mind:

- *Understand what the test claims to measure.* Standard personality measures are accompanied by information that discusses how the test was developed, to whom it is most applicable, and how the results should be interpreted. Read any explanations of the test; they will help you understand the results.

- *Base no decision only on the results of any one test.* Test results should be interpreted in the context of other information—academic records, social interests, and home and community activities.

- *Remember that test results are not always accurate.* The results may be in error; the test may be unreliable or invalid. You may, for example, have had a "bad day" when you took the test, or the person scoring and interpreting the test may have made a mistake. You should not place too much significance on the results of a single administration of any test.

In sum, it is important to keep in mind the complexity of human behavior—particularly your own. No single test can provide an understanding of the intricacies of someone's personality without considering a good deal more information than can be provided in a single testing session (Gladwell, 2004; Paul, 2004; Hogan, Davies, & Hogan, 2007).

RECAP/EVALUATE/RETHINK

RECAP

How can we most accurately assess personality?

- Psychological tests such as the MMPI are standard assessment tools that measure behavior objectively. They must be reliable (measuring what they are trying to measure consistently) and valid (measuring what they are supposed to measure). (p. 469)

What are the major types of personality measures?

- Self-report measures ask people about a sample range of their behaviors. These reports are used to infer the presence of particular personality characteristics. (p. 471)

- Projective personality tests (such as the Rorschach and the Thematic Apperception Test) present an ambiguous stimulus; the test administrator infers information about the test taker from his or her responses. (p. 473)

- Behavioral assessment is based on the principles of learning theory. It employs direct measurement of an individual's behavior to determine characteristics related to personality. (p. 474)

EVALUATE

1. _____ is the consistency of a personality test; _____ is the ability of a test to actually measure what it is designed to measure.

2. _____ are standards used to compare scores of different people taking the same test.

3. Tests such as the MMPI-2, in which a small sample of behavior is assessed to determine larger patterns, are examples of
   a. Cross-sectional tests
   b. Projective tests
   c. Achievement tests
   d. Self-report tests

4. A person shown a picture and asked to make up a story about it would be taking a _____ personality test.

RETHINK

1. Should personality tests be used for personnel decisions? Should they be used for other social purposes, such as identifying individuals at risk for certain types of personality disorders?

2. *From the perspective of a politician:* Imagine that you had to vote on a law that would require institutions and organizations to perform race norming procedures on standardized performance tests. Would you support such a law? Why or why not? In addition to race, should norming procedures take other factors into account? Which ones and why?

Answers to Evaluate Questions

1. reliability, validity; 2. norms; 3. d; 4. projective

KEY TERMS

psychological tests p. 469
self-report measures p. 471
Minnesota Multiphasic
   Personality Inventory-2
   (MMPI-2) p. 471

test standardization p. 472
projective personality
   test p. 472
Rorschach test p. 473

Thematic Apperception Test
   (TAT) p. 474
behavioral assessment p. 474

Psychology on the Web

1. Sigmund Freud is one of the towering figures in psychology. His influence extends far beyond his psychoanalytic work. Find information about Freud on the Web. Pick one aspect of his work or influence (for example, on therapy, medicine, literature, film, or culture and society) and summarize in writing what you have found, including your attitude toward your findings.

2. Find a Web site that links to personality tests and take one or two tests—remembering to take them with skepticism. For each test, summarize in writing the aspects of personality that were tested, the theoretical approach the test appeared to be based on, and your assessment of the trustworthiness of the results.

Epilogue

We have discussed the different ways in which psychologists have interpreted the development and structure of personality. The perspectives we examined ranged from Freud's analysis of personality based primarily on internal, unconscious factors to the externally based view of personality as a learned set of traits and actions that is championed by learning theorists. We also noted that there are many ways to interpret personality, and by no means does a consensus exist on what the key traits are that are central to personality.

Return to the prologue and consider Google's plan to predict job performance from a personality profile. Use your understanding of personality to consider the following questions.

1. Which approach to personality does Google seem to be applying with its personnel selection method?

2. Why do you think Google doesn't just use standard personality measures such as the Big Five factor dimensions or MMPI?

3. If engineers who own dogs are better at their jobs than engineers without dogs, would dog ownership alone be a good criterion for hiring new engineers? What important information is likely to be missed by Google's questionnaire?

4. Would projective tests work as well as Google's questionnaire? Why or why not?

CHAPTER 14

Health Psychology: Stress, Coping, and Well-Being

Key Concepts for Chapter 14

Prologue *Never a Moment's Rest*

Seventeen-year-old Alex Capp of Grosse Pointe, Michigan, hopes his senior year of high school will be less stressful than his junior year.

"It was a pretty overwhelming workload," he says.

Besides taking two Advanced Placement classes, honors chemistry, math, and electives, he served on the student council organizing community service projects, took a cultural diversity class at a community college for college credit, participated in his school's alcohol awareness group, did volunteer work, took tennis lessons, and held down a part-time job.

He hasn't had too much rest this summer, either; it was largely spent building up his credentials for college. He took a summer school class, volunteered, worked at his dad's office, and completed parts of the Common Application for the 10 or so colleges he's applying to. (Jayson, 2006)

Looking Ahead

It's not hard to understand why Alex Capp is looking forward to experiencing less stress. For people like him—and that probably includes most of us—the intensity of juggling multiple roles leads to feelings of never having sufficient time and, in some cases, takes a toll on both physical and psychological well-being.

Stress and how we cope with it have long been central topics of interest for psychologists. However, in recent years the focus has broadened as psychology has come to view stress in the broader context of one of psychology's newer subfields: health psychology. **Health psychology** investigates the psychological factors related to wellness and illness, including the prevention, diagnosis, and treatment of medical problems. Health psychologists investigate the effects of psychological factors such as stress on illness. They examine the psychological principles underlying treatments for disease and illness. They also study prevention: how more healthful behavior can help people avoid and reduce health problems such as stress and heart disease.

Health psychologists take a decisive stand on the enduring mind-body issue that philosophers, and later psychologists, have debated since the time of the ancient Greeks. In their view, the mind and the body are clearly linked, rather than representing two distinct systems (Sternberg, 2000; Dalal & Misra, 2006).

Health psychologists recognize that good health and the ability to cope with illness are affected by psychological factors such as thoughts, emotions, and the ability to manage stress. They have paid particular attention to the *immune system*, the complex of organs, glands, and cells that constitute our bodies' natural line of defense in fighting disease.

In fact, health psychologists are among the primary investigators in a growing field called **psychoneuroimmunology**, or **PNI**, the study of the relationship among psychological factors, the immune system, and the brain. PNI has led to discoveries such as the existence of an association between a person's emotional state and the success of the immune system in fighting disease (Dickerson et al., 2004; Kemeny, 2007).

In sum, health psychologists view the mind and the body as two parts of a whole human being that cannot be considered independently. This more recent view marks a sharp departure from earlier thinking. Previously, disease was seen as a purely biological phenomenon, and psychological factors were of little interest to most health-care workers. In the early 20th century, the primary causes of death were short-term infections from which one either rapidly recovered—or died. Now, however, the major causes of death, such as heart disease, cancer, and diabetes, are chronic illnesses that—because they often cannot be cured and may linger for years—pose significant psychological issues (Bishop, 2005; Rotan & Ospina-Krammerer, 2007).

Advances in health psychology have had an impact across a variety of disciplines and professions. For instance, medical professionals such as physicians and nurses, social workers, dieticians, pharmacists, occupational therapists, and even clergy are increasingly likely to receive training in health psychology.

In the three modules that follow we discuss the ways in which psychological factors affect health. We first focus on the causes and consequences of stress, as well as on the means of coping with it. Next, we explore the psychological aspects of several major health problems, including heart disease, cancer, and ailments resulting from smoking. Finally, we examine the ways in which patient-physician interactions influence our health and offer suggestions for increasing people's compliance with recommendations about behavior that will improve their well-being.

Health psychology: The branch of psychology that investigates the psychological factors related to wellness and illness, including the prevention, diagnosis, and treatment of medical problems.

Psychoneuroimmunology (PNI): The study of the relationship among psychological factors, the immune system, and the brain.

Stress and Coping

Anthony Lepre started feeling awful almost as soon as [U.S. Homeland Security Secretary] Tom Ridge put the nation on high alert for a terrorist attack. . . . He awoke in the middle of the night short of breath, his heart pounding. And the sound of his telephone seemed a sure sign of bad news. By midweek, he was rushing off to Costco to stock up on fruit juice, bottle water, peanut butter, canned tuna, "and extra food for my cats Monster, Monkey and Spike." He also picked up a first-aid kit, six rolls of duct tape, and a bulk package of plastic wrap to seal his windows. "The biggest problem was that I felt helpless," he says, "completely powerless over the situation" (Cowley, 2003, pp. 43-44).

Key Concepts

How is health psychology a union between medicine and psychology?

What is stress, how does it affect us, and how can we best cope with it?

Stress: Reacting to Threat and Challenge

Most of us need little introduction to the phenomenon of **stress**, people's response to events that threaten or challenge them. Whether it is a paper or an exam deadline, a family problem, or even the ongoing threat of a terrorist attack, life is full of circumstances and events, known as *stressors*, that produce threats to our well-being. Even pleasant events—such as planning a party or beginning a sought-after job— can produce stress, although negative events result in greater detrimental consequences than do positive ones.

Stress: A person's response to events that are threatening or challenging

All of us face stress in our lives. Some health psychologists believe that daily life actually involves a series of repeated sequences of perceiving a threat, considering ways to cope with it, and ultimately adapting to the threat, with greater or lesser success. Although adaptation is often minor and occurs without our awareness, adaptation requires a major effort when stress is more severe or longer lasting. Ultimately, our attempts to overcome stress may produce biological and psychological responses that result in health problems (Boyce & Ellis, 2005; Dolbier, Smith, & Steinhardt, 2007).

THE NATURE OF STRESSORS: MY STRESS IS YOUR PLEASURE

Stress is a very personal thing. Although certain kinds of events, such as the death of a loved one or participation in military combat, are universally stressful, other situations may or may not be stressful to a specific person.

Consider, for instance, bungee jumping. Some people would find jumping off a bridge while attached to a slender rubber tether extremely stressful. However, there are individuals who

Even positive events can produce significant stress.

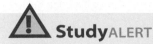

Cataclysmic events: Strong stressors that occur suddenly, affecting many people at once (e.g., natural disasters).

Personal stressors: Major life events, such as the death of a family member, that have immediate negative consequences that generally fade with time.

Posttraumatic stress disorder (PTSD): A phenomenon in which victims of major catastrophes or strong personal stressors feel long-lasting effects that may include reexperiencing the event in vivid flashbacks or dreams.

see such an activity as challenging and fun-filled. Whether bungee jumping is stressful depends in part, then, on a person's perception of the activity.

For people to consider an event stressful, they must perceive it as threatening or challenging and must lack all the resources to deal with it effectively. Consequently, the same event may at some times be stressful and at other times provoke no stressful reaction at all. A young man may experience stress when he is turned down for a date—if he attributes the refusal to his unattractiveness or unworthiness. But if he attributes it to some factor unrelated to his self-esteem, such as a previous commitment by the woman he asked, the experience of being refused may create no stress at all. Hence, a person's interpretation of events plays an important role in the determination of what is stressful (Folkman & Moskowitz, 2000; Giacobbi Jr., et al., 2004; Friborg et al., 2007).

CATEGORIZING STRESSORS

What kinds of events tend to be seen as stressful? There are three general types of stressors: cataclysmic events, personal stressors, and background stressors.

Cataclysmic events are strong stressors that occur suddenly and typically affect many people simultaneously. Disasters such as tornadoes and plane crashes, as well as terrorist attacks, are examples of cataclysmic events that can affect hundreds or thousands of people simultaneously.

Although it might seem that cataclysmic events would produce potent, lingering stress, in many cases they do not. In fact, cataclysmic events involving natural disasters may produce less stress in the long run than do events that initially are not as devastating. One reason is that natural disasters have a clear resolution. Once they are over, people can look to the future knowing that the worst is behind them. Moreover, the stress induced by cataclysmic events is shared by others who also experienced the disaster. Such sharing permits people to offer one another social support and a first-hand understanding of the difficulties others are going through (Hobfoll et al., 1996; Benight, 2004; Yesilyaprak, Kisac, & Sanlier, 2007).

In contrast, terrorist attacks like the one on the World Trade Center in 2001, are cataclysmic events that produce considerable stress. Terrorist attacks are deliberate, and victims (and observers) know that future attacks are likely. Government warnings in the form of heightened terror alerts may further increase the stress (Murphy, Wismar, & Freeman, 2003; Laugharne, Janca, & Widiger, 2007).

The second major category of stressor is the personal stressor. **Personal stressors** include major life events such as the death of a parent or spouse, the loss of one's job, a major personal failure, or even something positive such as getting married. Typically, personal stressors produce an immediate major reaction that soon tapers off. For example, stress arising from the death of a loved one tends to be greatest just after the time of death, but people begin to feel less stress and are better able to cope with the loss after the passage of time.

Some victims of major catastrophes and severe personal stressors experience **posttraumatic stress disorder**, or **PTSD**, in which a person has experienced a significantly stressful event that has long-lasting effects that may include reexperiencing the event in vivid flashbacks or dreams. An episode of PTSD may be triggered by an otherwise innocent stimulus, such as the sound of a honking horn, that leads someone to reexperience a past event that produced considerable stress.

Symptoms of posttraumatic stress disorder also include emotional numbing, sleep difficulties, interpersonal problems, alcohol and drug abuse, and—in some cases—suicide. For instance, the suicide rate for veterans of the Vietnam War is as much as 25 percent higher than it is for the general population (McKeever & Huff, 2003; Dohrenwend et al., 2006; Pole, 2007).

Around 16 percent of soldiers returning from Iraq show symptoms of PTSD. Furthermore, those who have experienced child abuse or rape, rescue workers facing overwhelming situations, and victims of sudden natural disasters or accidents that produce feelings of helplessness and shock may suffer from the same disorder (Ozer & Weiss, 2004; Hoge & Castro, 2006; Friedman, 2006).

Terrorist attacks produce high incidences of PTSD. For example, 11 percent of people in New York City had some form of PTSD in the months after the September 11 terrorist attacks. But the responses varied significantly with a resident's proximity to the attacks, as illustrated in Figure 1; the closer someone lived to ground zero, the greater the likelihood of PTSD (Susser, Herman, & Aaron, 2002; Lee, Isaac, & Mohan, 2007; Marshall et al., 2007).

Background stressors, or more informally, *daily hassles*, are the third major category of stressors. Exemplified by standing in a long line at a bank and getting stuck in a traffic jam, daily hassles are the minor irritations of life that we all face time and time again. Another type of background stressor is a long-term, chronic problem, such as experiencing dissatisfaction with school or a job, being in an unhappy relationship, or living in crowded quarters without privacy (Lazarus, 2000; Weinstein et al., 2004).

By themselves, daily hassles do not require much coping or even a response on the part of the individual, although they certainly produce unpleasant emotions and

StudyALERT

Remember the three categories of stressors: cataclysmic events, personal stressors, and background stressors—and that they produce different levels of stress.

Background stressors ("daily hassles"): Everyday annoyances, such as being stuck in traffic, that cause minor irritations and may have long-term ill effects if they continue or are compounded by other stressful events.

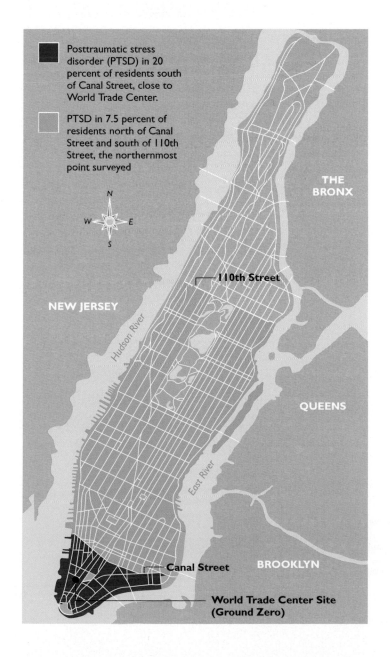

Posttraumatic stress disorder (PTSD) in 20 percent of residents south of Canal Street, close to World Trade Center.

PTSD in 7.5 percent of residents north of Canal Street and south of 110th Street, the northernmost point surveyed

110th Street

THE BRONX

NEW JERSEY

Hudson River

QUEENS

East River

Canal Street   BROOKLYN

World Trade Center Site (Ground Zero)

FIGURE 1 The closer people lived to the site of the World Trade Center terrorist attack, the greater the rate of posttraumatic stress disorder. (Source: Susser, Herman, & Aaron, 2002.)

moods. Yet daily hassles add up—and ultimately they may take as great a toll as a single, more stressful incident does. In fact, the *number* of daily hassles people face is associated with psychological symptoms and health problems such as flu, sore throat, and backaches.

The flip side of hassles is *uplifts*, the minor positive events that make us feel good—even if only temporarily. As indicated in Figure 2, uplifts range from relating well to a companion to finding one's surroundings pleasing. What is especially intriguing about uplifts is that they are associated with people's psychological health in just the opposite way that hassles are: The greater the number of uplifts we experience, the fewer the psychological symptoms we report later (Chamberlain & Zika, 1990; Ravindran et al., 2002; Jain et al., 2007).

FIGURE 2 The most common everyday hassles and uplifts (hassles: Chamberlain & Zika, 1990; uplifts: Kanner et al., 1981.) How many of these are part of your life, and how do you cope with them?

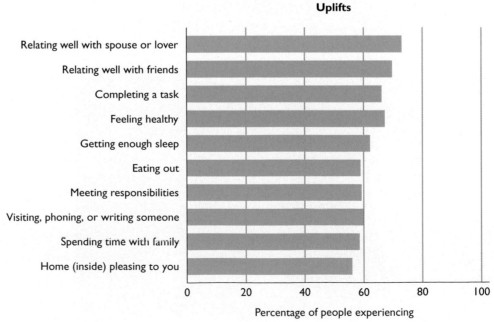

THE HIGH COST OF STRESS

Stress can produce both biological and psychological consequences. Often the most immediate reaction to stress is a biological one. Exposure to stressors generates a rise in hormone secretions by the adrenal glands, an increase in heart rate and blood pressure, and changes in how well the skin conducts electrical impulses. On a short-term basis, these responses may be adaptive because they produce an "emergency reaction," in which the body prepares to defend itself through activation of the sympathetic nervous system. Those responses may allow more effective coping with the stressful situation (Akil & Morano, 1996; McEwen, 1998).

However, continued exposure to stress results in a decline in the body's overall level of biological functioning because of the constant secretion of stress-related hormones. Over time, stressful reactions can promote deterioration of body tissues such as blood vessels and the heart. Ultimately, we become more susceptible to disease as our ability to fight off infection is lowered (Kemeny, 2003; Brydon et al., 2004; Dean-Borenstein, 2007).

Furthermore, an entire class of physical problems known as **psychophysiological disorders** often result from or are worsened by stress. Once referred to as *psychosomatic disorders* (a term dropped because people assumed that the disorders were somehow unreal), psychophysiological disorders are actual medical problems that are influenced by an interaction of psychological, emotional, and physical difficulties. The more common psychophysiological disorders range from major problems, such as high blood pressure, to usually less serious conditions, such as headaches, backaches, skin rashes, indigestion, fatigue, and constipation. Stress has even been linked to the common cold (Cohen et al., 2003; Andrasik, 2006).

On a psychological level, high levels of stress prevent people from adequately coping with life. Their view of the environment can become clouded (for example, a minor criticism made by a friend is blown out of proportion). Moreover, at the highest levels of stress, emotional responses may be so extreme that people are unable to act at all. People under a lot of stress also become less able to deal with new stressors.

In short, stress affects us in multiple ways. It may increase the risk that we will become ill, it may directly cause illness, it may make us less able to recover from a disease, and it may reduce our ability to cope with future stress. (See Figure 3 to get a measure of your own level of stress.)

Everyone confronts daily hassles, or background stressors, at some point. At what point do daily hassles become more than mere irritants?

Psychophysiological disorders: Medical problems influenced by an interaction of psychological, emotional, and physical difficulties.

THE GENERAL ADAPTATION SYNDROME MODEL: THE COURSE OF STRESS

The effects of long-term stress are illustrated in a series of stages proposed by Hans Selye (pronounced "sell-yay"), a pioneering stress theorist (Selye, 1976, 1993). This model, the **general adaptation syndrome (GAS)**, suggests that the physiological response to stress follows the same set pattern regardless of the cause of stress.

As shown in Figure 4, the GAS has three phases. The first stage—*alarm and mobilization*—occurs when people become aware of the presence of a stressor. On a biological level, the sympathetic nervous system becomes energized, helping a person cope initially with the stressor.

However, if the stressor persists, people move into the second response stage: *resistance*. During this stage, the body prepares to fight the stressor. During resistance, people use a variety of means to cope with the stressor—sometimes successfully but at a cost of some degree of physical or psychological well-being. For example, a student who faces the stress of failing several courses might spend long hours studying, seeking to cope with the stress.

General adaptation syndrome (GAS): A theory developed by Selye that suggests that a person's response to a stressor consists of three stages: alarm and mobilization, resistance, and exhaustion.

How Stressful Is Your Life?

Test your level of stress by answering these questions, and adding the score from each box. Questions apply to the last month only. A key below will help you determine the extent of your stress.

1. How often have you been upset because of something that happened unexpectedly?

   0 = never, 1 = almost never, 2 = sometimes, 3 = fairly often, 4 = very often

2. How often have you felt that you were unable to control the important things in your life?

   0 = never, 1 = almost never, 2 = sometimes, 3 = fairly often, 4 = very often

3. How often have you felt nervous and "stressed"?

   0 = never, 1 = almost never, 2 = sometimes, 3 = fairly often, 4 = very often

4. How often have you felt confident about your ability to handle your personal problems?

   4 = never, 3 = almost never, 2 = sometimes, 1 = fairly often, 0 = very often

5. How often have you felt that things were going your way?

   4 = never, 3 = almost never, 2 = sometimes, 1 = fairly often, 0 = very often

6. How often have you been able to control irritations in your life?

   4 = never, 3 = almost never, 2 = sometimes, 1 = fairly often, 0 = very often

7. How often have you found that you could not cope with all the things that you had to do?

   0 = never, 1 = almost never, 2 = sometimes, 3 = fairly often, 4 = very often

8. How often have you felt that you were on top of things?

   4 = never, 3 = almost never, 2 = sometimes, 1 = fairly often, 0 = very often

9. How often have you been angered because of things that were outside your control?

   0 = never, 1 = almost never, 2 = sometimes, 3 = fairly often, 4 = very often

10. How often have you felt difficulties were piling up so high that you could not overcome them?

    0 = never, 1 = almost never, 2 = sometimes, 3 = fairly often, 4 = very often

How You Measure Up:

Stress levels vary among individuals—compare your total score to the averages below:

AGE		GENDER	
18–29	14.2	Men	12.1
30–44	13.0	Women	13.7
45–54	12.6		
55–64	11.9		
65 & over	12.0		

MARITAL STATUS	
Widowed	12.6
Married or living with a partner	12.4
Single or never wed	14.1
Divorced	14.7
Separated	16.6

FIGURE 3 To get a sense of the level of stress in your life, complete this questionnaire. (Source: Cohen, 1999.)

Stressor

1. Alarm and mobilization
   Meeting and resisting stressor.

2. Resistance
   Coping with stress and resistance to stressor.

3. Exhaustion
   Negative consequences of stress (such as illness) occur when coping is inadequate.

FIGURE 4 The general adaptation syndrome (GAS) suggests that there are three major stages to stress responses. (Source: Selye, 1976.)

If resistance is inadequate, people enter the last stage of the GAS: *exhaustion*. During the exhaustion stage, a person's ability to adapt to the stressor declines to the point where negative consequences of stress appear: physical illness and psychological symptoms in the form of an inability to concentrate, heightened irritability, or, in severe cases, disorientation and a loss of touch with reality. In a sense, people wear out, and their physical reserves are used up.

How do people move out of the third stage after they have entered it? In some cases, exhaustion allows people to avoid a stressor. For example, people who become ill from overwork may be excused from their duties for a time, giving them a temporary respite from their responsibilities. At least for a time, then, the immediate stress is reduced.

Although the GAS has had a substantial impact on our understanding of stress, Selye's theory has not gone unchallenged. For example, whereas the theory suggests that regardless of the stressor, the biological reaction is similar, some health psychologists disagree. They believe that people's biological responses are specific to the way they appraise a stressful event. If a stressor is seen as unpleasant but not unusual, then the biological response may be different from that if the stressor is seen as unpleasant, out of the ordinary, and unanticipated. This perspective has led to an increased focus on psychoneuroimmunology (Taylor et al., 2000; Gaab, Rohleder, Nater, & Ehlert, 2005).

PSYCHONEUROIMMUNOLOGY AND STRESS

Contemporary health psychologists specializing in psychoneuroimmunology (PNI) have taken a broader approach to stress. Focusing on the outcomes of stress, they have identified three main consequences (see Figure 5).

First, stress has direct physiological results, including an increase in blood pressure, an increase in hormonal activity, and an overall decline in the functioning of the immune system. Second, stress leads people to engage in behaviors that are harmful to their health, including increased nicotine, drug, and alcohol use; poor eating habits; and decreased sleep. Finally, stress produces indirect consequences that result in declines in health: a reduction in the likelihood of obtaining health care and decreased compliance with medical advice when it is sought (Sapolsky, 2003; Broman, 2005; Lindblad et al., 2006).

Why is stress so damaging to the immune system? One reason is that stress may overstimulate the immune system. Rather than fighting invading bacteria,

FIGURE 5 Three major types of consequences result from stress: direct physiological effects, harmful behaviors, and indirect health-related behaviors.
(Source: Adapted from Baum, 1994.)

The ability to fight off disease is related to psychological factors. Here a cell from the body's immune system engulfs and destroys disease-producing bacteria.

Coping: The efforts to control, reduce, or learn to tolerate the threats that lead to stress.

viruses, and other foreign invaders, it may begin to attack the body itself, damaging healthy tissue. When that happens, it can lead to disorders such as arthritis and an allergic reaction.

Stress can also decrease the immune system response, permitting germs that produce colds to reproduce more easily or allowing cancer cells to spread more rapidly. In normal circumstances, our bodies produce *lymphocytes*, specialized white blood cells that fight disease, at an extraordinary rate—some 10 million every few seconds—and it is possible that stress can alter this level of production (Cohen et al., 2002; Segerstrom & Miller, 2004; Dougall & Baum, 2004).

Coping with Stress

Stress is a normal part of life—and not necessarily a completely bad part. For example, without stress, we might not be sufficiently motivated to complete the activities we need to accomplish. However, it is also clear that too much stress can take a toll on physical and psychological health. How do people deal with stress? Is there a way to reduce its negative effects?

Efforts to control, reduce, or learn to tolerate the threats that lead to stress are known as **coping**. We habitually use certain coping responses to deal with stress. Most of the time, we're not aware of these responses—just as we may be unaware of the minor stressors of life until they build up to harmful levels (Wrzesniewski & Chylinska, 2007).

We also have other, more direct, and potentially more positive ways of coping with stress, which fall into two main categories (Folkman & Moskowitz, 2000, 2004):

- **Emotion-focused coping**. In *emotion-focused coping*, people try to manage their emotions in the face of stress, seeking to change the way they feel about or perceive a problem. Examples of emotion-focused coping include strategies such as accepting sympathy from others and looking at the bright side of a situation.

- **Problem-focused coping**. *Problem-focused coping* attempts to modify the stressful problem or source of stress. Problem-focused strategies lead to changes in behavior or to the development of a plan of action to deal with stress. Starting a study group to improve poor classroom performance is an example of problem-focused coping. In addition, one might take a time-out from stress by creating positive events. For example, taking a day off from caring for a relative with a serious, chronic illness to go a health club or spa can bring significant relief from stress.

People often employ several types of coping strategies simultaneously. Furthermore, they use emotion-focused strategies more frequently when they perceive circumstances as being unchangeable and problem-focused approaches more often in situations they see as relatively modifiable (Stanton et al., 2000; Penley, Tomaka, & Wiebe, 2002).

Some forms of coping are less successful. One of the least effective forms of coping is avoidant coping. In *avoidant coping*, a person may use wishful thinking to reduce stress or use more direct escape routes, such as drug use, alcohol use, and overeating. An example of wishful thinking to avoid a test would be to say to oneself, "Maybe it will snow so hard tomorrow that the test will be canceled." Alternatively, a person might get drunk to avoid a problem. Either way, avoidant coping usually results in a postponement of dealing with a stressful situation, and this often makes the problem even worse (Roesch et al., 2005; Hutchinson, Baldwin, & Oh, 2006).

Another way of dealing with stress occurs unconsciously through the use of defense mechanisms. As we discussed in the chapter on personality, *defense mechanisms* are unconscious strategies that people use to reduce anxiety by concealing the source from themselves and others. Defense mechanisms permit people to avoid stress by acting as if the stress were not even there. For example, one study examined California college students who lived in dormitories close to a geological fault. Those who lived in dorms that were known to be unlikely to withstand an earthquake were significantly *more* likely to doubt experts' predictions of an impending earthquake than were those who lived in safer structures (Lehman & Taylor, 1988).

Another defense mechanism used to cope with stress is *emotional insulation*, in which a person stops experiencing any emotions at all, thereby remaining unaffected and unmoved by both positive and negative experiences. The problem with defense mechanisms, of course, is that they do not deal with reality but merely hide the problem.

LEARNED HELPLESSNESS

Have you ever faced an intolerable situation that you just couldn't resolve, and you finally simply gave up and accepted things the way they were? This example illustrates one of the possible consequences of being in an environment in which control over a situation is not possible—a state that produces learned helplessness. **Learned helplessness** occurs when people conclude that unpleasant or aversive stimuli cannot be controlled—a view of the world that becomes so ingrained that they cease trying to remedy the aversive circumstances, even if they actually can exert some influence on the situation (Seligman, 1975, 2007; Aujoulat, Luminet, & Deccache, 2007).

Victims of learned helplessness have concluded that there is no link between the responses they make and the outcomes that occur. People experience more physical symptoms and depression when they perceive that they have little or no control than they do when they feel a sense of control over a situation (Chou, 2005; Bjornstad, 2006).

Learned helplessness: A state in which people conclude that unpleasant or aversive stimuli cannot be controlled—a view of the world that becomes so ingrained that they cease trying to remedy the aversive circumstances, even if they actually can exert some influence.

COPING STYLES: THE HARDY PERSONALITY

Most of us cope with stress in a characteristic manner, employing a *coping style* that represents our general tendency to deal with stress in a specific way. For example, you may know people who habitually react to even the smallest amount of stress with hysteria, and others who calmly confront even the greatest stress in an unflappable manner. These kinds of people clearly have very different coping styles (Taylor, 2003; Kato & Pedersen, 2005).

Among those who cope with stress most successfully are people who are equipped with **hardiness**, a personality characteristic associated with a lower rate of stress-related illness. Hardiness consists of three components (Baumgartner, 2002; Maddi, 2007):

Hardiness: A personality characteristic associated with a lower rate of stress-related illness, consisting of three components: commitment, challenge, and control.

- *Commitment.* Commitment is a tendency to throw ourselves into whatever we are doing with a sense that our activities are important and meaningful.

- *Challenge.* Hardy people believe that change, rather than stability, is the standard condition of life. To them, the anticipation of change serves as an incentive rather than a threat to their security.

- *Control.* Hardiness is marked by a sense of control—the perception that people can influence the events in their lives.

Hardy individuals approach stress in an optimistic manner and take direct action to learn about and deal with stressors, thereby changing stressful events into less threatening ones. As a consequence, hardiness acts as a defense against stress-related illness.

For those who confront the most profound difficulties, such as the death of a loved one or a permanent injury such as paralysis after an accident, a key ingredient in their psychological recovery is their degree of resilience. *Resilience* is the ability to withstand, overcome, and actually thrive after profound adversity (Bonanno, 2004; Norlander et al., 2005; Jackson, 2006).

Resilient people are generally easygoing and good-natured and have good social skills. They are usually independent, and they have a sense of control over their own destiny—even if fate has dealt them a devastating blow. In short, they work with what they have and make the best of whatever situation they find themselves in (Humphreys, 2003; Spencer, 2003; Deshields et al., 2005; Friborg, Barlaug, Martinussen, Rosenvinge, & Hjemdal, 2005).

"Today, we examined our life style, we evaluated our diet and our exercise program, and we also assessed our behavioral patterns. Then we felt we needed a drink."

SOCIAL SUPPORT: TURNING TO OTHERS

Social support: A mutual network of caring, interested others.

Our relationships with others also help us cope with stress. Researchers have found that **social support**, the knowledge that we are part of a mutual network of caring, interested others, enables us to experience lower levels of stress and be better able to cope with the stress we do undergo (Cohen, 2004; Martin & Brantley, 2004; Boliger & Amarel, 2007).

The social and emotional support people provide each other helps in dealing with stress in several ways. For instance, such support demonstrates that a person is an important and valued member of a social network. Similarly, other people can provide information and advice about appropriate ways of dealing with stress (Day & Livingstone, 2003; Lindorff, 2005).

Finally, people who are part of a social support network can provide actual goods and services to help others in stressful situations. For instance, they can supply temporary living quarters to a person whose house has burned down, or they can offer study help to a student who is experiencing stress because of poor academic performance (Natvig, Albrektsen, & Ovamstrom, 2003; Takizawa et al., 2007).

The importance of social support is also illustrated by findings that attendance at religious services (as well as spirituality in general) provides health-related benefits. For example, healthy people who regularly attend religious services have lower death rates than those who do not attend regularly (Miller & Thoresen, 2003; Powell, Shahabi, & Thoresen, 2003; Gilbert, 2007).

Recent research is also beginning to identify how social support affects brain processing. For instance, one experiment found that activation of the areas of the brain reflecting stress was reduced when social support—simply being able to hold the hand of another person—was available (see **Neuroscience in Your Life**, Figure 6; Coan, Schaefer, & Davidson, 2006).

Neuroscience in Your Life

FIGURE 6 When participants in a study were threatened by being told they would be receiving a shock, activation of the areas of the brain that reflect stress was reduced when social support was provided. Specifically, social support in this study was having either a stranger or a participant's spouse hold his or her hand. In the figure, green areas highlight brain areas that show reductions in activity with spouse hand-holding while blue clusters highlight brain areas that show reductions in activity with spouse and stranger hand-holding. (Source: Coan, Schaefer, & Davidson, 2006, Figure 3.)

How can we deal with the stress in our lives? Although there is no universal solution, because effective coping depends on the nature of the stressor and the degree to which it can be controlled, here are some general guidelines (Aspinwall & Taylor, 1997; Folkman & Moskowitz, 2000):

BECOMING
AN INFORMED CONSUMER

of Psychology
Effective Coping Strategies

- *Turn a threat into a challenge.* When a stressful situation might be controllable, the best coping strategy is to treat the situation as a challenge, focusing on ways to control it. For instance, if you experience stress because your car is always breaking down, you might take a course in auto mechanics and learn to deal directly with the car's problems.

- *Make a threatening situation less threatening.* When a stressful situation seems to be uncontrollable, you need to take a different approach. It is possible to change your appraisal of the situation, view it in a different light, and modify your attitude toward it. The old truism "Look for the silver lining in every cloud" is supported by research (Smith & Lazarus, 2001; Cheng & Cheung, 2005).

- *Change your goals.* If you are faced with an uncontrollable situation, a reasonable strategy is to adopt new goals that are practical in view of the particular situation. For example, a dancer who has been in an automobile accident and has lost full use of her legs may no longer aspire to a career in dance but might modify her goals and try to become a choreographer.

- *Take physical action.* Changing your physiological reaction to stress can help with coping. For example, biofeedback (in which a person learns to control internal physiological processes through conscious thought) can alter basic physiological processes, allowing people to reduce blood pressure, heart rate, and other consequences of heightened stress. Exercise can also be effective in reducing stress (Langreth, 2000; Spencer, 2003; Hamer, Taylor, & Steptoe, 2006).

- *Prepare for stress before it happens.* A final strategy for coping with stress is *proactive coping*, anticipating and preparing for stress *before* it is encountered. For example, if you're expecting to go through a one-week period in which you must take a number of major tests, you can try to arrange your schedule so you have more time to study (Aspinwall & Taylor, 1997; Bode et al., 2007).

RECAP/EVALUATE/RETHINK

RECAP

How is health psychology a union between medicine and psychology?

- The field of health psychology considers how psychology can be applied to the prevention, diagnosis, and treatment of medical problems. (p. 480)

What is stress, how does it affect us, and how can we best cope with it?

- Stress is a response to threatening or challenging environmental conditions. People encounter stressors—the circumstances that produce stress—of both a positive and a negative nature. (p. 481)

- The way an environmental circumstance is interpreted affects whether it will be considered stressful. Still, there are general classes of events that provoke stress: cataclysmic events, personal stressors, and background stressors (daily hassles). (p. 482)

- Stress produces immediate physiological reactions. In the short term those reactions may be adaptive, but in the long term they may have negative consequences, including the development of psychophysiological disorders. (p. 485)

- The consequences of stress can be explained in part by Selye's general adaptation syndrome (GAS), which suggests that there are three stages in stress responses: alarm and mobilization, resistance, and exhaustion. (p. 485)

- Stress can be reduced by developing a sense of control over one's circumstances. In some cases, however, people develop a state of learned helplessness. (p. 489)

- Coping with stress can take a number of forms, including the unconscious use of defense mechanisms and the use of emotion-focused or problem-focused coping strategies. (p. 490)

EVALUATE

1. _____ is defined as a response to challenging or threatening events.
2. Match each portion of the GAS with its definition.
   1. Alarm and mobilization
   2. Exhaustion
   3. Resistance
   a. Ability to adapt to stress diminishes; symptoms appear.
   b. Activation of sympathetic nervous system.
   c. Various strategies are used to cope with a stressor.
3. Stressors that affect a single person and produce an immediate major reaction are known as
   a. Personal stressors
   b. Psychic stressors
   c. Cataclysmic stressors
   d. Daily stressors
4. People with the personality characteristic of _____ seem to be better able to successfully combat stressors.

RETHINK

1. Why are cataclysmic stressors less stressful in the long run than are other types of stressors? Does the reason relate to the coping phenomenon known as social support? How?
2. *From the perspective of a social worker:* How would you help people deal with and avoid stress in their everyday lives? How might you encourage people to create social support networks?

Answers to Evaluate Questions

1. stress; 2. 1-b; 2-a; 3-c; 3. a; 4. hardiness

KEY TERMS

health psychology p. 480
psychoneuroimmunology (PNI) p. 480
stress p. 481
cataclysmic events p. 482

personal stressors p. 482
posttraumatic stress disorder (PTSD) p. 482
background stressors ("daily hassles") p. 483

psychophysiological disorders p. 485
general adaptation syndrome (GAS) p. 485
coping p. 488

learned helplessness p. 489
hardiness p. 489
social support p. 490

Psychological Aspects of Illness and Well-Being

Once a week they meet to talk, to cry, sometimes to laugh together. "Is the pain still worse in the mornings?" Margaret asks Kate today.

A petite, graceful woman in her late forties, Kate shakes her head no. "It's getting bad all the time," she says in a voice raw with worry and fatigue. . . . They nod in tacit understanding, eight women sitting in a loose circle of chairs here in a small, sparely furnished room at Stanford University Medical Center. They know. All of them have been diagnosed with recurrent breast cancer. . . .

They gather here each Wednesday afternoon to talk with each other and to listen. It's a chance to discuss their fears and find some small comfort, a time to feel they're not alone. And in some way that no one has been able to explain, it may be keeping them alive. (Jaret, 1992, p. 87)

As recently as two decades ago, most psychologists and health-care providers would have scoffed at the notion that a discussion group could improve a cancer patient's chances of survival. Today, however, such methods have gained increasing acceptance.

Growing evidence suggests that psychological factors have a substantial impact both on major health problems that were once seen in purely physiological terms and on our everyday sense of health, well-being, and happiness. We'll consider the psychological components of three major health problems—heart disease, cancer, and smoking—and then consider the nature of people's well-being and happiness.

The As, Bs, and Ds of Coronary Heart Disease

Tim knew it wasn't going to be his day when he got stuck in traffic behind a slow-moving farm truck. How could the driver dawdle like that? Didn't he have anything of any importance to do? Things didn't get any better when Tim arrived on campus and discovered the library didn't have the books he needed. He could almost feel the tension rising.

"I need that material to finish my paper," he thought to himself.

He knew that meant he wouldn't be able to get his paper done early, and that meant he wouldn't have the time he wanted to revise the paper. He wanted it to be a first-class paper. This time Tim wanted to get a better grade than his roommate, Luis; although Luis didn't know it, Tim felt they were in competition and was always trying to better him, whether it was academically or just playing cards.

"In fact," Tim mused to himself, "I feel like I'm in competition with everyone, no matter what I'm doing."

Have you, like Tim, ever seethed impatiently at being caught behind a slow-moving vehicle, felt anger and frustration at not finding material you needed at the library, or experienced a sense of competitiveness with your classmates?

Key Concept

How do psychological factors affect health-related problems such as coronary heart disease, cancer, and smoking?

Type A behavior pattern: A cluster of behaviors involving hostility, competitiveness, time urgency, and feeling driven.

Type B behavior pattern: A cluster of behaviors characterized by a patient, cooperative, noncompetitive manner.

⚠️ **Study**ALERT

It's important to distinguish among Type A (hostility, competitiveness), Type B (patience, cooperativeness), and Type D (distressed) behaviors.

Many of us experience these sorts of feelings at one time or another, but for some people they represent a pervasive, characteristic set of personality traits known as the Type A behavior pattern. The **Type A behavior pattern** is a cluster of behaviors involving hostility, competitiveness, time urgency, and feeling driven. In contrast, the **Type B behavior pattern** is characterized by a patient, cooperative, noncompetitive, and nonaggressive manner. It's important to keep in mind that Type A and Type B represent the ends of a continuum, and most people fall somewhere in between the two endpoints. Few people are purely a Type A or a Type B.

The importance of the Type A behavior pattern lies in its links to coronary heart disease. Men who display the Type A pattern develop coronary heart disease twice as often and suffer significantly more fatal heart attacks than do those classified as having the Type B pattern. Moreover, the Type A pattern predicts who is going to develop heart disease at least as well as—and independently of—any other single factor, including age, blood pressure, smoking habits, and cholesterol levels in the body (Rosenman et al., 1994; Wielgosz & Nolan, 2000; Beresnevaité, Taylor, & Bagby, 2007).

Hostility is the key component of the Type A behavior pattern that is related to heart disease. Although competition, time urgency, and feelings of being driven may produce stress and potentially other health and emotional problems, they aren't linked to coronary heart disease in the way that hostility is (Williams et al., 2000; Boyle et al., 2005; Ohira et al., 2007).

Why is hostility so toxic? The key reason is that hostility produces excessive physiological arousal in stressful situations. That arousal, in turn, results in increased production of the hormones epinephrine and norepinephrine, as well as increases in heart rate and blood pressure. Such an exaggerated physiological response ultimately produces an increased incidence of coronary heart disease (Eaker et al., 2004; Demaree & Everhart, 2004; Myrtek, 2007).

It's important to keep in mind that not everyone who displays Type A behaviors is destined to have coronary heart disease. For one thing, a firm association between Type A behaviors and coronary heart disease has not been established for women; most findings pertain to males, not to females, in part because until recently, most research was done on men. In addition, other types of negative emotions, besides the hostility found in Type A behavior, appear to be related to heart attacks. For example, psychologist Johan Denollet has found evidence that what he calls *Type D*—for "distressed"—behavior is linked to coronary heart disease. In his view, insecurity, anxiety, and the negative outlook displayed by Type Ds puts them at risk for repeated heart attacks (Denollet & Brutsaert, 1998; Denollet, 2005; Schiffer et al., 2005). (For more on the links between psychological factors and coronary heart disease, see the *Applying Psychology in the 21st Century* box.)

Psychological Aspects of Cancer

Hardly any disease is feared more than cancer. Most people think of cancer in terms of lingering pain, and being diagnosed with the disease is typically viewed as receiving a death sentence.

Although a diagnosis of cancer is not as grim as we might at first suspect—several kinds of cancer have a high cure rate if detected early enough—cancer remains the second leading cause of death after coronary heart disease. The precise trigger for the disease is not well understood, but the process by which cancer spreads is straightforward. Certain cells in the body become altered and multiply rapidly in an uncontrolled fashion. As those cells grow, they form tumors, which, if left unchecked, suck nutrients from healthy cells and body tissue, ultimately destroying the body's ability to function properly.

Although the processes involved in the spread of cancer are basically physiological, accumulating evidence suggests that the emotional responses of cancer patients to their disease may have a critical effect on its course. For example, one experiment

Scared to Death: The Link Between Stress and Coronary Heart Disease

You can call it the Northridge Effect, after the powerful earthquake that struck near Los Angeles at 4:30 on a January morning in 1994. Within an hour, and for the rest of the day, medics responding to people crushed or trapped inside buildings faced a second wave of deaths from heart attacks among people who had survived the tremor unscathed. In the months that followed, researchers at two universities examined coroners' records from Los Angeles County and found an astonishing jump in cardiovascular deaths, from 15.6 on an average day to 51 on the day of the quake itself. Most of these people turned out to have a history of coronary disease, or risk factors such as high blood pressure. But those who died were not involved in rescue efforts or trying to dig themselves out of the rubble. Why did they die? (Underwood, 2005, p. 49)

Heart specialists have focused much of their attention on the major physiological risk factors for heart disease, which include smoking, obesity, high blood pressure, high levels of serum cholesterol, diabetes, and lack of exercise. But a growing body of research makes a compelling case that psychological stress can be just as harmful to the heart as many of these sources of physiological stress are (Matthews, 2005; Janicki-Deverts et al., 2007).

In one study, researchers examined the medical records of thousands of adult hospital patients for indications of heart

Survivors of natural disasters are at greater risk for subsequent coronary heart disease. Why?

disease, including heart attacks. The patients were asked to complete surveys in which they reported whether they had experienced certain traumatic events in childhood, such as domestic violence, physical abuse, or neglect. They also indicated whether they had endured the stress of living with a family member who was sent to prison, who abused drugs or alcohol, or who was mentally ill. Having such troublesome childhood experiences dramatically increased the participants' risk of heart disease later in life—as much as doubling it for those who experienced many of these events (Dong et al., 2004).

In another study, this one conducted across the globe, researchers examined thousands of hospital patients across 52 countries who had been treated for a first-time heart attack. Patients were asked about the presence of a variety of personal and familial risk factors for heart disease and compared to controls. Not surprisingly, the strongest predictors of heart attack were smoking, cholesterol profile, high blood pressure, diabetes, and obesity (which together accounted for roughly 80% of the population risk). What was surprising was the contribution

of psychosocial risk factors such as life, work, or financial stress or depression (as experienced in the year prior to the heart attack). Taken individually, these factors accounted for 8% to 18% of the population risk of heart attack; taken together, they accounted for over 30%—a level comparable to high blood pressure and obesity. These findings held equally for men and women, across all ages and geographic regions (Yusuf et al., 2004).

How does stress lead to heart attacks? One way is by affecting risk-related behavior such as smoking and poor eating habits. But stress has direct effects on the heart, too. Stress hormones increase blood pressure, induce inflammation, and cause other physiological changes that damage blood vessels over time—including the coronary arteries (Underwood, 2005).

Considering that the stresses of modern life aren't easily avoided, this research may seem, well, distressing. But take heart! Other research suggests that activities that reduce stress may have a protective effect. In one study, students who were about to have a stressful experience spent a few minutes thinking about a supportive friend; their subsequent stress reactions were less pronounced than those of a control group. In another study, participants who spent 15 minutes laughing at a funny movie had relaxed arteries and better blood flow as long as 45 minutes afterward, much as if they had spent time exercising (Blor et al., 2004, Miller, 2005).

- How does chronic stress take its toll on the heart?
- What are some ways in which people might reduce the impact of stress on their hearts?

found that people who adopt a fighting spirit are more likely to recover than are those who pessimistically suffer and resign themselves to death (Pettingale et al., 1985). The study analyzed the survival rates of women who had undergone the removal of a breast because of cancer.

The results suggested that the survival rates were related to the psychological response of the women three months after surgery (see Figure 1). Women who stoically accepted their fate, trying not to complain, and those who felt the situation was

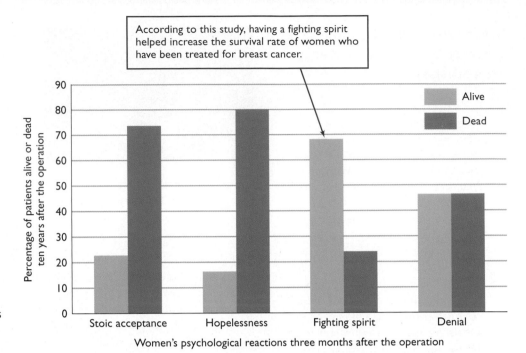

According to this study, having a fighting spirit helped increase the survival rate of women who have been treated for breast cancer.

FIGURE 1 The relationship between women's psychological response to breast cancer 3 months after surgery and their survival 10 years after the operation (Pettingale et al., 1985). What implications do these findings have for the treatment of people with cancer?

hopeless and that nothing could be done showed the lowest survival rates; most of those women were dead after 10 years. In comparison, the survival rates of women who showed a fighting spirit (predicting that they would overcome the disease and planning to take steps to prevent its recurrence) and the survival rates of women who (erroneously) denied that they had ever had cancer (saying that the breast removal was merely a preventive step) were significantly higher. In sum, according to this study, cancer patients with a positive attitude were more likely to survive than were those with a more negative one.

On the other hand, other research contradicts the notion that the course of cancer is affected by patients' attitudes and emotions. For example, some findings show that although a "fighting spirit" leads to better coping, the long-term survival rate is no better than it is for patients with a less positive attitude (Watson et al., 1999).

Despite the conflicting evidence, health psychologists believe that patients' emotions may at least partially determine the course of their disease. In the case of cancer, it is possible that positive emotional responses may help generate specialized "killer" cells that help control the size and spread of cancerous tumors. Conversely, negative emotions may suppress the ability of those cells to fight tumors (Schedlowski & Tewes, 1999; Noy, 2006).

Is a particular personality type linked to cancer? Some researchers suggest that cancer patients are less emotionally reactive, suppress anger, and lack outlets for emotional release. However, the data are too tentative and inconsistent to suggest firm conclusions about a link between personality characteristics and cancer. Certainly no conclusive evidence suggests that people who develop cancer would not have done so if their personality had been of a different sort or if their attitudes had been more positive (Smith, 1988; Zevon & Corn, 1990; Holland & Lewis, 2001).

What is increasingly clear, however, is that certain types of psychological therapy have the potential for extending the lives of cancer patients. For example, the results of one study showed that women with breast cancer who received psychological treatment lived at least a year and a half longer, and experienced less anxiety and pain, than did women who did not participate in therapy. Research on patients with other health problems, such as heart disease, also has found that therapy can be beneficial, both psychologically and medically (Spiegel, 1993, 1996b; Galavotti et al., 1997; Frasure-Smith, Lesperance, & Talajic, 2000).

Smoking

Would you walk into a convenience store and buy an item with a label warning you that its use could kill you? Although most people would probably answer no, millions make such a purchase every day: a pack of cigarettes. Furthermore, they do this despite clear, well-publicized evidence that smoking is linked to cancer, heart attacks, strokes, bronchitis, emphysema, and a host of other serious illnesses. Smoking is the greatest preventable cause of death in the United States; one in five U.S. deaths is caused by smoking. Worldwide, close to 5 million people die each year from the effects of smoking (Ezzati, 2005).

WHY PEOPLE SMOKE

Why do people smoke despite all the evidence showing that it is bad for their health? It is not that they are somehow unaware of the link between smoking and disease; surveys show that most *smokers* agree with the statement "Cigarette smoking frequently causes disease and death." And almost three-quarters of the 48 million smokers in the United States say they would like to quit (CDC, 1994; Wetter et al., 1998).

Heredity seems to determine, in part, whether people will become smokers, how much they will smoke, and how easily they can quit. Genetics also influences how susceptible people are to the harmful effects of smoking. For instance, there is an almost 50 percent higher rate of lung cancer in African-American smokers than in white smokers. This difference may be due to genetically produced variations in the efficiency with which enzymes are able to reduce the effects of the cancer-causing chemicals in tobacco smoke (Heath & Madden, 1995; Pomerlau, 1995; Li et al., 2003).

However, although genetics plays a role in smoking, most research suggests that environmental factors are the primary cause of the habit. Smoking at first may be seen as "cool" or sophisticated, as a rebellious act, or as facilitating calm performance in stressful situations. Greater exposure to smoking in media such as film also leads to a higher risk of becoming an established smoker. In addition, smoking a cigarette is sometimes viewed as a "rite of passage" for adolescents, undertaken at the urging of friends and viewed as a sign of growing up (Wagner & Atkins, 2000; Sargent et al., 2007).

Ultimately, smoking becomes a habit. People begin to label themselves smokers, and smoking becomes part of their self-concept. Moreover, they become dependent physiologically as a result of smoking, because nicotine, a primary ingredient of tobacco, is highly addictive. A complex relationship develops among smoking, nicotine levels, and a smoker's emotional state, in which a certain nicotine level becomes associated with a positive emotional state. As a result, people smoke in an effort to regulate *both* emotional states and nicotine levels in the blood (Amos et al., 2006; Kassel et al., 2007).

QUITTING SMOKING

Because smoking has both psychological and biological components, few habits are as difficult to break. Long-term successful treatment typically occurs in just 15 percent of those who try to stop smoking, and once smoking becomes a habit, it is as hard to stop as an addiction to cocaine or heroin. In fact, some of the biochemical reactions to nicotine are similar to those to cocaine, amphetamines, and morphine. Many people try to quit and fail (Vanasse, Niyonsenga, & Courteau, 2004; Foulds, 2006).

Among the most effective tools for ending the smoking habit are drugs that replace the nicotine found in cigarettes. Whether in the form of gum, patches, nasal sprays, or inhalers, these products provide a dose of nicotine that reduces dependence on cigarettes. Another approach is exemplified by the drugs Zyban and Chantrix, which, rather than replacing nicotine, reduce the pleasure from smoking and suppress withdrawal symptoms that smokers experience when they try to stop (Dalsgaro et al., 2004; Garwood & Potts, 2007; Shiffman, 2007).

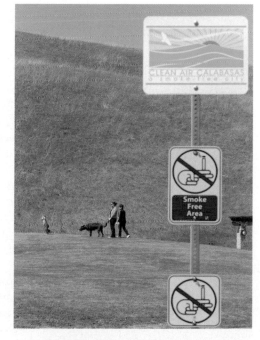

Although smoking is prohibited in an increasing number of places, it remains a substantial social problem.

FIGURE 2 Although smoking among teenagers is lower than it was 20 years ago, a significant number still report smoking regularly. What factors might account for the continued high use of tobacco by teenagers, despite the increase in antismoking advertising? (Source: Monitoring the Future Study, 2006.)

Behavioral strategies, which view smoking as a learned habit and concentrate on changing the smoking response, can also be effective. Initial "cure" rates of 60 percent have been reported, and one year after treatment more than half of those who quit have not resumed smoking. Counseling, either individually or in groups, also increases the rate of success in breaking the habit. The best treatment seems to be a combination of nicotine replacement and counseling. What doesn't work? Going it alone: Only 5 percent of smokers who quit cold-turkey on their own are successful (Noble, 1999; Rock, 1999; Woodruff, Conway, & Edwards, 2007).

In the long term, the most effective means of reducing smoking may be changes in societal norms and attitudes toward the habit. For instance, many cities and towns have made smoking in public places illegal, and legislation banning smoking in places such as college classrooms and buildings—based on strong popular sentiment—is being passed with increasing frequency (Hamilton, Biener, & Brennan, 2007).

The long-term effect of the barrage of information regarding the negative consequences of smoking on people's health has been substantial; overall, smoking has declined over the last two decades, particularly among males. Still, more than one-fourth of students enrolled in high school are active smokers by the time they graduate, and there is evidence that the decline in smoking is leveling off. Among these students, around 10 percent become active smokers as early as the eighth grade (see Figure 2; Johnston, O'Malley, & Bachman, 2006; Fichtenberg & Glantz, 2006).

Exploring DIVERSITY

Hucksters of Death: Promoting Smoking Throughout the World

A Jeep decorated with the Camel logo pulls up to a high school in Buenos Aires. A woman begins handing out free cigarettes to 15- and 16-year-olds during their lunch recess. At a video arcade in Taipei, free American cigarettes are strewn atop each game. At a disco filled with high school students, free packs of Salems are on each table. (Ecenbarger, 1993, p. 50)

As the number of smokers has declined in the United States, cigarette manufacturers have turned to new markets in an effort to increase the number of people who smoke. In the process, they have employed some dubious marketing techniques.

For instance, the tobacco company RJ Reynolds developed a new cigarette brand it named Uptown in the early 1990s. Because of the nature of the advertising that initiated the distribution of the cigarette, it soon became apparent that the product was targeted at African Americans (Jhally et al., 1995; Ringold, 1996; Balbach, Gasior, & Barbeau, 2003). Given the questionable ethics of targeting a potentially life-threatening product to a minority population, the product introduction caused considerable controversy. Ultimately, the secretary of the U.S. Department of Health and Human Services condemned the tactic, and the manufacturer stopped distributing the brand soon afterward.

Because of legal constraints on smoking in the United States, manufacturers have turned their sights to other parts of the world, where they see a fertile market of non-smokers. Although they must often sell cigarettes more cheaply than they do in the United States, the huge number of potential smokers still makes it financially worthwhile for the tobacco companies. The United States is now the world's largest exporter of cigarettes (Bartecchi, MacKenzie, & Schrier, 1995; Brown, 2001).

Clearly, the push into worldwide markets has been successful. In some Latin American cities, as many as 50 percent of teenagers smoke. Children as young as age 7 smoke in Hong Kong, and 30 percent of children smoked their first whole cigarette before the age of 10 in India, Ghana, Jamaica, and Poland. The World Health Organization predicts that smoking will prematurely kill some 200 million of the world's children, and that ultimately 10 percent of the world's population will die as a result of smoking. Of everyone alive today, 500 million will eventually die from tobacco use (Mackay & Eriksen, 2002).

In some countries, children as young as 6 smoke regularly.

RECAP/EVALUATE/RETHINK

RECAP

How do psychological factors affect health-related problems such as coronary heart disease, cancer, and smoking?

- Hostility, a key component of the Type A behavior pattern, is linked to coronary heart disease. The Type A behavior pattern is a cluster of behaviors involving hostility, competitiveness, time urgency, and feeling driven. (p. 493)

- Increasing evidence suggests that people's attitudes and emotional responses affect the course of cancer through links to the immune system. (p. 494)

- Smoking, the leading preventable cause of health problems, has proved to be difficult to quit, even though most smokers are aware of the dangerous consequences of the behavior. (p. 496)

EVALUATE

1. Type _____ behavior is characterized by cooperativeness and by being easy going; Type _____ behavior is characterized by hostility and competitiveness.

2. The Type A behavior pattern is known to directly cause heart attacks. True or false?

3. A cancer patient's attitude and emotions may affect that person's _____ system, helping or hindering the patient's fight against the disease.

4. Smoking is used to regulate both nicotine levels and emotional states in smokers. True or false?

RETHINK

1. Is there a danger of "blaming the victim" when we argue that the course of cancer can be improved if a person with the disease holds positive attitudes or beliefs, particularly when we consider people with cancer who are not recovering? Explain your answer.

2. *From the perspective of a health-care provider:* What type of advice would you give to your patients about the connections between personality and disease? For example, would you encourage Type A people to become "less Type A" in order to decrease their risk of heart disease?

Answers to Evaluate Questions

1. B, A; 2. false; Type A behavior is related to a higher incidence of coronary heart disease but does not necessarily cause it directly; 3. immune; 4. true

KEY TERMS

Type A behavior pattern
 p. 494

Type B behavior pattern
 p. 494

Promoting Health and Wellness

When Stuart Grinspoon first noticed the small lump in his arm, he assumed it was just a bruise from the touch football game he had played the previous week. But as he thought about it more, he considered more serious possibilities and decided that he'd better get it checked out at the university health service. But the visit was less than satisfactory. A shy person, Stuart felt embarrassed talking about his medical condition. Even worse, after answering a string of questions, he couldn't even understand the physician's diagnosis and was too embarrassed to ask for clarification.

Stuart Grinspoon's attitudes toward health care are shared by many of us. We approach physicians the same way we approach auto mechanics. When something goes wrong with the car, we want the mechanic to figure out the problem and then fix it. In the same way, when something isn't working right with our bodies, we want a diagnosis of the problem and then a (we hope, quick) repair.

Yet such an approach ignores the fact that—unlike auto repair—good health care requires taking psychological factors into account. Health psychologists have sought to determine the factors involved in the promotion of good health and, more broadly, a sense of well-being and happiness. Let's take a closer look at two areas they have tackled: producing compliance with health-related advice and identifying the determinants of well-being and happiness.

Key Concepts

How do our interactions with physicians affect our health and compliance with medical treatment?

How does a sense of well-being develop?

Following Medical Advice

We're not very good at taking medical advice. Consider these figures:

- As many as 85 percent of patients do not fully comply with a physician's recommendations.

- Between 14 and 21 percent of patients don't ever fill their drug prescriptions.

- Some 10 percent of adolescent pregnancies result from noncompliance with birth control practices.

- Sixty percent of all patients cannot identify their own medicines.

- From 30 percent to 50 percent of all patients ignore instructions or make errors in taking medication (Christensen & Johnson, 2002; Health Pages, 2003; Colland et al., 2004).

Noncompliance with medical advice can take many forms. For example, patients may fail to show up for scheduled appointments, not follow diets or not give up smoking, or discontinue medication during treatment. In some cases, they fail to take prescribed medicine at all.

Patients also may practice *creative nonadherence*, in which they adjust a treatment prescribed by a physician, relying on their own medical judgment and experience. In many cases patients' lack of medical knowledge may be harmful (Taylor, 1995; Hamani et al., 2007).

Noncompliance is sometimes a result of psychological reactance. **Reactance** is a negative emotional and cognitive reaction that results from the restriction of one's

Reactance: A disagreeable emotional and cognitive reaction that results from the restriction of one's freedom.

501

freedom. People who experience reactance feel hostility and anger. Because of such emotions, they may seek to restore their sense of freedom, but in a self-destructive manner by refusing to accept medical advice and perhaps acting in a way that worsens their medical condition. For instance, a man who is placed on a strict diet may experience reactance and tend to eat even more than he did before his diet was restricted (Fogarty & Young, 2000; Dillard & Shen, 2004).

COMMUNICATING EFFECTIVELY WITH HEALTH-CARE PROVIDERS

> I was lying on a gurney, trying to prepare myself for a six-hour breast-reconstruction surgery. A few months earlier, I'd had a mastectomy for breast cancer. Because I'm small-boned, my doctor told me I needed to have a muscle sliced from my back and moved to my chest to create a proper foundation for an implant. I knew the operation would slow me down—bad news for someone who swims, runs, and chases three young kids. But as the surgeon diagrammed incision points on my chest with a felt-tip pen, my husband asked a question: "Is it really necessary to transfer this back muscle?" (Halpert, 2003, p. 63)

The surgeon's answer shocked the patient: No, it wasn't necessary. And if she didn't have the procedure, her recovery time would be cut in half. The surgeon had simply assumed, without asking the patient, that she would prefer the more complicated procedure, because cosmetically it would be preferable. But after a hurried consultation with her husband, the patient opted for the less invasive procedure.

Lack of communication between medical care providers and patients can be a major obstacle to good medical care. Such communication failures occur for several reasons. One is that physicians make assumptions about what patients prefer, or they push a specific treatment that they prefer without consulting patients. Furthermore, the relatively high prestige of physicians may intimidate patients. Patients may also be reluctant to volunteer information that might cast them in a bad light, and physicians may have difficulties encouraging their patients to provide information. In many cases, physicians dominate an interview with questions of a technical nature, whereas patients attempt to communicate a personal sense of their illness and the impact it is having on their lives, as illustrated in Figure 1 (Ihler, 2003; Schillinger et al., 2004; Wain et al., 2006).

Furthermore, the view held by many patients that physicians are "all-knowing" can result in serious communication problems. Many patients do not understand their treatments yet fail to ask their physicians for clear explanations of a prescribed course of action. About half of all patients are unable to report accurately how long they are to continue taking a medication prescribed for them, and about a quarter do not even know the purpose of the drug. In fact, some patients are not even sure, as they are about to be rolled into the operating room, why they are having surgery (Svarstad, 1976; Atkinson, 1997; Halpert, 2003)!

Sometimes patient-physician communication difficulties occur because the material that must be communicated is too technical for patients, who may lack fundamental knowledge about the body and basic medical practices. In response to this problem, some health-care providers routinely use baby talk (calling patients "honey" or telling them to go "night-night") and assume that patients are unable to understand even simple information (Whitbourne & Wills, 1993; Mika et al., 2007).

The amount of physician-patient communication also is related to the sex of a physician and patient. Overall, female primary care physicians provide more patient-centered communications than do male primary care physicians. Furthermore, patients often prefer same-sex physicians (Roter, Hall, & Aoki, 2002; Kiss, 2004; Schnatz et al., 2007).

Cultural values and expectations also contribute to communication barriers between patients and their physicians.

"There's no easy way I can tell you this, so I'm sending you to someone who can."

A Patient Talks to Her Physician

The following excerpt from a case study used at the Harvard Medical School is an example of poor interviewing technique on the part of the physician.

Patient: I can hardly drink water.

Doctor: Um hum.

Patient: Remember when it started? . . . It was pains in my head. It must have been then.

Doctor: Um-hum.

Patient: I don't know what it is. The doctor looked at it . . . said something about glands.

Doctor: Ok. Um-hum, aside from this, how have you been feeling?

Patient: Terrible.

Doctor: Yeah.

Patient: Tired . . . there's pains . . . I don't know what it is.

Doctor: Ok. . . . Fever or chills?

Patient: No.

Doctor: Ok. . . . Have you been sick to your stomach or anything?

Patient: (Sniffles, crying) I don't know what's going on. I get up in the morning tired. The only time I feel good . . . maybe like around suppertime . . . and everything (crying) and still the same thing.

Doctor: Um-hum. You're getting the nausea before you eat or after? (Goleman, 1988, p. B16)

Although the frequent "um-hums" suggest that the physician is listening to the patient, in fact he does not encourage the patient to disclose more pertinent details. Even more, late in the interview, the physician ignores the patient's emotional distress and coldly continues through the list of questions.

FIGURE 1 Effective communication between patient and physician is important, but often proves frustrating for both. (Source: From Daniel Goleman, "Doctor and Patient; Physicians May Bungle Key Part of Treatment: The Medical Interview." From *The New York Times*, January 21, 1988, p. B16. © 1988 The New York Times. All rights reserved. Used by permission and protected by the Copyright Laws of the United States. The printing, copying, redistribution, or retransmission of the Material without express written permission is prohibited. www.nytimes.com.)

Providing medical advice to a patient whose native language is not English may be problematic. Furthermore, medical practices differ between cultures, and medical practitioners need to be familiar with a patient's culture in order to produce compliance with medical recommendations (Whaley, 2000; Ho et al., 2004; Culhane-Pera, Borkan, & Patten, 2007).

What can patients do to improve communication with health-care providers? Here are some tips provided by physician Holly Atkinson (Atkinson, 2003):

- Make a list of health-related concerns before you visit a health-care provider.
- Before a visit, write down the names and dosages of every drug you are currently taking.
- Determine if your provider will communicate with you via e-mail and under what circumstances.
- If you find yourself intimidated, take along an advocate—a friend or relative—who can help you communicate more effectively.
- Take notes during the visit.

INCREASING COMPLIANCE WITH ADVICE

Although compliance with medical advice does not guarantee that a patient's medical problems will go away, it does optimize the possibility that the patient's condition will improve. What, then, can health-care providers do to produce greater compliance on the part of their patients? One strategy is to provide clear instructions to patients regarding drug regimens. Maintaining good, warm relations between physicians and patients also leads to increased compliance (Cramer, 1995; Cheney, 1996).

In addition, honesty helps. Patients generally prefer to be well informed—even if the news is bad—and their degree of satisfaction with their medical care is linked to

Positively framed messages suggest that a change in behavior will lead to a health-related gain.

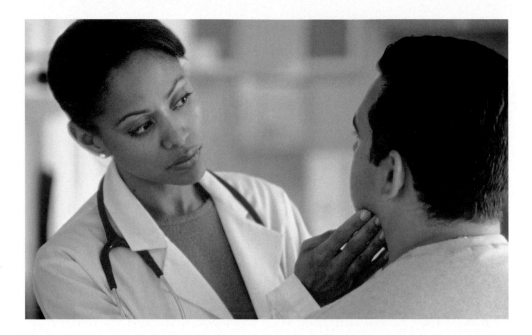

how well and how accurately physicians are able to convey the nature of their medical problems and treatments (Haley, Clair, & Saulsberry, 1992; Zuger, 2005).

The way in which a message is framed also can result in more positive responses to health-related information. *Positively framed messages* suggest that a change in behavior will lead to a gain, emphasizing the benefits of carrying out a health-related behavior. For instance, suggesting that skin cancer is curable if it is detected early, and that you can reduce your chances of getting the disease by using a sunscreen, places information in a positive frame. In contrast, *negatively framed messages* highlight what you can lose by not performing a behavior. For instance, a physician might say that if you don't use sunscreen, you're more likely to get skin cancer, which can kill you if it's not detected early—an example of a negative frame.

What type of message is more effective? According to psychologists Alex Rothman and Peter Salovey, it depends on the type of health behavior the health provider is trying to bring about. Positively framed messages are best for motivating *preventive* behavior. However, negatively framed messages are most effective in producing behavior that will lead to the detection of a disease (Rothman & Salovey, 1997; Apanovich, McCarthy, & Salovey, 2003; McCaul, Johnson, & Rothman, 2003; Lee & Aaker, 2004).

Well-Being and Happiness

What makes for a good life?

This is a question that philosophers and theologians have pondered for centuries, and now health psychologists are turning their spotlight on the question. They are doing that by investigating **subjective well-being**, people's evaluations of their lives in terms of both their thoughts and their emotions. Considered another way, subjective well-being is the measure of how happy people are (Diener, Lucas, & Oishi, 2002; Dolan & White, 2007; Tsaousis et al., 2007).

Subjective well-being: People's own evaluation of their lives in terms of both their thoughts and their emotions.

WHAT ARE THE CHARACTERISTICS OF HAPPY PEOPLE?

Research on the subject of well-being shows that happy people share several characteristics (Myers, 2000; Diener & Seligman, 2002; Otake et al., 2006):

- *Happy people have high self-esteem.* Particularly in Western cultures, which emphasize the importance of individuality, people who are happy like themselves.

They see themselves as more intelligent and better able to get along with others than is the average person. In fact, they often hold *positive illusions* or moderately inflated views of themselves as good, competent, and desirable (Taylor et al., 2000; Boyd-Wilson, McClure, & Walkey, 2004).

- *Happy people have a firm sense of control.* They feel more in control of events in their lives, unlike those who feel they are the pawns of others and who experience learned helplessness.

- *Happy individuals are optimistic.* Their optimism permits them to persevere at tasks and ultimately to achieve more. In addition, their health is better (Peterson, 2000).

- *Happy people like to be around other people.* They tend to be extroverted and have a supportive network of close relationships.

Perhaps most important, most people are at least moderately happy most of the time. In both national and international surveys, people living in a wide variety of circumstances report being happy. Furthermore, life-altering events that one might expect would produce long-term spikes in happiness, such as winning the lottery, probably won't make you much happier than you already are, as we discuss next.

DOES MONEY BUY HAPPINESS?

If you were to win the lottery, would you be happier?

Probably not. At least that's the implication of health psychologists' research on subjective well-being. That research shows that although winning the lottery brings an initial surge in happiness, a year later winners' level of happiness seems to return to what it was before. The converse phenomenon occurs for people who have had serious injuries in accidents: Despite an initial decline in happiness, in most cases victims return to their prior levels of happiness after the passage of time (Diener & Biswas Diener, 2002; Nissle & Bschor, 2002; Spinella & Lester, 2006).

Why is the level of subjective well-being so stable? One explanation is that people have a general *set point* for happiness, a marker that establishes the tone for one's life. Although specific events may temporarily elevate or depress one's mood (a surprise promotion or a job loss, for example), ultimately people return to their general level of happiness.

Although it is not certain how people's happiness set points are initially established, some evidence suggests that the set point is determined at least in part by genetic factors. Specifically, identical twins who grow up in widely different circumstances turn out to have very similar levels of happiness (Kahneman, Diener, & Schwarz, 1998; Diener, Lucas, & Scollon, 2006).

Most people's well-being set point is relatively high. For example, some 30 percent of people in the United States rate themselves as "very happy," and only one in ten rates himself or herself as "not too happy." Most people declare themselves to be "pretty happy." Such feelings are graphically confirmed by people who are asked to place themselves on the measure of happiness illustrated in Figure 2. The scale clearly illustrates that most people view their lives quite positively.

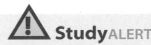

StudyALERT

Remember the concept that individuals have a set point (a general, consistent level) relating to subjective well-being.

Faces Scale: "Which face comes closest to expressing how you feel about your life as a whole?"

| 20% | 46% | 27% | 4% | 2% | 1% | 0% |

FIGURE 2 Most people in the United States rate themselves as happy, while only a small minority indicate they are "not too happy." (Source: Myers, 2000, p. 57, drawn from Social Indicators of Well-Being: Americans' Perceptions of Life Quality (pp. 207 and 306), by F. M. Andrews and S. B. Withey, 1976. New York, Plenum. Copyright 1976 by Plenum.)

Similar results are found when people are asked to compare themselves with others. For example, when asked, "Who of the following people do you think is the happiest?" survey respondents answered "Oprah Winfrey" (23 percent), "Bill Gates" (7 percent), "the Pope" (12 percent), and "yourself" (49 percent), with 6 percent saying they didn't know (Black & McCafferty, 1998).

Few differences exist between members of different demographic groups. Men and women report being equally happy, and African Americans are only slightly less likely than European Americans to rate themselves as "very happy." Furthermore, happiness is hardly unique to U.S. culture. Even countries that are not economically prosperous have, on the whole, happy residents (Myers & Diener, 1996; Diener & Clifton, 2002; Suh, 2002; Suhail & Chaudhry, 2004).

The bottom line: Money does *not* seem to buy happiness. Despite the ups and downs of life, most people tend to be reasonably happy, and they adapt to the trials and tribulations—and joys and delights—of life by returning to a steady-state level of happiness. That habitual level of happiness can have profound—perhaps life-prolonging—implications (Diener & Seligman, 2004; Hecht, 2007).

RECAP/EVALUATE/RETHINK

RECAP

How do our interactions with physicians affect our health and compliance with medical treatment?

- Although patients would often like physicians to base a diagnosis only on a physical examination, communicating one's problem to the physician is equally important. (p. 501)

- Patients may find it difficult to communicate openly with their physicians because of the high social prestige of physicians and the technical nature of medical information. (p. 502)

How does a sense of well-being develop?

- Subjective well-being, the measure of how happy people are, is highest in people with high self-esteem, a sense of control, optimism, and a supportive network of close relationships. (p. 504)

EVALUATE

1. Health psychologists are most likely to focus on which of the following problems with health care?
   a. Incompetent health-care providers
   b. Rising health-care costs
   c. Ineffective communication between physician and patient
   d. Scarcity of medical research funding

2. If you want people to floss more to prevent gum disease, the best approach is to
   a. Use a negatively framed message
   b. Use a positively framed message
   c. Have a dentist deliver an encouraging message on the pleasures of flossing
   d. Provide people with free dental floss

3. Winning the lottery is likely to
   a. Produce an immediate and long-term increase in the level of well-being
   b. Produce an immediate, but not lingering, increase in the level of well-being
   c. Produce a decline in well-being over the long run
   d. Lead to an increase in greed over the long run

RETHINK

1. Do you think stress plays a role in making communication between physicians and patients difficult? Why?

2. *From the perspective of a health-care provider:* How would you try to better communicate with your patients? How might your techniques vary depending upon the patient's background, gender, age, and culture?

Answers to Evaluate Questions

1. c; 2. a; 3. b

KEY TERMS

Psychology on the Web

1. Find three or more Web sites that deal with stress reduction. Gather at least five techniques for reducing stress and summarize them. Write a critique and evaluation of those techniques, using the information you have learned about stress. Which ones seem to have a sound basis in psychological theory and/or research?

2. Are you closer to a Type A or a Type B personality? Find two Web sites offering tests that claim to provide the answer. Summarize the quality of the tests from a scientific point of view and compare the results you received from each one.

Epilogue

In this set of modules, we have explored the intersection of psychology and biology. We have seen how the emotional and psychological experience of stress can lead to physical symptoms of illness, how personality factors may be related to major health problems, and how psychological factors can interfere with effective communication between physician and patient. We have also looked at the other side of the coin, noting that some relatively simple strategies can help us control stress, affect illness, and improve our interactions with physicians.

Turn back to the prologue of this set of modules, about Alex Capp and his hectic schedule and use your understanding of health psychology and stress to consider these questions.

1. Does Capp's hectic schedule necessarily mean that he is under stress? Why or why not?
2. What seem to be the personal stressors in Capp's life? What daily hassles and uplifts might he encounter?
3. Following the model of general adaptation syndrome, how might Capp be engaged in resistance? What would determine whether he enters the exhaustion stage?
4. What forms of emotion-focused and problem-focused coping could Capp use to reduce his stress?

CHAPTER 15

Psychological Disorders

Key Concepts for Chapter 15

Prologue *Chris Coles*

Chris Coles heard the voice in his head for the first time late one evening. The voice told him to meet a friend at that moment, and to apologize to the friend for planning to date the friend's girlfriend.

Although Chris had never thought about dating the girlfriend, he nonetheless did as he was told, arriving at the beach at two o'clock in the morning. No one was there.

Chris put the incident out of his mind, attributing it to a trick of imagination, like something in a dream. However, the voice kept intruding in Chris's thoughts. And then he started to see visions. He would see whales and dolphins swimming up to the beach, and there would be a golden Buddha shining from the bushes. He also began to think he could control nature.

As Chris later said, "I felt that I had power over things in nature, influence over the whales and dolphins and waves. I thought I could make things happen magically in the water." (Begley, 2002, p. 44)

Looking **Ahead**

Chris Coles was losing his grip on reality. It turned out that he was suffering from schizophrenia, one of the more severe psychological disorders. Although drug treatments eventually stilled the voices that ran through his head, his experience raises several questions. What caused his disorder? Were genetic factors involved, or were stressors in his life primarily responsible? Were there signs that family and friends should have noticed earlier? Could his schizophrenia have been prevented? And, more generally, how do we distinguish normal from abnormal behavior, and how can Chris's behavior be categorized and classified in such a way as to pinpoint the specific nature of his problem?

We address the issues raised by Chris Coles's case in this set of modules. We begin by discussing the difference between normal and abnormal behavior, which can be surprisingly indistinct. We then turn to a consideration of the most significant kinds of psychological disorders. Finally, we'll consider ways of evaluating behavior—one's own and that of others—to determine whether seeking help from a mental health professional is warranted.

Normal Versus Abnormal: Making the Distinction

Universally that person's acumen is esteemed very little perceptive concerning whatsoever matters are being held as most profitable by mortals with sapience endowed to be studied who is ignorant of that which the most in doctrine erudite and certainly by reason of that in them high mind's ornament deserving of veneration constantly maintain when by general consent they affirm that other circumstances being equal by no exterior splendour is the prosperity of a nation . . .

It would be easy to conclude that these words are the musings of a madman. To most people, the passage does not seem to make any sense at all. But literary scholars would disagree. Actually, this passage is from James Joyce's classic *Ulysses*, hailed as one of the major works of 20th-century literature (Joyce, 1934, p. 377).

As this example illustrates, casually examining a person's writing is insufficient to determine the degree to which that person is "normal." But even when we consider more extensive samples of a person's behavior, we will find that there may be only a fine line between behavior that is considered normal and that which is considered abnormal.

Key Concepts

How can we distinguish normal from abnormal behavior?

What are the major perspectives on psychological disorders used by mental health professionals?

What are the major categories of psychological disorders?

Defining Abnormality

Because of the difficulty in distinguishing normal from abnormal behavior, psychologists have struggled to devise a precise, scientific definition of "abnormal behavior." For instance, consider the following definitions, each of which has advantages and disadvantages:

- *Abnormality as deviation from the average.* To employ this statistically based approach, we simply observe what behaviors are rare or occur infrequently in a specific society or culture and label those deviations from the norm "abnormal."

  The difficulty with this definition is that some statistically rare behaviors clearly do not lend themselves to classification as abnormal. If most people prefer to have cornflakes for breakfast but you prefer raisin bran, this deviation hardly makes your behavior abnormal. Similarly, such a concept of abnormality would unreasonably label a person who has an unusually high IQ as abnormal, simply because a high IQ is statistically rare. In short, a definition of abnormality that rests on deviation from the average is insufficient.

- *Abnormality as deviation from the ideal.* An alternative approach considers abnormality in relation to the standard toward which most people are striving—the ideal. This sort of definition considers behavior abnormal if it deviates enough from some kind of ideal or cultural standard. However, society has few standards on which people universally agree. (For example, we would be hard-pressed to find agreement on whether the New Testament, the Koran, the Talmud, or the Book of Mormon provides the most reasonable standards.)

Andrea Yates was sane when she drowned her five children in a bathtub, according to the first jury that heard her case. At a later trial, however, she was found not guilty by reason of insanity.

StudyALERT

Remember the different definitions of abnormality (deviation from the average, deviation from the ideal, a sense of personal discomfort, inability to function effectively, and abnormality as a legal concept).

Abnormal behavior: Behavior that causes people to experience distress and prevents them from functioning in their daily lives.

Furthermore, standards that do arise change over time and vary across cultures. Thus, the deviation-from-the-ideal approach is also inadequate.

- *Abnormality as a sense of personal discomfort.* A more useful definition concentrates on the psychological consequences of the behavior for the individual. In this approach, behavior is considered abnormal if it produces a sense of personal distress, anxiety, or guilt in an individual—or if it is harmful to others in some way.

  Even a definition that relies on personal discomfort has drawbacks, though, because in some especially severe forms of mental disturbance, people report feeling wonderful, even though their behavior seems bizarre to others. In such cases, a personal state of well-being exists, yet most people would consider the behavior abnormal. For example, most of us would think that a woman who says she is hearing uplifting messages from Martians would be considered to be displaying abnormal behavior, even though she may say that the messages make her feel happy.

- *Abnormality as the inability to function effectively.* Most people are able to feed themselves, hold a job, get along with others, and in general live as productive members of society. Yet there are those who are unable to adjust to the demands of society or function effectively.

  According to this view of abnormality, people who are unable to function effectively and to adapt to the demands of society are considered abnormal. For example, an unemployed, homeless woman living on the street may be considered unable to function effectively. Therefore, her behavior can be viewed as abnormal, even if she has chosen to live this way. Her inability to adapt to the requirements of society is what makes her "abnormal," according to this approach.

- *Abnormality as a legal concept.* According to the jury that first heard her case, Andrea Yates, a woman who drowned her five children in a bathtub, was sane. She was sentenced to life in prison for her act.

  Although you might question this view (and a later appeals jury overturned the conviction), the initial verdict reflected the way in which the law defines abnormal behavior. To the judicial system, the distinction between normal and abnormal behavior rests on the definition of insanity, which is a legal, but not a psychological, term. The definition of insanity varies from one jurisdiction to another. In some states, insanity simply means that defendants cannot understand the difference between right and wrong at the time they commit a criminal act. Other states consider whether defendants are substantially incapable of understanding the criminality of their behavior or unable to control themselves. And in some jurisdictions pleas of insanity are not allowed at all (Weiner & Wettstein, 1993; Frost & Bonnie, 2001; Sokolove, 2003).

Clearly, none of the previous definitions is broad enough to cover all instances of abnormal behavior. Consequently, the distinction between normal and abnormal behavior often remains ambiguous even to trained professionals. Furthermore, to a large extent, cultural expectations for "normal" behavior in a particular society influence the understanding of "abnormal behavior" (Scheff, 1999; Sanderson, 2007; also see the *Applying Psychology in the 21st Century* box).

Given the difficulties in precisely defining the construct, psychologists typically define **abnormal behavior** broadly, considering it to be behavior that causes people to experience distress and prevents them from functioning in their daily lives (Nolen-Hoeksema, 2007). Because of the imprecision of this definition, it's best to view abnormal behavior and normal behavior as marking two ends of a continuum rather than as absolute states. Behavior should be evaluated in terms of gradations, ranging from fully normal functioning to extremely abnormal behavior. Behavior typically falls somewhere between those extremes.

Terrorist Suicide Bombers: Normal or Abnormal?

What kinds of people are willing to strap explosives to their bodies and blow themselves—and as many others as possible—to smithereens? Sounds crazy ... but is their behavior abnormal?

According to most psychologists studying the issue, the answers to these questions are clear: Suicide bombers are *not* psychologically disordered. Almost no real-life suicide attackers are deranged, maniacal loners like the ones portrayed in movies and on television, nor are they suicidal in the traditional way the term is used (Townsend, 2007).

For example, studies of Palestinian and Lebanese suicide bombers show that they are usually males in their early twenties who come from a wide range of backgrounds. Some bombers are wealthy, whereas others are poor; and some are highly educated, whereas others are uneducated. Although suicide bombers are generally unmarried, they are otherwise similar to the average members of their societies (Gathérias, 2006; Merari, 2007; Townsend, 2007).

Far from being loners, most suicide bombers are sociable. They have close friends and family members, and people who know them often say they are extroverted. Moreover, their psychological functioning seems generally normal: Before their attacks, they show no suicidal symptoms, and they do not express feelings of hopelessness or of having nothing to lose. In short, psychological studies of suicide bombers provide little evidence that those individuals are suffering from any type of

Are suicide bombers psychologically disordered? Most research suggests that they are not.

diagnosable psychological disorder (Atran, 2003; Berko & Yuval, 2007).

Furthermore, terrorists are motivated by commitment to a particular group or cause. Religious ties are particularly important. Suicide bombers often belong to religious groups whose leaders consistently seek to inspire potential bombers' loyalty to their religion. They feel that their goal is moral and just, and in their eyes the objective of attaining a just and fair society justifies any act (Palermo, 2006; Moghaddam, 2007; Rogers et al., 2007).

Ultimately, situational pressures, rather than personality factors, may drive suicide bombers. Terrorists typically are part of a small, four- or five-person cell that becomes the focus of their lives and in some ways acts as a substitute family. The group pressure generated by such cells may be enormously influential—strong enough to lead to the ultimate act of self-sacrifice for the good of the group (Plous & Zimbardo, 2004; McCauley, 2007; Palmer, 2007).

For those charged with stopping suicide bombers' attacks and other types of terrorism, it is problematic that suicide attackers are driven not by a psychological disorder, but by a complex web of emotions, loyalties, and politics. Terrorist attacks motivated by mental illness probably would be a much simpler problem to solve than are terrorist attacks inflamed by emotional, political, and religious group conflict.

RETHINK

- If it were your job to combat suicide bombings, how would you do it?
- What kinds of psychological, political, or social interventions might help discourage potential suicide attackers from volunteering?

Perspectives on Abnormality: From Superstition to Science

Throughout much of human history, people linked abnormal behavior to superstition and witchcraft. Individuals who displayed abnormal behavior were accused of being possessed by the devil or some sort of demonic god. Authorities felt justified in "treating" abnormal behavior by attempting to drive out the source of the problem. This typically involved whipping, immersion in hot water, starvation, or other forms of torture in which the cure was often worse than the affliction (Howells & Osborn, 1984; Berrios, 1996).

Perspectives on Psychological Disorders		
Perspective	**Description**	**Possible Application of Perspective to Chris Coles's Case**
Medical perspective	Assumes that physiological causes are at the root of psychological disorders	Examine Coles for medical problems, such as brain tumor, chemical imbalance in the brain, or disease
Psychoanalytic perspective	Argues that psychological disorders stem from childhood conflicts	Seek out information about Coles's past, considering possible childhood conflicts
Behavioral perspective	Assumes that abnormal behaviors are learned responses	Concentrate on rewards and punishments for Coles's behavior, and identify environmental stimuli that reinforce his behavior
Cognitive perspective	Assumes that cognitions (people's thoughts and beliefs) are central to psychological disorders	Focus on Coles's perceptions of self and his environment
Humanistic perspective	Emphasizes people's responsibility for their own behavior and the need to self-actualize	Consider Coles's behavior in terms of his choices and efforts to reach his potential
Sociocultural perspective	Assumes that behavior is shaped by family, society, and culture	Focus on how societal demands contributed to Coles's disorder

FIGURE 1 In considering the case of Chris Coles, discussed in the prologue, we can employ each of the different perspectives on abnormal behavior. Note, however, that because of the nature of his psychological disorder, some of the perspectives are more applicable than others.

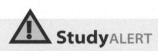

StudyALERT

Use Figure 1 to review the six major perspectives on abnormality and consider how they relate to the major perspectives on the field of psychology that we discussed in Chapter 1.

Medical perspective: The perspective that suggests that when an individual displays symptoms of abnormal behavior, the root cause will be found in a physical examination of the individual, which may reveal a hormonal imbalance, a chemical deficiency, or a brain injury.

Psychoanalytic perspective: The perspective that suggests that abnormal behavior stems from childhood conflicts over opposing wishes regarding sex and aggression.

Contemporary approaches take a more enlightened view. Today, six major perspectives are used to understand psychological disorders. These perspectives suggest not only different causes of abnormal behavior but different treatment approaches as well. Furthermore, some perspectives are more applicable to specific disorders than are others. Figure 1 summarizes the perspectives and the way in which they can be applied to the experience of Chris Coles, described in the prologue.

MEDICAL PERSPECTIVE

When people display the symptoms of tuberculosis, medical professionals can generally find tubercular bacteria in their body tissue. Similarly, the **medical perspective** suggests that when an individual displays symptoms of abnormal behavior, the fundamental cause will be found through a physical examination of the individual, which may reveal a hormonal imbalance, a chemical deficiency, or a brain injury. Indeed, when we speak of mental "illness," "symptoms" of abnormal behavior, and mental "hospitals," we are using terminology associated with the medical perspective.

Because many abnormal behaviors have been linked to biological causes, the medical perspective is a reasonable approach, yet serious criticisms have been leveled against it. For one thing, no biological cause has been identified for many forms of abnormal behavior. In addition, some critics have argued that the use of the term *illness* implies that people who display abnormal behavior have no responsibility for their actions (Szasz, 1994, 2004, 2006).

Still, recent advances in our understanding of the biological bases of behavior underscore the importance of considering physiological factors in abnormal behavior. For instance, some of the more severe forms of psychological disturbance, such as major depression and schizophrenia, are influenced by genetic factors and malfunctions in neurotransmitter signals (Pennington, 2002, 2003; Plomin & McGuffin, 2003).

PSYCHOANALYTIC PERSPECTIVE

Whereas the medical perspective suggests that biological causes are at the root of abnormal behavior, the **psychoanalytic perspective** holds that abnormal behavior stems from childhood conflicts over opposing wishes regarding sex and aggression.

According to Freud, children pass through a series of stages in which sexual and aggressive impulses take different forms and produce conflicts that require resolution. If these childhood conflicts are not dealt with successfully, they remain unresolved in the unconscious and eventually bring about abnormal behavior during adulthood.

To uncover the roots of people's disordered behavior, the psychoanalytic perspective scrutinizes their early life history. However, because there is no conclusive way to link people's childhood experiences with the abnormal behaviors they display as adults, we can never be sure that the causes suggested by psychoanalytic theory are accurate. Moreover, psychoanalytic theory paints a picture of people as having relatively little control over their behavior, because much of it is guided by unconscious impulses. In the eyes of some critics, this perspective suggests that people have little responsibility for their own behavior.

On the other hand, the contributions of psychoanalytic theory have been significant. More than any other approach to abnormal behavior, this perspective highlights the fact that people can have a rich, involved inner life and that prior experiences can have a profound effect on current psychological functioning (Bornstein, 2003; Elliott, 2002; Rangell, 2007).

BEHAVIORAL PERSPECTIVE

Both the medical and psychoanalytic perspectives look at abnormal behaviors as *symptoms* of an underlying problem. In contrast, the **behavioral perspective** views the behavior itself as the problem. Using the basic principles of learning, behavioral theorists see both normal and abnormal behaviors as responses to various stimuli, responses that have been learned through past experience and that are guided in the present by stimuli in the individual's environment. To explain why abnormal behavior occurs, we must analyze how an individual has learned abnormal behavior and observe the circumstances in which it is displayed.

Behavioral perspective: The perspective that looks at the behavior itself as the problem.

The emphasis on observable behavior represents both the greatest strength and the greatest weakness of the behavioral approach to abnormal behavior. This perspective provides the most precise and objective approach for examining behavioral symptoms of specific disorders, such as attention-deficit hyperactivity disorder (ADHD), which we will discuss in a later module. At the same time, though, critics charge that the perspective ignores the rich inner world of thoughts, attitudes, and emotions that may contribute to abnormal behavior.

COGNITIVE PERSPECTIVE

The medical, psychoanalytic, and behavioral perspectives view people's behavior as the result of factors largely beyond their control. To many critics of these views, however, people's thoughts cannot be ignored.

In response to such concerns, some psychologists employ a **cognitive perspective**. Rather than considering only external behavior, as in traditional behavioral approaches, the cognitive approach assumes that *cognitions* (people's thoughts and beliefs) are central to a person's abnormal behavior. A primary goal of treatment using the cognitive perspective is to explicitly teach new, more adaptive ways of thinking.

Cognitive perspective: The perspective that suggests that people's thoughts and beliefs are a central component of abnormal behavior.

For instance, suppose that you develop the erroneous belief that "doing well on this exam is crucial to my entire future" whenever you take an exam. Through therapy, you might learn to hold the more realistic, and less anxiety-producing, thought "my entire future is not dependent on this one exam." By changing cognitions in this way, psychologists working within a cognitive framework help people free themselves from thoughts and behaviors that are potentially maladaptive (Clark, 2004; Everly & Lating, 2007).

The cognitive perspective is not without critics. For example, it is possible that maladaptive cognitions are the symptoms or consequences of disorders, rather than their cause. Furthermore, there are circumstances in which negative beliefs may not be irrational at all, but simply reflect the unpleasant environments in which people live—after all, there are times when a single exam may be extremely important. Still, cognitive theorists would argue that one can find a more adaptive way of framing beliefs even in the most negative circumstances.

HUMANISTIC PERSPECTIVE

Humanistic perspective: The perspective that emphasizes the responsibility people have for their own behavior, even when such behavior is abnormal.

Psychologists who subscribe to the **humanistic perspective** emphasize the responsibility people have for their own behavior, even when their behavior is considered abnormal. The humanistic perspective—growing out of the work of Carl Rogers and Abraham Maslow—concentrates on what is uniquely human—that is, a view of people as basically rational, oriented toward a social world, and motivated to seek self-actualization (Rogers, 1995).

Humanistic approaches focus on the relationship of the individual to society, considering the ways in which people view themselves in relation to others and see their place in the world. The humanistic perspective views people as having an awareness of life and of themselves that leads them to search for meaning and self-worth. Rather than assuming that individuals require a "cure," the humanistic perspective suggests that they can, by and large, set their own limits of what is acceptable behavior. As long as they are not hurting others and do not feel personal distress, people should be free to choose the behaviors in which they engage.

Although the humanistic perspective has been criticized for its reliance on unscientific, unverifiable information and its vague, almost philosophical formulations, it offers a distinctive view of abnormal behavior. It stresses the unique aspects of being human and provides a number of important suggestions for helping those with psychological problems.

SOCIOCULTURAL PERSPECTIVE

Sociocultural perspective: The perspective that assumes that people's behavior—both normal and abnormal—is shaped by the kind of family group, society, and culture in which they live.

The **sociocultural perspective** assumes that people's behavior—both normal and abnormal—is shaped by the kind of family group, society, and culture in which they live. According to this view, the nature of one's relationships with others may support abnormal behaviors and even cause them. Consequently, the kinds of stresses and conflicts people experience in their daily interactions with others can promote and maintain abnormal behavior.

This perspective finds statistical support for the position that sociocultural factors shape abnormal behavior given the fact that some kinds of abnormal behavior are far more prevalent among certain social classes than they are in others. For instance, diagnoses of schizophrenia tend to be higher among members of lower socioeconomic groups than among members of more affluent groups. Proportionally more African-American individuals are hospitalized involuntarily for psychological disorders than are whites. Furthermore, poor economic times seem to be linked to general declines in psychological functioning, and social problems such as homelessness are associated with psychological disorders (López & Guarnaccia, 2005; Conger et al., 2002; Nasir & Hand, 2006).

On the other hand, alternative explanations abound for the association between abnormal behavior and social factors. For example, people from lower socioeconomic levels may be less likely than those from higher levels to seek help, gradually reaching a point where their symptoms become severe and warrant a serious diagnosis. Furthermore, sociocultural explanations provide relatively little specific guidance for the treatment of individuals showing mental disturbance, because the focus is on broader societal factors (Paniagua, 2000).

"First off, you're not a nut. You're a legume."

Classifying Abnormal Behavior: The ABCs of *DSM*

Crazy. Whacked. Mental. Loony. Insane. Neurotic. Psycho. Strange. Demented. Odd. Possessed.

Society has long placed labels on people who display abnormal behavior. Unfortunately, most of the time these labels have reflected intolerance and have been used with little thought as to what each label signifies.

Providing appropriate and specific names and classifications for abnormal behavior has presented a major challenge to psychologists. It is not hard to understand why, given the difficulties discussed earlier in simply distinguishing normal from abnormal behavior. Yet psychologists and other care providers need to classify abnormal behavior in order to diagnose it and, ultimately, to treat it.

DSM-IV-TR: DETERMINING DIAGNOSTIC DISTINCTIONS

Over the years, mental health professionals have developed many different classification systems that vary in terms of their utility and the degree to which they have been accepted. However, one standard system, devised by the American Psychiatric Association, has emerged in the United States. Most professionals today use this classification system, known as the **Diagnostic and Statistical Manual of Mental Disorders, Fourth Edition, Text Revision (DSM-IV-TR)** to diagnose and classify abnormal behavior.

DSM-IV-TR presents comprehensive and relatively precise definitions for more than 200 disorders, divided into 17 major categories. It also includes five types of information, known as axes, that have to be considered in assessing a patient:

- **Axis I: Clinical Disorders.** Disorders that produce distress and impair functioning.

- **Axis II: Personality Disorders and Mental Retardation.** Enduring, rigid behavior patterns.

- **Axis III: General Medical Conditions.** Physical disorders that may be related to psychological disorders.

- **Axis IV: Psychosocial and Environmental Problems.** Problems in a person's life such as stressors or life events that may affect the diagnosis, treatment, and outcome of psychological disorders.

- **Axis V: Global Assessment of Functioning.** Overall level of mental, social, occupational, and leisure functioning.

By following the criteria presented in the *DSM-IV-TR* classification system, diagnosticians can identify the specific problem an individual is experiencing. (Figure 2 provides a brief outline of the major diagnostic categories.)

DSM-IV-TR is designed to be primarily descriptive and avoids suggesting an underlying cause for an individual's behavior and problems. For instance, the term *neurotic*—a label that is commonly used by people in their everyday descriptions of abnormal behavior—is not listed as a *DSM-IV-TR* category. Because the term *neurosis* refers to problems associated with a specific cause based in Freud's theory of personality, it is not included in *DSM-IV-TR*.

DSM-IV-TR has the advantage, then, of providing a descriptive system that does not specify the cause of or reason for a problem. Rather, it paints a picture of the behavior that is being displayed. Why should this approach be important? For one thing, it allows communication between mental health professionals of diverse backgrounds and theoretical approaches. In addition, precise classification enables researchers to explore the causes of a problem. Without reliable descriptions of abnormal behavior, researchers would be hard-pressed to find ways to investigate

Diagnostic and Statistical Manual of Mental Disorders, Fourth Edition, Text Revision (DSM-IV-TR): A system, devised by the American Psychiatric Association, used by most professionals to diagnose and classify abnormal behavior.

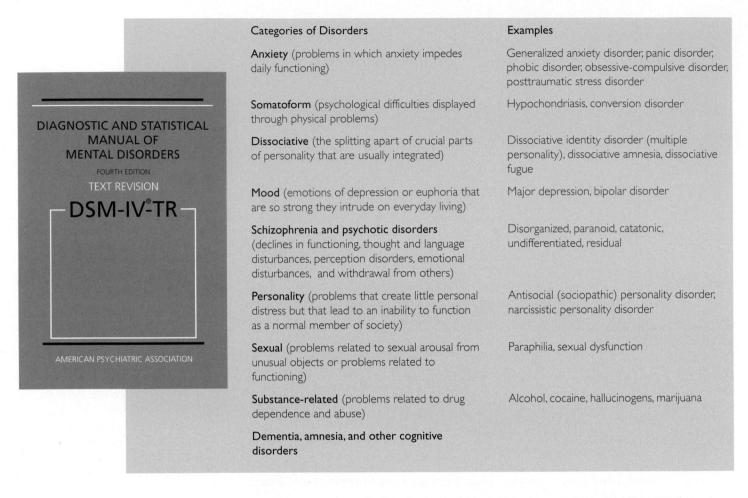

Categories of Disorders	Examples
Anxiety (problems in which anxiety impedes daily functioning)	Generalized anxiety disorder, panic disorder, phobic disorder, obsessive-compulsive disorder, posttraumatic stress disorder
Somatoform (psychological difficulties displayed through physical problems)	Hypochondriasis, conversion disorder
Dissociative (the splitting apart of crucial parts of personality that are usually integrated)	Dissociative identity disorder (multiple personality), dissociative amnesia, dissociative fugue
Mood (emotions of depression or euphoria that are so strong they intrude on everyday living)	Major depression, bipolar disorder
Schizophrenia and psychotic disorders (declines in functioning, thought and language disturbances, perception disorders, emotional disturbances, and withdrawal from others)	Disorganized, paranoid, catatonic, undifferentiated, residual
Personality (problems that create little personal distress but that lead to an inability to function as a normal member of society)	Antisocial (sociopathic) personality disorder, narcissistic personality disorder
Sexual (problems related to sexual arousal from unusual objects or problems related to functioning)	Paraphilia, sexual dysfunction
Substance-related (problems related to drug dependence and abuse)	Alcohol, cocaine, hallucinogens, marijuana
Dementia, amnesia, and other cognitive disorders	

FIGURE 2 This list of disorders represents the major categories from the *DSM-IV-TR*. It is only a partial list of the more than 200 disorders included there.

the disorder. Finally, *DSM-IV-TR* provides a kind of conceptual shorthand through which professionals can describe the behaviors that tend to occur together in an individual (Widiger & Clark, 2000; Frances, First, & Pincus, 2002).

CONNING THE CLASSIFIERS: THE SHORTCOMINGS OF *DSM-IV-TR*

When clinical psychologist David Rosenhan and eight colleagues sought admission to separate mental hospitals across the United States in the 1970s, each stated that he or she was hearing voices—"unclear voices" that said "empty," "hollow," and "thud"—and each was immediately admitted to the hospital. However, the truth was that they actually were conducting a study, and none of them was really hearing voices. Aside from these misrepresentations, *everything* else they did and said represented their true behavior, including the responses they gave during extensive admission interviews and their answers to the battery of tests they were asked to complete. In fact, as soon as they were admitted, they said they no longer heard any voices. In short, each of the pseudopatients acted in a "normal" way (Rosenhan, 1973).

We might assume that Rosenhan and his colleagues would have been quickly discovered as the impostors they were, but this was not the case. Instead, each of them was diagnosed as severely abnormal on the basis of observed behavior. Mental health professionals labeled most as suffering from schizophrenia and kept them in the hospital for 3 to 52 days, with the average stay being 19 days. Even when they were discharged, most of the "patients" left with the label *schizophrenia—in remission*, implying that the abnormal behavior had only temporarily subsided and could recur at any time. Most disturbing, no one on the hospital staff identified any of the pseudo-patients as impostors—although some of the actual patients figured out the ruse.

The results of Rosenhan's classic study illustrate that placing labels on individuals powerfully influences the way mental health workers perceive and interpret their actions. It also points out that determining who is psychologically disordered is not always a clear-cut or accurate process.

Although *DSM-IV-TR* was developed to provide more accurate and consistent diagnoses of psychological disorders, it has not been entirely successful. For instance, critics charge that it relies too much on the medical perspective. Because it was drawn up by psychiatrists—who are physicians—some condemn it for viewing psychological disorders primarily in terms of the symptoms of an underlying physiological disorder. It also does not fully take into account the advances in behavioral neuroscience that have identified the genetic underpinnings of some psychological disorders. Moreover, critics suggest that *DSM-IV-TR* compartmentalizes people into inflexible, all-or-none categories, rather than considering the degree to which a person displays psychologically disordered behavior (Schmidt, Kotov, & Joiner, 2004; Samuel & Widiger, 2006).

Other concerns with *DSM-IV-TR* are more subtle, but equally important. For instance, some critics argue that labeling an individual as abnormal provides a dehumanizing, lifelong stigma. (Think, for example, of political contenders whose candidacies have been terminated by the disclosure that they received treatment for severe psychological disorders.) Furthermore, after an initial diagnosis has been made, mental health professionals, who may concentrate on the initial diagnostic category, could overlook other diagnostic possibilities (Szasz, 1994; Duffy et al., 2002; Quinn, Kahng, & Crocker, 2004).

Still, despite the drawbacks inherent in any labeling system, *DSM-IV-TR* has had an important influence on the way in which mental health professionals view psychological disorders. It has increased both the reliability and the validity of diagnostic categorization. In addition, it offers a logical way to organize examination of the major types of mental disturbance.

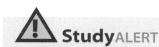 **Study**ALERT

It is important to understand the advantages and weaknesses of the *DSM* classification system.

RECAP/EVALUATE/RETHINK

RECAP

How can we distinguish normal from abnormal behavior?

- Definitions of abnormality include deviation from the average, deviation from the ideal, a sense of personal discomfort, the inability to function effectively, and legal conceptions. (p. 512)

- Although no single definition is adequate, abnormal behavior can be considered to be behavior that causes people to experience distress and prevents them from functioning in their daily lives. Most psychologists believe that abnormal and normal behavior should be considered in terms of a continuum. (p. 513)

What are the major perspectives on psychological disorders used by mental health professionals?

- The medical perspective views abnormality as a symptom of an underlying disease. (p. 514)

- Psychoanalytic perspectives suggest that abnormal behavior stems from childhood conflicts in the unconscious. (p. 514)

- Behavioral approaches view abnormal behavior not as a symptom of an underlying problem, but as the problem itself. (p. 515)

- The cognitive approach suggests that abnormal behavior is the result of faulty cognitions (thoughts and beliefs). In this view, abnormal behavior can be remedied by changing one's flawed thoughts and beliefs. (p. 515)

- Humanistic approaches emphasize the responsibility people have for their own behavior, even when such behavior is seen as abnormal. (p. 516)

- Sociocultural approaches view abnormal behavior in terms of difficulties arising from family and other social relationships. (p. 516)

What classification system is used to categorize psychological disorders?

- The most widely used system for classifying psychological disorders is *DSM-IV-TR—Diagnostic and Statistical Manual of Mental Disorders, Fourth Edition, Text Revision.* (p. 517)

EVALUATE

1. One problem in defining abnormal behavior is that
   a. Statistically rare behavior may not be abnormal.
   b. Not all abnormalities are accompanied by feelings of discomfort.
   c. Cultural standards are too general to use as a measuring tool.
   d. All of the above.
2. If abnormality is defined as behavior that causes personal discomfort or harms others, which of the following people is most likely to need treatment?
   a. An executive is afraid to accept a promotion because it would require moving from his ground-floor office to the top floor of a tall office building.
   b. A woman decides to quit her job and chooses to live on the street in order to live a "simpler life."
   c. A man believes that friendly spacemen visit his house every Thursday.
   d. A photographer lives with 19 cats in a small apartment, lovingly caring for them.
3. Virginia's mother thinks that her daughter's behavior is clearly abnormal because, despite being offered admission to medical school, Virginia decides to become a waitress. What approach is Virginia's mother using to define abnormal behavior?
4. Which of the following is a strong argument against the medical perspective on abnormality?
   a. Physiological abnormalities are almost always impossible to identify.
   b. There is no conclusive way to link past experience and behavior.

c. The medical perspective rests too heavily on the effects of nutrition.
   d. Assigning behavior to a physical problem takes responsibility away from the individual for changing his or her behavior.
5. Cheryl is painfully shy. According to the behavioral perspective, the best way to deal with her "abnormal" behavior is to
   a. Treat the underlying physical problem.
   b. Use the principles of learning theory to modify her shy behavior.
   c. Express a great deal of caring.
   d. Uncover her negative past experiences through hypnosis.

RETHINK

1. Do you agree or disagree that *DSM* should be updated every several years? Why? What makes abnormal behavior so variable?
2. *From the perspective of an employer:* Imagine that a well-paid employee was arrested for shoplifting a $15 sweater. What sort of explanation for this behavior would be provided by the proponents of *each* perspective on abnormality: the medical perspective, the psychoanalytic perspective, the behavioral perspective, the cognitive perspective, the humanistic perspective, and the sociocultural perspective? Based on the potential causes of the shoplifting, would you fire the employee? Why or why not?

Answers to Evaluate Questions

1. d; 2. a; 3. deviation from the ideal; 4. d; 5. b

KEY TERMS

abnormal behavior p. 512
medical perspective p. 514
psychoanalytic perspective
  p. 514
behavioral perspective p. 515
cognitive perspective p. 515

humanistic perspective
  p. 516
sociocultural perspective
  p. 516

Diagnostic and Statistical Manual of Mental Disorders, Fourth Edition, Text Revision (DSM-IV-TR) p. 517

The Major Psychological Disorders

Sally experienced her first panic attack out of the blue, 3 weeks after completing her senior year in college. She had just finished a job interview and was meeting some friends for dinner. In the restaurant, she began to feel dizzy. Within a few seconds, her heart was pounding, and she was feeling breathless, as though she might pass out. Her friends noticed that she did not look well and offered to drive her home. Sally suggested they stop at the hospital emergency room instead. Although she felt better by the time they arrived at the hospital, and tests indicated nothing wrong, Sally experienced a similar episode a week later while at a movie. . . .

Her attacks became more and more frequent. Before long, she was having several attacks per week. In addition, she constantly worried about having attacks. She began to avoid exercise and other activities that produced physical sensations. She also noticed the attacks were worse when she was alone. She began to avoid driving, shopping in large stores, and eating in all restaurants. Some weeks she avoided leaving the house completely. (Antony, Brown, & Barlow, 1992, p. 79)

Sally suffered from panic disorder, one of the specific psychological disorders we'll consider in this module. Keep in mind that although we'll be discussing these disorders in an objective manner, each represents a very human set of difficulties that influence, and in some cases considerably disrupt, people's lives.

Key Concept

What are the major psychological disorders?

Anxiety Disorders

All of us, at one time or another, experience *anxiety*, a feeling of apprehension or tension, in reaction to stressful situations. There is nothing "wrong" with such anxiety. It is a normal reaction to stress that often helps, rather than hinders, our daily functioning. Without some anxiety, for instance, most of us probably would not have much motivation to study hard, undergo physical exams, or spend long hours at our jobs.

But some people experience anxiety in situations in which there is no external reason or cause for such distress. When anxiety occurs without external justification and begins to affect people's daily functioning, mental health professionals consider it a psychological problem known as **anxiety disorder**. We'll discuss the four major types of anxiety disorders: phobic disorder, panic disorder, generalized anxiety disorder, and obsessive-compulsive disorder.

Anxiety disorder: The occurrence of anxiety without an obvious external cause, affecting daily functioning.

PHOBIC DISORDER

It's not easy moving through the world when you're terrified of electricity. "Donna," 45, a writer, knows that better than most. Get her in the vicinity of an appliance or a light switch or—all but unthinkable—a thunderstorm, and she is overcome by a terror so

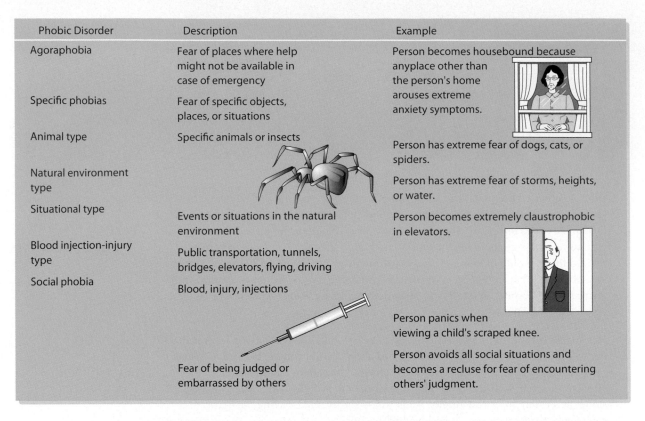

Phobic Disorder	Description	Example
Agoraphobia	Fear of places where help might not be available in case of emergency	Person becomes housebound because anyplace other than the person's home arouses extreme anxiety symptoms.
Specific phobias	Fear of specific objects, places, or situations	
Animal type	Specific animals or insects	Person has extreme fear of dogs, cats, or spiders.
Natural environment type		Person has extreme fear of storms, heights, or water.
Situational type	Events or situations in the natural environment	Person becomes extremely claustrophobic in elevators.
Blood injection-injury type	Public transportation, tunnels, bridges, elevators, flying, driving	
Social phobia	Blood, injury, injections	Person panics when viewing a child's scraped knee.
	Fear of being judged or embarrassed by others	Person avoids all social situations and becomes a recluse for fear of encountering others' judgment.

FIGURE 1 Phobic disorders differ from generalized anxiety and panic disorders because a specific stimulus can be identified. Listed here are a number of types of phobias and their triggers. (Source: Adapted from Nolen-Hoeksema, 2007).

blinding she can think of nothing but fleeing. That, of course, is not always possible, so over time, Donna has come up with other answers. When she opens the refrigerator door, rubber-sole shoes are a must. If a light bulb blows, she will tolerate the dark until someone else changes it for her. Clothes shopping is done only when necessary, lest static on garments send her running from the store. And swimming at night is absolutely out of the question, lest underwater lights electrocute her. (Kluger, 2001, p. 51)

Phobias: Intense, irrational fears of specific objects or situations.

Donna suffers from a **phobia**, an intense, irrational fear of a specific object or situation. For example, claustrophobia is a fear of enclosed places, acrophobia is a fear of high places, xenophobia is a fear of strangers, social phobia is the fear of being judged or embarrassed by others, and—as in Donna's case—electrophobia is a fear of electricity.

The objective danger posed by an anxiety-producing stimulus (which can be just about anything, as you can see in Figure 1) is typically small or nonexistent. However, to someone suffering from the phobia, the danger is great, and a full-blown panic attack may follow exposure to the stimulus. Phobic disorders differ from generalized anxiety disorders and panic disorders in that there is a specific, identifiable stimulus that sets off the anxiety reaction.

Phobias may have only a minor impact on people's lives if those who suffer from them can avoid the stimuli that trigger fear. Unless they are firefighters or window washers, for example, a fear of heights may have little impact on people's everyday lives (although it may prevent them from living in a high floor in an apartment). On the other hand, a *social phobia*, or a fear of strangers, presents a more serious problem. In one extreme case, a Washington woman left her home just three times in 30 years— once to visit her family, once for a medical operation, and once to purchase ice cream for a dying companion (Adler, 1984; Kimbrel, 2007).

PANIC DISORDER

In another type of anxiety disorder, **panic disorder**, *panic attacks* occur that last from a few seconds to several hours. Unlike phobias, which are stimulated by specific objects or situations, panic disorders do not have any identifiable stimuli. Instead, during an attack, such as the ones experienced by Sally in the case described earlier, anxiety suddenly—and often without warning—rises to a peak, and an individual feels a sense of impending, unavoidable doom. Although the physical symptoms differ from person to person, they may include heart palpitations, shortness of breath, unusual amounts of sweating, faintness and dizziness, gastric sensations, and sometimes a sense of imminent death. After such an attack, it is no wonder that people tend to feel exhausted (Rachman & deSilva, 2004; Laederach-Hofmann & Messerli-Buergy, 2007).

Panic attacks seemingly come out of nowhere and are unconnected to any specific stimulus. Because they don't know what triggers their feelings of panic, victims of panic attacks may become fearful of going places. In fact, some people with panic disorder develop a complication called *agoraphobia*, the fear of being in a situation in which escape is difficult and in which help for a possible panic attack would not be available. In extreme cases, people with agoraphobia never leave their homes (Marcaurelle, Belanger, & Marchand, 2003, 2005; Herrán et al., 2006).

In addition to the physical symptoms, panic disorder affects how information is processed in the brain. For instance, people with panic disorder have reduced reactions in the anterior cingulate cortex to stimuli (such as viewing a fearful face) that normally produce a strong reaction in those without the disorder (see Figure 2). It may be that recurring high levels of emotional arousal experienced by patients with panic disorder desensitizes them to emotional stimuli (Pillay et al., 2006; Pillay et al., 2007).

Acrophobia, the fear of heights, is not an uncommon phobia. What sort of behavior-modification approaches might be used to deal with acrophobia?

Panic disorder: Anxiety disorder that takes the form of panic attacks lasting from a few seconds to as long as several hours.

Neuroscience in Your Life

FIGURE 2 In this study healthy participants as well as those with panic disorder viewed fearful faces. The figure shows regions of the brain in which there is less activation (e.g., the anterior cingulate cortex) for patients with panic disorder as compared to people without the disorder when viewing fearful faces. The researchers hypothesize that recurring high levels of emotional arousal experienced by patients with panic disorder desensitizes them to emotional stimuli. (Source: Pillay et al., 2006, Figure 1.)

GENERALIZED ANXIETY DISORDER

Generalized anxiety disorder:
The experience of long-term, persistent anxiety and worry.

People with **generalized anxiety disorder** experience long-term, persistent anxiety and uncontrollable worry. Sometimes their concerns are about identifiable issues involving family, money, work, or health. In other cases, though, people with the disorder feel that something dreadful is about to happen but can't identify the reason, experiencing "free-floating" anxiety.

Because of persistent anxiety, people with generalized anxiety disorder cannot concentrate or set their worry and fears aside; their lives become centered on their worry. Furthermore, their anxiety is often accompanied by physiological symptoms such as muscle tension, headaches, dizziness, heart palpitations, or insomnia (Starcevic et al., 2007). Figure 3 shows the most common symptoms of generalized anxiety disorder.

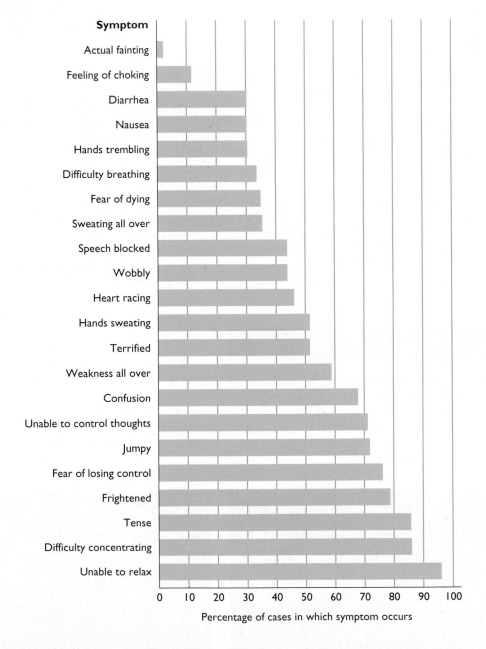

FIGURE 3 Frequency of symptoms in cases of generalized anxiety disorder. (Source: Adapted from Beck & Emery, 1985, pp. 87–88.)

Obsessive-Compulsive Disorder. In **obsessive-compulsive disorder**, people are plagued by unwanted thoughts, called obsessions, or feel that they must carry out actions, termed compulsions, against their will.

An **obsession** is a persistent, unwanted thought or idea that keeps recurring. For example, a student may be unable to stop thinking that she has neglected to put her name on a test and may think about it constantly for the two weeks it takes to get the paper back. A man may go on vacation and wonder the whole time whether he locked his house. A woman may hear the same tune running through her head over and over. In each case, the thought or idea is unwanted and difficult to put out of mind. Of course, many people suffer from mild obsessions from time to time, but usually such thoughts persist only for a short period. For people with serious obsessions, however, the thoughts persist for days or months and may consist of bizarre, troubling images (Lee & Kwon, 2003, 2005; Rassin & Muris, 2007).

As part of an obsessive-compulsive disorder, people may also experience **compulsions**, irresistible urges to repeatedly carry out some act that seems strange and unreasonable, even to them. Whatever the compulsive behavior is, people experience extreme anxiety if they cannot carry it out, even if it is something they want to stop. The acts may be relatively trivial, such as repeatedly checking the stove to make sure all the burners are turned off, or more unusual, such as continuously washing oneself (Carter, Pauls, & Leckman, 2000; Frost & Steketee, 2002; Clark, 2007).

For example, consider this case report of a 27-year-old woman with a cleaning ritual:

> Bess would first remove all of her clothing in a preestablished sequence. She would lay out each article of clothing at specific spots on her bed, and examine each one for any indications of "contamination." She would then thoroughly scrub her body, starting at her feet and working meticulously up to the top of her head, using certain washcloths for certain areas of her body. Any articles of clothing that appeared to have been "contaminated" were thrown into the laundry. Clean clothing was put in the spots that were vacant. She would then dress herself in the opposite order from which she took the clothes off. (Meyer & Osborne, 1987, p. 156)

Although such compulsive rituals lead to some immediate reduction of anxiety, in the long term the anxiety returns. In fact, people with severe cases lead lives filled with unrelenting tension (Goodman, Rudorfer, & Maser, 2000; Penzel, 2000).

THE CAUSES OF ANXIETY DISORDERS

We've considered the four major types of anxiety disorders, but there are others as well. For instance, *posttraumatic stress disorder* (in which a person reexperiences a stressful event in vivid flashbacks or dreams, and which we discussed when we considered stress) is classified as an anxiety disorder.

The variety of anxiety disorders means that no single explanation fits all cases. Genetic factors clearly are part of the picture. For example, if one member of a pair of identical twins has panic disorder, there is a 30 percent chance that the other twin will have it also. Furthermore, a person's characteristic level of anxiety is related to a specific gene involved in the production of the neurotransmitter serotonin. This is consistent with findings indicating that certain chemical deficiencies in the brain appear to produce some kinds of anxiety disorder (Rieder, Kaufmann, & Knowles, 1996; Holmes, Yang, Lesch, Crawley, & Murphy, 2003; Beidel & Turner, 2007).

Some researchers believe that an overactive autonomic nervous system may be at the root of panic attacks. Specifically, they suggest that poor regulation of the brain's locus ceruleus may lead to panic attacks, which cause the limbic system to become overstimulated. In turn, the overstimulated limbic system produces chronic anxiety, which ultimately leads the locus ceruleus to generate still more panic attacks (Gorman, Papp, & Coplan, 2000; Balaban, 2002).

Obsessive-compulsive disorder: A disorder characterized by obsessions or compulsions.

Obsession: A persistent, unwanted thought or idea that keeps recurring.

Compulsion: An irresistible urge to repeatedly carry out some act that seems strange and unreasonable.

Psychologists who employ the behavioral perspective have taken a different approach that emphasizes environmental factors. They consider anxiety to be a learned response to stress. For instance, suppose a dog bites a young girl. When the girl next sees a dog, she is frightened and runs away—a behavior that relieves her anxiety and thereby reinforces her avoidance behavior. After repeated encounters with dogs in which she is reinforced for her avoidance behavior, she may develop a full-fledged phobia regarding dogs.

Finally, the cognitive perspective suggests that anxiety disorders grow out of inappropriate and inaccurate thoughts and beliefs about circumstances in a person's world. For example, people with anxiety disorders may view a friendly puppy as a ferocious and savage pit bull, or they may see an air disaster looming every moment they are in the vicinity of an airplane. According to the cognitive perspective, people's maladaptive thoughts about the world are at the root of an anxiety disorder (Frost & Steketee, 2002; Wang & Clark, 2002).

Somatoform Disorders

Somatoform disorders: Psychological difficulties that take on a physical (somatic) form, but for which there is no medical cause.
Hypochondriasis: A disorder in which people have a constant fear of illness and a preoccupation with their health.

Somatoform disorders are psychological difficulties that take on a physical (somatic) form, but for which there is no medical cause. Even though an individual with a somatoform disorder reports physical symptoms, no biological cause exists, or if there is a medical problem, the person's reaction is greatly exaggerated.

One type of somatoform disorder is **hypochondriasis**, in which people have a constant fear of illness and a preoccupation with their health. These individuals believe that everyday aches and pains are symptoms of a dread disease. It is not that the "symptoms" are faked; rather, it is the misinterpretation of those sensations as evidence of some serious illness—often in the face of inarguable medical evidence to the contrary—that characterizes hypochondriasis (Noyes et al., 2003; Fallon & Feinstein, 2001; Abramowitz, Olatunji, & Deacon, 2007).

Conversion disorder: A major somatoform disorder that involves an actual physical disturbance, such as the inability to use a sensory organ or the complete or partial inability to move an arm or leg.

Another somatoform disorder is conversion disorder. Unlike hypochondriasis, in which there is no physical problem, **conversion disorders** involve an actual physical disturbance, such as the inability to see or hear or to move an arm or leg. The *cause* of such a physical disturbance is purely psychological; there is no biological reason for the problem. Some of Freud's classic cases involved conversion disorders. For instance, one of Freud's patients suddenly became unable to use her arm, without any apparent physiological cause. Later, just as abruptly, the problem disappeared.

Conversion disorders often begin suddenly. People wake up one morning blind or deaf, or they experience numbness that is restricted to a certain part of the body. A hand, for example, may become entirely numb, while an area above the wrist, controlled by the same nerves, remains sensitive to touch—something that is physiologically implausible. Mental health professionals refer to such a condition as "glove anesthesia," because the numb area is the part of the hand covered by a glove, not a region related to pathways of the nervous system (see Figure 4).

Surprisingly, people who experience conversion disorders frequently remain unconcerned about symptoms that most of us would expect to be highly anxiety-producing. For instance, a person in good health who wakes up blind may react in a bland, matter-of-fact way. Considering how most of us would feel if we woke up unable to see, this unemotional reaction (called *"la belle indifference,"* a French phrase meaning "a beautiful indifference") hardly seems appropriate (Brasic, 2002).

Dissociative Disorders

Dissociative disorders: Psychological dysfunctions characterized by the separation of different facets of a person's personality that are normally integrated.

The classic movie *The Three Faces of Eve* and the book *Sybil* (about a girl who allegedly had 16 personalities) represent a highly dramatic, rare, and controversial class of disorders: dissociative disorders. **Dissociative disorders** are characterized by the separation

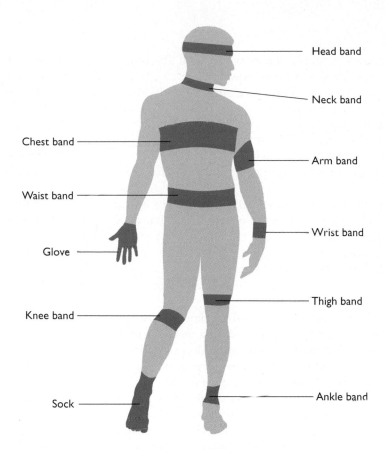

Head band

Neck band

Chest band

Arm band

Waist band

Wrist band

Glove

Thigh band

Knee band

Sock

Ankle band

FIGURE 4 Conversion disorders sometimes produce numbness in specific and isolated areas of the body (indicated by the shaded areas in the figure). For instance, in glove anesthesia, the area of the body covered by a glove feels numb. However, the condition is biologically implausible because of the nerves involved, suggesting that the problem results from a psychological disorder rather than from actual nerve damage.

(or dissociation) of different facets of a person's personality that are normally integrated and work together. By dissociating key parts of who they are, people are able to keep disturbing memories or perceptions from reaching conscious awareness, thereby reducing their anxiety (Maldonado & Spiegel, 2003; Houghtalen & Talbot, 2007).

Several dissociative disorders exist, although all of them are rare. A person with a **dissociative identity disorder (DID)** (once called *multiple personality disorder*) displays characteristics of two or more distinct personalities, identities, or personality fragments. Individual personalities often have a unique set of likes and dislikes and their own reactions to situations. Some people with multiple personalities even carry several pairs of glasses because their vision changes with each personality. Moreover, each individual personality can be well adjusted when considered on its own (Ellason & Ross, 2004; Stickely & Nickeas, 2006).

The diagnosis of dissociative identity disorder is controversial. It was rarely diagnosed before 1980, when, for the first time, it was added as a category in the third edition of *DSM*. At that point, the number of cases increased significantly. Some clinicians suggest the increase was due to more precise identification of the disorder, while others suggest the increase was due to an overreadiness to use the classification. In addition, widespread publicity about cases of DID may have influenced patients to report symptoms of more common personality disorders in ways that made it more likely that they would receive a diagnosis of DID. There are also significant cross-cultural differences in the incidence of DID (Kihlstrom, 2005; Xiao et al., 2006).

Dissociative amnesia is another dissociative disorder in which a significant, selective memory loss occurs. Dissociative amnesia is unlike simple amnesia, which involves an actual loss of information from memory, typically resulting from a physiological cause. In contrast, in cases of dissociative amnesia, the "forgotten" material is

Dissociative identity disorder (DID): A disorder in which a person displays characteristics of two or more distinct personalities.

Dissociative amnesia: A disorder in which a significant, selective memory loss occurs.

still present in memory—it simply cannot be recalled. The term *repressed memories* is sometimes used to describe the lost memories of people with dissociative amnesia.

In the most severe form of dissociative amnesia, individuals cannot recall their names, are unable to recognize parents and other relatives, and do not know their addresses. In other respects, though, they may appear quite normal. Apart from an inability to remember certain facts about themselves, they may be able to recall skills and abilities that they developed earlier. For instance, even though a chef may not remember where he grew up and received training, he may still be able to prepare gourmet meals.

In some cases of dissociative amnesia, the memory loss is profound. For example, in one dramatic case, Raymond Power Jr., an attorney, husband, father of two, and Boy Scout leader, left home to go to work one morning. Two days later he was homeless, living a new life a thousand miles away, with no memory of who he was or how he got there. Six months later, after being found, he still had no recollection of his previous life, including any knowledge of his wife of 30 years or that he even had children (Foderaro, 2006).

Dissociative fugue: A form of amnesia in which the individual leaves home and sometimes assumes a new identity.

A more unusual form of amnesia is a condition known as **dissociative fugue**. In this state, people take sudden, impulsive trips, and sometimes assume a new identity. After a period of time—days, months, or sometimes even years—they suddenly realize that they are in a strange place and completely forget the time they have spent wandering. Their last memories are those from the time just before they entered the fugue state.

The common thread among dissociative disorders is that they allow people to escape from some anxiety-producing situation. Either the person produces a new personality to deal with stress, or the individual forgets or leaves behind the situation that caused the stress as he or she journeys to some new—and perhaps less anxiety-ridden—environment (Putnam, 2000; Brown, 2006).

Mood Disorders

> From the time I woke up in the morning until the time I went to bed at night, I was unbearably miserable and seemingly incapable of any kind of joy or enthusiasm. Everything—every thought, word, movement—was an effort. Everything that once was sparkling now was flat. I seemed to myself to be dull, boring, inadequate, thick brained, unlit, unresponsive, chill skinned, bloodless, and sparrow drab. I doubted, completely, my ability to do anything well. It seemed as though my mind had slowed down and burned out to the point of being virtually useless. (Jamison, 1995a, p. 110)

We all experience mood swings. Sometimes we are happy, perhaps even euphoric; at other times we feel upset, saddened, or depressed. Such changes in mood are a normal part of everyday life. In some people, however, moods are so pronounced and lingering—like the feelings described above by writer (and psychiatrist) Kay Jamison—that they interfere with the ability to function effectively. In extreme cases, a mood may become life-threatening, and in other cases, it may cause the person to lose touch with reality. Situations such as these represent **mood disorders**, disturbances in emotional experience that are strong enough to intrude on everyday living.

Mood disorder: A disturbance in emotional experience that is strong enough to intrude on everyday living.

MAJOR DEPRESSION

President Abraham Lincoln. Queen Victoria. Newscaster Mike Wallace.

The common link among these people? Each suffered from periodic attacks of **major depression**, a severe form of depression that interferes with concentration, decision making, and sociability. Major depression is one of the more common forms of mood disorders. Some 15 million people in the United States suffer from major depression, and at any one time, 6 to 10 percent of the U.S. population is clinically depressed. Almost one in five people in the United States experiences major depression at some

Major depression: A severe form of depression that interferes with concentration, decision making, and sociability.

point in life, and 15 percent of college students have received a diagnosis of depression. The cost of depression is more than $80 billion a year in lost productivity (Winik, 2006; Scelfo, 2007).

Women are twice as likely to experience major depression as men, with one-fourth of all females apt to encounter it at some point during their lives. Furthermore, although no one is sure why, the rate of depression is going up throughout the world. Results of in-depth interviews conducted in the United States, Puerto Rico, Taiwan, Lebanon, Canada, Italy, Germany, and France indicate that the incidence of depression has increased significantly over previous rates in every area. In fact, in some countries, the likelihood that individuals will have major depression at some point in their lives is three times higher than it was for earlier generations. In addition, people are developing major depression at increasingly younger ages (Miller, 2003; Staley et al., 2006; Kendler et al., 2006).

When psychologists speak of major depression, they do not mean the sadness that comes from experiencing one of life's disappointments, something that we all have experienced. Some depression is normal after the breakup of a long-term relationship, the death of a loved one, or the loss of a job. It is normal even after less serious problems, such as doing badly on a test or having a romantic partner forget one's birthday.

People who suffer from major depression experience similar sorts of feelings, but the severity tends to be considerably greater. They may feel useless, worthless, and lonely and may think the future is hopeless and that no one can help them. They may lose their appetite and have no energy. Moreover, they may experience such feelings for months or even years. They may cry uncontrollably, have sleep disturbances, and be at risk for suicide. The depth and duration of such behavior are the hallmarks of major depression. (Figure 5 provides a self-assessment of depression.)

MANIA AND BIPOLAR DISORDER

While depression leads to the depths of despair, mania leads to emotional heights. **Mania** is an extended state of intense, wild elation. People experiencing mania feel intense happiness, power, invulnerability, and energy. They may become involved in

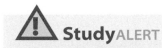

StudyALERT

Major depression differs from the normal depression that occasionally occurs during most people's lives; major depression is more intense, lasts longer, and may have no clear trigger.

Mania: An extended state of intense, wild elation.

A Test for Depression

To complete the questionnaire, count the number of statements with which you agree:

1. I feel downhearted, blue, and sad.
2. I don't enjoy the things that I used to.
3. I feel that others would be better off if I were dead.
4. I feel that I am not useful or needed.
5. I notice that I am losing weight.
6. I have trouble sleeping through the night.
7. I am restless and can't keep still.
8. My mind isn't as clear as it used to be.
9. I get tired for no reason.
10. I feel hopeless about the future.

Scoring: If you agree with at least five of the statements, including either item 1 or 2, and if you have had these symptoms for at least two weeks, help from a professional is strongly recommended. If you answer yes to number 3, you should get help immediately.

FIGURE 5 This is a version of a test distributed by mental health organizations during the annual National Depression Screening Day, a nationwide event that seeks to identify people who are suffering from depression that is severe enough to warrant psychological intervention. (Source: National Depression Screening Day, 2003.)

wild schemes, believing they will succeed at anything they attempt. Consider, for example, the following description of an individual who experienced a manic episode:

> Mr. O'Reilly took a leave of absence from his civil service job. He purchased a large number of cuckoo clocks and then an expensive car, which he planned to use as a mobile showroom for his wares, anticipating that he would make a great deal of money. He proceeded to "tear around town" buying and selling clocks and other merchandise, and when he was not out, he was continuously on the phone making "deals." . . . He was $3,000 in debt and had driven his family to exhaustion with his excessive activity and talkativeness. He said, however, that he felt "on top of the world." (Spitzer et al., 1983, p. 115)

Bipolar disorder: A disorder in which a person alternates between periods of euphoric feelings of mania and periods of depression.

Typically, people sequentially experience periods of mania and depression. This alternation of mania and depression is called **bipolar disorder** (a condition previously known as manic-depressive disorder). The swings between highs and lows may occur a few days apart or may alternate over a period of years. In addition, in bipolar disorder, periods of depression are usually longer than periods of mania.

Ironically, some of society's most creative individuals may have suffered from bipolar disorder. The imagination, drive, excitement, and energy that they display during manic stages allow them to make unusually creative contributions. For instance, historical analysis of the composer Robert Schumann's music shows that he was most prolific during periods of mania. In contrast, his output dropped off drastically during periods of depression (see Figure 6). On the other hand, the high output associated with mania does not necessarily lead to higher quality: Some of Schumann's greatest works were created outside his periods of mania (Ludwig, 1996; Szegedy-Maszak, 2003).

Despite the creative fires that may be lit by mania, persons who experience this disorder often show a recklessness that produces self-injury—emotionally and sometimes physically. They may alienate others with their talkativeness, inflated self-esteem, and indifference to the needs of others.

FIGURE 6 The number of pieces written by composer Robert Schumann in a given year is related to his periods of depression and mania (Slater & Meyer, 1959; reprinted in Jamison, 1993). Why do you think mania might be associated with creative productivity in some people?

CAUSES OF MOOD DISORDERS

Because they represent a major mental health problem, mood disorders—and, in particular, depression—have received a good deal of study. Several approaches have been used to explain the disorders.

Some mood disorders clearly have genetic and biochemical roots. In fact, most evidence suggests that bipolar disorders are caused primarily by biological factors. For instance, bipolar disorder (and some forms of major depression) clearly runs in some families. Furthermore, researchers have found that several neurotransmitters play a role in depression. For example, alterations in the functioning of serotonin and norepinephrine in the brain are related to the disorder (Plomin & McGuffin, 2003; Kato, 2007).

Other explanations for depression have also included a focus on psychological causes. For instance, proponents of psychoanalytic approaches see depression as the result of feelings of loss (real or potential) or of anger directed at oneself. One psychoanalytic approach, for instance, suggests that depression is produced by the loss or threatened loss of a parent early in life (Vanheule et al., 2006).

Behavioral theories of depression argue that the stresses of life produce a reduction in positive reinforcers. As a result, people begin to withdraw, which only serves to reduce positive reinforcers further. In addition, people receive attention for their depressive behavior, which further reinforces the depression (Lewinsohn & Essau, 2002; Lewinsohn et al., 2003).

Some explanations for mood disorders attribute them to cognitive factors. For example, psychologist Martin Seligman suggests that depression is largely a response to learned helplessness. *Learned helplessness* is a learned expectation that events in one's life are uncontrollable and that one cannot escape from the situation. As a consequence, people simply give up fighting aversive events and submit to them, thereby producing depression. Other theorists go a step further, suggesting that depression results from hopelessness, a combination of learned helplessness and an expectation that negative outcomes in one's life are inevitable (Kwon & Laurenceau, 2002; Maier & Watkins, 2000; Bjornstad, 2006).

Clinical psychologist Aaron Beck has proposed that faulty cognitions underlie people's depressed feelings. Specifically, his cognitive theory of depression suggests that depressed individuals typically view themselves as life's losers, blaming themselves whenever anything goes wrong. By focusing on the negative side of situations, they feel inept and unable to act constructively to change their environment. In sum, their negative cognitions lead to feelings of depression (Newman et al., 2002).

Brain imaging studies suggest that people with depression experience a general blunting of emotional reactions. For example, one study found that the brains of people with depression showed significantly less activation when they viewed photos of human faces displaying strong emotions than those without the disorder (see Figure 7; Gotlib et al., 2004).

Other explanations of depression derive from evolutionary psychology, which considers how behavior is influenced by our genetic inheritance from our ancestors. In the evolutionary view, depression is an adaptive response to unattainable goals. When people fruitlessly pursue an ever-elusive goal, depression begins, ending pursuit of the goal. Ultimately, when the depression lifts, people can turn to other, more reasonable goals. In this view, depression serves a positive function, in the long run increasing the chances of survival for particular individuals, who can then pass the behavior to their offspring. Such reasoning, of course, is highly speculative (Nesse, 2000, Siegert & Ward, 2002; Pfeffer, 2006).

The various theories of depression have not provided a complete answer to an elusive question that has dogged researchers: Why does depression occur in approximately twice as many women as men—a pattern that is similar across a variety of cultures?

FIGURE 7 The brains of those with depression (left) show significantly less activation in response to photos of sad, angry, and fearful faces than those of people without the disorder (right). (Source: Ian Gotlib, Stanford Mood and Anxiety Disorders Laboratory, 2005.)

One explanation suggests that the stress experienced by women may be greater than that experienced by men at certain points in their lives—such as when a woman must simultaneously earn a living and be the primary caregiver for her children. In addition, women have a higher risk for physical and sexual abuse, typically earn lower wages than men, report greater unhappiness with their marriages, and generally experience chronic negative circumstances. Furthermore, women and men may respond to stress with different coping mechanisms. For instance, men may abuse drugs, while women respond with depression (Antonucci et al., 2002; Holden, 2005; Nolen-Hoeksema, 2007).

Biological factors may also explain some women's depression. For example, because the rate of female depression begins to rise during puberty, some psychologists believe that hormones make women more vulnerable to the disorder. In addition, 25 to 50 percent of women who take oral contraceptives report symptoms of depression, and depression that occurs after the birth of a child is linked to hormonal changes. Finally, structural differences in men's and women's brains that we discussed in the neuroscience and behavior modules may be related to gender differences in depression (Holden, 2005; Graham et al., 2007).

It is clear, ultimately, that researchers have discovered no definitive solutions to the puzzle of depression, and there are many alternative explanations. Most likely, a complex interaction of several factors causes mood disorders.

Schizophrenia

I'm a doctor, you know. . . . I don't have a diploma, but I'm a doctor. I'm glad to be a mental patient, because it taught me how to be humble. I use Cover Girl creamy natural makeup. Oral Roberts has been here to visit me. . . . This place is where *Mad* magazine is published. The Nixons make Noxon metal polish. When I was a little girl, I used to sit and tell stories to myself. When I was older, I turned off the sound on the TV set and made up dialogue to go with the shows I watched. . . . I'm a week pregnant. I have schizophrenia— cancer of the nerves. My body is overcrowded with nerves. This is going to win me the

Nobel Prize for medicine. I don't consider myself schizophrenic anymore. There's no such thing as schizophrenia, there's only mental telepathy. I once had a friend named Camilla Costello. (Sheehan, 1982, pp. 72–73)

This excerpt illustrates the efforts of a woman with schizophrenia, one of the more severe forms of mental disturbance, to hold a conversation with a clinician. People with schizophrenia account for by far the largest percentage of those hospitalized for mental disorders. They are also in many respects the least likely to recover from their psychological difficulties.

Schizophrenia refers to a class of disorders in which severe distortion of reality occurs. Thinking, perception, and emotion may deteriorate; the individual may withdraw from social interaction; and the person may display bizarre behavior. Although there are several types of schizophrenia (see Figure 8), the distinctions between them are not always clear-cut. Moreover, the symptoms displayed by persons with schizophrenia may vary considerably over time, and people with schizophrenia show significant differences in the pattern of their symptoms even when they are labeled with the same diagnostic category. Nonetheless, a number of characteristics reliably distinguish schizophrenia from other disorders. They include the following:

Schizophrenia: A class of disorders in which severe distortion of reality occurs.

- *Decline from a previous level of functioning.* An individual can no longer carry out activities he or she was once able to do.

- *Disturbances of thought and language.* People with schizophrenia use logic and language in a peculiar way. Their thinking often does not make sense, and their information processing is frequently faulty. They also do not follow conventional linguistic rules (Penn et al., 1997). Consider, for example, the following response to the question "Why do you think people believe in God?"

Uh, let's, I don't know why, let's see, balloon travel. He holds it up for you, the balloon. He don't let you fall out, your little legs sticking down through the clouds. He's down to the smokestack, looking through the smoke trying to get the balloon gassed up you know. Way they're flying on top that way, legs sticking out. I don't know, looking down on the ground, heck, that'd make you so dizzy you just stay and sleep you know, hold down and sleep there. I used to be sleep outdoors, you know, sleep outdoors instead of going home. (Chapman & Chapman, 1973, p. 3)

FIGURE 8 The distinctions among the different types of schizophrenia are not always clear-cut, and symptoms may vary considerably over time.

Types of Schizophrenia

Type	Symptoms
Disorganized (hebephrenic) schizophrenia	Innappropriate laughter and giggling, silliness, incoherent speech, infantile behavior, strange and sometimes obscene behavior
Paranoid schizophrenia	Delusions and hallucinations of persecution or of greatness, loss of judgment, erratic and unpredictable behavior
Catatonic schizophrenia	Major disturbances in movement; in some phases, loss of all motion, with patient frozen into a single position, remaining that way for hours and sometimes even days; in other phases, hyperactivity and wild, sometimes violent, movement
Undifferentiated schizophrenia	Variable mixture of major symptoms of schizophrenia; classification used for patients who cannot be typed into any of the more specific categories
Residual schizophrenia	Minor signs of schizophrenia after a more serious episode

As this selection illustrates, although the basic grammatical structure may be intact, the substance of thinking characteristic of schizophrenia is often illogical, garbled, and lacking in meaningful content (Holden, 2003; Heinrichs, 2005; see Figure 9).

- *Delusions*. People with schizophrenia often have delusions, firmly held, unshakable beliefs with no basis in reality. Among the common delusions experienced by people with schizophrenia are the beliefs that they are being controlled by someone else, they are being persecuted by others, and their thoughts are being broadcast so that others know what they are thinking (Stompe et al., 2003; Coltheart, Langdon, & McKay, 2007).

- *Hallucinations and perceptual disorders*. People with schizophrenia do not perceive the world as most other people do. They also may have *hallucinations*, the experience of perceiving things that do not actually exist. Furthermore, they may see, hear, or smell things differently from others (see Figure 9) and do not even have a sense of their bodies in the way that others do, having difficulty determining where their bodies stop and the rest of the world begins (Copolov et al., 2003; Botvinick, 2004; Thomas et al., 2007).

- *Emotional disturbances*. People with schizophrenia sometimes show a lack of emotion in which even the most dramatic events produce little or no emotional response. Conversely, they may display emotion that is inappropriate to a situation. For example, a person with schizophrenia may laugh uproariously at a funeral or react with anger when being helped by someone.

- *Withdrawal*. People with schizophrenia tend to have little interest in others. They tend not to socialize or hold real conversations with others, although they may talk at another person. In the most extreme cases they do not even acknowledge the presence of other people, appearing to be in their own isolated world.

Usually, the onset of schizophrenia occurs in early adulthood, and the symptoms follow one of two primary courses. In *process schizophrenia*, the symptoms develop slowly and subtly. There may be a gradual withdrawal from the world, excessive daydreaming, and a blunting of emotion, until eventually the disorder reaches the point where others cannot overlook it. In other cases, known as *reactive schizophrenia*, the onset of symptoms is sudden and conspicuous. The treatment outlook for reactive schizophrenia is relatively favorable, but process schizophrenia has proved more difficult to treat.

FIGURE 9 This unusual art was created by an individual suffering from severe mental disturbance.

The symptoms of schizophrenia are classified into two types by *DSM-IV-TR*. Positive-symptom schizophrenia is indicated by the presence of disordered behavior such as hallucinations, delusions, and emotional extremes. In contrast, negative-symptom schizophrenia shows an absence or loss of normal functioning, such as social withdrawal or blunted emotions. Schizophrenia researchers sometimes speak of *Type I schizophrenia*, in which positive symptoms are dominant, and *Type II schizophrenia*, in which negative symptoms are more prominent (Buchanan et al., 2007; Levine & Rabinowitz, 2007).

The distinction between Type I and Type II schizophrenia is important because it suggests that two different processes might trigger schizophrenia, the cause of which remains one of the greatest mysteries facing psychologists who deal with disordered behavior.

SOLVING THE PUZZLE OF SCHIZOPHRENIA: BIOLOGICAL CAUSES

Although schizophrenic behavior clearly departs radically from normal behavior, its causes are less apparent. It does appear, however, that schizophrenia has both biological and environmental origins (Sawa & Snyder, 2002).

Let's first consider the evidence pointing to a biological cause. Because schizophrenia is more common in some families than in others, genetic factors seem to be involved in producing at least a susceptibility to or readiness for developing schizophrenia. For example, the closer the genetic link between a person with schizophrenia and another individual, the greater the likelihood that the other person will experience the disorder (see Figure 10; Brzustowicz et al., 2000; Plomin & McGuffin, 2003; Gottesman & Hanson, 2005).

However, if genetics alone were responsible for schizophrenia, the chance of both of two identical twins having schizophrenia would be 100 percent instead of just under 50 percent, because identical twins have the same genetic makeup. Moreover, attempts to find a link between schizophrenia and a particular gene have been only partly successful. Apparently, genetic factors alone do not produce schizophrenia (Franzek & Beckmann, 1996; Lenzenweger & Dworkin, 1998).

One intriguing biological hypothesis to explain schizophrenia is that the brains of people with the disorder may harbor either a biochemical imbalance or a structural abnormality. For example, the *dopamine hypothesis* suggests that schizophrenia occurs when there is excess activity in the areas of the brain that use dopamine as a neurotransmitter. This hypothesis came to light after the discovery that drugs that block dopamine action in brain pathways can be highly effective in reducing the symptoms

StudyALERT

In Type I schizophrenia, positive symptoms (in which hallucinations, delusions, and emotional extremes are present) are dominant; in Type II schizophrenia, negative symptoms (characterized by an absence or loss of normal functioning) are dominant.

Risk of Developing Schizophrenia, Based on Genetic Relatedness to a Person with Schizophrenia		
Relationship	Genetic Relatedness, %	Risk of Developing Schizophrenia, %
Identical twin	100	48
Child of two schizophrenic parents	100	46
Fraternal twin	50	17
Offspring of one schizophrenic parent	50	17
Sibling	50	9
Nephew or niece	25	4
Spouse	0	2
Unrelated person	0	1

FIGURE 10 The closer the genetic links between two people, the greater the likelihood that if one experiences schizophrenia, so will the other some time during his or her lifetime. However, genetics is not the full story, because if it were, the risk of identical twins having schizophrenia would be 100 percent, not the 48 percent shown in this figure. (Source: Gottesman, 1991.)

Neuroscience in Your Life

FIGURE 11 Changes in the brain have been found in people with schizophrenia. In the first MRI reconstruction of the brain of a patient with schizophrenia (left), the hippocampus (yellow) is shrunken, and the ventricles (gray) are enlarged and fluid-filled. In contrast, the brain of a person without the disorder (right) appears structurally different. (Source: N.C. Andreasen, University of Iowa.)

 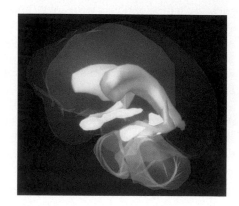

of schizophrenia. Other research suggests that glutamate, another neurotransmitter, may be a major contributor to the disorder (Remington, 2003; Baumeister & Francis, 2002; Javitt & Coyle, 2004; Ohara, 2007).

Some biological explanations propose that structural abnormalities exist in the brains of people with schizophrenia, perhaps as a result of exposure to a virus during prenatal development. For example, some research shows abnormalities in the neural circuits of the cortex and limbic systems of individuals with schizophrenia. Consistent with such research, people with schizophrenia and those without the disorder show different brain functioning (see Figure 11; Lenzenweger & Dworkin, 1998; Bartzokis et al., 2003; Reichenberg & Harvey, 2007).

Further evidence for the importance of biological factors shows that when people with schizophrenia hear voices during hallucinations, the parts of the brain responsible for hearing and language processing become active. When they have visual hallucinations, the parts of the brain involved in movement and color are active. At the same time, people with schizophrenia often have unusually low activity in the brain's frontal lobes—the parts of the brain involved with emotional regulation, insight, and the evaluation of sensory stimuli (Stern & Silbersweig, 2001).

ENVIRONMENTAL PERSPECTIVES ON SCHIZOPHRENIA

Although biological factors provide important pieces of the puzzle of schizophrenia, we still need to consider past and current experiences in the environments of people who develop the disturbance. For instance, psychoanalytic approaches suggest that schizophrenia is a form of regression to earlier experiences and stages of life. Freud believed that people with schizophrenia lack strong enough egos to cope with their unacceptable impulses. They regress to the oral stage—a time when the id and ego are not yet separated. Therefore, individuals with schizophrenia essentially lack an ego and act out impulses without concern for reality.

Although this reasoning is theoretically plausible, little evidence supports psychoanalytic explanations. Somewhat more convincing theories look toward the emotional and communication patterns of the families of people with schizophrenia. For instance, some researchers suggest that schizophrenia results from high levels of expressed emotion. *Expressed emotion* is an interaction style characterized by criticism, hostility, and emotional intrusiveness by family members. Other researchers suggest that faulty communication patterns lie at the heart of schizophrenia (Miklowitz & Tompson, 2003; Lobban, Barrowclough, & Jones, 2006).

Psychologists who take a cognitive perspective on schizophrenia suggest that the problems in thinking experienced by people with the disorder point to a cognitive cause. Some suggest that schizophrenia results from *overattention* to stimuli in the environment. Rather than being able to screen out unimportant or inconsequential stimuli and focus on the most important things in the environment, people with schizophrenia may be excessively receptive to virtually everything in their environment. As a consequence, their information-processing capabilities become overloaded and eventually break down. Other cognitive experts argue that schizophrenia results from *underattention* to certain stimuli. According to this explanation, people with schizophrenia fail to focus sufficiently on important stimuli, and pay attention to other, less important information in their surroundings (Braff, 1995).

Although it is plausible that overattention and underattention are related to different forms of schizophrenia, these phenomena do not explain the origins of such information-processing disorders. Consequently, cognitive approaches—like other environmental explanations—do not provide a full explanation of the disorder.

THE MULTIPLE CAUSES OF SCHIZOPHRENIA

The predominant approach used to explain the onset of schizophrenia today, the *predisposition model of schizophrenia*, incorporates a number of biological and environmental factors. This model suggests that individuals may inherit a predisposition or an inborn sensitivity to schizophrenia that makes them particularly vulnerable to stressful factors in the environment, such as social rejection or dysfunctional family communication patterns. The stressors may vary, but if they are strong enough and are coupled with a genetic predisposition, the result will be the onset of schizophrenia. Similarly, a strong genetic predisposition may lead to the onset of schizophrenia even when the environmental stressors are relatively weak.

In short, the models used today associate schizophrenia with several kinds of biological and environmental factors. It is increasingly clear, then, that no single factor, but a combination of interrelated variables, produces schizophrenia (Meltzer, 2000; McDonald & Murray, 2004).

StudyALERT

Remember that the multiple causes of schizophrenia include biological and environmental factors.

Personality Disorders

> I had always wanted lots of things; as a child I can remember wanting a bullet that a friend of mine had brought in to show the class. I took it and put it into my school bag and when my friend noticed it was missing, I was the one who stayed after school with him and searched the room, and I was the one who sat with him and bitched about the other kids and how one of them took his bullet. I even went home with him to help him break the news to his uncle, who had brought it home from the war for him.
>
> But that was petty compared with the stuff I did later. I wanted a Ph.D. very badly, but I didn't want to work very hard—just enough to get by. I never did the experiments I reported; hell, I was smart enough to make up the results. I knew enough about statistics to make anything look plausible. I got my master's degree without even spending one hour in a laboratory. I mean, the professors believed anything. I'd stay out all night drinking and being with my friends, and the next day I'd get in just before them and tell 'em I'd been in the lab all night. They'd actually feel sorry for me. (Duke & Nowicki, 1979, pp. 309–310)

Personality disorder: A disorder characterized by a set of inflexible, maladaptive behavior patterns that keep a person from functioning appropriately in society.

This excerpt provides a graphic first-person account of a person with a personality disorder. A **personality disorder** is characterized by a set of inflexible, maladaptive behavior patterns that keep a person from functioning appropriately in society. Personality disorders differ from the other problems we have discussed because those affected by them often have little sense of personal distress associated with the psychological maladjustment. In fact, people with personality disorders frequently lead seemingly normal lives. However, just below the surface lies a set of inflexible, maladaptive personality traits that do not permit these individuals to function as members of society (Millon & Davis, 1996, 1999; Clarkin & Lenzenweger, 2004; Friedman, Oltmanns, & Turkheimer, 2007).

StudyALERT

Unlike most psychological disorders, personality disorders produce little or no personal distress.

Antisocial personality disorder:
A disorder in which individuals show no regard for the moral and ethical rules of society or the rights of others.

The best-known type of personality disorder, illustrated by the case above, is the **antisocial personality disorder** (sometimes referred to as a sociopathic personality). Individuals with this disturbance show no regard for the moral and ethical rules of society or the rights of others. Although they can appear quite intelligent and likable (at least at first), upon closer examination they turn out to be manipulative and deceptive. Moreover, they lack any guilt or anxiety about their wrongdoing. When those with antisocial personality disorder behave in a way that injures someone else, they understand intellectually that they have caused harm but feel no remorse (Lykken, 1995; Goodwin & Hamilton, 2003; Hilarski, 2007).

People with antisocial personality disorder are often impulsive and lack the ability to withstand frustration. They can be extremely manipulative. They also may have excellent social skills; they can be charming, engaging, and highly persuasive. Some of the best con artists have antisocial personalities.

What causes such an unusual constellation of problem behaviors? A variety of factors have been suggested, ranging from an inability to experience emotions appropriately to problems in family relationships. For example, in many cases of antisocial behavior, the individual has come from a home in which a parent has died or left, or one in which there is a lack of affection, a lack of consistency in discipline, or outright rejection. Other explanations concentrate on sociocultural factors, because an unusually high proportion of people with antisocial personalities come from lower socioeconomic groups. Still, no one has been able to pinpoint the specific causes of antisocial personalities, and it is likely that some combination of factors is responsible (Nigg & Goldsmith, 1994; Rosenstein & Horowitz, 1996; Costa & Widiger, 2002).

Borderline personality disorder:
A disorder in which individuals have difficulty developing a secure sense of who they are.

People with **borderline personality disorder** have difficulty developing a secure sense of who they are. As a consequence, they tend to rely on relationships with others to define their identity. The problem with this strategy is that rejections are devastating. Furthermore, people with this disorder distrust others and have difficulty controlling their anger. Their emotional volatility leads to impulsive and self-destructive behavior. Individuals with borderline personality disorder often feel empty and alone. They may form intense, sudden, one-sided relationships, demanding the attention of another person and then feeling angry when they don't receive it. One reason for this behavior is that they may have a background in which others discounted or criticized their emotional reactions, and they may not have learned to regulate their emotions effectively (Linehan, Cochran, & Kehrer, 2001; Trull, Stepp, & Durrett, 2003; Links et al., 2007).

Narcissistic personality disorder:
A personality disturbance characterized by an exaggerated sense of self-importance.

Another example of a personality disturbance is the **narcissistic personality disorder**, which is characterized by an exaggerated sense of self-importance. Those with the disorder expect special treatment from others, while at the same time disregarding others' feelings. In some ways, in fact, the main attribute of the narcissistic personality is an inability to experience empathy for other people.

There are several other categories of personality disorder, ranging in severity from individuals who may simply be regarded by others as eccentric, obnoxious, or difficult to people who act in a manner that is criminal and dangerous to others. Although they are not out of touch with reality in the way that people with schizophrenia are, people with personality disorders lead lives that put them on the fringes of society (Millon et al., 2000; Trull & Widiger, 2003).

Childhood Disorders

We typically view childhood as a time of innocence and relative freedom from stress. In reality, though, almost 20 percent of children and 40 percent of adolescents experience significant emotional or behavioral disorders (Romano et al., 2003; Broidy et al., 2003; Nolen-Hoeksema, 2007).

For example, although major depression is more prevalent in adults, around 2.5 percent of children and more than 8 percent of adolescents suffer from the disorder. In fact, by the time they reach age 20, between 15 and 20 percent of children and adolescents will experience an episode of major depression (Garber & Horowitz, 2002).

Children do not always display depression in the same way adults do. Rather than showing profound sadness or hopelessness, childhood depression may produce the expression of exaggerated fears, clinginess, or avoidance of everyday activities. In older children, the symptoms may be sulking, school problems, and even acts of delinquency (Wenar, 1994; Seroczynski, Jacquez, & Cole, 2003; Koplewicz, 2002).

A considerably more common childhood disorder is **attention-deficit hyperactivity disorder**, or **ADHD**, a disorder marked by inattention, impulsiveness, a low tolerance for frustration, and generally a great deal of inappropriate activity. Although all children show such behavior some of the time, it is so common in children diagnosed with ADHD that it interferes with their everyday functioning (Barkley, 2005; Swanson, Harris, & Graham, 2003; Smith, Barkley, & Shapiro, 2006).

ADHD is surprisingly widespread, with estimates ranging between 3 and 5 percent of the school-age population—or some 3.5 million children under the age of 18 in the United States. Children diagnosed with the disorder are often exhausting to parents and teachers, and even their peers find them difficult to deal with.

The cause of ADHD is not known, although most experts feel that it is produced by dysfunctions in the nervous system. For example, one theory suggests that unusually low levels of arousal in the central nervous system cause ADHD. To compensate, children with ADHD seek out stimulation to increase arousal. Still, such theories are speculative. Furthermore, because many children occasionally show behaviors characteristic of ADHD, it often is misdiagnosed or, in some cases, overdiagnosed. Only the frequency and persistence of the symptoms of ADHD allow for a correct diagnosis, which can be done only by a trained professional (Hinshaw et al., 1997; Barkley, 2000).

Autism, a severe developmental disability that impairs children's ability to communicate and relate to others, is another childhood disorder that usually appears in the first three years and typically continues throughout life. Children with autism have difficulties in both verbal and nonverbal communication, and they may avoid social contact. About one in 150 children are now thought to have the disorder (Centers for Disease Control Prevention, 2007).

> **Attention-deficit hyperactivity disorder (ADHD):** A disorder marked by inattention, impulsiveness, a low tolerance for frustration, and a great deal of inappropriate activity.

> **Autism:** A severe developmental disability that impairs children's ability to communicate and relate to others.

Other Disorders

It's important to keep in mind that the various forms of psychological disorders described in *DSM-IV-TR* cover much more ground than we have been able to discuss in this module. Some relate to topics previously considered in other chapters. For example, *psychoactive substance-use disorder* relates to problems that arise from the use and abuse of drugs. Furthermore, *alcohol use disorders* are among the most serious and widespread problems. Both psychoactive substance-use disorder and alcohol use disorder co-occur with many other psychological disorders such as mood disorders, post-traumatic stress disorder, and schizophrenia, complicating treatment considerably (Salgado, Quinlan, & Zlotnick, 2007).

Another widespread problem is *eating disorders*. They include such disorders as *anorexia nervosa* and *bulimia*, which we considered in the chapter on motivation and emotion, as well as *binge-eating disorder*, characterized by binge eating without behaviors designed to prevent weight gain. Finally, *sexual disorders*, in which one's sexual activity is unsatisfactory, are another important class of problems. They include *sexual desire disorders*, *sexual arousal disorders*, and *paraphilias*, atypical sexual activities that may include nonhuman objects or nonconsenting partners.

Another important class of disorders is *organic mental disorders*, some of which we touched on previously. These are problems that have a purely biological basis, such as Alzheimer's disease and some types of mental retardation. Remember that there are other disorders that we have not mentioned at all, and each of the classes we have discussed can be divided into several subcategories (Kopelman & Fleminger, 2002; Pratt et al., 2003; Reijonen et al., 2003).

In the most severe cases of autism, children display self-injurious behavior and must wear protective head gear.

RECAP/EVALUATE/RETHINK

RECAP

What are the major psychological disorders?

- Anxiety disorders are present when a person experiences so much anxiety that it affects daily functioning. Specific types of anxiety disorders include phobic disorder, panic disorder, generalized anxiety disorder, and obsessive-compulsive disorder. (p. 521)

- Somatoform disorders are psychological difficulties that take on a physical (somatic) form, but for which there is no medical cause. Examples are hypochondriasis and conversion disorders. (p. 526)

- Dissociative disorders are marked by the separation, or dissociation, of different facets of a person's personality that are usually integrated. Major kinds of dissociative disorders include dissociative identity disorder, dissociative amnesia, and dissociative fugue. (p. 526)

- Mood disorders are characterized by emotional states of depression or euphoria so strong that they intrude on everyday living. They include major depression and bipolar disorder. (p. 528)

- Schizophrenia is one of the more severe forms of mental illness. Symptoms of schizophrenia include declines in functioning, thought and language disturbances, perceptual disorders, emotional disturbance, and withdrawal from others. (p. 533)

- Strong evidence links schizophrenia to genetic, biochemical, and environmental factors. According to the predisposition model, an interaction among various factors produces the disorder. (p. 535)

- People with personality disorders experience little or no personal distress, but they do suffer from an inability to function as normal members of society. These disorders include antisocial personality disorder, borderline personality disorder, and narcissistic personality disorder. (p. 537)

- Childhood disorders include major depression, attention-deficit hyperactivity disorder (ADHD), and autism. (p. 538)

EVALUATE

1. Kathy is terrified of elevators. She could be suffering from a(n)
   a. Obsessive-compulsive disorder
   b. Phobic disorder
   c. Panic disorder
   d. Generalized anxiety disorder
2. Carmen described an incident in which her anxiety suddenly rose to a peak and she felt a sense of impending doom. Carmen experienced a(n) _____ _____.
3. Troubling thoughts that persist for weeks or months are known as
   a. Obsessions
   b. Compulsions
   c. Rituals
   d. Panic attacks
4. An overpowering urge to carry out a strange ritual is called a(n) _____.
5. The separation of the personality, providing escape from stressful situations, is the key factor in _____ disorders.
6. States of extreme euphoria and energy paired with severe depression characterize _____ disorder.
7. _____ schizophrenia is characterized by symptoms that are sudden and of easily identifiable onset; _____ schizophrenia develops gradually over a person's life span.
8. The _____ states that schizophrenia may be caused by an excess of certain neurotransmitters in the brain.

RETHINK

1. What cultural factors might contribute to the rate of anxiety disorders found in a culture? How might the experience of anxiety differ among people of different cultures?
2. *From the perspective of a social worker:* Personality disorders are often not apparent to others, and many people with these problems seem to live basically normal lives and are not a threat to others. Because these people often appear from the outside to function well in society, why should they be considered psychologically disordered?

Answers to Evaluate Questions

1. b; 2. panic attack; 3. a; 4. compulsion; 5. dissociative; 6. bipolar; 7. reactive, process; 8. dopamine hypothesis

KEY TERMS

anxiety disorder p. 521
phobias p. 522
panic disorder p. 523
generalized anxiety disorder
   p. 524
obsessive-compulsive
   disorder p. 525
obsession p. 525
compulsion p. 525

somatoform disorders p. 526
hypochondriasis p. 526
conversion disorder p. 526
dissociative disorders p. 526
dissociative identity
   disorder (DID) p. 527
dissociative amnesia p. 527
dissociative fugue p. 527

mood disorder p. 528
major depression p. 528
mania p. 529
bipolar disorder p. 530
schizophrenia p. 533
personality disorder p. 537
antisocial personality
   disorder p. 538

borderline personality
   disorder p. 538
narcissistic personality
   disorder p. 538
attention-deficit hyperactivity
   disorder (ADHD) p. 539
autism p. 539

Psychological Disorders in Perspective

How common are the kinds of psychological disorders we've been discussing? Here's one answer: Every second person you meet in the United States is likely to suffer, at some point during his or her life, from a psychological disorder.

That's the conclusion drawn from a massive study on the prevalence of psychological disorders. In that study, researchers conducted face-to-face interviews with more than 8,000 men and women between the ages of 15 and 54 years. The sample was designed to be representative of the population of the United States. According to results of the study, 48 percent of those interviewed had experienced a disorder at some point in their lives. In addition, 30 percent experienced a disorder in any particular year, and the number of people who experienced simultaneous multiple disorders (known as *comorbidity*) was significant (Welkowitz et al., 2000; Kessler et al., 2005; Merikangas et al., 2007).

The most common disorder reported in the study was depression, with 17 percent of those surveyed reporting at least one major episode. Ten percent had suffered from depression during the current year. The next most common disorder was alcohol dependence, which occurred at a lifetime incidence rate of 14 percent. In addition, 7 percent of those interviewed had experienced alcohol dependence in the last year. Other frequently occurring psychological disorders were drug dependence, disorders involving panic (such as an overwhelming fear of talking to strangers and terror of heights), and posttraumatic stress disorder.

Although some researchers think the estimates of severe disorders may be too high (Narrow et al., 2002), the national findings are consistent with studies of college students and their psychological difficulties. For example, in one study of the problems of students who visited a college counseling center, more than 40 percent of students reported being depressed (see Figure 1). These figures include only students who sought help from the counseling center, not those who did not seek treatment. Consequently, the figures are not representative of the entire college population (Benton et al., 2003).

The significant level of psychological disorders is a problem not only in the United States; according to the World Health Organization, mental health difficulties are also a global concern. Throughout the world, psychological disorders are widespread. Furthermore, there are economic disparities in treatment, such that more affluent people with mild disorders receive more and better treatment than poor people who have more severe disorders. In fact, psychological disorders make up 14 percent of global illness, and 90 percent of people in developing countries receive no care at all for their disorders (see Figure 2 on page 543; The WHO World Mental Health Survey Consortium, 2004; Jacob et al., 2007; Wang et al., 2007).

Also, keep in mind that the incidence of specific disorders varies significantly in other cultures. For instance, cross-cultural surveys show that the incidence of major depression varies significantly from one culture to another. The probability of having at least one episode of depression is only 1.5 percent in Taiwan and 2.9 percent in Korea, compared with 11.6 percent in New Zealand and 16.4 percent in France. Such notable differences underscore the importance of considering the cultural context of psychological disorders (Weissman et al., 1997; Howarth & Weissman, 2000; Tseng, 2003).

Key Concepts

How prevalent are psychological disorders?

What indicators signal a need for the help of a mental health practitioner?

StudyALERT

Remember that the incidence of various types of psychological disorders in the general population is surprisingly high.

FIGURE 1 The problems reported by students visiting a college counseling center. Would you have predicted this pattern of psychological difficulties? (Source: Benton et al., 2003.)

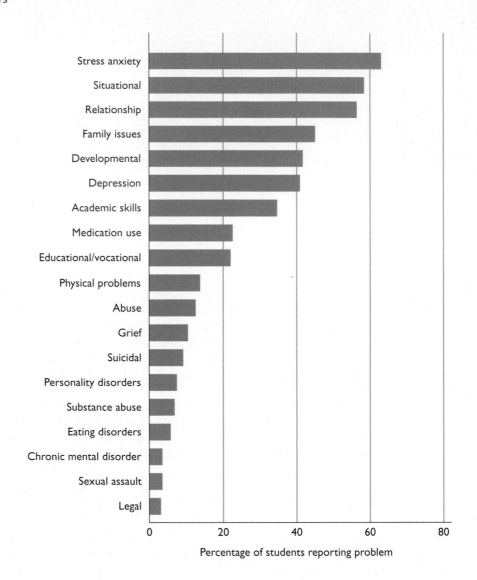

Percentage of students reporting problem

The Social and Cultural Context of Psychological Disorders

In considering the nature of the psychological disorders described in *DSM-IV-TR*, it's important to keep in mind that the specific disorders reflect turn-of-the-21st century Western cultures. The classification system provides a snapshot of how its authors viewed mental disorder when it was published. In fact, the development of the most recent version of *DSM* was a source of great debate, in part reflecting issues that divide society.

For example, two disorders caused particular controversy during the revision process. One, known as *self-defeating personality disorder*, was ultimately removed from the appendix, where it had appeared in the previous revision. The term *self-defeating personality disorder* had been applied to cases in which people who were treated unpleasantly or demeaningly in relationships neither left nor took other action. It was typically used to describe people who remained in abusive relationships.

Although some clinicians argued that it was a valid category, one that they observed in clinical practice, the disorder seemed to lack enough research evidence to support its designation as a disorder in *DSM*. Furthermore, some critics complained that use of the label had the effect of condemning targets of abuse for their

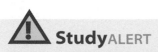

StudyALERT

It is important to understand that the *DSM* is a living document that presents a view of disorders that reflects the culture and historical context of its authors.

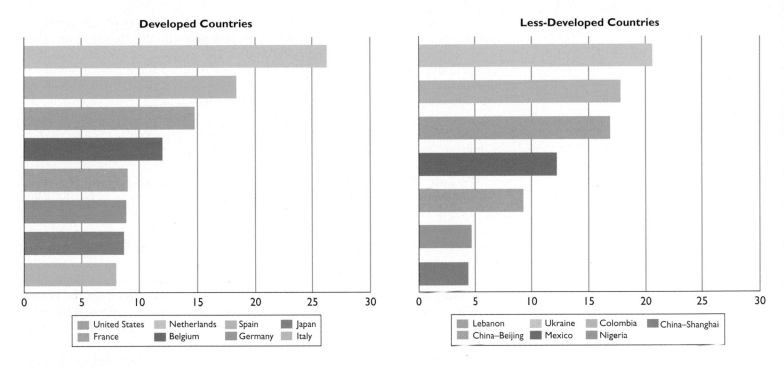

FIGURE 2 According to a global survey conducted by the World Health Organization, the prevalence of psychological disorders is widespread. These figures show the prevalence of any psychological disorder within the last 12 months. (Source: The WHO World Mental Health Survey Consortium, 2004, Table 3.)

plight—a blame-the-victim phenomenon—and as a result, the category was removed from the manual.

A second and even more controversial category was "premenstrual dysphoric disorder." That disorder is characterized by severe, incapacitating mood changes or depression related to a woman's menstrual cycle. Some critics argued that the classification simply labels normal female behavior as a disorder. Former U.S. Surgeon General Antonia Novello suggested that what "in women is called PMS [premenstrual syndrome, a similar classification] in men is called healthy aggression and initiative" (Cotton, 1993, p. 270). Advocates for including the disorder prevailed, however, and "premenstrual dysphoric disorder" appears in the appendix of *DSM-IV-TR* (Hartung & Widiger, 1998).

Such controversies underline the fact that our understanding of abnormal behavior reflects the society and culture in which we live. Future revisions of *DSM* may include a different catalog of disorders. Even now, other cultures might include a list of disorders that look very different from the list that appears in the current *DSM*, as we discuss next.

In most people's estimation, a person who hears voices of the recently deceased is probably a victim of a psychological disturbance. Yet some Plains Indians routinely hear the voices of the dead calling to them from the afterlife.

This is only one example of the role of culture in labeling behavior as "abnormal." In fact, among all the major adult disorders included in the *DSM* categorization, just four are found across all cultures of the world: schizophrenia, bipolar disorder, major depression, and anxiety disorders. *All* the rest are specific to North America and Western Europe (Kleinman, 1996; Cohen et al., 1999; López & Guarnaccia, 2000).

Exploring DIVERSITY

DSM and Culture—and the Culture of *DSM*

Take, for instance, anorexia nervosa, the disorder in which people develop inaccurate views of their body appearance, become obsessed with their weight, and refuse to eat, sometimes starving to death in the process. This disorder occurs only in cultures that hold the societal standard that slender female bodies are the most desirable. In most of the world, where such a standard does not exist, anorexia nervosa does not occur. Interestingly, there is no anorexia nervosa in all of Asia, with two exceptions: the upper and upper-middle classes of Japan and Hong Kong, where Western influence tends to be great. In fact, anorexia nervosa developed fairly recently even in Western cultures. In the 1600s and 1700s it did not occur because the ideal female body in Western cultures at that time was a full-figured one.

Similarly, dissociative identity (multiple personality) disorder makes sense as a problem only in societies in which a sense of self is fairly concrete. In India, the self is based more on external factors that are relatively independent of the person. There, when an individual displays symptoms of what people in a Western society would call dissociative identity disorder, Indians assume that that person is possessed either by demons (which they view as a malady) or by gods (which does not require treatment).

Furthermore, even though disorders such as schizophrenia are found throughout the world, cultural factors influence the specific symptoms of the disorder. Hence, catatonic schizophrenia, in which unmoving patients appear to be frozen in the same position, sometimes for days, is rare in North America and Western Europe. In contrast, in India, 80 percent of those with schizophrenia are catatonic.

Other cultures have disorders that do not appear in the West. For example, in Malaysia, a behavior called *amok* is characterized by a wild outburst in which a person, usually quiet and withdrawn, kills or severely injures another. *Koro* is a condition found in Southeast Asian males who develop an intense panic that the penis is about to withdraw into the abdomen. Some West African men develop a disorder when they first attend college that they call "brain fag"; it includes feelings of heaviness or heat in the head, as well as depression and anxiety. Finally, *ataque de nervios* is a disorder found most often among Latinos from the Caribbean. It is characterized by trembling, crying, uncontrollable screams, and incidents of verbal or physical aggression (Cohen et al., 1999; López & Guarnaccia, 2000; Adams, 2007).

Explanations for psychological disorders also differ among cultures. For example, in China, psychological disorders are commonly viewed as a weakness of the heart, a concept that derives from thousands of years of traditional Chinese medicine. Many terms used to describe emotions and symptoms of psychological disorders make direct reference to the heart—but the association isn't simply a metaphorical one. Chinese people are more likely than people in Western cultures to express their emotional anguish in terms of physical symptoms such as heart pain, "heart panic," or "heart vexed." They may also see their emotional pain as merely a side effect of some underlying physical cause, or even focus more on the effects that their symptoms are having on their relationships with friends and family members (Miller, 2006; Lee, Kleinman, & Kleinman, 2007).

In sum, we should not assume that the *DSM* provides the final word on psychological disorders. The disorders it includes are very much a creation and function of Western cultures at a particular moment in time, and its categories should not be seen as universally applicable (Tseng, 2003).

BECOMING AN INFORMED CONSUMER
of Psychology
Deciding When You Need Help

After you've considered the range and variety of psychological disturbances that can afflict people, you may begin to feel that you suffer from one (or more) of the problems we have discussed. In fact, this perception has a name: *medical student's disease*. Although in this case it might more aptly be labeled "psychology student's disease," the basic symptoms are the same: feeling that you suffer from the same sorts of problems you are studying.

Most often, of course, your concerns will be unwarranted. As we have discussed, the differences between normal and abnormal behavior are often so fuzzy that it is easy to jump to the conclusion that you might have the same symptoms that are involved in serious forms of mental disturbance.

Before coming to such a conclusion, though, keep in mind that from time to time we all experience a wide range of emotions, and it is not unusual to feel deeply unhappy, fantasize about bizarre situations, or feel anxiety about life's circumstances. It is the persistence, depth, and consistency of such behavior that set normal reactions apart from abnormal ones. If you have not previously had serious doubts about the normality of your behavior, it is unlikely that reading about others' psychological disorders will prompt you to reevaluate your earlier conclusion.

On the other hand, many people do have problems that merit concern, and in such cases, it is important to consider the possibility that professional help is warranted. The following list of symptoms can serve as a guideline to help you determine whether outside intervention might be useful (Engler & Goleman, 1992):

- Long-term feelings of distress that interfere with your sense of well-being, competence, and ability to function effectively in daily activities
- Occasions in which you experience overwhelmingly high stress, accompanied by feelings of inability to cope with the situation
- Prolonged depression or feelings of hopelessness, especially when they do not have any clear cause (such as the death of someone close)
- Withdrawal from other people
- Thoughts of inflicting harm on oneself or suicide
- A chronic physical problem for which no physical cause can be determined
- A fear or phobia that prevents you from engaging in everyday activities
- Feelings that other people are out to get you or are talking about and plotting against you
- Inability to interact effectively with others, preventing the development of friendships and loving relationships

This list offers a rough set of guidelines for determining when the normal problems of everyday living have escalated beyond your ability to deal with them by yourself. In such situations, the *least* reasonable approach would be to pore over the psychological disorders we have discussed in an attempt at self-diagnosis. A more reasonable strategy is to consider seeking professional help.

RECAP/EVALUATE/RETHINK

RECAP

How prevalent are psychological disorders?

- About half the people in the United States are likely to experience a psychological disorder at some point in their lives: 30 percent experience a disorder in any specific year. (p. 541)

What indicators signal a need for the help of a mental health practitioner?

- The signals that indicate a need for professional help include long-term feelings of psychological distress, feelings of inability to cope with stress, withdrawal from other people, thoughts of inflicting harm on oneself or suicide, prolonged feelings of hopelessness, chronic physical problems with no apparent causes, phobias and compulsions, paranoia, and an inability to interact with others. (p. 544)

EVALUATE

1. The latest version of *DSM* is considered to be the conclusive guideline on defining psychological disorders. True or false?

2. _____ _____ _____, characterized by severe, incapacitating mood changes or depression related to a woman's menstrual cycle, was eventually added to the appendix of *DSM-IV-TR* despite controversy surrounding its inclusion.

3. Match the disorder with the culture in which it is most common:
   1. amok
   2. anorexia nervosa
   3. brain fag
   4. catatonic schizophrenia
      a. India
      b. Malaysia
      c. United States
      d. West Africa

RETHINK

1. Why is inclusion in the *DSM-IV-TR* of "borderline" disorders such as self-defeating personality disorder and premenstrual dysphoric disorder so controversial and political? What disadvantages does inclusion bring? Does inclusion bring any benefits?

2. *From the perspective of a college counselor:* What indicators might be most important in determining whether a college student is experiencing a psychological disorder? Do you believe that all students who show signs of a psychological disorder should seek professional help? How might your responses change if the student were from a different culture (e.g., an African society)?

Answers to Evaluate Questions

1. false; the development of the latest version of *DSM* was a source of great controversy, in part reflecting issues that divide society; 2. premenstrual dysphoric disorder; 3. 1-b, 2-c, 3-d, 4-a

Psychology on the Web

1. On the Web, research the insanity defense as it is used in U.S. courts of law, consulting at least two sources. Summarize your findings, evaluating them against the perspectives on psychological disorders. Are there differences between legal and psychological interpretations of "sanity"? If so, what are they? Do you think such differences are appropriate?

2. Find information on the Web about the controversy surrounding dissociative (or multiple) personality disorder. Summarize both sides of the controversy. Using your knowledge of psychology, state your opinion on the matter.

Epilogue

We've discussed some of the many types of psychological disorders to which people are prone, noting the difficulty psychologists and physicians have in clearly differentiating normal from abnormal behavior and looking at some of the approaches mental health professionals have taken to explain and treat psychological disorders. We considered today's most commonly used classification scheme, categorized in *DSM-IV-TR*, and examined some of the more prevalent forms of psychological disorders. To gain a perspective on the topic of psychological disorders, we discussed the surprisingly broad incidence of psychological disorders in U.S. society and the cultural nature of such disorders.

Turn back to the prologue, in which the case of Chris Coles was described. Using the knowledge you've gained about psychological disorders, consider the following questions.

1. Coles was diagnosed as suffering from schizophrenia. What elements of his behavior seem to fit the description of schizophrenia provided by *DSM-IV-TR*?

2. From which type of schizophrenia (i.e., disorganized, paranoid, catatonic, undifferentiated, or residual) do you think Coles was probably suffering? Why?

3. Which perspective (i.e., medical, psychoanalytic, behavioral, cognitive, humanistic, or sociocultural) provides the most useful explanation for Coles's case, in your opinion? Why?

4. What advantages might there be in using multiple perspectives to address Coles's case?

CHAPTER 16

Treatment of Psychological Disorders

Key Concepts for Chapter 16

What are the goals of psychologically and biologically based treatment approaches?
● What are the psychodynamic, behavioral, and cognitive approaches to treatment?

Psychotherapy: Psychodynamic, Behavioral, and Cognitive Approaches to Treatment

Psychodynamic Approaches to Therapy

Behavioral Approaches to Therapy

Cognitive Approaches to Therapy

What are the humanistic approaches to treatment? ● What is interpersonal therapy? ● How does group therapy differ from individual types of therapy? ● How effective is psychotherapy, and which kind of psychotherapy works best in a given situation?

Psychotherapy: Humanistic, Interpersonal, and Group Approaches to Treatment

Humanistic Therapy

Interpersonal Therapy

Group Therapy, Family Therapy, and Self-Help Groups

Evaluating Psychotherapy: Does Therapy Work?

Exploring Diversity: Racial and Ethnic Factors in Treatment: Should Therapists Be Color-Blind?

How are drug, electroconvulsive, and psychosurgical techniques used today in the treatment of psychological disorders?

Biomedical Therapy: Biological Approaches to Treatment

Drug Therapy

Electroconvulsive Therapy (ECT)

Psychosurgery

Biomedical Therapies in Perspective

Applying Psychology in the 21st Century: Prescription: Stay Involved with Work and Family

Community Psychology: Focus on Prevention

Becoming an Informed Consumer of Psychology: Choosing the Right Therapist

Next thing I know I am waking up. I am back on an upper floor of Massachusetts General Hospital, in the unit where I slept last night. I feel light-headed, groggy, the way you do when anesthesia is wearing off and you are floating in the abyss between sleep and wakefulness. I vaguely recall the anesthesiologist having had me count to ten, but I never got beyond three or four. I remember Charlie Welch and his ECT [electroconvulsive Therapy] team, but am not sure I got the treatment. One clue is a slight headache, which they told me ECT might cause but which could have come from the anesthesia. Another is the goo on my hair, where they must have attached the electrodes.

There is one more sign that I did in fact have my first session of seizure therapy: I feel good—I feel alive. (From *Shock: The Healing Power of Electroconvulsive Therapy* by Kitty Dukakis and Larry Tye, copyright © 2006 by Kitty Dukakis & Larry Tye. Used by permission of Avery Publishing, an imprint of Penguin Group (USA) Inc.)

Looking Ahead

The procedure that has brought new life to former first lady of Massachusetts Kitty Dukakis is just one of many that, along with other new treatment approaches, have revolutionized the treatment of psychological disorders. Although treatment can take dozens of different approaches, ranging from one-meeting informal counseling sessions to long-term drug therapy to more invasive procedures such as that experienced by Dukakis, all the approaches have a common objective: the relief of psychological disorders, with the ultimate aim of enabling individuals to achieve richer, more meaningful, and more fulfilling lives.

Despite their diversity, approaches to treating psychological disorders fall into two main categories: psychologically based and biologically based therapies. Psychologically based therapy, or **psychotherapy**, is treatment in which a trained professional—a therapist—uses psychological techniques to help someone overcome psychological difficulties and disorders, resolve problems in living, or bring about personal growth. In psychotherapy, the goal is to produce psychological change in a person (called a "client" or "patient") through discussions and interactions with the therapist. In contrast, **biomedical therapy** relies on drugs and medical procedures to improve psychological functioning.

As we describe the various approaches to therapy, keep in mind that although the distinctions may seem clear-cut, the classifications and procedures overlap a good deal. In fact, many therapists today use a variety of methods with an individual patient, taking an *eclectic approach to therapy*. Assuming that both psychological and biological processes often produce psychological disorders, eclectic therapists may draw from several perspectives simultaneously to address both the psychological and the biological aspects of a person's problems (Goin, 2005; Berman, Jobes, & Silverman, 2006).

Psychotherapy: Treatment in which a trained professional—a therapist—uses psychological techniques to help a person overcome psychological difficulties and disorders, resolve problems in living, or bring about personal growth.

Biomedical therapy: Therapy that relies on drugs and other medical procedures to improve psychological functioning.

Psychotherapy: Psychodynamic, Behavioral, and Cognitive Approaches to Treatment

Therapists use some 400 different varieties of psychotherapy, approaches to therapy that focus on psychological factors. Although diverse in many respects, all psychological approaches see treatment as a way of solving psychological problems by modifying people's behavior and helping them gain a better understanding of themselves and their past, present, and future.

In light of the variety of psychological approaches, it is not surprising that the people who provide therapy vary considerably in educational background and training (see Figure 1). Many have doctoral degrees in psychology (that is, they have attended graduate school, learned clinical and research techniques, and held an internship). But therapy is also provided by people in fields allied with psychology, such as psychiatry and social work.

Regardless of their specific training, almost all psychotherapists employ one of four major approaches to therapy: psychodynamic, behavioral, cognitive, and humanistic treatments. These approaches are based on the models of personality and psychological disorders developed by psychologists. Here we'll consider the psychodynamic, behavioral, and cognitive approaches in turn. In the next module, we'll explore the humanistic approach, as well as interpersonal psychotherapy and group therapy, and evaluate the effectiveness of psychotherapy.

Key Concepts

What are the goals of psychologically and biologically based treatment approaches?

What are the psychodynamic, behavioral, and cognitive approaches to treatment?

Getting Help from the Right Person

Clinical Psychologists

Psychologists with a Ph.D. or Psy.D. who have also completed a postgraduate internship. They specialize in assessment and treatment of psychological difficulties.

Counseling Psychologists

Psychologists with a Ph.D. or Ed.D. who typically treat day-to-day adjustment problems, often in a university mental health clinic.

Psychiatrists

M.D.s with postgraduate training in abnormal behavior. Because they can prescribe medication, they often treat the most severe disorders.

Psychoanalysts

Either M.D.s or psychologists who specialize in psychoanalysis, the treatment technique first developed by Freud.

Licensed Professional Counselors or Clinical Mental Health Counselors

Professionals with a master's degree who provide therapy to individuals, couples, and families and who hold a national or state certification.

Clinical or Psychiatric Social Workers

Professionals with a master's degree and specialized training who may provide therapy, usually regarding common family and personal problems.

FIGURE 1 A variety of professionals provide therapy and counseling. Each could be expected to give helpful advice and direction. However, the nature of the problem a person is experiencing may make one or another therapy more appropriate. For example, a person who is suffering from a severe disturbance and who has lost touch with reality will typically require some sort of biologically based drug therapy. In that case, a psychiatrist—who is a physician—would be the professional of choice. In contrast, those suffering from milder disorders, such as difficulty adjusting to the death of a family member, have a broader choice that might include any of the professionals listed in the figure. The decision can be made easier by initial consultations with professionals in mental health facilities in communities, colleges, and health organizations, who can provide guidance in selecting an appropriate therapist.

"Look, call it denial if you like, but I think what goes on in my personal life id none of my own damn business."

Psychodynamic Approaches to Therapy

Psychodynamic therapy seeks to bring unresolved past conflicts and unacceptable impulses from the unconscious into the conscious, where patients may deal with the problems more effectively. Psychodynamic approaches are based on Freud's psychoanalytic approach to personality, which holds that individuals employ *defense mechanisms*, psychological strategies to protect themselves from unacceptable unconscious impulses.

The most common defense mechanism is repression, which pushes threatening conflicts and impulses back into the unconscious. However, since unacceptable conflicts and impulses can never be completely buried, some of the anxiety associated with them can produce abnormal behavior in the form of what Freud called *neurotic symptoms*.

How do we rid ourselves of the anxiety produced by unconscious, unwanted impulses and drives? To Freud, the answer was to confront the conflicts and impulses by bringing them out of the unconscious part of the mind and into the conscious part. Freud assumed that this technique would reduce anxiety stemming from past conflicts and that the patient could then participate in his or her daily life more effectively.

A psychodynamic therapist, then, faces the challenge of finding a way to assist patients' attempts to explore and understand the unconscious. The technique that has evolved has a number of components, but basically it consists of guiding patients to consider and discuss their past experiences, in explicit detail, from the time of their first memories. This process assumes that patients will eventually stumble upon long-hidden crises, traumas, and conflicts that are producing anxiety in their adult lives. They will then be able to "work through"—understand and rectify—those difficulties.

PSYCHOANALYSIS: FREUD'S THERAPY

Classic Freudian psychodynamic therapy, called psychoanalysis, tends to be a lengthy and expensive affair. **Psychoanalysis** is Freudian psychotherapy in which the goal is to release hidden unconscious thoughts and feelings in order to reduce their power in controlling behavior.

In psychoanalysis, patients may meet with a therapist with considerable frequency, sometimes as much as 50 minutes a day, four to five days a week, for several years. In their sessions, they often use a technique developed by Freud called *free association*. Psychoanalysts using this technique tell patients to say aloud whatever comes to mind, regardless of its apparent irrelevance or senselessness, and the analysts attempt to recognize and label the connections between what a patient says and the patient's unconscious. Therapists also use *dream interpretation*, examining dreams to find clues to unconscious conflicts and problems. Moving beyond the surface description of a dream (called the *manifest content*), therapists seek its underlying meaning (the *latent content*), thereby revealing the true unconscious meaning of the dream (Galatzer-Levy & Cohler, 1997; Auld, Hyman, & Rudzinski, 2005; Bodin, 2006).

The processes of free association and dream interpretation do not always move forward easily. The same unconscious forces that initially produced repression may keep past difficulties out of the conscious mind, producing resistance. *Resistance* is an inability or unwillingness to discuss or reveal particular memories, thoughts, or motivations. Patients can express resistance in many ways. For instance, patients may be discussing a childhood memory and suddenly forget what they were saying, or they may change the subject completely. It is the therapist's job to pick up instances of resistance and interpret their meaning, as well as to ensure that patients return to the subject—which is likely to hold difficult or painful memories for the patients.

Psychodynamic therapy: Therapy that seeks to bring unresolved past conflicts and unacceptable impulses from the unconscious into the conscious, where patients may deal with the problems more effectively.

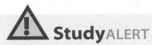

Study ALERT

To better understand how psychodynamic therapy works, review Freud's psychoanalytic theory, discussed in the chapter on personality.

Psychoanalysis: Freudian psychotherapy in which the goal is to release hidden unconscious thoughts and feelings in order to reduce their power in controlling behavior.

Because of the close, almost intimate interaction between patient and psychoanalyst, the relationship between the two often becomes emotionally charged and takes on a complexity unlike most other relationships. Patients may eventually think of the analyst as a symbol of a significant other in their past, perhaps a parent or a lover, and apply some of their feelings for that person to the analyst—a phenomenon known as transference. **Transference** is the transfer to a psychoanalyst feelings of love or anger that had been originally directed to a patient's parents or other authority figures (Van Beekum, 2005; Evans, 2007).

A therapist can use transference to help a patient re-create past relationships that were psychologically difficult. For instance, if a patient undergoing transference views her therapist as a symbol of her father—with whom she had a difficult relationship—the patient and therapist may "redo" an earlier interaction, this time including more positive aspects. Through this process, the patient may resolve conflicts regarding her real father—something that is beginning to happen in the following therapy session:

The close and intense relationship between therapist and patient may become highly complex.

> Sandy: My father . . . never took any interest in any of us. . . . It was my mother—rest her soul—who loved us, not our father. He worked her to death. Lord, I miss her. . . . I must sound angry at my father. Don't you think I have a right to be angry?
>
> Therapist: Do you think you have a right to be angry?
>
> Sandy: Of course, I do! Why are you questioning me? You don't believe me, do you?
>
> Therapist: You want me to believe you.
>
> Sandy: I don't care whether you believe me or not. . . . I know what you're thinking—you think I'm crazy—you must be laughing at me—I'll probably be a case in your next book! You're just sitting there—smirking—making me feel like a bad person—thinking I'm wrong for being mad, that I have no right to be mad.
>
> Therapist: Just like your father.
>
> Sandy: Yes, you're just like my father.—Oh my God! Just now—I—I— thought I was talking to him. (Sue, Sue, & Sue, 1990, pp. 514–515)

Transference: The transfer of feelings to a psychoanalyst of love or anger that had been originally directed to a patient's parents or other authority figures.

CONTEMPORARY PSYCHODYNAMIC APPROACHES

Few people have the time, money, or patience to participate in years of traditional psychoanalysis. Moreover, no conclusive evidence shows that psychoanalysis, as originally conceived by Freud in the 19th century, works better than other, more recent forms of psychodynamic therapy.

Today, psychodynamic therapy tends to be of shorter duration, usually lasting no longer than three months or 20 sessions. The therapist takes a more active role than Freud would have liked, controlling the course of therapy and prodding and advising the patient with considerable directness. Finally, the therapist puts less emphasis on a patient's past history and childhood, concentrating instead on an individual's current relationships and specific complaints (Goode, 2003b; Charman, 2004; Wolitzky, 2006).

EVALUATING PSYCHODYNAMIC THERAPY

Even with its current modifications, psychodynamic therapy has its critics. In its longer versions, it can be time-consuming and expensive, especially in comparison with other forms of psychotherapy, such as behavioral and cognitive approaches. Furthermore, less articulate patients may not do as well as more verbal ones do.

Ultimately, the most important concern about psychodynamic treatment is whether it actually works, and there is no simple answer to this question. Psychodynamic treatment techniques have been controversial

"And when did you first realize you weren't like other precipitation?"

since Freud introduced them. Part of the problem is the difficulty in establishing whether patients have improved after psychodynamic therapy. Determining effectiveness depends on reports from the therapist or the patients themselves, reports that are obviously open to bias and subjective interpretation.

Furthermore, critics have questioned the entire theoretical basis of psychodynamic theory, maintaining that constructs such as the unconscious have not been scientifically confirmed. Despite the criticism, though, the psychodynamic treatment approach has remained viable. For some people, it provides solutions to difficult psychological issues, provides effective treatment for psychological disturbance, and also permits the potential development of an unusual degree of insight into one's life (Clay, 2000; Ablon & Jones, 2005; Bond, 2006).

Behavioral Approaches to Therapy

Perhaps, when you were a child, your parents rewarded you with an ice cream cone when you were especially good . . . or sent you to your room if you misbehaved. Sound principles back up such a child-rearing strategy: Good behavior is maintained by reinforcement, and unwanted behavior can be eliminated by punishment.

These principles represent the basic underpinnings of **behavioral treatment approaches**. Building on the basic processes of learning, behavioral treatment approaches make this fundamental assumption: Both abnormal behavior and normal behavior are *learned*. People who act abnormally either have failed to learn the skills they need to cope with the problems of everyday living or have acquired faulty skills and patterns that are being maintained through some form of reinforcement. To modify abnormal behavior, then, proponents of behavioral approaches propose that people must learn new behavior to replace the faulty skills they have developed and unlearn their maladaptive behavior patterns (Bergin & Garfield, 1994; Agras & Berkowitz, 1996; Krijn, Emmelkamp, Olafsson, & Biemond, 2004; Norton & Price, 2007).

Behavioral psychologists do not need to delve into people's pasts or their psyches. Rather than viewing abnormal behavior as a symptom of an underlying problem, they consider the abnormal behavior as the problem in need of modification. The goal of therapy is to change people's behavior to allow them to function more effectively. In this view, then, there is no problem other than the maladaptive behavior itself, and if you can change that behavior, treatment is successful.

CLASSICAL CONDITIONING TREATMENTS

Suppose you bite into your favorite candy bar and find that not only is it infested with ants but you've also swallowed a bunch of them. You immediately become sick to your stomach and throw up. Your long-term reaction? You never eat that kind of candy bar again, and it may be months before you eat any type of candy. You have learned, through the basic process of classical conditioning, to avoid candy so that you will not get sick and throw up.

Aversive Conditioning. This simple example illustrates how a person can be classically conditioned to modify behavior. Behavior therapists use this principle when they employ **aversive conditioning**, a form of therapy that reduces the frequency of undesired behavior by pairing an aversive, unpleasant stimulus with undesired behavior. For example, behavior therapists might use aversive conditioning by pairing alcohol with a drug that causes severe nausea and vomiting. After the two have been

Behavioral treatment approaches: Treatment approaches that build on the basic processes of learning, such as reinforcement and extinction, and assume that normal and abnormal behavior are both learned.

Aversive conditioning: A form of therapy that reduces the frequency of undesired behavior by pairing an aversive, unpleasant stimulus with undesired behavior.

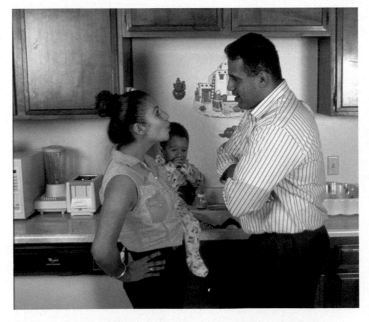

Behavioral approaches to treatment would seek to modify the behavior of this couple, rather than focusing on the underlying causes of the behavior.

paired a few times, the person associates the alcohol alone with vomiting and finds alcohol less appealing.

Although aversion therapy works reasonably well in inhibiting substance-abuse problems such as alcoholism and certain kinds of sexual disorders, critics question its long-term effectiveness. Also, important ethical concerns surround aversion techniques that employ such potent stimuli as electric shock, which therapists use only in the most extreme cases, such as patient self-mutilation. Clearly, though, aversion therapy offers an important procedure for eliminating maladaptive responses for some period of time—a respite that provides, even if only temporarily, an opportunity to encourage more adaptive behavior patterns (Bordnick, Elkins, Orr, Walters, & Thyer, 2004; Delgado, Labouliere, & Phelps, 2006).

Systematic Desensitization. Another treatment to grow out of the classical conditioning is systematic desensitization. In **systematic desensitization**, gradual exposure to an anxiety-producing stimulus is paired with relaxation to extinguish the response of anxiety (McGlynn, Smitherman, & Gothard, 2004; Pagoto et al., 2006; Choy, Fyer, & Lipsitz, 2007).

> Systematic desensitization: A behavioral technique in which gradual exposure to an anxiety-producing stimulus is paired with relaxation to extinguish the response of anxiety.

Suppose, for instance, you were extremely afraid of flying. The very thought of being in an airplane would make you begin to sweat and shake, and you couldn't get yourself near enough to an airport to know how you'd react if you actually had to fly somewhere. Using systematic desensitization to treat your problem, you would first be trained in relaxation techniques by a behavior therapist, learning to relax your body fully—a highly pleasant state, as you might imagine (see Figure 2).

The next step would involve constructing a *hierarchy of fears*—a list, in order of increasing severity, of the things you associate with your fears. For instance, your hierarchy might resemble this one:

1. Watching a plane fly overhead.
2. Going to an airport.
3. Buying a ticket.
4. Stepping into the plane.
5. Seeing the plane door close.
6. Having the plane taxi down the runway.
7. Taking off.
8. Being in the air.

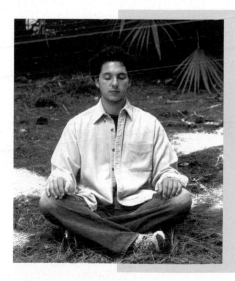

Step 1. Pick a focus word or short phrase that's firmly rooted in your personal belief system. For example, a nonreligious individual might choose a neutral word like *one* or *peace* or *love*. A Christian person desiring to use a prayer could pick the opening words of Psalm 23. *The Lord is my shepherd*; a Jewish person could choose *Shalom*.

Step 2. Sit quietly in a comfortable position.

Step 3. Close your eyes.

Step 4. Relax your muscles.

Step 5. Breathe slowly and naturally, repeating your focus word or phrase silently as you exhale.

Step 6. Throughout, assume a passive attitude. Don't worry about how well you're doing. When other thoughts come to mind, simply say to yourself, "Oh, well," and gently return to the repetition.

Step 7. Continue for 10 to 20 minutes. You may open your eyes to check the time, but do not use an alarm. When you finish, sit quietly for a minute or so, at first with your eyes closed and later with your eyes open. Then do not stand for one or two minutes.

Step 8. Practice the technique once or twice a day.

FIGURE 2 Following these basic steps will help you achieve a sense of calmness by employing the relaxation response.

StudyALERT

To help remember the concept of hierarchy of fears, think of something that you are afraid of and construct your own hierarchy of fears.

Exposure: A behavioral treatment for anxiety in which people are confronted, either suddenly or gradually, with a stimulus that they fear.

Once you had developed this hierarchy and had learned relaxation techniques, you would learn to associate the two sets of responses. To do this, your therapist might ask you to put yourself into a relaxed state and then imagine yourself in the first situation identified in your hierarchy. Once you could consider that first step while remaining relaxed, you would move on to the next situation, eventually moving up the hierarchy in gradual stages until you could imagine yourself being in the air without experiencing anxiety. Ultimately, you would be asked to make a visit to an airport and later to take a flight.

Exposure Treatments. Although systematic desensitization has proven to be a successful treatment, today it is often replaced with a less complicated form of therapy called exposure. **Exposure** is a behavioral treatment for anxiety in which people are confronted, either suddenly or gradually, with a stimulus that they fear. However, unlike systematic desensitization, relaxation training is omitted. Exposure allows the maladaptive response of anxiety or avoidance to extinguish, and research shows that this approach is generally as effective as systematic desensitization (Tyron, 2005; Havermans et al., 2007; Hoffmann, 2007).

In most cases, therapists use *graded exposure* in which patients are exposed to a feared stimulus in gradual steps. For example, a patient who is afraid of dogs might first view a video of dogs. Gradually the exposure escalates to seeing a live, leashed dog across the room, and then actually petting and touching the dog (Berle, 2007; Means & Edinger, 2007).

Exposure has proved to be an effective treatment for a number of problems, including phobias, anxiety disorders, and even impotence and fear of sexual contact. Through this technique, people can learn to enjoy the things they once feared (Tryon, 2005; Choy, Fyer, & Lipsitz, 2007; Franklin, March, & Garcia, 2007).

OPERANT CONDITIONING TECHNIQUES

Some behavioral approaches make use of the operant conditioning principles that we discussed earlier in the book when considering learning. These approaches are based on the notion that we should reward people for carrying out desirable behavior and extinguish undesirable behavior by either ignoring it or punishing it.

One example of the systematic application of operant conditioning principles is the *token system*, which rewards a person for desired behavior with a token such as a poker chip or some kind of play money. Although it is most frequently employed in institutional settings for individuals with relatively serious problems, and sometimes with children as a classroom management technique, the system resembles what parents do when they give children money for being well behaved—money that the children can later exchange for something they want. The desired behavior may range from simple things such as keeping one's room neat to personal grooming and interacting with other people. In institutions, patients can exchange tokens for some object or activity, such as snacks, new clothes, or, in extreme cases, being able to sleep in one's own bed rather than in a sleeping bag on the floor.

Contingency contracting, a variant of the token system, has proved quite effective in producing behavior modification. In *contingency contracting*, the therapist and client (or teacher and student, or parent and child) draw up a written agreement. The contract states a series of behavioral goals the client hopes to achieve. It also specifies the positive consequences for the client if the client reaches goals—usually an explicit reward such as money or additional privileges. Contracts frequently state negative consequences if the client does not meet the goals. For example, clients who are trying to quit smoking might write out a check to a cause they have no interest in supporting (for instance, the National Rifle Association if they are strong supporters of gun control). If the client smokes on a given day, the therapist will mail the check.

Behavior therapists also use *observational learning*, the process in which the behavior of other people is modeled, to systematically teach people new skills and ways of handling their fears and anxieties. For example, modeling helps when therapists are teaching basic social skills such as maintaining eye contact during conversation and acting assertively. Similarly, children with dog phobias have been able to overcome their fears by watching another child—called the "Fearless Peer"—repeatedly walk up to a dog, touch it, pet it, and finally play with it. Modeling, then, can play an effective role in resolving some kinds of behavior difficulties, especially if the model receives a reward for his or her behavior (Bandura, Grusec, & Menlove, 1967; Greer, Dudek-Singer, Gautreaux, 2006).

A "Fearless Peer" who models appropriate and effective behavior can help children overcome their fears.

DIALECTICAL BEHAVIOR THERAPY

In **dialectical behavior therapy**, the focus is on getting people to accept who they are, regardless of whether it matches their ideal. Even if their childhood has been dysfunctional or they have ruined relationships with others, that's in the past. What matters is who they wish to become (Manning, 2005; Lynch et al., 2007; Wagner, Rizvi, & Hamed, 2007).

Like treatment approaches based on the principles of classical and operant conditioning, dialectical behavior therapy is an outgrowth of behavioral approaches, but it also includes components of other perspectives. Therapists using dialectical behavior therapy seek to have patients realize that they basically have two choices: Either they remain unhappy, or they change. Once patients agree that they wish to change, it is up to them to modify their behavior. Patients are taught that even if they experience unhappiness, or anger, or any other negative emotion, it doesn't need to rule their behavior. It's their behavior that counts—not their inner life.

Dialectical behavior therapy teaches behavioral skills that help people behave more effectively and keep their emotions in check. Although it is a relatively new form of therapy, increasing evidence supports its effectiveness, particularly with certain person ality disorders (van den Bosch et al., 2005; Clarkin et al., 2007; Swales & Heard, 2007).

Dialectical behavior therapy: A form of treatment in which the focus is on getting people to accept who they are, regardless of whether it matches their ideal.

EVALUATING BEHAVIOR THERAPY

Behavior therapy works especially well for eliminating anxiety disorders, treating phobias and compulsions, establishing control over impulses, and learning complex social skills to replace maladaptive behavior. More than any of the other therapeutic techniques, it provides methods that nonprofessionals can use to change their own behavior. Moreover, it is efficient, because it focuses on solving carefully defined problems (Richard & Lauterbach, 2006; Barlow, 2007).

Critics of behavior therapy believe that because it emphasizes changing external behavior, people do not necessarily gain insight into thoughts and expectations that may be fostering their maladaptive behavior. On the other hand, neuroscientific evidence shows that behavioral treatments can produce actual changes in brain functioning, suggesting that behavioral treatments can produce changes beyond external behavior.

For example, one experiment looked at the neurological reactions of patients with borderline personality disorder who participated in a 12-week dialectical behavioral therapy program. Compared with a control group comprised of people who did not have the disorder, the patients showed significant changes in their reactions to highly arousing emotion-evoking stimuli. Following therapy, the patients' neurological functioning was more similar to those without the disorder than it was prior to therapy (see Figure 3).

FIGURE 3 This figure highlights areas of the brain that show a reduction in response to highly emotionally arousing pictures after behavioral therapy in patients with borderline personality disorder. The figure on the left shows areas of increased activity in those with borderline personality disorder as compared to healthy controls before treatment; the figure on the right shows this same comparison after treatment. The results suggests that the brains of those with borderline personality disorder react more similarly to healthy participants following behavioral therapy. (Source: Schnell & Herpertz, 2007, Figure 3.)

Cognitive treatment approaches: Treatment approaches that teach people to think in more adaptive ways by changing their dysfunctional cognitions about the world and themselves.

Cognitive-behavioral approach: A treatment approach that incorporates basic principles of learning to change the way people think.

Rational-emotive behavior therapy: A form of therapy that attempts to restructure a person's belief system into a more realistic, rational, and logical set of views by challenging dysfunctional beliefs that maintain irrational behavior.

Cognitive Approaches to Therapy

If you assumed that illogical thoughts and beliefs lie at the heart of psychological disorders, wouldn't the most direct treatment route be to teach people new, more adaptive modes of thinking? The answer is yes, according to psychologists who take a cognitive approach to treatment.

Cognitive treatment approaches teach people to think in more adaptive ways by changing their dysfunctional cognitions about the world and themselves. Unlike behavior therapists, who focus on modifying external behavior, cognitive therapists attempt to change the way people think as well as their behavior. Because they often use basic principles of learning, the methods they employ are sometimes referred to as the **cognitive-behavioral approach** (Beck & Rector, 2005; Butler et al., 2006; Friedberg, 2006).

Although cognitive treatment approaches take many forms, they all share the assumption that anxiety, depression, and negative emotions develop from maladaptive thinking. Accordingly, cognitive treatments seek to change the thought patterns that lead to getting "stuck" in dysfunctional ways of thinking. Therapists systematically teach clients to challenge their assumptions and adopt new approaches to old problems.

Cognitive therapy is relatively short-term, usually lasting a maximum of 20 sessions. Therapy tends to be highly structured and focused on concrete problems. Therapists often begin by teaching the theory behind the approach and then continue to take an active role throughout the course of therapy, acting as a combination of teacher, coach, and partner.

One good example of cognitive treatment, **rational-emotive behavior therapy**, attempts to restructure a person's belief system into a more realistic, rational, and logical set of views. According to psychologist Albert Ellis (2002, 2004), many people lead unhappy lives and suffer from psychological disorders because they harbor irrational, unrealistic ideas such as these:

- We need the love or approval of virtually every significant other person for everything we do.
- We should be thoroughly competent, adequate, and successful in all possible respects in order to consider ourselves worthwhile.
- It is horrible when things don't turn out the way we want them to.

FIGURE 4 In the A-B-C model of rational-emotive behavior therapy, negative activating conditions (A) lead to the activation of an irrational belief system (B), which leads to emotional consequences (C). Those emotional consequences then feed back and support the belief system. At what steps in the model could change occur as a result of rational-emotive behavior therapy?

Such irrational beliefs trigger negative emotions, which in turn support the irrational beliefs, leading to a self-defeating cycle. Ellis calls it the A-B-C model, in which negative activating conditions (A) lead to the activation of an irrational belief system (B), which in turn leads to emotional consequences (C). For example, if a person experiences the breakup of a close relationship (A) and holds the irrational belief (B) that "I'll never be loved again," this triggers negative emotions (C) that in turn feed back into support of the irrational belief (see Figure 4).

Rational-emotive behavior therapy aims to help clients eliminate maladaptive thoughts and beliefs and adopt more effective thinking. To accomplish this goal, therapists take an active, directive role during therapy, openly challenging patterns of thought that appear to be dysfunctional. Consider this example:

> Martha: The basic problem is that I'm worried about my family. I'm worried about money. And I never seem to be able to relax.
>
> Therapist: Why are you worried about your family? . . .What's to be concerned about? They have certain demands which you don't want to adhere to.
>
> Martha: I was brought up to think that I mustn't be selfish.
>
> Therapist: Oh, we'll have to knock that out of your head!
>
> Martha: My mother feels that I shouldn't have left home—that my place is with them. There are nagging doubts about what I should—
>
> Therapist: Why are there doubts? Why should you?
>
> Martha: I think it's a feeling I was brought up with that you always have to give of yourself. If you think of yourself, you're wrong.
>
> Therapist: That's a belief. Why do you have to keep believing that—at your age? You believed a lot of superstitions when you were younger. Why do you have to retain them? Your parents indoctrinated you with this nonsense, because that's their belief. . . . Who needs that philosophy? All it's gotten you, so far, is guilt. (Ellis, 1974, pp. 223–286)

By poking holes in Martha's reasoning, the therapist is attempting to help her adopt a more realistic view of herself and her circumstances (Dryden, 1999; Ellis, 2002).

Another influential form of therapy that builds on a cognitive perspective is that of Aaron Beck (Beck, 1995, 2004). Like rational-emotive behavior therapy, Beck's cognitive therapy aims to change people's illogical thoughts about themselves and the world.

However, cognitive therapy is considerably less confrontational and challenging than rational-emotive behavior therapy. Instead of the therapist actively arguing with clients about their dysfunctional cognitions, cognitive therapists more often play the role of teacher. Therapists urge clients to obtain information on their own that will lead them to discard their inaccurate thinking through a process of cognitive appraisal. In *cognitive appraisal*, clients are asked to evaluate situations, themselves, and others in terms of their memories, values, beliefs, thoughts, and expectations. During the course of treatment, therapists help clients discover ways of thinking more appropriately about themselves and others (Rosen, 2000; Beck, Freeman, & Davis, 2004; Moorey, 2007).

EVALUATING COGNITIVE APPROACHES TO THERAPY

Cognitive approaches to therapy have proved successful in dealing with a broad range of disorders, including anxiety disorders, depression, substance abuse, and eating disorders. Furthermore, the willingness of cognitive therapists to incorporate additional treatment approaches (e.g., combining cognitive and behavioral techniques in cognitive behavioral therapy) has made this approach a particularly effective form of treatment (McMullin, 2000; Mitte, 2005; Ishikawa et al., 2007).

At the same time, critics have pointed out that the focus on helping people to think more rationally ignores the fact that life is, in reality, sometimes irrational. Changing one's assumptions to make them more reasonable and logical thus may not always be helpful—even assuming it is possible to bring about true cognitive change. Still, the success of cognitive approaches has made it one of the most frequently employed therapies (Leahy, 2003; Beck, 2005).

RECAP/EVALUATE/RETHINK

RECAP

What are the goals of psychologically and biologically based treatment approaches?

- Psychotherapy (psychologically based therapy) and bio-medical therapy (biologically based therapy) share the goal of resolving psychological problems by modifying people's thoughts, feelings, expectations, evaluations, and ultimately behavior. (p. 550)

What are the basic kinds of psychotherapies?

- Psychoanalytic approaches seek to bring unresolved past conflicts and unacceptable impulses from the unconscious into the conscious, where patients may deal with the problems more effectively. To do this, therapists use techniques such as free association and dream interpretation. (p. 552)

- Behavioral approaches to treatment view abnormal behavior as the problem, rather than viewing that behavior as a symptom of some underlying cause. To bring about a "cure," this view suggests that the outward behavior must be changed by using methods such as aversive conditioning, systematic desensitization, observational learning, token systems, contingency contracting, and dialectical behavior therapy. (p. 554)

- Cognitive approaches to treatment consider the goal of therapy to be to help a person restructure his or her faulty belief system into a more realistic, rational, and logical view of the world. Two examples of cognitive treatments are the rational-emotive behavior therapy and cognitive therapy. (p. 558)

EVALUATE

1. Match the following mental health practitioners with the appropriate description.
   1. Psychiatrist
   2. Clinical psychologist
   3. Counseling psychologist
   4. Psychoanalyst
   a. Ph.D. specializing in the treatment of psychological disorders
   b. Professional specializing in Freudian therapy techniques
   c. M.D. trained in abnormal behavior
   d. Ph.D. specializing in the adjustment of day-to-day problems

2. According to Freud, people use _____ _____ as a means of preventing unwanted impulses from intruding on conscious thought.

3. In dream interpretation, a psychoanalyst must learn to distinguish between the _____ content of a dream, which is what appears on the surface, and the _____ content, its underlying meaning.

4. Which of the following treatments deals with phobias by gradual exposure to the item producing the fear?
   a. Systematic desensitization
   b. Partial reinforcement
   c. Behavioral self-management
   d. Aversion therapy

RETHINK

1. In what ways are psychoanalysis and cognitive therapy similar, and how do they differ?

2. *From the perspective of a child-care provider:* How might you use systematic desensitization to help children overcome their fears?

Answers to Evaluate Questions

1. 1-c, 2-a, 3-d, 4-b; 2. defense mechanisms; 3. manifest, latent; 4. a

KEY TERMS

psychotherapy p. 550
biomedical therapy p. 550
psychodynamic therapy p. 552
psychoanalysis p. 552
transference p. 553

behavioral treatment
   approaches p. 554
aversive conditioning p. 554
systematic desensitization
   p. 555

exposure p. 556
dialectical behavior therapy
   p. 557
cognitive treatment
   approaches p. 558

cognitive-behavioral
   approach p. 558
rational-emotive behavior
   therapy p. 558

Psychotherapy: Humanistic, Interpersonal, and Group Approaches to Treatment

Humanistic Therapy

As you know from your own experience, a student cannot master the material covered in a course without some hard work, no matter how good the teacher and the textbook are. *You must* take the time to study, memorize the vocabulary, and learn the concepts. Nobody else can do it for you. If you choose to put in the effort, you'll succeed; if you don't, you'll fail. The responsibility is primarily yours.

Humanistic therapy draws on this philosophical perspective of self-responsibility in developing treatment techniques. The many different types of therapy that fit into this category have a similar rationale: We have control of our own behavior, we can make choices about the kinds of lives we want to live, and it is up to us to solve the difficulties we encounter in our daily lives.

Instead of acting in the more directive manner of some psychodynamic and behavioral approaches, humanistic therapists view themselves as guides or facilitators. Therapists using humanistic techniques seek to help people understand themselves and find ways to come closer to the ideal they hold for themselves. In this view, psychological disorders result from the inability to find meaning in life and from feelings of loneliness and a lack of connection to others (Cain, 2002).

Humanistic approaches have produced many therapeutic techniques. Among the most important is person-centered therapy.

PERSON-CENTERED THERAPY

Consider the following therapy session excerpt:

> Alice: I was thinking about this business of standards. I somehow developed a sort of a knack, I guess, of—well—habit—of trying to make people feel at ease around me, or to make things go along smoothly. . . .
>
> Therapist: In other words, what you did was always in the direction of trying to keep things smooth and to make other people feel better and to smooth the situation.
>
> Alice: Yes. I think that's what it was. Now the reason why I did it probably was—I mean, not that I was a good little Samaritan going around making other people happy, but that was probably the role that felt easiest for me to play. . . .
>
> Therapist: You feel that for a long time you've been playing the role of kind of smoothing out the frictions or differences or what not. . . .
>
> Alice: M-hm.
>
> Therapist: Rather than having any opinion or reaction of your own in the situation. Is that it? (Rogers, 1951, pp. 152–153)

Key Concepts

What are the humanistic approaches to treatment?

What is interpersonal therapy?

How does group therapy differ from individual types of therapy?

How effective is psychotherapy, and which kind of psychotherapy works best in a given situation?

Humanistic therapy: Therapy in which the underlying rationale is that people have control of their behavior, can make choices about their lives, and are essentially responsible for solving their own problems.

Humanistic therapy focuses on self-responsibility.

The therapist does not interpret or answer the questions the client has raised. Instead, the therapist clarifies or reflects back what the client has said (e.g., "In other words, what you did. . . ."; "You feel that. . . ."; "Is that it?"). This therapeutic technique, known as *nondirective counseling*, is at the heart of person-centered therapy, which was first practiced by Carl Rogers in the mid-20th century (Rogers, 1951, 1980; Raskin & Rogers, 1989).

Person-centered therapy: Therapy in which the goal is to reach one's potential for self-actualization.

Person-centered therapy (also called *client-centered therapy*) aims to enable people to reach their potential for self-actualization. By providing a warm and accepting environment, therapists hope to motivate clients to air their problems and feelings. In turn, this enables clients to make realistic and constructive choices and decisions about the things that bother them in their current lives (Bozarth, Zimring, & Tausch, 2002; Kirschenbaum, 2004; Bohart, 2006).

Instead of directing the choices clients make, therapists provide what Rogers calls *unconditional positive regard*—expressing acceptance and understanding, regardless of the feelings and attitudes the client expresses. By doing this, therapists hope to create an atmosphere that enables clients to come to decisions that can improve their lives (Kirschenbaum & Jourdan, 2005; Vieira & Freire, 2006).

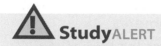 **Study**ALERT

To better remember the concept of unconditional positive regard, try offering it to a friend during a conversation by showing your support, acceptance, and understanding no matter what thought or attitude is being offered.

Furnishing unconditional positive regard does not mean that therapists must approve of everything their clients say or do. Rather, therapists need to communicate that they are caring, nonjudgmental, and *empathetic*—understanding of a client's emotional experiences (Fearing & Clark, 2000).

Person-centered therapy is rarely used today in its purest form. Contemporary approaches tend to be somewhat more directive, with therapists nudging clients toward insights rather than merely reflecting back their statements. However, therapists still view clients' insights as central to the therapeutic process.

EVALUATING HUMANISTIC APPROACHES TO THERAPY

The notion that psychological disorders result from restricted growth potential appeals philosophically to many people. Furthermore, when humanistic therapists acknowledge that the freedom we possess can lead to psychological difficulties, clients find an unusually supportive environment for therapy. In turn, this atmosphere can help clients discover solutions to difficult psychological problems.

However, humanistic treatments lack specificity, a problem that has troubled their critics. Humanistic approaches are not very precise and are probably the least scientifically and theoretically developed type of treatment. Moreover, this form of treatment works best for the same type of highly verbal client who profits most from psychoanalytic treatment.

Interpersonal Therapy

Interpersonal therapy (IPT): Short-term therapy that focuses on the context of current social relationships.

Interpersonal therapy (IPT) considers therapy in the context of social relationships. Although its roots stem from psychodynamic approaches, interpersonal therapy concentrates more on the here and now with the goal of improving a client's current relationships. It typically focuses on interpersonal issues such as conflicts with others, social skills issues, role transitions (such as divorce), or grief (Weissman, Markowitz, & Klerman, 2007).

Interpersonal therapy is more active and directive than traditional psychodynamic approaches, and sessions are more structured. The approach makes no assumptions about the underlying causes of psychological disorders, but focuses on the interpersonal context in which a disorder is developed and maintained. It also tends to be shorter than traditional psychodynamic approaches, typically lasting only 12 to 16 weeks. During those sessions, therapists make concrete suggestions on improving relations with others, offering recommendations and advice.

Because interpersonal therapy is short and structured, researchers have been able to demonstrate its effectiveness more readily than longer-term types of therapy. Evaluations of the approach have shown that interpersonal therapy is especially effective in dealing with depression, anxiety, addictions, and eating disorders (De Mello et al., 2005; Salsman, 2006; Grigoriadis & Ravitz, 2007).

Group Therapy, Family Therapy, and Self-Help Groups

In group therapy, people with psychological difficulties meet with a therapist to discuss their problems.

Although most treatment takes place between a single individual and a therapist, some forms of therapy involve groups of people seeking treatment. In **group therapy**, several unrelated people meet with a therapist to discuss some aspect of their psychological functioning.

People typically discuss with the group their problems, which often center on a common difficulty, such as alcoholism or a lack of social skills. The other members of the group provide emotional support and dispense advice on ways in which they have coped effectively with similar problems (Alonso, Alonso, & Piper, 2003; Scaturo, 2004; Rigby & Waite, 2007).

Groups vary greatly in terms of the particular model they employ; there are psychoanalytic groups, humanistic groups, and groups corresponding to the other therapeutic approaches. Furthermore, groups also differ in regard to the degree of guidance the therapist provides. In some, the therapist is quite directive, while in others, the members of the group set their own agenda and determine how the group will proceed (Beck & Lewis, 2000; Stockton, Morran, & Krieger, 2004).

Because in group therapy several people are treated simultaneously, it is a much more economical means of treatment than individual psychotherapy. On the other hand, critics argue that group settings lack the individual attention inherent in one-to-one therapy, and that especially shy and withdrawn individuals may not receive the attention they need in a group setting.

Group therapy: Therapy in which people meet in a group with a therapist to discuss problems.

Family therapy: An approach that focuses on the family and its dynamics.

FAMILY THERAPY

One specialized form of group therapy is family therapy. As the name implies, **family therapy** involves two or more family members, one (or more) of whose problems led to treatment. But rather than focusing simply on the members of the family who present the initial problem, family therapists consider the family as a unit, to which each member contributes. By meeting with the entire family simultaneously, family therapists try to understand how the family members interact with one another (Cooklin, 2000; Strong & Tomm, 2007).

Family therapists view the family as a "system," and assume that individuals in the family cannot improve without understanding the conflicts found in interactions among family members. Thus, the therapist expects each member to contribute to the resolution of the problem being addressed.

Many family therapists believe that family members fall into rigid roles or set patterns of behavior, with one person acting as the scapegoat, another as a bully, and so forth. In their view, that system of roles perpetuates family disturbances. One goal of this type of therapy, then, is to get the family members to adopt new, more constructive roles and patterns of behavior (Minuchin, 1999; Sprenkle & Moon, 1996; Sori, 2006).

"So, would anyone in the group care to respond to what Clifford has just shared with us?"

SELF-HELP THERAPY

In many cases, group therapy does not involve a professional therapist. Instead, people with similar problems get together to discuss their shared feelings and experiences. For example, people who have recently experienced the death of a spouse might meet in a *bereavement support group*, or college students may get together to discuss their adjustment to college.

One of the best-known self-help groups is Alcoholics Anonymous (AA), designed to help members deal with alcohol-related problems. AA prescribes 12 steps that alcoholics must pass through on their road to recovery, beginning with an admission that they are alcoholics and powerless over alcohol. AA provides more treatment for alcoholics than any other therapy, and it and other 12-step programs (such as Narcotics Anonymous) can be as successful in treating alcohol and other substance-abuse problems (Bogenschutz, Geppert, & George, 2006; Galanter, 2007).

Evaluating Psychotherapy: Does Therapy Work?

Your best friend, Ben, comes to you because he just hasn't been feeling right about things lately. He's upset because he and his girlfriend aren't getting along, but his difficulties go beyond that. He can't concentrate on his studies, has a lot of trouble getting to sleep, and—this is what really bothers him—has begun to think that people are ganging up on him, talking about him behind his back. It seems that no one really cares about or understands him or makes any effort to see why he's become so miserable.

Ben knows that he ought to get *some* kind of help, but he is not sure where to turn. He is fairly skeptical of psychologists, thinking that a lot of what they say is just mumbo-jumbo, but he's willing to put his doubts aside and try anything to feel better. He also knows there are many different types of therapy, and he doesn't have a clue about which would be best for him. He turns to you for advice, because he knows you are taking a psychology course. He asks, "Which kind of therapy works best?"

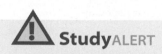

StudyALERT

Pay special attention to the discussion of (1) whether therapy is effective in general and (2) what specific types of therapy are effective, because it is a key issue for therapists.

IS THERAPY EFFECTIVE?

This question requires a complex response. In fact, identifying the single most appropriate form of treatment is a controversial, and still unresolved, task for psychologists specializing in psychological disorders. In fact, even before considering whether one form of therapy works better than another, we need to determine whether therapy in any form effectively alleviates psychological disturbances.

Until the 1950s, most people simply assumed that therapy was effective. But in 1952 psychologist Hans Eysenck published an influential study challenging that assumption. He claimed that people who received psychodynamic treatment and related therapies were no better off at the end of treatment than were people who were placed on a waiting list for treatment but never received it. Eysenck concluded that people would go into **spontaneous remission**, recovery without treatment, if they were simply left alone—certainly a cheaper and simpler process.

Although other psychologists quickly challenged Eysenck's conclusions, his review stimulated a continuing stream of better controlled, more carefully crafted studies on the effectiveness of psychotherapy, and today most psychologists agree: Therapy does work. Several comprehensive reviews indicate that therapy brings about greater improvement than does no treatment at all, with the rate of spontaneous remission being fairly low. In most cases, then, the symptoms of abnormal behavior do not go away by themselves if left untreated—although the issue continues to be hotly debated (Seligman, 1996; Westen, Novotny, & Thompson-Brenner, 2004; Lutz et al., 2006).

Spontaneous remission: Recovery without treatment.

WHICH KIND OF THERAPY WORKS BEST?

Although most psychologists feel confident that psychotherapeutic treatment *in general* is more effective than no treatment at all, the question of whether any specific form of treatment is superior to any other has not been answered definitively (Nathan, Stuart, & Dolan, 2000; Westen, Novotny, & Thompson-Brenner, 2004; Abboud, 2005).

For instance, one classic study comparing the effectiveness of various approaches found that although success rates vary somewhat by treatment form, most treatments show fairly equal success rates. As Figure 1 indicates, the rates ranged from about 70 to 85 percent greater success for treated compared with untreated individuals. Behavioral and cognitive approaches tended to be slightly more successful, but that result may have been due to differences in the severity of the cases treated (Smith, Glass, & Miller, 1980; Orwin & Condray, 1984).

Other research, relying on *meta-analysis*, in which data from a large number of studies are statistically combined, yields similar general conclusions. Furthermore, a large survey of 186,000 individuals found that respondents felt they had benefited substantially from psychotherapy (see Figure 2). However, there was little difference in "consumer satisfaction" on the basis of the specific type of treatment they had received (CR, 1995; Seligman, 1995; Strupp, 1996; Nielsen et al., 2004; Malouff, Thorsteinsson, & Schutte, 2007).

In short, converging evidence allows us to draw several conclusions about the effectiveness of psychotherapy (Strupp & Binder, 1992; Seligman, 1996; Gottfried & Pachankis, 2007):

- *For most people, psychotherapy is effective.* This conclusion holds over different lengths of treatment, specific kinds of psychological disorders, and various types of treatment. Thus, the question "Does psychotherapy work?" appears to have been answered convincingly: It does (Seligman, 1996; Spiegel, 1999; Westen, Novotny, & Thompson-Brenner, 2004).

- *On the other hand, psychotherapy doesn't work for everyone.* As many as 10 percent of people treated show no improvement or actually deteriorate (Boisvert & Faust, 2003; Pretzer & Beck, 2005; Coffman et al., 2007; Lilienfeld, 2007).

- *No single form of therapy works best for every problem, and certain specific types of treatment are better, although not invariably, for specific types of problems.* For example, cognitive therapy works especially well for panic disorders, and exposure therapy relieves specific phobias effectively. However, there are exceptions to

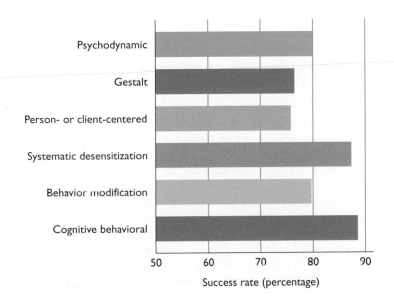

Success rate (percentage)

FIGURE 1 Estimates of the effectiveness of different types of treatment, in comparison to control groups of untreated people (adapted from Smith, Glass, & Miller, 1980). The percentile score shows how much more effective a specific type of treatment is for the average patient than is no treatment. For example, people given psychodynamic treatment score, on average, more positively on outcome measures than about three-quarters of untreated people.

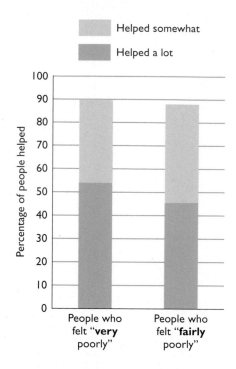

Helped somewhat

Helped a lot

FIGURE 2 A large survey of 186,000 individuals found that while the respondents had benefited substantially from psychotherapy, there was little difference in "consumer satisfaction" based on the specific type of treatment they had received. (Source: "Mental Health: Does Therapy Help?" Consumer Reports, 1995.)

these generalizations, and often the differences in success rates for different types of treatment are not substantial (Miller & Magruder, 1999; Westen, Novotny, & Thompson-Brenner, 2004).

- *Most therapies share several basic similar elements.* Despite the fact that the specific methods used in different therapies are very different from one another, there are several common themes that lead them to be effective. These elements include the opportunity for a client to develop a positive relationship with a therapist, an explanation or interpretation of a client's symptoms, and confrontation of negative emotions. The fact that these common elements exist in most therapies makes it difficult to compare one treatment against another (Norcross, 2002; Norcross, Beutler & Levant, 2006).

Consequently, there is no single, definitive answer to the broad question "Which therapy works best?" because of the complexity in sorting out the various factors that enter into successful therapy. Recently, however, clinicians and researchers have reframed the question by focusing on evidence-based psychotherapy practice. *Evidence-based psychotherapy practice* seeks to use the research literature to determine the best practices for treating a specific disorder. To determine best practices, researchers use clinical interviews, client self-reports of improvement in quality of life, reductions in symptoms, observations of behavior, and other outcomes to compare different therapies. By using objective research findings, clinicians are increasingly able to determine the most effective treatment for a specific disorder (APA Presidential Task Force, 2006; Fisher & O'Donohue, 2006; Goodheart, Kazdin, & Sternberg, 2006; Brownlee, 2007).

Because no single type of psychotherapy is invariably effective for every individual, some therapists use an eclectic approach to therapy. In an *eclectic approach to therapy*, therapists use a variety of techniques, integrating several perspectives, to treat a person's problems. By employing more than one approach, therapists can choose the appropriate mix of evidence-based treatments to match the specific needs of the individual. Furthermore, therapists with certain personal characteristics may work better with particular individuals and types of treatments, and—as we consider next—even racial and ethnic factors may be related to the success of treatment (Cheston, 2000; Chambless et al., 2006; Hays, 2008).

Exploring DIVERSITY

Racial and Ethnic Factors in Treatment: Should Therapists Be Color-Blind?

Consider the following case report, written by a school counselor about Jimmy Jones, a 12-year-old student who was referred to a counselor because of his lack of interest in schoolwork:

Jimmy does not pay attention, daydreams often, and frequently falls asleep during class. There is a strong possibility that Jimmy is harboring repressed rage that needs to be ventilated and dealt with. His inability to directly express his anger had led him to adopt passive aggressive means of expressing hostility, i.e., inattentiveness, daydreaming, falling asleep. It is recommended that Jimmy be seen for intensive counseling to discover the basis of the anger. (Sue & Sue, 1990, p. 44)

The counselor was wrong, however. Rather than suffering from "repressed rage," Jimmy lived in a poverty-stricken and disorganized home. Because of overcrowding at his house, he did not get enough sleep and consequently was tired the next day. Frequently, he was also hungry. In short, the stresses arising from his environment caused his problems, not any deep-seated psychological disturbances.

This incident underscores the importance of taking people's environmental and cultural backgrounds into account during treatment for psychological disorders. In particular, members of racial and ethnic minority groups, especially those who are also poor, may behave in ways that help them deal with a society that discriminates against them. As a consequence, behavior that may signal psychological disorder in middle- and upper-class whites may simply be adaptive in people from other racial and socioeconomic groups. For instance, characteristically suspicious and distrustful people may be displaying a survival strategy to protect themselves from psychological and physical injury, rather than suffering from a psychological disturbance (Paniagua, 2000; Tseng, 2003; Pottick et al., 2007).

In fact, therapists must question some basic assumptions of psychotherapy when dealing with racial, ethnic, and cultural minority-group members. For example, compared with the dominant culture, Asian and Latino cultures typically place much greater emphasis on the group, family, and society. When an Asian or Latino faces a critical decision, the family helps make it—a cultural practice suggesting that family members should also play a role in psychological treatment. Similarly, the traditional Chinese recommendation for dealing with depression or anxiety is to urge people who experience such problems to avoid thinking about whatever is upsetting them. Consider how this advice contrasts with treatment approaches that emphasize the value of insight (Ponterotto et al., 2001; McCarthy, 2005; Leitner, 2007).

Clearly, therapists *cannot* be "color-blind." Instead, they must take into account the racial, ethnic, cultural, and social class backgrounds of their clients in determining the nature of a psychological disorder and the course of treatment (Aponte & Wohl, 2000; Pedersen et al., 2002; Hayes, 2008).

Therapists' interpretation of their clients' behavior is influenced by racial, ethnic, cultural, and social class backgrounds of the clients.

RECAP/EVALUATE/RETHINK

RECAP

What are humanistic approaches to treatment?

- Humanistic therapy is based on the premise that people have control of their behavior, that they can make choices about their lives, and that it is up to them to solve their own problems. Humanistic therapies, which take a nondirective approach, include person-centered therapy. (p. 563)

What is interpersonal therapy?

- Interpersonal therapy focuses on interpersonal relationships and strives for immediate improvement during short-term therapy. (p. 564)

How does group therapy differ from individual types of therapy?

- In group therapy, several unrelated people meet with a therapist to discuss some aspect of their psychological functioning, often centering on a common problem. (p. 565)

How effective is psychotherapy, and which kind of psychotherapy works best in a given situation?

- Most research suggests that, in general, therapy is more effective than no therapy, although how much more effective is not known. (p. 566)

- The more difficult question of which therapy works best is harder to answer, but it is clear particular kinds of therapy are more appropriate for some problems than for others. (p. 567)

- Because no single type of psychotherapy is invariably effective, eclectic approaches, in which a therapist uses a variety of techniques, integrating several perspectives, are sometimes used. (p. 568)

EVALUATE

1. Match each of the following treatment strategies with the statement you might expect to hear from a therapist using that strategy.
   1. Group therapy
   2. Unconditional positive regard
   3. Behavioral therapy
   4. Nondirective counseling
   a. "In other words, you don't get along with your mother because she hates your girlfriend, is that right?"
   b. "I want you all to take turns talking about why you decided to come and what you hope to gain from therapy."
   c. "I can understand why you wanted to wreck your friend's car after she hurt your feelings. Now tell me more about the accident."
   d. "That's not appropriate behavior. Let's work on replacing it with something else."

2. _____ therapies assume that people should take responsibility for their lives and the decisions they make.

3. One of the major criticisms of humanistic therapies is that
   a. They are too imprecise and unstructured.
   b. They treat only the symptom of the problem.
   c. The therapist dominates the patient-therapist interaction.
   d. They work well only on clients of lower socioeconomic status.
4. In a controversial study, Eysenck found that some people go into _____ _____, or recovery without treatment, if they are simply left alone instead of treated.

1. How can people be successfully treated in group therapy when individuals with the "same" problem are so different? What advantages might group therapy offer over individual therapy?
2. *From the perspective of a social worker:* How might the types of therapies you employ vary depending on a client's cultural and socioeconomic background?

Answers to Evaluate Questions

1. 1-b, 2-c, 3-d, 4-a; 2. humanistic; 3. a; 4. spontaneous remission

KEY TERMS

humanistic therapy p. 563
person-centered therapy
    p. 564

interpersonal therapy
    (IPT) p. 564
group therapy p. 565

family therapy p. 565
spontaneous remission
    p. 566

Biomedical Therapy: Biological Approaches to Treatment

If you get a kidney infection, your doctor gives you an antibiotic, and with luck, about a week later your kidney should be as good as new. If your appendix becomes inflamed, a surgeon removes it and your body functions normally once more. Could a comparable approach, focusing on the body's physiology, be effective for psychological disturbances?

According to biological approaches to treatment, the answer is yes. Therapists routinely use biomedical therapies. This approach suggests that rather than focusing on a patient's psychological conflicts or past traumas, or on environmental factors that may produce abnormal behavior, focusing treatment directly on brain chemistry and other neurological factors may be more appropriate. To do this, therapists can use drugs, electric shock, or surgery to provide treatment.

Key Concept

How are drug, electroconvulsive, and psychosurgical techniques used today in the treatment of psychological disorders?

Drug Therapy

Drug therapy, the control of psychological disorders through drugs, works by altering the operation of neurotransmitters and neurons in the brain. Some drugs operate by inhibiting neurotransmitters or receptor neurons, reducing activity at particular synapses, the sites where nerve impulses travel from one neuron to another. Other drugs do just the opposite: They increase the activity of certain neurotransmitters or neurons, allowing particular neurons to fire more frequently (see Figure 1).

Drug therapy: Control of psychological disorders through the use of drugs.

ANTIPSYCHOTIC DRUGS

Probably no greater change has occurred in mental hospitals than the successful introduction in the mid-1950s of **antipsychotic drugs**—drugs used to reduce severe symptoms of disturbance, such as loss of touch with reality and agitation. Previously, the typical mental hospital wasn't very different from the stereotypical 19th-century insane asylum, giving mainly custodial care to screaming, moaning, clawing patients who displayed bizarre behaviors. Suddenly, in just a matter of days after hospital staff members administered antipsychotic drugs, the wards became considerably calmer environments in which professionals could do more than just try to get patients through the day without causing serious harm to themselves or others.

This dramatic change came about through the introduction of the drug *chlorpromazine*. Along with other similar drugs, chlorpromazine rapidly became the most popular and successful treatment for schizophrenia. Today drug therapy is the preferred treatment for most cases of severely abnormal behavior and, as such, is used for most patients hospitalized with psychological disorders. The newest generation of antipsychotics, referred to as *atypical antipsychotics*, which have fewer side effects, include *rizperidone, olanzapine,* and *paliperidone* (Anand & Burton, 2003; Lublin, Eberhard, & Levander, 2005; Savas et al., 2007).

How do antipsychotic drugs work? Most block dopamine receptors at the brain's synapses. Atypical antipsychotics effect both serotonin and dopamine levels in certain parts of the brain, such as those related to planning and goal-directed activity (Sawa & Snyder, 2002; Advokat, 2005).

Antipsychotic drugs: Drugs that temporarily reduce psychotic symptoms such as agitation, hallucinations, and delusions.

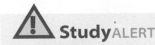 **Study** ALERT

To help organize your study of different drugs used in therapy, review Figure 1, which classifies them according to the categories of antipsychotic, atypical antipsychotic, antidepressant, mood stabilizing, and antianxiety drugs.

Drug Treatments			
Class of Drug	**Effects of Drug**	**Primary Action of Drug**	**Examples**
Antipsychotic Drugs, Atypical Antipsychotic Drugs	Reduction in loss of touch with reality, agitation	Block dopamine receptors	Antipsychotic: Chlorpromazine (Thorazine), clozapine (Clozaril), haloperidol (Haldol) Atypical Antipsychotic: rizperadine, olanzapine
Antidepressant Drugs			
Tricyclic antidepressants	Reduction in depression	Permit rise in neurotransmitters such as norepinepherine	Trazodone (Desyrel), amitriptyline (Elavil), desipramine (Norpamin)
MAO inhibitors	Reduction in depression	Prevent MAO from breaking down neurotransmitters	Phenelzine (Nardil), tranylcypromine (Parnate)
Selective serotonin reuptake inhibitors (SSRIs)	Reduction in depression	Inhibit reuptake of serotonin	Fluoxetine (Prozac), Luvox, Paxil, Celexa, Zoloft, nefazodone (Serzone)
Mood Stabilizers			
Lithium	Mood stabilization	Can alter transmission of impulses within neurons	Lithium (Lithonate), Depakote, Tegretol
Antianxiety Drugs	Reduction in anxiety	Increase activity of neurotrasmitter GABA	Benzodiazepines (Valium, Xanax)

FIGURE 1 The major classes of drugs used to treat psychological disorders have different effects on the brain and nervous system.

Despite the effectiveness of antipsychotic drugs, they do not produce a "cure" in the same way that, say, penicillin cures an infection. Most of the time, when the drug is withdrawn, the symptoms reappear. Furthermore, such drugs can have long-term side effects, such as dryness of the mouth and throat, dizziness, and sometimes tremors and loss of muscle control, which may continue after drug treatments are stopped (Voruganti et al., 2007).

Antidepressant drugs: Medications that improve a severely depressed patient's mood and feeling of well-being.

Prozac is a widely prescribed—but still controversial—antidepressant.

ANTIDEPRESSANT DRUGS

As their name suggests, **antidepressant drugs** are a class of medications used in cases of severe depression to improve the moods of patients. They are also sometimes used for other disorders, such as anxiety disorders and bulimia (Walsh et al., 2006; Hedges, 2007).

Most antidepressant drugs work by changing the concentration of specific neurotransmitters in the brain. For example, *tricyclic drugs* increase the availability of norepinephrine at the synapses of neurons, whereas *MAO inhibitors* prevent the enzyme monoamine oxidase (MAO) from breaking down neurotransmitters. Newer antidepressants—such as Lexapro—are *selective serotonin reuptake inhibitors (SSRIs)*. SSRIs target the neurotransmitter serotonin, permitting it to linger at the synapse. Some antidepressants produce a combination of effects. For instance, nefazodone (Serzone) blocks serotonin at some receptor sites but not others, while bupropion (Wellbutrin and Zyban) affects the norepinephrine and dopamine systems (see Figure 2; Anand, 2002; Lucki & O'Leary, 2004; Robinson, 2007).

The overall success rates of antidepressant drugs is good. Unlike antipsychotic drugs, antidepressants can produce lasting, long-term recovery from depression. In many cases, even after patients stop taking the drugs, their depression does not return. On the other hand, antidepressant drugs may produce side effects such as drowsiness and faintness, and there is evidence that SSRI antidepressants can increase the risk of suicide in children and adolescents (Gibbons et al., 2007; Leckman & King, 2007).

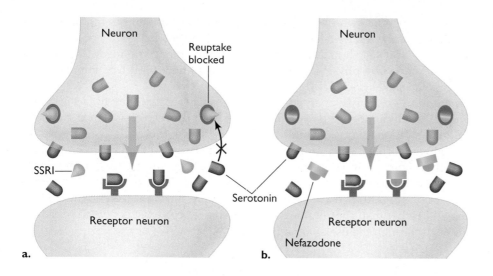

a.   **b.**

FIGURE 2 In (a), selective serotonin reuptake inhibitors (SSRIs) reduce depression by permitting the neurotransmitter serotonin to remain in the synapse. In (b), a newer antidepressant, Nefazodone (Serzone), operates more selectively to block serotonin at some sites but not others, helping to reduce the side effects of the drug. (Source: Based on Mischoulon, 2000.)

Consumers spend billions of dollars each year on antidepressant drugs. In particular, the antidepressant *Fluoxetine*, sold under the trade name *Prozac*, has been highlighted on magazine covers and has been the topic of best-sellers.

Does Prozac deserve its acclaim? In some respects, yes. It is effective and has relatively few side effects. Furthermore, many people who do not respond to other types of antidepressants do well on Prozac. On the other hand, 20 to 30 percent of users report experiencing nausea and diarrhea, and a smaller number report sexual dysfunctions (Kramer, 1993; Brambilla, Cipriani, Hotopf, & Barbui, 2005; Fenter, 2006).

Another drug that has received a great deal of publicity is *St. John's wort*, an herb that some have called a "natural" antidepressant. Although it is widely used in Europe for the treatment of depression, the U.S. Food and Drug Administration considers it a dietary supplement, and therefore the substance is available here without a prescription.

Despite the popularity of St. John's wort, definitive clinical tests have found that the herb is ineffective in the treatment of depression. However, because some research shows that the herb successfully reduces certain psychological symptoms, some proponents argue that using it is reasonable. In any case, people should not use St. John's wort to medicate themselves without consulting a mental health care professional (Williams et al., 2000; Shelton et al., 2002; Thachil, Mohan & Bhugra, 2007).

MOOD STABILIZERS

Mood stabilizers are used to treat mood disorders. For example, the drug *lithium*, a form of mineral salts, has been used very successfully in patients with bipolar disorders. Although no one knows definitely why, lithium and other mood stabilizers such as divalproex sodium (*Depakote*) and carbamazepine (*Tegretol*) effectively reduce manic episodes. However, they do not effectively treat depressive phases of bipolar disorder, so antidepressants are usually prescribed during those phases (Dubovsky, 1999; Fountoulakis et al., 2005; Abraham & Calabrese, 2007).

Lithium and similar drugs have a quality that sets them apart from other drug treatments: They can be a *preventive* treatment, blocking future episodes of manic depression. Often, people who have had episodes of bipolar disorder can take a daily dose of lithium to prevent a recurrence of their symptoms. Most other drugs are useful only when symptoms of psychological disturbance occur.

Mood stabilizers: Drugs used to treat mood disorders that prevent manic episodes of bipolar disorder.

ANTIANXIETY DRUGS

As the name implies, **antianxiety drugs** reduce the level of anxiety a person experiences and increase feelings of well-being. They are prescribed not only to reduce

Antianxiety drugs: Drugs that reduce the level of anxiety a person experiences, essentially by reducing excitability and increasing feelings of well-being.

general tension in people who are experiencing temporary difficulties but also to aid in the treatment of more serious anxiety disorders (Zito, 1993).

Antianxiety drugs such as Xanax and Valium are among the medications most frequently prescribed by physicians. In fact, more than half of all U.S. families have someone who has taken such a drug at one time or another.

Although the popularity of antianxiety drugs suggests that they hold few risks, they can produce a number of potentially serious side effects. For instance, they can cause fatigue, and long-term use can lead to dependence. Moreover, when taken in combination with alcohol, some antianxiety drugs can be lethal. But a more important issue concerns their use to suppress anxiety. Almost every therapeutic approach to psychological disturbance views continuing anxiety as a signal of some other sort of problem. Thus, drugs that mask anxiety may simply be hiding other difficulties. Consequently, rather than confronting their underlying problems, people may be hiding from them through the use of antianxiety drugs.

Electroconvulsive Therapy (ECT)

Electroconvulsive therapy (ECT): A procedure used in the treatment of severe depression in which an electric current of 70 to 150 volts is briefly administered to a patient's head.

First introduced in the 1930s, **electroconvulsive therapy (ECT)** is a procedure used in the treatment of severe depression. In the procedure, an electric current of 70 to 150 volts is briefly administered to a patient's head, causing a loss of consciousness and often causing seizures. Typically, health professionals sedate patients and give them muscle relaxants before administering the current, and such preparations help reduce the intensity of muscle contractions produced during ECT. The typical patient receives about 10 such treatments in the course of a month, but some patients continue with maintenance treatments for months afterward (Greenberg & Kellner, 2005; Stevens & Harper, 2007).

ECT is a controversial technique. Apart from the obvious distastefulness of a treatment that evokes images of electrocution, side effects occur frequently. For instance, after treatment patients often experience disorientation, confusion, and sometimes memory loss that may remain for months. Furthermore, ECT often does not produce long-term improvement; one study found that without follow-up medication, depression returned in most patients who had undergone ECT treatments. Finally, even when ECT does work, we do not know why, and some critics believe it may cause permanent brain damage (Valente, 1991; Sackeim et al., 2001; Frank, 2002).

In light of the drawbacks to ECT, why do therapists use it at all? Basically, they use it because, in many severe cases of depression, it offers the only quickly effective treatment—as in the case of Kitty Dukakis, which began the chapter. For instance, it may prevent depressed, suicidal individuals from committing suicide, and it can act more quickly than antidepressive medications.

The use of ECT has risen in the last decade, with more than 100,000 people undergoing it each year. Still, ECT tends to be used only when other treatments have proved ineffective, and researchers continue to search for alternative treatments (Fink, 2000; Eranti & McLoughlin, 2003; Pandya, Pozuelo, & Malone, 2007).

Transcranial magnetic stimulation (TMS): A depression treatment in which a precise magnetic pulse is directed to a specific area of the brain.

One new and promising alternative to ECT is **transcranial magnetic stimulation (TMS)**. TMS creates a precise magnetic pulse in a specific area of the brain. By activating particular neurons, TMS has been found to be effective in relieving the symptoms of depression in a number of controlled experiments. However, the therapy can produce side effects, such as seizures and convulsions, and it is still considered experimental by the government (Simons, 2005; Lefaucheur et al., 2007; Leo & Latif, 2007).

Psychosurgery

Psychosurgery: Brain surgery once used to reduce the symptoms of mental disorder but rarely used today.

If ECT strikes you as a questionable procedure, the use of **psychosurgery**—brain surgery in which the object is to reduce symptoms of mental disorder—probably appears even more dubious. A technique used only rarely today, psychosurgery was introduced as a "treatment of last resort" in the 1930s.

The initial form of psychosurgery, a *prefrontal lobotomy*, consisted of surgically destroying or removing parts of a patient's frontal lobes, which, surgeons thought, controlled emotionality. In the 1930s and 1940s, surgeons performed the procedure on thousands of patients, often with little precision. For example, in one common technique, a surgeon would jab an ice pick under a patient's eyeball and swivel it back and forth (El-Hai, 2005; Ogren & Sandlund, 2007).

Psychosurgery often did improve a patient's behavior—but not without drastic side effects. Along with remission of the symptoms of the mental disorder, patients sometimes experienced personality changes, becoming bland, colorless, and unemotional. In other cases, patients became aggressive and unable to control their impulses. In the worst cases, treatment resulted in the death of the patient.

With the introduction of effective drug treatments—and the obvious ethical questions regarding the appropriateness of forever altering someone's personality—psychosurgery became nearly obsolete. However, it is still used in very rare cases when all other procedures have failed and the patient's behavior presents a high risk to the patient and others. Today, surgeons sometimes use a more precise form of psychosurgery called a *cingulotomy* in rare cases of obsessive-compulsive disorder. Occasionally, dying patients with severe, uncontrollable pain also receive psychosurgery. Still, even these cases raise important ethical issues, and psychosurgery remains a highly controversial treatment (Mashour, Walker, & Martuza, 2005; Steele et al., 2007).

Biomedical Therapies in Perspective

In some respects, no greater revolution has occurred in the field of mental health than biological approaches to treatment. As previously violent, uncontrollable patients have been calmed by the use of drugs, mental hospitals have been able to concentrate more on actually helping patients and less on custodial functions. Similarly, patients whose lives have been disrupted by depression or bipolar episodes have been able to function normally, and other forms of drug therapy have also shown remarkable results.

The use of biomedical therapy for everyday problems is rising. For example, one survey of users of a college counseling service found that from 1989 to 2001, the proportion of students receiving treatment who were taking medication for psychological disorders increased from 10 percent to 25 percent (Benton et al., 2003).

Furthermore, new forms of biomedical therapy are promising. For example, the newest treatment possibility—which remains experimental at this point—is gene therapy. As we discussed when considering behavioral genetics, specific genes may be introduced to particular regions of the brain. These genes then have the potential to reverse or even prevent biochemical events that give rise to psychological disorders (Lymberis et al., 2004; Sapolsky, 2003; Tuszynski, 2007).

Despite their current usefulness and future promise, biomedical therapies do not represent a cure-all for psychological disorders. For one thing, critics charge that such therapies merely provide relief of the *symptoms* of mental disorder; as soon as the drugs are withdrawn, the symptoms return. Although it is considered a major step in the right direction, biomedical treatment may not solve the underlying problems that led a patient to therapy in the first place. Biomedical therapies also can produce side effects, ranging from minor to serious physical reactions to the development of *new* symptoms of abnormal behavior. Finally, as we discuss in the *Applying Psychology in the 21st Century* box, an overreliance on biomedical therapies may lead therapists to overlook alternative forms of treatment that may be helpful.

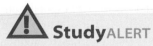

StudyALERT

Remember that biomedical treatments have both benefits and drawbacks.

Still, biomedical therapies—sometimes alone and more often in conjunction with psychotherapy—have permitted millions of people to function more effectively. Furthermore, although biomedical therapy and psychotherapy appear distinct, research shows that biomedical therapies ultimately may not be as different from talk therapies as one might imagine, at least in terms of their consequences.

Specifically, measures of brain functioning as a result of drug therapy compared with psychotherapy show little difference in outcomes. For example, one study

Prescription: Stay Involved with Work and Family

Incense wafts around two dozen men standing in a circle stomping, clapping, and chanting to the rhythm of a drum. This ceremony for the Hindu god Krishna wouldn't seem out of place in a temple, but this evening the venue is a rehab clinic, and the men are patients with schizophrenia. Earlier, the men were hard at work here at the Schizophrenia Research Foundation (SCARF), making chalk sticks or fashioning sturdy shopping bags from old newspapers. The clinic sells the items, along with dolls and candles made by female patients, to local shops in Chennai, a sweltering city of 6 million on India's southeast coast, and shares the proceeds with the patients. The buzz of activity makes SCARF feel more like a summer camp than a psychiatric ward. (Miller, 2006, p. 464)

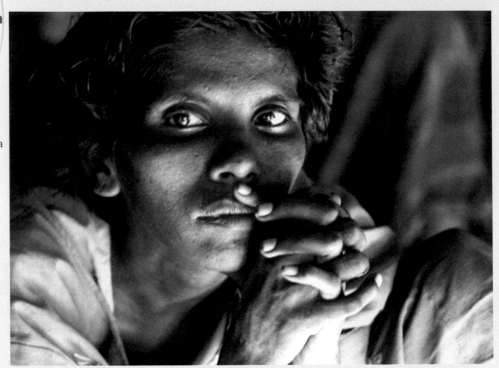

Work and family involvement are key components of treatment of schizophrenia in an approach developed in India.

Although India has very limited resources for services to those with severe psychological disturbances—for example, only one hospital bed is available for roughly every 600 people with psychological disorders who need one—it does a notable job of rehabilitating patients with schizophrenia who do receive care. In fact, outcomes for patients with schizophrenia in terms of longer remission and fewer relapses are better in India than in the United States and other developed countries (Thara, 2004; Miller, 2006).

India's success rests on the kind of treatment made available at SCARF and other similar clinics. Although the patients take antipsychotic drugs, they also engage in activities that emphasize maintaining social and family ties. For example, in addition to developing useful job skills, patients might play competitive sports together, receive social skills training, and work at actual jobs that were developed specifically for them. The patients' work experience is especially useful for maintaining connectedness with the community, for developing marketable skills,

and for gaining a sense of purpose in their lives. Maintaining a job is considered a necessary part of the treatment program at SCARF. By comparison, fewer than one in five patients with schizophrenia in the United States are able to find work, even though most want to (Mueser, Salyers, & Mueser, 2001; Miller, 2006).

The role of families in the treatment of schizophrenia patients is another distinction between India and many developed countries. In India, almost all people with schizophrenia live with their families—a situation more out of necessity than for therapeutic reasons. In developed countries, most schizophrenia patients are treated in hospitals or other facilities, removed from the family context. But having a family member with schizophrenia affects the entire family, and maintaining social ties is helpful for getting patients reintegrated into society (Thara, 2004; Miller, 2006).

Given the encouraging evidence of improved outcomes for patients, why

aren't more community-based interventions employed more often in the United States? One reason is the medical culture in the United States, which tends to focus on physical causes rather than the social context. Consequently, an overreliance on drug therapies may inhibit the use of other options.

In terms of treating schizophrenia, then, cultural differences between the United States and India have given rise to quite different approaches. The challenge is for wealthier countries to be open to approaches emerging from developing nations, making use of promising practices that might supplement traditional care.

- Why might everyday activities of work and family life assist in the treatment of schizophrenia?
- What might be some of the barriers to adopting the Indian approach to treating schizophrenia in the United States?

compared the reactions of patients with major depression who received either an anti-depressant drug or psychotherapy. After six weeks of either therapy, activity in the portion of the brain related to the disorder—the basal ganglia—had changed in similar ways, and that area appeared to function more normally. Although such research is not definitive, it does suggest that at least for some disorders, psychotherapy may be just as effective as biomedical interventions—and vice versa. Research also makes it clear that no single treatment is effective universally, and that each type of treatment has both advantages and disadvantages (Hollon, Thase, & Markowitz, 2002; DeRubeis, Hollon, & Shelton, 2003; Pinquart, Duberstein, & Lyness, 2006).

Community Psychology: Focus on Prevention

Each of the treatments we have reviewed has a common element: It is a "restorative" treatment, aimed at alleviating psychological difficulties that already exist. However, an approach known as **community psychology** has a different aim: to prevent or minimize the incidence of psychological disorders.

Community psychology came of age in the 1960s, when mental health profession-als developed plans for a nationwide network of community mental health centers. The hope was that those centers would provide low-cost mental health services, including short-term therapy and community educational programs. In another devel-opment, the population of mental hospitals has plunged as drug treatments made physical restraint of patients unnecessary.

This transfer of former mental patients out of institutions and into the community—a process known as **deinstitutionalization**—was encouraged by the growth of the community psychology movement (see Figure 3). Proponents of deinstitutionalization wanted to ensure not only that deinstitutionalized patients received proper treatment but also that their civil rights were maintained (Wolff, 2002; St. Dennis et al., 2007).

Unfortunately, the promise of deinstitutionalization has not been met, largely because insufficient resources are provided to deinstitutionalized patients. What started as a worthy attempt to move people out of mental institutions and into the community ended, in many cases, with former patients being dumped into the

While deinstitutionalization has had many successes, it has also contributed to the release of mental patients into the community with little or no support. As a result many have become homeless.

Community psychology: A branch of psychology that focuses on the pre-vention and minimization of psycho-logical disorders in the community.
Deinstitutionalization: The transfer of former mental patients from institu-tions to the community.

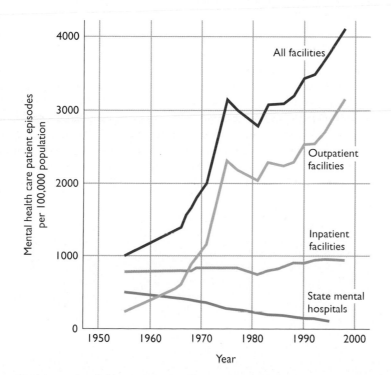

FIGURE 3 As deinstitutionalization has become more prevalent over the last fifty years, the number of patients being treat-ed in state mental hospitals has declined significantly, while the number of outpa-tient facilities has increased.
(Source: National Mental Health Information Center, U.S. Department of Health and Human Services, reprinted in *Scientific American*, December, 2002, p. 38.)

community without any real support. Many became homeless—between a third and a half of all homeless adults are thought to have a major psychological disorder—and some became involved in illegal acts caused by their disorders. In short, many people who need treatment do not get it, and in some cases care for people with psychological disorders has simply shifted from one type of treatment site to another (Doyle, 2002; Lamb & Weinberger, 2005; Shinn et al., 2007).

On the other hand, the community psychology movement has had some positive outcomes. Telephone "hot lines" are now common. At any time of the day or night, people experiencing acute stress can call a trained, sympathetic listener who can provide immediate—although obviously limited—treatment (Reese, Conoley, & Brossart, 2002; Paukert, Stagner, & Hope, 2004; Cauce, 2007).

College and high school crisis centers are another innovation that grew out of the community psychology movement. Modeled after suicide prevention hot-line centers (services that enable potential suicide victims to call and speak to someone about their difficulties), crisis centers give callers an opportunity to discuss life crises with a sympathetic listener, who is often a volunteer.

BECOMING AN INFORMED CONSUMER of Psychology

Choosing the Right Therapist

If you decide to seek therapy, you're faced with a daunting task. Choosing a therapist is not a simple matter. One place to begin the process of identifying a therapist is at the "Help Center" of the American Psychological Association at http://locator.apahelpcenter.org or 1-800-964-2000. And, if you start therapy, several general guidelines can help you determine whether you've made the right choice:

You and your therapist should agree on the goals for treatment. They should be clear, specific, and attainable.

- *You should feel comfortable with your therapist.* You should not be intimidated by, or in awe of, a therapist. Rather, you should trust the therapist and feel free to discuss the most personal issues without fearing a negative reaction. In sum, the "personal chemistry" should be right.

- *Therapists should have appropriate training and credentials and should be licensed by appropriate state and local agencies.* Check therapists' membership in national and state professional associations. In addition, the cost of therapy, billing practices, and other business matters should be clear. It is not a breach of etiquette to put these matters on the table during an initial consultation.

- *You should feel that you are making progress after therapy has begun, despite occasional setbacks.* If you have no sense of improvement after repeated visits, you and your therapist should discuss this issue frankly. Although there is no set timetable, the most obvious changes resulting from therapy tend to occur relatively early in the course of treatment. For instance, half of patients in psychotherapy improve by the 8th session, and three-fourths by the 26th session (see Figure 4). The average number of sessions with college students is just five (Crits-Cristoph, 1992; HMHL, 1994b; Lazarus, 1997).

"Looking good!"

FIGURE 4 For most clients, improvements in psychological functioning occur relatively soon after therapy has begun. (Source: Howard et al., 1986a.)

Be aware that you will have to put in a great deal of effort in therapy. Although our culture promises quick cures for any problem, in reality, solving difficult problems is not easy. You must be committed to making therapy work and should know that it is you, not the therapist, who must do most of the work to resolve your problems. The effort has the potential to pay off handsomely—as you experience a more positive, fulfilling, and meaningful life.

RECAP/EVALUATE/RETHINK

RECAP

How are drug, electroconvulsive, and psychosurgical techniques used today in the treatment of psychological disorders?

- Biomedical treatment approaches suggest that therapy should focus on the physiological causes of abnormal behavior, rather than considering psychological factors. Drug therapy, the best example of biomedical treatments, has brought about dramatic reductions in the symptoms of mental disturbance. (p. 571)

- Antipsychotic drugs such as chlorpromazine very effectively reduce psychotic symptoms. Antidepressant drugs such as Prozac reduce depression so successfully that they are used very widely. Antianxiety drugs, or minor tranquilizers, are among the most frequently prescribed medications of any sort. (p. 571)

- In electroconvulsive therapy (ECT), used in severe cases of depression, a patient receives a brief electric current of 70 to 150 volts. (p. 574)

- Psychosurgery typically consists of surgically destroying or removing certain parts of a patient's brain. (p. 574)

- The community psychology approach encouraged deinstitutionalization, in which previously hospitalized mental patients were released into the community. (p. 577)

EVALUATE

1. Antipsychotic drugs have provided effective, long-term, and complete cures for schizophrenia. True or false?
2. One highly effective biomedical treatment for a psychological disorder, used mainly to arrest and prevent manic-depressive episodes, is
   a. Chlorpromazine
   b. Lithium
   c. Librium
   d. Valium
3. Psychosurgery has grown in popularity as a method of treatment as surgical techniques have become more precise. True or false?

4. The trend toward releasing more patients from mental hospitals and into the community is known as _____.

RETHINK

1. One of the main criticisms of biological therapies is that they treat the symptoms of mental disorder without uncovering and treating the underlying problems from which people are suffering. Do you agree with this criticism? Why?

2. *From the perspective of a politician:* How would you go about regulating the use of electroconvulsive therapy and psychosurgery? Would you restrict their use or make either one completely illegal? Why?

Answers to Evaluate Questions

1. false; schizophrenia can be controlled, but not cured, by medication; 2. b; 3. false; psychosurgery is now used only as a treatment of last resort; 4. deinstitutionalization

KEY TERMS

drug therapy p. 571
antipsychotic drugs p. 571
antidepressant drugs p. 572
mood stabilizers p. 573

antianxiety drugs p. 573
electroconvulsive therapy (ECT) p. 574

transcranial magnetic stimulation (TMS) p. 574
psychosurgery p. 574

community psychology p. 577
deinstitutionalization p. 577

Psychology on the Web

1. Investigate computer-assisted psychotherapy on the Web. Locate (a) a computerized therapy program, such as ELIZA, which offers "therapy" over the Internet, and (b) a report on "cybertherapy," in which therapists use the Web to interact with patients. Compare the two approaches, describing how each one works and relating it to the therapeutic approaches you have studied.

2. Find more information on the Web about deinstitutionalization. Try to find pro and con arguments about it and summarize the arguments, including your judgment of the effectiveness and advisability of deinstitutionalization as an approach to dealing with mental illness.

Epilogue

We have examined how psychological professionals treat people with psychological disorders. We have considered a range of approaches, including both psychologically based and biologically based therapies. Clearly, the field has made substantial progress in recent years both in treating the symptoms of mental disorders and in understanding their underlying causes.

Before we leave the topic of treatment of psychological disorders, turn back to the prologue, in which Kitty Dukakis describes how electroconvulsive therapy relieved her depression. On the basis of your understanding of the treatment of psychological disorders, consider the following questions.

1. How would Dukakis's treatment have proceeded if she had undergone Freudian psychoanalysis? What sorts of issues might a psychoanalyst have asked about?

2. Do you think any behavioral therapies would have been helpful in treating Dukakis's depression? What behaviors might such therapies have focused on?

3. Dukakis describes some side effects of her treatment, including headaches and short-term memory loss. Do you think the benefits of electroconvulsive therapy outweigh these drawbacks?

4. Given that the mechanism by which electroconvulsive therapy works is not well understood and that the relief from depression that it provides is usually only temporary, it is often considered a treatment of last resort. What alternative treatments to depression exist? Under what circumstances would electroconvulsive therapy be best justified?

5. What are some of the drawbacks to drug therapy that Dukakis hints at?

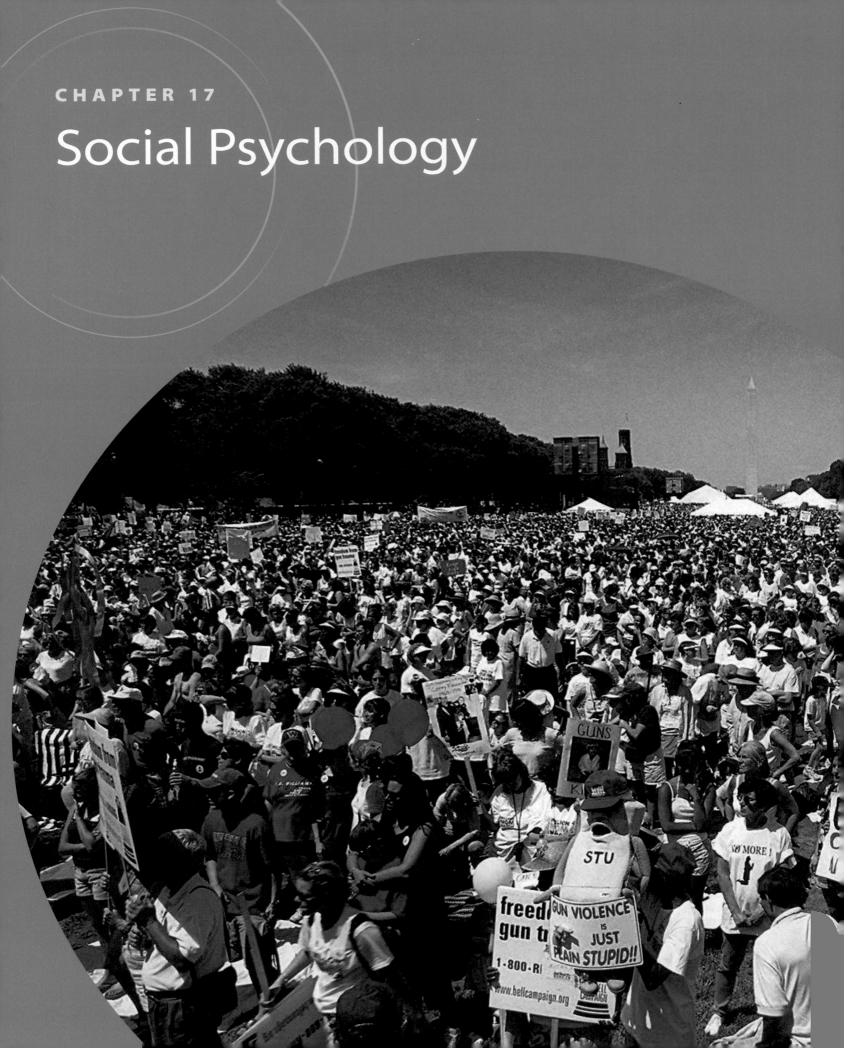

Social Psychology

Key Concepts for Chapter 17

Prologue *A Gift of Life*

It was every subway rider's nightmare, times two.

Who has ridden along New York's 656 miles of subway lines and not wondered: "What if I fell to the tracks as a train came in? What would I do?"

And who has not thought: "What if someone else fell? Would I jump to the rescue?"

Wesley Autrey, a 50-year-old construction worker and Navy veteran, faced both those questions in a flashing instant yesterday, and got his answers almost as quickly.

Mr. Autrey was waiting for the downtown local at 137th Street and Broadway in Manhattan around 12:45 p.m. He was taking his two daughters, Syshe, 4, and Shuqui, 6, home before work.

Nearby, a man collapsed, his body convulsing. Mr. Autrey and two women rushed to help, he said. The man, Cameron Hollopeter, 20, managed to get up, but then stumbled to the platform edge and fell to the tracks, between the two rails.

The headlights of the No. 1 train appeared. "I had to make a split decision," Mr. Autrey said.

So he made one, and leapt.

Mr. Autrey lay on Mr. Hollopeter, his heart pounding, pressing him down in a space roughly a foot deep. The train's brakes screeched, but it could not stop in time.

Five cars rolled overhead before the train stopped, the cars passing inches from his head, smudging his blue knit cap with grease. Mr. Autrey heard onlookers' screams. "We're O.K. down here," he yelled, "but I've got two daughters up there. Let them know their father's O.K." He heard cries of wonder, and applause. . . .

"I don't feel like I did something spectacular; I just saw someone who needed help," Mr. Autrey said. "I did what I felt was right." (From Cara Buckley, "Man Is Rescued by Stranger on Subway Tracks." From *The New York Times*, January 3, 2007, p. A1. © 2007 The New York Times. All rights reserved. Used by permission and protected by the Copyright Laws of the United States. The printing, copying, redistribution, or retransmission of the Material without express written permission is prohibited. www.nytimes.com.)

Looking Ahead

What led Wesley Autrey to behave so heroically? Was it simply the circumstances, or was it something about the kind of person Autrey was? What, in general, drives some people to help others—and conversely, why do other people show no concern for the welfare of others? More broadly, how can we improve social conditions so that people can live together in harmony?

We can fully answer these questions only by taking into account findings from the field of social psychology, the branch of psychology that focuses on the aspects of human behavior that unite—and separate—us from one another. **Social psychology** is the scientific study of how people's thoughts, feelings, and actions are affected by others. Social psychologists consider the kinds and causes of the behavior of the individual in social situations. They examine how the nature of situations in which we find ourselves influences our behavior in important ways.

The broad scope of social psychology is conveyed by the kinds of questions social psychologists ask, such as: How can we convince people to change their attitudes or adopt new ideas and values? In what ways do we come to understand what others are like? How are we influenced by what others do and think? Why do some people display so much violence, aggression, and cruelty toward others that people throughout the world live in fear of annihilation at their hands? And why, in comparison, do some people place their own lives at risk to help others? In exploring these and other questions, we also discuss strategies for confronting and solving a variety of problems and issues that all of us face—ranging from achieving a better understanding of persuasive tactics to forming more accurate impressions of others.

We begin with a look at how our attitudes shape our behavior and how we form judgments about others. We'll discuss how we are influenced by others, and we will consider prejudice and discrimination, focusing on their roots and the ways in which we can reduce them. After examining what social psychologists have learned about the ways in which people form friendships and relationships, we'll conclude with a look at the determinants of aggression and helping—two opposing sides of human behavior.

Social psychology: The scientific study of how people's thoughts, feelings, and actions are affected by others.

Attitudes and Social Cognition

What do Tiger Woods, Rachel Ray, and Tom Brady have in common?

Each has appeared in advertisements designed to mold or change our attitudes. Such commercials are part of the barrage of messages we receive each day from sources as varied as politicians, sales staff in stores, and celebrities, all of which are meant to influence us.

Persuasion: Changing Attitudes

Persuasion is the process of changing attitudes, one of the central concepts of social psychology. **Attitudes** are evaluations of a particular person, behavior, belief, or concept. For example, you probably hold attitudes toward the U.S. president (a person), abortion (a behavior), affirmative action (a belief), or architecture (a concept) (Perloff, 2003; Brock & Green, 2005; Hegarty & Massey, 2007).

The ease with which we can change our attitudes depends on a number of factors, including:

- *Message source.* The characteristics of a person who delivers a persuasive message, known as an *attitude communicator*, have a major impact on the effectiveness of that message. Communicators who are physically and socially attractive produce greater attitude change than those who are less attractive. Moreover, the expertise and trustworthiness of a communicator are related to the impact of a message—except in situations in which the audience believes the communicator has an ulterior motive (Ziegler, Diehl, & Ruther, 2002; Ariyanto, Hornsey, & Gallois, 2006; McClure, Sutton, & Sibley, 2007).

- *Characteristics of the message.* It is not just *who* delivers a message but what the message is like that affects attitudes. Generally, two-sided messages—which include both the communicator's position and the one he or she is arguing against—are more effective than one-sided messages, given the assumption that the arguments for the other side can be effectively refuted and the audience is knowledgeable about the topic. In addition, fear-producing messages ("If you don't practice safer sex, you'll get AIDS") are generally effective when they provide the audience with a means for reducing the fear. However, if the fear that is aroused is too strong, messages may evoke people's defense mechanisms and be ignored (Perloff, 2003).

- *Characteristics of the target.* Once a communicator has delivered a message, characteristics of the *target* of the message may determine whether the message will be accepted. For example, intelligent people are more resistant to persuasion than are those who are less intelligent. Gender differences in persuasibility also seem to exist. In public settings, women are somewhat more easily persuaded than men, particularly when they have less knowledge about the message's topic. However, they are as likely as men to change their private attitudes. In fact, the magnitude of the differences in resistance to persuasion between men and women is not large (Wood, 2000; Guadagno & Cialdini, 2002).

Key Concepts

What are attitudes, and how are they formed, maintained, and changed?

How do people form impressions of what others are like and of the causes of their behavior?

What are the biases that influence the ways in which people view others' behavior?

Attitudes: Evaluations of a particular person, behavior, belief, or concept.

Companies use sports stars such as Tiger Woods to persuade consumers to buy their products. Can celebrities really affect the purchasing habits of consumers? How?

"I'm neither a good cop nor a bad cop, Jerome. Like yourself, I'm a complex amalgam of positive and negative personality traits that emerge or not, depending on circumstances."

Central route processing: Message interpretation characterized by thoughtful consideration of the issues and arguments used to persuade.
Peripheral route processing: Message interpretation characterized by consideration of the source and related general information rather than of the message itself.

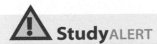 **Study**ALERT

Central route processing involves the **c**ontent of the message; **p**eripheral route processing involves how the message is **p**rovided.

ROUTES TO PERSUASION

Recipients' receptiveness to persuasive messages relates to the type of information-processing they use. Social psychologists have discovered two primary information-processing routes to persuasion: central route and peripheral route processing. **Central route processing** occurs when the recipient thoughtfully considers the issues and arguments involved in persuasion. In central route processing, people are swayed in their judgments by the logic, merit, and strength of arguments.

In contrast, **peripheral route processing** occurs when people are persuaded on the basis of factors unrelated to the nature or quality of the content of a persuasive message. Instead, factors that are irrelevant or extraneous to the issue, such as who is providing the message, how long the arguments are, or the emotional appeal of the arguments, influence them (Petty et al., 2005; Wegener et al., 2004; Warden, Wu, & Tsai, 2006).

In general, people who are highly involved and motivated use central route processing to comprehend a message. However, if a person is uninvolved, unmotivated, bored, or distracted, the nature of the message becomes less important, and peripheral factors become more critical (see Figure 1). Although both central route and peripheral route processing lead to attitude change, central route processing generally leads to stronger, more lasting attitude change.

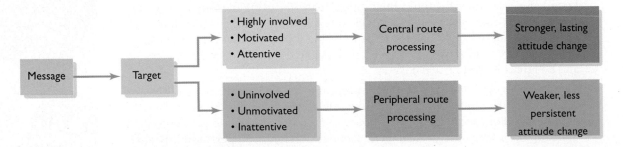

FIGURE 1 Routes to persuasion. Targets who are highly involved, motivated, and attentive use central route processing when they consider a persuasive message, which leads to a more lasting attitude change. In contrast, uninvolved, unmotivated, and inattentive targets are more likely to use peripheral route processing, and attitude change is likely to be less enduring. Can you think of specific advertisements that try to produce central route processing?

The Need for Cognition

Which of the following statements apply to you?

1. I really enjoy a task that involves coming up with new solutions to problems.
2. I would prefer a task that is intellectual, difficult, and important to one that is somewhat important but does not require much thought.
3. Learning new ways to think doesn't excite me very much.
4. The idea of relying on thought to make my way to the top does not appeal to me.
5. I think only as hard as I have to.
6. I like tasks that require little thought once I've learned them.
7. I prefer to think about small, daily projects rather than long-term ones.
8. I would rather do something that requires little thought than something that is sure to challenge my thinking abilities.
9. I find little satisfaction in deliberating hard and for long hours.
10. I don't like to be responsible for a situation that requires a lot of thinking.

Scoring: The more you agree with statements 1 and 2, and disagree with the rest, the greater the likelihood that you have a high need for cognition.

FIGURE 2 This simple questionnaire will give you a general idea of the level of your need for cognition. (Source: Cacioppo et al., 1996.)

Are some people more likely than others to use central route processing rather than peripheral route processing? The answer is yes. People who have a high *need for cognition*, a person's habitual level of thoughtfulness and cognitive activity, are more likely to employ central route processing. Consider the statements shown in Figure 2. People who agree with the first two statements and disagree with the rest have a relatively high need for cognition (Cacioppo et al., 1996; Dai & Wang, 2007).

People who have a high need for cognition enjoy thinking, philosophizing, and reflecting on the world. Consequently, they tend to reflect more on persuasive messages by using central route processing, and are likely to be persuaded by complex, logical, and detailed messages. In contrast, those who have a low need for cognition become impatient when forced to spend too much time thinking about an issue. Consequently, they usually use peripheral route processing and are persuaded by factors other than the quality and detail of messages (Dollinger, 2003; VanOverwalle & Siebler, 2005).

THE LINK BETWEEN ATTITUDES AND BEHAVIOR

Not surprisingly, attitudes influence behavior. The strength of the link between particular attitudes and behavior varies, of course, but generally people strive for consistency between their attitudes and their behavior. Furthermore, people hold fairly consistent attitudes. For instance, you would probably not hold the attitude that eating meat is immoral and still have a positive attitude toward hamburgers (Ajzen, 2002; Conner et al., 2003; Levi, Chan, & Pence, 2006).

Ironically, the consistency that leads attitudes to influence behavior sometimes works the other way around, for in some cases it is our behavior that shapes our attitudes. Consider, for instance, the following incident:

You've just spent what you feel is the most boring hour of your life, turning pegs for a psychology experiment. Just as you finally finish and are about to leave, the experimenter asks you to do him a favor. He tells you that he needs a helper for future experimental sessions to introduce subsequent participants to the peg-turning task. Your specific job will be to tell them that turning the pegs is an interesting, fascinating experience. Each time you tell this tale to another participant, you'll be paid $1.

If you agree to help the experimenter, you may be setting yourself up for a state of psychological tension called cognitive dissonance. According to social psychologist

Cognitive dissonance: The conflict that occurs when a person holds two contradictory attitudes or thoughts (referred to as cognitions).

Leon Festinger (1957), **cognitive dissonance** occurs when a person holds two contradictory attitudes or thoughts (referred to as *cognitions*).

If you participate in the situation just described, you are left with two contradictory thoughts: (1) I believe the task is boring, but (2) I said it was interesting with little justification ($1). These two thoughts should arouse dissonance. How can you reduce cognitive dissonance? You cannot deny having said that the task is interesting without breaking with reality. Relatively speaking, it is easier to change your attitude toward the task—and thus the theory predicts that participants will reduce dissonance by adopting more positive attitudes toward the task (Cooper, Mirabile, & Scher, 2005; Cooper, 2007).

A classic experiment (Festinger & Carlsmith, 1959) confirmed this prediction. The experiment followed essentially the same procedure outlined earlier, in which a participant was offered $1 to describe a boring task as interesting. In addition, in a comparison condition, some participants were offered $20 to say that the task was interesting. The reasoning behind this condition was that $20 was so much money that participants in this condition had a good reason to be conveying incorrect information; dissonance would not be aroused, and less attitude change would be expected. The results supported this notion. More of the participants who were paid $1 changed their attitudes (becoming more positive toward the peg-turning task) than did participants who were paid $20.

We now know that dissonance explains many everyday events involving attitudes and behavior. For example, smokers who know that smoking leads to lung cancer hold contradictory cognitions: (1) I smoke, and (2) smoking leads to lung cancer. The theory predicts that these two thoughts will lead to a state of cognitive dissonance. More important, it predicts that—assuming that they don't change their behavior by quitting smoking—smokers will be motivated to reduce their dissonance by one of the following methods: (1) modifying one or both of the cognitions, (2) changing the perceived importance of one cognition, (3) adding cognitions, or (4) denying that the two cognitions are related to each other. Hence, a smoker may decide that he really doesn't smoke all that much or that he'll quit soon (modifying the cognition), that the evidence linking smoking to cancer is weak (changing the importance of a cognition), that the amount of exercise he gets compensates for the smoking (adding cognitions), or that there is no evidence linking smoking and cancer (denial). Whichever technique the smoker uses results in reduced dissonance (see Figure 3).

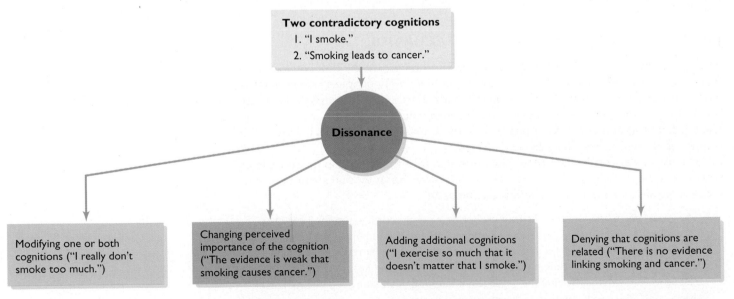

FIGURE 3 Cognitive dissonance. The simultaneous presence of two contradictory cognitions ("I smoke" and "Smoking leads to cancer") produces dissonance, which can be reduced through several methods. What are additional ways in which dissonance can be reduced?

Social Cognition: Understanding Others

Regardless of Bill Clinton's personal transgressions and impeachment trial, many Americans genuinely *liked* him when he was president, and his popularity remained high throughout his term in office. Cases like this illustrate the power of our impressions and attest to the importance of determining how people develop an understanding of others. One of the dominant areas in social psychology during the last few years has focused on learning how we come to understand what others are like and how we explain the reasons underlying others' behavior.

UNDERSTANDING WHAT OTHERS ARE LIKE

Consider for a moment the enormous amount of information about other people to which we are exposed. How can we decide what is important and what is not and make judgments about the characteristics of others? Social psychologists interested in this question study **social cognition**—the way people understand and make sense of others and themselves. Those psychologists have learned that individuals have highly developed **schemas**, sets of cognitions about people and social experiences. Those schemas organize information stored in memory, represent in our minds the way the social world operates, and give us a framework to recognize, categorize, and recall information relating to social stimuli such as people and groups (Brewer & Hewstone, 2003; Moskowitz, 2004; Smith & Semin, 2007).

We typically hold schemas for specific types of people. Our schema for "teacher," for instance, generally consists of a number of characteristics: knowledge of the subject matter he or she is teaching, a desire to impart that knowledge, and an awareness of the student's need to understand what is being said. Or we may hold a schema for "mother" that includes the characteristics of warmth, nurturance, and caring. Regardless of their accuracy, schemas are important because they organize the way in which we recall, recognize, and categorize information about others. Moreover, they help us predict what others are like on the basis of relatively little information, because we tend to fit people into schemas even when we do not have much concrete evidence to go on (Bargh & Chartrand, 2000; Ruscher, Fiske, & Schnake, 2000).

> **Social cognition:** The cognitive processes by which people understand and make sense of others and themselves.
> **Schemas:** Sets of cognitions about people and social experiences.

IMPRESSION FORMATION

How do we decide that Sayreeta is a flirt, Jacob is obnoxious, or Hector is a really nice guy? The earliest work on social cognition examined *impression formation*, the process by which an individual organizes information about another person to form an overall impression of that person. In a classic study, for instance, students learned that they were about to hear a guest lecturer (Kelley, 1950). Researchers told one group of students that the lecturer was "a rather warm person, industrious, critical, practical, and determined," and told a second group that he was "a rather cold person, industrious, critical, practical, and determined."

The simple substitution of "cold" for "warm" caused drastic differences in the way the students in each group perceived the lecturer, even though he gave the same talk in the same style in each condition. Students who had been told he was "warm" rated him considerably more positively than students who had been told he was "cold."

The findings from this experiment led to additional research on impression formation that focused on the way in which people pay particular attention to certain unusually important traits—known as **central traits**—to help them form an overall impression of others. According to this work, the presence of a central trait alters the meaning of other traits. Hence, the description of the lecturer as "industrious" presumably meant something different when it was associated with the central trait

> **Central traits:** The major traits considered in forming impressions of others.

"warm" than it meant when it was associated with "cold" (Widmeyer & Loy, 1988; Glicksohn & Nahari, 2007).

Other work on impression formation has used information-processing approaches to develop mathematically oriented models of how individual personality traits combine to create an overall impression. Generally, the results of this research suggest that in forming an overall judgment of a person, we use a psychological "average" of the individual traits we see, just as we would find the mathematical average of several numbers (Mignon & Mollaret, 2002).

We make such impressions remarkably quickly. In just a few seconds, using what have been called "thin slices of behavior," we are able to make judgments of people that are accurate and that match those of people who make judgments based on longer snippets of behavior (Choi, Gray, & Ambady, 2004; Pavitt, 2007).

Of course, as we gain more experience with people and see them exhibiting behavior in a variety of situations, our impressions of them become more complex. However, because our knowledge of others usually has gaps, we still tend to fit individuals into personality schemas that represent particular "types" of people. For instance, we may hold a "gregarious person" schema, made up of the traits of friendliness, aggressiveness, and openness. The presence of just one or two of those traits may be sufficient to make us assign a person to a particular schema.

However, our schemas are susceptible to error. For example, mood affects how we perceive others. Happy people form more favorable impressions and make more positive judgments than do people who are in a bad mood (Forgas & Laham, 2005).

Even when schemas are not entirely accurate, they serve an important function: They allow us to develop expectations about how others will behave. Those expectations permit us to plan our interactions with others more easily and serve to simplify a complex social world.

ATTRIBUTION PROCESSES: UNDERSTANDING THE CAUSES OF BEHAVIOR

> When Barbara Washington, a new employee at the Ablex Computer Company, completed a major staffing project two weeks early, her boss, Yolanda, was delighted. At the next staff meeting, she announced how pleased she was with Barbara and explained that *this* was an example of the kind of performance she was looking for in her staff. The other staff members looked on resentfully, trying to figure out why Barbara had worked night and day to finish the project not just on time but two weeks early. She must be an awfully compulsive person, they decided.

At one time or another, most of us have puzzled over the reasons behind someone's behavior. Perhaps it was in a situation similar to the one above, or it may have been in more formal circumstances, such as being a judge on a student judiciary board in a cheating case. In contrast to theories of social cognition, which describe how people develop an overall impression of others' personality traits, **attribution theory** seeks to explain how we decide, on the basis of samples of an individual's behavior, what the specific causes of that person's behavior are.

The general process we use to determine the causes of behavior and other social occurrences proceeds in several steps, as illustrated in Figure 4. After first noticing that something unusual has happened—for example, golf star Tiger Woods has played a terrible round of golf—we try to interpret the meaning of the event. This leads us to formulate an initial explanation (maybe Woods stayed up late the night before the match). Depending on the time available, the cognitive resources on hand (such as the attention we can give to the matter), and our motivation (determined in part by how important the event is), we may choose to accept our initial explanation or seek to modify it (Woods was sick, perhaps). If we have the time, cognitive resources, and motivation, the event triggers deliberate problem solving as we seek a fuller explanation. During the problem formulation and resolution stage, we may try out several

Attribution theory: The theory of personality that seeks to explain how we decide, on the basis of samples of an individual's behavior, what the specific causes of that person's behavior are.

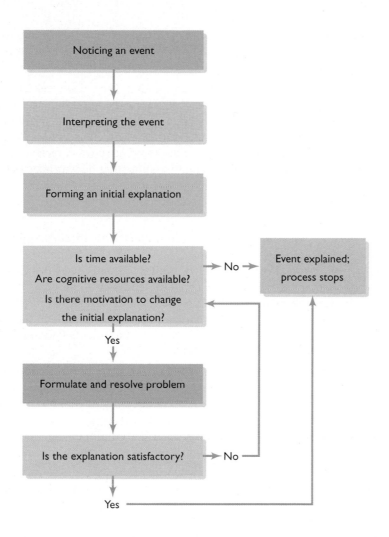

FIGURE 4 Determining why people behave the way they do. The general process we use to determine the causes of others' behavior proceeds in several steps. The kind of explanation we come up with depends on the time available to us, our cognitive resources, and our degree of motivation to come up with an accurate explanation. If time, cognitive resources, and motivation are limited, we'll make use of our first impression, which may be inaccurate. (Source: Adapted from Krull & Anderson, 1997, p. 2.)

possibilities before we reach a final explanation that seems satisfactory to us (Malle, 2004; Brown, 2006).

In seeking an explanation for behavior, we must answer one central question: Is the cause situational or dispositional? **Situational causes** are those brought about by something in the environment. For instance, someone who knocks over a quart of milk and then cleans it up probably does the cleaning not because he or she is necessarily a neat person but because the *situation* requires it. In contrast, a person who spends hours shining the kitchen floor probably does so because he or she is a neat person— hence, the behavior has a **dispositional cause**, prompted by the person's disposition (his or her internal traits or personality characteristics).

In our example involving Barbara Washington, her fellow employees attributed her behavior to her disposition rather than to the situation. But from a logical standpoint, it is equally plausible that something about the situation caused the behavior. If asked, Barbara might attribute her accomplishment to situational factors, explaining that she had so much other work to do that she just had to get the project out of the way, or that the project was not all that difficult and so it was easy to complete ahead of schedule. To her, then, the reason for her behavior might not be dispositional at all; it could be situational.

ATTRIBUTION BIASES: TO ERR IS HUMAN

If we always processed information in the rational manner that attribution theory suggests, the world might run a lot more smoothly. Unfortunately, although attribution theory generally makes accurate predictions, people do not always process

Situational causes (of behavior): Perceived causes of behavior that are based on environmental factors.

Dispositional causes (of behavior): Perceived causes of behavior that are based on internal traits or personality factors.

 StudyALERT

The central question in making an attribution is whether the cause of behavior is due to situational or dispositional factors.

information about others in as logical a fashion as the theory seems to suggest. In fact, research reveals consistent biases in the ways people make attributions. Typical ones include the following:

Halo effect: A phenomenon in which an initial understanding that a person has positive traits is used to infer other uniformly positive characteristics.

- *The halo effect.* Harry is intelligent, kind, and loving. Is he also conscientious? If you were to guess, your most likely response probably would be yes. Your guess reflects the **halo effect**, a phenomenon in which an initial understanding that a person has positive traits is used to infer other uniformly positive characteristics. The opposite would also hold true. Learning that Harry was unsociable and argumentative would probably lead you to assume that he was lazy as well. However, because few people have either uniformly positive or uniformly negative traits, the halo effect leads to misperceptions of others (Goffin, Jelley, & Wagner, 2003; Dennis, 2007).

Assumed-similarity bias: The tendency to think of people as being similar to oneself, even when meeting them for the first time.

- *Assumed-similarity bias.* How similar to you—in terms of attitudes, opinions, and likes and dislikes—are your friends and acquaintances? Most people believe that their friends and acquaintances are fairly similar to themselves. But this feeling goes beyond just people we know to a general tendency—known as the **assumed-similarity bias**—to think of people as being similar to oneself, even when meeting them for the first time. Given the range of people in the world, this assumption often reduces the accuracy of our judgments (Watson, Hubbard, & Wiese, 2000; Lemay, Clark, Feeney, 2007).

Self-serving bias: The tendency to attribute personal success to personal factors (skill, ability, or effort) and to attribute failure to factors outside oneself.

- *The self-serving bias.* When their teams win, coaches usually feel that the success is due to their coaching. But when they coach a losing team, coaches may think it's due to the poor skills of their players. Similarly, if you get an A on a test, you may think it's due to your hard work, but if you get a poor grade, it's due to the professor's inadequacies. The reason is the **self-serving bias**, the tendency to attribute success to personal factors (skill, ability, or effort) and attribute failure to factors outside oneself (Spencer et al., 2003; Bergeron, 2006).

Fundamental attribution error: A tendency to overattribute others' behavior to dispositional causes and the corresponding minimization of the importance of situational causes.

- *The fundamental attribution error.* One of the more common attribution biases is the tendency to overattribute others' behavior to dispositional causes and the corresponding failure to recognize the importance of situational causes. Known as the **fundamental attribution error**, this tendency is prevalent in Western cultures. We tend to exaggerate the importance of personality characteristics (dispositional causes) in producing others' behavior, minimizing the influence of the environment (situational factors). For example, we are more likely to jump to the

The assumed-similarity bias leads us to believe that others hold similar attitudes, opinions, and likes and dislikes.

conclusion that someone who is often late to work is too lazy to take an earlier bus (a dispositional cause) than to assume that the lateness is due to situational factors, such as the bus is always running behind schedule.

Why is the fundamental attribution error so common? One reason pertains to the nature of information available to the people making an attribution. When we view the behavior of another person in a particular setting, the most conspicuous information is the person's behavior. Because the individual's immediate surroundings remain relatively unchanged and less attention-grabbing, we center our attention on the person whose behavior we're considering. Consequently, we are more likely to make attributions based on personal dispositional factors and less likely to make attributions relating to the situation (Follett & Hess, 2002; Langdridge & Butt, 2004; Tal-Or & Papirman, 2007).

Despite the importance of the fundamental attribution error in shaping the perceptions of members of Western cultures, it turns out that it's not so fundamental when we looks at non-Western cultures, as we discuss next.

Attribution biases do not affect all of us in the same way. The culture in which we are raised clearly plays a role in the way we attribute others' behavior.

Exploring DIVERSITY

Attributions in a Cultural Context: How Fundamental Is the Fundamental Attribution Error?

Take, for example, the fundamental attribution error, the tendency to overestimate the importance of personal, dispositional factors and underattribute situational factors in determining the causes of others' behavior. The error is pervasive in Western cultures and not in Eastern societies. For instance, adults in India were more likely to use situational attributions than dispositional ones in explaining events. These findings are the opposite of those for the United States, and they contradict the fundamental attribution error (Miller, 1984, Lien et al., 2006).

One reason for the difference may lie in the norms and values of Eastern society, which emphasize social responsibility and societal obligations to a greater extent than in Western societies. In addition, the language spoken in a culture may lead to different sorts of attributions. For instance, a tardy person using English may say "I am late," suggesting a personal, dispositional cause ("I am a tardy person"). In contrast, users of Spanish who are late say, "The clock caused me to be late." Clearly, the statement in Spanish implies that the cause is a situational one (Zebrowitz-McArthur, 1988; Macduff, 2006; Alon & Brett, 2007).

Cultural differences in attributions may have profound implications. For example, parents in Asia tend to attribute good academic performance to effort and hard work (situational factors). In contrast, parents in Western cultures tend to deemphasize the role of effort and attribute school success to innate ability (a dispositional factor). As a result, Asian students in general may strive harder to achieve and ultimately outperform U.S. students in school (Stevenson, Lee, & Mu, 2000; Lien et al., 2006).

The difference in thinking between people in Asian and Western cultures is a reflection of a broader difference in the way the world is perceived. Asian societies generally have a *collectivistic orientation*, a worldview that promotes the notion of interdependence. People with a collectivistic orientation generally see themselves as parts of a larger, interconnected social network and as responsible to others. In contrast, people in Western cultures are more likely to hold an *individualist orientation*, that emphasizes personal identity and the uniqueness of the individual. They focus more on what sets them apart from others and what makes them special (Markus & Kitayama, 2003; Wang, 2004; Markus et al., 2007).

Students in Asian societies may perform exceptionally well in school because the culture emphasizes academic success and perseverance.

RECAP/EVALUATE/RETHINK

RECAP

What are attitudes, and how are they formed, maintained, and changed?

- Social psychology is the scientific study of the ways in which people's thoughts, feelings, and actions are affected by others and the nature and causes of individual behavior in social situations. (p. 584)

- Attitudes are evaluations of a particular person, behavior, belief, or concept. (p. 585)

- Cognitive dissonance occurs when an individual simultaneously holds two cognitions—attitudes or thoughts—that contradict each other. To resolve the contradiction, the person may modify one cognition, change its importance, add a cognition, or deny a link between the two cognitions, thereby bringing about a reduction in dissonance. (p. 588)

How do people form impressions of what others are like and of the causes of their behavior?

- Social cognition involves the way people understand and make sense of others and themselves. People develop schemas that organize information about people and social experiences in memory and allow them to interpret and categorize information about others. (p. 589)

- People form impressions of others in part through the use of central traits, personality characteristics that receive unusually heavy emphasis when we form an impression. (p. 589)

- Information-processing approaches have found that we tend to average together sets of traits to form an overall impression. (p. 590)

- Attribution theory tries to explain how we understand the causes of behavior, particularly with respect to situational or dispositional factors. (p. 590)

What are the biases that influence the ways in which people view others' behavior?

- Even though logical processes are involved, attribution is prone to error. For instance, people are susceptible to the halo effect, assumed-similarity bias, self-serving bias, and fundamental attribution error (the tendency to over-attribute others' behavior to dispositional causes and the corresponding failure to recognize the importance of situational causes). (p. 592)

EVALUATE

1. An evaluation of a particular person, behavior, belief, or concept is called a(n) _____.
2. One brand of peanut butter advertises its product by describing its taste and nutritional value. It is hoping to persuade customers through _____ route processing. In ads for a competing brand, a popular actor happily eats the product—but does not describe it. This approach hopes to persuade customers through _____ route processing.
3. Cognitive dissonance theory suggests that we commonly change our behavior to keep it consistent with our attitudes. True or false?
4. Sopan was happy to lend his textbook to a fellow student who seemed bright and friendly. He was surprised when his classmate did not return it. His assumption that the bright and friendly student would also be responsible reflects the _____ effect.

RETHINK

1. Joan sees Annette, a new co-worker, act in a way that seems abrupt and curt. Joan concludes that Annette is unkind and unsociable. The next day Joan sees Annette acting kindly toward another worker. Is Joan likely to change her impression of Annette? Why or why not? Finally, Joan sees several friends of hers laughing and joking with Annette, treating her in a very friendly fashion. Is Joan likely to change her impression of Annette? Why or why not?

2. *From the perspective of a marketing specialist:* Suppose you were assigned to develop a full advertising campaign for a product, including television, radio, and print ads. How might theories of persuasion guide your strategy to suit the different media?

Answers to Evaluate Questions

1. attitude; 2. central, peripheral; 3. false; we typically change our attitudes, not our behavior, to reduce cognitive dissonance; 4. halo

KEY TERMS

social psychology p. 584
attitudes p. 585
central route processing
  p. 586
peripheral route processing
  p. 586

cognitive dissonance p. 588
social cognition p. 589
schemas p. 589
central traits p. 589
attribution theory p. 590

situational causes (of
  behavior) p. 591
dispositional causes (of
  behavior) p. 591
halo effect p. 592

assumed-similarity bias
  p. 592
self-serving bias p. 592
fundamental attribution
  error p. 592

Social Influence and Groups

You have just transferred to a new college and are attending your first class. When the professor enters, your fellow classmates instantly rise, bow to the professor, and then stand quietly, with their hands behind their backs. You've never encountered such behavior, and it makes no sense to you. Is it more likely that you will (1) jump up to join the rest of the class or (2) remain seated?

On the basis of what research has told us about **social influence**, the process by which the actions of an individual or group affect the behavior of others, a person would almost always choose the first option. As you undoubtedly know from your own experience, pressures to conform can be painfully strong, and can bring about changes in behavior that otherwise never would have occurred.

Why can conformity pressures in groups be so strong? For one reason, groups, and other people generally, play a central role in our lives. As defined by social psychologists, **groups** consist of two or more people who (1) interact with one another; (2) perceive themselves as part of a group; and (3) are interdependent—that is, the events that affect one group member affect other members, and the behavior of members has significant consequences for the success of the group in meeting its goals.

Groups develop and hold *norms*, expectations regarding behavior appropriate to the group. Furthermore, we understand that not adhering to group norms can result in retaliation from other group members, ranging from being ignored to being overtly derided or even being rejected or excluded by the group. Thus, people conform to meet the expectations of the group (Baumeister, Twenge, & Nuss, 2002; Jetten, Hornsey, & Adarves-Yorno, 2006).

Groups exert considerable social influence over individuals, ranging from the mundane, such as the decision to wear a certain kind of jeans to the extreme cases such as the cruelty of guards at the Abu Ghraib prison in Iraq. We'll consider three types of social pressure: conformity, compliance, and obedience.

Conformity: Following What Others Do

Conformity is a change in behavior or attitudes brought about by a desire to follow the beliefs or standards of other people. Subtle or even unspoken social pressure results in conformity.

The classic demonstration of pressure to conform comes from a series of studies carried out in the 1950s by Solomon Asch (Asch, 1951). In the experiments, the participants thought they were taking part in a test of perceptual skills with six other people. The experimenter showed the participants one card with three lines of varying length and a second card that had a fourth line that matched one of the first three (see Figure 1). The task was seemingly straightforward: Each of the participants had to announce aloud which of the first three lines was identical in length to the "standard"

Key Concept

What are the major sources and tactics of social influence?

Social influence: The process by which the actions of an individual or group affect the behavior of others.

Group: Two or more people who interact with one another, perceive themselves as part of a group, and are interdependent.

 StudyALERT

The distinction between the three types of social pressure— conformity, compliance, and obedience—depends on the nature and strength of the social pressure brought to bear on a person.

Conformity: A change in behavior or attitudes brought about by a desire to follow the beliefs or standards of other people.

Standard line · Comparison lines

FIGURE 1 Which of the three comparison lines is the same length as the "standard" line?

line on the second card. Because the correct answer was always obvious, the task seemed easy to the participants.

Indeed, because the participants all agreed on the first few trials, the procedure appeared to be simple. But then something odd began to happen. From the perspective of the participant in the group who answered last on each trial, all the answers of the first six participants seemed to be wrong—in fact, unanimously wrong. And this pattern persisted. Over and over again, the first six participants provided answers that contradicted what the last participant believed to be correct. The last participant faced the dilemma of whether to follow his or her own perceptions or follow the group by repeating the answer everyone else was giving.

As you might have guessed, this experiment was more contrived than it appeared. The first six participants were actually confederates (paid employees of the experimenter) who had been instructed to give unanimously erroneous answers in many of the trials. And the study had nothing to do with perceptual skills. Instead, the issue under investigation was conformity.

Asch found that in about one-third of the trials, the participants conformed to the unanimous but erroneous group answer, with about 75 percent of all participants conforming at least once. However, he found strong individual differences. Some participants conformed nearly all the time, whereas others never did.

CONFORMITY CONCLUSIONS

Since Asch's pioneering work, literally hundreds of studies have examined conformity, and we now know a great deal about the phenomenon. Significant findings focus on:

- *The characteristics of the group.* The more attractive a group appears to its members, the greater is its ability to produce conformity. Furthermore, a person's relative **status**, the social rank held within a group, is critical: The lower a person's status in the group, the greater the power of the group over that person's behavior (Hogg & Hains, 2001).

- *The situation in which the individual is responding.* Conformity is considerably higher when people must respond publicly than it is when they can do so privately, as the founders of the United States noted when they authorized secret ballots in voting.

- *The kind of task.* People working on ambiguous tasks and questions (ones having no clear answer) are more susceptible to social pressure. Asked to give an opinion, such as what type of clothing is fashionable, a person will more likely yield to conformist pressures than he or she will if asked a question of fact. In addition, tasks at which an individual is less competent than others in the group make conformity more likely. For example, a person who is an infrequent computer user may feel pressure to conform to an opinion about computer brands when in a group of experienced computer users.

- *Unanimity of the group.* Groups that unanimously support a position show the most pronounced conformity pressures. But what of the case in which people with dissenting views have an ally in the group, known as a **social supporter**, who agrees with them? Having just one person present who shares the minority point of view is sufficient to reduce conformity pressures (Prislin, Brewer, & Wilson, 2002; Goodwin et al., 2004; Levine & Moreland, 2006).

Status: The social rank held within a group.

Social supporter: A group member whose dissenting views make nonconformity to the group easier.

GROUPTHINK: CAVING IN TO CONFORMITY

Although we usually think of conformity in terms of our individual relations with others, in some instances conformity pressures in organizations can lead to disastrous effects with long-term consequences. For instance, consider NASA's determination that the falling foam that hit the space shuttle *Columbia* when it took off in 2003 would

Groupthink may explain the poor decision-making of NASA engineers that led to the destruction of the space shuttle *Columbia*.

pose no significant danger when it was time for the *Columbia* to land. Despite the misgivings of some engineers, a consensus formed that the foam was not dangerous to the shuttle. Ultimately, that consensus proved wrong: The shuttle came apart as it attempted to land, killing all the astronauts on board (Schwartz & Wald, 2003).

In hindsight, NASA's decision was clearly wrong. How could such a poor decision have been made?

A phenomenon known as groupthink may provide an explanation. **Groupthink** is a type of thinking in which group members share such a strong motivation to achieve consensus that they lose the ability to critically evaluate alternative points of view. Groupthink is most likely to occur when a popular or powerful leader is surrounded by people of lower status—obviously the case with any U.S. president and his advisers, but also true in a variety of other organizations (Janis, 1997; Kowert, 2002; Baron, 2005; Henningsen et al., 2006).

Groupthink typically leads to poor decisions. Groups limit the list of possible solutions to just a few, and spend relatively little time considering any alternatives once the leader seems to be leaning toward a particular solution. In addition, groups may fall prey to *entrapment*, a circumstance in which commitments to a failing point of view or course of action are increased to justify investments in time and energy that have already been made (Weiss & Weiss, 2003; Turner, Pratkanis, & Struckman, 2007).

Ultimately, group members may completely ignore information that challenges a developing consensus. Because historical research suggests that many disastrous decisions reflect groupthink, it is important for groups to be on guard (Tetlock, 1997; Park, 2000; Kowert, 2002; Chapman, 2006).

Groupthink: A type of thinking in which group members share such a strong motivation to achieve consensus that they lose the ability to critically evaluate alternative points of view.

CONFORMITY TO SOCIAL ROLES

Another way in which conformity influences behavior is through social roles. *Social roles* are the behaviors that are associated with people in a given position. For example, the role of "student" is comprised of behaviors such as studying, listening to an instructor, and attending class. Like a theatrical role, social roles tell us what behavior is associated with a given position.

In some cases, though, social roles influence us so profoundly that we engage in behavior in entirely atypical—and damaging—ways. This fact was brought home in an influential experiment conducted by Philip Zimbardo and colleagues. In the study, the researchers set up a mock prison, complete with cells, solitary confinement cubicles, and a small recreation area. The researchers then advertised for participants who were willing to spend 2 weeks in a study of prison life. Once they identified the study participants, a flip of a coin designated who would be a prisoner and who would be a prison guard. Neither prisoners nor guards were told how to fulfill their roles (Zimbardo, 1973; Zimbardo, Maslach, & Haney, 2000; Zimbardo, 2007).

After just a few days in this mock prison, the students assigned to be guards became abusive to the prisoners, waking them at odd hours and subjecting them to arbitrary punishment. They withheld food from the prisoners and forced them into hard labor. On the other hand, the students assigned to the prisoner role soon became docile and submissive to the guards. They became extremely demoralized, and one slipped into a depression so severe he was released after just a few days. In fact, after only 6 days of captivity, the remaining prisoners' reactions became so extreme that the study was ended.

The experiment (which, it's important to note, drew criticism on both methodological and ethical grounds) provided a clear lesson: Conforming to a social role can have a powerful consequence on the behavior of even normal, well-adjusted people, inducing them to change their behavior in sometimes undesirable ways. This phenomenon may explain how the situation in which U.S. Army guards at the Iraq Abu Ghraib prison found themselves could have led to their abusive behavior toward the prisoners (Zimbardo, 2007).

Compliance: Submitting to Direct Social Pressure

When we refer to conformity, we usually mean a phenomenon in which the social pressure is subtle or indirect. But in some situations social pressure is much more obvious, with direct, explicit pressure to endorse a particular point of view or behave in a certain way. Social psychologists call the type of behavior that occurs in response to direct social pressure **compliance**.

Compliance: Behavior that occurs in response to direct social pressure.

Several specific techniques represent attempts to gain compliance. Those frequently employed include:

- *Foot-in-the-door technique.* A salesperson comes to your door and asks you to accept a small sample. You agree, thinking you have nothing to lose. A little later comes a larger request, which, because you have already agreed to the first one, you have a hard time turning down.

  The salesperson in this case is using a tried-and-true strategy that social psychologists call the foot-in-the-door technique. In the *foot-in-the-door technique,* you ask a person to agree to a small request and later ask that person to comply with a more important one. It turns out that compliance with the more important request increases significantly when the person first agrees to the smaller favor.

  Researchers first demonstrated the foot-in-the-door phenomenon in a study in which a number of experimenters went door to door asking residents to sign a petition in favor of safe driving (Freedman & Fraser, 1966). Almost everyone complied with that small, benign request. A few weeks later, different experimenters contacted the residents and made a much larger request: that the residents erect a huge sign reading "Drive Carefully" on their front lawns. The results were clear: 55 percent of those who had signed the petition agreed to the request to put up a sign, whereas only 17 percent of the people in a control group who had not been asked to sign the petition agreed to put up a sign.

Why does the foot-in-the-door technique work? For one reason, involvement with the small request leads to an interest in an issue, and taking an action—any action—makes the individual more committed to the issue, thereby increasing the likelihood of future compliance. Another explanation revolves around people's self-perceptions. By complying with the initial request, individuals may come to see themselves as people who provide help when asked. Then, when confronted with the larger request, they agree in order to maintain the kind of consistency in attitudes and behavior that we described earlier. Although we don't know which of these two explanations is more accurate, it is clear that the foot-in-the-door strategy is effective (Burger & Caldwell, 2003; Bloom et al., 2006).

- *Door in-the-face technique.* A fund-raiser asks for a $500 contribution. You laughingly refuse, telling her that the amount is way out of your league. She then asks for a $10 contribution. What do you do? If you are like most people, you'll probably be a lot more compliant than you would be if she hadn't asked for the huge contribution first. In this tactic, called the *door-in-the-face technique*, someone makes a large request, expecting it to be refused, and follows it with a smaller one. This strategy, which is the opposite of the foot-in-the-door approach, has also proved to be effective (Millar, 2002; Pascual & Gueguen, 2005, 2006).

  In a field experiment that demonstrates the success of this approach, experimenters stopped college students on the street and asked them to agree to a substantial favor—acting as unpaid counselors for juvenile delinquents 2 hours a week for 2 years (Cialdini et al., 1975). Not surprisingly, no one agreed to make such an enormous commitment. But when they were later asked the considerably smaller favor of taking a group of delinquents on a 2-hour trip to the zoo, half the people complied. In comparison, only 17 percent of a control group of participants who had not first received the larger request agreed.

  The use of this technique is widespread. You may have tried it at some point yourself, perhaps by asking your parents for a large increase in your allowance and later settling for less. Similarly, television writers, by sometimes sprinkling their scripts with obscenities that they know will be cut out by network censors, hope to keep other key phrases intact (Cialdini & Sagarin, 2005).

- *That's-not-all technique.* In this technique, a salesperson offers you a deal at an inflated price. But immediately after the initial offer, the salesperson offers an incentive, discount, or bonus to clinch the deal.

  Although it sounds transparent, this practice can be quite effective. In one study, the experimenters set up a booth and sold cupcakes for 75 cents each. In one condition, the experimenters directly told customers that the price was 75 cents. But in another condition, they told customers that the price was originally $1 but had been reduced to 75 cents. As we might predict, more people bought cupcakes at the "reduced" price—even though it was identical to the price in the other experimental condition (Burger, Reed, & DeCesare, 1999; Pratkanis, 2007).

- *Not-so-free sample.* If you ever receive a free sample, keep in mind that it comes with a psychological cost. Although they may not couch it in these terms, salespeople who provide samples to potential customers do so to instigate the norm of reciprocity. The *norm of reciprocity* is the well-accepted societal standard dictating that we should treat other people as they treat us. Receiving a *not-so-free sample*, then, suggests the need for reciprocation—in the form of a purchase, of course (Spiller & Wymer, 2001; Cialdini, 2006; Park & Antonioni, 2007).

Companies seeking to sell their products to consumers often use the techniques identified by social psychologists for promoting compliance. But employers also use them to bring about compliance and raise the

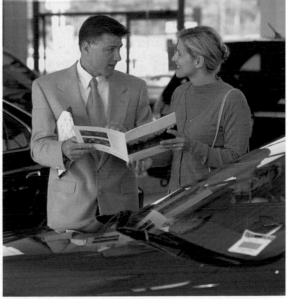

The persuasive techniques identified by social psychologists can be seen in practice at auto dealerships.

Industrial-organizational (I/O) psychology: The branch of psychology focusing on work- and job-related issues, including worker motivation, satisfaction, safety, and productivity.

Obedience: A change in behavior in response to the commands of others.

productivity of employees in the workplace. In fact, a close cousin to social psychology, **industrial-organizational (I/O) psychology**, considers issues such as worker motivation, satisfaction, safety, and productivity. I/O psychologists also focus on the operation and design of organizations, asking questions such as how decision making can be improved in large organizations and how the fit between workers and their jobs can be maximized.

Obedience: Following Direct Orders

Compliance techniques are used to gently lead people toward agreement with a request. In some cases, however, requests aim to produce **obedience**, a change in behavior in response to the commands of others. Although obedience is considerably less common than conformity and compliance, it does occur in several specific kinds of relationships. For example, we may show obedience to our bosses, teachers, or parents merely because of the power they hold to reward or punish us.

To acquire an understanding of obedience, consider for a moment how you might respond if a stranger said to you:

> I've devised a new way of improving memory. All I need is for you to teach people a list of words and then give them a test. The test procedure requires only that you give learners a shock each time they make a mistake on the test. To administer the shocks you will use a "shock generator" that gives shocks ranging from 15 to 450 volts. You can see that the switches are labeled from "slight shock" through "danger: severe shock" at the top level, where there are three red Xs. But don't worry; although the shocks may be painful, they will cause no permanent damage.

Presented with this situation, you would be likely to think that neither you nor anyone else would go along with the stranger's unusual request. Clearly, it lies outside the bounds of what we consider good sense.

Or does it? Suppose the stranger asking for your help were a psychologist conducting an experiment. Or suppose the request came from your teacher, your employer, or your military commander—all people in authority with a seemingly legitimate reason for the request.

If you still believe it's unlikely that you would comply—think again. The situation presented above describes a classic experiment conducted by social psychologist Stanley Milgram in the 1960s. In the study, an experimenter told participants to give increasingly stronger shocks to another person as part of a study on learning (see Figure 2). In reality, the experiment had nothing to do with learning; the real issue under consideration was the degree to which participants would comply with the experimenter's requests. In fact, the "learner" supposedly receiving the shocks was a confederate who never really received any punishment (Milgram, 2005).

Most people who hear a description of Milgram's experiment feel that it is unlikely that *any* participant would give the maximum level of shock—or, for that matter, any shock at all. Even a group of psychiatrists to whom the situation was described predicted that fewer than 2 percent of the participants would fully comply and administer the strongest shocks.

However, the actual results contradicted both experts' and nonexperts' predictions. Some 65 percent of the participants eventually used the highest setting on the shock generator—450 volts—to shock the learner. This obedience occurred even though the learner, who had mentioned at the start of the experiment that he had a heart condition, demanded to be released, screaming, "Let me out of here! Let me out of here! My heart's bothering me. Let me out of here!" Despite the learner's pleas, most participants continued to administer the shocks.

Why did so many individuals comply with the experimenter's demands? The participants, who were extensively interviewed after the experiment, said they obeyed primarily because they believed that the experimenter would be responsible for any

FIGURE 2 This fearsome-looking "shock generator" led participants to believe they were administering electric shocks to another person, who was connected to the generator by electrodes that were attached to the skin. (Source: Copyright 1965 by Stanley Milgram. From the film *Obedience*, distributed by the New York University Film Library and Pennsylvania State University, PCR.)

potential ill effects that befell the learner. The participants accepted the experimenter's orders, then, because they thought that they personally could not be held accountable for their actions—they could always blame the experimenter (Blass, 1996, 2004).

Although most participants in the Milgram experiment said later that they felt the knowledge gained from the study outweighed the discomfort they may have felt, the experiment has been criticized for creating an extremely trying set of circumstances for the participants, thereby raising serious ethical concerns. (Undoubtedly, the experiment could not be conducted today because of ethical considerations.) Other critics have suggested that Milgram's methods were ineffective in creating a situation that actually mirrored real-world obedience. For example, how often are people placed in a situation in which someone orders them to continue hurting a victim, while the victim's protests are ignored (Blass, 2000, 2004)?

Despite these concerns, Milgram's research remains the strongest laboratory demonstration of obedience. We need only consider actual instances of obedience to authority to witness some frightening real-life parallels. For instance, after World War II, the major defense that Nazi officers gave to excuse their participation in atrocities during the war was that they were "only following orders." Milgram's experiment, which was motivated in part by his desire to explain the behavior of everyday Germans during World War II, forces us to ask ourselves this question: Would we be able to withstand the intense power of authority?

 StudyALERT

Because of its graphic demonstration of obedience to authority, the Milgram experiment is one of the most famous and influential studies in social psychology.

RECAP/EVALUATE/RETHINK

RECAP

What are the major sources and tactics of social influence?

- Social influence is the area of social psychology concerned with situations in which the actions of an individual or group affect the behavior of others. (p. 595)

- Conformity refers to changes in behavior or attitudes that result from a desire to follow the beliefs or standards of others. (p. 595)

- Compliance is behavior that results from direct social pressure. Among the ways of eliciting compliance are the foot-in-the-door, door-in-the-face, that's-not-all, and not-so-free-sample techniques. (p. 598)

- Obedience is a change in behavior in response to the commands of others. (p. 600)

EVALUATE

1. A _____ _____, or person who agrees with the dissenting viewpoint, is likely to reduce conformity.
2. Who pioneered the study of conformity?
   a. Skinner
   b. Asch
   c. Milgram
   d. Fiala
3. Which of the following techniques asks a person to comply with a small initial request to enhance the likelihood that the person will later comply with a larger request?
   a. Door-in-the-face
   b. Foot-in-the-door
   c. That's-not-all
   d. Not-so-free sample

4. The _____-_____-_____-_____ technique begins with an outrageous request that makes a subsequent, smaller request seem reasonable.
5. _____ is a change in behavior that is due to another person's orders.

RETHINK

1. Why do you think the Milgram experiment is so controversial? What sorts of effects might the experiment have had on participants? Do you think the experiment would have had similar results if it had been conducted not in a laboratory setting, but among members of a social group (such as a fraternity or sorority) with strong pressures to conform?
2. *From the perspective of a sales representative:* Imagine that you have been trained to use the various compliance techniques described in this section. Because these compliance techniques are so powerful, should the use of certain such techniques be forbidden? Should consumers be taught defenses against such techniques? Is the use of such techniques ethically and morally defensible? Why?
3. *From the perspective of an educator:* Student obedience in the elementary and secondary classroom is a major issue for many teachers. How might you promote student obedience in the classroom? What are some of the potentially harmful ways that teachers could use their social influence to elicit student obedience?

Answers to Evaluate Questions

1. social supporter; 2. b; 3. b; 4. door-in-the-face; 5. obedience

KEY TERMS

social influence p. 595
group p. 595
conformity p. 595

status p. 596
social supporter p. 596
groupthink p. 597

compliance p. 598
industrial-organizational
  (I/O) psychology p. 600

obedience p. 600

Prejudice and Discrimination

What do you think when someone says, "He's African American," "She's Chinese," or "That's a woman driver"?

If you're like most people, you'll probably automatically form some sort of impression of what each person is like. Most likely your impression is based on a **stereotype**, a set of generalized beliefs and expectations about a specific group and its members. Stereotypes, which may be negative or positive, grow out of our tendency to categorize and organize the vast amount of information we encounter in our everyday lives. All stereotypes share the common feature of oversimplifying the world: We view individuals not in terms of their unique, personal characteristics, but in terms of characteristics we attribute to all the members of a particular group.

Stereotypes can lead to **prejudice**, a negative (or positive) evaluation of a group and its members. For instance, racial prejudice occurs when a member of a racial group is evaluated in terms of race and not because of his or her own characteristics or abilities. Although prejudice can be positive ("I love the Irish"), social psychologists have focused on understanding the roots of negative prejudice ("I hate immigrants").

Common stereotypes and forms of prejudice involve race, religion, ethnicity, and gender. Over the years, various groups have been called "lazy" or "shrewd" or "cruel" with varying degrees of regularity by those who are not members of that group. Even today, despite major progress toward reducing legally sanctioned forms of prejudice, such as school segregation, stereotypes remain (Eberhardt et al., 2004; Pettibrew, 2004; Hunt et al., 2006).

Even people who on the surface appear to be unprejudiced may harbor hidden prejudice. For example, when white participants in experiments are shown faces on a computer screen so rapidly that they cannot consciously perceive the faces, they react more negatively to black than to white faces—an example of what has been called *modern racism* (Dovidio, Gaertner, Pearson, 2005; Liu & Mills, 2006; Pearson, Dovidio, & Pratto, 2007).

Although usually backed by little or no evidence, stereotypes can have harmful consequences. Acting on negative stereotypes results in **discrimination**—behavior directed toward individuals on the basis of their membership in a particular group. Discrimination can lead to exclusion from jobs, neighborhoods, and educational opportunities, and may result in lower salaries and benefits for members of specific groups. Discrimination can also result in more favorable treatment to favored groups, as when an employer hires a job applicant of his or her own racial group because of the applicant's race.

Stereotyping not only leads to overt discrimination, but also can cause members of stereotyped groups to behave in ways that reflect the stereotype through a phenomenon known as the *self-fulfilling prophecy*. Self-fulfilling prophecies are expectations about the occurrence of a future event or behavior that act to increase the likelihood that the event or behavior will occur. For example, if people think that members of a specific group lack ambition, they may treat them in a way that actually brings about a lack of ambition. Furthermore, it can lead to a self-stereotyping phenomenon that we discuss in the *Applying Psychology in the 21st Century* box (Oskamp, 2000; Seibl & Forster, 2005; Madon et al., 2006).

Key Concepts

How do stereotypes, prejudice, and discrimination differ?

How can we reduce prejudice and discrimination?

Stereotype: A set of generalized beliefs and expectations about a particular group and its members.

Prejudice: A negative (or positive) evaluation of a particular group and its members.

Discrimination: Behavior directed toward individuals on the basis of their membership in a particular group.

 StudyALERT

Remember that *prejudice* relates to *attitudes* about a group and its members, while *discrimination* relates to *behavior* directed to a group and its members.

Decreasing the Damage of Negative Stereotypes

You're probably familiar with the stereotype that women don't do well in math and science, or that African-American people don't do well in school at all. Negative stereotypes such as these can harm members of the group that is being stereotyped—not just by making them feel badly or encouraging others to treat them in a prejudiced way, although those things happen, too. Group members know about these stereotypes, of course, and their fear of confirming them may ironically end up hindering their performance. This apparent confirmation of the self-doubt planted by the stereotype may eventually lead group members to give up even trying to succeed (Kiefer & Sekaquaptewa, 2007).

This phenomenon, known as *stereotype threat*, helps to explain academic achievement gaps between majority and minority groups. Students who are members of a minority group that is stereotyped as unintelligent or academically inferior are burdened with this threat that adds to their stress and anxiety, putting them at a disadvantage to students who are not negatively stereotyped. Therefore, reducing the threat by removing this source of disadvantage may be one approach to closing these academic achievement gaps (Aronson & Steele, 2005; Nussbaum & Steele, 2007).

Although the stereotypes themselves may be difficult to change, what can be changed is how members of minority groups respond to those stereotypes. If they don't allow the stereotype to undermine their confidence, their performance wouldn't be hindered by the threat of confirming the stereotype. New research suggests a surprisingly simple technique to do this: providing minority students with self-affirmation that reinforces their confidence in their abilities, thereby inoculating them against the fear and doubt triggered by negative stereotypes (Cohen et al., 2006; Wilson, 2006).

In one study, researchers had seventh-grade African-American and European-American students complete a simple assignment at the start of their school year in which they picked a value that was very important to them from a list and then wrote a short paragraph explaining why it was an important value. Examples of values that students could choose included relationships with friends or family or being good at art. The researchers expected that this activity would act as a self-affirmation, reinforcing students' sense of self-worth. A control group of students of both races chose and wrote about the value that was least important to them. This one-time intervention took only about 15 minutes and no other intervention was given for the rest of the school year (Cohen et al., 2006).

Amazingly, this very quick and simple exercise had profound effects on the African-American students' academic performance throughout the rest of the school year. On average, the year-end grades of African-American students who completed the self-affirmation improved by nearly a third of a grade point relative to controls; no effect was observed for the European-American students. Nearly 70% of the African-American students saw an improvement, including those who were previously performing poorly and those who were previously performing well. The overall improvement among African-American students resulting from this simple intervention actually reduced the observed academic achievement gap between African-American and European-American students in this sample by a staggering 40%!

How could such a remarkable improvement result from such a minor intervention? The researchers offered some theories to explain these seemingly disproportionate effects:

- First, stereotype threat and impaired performance might normally tend to feed back into one another in a downward-spiraling fashion. Even a small intervention that simply breaks the

cycle might therefore stave off this reciprocal process.
- Second, a small intervention that produces even a minor, temporary gain in performance might set off an opposite reciprocal process in which small performance gains and erosion of stereotype threat feed back into each other over time, producing strong long-term effects.
- Third, relatively small performance improvements were noted at various evaluations across the semester; even though each of these improvements was small, the cumulative effect of many small improvements may have led to large improvement in year-end grades.

This research offers great hope for combating the ill effects of stereotype threat, with the use of a simple intervention that can easily be done in the classroom in a very short amount of time. Moreover, there is no reason to think that the effect is limited to African-American students; any student who is affected by stereotype threat should see similar benefits. The intervention is harmless to those who don't need it, and since it takes little time and effort, it can simply be assigned to all students. Where the cost is so small and the potential benefit so profound, there seems to be no reason for schools not to give it a try.

- Does it make sense to you that other people's negative expectations can hinder your performance? Why or why not?
- Does having students write about an important value seem like a good way to bolster their self-worth? What other similar kinds of interventions do you think might be worth trying?

The Foundations of Prejudice

No one has ever been born disliking a specific racial, religious, or ethnic group. People learn to hate, in much the same way that they learn the alphabet.

According to *observational learning approaches* to stereotyping and prejudice, the behavior of parents, other adults, and peers shapes children's feelings about members of various groups. For instance, bigoted parents may commend their children for expressing prejudiced attitudes. Likewise, young children learn prejudice by imitating the behavior of adult models. Such learning starts at an early age: children as young as 3 years of age begin to show preferences for members of their own race (Schenider, 2003; Nesdale, Maass, & Durkin, 2005; Dovidio & Gaertner, 2006).

The mass media also provide information about stereotypes, not just for children but for adults as well. Even today, some television shows and movies portray Italians as Mafia-like mobsters, Jews as greedy bankers, and African Americans as promiscuous or lazy. When such inaccurate portrayals are the primary source of information about minority groups, they can lead to the development and maintenance of unfavorable stereotypes (Coltraine & Messineo, 2000; Ward, 2004; Do, 2006).

Other explanations of prejudice and discrimination focus on how being a member of a specific group helps to magnify one's sense of self-esteem. According to *social identity theory*, we use group membership as a source of pride and self-worth. Social identity theory suggests that people tend to be *ethnocentric*, viewing the world from their own perspective and judging others in terms of their group membership. Slogans such as "gay pride" and "Black is beautiful" illustrate that the groups to which we belong furnish us with a sense of self-respect (Rowley et al., 1998; Tajfel & Turner, 2004; Hogg, 2006).

However, the use of group membership to provide social respect produces an unfortunate outcome. In an effort to maximize our sense of self-esteem, we may come to think that our own group (our *ingroup*) is better than groups to which we don't belong (our *outgroups*). Consequently, we inflate the positive aspects of our ingroup—and, at the same time, devalue outgroups. Ultimately, we come to view members of outgroups as inferior to members of our ingroup (Tajfel & Turner, 2004). The end result is prejudice toward members of groups of which we are not a part.

Neither the observational learning approach nor the social identity approach provides a full explanation for stereotyping and prejudice. For instance, some psychologists argue that prejudice results when there is perceived competition for scarce societal resources. Thus, when competition exists for jobs or housing, members of majority groups may believe (however unjustly or inaccurately) that minority group members are hindering their efforts to attain their goals, and this belief can lead to prejudice. In addition, other explanations for prejudice emphasize human cognitive limitations that lead us to categorize people on the basis of visually conspicuous physical features such as race, sex, and ethnic group. Such categorization can lead to the development of stereotypes and, ultimately, to discriminatory behavior (Dovidio, 2001; Fiske, 2002; Mullen & Rice, 2003; Weeks & Lupfer, 2004).

The most recent approach to understanding prejudice comes from an increasingly important area within social psychology: social neuroscience. **Social neuroscience** seeks to identify the neural basis of social behavior. It looks at how we can illuminate our understanding of groups, interpersonal relations, and emotions by understanding their neuroscientific underpinnings (Cacioppo, Visser, & Pickett, 2005; Harmon-Jones & Winkielman, 2007).

In one example of the value of social neuroscience approaches, researchers examined activation of the *amygdala*, the structure in the brain that relates to emotion-evoking stimuli and situations, while viewing white and black faces.

Social neuroscience: The subfield of social psychology that seeks to identify the neural basis of social behavior.

Like father, like son: Social learning approaches to stereotyping and prejudice suggest that attitudes and behaviors toward members of minority groups are learned through the observation of parents and other individuals. How can this cycle be broken?

Neuroscience in Your Life

FIGURE 1 Both white and black participants showed greater activity in the amygdala when viewing black faces as compared to viewing white faces in this composite fMRI scan. The researchers hypothesized that negative cultural messages about blacks lead to higher activation of the amygdala while viewing black faces due to it's role in negative emotions. What other explanations might have produced the same findings? (Source: Lieberman et al., 2005, Figure 1b).

Because the amygdala is especially responsive to threatening, unusual, or highly arousing stimuli, the researchers hypothesized greater activation of the amygdala during exposure to black faces due to negative cultural associations with racial minorities (Lieberman et al., 2005; Lieberman, 2007).

As you can see in Figure 1, the hypothesis was confirmed: the amygdala showed more activation when participants saw a black face than when they saw a white one. Because both blacks and whites were participants in the study, it is unlikely that the amygdala activation was simply the result of the novelty of viewing members of a racial minority. Instead, the findings suggest that culturally learned societal messages about race led to the brain activation.

Measuring Prejudice and Discrimination: The Implicit Personality Test

A 34-year-old white woman sat down in her Washington office to take a psychological test. Her office decor attested to her passion for civil rights—as a senior activist at a national gay rights organization, and as a lesbian herself, fighting bias and discrimination is what gets her out of bed every morning. . . .

All [the test] asked her to do was distinguish between a series of black and white faces. When she saw a black face she was to hit a key on the left, when she saw a white face she was to hit a key on the right. Next, she was asked to distinguish between a series of positive and negative words. Words such as "glorious" and "wonderful" required a left key, words such as "nasty" and "awful" required a right key. The test remained simple when two categories were combined: The activist hit the left key if she saw either a white face or a positive word, and hit the right key if she saw either a black face or a negative word.

Then the groupings were reversed. The woman's index fingers hovered over her keyboard. The test now required her to group black faces with positive words, and white faces with negative words. She leaned forward intently. She made no mistakes, but it took her longer to correctly sort the words and images. (From Shankar Vedantam, "See No Bias." From *The Washington Post*, Magazine Section, January 23, 2005, p. W12. © 2005 The Washington Post. All rights reserved. Used by permission and protected by the Copyright Laws of the United States. The printing, copying, redistribution, or retransmission of the Material without express written permission is prohibited. www.washingtonpost.com.)

When she found out her results, the activist was shocked: The test revealed that she showed bias in favor of whites over blacks.

Could you, like this woman, be prejudiced and not even know it? The answer, according to the researchers who developed the *Implicit Association Test*, is probably yes. People often fool themselves, and they are very careful about revealing their true attitudes about members of various groups, not only to others but to themselves. However, even though they may truly believe that they are unprejudiced, the reality is that they actually routinely differentiate between people on the basis of race, ethnicity, and sexual orientation.

The Implicit Association Test, or IAT, is an ingenious measure of prejudice that permits a more accurate assessment of people's discrimination between members of different groups. It was developed, in part, as a reaction to the difficulty in finding a questionnaire that would reveal prejudice. Direct questions such as, "Would you prefer interacting with a member of Group X rather than Group Y?" typically identify only the most blatant prejudices, because people try to censor their responses (Greenwald et al., 2006; Rudman & Ashmore, 2007).

In contrast, the IAT makes use of the fact that people's automatic reactions often provide the most valid indicator of what they actually believe. Having grown up in a culture that teaches us to think about members of particular groups in specific ways, we tend to absorb associations about those groups that are reflective of the culture (Lane et al., 2007).

The results of the IAT show that almost 90 percent of test-takers have a pro-white implicit bias, and more than two-thirds of non-Arab, non-Muslim volunteers display implicit biases against Arab Muslims. Moreover, more than 80 percent of heterosexuals display an implicit bias against gays and lesbians (Wittenbrink & Schwarz, 2007).

Of course, having an implicit bias does not mean that people will overtly discriminate, a criticism that has been made of the test. Yet it does mean that the cultural lessons to which we are exposed have a considerable unconscious influence on us. (Interested in how you would perform on the IAT? Go to this Web site to take the test: https://implicit.harvard.edu/implicit).

 StudyALERT

Remember that the Implicit Association Test allows measurement of attitudes about which people might not be consciously aware, as well as attitudes they wish to keep hidden from others.

Reducing the Consequences of Prejudice and Discrimination

How can we diminish the effects of prejudice and discrimination? Psychologists have developed several strategies that have proved effective.

- *Increasing contact between the target of stereotyping and the holder of the stereotype.* In a groundbreaking 1954 ruling, the United States Supreme Court ruled that school segregation, in which whites and blacks attended separate schools, was unconstitutional. One rationale for the ruling was social psychological evidence that segregation had harmful consequences for the self-esteem and academic performance of minority students. By desegregating schools, the hope was that the contact in school between students of different races ultimately would reduce prejudice and discrimination.

  In fact, research consistently has shown that increasing the amount of interaction between people can reduce negative stereotyping. But only certain kinds of contact are likely to reduce prejudice and discrimination. Situations in which contact is relatively intimate, the individuals are of equal status, or participants must cooperate with one another or are dependent on one another are more likely to reduce stereotyping (Dovidio, Gaertner, & Kawakami, 2003; Tropp & Pettigrew, 2005; Pettigrew & Tropp, 2006).

- *Making values and norms against prejudice more conspicuous.* Sometimes just reminding people about the values they already hold regarding equality and fair treatment of others is enough to reduce discrimination. Similarly, people who hear others making strong, vehement antiracist statements are subsequently more likely to strongly condemn racism (Czopp & Monteith, 2005; Tropp & Bianchi, 2006).

- *Providing information about the targets of stereotyping.* Probably the most direct means of changing stereotypical and discriminatory attitudes is education: teaching people to be more aware of the positive characteristics of targets of stereotyping. For instance, when the meaning of puzzling behavior is explained to people who hold stereotypes, they may come to appreciate the actual significance of the behavior (Isbell & Tyler, 2003; Banks, 2006; Nagda, Tropp, & Paluck, 2006).

RECAP/EVALUATE/RETHINK

RECAP

How do stereotypes, prejudice, and discrimination differ?

- Stereotypes are generalized beliefs and expectations about a specific group and its members. Stereotyping can lead to prejudice and self-fulfilling prophecies. (p. 603)
- Prejudice is the negative (or positive) evaluation of a particular group and its members. (p. 603)
- Stereotyping and prejudice can lead to discrimination, behavior directed toward individuals on the basis of their membership in a particular group. (p. 603)
- According to observational learning approaches, children learn stereotyping and prejudice by observing the behavior of parents, other adults, and peers. Social identity theory suggests that group membership is used as a source of pride and self-worth, and this may lead people to think of their own group as better than others. (p. 604)
- Social neuroscientific approaches to prejudice examine the functioning of the brain and nervous system to understand the basis of prejudice. (p. 605)

How can we reduce prejudice and discrimination?

- Among the ways of reducing prejudice and discrimination are increasing contact, demonstrating positive values against prejudice, and education. (p. 607)

EVALUATE

1. Any expectation—positive or negative—about an individual solely on the basis of that person's membership in a group can be a stereotype. True or false?
2. The negative (or positive) evaluation of a group and its members is called
   a. Stereotyping
   b. Prejudice
   c. Self-fulfilling prophecy
   d. Discrimination
3. Paul is a store manager who does not expect women to succeed in business. He therefore offers important, high-profile responsibilities only to men. If the female employees fail to move up in the company, it could be an example of a _____-_____ prophecy.

RETHINK

1. Do you think women can be victims of stereotype vulnerability? In what topical areas might this occur? Can men be victims of stereotype vulnerability? Why?
2. *From the perspective of a corrections officer:* How might overt forms of prejudice and discrimination toward disadvantaged groups (such as African Americans) be reduced in a state or federal prison?

Answers to Evaluate Questions

1. true; 2. b; 3. self-fulfilling

KEY TERMS

Positive and Negative Social Behavior

Are people basically good or bad?

Like philosophers and theologians, social psychologists have pondered the basic nature of humanity. Is it represented mainly by the violence and cruelty we see throughout the world, or does something special about human nature permit loving, considerate, unselfish, and even noble behavior as well?

We turn to two routes that social psychologists have followed in seeking answers to these questions. We first consider what they have learned about the sources of our attraction to others, and we end with a look at two opposite sides of human behavior: aggression and helping.

Liking and Loving: Interpersonal Attraction and the Development of Relationships

Nothing is more important in most people's lives than their feelings for others. Consequently, it is not surprising that liking and loving have become a major focus of interest for social psychologists. Known more formally as the study of **interpersonal attraction** or **close relationships**, this area addresses the factors that lead to positive feelings for others.

HOW DO I LIKE THEE? LET ME COUNT THE WAYS

By far the greatest amount of research has focused on liking, probably because it is easier for investigators conducting short-term experiments to produce states of liking in strangers who have just met than to instigate and observe loving relationships over long periods. Consequently, research has given us a good deal of knowledge about the factors that initially attract two people to each other. The important factors considered by social psychologists are the following:

- *Proximity*. If you live in a dormitory or an apartment, consider the friends you made when you first moved in. Chances are that you became friendliest with those who lived geographically closest to you. In fact, this is one of the more firmly established findings in the literature on interpersonal attraction: *Proximity* leads to liking (Burgoon et al., 2002; Smith & Weber, 2005).

- *Mere exposure*. Repeated exposure to a person is often sufficient to produce attraction. Interestingly, repeated exposure to *any* stimulus—a person, picture, compact disc, or virtually anything—usually makes us like the stimulus more. Becoming familiar with a person can evoke positive feelings; we then transfer the positive feelings stemming from familiarity to the person him- or herself. There are exceptions, though. In cases of strongly negative initial interactions,

Key Concepts

Why are we attracted to certain people, and what progression do social relationships follow?

What factors underlie aggression and prosocial behavior?

Interpersonal attraction (or close relationship): Positive feelings for others; liking and loving.

"I'm attracted to you, but then I'm attracted to me, too."

repeated exposure is unlikely to cause us to like a person more. Instead, the more we are exposed to him or her, the more we may dislike the individual (Zajonc, 2001; Butler & Berry, 2004).

- *Similarity.* Folk wisdom tells us that birds of a feather flock together. However, it also maintains that opposites attract. Social psychologists have come up with a clear verdict regarding which of the two statements is correct: We tend to like those who are similar to us. Discovering that others have similar attitudes, values, or traits promotes our liking for them. Furthermore, the more similar others are, the more we like them. One reason similarity increases the likelihood of interpersonal attraction is that we assume that people with similar attitudes will evaluate us positively. Because we experience a strong **reciprocity-of-liking effect** (a tendency to like those who like us), knowing that someone evaluates us positively promotes our attraction to that person. In addition, we assume that when we like someone else, that person likes us in return (Bates, 2002; Umphress et al., 2007).

Reciprocity-of-liking effect: A tendency to like those who like us.

- *Physical attractiveness.* For most people, the equation *beautiful = good* is quite true. As a result, physically attractive people are more popular than are physically unattractive ones, if all other factors are equal. This finding, which contradicts the values that most people say they hold, is apparent even in childhood—with nursery-school-age children rating their peers' popularity on the basis of attractiveness—and continues into adulthood. Indeed, physical attractiveness may be the single most important element promoting initial liking in college dating situations, although its influence eventually decreases when people get to know each other better (Langlois et al., 2000; Zebrowitz & Montepare, 2005; Little, Burt, & Perrett, 2006).

These factors alone, of course, do not account for liking. For example, in one experiment that examined the desired qualities in a friendship, the top-rated qualities in a same-sex friend included sense of humor, warmth and kindness, expressiveness and openness, an exciting personality, and similarity of interests and leisure activities (Sprecher & Reagan, 2002).

HOW DO I LOVE THEE? LET ME COUNT THE WAYS

Whereas our knowledge of what makes people like one another is extensive, our understanding of love is more limited in scope and recently acquired. For some time, many social psychologists believed that love was too difficult to observe and study in a controlled, scientific way. However, love is such a central issue in most people's lives that eventually social psychologists could not resist its allure.

As a first step, researchers tried to identify the characteristics that distinguish between mere liking and full-blown love. They discovered that love is not simply a greater quantity of liking, but a qualitatively different psychological state. For instance, at least in its early stages, love includes relatively intense physiological arousal, an all-encompassing interest in another individual, fantasizing about the other, and relatively rapid swings of emotion. Similarly, love, unlike liking, includes elements of passion, closeness, fascination, exclusiveness, sexual desire, and intense caring. We idealize partners by exaggerating their good qualities and minimizing their imperfections (Garza-Guerrero, 2000; Murray, Holmes, & Griffin, 2004).

Passionate (or romantic) love: A state of intense absorption in someone that includes intense physiological arousal, psychological interest, and caring for the needs of another.

Companionate love: The strong affection we have for those with whom our lives are deeply involved.

Other researchers have theorized that there are two main types of love: passionate love and companionate love. **Passionate (or romantic) love** represents a state of intense absorption in someone. It includes intense physiological arousal, psychological interest, and caring for the needs of another. In contrast, **companionate love** is the strong affection we have for those with whom our lives are deeply involved. The love we feel for our parents, other family members, and even some close friends falls into the category of companionate love (Hendrick & Hendrick, 2003; Masuda, 2003; Regan, 2006).

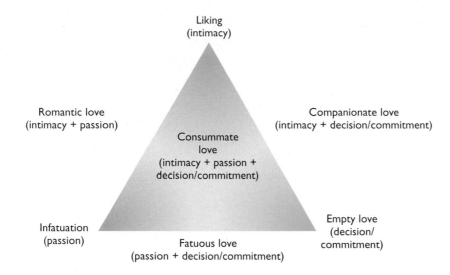

FIGURE 1 According to Sternberg, love has three main components: intimacy, passion, and decision/commitment. Different combinations of these components can create other types of love. Nonlove contains none of the three components.

Psychologist Robert Sternberg makes an even finer differentiation between types of love. He proposes that love consists of three parts:

- *Decision/commitment*, the initial thoughts that one loves someone and the longer-term feelings of commitment to maintain love.

- *Intimacy component*, feelings of closeness and connectedness.

- *Passion component*, the motivational drives relating to sex, physical closeness, and romance.

According to Sternberg, these three components combine to produce the different types of love. He suggests that different combinations of the three components vary over the course of relationships. For example, in strong, loving relationships the level of commitment peaks and then remains stable. Passion, on the other hand, peaks quickly, and then declines and levels off relatively early in most relationships. In addition, relationships are happiest in which the strength of the various components are similar between the two partners (Sternberg, Hojjat, & Barnes, 2001; Sternberg, 2004; Sternberg, 2006; see Figure 1).

Is love a necessary ingredient in a good marriage? Yes, if you live in the United States. In contrast, it's considerably less important in other cultures. Although mutual attraction and love are the two most important characteristics desired in a mate by men and women in the United States, men in China rated good health as most important, and women there rated emotional stability and maturity as most important. Among the Zulu in South Africa, men rated emotional stability first and women rated dependable character first (Buss et al., 1990; see Figure 2).

Liking and loving clearly show a positive side of human social behavior. Now we turn to behaviors that are just as much a part of social behavior: aggression and helping behavior.

Aggression and Prosocial Behavior: Hurting and Helping Others

Drive-by shootings, carjackings, and abductions are just a few examples of the violence that seem all too common today. Yet we also find examples of generous, unselfish, thoughtful behavior that suggest a more optimistic view of humankind. Consider, for instance, people such as Mother Teresa, who ministered to the poor in India. Or contemplate the simple kindnesses of life: lending a valued compact disc, stopping to help a child who has fallen off a bicycle, or merely sharing a candy bar with a friend.

Rank Ordering of Desired Characteristics in a Mate						
	United States		China		South Africa Zulu	
	Females	**Males**	**Females**	**Males**	**Females**	**Males**
Mutual attraction—love	1	1	8	4	5	10
Emotional stability and maturity	2	2	1	5	2	1
Dependable character	3	3	7	6	1	3
Pleasing disposition	4	4	16	13	3	4
Education and intelligence	5	5	4	8	6	6
Good health	9	6	3	1	4	5
Good looks	13	7	15	11	16	14
Sociability	8	8	9	12	8	11
Desire for home and children	7	9	2	2	9	9
Refinement, neatness	12	10	10	7	10	7
Ambition and industriousness	6	11	5	10	7	8
Similar education	10	12	12	15	12	12
Good cook and housekeeper	16	13	11	9	15	2
Favorable social status or rating	14	14	13	14	14	17
Similar religious background	15	15	18	18	11	16
Good financial prospect	11	16	14	16	13	18
Chastity (no prior sexual intercourse)	18	17	6	3	18	13
Similar political background	17	18	17	17	17	15

FIGURE 2 Although love may be an important factor in choosing a marriage partner if you live in the United States, other cultures place less importance on it. (Source: Buss et al., 1990.)

Such instances of helping are no less characteristic of human behavior than are the distasteful examples of aggression.

HURTING OTHERS: AGGRESSION

We need look no further than the daily paper or the nightly news to be bombarded with examples of aggression, both on a societal level (war, invasion, assassination) and on an individual level (crime, child abuse, and the many petty cruelties humans are capable of inflicting on one another). Is such aggression an inevitable part of the human condition? Or is aggression primarily a product of particular circumstances that, if changed, could lead to its reduction?

The difficulty of answering such knotty questions becomes apparent as soon as we consider how best to define the term *aggression*. Depending on the way we define the word, many examples of inflicted pain or injury may or may not qualify as aggression (see Figure 3). For instance, a rapist is clearly acting with aggression toward his victim. On the other hand, it is less certain that a physician carrying out an emergency medical procedure without an anesthetic, thereby causing incredible pain to the patient, should be considered aggressive.

Most social psychologists define *aggression* in terms of the intent and the purpose behind the behavior. **Aggression** is intentional injury of or harm to another person. By this definition, the rapist is clearly acting aggressively, whereas the physician causing pain during a medical procedure is not (Berkowitz, 2001).

We turn now to several approaches to aggressive behavior developed by social psychologists.

Aggression: The intentional injury of, or harm to, another person.

FIGURE 3 What is aggression? It depends on how the word is defined and in what context it is used. (Source: Adapted from Benjamin, 1985, p. 41.)

Is This Aggression?

To see for yourself the difficulties involved in defining aggression, consider each of the following acts and determine whether it represents aggressive behavior—according to your own definition of aggression.

1. A spider eats a fly. Yes _____ No _____
2. Two wolves fight for the leadership of the pack. Yes _____ No _____
3. A soldier shoots an enemy at the front line. Yes _____ No _____
4. The warden of a prison executes a convicted criminal. Yes _____ No _____
5. A man viciously kicks a cat. Yes _____ No _____
6. A man, while cleaning a window, knocks over a flower pot, which, in falling, injures a pedestrian. Yes _____ No _____
7. Mr. X, a notorious gossip, speaks disparagingly of many people of his acquaintance. Yes _____ No _____
8. A man mentally rehearses a murder he is about to commit. Yes _____ No _____
9. An angry son purposely fails to write to his mother, who is expecting a letter and will be hurt if none arrives. Yes _____ No _____
10. An enraged boy tries with all his might to inflict injury on his antagonist, a bigger boy, but is not successful in doing so. His efforts simply amuse the bigger boy. Yes _____ No _____
11. A senator does not protest the escalation of bombing to which she is normally opposed. Yes _____ No _____
12. A farmer beheads a chicken and prepares it for supper. Yes _____ No _____
13. A hunter kills an animal and mounts it as a trophy. Yes _____ No _____
14. A physician gives a flu shot to a screaming child. Yes _____ No _____
15. A boxer gives his opponent a bloody nose. Yes _____ No _____
16. A Girl Scout tries to assist an elderly woman but trips her by accident. Yes _____ No _____
17. A bank robber is shot in the back while trying to escape. Yes _____ No _____
18. A tennis player smashes her racket after missing a volley. Yes _____ No _____
19. A person commits suicide. Yes _____ No _____
20. A cat kills a mouse, parades around with it, and then discards it. Yes _____ No _____

INSTINCT APPROACHES: AGGRESSION AS A RELEASE

If you have ever punched an adversary in the nose, you may have experienced a certain satisfaction, despite your better judgment. Instinct theories, noting the prevalence of aggression not only in humans but in animals as well, propose that aggression is primarily the outcome of innate—or inborn—urges.

Sigmund Freud was one of the first to suggest, as part of his theory of personality, that aggression is a primary instinctual drive. Konrad Lorenz, an ethologist (a scientist who studies animal behavior), expanded on Freud's notions by arguing that humans, along with members of other species, have a fighting instinct, which in earlier times ensured protection of food supplies and weeded out the weaker of the species (Lorenz, 1966, 1974). Lorenz's instinct approach led to the controversial notion that aggressive energy constantly builds up within an individual until the person finally discharges it in a process called **catharsis**. The longer the energy builds up, says Lorenz, the greater will be the amount of the aggression displayed when it is discharged.

Probably the most controversial idea to come out of instinct theories of aggression is Lorenz's proposal that society should provide acceptable ways of permitting

Catharsis: The process of discharging built-up aggressive energy.

catharsis. For example, he suggested that participation in aggressive sports and games would prevent the discharge of aggression in less socially desirable ways. However, little research has found evidence for the existence of a pent-up reservoir of aggression that needs to be released. In fact, some studies flatly contradict the notion of catharsis, leading psychologists to look for other explanations for aggression (Bushman & Anderson, 2002; Bushman, Wang, & Anderson, 2005; Scheele & DuBois, 2006).

FRUSTRATION-AGGRESSION APPROACHES: AGGRESSION AS A REACTION TO FRUSTRATION

Suppose you've been working on a paper that is due for a class early the next morning, and your computer printer runs out of ink just before you can print out the paper. You rush to the store to buy more ink, only to find the sales clerk locking the door for the day. Even though the clerk can see you gesturing and begging him to open the door, he refuses, shrugging his shoulders and pointing to a sign that indicates when the store will open the next day. At that moment, the feelings you experience toward the sales clerk probably place you on the verge of real aggression, and you are undoubtedly seething inside.

Frustration-aggression theory tries to explain aggression in terms of events like this one. It suggests that *frustration* (the reaction to the thwarting or blocking of goals) produces anger, leading to a readiness to act aggressively. Whether actual aggression occurs depends on the presence of *aggressive cues,* stimuli that have been associated in the past with actual aggression or violence and that will trigger aggression again (Berkowitz, 2001).

What kinds of stimuli act as aggressive cues? They can range from the most explicit, such as the presence of weapons, to more subtle cues, such as the mere mention of the name of an individual who behaved violently in the past. For example, angered participants in experiments behave significantly more aggressively when in the presence of a gun than a comparable situation in which no guns are present. Similarly, frustrated participants who view a violent movie are more physically aggressive toward a confederate with the same name as the star of the movie than they are toward a confederate with a different name. It appears, then, that frustration does lead to aggression, at least when aggressive cues are present (Berkowitz, 2001; Marcus-Newhall, Pederson, & Carlson, 2000).

OBSERVATIONAL LEARNING APPROACHES: LEARNING TO HURT OTHERS

Do we learn to be aggressive? The observational learning (sometimes called social learning) approach to aggression says that we do. Taking an almost opposite view from instinct theories, which focus on innate explanations of aggression, observational learning theory emphasizes that social and environmental conditions can teach individuals to be aggressive. The theory sees aggression not as inevitable, but rather as a learned response that can be understood in terms of rewards and punishments.

Observational learning theory pays particular attention not only to direct rewards and punishments that individuals themselves receive, but also to the rewards and punishments that models—individuals who provide a guide to appropriate behavior—receive for their aggressive behavior. According to observational learning theory, people observe the behavior of models and the subsequent consequences of that behavior. If the consequences are positive, the behavior is likely to be imitated when observers find themselves in a similar situation.

Suppose, for instance, a girl hits her younger brother when he damages one of her new toys. Whereas instinct theory would suggest that the aggression had been pent up and was now being discharged, and frustration-aggression theory would examine the girl's frustration at no longer being able to use her new toy, observational learning theory

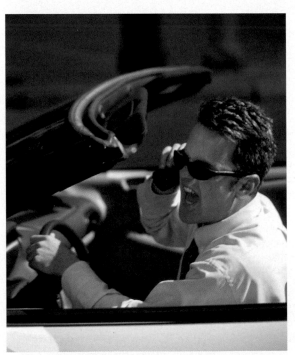

Is road rage a result of frustration? According to frustration-aggression approaches, frustration is a likely cause.

would look to previous situations in which the girl had viewed others being rewarded for their aggression. For example, perhaps she had watched a friend get to play with a toy after he painfully twisted it out of the hand of another child.

Observational learning theory has received wide research support. For example, nursery-school-age children who have watched an adult model behave aggressively and then receive reinforcement for it later display similar behavior themselves if they have been angered, insulted, or frustrated after exposure. Furthermore, a significant amount of research links watching television shows containing violence with subsequent viewer aggression (Coyne & Archer, 2005; Winerman, 2005; Greer, Dudek-Singer, & Gautreaux, 2006).

StudyALERT

Understand the distinction between the instinctual, frustration-aggression, and observational learning approaches to aggression.

Helping Others: The Brighter Side of Human Nature

Turning away from aggression, we move now to the opposite—and brighter—side of human nature: helping behavior. Helping behavior, or **prosocial behavior** as it is more formally known, has been considered under many different conditions. However, the question that psychologists have looked at most closely relates to bystander intervention in emergency situations. What are the factors that lead someone to help a person in need?

One critical factor is the number of others present. When more than one person witnesses an emergency situation, a sense of **diffusion of responsibility** can arise among the bystanders (as we discussed earlier in the book when we considered research methods). Diffusion of responsibility is the tendency for people to feel that responsibility for acting is shared, or diffused, among those present. The more people who are present in an emergency, the less personally responsible each individual feels—and therefore the less help he or she provides (Blair, Thompson, & Wuensch, 2002; Barron & Yechiam, 2002; Gray, 2006).

For example, think back to the classic case of Kitty Genovese that we described when discussing the topic of research early in the book. Genovese was stabbed multiple times, and no one offered help, despite purportedly close to 40 people who lived in nearby apartments having heard her screams for help. The lack of help has been attributed to diffusion of responsibility: the fact that there were so many potential helpers led each individual to feel diminished personal responsibility (Rogers & Eftimiades, 1995; Rosenthal, 2008).

Although most research on helping behavior supports the diffusion-of-responsibility explanation, other factors are clearly involved in helping behavior. According to a model of the helping process, the decision to give aid involves four basic steps (Latané and Darley, 1970; Garcia et al., 2002; see Figure 4):

- *Noticing a person, event, or situation that may require help.*

- *Interpreting the event as one that requires help.* Even if we notice an event, it may be sufficiently ambiguous for us to interpret it as a nonemergency situation. It is here that the presence of others first affects helping behavior. The presence of inactive others may indicate to us that a situation does not require help—a judgment we do not necessarily make if we are alone.

- *Assuming responsibility for helping.* It is at this point that diffusion of responsibility is likely to occur if others are present. Moreover, a bystander's particular expertise is likely to play a role in determining whether he or she helps. For instance, if people with training in medical aid or lifesaving techniques are present, untrained bystanders are less likely to intervene because they feel they have less expertise.

- *Deciding on and implementing the form of helping.* After we assume responsibility for helping, we must decide how to provide assistance. Helping can range from very indirect forms of intervention, such as calling the police, to more direct

Prosocial behavior: Helping behavior.

Diffusion of responsibility: The tendency for people to feel that responsibility for acting is shared, or diffused, among those present.

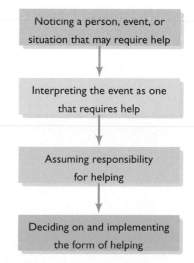

FIGURE 4 The basic steps of helping. (Source: Latané, Bibb; Darley, John M., *The Unresponsive Bystander: Why Doesn't He Help?* 1st ed., © 1970. Reproduced in print and electronic formats by permission of Pearson Education, Inc., Upper Saddle River, New Jersey.).

forms, such as giving first aid or taking the victim to a hospital. Most social psychologists use a *rewards-costs approach* for helping to predict the nature of the assistance a bystander will choose to provide. The general notion is that the rewards for helping, as perceived by the bystander, must outweigh the costs if helping is to occur, and most research tends to support this notion (Koper & Jaasma, 2001; Bartlett & DeSteno, 2006; Lin & Lin, 2007).

After determining the nature of the assistance needed, the actual help must be implemented. A rewards-costs analysis suggests that we are most likely to use the least costly form of implementation. However, this is not always the case: In some situations, people behave altruistically. **Altruism** is helping behavior that is beneficial to others but clearly requires self-sacrifice. For example, people who helped strangers escape from the burning World Trade Center towers during the 9-11 terrorist attack, putting themselves at mortal risk, would be considered altruistic (Krueger, Hicks, & McGue, 2001; Batson & Powell, 2003; Manor & Gailliot, 2007).

People who intervene in emergency situations tend to possess certain personality characteristics that differentiate them from nonhelpers. For example, helpers are more self-assured, sympathetic, and emotionally understanding, and they have greater *empathy* (a personality trait in which someone observing another person experiences the emotions of that person) than are nonhelpers (Batson, 2006; Graziano et al., 2007; Walker & Frimer, 2007).

Still, most social psychologists agree that no single set of attributes differentiates helpers from nonhelpers. For the most part, temporary situational factors (such as the mood we're in) determine whether we will intervene in a situation requiring aid (Eisenberg, Guthrie, & Cumberland, 2002; Dovidio et al., 2006).

Altruism: Helping behavior that is beneficial to others but clearly requires self-sacrifice.

StudyALERT

The distinction between *prosocial behavior* and *altruism* is important. Prosocial behavior need not have a self-sacrificing component; altruism, by definition, contains an element of self-sacrifice.

Altruism is often the only bright side of a natural disaster.

At one time or another, almost everyone feels angry. The anger may result from a frustrating situation, or it may be due to the behavior of another individual. The way we deal with anger may determine the difference between a promotion and a lost job or a broken relationship and one that mends itself.

Social psychologists who have studied the topic suggest several good ways to deal with anger, strategies that maximize the potential for positive consequences (Ellis & Tafrate, 2000; Nelson & Finch, 2000). Among the most useful strategies are the following:

**BECOMING
AN INFORMED CONSUMER
of Psychology**
Dealing Effectively with Anger

- *Look again at the anger-provoking situation from the perspective of others.* By taking others' points of view, you may be able to understand the situation better, and with increased understanding you may become more tolerant of the apparent shortcomings of others.

- *Minimize the importance of the situation.* Does it really matter that someone is driving too slowly and that you'll be late to an appointment as a result? Reinterpret the situation in a way that is less bothersome.

- *Fantasize about getting even—but don't act on it.* Fantasy provides a safety valve. In your fantasies, you can yell at that unfair professor all you want and suffer no consequences at all. However, don't spend too much time brooding: Fantasize, but then move on.

- *Relax.* By teaching yourself the kinds of relaxation techniques used in systematic desensitization (discussed in the module on treatment of psychological disorders), you can help reduce your reactions to anger. In turn, your anger may dissipate.

No matter which of these strategies you try, above all, don't ignore your anger. People who always try to suppress their anger may experience a variety of consequences, such as self-condemnation, frustration, and even physical illness (Finney, Stoney, & Engebretson, 2002; Burns et al., 2007; Quartana & Burns, 2007).

RECAP/EVALUATE/RETHINK

RECAP

Why are we attracted to certain people, and what progression do social relationships follow?

- The primary determinants of liking include proximity, exposure, similarity, and physical attractiveness. (p. 609)

- Loving is distinguished from liking by the presence of intense physiological arousal, an all-encompassing interest in another, fantasies about the other, rapid swings of emotion, fascination, sexual desire, exclusiveness, and strong feelings of caring. (p. 610)

- Love can be categorized as passionate or companionate. In addition, love has several components: intimacy, passion, and decision/commitment. (p. 611)

What factors underlie aggression and prosocial behavior?

- Aggression is intentional injury of or harm to another person. (p. 612)

- Explanations of aggression include instinct approaches, frustration-aggression theory, and observational learning. (p. 613)

- Helping behavior in emergencies is determined in part by the phenomenon of diffusion of responsibility, which results in a lower likelihood of helping when more people are present. (p. 615)

- Deciding to help is the outcome of a four-stage process consisting of noticing a possible need for help, interpreting the situation as requiring aid, assuming responsibility for taking action, and deciding on and implementing a form of assistance. (p. 615)

EVALUATE

1. We tend to like people who are similar to us. True or false?

2. Which of the following sets are the three components of love proposed by Sternberg?
   a. Passion, closeness, sexuality
   b. Attraction, desire, complementarity
   c. Passion, intimacy, decision/commitment
   d. Commitment, caring, sexuality

3. Based on research evidence, which of the following might be the best way to reduce the amount of fighting a young boy does?
   a. Take him to the gym and let him work out on the boxing equipment.
   b. Make him repeatedly watch violent scenes from the film *The Matrix Reloaded* in the hope that it will provide catharsis.
   c. Reward him if he doesn't fight during a certain period.
   d. Ignore it and let it die out naturally.

4. If a person in a crowd does not help in an apparent emergency situation because many other people are present, that person is falling victim to the phenomenon of _____ _____.

RETHINK

1. Can love be studied scientifically? Is there an elusive quality to love that makes it at least partially unknowable? How would you define "falling in love"? How would you study it?

2. *From the perspective of a criminal justice worker:* How would the aggression of Eric Rudolph, who was convicted of exploding a bomb during the 1996 Summer Olympics in Atlanta and later attacking several women's clinics, be interpreted by proponents of the three main approaches to the study of aggression: instinct approaches, frustration-aggression approaches, and observational learning approaches? Do you think any of these approaches fits the Rudolph case more closely than the others?

Answers to Evaluate Questions

1. true; 2. c; 3. c; 4. diffusion of responsibility

KEY TERMS

interpersonal attraction (or close relationship) p. 609
reciprocity-of-liking effect p. 610

passionate (or romantic) love p. 610
companionate love p. 610
aggression p. 612

catharsis p. 613
prosocial behavior p. 615
diffusion of responsibility p. 615

altruism p. 616

Psychology on the Web

1. Find examples on the Web of advertisements or other persuasive messages that use central route processing and peripheral route processing. What type of persuasion appears to be more prevalent on the Web? For what type of persuasion does the Web appear to be better suited? Is there a difference between Web-based advertising and other forms of advertising?

2. Is "hate crimes legislation" a good idea? Use the Web to find at least two discussions of hate crimes legislation—one in favor and one opposed—and summarize in writing the main issues and arguments presented. Using your knowledge of prejudice and aggression, evaluate the arguments for and against hate crimes legislation. State your opinion about whether this type of legislation is advisable.

Epilogue

We have touched on some of the major ideas, research topics, and experimental findings of social psychology. We examined how people form, maintain, and change attitudes and how they form impressions of others and assign attributions to them. We also saw how groups, through conformity and tactics of compliance, can influence individuals' actions and attitudes. Finally, we discussed interpersonal relationships, including both liking and loving, and looked at the two sides of a coin that represent the extremes of social behavior: aggression and prosocial behavior.

Turn back to the prologue of this set of modules, which describes the heroism of Wesley Autrey. Use your understanding of social psychology to consider the following questions.

1. What factors would a social psychologist consider in examining why Autrey jumped onto the subway tracks and helped a stranger?

2. Given what social psychologists know about the factors that lead people to be helpful, do you believe that Autrey's helpfulness was caused by situational factors or that it had more to do with his personality? Why?

3. Prior to the victim's falling onto the tracks, he had suffered a seizure on the subway platform, and Autrey had come to his aide at that point. Do you think the fact that Autrey had helped the victim initially made it more likely that he would react as he did when the man subsequently fell onto the tracks? Why?

4. Do you think Autrey would have reacted in a similar manner if he had had more time to think about acting? Why or why not?

5. What are some ways in which the incidence of helping behavior can be increased and the incidence of aggressive and antisocial behavior can be discouraged?

MASTERING attitude change

Persuasion can lead to attitude change in a variety of ways, including central and peripheral route processing. Use this visual guide to understand how attitude change occurs. Then answer the questions below to test your understanding of the concepts.

1 Attitude change starts with a message and a source. If the person delivering the message is perceived as attractive, trustworthy, and knowledgeable, and if different sides of an issue are presented, the message is more likely to be accepted. Additionally, the characteristics of the target audience affect their willingness to be persuaded.

Central route processing

2 In central route processing, we carefully consider the issues and arguments used to persuade us. People who are motivated, highly involved, and attentive are more receptive to central route processing. Central route processing can lead to commitment and more lasting attitude change.

EVALUATE

1 In the example above _____ evokes central route processing.
   a attending an expert's lecture on global warning
   b observing a student demonstration on global warming
   c watching a weather report
   d hearing a friend talk about how hot it was last summer

2 In this example, peripheral route processing might be occurring when
   a attending an expert's lecture on global warning
   b hearing a friend talk about how hot it was last summer
   c watching a weather report
   d observing a student demonstration on global warming

3 In peripheral route processing, we consider the source of the information and related information, rather than the message itself. Uninvolved, unmotivated, and inattentive individuals are more likely to use peripheral route processing. Although they might be persuaded initially, especially if the message comes from an attractive and famous person, their change in attitude is often weaker and less likely to last.

Peripheral route processing

3 Central route processing generally leads to more lasting attitude change than peripheral route processing. True or false?

RETHINK

1 An advertising company wants to produce peripheral route processing when viewers watch a television commercial for clam chowder. Why would the advertiser want to do this, and what elements might the commercial include to evoke peripheral route processing?

Answers to Evaluate questions: 1. a; 2. d; 3. True

Going by the Numbers: Statistics in Psychology

Key Concepts for Appendix

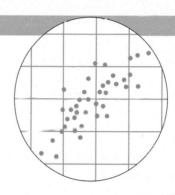

Prologue *Selma Vorwerk*

As the boat moved nearer to shore, the outline of the Statue of Liberty was plainly visible in the distance. Closer and closer it came, sending a chill down the spine of Selma Vorwerk. A symbol of America, the statue represented the hopes she carried from her native Europe in the early 1900s—hopes of liberty, of success, of a life free of economic and social strain.

Yet as the boat sailed closer to Ellis Island, the first point of arrival in the United States, Vorwerk did not realize that her very presence—and that of the other thousands of immigrants seeking their fortune in a land of opportunity—was threatened. A strong political movement was growing in the country on which she was pinning her hopes. That movement sought, by using information collected by psychologists, to stem the flow of immigrants through "scientific" analysis of data.

The major claim of the group was that a flood of "mentally deficient" immigrants was poisoning the intellectual capacity of the United States. To supporters of that view, unless drastic measures were taken, it would not be too many years before Western civilization collapsed from a lack of intelligence.

To support this assertion, Lathrop Stoddard, a member of the anti-immigration movement, reported the results of a study of intelligence in which tests were administered to a group of 82 children and 400 adults. On the basis of those test results, he concluded that the average mental age of people in the United States was only 14 years—proof to him that unlimited immigration had already produced a serious decline in the country's intelligence.

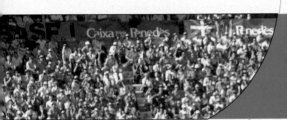

Looking Ahead

Fortunately for immigrants such as Selma Vorwerk, observers in favor of immigration pointed out the fallacy of using data from a relatively small sample—when a considerably larger set of intelligence test data was available. The U.S. Army had been collecting intelligence data for years and had the test scores of 1.7 million men available. When those scores were analyzed, it immediately became apparent that the claim that the average mental age of American adults was 14 years was completely without merit.

A debate reminiscent of this one rages today, as some observers suggest that an unrestrained flow of immigrants—this time from Latin America and Asia—will seriously damage the United States. This time, though, the debate is based more on analyses of social and economic statistics, with opponents of immigration suggesting that the social fabric of the country will be changed and that jobs are being taken away from longer-term residents because of the influx of immigrants. Equally vehement proponents of immigration suggest that the relevant statistics are being misinterpreted, and that their analyses of the situation result in a very different conclusion.

Descriptive Statistics

Statistics, the branch of mathematics concerned with collecting, organizing, analyzing, and drawing conclusions from numerical data, is a part of all of our lives. For instance, we are all familiar with the claims and counterclaims regarding the effects of smoking. The U.S. government requires that cigarette manufacturers include a warning that smoking is dangerous to people's health on every package of cigarettes and in their advertisements; the government's data show clear statistical links between smoking and disease. At the same time, the tobacco industry has long minimized the negative effects of smoking.

Statistics is also at the heart of a considerable number of debates in the field of psychology. How do we determine the nature and strength of the effects of heredity on behavior? What is the relationship between learning and schedules of reinforcement? How do we know if the "double standard" regarding male and female sexual practices has shifted over time? These questions, and most others of interest to psychologists, cannot be answered without a reliance on statistics (Leblanc, 2004).

In this set of modules, we consider the basic approaches to statistical measurement. We first discuss approaches to summarizing data that allow us to describe sets of observations. Next, we consider techniques for deciding how different one set of scores is from another. Finally, we examine approaches to measuring the relationship between two sets of scores.

Suppose, as an instructor of college psychology, you wanted to evaluate your class's performance on its initial exam. Where might you begin?

You would probably start by using **descriptive statistics**, the branch of statistics that provides a means of summarizing data, presenting the data in a usable and convenient form. For instance, you might first simply list the scores the pupils had received on the test:

72	78	78	92	69	73	85	49
86	86	72	59	58	85	89	
80	83	69	78	90	90	96	83

Viewed in this way, the scores are a jumble of numbers of which it is difficult to make any sense. However, there are several methods by which you could begin to organize the scores in a more meaningful way. For example, you might sort them in order of highest score to lowest score, as is done in Figure 1. By indicating the number of people who obtained each score, you would have produced what is called a **frequency distribution**, an arrangement of scores from a sample that indicates how often a particular score is present.

Another way of summarizing the scores is to consider them visually. For example, you could construct the **histogram**, or bar graph, shown in Figure 2. In that histogram, the number of people obtaining a given score is represented pictorially. The scores are ordered along one dimension of the graph, and the number of people obtaining each score along the other dimension.

Key Concept

What measures can we use to summarize sets of data?

Statistics: The branch of mathematics concerned with collecting, organizing, analyzing, and drawing conclusions from numerical data.

Descriptive statistics: The branch of statistics that provides a means of summarizing data.

Frequency distribution: An arrangement of scores from a sample that indicates how often a particular score is present.

Histogram: Bar graph.

"*Meaningless statistics were up one-point-five percent this month over last month.*"

A Sample Frequency Distribution

Test Score	Number of Students Attaining That Score
96	1
92	1
90	2
89	1
86	2
85	2
83	2
80	1
78	3
73	1
72	2
69	2
59	1
58	1
49	1

FIGURE 1 Example of a frequency distribution, which arranges scores from a sample and indicates how often a particular score is present.

Arranging the scores from the highest to the lowest allows us to visually inspect the data. Most often, however, visual inspection is insufficient. For one thing, there may be so many scores in a sample that it is difficult to construct a meaningful visual representation. For another, our interpretations of patterns on a graph or table are often biased and inaccurate; more precise, mathematically based measures would seem to be preferable. In cases in which a precise means of summarizing the data is desirable, psychologists turn to measures of central tendency. **Central tendency** is an index of the central location within a distribution of scores. There are three major measures of central tendency: the mean, the median, and the mode.

The Mean: Finding the Average

The most familiar measure of central tendency is the **mean**. A mean is the technical term for an average, which is simply the sum of all the scores in a set, divided by the number of scores making up the set. For example, to calculate the mean of the sample we have been using, begin by adding each of the numbers (96 + 92 + 90 + 90 + 89 + . . . and so forth). When you have the total, divide that sum by the number of scores, which is 23. This calculation, 1,800/23 = 78.26, produces a mean score, or average, for our sample.

In general, the mean is an accurate reflection of the central score in a set of scores; as you can see from the histogram in Figure 2, our mean of 78.26 falls roughly in the center of the distribution of scores. Yet the mean does not always provide the best measure of central tendency. For one thing, the mean is very sensitive to extreme scores. As an example, imagine that we added two scores of 20 and 22 to our sample scores. The mean would now become 1,842/25, or 73.68, a drop of almost five points. Because of its sensitivity to extreme scores, then, the mean can sometimes present a deceptive picture of a set of scores, especially in cases where the mean is based on a relatively small number of scores.

FIGURE 2 In this histogram, the number of students obtaining each score is represented by a bar.

The Median: Finding the Middle

A measure of central tendency that is less sensitive to extreme scores than the mean is the median. The **median** is the point in a distribution of scores that divides the distribution exactly in half. If we arrange all the scores in order from the highest to the lowest, the median lies in the middle of the distribution.

For example, consider a distribution of five scores: 10, 8, 7, 4, and 3. The point that divides the distribution exactly in half is the score 7: Two scores in the distribution lie above the 7 score, and two scores lie below it. If there are an even number of scores in a distribution—in which case there will be no score lying in the middle—the two middle scores are averaged. If our distribution consisted of scores of 10, 8, 7, 6, 4, and 3, then, we would average the two middle scores of 7 and 6 to form a median of 7 + 6 divided by 2, or 13/2 = 6.5.

In our original sample test scores, there are 23 scores. The score that divides the distribution exactly in half will be the 12th score in the frequency distribution of scores, because the 12th score has 11 scores above it and 11 below it. If you count down to the 11th score in the distribution depicted in Figure 1, you will see that the score is 80. Therefore, the median of the distribution is 80.

One feature of the median as a measure of central tendency is that it is insensitive to extreme scores. For example, adding the scores of 20 and 22 to our distribution would change the median no more than would adding scores of 48 and 47 to the distribution. The reason is clear: The median divides a set of scores in half, and the magnitude of the scores is of no consequence in this process.

The median is often used instead of the mean when extreme scores might be misleading. For example, government statistics on income are typically presented using the median as the measure of central tendency, because the median corrects for the small number of extreme cases of very wealthy individuals, whose high incomes might otherwise inflate the mean income.

The Mode: Finding What Is Most Frequent

The final measure of central tendency is the **mode**. The mode is the most frequently occurring score in a set of scores. If you return to the distribution in Figure 1, you can see that three people scored 78, and the frequency of all the other scores is either 2 or 1. The mode for the distribution, then, is 78.

Some distributions, of course, may have more than one score occurring most frequently. For instance, we could imagine that if the distribution had a score of 86 added to the two that are already there, there would be two most frequently occurring categories: 78 and now 86. In this instance, we would say there are two modes—a case known as a *bimodal distribution*.

The mode is often used as a measure of preference or popularity. For instance, if teachers wanted to know who was the most popular child in their elementary school classrooms, they might develop a questionnaire that asked the students to choose someone with whom they would like to participate in some activity. After the choices were tallied, the mode probably would provide the best indication of which child was the most popular.

Central tendency: An index of the central location within a distribution of scores; the most representative score in a distribution of scores (the mean, median, and mode are measures of central tendency).

Mean: The average of all scores, arrived at by adding scores together and dividing by the number of scores.

Median: The point in a distribution of scores that divides the distribution exactly in half when the scores are listed in numerical order.

Mode: The most frequently occurring score in a set of scores.

FIGURE 3 In a normal distribution, the mean, median, and mode are identical, falling at the center of the distribution.

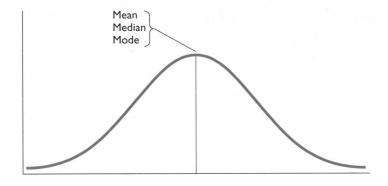

Mean
Median
Mode

Comparing the Three M's: Mean Versus Median Versus Mode

Normal distribution: A distribution of scores that produces a symmetrical, bell-shaped curve in which the right half mirrors the left half and in which the mean, median, and mode all have the same value.

If a sample is sufficiently large, there is generally little difference between the mean, median, and mode. The reason is that with large samples, scores typically form what is called a normal distribution. A **normal distribution** is a distribution of scores that produces a symmetrical, bell-shaped curve, such as the one displayed in Figure 3, in which the right half mirrors the left half, and in which the mean, median, and mode all have the same value.

Most large distributions, those containing many scores, produce a normal curve. For instance, if you asked a large number of students how many hours a week they studied, you might expect to find that most studied within a similar range of hours, and there would be a few who studied many, many hours, and a very few who studied not at all. There would be many scores hovering around the center of the distribution of scores, then, and only a few at the extremes—producing a normal distribution. Many phenomena of interest to psychologists produce a normal curve when graphed. For example, the distribution of IQ scores among the general population falls into a normal distribution.

The mean, median, and mode fall at exactly the same point in a normal distribution. This means that in a normal distribution of scores, the mean score will divide the distribution exactly in half (making it the median), and it will be the most frequently occurring score in the distribution (making it the mode).

The mean, median, and mode differ, however, when distributions are not normal. In cases in which the distributions are *skewed*, or not symmetrical, there is a "hump" at one end or the other (see Figures 4 and 5). For instance, if we gave a calculus exam to a group of students enrolled in an elementary algebra class, we would expect that most of the students would fail the test, leading to low scores being overrepresented in the distribution, as in Figure 4. On the other hand, if we gave the same students a

FIGURE 4 In this skewed distribution, most scores are low.

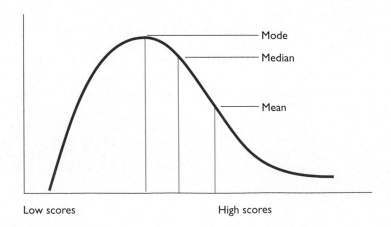

Mode

Median

Mean

Low scores   High scores

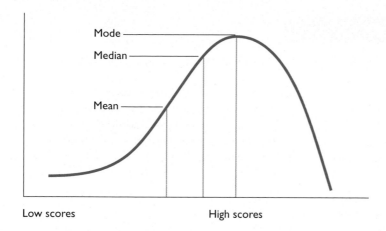

Low scores   High scores

FIGURE 5 In this example of a skewed distribution, there tend to be more high scores than low scores.

test of elementary addition problems, the scores would probably form a distribution in which high scores predominated, as in Figure 5. Both distributions are skewed, although in opposite directions, and the mean, median, and mode are different from one another.

RECAP/EVALUATE/RETHINK

RECAP

What measures can we use to summarize sets of data?

- Statistics is concerned with collecting, organizing, analyzing, and drawing conclusions from numerical data. (p. A-2)

- Descriptive statistics provides a means of summarizing data and presenting the data in a usable and convenient form. (p. A-2)

- A frequency distribution arranges scores from a sample by indicating how often a particular score is presented. A histogram, or bar graph, presents the same data pictorially. (p.A-2)

- Central tendency is the most representative score in a distribution of scores. The mean (or average) is generally the best measure of central tendency. The median is the point or score in a distribution that divides the distribution in half so that half the scores are higher and half are lower. The third measure of central tendency is the mode, the most frequently occurring score in a distribution of scores. (p. A-7)

EVALUATE

1. A frequency distribution of numbers could be displayed pictorially by constructing a bar graph, or _____.
2. Match each item in the left-hand column with the corresponding item in the right-hand column.
   1. Mean = 10   **a.** 2, 8, 10, 12, 13, 18
   2. Median = 11   **b.** 4, 5, 10, 10, 15, 16
   3. Mode = 12   **c.** 4, 5, 12, 12, 12, 16

3. The mean, median, and mode are measures of _____ _____.
4. Professor Garcia explains to the class that most of the 40 exam scores fell within a B range, but there were two extremely high scores. Should she report the median or the mean as a measure of central tendency?
5. The mean, median, and mode will differ in a normal distribution. True or false?

RETHINK

1. Government statistics on family income are presented in a variety of ways. What would be the most useful way of providing a summary of family incomes across the country: the mean, median, or mode? Why might providing only the mean be misleading?

Answers to Evaluate Questions

1. histogram; 2. 1-b, 2-a, 3-c; 3. central tendency; 4. the median; the mean is too sensitive to extreme scores; 5. false; they will be equal

KEY TERMS

statistics p. A-2
descriptive statistics p. A-2
frequency distribution p. A-2

histogram p. A-2
central tendency p. A-7
mean p. A-7

median p. A-7
mode p. A-7
normal distribution p. A-8

Measures of Variability

Although measures of central tendency provide information about where the center of a distribution lies, often this information is insufficient. For example, suppose a psychologist was interested in determining the nature of people's eye movements while they were reading in order to perfect a new method to teach reading. It would not be enough to know how *most* people moved their eyes (information that a measure of central tendency would provide); it would also be important to know how much individual people's eye movements differed or varied from one another.

A second important characteristic of a set of scores provides this information: variability. **Variability** is a term that refers to the spread, or dispersion, of scores in a distribution. Figure 1 contains two distributions of scores that have identical means but differ in variability. Measures of variability provide a way to describe the spread of scores in a distribution.

The Range: Highest Minus Lowest

The simplest measure of variability is the **range**. The range is the difference between the highest score in a distribution and the lowest score. In the set of scores

96	92	90	90	89	86
86	85	85	83	83	80
78	78	78	73	72	72
69	69	59	58	49	

the distribution has a range of 47 (96 − 49 = 47).

The fact that a range is simple to calculate is about its only virtue. The problem with this particular measure of variability is that it is based entirely on extreme scores, and a single score that is very different from the others in a distribution can distort the picture of the distribution as a whole. For example, the addition of a score of 20 to the test score distribution we are considering would almost double the range, even though the variability of the remaining scores in the distribution would not have changed at all.

The Standard Deviation: Differences from the Mean

The most frequently used method of characterizing the variability of a distribution of scores is the standard deviation. The standard deviation bears a conceptual relationship to a mean. You will recall that the mean is the average score in a distribution of scores. A **standard deviation** is an index of the average deviation of a set of scores from the center of the distribution.

Key Concept

How can we assess the variability of a set of data?

Variability: The spread, or dispersion, of scores in a distribution.

Range: The difference between the highest score and the lowest score in a distribution.

Standard deviation: An index of the average deviation of a set of scores from the center of the distribution.

FIGURE 1 Although the mean is identical in these two distributions, the variability, or spread of scores, is very different. Specifically, the variability is considerably greater in (a) than in (b).

a.

b.

Consider, for instance, the distributions in Figure 1. The distribution on the left is widely dispersed, and on the average an individual score in the distribution can be thought of as deviating quite a bit from the center of the distribution. Certainly the scores in the distribution on the left are going to deviate more from the center of the distribution than those in the distribution on the right.

In contrast, in the distribution on the right, the scores are closely packed together and there is little deviation of a typical score from the center of the distribution. On the basis of this analysis, then, it would be expected that a good measure of variability would yield a larger value for the distribution on the left than it would for the one on the right—and, in fact, a standard deviation would do exactly this by indicating how far away a typical score lies from the center of the distribution.

In a normal distribution, 68 percent of the scores fall within one standard deviation of the mean (34 percent on either side of it), 95 percent of the scores fall within two standard deviations, and 99.7 percent fall within three standard deviations. In the general population, IQ scores of intelligence fall into a normal distribution, and they have a mean of 100 and a standard deviation of 15. Consequently, an IQ score of 100 does not deviate from the mean, whereas an IQ score that is three standard deviations above the mean (or 145) is very unusual (higher than 99 percent of all IQ scores).

The calculation of the standard deviation follows the logic of calculating the difference of individual scores from the mean of the distribution (see Figure 2). Not only does the standard deviation provide an excellent indicator of the variability of a set of scores, it provides a means for converting initial scores on standardized tests such as the SAT (the college admissions exam) into the scales used to report results. In this

FIGURE 2 How to calculate a standard deviation.

Calculating a Standard Deviation

1. The calculation of a standard deviation begins with the calculation of the mean of distribution. In the following distribution of scores on a psychology student's weekly quizzes, the mean is 84.5: 82, 88, 71, 86, 96, 84. (As you recall, the mean is the sum of the scores divided by the number of scores in the distribution, or $507 \div 6 = 84.5$.)

2. The next step is to produce a deviation score for each score in the distribution. A deviation score is simply an original score minus the mean of all the scores in a distribution. This has been done in the second column below:

Original Score	Deviation Score	Deviation Score Squared
82	−2.5	6.25
88	3.5	12.25
71	−13.5	182.25
86	1.5	2.25
96	11.5	132.25
84	−.5	.25

3. In the third step, the deviation scores are squared (multiplied by themselves) to eliminate negative numbers. This has been carried out in the third column above.

4. The squared deviation scores are then added together; and this sum is divided by the number of scores. In the example above, the sum of the squared deviation scores is $6.25 + 12.25 + 182.25 + 2.25 + 132.25 + .25 = 335.50$, and $335.50 \div 6 = 55.916$.

5. The final step is to take the square root of the resulting number. The square root of 55.916 is 7.4777—which is the standard deviation of the distribution of scores.

6. To summarize, the standard deviation is calculated using the formula

$$\sqrt{\frac{\sum(\text{score} - \text{mean})^2}{N}}$$

Original score minus the mean of 84.5

(Note: Because this formula provides the standard deviation for a sample, the sum of the deviation scores is divided by the number of scores, N. However, in some cases, in which we might wish to generalize beyond the specific sample to a larger population, the standard deviation is calculated by using the number of scores minus 1, or $N-1$.)

way, it is possible to make a score of 585 on the verbal section of the SAT exam, for example, equivalent from one year to the next, even though the specific test items differ from year to year.

RECAP/EVALUATE/RETHINK

RECAP

How can we assess the variability of a set of data?

- The range and standard deviation are two measures of variability, which is the spread, or dispersion, of scores in a distribution. The range is the distance between the largest score in a distribution and the smallest score. The standard deviation is an index of the extent to which the average score in a distribution deviates from the center of the distribution. (p. A-11)

EVALUATE

1. A measure of variability based solely on the distance between the most extreme scores is the
   a. Spread
   b. Standard deviation
   c. Deviation score
   d. Range

KEY TERMS

variability p. A-11   range p. A-11   standard deviation p. A-11

2. By simply eyeing the following sets of numbers, predict which will have a higher standard deviation and why:
   a.   6, 8, 10, 10, 11, 12, 13
   b.   2, 5, 8, 11, 16, 17, 18
3. Calculate the mean and standard deviation for sets a and b in Question 2.

RETHINK

1. If you were interested in understanding the number of people living below the poverty line in the United States, why might the range and the standard deviation provide you with a better understanding of the extent of poverty than would measures of central tendency (the mean, median, and mode)?

Answers to Evaluate Questions

1. d; 2. b, because the numbers are more widely dispersed; 3a. mean = 10, standard deviation = 2.20; 3b. mean = 11, standard deviation = 5.80

Using Statistics to Answer Questions: Inferential Statistics and Correlation

Suppose you were a psychologist who was interested in whether there is a relationship between smoking and anxiety. Would it be reasonable to simply look at a group of smokers and measure their anxiety by using some rating scale? Probably not. It clearly would be more informative if you compared their anxiety with the anxiety exhibited by a group of nonsmokers.

Once you decided to observe anxiety in two groups of people, you would have to determine just who would be your subjects. In an ideal world with unlimited resources, you might contact every smoker and nonsmoker, because these are the two populations with which you are concerned. A **population** consists of all the members of a group of interest. Obviously, however, this would be impossible because of the all-encompassing size of the two groups; instead, you would limit your subjects to a sample of smokers and nonsmokers. A **sample**, in formal statistical terms, is a sub-group of a population of interest that is intended to be representative of the larger population. Once you had identified samples representative of the population of inter-est to you, it would be possible to carry out your study, yielding two distributions of scores—one from the smokers and one from the nonsmokers (Fowler, 2001).

The obvious question is whether the two samples differ in the degree of anxiety displayed by their members. The statistical procedures that we discussed earlier are helpful in answering this question, because each of the two samples can be examined in terms of central tendency and variability. The more important question, though, is whether the magnitude of difference between the two distributions is sufficient to conclude that the distributions truly differ from one another, or if, instead, the differ-ences are attributable merely to chance.

To answer the question of whether samples are truly different from one another, psychologists use inferential statistics. **Inferential statistics** is the branch of statistics that uses data from samples to make predictions about a larger population, permitting generalizations to be drawn. To take a simple example, suppose you had two coins that both were flipped 100 times. Suppose further that one coin came up heads 41 times and the other came up heads 65 times. Are both coins fair? We know that a fair coin should come up heads about 50 times in 100 flips. But a little thought would also suggest that it is unlikely that even a fair coin would come up heads exactly 50 times in 100 flips. The question is, then, how far a coin could deviate from 50 heads before that coin would be considered unfair.

Questions such as this—as well as whether the results found are due to chance or represent unexpected, nonchance findings—revolve around how "probable" certain events are. Using coin flipping as an example, 53 heads in 100 flips would be a highly probable outcome because it departs only slightly from the expected outcome of 50 heads. In contrast, if a coin was flipped 100 times and 90 of those times it came up heads, that would be a highly improbable outcome. In fact, 90 heads out of 100 flips should occur by chance only once in 2 million trials of 100 flips of a fair coin. Ninety heads in 100 flips, then, is an extremely improbable outcome; if 90 heads did appear, the odds would be that the coin or the flipping process was rigged.

Inferential statistics are used to mathematically determine the probability of observed events. By using inferential statistics to evaluate the result of an experiment, psychologists are able to calculate the likelihood that the difference is a reflection of a true difference between populations. For example, suppose we find that the mean on

Key Concepts

How do we generalize from data?

How can we determine the nature of a relationship, and the significance of differences, between two sets of scores?

Population: All the members of a group of interest.
Sample: A representative subgroup of a population of interest.

Inferential statistics: The branch of statistics that uses data from samples to make predictions about the larger population from which the sample is drawn.

an anxiety scale is 68 for smokers and 48 for nonsmokers. Inferential statistical procedures allow us to determine whether this difference is really meaningful, or whether we might expect the same difference to occur merely because of chance factors (Cohen & Lea, 2003; Gaffney & Henry, 2007).

The results of inferential statistical procedures are described in terms of measures of significance. To a psychologist, a **significant outcome** is one in which the observed outcome would be expected to have occurred only by chance with a probability of .05 or less. Put another way, a significant difference between two means says that there are only 5 chances out of 100 (or less) that the difference an experimenter has found is due to chance, rather than to an actual difference between the means.

Obtaining a significant outcome in a study does not necessarily imply that the results of an experiment have real-world importance. An experiment may demonstrate that two groups differ significantly from one another, but the meaning of the differences in terms of what occurs outside the laboratory may be limited. Still, finding a significant outcome tells us something important: The differences a researcher has found are overwhelmingly likely to be true differences, not only due to chance (Lehmann & Romano, 2004; Bakeman, 2006).

Significant outcome: An outcome in which the observed outcome would be expected to have occurred by chance with a probability of .05 or less.

The Correlation Coefficient: Measuring Relationships

How do we know if television viewing is related to aggression, if reading romance novels is related to sexual behavior, or if mothers' IQs are related to their daughters' IQs?

Each of these questions revolves around the issue of the degree of relationship between two variables. One way of answering them is to draw a *scatterplot*, a means of graphically illustrating the relationship between two variables. We would first collect two sets of paired measures and assign one score to the horizontal axis (variable *x*) and the other score to the vertical axis (variable *y*). Then we would draw a dot at the place where the two scores meet on the graph. The first two scatterplots in Figure 1 present typical situations. In (a) and (b), there is a **positive relationship**, in which high values of variable *x* are associated with high values of variable *y* and low values of *x* are associated with low values of *y*. In (c) and (d), there is a **negative relationship**: As values of variable *x* increase, the values of variable *y* decrease. In (e), no clear relationship exists between variable *x* and variable *y*.

It is also possible to consider scores in terms of their mathematical relationship to one another, rather than simply the way they appear on a scatterplot. Suppose, for example, a psychologist was interested in the degree to which a daughter's IQ was related to her mother's IQ—specifically, if a mother with a high IQ tended to have a daughter who also had a high IQ, and whether a mother with a low IQ tended to have a daughter with a low IQ. To examine the issue, suppose the psychologist measured the IQs of 10 mothers and daughters and arranged their IQs as presented in Figure 2.

Looking at the data in the table, it is obvious that mothers and daughters do not have identical IQs. Moreover, they do not even have IQs that are rank-ordered the same in the two columns. For example, the mother with the highest IQ does not have the daughter with the highest IQ, and the mother with the lowest IQ does not have the daughter with the lowest IQ. It is apparent, then, that there is not a *perfect* relationship between the IQ of a mother and the IQ of a daughter. However, it would be a mistake to conclude that there is a zero, or no, relationship between the IQs of the mothers and daughters, because it is clear that there is a tendency for mothers who have high IQs to have daughters with high IQs, and that mothers with low IQs tend to have daughters with low IQs.

The statistic that provides a precise mathematical index of the degree to which two variables are related is the correlation coefficient. A **correlation coefficient** is a numerical measure that indicates the extent of the relationship between two variables. It ranges in value from + 1.00 to − 1.00. A value of + 1.00 would indicate that

Positive relationship: A relationship established by data that shows high values of one variable corresponding with high values of another, and low values of the first variable corresponding with low values of the other.

Negative relationship: A relationship established by data that shows high values of one variable corresponding with low values of the other.

Correlation coefficient: A numerical measure that indicates the extent of the relationship between two variables.

FIGURE 1 These scatterplots show relationships of different strengths. In (a) and (b), the relationships are positive, although in (a) the relationship is considerably stronger than in (b). In contrast, the relationships in (c) and (d) are negative, with (d) representing a stronger negative relationship. Finally, (e) illustrates a case where no systematic relationship exists between the variables.

two variables had a perfect positive relationship with one another, meaning that the highest score on one variable would be associated with the highest score on the other variable, the second highest score on the first variable would be associated with the second highest score on the second variable, and so on. A value of −1.00 would indicate that there was a perfect negative relationship between the two variables; the highest score on the first variable would be associated with the lowest score on the second variable, the second highest score would be associated with the second lowest score, and so forth.

Correlation coefficients at or only slightly greater or slightly less than zero indicate that there is no relationship between the two variables. In such cases, there is no tendency for high values on one variable to be associated with either high or low values on the second variable.

Correlation coefficients that range between zero and +/−1.00 reflect varying degrees of relationship between the two variables. For instance, a value of +.20 or −.20 would indicate that there was a slight relationship between the two variables, a value

IQ Scores of Mothers and Daughters

Mother's IQ	Daughter's IQ
135	122
128	130
125	110
120	132
114	100
110	116
102	108
96	89
90	84
86	92

FIGURE 2 In this distribution, each mother's IQ score is compared to her daughter's IQ score. Using a correlation coefficient, we can calculate the strength of the relationship between the set of pairs of scores.

of around +.50 or −.50 would indicate a moderate relationship, and a value of +.80 or −.80 would indicate a relatively strong relationship. As an example, if we were to calculate the correlation of the two sets of variables in Figure 2 (most advanced calculators do the necessary calculations automatically), we would find a correlation that is quite strong: The coefficient is +.86.

It is important to note that finding a strong correlation between two variables does *not* in any way indicate that changes in one variable *cause* changes in another—only that the variables are associated with one another. Although it may seem plausible to us, for example, that it is the mother's intelligence that causes higher intelligence in a daughter, it is just as possible that a daughter's intelligence affects how the mother performs on an IQ test. (Perhaps the daughter's behavior affects the general home environment, influencing the mother's performance on IQ tests.) It is even plausible that some unmeasured—and previously unconsidered—third variable is causing both mother's and daughter's IQs to increase or decrease simultaneously. In a clear example of this possibility, even if we found that ice cream sales and rates of violent crime are positively correlated with one another (as they happen to be), we would not presume that they are causally related. In this case, it is likely that both are influenced by a third factor—the weather.

The crucial point is that even if we find a perfect correlation between two sets of variables, we will not be able to say that the two variables are linked causally—only that they are strongly related to one another (Good, 2003).

RECAP/EVALUATE/RETHINK

RECAP

How do we generalize from data?

- Inferential statistics—techniques that use data from samples to make predictions about a larger population—are useful in deciding whether differences between distributions of data are attributable to real differences or to chance variation. (p. A-15)

How can we determine the nature of a relationship, and the significance of differences, between two sets of scores?

- Measures of relationship provide a numerical index of the extent to which two variables are related. The correlation coefficient ranges in value from +1.00 to –1.00, with +1.00 indicating a perfect positive relationship and –1.00 indicating a perfect negative relationship. Correlations close to or at zero indicate there is little or no relationship between two variables. (p. A-16)

EVALUATE

1. Researchers would like to estimate the level of stress for first-year college students for a given year at a large university. A stress index is given to a randomly assigned group of 500 first-year students. The class size is 6,000 for that year. In this example the group of 500 is known as a _____, and the entire class of first-year students is known as the _____.

2. Dr. Sanders states that the results of his experiment show a difference between the two groups, and that there is a 90 percent probability that the results are due to a true difference between the groups and not to chance. Are his results statistically significant in the way the term *significant* typically is used by psychologists?

3. A hypothetical set of data drawn from a sample of college sophomores at a university found that as the rate of caffeine consumption increases, the amount of sleep decreases. The scatterplot for these data is apt to show a _____ relationship.

4. What would the value of the correlation coefficient be for the following?
   a. A perfect negative relationship
   b. A perfect positive relationship
   c. No relationship

5. If we observed a correlation coefficient of –.90 in Question 3, we would probably be safe in saying that caffeine consumption causes lack of sleep in college students. True or false?

6. The researchers in Question 3 decide to extend the findings they obtain from their sample of college sophomores to all adults. Would you accept their generalization? Why or why not?

RETHINK

1. For many years, cigarette manufacturers argued that because the data linking smoking and disease was correlational, one could not infer that there was a causal connection between them and therefore no reason not to smoke. Did the manufacturers have a valid argument? How could you refute their argument?

Answers to Evaluate Questions

1. sample, population; 2. no, at least not at the .05 level typically required by psychologists who wish to claim a result is significant; 3. negative; 4. a. –1.00, b. +1.00, c. 0; 5. false; we cannot assume a causal relation, only an association; 6. no; the sample (drawn from college sophomores) does not represent the population (all adults)

KEY TERMS

population p. A-15

sample p. A-15

inferential statistics p. A-15

significant outcome p. A-16

positive relationship p. A-16

negative relationship p. A-16

correlation coefficient
  p. A-16

Psychology on the Web

1. Search the Web for the results of a recent survey, such as one conducted by the Gallup polling organization (www.gallup.com). Describe the results, summarizing the methodology and the sample size for the survey. How does the sample address the population to which the survey is being generalized?

Epilogue

In this group of modules, we've seen how statistical methods are used by psychologists to summarize data and support hypotheses. Return, for a moment, to the prologue about Selma Vorwerk, who immigrated to this country in the early 1900s, and use the statistical concepts that we covered to answer the following questions.

1. What was the sample size used by anti-immigrationist Lathrop Stoddard, and to what population was he generalizing?
2. What are the statistical flaws in the arguments made by critics of immigration in the early 1900s?
3. What statistical methods would you find useful in refuting Stoddard's conclusions about immigrants?

Glossary

abnormal behavior Behavior that causes people to experience distress and prevents them from functioning in their daily lives (Module 46)

absolute threshold The smallest intensity of a stimulus that must be present for the stimulus to be detected (Module 10)

achievement test A test designed to determine a person's level of knowledge in a given subject area (Module 26)

acquired immune deficiency syndrome (AIDS) A fatal, sexually transmitted infection caused by a virus that destroys the body's immune system (Module 34)

action potential An electric nerve impulse that travels through a neuron when it is set off by a "trigger," changing the neuron's charge from negative to positive (Module 7)

activation-synthesis theory J. Allan Hobson's theory that the brain produces random electrical energy during REM sleep that stimulates memories lodged in various portions of the brain (Module 14)

activity theory of aging A theory that suggests that the elderly who are more successful while aging are those who maintain the interests and activities they had during middle age (Module 39)

adaptation An adjustment in sensory capacity after prolonged exposure to unchanging stimuli (Module 10)

addictive drugs Drugs that produce a biological or psychological dependence in the user so that withdrawal from them leads to a craving for the drug that, in some cases, may be nearly irresistible (Module 16)

adolescence The developmental stage between childhood and adulthood (Module 38)

age of viability The point at which a fetus can survive if born prematurely (Module 36)

aggression The intentional injury of, or harm to, another person (Module 56)

algorithm A rule that, if applied appropriately, guarantees a solution to a problem (Module 23)

all-or-none law The rule that neurons are either on or off (Module 7)

altruism Helping behavior that is beneficial to others but clearly requires self-sacrifice (Module 57)

Alzheimer's disease A progressive brain disorder that leads to a gradual and irreversible decline in cognitive abilities (Module 22, Module 39)

amnesia Memory loss that occurs without other mental difficulties (Module 22)

anal stage According to Sigmund Freud, a stage from age 12 to 18 months to 3 years of age, in which a child's pleasure is centered on the anus (Module 40)

androgens Male sex hormones secreted by the testes (Module 33)

androgynous Characterized by gender roles that encompass psychological and behavioral traits thought typical of both sexes (Module 33)

anorexia nervosa A severe eating disorder in which people may refuse to eat while denying that their behavior and appearance—which can become skeletonlike—are unusual (Module 30)

anorgasmia (an-or-GAZ-mee-uh) A female's lack of orgasm (Module 34)

anterograde amnesia Amnesia in which memory is lost for events that follow an injury (Module 22)

antianxiety drugs Drugs that reduce the level of anxiety a person experiences, essentially by reducing excitability and increasing feelings of well-being (Module 51)

antidepressant drugs Medications that improve a severely depressed patient's mood and feeling of well-being (Module 51)

antipsychotic drugs Drugs that temporarily reduce psychotic symptoms such as agitation, hallucinations, and delusions (Module 51)

antisocial personality disorder A disorder in which individuals show no regard for the moral and ethical rules of society or the rights of others (Module 47)

anxiety disorder The occurrence of anxiety without an obvious external cause, affecting daily functioning (Module 47)

aptitude test A test designed to predict a person's ability in a particular area or line of work (Module 26)

archetypes According to Carl Jung, universal symbolic representations of a particular person, object, or experience (such as good and evil) (Module 40)

archival research Research in which existing data, such as census documents, college records, and newspaper clippings, are examined to test a hypothesis (Module 5)

arousal approaches to motivation The belief that we try to maintain certain levels of stimulation and activity, increasing or reducing them as necessary (Module 29)

association areas One of the major regions of the cerebral cortex; the site of the higher mental processes, such as thought, language, memory, and speech (Module 9)

assumed-similarity bias The tendency to think of people as being similar to oneself, even when meeting them for the first time (Module 52)

attachment The positive emotional bond that develops between a child and a particular individual (Module 37)

attention deficit hyperactivity disorder (ADHD) A disorder marked by inattention, impulsiveness, a low tolerance for frustration, and a great deal of inappropriate activity (Module 47)

attitudes Evaluations of a particular person, behavior, belief, or concept (Module 52)

attribution theory The theory of personality that seeks to explain how we decide, on the basis of samples of an individual's behavior, what the specific causes of that person's behavior are (Module 52)

authoritarian parents Parents who are rigid and punitive and value unquestioning obedience from their children (Module 37)

authoritative parents Parents who are firm, set clear limits, reason with their children, and explain things to them (Module 37)

autism A severe developmental disability that impairs children's ability to communicate and relate to others (Module 47)

autobiographical memories Our recollections of circumstances and episodes from our own lives (Module 21)

autonomic division The part of the peripheral nervous system that controls involuntary movement of the heart, glands, lungs, and other organs (Module 8)

autonomy-versus-shame-and-doubt stage The period which, according to Erik Erikson, toddlers (ages 1½ to 3 years) develop independence and autonomy if exploration and freedom are encouraged, or shame and self-doubt if they are restricted and overprotected (Module 37)

aversive conditioning A form of therapy that reduces the frequency of undesired behavior by pairing an aversive, unpleasant stimulus with undesired behavior (Module 49)

axon The part of the neuron that carries messages destined for other neurons (Module 7)

babble Meaningless speechlike sounds made by children from around the age of 3 months through 1 year (Module 25)

background stressors ("daily hassles") Everyday annoyances, such as being stuck in traffic, that cause minor irritations and may have long-term ill effects if they continue or are compounded by other stressful events (Module 45)

basilar membrane A vibrating structure in the ear that runs through the center of the cochlea, dividing it into an upper chamber and a lower chamber and containing sense receptors for sound (Module 12)

behavior modification A formalized technique for promoting the frequency of desirable behaviors and decreasing the incidence of unwanted ones (Module 18)

behavioral assessment Direct measures of an individual's behavior used to describe personality characteristics (Module 42)

behavioral genetics The study of the effects of heredity on behavior (Module 8)

behavioral neuroscientists (or biopsychologists) Psychologists who specialize in considering the ways in which the biological structures and functions of the body affect behavior (Module 7)

behavioral perspective The approach that suggests that observable, measurable behavior should be the focus of study (Modules 2, 46)

behavioral perspective on psychological disorders The perspective that looks at the behavior itself as the problem (Module 48)

behavioral treatment approaches Treatment approaches that build on the basic processes of learning, such as reinforcement and extinction, and assume that normal and abnormal behavior are both learned (Module 49)

biofeedback A procedure in which a person learns to control through conscious thought internal physiological processes such as blood pressure, heart and respiration rate, skin temperature, sweating, and the constriction of particular muscles (Module 9)

biological and evolutionary approaches to personality Theories that suggest that important components of personality are inherited (Module 41)

biomedical therapy Therapy that relies on drugs and other medical procedures to improve psychological functioning (Module 49)

biopsychologists *See* behavioral neuroscientists (Module 7)

bipolar disorder A disorder in which a person alternates between periods of euphoric feelings of mania and periods of depression (Module 47)

bisexuals Persons who are sexually attracted to people of the same sex and the other sex (Module 34)

borderline personality disorder A disorder in which individuals have difficulty developing a secure sense of who they are (Module 47)

bottom-up processing Perception that consists of the progression of recognizing and processing information from individual components of a stimuli and moving to the perception of the whole (Module 13)

bulimia An eating disorder in which a person binges on incredibly large quantities of food (Module 30)

Cannon-Bard theory of emotion The belief that both physiological arousal and emotional experience are produced simultaneously by the same nerve stimulus (Module 31)

case study An in-depth, intensive investigation of an individual or small group of people (Module 5)

cataclysmic events Strong stressors that occur suddenly, affecting many people at once (e.g., natural disasters) (Module 45)

catharsis The process of discharging built-up aggressive energy (Module 56)

central core The "old brain," which controls basic functions such as eating and sleeping and is common to all vertebrates (Module 9)

central nervous system (CNS) The part of the nervous system that includes the brain and spinal cord (Module 8)

central route processing Message interpretation characterized by thoughtful consideration of the issues and arguments used to persuade (Module 52)

central tendency An index of the central location within a distribution of scores; the most representative score in a distribution of scores (the mean, median, and mode are measures of central tendency) (Module 56)

central traits The major traits considered in forming impressions of others (Module 52)

cerebellum (ser uh BELL um) The part of the brain that controls bodily balance (Module 9)

cerebral cortex The "new brain," responsible for the most sophisticated information processing in the brain; contains four lobes (Module 9)

chromosomes Rod-shaped structures that contain all basic hereditary information (Module 36)

chunk A meaningful grouping of stimuli that can be stored as a unit in short-term memory (Module 20)

circadian rhythms Biological processes that occur regularly on approximately a twenty-four-hour cycle (Module 14)

classical conditioning A type of learning in which a neutral stimulus comes to bring about a response after it is paired with a stimulus that naturally brings about that response (Module 17)

cochlea (KOKE lee uh) A coiled tube in the ear filled with fluid that vibrates in response to sound (Module 12)

cognitive approaches to motivation Theories suggesting that motivation is a product of people's thoughts and expectations—their cognitions (Module 29)

cognitive development The process by which a child's understanding of the world changes as a function of age and experience (Module 37)

cognitive dissonance The conflict that occurs when a person holds two contradictory attitudes or thoughts (referred to as *cognitions*) (Module 52)

cognitive learning theory An approach to the study of learning that focuses on the thought processes that underlie learning (Module 19)

cognitive perspective The approach that focuses on how people think, understand, and know about the world (Modules 2, 46)

cognitive perspective on psychological disorders The perspective that suggests that people's thoughts and beliefs are a central component of abnormal behavior (Module 48)

cognitive psychology The branch of psychology that focuses on the study of higher mental processes, including thinking, language, memory, problem solving, knowing, reasoning, judging, and decision making (Module 23)

cognitive treatment approaches Treatment approaches that teach people to think in more adaptive ways by changing their dysfunctional cognitions about the world and themselves (Module 49)

cognitive-behavioral approach A treatment approach that incorporates basic principles of learning to change the way people think (Module 49)

collective unconscious According to Carl Jung, a common set of ideas, feelings, images, and symbols that we inherit from our ancestors, the whole human race, and even nonhuman ancestors from the distant past (Module 40)

community psychology A branch of psychology that focuses on the prevention and minimization of psychological disorders in the community (Module 51)

companionate love The strong affection we have for those with whom our lives are deeply involved (Module 55)

compliance Behavior that occurs in response to direct social pressure (Module 53)

compulsion An irresistible urge to carry out some act that seems strange or unreasonable (Module 47)

concepts Categorizations of objects, events, or people that share common properties (Module 23)

concrete operational stage According to Jean Piaget, the period from 7 to 12 years of age that is characterized by logical thought and a loss of egocentrism (Module 37)

conditioned response (CR) A response that, after conditioning, follows a previously neutral stimulus (e.g., salivation at the ringing of a bell) (Module 17)

conditioned stimulus (CS) A once-neutral stimulus that has been paired with an unconditioned stimulus to bring about a response formerly caused only by the unconditioned stimulus (Module 17)

cones Cone-shaped, light-sensitive receptor cells in the retina that are responsible for sharp focus and color perception, particularly in bright light (Module 11)

confirmation bias The tendency to favor information that supports one's initial hypotheses and ignore contradictory information that supports alternative hypotheses or solutions (Module 24)

conformity A change in behavior or attitudes brought about by a desire to follow the beliefs or standards of other people (Module 53)

consciousness The awareness of sensations, thoughts, and feelings being experienced at a given moment (Module 14)

constructive processes Processes in which memories are influenced by the meaning we give to events (Module 21)

continuous reinforcement schedule Reinforcing of a behavior every time it occurs (Module 18)

control group A group participating in an experiment that receives no treatment (Module 5)

convergent thinking The ability to produce responses that are based primarily on knowledge and logic (Module 24)

conversion disorder A major somatoform disorder that involves an actual physical disturbance, such as the inability to use a sensory organ or the complete or partial inability to move an arm or a leg (Module 47)

coping The efforts to control, reduce, or learn to tolerate the threats that lead to stress (Module 43)

correlation coefficient A numerical measure that indicates the extent of the relationship between two variables (Module 58)

correlational research Research in which the relationship between two sets of variables is examined to determine whether they are associated, or "correlated" (Module 5)

creativity The ability to generate original ideas or solve problems in novel ways (Module 24)

cross-sectional research A research method that compares people of different ages at the same point in time (Module 35)

crystallized intelligence The accumulation of information, skills, and strategies that are learned through experience and can be applied in problem-solving situations (Module 26)

cue-dependent forgetting Forgetting that occurs when there are insufficient retrieval cues to rekindle information that is in memory (Module 22)

culture-fair IQ test A test that does not discriminate against the members of any minority group (Module 28)

daily hassles *See* background stressors (Module 45)

date rape Rape in which the rapist is either a date or a romantic acquaintance (Module 34)

daydreams Fantasies that people construct while awake (Module 14)

decay The loss of information in memory through its nonuse (Module 22)

declarative memory Memory for factual information, names, faces, dates, and the like (Module 20)

defense mechanisms In Freudian theory, unconscious strategies that people use to reduce anxiety by concealing the source of the anxiety from themselves and others (Module 40)

deinstitutionalization The transfer of former mental patients from institutions to the community (Module 51)

dendrite A cluster of fibers at one end of a neuron that receive messages from other neurons (Module 7)

dependent variable The variable that is measured and is expected to change as a result of changes caused by the experimenter's manipulation of the independent variable (Module 5)

depressants Drugs that slow down the nervous system (Module 16)

depth perception The ability to view the world in three dimensions and to perceive distance (Module 13)

descriptive research An approach to research designed to systematically investigate a person, group, or patterns of behavior (Module 5)

descriptive statistics The branch of statistics that provides a means of summarizing data (Module 56)

determinism The idea that people's behavior is produced primarily by factors outside of their willful control (Module 3)

developmental psychology The branch of psychology that studies the patterns of growth and change that occur throughout life (Module 35)

Diagnostic and Statistical Manual of Mental Disorders, Fourth Edition, Text Revision (DSM-IV-TR) A system, devised by the American Psychiatric Association, used by most professionals to diagnose and classify abnormal behavior (Module 46)

dialectical behavior therapy A form of treatment in which the focus is on getting people to accept who they are, regardless of whether it matches their ideal (Module 49)

difference threshold (just noticeable difference) The smallest level of added or reduced stimulation required to sense that a change in stimulation has occurred (Module 10)

diffusion of responsibility The tendency for people to feel that responsibility for acting is shared, or diffused, among those present (Module 55)

discrimination Behavior directed toward individuals on the basis of their membership in a particular group (Module 54)

disengagement theory of aging A theory that suggests that aging produces a gradual withdrawal from the world on physical, psychological, and social levels (Module 39)

display rules Guidelines that govern the appropriateness of showing emotion nonverbally (Module 32)

dispositional causes (of behavior) Perceived causes of behavior that are based on internal traits or personality factors (Module 52)

dissociative amnesia A disorder in which a significant, selective memory loss occurs (Module 47)

dissociative disorders Psychological dysfunctions characterized by the separation of critical personality facets that are normally integrated, allowing stress avoidance through escape (Module 47)

dissociative fugue A form of amnesia in which the individual leaves home and sometimes assumes a new identity (Module 47)

dissociative identity disorder (or multiple personality disorder) A disorder in which a person displays characteristics of two or more distinct personalities (Module 47)

divergent thinking The ability to generate unusual, yet nonetheless appropriate, responses to problems or questions (Module 24)

double standard The view that premarital sex is permissible for males but not for females (Module 34)

Down syndrome A cause of mental retardation resulting from the presence of an extra chromosome (Module 28)

dreams-for-survival theory The theory suggesting that dreams permit information that is critical for our daily survival to be reconsidered and reprocessed during sleep (Module 14)

drive Motivational tension, or arousal, that energizes behavior to fulfill a need (Module 29)

drive-reduction approaches to motivation Theories suggesting that a lack of a basic biological requirement such as water produces a drive to obtain that requirement (in this case, the thirst drive) (Module 29)

drug therapy Control of psychological disorders through the use of drugs (Module 51)

eardrum The part of the ear that vibrates when sound hits it (Module 12)

eclectic approach to therapy An approach to therapy that uses techniques taken from a variety of treatment methods, rather than just one (Module 52)

ego The part of the personality that provides a buffer between the id and the outside world (Module 40)

egocentric thought A way of thinking in which a child views the world entirely from his or her own perspective (Module 37)

ego-integrity-versus-despair stage According to Erik Erikson, a period from late adulthood until death during which we review life's accomplishments and failures (Module 40)

electroconvulsive therapy (ECT) A procedure in which an electric current of 70 to 150 volts is briefly administered to a patient's head, causing a loss of consciousness and often causing seizures (Module 51)

embryo A developed zygote that has a heart, a brain, and other organs (Module 36)

emotional intelligence The set of skills that underlie the accurate assessment, evaluation, expression, and regulation of emotions (Module 26)

emotions Feelings that generally have both physiological and cognitive elements and that influence behavior (Module 31)

endocrine system A chemical communication network that sends messages throughout the body via the bloodstream (Module 8)

episodic memory Memory for events that occur in a particular time, place, or context (Module 20)

erectile dysfunction The inability of a male to achieve or maintain an erection (Module 34)

erogenous zones Areas of the body that are particularly sensitive because of the presence of an unusually rich array of nerve receptors (Module 33)

estrogens Class of female sex hormones (Module 33)

evolutionary psychology The branch of psychology that seeks to identify behavior patterns that are a result of our genetic inheritance from our ancestors (Module 8)

excitatory message A chemical message that makes it more likely that a receiving neuron will fire and an action potential will travel down its axon (Module 7)

experiment The investigation of the relationship between two (or more) variables by deliberately producing a change in one variable in a situation and observing the effects of that change on other aspects of the situation (Module 5)

experimental bias Factors that distort how the independent variable affects the dependent variable in an experiment (Module 6)

experimental group Any group participating in an experiment that receives a treatment (Module 5)

experimental manipulation The change that an experimenter deliberately produces in a situation (Module 5)

explicit memory Intentional or conscious recollection of information (Module 21)

extinction A basic phenomenon of learning that occurs when a previously conditioned response decreases in frequency and eventually disappears (Module 17)

extramarital sex Sexual activity between a married person and someone who is not his or her spouse (Module 34)

facial-affect program Activation of a set of nerve impulses that make the face display the appropriate expression (Module 31)

facial-feedback hypothesis The hypothesis that facial expressions not only reflect emotional experience but also help determine how people experience and label emotions (Module 31)

familial retardation Mental retardation in which no apparent biological defect exists, but there is a history of retardation in the family (Module 27)

family therapy An approach that focuses on the family and its dynamics (Module 50)

feature analysis An approach to perception suggesting that we perceive a shape, pattern, object, or scene through the reaction of specific neurons to the individual elements that make up the stimulus (Module 13)

feature detection The activation of neurons in the cortex by visual stimuli of specific shapes or patterns (Module 11)

fetal alcohol syndrome The most common cause of mental retardation in newborns, occurring when the mother uses alcohol during pregnancy (Module 27)

fetus A developing individual, from eight weeks after conception until birth (Module 36)

fixations Conflicts or concerns that persist beyond the developmental period in which they first occur (Module 40)

fixed-interval schedule A schedule that provides reinforcement for a response only if a fixed time period has elapsed, making overall rates of response relatively low (Module 18)

fixed-ratio schedule A schedule by which reinforcement is given only after a specific number of responses are made (Module 18)

flashbulb memories Memories centered on a specific, important, or surprising event that are so vivid it is as if they represented a snapshot of the event (Module 21)

fluid intelligence Intelligence that reflects information-processing capabilities, reasoning, and memory (Module 26)

formal operational stage According to Jean Piaget, the period from age 12 to adulthood that is characterized by abstract thought (Module 37)

free will The idea that behavior is caused primarily by choices that are made freely by the individual (Module 3)

frequency distribution An arrangement of scores from a sample that indicates how often a particular score is present (Module 56)

frequency theory of hearing The theory that the entire basilar membrane acts like a microphone, vibrating as a whole in response to sound (Module 12)

frustration The thwarting or blocking of some ongoing, goal-directed behavior (Module 57)

functional fixedness The tendency to think of an object only in terms of its typical use (Module 24)

functionalism An early approach to psychology that concentrated on what the mind does—the functions of mental activity—and the role of behavior in allowing people to adapt to their environments (Module 2)

fundamental attribution error A tendency to overattribute others' behavior to dispositional causes and the corresponding minimization of the importance of situational causes (Module 52)

g or g-factor The single, general factor for mental ability assumed to underlie intelligence in some early theories of intelligence (Module 26)

gate-control theory of pain The theory that particular nerve receptors lead to specific areas of the brain related to pain (Module 12)

gender The perception of being male or female (Module 32)

gender roles The set of expectations, defined by a particular society, that indicate what is appropriate behavior for men and women (Module 32)

gender schema A mental framework that organizes and guides a child's understanding of information relevant to gender (Module 32)

general adaptation syndrome (GAS) A theory developed by Hans Selye that suggests that a person's response to a stressor consists of three stages: alarm and mobilization, resistance, and exhaustion (Module 43)

generalized anxiety disorder The experience of long-term, persistent anxiety and worry (Module 47)

generativity-versus-stagnation stage According to Erik Erikson, a period in middle adulthood during which we take stock of our contributions to family and society (Module 38)

genes The parts of the chromosomes through which genetic information is transmitted (Module 36)

genetic preprogramming theories of aging Theories that suggest that human cells have a built-in time limit to their reproduction, and that after a certain time they are no longer able to divide (Module 39)

genital stage According to Freud, the period from puberty until death, marked by mature sexual behavior (that is, sexual intercourse) (Module 40)

genitals The male and female sex organs (Module 33)

gestalt (geh SHTALLT) laws of organization A series of principles that describe how we organize bits and pieces of information into meaningful wholes (Module 13)

gestalt psychology An approach to psychology that focuses on the organization of perception and thinking in a "whole" sense rather than on the individual elements of perception (Module 2)

gestalt therapy A treatment approach in which people are led to examine their earlier experiences and complete any "unfinished business" from their past that may still affect and color present-day relationships (Module 52)

grammar The system of rules that determine how our thoughts can be expressed (Module 25)

group Two or more people who interact with one another; perceive themselves as part of a group, and are interdependent (Module 53)

group therapy Therapy in which people meet with a therapist to discuss problems with a group (Module 50)

groupthink A type of thinking in which group members share such a strong motivation to achieve consensus that they lose the ability to critically evaluate alternative points of view (Module 53)

habituation The decrease in response to a stimulus that occurs after repeated presentations of the same stimulus (Module 37)

hair cells Tiny cells covering the basilar membrane that, when bent by vibrations entering the cochlea, transmit neural messages to the brain (Module 12)

hallucinogen A drug that is capable of producing hallucinations, or changes in the perceptual process (Module 16)

halo effect A phenomenon in which an initial understanding that a person has positive traits is used to infer other uniformly positive characteristics (Module 52)

hardiness A personality characteristic associated with a lower rate of stress-related illness, consisting of three components: commitment, challenge, and control (Module 43)

health psychology The branch of psychology that investigates the psychological factors related to wellness and illness, including the prevention, diagnosis, and treatment of medical problems (Module 43)

hemispheres Symmetrical left and right halves of the brain that control the side of the body opposite to their location (Module 9)

heritability A measure of the degree to which a characteristic is related to genetic, inherited factors (Module 28)

heterosexuality Sexual attraction and behavior directed toward the other sex (Module 34)

heuristic A cognitive shortcut that may lead to a solution (Module 23)

histogram Bar graph (Module 56)

homeostasis The body's tendency to maintain a steady internal state (Module 29)

homosexuals Persons who are sexually attracted to members of their own sex (Module 34)

hormones Chemicals that circulate through the blood and regulate the functioning or growth of the body (Module 8)

humanistic approaches to personality Theories that emphasize people's innate goodness and desire to achieve higher levels of functioning (Module 41)

humanistic perspective The approach that suggests that all individuals naturally strive to grow, develop, and be in control of their lives and behavior (Modules 2, 46)

humanistic perspective on psychological disorders The perspective that emphasizes the responsibility people have for their own

behavior, even when such behavior is abnormal (Module 48)

humanistic therapy Therapy in which the underlying rationale is that people have control of their behavior, can make choices about their lives, and are essentially responsible for solving their own problems (Module 50)

hypnosis A trancelike state of heightened susceptibility to the suggestions of others (Module 15)

hypochondriasis A disorder in which people have a constant fear of illness and a preoccupation with their health (Module 47)

hypothalamus A tiny part of the brain, located below the thalamus, that maintains homeostasis and produces and regulates vital behavior, such as eating, drinking, and sexual behavior (Module 9)

hypothesis A prediction, stemming from a theory, stated in way that allows it to be tested (Module 4)

id The raw, unorganized, inborn part of personality whose sole purpose is to reduce tension created by primitive drives related to hunger, sex, aggression, and irrational impulses (Module 40)

identical twins Twins who are genetically identical (Module 35)

identification The process of wanting to be like another person as much as possible, imitating that person's behavior and adopting similar beliefs and values (Module 42)

identity The distinguishing character of the individual: who each of us is, what our roles are, and what we are capable of (Module 38)

identity-versus-role-confusion stage According to Erik Erikson, a time in adolescence of major testing to determine one's unique qualities (Module 40)

implicit memory Memories of which people are not consciously aware, but which can affect subsequent performance and behavior (Module 21)

incentive approaches to motivation Theories suggesting that motivation stems from the desire to obtain valued external goals, or incentives (Module 29)

independent variable The variable that is manipulated by an experimenter (Module 5)

industrial-organizational (I/O) psychology The branch of psychology focusing on work and job-related issues, including worker motivation, satisfaction, safety, and productivity (Module 53)

industry-versus-inferiority stage According to Erik Erikson, the last stage of childhood, during which children age 6 to 12 years may develop positive social interactions with others or may feel inadequate and become less sociable (Module 37)

inferential statistics The branch of statistics that uses data from samples to make predictions about the larger population from which the sample is drawn (Module 58)

inferiority complex According to Alfred Adler, a problem affecting adults who have not

been able to overcome the feelings of inferiority that they developed as children, when they were small and limited in their knowledge about the world (Module 40)

information processing The way in which people take in, use, and store information (Module 37)

informed consent A document signed by participants affirming that they have been told the basic outlines of the study and are aware of what their participation will involve (Module 6)

inhibited ejaculation The inability of a male to ejaculate when he wants to, if at all (Module 34)

inhibited sexual desire A sexual dysfunction in which the motivation for sexual activity is restrained or lacking entirely (Module 34)

inhibitory message A chemical message that prevents or decreases the likelihood that a receiving neuron will fire (Module 7)

initiative-versus-guilt stage According to Erik Erikson, the period during which children ages 3 to 6 years experience conflict between independence of action and the sometimes negative results of that action (Module 37)

insight A sudden awareness of the relationships among various elements that had previously appeared to be independent of one another (Module 24)

instincts Inborn patterns of behavior that are biologically determined rather than learned (Module 29)

intellectually gifted The 2 to 4 percent of the population who have IQ scores greater than 130 (Module 27)

intelligence The capacity to understand the world, think rationally, and use resources effectively when faced with challenges (Module 26)

intelligence quotient (IQ) A score that takes into account an individual's mental and chronological ages (Module 26)

intelligence tests Tests devised to quantify a person's level of intelligence (Module 26)

interactionist approach (to language development) The view that language development is produced through a combination of genetically determined predispositions and environmental circumstances that help teach language (Module 25)

interference The phenomenon by which information in memory disrupts the recall of other information (Module 22)

interneurons Neurons that connect sensory and motor neurons, carrying messages between the two (Module 8)

interpersonal attraction (or close relationship) Positive feelings for others; liking and loving (Module 55)

interpersonal therapy (IPT) Short-term therapy that focuses on the context of current social relationships (Module 50)

intimacy-versus-isolation stage According to Erik Erikson, a period during early adulthood that focuses on developing close relationships (Module 38)

introspection A procedure used to study the structure of the mind in which subjects are asked to describe in detail what they are experiencing when they are exposed to a stimulus (Module 2)

James-Lange theory of emotion The belief that emotional experience is a reaction to bodily events occurring as a result of an external situation ("I feel sad because I am crying") (Module 31)

just noticeable difference *See* difference threshold (Module 10)

Korsakoff's syndrome A disease that afflicts long-term alcoholics, leaving some abilities intact, but including hallucinations and a tendency to repeat the same story (Module 22)

language The communication of information through symbols arranged according to systematic rules (Module 25)

language-acquisition device A neural system of the brain hypothesized by Noam Chomsky to permit understanding of language (Module 25)

latency period According to Sigmund Freud, the period between the phallic stage and puberty during which children's sexual concerns are temporarily put aside (Module 40)

latent content of dreams According to Sigmund Freud, the "disguised" meaning of dreams, hidden by more obvious subjects (Module 14)

latent learning Learning in which a new behavior is acquired but is not demonstrated until some incentive is provided for displaying it (Module 19)

lateralization The dominance of one hemisphere of the brain in specific functions, such as language (Module 9)

learned helplessness A state in which people conclude that unpleasant or aversive stimuli cannot be controlled—a view of the world that becomes so ingrained that they cease trying to remedy the aversive circumstances, even if they actually can exert some influence (Module 43)

learning A relatively permanent change in behavior brought about by experience (Module 17)

learning-theory approach (to language development) The theory suggesting that language acquisition follows the principles of reinforcement and conditioning (Module 25)

levels-of-processing theory The theory of memory that emphasizes the degree to which new material is mentally analyzed (Module 21)

life review The process by which people examine and evaluate their lives (Module 39)

limbic system The part of the brain that controls eating, aggression, and reproduction (Module 9)

linguistic-relativity hypothesis The notion that language shapes and may determine the

way people in a particular culture perceive and understand the world (Module 25)

lithium A drug made up of mineral salts that is used to treat and prevent manic episodes of bipolar disorder (Module 53)

lobes The four major sections of the cerebral cortex: frontal, parietal, temporal, and occipital (Module 9)

longitudinal research A research method that investigates behavior as participants age (Module 35)

long-term memory Memory that stores information on a relatively permanent basis, although it may be difficult to retrieve (Module 20)

major depression A severe form of depression that interferes with concentration, decision making, and sociability (Module 47)

mania An extended state of intense, wild elation (Module 49)

manifest content of dreams According to Sigmund Freud, the apparent story line of dreams (Module 14)

masturbation Sexual self-stimulation (Module 34)

mean The average of all scores, arrived at by adding scores together and dividing by the number of scores (Module 56)

means-ends analysis Repeated testing for differences between the desired outcome and what currently exists (Module 24)

median The point in a distribution of scores that divides the distribution exactly in half when the scores are listed in numerical order (Module 56)

medical perspective The perspective that suggests that when an individual displays symptoms of abnormal behavior, the root cause will be found in a physical examination of the individual, which may reveal a hormonal imbalance, a chemical deficiency, or a brain injury (Module 46)

meditation A learned technique for refocusing attention that brings about an altered state of consciousness (Module 15)

memory The process by which we encode, store, and retrieve information (Module 20)

memory trace A physical change in the brain that occurs when new material is learned (Module 22)

menopause The period during which women stop menstruating and are no longer fertile (Module 39)

mental age The average age of individuals who achieve a particular level of performance on a test (Module 26)

mental images Representations in the mind that resemble the object or event being represented (Module 23)

mental retardation or intellectual disability A condition characterized by significant limitations both in intellectual functioning and in conceptual, social, and practical adaptive skills (Module 27)

mental set The tendency for old patterns of problem solving to persist (Module 24)

metabolism The rate at which food is converted to energy and expended by the body (Module 30)

metacognition An awareness and understanding of one's own cognitive processes (Module 37)

Minnesota Multiphasic Personality Inventory-2 (MMPI-2) A widely used self-report test that identifies people with psychological difficulties and is employed to predict some everyday behaviors (Module 42)

mirror neurons Specialized neurons that fire not only when a person enacts a particular behavior, but also when a person simply observes *another* individual carrying out the same behavior (Module 7)

mode The most frequently occurring score in a set of scores (Module 56)

mood disorder An emotional disturbance that is strong enough to intrude on everyday living (Module 47)

mood stabilizers Drugs used to treat mood disorders that prevent manic episodes of bipolar disorder (Module 51)

motivation The factors that direct and energize the behavior of humans and other organisms (Module 29)

motor area The part of the cortex that is largely responsible for the body's voluntary movement (Module 9)

motor (efferent) neurons Neurons that communicate information from the nervous system to muscles and glands (Module 8)

multiple personality disorder *See* dissociative identity disorder (Module 47)

myelin sheath A protective coat of fat and protein that wraps around the neuron (Module 7)

narcissistic personality disorder A personality disturbance characterized by an exaggerated sense of self-importance (Module 47)

narcotics Drugs that increase relaxation and relieve pain and anxiety (Module 16)

nativist approach (to language development) The theory that a genetically determined, innate mechanism directs language development (Module 25)

naturalistic observation Research in which an investigator simply observes some naturally occurring behavior and does not make a change in the situation (Module 5)

nature–nurture issue The issue of the degree to which environment and heredity influence behavior (Module 35)

need for achievement A stable, learned characteristic in which a person obtains satisfaction by striving for and attaining a level of excellence (Module 30)

need for affiliation An interest in establishing and maintaining relationships with other people (Module 30)

need for power A tendency to seek impact, control, or influence over others, and to be seen as a powerful individual (Module 30)

negative reinforcer An unpleasant stimulus whose *removal* leads to an increase in the probability that a preceding response will be repeated in the future (Module 18)

negative relationship A relationship established by data that shows high values of one variable corresponding with low values of the other (Module 58)

neo-Freudian psychoanalysts Psychoanalysts who were trained in traditional Freudian theory but who later rejected some of its major points (Module 40)

neonate A newborn child (Module 37)

neurons Nerve cells, the basic elements of the nervous system (Module 7)

neuroplasticity Changes in the brain that occur throughout the life span relating to the addition of new neurons, new interconnections between neurons, and the reorganization of information-processing areas (Module 9)

neuroscience perspective The approach that views behavior from the perspective of the brain, the nervous system, and other biological functions (Module 2)

neurotransmitters Chemicals that carry messages across the synapse to the dendrite (and sometimes the cell body) of a receiver neuron (Module 7)

neutral stimulus A stimulus that, before conditioning, does not naturally bring about the response of interest (Module 17)

normal distribution A distribution of scores that produces a symmetrical, bell-shaped curve in which the right half mirrors the left half and in which the mean, median, and mode all have the same value (Module 56)

norms Standards of test performance that permit the comparison of one person's score on a test with the scores of other individuals who have taken the same test (Module 26)

obedience A change in behavior in response to the commands of others (Module 53)

obesity Body weight that is more than 20 percent above the average weight for a person of a particular height (Module 30)

object permanence The awareness that objects—and people—continue to exist even if they are out of sight (Module 37)

observational learning Learning by observing the behavior of another person, or model (Module 19)

obsession A persistent, unwanted thought or idea that keeps recurring (Module 47)

obsessive-compulsive disorder A disorder characterized by obsessions or compulsions (Module 47)

Oedipal conflict A child's sexual interest in his or her opposite-sex parent, typically resolved through identification with the same-sex parent (Module 40)

operant conditioning Learning in which a voluntary response is strengthened or weak-

ened, depending on its favorable or unfavorable consequences (Module 18)

operational definition The translation of a hypothesis into specific, testable procedures that can be measured and observed (Module 5)

opponent-process theory of color vision The theory that receptor cells for color are linked in pairs, working in opposition to each other (Module 11)

optic nerve A bundle of ganglion axons that carry visual information to the brain (Module 11)

oral stage According to Sigmund Freud, a stage from birth to age 12 to 18 months, in which an infant's center of pleasure is the mouth (Module 40)

orgasm The peak of sexual excitement, during which rhythmic muscular contractions occur in the genitals (Module 33)

otoliths Tiny, motion-sensitive crystals within the semicircular canals that sense body acceleration (Module 12)

overgeneralization The phenomenon by which children apply language rules even when the application results in an error (Module 25)

ovulation The point at which an egg is released from the ovaries (Module 33)

panic disorder Anxiety disorder that takes the form of panic attacks lasting from a few seconds to as long as several hours (Module 47)

parasympathetic division The part of the autonomic division of the nervous system that acts to calm the body after an emergency [or a stressful situation] has ended (Module 8)

partial (or intermittent) reinforcement schedule Reinforcing of a behavior some but not all of the time (Module 18)

passionate (or romantic) love A state of intense absorption in someone that includes intense physiological arousal, psychological interest, and caring for the needs of another (Module 55)

perception The sorting out, interpretation, analysis, and integration of stimuli by the sense organs and brain (Module 10)

peripheral nervous system The part of the nervous system that includes the autonomic and somatic subdivisions; made up of neurons with long axons and dendrites, it branches out from the spinal cord and brain and reaches the extremities of the body (Module 8)

peripheral route processing Message interpretation characterized by consideration of the source and related general information rather than of the message itself (Module 52)

permissive parents Parents who give their children relaxed or inconsistent direction and, although warm, require little of them (Module 37)

personal stressors Major life events, such as the death of a family member, that have immediate consequences that generally fade with time (Module 43)

personality The pattern of enduring characteristics that produce consistency and individuality in a given person (Module 40)

personality disorder A disorder characterized by a set of inflexible, maladaptive behavior patterns that keep a person from functioning appropriately in society (Module 47)

person-centered therapy Therapy in which the goal is to reach one's potential for self-actualization (Module 50)

phallic stage According to Sigmund Freud, a period beginning around age 3 during which a child's pleasure focuses on the genitals (Module 42)

phobias Intense, irrational fears of specific objects or situations (Module 47)

phonemes The smallest units of speech that affect meaning (Module 25)

phonology The study of the smallest units of speech, called phonemes (Module 25)

pituitary gland The major component of the endocrine system, or "master gland," which secretes hormones that control growth and other parts of the endocrine system (Module 8)

place theory of hearing The theory that different areas of the basilar membrane respond to different frequencies (Module 12)

placebo A false treatment, such as a pill, "drug," or other substance, without any significant chemical properties or active ingredient (Module 6)

plateau phase The period in which the maximum level of arousal is attained, the penis and clitoris swell with blood, and the body prepares for orgasm (Module 33)

population All the members of a group of interest (Module 58)

positive reinforcer A stimulus added to the environment that brings about an increase in a preceding response (Module 18)

positive relationship A relationship established by data that shows high values of one variable corresponding with high values of another, and low values of the first variable corresponding with low values of the other (Module 50)

posttraumatic stress disorder (PTSD) A phenomenon in which victims of major catastrophes or strong personal stressors feel long-lasting effects that may include reexperiencing the event in vivid flashbacks or dreams (Module 43)

practical intelligence According to Robert Sternberg, intelligence related to overall success in living (Module 26)

prejudice A negative (or positive) evaluation of a particular group and its members (Module 53)

premature ejaculation The inability of a male to delay orgasm as long as he wishes (Module 34)

preoperational stage According to Jean Piaget, the period from 2 to 7 years of age that is characterized by language development (Module 37)

priming A phenomenon in which exposure to a word or concept (called a *prime*) later makes it easier to recall related information, even when there is no conscious memory of the word or concept (Module 21)

principle of conservation The knowledge that quantity is unrelated to the arrangement and physical appearance of objects (Module 37)

proactive interference Interference in which information learned earlier disrupts the recall of newer information (Module 22)

procedural memory Memory for skills and habits, such as riding a bike or hitting a baseball, sometimes referred to as *nondeclarative memory* (Module 20)

progesterone A female sex hormone secreted by the ovaries (Module 34)

projective personality test A test in which a person is shown an ambiguous stimulus and asked to describe it or tell a story about it (Module 42)

prosocial behavior Helping behavior (Module 55)

prototypes Typical, highly representative samples of a concept (Module 23)

psychoactive drugs Drugs that influence a person's emotions, perceptions, and behavior (Module 16)

psychoanalysis Freudian psychotherapy in which the goal is to release hidden unconscious thoughts and feelings in order to reduce their power in controlling behavior (Module 49)

psychoanalytic perspective on psychological disorders The perspective that suggests that abnormal behavior stems from childhood conflicts over opposing wishes regarding sex and aggression (Module 46)

psychoanalytic theory Sigmund Freud's theory that unconscious forces act as determinants of personality (Module 40)

psychodynamic approaches to personality Approaches that assume that personality is motivated by inner forces and conflicts about which people have little awareness and over which they have no control (Module 40)

psychodynamic perspective The approach based on the view that behavior is motivated by unconscious inner forces over which the individual has little control (Module 2)

psychodynamic therapy Therapy that seeks to bring unresolved past conflicts and unacceptable impulses from the unconscious into the conscious, where patients may deal with the problems more effectively (Module 49)

psychological tests Standard measures devised to assess behavior objectively; used by psychologists to help people make decisions about their lives and understand more about themselves (Module 42)

psychology The scientific study of behavior and mental processes (Module 1)

psychoneuroimmunology (PNI) The study of the relationship among psychological factors, the immune system, and the brain (Module 43)

psychophysics The study of the relationship between the physical aspects of stimuli and our psychological experience of them (Module 10)

psychophysiological disorders Medical problems influenced by an interaction of psychological, emotional, and physical difficulties (Module 43)

psychosexual stages Developmental periods that children pass through during which they encounter conflicts between the demands of society and their own sexual urges (Module 40)

psychosocial development Development of individuals' interactions and understanding of each other and of their knowledge and understanding of themselves as members of society (Module 37)

psychosurgery Brain surgery once used to reduce the symptoms of mental disorder but rarely used today (Module 51)

psychotherapy Treatment in which a trained professional—a therapist—uses psychological techniques to help a person overcome psychological difficulties and disorders, resolve problems in living, or bring about personal growth (Module 49)

puberty The period at which maturation of the sexual organs occurs, beginning at about age 11 or 12 for girls and 13 or 14 for boys (Module 40)

punishment A stimulus that decreases the probability that a previous behavior will occur again (Module 18)

random assignment to condition A procedure in which participants are assigned to different experimental groups or "conditions" on the basis of chance and chance alone (Module 5)

range The difference between the highest score and the lowest score in a distribution (Module 57)

rape The act by which one person forces another person to submit to sexual activity (Module 34)

rapid eye movement (REM) sleep Sleep occupying 20 percent of an adult's sleeping time, characterized by increased heart rate, blood pressure, and breathing rate; erections (in males); eye movements; and the experience of dreaming (Module 14)

rational-emotive behavior therapy A form of therapy that attempts to restructure a person's belief system into a more realistic, rational, and logical set of views by challenging dysfunctional beliefs that maintain irrational behavior (Module 49)

reactance A disagreeable emotional and cognitive reaction that results from the restriction of one's freedom and that can be associated with medical regimens (Module 45)

recall Memory task in which specific information must be retrieved (Module 21)

reciprocity-of-liking effect A tendency to like those who like us (Module 55)

recognition Memory task in which individuals are presented with a stimulus and asked whether they have been exposed to it in the past or to identify it from a list of alternatives (Module 21)

reflex An automatic, involuntary response to an incoming stimulus (Module 8, Module 37)

refractory period A temporary period that follows the resolution stage and during which the male cannot develop an erection again (Module 33)

rehearsal The repetition of information that has entered short-term memory (Module 20)

reinforcement The process by which a stimulus increases the probability that a preceding behavior will be repeated (Module 18)

reinforcer Any stimulus that increases the probability that a preceding behavior will occur again (Module 18)

reliability The property by which tests measure consistently what they are trying to measure (Module 26)

replicated research Research that is repeated, sometimes using other procedures, settings, and groups of participants, to increase confidence in prior findings (Module 5)

repression The primary defense mechanism in which unacceptable or unpleasant id impulses are pushed back into the unconscious (Module 40)

resolution phase The interval after orgasm in which the body returns to its unaroused phase, reversing the changes brought about by arousal (Module 33)

resting state The state in which there is a negative electrical charge of about 270 millivolts within a neuron (Module 7)

reticular formation The part of the brain extending from the medulla through the pons and made up of groups of nerve cells that can immediately activate other parts of the brain to produce general bodily arousal (Module 9)

retina The part of the eye that converts the electromagnetic energy of light to electrical impulses for transmission to the brain (Module 11)

retroactive interference Interference in which there is difficulty in the recall of information learned earlier because of later exposure to different material (Module 22)

retrograde amnesia Amnesia in which memory is lost for occurrences prior to a certain event (Module 22)

reuptake The reabsorption of neurotransmitters by a terminal button (Module 7)

rods Thin, cylindrical receptor cells in the retina that are highly sensitive to light (Module 11)

Rorschach test A test that involves showing a series of symmetrical visual stimuli to people who then are asked what the figures represent to them (Module 42)

sample A representative subgroup of a population of interest (Module 58)

Schachter-Singer theory of emotion The belief that emotions are determined jointly by a nonspecific kind of physiological arousal and its interpretation, based on environmental cues (Module 31)

schedules of reinforcement Different patterns of frequency and timing of reinforcement following desired behavior (Module 18)

schemas Organized bodies of information stored in memory that bias the way new information is interpreted, stored, and recalled. In social cognition, sets of cognitions about people and social experiences (Modules 21, 52)

schizophrenia A class of disorders in which severe distortion of reality occurs (Module 47)

scientific method The approach through which psychologists systematically acquire knowledge and understanding about behavior and other phenomena of interest (Module 4)

self-actualization A state of self-fulfillment in which people realize their highest potential, each in their own unique way (Modules 29, 41)

self-efficacy Belief in one's personal capabilities. Self-efficacy underlies people's faith in their ability to carry out a particular behavior or produce a desired outcome (Module 41)

self-esteem The component of personality that encompasses our positive and negative self-evaluations (Module 41)

self-report measures A method of gathering data about people by asking them questions about a sample of their behavior (Module 42)

self-serving bias The tendency to attribute personal success to personal factors (skill, ability, or effort) and to attribute failure to factors outside oneself (Module 52)

semantic memory Memory for general knowledge and facts about the world, as well as memory for the rules of logic that are used to deduce other facts (Module 20)

semantic networks Mental representations of clusters of interconnected information (Module 20)

semantics The rules governing the meaning of words and sentences (Module 25)

semicircular canals Three tubelike structures of the inner ear containing fluid that sloshes through them when the head moves, signaling rotational or angular movement to the brain (Module 12)

sensation The activation of the sense organs by a source of physical energy (Module 10)

sensorimotor stage According to Jean Piaget, the stage from birth to 2 years, during which a child has little competence in representing the environment by using images, language, or other symbols (Module 37)

sensory (afferent) neurons Neurons that transmit information from the perimeter of the body to the central nervous system (Module 8)

sensory area The site in the brain of the tissue that corresponds to each of the senses, with the degree of sensitivity related to the amount of the tissue allocated to that sense (Module 9)

sensory memory The initial, momentary storage of information, lasting only an instant (Module 20)

sequential research A research method that combines cross-sectional and longitudinal research by considering a number of different age groups and examining them at several points in time (Module 35)

sexism Negative attitudes and behavior toward a person based on that person's gender (Module 32)

sexually transmitted infection (STI) A disease transmitted through sexual contact (Module 34)

shaping The process of teaching a complex behavior by rewarding closer and closer approximations of the desired behavior (Module 18)

short-term memory Memory that holds information for fifteen to twenty-five seconds (Module 20)

significant outcome Meaningful results that make it possible for researchers to feel confident that they have confirmed their hypotheses. In statistics, an outcome in which the observed outcome would be expected to have occurred by chance with a probability of .05 or less (Modules 5, 58)

situational causes (of behavior) Perceived causes of behavior that are based on environmental factors (Module 52)

skin senses The senses of touch, pressure, temperature, and pain (Module 12)

social cognition The cognitive processes by which people understand and make sense of others and themselves (Module 52)

social cognitive approaches to personality Theories that emphasize the influence of a person's cognitions—thoughts, feelings, expectations, and values—as well as observation of others' behavior, in determining personality (Module 41)

social influence The process by which the actions of an individual or group affect the behavior of others (Module 53)

social psychology The scientific study of how people's thoughts, feelings, and actions are affected by others (Module 52)

social neuroscience The subfield of social psychology that seeks to identify the neural basis of social behavior (Module 54)

social support A mutual network of caring, interested others (Module 43)

social supporter A group member whose dissenting views make nonconformity to the group easier (Module 53)

sociocultural perspective The perspective that assumes that people's behavior—both normal and abnormal—is shaped by the kind of family group, society, and culture in which they live (Module 46)

somatic division The part of the peripheral nervous system that specializes in the control of voluntary movements and the communication of information to and from the sense organs (Module 8)

somatoform disorders Psychological difficulties that take on a physical (somatic) form, but for which there is no medical cause (Module 47)

sound The movement of air molecules brought about by a source of vibration (Module 12)

spinal cord A bundle of neurons that leaves the brain and runs down the length of the back and is the main means for transmitting messages between the brain and the body (Module 8)

spontaneous recovery The reemergence of an extinguished conditioned response after a period of rest and with no further conditioning (Module 17)

spontaneous remission Recovery without treatment (Module 50)

stage 1 sleep The state of transition between wakefulness and sleep, characterized by relatively rapid, low-amplitude brain waves (Module 14)

stage 2 sleep A sleep deeper than that of stage 1, characterized by a slower, more regular wave pattern, along with momentary interruptions of sleep spindles (Module 14)

stage 3 sleep A sleep characterized by slow brain waves, with greater peaks and valleys in the wave pattern than in stage 2 sleep (Module 14)

stage 4 sleep The deepest stage of sleep, during which we are least responsive to outside stimulation (Module 14)

standard deviation An index of the average deviation of a set of scores from the center of the distribution (Module 57)

statistics The branch of mathematics concerned with collecting, organizing, analyzing, and drawing conclusions from numerical data (Module 58)

status The social rank held within a group (Module 53)

stereotype A set of generalized beliefs and expectations about a particular group and its members (Module 54)

stimulants Drugs that have an arousal effect on the central nervous system, causing a rise in heart rate, blood pressure, and muscular tension (Module 16)

stimulus Energy that produces a response in a sense organ (Module 10)

stimulus discrimination The process that occurs if two stimuli are sufficiently distinct from one another that one evokes a conditioned response but the other does not; the ability to differentiate between stimuli (Module 17)

stimulus generalization Occurs when a conditioned response follows a stimulus that is similar to the original conditioned stimulus; the more similar the two stimuli are, the more likely generalization is to occur (Module 17)

stress A person's response to events that are threatening or challenging (Module 45)

structuralism Wilhelm Wundt's approach, which focuses on uncovering the fundamental mental components of consciousness, thinking, and other kinds of mental states and activities (Module 2)

subjective well-being People's own evaluation of their lives in terms of both their thoughts and their emotions (Module 45)

superego According to Sigmund Freud, the final personality structure to develop; it represents the rights and wrongs of society as handed down by a person's parents, teachers, and other important figures (Module 40)

survey research Research in which people chosen to represent a larger population are asked a series of questions about their behavior, thoughts, or attitudes (Module 5)

syllogistic reasoning Formal reasoning in which a person draws a conclusion from a set of assumptions (Module 23)

sympathetic division The part of the autonomic division of the nervous system that acts to prepare the body for action in stressful situations, engaging all the organism's resources to respond to a threat (Module 8)

synapse The space between two neurons where the axon of a sending neuron communicates with the dendrites of a receiving neuron by using chemical messages (Module 7)

syntax Ways in which words and phrases can be combined to form sentences (Module 25)

systematic desensitization A behavioral technique in which gradual exposure to an anxiety-producing stimulus is paired with relaxation to extinguish the response of anxiety (Module 49)

telegraphic speech Sentences in which words not critical to the message are left out (Module 25)

temperament Basic, innate disposition that emerges early in life (Modules 37, 41)

teratogens Environmental agents such as a drug, chemical, virus, or other factor that produce a birth defect (Module 38)

terminal buttons Small bulges at the end of axons that send messages to other neurons (Module 7)

test standardization A technique used to validate questions in personality tests by studying the responses of people with known diagnoses (Module 42)

thalamus The part of the brain located in the middle of the central core that acts primarily to relay information about the senses (Module 9)

Thematic Apperception Test (TAT) A test consisting of a series of pictures about which a person is asked to write a story (Module 42)

theories Broad explanations and predictions concerning phenomena of interest (Module 4)

theory of multiple intelligences Howard Gardner's theory that proposes that there are eight distinct spheres of intelligence (Module 26)

thinking The manipulation of mental representations of information (Module 23)

tip-of-the-tongue phenomenon The inability to recall information that one realizes one knows—a result of the difficulty of retrieving information from long-term memory (Module 21)

top-down processing Perception that is guided by higher-level knowledge, experience, expectations, and motivations (Module 13)

trait theory A model of personality that seeks to identify the basic traits necessary to describe personality (Module 41)

traits Consistent personality characteristics and behaviors displayed in different situations (Module 41)

transcranial magnetic stimulation (TMS) A depression treatment in which a precise magnetic pulse is directed to a specific area of the brain (Module 51)

transference The transfer of feelings to a psychoanalyst of love or anger that had been originally directed to a patient's parents or other authority figures (Module 49)

transsexual Persons who believe they were born with the body of the other gender (Module 34)

treatment The manipulation implemented by the experimenter (Module 5)

trichromatic theory of color vision The theory that there are three kinds of cones in the retina, each of which responds primarily to a specific range of wavelengths (Module 11)

trust-versus-mistrust stage According to Erik Erikson, the first stage of psychosocial development, occurring from birth to age 1½ years, during which time infants develop feelings of trust or lack of trust (Module 37)

Type A behavior pattern A cluster of behaviors involving hostility, competitiveness, time urgency, and feeling driven (Module 44)

Type B behavior pattern A cluster of behaviors characterized by a patient, cooperative, noncompetitive, and nonaggressive manner (Module 44)

unconditional positive regard An attitude of acceptance and respect on the part of an observer, no matter what a person says or does (Module 41)

unconditioned response (UCR) A response that is natural and needs no training (e.g., salivation at the smell of food) (Module 17)

unconditioned stimulus (UCS) A stimulus that naturally brings about a particular response without having been learned (Module 17)

unconscious A part of the personality that contains the memories, knowledge, beliefs, feelings, urges, drives, and instincts of which the individual is not aware (Module 40)

unconscious wish fulfillment theory Sigmund Freud's theory that dreams represent unconscious wishes that dreamers desire to see fulfilled (Module 14)

uninvolved parents Parents who show little interest in their children and are emotionally detached (Module 37)

universal grammar Noam Chomsky's theory that all the world's languages share a common underlying structure (Module 25)

validity The property by which tests actually measure what they are supposed to measure (Module 26)

variability The spread, or dispersion, of scores in a distribution (Module 57)

variable Behaviors, events, or other characteristics that can change, or vary, in some way (Module 5)

variable-interval schedule A schedule by which the time between reinforcements varies around some average rather than being fixed (Module 18)

variable-ratio schedule A schedule by which reinforcement occurs after a varying number of responses rather than a fixed number (Module 18)

visual illusions Physical stimuli that consistently produce errors in perception (Module 13)

wear-and-tear theories of aging Theories that suggest that the mechanical functions of the body simply stop working efficiently (Module 39)

Weber's law A basic law of psychophysics stating that a just noticeable difference is in constant proportion to the intensity of an initial stimulus (Module 10)

weight set point The particular level of weight that the body strives to maintain (Module 30)

working memory A set of active, temporary memory stores that actively manipulate and rehearse information (Module 20)

zone of proximal development (ZPD) According to Lev Vygotsky, the level at which a child can almost, but not fully, comprehend or perform a task on his or her own (Module 37)

zygote The new cell formed by the union of an egg and sperm (Module 38)

References

Aartsen, M. J., Martin, M., & Zimprich, D. (2002). Gender differences in level and change in cognitive functioning: Results from the longitudinal aging study Amsterdam. *Gerontology, 50,* 35–38.

Aazh, H., & Moore, B. C. J. (2007). Dead regions in the cochlea at 4 kHz in elderly adults: Relation to absolute threshold, steepness of audiogram, and pure-tone average. *Journal of the American Academy of Audiology, 18,* 97–106.

Abboud, L. (2005, July 27). The next phase in psychiatry. *The Wall Street Journal,* pp. D1, D5.

Abelman, R.,(2007). Fighting the war on indecency: Mediating TV, Internet, and video-game usage among achieving and underachieving gifted children. *Roeper Review, 29,* 100–112.

Ablon, J. S., & Jones, E. E. (2002). Validity of controlled clinical trials of psychotherapy: Findings from the NIMH Treatment of Depression Collaborative Research Program. *American Journal of Psychiatry, 159,* 775–783.

Ablon, J. S., & Jones, E. E. (2005). On analytic process. *Journal of the American Psychoanalytic Association, 53,* 541–568.

Aboitiz, F., Garcia, R., & Brunetti, E. (2006). The origin of Broca's area and its connections from an ancestral working memory network. In Y. Grodzinsky, & K. Amunts, *Broca's region.* New York: Oxford University Press.

Abraham, P. F., & Calabrese, J. R. (2007). Review of: Lithium treatment of mood disorders: A practical guide, 6th rev. ed. *Bipolar Disorders, 9,* 548.

Abraham, S. F., Boyd, C., Luscombe, G., Hart, S., & Russell, J. (2007). When energy in does not equal energy out: Disordered energy control. *Eating Behaviors, 8,* 350–356.

Abramowitz, J. S., Olatunji, B. O., & Deacon, B. J. (2007). Health anxiety, hypochondriasis, and the anxiety disorders. *Behavior Therapy, 38,* 86–94.

Abrams, R. L., Klinger, M. R., & Greenwald, A. G. (2002). Subliminal words activate semantic categories (not automated responses). *Psychonomic Bulletin & Review, 9,* 100–106.

Abramson, L. Y., Alloy, L. B., Hogan, M. E., Whitehouse, W. G., Donova, P., Rose, D. T., Panzarella, C., & Raniere, D. (2002). Cognitive vulnerability to depression: Theory and evidence. In R. L. Leahy & E. T. Dowd (Eds.), *Clinical advances in cognitive psychotherapy: Theory and Application* (pp. 75–92). New York: Springer.

Abt, S. (1999, July 26). Armstrong wins tour and journey. *The New York Times,* pp. D1, D4.

Accardo, P. J., & Capute, A. J. (1998). Mental retardations. *Mental Retardation & Developmental Disabilities Research Reviews, 4,* 2–5.

Ackard, D. M., & Neumark-Sztainer, D. (2002). Date violence and date rape among adolescents: Associations with disordered eating behaviors and psychological health. *Child Abuse and Neglect, 26,* 455–473.

Adams, B., & Parker, J. D. (1990). Maternal weight gain in women with good pregnancy outcome. *Obstetrics and Gynecology, 76,* 1–7.

Adams, G., & Dzokoto, V. A. (2007). Genital-shrinking panic in Ghana: A cultural psychological analysis. *Culture & Psychology, 13,* 83–104.

Adams, K. B. (2004). Changing investment in activities and interests in elders' lives: Theory and measurement. *International Journal of Aging and Human Development, 58,* 87–108.

Adams, L., & Russakoff, D. (1999, June 12). Dissecting Columbine's cult of the athlete. *The Washington Post,* A1.

Adams, M., Zuniga, X., Hackman, H. W., Castaneda, C. R., & Blumenfeld, W. J. (2000). *Readings for diversity and social justice: An anthology on racism, sexism, anti-Semitism, heterosexism, classism, and ableism.* New York: Routledge.

Adams-Byers, J., Squilkr Witsell, S. & Moon, S. M. (2004). Gifted students' perceptions of the academic and social/emotional effects of homogeneous and heterogeneous grouping. *Gifted Child Quarterly, 48,* 7–20.

Addolorato, G., Leggio, L., Abenavoli, L., & Gasbarrini, G. (2005). Neurobiochemical and clinical aspects of craving in alcohol addiction: A review. *Addictive Behaviors, 30,* 1209–1224.

Adelson, R. (2005, May) Only the lonely. *Monitor on Psychology,* pp. 26–27.

Ader, R., Felten, D., & Cohen, N. (2001). *Psychoneuroimmunology* (3rd ed.). San Diego: Academic Press.

Addus, A. A., Chen, D., & Khan, A. S. (2007). Academic performance and advisement of university students: A case study. *College Student Journal, 41,* 316–326.

Adkins, E., and Keel, P. (2005). Does 'excessive' or 'compulsive' best describe exercise as a symptom of bulimia nervosa? *International Journal of Eating Disorders, 38,* 24–29.

Adler, J. (1984, April 23). The fight to conquer fear. *Newsweek,* pp. 66–72.

Adolphs, R. (2002). Neural systems for recognizing emotion. *Current Opinion in Neurobiology, 12,* 169–177.

Advokat, C. (2005). Differential effects of clozapine versus other antipsychotics on clinical outcome and dopamine release in the brain. *Essential Psychopharmacology, 6,* 73–90.

Affleck, G., Tennen, H., Urrows, S., & Higgins, P. (1994). Person and contextual features of daily stress reactivity: Individual differences in relations of undesirable daily events with mood disturbance and chronic pain intensity. *Journal of Personality and Social Psychology, 66,* 329–340.

Aftanas, L., & Golosheykin, S. (2005). Impact of regular meditation practice on EEG activity at rest and during evoked negative emotions. *International Journal of Neuroscience, 115,* 893–909.

Aghajanian, G. K. (1994). Serotonin and the action of LSD in the brain. *Psychiatric Annals, 24,* 137–141.

Agras, W. S., Berkowitz, R. I. (1996). Behavior therapy. In R. E. Hales & S. C. Yudofsky (Eds.), *The American Psychiatric Press synopsis of psychiatry.* Washington, DC: American Psychiatric Press.

Ahiima, R. S., & Osei, S. Y. (2004). Leptin signaling. *Physiology and Behavior, 81,* 223–241.

Ahissar, M., Ahissar, E., Bergman, H., & Vaadia, E. (1992). Encoding of sound-source location and movement: Activity of single neurons and interactions between adjacent neurons in the monkey auditory cortex. *Journal of Neurophysiology, 67,* 203–215.

Ahrons, C. (1995). *The good divorce: Keeping your family together when your marriage comes apart.* New York: HarperPerennial.

Aiello, R. J. (2006). Hypermasculinity and psychosocial development as predictors of potential date-rape perpetration on campus. *Dissertation Abstracts International: Section B: The Sciences and Engineering, 67(2-B),* 1178.

Aiken, L. (2000). *Dying, death, and bereavement* (4th ed.). Mahwah, NJ: Erlbaum.

Aiken, L. R. (1996). *Assessment of intellectual functioning* (2nd ed.). New York: Plenum.

Aiken, L. R. (1997). *Psychological testing and assessment* (9th ed.). Needham Heights, MA: Allyn & Bacon.

Aiken, L. R. (2000). *Personality: Theories, assessment, research, and applications.* Springfield, IL: Charles C. Thomas.

Ainsworth, M. D. S., Blehar, M. C., Waters, E., & Wall, S. (1978). *Patterns of attachment: A psychological study of the strange situation.* Hillsdale, NJ: Erlbaum.

Ajzen, I. (2002). Residual effects of past on later behavior: Habituation and reasoned action perspectives. *Personality and Social Psychology Review, 6,* 107–122.

Akil, H., & Morano, M. I. (1996). The biology of stress: From periphery to brain. In S. J. Watson (Ed.), *Biology of schizophrenia and affective disease.* Washington, DC: American Psychiatric Press.

Akirav, I., Raizel, H., & Maroun, M. (2006). Enhancement of conditioned fear extinction by infusion of the GABA-sub(A) agonist muscimol into the rat prefrontal cortex and amygdala. *European Journal of Neuroscience, 23,* 758–764.

Akman, I., Ozek, E., Bilgen, H., Ozdogan, T., & Cebeci, D. (2002). Sweet solutions and pacifiers for pain relief in newborn infants. *Journal of Pain, 3,* 199–202.

Akutsu, P. D., Sue, S., Zane, N. W. S., & Nakamura, C. Y. (1989). Ethnic differences in alcohol consumption among Asians and Caucasians in the United States: An investigation of cultural and physiological factors. *Journal of Studies on Alcohol, 50*, 261–267.

Alford, B. A., & Beck, A. T. (1997). *The integrative power of cognitive therapy.* New York: Guilford Press.

Allan, G. (2004). Being unfaithful: His and her affairs. In J. Duncombe., K. Harrison., G. Allan. & D. Marsden (Eds.), *The state of affairs: Explorations in infidelity and commitment.* Mahwah, NJ: Lawrence Erlbaum Associates Publishers

Allhoff, F. (2005). Germ-line genetic enhancement and Rawlsian primary goods. *Kennedy Institute of Ethics Journal, 15*, 39–56.

Allison, B. Z., Wolpaw, E. W., & Wolpaw, J. R. (2007). Brain-computer interface systems: progress and prospects. *Expert Review of Medical Devices, 4*, 463–474.

Alloy, L. B., Jacobson, N. S., & Acocella, J. (1999). *Abnormal psychology* (8th ed.). New York: McGraw-Hill.

Allport, G. W. (1961). *Pattern and growth in personality.* New York: Holt, Rinehart and Winston.

Allport, G. W. (1966). Traits revisited. *American Psychologist, 21*, 1–10.

Allport, G. W., & Postman, L. J. (1958). The basic psychology of rumor. In E. D. Maccoby, T. M. Newcomb, & E. L. Hartley (Eds.), *Readings in social psychology* (3rd ed.). New York: Holt, Rinehart and Winston.

Allwood, M. A. (2007). The relations of violence exposure, trauma symptoms and aggressive cognitions to youth violent behavior. *Dissertation Abstracts International: Section B: The Sciences and Engineering, 67*, 5387.

Aloia, M. S., Smith, K., & Arnedt, J. T. (2007). Brief behavioral therapies reduce early positive airway pressure discontinuation rates in sleep apnea syndrome: Preliminary findings *Behavioral Sleep Medicine, 5*, 89–104.

Alon, I., & Brett, J. M. (2007). Perceptions of time and their impact on negotiations in the Arabic-speaking Islamic world. *Negotiation Journal, 23*, 55–73.

Alonso, A., Alonso, S., & Piper, W. (2003). Group psychotherapy. In G. Stricker & T. A. Widiger, et al. (Eds.), *Handbook of psychology: Clinical psychology* (Vol. 8). New York: Wiley.

Altman, N. (1996). The accommodation of diversity in psychoanalysis. In R. P. Foster, M. Moskowitz, & R. A. Javier (Eds.), *Reaching across boundaries of culture and class: Widening the scope of psychotherapy.* Northvale, NJ: Jason Aronson.

Amabile, T., Barsade, S., Mueller, J., and Staw, B. (2005). Affect and creativity at work. *Administrative Science Quarterly, 50*, 267–403.

Amato, L., Davoili, M., Perucci, C. A., Ferri, M., Faggiano, F., & Mattick R. P. (2005). An overview of systematic reviews of the effectiveness of opiate maintenance therapies: Available evidence to inform clinical practice and research. *Journal of Substance Abuse Treatment, 28*, 321–329.

American Academy of Pediatrics. (1999, July 26). *Circumcision: Information for parents.* Retrieved from http://www.aap.org/family/circ.htm.

American Association of Mental Retardation (AAMR). (2002). *Mental retardation. Definition, classification, and systems of supports* (10th ed.). Washington, DC.: AAMR.

American Association of University Women (AAUW). (1992). *How schools shortchange women: The A.A.U.W. Report.* Washington, DC: AAUW Educational Foundation.

American Association of University Women (AAUW). (1993). *Hostile hallways: The AAUW survey on sexual harassment in American schools.* Washington, DC. AAUW Educational Foundation.

American Association of University Women (AAUW). (2001). *Hostile hallways: Bullying, teasing, and sexual harassment in school.* Washington, DC: American Association of University Women.

American College Health Association (2006). *Acquaintance and date rape: What everyone should know.* Baltimore, MD: American College Health Association.

American Insomnia Association (2005). Causes of insomnia. In L. Vande Creek (Ed.), *Innovations in clinical practice: Focus on adults.* Sarasota, FL: Professional Resource Press/Professional Resource Exchange.

American Psychiatric Association. (2000). *Diagnostic and statistical manual of mental disorders DSM-IV-TR, 4th Edition.* Arlington, VA: American Psychiatric Association.

American Psychological Association (APA). (1988). *Behavioral research with animals.* Washington, DC: American Psychological Association.

American Psychological Association (APA). (1993a). *Employment survey.* Washington, DC: American Psychological Association.

American Psychological Association. (APA). (1993b, January/February). Subgroup norming and the Civil Rights Act. *Psychological Science Agenda, 5*, 6.

American Psychological Association (APA). (1994). *Careers in psychology.* Washington, DC: American Psychological Association.

American Psychological Association (APA). (1999). *Talk to someone who can help.* Washington, DC: American Psychological Association.

American Psychological Association (APA). (2002, August 21). *APA ethics code, 2002.* Washington, DC: American Psychological Association.

American Psychological Association Task Force on Intelligence. (1996). *Intelligence: Knowns and unknowns.* Washington, DC: American Psychological Association.

Amos, A., Wiltshire, S., & Haw, S. (2006). Ambivalence and uncertainty: Experiences of and attitudes towards addiction and smoking cessation in the mid-to-late teens. *Health Education Research, 21*, 181-191.

Anand, G., & Burton, T. M. (2003, April 11). Drug debate: New antipsychotics pose a quandary for FDA, doctors. *The Wall Street Journal*, pp. A1, A8.

Anastasi, A., & Urbina, S. (1997). *Psychological testing* (7th ed.).Englewood Cliffs, NJ: Prentice Hall.

Andersen, B. L., Kiecolt-Glaser, J. K., & Glaser, R. (1994). A biobehavioral model of cancer stress and disease course. *American Psychologist, 49*, 389–404.

Anderson, B. F. (1980). *The complete thinker: A handbook of techniques for creative and critical problem solving.* Englewood Cliffs, NJ: Prentice Hall.

Anderson, C., & Home, J. A. (2006). Sleepiness enhances distraction during monotonous task. *Sleep: Journal of Sleep and Sleep Disorders Research, 29*, 573–576.

Anderson, C. A., & Bushman, B. J. (2002, March 29). The effects of media violence on society. *Science, 295*, 2377–2378.

Anderson, C. A., & Dill, K. E. (2000). Video games and aggressive thoughts, feelings, and behavior in the laboratory and in life. *Journal of Personality and Social Psychology, 78*, 772–790.

Anderson, C. A., Carnagey, N. L., & Eubanks, J. (2003). Exposure to violent media: The effects of songs with violent lyrics on aggressive thoughts and feelings. *Journal of Personality and Social Psychology, 84*, 960–971.

Anderson, C. A., Carnagey, N. L., Flanagan, M., Benjamin, A. J., Jr., Eubanks, J., & Valentine, J. C. (2004). Violent video games: Specific effects of violent content on aggressive thoughts and behavior. In M. P. Zanna (Ed.), *Advances in experimental social psychology* (Vol. 36). San Diego, CA: Elsevier Academic Press.

Anderson, J. (1988). Cognitive styles and multicultural populations. *Journal of Teacher Education, 39*, 2–9.

Anderson, J. A., & Adams, M. (1992). Acknowledging the learning styles of diverse student populations: Implications for instructional design. *New Directions for Teaching and Learning, 49*, 19–33.

Anderson, J. R. (1981). Interference: The relationship between response latency and response accuracy. *Journal of Experimental Psychology: Human Learning and Memory, 7*, 311–325.

Anderson, J. R., & Bower, G. H. (1972). Recognition and retrieval processes in free recall. *Psychological Review, 79*, 97–123.

Anderson, K. B., Cooper, H., & Okamura, L. (1997). Individual differences and attitudes toward rape: A meta-analytic review. *Personality and Social Psychology Bulletin, 23*, 295–315.

Anderson, N. H. (1996). *A functional theory of cognition.* Mahwah, NJ: Erlbaum.

Anderson, R. N., & Smith, B. L. (2003). Deaths: leading causes for 2001. *National Vital Statistics Report 2003, 52*, 1–86.

Anderson, T., & Magnusson, D. (1990). Biological maturation in adolescence and the development of drinking habits and alcohol abuse among young males: A prospective longitudinal study. *Journal of Youth and Adolescence, 19*, 33–42.

Andersson, M., Wehling, E., Hugdahl, K. & Lundervold, A. (2006). Age and gender effect in information processing: A dichotic listening study. *Alzheimer's and Dementia, 2*, S377–S378.

Andrasik, F. (2006). Psychophysiological disorders: Headache as a case in point. In F. Andrasik, *Comprehensive handbook of personality and psychopathology: Vol. 2: Adult Psychopathology.* Hoboken, NJ: John Wiley & Sons.

Andrasik, F. (2007). What does the evidence show? Efficacy of behavioural treatments for recurrent headaches in adults. *Neurological Science, 28, Supplement*, S70–S77.

Andreasen, N. C. (2005). *Research advances in genetics and genomics: Implications for psychiatry.* Washington, DC: American Psychiatric Publishing.

Andrews, F. M., & Withey, S. B. (1976). *Social indicators of well-being: Americans' perceptions of life quality* (pp. 207, 306). New York: Plenum.

Angier, N. (1991, January 22). A potent peptide prompts an urge to cuddle. *The New York Times*, p. C1.

Angier, N. (1996, November 1). Maybe gene isn't to blame for thrill-seeking manner. *The New York Times*, p. A12.

Angier, N., & Chang, K. (2005, January 24). Gray matter and the sexes: Still a scientific gray area. *The New York Times*, pp. A1, A15.

Angoff, W. H. (1988). The nature-nurture debate, aptitudes, and group differences. *American Psychologist, 43*, 713–720.

Ansaldo, A. I., Arguin, M., & Roch Locours, L. A. (2002). The contribution of the right cerebral hemisphere to the recovery from aphasia: A single longitudinal case study. *Brain Languages, 82*, 206–222.

Antonucci, T.C., Lansford, J.E., Akiyama, H., Smith, J., Baltes, M.M., Takahashi, K., et al. (2002). Differences between men and women in social relations, resource deficits, and depressive symptomatology during later life in four nations. *Journal of Social Issues, 58*, 767–783.

Antony, M. M., Brown, T. A., & Barlow, D. H. (1992). Current perspectives on panic and panic disorder. *Current Directions in Psychological Science, 1*, 79–82.

APA Presidential Task Force on Evidence-Based Practice. (2006). Evidence-based practice in psychology, 61, *271–285*.

Apanovich, A. M., McCarthy, D., & Salovey, P. (2003). Using message framing to motivate HIV testing among low-income, ethnic minority women. *Health Psychology, 22*, 88–94.

Apkarian, A. V., Bushnell, M. C., Treede, R. D., & Zubeita, J. K. (2005). Human brain mechanisms of pain perception and regulation in health and disease. *European Journal of Pain, 9*, 463–484.

Aponte, J. F., & Wohl, J. (2000). *Psychological intervention and cultural diversity.* Needham Heights, MA: Allyn & Bacon.

Appelhans, B. M., & Schmeck, R. R. (2002). Learning styles and approach versus avoidant coping during academic exam preparation. *College Student Journal, 36*, 157–160.

Appleyard, D. (2007, February 3). The bright stuff. *Daily Mail (London)*, p. 10.

Arafat, I., & Cotton, W. L. (1974). Masturbation practices of males and females. *Journal of Sex Research, 10*, 293–307.

Arambula, P., Peper, E., Kawakami, M., & Gibney, K. H. (2001). The physiological correlates of Kundalini yoga meditation: A study of a yoga master. *Applied Psychophysiology & Biofeedback, 26*, 147–153.

Arangure, J., Jr. (2005, August 2). Orioles star denied use before Congress. *Washington Post*, p. A01.

Arangure, J., Jr. (2005, August 2). Palmeiro suspended for steroid violation. *Washington Post*, p. C2.

Archambault, D. L. (1992). Adolescence: A physiological, cultural, and psychological no man's land. In G. W. Lawson & A. W. Lawson (Eds.), *Adolescent substance abuse: Etiology, treatment, and prevention.* Gaithersburg, MD: Aspen.

Archer, J., & Lloyd, B. B. (2002). *Sex and gender* (2nd ed.). New York: Cambridge University Press.

Arena, J. M. (1984, April). A look at the opposite sex. *Newsweek on Campus*, p. 21.

Arlin, P. K. (1989). The problem of the problem. In J. D. Sinnott (Ed.), *Everyday problem solving: Theory and applications.* New York: Praeger.

Ariyanto, A., Hornsey, M. J., & Gallois, C. (2006). Group-directed criticism in Indonesia: Role of message source and audience. *Asian Journal of Social Psychology, 9*, 96–102.

Armstrong, T. (2000). *Multiple intelligences in the classroom* (2nd ed.). Washington, DC: Association for Supervision & Curriculum Development.

Armstrong, T. (2003). *The multiple intelligences of reading and writing: Making the words come alive* (2nd ed.). Washington, DC: Association for Supervision & Curriculum Development.

Aronow, E., Reznikoff, M., & Moreland, K. (1994). *The Rorschach technique: Perceptual basics, content interpretation, and applications.* Boston: Longwood.

Aronson, J. & Steele, Claude M. (2005). Stereotypes and the fragility of academic competence, motivation, and self-concept. In A.J. Elliot & C.S. Dweck (Eds.), *Handbook of competence and motivation.* New York, NY: Guilford Publications.

Asch, S. E. (1946). Forming impressions of personality. *Journal of Abnormal and Social Psychology, 41*, 258–290.

Asch, S. E. (1951). Effects of group pressure upon the modification and distortion of judgments. In H. Guetzkow (Ed.), *Groups, leadership, and men.* Pittsburgh: Carnegie Press.

Aschcraft, M. H. (1994). *Human memory and cognition* (2nd ed.). New York: Harper-Collins.

Asher, S. R., & Parker, J. G. (1991). Significance of peer relationship problems in childhood. In B. H. Schneider, G. Attili, J. Nadel, & R. P. Weissberg (Eds.), *Social competence in developmental perspective.* Amsterdam, Netherlands: Kluwer Academic.

Aspinwall, L. G., & Taylor, S. E. (1997). A stitch in time: Self-regulation and proactive coping. *Psychological Bulletin, 121*, 417–436.

Astbury-Ward, E. (2002). From Kama Sutra to dot.com: The history, myths and management of premature ejaculation. *Sexual and Relationship Therapy, 17*, 367–380.

Atkinson, H. (Ed.). (1997, January 21). Understanding your diagnosis. *HealthNews*, p. 3.

Atkinson, H. G. (2003, August). Are you a "good" patient? *HealthNews*, p. 5.

Atkinson, J. W., & Feather, N. T. (1966). *Theory of achievement motivation.* New York: Krieger.

Atkinson, R. C., & Shiffrin, R. M. (1968). Human memory: A proposed system and its control processes. In K. W. Spence & J. T. Spence (Eds.), *The psychology of learning and motivation: Advances in research and theory* (Vol. 2, pp. 80–195). New York: Academic Press.

Atkinson, R. C., & Shiffrin, R. M. (1971). The control of short-term memory. *Scientific American, 225*, 82–90.

Atran, S. (2003). Genesis of suicide terrorism. *Science, 299*, 1534–1539.

Attree, E., A., Brooks, B. M., & Rose, F. D. (2005). Use of virtual environments in training and rehabilitation: International perspectives [Special issue]. *CyberPyschology & Behavior, 8*, 185–186.

Auer, J. A., Goodship, A., Arnoczky, S., Pearce, S., Price, J., Claes, L., von Rechenberg, B., Hofmann-Amtenbrinck, M., Schneider, E., Muller-Terpitz, R., Thiele, F., Rippe, K. P., & Grainger, D. W. (2007). Refining animal models in fracture research: seeking consensus for changing the agenda in optimising both animal welfare and scientific validity for appropriate biomedical use. *BMC Musculoskeletal Disorders, 8*, 72.

Auerbach, S. M., Kiesler, D. J., Strentz, T., Schmidt, J., & Serio, C. (1994). Interpersonal impacts and adjustment to the stress of simulated captivity: An empirical test of the Stockholm Syndrome. *Journal of Social and Clinical Psychology, 13*, 207–221.

Aujoulat, I., Luminet, O., & Deccache, A. (2007). The perspective of patients on their experience of powerlessness. *Quality Health Research, 17*, 772–785.

Auld, F., Hyman, M., & Rudzinski, D. (2005). Theory and strategy of dream interpretation. In F. Auld & M. Hyman (Eds.), *Resolution of inner conflict: An introduction to psychoanalytic therapy* (2nd ed.). Washington, DC: American Psychological Association.

Ausilloux, C., & Bagdadli, A. (2006). Handicap mental et société: Soigner, éduquer, intégrer. Mental handicap and society. *Neuropsychiatrie de l'Enfance et de l'Adolescence, 54*, 336–340.

Austin, L. S. (2000). *What's holding you back? Eight critical choices for women's success.* New York: Basic Books.

Avenell, A. Brown, T. J., McGee, M. A., Campbell, M. K., Grant, A. M., Broom, J., Jung, R. T., & Smith, W. C. S. (2004). What are the long-term benefits of weight reducing diets in adults? A systematic review of randomized controlled trials. *Journal of Human Nutrition and Dietetics, 17*, 317–335.

Averill, J. R. (1975). A semantic atlas of emotional concepts. *Catalog of Selected Documents in Psychology, 5*, 330.

Averill, J. R. (1994). Emotions are many splendored things. In P. Ekman & R. J. Davidson (Eds.), *The nature of emotion: Fundamental questions.* New York: Oxford University Press.

Averill, J.R., Ekman, P., Panksepp, J., Scherer, K. R., Shweder, R.A., Davidson, R.J., et al. (1994). Are there basic emotions? In P. Ekman & R.J. Davidson (Eds*.), The nature of emotion: Fundamental questions.* New York, NY, US: Oxford University Press,

Ayyash-Abdo, H. (2002). Adolescent suicide: An ecological approach. *Psychology in the Schools, 39*, 459–475.

Babkina, A. M., & Bondi, K. M. (Eds.). (2003). *Affirmative action: An annotated bibliography* (2nd ed.). New York: Nova Science.

Bacchiochi, J. R. (2006). Development and validation of the Malingering Discriminant Function Index (M-DFI) for the Minnesota Multiphasic Personality Inventory-2 (MMPI-2). *Dissertation Abstracts International: Section B: The Sciences and Engineering, 66(10-B)*, 5673.

Baddeley, A., & Wilson, B. (1985). Phonological coding and short-term memory in patients without speech. *Journal of Memory and Language, 24*, 490–502.

Baddeley, A., Gathercole, S., & Papagno, C. (1998). The phonological loop as a language learning device. *Psychological Review, 105*, 158–173.

Baddeley, A. D. (1990). *Human memory: Theory and practice.* Boston: Allyn & Bacon.

Baer, J. (1993). *Creativity and divergent thinking: A task-specific approach.* Hillsdale, NJ: Erlbaum.

Baer, J. S., Sampson, P. D., Barr, H. M., Connor, P. D., & Streissguth, A. P. (2003). A 21-year longitudinal analysis of the effects of prenatal alcohol exposure on young adult drinking. *Obstetrical and Gynecological Survey, 58*, 638–639.

Baer, L., Rauch, S. L., Callantine, T., Martuza, R., et al. (1995). Cingulotomy for intractable obsessive-compulsive disorder: Prospective long-term follow-up of 18 patients. *Archives of General Psychiatry, 52*, 384–392.

Bahrick, H. P. (1998). Loss and distortion of autobiographical memory content. In C. P. Thompson & D. J. Herrmann (Eds.), *Autobiographical memory: Theoretical and applied perspectives* (pp. 69–78). Mahwah, NJ: Lawrence Erlbaum.

Bai, L. (2005). Children at play: A childhood beyond the Confucian shadow. *Childhood: A Global Journal of Child Research, 12,* 9–32.

Bailey, J. M., Pillard, R. C., Kitzinger, C., & Wilkinson, S. (1997). Sexual orientation: Is it determined by biology? In M. R. Walsh (Ed.), *Women, men, and gender: Ongoing debates.* New Haven, CT: Yale University Press.

Bains, O. S. (2006). Insomnia: Difficulty falling and staying asleep. In N. F. Watson, & B. V. Bradley, *Clinician's guide to sleep disorders.* Philadelphia: Taylor & Francis.

Bair, D. (2003). *Jung: A biography.* New York: Little, Brown, and Company.

Baker, H. (2001). Hypnosis for anxiety reduction and ego-enhancement. *Australian Journal of Clinical and Experimental Hypnosis, 29,* 147–151.

Baker, S. E., Johnson, P. J., & Slater, D. (2007). Learned food aversion with and without an odour cue for protecting untreated baits from wild mammal foraging. *Applied Animal Behaviour Science, 102, Special issue: Conservation, enrichment and animal behavior,* 410–428.

Bakermans-Kranenburg, M. J., van Ijzendoorn, M. H., & Juffer, F. (2003). Less is more: Meta-analyses of sensitivity and attachment interventions in early childhood. *Psychological Bulletin, 129,* 195–215.

Balaban, C. D. (2002). Neural substrates linking balance control and anxiety [Special issue: The Pittsburgh special issue]. *Physiology and Behavior, 77,* 469–475.

Balaban, C. D., McBurney, D. H., & Affeltranger, M. A. (2005). Three distinct categories of time course of pain produced by oral capsaicin *The Journal of Pain, 6,* 315–322.

Balbach, E. D., Gasior, R. J., & Barbeau, E. M. (2003). R. J. Reynolds' targeting of African Americans: 1988–2000. *American Journal of Public Health, 93,* 822–827.

Ball, D. (2004). Genetic approaches to alcohol dependence. *British Journal of Psychiatry, 185,* 449–451.

Baltes, P. B., & Kunzmann, U. (2003). Wisdom. *Psychologist, 16,* 131–133.

Bandura, A. (1977). *Social learning theory.* Englewood Cliffs, NJ: Prentice Hall.

Bandura, A. (1986). *Social foundations of thought and action: A social cognitive theory.* Englewood Cliffs, NJ: Prentice Hall.

Bandura, A. (1988). Self-regulation of motivation and action through goal systems. In V. Hamilton and H. Gordon (Eds.), *Cognitive perspectives on emotion and motivation.* Dordrecht, Netherlands: Kluwer Academic.

Bandura, A. (1994). Social cognitive theory of mass communication. In J. Bryant, & D. Zillmann (Eds.), *Media effects: Advances in theory and research: LEA's communication series.* Hillsdale, NJ: Erlbaum.

Bandura, A. (1997). *Self-efficacy: The exercise of control.* New York: W. H. Freeman.

Bandura, A. (1999). Social cognitive theory of personality. In D. Cervone & Y. Shod (Eds.), *The coherence of personality.* NY: Guilford.

Bandura, A. (2000). Self-efficacy: The foundation of agency. In W. J. Perrig and A. Grob (Eds.), *Control of human behavior, mental processes, and consciousness: Essays in honor of the 60th birthday of August Flammer.* Mahwah, NJ: Erlbaum.

Bandura, A. (2001). Social cognitive theory: An agentic perspective. *Annual Review of Psychology, 52,* 1–26.

Bandura, A. (2004). Swimming against the mainstream: The early years from chilly tributary to transformative mainstream. *Behaviour Research and Therapy, 42,* 613–630.

Bandura, A., Grusec, J. E., & Menlove, F. L. (1967). Vicarious extinction of avoidance behavior. *Journal of Personality and Social Psychology, 5,* 16–23.

Bandura, A., & Locke, E. A. (2003). Negative self-efficacy and goal effects revisited. *Journal of Applied Psychology, 88,* 87–99.

Bandura, A., Ross, D., & Ross, S. (1963a). Imitation of film-mediated aggressive models. *Journal of Abnormal and Social Psychology, 66,* 3–11.

Bandura, A., Ross, D., & Ross, S. (1963b). Vicarious reinforcement and imitative learning. *Journal of Abnormal and Social Psychology, 67,* 601–607.

Banerjee, N. (2007, April 20). Massacre in Virginia: On a stunned campus, longing for the normal but enveloped by grief. *The Washington Post,* p. 20.

Banich, T., & Heller, W. (1998). Evolving perspectives on lateralization of function. *Current Directions in Psychological Science, 7,* 1–2.

Banks, J. A. (2006). Improving race relations in schools: From theory and research to practice. *Journal of Social Issues, 62,* 607–614.

Bannon, L. (2000, February 14). Why boys and girls get different toys. *The Wall Street Journal,* pp. B1, B4.

Baraas, R. C., Foster, D. H., & Amano, K. (2006). Anomalous trichromats' judgments of surface color in natural scenes under different daylights. *Neuroscience, 23,* 629–635.

Barandiaran, A. A., Pascual, A. C., & Samaniego, C. M. (2006). Una aportación crítica a la teoría kohlberiana: El desarrollo moral en adultos e implicaciones educativas. A criticism of the Kohlberg theory: The moral development in adults and educative implications. *Revista de Psicología General y Aplicada, 59,* 165–182.

Barber, J. (2001). Freedom from smoking: Integrating hypnotic methods and rapid smoking to facilitate smoking cessation. *International Journal of Clinical & Experimental Hypnosis, 49,* 257–266.

Barber, S., & Lane, R. C. (1995). Efficacy research in psychodynamic therapy: A critical review of the literature. *Psychotherapy in Private Practice, 14,* 43–69.

Bargh, J. A., & Chartrand, T. L. (2000). The mind in the middle: A practical guide to priming and automaticity research. In H. T. Reis & C. M. Judd (Eds.), *Handbook of research methods in social and personality psychology.* New York: Cambridge University Press.

Barkley, R. (2000). *Taking charge of ADHD* (rev. ed.). New York: Guilford Press.

Barkley, R. (2005). *ADHD and the nature of self-control.* New York: Guildford.

Barkow, J. H., Cosmides, L., & Tooby, J. (Eds.). (1992). *The adapted mind.* New York: Oxford University Press.

Barlow, D. H. (2007). *Clinical handbook of psychological disorders, fourth edition: A step-by-step treatment manual.* New York: Guilford Press.

Barmeyer, C. I. (2004). Learning styles and their impact on cross-cultural training. An international comparison in France, Germany and Quebec. *International Journal of Intercultural Relations, 28,* 577–594.

Barnard, N. D., & Kaufman, S. R. (1997, February). Animal research is wasteful and misleading. *Scientific American, 276,* 80–82.

Barnes, T., & Eardley, I. (2007). Premature ejaculation: The scope of the problem. *Journal of Sex & Marital Therapy, 33,* 151–170.

Barnes, V. A., Davis, H. C., Murzynowski, J., & Treiber, F. A. (2004). Impact of meditation on resting and ambulatory blood pressure and heart rate in youth. *Medicine, 66,* 909–914.

Barnett, J. E., Wise, E. H., & Johnson-Greene, D. (2007). Informed consent: Too much of a good thing or not enough? *Professional Psychology: Research and Practice, 38,* 179–186.

Barnett, R. C. (2004). Woman and work: Where are we, where did we come from, and where are we going? [Preface]. *Journal of Social Issues, 60,* 667–674.

Baron, R. S. (2005). So right it's wrong: Groupthink and the ubiquitous nature of polarized group decision making. In M. P. Zanna (Ed.), *Advances in experimental social psychology* (Vol. 37). San Diego, CA: Elsevier Academic Press.

Barresi, J. (2007). Consciousness and intentionality. *Journal of Consciousness Studies, 14, Special issue: Concepts of Consciousness: Integrating an Emerging Science,* 77–93.

Barrett, D. (2001). *The committee of sleep.* New York: Crown Publishers.

Barrett, L. F., & Salovey, P. (Eds). (2002). *The wisdom in feeling: Psychological processes in emotional intelligence.* New York: Guilford Press.

Barrett, L. F., & Wager, T. D. (2006). *Current Directions in Psychological Science, 15,* 79–83.

Barrett, M. (1999). *The development of language.* Philadelphia: Psychology Press.

Barringer, T. A., & Weaver, E. M. (2002). Does long-term bupropion (Zyban) use prevent smoking relapse after initial success at quitting smoking? *Journal of Family Practice, 51,* 172.

Barron, G., & Yechiam, E. (2002). Private e-mail requests and the diffusion of responsibility. *Computers in Human Behavior, 18,* 507–520.

Bartecchi, C. E., MacKenzie, T. D., & Schrier, R. W. (1995, May). The global tobacco epidemic. *Scientific American,* pp. 44–51.

Bartholow, B. D., & Anderson, C. A. (2002). Effects of violent video games on aggressive behavior: Potential sex differences. *Journal of Experimental Social Psychology, 38,* 283–290.

Bartholow, B. D., Bushman, B. J., & Sestir, M. A. (2005). Chronic violent video game exposure and desensitization to violence: Behavioral and event-related brain potential data. *Journal of Experimental Social Psychology, 42,* 532–539.

Bartlett, F. (1932). *Remembering: A study in experimental and social psychology.* Cambridge, England: Cambridge University Press.

Bartlett, M. Y., & DeSteno, D. (2006). Gratitude and prosocial behavior: Helping when it costs you. *Psychological Science, 17,* 319–325.

Bartocci, G. (2004). Transcendence techniques and psychobiological mechanisms underlying religious experience. *Mental Health, Religion and Culture, 7,* 171–181.

Bartoshuk, L. (2000, July/August). The bitter with the sweet. *APS Observer, 11,* 33.

Bartoshuk, L., & Drewnowski, A. (1997, February). Symposium presented at the annual meeting of the American Association for the Advancement of Science, Seattle.

Bartoshuk, L., & Lucchina, L. (1997, January 13) Are you a supertaster? *U.S. News & World Report,* pp. 58–59.

Bartzokis, G., Nuechterlein, K. H., Lu, P. H., Gitlin, M., Rogers, S., & Mintz, J. (2003).

Dysregulated brain development in adult men with schizophrenia: A magnetic resonance imaging study. *Biological Psychiatry, 53,* 412–421.

Baruss, I. (2003). *Alterations of consciousness: An empirical analysis for social scientists.* Washington, DC: American Psychological Association.

Basch, M. F. (1996). Affect and defense. In D. L. Nathanson (Ed.), *Knowing feeling: Affect, script, and psychotherapy.* New York: W. W. Norton.

Bass, A. (1996, April 21). Is anger good for you? *Boston Globe Magazine,* pp. 20–41.

Bassottdi, G., Villanacci, V., Fisogni, S., Rossi, E., Baronio, P., Clerici, C., Maurer, C. A., Cathomas, G., Antonelli, E. (2007). Enteric glial cells and their role in gastrointestinal motor abnormalities: Introducing the neurogliopathies. *World Journal of Gastroenterology, 14,* 4035–4041.

Bates, E. (2005). Plasticity, localization, and language development. In S. T. Parker and J. Langer (Eds.), *Biology and knowledge revisited: From neurogenesis to psychogenesis.* Mahwah, NJ: Lawrence Erlbaum Associates.

Bates, P. E., Cuvo, T., Miner, C. A., & Korabek, C. A. (2001). Simulated and community-based instruction involving persons with mild and moderate mental retardation. *Research in Developmental Disabilities, 22,* 95–115.

Bates, R. (2002). Liking and similarity as predictors of multi-source ratings. *Personnel Review, 31,* 540–552.

Batson, C. D. (2006). 'Not all self-interest after all': Economics of empathy-induced altruism. In D. De Cremer, M. Zeelenberg, & J. K. Murnighan, *Social psychology and economics.* Mahwah, NJ: Lawrence Erlbaum Associates.

Batson, C. D., & Powell, A. A. (2003). Altruism and prosocial behavior. In T. Millon & M. J. Lerner (Eds.), *Handbook of psychology: Personality and social psychology* (Vol. 5). New York: Wiley.

Batson, C. D., Ahmad, N., Lishner, D. A., & Tsang, J. A. (2002). Empathy and altruism. In C. R. Snyder & S. J. Lopez (Eds.), *Handbook of positive psychology,* pp. 485–498. London: Oxford University Press.

Bauer, P. J. (1996). What do infants recall of their lives? Memory for specific events by one- to two-year-olds. 102nd Annual Convention of the American Psychological Association. (1994, Los Angeles, California, U.S.). *American Psychologist, 51,* 29–41.

Baum, A. (1994). Behavioral, biological, and environmental interactions in disease processes. In S. Blumenthal, K. Matthews, & S. Weiss (Eds.), *New research frontiers in behavioral medicine: Proceedings of the National Conference.* Washington, DC: NIH Publications.

Baum, A. S., Revenson, R. A., & Singer, J. E. (Eds.). (2002). *Handbook of health psychology.* Mahwah, NJ: Erlbaum.

Bauman, S., & Kopp, T. G. (2006). Integrating a humanistic approach in outpatient sex offender groups. *Journal for Specialists in Group Work, 31,* 247–261.

Baumeister, A. A., & Francis, J. L. (2002). Historical development of the dopamine hypothesis of schizophrenia. *Journal of the History of the Neurosciences, 11,* 265–277.

Baumeister, R. F. (1998). The self. In D. T. Gilbert & S. T. Fiske (Eds.), *The handbook of social psychology* (Vol. 1, 4th ed.). Boston: McGraw-Hill.

Baumeister, R. F., Campbell, J. D., & Krueger, J. I. (2003). Does high self-esteem cause better performance, interpersonal success, happiness, or healthier lifestyles? *Psychological Science in the Public Interest, 4,* 1–44.

Baumeister, R. F., DeWall, C. N., & Ciarocco, N. J. (2005) Social exclusion impairs self-regulation. *Journal of Personality and Social Psychology, 88,* 589–604.

Baumeister, R. F., & Stillman, T. (2006). Erotic plasticity: nature, culture, gender, and sexuality. In R. D. McAnulty, & M. M. Burnette, *Sex and sexuality, Vol 1: Sexuality today: Trends and controversies.* Westport, CT: Praeger Publishers/Greenwood Publishing.

Baumeister, R. F., & Twenge, J. M. (2002). Cultural suppression of female sexuality. *Review of General Psychology, 6,* 166–203.

Baumeister, R. F., Twenge, J. M., & Nuss, C. K. (2002). Effects of social exclusion on cognitive processes: Anticipated aloneness reduces intelligent thought. *Journal of Personality and Social Psychology, 83,* 817–827.

Baumgartner, F. (2002). The effect of hardiness in the choice of coping strategies in stressful situations. *Studia Psychologica, 44,* 69–75.

Baumrind, D. (1971). Current patterns of parental authority. *Developmental Psychology Monographs, 4* (1, pt. 2).

Baumrind, D. (1980). New directions in socialization research. *Psychological Bulletin, 35,* 639–652.

Baumrind, D. (2005). Patterns of parental authority and adolescent autonomy. *New Directions for Child and Adolescent Development, 108,* 61–69.

Baumrind, D., Larzelere, R. E., & Cowan, P. A. (2002). Ordinary physical punishment: Is it harmful? Comment on Gershoff (2002). *Psychological Bulletin, 32,* 42–51.

Bayer, D. L. (1996). Interaction in families with young adults with a psychiatric diagnosis. *American Journal of Family Therapy, 24,* 21–30.

Bayliss, D. M., Jarrold, C., Baddeley, A. D., & Gunn, D. M. (2005a). The relationship between short-term memory and working memory: Complex span made simple? *Memory, 13,* 414–421.

Bayliss, D. M., Jarrold, C., Baddeley, A. D., Gunn, D. M., & Leigh, E. (2005b). Mapping the developmental constraints on working memory span performance. *Developmental Psychology, 41,* 579–597.

Bayne, R. (2005). *Ideas and evidence: Critical reflections on MBTI® theory and practice.* Gainesville, FL: Center for Applications of Psychological Type, CAPT.

Baynes, K., Eliassenk J. C., Lutsep, H. L., & Gazzaniga, M. S. (1998, May 8). Modular organization of cognitive systems marked by interhemispheric integration. *Science, 280,* 902–905.

Bazell, B. (1998, August 25). Back pain goes high-tech. *Slate,* pp. 1–4. Bearman, P. S., Moody, J., & Stovel, K. (2004). Chains of affection: The structure of adolescent romantic and sexual networks. *American Journal of Sociology, 110,* 44-91.

Bearman, C. R., Ball, L. J., & Ormerod, T. C. (2007). The structure and function of spontaneous analogising in domain-based problem solving. *Thinking & Reasoning, 13,* 273-294.

Beatty, J. (2000). *The human brain: Essentials of behavioral neuroscience.* Thousand Oaks, CA: Sage.

Beatty, W. W. (2002). Sex difference in geographical knowledge: Driving experience is not essential. *Journal of the International Neuropsychological Society, 8,* 804–810.

Beck, A. P., & Lewis, C. M. (Eds.). (2000). *The process of group psychotherapy: Systems for analyzing change.* Washington, DC: American Psychological Association.

Beck, A. T. (1991). Cognitive therapy: A 30-year perspective. *American Psychologist, 46,* 368–375.

Beck, A. T. (1995). Cognitive therapy: Past, present, and future. In M. J. Mahoney (Ed.), *Cognitive and constructive psychotherapies: Theory, research, and practice.* New York: Springer.

Beck, A. T. (2004). Cognitive therapy, behavior therapy, psychoanalysis, and pharmacotherapy: A cognitive continuum. In A. Freeman, M. J. Mahoney, P. Devito, & D. Martin (Eds.), *Cognition and Psychotherapy* (2nd ed.). New York: Springer Publishing Co.

Beck, A. T., & Emery, G., with Greenberg, R. L. (1985). *Anxiety disorders and phobias: A cognitive perspective.* New York: Basic Books.

Beck, A. T., Freeman, A., & Davis, D. D. (2004). *Cognitive therapy of personality disorders* (2nd ed.). New York: Guilford Press.

Beck, A. T., & Rector, N. A. (2005). Cognitive approaches to schizophrenia: theory and therapy. *Annual Review of Clinical Psychology, 1,* 577–606.

Becker, B. E., & Luthar, S. S. (2007). Peer-perceived admiration and social preference: Contextual correlates of positive peer regard among suburban and urban adolescents. *Journal of Research on Adolescence, 17,* 117–144.

Becker, T. (2003). Is emotional intelligence a viable concept? *Academy of Management Review, 28,* 192–195.

Beckham, E. E., & Leber, W. R. (Eds.). (1997). *Handbook of depression* (2nd ed.). New York: Guilford Press.

Bedard, W. W., & Parsinger, M. A. (1995). Prednisolone blocks extreme intermale social aggression in seizure-induced, brain-damaged rats: Implications for the amygdaloid central nucleus, corticotrophin-releasing factor, and electrical seizures. *Psychological Reports, 77,* 3–9.

Beersma, D. G. M., & Gordijn, M. C. M. (2007). Circadian control of the sleep-wake cycle. *Physiology & Behavior, 90.*

Begg, D., & Langley, J. (2001). Changes in risky driving behavior from age 21 to 26 years. *Journal of Safety Research, 32,* 491–499.

Begley, S. (2002, September 13). The memory of September 11 is seared in your mind; but is it really true? *The Wall Street Journal,* p. B1.

Begley, S. (2003, April 4). Likely suicide bombers include some profiles you'd never suspect. *The Wall Street Journal,* p. B1.

Begley, S. (2004, October 1). New ethical minefield: Drugs to boost memory and sharpen attention. *The Wall Street Journal,* p. B1.

Begley, S. (2005a, April 29). Evolution psychology may not help explain our behavior after all. *The Wall Street Journal,* p. D1.

Begley, S. (2005b, August 19). A spotless mind may ease suffering but erase identity. *The Wall Street Journal,* p. B1.

Beidel, D. C., & Turner, S. M. (2007). Etiology of social anxiety disorder. In D. C. Beidel, & S. M. Turner, *Shy children, phobic adults: Nature and treatment of social anxiety disorders* (2nd ed.). Washington, DC: American Psychological Association.

Beilin, H. (1996). Mind and meaning: Piaget and Vygotsky on causal explanation. *Human Development, 39,* 277–286.

Beilock, S. L., & Carr, T. H. (2005). When high-powered people fail: Working memory and "choking under pressure" in math. *Psychological Science, 16,* 101–105.

Bell, J., Grekul, J., Lamba, N., & Minas, C. (1995). The impact of cost on student helping behavior. *Journal of Social Psychology, 135,* 49–56.

Bellack, A. S., Hersen, M., & Kazdin, A. E. (1990). *International handbook of behavior modification and therapy.* New York: Plenum.

Bellezza, F. S. (2000). Mnemonic devices. In A. E. Kazdin (Ed.), *Encyclopedia of psychology: Vol. 5* (pp. 286–287). Washington, DC: American Psychological Association.

Bellezza, F. S., Six, L. S., & Phillips, D. S. (1992). A mnemonic for remembering long strings of digits. *Bulletin of the Psychonomic Society, 30,* 271–274.

Belli, R. F., & Loftus, E. F. (1996). The pliability of autobiographical memory: Misinformation and the false memory problem. In D. C. Rubin (Ed.), *Remembering our past: Studies in autobiographical memory* (pp. 157–179). New York: Cambridge University Press.

Belsky, J. (2002). Quantity counts: Amount of child care and children's socioemotional development. *Journal of Developmental and Behavioral Pediatrics, 23,* 167–170.

Belsky, J., Burchinal, M., & McCartney, K. (2007). Are there long-term effects of early child care? *NICHD Early Child Care Research Network; Child Development, 78,* 681–701.

Belsky, J., & Rovine, M. (1988). Non-maternal care in the first year of life and infant-parent attachment security. *Child Development, 59,* 157–167.

Bem, D. J. (1996). Exotic becomes erotic: A developmental theory of sexual orientation. *Psychological Review, 103,* 320–335.

Bem, D. J., & Honorton, C. (1994). Does psi exist? Replicable evidence for an anomalous process of information transfer. *Psychological Bulletin, 115,* 4–18.

Bem, S. L. (1993). *Lenses of gender.* New Haven, CT: Yale University Press.

Bem, S. L. (1998). *An unconventional family.* New Haven, CT: Yale University Press.

Benbow, C. P., Lubinski, D., & Hyde, J. S. (1997). Mathematics: Is biology the cause of gender differences in performance? In M. R. Walsh (Ed.), *Women, men, and gender: Ongoing debates.* New Haven, CT: Yale University Press.

Benca, R. M. (2005). Diagnosis and treatment of chronic insomnia: A review. *Psychiatric Services, 56,* 332–343.

Benderly, B. L. (2004). Looking beyond the SAT. *American Psychological Society, 17,* 12–18.

Benet-Martinez, V., Lee, F., & Leu, J. (2006). Biculturalism and cognitive complexity: Expertise in cultural representations. *Journal of Cross-Cultural Psychology, 37,* 386–407.

Benham, G., Woody, E. Z., & Wilson, K. S. (2006). Expect the unexpected: Ability, attitude, and responsiveness to hypnosis. *Journal of Personality and Social Psychology, 91,* 342–350.

Benight, C. C. (2004). Collective efficacy following a series of natural disasters. *Stress and Coping: An International Journal, 17,* 401–420.

Benjamin, L. T., Jr. (1985, February). Defining aggression: An exercise for classroom discussion. *Teaching of Psychology, 12* (1), 40–42.

Bennett, M. R. (2000). The concept of long term potentiation of transmission of synapses. *Progress in Neurobiology, 60,* 109–137.

Benson, E. (2003, April). The science of sexual arousal. *Monitor on Psychology,* pp. 50–56.

Benson, H. (1993). The relaxation response. In D. Goleman & J. Guerin (Eds.), *Mind-body medicine: How to use your mind for better health.* Yonkers, NY: Consumer Reports Publications.

Benson, H., Kornhaber, A., Kornhaber, C., LeChanu, M. N., et al. (1994). Increases in positive psychological characteristics with a new relaxation-response curriculum in high school students. *Journal of Research and Development in Education, 27,* 226–231.

Bentall, R. P. (1992). The classification of schizophrenia. In D. J. Kavanagh (Ed.), *Schizophrenia: An overview and practical handbook.* London: Chapman & Hall.

Benton, S. A., Robertson, J. M., Tseng, W. C., Newton, F. B., & Benton, S. L. (2003). Changes in counseling center client problems across 13 years. *Professional Psychology: Research and Practice, 34,* 66–72.

Beresnevaité, M., Taylor, G. J., & Bagby, R. M. (2007). Assessing alexithymia and type A behavior in coronary heart disease patients: A multimethod approach. *Psychotherapy and Psychosomatics, 76,* 186–192.

Bergeron, J. M. (2006). Self-serving bias: A possible contributor of construct-irrelevant variance in high-stakes testing. *Dissertation Abstracts International Section A: Humanities and Social Sciences, 67(1-A),* 88.

Bergh, C., Sjostedt, S., Hellers, G., Zandian, M., & Sodersten, P. (2003). Meal size, satiety and cholecystokinin in gastrectomized humans. *Physiological Behavior, 78,* 143–147.

Bergin, A. E., & Garfield, S. L. (Eds.). (1994). *Handbook of psychotherapy and behavior change* (4th ed.). New York: Wiley.

Berguier, A., & Ashton, R. (1992). Characteristics of the frequent nightmare sufferer. *Journal of Abnormal Psychology, 101,* 246–250.

Berk, L. E. (2005). Why parenting matters. In S. Olfman (Ed.), *Childhood lost: How American culture is failing our kids* (pp. 19–53). Westport, CT: Praeger Publishers/Greenwood Publishing Group.

Berko, A., & Yuval, E. (2007). *The path to paradise: The inner world of suicide bombers and their dispatchers.* Westport, CT: Praeger Security International.

Berkowitz, C. D. (2000). The long-term medical consequences of sexual abuse. In R. M. Reece, et al. (Eds.), *Treatment of child abuse: Common ground for mental health, medical, and legal practitioners.* Baltimore: Johns Hopkins University Press.

Berkowitz, L. (1989). Frustration-aggression hypothesis. *Psychological Bulletin, 106,* 59–73.

Berkowitz, L. (1990). On the formation and regulation of anger and aggression: A cognitive-neoassociationistic analysis. *American Psychologist, 45,* 494–503.

Berkowitz, L. (1993). *Aggression: Its causes, consequences, and control.* New York: McGraw-Hill.

Berkowitz, L. (2001). On the formation and regulation of anger and aggression: A cognitive-neoassociationistic analysis. In W. G. Parrott (Ed.), *Emotions in social psychology: Essential readings.* New York: Psychology Press.

Berkowitz, L., & Geen, R. G. (1966). Film violence and the cue properties of available targets. *Journal of Personality and Social Psychology, 3,* 525–530.

Berkowitz, L., & LePage, A. (1967). Weapons as aggression-eliciting stimuli. *Journal of Personality and Social Psychology, 7,* 202–207.

Berle, D. (2007). Graded exposure therapy for long-standing disgust-related cockroach avoidance in an older male. *Clinical Case Studies, 6,* 339–347.

Berliner, L., & Elliott, D. M. (2002). Sexual abuse of children. In J. E. B. Myers & L. Berliner, et al. (Eds.), *The APSAC handbook on child maltreatment* (2nd ed., pp. 55–78). Thousand Oaks, CA: Sage.

Berlyne, D. (1967). Arousal and reinforcement. In D. Levine (Ed.), *Nebraska symposium on motivation.* Lincoln: University of Nebraska Press.

Berman, A. L., Jobes, D. A., & Silverman, M. M. (2006). An integrative-eclectic approach to treatment. In A. L. Berman, D. A. Jobes, & M. M. Silverman, *Adolescent suicide: Assessment and intervention* (2nd ed.). Washington, DC: American Psychological Association.

Berman, R. M., Krystal, J. H., & Charney, D. S. (1996). Mechanism of action of antidepressants: Monoamine hypotheses and beyond. In S. J. Watson (Ed.), *Biology of schizophrenia and affective disease.* Washington, DC: American Psychiatric Press.

Bernal, G., Trimble, J. E., Burlew, A. K., & Leong, F. T. (Eds.) (2002). *Handbook of racial and ethnic minority psychology.* Thousand Oaks, CA: Sage.

Bernard, L. L. (1924). *Instinct: A study in social psychology.* New York: Holt.

Bernstein, D. M., Loftus, G. R., & Meltzoff, A. N. (2005). Object identification in preschool children and adults. *Developmental Science, 8,* 151–161.

Bernston, G. G., Bechara, A., & Damasio, H. (2007). Amygdala contribution to selective dimensions of emotion. *Social Cognitive and Affective Neuroscience, 2,* 123–129.

Berntsen, D., & Rubin, D. C. (2004). Cultural life scripts structure recall from autobiographical memory. *Memory and Cognition, 32,* 427–442.

Berntsen, D., & Thomsen, D. K. (2005). Personal memories for remote historical events: Accuracy and clarity of flashbulb memories related to World War II. *Journal of Experimental Psychology: General, 134,* 242–257.

Berrettini, W. H. (2000). Are schizophrenic and bipolar disorders related? A review of family and molecular studies [Special issue: A special issue on bipolar disorder] *Biological Psychiatry, 48,* 531–538.

Berridge, K. C. (2004). Motivation concepts in behavioral neuroscience. *Physiology and Behavior, 81,* 179–209.

Berrios, G. E. (1996). *The history of mental symptoms: Descriptive psychopathology since the 19th century.* Cambridge, England: Cambridge University Press.

Berry, J. W. (2006). Acculturative stress. In P. T. P. Wong, & C. J. L. Wong, *Handbook of multicultural perspectives on stress and coping.* Dallas, TX: Spring Publications.

Bersoff, D. M. (1999). Why good people sometimes do bad things: Motivated reasoning and unethical behavior. *Personality and Social Psychology Bulletin, 25,* 28–39.

Berthoud, H. R. (2002). Multiple neural systems controlling food intake and body weight. *Neuroscience and Biobehavioral Reviews, 26,* 393–428.

Betancourt, H., & Lopez, S. R. (1993). The study of culture, ethnicity, and race in American psychology. *American Psychologist, 48,* 1586–1596.

Beutler, L. E., Brown, M. T., Crothers, L., Booker, K., et al. (1996). The dilemma of factitious demographic distinctions in psychological research. *Journal of Consulting and Clinical Psychology, 64,* 892–902.

Bevene, Y., Gilliss, C., & Lee, K. (2007). "I take the good with the bad, and I moisturize": Defying middle age in the new millennium. *Menopause, 14,* 734–741.

Beyene, Y. (1989). *From menarche to menopause: Reproductive lives of peasant women in two cultures.* Albany, NY: State University of New York Press.

Beyene, Y. (1992). Menopause: A biocultural event. In A. J. Dan, & L. L. Lewis (Eds.), *Menstrual health in women's lives.* Chicago: University of Illinois Press.

Bhardwaj, R. D., Curtis, M. A., Spalding, K. L., Buchholz, B. A., Fink, D., Bjork-Eriksson, T., Nordborg, C., Gage, F. H., Druid, H., Eriksson, P. S., & Frisen, J. (2006). Neocortical neurogenesis in humans is restricted to development. *Proceedings of the National Academy of Sciences, 103,* 12564–12568.

Bialystok, E., & Martin, M. M. (2004). Attention and inhibition in bilingual children: Evidence from the dimensional change card sort task. *Developmental Science, 7,* 325–339.

Bianchi, S. M., & Casper, L. M. (2000). American families. *Population Bulletin, 55*(4).

Biederman, I. (1987). Recognition-by-components: A theory of human image understanding. *Psychological Review, 94,* 115–147.

Biederman, I. (1990). Higher-level vision. In D. N. Osherson, S. Kosslyn, & J. Hollerbach (Eds.), *An invitation to cognitive science: Visual cognition and action.* Cambridge, MA: MIT.

Biernat, M. (2003). Toward a broader view of social stereotyping. *American Psychologist, 58,* 1019–1027.

Binet, A., & Simon, T. (1916). *The development of intelligence in children (The Binet-Simon Scale).* Baltimore: Williams & Wilkins.

Bingenheimer, J. B., Brennan, R. T., & Earls, F. J. (2005, May 27). Firearm violence exposure and serious violent behavior. *Science, 308,* 1323–1327.

Binstock, R., & George, L. K. (Eds.). (1996). *Handbook of aging and the social sciences* (4th ed.). San Diego, CA: Academic Press.

Birch, H. G. (1945). The role of motivation factors in insightful problem solving. *Journal of Comparative Psychology, 38,* 295–317.

Birren, J. E. (Ed.). (1996). *Encyclopedia of gerontology: Age, aging and the aged.* San Diego, CA: Academic Press.

Bishop, M. (2005). Quality of life and psychosocial adaptation to chronic illness and disability: Preliminary analysis of a conceptual and theoretical synthesis. *Rehabilitation Counseling Bulletin, 48,* 219–231.

Bitterman, M. E. (2006). Classical conditioning since Pavlov. *Review of General Psychology, 10,* 365–376.

Bittles, A. H., Bower, C., & Hussain, R. (2007). The four ages of Down syndrome. *European Journal of Public Health, 17,* 121–225.

Bjork, R. A., & Richardson-Klarehn, A. (1989). On the puzzling relationship between environmental context and human memory. In C. Izawa (Ed.), *Current issues in cognitive processes: The Tulane-Floweree symposium on cognition.* Hillsdale, NJ: Erlbaum.

Bjorklund, D. F., & Ellis, B. J. (2005). *Evolutionary psychology and child development: An emerging synthesis.* New York: Guilford Press.

Bjornstad, R. (2006). Learned helplessness, discouraged workers, and multiple unemployment equilibria. *The Journal of Socio-Economics, 35,* 458–475.

Black, A.L. & McCafferty, D. (1998, July 3–5). The age of contentment. *USA Weekend,* pp. 4–6.

Black, B. M., & Weisz, A. N. (2004). Dating violence: A qualitative analysis of Mexican American youths' views. *Journal of Ethnic and Cultural Diversity in Social Work, 13,* 69–90.

Black, P. (2006). Thrust to wholeness: The nature of self-protection. *Review of General Psychology, 10,* 191–209.

Black, P. H., & Barbutt, L. D. (2002). Stress, inflammation and cardiovascular disease. *Journal of Psychosomatic Research, 52,* 1–23.

Blackwell, T., & Gayle, V. (2006). Factors which influence the academic motivation and disengagement of adolescent, African American males within a social-historical and psychological context. *Dissertation Abstracts International Section A: Humanities and Social Sciences, 67(5-A),* 1654.

Blagrove, M., Farmer, L., & Williams, E. (2004). The relationship of nightmare frequency and nightmare distress to well-being. *Journal of Sleep Research, 13,* 129–136.

Blair, C. A., Thompson, L. F., & Wuensch, K. L. (2005). Electronic helping behavior: The virtual presence of others makes a difference. *Basic and Applied Social Psychology, 27,* 171–178.

Blais, F. C., Morin, C. M., Boisclair, A., Grenier, V., & Guay, B. (2001). Insomnia: Prevalence and treatment of patients in general practice [Article in French]. *Canadian Family Physician, 47,* 759–767.

Blakeslee, S. (1991, August 7). Levels of caffeine in various foods. *The New York Times.*

Blakeslee, S. (1992, August 11). Finding a new messenger for the brain's signals to the body. *The New York Times,* p. C3.

Blakeslee, S. (2000, January 4). A decade of discovery yields a shock about the brain. *The New York Times,* p. D1.

Blass, T. (1996). Attribution of responsibility and trust in the Milgram obedience experiment. *Journal of Applied Social Psychology, 26,* 1529–1535.

Blass, T. (2004). *The man who shocked the world: The life and legacy of Stanley Milgram.* New York: Basic Books.

Blass, T. (Ed.) (2000). *Obedience to authority: Current perspectives on the Milgram Paradigm.* Mahwah, NJ: Erlbaum.

Blatter, K., & Cajochen, C. (2007). Circadian rhythms in cognitive performance: Methodological constraints, protocols, theoretical underpinnings. *Physiology & Behavior, 90,* 196–208.

Blau, Z. S. (1973). *Old age in a changing society.* New York: New Viewpoints. Blewett, A. E. (2000). Help cards for patients. *Psychiatric Bulletin, 24,* 276.

Blixen, C. E., Singh, A., & Xu, M. (2006). What women want: Understanding obesity and preferences for primary care weight reduction interventions among African-American and Caucasian women. *Journal of the National Medical Association, 98,* 1160–1170.

Block, R. I., O'Leary, D. S., Ehrhardt, J. C., Augustinack, J. C., Ghoneim, M. M., Arndt, S., & Hall, J. A. (2000). Effects of frequent marijuana use on brain tissue volume and composition. *Neuroreport 11,* 491–496.

Bloom, P. N., McBride, C. M., & Pollak, K. I. (2006). Recruiting teen smokers in shopping malls to a smoking-cessation program using the foot-in-the-door technique. *Journal of Applied Social Psychology, 36,* 1129–1144.

Bloor, L., Uchino, B., Hicks, A., and Smith, T.W. (2004). Social relationships and physiological functions: The effects of recalling social relationships on cardiovascular reactivity. *Annals of Behavioral Medicine, 28,* 29–38.

Blum, D. (2002). *Love at goon park: Harry Harlow and the science of affection.* Cambridge, MA: Perseus.

Blume, S. B. (1998, March). Alcoholism in women. *The Harvard Mental Health Letter,* pp. 5–7.

Boahen, K. (2005, May). Neuromorphic microchips. *Scientific American,* pp. 56–64.

Bode, C., de Ridder, D. T., Kuijer, R. G., & Bensing, J. M. (2007). Effects of an intervention promoting proactive coping competencies in middle and late adulthood. *Gerontologist, 47,* 42–51.

Boden, J. M., Fergusson, D. M., & Horwood, L. J. (2007). Anxiety disorders and suicidal behaviours in adolescence and young adulthood: Findings from a longitudinal study. *Psychological Medicine, 37,* 431–440.

Bodin, G. (2006). Review of harvesting free association. *Psychoanalytic Quarterly, 75,* 629–632.

Boehm, K. E., & Campbell, N. B. (1995). Suicide: A review of calls to an adolescent peer listening phone service. *Child Psychiatry and Human Development, 26,* 61–66.

Bogart, R. K., McDaniel, R. J., Dunn, W. J., Hunter, C., Peterson, A. L., & Write, E. E. (2007). Efficacy of group cognitive behavior therapy for the treatment of masticatory myofascial pain. *Military Medicine, 172,* 169–174.

Bogenschutz, M. P., Geppert, C. M., & George, J. (2006). The role of twelve-step approaches in dual diagnosis treatment and recovery. *American Journal of Addiction, 15,* 50–60.

Bohart, A. C. (2006). Understanding person-centered therapy: A review of Paul Wilkins' Person-centered therapy in focus. *Person-Centered and Experiential Psychotherapies, 5,* 138–143.

Bohn, A., Berntsen, D. (2007). Pleasantness bias in flashbulb memories: positive and negative flashbulb memories of the fall of the Berlin Wall among East and West Germans. *Memory and Cognition,35,* 565–577.

Boisvert, C.M., & Faust, D. (2003). Leading researchers' consensus on psychotherapy research findings: Implications for the teaching and conduct of psychotherapy. *Professional Psychology: Research and Practice, 34,* 508–513.

Boles, D. B. (2005). A large-sample study of sex differences in functional cerebral lateralization. *Journal of Clinical and Experimental Neuropsychology, 27,* 759–768.

Bolger, N., & Amarel, D. (2007). Effects of social support visibility on adjustment to stress: experimental evidence. *Journal of Personality and Social Psychology, 92,* 458–475.

Bolger, N., Zuckerman, A., & Kessler, R. C. (2000). Invisible support and adjustment to stress. *Journal of Personality and Social Psychology, 79,* 953–961.

Bolla, K. I., Cadet, J. L., & London, E. D. (1998). The neuropsychiatry of chronic cocaine abuse. *Journal of Neuropsychiatry and Clinical Neurosciences, 10,* 280–289.

Boller, F. (2004). Rational basis of rehabilitation following cerebral lesions: A review of the concept of cerebral plasticity. *Functional Neurology: New Trends in Adaptive and Behavioral Disorders, 19,* 65–72.

Bolonna, A. A., & Kerwin, R. W. (2005). Partial agonism and schizophrenia. *British Journal of Psychiatry, 186,* 7–10.

Bonanno, G.A. (2004). Loss, trauma, and human resilence: Have we underestimated the human capacity to thrive after extremely aversive events? *American Psychologist, 59,* 20–28.

Bond, J. T., Thompson, C., Galinsky, E., & Prottas, D. (2003). *Highlights of the 2002 national survey of the changing workforce (No. 3).* New York: Families and Work Institute.

Bond, M. (2006).Psychodynamic psychotherapy in the treatment of mood disorders. *Current Opinion in Psychiatry, 19,* 40–43.

Bonham, V. L., Warshauer-Baker, E., & Collins, F. S. (2005). Race and ethnicity in the genome era: The complexity of the constructs. *American Psychologist, 60,* 9–15.

Bonnardel, V. (2006). Color naming and categorization in inherited color vision deficiencies. *Visual Neuroscience, 23,* 637–643.

Borbely, A. (1986). *Secrets of sleep* (p. 43, graph). New York: Basic Books.

Bordnick, P. S., Elkins, R. L., Orr, T. E., Walters, P., & Thyer, B. A. (2004). Evaluating the relative effectiveness of three aversion therapies designed to reduce craving among cocaine abusers. *Behavioral Interventions, 19,* 1–24.

Borisenko, J. (2007). Fatherhood as a personality development factor in men. *The Spanish Journal of Psychology, 10,* 82–90.

Bornstein, M. H., & Arterberry, M. (1999) Perceptual development. In M. Bornstein & M. Lamb (Eds.), *Developmental psychology.* Mahwah, NJ: Erlbaum.

Bornstein, R. F. (2001). The impending death of psychoanalysis. *Psychoanalytic Psychology, 18,* 3–20.

Bornstein, R. F. (2003). Psychodynamic models of personality. In T. Millon & M. J. Lerner (Eds.), *Handbook of psychology: Personality and social psychology* (Vol. 5). New York: Wiley.

Bortfeld, H., & Whitehurst, G. J. (2001). Sensitive periods in first language acquisition. In D. B. Bailey, Jr., J. T. Bruer, et al. (Eds.), *Critical thinking about critical periods,* pp. 173–192. Baltimore, MD: Paul H. Brookes.

Bosma, H., van Boxtel, M. P. J., Ponds, R. W. H. M., Houx, P. J. H., Burdorf, A., & Jolles, J. (2002). Mental work demands protect against cognitive impairment: MAAS prospective cohort study. *Experimental Aging Research, 29,* 33–45.

Bosman, A. J., Snik, A. F. M., & Mylanus, E. A. M. (2006). Fitting range of the BAHA Cordelle. *International Journal of Audiology, 45,* 429–437.

Botting, J. H., & Morrison, A. R. (1997, February). Animal research is vital to medicine. *Scientific American, 276,* 83–86.

Botvinick, M. (2004, August 6). Probing the neural basis of body ownership. *Science, 305,* 782–783.

Bouchard, C., & Bray, G. A. (Eds.). (1996). *Regulation of body weight: Biological and behavioral mechanisms.* New York: Wiley.

Bouchard, T. J., Jr. (2004). Genetic influence on human psychological traits: A survey. *Current Directions in Psychological Science, 13,* 148–151.

Bouchard, T. J., Segal, N. L., & Tellegen, A. (2004). Genetic influence on social attitudes: Another challenge to psychology from behavior genetics. In L. F. DiLalla (Ed.), *Behavior genetics principles: Perspectives in development, personality, and psychopathology.* Washington, DC: American Psychological Association.

Bouchard, T. J. Jr., Segal, N. L., Tellegen, A., McGue, M., Keyes, M. & Krueger, R. (2004). Genetic influence on social attitudes: Another challenge to psychology from behavior genetics. In L.F. DiLalla (Ed.), *Behavior genetics principles: Perspectives in development, personality, and psychopathology.* Washington, DC: American Psychological Association.

Bourke, P. A., & Duncan, J. (2005). Effect of template complexity on visual search and dual-task performance. *Psychological Science, 16,* 208–213.

Bourne, L. E., Dominowski, R. L., Loftus, E. F., & Healy, A. F. (1986). *Cognitive processes* (2nd ed.). Englewood Cliffs, NJ: Prentice Hall.

Bower, G. H., Thompson, S. S., & Tulving, E. (1994). Reducing retroactive interference: An interference analysis. *Journal of Experimental Psychology Learning, Memory, and Cognition, 20,* 51–66.

Bower, J. M., & Parsons, L. M. (2003, August). Rethinking the "lesser brain." *Scientific American,* pp. 51–57.

Bower, J. M., & Parsons, L. M. (2007). Rethinking the "lesser brain." In F. E. Bloom *Best of the brain from Scientific American.* Washington, DC: Dana Press.

Boyce, W. T., & Ellis, B. J. (2005). Biological sensitivity to context: An evolutionary-developmental theory of the origins and functions of stress reactivity. *Development and Psychopathology, 17,* 271–301.

Boyd-Wilson, B. M., McClure, J., & Walkey, F. H. (2004). Are well-being and illusory perceptions linked? The answer may be yes, but. . . . *Australian Journal of Psychology, 56,* 1–9.

Boyle, G. J., Goldman, R., Svoboda, J. S., & Fernandez, E. (2002). Male circumcision: Pain, trauma and psychosexual sequelae. *Journal of Health Psychology, 7,* 329–343.

Boyle, S. H., Williams, R. B., Mark, D. B., Brummett, B. H., Siegler, I. C., & Barefoot, J. C. (2005). Hostility, age, and mortality in a sample of cardiac patients. *American Journal of Cardiology, 96,* 64–72.

Bozarth, J. D., Zimring, F. M., & Tausch, R. (2002). Client-centered therapy: The evolution of a revolution. In D. J. Cain (Ed.), *Humanistic psychotherapies: Handbook of research and practice* (pp. 147–188). Washington, DC: American Psychological Association.

Brady, N., Campbell, M., & Flaherty, M. (2005). Perceptual asymmetries are preserved in memory for highly familiar faces of self and friend. *Brain and Cognition, 58,* 334–342.

Brambilla, P., Cipriani, A., Hotopf, M., & Barbui, C. (2005) Side-effect profile of fluoxetine in comparison with other SSRIs, tricyclic and newer antidepressants: A meta-analysis of clinical trial data. *Pharmacopsychiatry, 38,* 69–77.

Brasic, J. R. (2002). Conversion disorder in childhood. *German Journal of Psychiatry, 5,* 54–61.

Braun, A. R., Balkin, T. J., Wesensten, N. J., Gwadry, F., Carson, R. E., Varga, M., Baldwin, P., Belenky, G., & Herscovitch, P. (1998). Dissociated pattern of activity in visual cortices and their projections during human rapid eye movement sleep. *Science, 279,* 91–95.

Brazelton, T. B. (1969). *Infants and mothers: Differences in development.* New York: Dell.

Breakwell, G. M., Hammond, S., & Fife-Schaw, C. (Eds.). (1995). *Research methods in psychology.* Newbury Park, CA: Sage.

Brefczynski-Lewis, J. A., Lutz, A., Schaefer, H. S., Levinson, D. B., & Davidson, R. J. (2007, July 3). Neural correlates of attentional expertise in long-term and meditation practitioners. *Proceedings of the National Academy of Sciences, 104,* 11483–11488.

Brehm, J. W., & Self, E. A. (1989). The intensity of motivation. *Annual Review of Psychology, 40,* 109–131.

Breland, K., & Breland, M. (1961). Misbehavior of organisms. *American Psychologist, 16,* 681–684.

Brendgen, M., Vitaro, F., & Bukowski, W. M. (2000). Stability and variability of adolescents' affiliation with delinquent friends: Predictors and consequences. *Social Development, 9,* 205–225.

Brewer, J. B., Zhao, Z., Desmond, J. E., Glover, G. H., & Gabrieli, J. D. E. (1998, August 21). Making memories: Brain activity that predicts how well visual experience will be remembered. *Science, 281,* 1185–1187.

Brewer, M. B., & Hewstone, M. (Eds.). (2003). *Social cognition.* Malden, MA: Blackwell Publishers.

Bright, P., Buckman, J., & Fradera, A. (2006). Retrograde amnesia in patients with hippocampal, medial temporal, temporal lobe, or frontal pathology. *Learning & Memory, 13,* 545–557.

Brislin, R. (1993). *Understanding culture's influence on behavior.* Fort Worth, TX: Harcourt Brace Jovanovich.

Brislin, R., Worthley, R., & Macnab, B. (2006). Cultural intelligence: understanding behaviors that serve people's goals. *Group & Organization Management, 31,* 40–55.

Brock, T. C., & Green, M. C. (Eds). (2005). *Persuasion: Psychological insights and perspectives* (2nd ed.). Thousand Oaks, CA: Sage Publications.

Bröder , A., & Schiffer, S. (2006). Stimulus format and working memory in fast and frugal strategy selection. *Journal of Behavioral Decision Making, 19,* 361–380.

Brody, A. L., Saxena, S., Stoessel, P., Gillies, L. A., Fairbanks, L. A., Alborzian, L., Phelps, M. E., Huang, S-C., Wu, H-M., Ho, M. L., Ho, M. K., Au, S. C., Maidment, K., & Baxter, L. R., Jr. (2001). Regional brain metabolic changes in patients with major depression treated with either paroxetine or interpersonal therapy. *Archives of General Psychiatry, 58,* 631–640.

Broidy, L. M., Nagin, D. S., & Tremblay, R. E. (2003). Developmental trajectories of childhood disruptive behaviors and adolescent delinquency: A six-site, cross-national study. *Developmental Psychology, 39,* 222–245.

Broman, C. L. (2005). Stress, race and substance use in college. *College Student Journal, 39,* 340–352.

Bronner, E. (1998, November 24). Study casts doubt on the benefits of S.A.T. coaching courses. *The New York Times,* p. A19.

Brookhiser, R. (1997, January 13). Lost in the weed. *U.S. News & World Report,* p. 9.

Brooks-Gunn, J., Han, W., & Waldfogel, J. (2002). Maternal employment and child cognitive outcomes in the first three years of life: The NICHD study of early child care. *Child Development, 73,* 1052–1072.

Brown, A. S., Susser, E. S., Butler, P. D., Andrews, R. R., et al. (1996). Neurobiological plausibility of prenatal nutritional deprivation as a risk factor for schizophrenia. *Journal of Nervous and Mental Disease, 184,* 71–85.

Brown, D. C. (1994). Subgroup norming: Legitimate testing practice or reverse discrimination? *American Psychologist, 49,* 927–928.

Brown, E. (2001, September 17). The World Health Organization takes on big tobacco (but don't hold your breath): Anti-smoking advocates are mounting a global campaign: It's going to be a long, hard fight. *Forbes,* pp. 37–41.

Brown, J. (2006). Attribution: Theories, affect and evolution. *Dissertation Abstracts International: Section B: The Sciences and Engineering, 67(2-B),* 1201.

Brown, M. B., (2000). Diagnosis and treatment of children and adolescents with attention-deficit/hyperactivity disorder. *Journal of Counseling & Development, 78,* 195–203.

Brown, L. S., & Pope, K. S. (1996). *Recovered memories of abuse: Assessment, therapy, forensics.* Washington, DC: American Psychological Association.

Brown, P. K., & Wald, G. (1964). Visual pigments in single rod and cones of the human retina. *Science, 144,* 45–52.

Brown, R. (1958). How shall a thing be called? *Psychological Review, 65,* 14–21.

Brown, R. J. (2006). Different types of "dissociation" have different psychological mechanisms. *Journal of Trauma Dissociation, 6,* 7–28.

Brown, S., & Martinez, M. J. (2007). Activation of premotor vocal areas during musical discrimination. *Brain and Cognition, 63,* 9–69.

Brown, S., Martinez, M. J., Parson, L. M. (2006). Music and language side by side in the brain: A PET study of the generation of melodies and sentences. *European Journal of Neuroscience, 23,* 2791–2803.

Brown, S. I., & Walter, M. I. (Eds.). (1993). *Problem posing: Reflections and applications.* Hillsdale, NJ: Erlbaum.

Brownlee, K. (2007). What works for whom? (2nd ed.). A critical review of psychotherapy research. *Psychiatric Rehabilitation Journal, 30,* 239–240.

Bruce, B., & Wilfley, D. (1996). Binge eating among the overweight population: A serious and prevalent problem. *Journal of the American Dietetic Association, 96,* 58–61.

Bruce, V., Green, P. R., & Georgeson, M. (1997). *Visual perception: Physiology, psychology and ecology* (3rd ed.). Mahwah, NJ: Erlbaum.

Bruehl, S., & Chung, O. K. (2004). *Psychological interventions for acute pain.* Mahwah, NJ: Lawrence Erlbaum Associates.

Bruer, J. T. (2001). A critical and sensitive period primer. In D. B. Bailey, Jr., J. T. Bruer, et al. (Eds.), *Critical thinking about critical periods,* pp. 173–192. Baltimore, MD: Paul H. Brookes.

Bruggeman, H., Yonas, A., & Konczak, J. (2007). The processing of linear perspective and binocular information for action and perception. *Neuropsychologia, 45,* 1420–1426.

Brunet, A., Orr, S. P., Tremblay, J., Robertson, K., Nader, K., & Pitman, R. K. (2007). Effect of post-retrieval propranolol on psychophysiologic responding during subsequent script-driven traumatic imagery in post-traumatic stress disorder. *Journal of Psychiatric Research, 22,* 301–315.

Bryant, R. M., Coker, A. D., Durodoye, B. A., McCollum, V. J., Pack-Brown, S. P., Constantine, M. G., & O'Bryant, B. J. (2005). Having our say: African American women, diversity, and counseling. *Journal of Counseling and Development, 83,* 313–319.

Brydon, L., Edwards, S., Mohamed-Ali, V., & Steptoe, A. (2004). Socioeconomic status and stress-induced increases in interleukin-6. *Brain, Behavior, and Immunity, 18,* 281–290.

Brzustowicz, L. M., Hodgkinson, K. A., Chow, E. W. C., Honer, W. G., & Bassett, A. S. (2000, April 28). Location of major susceptibility locus for familial schizophrenia on chromosome 1q21–q22. *Science, 288,* 678–682.

Buboltz, W. C., Loveland, J., & Jenkisn, S. M. (2006). College student sleep: Relationship to health and academic performance. In M. V. Landow, *College students: Mental health and coping strategies.* Hauppauge, NY: Nova Science Publishers.

Buchanan, R. W., Javitt, D. C., Marder, S. R., Schooler, N. R., Gold, J. M., McMahon, R. P., Heresco-Levy, U., & Carpenter, W. T. (2007). The Cognitive and Negative Symptoms in Schizophrenia Trial (CONSIST): The efficacy of glutamatergic agents for negative symptoms and cognitive impairments. *American Journal of Psychiatry, 164,* 1593–1602.

Buchanan, T. W., & Adolphs, R. (2004). The neuroanatomy of emotional memory in humans. In D. Reisberg & P. Hertel (Eds.), *Memory and emotion* (pp. 42–75). London: Oxford University Press.

Buchert, R., Thomasius, R., Wilke, F., Petersen, K., Nebeling, B., Obrocki, J., Schulze, O., Schmidt, U., & Clausen, M. (2004). A voxel-based PET investigation of the long-term effects of "ecstasy" consumption on brain serotonin transporters. *American Journal of Psychiatry, 161,* 1181–1189.

Buckley, C. (2007, January 3). A man down, a train arriving, and a stranger makes a choice. *The New York Times,* p. 1.

Buckout, R. (1974). Eyewitness testimony. *Scientific American, 231,* pp. 23–31.

Buehner, M., Krumm, S., & Ziegler, M. (2006). Cognitive abilities and their interplay: Reasoning, crystallized intelligence, working memory components, and sustained attention. *Journal of Individual Differences, 27,* 57–72.

Buhs, E., Ladd, G., & Herald, S. (2006). Peer exclusion and victimization: Processes that mediate the relation between peer group rejection and children's classroom engagement and achievement? *Journal of Educational Psychology, 98,* 1–13.

Bukowski, W. M., Newcomb, A. F., & Hartup, W. W. (Eds.). (1996). *The company they keep: Friendship in childhood and adolescence.* New York: Cambridge University Press.

Bulik, C. M., Tozzi, F., Anderson, C., Mazzeo, S. E., Aggen, S., & Sullivan, P. F. (2003). The relation between eating disorders and components of perfectionism. *American Journal of Psychiatry, 160,* 366–368.

Bull, P. (2006). Review of Detecting lies and deceit: The psychology of lying and the implications for professional practice. *Journal of Community & Applied Social Psychology, 16,* 166–167.

Bunge, S. A., & Wallis, J. D. (2008). *Neuroscience of rule-guided behavior.* New York: Oxford University Press.

Bunting, M. (2006). Proactive interference and item similarity in working memory. *Journal of Experimental Psychology: Learning, Memory, and Cognition, 32,* 183–196.

Burbach, M. E., Matkin, G. S., & Fritz, S. M. (2004). Teaching critical thinking in an introductory leadership course utilizing active learning strategies: A confirmatory study. *College Student Journal, 38,* 482–493.

Burchinal, M. R., Roberts, J. E., & Riggins, R., Jr. (2000). Relating quality of center-based child care to early cognitive and language development longitudinally. *Child Development, 71,* 338–357.

Burd, L., Cotsonas-Hassler, T. M., Martsolf, J. T., & Kerbeshian, J. (2003). Recognition and management of fetal alcohol syndrome. *Neurotoxicological Teratology, 25,* 681–688.

Bureau of Labor Statistics. (2007). American Time Use Survey. Washington, DC: Bureau of Labor Statistics.

Burger, J. M. (1986). Increasing compliance by improving the deal: The that's-not-all technique. *Journal of Personality and Social Psychology, 51,* 277–283.

Burger, J. M., & Caldwell, D. F. (2003). The effects of monetary incentives and labeling on the foot-in-the-door effect: Evidence for a self-perception process. *Basic and Applied Social Psychology, 25,* 235–241.

Burger, J. M., Reed, M., & DeCesare, K. (1999). The effects of initial request size on compliance: More about the that's-not-all technique.

Basic and Applied social Psychology, 21, 243–249.

Burgess, D., & Borgida, E. (1997). Sexual harassment: An experimental test of sex-role spillover theory. *Personality and Social Psychology Bulletin, 23,* 63–75.

Burgoon, J. K., & Bacue, A. E. (2003). Nonverbal communication skills. In J. O. Greene & B. R. Burleson (Eds.), *Handbook of communication and social interaction skills* (pp. 179–219). Mahwah, NJ: Lawrence Erlbaum.

Burgoon, J. K., Bonito, J. A., Ramirez, A. J. R., Dunbar, N. E., Kam, K., & Fischer, J. (2002). Testing the interactivity principle: Effects of mediation, propinquity, and verbal and nonverbal modalities in interpersonal interaction [Special Issue: Research on the relationship between verbal and nonverbal communication: Emerging integrations]. *Journal of Communication, 52,* 657–677.

Burke, C. & McDaniel, J. (2001). *A special kind of hero.* Lincoln, NE: Doubleday.

Burke, D. M., & Shafto, M. A. (2004). Aging and language production. *Current Directions in Psychological Science, 13,* 21–25.

Burns, J. W., Quartana, P. J., & Bruehl, S. (2007). Anger management style moderates effects of emotion suppression during initial stress on pain and cardiovascular responses during subsequent pain-induction. *Annals of Behavioral Medicine, 34,* 154–165.

Burns, NJ. R., Bryan, J., & Nettelbeck, T. (2006). Ginkgo biloba: No robust effect on cognitive abilities or mood in healthy young or older adults. *Human Psychopharmacology: Clinical and Experimental, 21,* 27–37.

Buschman, T. J., & Miller, E. K. (2007, March 30). Top-down versus bottom-up control of attention in the prefrontal and posterior parietal cortices. *Science, 315,* 1860–1862.

Bushman, B. J. (1993). Human aggression while under the influence of alcohol and other drugs: An integrative research review. *Current Directions in Psychological Science, 2,* 148–152.

Bushman, B. J., & Anderson, C. A. (2001). Media violence and the American public: Scientific facts versus media misinformation. *American Psychologist, 56,* 477–489.

Bushman, B. J., & Anderson, C. A. (2002). Violent video games and hostile expectations: A test of the general aggression model. *Personality and Social Psychology Bulletin, 28,* 1679–1686.

Bushman, B. J., Baumeister, R. F., Phillips, C. M. (2001). Do people aggress to improve their mood? Catharsis beliefs, affect regulation opportunity, and aggressive responding. *Journal of Personality and Social Psychology, 81,* 17–32.

Bushman, B. J., Wang, M. C., & Anderson, C. A. (2005). Is the curve relating temperature to aggression linear or curvilinear? Assaults and temperature in Minneapolis reexamined. *Journal of Personality and Social Psychology, 89,* 62–66.

Busey, T. A., & Loftus, G. R. (2007). Cognitive science and the law. *Trends in Cognitive Science, 11,* 111–117.

Buss, D. (2003). *Evolutionary psychology.* Boston: Allyn & Bacon.

Buss, D. M. (2000). The evolution of happiness. *American Psychologist, 55,* 15–23.

Buss, D. M. (2001). Human nature and culture: An evolutionary psychological perspective. *Journal of Personality, 69,* 955–978.

Buss, D. M. (2003a) *The evolution of desire: Strategies of human mating.* New York: Basic Books.

Buss, D. M. (2003b). Sexual strategies: A journey into controversy. *Psychological Inquiry, 14,* 219–226.

Buss, D. M. (2004). Sex differences in human mate preferences: Evolutionary hypotheses tested in 37 cultures. In H. T. Reis & C. E. Rusbult (Eds.), *Close relationships: Key readings.* Philadelphia, PA: Taylor & Francis.

Buss, D. M., Abbott, M., & Angleitner, A. (1990). International preferences in selecting mates: A study of 37 cultures. *Journal of Cross-Cultural Psychology, 21,* 5–47.

Buss, D. M., & Kenrick, D. T. (1998). Evolutionary social psychology. In D. T. Gilbert, S. T. Fiske, & G. Lindzey (Eds.), *The handbook of social psychology* (Vol. 2, 4th ed.). Boston: McGraw-Hill.

Buss, D. M., Larsen, R. J., Westen, D., & Semmelroth, J. (1992). Sex differences in jealousy: Evolution, physiology, and psychology. *Psychological Science, 3,* 251–255.

Butcher, J. N. (1995). Interpretation of the MMPI-2. In L. E. Beutler, & M. R. Berren (Eds.), *Integrative assessment of adult personality.* New York: Guilford Press.

Butcher, J. N. (2005). *A beginner's guide to the MMPI-2* (2nd ed.). Washington, DC: American Psychological Association.

Butcher, J. N., Graham, J. R., Dahlstrom, W. G., & Bowman, E. (1990). The MMPI-2 with college students. *Journal of Personality Assessment, 54,* 1–15.

Butler, A. C., Chapman, J. E., Forman, E. M., & Beck, A. T. (2006). The empirical status of cognitive-behavioral therapy: A review of meta-analyses. *Clinical Psychology Review, 26,* 17–31.

Butler, L. T., & Berry, D. C. (2004). Understanding the relationship between repetition priming and mere exposure. *British Journal of Psychology, 95,* 467–487.

Byne, W. (1996). Biology and homosexuality: Implications of neuroendocrinological and neuroanatomical studies. In R. P. Cabaj & T. S. Stein (Eds.), *Textbook of homosexuality and mental health.* Washington, DC: American Psychiatric Press.

Byrne, B. M., & Watkins, D. (2003). The issue of measurement invariance revisited. *Journal of Cross-Cultural Psychology, 34,* 155–175.

Byrne, R. (2005, July 10). It's man vs. machine again, and man comes out limping. *New York Times,* p. 29.

Cabanac, M., & Frankham, P. (2002). Evidence that transient nicotine lowers the body weight set point. *Physiology & Behavior, 76,* 539–542.

Cachelin, F. M., & Regan, P. C. (2006). Prevalence and correlates of chronic dieting in a multi-ethnic U.S. community sample. *Eating and Weight Disorders, 11,* 91–99.

Cacioppo, J. T., & Berntson, G. G. (Eds.) (2004). *Essays in social neuroscience.* Cambridge, MA: MIT.

Cacioppo, J. T., Berntson, G. G., & Crites, S. L., Jr. (1996). Social neuroscience: Principles of psychophysiological arousal and response. In E. T. Higgins & A. W. Kruglanski (Eds.), *Social psychology: Handbook of basic principles.* New York: Guilford.

Cacioppo, J. T., Visser, P. S., & Picket, C. L. (2005). *Social neuroscience: People thinking about thinking people.* Cambridge, MA: MIT Press.

Cadenhead, K. & Braff, D.L. (1995). Neurophysiology of schizophrenia: Attention, information processing, and inhibitory processes in schizophrenia. In J.A.

Den Boer., H.G.M. Westenberg & H.M. van Praag (Eds.), *Advances in the neurobiology of schizophrenia* (pp. 329–342). Oxford, England: John Wiley & Sons.

Cadinu, M., Maass, A., & Rosabianca, A. (2005). Why do women underperform under stereotype threat? Evidence for the role of negative thinking. *Psychological Science, 16,* 572–578.

Caelian, C. F. (2006).The role of perfectionism and stress in the suicidal behaviour of depressed adolescents. *Dissertation Abstracts International: Section B: The Sciences and Engineering, 66(12-B),* 6915.

Cahill, L. (2005, May). His brain, her brain. *Scientific American,* pp. 40–47.

Cain, D. J. (Ed.). (2002). *Humanistic psychotherapies: Handbook of research and practice.* Washington, DC: American Psychological Association.

Calderon, M. E., & Minaya-Rowe, L. (2003). *Designing and implementing two-way bilingual programs: A step-by-step guide for administrators, teachers, and parents.* Thousand Oaks, CA: Corwin Press.

Calin-Jageman, R. J., Fischer, T. M. (2007). Behavioral adaptation of the aplysia siphon-withdrawal response is accompanied by sensory adaptation. *Behavioral Neuroscience, 121,* 200–211.

Calle, E. E., & Kaaks, R. (2004). Overweight, obesity and cancer: Epidemiological evidence and proposed mechanisms. *Nature Reviews Cancer 4,* 579–591.

Calmes, J. (1998, March 5). Americans retain puritan attitudes on matters of sex. *The Wall Street Journal,* p. A12.

Cameron, O. G. (2002). *Visceral sensory neuroscience: Interoception.* London: Oxford University Press.

Campfield, L. A., Smith, F. J., Rosenbaum, M., & Hirsch, J. (1996). Human eating: Evidence for a physiological basis using a modified paradigm [Special issue: Society for the Study of Ingestive Behavior, Second Independent Meeting]. *Neuroscience and Biobehavioral Reviews, 20,* 133–137.

Cannon, W. B. (1929). Organization for physiological homeostatics. *Physiological Review, 9,* 280–289.

Canteras, N. S. (2002). The medial hypothalamic defensive system: Hodological organization and functional implications [Special issue: Functional role of specific systems within the extended amygdala and hypothalamus]. *Pharmacology, Biochemistry and Behavior, 71,* 481–491.

Cantwell, R. H., & Andrews, B. (2002). Cognitive and psychological factors underlying secondary school students' feelings towards group work. *Educational Psychology, 22,* 75–91.

Capaldi, E. D. (Ed.). (1996). *Why we eat what we eat: The psychology of eating.* Washington, DC: American Psychological Association.

Caplan, D., & Waters, G., & Kennedy, D. (2007). A study of syntactic processing in aphasia II: Neurological aspects. *Brain and Language, 101,* 151–177.

Caplan, D., Waters, G., & DeDe, G. (2007). A study of syntactic processing in aphasia I: Behavioral (psycholinguistic) aspects. *Brain and Language, 101,* 103–150.

Caralho, F. M., Pereira, S. R. C., Pires, R. G. W. (2006). Thiamine deficiency decreases glutamate uptake in the prefrontal cortex and impairs spatial memory performance in a water maze test. *Pharmacology, Biochemistry and Behavior, 83,* 481–489.

Cardemil, E. V., Pinedo, T. M., & Miller, I. W. (2005). Developing a culturally appropriate depression prevention program: The family coping skills program. *Cultural Diversity and Ethnic Minority Psychology, 11,* 99–112.

Carey, B. (2004, December 21). When pressure is on, good students suffer. *The New York Times,* p. D7.

Carhart-Harris, R., (2007). Speed > Ecstasy > Ritalin: The science of amphetamines. *Journal of Psychopharmacology, 21,* 225.

Carli, L.L. & Bukatko, D. (2000). Gender, communication, and social influence: A developmental perspective. In T. Eckes. & H.M. Trautner (Eds.), *The developmental social psychology of gender.* Mahwah, NJ: Lawrence Erlbaum Associates Publishers.

Carmichael, M. (2004, December 6). Medicine's next level. *Newsweek,* pp. 45–49.

Carnagey, N. L., Anderson, C. A., & Bushman, B. J. (2007). The effect of video game violence on physiological desensitization to real-life violence. *Journal of Experimental Social Psychology, 43,* 489–496.

Carnegie Council on Adolescent Development. (1995). *Great transitions: Preparing adolescents for a new century.* New York: Carnegie Corporation of New York.

Carnegie Task Force on Meeting the Needs of Young Children. (1994). *Starting points: Meeting the needs of our youngest children.* New York: Carnegie Corporation.

Carney, R. N., & Levin, J. R. (1998). Coming to terms with the keyword method in introductory psychology: A "neuromnemonic" example. *Teaching of Psychology, 25,* 132–135.

Carney, R. N., & Levin, J. R. (2003). Promoting higher-order learning benefits by building lower-order mnemonic connections. *Applied Cognitive Psychology, 17,* 563–575.

Carpenter, S. (2001). Sleep deprivation may be undermining teen health. *APA Monitor, 32,* 42–45.

Carpenter, S. (2002, April). What can resolve the paradox of mental health disparities? *APA Monitor, 33,* 18.

Carpenter, J., & Maciel, O. (2004, July 6). Disabled man relies on monkey. *Orange County Register,* p. 1.

Carr, A. (2002). *Avoiding risky sex in adolescence.* New York: Blackwell.

Carroll, J. M., & Russell, J. A. (1997). Facial expressions in Hollywood's portrayal of emotion. *Journal of Personality and Social Psychology, 72,* 164–176.

Carter, A. S., O'Donnell, D. A., Schultz, R. T., Scahill, L., Leckman, J. F., & Pauls, D. (2000). Social and emotional adjustment in children affected with Gilles de la Tourette's Syndrome: Associations with ADHD and family functioning. *Journal of Child Psychology and Psychiatry, 41,* 215–223.

Carter, R. T. (2003). Becoming racially and culturally competent: The racial-cultural counseling laboratory. *Journal of Multicultural Counseling and Development, 31,* 20–30.

Cartwright, R. (2006). A neuroscientist looks at how the brain makes up our minds. *PsycCRITIQUES, 51,* 35–41.

Cartwright, R., Agargum, M. Y., & Kirkby, J. (2006). Relation of dreams to waking concerns. *Psychiatry Research, 141,* 261–270.

Carvalho, F. M., Pereira, S. R., C., Pires, R. G. W., Ferraz, V. P., Romano-Silva, M. A., Oliveira-Silva, I. F., & Ribeiro, A. M. (2006). Thiamine deficiency decreases glutamate uptake in the prefrontal cortex and impairs spatial memory performance in a water maze test.

Pharmacology, Biochemistry and Behavior, 83, 481–489.

Carver, C., & Scheier, M. (2002). Coping processes and adjustment to chronic illness. In A. Christensen and M. Antoni (Eds.), *Chronic physical disorders: Behavioral medicine's perspective.* Malden: Blackwell Publishers.

Carver, C. S., Harris, S. D., Lehman, J. M., Durel, L. A., Antoni, M. H., Spencer, S. M., & Pozo-Kaderman, C. (2000). How important is the perception of personal control? Studies of early stage breast cancer patients. *Personality and Social Psychology Bulletin, 26,* 139–149.

Cary, P. (2007). A brief history of the concept of free will: Issues that are and are not germane to legal reasoning. *Behavioral Sciences & the Law, 25, Special issue: Free will,* 165–181.

Casad, B. J. (2007). Gender stereotype violation among job applicants: An examination of theory and measurement. *Dissertation Abstracts International: Section B: The Sciences and Engineering, 67(7-B),* 4154.

Case, R., & Okamoto, Y. (1996). The role of central conceptual structures in the development of children's thought. *Monographs of the Society for Research in Child Development, 61,* v–265.

Casey, B. J. (2002, May 24). Windows into the human brain. *Science, 296,* 1408–1409.

Casey, D. (2006, Fall). Eyeing the future: One patient's story. *Artificial Retina News,* p. 1.

Casey, S. D., Cooper-Brown, L. J., & Wacher, D. P. (2006). The use of descriptive analysis to identify and manipulate schedules of reinforcement in the treatment of food refusal. *Journal of Behavioral Education, 15,* 41–52.

Cashon, C. H., & Cohen, L. B. (2004). Beyond U-shaped development in infants' processing of faces: An information-processing account. *Journal of Cognition and Development, 5,* 59–80.

Caspi, A., Harrington, H., & Milne, B. (2003). Children's behavioral styles at age 3 are linked to their adult personality traits at age 26. *Journal of Personality, 71,* 495–513.

Cassells, J. V. S. (2007). The virtuous roles of truth and justice in integral dialogue: Research, theory, and model practice of the evolution of collective consciousness. *Dissertation Abstracts International Section A: Humanities and Social Sciences, 67(10-A),* 4005.

Cassidy, C., O'Connor, R. C., Howe, C., & Warden, D. (2004). Perceived discrimination and psychological distress: The role of personal and ethnic self-esteem. *Journal of Counseling Psychology, 51,* 329–339.

Catalano, S. M. (2006, September). Criminal Victimization, 2005. *Bureau of Justice Statistics Bulletin.* Washington, DC: Bureau of Justice Statistics.

Cattell, R. B. (1965). *The scientific analysis of personality.* Chicago: Aldine.

Cattell, R. B. (1998). Where is intelligence? Some answers from the triadic theory. In J. J. McArdle & R. W. Woodcock (Eds.), *Human cognitive abilities in theory and practice* (pp. 29–38). Mahwah, NJ: Lawrence Erlbaum.

Cattell, R. B., Cattell, A. K., & Catell, H. E. P. (1993). *Sixteen personality factor questionnaire (16PF)* (5th ed.). San Antonio, TX: Harcourt Brace.

Cattell, R. B., Cattell, A. K., & Cattell, H. E. P. (2000). *The sixteen personality factor™ (16PF®) questionnaire.* Champaign, IL: Institute for Personality and Ability Testing.

Cattell, R. B., Eber, L., & Tatsuoka, M. (1970, 1988, 1992). *Handbook for the 16PF.* Champaign, IL: Institute for Personality and Ability Testing.

Cauce, A. M. (2007). Bringing community psychology home: The leadership, community and values initiative. *American Journal of Community Psychology, 39,* 1–11.

Cavallini, E., Pagnin, A., and Vecchi, T. (2003). Aging and everyday memory: The beneficial effect of memory training. *Archives of Gerontology & Geriatrics, 37,* 241–257.

Cavenett, T., & Nixon, R. D. V. (2006). The effect of arousal on memory for emotionally-relevant information: A study of skydivers. *Behaviour Research and Therapy, 44,* 1461–1469.

Center on Addiction and Substance Abuse. (1994). *Report on college drinking.* New York: Columbia University Press.

Centers for Disease Control (CDC). (1992). *Most students sexually active: Survey of sexual activity.* Atlanta, GA: Centers for Disease Control.

Centers for Disease Control (CDC). (2000). *Suicide prevention fact sheet, National Center for Injury Prevention and Control.* Atlanta, GA: Centers for Disease Control and Prevention.

Centers for Disease Control (CDC). (2004a). *Chlamydia—CDC fact sheet.* Washington, DC: Centers for Disease Control and Prevention.

Centers for Disease Control (CDC). (2004b, June 11). Suicide and attempted suicide. *MMWR, 53,* 471.

Centers for Disease Control and Prevention (2003). *STD surveillance tables.* Atlanta, GA: Centers for Disease Control and Prevention.

Centers for Disease Control and Prevention. (2007). Physical activity and good nutrition: Essential elements to prevent chronic diseases and obesity, 2007. http://www.cdc.gov/nccdphp/publications/aag/pdf/dnpa.pdf.

Chamberlain, K., & Zika, S. (1990). The minor events approach to stress: Support for the use of daily hassles. *British Journal of Psychology, 81,* 469–481.

Chamberlin, J. (2000, February). Where are all these students coming from? *Monitor on Psychology,* pp. 32–34.

Chambless, D. L., Crits-Christoph, P., Wampold, B. E., Norcross, J. C., Lambert, M. J., Bohart, A. C., Beutler, L. E., & Johannsen, B. E. (2006). What should be validated? In J. C. Norcross, L. E. Beutler, & R. F. Levant, (Eds). *Evidence-based practices in mental health: Debate and dialogue on the fundamental questions.* Washington, DC: American Psychological Association.

Chandler, M. J. (1976). Social cognition and life-span approaches to the study of child development. In H. W. Reese & L. P. Lipsitt (Eds.), *Advances in child development and behavior* (Vol. 11). New York: Academic Press.

Chandra, P. (2007). Review of Language, mind, and brain: Some psychological and neurological constraints on theories of grammar. *Cognitive Systems Research, 8,* 53–56.

Chandran, S., & Menon, G. (2004). When a day means more than a year: Effects of temporal framing on judgments of health risk. *Journal of Consumer Research, 31,* 375–389.

Chang, J., & Sue, S. (2005). Culturally sensitive research: Where have we gone wrong and what do we need to do now? In M. G. Constantine, *Strategies for building multicultural competence in mental health and educational settings.* Hoboken, NJ: John Wiley & Sons.

Chang, L., & Geary, D. C. (2007). The future of psychology: Evolutionary approach to scientific psychology. *Acta Psychologica Sinica, 39, Special issue: Evolutionary Psychology,* 381–382.

Chang, S. W., & Ansley, T. N. (2003). A comparative study of item exposure control methods in computerized adaptive testing. *Journal of Educational Measurement, 40,* 71–103.

Chao, R. K. (2000). Cultural explanations for the role of parenting in the school success of Asian-American children. In R. D. Taylor & M. C. Wang (Eds.), *Resilience across contexts: Family, work, culture, and community* (pp. 333–363). Mahwah, NJ: Erlbaum.

Chapelot, D., Marmonier, C., Aubert, R., Gausseres, N., & Louis-Sylvestre, J. (2004). A role for glucose and insulin preprandial profiles to differentiate meals and snacks. *Physiology and Behavior, 80,* 721–731.

Chapman, J. (2006). Anxiety and defective decision making: An elaboration of the groupthink model. *Management Decision, 44,* 1391–1404.

Chapman, L. J., & Chapman, J. P. (1973). *Disordered thought in schizophrenia.* New York: Appleton-Century-Crofts.

Charles, N., Cheakalos, C., Hubbard, K., Miller, S., & Schindehette, S. (2001, December 10). Beyond the call. *People,* pp. 88–106.

Charles, S. T., Reynolds, C. A., & Gatz, M. (2001). Age-related differences and change in positive and negative affect over 23 years. *Journal of Personality and Social Psychology, 80,* 136–151.

Charman, D. P. (2004). *Core processes in brief psychodynamic psychotherapy: Advancing effective practice.* Mahwah, NJ: Lawrence Erlbaum Associates.

Chase, M. (1993, October 13). Inner music: Imagination may play role in how the brain learns muscle control. *Wall Street Journal,* pp. A1, A6.

Chastain, G., & Landrum, R. E. (Eds.). (1999). *Protecting human subjects: Departmental subject pools and institutional review boards.* Washington, DC: American Psychological Association.

Chatterjee, A. (2004). Cosmetic neurology: the controversy over enhancing movement, mentation, and mood. *Neurology, 28,* 968–974.

Chatterjee, A. (2006). The promise and predicament of cosmetic neurology. *Journal of Medical Ethics, 32,* 110–113.

Cheakalos, C., & Heyn, E. (1998, November 2). Mercy mission. *People Weekly,* pp. 149–150.

Chen, A., Zhou, Y., & Gong, H. (2004). Firing rates and dynamic correlated activities of ganglion cells both contribute to retinal information processing. *Brain Research, 1017,* 13–20.

Chen, C., & Stevenson, H. W. (1995). Motivation and mathematics achievement: A comparative study of Asian-American, Caucasian-American, and East Asian high school students. *Child Development, 66,* 1215–1234.

Cheney, C. D. (1996). Medical nonadherence: A behavior analysis. In J. R. Cautela & W. Ishaq (Eds.), *Contemporary issues in behavior therapy: Improving the human condition: Applied Clinical Psychology.* New York: Plenum Press.

Cheng, C., & Cheung, M. L. (2005). Cognitive processes underlying coping flexibility: Differentiation and integration. *Journal of Personality, 73,* 859–886.

Cheng, H., Cao, Y., & Olson, L. (1996, July 26). Spinal cord repair in adult paraplegic rats: Partial restoration of hind limb function. *Science, 273,* 510–513.

Cherry, B. J., Buckwalter, J. G., & Henderson, V. W. (2002). Better preservation of memory span relative to supraspan immediate recall in Alzheimer's disease. *Neuropsychologia, 40,* 846–852.

Chess, S. (1997). Temperament: Theory and clinical practice. *Harvard Mental Health Letter.*

Cheston, S. E. (2002). A new paradigm for teaching counseling theory and practice. *Counselor Education & Supervision, 39,* 254–269.

Chi-Ching, Y., & Noi, L. S. (1994). Learning styles and their implications for cross-cultural management in Singapore. *Journal of Social Psychology, 134,* 593–600.

Chin, S. B., & Pisoni, D. B. (1997). *Alcohol and speech.* New York: Academic Press.

Chisholm, E., Bapat, U., Chisholm, C., Alusi, G., & Vassaux, G. (2007). Gene therapy in head and neck cancer: A review. *Postgraduate Medical Journal, 83,* 731-737.

Cho, A. (2000, June 16). What's shakin' in the ear? *Science, 288,* 1954–1955.

Cho, S. H., Shin, H. K., Kwon, Y. H., Lee, M. Y., Lee, Y. H., Lee, C. H., Yang, D. S., & Jang, S. H. Cortical activation changes induced by visual biofeedback tracking training in chronic stroke patients. *Neurorehabilitation and Neural Repair, 22,* 77–84.

Cho, S., Holyoak, K. J., & Cannon, T. D. (2007). Analogical reasoning in working memory: Resources shared among relational integration, interference resolution, and maintenance. *Memory & Cognition, 35,* 1445–1455.

Choi, Y. S., Gray, H., & Ambady, N. (2004). Glimpses of others: Unintended communication and unintended perception. In J. Bargh, J. Uleman, & R. Hassin (Eds.), *Unintended thought* (2nd ed.). New York: Oxford University Press.

Chomsky, N. (1968). *Language and mind.* New York: Harcourt Brace Jovanovich.

Chomsky, N. (1978). On the biological basis of language capacities. In G. A. Miller & E. Lennenberg (Eds.), *Psychology and biology of language and thought.* New York: Academic Press.

Chomsky, N. (1991). Linguistics and cognitive science: Problems and mysteries. In A. Kasher (Ed.), *The Chomskyan turn.* Cambridge, MA: Blackwell.

Chou, K. (2005). Everyday competence and depressive symptoms: Social support and sense of control as mediators or moderators? *Aging and Mental Health, 9,* 177–183.

Choudhary, M. I., Nawaz, S. A., Zaheerul-Haq, A., Azim, M. K., Ghayur, M. N., Lodhi, M. A., Jalil, S., Khalid, A., Ahmed, A., Rode, B. M., AttaurRahman, R., Gilani, A. U., & Ahmad, V. U. (2005, July 15). Juliflorine: A potent natural peripheral anionic-site-binding inhibitor of acetylcholinesterase with calcium-channel blocking potential, a leading candidate for Alzheimer's disease therapy. *Biochemical and Biophysical Research Communications, 15,* 1171–1177.

Chow, A. Y., Chow, V. Y., Packo, K. H., Pollack, J. S., Peyman, G. A., & Schuchard, R. (2004). The artificial silicon retina microchip for the treatment of vision loss from retinitis pigmentosa. *Archives of Ophthalmology, 122,* 460–469.

Choy, Y., Fyer, A.J. & Lipsitz, J.D. (2007). Treatment of specific phobia in adults. *Clinical Psychology Review, 27,* 266–286.

Christ, S. E., Steiner, R. D., & Grange, D. K. (2006). Inhibitory control in children with phenylketonuria. *Developmental Neuropsychology, 30,* 845–864.

Christensen, A. J., & Johnson, J. A. (2002). Patient adherence with medical treatment regimens: An interactive approach. *Current Directions in Psychological Science, 11,* 94–101.

Christensen, T. C., Wood, J. V., & Barrett, L. F. (2003). Remembering everyday experience

through the prism of self-esteem. *Personality and Social Psychology Bulletin, 29,* 51–62.

Chronicle, E. P., MacGregor, J. N., & Ormerod, T. C. (2004). What makes an insight problem? The roles of heuristics, goal conception, and solution recoding in knowledge-lean problems. *Journal of Experimental Psychology: Learning, Memory, and Cognition, 30,* 14–27.

Chrysikou, E. G. (2006). When a shoe becomes a hammer: Problem solving as goal-derived, ad hoc categorization. *Dissertation Abstracts International: Section B: The Sciences and Engineering, 67(1-B),* 569.

Cialdini, R. B. (1988). *Influence: Science and practice* (2nd ed.). Glenview, IL: Scott, Foresman.

Cialdini, R. B. (2006). *Influence: The psychology of persuasion.* New York: Collins.

Cialdini, R. B., & Sagarin, B. J. (2005). Principles of interpersonal influence. In T. C. Brock & M. C. Green (Eds.), *Persuasion: Psychological insights and perspectives* (2nd ed.). Thousand Oaks, CA: Sage Publications.

Cialdini, R. B., Schaller, M., Houlihan, D., Arps, K., Fultz, J., & Beaman, A. L. (1975). Reciprocal concessions procedure for inducing compliance: The door-in-the-face technique. *Journal of Personality and Social Psychology, 31,* 206–215.

Cicero, F. R., & Pfadt, A. (2002). Investigation of a reinforcement-based toilet training procedure for children with autism. *Research in Developmental Disabilities, 23,* 319–331.

Cipolli, C., Fagioli, I., Mazzetti, M., & Tuozzi, G. (2005). Consolidation effect of the processing of declarative knowledge during human sleep: Evidence from long-term retention of interrelated contents of mental sleep experiences. *Brain Research Bulletin, 65,* 97–104.

Cisek, P., & Kalaska, J. F. (2004). Neural correlates of mental rehearsal in dorsal premotor cortex. *Nature, 431,* 993–996.

Clancy, S. A., Schacter, D. L., McNally, R. J., & Pitman, R. K. (2000). False recognition in women reporting recovered memories of sexual abuse. *Psychological Science, 7,* 26–33.

Clark, D. A. (2004). *Cognitive-behavioral therapy for OCD.* New York: Guilford.

Clark, D. A. (2007). Obsessions and compulsions. In N. Kazantzis, & L. L'Abate, *Handbook of homework assignments in psychotherapy: Research, practice, prevention.* New York: Springer Science + Business Media.

Clark, L., & Watson, R. (1999). Temperament. In L. A. Pervin & O. P. John (Eds.), *Handbook of personality: Theory and research* (2nd ed.). New York: Guilford.

Clark, R. E., & Squire, L. R. (1998, April 3). Classical conditioning and brain systems: The role of awareness. *Science, 280,* 77–81.

Clark, R., Anderson, N. B., Clark, V. R., & Williams, D. R. (1999). Racism as a stressor for African Americans: A biopsychosocial model. *American Psychologist, 54,* 805–816.

Clarke-Stewart, K. A., & Friedman, S. (1987). *Child development: Infancy through adolescence* New York: Wiley.

Clarke-Stewart, K.A., Vandell, D.L., McCartney, K., Owen, M.T. & Booth, C. (2000). Effects of parental separation and divorce on very young children. *Journal of Family Psychology, 14,* 304–326.

Clarkin, J. F., & Lenzenweger, M. F. (Eds.) (2004). *Major theories of personality disorders* (2nd ed.). New York: Guilford.

Clarkin, J. F., Levy, K. N., Lenzenweger, M. F., & Kernberg, O. F. (2007). Evaluating three treatments for borderline personality disorder: A multiwave study. *American Journal of Psychiatry, 164,* 922–928.

Clay D. L. (2000). Commentary: Rethinking our interventions in pediatric chronic pain and treatment research. *Journal of Pediatric Psychology, 25,* 53–55.

Cleary, A. M. (2006). Relating familiarity-based recognition and the tip-of-the-tongue phenomenon: Detecting a word's recency in the absence of access to the word. *Memory & Cognition, 34,* 804–816.

Clements, A., M., Rimrodt, S. L., & Abel, J. R. (2006). Sex differences in cerebral laterality of language and visuospatial processing. *Brain and Language, 98,* 150–158.

Clements, M (1994, August 7). Making love, how old, how often. *Parade,* p. 18.

Clemons, T. L. (2006). Underachieving gifted students: A social cognitive model. *Dissertation Abstracts International Section A: Humanities and Social Sciences, 66(9-A),* 3208.

Cloud, J. (2000, June 5). The lure of ecstasy. *Time,* pp. 60–68.

Coan, J.A., Schaefer, H.S. & Davidson, R.J. (2006). Lending a hand: Social regulation of the neural response to threat. *Psychological Science, 17,* 1032–1039.

Coates, S. L., Butler, L. T., & Berry, D. C. (2006). Implicit memory and consumer choice: The mediating role of brand familiarity. *Applied Cognitive Psychology, 20,* 1101–1116.

Coats, E. J., & Feldman, R. S. (1996). Gender differences in nonverbal correlates of social status. *Personality and Social Psychology Bulletin, 22,* 1014–1022.

Cobos, P., Sanchez, M., Garcia, C., Vera, M. N., & Vila, J. (2002). Revisiting the James versus Cannon debate on emotion: Startle and autonomic modulation in patients with spinal cord injuries. *Biological Psychology, 61,* 251–269.

Cochran, S. D. (2000). Emerging issues in research on lesbians' and gay men's mental health: Does sexual orientation really matter? *American Psychologist, 56,* 33–41.

Coffey, C. E., Saxton, J. A., & Ratcliff, G. (1999). Relation of education to brain size in normal aging: Implications for the reserve hypothesis. *Neurology, 53,* 189–196.

Coffman, S. J., Martell, C. R., Dimidjian, S., Gallop, R., & Holon, S. D. (2007). Extreme nonresponse in cognitive therapy: Can behavioral activation succeed where cognitive therapy fails? *Journal of Consulting Clinical Psychology, 75,* 531–545.

Cohen, B. H. (2002). *Explaining psychological statistics* (2nd ed.). New York: Wiley.

Cohen, B. H., & Lea, R. B. (2003). *Essentials of statistics for the social and behavioral sciences.* New York: Wiley.

Cohen, D. (1996). Law, social policy, and violence: The impact of regional cultures. *Journal of Personality and Social Psychology, 70,* 961–978.

Cohen, J. (2003). Things I have learned (so far). In A. E. Kazdin (Ed.), *Methodological issues and strategies in clinical research* (3rd ed.). Washington, DC: American Psychological Association.

Cohen, L., & Cashon, C. (2003). Infant perception and cognition. In R. Lerner and M. Easterbrooks (Eds.), *Handbook of psychology: Developmental psychology* (Vol. 6). New York: Wiley.

Cohen, P., Slomkowski, C., & Robins, L. N. (Eds.). (1999). *Historical and geographical influences on psychopathology.* Mahwah, NJ: Erlbaum.

Cohen, S. (2004, November). Social relationships and health. *American Psychologist,* 676–684.

Cohen, S., Doyle, W. J., Turner, R., Alper, C. M., & Skoner, D. P. (2003). Sociability and susceptibility to the common cold. *Psychological Science, 14*, 389–395.

Cohen, S., Hamrick, N., & Rodriguez, M. (2002). Reactivity and vulnerability to stress-associated risk for upper respiratory illness. *Psychosomatic Medicine, 64*, 302–310.

Col, N., & Komaroff, A. L. (2004, May 10). How to think about HT. *Newsweek, 143*, 80–81.

Cole, M., Levitin, K., & Luria, A. (2006). *The autobiography of Alexander Luria: A dialogue with the making of mind.* Mahwah, NJ: Erlbaum.

Coleman, E. (2002). Masturbation as a means of achieving sexual health. *Journal of Psychology and Human Sexuality, 14*, 5–16.

Coles, C. D., Platzman, K. A., & Lynch, M. E. (2003). Auditory and visual sustained attention in adolescents parentally exposed to alcohol. *Clinical and Experimental Research, 26*, 263–271.

Coles, R. (1997). *The moral intelligence of children.* New York: Random House.

Coles, R., & Stokes, G. (1985). *Sex and the American teenager.* New York: Harper & Row.

Colland, V. T., Van Essen-Zandvliet, L. E. M., Lans, C., Denteneer, A., Westers, P., & Brackel, H. J. L. (2004). Poor adherence to self-medication instructions in children with asthma and their parents. *Patient Education and Counseling, 55*, 416–421.

Collins, A. M., & Loftus, E. F. (1975). A spreading-activation theory of semantic processing. *Psychological Review, 82*, 407–428.

Collins, A. M., & Quillian, M. R. (1969). Retrieval times from semantic memory. *Journal of Verbal Learning and Verbal Behavior, 8*, 240–247.

Collins, S. L., & Izenwasser, S. (2004). Chronic nicotine differentially alters cocaine-induced locomotor activity in adolescent vs. adult male and female rats. *Neuropharmacology, 46*, 349–362.

Colom, R., Jung, R. E., & Haier, R. J. (2006). Finding the g-factor in brain structure using the method of correlated vectors. *Intelligence, 34*, 561–570.

Coltheart, M., Langdon, R., & McKay, R. (2007). Schizophrenia and monothematic delusions. *Schizophrenia Bulletin, 33*, 642–647.

Coltraine, S., & Messineo, M. (2000). The perpetuation of subtle prejudice: Race and gender imagery in 1990s television advertising. *Sex Roles, 42*, 363–389.

Colwell, M. J., & Lindsey, E. W. (2005). Preschool children's pretend and physical play and sex of play partner: Connections to peer competence. *Sex Roles, 52*, 497–509.

Combrink-Graham, L., & McKenna, S. B. (2006). Families with children with disrupted attachments. In L. Combrink-Graham, *Children in family contexts: Perspectives on treatment.* New York: Guilford Press.

Combris, M. (2006). Utilisation de la réalité virtuelle dans la prise en charge en thérapie cognitive et comportementale d'une phobie de l'avion. Using virtual reality in standard cognitive and behavioral therapy of a plane phobia. *Revue Francophone de Clinique Comportementale et Cognitive, 11*, 11–18.

Committee to Review the Scientific Evidence on the Polygraph. (2003). *The polygraph and lie detection.* Washington, DC: National Academies Press.

Compagni, A., & Manderscheid, R. W. (2006). A neuroscientist-consumer alliance to transform mental health care, *Journal of Behavioral Health Services & Research, 33*, 265–274.

Comuzzie, A. G., & Allison, D. B. (1998, May 29). The search for human obesity genes. *Science, 280*, 1374–1377.

Conduit, R., Crewther, S. G., & Coleman, G. (2004). Spontaneous eyelid movements (ELMS) during sleep are related to dream recall on awakening. *Journal of Sleep Research, 13*, 137–144.

Conger, R. D., Wallace, L. E., Sun, Y., Simons, R. L., McLoyd, V. C., & Brody, G. H. (2002). Economic pressure in African American families: A replication and extension of the family stress model. *Developmental Psychology, 38*, 179–193.

Conner, M., Povey, R., Sparks, P., James, R., & Shepherd, R. (2003). Moderating role of attitudinal ambivalence within the theory of planned behaviour. *British Journal of Social Psychology, 42*, 75–94.

Connolly, A. C. (2007). Concepts and their features: Can cognitive science make good on the promises of concept empiricism? *Dissertation Abstracts International: Section B: The Sciences and Engineering, 67(7-B)*, 4125.

Consumer Reports (CR). (1993, June). Dieting and weight loss, p. 347.

Consumer Reports (CR). (1995, November). Mental health: Does therapy help? pp. 734–739.

Conway, M. A. (1997). *Cognitive models of memory.* Cambridge, MA: MIT.

Conway, M. A. (Ed) (2002). *Levels of processing 30 years on special issue of memory.* Hove, UK: Psychology Press.

Cooke, J. R., & Ancoli-Israel, S. (2006). Sleep and its disorders in older adults. *Psychiatric Clinics of North America, 29*, 1077–1093.

Cooklin, A. (2000). Therapy, the family and others. In H. Maxwell, *Clinical psychotherapy for health professionals.* Philadelphia: Whurr Publishers.

Cookson, R. (2005, March 10). A noise for danger: Ten years ago, a Belgian rodent-lover decided that rats were smart. *The Independent* (London), p. F7.

Cooper, E. O. (2004). Candid camera: Computer-based facial recognition system spots terrorists entering the U.S. *Quest Summer, 7*, 33–39.

Cooper, J. (2007). *Cognitive dissonance: Fifty years of a classic theory.* Thousand Oaks, CA: Sage Publications.

Cooper, J., Mirabile, R., & Scher, S. J. (2005). Actions and attitudes: The theory of cognitive dissonance. In T. C. Brock & M. C. Green (Eds.), *Persuasion: Psychological insights and perspectives* (2nd ed.). Thousand Oaks, CA: Sage Publications.

Cooper, N. R., Kalaria, R. N., McGeer, P. L., & Rogers, J. (2000). Key issues in Alzheimer's disease inflammation. *Neurobiology of Aging, 21*, 451–453.

Cope, D. (2001). *Virtual music.* Cambridge, MA: MIT.

Cope, D. (2003). Computer analysis of musical allusions. *Computer Music Journal, 27*, 11–28.

Copeland, J. B., & Proudfoot, D. (2007). Artificial intelligence: history, foundations, and philosophical issues. In P. Thagard, *Philosophy of psychology and cognitive science.* Amsterdam, Netherlands: North Holland/Elsevier, 429–482.

Copolov, D. L., Seal, M. L., Maruff, P., Ulusoy, R., Wong, M. T. H., TochonDanguy, H. J., & Egan, G. F. (2003). Cortical activation associated with the human experience of auditory hallucinations and perception of human speech in schizophrenia: A PET correlation study. *Psychiatry Research: Neuroimaging, 123*, 139–152.

Corbetta, M., Kincade, J. M., & Shulman, G. L. (2002). Neural systems for visual orienting and their relationships to spatial working memory. *Journal of Cognitive Neuroscience, 14*, 508–523.

Corcoran, B. (2005, July 5). Large African rats being used to find landmines in Mozambique. *The Irish Times*, p. 10.

Cordnoldi, C., De Beni, R., & Helstrup, T. (2007). Memory sensitivity in autobiographical memory. In S. Magnussen, & T. Helstrup, *Everyday memory.* New York: Psychology Press.

Coren, S. (1992). The moon illusion: A different view through the legs. *Perceptual and Motor Skills, 75*, 827–831.

Coren, S. (2004). Sensation and perception. In I. B. Weiner. *Handbook of Psychology, Vol 1*, Hoboken, NJ: John Wiley & Sons.

Coren, S., & Ward, L. M. (1989). *Sensation and perception* (3rd ed.). San Diego, CA: Harcourt Brace Jovanovich.

Coren, S., Porac, C., & Ward, L. M. (1984). *Sensation and perception* (2nd ed.). New York: Academic Press.

Cornelius, M. D., Taylor, P. M., Geva, D., & Day, N. L. (1995). Prenatal tobacco and marijuana use among adolescents: Effects on offspring gestational age, growth, and morphology. *Pediatrics, 95*, 57–68.

Cornell, C. B. (2006). A graduated scale for determining mental age. *Dissertation Abstracts International: Section B: The Sciences and Engineering, 66(9-B)*, 5121.

Corsello, A. (2005). The wronged man. In *The best American magazine writing, 2005.* New York: Columbia University Press.

Cosmides, L., & Tooby, J. (2004). Social exchange: The evolutionary design of a neurocognitive system. In M. S. Gazzaniga (Ed.), *Cognitive neurosciences* (3rd ed.). Cambridge, MA: MIT.

Cosser, C. (2002). Hypnosis in the treatment of chronic pain: An ecosystemic approach. *Australian Journal of Clinical and Experimental Hypnosis, 30*, 156–169.

Costa, P. T., Jr., & Widiger, T. A. (Eds.). (2002). *Personality disorders and the five-factor model of personality* (2nd ed.). Washington, DC: American Psychological Association.

Cothran, M. M., & White, J. P. (2002). Adolescent behavior and sexually transmitted diseases: The dilemma of human papillomavirus [Special issue: Adolescent women's health]. *Health Care for Women International, 23*, 306–319.

Cotton, P. (1993, July 7). Psychiatrists set to approve DSM-IV. *Journal of the American Medical Association, 270*, 13–15.

Cottraux, J. (2005). Recent developments in research and treatment for social phobia (social anxiety disorder). *Current Opinion in Psychiatry, 18*, 51–54.

Council of National Psychological Associations for the Advancement of Ethnic Minority Interests (CNPAAEMI). (2000, January). *Guidelines for research in ethnic minority communities.* Washington, DC: American Psychological Association.

Couturier, J., & Lock, J. (2006). Eating disorders: Anorexia nervosa, bulimia nervosa, and binge eating disorder. In T. G. Plante, *Mental disorders of the new millennium: Biology and function (Vol 3.).* Westport, CT: Praeger Publishers/Greenwood Publishing.

Coventry, K. R., Venn, S. F., Smith, G. D., & Morley, A. M. (2003). Spatial problem solving and functional relations. *European Journal of Cognitive Psychology, 15*, 71–99.

Cowan, N., Towse, J. N., Hamilton, Z., Saults, J. S., Elliott, E. M., Lacey, J. F., Moreno, M. V., & Hitch, G. J. (2003). Children's working-memory processes: A response-timing analysis. *Journal of Experimental Psychology: General, 132*, 113–132.

Cowley, G. (2000, January 31). Alzheimer's: Unlocking the mystery. *Time*, pp. 46–54.

Cowley, G. (2003, February 24). Our Bodies, Our Fears. *Newsweek*, 43–44.

Cox, J. (2003, May 6). How far would you go to save your life? *Denver Post*, p. F1.

Cox, R., Baker, S. E., Macdonald, D. W., & Berdoy, M. (2004). Protecting egg prey from carrion crows: The potential of aversive conditioning. *Applied Animal Behaviour Science, 87*, 325–342.

Coyle, D. (2005). *Lance Armstrong's war: One man's battle against fate, fame, love, death, scandal, and a few other rivals on the road to the Tour de France*. New York: HarperCollins.

Coyle, N. (2006). The hard work of living in the face of death. *Journal of Pain and Symptom Management, 32*, 266–274.

Coyle, T. R. (2006). Test-retest changes on scholastic aptitude tests are not related to g. *Intelligence, 34*, 15–27.

Coyne, S. M., & Archer, J. (2005). The relationship between indirect and physical aggression on television and in real life. *Social Development, 14*, 324–338.

Craig, R. J. (1999). *Interpreting personality tests: A clinical manual for the MMPI-2, MCMI-III, CPI-R, and 16PF*. New York: Wiley.

Craik, F. I. M. (1990). Levels of processing. In M. E. Eysenck (Ed.), *The Blackwell dictionary of cognitive psychology*. London: Blackwell.

Craik, F. I., & Lockhart, R. S. (1972). Levels of processing: A framework for memory research. *Journal of Verbal Behavior, 11*, 671–684.

Cramer, J. A. (1995). Optimizing long-term patient compliance. *Neurology, 45*, s25–s28.

Cramer, P. (2000a). Thematic apperception test. In A. E. Kazdin (Ed.), *Encyclopedia of psychology* (Vol. 8). Washington, DC: American Psychological Association.

Cramer, P. (2000b). Defense mechanisms in psychology today: Further process for adaptation. *American Psychologist, 55*, 637–646.

Cramer, P. (2007). Longitudinal study of defense mechanisms: Late childhood to late adolescence. *Journal of Personality, 75*, 1–23.

Crawford, M., & Unger, R. (2004). *Women and gender: A feminist psychology* (4th ed.). New York: McGraw-Hill.

Crawford, N. (2002). Science-based program curbs violence in kids. *APA Monitor, 33*, 38–39.

Creasey, G. L. (2005). *Research methods in lifespan development* (6th ed.). Boston: Allyn & Bacon.

Crews, F. (1996). The verdict on Freud. *Psychological Science, 7*, 63–68.

Crits-Christoph, P. (1992). The efficacy of brief dynamic psychotherapy: A meta-analysis. *American Journal of Psychiatry, 149*, 151–158.

Crocker, J., & Park, L. E. (2004). The costly pursuit of self-esteem. *Psychological Bulletin, 130*, 392–414.

Crombag, H. S., & Robinson, R. E. (2004). Drugs, environment, brain, and behavior. *Current Directions in Psychological Science, 13*, 107–111.

Cropley, A. (2006). In praise of convergent thinking. *Creativity Research Journal, 18*, 391–404.

Crosby, F. J., Williams, J. C., & Biernat, M. (2004). The maternal wall. *Journal of Social Issues, 60*, 675–682.

Crosnoe, R., & Elder, G. H., Jr. (2002). Successful adaptation in the later years: A life course approach to aging. *Social Psychology Quarterly, 65*, 309–328.

Crum, A. J., & Langer, E. J. (2007). Mind-set matters: Exercise and the placebo effect. *Psychological Science, 18*, 165–171.

Cruz, A., & Green, B. G. (2000). Thermal stimulation of taste. *Nature, 403*, 889–892.

Csikszentmihalyi, M. (1997). *Creativity: Flow and the psychology of discovery and invention*. New York: BasicBooks/Mastermind Series.

Cuddy, A. J. C., Fiske, S. T., & Glick, P. (2004). When professionals become mothers, warmth doesn't cut the ice. *Journal of Social Issues, 60*, 701–718.

Culhane-Pera, K. A., Borkan, J. M., & Patten, S. (2007). Culture and ethnicity. In O. J. Z. Sahler, & J. E. Carr, *The behavioral sciences and health care* (2nd rev. and updated ed.). Ashland, OH: Hogrefe & Huber Publishers.

Cullinane, C. A., Chu, D. Z. J., & Mamelak, A. N. (2002). Current surgical options in the control of cancer pain. *Cancer Practice, 10*, s21–s26.

Cummings, A., Ceponiene, R., & Koyama, A. (2006). Auditory semantic networks for words and natural sounds. *Brain Research, 1115*, 92–107.

Cummings, E., & Henry, W. F. (1961). *Growing old*. New York: Basic Books.

Cummings, J., & Hall, C. (2002). Athletes' use of imagery in the off-season. *Sport Psychologist, 16*, 160–172.

Cunningham, P. (2006). Early years teachers and the influence of Piaget: Evidence from oral history. *Early Years An International Journal of Research and Development, 26*, 5–16.

Cutler, B., & Saporta, L. R. (2003). *Closing argument: Defending and befriending John Gotti, and other legal battles I have waged*. New York: Diane Publishing.

Cwikel, J., Behar, L., & Rabson-Hare, J. (2000). A comparison of a vote count and a meta-analysis review of intervention research with adult cancer patients. *Research on Social Work Practice, 10*, 139–158.

Cynkar, A. (2007). The changing gender composition of psychology. *Monitor on Psychology, 38*, 46-48.

Czeisler, C. A., Duffy, J. F., Shanahan, T. L., Brown, E. N., Mitchell, J. F., Rimmer, . W., Ronda, J. M., Silva, E. J., Allan, J. S., Emens, J. S., Dijk, D. J., & Kronauer, R. E. (1999, June 25). Stability, precision, and near-24-hour period of the human circadian pacemaker. *Science, 284*, 2177–2181.

Czopp, A.M., Monteith, M.J. & Mark, A.Y. (2006). Standing up for a change: reducing bias through interpersonal confrontation. *Journal of Personality and Social Psychology, 90*, 784–803.

D'Arcy, R., C. N., Bolster, R., B., & Ryner, L. (2007). A site directed fMRI approach for evaluating functional status in the anterolateral temporal lobes. *Neuroscience Research, 57*, 120–128.

Daftary, F., & Meri, J. W. (2002). *Culture and memory in medieval Islam*. London: I. B. Tauris.

Dai, D. Y., & Wang, X. (2007). The role of need for cognition and reader beliefs in text comprehension and interest development. *Contemporary Educational Psychology, 32*, 332–347.

Daines, B. (2006). Violations of agreed and implicit sexual and emotional boundaries in couple relationships—some thoughts arising from Levine's 'A clinical perspective on couple infidelity.' *Sexual and Relationship Therapy, 21*, 45–53.

Dalal, A. K., & Misra, G. (2006). Psychology of health and well-being: Some emerging perspectives. *Psychological Studies, 51, Special issue: Psychology of Health and Well-Being*, 91–104.

Dale, A. (2006). Quality issues with survey research. *International Journal of Social Research Methodology: Theory & Practice, 9, Special issue: Quality in Social Research*, 143–158.

Dale, J. W., & von Schantz, M. (2007). *From genes to genomes: Concepts and applications of DNA technology*. New York: John Wiley & Sons.

Dalsgaro, O. J., Hansen, N. G., Soes-Petersen, U., Evald, T., Hoegholm, A., Barber, J., & Vestbo, J. (2004). A multicenter, randomized, double-blind, placebo-controlled, 6-month trial of bupropion hydrochloride sustained-release tablets as an aid to smoking cessation in hospital employees. *Nicotine and Tobacco Research, 6*, 55–61.

Damasio, A. (1999). *The feeling of what happens: Body and emotion in the making of consciousness*. New York: Harcourt Brace.

Damasio, A. (2003, May 15). Mental self: The person within. *Nature, 423*, 227.

Damon, W. (1999, August). The moral development of children. *Scientific American*, pp. 72–78.

Danaei, G., Vender Hoorn, S., Lopez, A.D., Murray, C.J.L. & Ezzati, M. (2005). Causes of cancer in the world: Comparative risk assessment of nine behavioural and environmental risk factors. Comparative Risk Assessment collaborating group (Cancers). *Lancet, 366*, 1784–1793.

D'Argembeau, A., Comblain, C., &Van der Linden, M. (2003). Phenomenal characteristics of autobiographical memories for positive, negative, and neutral events. *Applied Cognitive Psychology, 17*, 281–294.

Darley, J. M. (1995). Constructive and destructive obedience: A taxonomy of principal-agent relationships. *Journal of Social Issues, 51*, 125–154.

Darley, J. M., & Latané, B. (1968). Bystanders intervention in emergencies: Diffusion of responsibility. *Journal of Personality and Social Psychology, 8*, 377–383.

Darwin, C. J., Turvey, M. T., & Crowder, R. G. (1972). An auditory analogue of the Sperling partial-report procedure: Evidence for brief auditory storage. *Cognitive Psychology, 3*, 255–267.

Das, A. (2007). Masturbation in the United States. *Journal of Sex & Marital Therapy, 33*, 301–317.

Davidson, J. E., Deuser, R., & Sternberg, R. J. (1994). The role of metacognition in problem solving. In J. Metcalfe & A. P. Shimamura (Eds.), *Metacognition: Knowing about knowing*. Cambridge, MA: MIT.

Davidson, P. S. R., & Glisky, E. L. (2002). Is flashbulb memory a special instance of source memory? Evidence from older adults. *Memory, 10*, 99–111.

Davidson, R. J., Gray, J. A., LeDoux, J. E., Levenson, R. W., Pankseep, J., & Ekman, P. (1994). Is there emotion-specific physiology? In P. Ekman & R. J. Davidson, New York, NY: Oxford University Press

Davidson (Eds.), *The nature of emotion*. New York: Oxford University Press.

Davis, C., Aronson, J., & Salinas, M. (2006). Shades of threat: Racial identity as a moderator of stereotype threat. *Journal of Black Psychology, 32*, 399–417.

Davis, S. F. (2007). The nose knows best. *PsycCRITIQUES, 52*, 22–31.

Davolt, S. (2006, July 1). Employers got game: Tedium-battling businesses use online motivational games. *Employee Benefit News.* http://ebn.benefitnews.com/.

Day, A. L., & Livingstone, H. A. (2003). Gender differences in perceptions of stressors and utilization of social support among university students. *Canadian Journal of Behavioural Science, 35*, 73–83.

Day, R. D., & Lamb, M. E. (2004). *Conceptualizing and measuring father involvement.* Mahwah, NJ: Lawrence Erlbaum Associates.

De Bini, R., Pazzaglia, F., & Gardini, S. (2007). The generation and maintenance of visual mental images: Evidence from image type and aging. *Brain and Cognition, 63*, 271–278.

Dean, C., & Dresbach, T. (2006). Neuroligins and neurexins: Linking cell adhesion, synapse formation and cognitive function. *International Journal of Psychiatry in Clinical Practice, 10 (Suppl)*, 5–11.

Dean-Borenstein, M. T. (2007). The long-term psychosocial effects of trauma on survivors of human-caused extreme stress situations. *Dissertation Abstracts International: Section B: The Sciences and Engineering, 67(11-B)*, 6733.

DeAngelis, T. (2002, March). Promising treatments for anorexia and bulimia. *Monitor on Psychology*, pp. 38–41.

de Araujo, I. E. T., Kringelbach, M. L., & Rolls, E. T. (2003). Representation of umami taste in the human brain. *Journal of Neurophysiology, 90*, 313–319.

Deary, I. J., & Der, G. (2005). Reaction time, age, and cognitive ability: Longitudinal findings from age 16 to 63 years in representative population samples. *Aging, Neuropsychology, & Cognition, 12*, 187–215.

Deater-Deckard, K., Ivy, L., & Smith, J. (2005). Resilience in gene-environment transactions. In S. Goldstein and R. B. Brooks (Eds.), *Handbook of resilience in children* (pp. 49–63). New York: Kluwer Academic/Plenum Publishers.

Deaux, K. (1995). How basic can you be? The evolution of research on gender stereotypes. *Journal of Social Issues, 51*, 11–20.

Debiec, J., Doyère, V., and Nader, K. (2006). Directly reactivated, but not indirectly reactivated, memories undergo reconsolidation in the amygdala. *PNAS Proceedings of the National Academy of Sciences of the United States of America, 103*, 3428–3433.

deCharms, R. C., Blake, D. T., & Merzenich, M. M. (1998, May 29). Optimizing sound features for cortical neurons. *Science, 280*, 1439–1440.

Deci, E. L., Koestner, R., & Ryan, R. M. (2001). Extrinsic rewards and intrinsic motivation in education: Reconsidered once again. *Review of Educational Research, 71*, 1–27.

Deckersbach, T., Miller, K. K., Klibanski, A., Fischman, A., Dougherty, D. D., Blais, M. A., Herzog, D. B., & Rauch, S. L. (2006). Regional cerebral brain metabolism correlates of neuroticism and extraversion. *Depression and Anxiety, 23*, 133–138.

DeCoster, V. A. (2003). Predicting emotions in everyday social interactions: A test and comparison of affect control and social interactional theories. *Journal of Human Behavior in the Social Environment, 6*, 53–73.

Dediu, D., & Ladd, D. R. (2007). From the Cover: Linguistic tone is related to the population frequency of the adaptive haplogroups of two brain size genes, ASPM and Microcephalin. *Proceedings of the National Academy of Sciences, 104*, 10944–10949.

Deffenbacher, J. L. (1988). Cognitive relaxation and social skills treatments of anger: A year later. *Journal of Consulting Psychology, 35*, 309–315.

Deffenbacher, J. L. (1996). Cognitive-behavioral approaches to anger reduction. In K. S. Dobson & K. D. Craig (Eds.), *Advances in cognitive-behavioral therapy* (Vol. 2). Thousand Oaks, CA: Sage Publications.

de Fockert, J. W., Rees, G., Frith, C. D., & Lavie, N. (2001, March 2). The role of working memory in visual selective attention. *Science, 291*, 1803–1806.

DeGaton, J. F., Weed, S., & Jensen, L. (1996). Understanding gender differences in adolescent sexuality. *Adolescence, 31*, 217–231.

deGroot, A. (1978). *Thought and choice in chess.* Paris: Mouton de Gruyter.

deGroot, A. D. (1966). Perception and memory versus thought: Some old ideas and recent findings. In B. Kleinmuntz (Ed.), *Problem solving: Research, method, and theory.* New York: Wiley.

del Rosal, E., Alonso, L., & Moreno, R. (2006). Simulation of habituation to simple and multiple stimuli. *Behavioural Processes, 73*, 272–277.

Delahanty, D., & Baum, A. (2000). Stress and breast cancer. In A. S. Baum, R. A. Revenson, & J. E. Singer (Eds.), *Handbook of health psychology.* Mahwah, NJ: Erlbaum.

DeLamater, J. D., & Sill, M. (2005). Sexual desire in later life. *Journal of Sex Research, 42*, 138–149.

Delcourt, M. A. B., Cornell, D. G., & Goldberg, M. D. (2007). Cognitive and affective learning outcomes of gifted elementary school students. *The Gifted Child Quarterly, 51*, 359–382.

Delgado, M. R., Labouliere, C. D., & Phelps, E. A. (2006). Fear of losing money? Aversive conditioning with secondary reinforcers. *Social Cognitive and Affective Neuroscience, 1, Special issue: Genetic, Comparative and Cognitive Studies of Social Behavior*, 250–259.

Delinsky, S. S., Latner, J. D., & Wilson, G. T. (2006). Binge eating and weight loss in a self-help behavior modification program. *Obesity, 14*, 1244–1249.

Demaree, H. A., & Everhart, D. E. (2004). Healthy high-hostiles: Reduced para-sympathetic activity and decreased sympathovagal flexibility during negative emotional processing. *Personality and Individual Differences, 36*, 457–469.

Demir, E., & Dickson, B. J. (2005). Fruitless splicing specifies male courtship behavior in *Drosophila. Cell 121*, 785–794.

De Mello, M. F., De Jesus Mari, J., Bacaltchuk, J., Verdeli, H., & Neugebauer, R. (2005). A systematic review of research findings on the efficacy of interpersonal therapy for depressive disorders. *European Archives of Psychiatry and Clinical Neuroscience, 255*, 75–82.

Dement, W. C. (1999). *The promise of sleep.* New York: Delacorte Press.

Dement, W. C., & Wolpert, E. A. (1958). The relation of eye movements, body mobility, and external stimuli to dream content. *Journal of Experimental Psychology, 55*, 543–553.

Dempster, F. N. (1981). Memory span: Sources for individual and developmental differences. *Psychological Bulletin, 89*, 63–100.

Denmark, G. L., & Fernandez, L. C. (1993). Historical development of the psychology of women. In F. L. Denmark & M. A. Paludi (Eds.), *A handbook of issues and theories.* Westport, CT: Greenwood Press.

Dennett, D. C. (2003). *Freedom evolves.* New York: Viking.

Dennis, I. (2007). Halo effects in grading student projects. *Journal of Applied Psychology, 92*, 1169–1176.

Dennis, T. A., Cole, P. M., Zahn-Waxler, C., & Mizuta, I. (2002). Self in context: Autonomy and relatedness in Japanese and U.S. mother-preschooler dyads. *Child Development, 73*, 1803–1817.

Denollet, J. (2005). DS14: standard assessment of negative affectivity, social inhibition, and Type D personality. *Psychosomatic Medicine, 67*, 89–97.

Denollet J., & Brutsaert, D. L. (1998). Personality, disease severity, and the risk of long-term cardiac events in patients with a decreased ejection fraction after myocardial infarction. *Circulation, 97*, 167–173.

Dentzer, S. (1986, May 5). Can you pass the job test? *Newsweek*, pp. 46–53.

Deouell, L. Y., Parnes, A., & Pickard, N. (2006). Spatial location is accurately tracked by human auditory sensory memory: Evidence from the mismatch negativity. *European Journal of Neuroscience, 24*, 1488–1494.

DePaulo, B. M., & Morris, W. L. (2005). Discerning lies from truths: Behavioral cues to deception and the indirect pathway of intuition. In P. A. Granhag & L. A. Stromwall (Eds.), *Deception detection in forensic contexts.* Cambridge: Cambridge University Press.

DePaulo, B. M., Lindsay, J. J., Malone, B. E., Muhlenbruck, L., Charlton, K., & Cooper, H. (2003). Cues to deception. *Psychological Bulletin, 129*, 74–118.

Deregowski, J. B. (1973). Illusion and culture. In R. L. Gregory & G. H. Combrich (Eds.), *Illusion in nature and art*, pp. 161–192. New York: Scribner.

Derryberry, W. P. (2006). Review of social motivation: conscious and unconscious processes. *Journal of Moral Education, 35*, 276–278.

DeRubeis, R., Hollon, S., & Shelton, R. (2003, May 23). Presentation, American Psychiatric Association meeting, Philadelphia.

Deshields, T., Tibbs, T., Fan, M. Y., & Taylor, M. (2006). Differences in patterns of depression after treatment for breast cancer [Electronic article published August 12, 2005]. *Psycho-Oncology, 15(5)*, 398–406.

Desimone, R. (1992, October 9). The physiology of memory: Recordings of things past. *Science, 258*, 245–255.

Des Jarlis, D. C., Sloboda, A., Friedman, S. R., Tempakski, B., McKnight, C., & Braine, N. (2006). Diffusion of the *D.A.R.E* and Syringe Exchange Programs. *American Journal of Public Health, 96*, 1354–1357.

DeSouza, E., Fansler, A. G. (2003). Contrapower sexual harassment: A survey of students and faculty members. *Sex Roles, 48*, 519–542.

Dessing, J. C., Peper, C. E., Bullock, D., & Beek, P. J. (2005). How position, velocity, and temporal information combine in the prospective control of catching: Data and model. *Journal of Cognitive Neuroscience, 17*, 668–686.

DeSteno, D., Bartlett, M. Y., & Braverman, J. (2002). Sex differences in jealousy: Evolutionary mechanism or artifact of measurement? *Journal of Personality and Social Psychology, 83*, 1103–1116.

Detoledo-Morrell, L., Stoub, T. R., & Wang, C. (2007). Hippocampal atrophy and disconnection in incipient and mild Alzheimer's disease. *Progressive Brain Research, 163C*, 741–823.

Detterman, D. K., Gabriel, L. T., & Ruthsatz, J. M. (2000). Intelligence and mental retardation. In R. J. Sternberg, et al. (Eds.), *Handbook of intelligence.* New York: Cambridge University Press.

de Valois, R. L., & de Valois, K. K. (1993). A multi-stage color model. *Vision Research, 33,* 1053–1065.

Devi, G. (2002). *Take a measure of your memory.* Dr. Gayatri Devi. Personal Communication.

deVilliers, J. G., & deVilliers, P. A. (1999). Language development. In M. H. Bronstein & M. E. Lamb (Eds.), *Developmental psychology.* Mahwah, NJ: Erlbaum.

Devonport, J. J., & Lane, A. M. (2006). Relationships between self-efficacy, coping and student retention. *Social Behavior and Personality, 34,* 127–138.

de Waal, F. B. M. (1999, December). The end of nature versus nurture. *Scientific American,* pp. 94–99.

Dey, E. L., Astin, A. W., Korn, W. S., & Berz, E. R. (1990). *The American freshman: National norms for fall, 1990.* Los Angeles: Higher Education Research Institute, Graduate School of Education, UCLA.

Diaz-Guerrero, R. (1979). Culture and personality revisited. *Annals of the New York Academy of Sciences, 285,* 119–130.

DiCano, P., & Everitt, B. J. (2002). Reinstatement and spontaneous recovery of cocaine-seeking following extinction and different durations of withdrawal. *Behavioural Pharmacology, 13,* 397–406.

Dickens, W. T., & Flynn, J. R. (2001). Heritability estimates versus large environmental effects: The IQ paradox resolved. *Psychological Review, 108,* 291–310.

Dickerson, S. S., Kemeny, M. E., Aziz, N., Kim, K. H., & Fahey, J. L. (2004). Immunological effects of induced shame and guilt. *Psychosomatic Medicine, 66,* 124–131.

Diefendorff, J. M., & Richard, E. M. (2003). Antecedents and consequences of emotional display rule perceptions. *Journal of Applied Psychology, 88,* 284–294.

Diener, E. (2000). Subjective well-being: The science of happiness and a proposal for a national index. *American Psychologist, 55,* 34–43.

Diener, E., & Biswas-Diener, R. (2002). Will money increase subjective well-being? *Social Indicators Research, 57,* 119–169.

Diener, E., & Clifton, D. (2002). Life satisfaction and religiosity in broad probability samples. *Psychological Inquiry, 13,* 206–209.

Diener, E., & Seligman, M. E. P. (2002). Very happy people. *Psychological Science, 18,* 81–84.

Diener, E., & Seligman, M.E.P. (2004). Beyond money: Toward an economy of well-being. *Psychological Science in the Public Interest, 5,* 1–31.

Diener, E., Lucas, R. E., & Oishi, S. (2002). Subjective well-being: The science of happiness and life satisfaction. In C. R. Snyder & S. J. Lopez (Eds.), *Handbook of positive psychology,* pp. 463–73. London: Oxford University Press.

Diener, E., Lucas, R. E., & Scollon, C. N. (2006). Beyond the hedonic treadmill: Revising the adaptation theory of well-being. *American Psychologist, 61,* 305–314.

Difede, J., & Hoffman, H. G. (2002). Virtual reality exposure therapy for World Trade Center post-traumatic stress disorder: A case report. *CyberPsychology and Behavior, 5,* 529–535.

DiGiovanna, A. G. (1994). *Human aging: Biological perspectives.* New York: McGraw-Hill.

Dijksterhuis, A., Chartrand, T. L., & Aarts, H. (2007). Effects of priming and perception on social behavior and goal pursuit. In J. A. Bargh, *Social psychology and the unconscious: The automaticity of higher mental processes.* New York: Psychology Press.

Dillard, J. P., & Shen, L. (2004). On the nature of reactance and its role in persuasive health communication. *Communication Monographs, 72,* 144–168.

Dillard, J. P., & Shen, L. (2007). Self-report measures of discrete emotions. In R. A. Reynolds, R. Woods, & J. D. Baker, *Handbook of research on electronic surveys and measurements.* Hershey, PA: Idea Group Reference/IGI Global, 2007.

DiLorenzo, P. M., & Yougentob, S. L. (2003). Olfaction and taste. In M. Gallagher & R. J. Nelson, *Handbook of psychology: Biological psychology* (Vol 3). New York: Wiley.

DiMatteo, M. R. (1997). Health behaviors and care decisions: An overview of professional-patient communications. In D. S. Gochman (Ed.), *Handbook of health behavior research.* New York: Plenum.

Dinges, D. F., Pack, F., Wiliams, K., Gillen, K. A., Powell, J. W., G. E., Aptowicz, C., & Pack, A. I. (1997). Cumulative sleepiness, mood disturbance, and psychomotor vigilance performance decrements during a week of sleep restricted to 4–5 hours per night. *Sleep, 20,* 267–273.

Dixon, R. A., & Cohen, A. L. (2003). Cognitive development in adulthood. In R. M. Lerner, M. A. Easterbrooks, et al. (Eds.), *Handbook of psychology: Developmental psychology* (Vol. 6, pp. 443–461). New York: Wiley.

Dixon, R. A., Rust, T. B., & Feltmate, S. E. (2007). Memory and aging: Selected research directions and application issues. *Canadian Psychology Psychologie Canadienne, 48,* 67–76.

Do, V. T. (2006). Asian American men and the media: The relationship between ethnic identity, self-esteem, and the endorsement of stereotypes. *Dissertation Abstracts International: Section B: The Sciences and Engineering, 67(6-B),* 3446.

Dobbins, A. C., Jeo, R. M., Fiser, J., & Allman, J. M. (1998, July 24). Distance modulation of neural activity in the visual cortex. *Science, 281,* 552–555.

Dobbs, D. (2006, April 2). A depression switch? *The New York Times,* B1.

Dobelle, W. H. (2000). Artificial vision for the blind by connecting a television camera to the visual cortex. *ASAIO Journal, 46,* 3–9.

Dodge, K. A. (2004). The nature-nurture debate and public policy. *Merrill-Palmer Quarterly, 50,* 418–427.

Dohrenwend, B. P., Turner, J. B., Turse, N. A., Adams, B. G., Koenen, K. C., & Marshall, R. (2006, August 18). The psychological risks of Vietnam for U.S. veterans: A revisit with new data and methods. *Science, 313,* 979–982.

Doi, T. (1990). The cultural assumptions of psychoanalysis. In J. W. Stigler, R. A. Shweder, & G. Herdt (Eds.), *Cultural psychology: Essays on comparative human development.* New York: Cambridge University Press.

Dolan, P., & White, M. P. (2007). How can measures of subjective well-being be used to inform public policy? *Perspectives on Psychological Science, 2,* 71–85.

Dolan, R. J. (2002, November 8). Emotion, cognition, and behavior. *Science, 298,* 1191–1194.

Dolbier, C. L., Smith, S. E., & Steinhardt, M. A. (2007). Relationships of protective factors to stress and symptoms of illness. *American Journal of Health Behavior, 31,* 423–433.

Dollard, J., Doob, L., Miller, N., Mower, O. H., & Sears, R. R. (1939). *Frustration and aggression.* New Haven, CT: Yale University Press.

Dollinger, S. J. (2003). Need for uniqueness, need for cognition and creativity. *Journal of Creative Behavior, 37,* 99–116.

Domhoff, G. W. (1996). *Finding meaning in dreams: A quantitative approach.* New York: Plenum Press.

Domhoff, G. W. (2001). A new neurocognitive theory of dreams. *Dreaming, 11,* 13–33.

Domhoff, G. W. (2003). *The scientific study of dreams: Neural networks, cognitive development, and content analysis.* Washington, DC: American Psychological Association.

Donahoe, J. W. (2003). Selectionism. In K. A. Lattal, & P. N. Chase (Eds.), *Behavior theory and philosophy.* New York: Kluwer Academic/Plenum Publishers.

Donahoe, J. W., & Vegas, R. (2004). Pavlovian Conditioning: The CSUR Relation. *Journal of Experimental Psychology: Animal Behavior Processes, 30,* 17–33.

Dong, M., Giles, W., Felitti, V., Dube, S. Williams, J., Chapman, D., and Anda, R. (2004). Insights into causal pathways for ischemic heart disease: Adverse childhood experiences study. *Circulation, 110,* 1761–1766.

Dooren, J. C. (2005, March 29). Talking yourself to sleep. *The Wall Street Journal,* pp. D1–D2.

Dorion, A. A. (2000). Hemispheric asymmetry and corpus callosum morphometry: A magnetic resonance imaging study. *Neuroscience Research, 36,* 9–13.

Dortch, S. (1996, October). Our aching heads. *American Demographics,* pp. 4–8.

Doty, R. L., Green, P. A., Ram, C., & Yankell, S. L. (1982). Communication of gender from human breath odors: Relationship to perceived intensity and pleasantness. *Hormones and Behavior, 16,* 13–22.

Dougall, A. L., & Baum, A. (2004). Psychoneuroimmunology and trauma. In P. P. Schnurr and B. L. Green (Eds.), *Trauma and health: Physical health consequences of exposure to extreme stress* (pp. 129–155). Washington, DC: American Psychological Association.

Douglas Brown, R., Goldstein, E., & Bjorklund, D. F. (2000). The history and zeitgeist of the repressed-false-memory debate: Scientific and sociological perspectives on suggestibility and childhood memory. In D. F. Bjorklund (Ed.), *False-memory creation in children and adults: Theory, research, and implications* (pp. 1–30). Mahwah, NJ: Lawrence Erlbaum.

Doumas, M., Praamstra, P., & Wing, A. M. (2005). Low frequency rTMS effects on sensorimotor synchronization. *Experimental Brain Research, 88,* 1–8.

Dovidio, J. F. (2001). On the nature of contemporary prejudice: The third wave. *Journal of Social Issues, 57,* 829–849.

Dovidio, J. F., & Gaertner, S. L. (2006). A multi-level perspective on prejudice: Crossing disciplinary boundaries. In P. A. M. Van Lange, *Bridging social psychology: Benefits of transdisciplinary approaches.* Mahwah, NJ: Lawrence Erlbaum Associates.

Dovidio, J. F., & Penner, L. A. (2004). Helping and altruism. In M. B. Brewer & M. Hewstone (Eds.), *Emotion and motivation.* Malden, MA: Blackwell Publishers.

Dovidio, J. F., Gaertner, S. L., & Kawakami, K. (2003). Intergroup contact: The past, present, and the future. *Group Processes and Intergroup Relations, 6,* 5–20.

Dovidio, J. F., Gaertner, S. L., & Pearson, A. R. (2005). On the nature of prejudice: The psychological foundations of hate. In R. J. Sternberg (Ed.), *Psychology of hate.* Washington, DC: American Psychological Association.

Dovidio, J. F., Kawakami, K., & Gaertner, S. L. (2000). Reducing contemporary prejudice: Combating explicit and implicit bias at the individual and intergroup level. In S. Oskamp (Ed.), *Reducing prejudice and discrimination: The Claremont Symposium on Applied Social Psychology* (pp. 137–163). Mahwah, NJ: Erlbaum.

Dovidio, J. F., Piliavin, J. A., Schroeder, D.. A., & Penner, L. A. (2006). *The social psychology of prosocial behavior.* Mahwah, NJ: Lawrence Erlbaum Associates.

Doyle, K. A. (2002). Rational Emotive Behavior Therapy and its application to women's groups. In W. Dryden, & M. Neenan (Eds.), *Rational emotive behaviour group therapy.* London: Whurr Publishers.

Dreman, S. (1997). *The family on the threshold of the 21st century.* Mahwah, NJ: Erlbaum.

Dressler, W. W., & Oths, K. S. (1997). Cultural determinants of health behavior. In D. S. Gochman (Ed.), *Handbook of health behavior research.* New York: Plenum.

Drewes, A. A. (2005). Play in selected cultures: Diversity and universality. In E. Gil and A. A. Drewes, *Cultural issues in play therapy* (pp. 26–71). New York: Guilford Press.

Drob, S. (2005). The mystical symbol: Some comments on Ankor, Giegerich, Scholem, and Jung. *Journal of Jungian Theory & Practice, 7,* 25–29.

Drogin, E. (2005). Civil and criminal trial matters. In E. Drogin, *Law & mental health professionals: Kentucky.* Washington, DC: American Psychological Association.

Druckman, D., & Bjork, R. A. (1991). *In the mind's eye: Enhancing human performance.* Washington, DC: National Academy Press.

Drummond, D. C., Tiffany, S. T., Glautier, S., & Remington, B. (Eds.). (1995). *Addictive behaviour: Cue exposure theory and practice.* Chichester, England: Wiley.

Dryden, W. (1999). *Rational emotive behavior therapy: A training manual.* New York: Springer.

Dryden, W. (2003). *Overcoming depression.* London: Sheldon Press.

DuBois, J. M. (2002). When is informed consent appropriate in educational research? *IRB: A Review of Human Subjects Research, 24,* 1–8.

Dubovsky, S. (1999, February 25). Tuning in to manic depression. *HealthNews, 5,* p. 8.

Ducharme, J. M., Sanjuan, E., & Drain, T. (2007). Errorless compliance training: Success-focused behavioral treatment of children with Asperger syndrome. *Behavior Modification, 31,* 329–344.

Duckworth, A., and Seligman, M. (2005). Self-discipline outdoes IQ in predicting academic performance of adolescents. *Psychological Science, 16,* 939–944.

Duffy, M., Gillig, S. E., Tureen, R. M., & Ybarra, M. A. (2002). A critical look at the DSM-IV. *Journal of Individual Psychology, 58,* 363–373.

Dufur, M. J., & Troutman, K. P. (2006). Family structure and adolescent labor market participation: Examining the motives for and effects of at-risk students' work for pay during high school. In L. Kowalski-Jones, & N. H. Wolfinger, *Fragile families and the marriage agenda.* New York: Springer Science + Business Media.

Dugger, C. W. (1996, December 28). Tug of taboos: African genital rite vs. U.S. law. *The New York Times,* pp. 1, 9.

Dukakis, K., and Tye, L. (2006, September 18). I feel good, I feel fine. *Newsweek,* 62–63.

Duke, M., & Nowicki, S., Jr. (1979). *Abnormal psychology: Perspectives on being different.* Monterey, CA: Brooks/Cole.

Duncan, J. (2005). Frontal lobe function and general intelligence: Why it matters. *Cortex, 41,* 215–217.

Duncan, J., Seitz, R. J., Kolodny, J., Bor, D., Herzog, H., Ahmed, A., Newell, F. N., & Emslie, H. (2000, July 21). A neural basis for general intelligence. *Science, 289,* 457–459.

Duncan, P. D., et al. (1985). The effects of pubertal timing on body image, school behavior, and deviance [Special Issue: Time of maturation and psychosocial functioning in adolescence: I]. *Journal of Youth and Adolescence, 14,* 227–235.

Duncker, K. (1945). On problem solving. *Psychological Monographs, 58* (5, whole no. 270).

Duncombe, J., Harrison, K., Allan, G. & Marsden, D. (2004). *The state of affairs: Explorations in infidelity and commitment.* Mahwah, NJ: Lawrence Erlbaum Associates Publishers.

Dunham, R. M., Kidwell, J. S., & Wilson, S. M. (1986). Rites of passage at adolescence: A ritual process paradigm. *Journal of Adolescent Research, 1,* 139–153.

Duret, F., Brelen, M. E., & Lambert, V. (2006). Object localization, discrimination, and grasping with the optic nerve visual prosthesis. *Restorative Neurology and Neuroscience, 24,* 31–40.

Durik, A. M., Hyde, J. S., & Marks, A. C. Ethnicity and gender stereotypes of emotion. *Sex Roles, 54,* 429–445.

Dutton, D. G., & Aron, A. P. (1974). Some evidence for heightened sexual attraction under conditions of high anxiety. *Journal of Personality and Social Psychology, 30,* 510–517.

Duvarci, S., ben Mamou, C., and Nader, K. (2006). Extinction is not a sufficient condition to prevent fear memories from undergoing reconsolidation in the basolateral amygdala. *European Journal of Neuroscience, 24,* 249–260.

Dweck, C. S., Mangels, J., & Good, C. (2004). Motivational Effects on attention, cognition, and performance. In D. Y. Dai & R. J. Sternberg (Eds.), *Motivation, emotion, and cognition: Integrated perspectives on intellectual functioning.* Mahwah, NJ: Erlbaum. Annual Meeting of the American Psychological Society, May 2004, Chicago.

Dworkin, J. B., Larson, R., & Hansen, D. (2003). Adolescents' accounts of growth experiences in youth activities. *Journal of Youth and Adolescence, 32,* 17–26.

Eagles, J. M. (2001). SAD—help arrives with the dawn? *Lancet, 358,* p. 2100.

Eagly, A., & Chaiken, S. (1998). Attitude structure and function. In D. T. Gilbert & S. T. Fiske (Eds.), *Handbook of social psychology* (Vol. 1, 4th ed.). New York: McGraw-Hill.

Eagly, A. H., Beall, A. & Sternberg, R. S. (Eds.). (2004). *The psychology of gender* (2nd ed.). New York: Guilford Press.

Eagly, A. H., & Wood, W. (2003). The origins of sex differences in human behavior: Evolved dispositions versus social roles. In C. B. Travis (Ed.), *Evolution, gender, and rape* (pp. 265–304). Cambridge, MA: MIT.

Eaker, E. D., Sullivan, L. M., Kelly-Hayes, M., D'Agostino, R. B., Sr., & Benjamin, E. J. (2004). Anger and hostility predict the development of atrial fibrillation in men in the Framingham Offspring Study. *Circulation, 109,* 1267–1271.

Earley, J. (1999). *Interactive group therapy: Integrating interpersonal, action-oriented and psychodynamic approaches.* New York: Brunner/Mazel.

Ebbinghaus, H. (1885/1913). *Memory: A contribution to experimental psychology* (H. A. Roger & C. E. Bussenius, Trans.). New York: Columbia University Press.

Eberhard, K. M., Cutting, J. C., & Bock, K. (2005). Making syntax of sense: Number agreement in sentence production. *Psychological Review, 112,* 531–559.

Eberhardt, J. L., Goff, P. A., Purdie, V. J., & Davies, P. G. (2004). Seeing black: Race, crime, and visual processing. *Journal of Personality and Social Psychology, 87,* 876–893.

Ebstein, R. P., Benjamin, J., & Belmaker, R. H. (2003). Behavioral genetics, genomics, and personality. In R. Plomin & J. C. DeFries (Eds.), *Behavioral genetics in the postgenomic era* (pp. 365–388). Washington, DC: American Psychological Association.

Eccles, J. S., Lord, S. E., & Roeser, R. W. (1996). Round holes, square pegs, rocky roads, and sore feet: The impact of stage-environment fit on young adolescents' experiences in schools and families. In D. Cicchetti & S. L. Toth (Eds.), *Adolescence: Opportunities and challenges: Rochester symposium on developmental psychopathology* (Vol. 7). Rochester, NY: University of Rochester Press.

Ecenbarger, W. (1993, April 1). America's new merchants of death. *The Reader's Digest,* p. 50.

Eckardt, M. H. (2005). Karen Horney: A portrait: The 120th anniversary, Karen Horney, September 16, 1885. *American Journal of Psychoanalysis, 65,* 95–101.

Ecklund, A. (1999, July 12). Cochlear implant. *People Weekly,* p. 68.

Edwards, R. R., & Fillingim, R. B. (2007). Self-reported pain sensitivity: Lack of correlation with pain threshold and tolerance. *European Journal of Pain, 11,* 594–598.

Edinger, J. D., Wohlgemuth, W. K., Radtke, R. A., Marsh, G. R., & Quillian, R. E. (2001). Cognitive behavioral therapy for treatment of chronic primary insomnia A randomized controlled trial. *Journal of the American Medical Association, 285,* 1856–1864.

Egan, K. (2005). Students' development in theory and practice: The doubtful role of research. *Harvard Educational Review, 75,* 25–41.

Eichenbaum, H. (2004). Toward an information processing framework for memory representation by the hippocampus. In M. S. Gazzaniga (Ed.), *Cognitive neurosciences* (3rd ed., pp. 679–690). Cambridge, MA: MIT.

Einarsson, C., & Granstroem, K. (2002). Gender-biased interaction in the classroom: The influence of gender and age in the relationship between teacher and pupil. *Scandinavian Journal of Educational Research, 46,* 117–127.

Eisenberg, N., Guthrie, I. K., & Cumberland, A. (2002). Prosocial development in early adulthood: A longitudinal study. *Journal of Personality and Social Psychology, 82,* 993–1006.

Eizenberg, M. M., & Zaslavsky, O. (2004). Students' verification strategies for combinatorial problems. *Mathematical Thinking and Learning, 6,* 15–36.

Ekman, P. (1972). Universals and cultural differences in facial expressions of emotion. In J. Cole (Ed.), *Darwin and facial expression: A cen-*

tury of research in review (pp. 169–222). New York: Academic Press.

Ekman, P. (1994a). All emotions are basic. In P. Ekman & R. J. Davidson (Eds.), *The nature of emotion: Fundamental questions.* New York: Oxford University Press.

Ekman, P. (1994b). Strong evidence for universals in facial expressions: A reply to Russell's mistaken critique. *Psychological Bulletin, 115,* 268–287.

Ekman, P. (2003). *Emotions revealed: Recognizing faces and feelings to improve communication and emotional life.* New York: Times Books.

Ekman, P., & O'Sullivan, M. (1991). Facial expression: Methods, means, and moues. In R. S. Feldman & B. Rimé (Eds.), *Fundamentals of nonverbal behavior.* Cambridge, England: Cambridge University Press.

Ekman, P., Davidson, R. J., & Friesen, W. V. (1990). Emotional expression and brain physiology: II. The Duchenne smile. *Journal of Personality and Social Psychology, 58,* 342–353.

Ekman, P., Levenson, R. W., & Friesen, W. V. (1983, September 16). Autonomic nervous system activity distinguishes among emotions. *Science, 223,* 1208–1210.

Ekstrom, S. R. (2004). The mind beyond our immediate awareness: Freudian, Jungian, and cognitive models of the unconscious. *Journal of Analytical Psychology, 49,* 657–682.

Elfenbein, H. A. (2005). It takes one to know one better: Controversy about the cultural in-group advantage in communicating emotion as a theoretical rather than methodological issue. In U. Hess & P. Philippot (Eds.), *Group dynamics and emotional expression.* Cambridge, England: Cambridge University Press.

Elfenbein, H. A., & Ambady, N. (2003). Universals and cultural differences in recognizing emotions. *Current Directions in Psychological Science, 12,* 159–164.

Elfenbein, H. A., Beaupré, M., & Lévesque, M. (2007). Toward a dialect theory: Cultural differences in the expression and recognition of posed facial expressions. *Emotion, 7,* 131–146.

Elfenbein, H. A., Mandal, M., Ambady, N., Harizuka, S., & Kumar, S. (2004). Hemifacial differences in the in-group advantage in emotion recognition. *Cognition and Emotion, 18,* 613–629.

Elfhag, K., Tynelius, P., & Rasmussen, F. (2007). Sugar-sweetened and artificially sweetened soft drinks in association to restrained, external and emotional eating. *Physiology & Behavior, 91,* 191–195.

El-Hai, J. (2005). *The lobotomist: A maverick medical genius and his tragic quest to rid the world of mental illness.* New York: Wiley.

Elkind, D. (1985) Cognitive development and adolescent disabilities. *Journal of Adolescent Health Care, 6,* 84–89.

Elkind, D. (1998). *All grown up and no place to go: Teenagers in crisis.* New York: Da Capo Press.

Elkins, G., Marcus, J., Bates, J., Hasan, R. M., & Cook, T. (2006). Intensive hypnotherapy for smoking cessation: a prospective study. *International Journal of Clinical Experimental Hypnosis, 54,* 303–315.

Elkins, G. R., & Rajab, M. H. (2004). Clinical hypnosis for smoking cessation: Preliminary results of a three-session intervention. *International Journal of Clinical and Experimental Hypnosis, 52,* 73–81.

Ellason, J. W., & Ross, C. A. (2004). SCL-90-R norms for dissociative identity disorder. *Journal of Trauma and Dissociation, 5,* 85–91.

Elliott, A. (2002). *Psychoanalytic theory: An introduction* (2nd ed.). Durham, NC: Duke University Press.

Elliott, J., Berman, H., & Kim, S. (2002). Critical ethnography of Korean Canadian women's menopause experience. *Health Care for Women International, 23,* 377–388.

Ellis, A. (1974). *Growth through reason.* Hollywood, CA: Wilshire Books. Ellis, A. (2002). *Overcoming resistance: A rational emotive behavior therapy integrated approach* (2nd ed.). New York: Springer.

Ellis, A. (2000). *How to control your anger before it controls you.* New York: Citadel.

Ellis, A. (2004). Expanding the ABCs of rational emotive behavior therapy. In A. Freeman, M. J. Mahoney, P. Devito, & D. Martin (Eds.), *Cognition and psychotherapy* (2nd ed.). New York: Springer Publishing Co.

Ellis, B. J., & Bjorklund, D. F. (2005). *Origins of the social mind: Evolutionary psychology and child development.* New York, NY: Guilford.

El-Mallakh, R. S., & Abraham, H. D. (2007). MDMA (Ecstasy). *Annals of Clinical Psychiatry, 19,* 45–52.

Elsner, D., (2006). Just another reproductive technology? The ethics of human reproductive cloning as an experimental medical procedure. *Journal of Medical Ethics, 32,* 596–600.

Embretson, S. E. (2005). Measuring human intelligence with artificial intelligence: Adaptive item generation. In R. J. Sternberg & J. E. Pretz (Eds.), *Cognition and intelligence: Identifying the mechanisms of the mind* (pp. 251–267). New York: Cambridge University Press.

Emick, J., & Welsh, M. (2005). Association between formal operational thought and executive function as measured by the Tower of Hanoi-Revised. *Learning and Individual Differences, 15,* 177–188.

Enard, W., Przeworski, M., Fisher, S. E., Lai, C. S. L., Wiebe, V., Kitano, T., Monaco, A. P., & Pääbo, S. (2002, August 14). Molecular evolution of FOXP2, a gene involved in speech and language. *Nature, 300,* 14.

Endres, T., & Fendt, M. (2007). Conditioned behavioral responses to a context paired with the predator odor trimethylthiazoline. *Behavioral Neuroscience, 121,* 594–601.

Engen, T. (1987). Remembering odors and their names. *American Scientist, 75,* 497–503.

Engle-Friedman, M., Baker, A., & Bootzin, R. R. (1985). Reports of wakefulness during EEG identified stages of sleep. *Sleep Research, 14,* 152.

Engler, J., & Goleman, D. (1992). *The consumer's guide to psychotherapy.* New York: Simon & Schuster.

Enserink, M. (1999, April 9). Can the placebo be the cure? *Science, 284,* 238–240.

Enserink, M. (2000, April, 21). Are placebo-controlled drug trials ethical? *Science, 288,* 416.

Epstein, R. (1987). The spontaneous interconnection of four repertoires of behavior in a pigeon. *Journal of Comparative Psychology, 101,* 197–201.

Epstein, R. (1996). *Cognition, creativity, and behavior: Selected essays.* Westport, CT: Praeger/ Greenwood.

Eranti, S. V., & McLoughlin, D. M. (2003). Electroconvulsive therapy: State of the art. *British Journal of Psychiatry, 182,* 8–9.

Erikson, E.H. (1963). *Childhood and society.* New York: Norton.

Ervik, S., Abdelnoor, M., & Heier, M. S. (2006). Health-related quality of life in narcolepsy. *Acta Neurologica Scandinavica, 114,* 198–204.

Etchegary, H. (2004). Psychological aspects of predictive genetic-test decision: What do we know so far? *Analyses of Social Issues and Public Policy, 4,* 13–31.

Evans, A. M. (2007). Transference in the nurse-patient relationship. *Journal of Psychiatric and Mental Health Nursing, 14,* 189–195.

Evans, D. E., & Rothbart, M. K. (2007). Developing a model for adult temperament. *Journal of Research in Personality, 41,* 868–888.

Evans, J. B. T. (2004). Informal reasoning: Theory and method. *Canadian Journal of Experimental Psychology, 58,* 69–74.

Evans, J. B. T., & Feeney, A. (2004). The role of prior belief in reasoning. In J. P. Leighton (Ed.), *Nature of reasoning.* New York: Cambridge University Press.

Evcik, D., Kavuncu, V., Cakir, T., Subasi, V., & Yaman, M. (2007). Laser therapy in the treatment of carpal tunnel syndrome: A randomized controlled trial. *Photomedical Laser Surgery, 25,* 34–39.

Everly, G. S., Jr., & Lating, J. M. (2007). Psychotherapy: A cognitive perspective. In A. Monat, R. S. Lazarus, & G. Reevy, *The Praeger handbook on stress and coping* (Vol. 2). Westport, CT: Praeger Publishers/ Greenwood Publishing.

Eysenck, H. J. (1990). Biological dimensions of personality. In L. A. Pervin (Ed.), *Handbook of personality: Theory and research,* p. 246. New York: Guilford Press.

Eysenck, H. J. (1994). The Big Five or giant three: Criteria for a paradigm. In C. F. Halverson, Jr., G. A. Kohnstamm, & R. P. Martin (Eds.), *The developing structure of temperament and personality from infancy to adulthood.* Hillsdale, NJ: Erlbaum.

Eysenck, H. J. (1995). *Eysenck on extraversion.* New York: Wiley.

Eysenck, H. J., Barrett, P., Wilson, G., & Jackson, C. (1992). Primary trait measurement of the 21 components of the P-E-N system. *European Journal of Psychological Assessment, 8,* 109–117.

Ezzell, C. (September 2002). Clocking cultures. *Scientific American,* pp. 74–75.

Fagan, J. F., & Holland, C. R. (2002). Equal opportunity and racial differences in IQ. *Intelligence, 30,* 361–387.

Fagan, J. F., & Holland, C. R. (2007). Racial equality in intelligence: Predictions from a theory of intelligence as processing. *Intelligence, 35,* 319–334.

Falck-Ytter, T., & Gredebäck, G. (2006). Infants predict other people's action goals. *Nature Neuroscience, 9,* 878–879.

Falk, D., Forese, N., Sade, D. S., & Dudek, B. C. (1999). Sex differences in brain/body relationships of Rhesus monkeys and humans. *Journal of Human Evolution, 36,* 233–238.

Fallon, A. (2006). Informed consent in the practice of group psychotherapy. *International Journal of Group Psychotherapy, 56,* 431–453.

Fallon, B. A., & Feinstein, S. (2001). Hypochondriasis. In K. A. Phillips (Ed.), *Somatoform and factitious disorders.* Washington, DC: American Psychiatric Association.

Fanselow, M. S., & Poulos, A. M. (2005). The neuroscience of mammalian associative learning. *Annual Review of Psychology, 56,* 207–234.

Farber, B. A., Brink, D. C., & Raskin, P. M. (Eds.). (1996). *The psychotherapy of Carl Rogers: Cases and commentary.* New York: Guilford Press.

Farkas, R. (2004, February 24). Ray Farkas stayed awake during brain surgery for Parkinson's—and filmed it. *People,* pp. 99–100.

Farley, F. (1986, May). The big T in personality. *Psychology Today,* pp. 44–52.

Farrell, E. F. (2005, July 15). To test or not to test? *The Chronicle of Higher Education*, pp. A39–A40.

Farver, J. M., & Lee-Shin, Y. (2000). Acculturation and Korean-American children's social and play behavior. *Social Development, 9*, 316–336.

Farver, J. M., Kim, Y. K., & Lee-Shin, Y. (1995). Cultural differences in Korean-and Anglo-American preschoolers' social interaction and play behaviors. *Child Development, 66*, 1088–1099.

Fearing, V. G., & Clark, J. (Eds.). (2000). *Individuals in context: A practical guide to client-centered practice.* Chicago: Slack Publishing.

Fee, E., Brown, T. M., Lazarus, J., & Theerman, P. (2002). Exploring acupuncture: Ancient ideas, modern techniques. *American Journal of Public Health, 92*, 1592.

Feeley, T. H. (2002). Comment on halo effects in rating and evaluation research [Special issue: Statistical and methodological issues in communication research]. *Human Communication Research, 28*, 578–586.

Feinberg, A. W. (2002, April). Homo-cysteine may raise Alzheimer's risk: A physician's perspective. *HealthNews*, p. 4.

Feingold, A. (1994). Gender differences in personality: A meta-analysis. *Psychological Bulletin, 116*, 429–456.

Feldhusen, J. F., (2006). The role of the knowledge base in creative thinking. In J. C. Kaufman, & J. Baer, *Creativity and reason in cognitive development.* New York: Cambridge University Press.

Feldman, D. H. (2003). Cognitive development in childhood. In R. M. Lerner, M. A. Easterbrooks, et al. (Eds.), *Handbook of psychology: Developmental psychology* (Vol. 6, pp. 195–210). New York: Wiley.

Feldman, D. H. (2004). Piaget's stages: The unfinished symphony of cognitive development. *New Ideas in Psychology, 22*, 175–231.

Feldman, R. S. (Ed.). (1982). *Development of nonverbal behavior in children.* New York: Springer-Verlag.

Feldman, R. S. (Ed.). (1993). *Applications of nonverbal behavioral theories and research.* Hillsdale, NJ: Erlbaum.

Feldman, R. S. (2003). *P.O.W.E.R. learning* (2nd ed.). New York: McGraw-Hill.

Feldman, R. S., & Tyler, J. M. (2005). *Lying to look good: Using deceptive behavior as a self-presentational strategy.* Mahwah, NJ, Lawrence Erlbaum.

Feldman, R. S., Coats, E. J., & Schwartzberg, S. (1994). *Case studies and critical thinking about psychology.* New York: McGraw-Hill.

Feldman, R. S., Forrest, J. A., & Happ, B. R. (2002). Self-presentation and verbal deception: Do self-presenters lie more? *Basic and Applied Social Psychology, 24*, 163–170.

Feldt, L. S. (2004). Estimating the reliability of a test battery composite or a test score based on weighted item scoring. *Measurement & Evaluation in Counseling & Development, 37*, 184–191.

Fellous, J. M., & Arbib, M. A. (2005). *Who needs emotions? The brain meets the robot.* New York: Oxford University Press, 2005.

Fenn, K. M., Nusbaum, H. C., & Margoliash, D. (2003, October 9). Consolidation during sleep of perceptual learning of spoken language. *Nature, 425*, 614–616.

Fenter, V. L. (2006). Concerns about Prozac and direct-to-consumer advertising of prescription drugs. *International Journal of Risk & Safety in Medicine, 18*, 1–7.

Feret, A., Steinweg, S., Griffin, H. C., & Glover, S. (2007). Macular degeneration: types, causes, and possible interventions. *Geriatric Nursing, 28*, 387–392.

Fernandez, A. M., Vera-Villarroel, P., & Sierra, J. C. (2007). Distress in response to emotional and sexual infidelity: evidence of evolved gender differences in Spanish students. *Journal of Psychology: Interdisciplinary and Applied, 141*, 17–24.

Festinger, L. (1957). *A theory of cognitive dissonance.* Stanford, CA: Stanford University Press.

Festinger, L., & Carlsmith, J. M. (1959). Cognitive consequences of forced compliance. *Journal of Abnormal and Social Psychology, 58*, 203–210.

Festinger, L., Schachter, S., & Back, K. W. (1950). *Social pressure in informal groups.* New York: Harper.

Fichtenberg, C. M., & Glantz, S. A. (2006). Association of the California tobacco control program with declines in cigarette consumption and mortality from heart disease. In K. E. Warner, *Tobacco control policy.* San Francisco, CA: Jossey-Bass.

Fields, R. D. (2004, April). The other half of the brain. *Scientific American*, pp. 55–61.

Fields, R. D. (2005, February). Making memories stick. *Scientific American*, 75–81.

Fields-Meyer, T. (1995, September 25). Having their say. *People*, 50–60.

Fields-Meyer, T. (1999, October 25). The whiz kids. *People*, pp. 59–63.

Fields-Meyer, T., & Haederle, M. (1996, June 24). Married to a stranger. *People*, pp. 48–51.

Fields-Meyer, T., & Lambert, P. (2004, November 15). Land of the Brave: These extraordinary Americans took on riptides, savage dogs—even an avalanche. *People Weekly*, p. 100.

Fields-Meyer, T., & Wihlborg, U. (2003, March 17). Gender jump. *People Magazine*, 109–111.

Fine, L. (1994). Personal communication.

Fine, R., & Fine, L. (2003). *Basic chess endings.* New York: Random House.

Fineran, S. (2002). Adolescents at work: Gender issues and sexual harassment. *Violence against Women, 8*, 953–967.

Fingelkurts, A., Fingelkurts, A. A., & Kallio, S. (2007). Hypnosis induces a changed composition of brain oscillations in EEG: A case study. *Contemporary Hypnosis, 24*, 3–18.

Fink, B., Manning, J. T., & Williams J. H. G. (2007). The 2nd to 4th digit ratio and developmental psychopathology in school-aged children. *Personality and Individual Differences, 42*, 369–379.

Fink, G. (Ed.). (2000) *Encyclopedia of stress.* New York: Academic Press.

Fink, M. (1999). *Electroshock: Restoring the mind.* New York: Oxford University Press.

Fink, M. (2000). Electroshock revisited. *American Scientist, 88*, 162–167.

Finke, R. A. (1995). Creative insight and preinventive forms. In R. J. Sternberg & J. E. Davidson (Eds.), *The nature of insight.* Cambridge, MA: MIT.

Finkelhor, D., & Jones, L.M. (2004, January). Explanations for the decline in child sexual abuse cases. *Juvenile Justice Bulletin.* Washington, DC: Office of Juvenile Justice and Delinquency Prevention.

Finkelhor, D., Ormrod, R., & Turner, H. (2005). The victimization of children and youth: A comprehensive, national survey. *Child Maltreatment: Journal of the American Professional Society on the Abuse of Children, 10*, 5–25.

Finkler, K. (2004). Traditional healers in Mexico: The effectiveness of spiritual practices. In U. P. Gielen, J. M. Fish, & J. G. Draguns (Eds.), *Handbook of culture, therapy, and healing.* Mahwah, NJ: Lawrence Erlbaum Associates.

Finlay, F. O., Jones, R., & Coleman, J. (2002). Is puberty getting earlier? The views of doctors and teachers. *Child: Care, Health and Development, 28*, 205–209.

Finley, C. L., & Cowley, B. J. (2005). The effects of a consistent sleep schedule on time taken to achieve sleep. *Clinical Case Studies, 4*, 304–311.

Finney, M. L., Stoney, C. M., & Engebretson, T. O. (2002). Hostility and anger expression in African American and European American men is associated with cardiovascular and lipid reactivity. *Psychophysiology, 39*, 340–349.

Firestein, B. A. (Ed.). (1996). *Bisexuality: The psychology and politics of an invisible minority.* Thousand Oaks, CA: Sage.

First, M. B., Frances, A., & Pincus, H. A. (2002). *DSM-IV-TR handbook of differential diagnosis.* Washington, DC: American Psychiatric Publishing.

Fischer, K. W., Shaver, P. R., & Carnochan, P. (1990). How emotions develop and how they organize development. *Cognition and Emotion, 4*, 81–127.

Fish, J. M. (Ed.) (2002). *Race and intelligence: Separating science from myth.* Mahwah, NJ: Erlbaum.

Fishbach, A., Dhar, R., & Zhang, Y. (2006). Subgoals as substitutes or complements: The role of goal accessibility. *Journal of Personality and Social Psychology, 91*, 232–242.

Fisher, C. B. (2003). *Decoding the ethics code: A practical guide for psychologists.* Thousand Oaks, CA: Sage.

Fisher, C. B., Hoagwood, K., Boyce, C., Duster, T., Frank, D. A., Grisso, T., Levine, R. J., Macklin, R., Spencer, M. B., Takanishi, R., Trimble, J. E., & Zayas, L. H. (2002). Research ethics for mental health science involving ethnic minority children and youths. *American Psychologist, 57*, 1024–1040.

Fisher, J. E., & O'Donohue, W. T. (2006). *Practitioner's guide to evidence-based psychotherapy.* New York: Springer Science + Business Media.

Fisk, J. E., Bury, A. S., & Holden, R. (2006). Reasoning about complex probabilistic concepts in childhood. *Scandinavian Journal of Psychology, 47*, 497–504.

Fisk, J. E., & Sharp, C. (2002). Syllogistic reasoning and cognitive ageing. *Quarterly Journal of Experimental Psychology: Human Experimental Psychology, 55A*, 1273–1293.

Fiske, S. T. (2002). What we know now about bias and intergroup conflict, the problem of the century. *Current Directions in Psychological Science, 11*, 123–128.

Fiske, S. T., & Taylor, S. E. (1991). *Social cognition* (2nd ed.). New York: McGraw-Hill.

Fitch, K. L., & Sanders, R. E. (2005). *Handbook of language and social interaction.* Mahwah, NJ: Lawrence Erlbaum Associates.

Fitzgerald, H., Mann, T., Cabrera, N., & Wong, M. M. (2003). Diversity in caregiving contexts. In R. M. Lerner, M. A. Easterbrooks, et al. (Eds.), *Handbook of psychology: Developmental psychology* (Vol. 6, pp. 135–167). New York: Wiley.

Fitzgerald, L. F. (2003). Sexual harassment and social justice: Reflections on the distance yet to go. *American Psychologist, 58*, 915–924.

Flam, F. (1991, June 14). Queasy riders. *Science, 252*, 1488.

Flavell, J. H. (2002). Development of children's knowledge about the mental world. In W. W. Hartup & R. K. Silbereisen (Eds.), *Growing points in developmental science: An introduction*, pp. 102–122. New York, NY: Psychology Press.

Flavell, S. W., Cowan, C. W., Kim, T., Greer, P. L., Lin, Y., Paradis, S., Griffith, E. C., Hu, L. S., Chen, C., & Greenberg, M. E. (2006, February 17). Activity-dependent regulation of MEF2 transcription factors suppresses excitatory synapse number. *Science, 311*, 1008–1010.

Fleischman, D. A., Wilson, R. S., Gabrieli, J. D. E., Bienias, J. L., & Bennett, D. A. (2004). A longitudinal study of implicit and explicit memory in old persons. *Psychology and Aging, 19*, 617–625.

Fleming, J. (2000). Affirmative action and standardized test scores. *Journal of Negro Education, 69*, 27–37.

Flynn, J. R. (1999). Searching for justice: The discovery of IQ gains over time. *American Psychologist, 54*, 5–20.

Flynn, J. R. (2000). IQ gains and fluid g. *American Psychologist, 55*, 543.

Foderaro, L. W. (2006, February 16). Westchester lawyer, his memory lost, is found in Chicago shelter after 6 months. *The New York Times*, p. B3.

Fogarty, J. S., & Young, G. A., Jr. (2000). Patient-physician communication. *Journal of the American Medical Association, 289*, 92.

Folkman, S., & Moskowitz, J. T. (2000). Stress, positive emotion, and coping. *Current Directions in Psychological Science, 9*, 115–118

Folkman, S., & Moskowitz, J. T. (2004). Coping: Pitfalls and promise. *Annual Review of Psychology, 55*, 745–774.

Follett, K., & Hess, T. M. (2002). Aging, cognitive complexity, and the fundamental attribution error. *Journal of Gerontology: Series B: Psychological Sciences and Social Sciences, 57B*, P312–P323.

Forbes, G. B., Jung, J., & Haas, K. B. (2006). Benevolent sexism and cosmetic use: A replication with three college samples and one adult sample. *Journal of Social Psychology, 146*, 635–640.

Ford, C. S., & Beach, F. A. (1951). *Patterns of sexual behavior*. New York: Harper.

Forer, B. (1949). The fallacy of personal validation: A classroom demonstration of gullibility. *Journal of Abnormal and Social Psychology, 44*, 118–123.

Forgas, J. P., & Laham, S. M. (2005). The interaction between affect and motivation in social judgments and behavior. In J. P. Forgas, K. P. Williams, S. M. Laham (Eds.), *Social motivation: Conscious and unconscious processes*. New York: Cambridge University Press.

Forlenza, M. J., & Baum, A. (2004). Psychoneuroimmunology. In T. J. Boll & R. G. Frank (Eds.), *Handbook of clinical health psychology: Volume 3. Models and perspectives in health psychology*. Washington, DC: American Psychological Association.

Foster, K. M. (2005). Introduction: John Uzo Ogbu (1939–2003): How do you ensure the fair consideration of a complex ancestor? Multiple approaches to assessing the work and legacy of John Uzo Ogbu. *International Journal of Qualitative Studies in Education, 18*, 559–564.

Foulds, J., Gandhi, K. K., & Steinberg, M. B. (2006). Factors associated with quitting smoking at a tobacco dependence treatment clinic. *American Journal of Health Behavior, 30*, 400–412.

Fountas, K. N., & Smith, J. R. (2007). Historical evolution of stereotactic amygdalotomy for the management of severe aggression. *Journal of Neurosurgery, 106*, 716–713.

Fountoulakis, K. N., Vieta, E., Sanchez-Moreno, J., Kaprinis, S. G., Goikolea, J. M., & Kaprinis, G. S. (2005). Treatment guidelines for bipolar disorder: A critical review. *Journal of Affective Disorders, 86*, 1–10.

Fowler, F. J., Jr. (2001). *Survey research methods*. Thousand Oaks, CA: Sage.

Fowler, R. D. (February 2002). APA's directory tells us who we are. *Monitor on Psychology*, 9.

Fox, C. R. (2006). The availability heuristic in the classroom: How soliciting more criticism can boost your course ratings. *Judgment and Decision Making, 1*, 86–90.

Fox, S., & Spector, P. E. (2000). Relations of emotional intelligence, practical intelligence, general intelligence, and trait affectivity with interview outcomes: It's not all just "G." *Journal of Organizational Behavior, 21*, 203–220.

Fraley, R. C., & Spieker, S. J. (2003). Are infant attachment patterns continuously or categorically distributed? A taxometric analysis of strange situation behavior. *Developmental Psychology, 39*, 387–404.

Frances, A., First, M. B., & Pincus, H. A. (1995). *DSM-IV guidebook*. Washington, DC: American Psychiatric Press.

Frank, L. R. (2002). Electroshock: A crime against the spirit. *Ethical Human Sciences and Services, 4*, 63–71.

Frankenberg, W. K., et al., 1992. *Denver II training manual*. Denver: Denver Developmental Materials.

Frankenberger, K. D. (2004). Adolescent egocentrism, risk perceptions, and sensation seeking among smoking and nonsmoking youth. *Journal of Adolescent Research, 19*, 576–590.

Franklin, A., Pilling, M., & Davies, I. (2005). The nature of infant color categorization: Evidence from eye movements on a target decision task. *Journal of Experimental Child Psychology, 91*, 227–248.

Franko, D., and Striegel-Moore, R. (2002). The role of body dissatisfaction as a risk factor for depression in adolescent girls: Are the differences Black and White? *Journal of Psychosomatic Research, 53*, 975–983.

Franks, D. D., & Smith, T. S. (1999) (Eds.). *Mind, brain, and society: Toward a neuro-sociology of emotion*. Stamford, CT: JAI Press.

Franzek, E., & Beckmann, H. (1996). Gene-environment interaction in schizophrenia: Season-of-birth effect reveals etiologically different subgroups. *Psychopathology, 29*, 14–26.

Frasure-Smith, N., Lesperance, F., & Talajic, M. (2000). The prognostic importance of depression, anxiety, anger, and social support following myocardial infarction: Opportunities for improving survival. In P. M McCabe, N. Schneiderman, T. M. Field, & A. R. Wellens (Eds.), *Stress, coping, and cardiovascular disease*. Mahwah, NJ: Erlbaum.

Fredrickson, B. L., Tugade, M. M., & Waugh, C. E. (2003). What good are positive emotions in crisis? A prospective study of resilience and emotions following the terrorist attacks on the United States on September 11th, 2001. *Journal of Personality & Social Psychology, 84*, 365–376.

Fredrickson, B. L., & Branigan, C. (2005). Positive emotions broaden the scope of attention and thought-action repertoires. *Cognition and Emotion, 19*, 313–332.

Free, M. L. (2000). *Cognitive therapy in groups: Guidelines and resources for practice*. New York: Wiley.

Freedman, D. S. (1995). The importance of body fat distribution in early life. *American Journal of the Medical Sciences, 310*, S72–S76.

Freedman, J. L., & Fraser, S. C. (1966). Compliance without pressure: The foot-in-the-door technique. *Journal of Personality and Social Psychology, 4*, 195–202.

Freeman, C. E. (2004). *Trends in educational equity of girls & women: 2004* (NCES 2005–016). U.S. Department of Education, National Center for Education Statistics. Washington, DC: U.S. Government Printing Office.

Freeman, J. E. (2006). Psychology of race and ethnicity. In W. Buskit, & S. F. Davis. *Handbook of the teaching of psychology*. Malden, MA: Blackwell Publishing.

Freeman, P. (1990, December 17). Silent no more. *People Weekly*, pp. 94–104.

Fregni, F., & Pascual-Leone, A. (2007). Technology insight: noninvasive brain stimulation in neurology-perspectives on the therapeutic potential of rTMS and tDCS. *Nature Clinical Practice Neurology, 3*, 383–393.

French, H. W. (1997, February 2). Africa's culture war: Old customs, new values. *The New York Times*, pp. 1E, 4E.

Frensch, P. A., & Rünger, D. (2003). Implicit learning. *Current Directions in Psychological Science, 12*, 13–18.

Freud, S. (1900). *The interpretation of dreams*. New York: Basic Books.

Freud, S. (1922/1959). *Group psychology and the analysis of the ego*. London: Hogarth.

Friborg, O., Barlaug, D., Martinussen, M., Rosenvinge, J. H., & Hjemdal, O. (2005). Resilience in relation to personality and intelligence. *International Journal of Methods in Psychiatric Research, 14*, 29–42.

Friborg, O., Hjemdal, O., & Rosenvinge, J. H. (2006). Resilience as a moderator of pain and stress. *Journal of Psychosomatic Research, 61*, 213–219.

Friedberg, R. D. (2006). A cognitive-behavioral approach to family therapy. *Journal of Contemporary Psychotherapy, 36*, 159–165.

Friedman, A. F., Lewak, R., Nichols, D. S., & Webb, J. T. (2000). *Psychological assessment with the MMPI-2*. Mahwah, NJ: Erlbaum.

Friedman, D. E. (2004). *The new economics of pre-school*. Washington, DC: Early Childhood Funders' Collaborative/NAEYC.

Friedman, J. M. (2003, February 7). A war on obesity, not the obese. *Science, 299*, 856–858.

Friedman, J. N. W., Oltmanns, T. F., & Turkheimer, E. (2007). Interpersonal perception and personality disorders: Utilization of a thin slice approach. *Journal of Research in Personality, 41*, 667–688.

Friedman, M. J. (2006). Posttraumatic stress disorder among military returnees from Afghanistan and Iraq. *American Journal of Psychiatry, 163*, 586–593.

Frijda, N. H. (2005). Emotion experience. *Cognition and Emotion, 19*, 473–497.

Frincke, J. L., & Pate, W. E., II. (2004, March). *Yesterday, today, and tomorrow. Careers in Psychology 2004, what students need to know*. Paper presented at the Annual Convention of the Southeastern Psychological Association, Atlanta, GA.

Frings, L., Wagner, K., Unterrainer, J., Spreer, J., Halsband, U., & Schulze-Bonhage, A. (2006). Gender-related differences in lateralization of hippocampal activation and cognitive strategy. *Neuroreport, 17*, 417–421.

Fritsch, J. (1999, October 5). Scientists unmask diet myth: Willpower. *The New York Times*, pp. D1, D9.

Fritsch, T., McClendon, M. J., Smyth, K. A., Lerner, A. J., Friedland, R. P., & Larsen, J. D. (2007). Cognitive functioning in healthy aging: The role of reserve and lifestyle factors early in life. *Gerontologist, 47*, 307–322.

Fromkin, V. A. (2000). On the uniqueness of language. In K. Emmorey, H. Lane, et al. (Eds.), *The signs of language revisited: An anthology to honor Ursula Bellugi and Edward Klima.* Mahwah, NJ: Erlbaum.

Fromm, E., & Nash, M. (Eds.) (1992). *Contemporary hypnosis research.* New York: Guilford.

Frost, L. E., & Bonnie, R. J. (Eds.). (2001). *The evolution of mental health law.* Washington, DC: American Psychological Association.

Frost, R. O., & Steketee, G. (Eds.). (2002). *Cognitive approaches to obsessions and compulsions: Theory, assessment, and treatment.* New York: Pergamon Press.

Frot, M., Feine, J. S., & Bushnel, M. C. (2004). Sex differences in pain perception and anxiety. A psychophysical study with topical capsaicin. *Pain, 108*, 230–236.

Frueh, B. C., Elhai, J. D., & Grubaugh, A. L. (2005). Documented combat exposure of US veterans seeking treatment for combat-related post-traumatic stress disorder. *British Journal of Psychiatry, 186*, 467–472.

Fuller, A. (2006). Hypnosis and ideomotor compliance in the treatment of smoking tobacco and cannabis. *Australian Journal of Clinical Hypnotherapy and Hypnosis, 27*, 14–18.

Funder, D. C. (1991). Global traits: A neoAllportian approach to personality. *Psychological Science, 2*, 31–39.

Funder, D. C. (1997). *The personality puzzle.* New York: W. W. Norton.

Funk, J. B. (2005). Children's exposure to violent video games and desensitization to violence. *Child and Adolescent Psychiatric Clinics of North America, 14*, 387–404.

Funk, M. S. (1996). Development of object permanence in the New Zealand parakeet (*Cyanoramphus auriceps*). *Animal Learning and Behavior, 24*, 375–383.

Furnham, A. (1995). The relationship of personality and intelligence to cognitive learning style and achievement. In D. H. Saklofske & M. Zeidner (Eds.), *International handbook of personality and intelligence. Perspectives on individual differences.* New York: Plenum.

Furnham, A., & Crump, J. (2005). Personality traits, types, and disorders: An examination of the relationship between three self-report measures. *European Journal of Personality, 19*, 167–184.

Furnham, A., Pallangyo, A. E., & Gunter, B. (2001). Gender-role stereotyping in Zimbabwean television advertisements. *South African Journal of Psychology, 31*, 21–29.

Furnham, A., & Swami, V. (2007). Perception of female buttocks and breast size in profile. *Social Behavior and Personality, 35*, 1–8.

Furst, P. T. (1977). "High states" in culture-historical perspective. In N. E. Zinberg (Ed.), *Alternate states of consciousness.* New York: Free Press.

Furumoto, L., & Scarborough, E. (2002). Placing women in the history of psychology: The first American women psychologists. In W. E. Pickren (Ed.), *Evolving perspectives on the history of psychology* (pp. 527–543). Washington, DC: American Psychological Association.

Gaab, J., Rohleder, N., Nater, U. M., & Ehlert, U. (2005). Psychological determinants of the cortisol stress response: The role of anticipatory cognitive appraisal. *Psychoneuroendocrinology, 30*, 599–610.

Gagnon, G. H. (1977). *Human sexualities.* Glenview, IL: Scott, Foresman.

Galanter, E. (1962). Contemporary psychophysics. In R. Brown, E. Galanter, E. Hess, & G. Maroler (Eds.), *New directions in psychology* (pp. 87–157). New York: Holt.

Galanter, M. (2007). Spirituality and recovery in 12-step programs: an empirical model. *Journal of Substance Abuse Treatment, 33*, 265–272.

Galanter, M., & Kleber, H. D. (Eds.). (1999). *The American Psychiatric Press textbook of substance abuse: Abuse treatment* (2nd ed.). Washington, DC: American Psychiatric Press.

Galatzer-Levy, R. M., & Cohler, B. J. (1997). *Essential psychoanalysis: A contemporary introduction.* New York: Basic Books.

Galavotti, C., Saltzman, L. E., Sauter, S. L., & Sumartojo, E. (1997, February). Behavioral science activities at the Center for Disease Control and Prevention: A selected overview of exemplary programs. *American Psychologist, 52*, 154–166.

Galef, D. (2001, April 27). The information you provide is anonymous, but what was your name again? *The Chronicle of Higher Education, 47*, p. B5.

Gallagher, A. M., & Kaufman, J. C. (2005). *Gender differences in mathematics: An integrated psychological approach.* Cambridge, England: Cambridge University Press.

Gallagher, D. J. (1996). Personality, coping, and objective outcomes: Extraversion, neuroticism, coping styles, and academic performance. *Personality & Individual Differences, 21*, 421–429.

Gallagher, J. J. (1994). Teaching and learning: New models. *Annual Review of Psychology, 45*, 171–195.

Gallagher, M., & Rapp, R. R. (1997). The use of animal models to study the effects of aging on cognition. *Annual Review of Psychology, 48*, 339–370.

Gallup News Service (1998). *Adults who find that premarital sex is not wrong.* Washington, DC: Gallup News Service.

Gallup Poll. (2001, June 8). *American's belief in psychic and paranormal phenomena is up over last decade.* Washington, DC: The Gallup Organization.

Gami, A. S., Howard, D. E., Olson, E. J., Somers, V. K. (2005). Day-night pattern of sudden death in obstructive sleep apnea. *New England Journal of Medicine, 353*, 1206–1214.

Gangestad, S. W., Simpson, J. A., Cousins, A. J., Garver-Apgar, C. E., & Christensen, P. N. (2004). Women's preferences for male behavioral displays change across the menstrual cycle. *Psychological Science, 15*, 203–207.

Ganong, L. H., & Coleman, M. (1999). *Changing families, changing responsibilities: Family obligations following divorce and remarriage.* Mahwah, NJ: Erlbaum.

Garb, H. N. (2002). Practicing psychological assessment. *American Psychologist, 57*, 990–991.

Garb, H. N. (2003). Observations on the validity of neuropsychological and personality assessment testing. *Australian Psychologist, 38*, 14–21.

Garb, H. N., Wood, J. M., Lilenfeld, S. O., & Nezworski, M. T. (2005). Roots of the Rorschach controversy. *Clinical Psychology Review, 25*, 97–118.

Garber, J., & Horowitz, J. L. (2002). Depression in children. In I. H. Gotlib & C. L. Hammen (Eds.), *Handbook of depression.* New York: Guilford Press.

Garcia, J. (1990). Learning without memory. *Journal of Cognitive Neuroscience, 2*, 287–305.

Garcia, J. (2003). Psychology is not an enclave. In R. J. Sternberg (Ed.), *Psychologists defying the crowd: Stories of those who battled the establishment and won.* Washington, DC: American Psychological Association.

Garcia, J., Hankins, W. G., & Rusiniak, K. W. (1974). Behavioral regulation of the milieu intern in man and rat. *Science, 185*, 824–831.

Garcia, S. M., Weaver, K., Moskowitz, G. B., & Darley, J. M. (2002). Crowded minds: The implicit bystander effect. *Journal of Personality and Social Psychology, 83*, 843–853.

Garcia-Andrade, C., Wall, T. L., & Ehlers, C. L. (1997). The firewater myth and response to alcohol in Mission Indians. *Journal of Psychiatry, 154*, 983–988.

Garcia-Palacios, A., Hoffman, H., & Carlin, A. (2002). Virtual reality in the treatment of spider phobia: A controlled study. *Behavior Research & Therapy, 40*, 983–993.

Gardner, E. P., & Kandel, E. R. (2000). Touch. In E. R. Kandel, J. H. Schwartz, & T. M. Jessell (Eds.), *Principles of neural science* (4th ed.). New York: McGraw-Hill.

Gardner, H. (1975). *The shattered mind: The person after brain damage.* New York: Knopf.

Gardner, H. (1999). *Intelligence reframed: Multiple intelligences for the 21st century.* New York, NY: Basic Books.

Gardner, H. (2005). Scientific psychology: Should we bury it or praise it? In R. J. Sternberg (Ed.), *Unity in psychology: Possibility or pipe dream?* (pp. 77–90). Washington, DC: American Psychological Association.

Gardner, R. A., & Gardner, B. T. (1969). Teaching sign language to a chimpanzee. *Science, 165*, 664–672.

Garlow, S. J., Purselle, D. C., & Heninger, M. (2007). Cocaine and alcohol use preceding suicide in African American and White adolescents. *Journal of Psychiatric Research, 41*, 530–536.

Garwick, G. B. (2007). Intelligence-related terms in mental retardation, learning disability, and gifted/talented professional usage, 1983–2001: The 1992 mental retardation redefinition as natural experiment. *Dissertation Abstracts International Section A: Humanities and Social Sciences, 67*(9-A), 3296.

Garwood, C. L., & Potts, L. A. (2007). Emerging pharmacotherapies for smoking cessation. *American Journal of Health Systems Pharmacology, 64*, 1693–1698.

Garza-Guerrero, C. (2000). Idealization and mourning in love relationships: Normal and pathological spectra. *Psychoanalytic Quarterly, 69*, 121–150.

Gaser, C. & Schlaug, G. (2003). Brain structures differ between musicians and non-musicians. *Journal of Neuroscience, 23*, 9240–9245.

Gass, C. S., Luis, C. A., Meyers, T. L., & Kuljis, R. O. (2000). Familial Creutzfeldt-Jakob disease: A neuro-psychological case study. *Archives of Clinical Neuropsychology, 15*, 165–175.

Gassio, R., Artuch, R., Vilaseca, M. A., Fuste, E., Boix, C., Sans, A., & Campistol, J. (2005). Cognitive functions in classic phenylketonuria and mild hyperphenylalaninaemia: Experience in a paediatric population. *Developmental Medicine and Child Neurology, 47*, 443–448.

Gatchel, R. J., & Baum, A. (1983). *An introduction to health psychology.* Reading, MA: Addison-Wesley.

Gatchel, R. J., & Oordt. M. S. (2003). Obesity. In R. J. Gatchel & M. S. Oordt, *Clinical health psychology and primary care: Practical advice and clinical guidance for successful collaboration* (pp. 149–167). Washington, DC: American Psychological Association.

Gatchel, R. J., & Turk, D. C. (Eds.). (1996). *Psychological approaches to pain management: A practioner's handbook.* New York: Guilford.

Gatchel, R. J. & Weisberg, J. N. (2000). *Personality characteristics of patients with pain.* Washington, DC: APA Books.

Gathérias, F. (2006). Psychologie succincte des auteurs d'attentat suicide. Brief psychological analysis of suicide bombers. *Revue Francophone Du Stress et du Trauma, 6,* 47–52.

Gathercole, S. E., & Baddeley, A.D. (1993). *Working memory and language processing.* Hillsdale, NJ: Erlbaum.

Gazzaniga, M. S. (1998, July). The split brain revisited. *Scientific American,* 50–55.

Gazzaniga, M. S., Ivry, R. B., & Mangun, G. R. (2002). *Cognitive neuroscience: The biology of the mind* (2nd ed.). New York: W. W. Norton.

Ge, X., Conger, R. D., & Elder, G. H., Jr. (1996). Coming of age too early: Pubertal influences on girls' vulnerability to psychological distress. *Child Development, 67,* 3386–3400.

Ge, X., Kim, I. J., Brody, G. H., Conger, R. D., Simons, R. L., Gibbons, F. X., & Cutrona, C. E. (2003). It's about timing and change: Pubertal transition effects on symptoms of major depression among African American youths. *Developmental Psychology, 39,* 430–439.

Geen, R. G., & Donnerstein, E. (1983). *Aggression: Theoretical and empirical reviews.* New York: Academic Press.

Geen, R., & Donnerstein, E. (1998). *Human aggression: Theories, research, and implications for social policy.* San Diego, CA: Academic Press.

Gegax, T. (2005, June 6). An end to 'power hour.' *Newsweek,* p. 28.

Gegenfurtner, K. R. (2003). Color vision. *Annual Review of Neuroscience, 26,* 181–206.

Geiselman, R. E., Fisher, R. P., MacKinnon, D. P., & Holland, H. L. (1985). Eyewitness memory enhancement in the police interview: Cognitive retrieval mnemonics versus hypnosis. *Journal of Applied Psychology, 70,* 401–412.

Gelfand, M. M. (2000). Sexuality among older women. *Journal of Women's Health and Gender Based Medicine, 9*(Suppl. 1), S15–S20.

Gelman, D. (1994, April 18). The mystery of suicide. *Newsweek,* pp. 44–49.

Gelman, R., & Baillargeon, R. (1983). A review of some Piagetian concepts. In J. H. Flavell & E. M. Markman (Eds.), *Handbook of child psychology, Vol. 3: Cognitive development* (4th ed.). New York: Wiley.

Gelman, R., & Kit-Fong Au, T. (Eds.). (1996). *Perceptual and cognitive development.* New York: Academic Press.

Gennaro, R. J. (2004). *Higher-order theories of consciousness: An anthology.* Amsterdam, Netherlands: John Benjamins.

Genovese, J. E. C. (2006). Piaget, pedagogy, and evolutionary psychology. *Evolutionary Psychology, 4,* 2127–2137.

Gentner, D., Goldin, S., & Goldin-Meadow, S. (Eds.). (2003). *Language in mind: Advances in the study of language and cognition.* Cambridge, MA: MIT.

Genuis, M., & Violato, C. (2000). Attachment security to mother, father, and the parental unit. In C. Violato, & E. Oddone-Paolucci (Eds.), *The changing family and child development.* Aldershot, England: Ashgate Publishing.

George, M. S. (2003, September). Stimulating the brain. *Scientific American,* pp. 66–73.

George, M. S., Wassermann, E. M., Williams, W. A., Callahan, A., et al. (1995). Daily repetitive transcranial magnetic stimulations (rTMS) improves mood in depression. *Neuroreport: An International Journal for the Rapid Communication of Research in Neuroscience, 6,* 1853–1856.

George, S., & Moselhy, H. (2005). Cocaine-induced trichotillomania. *Addiction, 100,* 255–256.

George, T. P. (1999). Design, measurement, and analysis in developmental research. In M. Bornstein & M. Lamb, *Developmental psychology.* Mahwah, NJ: Erlbaum.

Georgiou, G. A., Bleakley, C., Hayward, J., Russo, R., Dutton, K., Eltiti, S., & Fox, E. (2005). Focusing on fear: Attentional disengagement from emotional faces. *Visual Cognition, 12,* 145–158.

Gershkoff-Stowe, L., Connell, B., & Smith, L. (2006). Priming overgeneralizations in two- and four-year-old children. *Journal of Child Language, 33,* 461–486.

Gershoff, E. T. (2002). Corporal punishment by parents and associated child behaviors and experiences: A meta-analytic and theoretical review. *Psychological Bulletin, 128,* 539–579.

Gerstel, N. (2005, April 8). In search of time. *Science, 308,* 204–205.

Getner, D., & Holyoak, K. J. (1997, January). Reasoning and learning by analogy. *American Psychologist, 52,* 32–34.

Gevirtz, R. (2000). The physiology of stress. In D. T. Kenny, J. G. Carlson, et al. (Eds.), *Stress and health: Research and clinical applications* (pp. 53–71). Amsterdam, Netherlands: Harwood Academic.

Ghaemi, S. N. (2003). *Mood disorders: A practical guide. Practical Guides in Psychiatry.* New York: Lippincott Williams & Wilkins.

Ghazvini, A., & Mullis, R. L. (2002). Center-based care for young children: Examining predictors of quality. *Journal of Genetic Psychology, 163,* 112–125.

Giacobbi, P. R., Jr., Lynn, T. K. Wetherington, J. M., Jenkins, J., Bodendorf, M., & Langley, B. (2004). Stress and coping during the transition to university for first-year female athletes. *Sports Psychologist, 18,* 1–20.

Giacomini, M., Baylis, F., & Robert, J. (2007). Banking on it: Public policy and the ethics of stem cell research and development. *Social Sciences Medicine, 22,* 88–84.

Gibb, K., Tunbridge, D., Chua, A., & Frederickson, N. (2007). Pathways to inclusion: Moving from special school to mainstream. *Educational Psychology in Practice, 23,* 109–127.

Gibbons, R. D., Brown, C. H., Hur, K., Marcus, S. M., Bhamik, D. K., Erkens, J. A., Herrings, R. M. C., & Mann, J. J. (2007). Early evidence on the effects of regulators' suicidally warnings on SSRI prescriptions and suicide in children and adolescents. *American Journal of Psychiatry, 164,* 1356–1363.

Gibbs, N. (2005, August 8). Being 13. *Time,* pp. 41–55.

Gibbs, W. W. (2002, August.) From mouth to mind. *Scientific American,* p. 26.

Gibson, B. (1997). Smoker-nonsmoker conflict: Using a social psychological framework to understand a current social controversy. *Journal of Social Issues, 53,* 97–112.

Gibson, H. B. (1995). A further case of the misuse of hypnosis in a police investigation. *Contemporary Hypnosis, 12,* 81–86.

Gilberson, T. A., Damak, S., & Margolskee, R. F. (2000). The molecular physiology of taste transduction. *Current Opinion in Neurobiology, 10,* 519–527.

Gilbert, B. (1996). New ideas in the air at the National Zoo. *Smithsonian,* pp. 32–43.

Gilbert, D. G. (1995). *Smoking: Individual differences, psychopathology, and emotion.* Philadelphia: Taylor & Francis.

Gilbert, D. T., Miller, A. G., & Ross, L. (1998). Speeding with Ned: A personal view of the correspondence bias. In J. M. Darley & J. Cooper (Eds.), *Attribution and social interaction: The legacy of Edward E. Jones.* Washington, DC: American Psychological Association.

Gilbert, D. T., McNulty, S. E., Guiliano, T. A., & Benson, J. F. (1992). Blurry words and fuzzy deeds: The attribution of obscure behavior. *Journal of Personality and Social Psychology, 62,* 18–25.

Gilbert, P. D. (2007). Spirituality and mental health: A very preliminary overview. *Current Opinions in Psychiatry, 20,* 594–598.

Gilboa, A., Winocur, G., & Rosenbaum, R. S. (2006). Hippocampal contributions to recollection in retrograde and anterograde amnesia. *Hippocampus, 16,* 966–980.

Gilligan, C. (1996). The centrality of relationships in psychological development: A puzzle, some evidence, and a theory. In G. G. Noam & K. W. Fischer (Eds.), *Development and vulnerability in close relationships.* Hillsdale, NJ: Erlbaum.

Gillyatt, P. (1997, February). When the nose doesn't know. *Harvard Health Letter,* pp. 6–7.

Gilovich, T., Griffin, D., & Kahneman, D. (Eds.) (2002). *Heuristics and biases: The psychology of intuitive judgment.* Cambridge, England: Cambridge University Press.

Gladwell, M. (2002, August 5). The naked face: Can you read people's thoughts just by looking at them? *The New Yorker,* pp. 38–49.

Gladwell, M. (2004, September 20). Annals of psychology: Personality, plus how corporations figure out who you are. *The New Yorker,* 42–45.

Gladwin, T. (1964). Culture and logical process. In N. Goodenough (Ed.), *Explorations in cultural anthropology: Essays in honor of George Peter Murdoch.* New York: McGraw-Hill.

Glassman, A. H., & Koob, G. F. (1996, February 22). Neuropharmacology: Psychoactive smoke. *Nature, 379,* 677–678.

Glenmullen, J. (2000). *Prozac backlash: Overcoming the dangers of Prozac, Zoloft, Paxil, and other antidepressants with safe, effective alternatives.* New York: Simon & Schuster.

Glenn, D. (2004, June 1). Students' performance on tests is tied to their views of their innate intelligence, researchers say. *The Chronicle of Higher Education,* p. 28.

Glick, P., & Fiske, S. T. (2001). An ambivalent alliance: Hostile and benevolent sexism as complementary justifications for gender inequality. *American Psychologist, 56,* 109–118.

Glick, P., Lameiras, M., Fiske, S. T., Eckes, T., Masser, B., Volpato, C., Huang, L. L., Sakalli-Ugurlu, N., Castro, Y. R., Pereira, M. L. D., Willemsen, T. M., Brunner, A., Six-Materna, I., & Wells, R. (2004). Bad but bold: Ambivalent attitudes toward men predict gender inequality in 16 nations. *Journal of Personality and Social Psychology, 86,* 713–728.

Glickler, J. (2006). Advancing in advancement: A self-efficacy study of development practitioners in higher education. *Dissertation Abstracts International: Section B: The Sciences and Engineering, 67(2-B),* 1190.

Glicksohn, J., & Nahari, G. (2007). Interacting personality traits? Smoking as a test case. *European Journal of Personality, 21,* 225–234.

Glisky, E. L. (2007). Changes in cognitive function in human aging. In D. R. Riddle, *Brain aging: Models, methods, and mechanisms.* Boca Raton, FL: CRC Press.

Goffin, R. D., Jelley, R. B., & Wagner, S. H. (2003). Is halo helpful? Effects of inducing halo on performance rating accuracy. *Social Behavior and Personality, 31,* 625–636.

Goin, M. K. (2005). A current perspective on the psychotherapies. *Psychiatric Services, 56,* 255–257.

Gold, P. E., Cahill, L., & Wenk, G. L. (2002). Ginkgo biloba: A cognitive enhancer? *Psychological Science in the Public Interest, 3,* 2–7.

Goldberg, C. (2003, May 1). Some fear loss of privacy as science pries into brain. *The Boston Globe,* p. S1.

Goldberg. C. (2007, August 2). Implants offer hope in brain injury cases. *Boston Globe,* p. A1.

Golden, A. M., Daigleish, T., & Spinks, H. (2006). Dysfunctional attitudes in seasonal affective disorder. *Behaviour Research and Therapy, 44,* 1159–1164.

Golden, W. L. (2006). Hypnotherapy for anxiety, phobias and psychophysiological disorders. In R. A. Chapman, *The clinical use of hypnosis in cognitive behavior therapy: A practitioner's casebook.* New York: Springer Publishing.

Golden, R. N., Gaynes, B. N., Ekstrom, R. D., Hamer, R. M., Jacobsen, F. M., Suppes, T., Wisner, K. L., & Nemeroff, C. B. (2005). The efficacy of light therapy in the treatment of mood disorders: A review and meta-analysis of the evidence. *American Journal of Psychiatry, 162,* 656–662.

Goldfried, M. R., & Pachankis, J. E. (2007). On the next generation of process research. *Clinical Psychological Review, 27,* 760–768.

Goldner, E. M., Cockell, S. J., & Srikameswaran, S. (2002).Perfectionism and eating disorders. In G. L. Flett & P. L. Hewitt (Eds.), *Perfectionism: Theory, research, and treatment,* pp. 319–340. Washington, DC: American Psychological Association.

Goldstein, E. B. (1984). *Sensation and perception* (2nd ed.). Pacific Grove, CA: Brooks/Cole.

Goldstein, G., Beers, S. R., Longmore, S., & McCue, M. (1996). Efficacy of memory training: A technological extension and replication. *Clinical Neuropsychologist, 10,* 66–72.

Goldstein, I. (2000). Female sexual arousal disorder: New insights. *International Journal of Impotence Research, 12*(Suppl. 4), S152–S157.

Goldstein, J. (2003). People @ play: Electronic games. In van Oostendorp, H., *Cognition in a digital world* (pp. 25–45). Mahwah, NJ: Lawrence Erlbaum Associates.

Goldstein, S. N. (2006). The exploration of spirituality and identity status in adolescence. *Dissertation Abstracts International: Section B: The Sciences and Engineering, 67(6-B),* 3481.

Goldston, D. B. (2003). *Measuring suicidal behavior and risk in children and adolescents.* Washington, DC: American Psychological Association.

Goldstone, R. L., & Kersten, A. (2003). Concepts and categorization. In A. F. Healy & R. W. Proctor (Eds.), *Handbook of psychology:*
Experimental psychology (Vol. 4, pp. 599–621). New York: Wiley.

Goleman, D. (1993, July 21). "Expert" babies found to teach others. *The New York Times,* p. C-10.

Goleman, D. (1995). *Emotional intelligence.* New York: Bantam.

Golimbet, V. E., Alfimova, M. V., Gritsenko, I. K., & Ebstein, R. P. (2007). Relationship between dopamine system genes and extraversion and novelty seeking. *Neuroscience Behavior and Physiology, 37,* 601–606.

Gontkovsky, S. T. (2005). Neurobiological bases and neuropsychological correlates of aggression and violence. In J. P. Morgan (Ed.), *Psychology of aggression.* Hauppauge, NY: Nova Science Publishers.

Gontkovsky, S. T., & Beatty, W. W. (2006). Practical methods for the clinical assessment of information processing speed. *International Journal of Neuroscience, 116,* 1317–1325.

Good, C., Aronson, J., & Inzlicht, M. (2003). Improving adolescents' standardized test performance: An intervention to reduce the effects of stereotype threat. *Journal of Applied Developmental Psychology, 24,* 645–662.

Good, P. I. (2003). *Common errors in statistics and how to avoid them.* New York: Wiley.

Goode, E. (1999, April 13). If things taste bad, "phantoms" may be at work. *The New York Times,* pp. D1–D2.

Goode, E. (2001, September 12). Suicide attackers are sane, not suicidal in the normal sense, experts say. *The New York Times,* p. A13.

Goode, E. (2003, January 28). Even in the age of Prozac, some still prefer the couch. *The New York Times,* Section F, p. 1.

Goodheart, C. D., Kazdin, A. E., & Sternberg, R. J. (Eds). (2006). *Evidence-based psychotherapy: Where practice and research meet.* Washington, DC: American Psychological Association.

Goodman, G. S., Batterman-Faunce, J. M., Schaaf, J. M., & Kenney, R. (2002). Nearly 4 years after an event: Children's eyewitness memory and adults' perceptions of children's accuracy. *Child Abuse and Neglect, 26,* 849–884.

Goodman, G. S., Ghetti, S., Quas, J. A., Edelstein, R. S., Alexander K. W., Redlich, A. D., Cordon, I. M., & Jones, D. P. H. (2003). A prospective study of memory for child sexual abuse: New findings relevant to the repressed-memory controversy. *Psychological Science, 14,* 113–117.

Goodman, W., K., Rudorfer, M. V., & Maser, J. D. (2000). *Obsessive-compulsive disorder: Contemporary issues in treatment.* Mahwah, NJ: Lawrence Erlbaum Associates.

Goodwin, R., Costa, P., & Adonu, J. (2004). Social support and its consequences: 'Positive' and 'deficiency' values and their implications for support and self-esteem. *British Journal of Social Psychology, 43,* 465–474.

Goodwin, R. D., & Hamilton, S. P. (2003). Lifetime comorbidity of antisocial personality disorder and anxiety disorders among adults in the community. *Psychiatry Research, 117,* 159–166.

Gooren, L. (2006). The biology of human psychosexual differentiation. *Hormones and Behavior, 50,* 589–601.

Goossens, L., Beyers, W., Emmen, M., & van Aken, M. (2002). The imaginary audience and personal fable: Factor analyses and concurrent validity of the "New Look" measures. *Journal of Research on Adolescence, 12,* 193–215.

Gordon, E. F. (2000). *Mockingbird years: A life in and out of therapy.* New York: Basic Books.

Gordon, P. (2004). Numerical cognition without words: Evidence from Amazonia. *Science,* 306, 496–499. First appeared in *Science Express,* online publication August 16, 2004.

Gotlib, I. H., Krasnoperova, E., Yue, D. N., & Joorman, J. (2004). Attentional biases for negative interpersonal stimuli in clinical depression. *Journal of Abnormal Psychology, 113,* 127–135.

Gottesman, I. I. (1991). *Schizophrenia genesis: The origins of madness.* New York: Freeman.

Gottesman, I. I. (1997, June 6). Twin: En route to QTLs for cognition. *Science, 276,* 1522–1523.

Gottesman, I. I., & Hanson, D. R. (2005). Human development: Biological and genetic processes. *Annual Review of Psychology, 56,* 263–286.

Gottfredson, L. S. (2004). Schools and the *g* factor. *Wilson Quarterly,* pp. 35–45.

Gottfredson, L. S., & Deary, I. J. (2004). Intelligence predicts health and longevity, but why? *Current Directions in Psychological Science, 13,* 1–4.

Gottlieb, D. A. (2004). Acquisition with partial and continuous reinforcement in pigeon autoshaping. *Learning and Behavior, 32,* 321–334.

Gottlieb, D. A. (2006). Effects of partial reinforcement and time between reinforced trials on terminal response rate in pigeon autoshaping. *Behavioural Processes, 72,* 6–13.

Gottlieb, G., & Lickliter, R. (2004). The various roles of animal models in understanding human development. *Social Development, 13,* 311–325.

Gould, E., Reeves, A. J., Graziano, M. S. A., & Gross, C. G. (1999, October 15). Neurogenesis in the neocortex of adult primates. *Science,* 548–552.

Gould, R. L. (1978). *Transformations.* New York: Simon & Schuster.

Govindarajan, A., Kelleher, R. J., & Tonegawa, S. (2006). A clustered plasticity model of long-term memory engrams. *Nature Reviews Neuroscience, 7,* 575-583.

Gowaty, P. A. (2003). Power asymmetries between the sexes, mate preferences, and components of fitness. In C. B. Travis (Ed.), *Evolution, gender, and rape* (pp. 61–86). Cambridge, MA: MIT.

Gowing, L. R., Henry-Edwards, S. M., Irvine, R. J., & Ali, R. L. (2002). The health effects of ecstasy: A literature review. *Drug and Alcohol Review, 21,* 53–63.

Grady, D. (2002, November 26). Why we eat (and eat and eat). *The New York Times,* pp. D1, D4.

Grady, D., & Kolata, G. (2003, August, 29). Gene therapy used to treat patient with Parkinson's. *The New York Times,* pp. A1, A18.

Graf, P. (1990). Life-span changes in implicit and explicit memory. *Bulletin of the Psychonomic Society, 28,* 353–358.

Graffin, N. F., Ray, W. J., & Lundy, R. (1995). EEG concomitants of hypnosis and hypnotic susceptibility. *Journal of Abnormal Psychology, 104,* 123–131.

Graham, C. A., Bancroft, J., & Doll, H. A. (2007). Does oral contraceptive-induced reduction in free testosterone adversely affect the sexuality or mood of women? *Psychoneuroendocrinology, 32,* 246–255.

Graham, J. R. (1999). *MMPI-2: Assessing personality and psychopathology* (3rd ed.). New York: Oxford University Press.

Graham, S. (1992). "Most of the subjects were white and middle class": Trends in published research on African Americans in selected APA journals, 1970–1989. *American Psychologist, 47*, 629–639.

Graham, S. (2001, November 12). *9/11: The psychological aftermath*. Retrieved from the *Scientific American* Web site http://www.sciam.com/explorations/2001/111201anxiety/index.html.

Grand Rapids Press. (2007, May 15). Police say bystanders did nothing to stop attack on senior. *The Grand Rapids Press*, B6.

Granic, I., Hollenstein, T., & Dishion, T. (2003). Longitudinal analysis of flexibility and reorganization in early adolescence: A dynamic systems study of family interactions. *Developmental Psychology, 39*, 606–617.

Grann, J. D. (2007). Confidence in knowledge past: An empirical basis for a differential decay theory of very long-term memory monitoring. *Dissertation Abstracts International Section A: Humanities and Social Sciences, 67*, 2462.

Graswich, R. E. (2004, December 10). The bystander's dilemma: For light-rail attack victim, bystander apathy worse than thugs' blows. *The Sacramento Bee*, p. B1.

Graugaard, P. K., Eide, H., & Finset, A. (2003). Interaction analysis of physician-patient communication: The influence of trait anxiety on communication and outcome. *Patient Education and Counseling, 49*, 149–156.

Gray, G. C. (2006). The regulation of corporate violations: punishment, compliance, and the blurring of responsibility. *British Journal of Criminology, 46*, 875–892.

Gray, J. R., Chabris, C. F., & Braver, T. S. (2003, February 18). Neural mechanisms of general fluid intelligence. *Nature: Neurosciences* Retrieved from http://www.nature.com/cgitaf/DynaPage.taf?file=/neuro/journal/vaop/ncurrent/abs/nn1014.html.

Graziano, M. S., Taylor, C. S., & Moore, T. (2002). Complex movements evolved by microstimulation of precentral cortex. *Neuron, 34*, 841–851.

Graziano, W. G., Habashi, M. M., Sheese, B. E., & Tobin, R. M. (2007). Agreeableness, empathy, and helping: A person situation perspective. *Journal of Personality and Social Psychology, 93*, 583–599.

Green, B. G., & Pravin, G. (2004). Thermal taste predicts higher responsiveness to chemical taste and flavor. *Chemical Senses, 29*, 617–628.

Green, J. S., Henderson, F. R., & Collinge, M. D. (2003). *Prevention and control of wildlife damage: Coyotes*. Lincoln: University of Nebraska, Institute of Agriculture and Natural Resources. Retrieved from http://wildlifedamage.unl.edu/handbook/handbook/carnivor/ca_c51.pdf.

Greenberg, R. L. (2000). The creative client in cognitive therapy [Special issue: Creativity in the context of cognitive therapy]. *Journal of Cognitive Psychotherapy, 14*, 163–174.

Greenberg, R. M., & Kellner, C. H. (2005). Electroconvulsive therapy: A selected review. *American Journal of Geriatric Psychiatry, 13*, 268–281.

Greene, B., & Herek, G. (1994). *Lesbian and gay psychology: Theory, research, and clinical applications*. Newbury Park, CA: Sage.

Greene, J. D., Sommerville, R. B., Nystrom, L. E., Darley, J. M., & Cohen, J. D. (2001, September 14). An fMRI investigation of emotional engagement in moral judgment. *Science, 293*, 2105–2108.

Greene, M., Scholl, K., Takahaski, S., Bateman-House, A., Beauchamp, T., Bok, H., Cheney, D., Coyle, J., Deacon, T., Dennett, D.,

Donovan, P., Flanagan, O., Goldman, S., Greely, H., Martin, L., Miller, E., Mueller, D., Siegel, A., Solter, D., Gearhart, McKhann, G., & Faden, R. (2005, July 15). Moral issues of human-non-human primate neural grafting. *Science, 309*, 385–386.

Greene, R. L., & Clopton, J. R. (2004). Minnesota Multiphasic Personality Inventory-2 (MMPI-2). In M. E. Maruish (Ed.), *Use of psychological testing for treatment planning and outcomes assessment: Instruments for adults* (Vol. 3, 3rd ed.). Mahwah, NJ: Lawrence Erlbaum Associates.

Greenfield, P. M. (1997) You can't take it with you: Why ability assessments don't cross cultures. *American Psychologist, 52*, 1115–1124.

Greenlaw, P. S., & Jensen, S. S. (1996). Race-norming and the Civil Rights Act of 1991. *Public Personnel Management, 25*, 13–24.

Greenspan, S. (2006). Functional concepts in mental retardation: Finding the natural essence of an artificial category. *Exceptionality, 14*, 205–224.

Greenwald, A. G., Banaji, M. R., Rudman, L. A., Farnham, S. D., Nosek, B. A., & Mellott, D. S. (2002). A unified theory of implicit attitudes, stereotypes, self-esteem, and self-concept. *Psychological Review, 109*, 3–25.

Greenwald, A. G., Draine S. C., & Abrams, R. L. (1996, September 20). Three cognitive markers of unconscious semantic activation. *Science, 272*, 1699–1702.

Greenwald, A.G., Nosek, B. A., & Banaji, M. R. (2003). Understanding and using the Implicit Association Test: 1. An improved scoring algorithm. *Journal of Personality and Social Psychology 85*, 197–216.

Greenwald, A. G., Nosek, B. A., & Sriram, N. (2006). Consequential validity of the implicit association test: Comment on Blanton and Jaccard. *American Psychologist, 61*, 56–61.

Greenwald, A. G., Rudman, L. A., Nosek, B. A., & Zayas, V. (2006). Why so little faith? A reply to Blanton and Jaccard's (2006) Skeptical view of testing pure multiplicative theories. *Psychological Review, 113*, 170–180.

Greenwald, A. G., Spangenberg, E. R., Pratkanis, A. R., & Eskenzai, J. (1991). Double-blind tests of subliminal self-help audiotapes. *Psychological Science, 2*, 119–122.

Greenwood, C. R., Carta, J. J., Hart, B., Kamps, D., Terry, B., Arreaga-Mayer, C., Atwater, J., Walker, D., Risley, T., & Delquadri, J. C. (1992). Out of the laboratory and into the community: 26 years of applied behavior analysis at the Juniper Gardens children's project. *American Psychologist, 47*, 464–1474.

Greer, R. D., Dudek-Singer, J., & Gautreaux, G. (2006). Observational learning. *International Journal of Psychology, 41*, 486–499.

Gregg, J. P., Lit, L., Baron, C. A., Hertz-Picciotto, I., Walker, W., Davis, R. A., Croen, L. A., Ozonoff, S., Hansen, R., Pessah, I. N., & Sharp, F. R. (2007). Gene expression changes in children with autism. *Genomics, 12*, 88–97.

Gregory, R. L. (1978). *The psychology of seeing* (3rd ed.). New York: McGraw-Hill.

Gregory, S. (1856). *Facts for young women*. Boston.

Gregory, S. S. (1994, March 21). At risk of mutilation. *Time*, pp. 45–46.

Greist-Bousquet, S., & Schiffman, H. R. (1986). The basis of the Poggendorff effect: An additional clue for Day and Kasperczyk. *Perception and Psychophysics, 39*, 447–448.

Grezes, J., Frith, C., Passingham, R. E. (2004). Inferring false beliefs from the actions of oneself and others: An fMRI study. *Neuroimage, 21*, 744–750.

Grigorenko, E. L. (2000). Heritability and intelligence. In R. J. Sternberg, et al. (Eds.), *Handbook of intelligence*. New York: Cambridge University Press.

Grigoriadis, S., & Ravitz, P. (2007). An approach to interpersonal psychotherapy for postpartum depression: Focusing on interpersonal changes. *Canadian Family Physician, 53*, 1469–1475.

Grilo, C M., Sanislow, C. A., Skodol, A. E., Gunderson, J. G., Stout, R. L., Shea, M. T., Zanarini, M. C., Bencer, D. S., Morey, L. C., Dyck, I. R., & McGlashan, T. H. (2003). Do eating disorders co-occur with personality disorders? Comparison groups matter. *International Journal of Eating Disorders, 33*, 155–164.

Grindstaff, J. S., & Fisher, L. A. (2006). Sport psychology consultants' experience of using hypnosis in their practice: An exploratory investigation. *The Sport Psychologist, 20*, 368–386.

Gron, G., Kirstein, M., Thielscher, A., Riepe, M. W., & Spitzer, M. (2005, July). Cholinergic enhancement of episodic memory in healthy young adults. *Psychopharmacology (Berlin)*, 1–10.

Gronholm, P., Rinne, J. O., Vorobyev, V., & Laine, M. (2005). Naming of newly learned objects: A PET activation study. *Brain Research and Cognitive Brain Research, 14*, 22–28.

Gross, D. M. (2006). *The secret history of emotion: From Aristotle's Rhetoric to modern brain science*. Chicago: University of Chicago Press.

Grossi, G., Semenza, C., Corazza, S., & Volterra, V. (1996). Hemispheric specialization for sign language. *Neuropsychologia, 34*, 737–740.

Grossmann, T., Striano, T., & Friederici, A. D. (2007). Developmental changes in infants' processing of happy and angry facial expressions: A neurobehavioral study. *Brain and Cognition, 64*, 30–41.

Groth-Marnat, G. (1996). *Handbook of psychological assessment* (3rd ed.). Somerset, NJ: Wiley.

Groves, R. M., Singer, E., Lepkowski, J. M., Heeringa, S. G., & Alwin, D. F. In S. J. House, F. T. Juster, R. L. Kahn, H. Schuman, & E. Singer. (2004). *A telescope on society: Survey research and social science at the University of Michigan and beyond*. Ann Arbor, MI: University of Michgan Press.

Gruneberg, M. M., & Pascoe, K. (1996). The effectiveness of the keyword method for receptive and productive foreign vocabulary learning in the elderly. *Contemporary Educational Psychology, 21*, 102–109.

Grunwald, T., Boutros, N. N., Pezer, N., von Oertzen, J., Fernandez, G., Schaller, C., & Elger, C. E. (2003). Neuronal substrates of sensory gating within the human brain. *Biological Psychiatry, 15*, 511–519.

Guadagno, R. E., & Cialdini, R. B. (2002). Online persuasion: An examination of gender differences in computer-mediated interpersonal influence [Special issue: Groups and Internet]. *Group Dynamics, 6*, 38–51.

Guadagno, R. E., Asher, T., Demaine, L. J., & Cialdini, R. B. (2001). When saying yes leads to saying no: Preference for consistency and the reverse foot-in-the-door effect. *Personality and Social and Social Psychology Bulletin, 27*, 859–867.

Gualtiere, C. T. (2003). Brain injury and mental retardation: Psycho-pharmacology and neuropsychiatry. *Human Psychopharmacology: Clinical and Experimental, 18*, 151.

Gueguen, N. (2002). Foot-in-the-door technique and computer-mediated communication. *Computers in Human Behavior, 18*, 11–15.

Guilford, J. P. (1982). Cognitive psychology's ambiguities: Some suggested remedies. *Psychological Review, 89*, 48–59.

Guilleminault, C., Kirisoglu, C., Bao, G., Arias, V., Chan, A., & Li, K. K. (2005). Adult chronic sleepwalking and its treatment based on polysomnography. *Brain, 128* (Pt. 5), 1062–1069.

Gullotta, T., Adams, G., & Markstrom, C. (1999). *The adolescent experience*. Orlando, FL: Academic Press.

Gur, R. C. (1996, March). Paper presented at the annual meeting of the American Association for the Advancement of Science, Baltimore, Maryland.

Gur, R. C., Gur, R. E., Obrist, W. D., Hungerbuhler, J. P., Younkin, D., Rosen, A. D., Skilnick, B. E., & Reivich, M. (1982). Sex and handedness differences in cerebral blood flow during rest and cognitive activity. *Science, 217*, 659–661.

Gur, R. C., Mozley, L. H., Mozley, P. D., Resnick, S. M., Karp, J. S., Alavi, A., Arnold, S. E., & Gur, R. E. (1995, January 27). Sex differences in regional cerebral glucose metabolism during a resting state. *Science, 267*, 528–531.

Guralnick, M. J., Connor, R. T., Hammond, M., Gottman, J. M., et al. (1996). Immediate effects of mainstreamed settings on the social interactions and social integration of preschool children. *American Journal on Mental Retardation, 100*, 359–377.

Gurin, P. (2006). Informing theory from practice and applied research. *Journal of Social Issues, 62*, 621–628.

Gutek, B. A., Cohen, A. G., & Tsui, A. (1996). Reactions to perceived sex discrimination. *Human Relations, 49*, 791–813.

Guterl, F. (2002, November 11). What Freud got right. *Newsweek*, pp. 50–51.

Guterman, L. (2005, November 21). Placebos could play a role in treating some conditions, scientists say. *The Chronicle of Higher Education*, 12–14.

Guthrie, R. V. (1998). *Even the rat was white: A historical view of psychology* (2nd ed.). Needham Heights, MA: Allyn and Bacon.

Gutierrez, P. M., Muehlenkamp, J. L., Konick, L. C., & Osman, A. (2005). What role does race play in adolescent suicidal ideation? *Archives of Suicide Research, 9*, 177–192.

Guttman, M. (1995, March 3–5). She had electroshock therapy. *USA Weekend*, p. 16.

Gwynn, M. I., & Spanos, N. P. (1996). Hypnotic responsiveness, nonhypnotic suggestibility, and responsiveness to social influence. In R. G. Kunzendorf, N. P. Spahos, & B. Wallace (Eds.), *Hypnosis and imagination*. Amityville, NY: Baywood.

Haberstick, B. C., Schmitz, S., Young, S. E., & Hewitt, J. K. (2005).Contributions of genes and environments to stability and change in externalizing and internalizing problems during elementary and middle school. *Behavior Genetics, 35*, 381–396.

Haberstick, B. C., Timberlake, D., & Ehringer, M. A. (2007). Genes, time to first cigaratte and nicotine dependence in a general population sample of young adults. *Addiction, 102*, 655–665.

Hackam, D. G. (2007). Translating animal research into clinical benefit. *British Medical Journal, 334*, 163–1644.

Hackett, T. A., & Kaas, J. H. (2003). Auditory processing in the primate brain. In M. Gallagher &

R. J. Nelson (Eds.), *Handbook of psychology: Biological psychology* (Vol. 3). New York: Wiley.

Hadjistavropoulos, T., Craig, K. D., & Fuchs-Lacelle, S. (2004). *Social influences and the communication of pain*. Mahwah, NJ: Lawrence Erlbaum Associates.

Haier, R. J. (2003). Brain imaging studies of intelligence: Individual differences and neurobiology. In R. J. Sternberg & J. Lautrey (Eds.), *Models of intelligence: International perspectives* (pp. 185–193). Washington, DC: American Psychological Association.

Haley, W. E., Clair, J. M., & Saulsberry, K. (1992). Family caregiver satisfaction with medical care of their demented relatives. *Gerontologist, 32*, 219–226.

Halford, S. (2006). Collapsing the boundaries? Fatherhood, organization and home-working. *Gender, Work & Organization, 13*, 383–402.

Halgin, R. P., & Whitbourne, S. K. (1994). *Abnormal psychology*. Fort Worth, TX: Harcourt Brace.

Hall, G. C. N. (1996). *Theory-based assessment, treatment, and prevention of sexual aggression*. New York: Oxford University Press.

Hall, J., & Bernieri, F. (Eds.). (2001). *Interpersonal sensitivity*. Mahwah, NJ: Lawrence Erlbaum Associates.

Hall, J. A., Roter, D. L., & Katz, N. R. (1988). Task versus socioemotional behaviors in physicians. *Medical Care, 25*, 399–412.

Hall, R. E. (2002). *The Bell Curve*: Implications for the performance of black/white athletes. *Social Science Journal, 39*, 113–118.

Hall, S. S. (2003, September). The quest for a smart pill. *Scientific American*, pp. 54–63.

Halling, S., & Goldfarb, M. (1996). The new generation of diagnostic manuals (DSM-III, DSM-III-R, and DSM-IV): An overview and a phenomenologically based critique. *Journal of Phenomenological Psychology, 27*, 49–71.

Hallschmid, M., Benedict, C., Born, J., Fehm, H., & Kern, W. (2004). Manipulating central nervous mechanisms of food intake and body weight regulation by intranasal administration of neuropeptides in man. *Physiology and Behavior, 83*, 55–64.

Halpern, D. F. (1998). Teaching critical thinking for transfer across domains. *American Psychologist, 53*, 449–455.

Halpern, D. F. (2000). *Sex differences in cognitive abilities* (3rd ed.). Mahwah, NJ: Erlbaum.

Halpern, D. F. (2005). Psychology at the intersection of work and family: Recommendations for employers, working families, and policymakers. *American Psychologist, 60*, 397–409.

Halpern, D., & Riggio, H. (2002). *Thinking critically about critical thinking*. Mahwah, NJ: Erlbaum.

Halpert, J. (2003, April 28). What do patients want? *Newsweek*, pp. 63–64.

Hamani, Y., Sciaki-Tamir, Y., Deri-Hasid, R., Miller-Pogrund, T., Milwidsky, A., & Haimov-Kochman, R. (2007). Misconceptions about oral contraception pills among adolescents and physicians. *Human Reproduction, 22*, 3078–3083.

Hamann, S. (2001). Cognitive and neural mechanisms of emotional memory. *Trends in Cognitive Sciences, 5*, 394–400.

Hamann, S. B., Ely, T. D., Hoffman, J. M., & Kilts, C. D. (2002). Ecstasy and agony: Activation of human amygdala in positive and negative emotion. *Psychological Science, 13*, 135–141.

Hamann, S., Herman, R. A., Nolan, C. L., & Wallen, K. (2004). Men and women differ in amygdala response to visual sexual stimuli. *Nature Neuroscience, 7*, 411–416.

Hambleton, R. K. (2006). Psychometric models, test designs and item types for the next generation of educational and psychological tests. In D. Bartram, & R. K. Hambleton, *Computer-based testing and the Internet: Issues and advances*. New York: John Wiley & Sons.

Hamel, S., Leclerc, G., & Lefrancois, R. (2003). A psychological outlook on the concept of transcendent actualization. *International Journal of the Psychology of Religion, 13*, 3–15.

Hamer, D. H., Hu, S., Magnuson, V. L., Hu, N., & Pattatucci, A. M. L. (1993, July 16). A linkage between DNA markers on the X chromosome and male sexual orientation. *Science, 261*, 321–327.

Hamer, M., Taylor, A., & Steptoe, A. (2006). The effect of acute aerobic exercise on stress related blood pressure responses: A systematic review and meta-analysis. *Biological Psychology, 71*, 183–190.

Hamilton, A. C., & Martin, R. C. (2007). Semantic short-term memory deficits and resolution of interference: A case for inhibition? In D. S. Gorfein, & C. M. Macleod, *Inhibition in cognition*. Washington, DC: American Psychological Association.

Hamilton, C. E. (2000). Continuity and discontinuity of attachment from infancy through adolescence. *Child Development, 71*, 690–694.

Hamilton, W. L., Biener, L., & Brennan, R. T. (2007). Do local tobacco regulations influence perceived smoking norms? Evidence from adult and youth surveys in Massachusetts. *Health Education Research,* Health Education Research Advance Access published online on October 18, 2007 Health Education Research, doi:10.1093/her/cym054

Hammond, D. C. (2007). Review of the efficacy of clinical hypnosis with headaches and migraines. *International Journal of Clinical and Experimental Hypnosis, 55, April 2007. Special issue: Evidence-based practice clinical hypnosis—part 1*, 207–219.

Hanley, S. J., & Abell, S. C. (2002). Maslow and relatedness: Creating an interpersonal model of self-actualization. *Journal of Humanistic Psychology, 42*, 37–56.

Hanna, J. L. (1984). Black/white nonverbal differences, dance, and dissonance: Implications for desegregation. In A. Wolfgang (Ed.), *Nonverbal behavior: Perspectives, applications, intercultural insights*. Lewiston, NY: Hogrefe.

Hannon, E. E., & Johnson, S. P. (2005). Infants use meter to categorize rhythms and melodies: Implications for musical structure learning. *Cognitive Psychology, 50*, 354–377.

Hansell, S. (2007, January 3). Google answer to filling jobs is an algorithm. *The New York Times*, p. A1.

Harden, B. (2000, January 9). Very young, smart, and restless. *New York Times Education Life*, pp. 28–31.

Hardison, D. M. (2006). Review of Phonetics and phonology in language comprehension and production: Differences and similarities. *Studies in Second Language Acquisition, 28*, 138–140.

Hardy, J., & Selkoe, D. J. (2002, July 19). The amyloid hypothesis of Alzheimer's disease: Progress and problems on the road to therapeutics. *Science, 297*, 353–356.

Hardy, L. T., (2007). Attachment theory and reactive attachment disorder: theoretical perspectives and treatment implications. *Journal of Child and Adolescent Psychiatric Nursing, 20*, 27–39.

Harlaar, N., Spinath, F. M., Dale, P. S., & Plomin, R. (2005). Genetic influences on early word recognition abilities and disabilities: A study of 7-year-old twins. *Journal of Child Psychology and Psychiatry, 46,* 373–384.

Harlow, H. F., & Zimmerman, R. R. (1959). Affectional responses in the infant monkey. *Science, 130,* 421–432.

Harlow, J. M. (1869). Recovery from the passage of an iron bar through the head. *Massachusetts Medical Society Publication, 2,* 329–347.

Harmon-Jones, E., Peterson, H., & Vaughn, K. (2003). The dissonance-inducing effects of an inconsistency between experienced empathy and knowledge of past failures to help: Support for the action-based model of dissonance. *Basic and Applied Social Psychology, 25,* 69–78.

Harmon-Jones, E., & Winkielman, P. (2007). *Social neuroscience: Integrating biological and psychological explanations of social behavior.* New York, NY: Guilford Press.

Harold, G. T., Fincham, F. D., Osborne, L. N., & Conger, R. D. (1997). Mom and dad are at it again: Adolescent perceptions of marital conflict and adolescent psychological distress. *Developmental Psychology, 33,* 333–350.

Harper, T. (1978, November 15). It's not true about people 65 or over. *Green Bay Press-Gazette* (Wisconsin), p. D-1.

Harris, C. R., & Christenfeld, N. (1996). Gender, jealousy, and reason. *Psychological Science, 7,* 364–366.

Harris, J. (2005). *On cloning.* New York: Routledge.

Harris Poll. (2000, February 2). *The power of tobacco addiction.* New York: Harris Interactive.

Harrison, J. A., & Wells, R. B. (1991). Bystander effects on male helping behavior: Social comparison and diffusion of responsibility. *Representative Research in Social Psychology, 19,* 53–63.

Hart, B., & Risley, T. R. (1997). Use of language by three-year-old children. Courtesy of Drs. Betty Hart and Todd Risley, University of Kansas.

Hartmann, E. (1967). *The biology of dreaming.* Springfield, IL: Thomas.

Harton, H. C., & Lyons, P. C. (2003). Gender, empathy, and the choice of the psychology major. *Teaching of Psychology, 30,* 19–24.

Hartung, C. M., & Widiger, T. A. (1998). Gender differences in the diagnosis of mental disorders: Conclusions and controversies of the DSM-IV. *Psychological Bulletin, 123,* 260–278.

Harvard Mental Health Letter (HMHL). (1994, March). Brief psychodynamic therapy—Part I. *Harvard Mental Health Letter,* p. 10.

Harvey, J. H., & Weber, A. L. (2002). *Odyssey of the heart: Close relationships in the 21st century* (2nd ed.). Mahwah, NJ: Erlbaum.

Harvey, J. H., & Wenzel, A. (2004). *The handbook of sexuality in close relationships.* Mahwah, NJ: Lawrence Erlbaum.

Hasselmo, M. E. (2006). The role of acetylcholine in learning and memory. *Opinion in Neurobiology, 16,* 710–715.

Hassold, T. J., & Patterson, D. (1999). *Down syndrome: A promising future, together.* New York, NY: Wiley-Liss.

Hasson, U., Nir, Y., Levy, I., Fuhrmann, G., & Malach, R. (2004, March 12). Intersubject synchronization of cortical activity during natural vision. *Science, 303,* 1634–1637.

Hastings, R. P., & Oakford, S. (2003). Student teachers' attitudes towards the inclusion of children with special needs. *Educational Psychology, 23,* 87–94.

Haugtvedt, C. P., Petty, R. E., & Cacioppo, J. T. (1992). Need for cognition and advertising: Understanding the role of personality variables in consumer behavior. *Journal of Consumer Psychology, 1,* 239–260.

Hauke, C. (2006). The unconscious: Personal and collective. In R. K. Papadopoulos, *The handbook of Jungian psychology: Theory, practice and applications.* New York: Routledge.

Hausenblas, H., and Downs, D. (2002). Relationship among sex, imagery and exercise dependence symptoms. *Psychology of Addictive Behaviors, 16,* 169–172.

Hauser, M. D. (2000). The sound and the fury: Primate vocalizations as reflections of emotion and thought. In N. L. Wallin & B. Merker (Eds.), *The origins of music.* Cambridge, MA: MIT.

Hauser, M. D., Chomsky, N., & Fitch, W. T. (2002, November, 22). The faculty for language: What is it, who has it, and how did it evolve? *Science, 298,* 1569–1579.

Havermans, R. C., Mulkens, S., Nederkoorn, C., & Jansen, A. (2007). The efficacy of cue exposure with response prevention in extinguishing drug and alcohol cue reactivity. *Behavioral Interventions, 22,* 121–135.

Haviland-Jones, J., & Chen, D. (1999, April 17). *Human olfactory perception.* Paper presented at the Association for Chemoreception Sciences, Sarasota, Florida.

Hawke, J. M., Jainchill, N., & De Leon, G. (2000). The prevalence of sexual abuse and its impact on the onset of drug use among adolescents in therapeutic community drug treatment. *Journal of Child & Adolescent Substance Abuse, 9,* 35–49.

Haxby, J. V., Gobini, M. I., Furey, M. L., Ishai, A., Schouten, J. L., & Pietrini, P. (2001, September 28). Distributed and overlapping representations of faces and objects in ventral temporal cortex. *Science, 293,* 2425–2430.

Hayes, J. R. (1966). Memory, goals, and problem solving. In B. Kleinmuntz (Ed.), *Problem solving: Research, method, and theory.* New York: Wiley.

Hayflick, L. (1994). *How and why we age.* New York: Ballantine.

Hayflick, L. (2007). Biological aging is no longer an unsolved problem. *Annals of the New York Academy of Sciences, 1100,* 1–13

Hays, P. A. (2008). *Addressing cultural complexities in practice: Assessment, diagnosis, and therapy* (2nd ed.). Washington, DC: American Psychological Association.

Health Pages. (2003, March 13). Just what the doctor ordered. Retrieved from http://www.thehealthpages.com/articles/ar-drord.html *HealthNews.* (1999, November 20). Losing weight: A little goes a long way. *HealthNews,* p. 1.

Heath, A. C., & Madden, P. A. F. (1995). Genetic influences on smoking behavior. In J. R. Turner, L. R. Cardon, & J. K. Hewitt (Eds.), *Behavior genetic approaches in behavioral medicine: Perspectives on individual differences.* New York: Plenum.

Heath, R. A. (2006). *The Praeger handbook of transsexuality: Changing gender to match mindset.* Westport, CT: Praeger Publishers/Greenwood Publishing.

Hecht, J. M. (2007). The happiness myth: Why what we think is right is wrong. A history of what really makes us happy. New York: HarperSanFrancisco/HarperCollins.

Hedgepeth, E. (2005). Different lenses, different vision. *School Administrator, 62,* 36–39.

Hedges, D. W., Brown, B. L. Shwalk, D. A., Godfrey, K., & Larcher, A. M. (2007). The efficacy of selective serotonin reuptake inhibitors in adult social anxiety disorder: A meta-analysis of double-blind, placebo-controlled trials. *Journal of Psychopharmacology, 21,* 102–111.

Hedges, L. V., & Nowell, A. (July 7, 1995). Sex differences in mental test scores, variability, and numbers of high-scoring individuals. *Science, 269,* 41–45.

Hegarty, P. (2007). From genius inverts to gendered intelligence: Lewis Terman and the power of the norm. *History of Psychology, 10,* Special issue: Power matters: Knowledge politics in the history of psychology, 132–155.

Hegarty, P., & Massey, S. (2007). Anti-homosexual prejudice . . . as opposed to what? Queer theory and the social psychology of anti-homosexual attitudes. *Journal of Homosexuality, 52,* 47–71.

Heider, F. (1958). *The psychology of interpersonal relations.* New York: Wiley.

Heikkinen, H., Nutt, J. G., & LeWitt, P. A. (2001). The effects of different repeated doses of entacapone on the pharmacokinetics of L-dopa and on the clinical response to L-dopa in Parkinson's disease. *Clinical Neuropharmacology, 24,* 150–157.

Heinrichs, R. W. (2005). The primacy of cognition in schizophrenia. *American Psychologist, 60,* 229–242.

Helgeson, V. S., Snyder, P., & Seltman, H. (2004). Psychological and physical adjustment to breast cancer over 4 years: Identifying distinct trajectories of change. *Health Psychology, 23,* 3–15.

Heller, S. (2005). *Freud A to Z.* New York: Wiley.

Helms, J. E. (1992). Why is there no study of cultural equivalence in standardized cognitive ability testing? *American Psychologist, 47,* 1083–1101.

Helmuth, L. (2000, August 25). Synapses shout to overcome distance. *Science, 289,* 1273.

Helmuth, L. (2003, October 31). In sickness or in health? *Science, 302,* 808–810.

Helps, S., Fuggle, P., Udwin, O., & Dick M. (2003). Psychosocial and neuro-cognitive aspects of sickle cell disease. *Child and Adolescent Mental Health, 8,* 11–17.

Henderlong, J., & Lepper, M. R. (2002). The effects of praise on children's intrinsic motivation: A review and synthesis. *Psychological Bulletin, 128,* 774–795.

Henderson, J., Kesmodel, U., & Gray, R. (2007). Systematic review of the fetal effects of prenatal binge-drinking. *Journal of Epidemiology and Community Health, 61,* 1069–1073.

Henderson, N. D. (1982). Correlations in IQ for pairs of people with varying degrees of genetic relatedness and shared environment. *Annual Review of Psychology, 33,* 219–243.

Hendrick, C., & Hendrick, S. S. (2003). Romantic love: Measuring cupid's arrow. In S. J. Lopez & C. R. Snyder (Eds.), *Positive psychological assessment: A handbook of models and measures.* Washington, DC: American Psychological Association.

Henningsen, D. D., Henningsen, M. L., & Eden, J. (2006). Examining the symptoms of groupthink and retrospective sensemaking. *Small Group Research, 37,* 36–64.

Hentschel, U., Smith, G., Draguns, J. G., & Elhers, W. (2004). *Defense mechanisms: Theoretical, research and clinical perspectives.* Oxford, England: Elsevier Science.

Hermann, D., Raybeck, D., & Gruneberg, M. M. (2002). *Improving memory and study skills: Advances in theory and practice.* Cambridge, MA: Hogrefe & Huber.

Herrán, A., Carrera, M., & Sierra-Biddle, D. (2006). Panic disorder and the onset of agoraphobia. *Psychiatry and Clinical Neurosciences, 60,* 395–396.

Herrington, D. M., & Howard, T. D. (2003). From presumed benefit to potential harm—Hormone therapy and heart disease. *New England Journal of Medicine, 349,* 519–521.

Herrnstein, R. J., & Murray, D. (1994). *The bell curve.* New York: Free Press.

Hertlein, K. M., Weeks, G. R., & Gambescia, N. (2007). The treatment of hypoactive sexual desire disorder: An intersystem approach. In L. VandeCreek, F. L. Peterson, Jr., & J. W. Bley, *Innovations in clinical practice: Focus on sexual health.* Sarasota, FL: Professional Resource Press/Professional Resource Exchange.

Herzog, H. A. (2005). Dealing with the animal research controversy. In C. K. Akins & S. Panicker (Eds.), *Laboratory animals in research and teaching: Ethics, care, and methods.* Washington, DC: American Psychological Association.

Heshka, S., Anderson, J. W., Atkinson, R. L., Greenway, F. L., Hill, J. O., Phinney, S. D., Kolotkin, R. L., Miller-Kovach, K., & Pi-Sunyer, F. X. (2003). Weight loss with self-help compared with a structured commercial program: A randomized trial. *Journal of the American Medical Association, 289,* 1792–1798.

Hess, D. W., Kolakowsky-Hayner, S. A., Cifu, D. X., & Huang, M. E. (2000). A comparative study of outcomes and expenses following tetraplegia and paraplegia. *Journal of Spinal Cord Medicine, 23,* 228–233.

Hess, T. M., Hinson, J. T., & Statham, J. A. (2004). Explicit and implicit stereotype activation effects on memory: Do age and awareness moderate the impact of priming? *Psychology and Aging, 19,* 495–505.

Hetherington, E. M. (Ed.). (1999). *Coping with divorce, single parenting, and remarriage: A risk and resiliency perspective.* Mahwah, NJ: Erlbaum.

Heuser, S. (2006, April 2). A case of mind over matter. *Boston Globe,* p. A1.

Heward, W. L., & Orlansky, M. D. (1988). *Exceptional children* (3rd ed.). Columbus, OH: Merrill.

Hewitt, B., Gose, S. G., & Birkbeck, M. (2000, December 11). House divided. *People Weekly, 54,* 138–144.

Heyman, G. D., & Diesendruck, G. (2002). The Spanish *ser/estar* distinction in bilingual children's reasoning about human psychological characteristics. *Developmental Psychology, 38,* 407–417.

Heywood, S., & McCabe, M. P. (2006). Negative affect as a mediator between body dissatisfaction and extreme weight loss and muscle gain behaviors. *Journal of Health Psychology, 11,* 833–844.

Hiby, E. F. Rooney, N. J., & Bradshaw, J. W. S. (2004). Dog training methods: Their use, effectiveness and interaction with behaviour and welfare. *Animal Welfare, 13,* 63–69.

Hicks, T. V., & Leitenberg, H. (2001). Sexual fantasies about one's partner versus someone else: Gender differences in incidence and frequency. *Journal of Sex Research, 38,* 43–50.

Hilarski, C. (2007). Antisocial personality disorder. In B. A. Thyer, & J. S. Wodarski, *Social work in mental health: An evidence-based approach.* Hoboken, NJ: John Wiley & Sons.

Hilgard, E. (1992). Disassociation and theories of hypnosis. In E. Fromm & M. E. Nash (Eds.), *Contemporary hypnosis research.* New York: Guilford.

Hilgard, E. R. (1975). Hypnosis. *Annual Review of Psychology, 26,* 19–44.

Hill, J. O., & Peters, J. C. (1998). Environmental contributions to the obesity epidemic. *Science, 280,* 1371–1374.

Hill, J. O., Catenacci, V., & Wyatt, H. R. (2005). Obesity: Overview of an epidemic. *Psychiatric Clinics of North America, 28,* 1–23.

Hill, J. O., Wyatt, H. R., Reed, G. W., & Peters, J. C. (2003, February 7). Obesity and the environment: Where do we go from here? *Science, 299,* 853–855.

Hillix, W. A. (2007). The past, present, and possible futures of animal language research. In D. A. Washburn, *Primate perspectives on behavior and cognition.* Washington, DC: American Psychological Association.

Hines, M. (2004) *Brain gender.* New York: Oxford University Press.

Hines, M., Golombok, S., Rust, J., Johnston, K. J., Golding, J., & Avon Longitudinal Study of Parents and Children Study Team. (2002). Testosterone during pregnancy and gender role behavior of preschool children: A longitudinal, population study. *Child Development, 73,* 1678–1687.

Hinshaw, S. P., Zupan, B. A., Simmel, C., Nigg, J. T., & Melnick, S. (1997). Peer status in boys with and without attention-deficit hyperactivity disorder: Predictions from overt and covert antisocial behavior, social isolation, and authoritative parenting beliefs. *Child Development, 68,* 880–896.

Hinterberger, T., Birbaumer, N., & Flor, H. (2005). Assessment of cognitive function and communication ability in a completely locked-in patient. *Neurology, 64,* 1307.

Hipkiss, R. A. (1995). *Semantics: Defining the discipline.* Mahwah, NJ: Erlbaum.

Hirschler, B. (2007, May 1). Doctors test gene therapy to treat blindness. *Reuters,* p. 9.

Hirsh, I. J., & Watson, C. S. (1996). Auditory psychophysics and perception. *Annual Review of Psychology, 47,* 461–484.

Hjemdal, O., Aune, T., Reinfjell, T., Stiles, T.C. & Friborg, O. (2007). Resilience as a predictor of depressive symptoms: A correlational study with young adolescents. *Clinical Child Psychology and Psychiatry, 12,* 91–104.

Ho, S. M. Y., Saltel, P., Machavoine, J., Rapoport-Hubschman, N., & Spiegel, D. (2004). Cross-cultural aspects of cancer care. In National Institutes of Health and Stanford University School of Medicine, *Cancer, culture, and communication.* New York: Kluwer Academic/Plenum Publishers.

Ho, W. (2004). Using Kohonen neural network and principle component analysis to characterize divergent thinking. *Creativity Research Journal, 16,* 283–292.

Hobfoll, S. E., Freedy, J. R., Green B. L., & Solomon, S. D. (1996). Coping in reaction to extreme stress: The roles of resource loss and resource availability. In M. Zeidner & N. S. Endler (Eds.), *Handbook of coping: Theory, research, applications.* New York: Wiley.

Hobfoll, S. E., Hall, B. J., & Canetti-Nisim, D. (2007). Refining our understanding of traumatic growth in the face of terrorism: Moving from meaning cognitions to doing what is meaningful. *Applied Psychology: An International Review, 56,* 345–366.

Hobson, J. A. (1988). *The dreaming brain.* New York: Basic Books.

Hobson, J. A. (1996, February). How the brain goes out of its mind. *Harvard Mental Health Letter,* pp. 3–5.

Hobson, J. A. (2005). In bed with Mark Solms? What a nightmare! A reply to Domhoff (2005). *Dreaming, 15,* 21–29.

Hobson, J. A., & Silverstri, L. (1999, February). Parasomnias. *The Harvard Mental Health Letter,* pp. 3–5.

Hochschild, A. (2001, February). A generation without public passion. *Atlantic Monthly,* pp. 33–42.

Hochschild, A. R. (1990). The second shift: Employed women and putting in another day of work at home. *Utne Reader, 38,* 66–73.

Hochschild, A. R., & Machung, A. (2001). *The second shift: Working parents and the revolution at home.* New York: Viking.

Hock, H. S., & Ploeger, A. (2006) Linking dynamical perceptual decisions at different levels of description in motion pattern formation: Psychophysics. *Perception & Psychophysics, 68,* 505–514.

Hoff, E. (2003). Language development in childhood. In R. M. Lerner, M. A. Easterbrooks, et al. (Eds.), *Handbook of psychology: Developmental psychology* (Vol. 6, pp. 171–193). New York: Wiley.

Hoff, E. (2008). *Language development.* New York: Wadsworth.

Hoffer, T. B., et al. (2005, March 8). *Doctorate recipients from United States universities: Summary report 2003.* Chicago: NORC at the University of Chicago.

Hoffman, E. (2001). *Psychological testing at work: How to use, interpret, and get the most out of the newest tests in personality, learning style, aptitudes, interests, and more!* New York: McGraw-Hill.

Hoffman, H. G. (2004, August). Virtual-reality therapy. *Scientific American,* pp. 58–65.

Hoffman, J. P., Baldwin, S. A., & Cerbone, F. G. (2003). Onset of major depressive disorder among adolescents. *Journal of the American Academy of Child and Adolescent Psychiatry, 42,* 217–224.

Hofmann, S. G. (2007). Enhancing exposure-based therapy from a translational research perspective. *Behaviour Research and Therapy, 45,* 1987–2001.

Hogan, J., Davies, S., & Hogan, R. (2007). Generalizing personality-based validity evidence. In S. M. McPhail, *Alternative validation strategies: Developing new and leveraging existing validity evidence.* Hoboken, NJ: John Wiley & Sons.

Hogan, R., Hogan, J., & Roberts, B. W. (1996). Personality measurement and employment decisions: Questions and answers. *American Psychologist, 51,* 469–477.

Hoge, C. W., & Castro, C. A. (2006, September 2). Post-traumatic stress disorder in UK and US forces deployed to Iraq. *Lancet, 368,* 837.

Hoge, C. W., Castro, C. A., Messer, S. C., McGurk, D., Cotting, D. I., & Koffman, R. L. (2004). Combat duty in Iraq and Afghanistan, mental health problems and barriers to care. *New England Journal of Medicine, 351,* 13–22.

Hogg, M. A. (2006). Social identity theory. In P. J. Burke, *Contemporary social psychological theories.* Stanford University Press.

Hogg, M. A., & Hains, S. C. (2001). Intergroup relations and group solidarity: Effects of group identification and social beliefs on depersonalized attraction. In M. A. Hogg & D. Abrams (Eds.), *Intergroup relations: Essential readings.* New York: Psychology Press.

Holden, C. (2003, January 17). Deconstructing schizophrenia. *Science, 299,* 333–335.

Holden, C. (2005, June 10). Sex and the suffering brain. *Science, 308,* 1574–1577.

Holden, C. (2007, June 29). Embryonic stem cells. Stem cell science advances as politics stall. *Science, 316*, 1825.

Holden, G. W. (2002). Perspectives on the effects of corporal punishment: Comment on Gershoff (2002). *Psychological Bulletin, 128*, 590–595.

Holden, R. R. (2000). Are there promising MMPI substitutes for assessing psychopathology and personality? Review and prospect. In R. H. Dana, et al. (Eds.). *Handbook of cross-cultural and multicultural personality assessment. Personality and clinical psychology series.* Mahwah, NJ: Lawrence Erlbaum.

Holland, J. C., & Lewis, S. (2001). *The human side of cancer: Living with hope, coping with uncertainty.* New York: Quill.

Holler, G. D. (2006). Relations of hypnotic susceptibility, absorption, imagery, sexual fantasy, sexual daydreaming, and social desirability to sexual satisfaction. *Dissertation Abstracts International: Section B: The Sciences and Engineering, 67*, 3453.

Hollingworth, H. L. (1943/1990). *Leta Stetter Hollingworth: A biography.* Boston: Anker.

Hollins, K. (2007). Consequences of antenatal mental health problems for child health and development. *Current Opinions on Obstetric Gynecology, 19*, 568–573.

Hollis, K. L. (1997, September). Contemporary research on Pavlovian conditioning: A "new" functional analysis. *American Psychologist, 52*, 956–965.

Hollon, S. D., Thase, M. E., & Markowitz, J. C. (2002). Treatment and prevention of depression. *Psychological Science in the Public Interest, 3*, 39–77.

Holloway, L. (2000, December 16). Chief of New York City schools plans to revamp bilingual study. *The New York Times*, p. A1.

Holmes, A., Yang, R. J., Lesch, K. P., Crawley, J. N., & Murphy, D. L. (2003). Mice lacking the Serotonin Transporter Exhibit 5-HT sub(1A) receptor-mediated abnormalities in tests for anxiety-like behavior. *Neuropsychopharmacology, 28*, 2077–2088.

Holmes, C. T., & Keffer, R. L. (1995). A computerized method to teach Latin and Greek root words: Effect on verbal SAT scores. *Journal of Educational Research, 89*, 47–50.

Holowka, S., & Pettito, L. A. (2002, August 30). Left hemisphere cerebral specialization for babies while babbling. *Science, 297*, 1515.

Holt, M., & Jahn, R. (2004, March, 26). Synaptic vesicles in the fast lane. *Science, 303*, 1986–1987.

Holy, T. E., Dulac, C., & Meister, M. (2000, September 1). Responses of vomeronasal neurons to natural stimuli. *Science, 289*, 1569–1572.

Hong, E., Milgram, R. M., & Gorsky, H. (1995). Original thinking as a predictor of creative performance in young children. *Roeper Review, 18*, 147–149.

Hong, S. (2000). Exercise and psychoneuroimmunology [Special issue: Exercise psychology]. *International Journal of Sport Psychology, 31*, 204–227.

Hong, Y., Morris, M., Chiu, C., & Benet-Martinez, V. (2000). Multicultural minds. *American Psychologist, 55*, 709–720.

Hongchun, W., & Mind, L. (2006). About the research on suggestibility and false memory. *Psychological Science (China), 29*, 905–908.

Hoover, E. (2004). More college students report diagnoses of depression, survey finds. *The Chronicle of Higher Education.* Retrieved from http://chronicle.com/daily/2004/11/2004113004n.htm.

Hopkin, M. (2007, August 2). Implant boosts activity in injured brain. *Nature, 448*, 522.

Horgan, J. (1993, December). Fractured functions: Does the brain have a supreme integrator? *Scientific American*, pp. 36–37.

Horgan, J. (1995, November). Get smart, take a test. *Scientific American*, pp. 12–14.

Horgan, J. (1996, December). Why Freud isn't dead. *Scientific American*, pp. 106–111.

Horinek, D., Varjassyová, A., & Hort, J. (2007). Magnetic resonance analysis of amygdalar volume in Alzheimer's disease. *Current Opinion in Psychiatry, 20*, 273–277.

Horn, J. L. (2002). Selections of evidence, misleading assumptions, and over-simplifications: The political message of *The Bell Curve*. In J. M. Fish (Ed.), *Race and intelligence: Separating science from myth*, pp. 297–325. Mahwah, NJ: Erlbaum.

Horney, K. (1937). *Neurotic personality of our times.* New York: Norton.

Horton, K. D., Wilson, D. E., Vonk, J., Kirby, S. L., & Nielsen, T. (2005). Measuring automatic retrieval: A comparison of implicit memory, process dissociation, and speeded response procedures. *Acta Psychologica, 119*, 235–263.

Houghtalen, R. P., & Talbot, N. (2007). Dissociative disorders and cognitive disorders. In O. J. Z. Sahler, & J. E. Carr, *The behavioral sciences and health care* (2nd rev. and updated ed.). Ashland, OH: Hogrefe & Huber Publishers, 2007.

Hovland, C., Janis, I., & Kelly, H. H. (1953). *Communication and persuasion.* New Haven, CT: Yale University Press.

Howatt, W. A. (2005). Cognitive-behavioral models. In R. H. Coombs (Ed.), *Addiction counseling review: Preparing for comprehensive, certification, and licensing examinations.* Mahwah, NJ: Lawrence Erlbaum Associates.

Howe, C. J. (2002). The countering of overgeneralization. *Journal of Child Language, 29*, 875–895.

Howells, J. G., & Osborn, M. L. (1984). *A reference companion to the history of abnormal psychology.* Westport, CT: Greenwood Press.

Howitt, D., & Cramer, D. (2000). *First steps in research and statistics: A practical workbook for psychology students.* Philadelphia: Psychology Press.

Hrabosky, J. I., White, M. A., Masheb, R. M., & Grilo, C. M. (2007). Physical activity and its correlates in treatment-seeking obese patients with binge eating disorder. *International Journal of Eating Disorders, 40*, 72–76.

Hsu, B., Koing, A., Kessler, C., Knapke, K., et al. (1994). Gender differences in sexual fantasy and behavior in a college population: A ten-year replication. *Journal of Sex and Marital Therapy, 20*, 103–118.

Hu, F. B., Li, T. Y., Colditz, G. A., Willett, W. C., & Manson, J. E. (2003). Television watching and other sedentary behaviors in relation to risk of obesity and type 2 diabetes mellitus in women. *Journal of the American Medical Association, 289*, 1785–1791.

Hubbard, K., O'Neill, A., & Cheakalos, C. (1999, April 12). Out of control. *People*, pp. 52–72.

Hubble, M. A., Duncan, B. L., & Miller, S. D. (Eds.). (1999). *The heart and soul of change: What works in therapy.* Washington, DC: American Psychological Association.

Hubel, D. H., & Wiesel, T. N. (2004). *Brain and visual perception. The story of a 25-year collaboration.* New York: Oxford University Press.

Huber, F., Beckmann, S. C., & Herrmann, A. (2004). Means-end analysis: Does the affective state influence information processing style? *Psychology and Marketing, 21*, 715–737.

Hudson, W. (1960). Pictorial depth perception in subcultural groups in Africa. *Journal of Social Psychology, 52*, 183–208.

Hudspeth, A. J. (2000). Hearing. In E. R. Kandel, J. H. Schwartz, & T. M. Jessell (Eds.), *Principles of neural science* (4th ed.). New York: McGraw-Hill.

Huerta, M., Cortina, L. M., & Pang, J. S. (2006). Sex and power in the academy: Modeling sexual harassment in the lives of college women. *Personality and Social Psychology Bulletin, 32*, 616–628.

Huesmann, L. R., Moise-Titus, J., Podolski, C. L., & Eron, L. D. (2003). Longitudinal relations between children's exposure to TV violence and their aggressive and violent behavior in young adulthood: 1977–1992 [Special issue: Violent children]. *Developmental Psychology, 39*, 201–221.

Huff, C. (2004, September). The baggage screener's brain scan. *Monitor on Psychology*, pp. 34–36.

Huffman, C. J., Matthews, T. D., & Gagne, P. E. (2001). The role of part-set cuing in the recall of chess positions: Influence of chunking in memory. *North American Journal of Psychology, 3*, 535–542.

Hughes, J. O., & Sandler, B. R. (1987). *In case of sexual harassment: A guide for women students.* Washington, D.C: Association of American Colleges.

Huijie, T. (2006). The measurement and assessment of mental health: A longitudinal and cross-sectional research on undergraduates, adults and patients. *Psychological Science (China), 29*, 419–422.

Hull, C. L. (1943). *Principles of behavior.* New York: Appleton-Century-Crofts.

Humayun, M., Dagnelie, G. Greenberg, R., Propst, R., & Phillips, D. (1966). Visual perception elicited by electrical stimulation of retina in blind humans. *Archive of Ophthalmology, 114*, 40–46.

Humphrey, N., Curran, A., & Morris, E. (2007). Emotional intelligence and education: A critical review. *Educational Psychology, 27*, 235–254.

Humphreys, G. W., & Müller, H. (2000). A search asymmetry reversed by figure-ground assignment. *Psychological Science, 11*, 196–200.

Humphreys, J. (2003). Resilience in sheltered battered women. *Issues in Mental Health Nursing, 24*, 137–152.

Hunt, E. (1994). Problem solving. In R. J. Sternberg (Ed.), *Thinking and problem solving: Handbook of perception and cognition* (2nd ed.). San Diego, CA: Academic Press.

Hunt, E. (2005). Information processing and intelligence: Where we are and where we are going. In R. J. Sternberg & J. E. Pretz, *Cognition and intelligence: Identifying the mechanisms of the mind.* New York: Cambridge University Press.

Hunt, J. S., Seifert, A. L., & Armenta, B. E. (2006). Stereotypes and prejudice as dynamic constructs: reminders about the nature of intergroup bias from the hurricane Katrina relief efforts. *Analyses of Social Issues and Public Policy (ASAP), 6*, 237–253.

Hunt, M. (1974). *Sexual behaviors in the 1970s.* New York: Dell.

Huston, A. C., Donnerstein, E., Fairchild, H. H., Feshback, N. D., Katz, P., Murray, J. P., Rubinstein, E. A., Wilcox, B. L., & Zuckerman, D. (1992). Big world, small screen: The role of television in American society. Omaha, NE: University of Nebraska Press.

Hutchinson, S. L., Baldwin, C. K., & Oh, S-S. (2006). Adolescent coping: Exploring adolescents' leisure-based responses to stress. *Leisure Sciences, 28,* 115–131.

Hyde, J. (2004). *Half the human experience: The psychology of women* (6th ed.). Boston: Houghton Mifflin.

Hyde, J. S. (1994). *Understanding human sexuality* (5th ed.). New York: McGraw-Hill.

Hyde, J. S. (2005). The gender similarities hypothesis. *American Psychologist, 50,* 581-592.

Hyde, J.S. & Grabe, S. (2008). Meta-analysis in the psychology of women. In F.L. Denmark & M.A. Paludi (Eds.), *Psychology of women: A handbook of issues and theories* (2nd ed.). Westport, CT: Praeger Publishers/ Greenwood Publishing Group.

Hyde, J. S., & Linn, M. C. (1988). Gender differences in verbal ability: A meta-analysis. *Psychological Bulletin, 104,* 53–69.

Hyde, J. S., DeLamater, J. D., & Byers, E. S. (2006). *Understanding human sexuality* (3rd ed). New York: McGraw-Hill.

Hyde, J. S., Fennema, E., & Lamon, S. J. (1990). Gender differences in mathematics performance: A meta-analysis. *Psychological Bulletin, 107,* 139–155.

Hyman, R. (1994). Anomaly or artifact? Comments on Bem and Honorton. *Psychological Bulletin, 115,* 19–24.

Hyman, S. E. (2003, September). Diagnosing disorders. *Scientific American,* pp. 96–103.

Iachini, T., & Giusberti, F. (2004). Metric properties of spatial images generated from locomotion: The effect of absolute size on mental scanning. *European Journal of Cognitive Psychology, 16,* 573–596.

Ievers-Landis, C. E., Hoff, A. L., Brez, C., Cancilliere, M. K., McConnell, J., & Kerr, D. (2005). Situational analysis of dietary challenges of the treatment regimen for children and adolescents with phenylketonuria and their primary caregivers. *Journal of Developmental and Behavioral Pediatrics, 26,* 186–193.

Iglesias, A. (2005). Awake-alert hypnosis in the treatment of panic disorder: A case report. *American Journal of Clinical Hypnosis, 47,* 249–257.

Igo, S. E. (2006). Review of A telescope on society: Survey research and social science at the University of Michigan and beyond. *Journal of the History of the Behavioral Sciences, 42,* 95–96.

Ihler, E. (2003). Patient-physician communication. *Journal of the American Medical Association, 289,* 92.

Ikonomidou, C., Bittigau, P., Ishimaru, M. J., Wozniak, D. F., Koch, C., Genz, K., Price, M. T., Stefovska, V., Hörster, F., Tenkova, T., Dikranian, K., & Olney, J. W. (2000, February 11). Ethanol-induced apoptotic neurodegeneration and fetal alcohol syndrome. *Science, 287,* 1056–1060.

Ilies, R., Arvey, R. D., & Bouchard, T. J., Jr. (2006). Darwinism, behavioral genetics, and organizational behavior: A review and agenda for future research. *Journal of Organizational Behavior, 27,* Special issue: Darwinian Perspectives on Behavior in Organizations, 96–123.

Ilies, R., Arvey, R. D., & Bouchard, T. J., Jr. (2006). Darwinism, behavioral genetics, and organizational behavior: A review and agenda for future research. *Journal of Organizational Behavior, 27,* Special issue: *Darwinian Perspectives on Behavior in Organizations,* 121–141.

Imamura, M., & Nakamizo, S. (2006). An empirical test of formal equivalence between Emmert's Law and the size-distance invariance hypothesis. *The Spanish Journal of Psychology, 9(2),* 295–299.

Innocenti, G. M. (2007). Subcortical regulation of cortical development: some effects of early, selective deprivations. *Progressive Brain Research, 164,* 23–37.

Irwin, R. R. (2006). Spiritual development in adulthood: Key concepts and models. In C. Hoare, *Handbook of adult development and learning* New York: Oxford University Press.

Isay, R. A. (1994). *Being homosexual: Gay men and their development.* Lanham, MD: Jason Aronson.

Isbell, L. M., & Tyler, J. M. (2003). Teaching students about in-group favoritism and the minimal groups paradigm. *Teaching of Psychology, 30,* 127–130.

Ishikura, R., & Tashiro, N. (2002). Frustration and fulfillment of needs in dissociative and conversion disorders. *Psychiatry and Clinical Neurosciences, 56,* 381–390.

Iverson, L. (2000). *The science of marijuana.* Oxford, England: Oxford University Press.

Iverson, P., Kuhl, P. K., Reiko, A. Y., Diesch, E., Tohkura, Y., Ketterman, A., & Siebert, C. (2003). A perceptual interference account of acquisition difficulties for non-native phonemes. *Cognition, 87,* B47–B57.

Iverson, S. D, & Iversen, L. L. (2007). Dopamine: 50 years in perspective. *Trends in Neurosciences, 30,* 188–191.

Izard, C. E. (1990). Facial expressions and the regulation of emotions. *Journal of Personality and Social Psychology, 58,* 487–498.

Izard, C. E. (1994). Innate and universal facial expressions: Evidence from developmental and cross-cultural research. *Psychological Bulletin, 115,* 288–299.

Izard, C. E., & Abe, J. A. (2004). Developmental changes in facial expressions of emotions in the strange situation during the second year of life. *Emotion, 4,* 251–265.

Jackson, D. N., & Rushton, J. P. (2006). Males have greater g: Sex differences in general mental ability from 100,000 17- to 18-year-olds on the Scholastic Assessment Test. *Intelligence, 34,* 479–486.

Jackson, J. D. (2006). Trauma, attachment, and coping: Pathways to resilience. *Dissertation Abstracts International: Section B: The Sciences and Engineering, 67(1-B),* 547.

Jackson, T. L. (Ed.). (1996). *Acquaintance rape: Assessment, treatment, and prevention.* Sarasota, FL: Professional Resource Press/ Professional Resource Exchange.

Jacobs, J. A., & Gerson, K. (2004). *The time divide: Work, family, and gender inequality.* Cambridge, MA: Harvard University Press.

Jacobson, P. D., Wasserman, J., & Anderson, J. R. (1997). Historical overview of tobacco legislation and regulation. *Journal of Social Issues, 53,* 75–95.

Jacoby, L. L., Bishara, A. J., Hessels, S., & Hughes, A. (2007). Probabilistic retroactive interference: The role of accessibility bias in interference effects. *Journal of Experimental Psychology: General, 136,* 200–216.

Jaffé, A., Prasad, S. A., & Larcher, V. (2006). Gene therapy for children with cystic fibrosis— Who has the right to choose? *Journal of Medical Ethics, 32,* 361–364.

Jaffe, S., & Hyde, J. S. (2000). Gender differences in moral orientation: A meta-analysis. *Psychological Bulletin, 126,* 703–726.

Jain, S., Mills, P. J., & Von Känel, R. (2007). Effects of perceived stress and uplifts on inflammation and coagulability. *Psychophysiology, 44,* 154–160.

James, J. E. (1997). *Understanding caffeine: A biobehavioral analysis.* Newbury Park, CA: Sage.

James, H. S., Jr. (2005). Why did you do that? An economic examination of the effect of extrinsic compensation on intrinsic motivation and performance. *Journal of Economic Psychology, 26,* 549–566.

James, W. (1890). *The principles of psychology.* New York: Holt.

Jamieson, G. A. (2007). *Hypnosis and conscious states: The cognitive neuroscience perspective.* New York: Oxford University Press.

Jamison, K. R. (1993). *Touched with fire: Manic depressive illness and the artistic temperament.* New York: Free Press.

Jamison, K. R. (1995a). *An unquiet mind: A memoir of moods and madness.* New York: Knopf.

Jamison, K. R. (1995b, February). Manic-depressive illness and creativity. *Scientific American,* pp. 62–67.

Jang, S. J., You, S. H., & Ahn, S. H. (2007). Neurorehabilitation-induced cortical reorganization in brain injury: A 14-month longitudinal follow-up study. *NeuroRehabilitation, 22,* 117–122.

Janicki-Deverts, D., Cohen, S., Adler, N. E., Schwartz, J. E., Matthews, K. A., & Seeman, T. E. (2007). Socioeconomic status is related to urinary catecholamines in the Coronary Artery Risk Development in Young Adults (CARDIA) study. *Psychosomatic Medicine, 69,* 514–520.

Janis, I. L. (1989). *Crucial decisions: Leadership in policy-making management.* New York: Free Press.

Janis, I. L. (1997). Groupthink. In R. P. Vecchio, *Leadership: Understanding the dynamics of power and influence in organizations.* Notre Dame, IN: University of Notre Dame Press.

Jaret, P. (1992, November/December). Mind over malady. *Health,* pp. 87–94.

Jarlais, D. C. D., Arasteh, K., & Perlis, T. (2007). The transition from injection to non-injection drug use: Long-term outcomes among heroin and cocaine users in New York City. *Addiction, 102,* 778–785.

Javitt, D. C., & Coyle, J. T. (January 2004). Decoding schizophrenia. *Scientific American,* pp. 46–55.

Jayson, S. (2006, August 21). Gen Nexters have their hands full. *USA Today,* p. 1D.

Jefferson, D. J. (2005, August 8). American's most dangerous drug. *Newsweek,* pp. 41–47.

Jenike, M. A. (1998). Neurosurgical treatment of obsessive-compulsive disorder. *British Journal of Psychiatry, 173*(Suppl. 35), 79–90.

Jenkins, A. M., Albee, G. W., Paster, V. S., Sue, S., Baker, D. B., Comas-Diaz, L., Puente, A. E., Suinn, R. M., Caldwell-Colbert, A. T., Williams, V. M., & Root, M. P. P. (2003). Ethnic minorities. In D. K. Freedheim, *Handbook of psychology: History of Psychology, Vol. 1.* Hoboken, NJ: John Wiley & Sons.

Jenkins, C. D., Zyzanski, S. J., & Rosenman, R. H. (1978). Coronary-prone behavior: One pattern or several? *Psychosomatic Medicine, 40,* 25–43.

Jenkins, L. S., & Gortner, S. R. (1998). Correlates of self-efficacy expectation and prediction of walking behavior in cardiac surgery elders. *Annals of Behavioral Medicine, 20,* 99–103.

Jenkins, S. (2004, October 29). Mystics all-star cites depression for her absence. *The Washington Post*, p. A1.

Jenkins, S. R. (1994). Need for power and women's careers over 14 years: Structural power, job satisfaction, and motive change. *Journal of Personality and Social Psychology, 66*, 155–165.

Jensen, A. R. (2002). Galton's legacy to research on intelligence. *Journal of Biosocial Science, 34*, 145–172.

Jensen, A. R. (2003). Do age-group differences on mental tests imitate racial differences? *Intelligence, 31*, 107–121.

Jensen, A. R. (2005). Psychometric g and mental chronometry. *Cortex, 41*, 230–231.

Jequier, E. (2002). Pathways to obesity. *International Journal of Obesity and Related Metabolic Disorders, 26*, S12–S17.

Jetten, J., Hornsey, M. J., & Adarves-Yorno, I. (2006). When group members admit to being conformist: The role of relative intragroup status in conformity self-reports. *Personality and Social Psychology Bulletin, 32*, 162–173.

Jha, A. (2006, February 3). Pill could make painful memories a thing of past: Common drug may help to fight post traumatic stress. *The Guardian* (London), p. 15.

Jhally, S., Goldman, R., Cassidy, M., Katula, R., Seiter, E., Pollay, R. W., Lee, J. S., Carter-Whitney, D., Steinem, G., et al. (1995). Advertising. In G. Dines & J. M. Humez (Eds.), *Gender, race, and class in media: A text reader*. Thousand Oaks, CA: Sage.

Joacoby, L. L., Bishara, A. J., & Hessels, S. (2007). Probabilistic retroactive interference: The role of accessibility bias in interference effects. *Journal of Experimental Psychology: General, 136*, 200–216.

Joe, G. W., Flynn, P. M., & Broome, K. M. (2007). Patterns of drug use and expectations in methadone patients. *Addictive Behaviors, 32*, 1640–1656.

Johns, M., Schmader, T., & Martens, A. (2005). Knowing is half the battle: Teaching stereotype threat as a means of improving women's math performance. *Psychological Science, 16*, 175–179.

Johnsdotter, S., & Essén, B. (2005). It is only a tradition: Making sense of Swedish Somalis' narratives of female circumcision and avoiding submission to hegemonic political discourse. *Critical Social Policy, 25*, 577–589.

Johnson, D. M., Parrott, G. R., & Stratton, R. P. (1968). Production and judgment of solutions to five problems. *Journal of Educational Psychology Monograph Supplement, 59* (6, pt. 2).

Johnson, G. B. (2000). *The Living World*, p. 600. Boston: McGraw-Hill.

Johnson, H. D. (2004). Gender, grade and relationship differences in emotional closeness within adolescent friendships. *Adolescence, 39*, 243–255.

Johnson, J. G., Cohen, P., Smailes, E. M., Kasen, S., & Brook, J. S. (2002, March 29). Television viewing and aggressive behavior during adolescence and adulthood. *Science, 295*, 2468–2471.

Johnson, S. P. (2004). Development of perceptual completion in infancy. *Psychological Science, 15*, 769–775.

Johnson, S. P., Bremner, J. G., Slater, A., Mason, U., Foster, K., & Cheshire, A. (2003). Infants' perception of object trajectories. *Child Development, 74*, 94–108.

Johnson-Laired, P. N. (2006). *How we reason*. Oxford, England: Oxford University Press.

John-Steiner, V., & Mahn, H. (2003). Sociocultural contexts for teaching and learn-

ing. In W. M. Reynolds & G. E. Miller (Eds.), *Handbook of psychology: Educational psychology* (Vol. 7, pp. 125–151). New York: Wiley.

Johnston, L. D., O'Malley, P. M., & Bachman, J. G. (2003). *Monitoring the future: National results on adolescent drug use: Overview of key findings, 2002.* Bethesda MD: National Institute on Drug Abuse.

Johnston, L. D., O'Malley, P. M., & Bachman. J. G. (2002, December 16). *Ecstasy use among American teens drops for the first time in recent years, and overall drug and alcohol use also decline in the year after 9/11.* Ann Arbor, MI: University of Michigan News and Information Services. www.monitoringthefuture.org; accessed December 26, 2002.

Johnston, L. D., O'Malley, P. M., Bachman, J. G., & Schulenberg, J. E. (2004, December 21). *Overall teen drug use continues gradual decline; but use of inhalants rises.* University of Michigan News and Information Services: Ann Arbor, MI. Retrieved August 23, 2005, from http://www.monitoringthefuture.org.

Johnston, L. D., O'Malley, P. M., Bachman, J. G., & Schulenberg, J. E. (2006). *Monitoring the Future national results on adolescent drug use: Overview of key findings, 2006.*

Johnston, L. D., O'Malley, P. M., Bachman, J. G., & Schulenberg, J. E. (2007). *Monitoring the Future national results on adolescent drug use: Overview of key findings, 2007.* Ann Arbor, MI: University of Michigan.

Johnston, M. V. (2004). Clinical disorders of brain plasticity. *Brain and Development, 26*, 73–80.

Joiner, T. E., & Wagner, K. D. (1995). Attribution style and depression in children and adolescents: A meta-analytic review. *Clinical Psychology Review, 15*, 777–798.

Jones, A., & Crandall, R. (Eds.). (1991). Handbook of self-actualization. *Journal of Social Behavior and Personality, 6*, 1–362.

Jones, A. L. (2006). The contemporary psychoanalyst: Karen Horney's theory applied in today's culture. *PsycCRITIQUES, 51*, 127–134.

Jones, J. C., & Barlow, D. H. (1990). Self-reported frequency of sexual urges, fantasies, and masturbatory fantasies in heterosexual males and females. *Archives of Sexual Behavior, 19*, 269–279.

Jones, J. E., & Corp, E. S. (2003). Effect of naltrexone on food intake and body weight in Syrian hamsters depends on metabolic status. *Physiology and Behavior, 78*, 67–72.

Jones, J. M. (2007). Exposure to chronic community violence: Resilience in African American children. *Journal of Black Psychology, 33*, 125–149.

Jones, K. M., & Friman, P. C. (1999). A case study of behavioral assessment and treatment of insect phobia. *Journal of Applied Behavior Analysis, 32*, 95–98.

Jones, R. K., Darroch, J. E., Singh, S. (2005). Religious differentials in the sexual and reproductive behaviors of young women in the United States. *Journal of Adolescent Health, 36*, 279–288.

Jorgensen, G. (2006). Kohlberg and Gilligan: duet or duel? *Journal of Moral Education, 35*, 179–196.

Jorgenson, L. M., & Wahl, K. M. (2000). Psychiatrists as expert witnesses in sexual harassment cases under *Daubert* and *Kumho. Psychiatric Annals, 30*, 390–396.

Joyce, J. (1934). *Ulysses.* New York: Random House.

Julesz, B. (1986). Stereoscopic vision. *Vision Research, 26*, 1601–1612.

Juliano, L. M., & Griffiths, R. R. (2004). A critical review of caffeine withdrawal: Empirical validation of symptoms and signs, incidence, severity, and associated features. *Psychopharmacology, 176*, 1–29.

Julien, R. M (2001). *A primer of drug action* (9th ed.). New York: Freeman.

Jung, C. G. (1961). *Freud and psychoanalysis.* New York: Pantheon.

Jung, J. (2002). *Psychology of alcohol and other drugs: A research perspective.* Thousand Oaks, CA: Sage.

Juster, F. T., Ono, H., & Stafford, F. (2002). *Report on housework and division of labor.* Ann Arbor, MI: Institute for Social Research.

Jylha, M. (2004). Old age and loneliness: Cross-sectional and longitudinal analyses in the Tampere longitudinal study on aging. *Canadian Journal on Aging/La Revue canadienne du vieillissement, 23*, 157–168.

Kaasinen, V., & Rinne, J. O. (2002). Functional imaging studies of dopamine system and cognition in normal aging and Parkinson's disease. *Neuroscience & Biobehavioral Reviews, 26*, 785–793.

Kahn, J. P. (2004). Hostility, coronary risk, and alpha-adrenergic to beta-adrenergic receptor density ratio. *Psychosomatic Medicine, 66*, 289–297.

Kahn, R. S., Davidson, M., & Davis, K. L. (1996). Dopamine and schizophrenia revisited. In S. J. Watson (Ed.), *Biology of schizophrenia and affective disease.* Washington, DC: American Psychiatric Press.

Kahneman, D., Diener, E., & Schwarz, N. (1998). *Well-being: The foundations of hedonic psychology.* New York: Russell Sage Foundation.

Kahng, S. W., Iwata, B. A., & Lewin, A. B. (2002). Behavioral treatment of self-injury, 1964 to 2000. *American Journal on Mental Retardation, 107*, 212–221.

Kalb, C. (2001a, April 9). Playing with pain killers. *Newsweek*, pp. 45–48.

Kalb, C. (2001b, February 26). DARE checks into rehab. *Newsweek*, pp. 56.

Kaller, C. P., Unterrainer, J. M., Rahm, B., & Halsband, U. (2004). The impact of problem structure on planning: Insights from the Tower of London task. *Cognitive Brain Research, 20*, 462–472.

Kallio, S., & Revonsuo, A. (2003). Hypnotic phenomena and altered states of consciousness: A multilevel framework of description and explanation. *Contemporary Hypnosis, 20*, 111–164.

Kamieniecki, G. W., & Lynd-Stevenson, R. M. (2002). Is it appropriate to use United States norms to assess the "intelligence" of Australian children? *Australian Journal of Psychology, 54*, 67–78.

Kaminski, P., Chapman, B. P, Haynes, S. D., & Own, L. (2005). Body image, eating behaviors, and attitudes toward exercise among gay and straight men. *Eating Behaviors, 6*, 179–187.

Kandel, E. R., Schwartz, J. H., & Jessell, T. M. (Eds.) (2000). *Principles of neural science* (4th ed.). New York: McGraw-Hill.

Kane, M. J., & Engle, R. W. (2002). The role of prefrontal cortex in working-memory capacity, executive attention, and general fluid intelligence: An individual-differences perspective. *Psychonomic Bulletin and Review, 9*, 637–671.

Kaniasty, K., & Norris, F. H. (1995, June). Mobilization and deterioration of social support following natural disasters. *Current Directions in Psychological Science, 4*, 94–98.

Kanner, A. D., Coyne, J. C., Schaefer, C., & Lazarus, R. (1981). Comparison of two modes of stress measurement: Daily hassles and uplifts versus major life events. *Journal of Behavioral Medicine, 4,* 14.

Kantrowitz, B. (2006, April 24). The quest for rest. *Newsweek,* p. 51.

Kantrowitz, B. (2007, February 26). "I never knew what to expect": Depressed parents often leave their children a legacy of fear and anxiety. *Newsweek,* p. 49.

Kantrowitz, B., & Underswood, A. (2007, June 25). The teen drinking dilemma. *Newsweek,* pp. 36–37.

Kaplan, H. S. (1974). *The new sex therapy.* New York: Brunner-Mazel.

Kaplan, J. R., & Manuck, S. B. (1989). The effect of propranolol on behavioral interactions among adult male cynomolgus monkeys (*Macaca fascicularis*) housed in disrupted social groupings. *Psychosomatic Medicine, 51,* 449–462.

Kaplan, R M., & Saccuzzo, D. P. (2001). *Psychological testing: Principles, applications, and issues* (5th ed.). Belmont, CA: Wadsworth/Thomson Learning.

Kapur, S., & Remington, G. (1996). Serotonin-dopamine interaction and its relevance to schizophrenia. *American Journal of Psychiatry, 153,* 466–476.

Karim, A., Hinterberger, T., Richter, J., Mellinger, J., Neumann, N., Flor, H., Kubler, A., and Birnaumer, N. (2006). Neural Internet: Web surfing with brain potentials for the completely paralyzed. *Neurorehabilitation and Neural Repair, 20,* 508–515.

Karni, A., Tanne, D., Rubenstein, B. S., Askenasy, J. J. M., & Sagi, D. (1994, July 29). Dependence on REM sleep of overnight improvement of a perceptual skill. *Science, 265,* 679–682.

Karni, A., Tanne, D., Rubenstein, B. S., Askenazy, J. J. M., & Sagi, D. (1992, October). No dreams—no memory: The effect of REM sleep deprivation on learning a new perceptual skill. *Society for Neuroscience Abstracts, 18,* 387.

Kassel, J. D., Evatt, D. P., Greenstein, J. E., Wardle, M. C., Yates, M. C., & Veilleux, J. C. (2007). The acute effects of nicotine on positive and negative affect in adolescent smokers. *Journal of Abnormal Psychology, 116,* 543–553.

Kassel, J. D., Stroud, L. R., & Paronis, C. A. (2003). Smoking, stress, and negative affect: Correlation, causation, and context across stages of smoking. *Psychological Bulletin, 129,* 270–304.

Kassin, S., M. (2005). On the psychology of confessions: Does innocence put innocents at risk? *American Psychologist, 60,* 215–228.

Kaštelan, A., Franciškovic, A., Tanja, M., & Moro, L. (2007). Psychotic symptoms in combat-related post-traumatic stress disorder. *Military Medicine, 172,* 273–277.

Katigbak, M. S., Church, A. T., GuanzonLapena, M. A., Carlota, A. J., & del Pilar, G. H. (2002). Are indigenous personality dimensions culture specific? Philippine inventories and the five-factor model. *Journal of Personality and Social Psychology, 82,* 89–101.

Kato, K., & Pedersen, N. L. (2005). Personality and coping: A study of twins reared apart and twins reared together. *Behavior Genetics, 35,* 147–158.

Kato, T. (2007). Molecular genetics of bipolar disorder and depression. *Psychiatry and Clinical Neurosciences, 61,* 3–19.

Katsiyannis, A., Zhang, D., & Archwamety, T. (2002). Place and exit patterns for students with mental retardation: An analysis of national trends. *Education and Training in Mental Retardation and Developmental Disabilities, 37,* 134–145.

Katsiyannis, A., Zhang, D., & Woodruff, N. (2005). Transition supports to students with mental retardation: An examination of data from the national longitudinal transition study 2. *Education and Training in Developmental Disabilities, 40,* 109–116.

Katz, A. N. (1989). Autobiographical memory as a reconstructive process: An extension of Ross's hypothesis. *Canadian Journal of Psychology, 43,* 512–517.

Katz, M. (2001). The implications of revising Freud's empiricism for drive theory. *Psychoanalysis and Contemporary Thought, 24,* 253–272.

Katz, P. A. (Ed.). (1976). *Towards the elimination of racism.* New York: Pergamon.

Kaufman, A.S. & Lichtenberger, E.O. (1999). *Essentials of WAIS-III assessment.* Hoboken, NJ: John Wiley & Sons Inc.

Kaufman, A. S., & Lichtenberger, E. O. (2000). *Essentials of WISC-III and WPPSI-R assessment.* New York: Wiley.

Kaufman, J. C. (2005). The door that leads into madness: Eastern European poets and mental illness. *Creativity Research Journal, 17,* 99–103.

Kaufman, J. C., & Baer, J. (2005). *Creativity across domains: Faces of the muse.* Mahwah, NJ: Lawrence Erlbaum Associates.

Kaufman, J. C., & Baer, J. *Creativity and reason in cognitive development.* New York: Cambridge University Press, 2006.

Kaufman, L., & Kaufman, J. H. (2000). From the cover: Explaining the moon illusion. *Proceedings of the National Academy of Science, 97,* 500–505.

Kausler, D. H. (1994). *Learning and memory in normal aging.* San Diego, CA: Academic Press.

Kavale, K. A. (2002). Mainstreaming to full inclusion: From orthogenesis to pathogenesis of an idea [Special issue: The slow learning child: 25 years on]. *International Journal of Disability, Development & Education, 49,* 201–214.

Kawasaki, C., Nugent, J. K., Miyashita, H., Miyahara, H., et al. (1994). The cultural organization of infants' sleep [Special issue: Environments of birth and infancy]. *Children's Environment, 11,* 135–141.

Kawashima, H., Izaki, Y., & Grace, A. A. (2006). Cooperativity between hippocampal-prefrontal short-term plasticity through associative long-term potentiation. *Brain Research, 1109,* 37–44.

Kay, P., & Regier, T. (2007). Color naming universals: the case of Berinmo. *Cognition, 102,* 289–298.

Kazar, D. B. (2006). Forensic psychology: Did we leave anything out? *PsycCRITIQUES, 51,* 88–97.

Kearns, K. P. (2005). Broca's aphasia. In L. L. LaPointe (Ed.), *Aphasia and related neurogenic language disorders* (3rd ed.). New York: Thieme New York.

Keating, D. P., & Clark, L. V. (1980). Development of physical and social reasoning in adolescence. *Developmental Psychology, 16,* 23–30.

Keillor, J. M., Barrett, A. M., Crucian, G. P., Kortenkamp, S., & Heilman, K. M. (2002). Emotional experience and perception in the absence of facial feedback. *Journal of the International Neuropsychological Society, 8,* 130–135.

Keller, J., (2007). Stereotype threat in classroom settings: The interactive effect of domain identification, task difficulty and stereotype threat on female students' math performance. *British Journal of Educational Psychology, 77,* 323–338.

Kelley, H. (1950). The warm-cold variable in first impressions of persons. *Journal of Personality and Social Psychology, 18,* 431–439.

Kelly, D., & Declan, T. (2006). Adapting to intelligence profile in an adaptive educational system. *Interacting with Computers, 18,* 385–409.

Kelly, E. S. (1997, January 22). The latest in take-at-home tests: I.Q. *New York Times,* p. B7.

Kelly, F. D. (1997). *The assessment of object relations phenomena in adolescents: TAT and Rorschach measures.* Mahwah, NJ: Erlbaum.

Kelly, J.B. (2000). Children's adjustment in conflicted marriage and divorce: A decade review of research. *Journal of the American Academy of Child & Adolescent Psychiatry, 39,* 963–973.

Keltikangas-Järvinen, L., Räikkönen, K., Ekelund, J., & Peltonen, L. (2004). Nature and nurture in novelty seeking. *Molecular Psychiatry, 9,* 308–311.

Kemeny, M. E. (2003). The psychobiology of stress. *Current Directions in Psychological Science, 12,* 124–129.

Kemeny, M. E. (2007). Psychoneuroimmunology. In H. S. Friedman, & R. C. Silver, *Foundations of health psychology.* New York: Oxford University Press.

Kempermann, G., & Gage, F. H. (1999, May). New nerve cells for the adult brain. *Scientific American,* pp. 48–53.

Kemps, E., & Tiggemann, M. (2007). Reducing the vividness and emotional impact of distressing autobiographical memories: The importance of modality-specific interference. *Memory, 15,* 412–422.

Kendler, K. S., Gatz, M., & Gardner, C. O. (21006). Personality and major depression. *Archives of General Psychiatry, 63,* 1113–1120.

Kendler, K. S., Myers, J., & Bardner, C. O. (2006). Caffeine intake, toxicity and dependence and lifetime risk for psychiatric and substance use disorders: An epidemiologic and co-twin control analysis. *Psychological Medicine, 36,* 1717–1725.

Kenneally, C. (2006, July 3). The deepest cut. How can someone live with only half a brain?

Kennedy, Q., Mather, M., & Carstensen, L. L. (2004). The role of motivation in the age-related positivity effect in autobiographical memory. *Psychological Science, 15,* 208–211.

Kennedy, J. E. (2004). A proposal and challenge for proponents and skeptics of psi. *Journal of Parapsychology, 68,* 157–167.

Kenshalo, D. R. (1968). *The skin senses.* Springfield, IL: Charles C. Thomas.

Kensinger, E. A., & Schacter, D. L. (2006). Neural processes underlying memory attribution on a reality-monitoring task. *Cerebral Cortex, 16,* 1126–1133.

Kenway, L., & Wilson, M. A. (2001). Temporally structured replay of awake hippocampal ensemble activity during rapid eye movement sleep. *Neuron, 29,* 145–156.

Kersting, K. (2004, March). How do you test on the web? Responsibly. *Monitor on Psychology,* pp. 26–27.

Kess, J. F., & Miyamoto, T. (1994). *Japanese psycholinguistics.* Amsterdam, Netherlands: John Benjamins.

Kessler, R. C., Berglund, P., & Demler, O. (2005). Lifetime prevalence and age-of-onset distributions of DSM-IV disorders in the National Comorbidity Survey replication. *Archives of General Psychiatry, 62,* 593–602.

Kettenmann, H., & Ransom, B. R. (2005). *Neuroglia* (2nd ed.). New York: Oxford University Press.

Ketterhargen, D., VandeVusse, L., & Berner, M. A. (2002). Self-hypnosis: Alternative anesthesia for childbirth. *American Journal of Maternal/Child Nursing, 27,* 335–341.

Kevenaar, T. A. M., Schrijen, G. J., van der Veen, M., Akkermans, A. H. M., & Zuo, F. (2005). Face recognition with renewable and privacy preserving binary templates. *Automatic Identification Advanced Technologies, 2005,* 21–26.

Key, W. B. (2003). Subliminal sexuality: The fountainhead for America's obsession. In T. Reichert & J. Lambaiase (Eds.), *Sex in advertising: Perspectives on the erotic appeal. LEA's communication series* (pp. 195–212). Mahwah, NJ: Lawrence Erlbaum.

Keyes, C. L., & Shapiro, A. D. (2004). Social well-being in the United States: A descriptive epidemiology. In O. G. Brim and C. D. Ryff, *How healthy are we? A national study of well-being at midlife.* Chicago: University of Chicago Press.

Kiecolt, J. K. (2003). Satisfaction with work and family life: No evidence of a cultural reversal. *Journal of Marriage and Family, 65,* 23–35.

Kiefer, A. K. (2006). The effects of stereotypes on performance attributions: How gender-math stereotypes lead women to internalize failure. *Dissertation Abstracts International: Section B: The Sciences and Engineering, 66(9-B),* 5140.

Kiefer, A. K., & Sekaquaptewa, D. (2006). Implicit stereotypes and women's math performance: How implicit gender-math stereotypes influence women's susceptibility to stereotype threat. *Journal of Experimental Social Psychology, 43,* 825–832.

Kiesler, C. A., & Simpkins, C. G. (1993). *The unnoticed majority in psychiatric inpatient care.* New York: Plenum.

Kiesler, D. J. (2000). *Beyond the disease model of mental disorders.* Westport, CT: Greenwood Publishing Group.

Kihlstrom, J. F. (2005). Is hypnosis an altered state of consciousness or what? Comment. *Contemporary Hypnosis, 22,* 34–38.

Kihlstrom, J. F. (2005). Dissociative disorders. *Annual Review of Clinical Psychology, 1,* 227–253.

Kihlstrom, J. F., Schacter, D. L., Cork, R. C., Hurt, C. A., & Behr, S. E. (1990). Implicit and explicit memory following surgical anesthesia. *Psychological Science, 1,* 303–306.

Kilpatrick, D. G., Edmunds, C. S., & Seymour, A. K. (1992, November 13). *Rape in America: A report to the nation.* Arlington, VA: National Victims Center and Medical University of South Carolina.

Kim, H. S. (2002). We talk, therefore we think? A cultural analysis of the effect of talking on thinking. *Journal of Personality and Social Psychology, 83,* 828–842.

Kim, K. H., Relkin, N. R., Lee, K. M., & Hirsch, J. (1997, July 10). Distinct cortical areas associated with native and second languages. *Nature, 388,* 171–174.

Kim, S-E., Kim, J-W, & Kim, J-J. (2007). The neural mechanism of imagining facial affective expression. *Brain Research, 1145,* 128–137.

Kim, S. Y. H., & Holloway, R. G. (2003). Burdens and benefits of placebos in antidepressant clinical trials: A decision and cost-effectiveness analysis. *American Journal of Psychiatry, 160,* 1272–1276.

Kim-Cohen, J., Caspi, A., & Moffitt, T. E. (2003). Prior juvenile diagnoses in adults with mental disorder: Developmental follow-back of a prospective-longitudinal cohort. *Archives of General Psychiatry, 60,* 709–717.

Kim-Cohen, J., Moffitt, T. E., Taylor, A., Pawlby, S. J., & Caspi, A. (2005). Maternal depression and children's antisocial behavior: Nature and nurture effects. *Archives of General Psychiatry, 62,* 173–181.

Kimbrel, N. A. (2007). A model of the development and maintenance of generalized social phobia. *Clinical Psychological Review, 8,* 69–75.

Kimura, D. (1992, September). Sex differences in the brain. *Scientific American,* pp. 119–125.

Kimura, D. (1999). *Sex and cognition.* Cambridge, MA: MIT.

Kinsey, A. C., Pomeroy, W. B., & Martin, C. E. (1948). *Sexual behavior in the human male.* Philadelphia: Saunders.

Kinsey, A. C., Pomeroy, W. B., Martin, C. E., & Gebhard, P. H. (1953). *Sexual behavior in the human female.* Philadelphia: Saunders.

Kirby, D. (1977). The methods and methodological problems of sex research. In J. S. DeLora & C. A. B. Warren (Eds.), *Understanding sexual interaction.* Boston: Houghton Mifflin.

Kirk, K. M., Bailey, J. M., & Martin, N. G. (2000). Etiology of male sexual orientation in an Australian twin sample. *Psychology, Evolution & Gender, 2,* 301–311.

Kirsch, I. (Ed.). (1999). *How expectancies shape experience.* Washington, DC: American Psychological Association.

Kirsch, I., & Braffman, W. (2001). Imaginative suggestibility and hypnotizability. *Current Directions in Psychological Science, 10,* 57–61.

Kirsch, I., & Lynn, S. J. (1995). The altered state of hypnosis: Changes in the theoretical landscape. *American Psychologist, 50,* 846–858.

Kirsch, I., & Lynn, S. J. (1998). Social-cognitive alternatives to dissociation theories of hypnotic involuntariness. *Review of General Psychology, 2,* 66–80.

Kirsch, I., Lynn, S. J., Vigorito, M, & Miller, R. R. (2004). The role of cognition in classical and operant conditioning. *Journal of Clinical Psychology, 60,* 369–392.

Kirschenbaum, H. (2004). Carl Rogers's life and work: An assessment on the 100th anniversary of his birth. *Journal of Counseling and Development, 82,* 116–124.

Kirschenbaum, H., & Jourdan, A. (2005). The current status of Carl Rogers and the person-centered approach. *Psychotherapy: Theory, Research, Practice, Training, 42,* 37–51.

Kish, S. J. (2002). Effects of dose, sex, and long-term abstention from use on toxic effects of MDMA (Ecstasy) on brain serotonin neurons: Comment. *Lancet, 359,* 1616.

Kiss, A. (2004). Does gender have an influence on the patient-physician communication? *Journal of Men's Health and Gender, 1,* 77–82.

Kitterle, F. L. (Ed.). (1991). *Cerebral laterality: Theory and research.* Hillsdale, NJ: Erlbaum.

Klein, M. (1998, February). Family chats. *American Demographics,* p. 37.

Kleinman, A. (1996). How is culture important for DSM-IV? In J. E Mezzich, A. Kleinman, H. Fabrega, Jr., & D. L. Parron (Eds.), *Culture and psychiatric diagnosis: A DSM-IV perspective.* Washington, DC: American Psychiatric Press.

Kleinman, A., & Cohen, A. (1997, March). Psychiatry's global challenge. *Scientific American,* pp. 86–89.

Kling, K. C., Ryff, C. D., Love, G. (2003). Exploring the influence of personality on depressive symptoms and self-esteem across a significant life transition. *Journal of Personality and Social Psychology, 85,* 922–932.

Klinke, R., Kral, A., Heid, S., Tillein, J., & Hartmann, R. (1999, September 10). Recruitment of the auditory cortex in congenitally deaf cats by long-term cochlear electrostimulation. *Science, 285,* 1729–1733.

Klinkenborg, V. (1997, January 5). Awakening to sleep. *The New York Times,* pp. 26–31, 41, 51, 55.

Klötz, F., Garle, M., & Granath, F. (2006). Criminality among individuals testing positive for the presence of anabolic androgenic steroids. *Archives of General Psychiatry, 63,* 1274–1279.

Kluft, R. P. (1999). An overview of the psychotherapy of dissociative identity disorder. *American Journal of Psychotherapy, 53,* 289–319.

Kluger, J. (2001, April 2). Fear not! *Time,* pp. 51–62.

Kluger, J. (2006, December 4). Why we worry about the things we shouldn't and ignore the things we should. *Time,* pp. 64–71.

Knight, G. P., Jonson, L. G., Carlo, G., & Eisenberg, N. (1994). A multiplicative model of the dispositional antecedents of a prosocial behavior: Predicting more of the people more of the time. *Journal of Personality and Social Psychology, 66,* 178–183.

Knight, S. C., & Meyer, R. G. (2007). Forensic hypnosis. In A. M. Goldstein, *Forensic psychology: Emerging topics and expanding roles.* Hoboken, NJ: John Wiley & Sons.

Knoblich, G., & Natalie, Sebanz. (2006). The social nature of perception and action. *Current Directions in Psychological Science, 15,* 99–111.

Knops, A., Nuerk, H. C., Fimm, B., Vohn, R, & Willmes, K. (2005). A special role for numbers in working memory? An fMRI study. *Neuroimage, 22,* 125–132.

Kobasa, S. C. O., Maddi, S. R., Puccetti, M. C., & Zola, M. A. (1994). Effectiveness of hardiness, exercise and social support as resources against illness. In A. Steptoe & J. Wardle (Eds.), *Psychosocial processes and health: A reader.* Cambridge, England: Cambridge University Press.

Kobayashi, F., Schallert, D. L., & Ogren, H. A. (2003). Japanese and American folk vocabularies for emotions. *Journal of Social Psychology, 143,* 451–478.

Koch, J. (2003). Gender issues in the classroom. In W. M. Reynolds & G. E. Miller (Eds.), *Handbook of psychology: Educational psychology* (Vol. 7, pp. 259–281). New York: Wiley.

Koenig, A. M., & Eagly, A. H. (2005). Stereotype threat in men on a test of social sensitivity. *Sex Roles, 52,* 489–496.

Kohlberg, L. (1984). *The psychology of moral development: Essays on moral development* (Vol. 2). San Francisco: Harper & Row.

Kohlberg, L., & Ryncarz, R. A. (1990). Beyond justice reasoning: Moral development and consideration of a seventh stage. In C. N. Alexander & E. J. Langer (Eds.), *Higher stages of human development: Perspectives on adult growth.* New York: Oxford University Press.

Kohler, C. G., Turner, T., Stolar, N. M., Bilker, W. B., Brensinger, C. M., Gur, R. E., & Gur, R. C. (2004). Differences in facial expressions of four universal emotions. *Psychiatry Research, 128,* 235–244.

Köhler, W. (1927). *The mentality of apes.* London: Routledge & Kegan Paul.

Kolata, G. (2002, December 2). With no answers on risks, steroid users still say "yes." *The New York Times*, p. 1A.

Kolb, B., Gibb, R., & Robinson, T. E. (2003). Brain plasticity and behavior. *Current Directions in Psychological Science, 12*, 1–5.

Konig, R. (2005). Introduction: Plasticity, learning, and cognition. In R. Konig., P. Heil., E. Budinger & H. Scheich (Eds.), *The auditory cortex: A synthesis of human and animal research.* Mahwah, NJ, US: Lawrence Erlbaum Associates Publishers, 2005.

Konijn, E., Bijvank, M. N., & Bushman, B. J. (2007). I wish I were a warrior: The role of wishful identification in the effects of violent video games on aggression in adolescent boys. *Developmental Psychology, 43*, 1038–1044.

Koocher, G. P., Norcross, J. C., & Hill, S. S. (2005). *Psychologists' desk reference* (2nd ed.). New York: Oxford University Press.

Kopelman, M. D., & Fleminger, S. (2002). Experience and perspectives on the classification of organic mental disorders. *Psychopathology, 35*, 76–81.

Koper, R. J., & Jaasma, M. A. (2001). Interpersonal style: are human social orientations guided by generalized interpersonal needs? *Communications Reports, 14*, 117–129.

Koplewicz, H. (2002). *More than moody: Recognizing and treating adolescent depression.* New York: Putnam.

Korecka, J. A., Verhaagen, J., & Hol, E. M. (2007). Cell-replacement and gene-therapy strategies for Parkinson's and Alzheimer's disease. *Regenerative Medicine, 2*, 425-426.

Kosfeld, M., Heinrich, M., Zak, P. J., Fischbacher, U., & Fehr, E. (2005, June 2). Oxytocin increases trust in humans. *Nature, 435*, 673–676.

Koss, M. P. (1993). Rape: Scope, impact, interventions, and public policy responses. *American Psychologist, 48*, 1062–1069.

Kosslyn, S. M. (2005). Mental images and the brain. *Cognitive Neuropsychology, 22*, 333–347.

Kosslyn, S. M., & Shin, L. M. (1994). Visual mental images in the brain: Current issues. In M. J. Farah & G. Ratcliff (Eds.), *The neuropsychology of high-level vision: Collected tutorial essays. Carnegie Mellon symposia on cognition.* Hillsdale, NJ: Erlbaum.

Kosslyn, S. M., Cacioppo, J. T., Davidson, R. J., Hugdahl, K., Lovallo, W. R., Spiegel, D., & Rose, R. (2002). Bridging psychology and biology. *American Psychologist, 57*, 341–351.

Kotre, J., & Hall, E. (1990). *Seasons of life.* Boston: Little, Brown.

Koval, J. J., Pederson, L. L., Mills, C. A., McGrady, G. A., & Carvajal, S. C. (2000). Models of the relationship of stress, depression, and other psychosocial factors to smoking behavior: A comparison of a cohort of students in grades 6 and 8. *Preventive Medicine: an International Devoted to Practice & Theory, 30*, 463–477.

Koveces, Z. (1987). *The container metaphor of emotion.* Paper presented at the University of Massachusetts, Amherst.

Kowert, P. A. (2002). *Groupthink or deadlock: When do leaders learn from their advisors? SUNY Series on the Presidency.* Albany: State University of New York Press.

Kozaric-Kovacic, D., & Borovecki, A. (2005). Prevalence of psychotic comorbidity in combat-related post-traumatic stress disorder. *Military Medicine, 170*, 223–226.

Kozulin, A., Gindis, B., Ageyev, V. S., & Miller, S. M. (2003). *Vygotsky's educational theory in cultural context.* New York: Cambridge University Press.

Kral, M. C., & Brown, R. T. (2004). Transcranial Doppler ultrasonography and executive dysfunction in children with sickle cell disease. *Journal of Pediatric Psychology, 29*, 185–195.

Kramer, P. (1993). *Listening to Prozac.* New York: Viking.

Kraus, S. J. (1995, January). Attitudes and the prediction of behavior: A meta-analysis of the empirical literature. *Personality and Social Psychology Bulletin, 21*, 58–75.

Krause, S. S. (2003). *Aircraft safety: Accident investigations, analyses, and applications* (2nd ed.). New York: McGraw-Hill.

Kremer, J. M. D., & Scully, D. M. (1994). *Psychology in sport.* London, England: Taylor & Francis.

Krijn, M., Emmelkamp, P. M. G., Olafsson, R. P., & Biemond, R. (2004). Virtual reality exposure therapy of anxiety disorders: A review. *Clinical Psychology Review, 24*, 259–281.

Krohne, H. W. (1996). Individual differences in coping. In M. Zeidner & N. S. Endler (Eds.), *Handbook of coping: Theory, research, applications.* New York: Wiley.

Krueger, R. G., Hicks, B. M., & McGue, M. (2001). Altruism and antisocial behavior: Independent tendencies, unique personality correlates, distinct etiologies. *Psychological Science, 12*, 397–402.

Krull, D. S., & Anderson, C. A. (1997). The process of explanation. *Current Directions in Psychological Science, 6*, 1–5.

Ku, L., St. Louis, M., Farshy, C., Aral, S., Turner, C. F., Lindberg, L. D., & Sonenstein, F. (2002). Risk behaviors, medical care, and chlamydial infection among young men in the United States. *American Journal of Public Health, 92*, 1140–1143.

Kubler, A., Winter, S., and Ludolph, A. (2005). Severity of depressive symptoms and quality of life in patients with amyotrophic lateral sclerosis. *Neurorehabilitation and Neural Repair, 19*, 182–193.

Kübler-Ross, E. (1969). *On death and dying.* New York: Macmillan.

Kubovy, M., Epstein, W., & Gepshtein, S. (2003). Foundations of visual perception. In A. F. Healy, & R. W. Proctor (Eds.). *Handbook of psychology: Experimental psychology* (Vol. 4). New York: Wiley.

Kulynych, J. J., Vladar, K., Jones, D. W., & Weinberger, D. R. (1994). Gender differences in the normal lateralization of the supratemporal cortex: MRI surface-rendering morphometry of Heschl's gyrus and the planum temporale. *Cerebral Cortex, 4*, 107–118.

Kunda, Z. (2000). The case for motivated reasoning. In D. T. Higgins & A. W. Kruglanski (Eds.), *Motivational science: Social and personality perspectives. Key readings in social psychology* (pp. 313–335). Philadelphia: Psychology Press.

Kuo, L. J. (2007). Effects of bilingualism on development of facets of phonological competence (China). *Dissertation Abstracts International Section A: Humanities and Social Sciences, 67(11-A)*, 4095.

Kuppens, P., Ceulemans, E., Timmerman, M. E., Diener, E., & Kim-Prieto, C. (2006). Universal intracultural and intercultural dimensions of the recalled frequency of emotional experience. *Journal of Cross Cultural Psychology, 37*, 491–515.

Kuriyama, K., Stickgold, R., & Walker, M. P. (2004). Sleep-dependent learning and motor-skill complexity. *Learning and Memory, 11*, 705–713.

Kushner, R. F., Blatner, D. J., & Jewell, D. E. (2006). The PPET study: people and pets exercising together. *Obesity, 14*, 1762–1770.

Kuther, T. L. (2003). *Your career in psychology: Psychology and the law.* New York: Wadsworth.

Kvavilashvili, L., & Fisher, L. (2007). Is time-based prospective remembering mediated by self-initiated rehearsals? Role of incidental cues, ongoing activity, age, and motivation. *Journal of Experimental Psychology: General, 136*, 112–132.

Kwan, V. S. Y., Bond, M. H., & Singelis, T. M. (1997). Pancultural explanations for life satisfaction: Adding relationship harmony to self-esteem. *Journal of Personality & Social Psychology, 73*, 1038–1051.

Kwate, N. O. A. (2001). Intelligence or misorientation? Eurocentrism in the WISC-III. *Journal of Black Psychology, 27*, 221–239.

Kwon, P., & Laurenceau, J. P. (2002). A longitudinal study of the hopelessness theory of depression: Testing the dia-thesis-stress model within a differential reactivity and exposure framework [Special issue: Reprioritizing the role of science in a realistic version of the scientist-practitioner model]. *Journal of Clinical Psychology, 50*, 1305–1321.

Laas, I. (2006). Self-actualization and society: A new application for an old theory. *Journal of Humanistic Psychology, 46*, 77–91.

Lacerda, F., von Hofsten, C., & Heimann, M. (2001). *Emerging cognitive abilities in early infancy.* Mahwah, NJ: Lawrence Erlbaum Associates.

Lacey, M. (2002, January 6). In Kenyan family, ritual for girls still divides. *The New York Times*, p. 6.

Laederach-Hofmann, K., & Messerli-Buergy, N. (2007). Chest pain, angina pectoris, panic disorder, and Syndrome X. In J. Jordan, B. Barde, & A. M. Zeiher, *Contributions toward evidence-based psychocardiology: A systematic review of the literature.* Washington, DC: American Psychological Association.

LaFrance, M., & Harris, J. L. (2004). Gender and verbal and nonverbal communication. In M. A. Paludi (Ed.), *Praeger guide to the psychology of gender.* Westport, CT: Praeger Publishers/Greenwood Publishing Group.

LaFromboise, T., Coleman, H. L. K., & Gerton, J. (1995). Psychological impact of biculturalism: Evidence and theory. In N. R. Goldberger & J. B. Veroff (Eds.), *The culture and psychology reader.* New York: New York University Press.

Lagacé-Séguin, D. G., & d'Entremont, M. L. (2006). The role of child negative affect in the relations between parenting styles and play. *Early Child Development and Care, 176*, 461–477.

Lahti, J., Räikkönen, K., Ekelund, J., Peltonen, L., Raitakari, O. T., & Keltikangas-Järvinen, L. (2005). Novelty seeking: Interaction between parental alcohol use and dopamine D4 receptor gene exon III polymorphism over 17 years. *Psychiatric Genetics, 15*, 133–139.

Laird, J. D., & Bressler, C. (1990). William James and the mechanisms of emotional experience. *Personality and Social Psychology Bulletin, 16*, 636–651.

Lal, S. (2002). Giving children security: Mamie Phipps Clark and the racialization of child psychology. *American Psychologist, 57*, 20–28.

Lamal, P. A. (1979). College students' common beliefs about psychology. *Teaching of Psychology, 6*, 155–158.

Lamb, H. R., & Weinberger, L. E. (2005). One-year follow-up of persons discharged from a locked intermediate care facility. *Psychiatric Services, 56*, 198–201.

Lamb, M. E. (1996). Effects of nonparental child care on child development: An update. *Canadian Journal of Psychiatry, 41*, 330–342.

Lamb, M. E., & Garretson, M. E. (2003), The effects of interviewer gender and child gender on the informativeness of alleged child sexual abuse victims in forensic interviews. *Law and Human Behavior, 27*, 157–171.

Lamb, R. J., Morral, A. R., Kirby, K. C., Iguchi, M. Y., & Galbicka, G. (2004). Shaping smoking cessation using percentile schedules. *Drug and Alcohol Dependence, 76*, 247–259.

Lambert, M. J., Shapiro, D. A., & Bergin, A. E. (1986). The effectiveness of psychotherapy. In S. L. Garfield & A. E. Bergin (Eds.), *Handbook of psychotherapy and behavior change* (3rd ed.). New York: Wiley.

Lana, R. E. (2002). The cognitive approach to language and thought [Special issue: Choice and chance in the formation of society: Behavior and cognition in social theory]. *Journal of Mind and Behavior, 23*, 51–57.

Lanctot, K.L., Herrmann, N. & Mazzotta, P. (2001). Role of serotonin in the behavioral and psychological symptoms of dementia. *Journal of Neuropsychiatry & Clinical Neurosciences, 13*, 5–21.

Landry, D. W. (1997, February). Immunotherapy for cocaine addiction. *Scientific American*, pp. 41–45.

Lane, K. A., Banaji, M. R., Nosek, B. A., & Greenwald, A. G. (Eds.). (2007). Understanding and using the implicit association test: iv: what we know (so far) about the method. In B. Wittenbrink, & N. Schwarz, *Implicit measures of attitudes*. New York: Guilford Press.

Lane, S. D., Cherek, D. R., & Tcheremissine, O. V. (2007). Response perseveration and adaptation in heavy marijuana-smoking adolescents. *Addictive Behaviors, 32*, 977–990.

Lang, A. J., Sorrell, J. T., & Rodgers, C. S. (2006). Anxiety sensitivity as a predictor of labor pain. *European Journal of Pain, 10*, 263–270.

Langan-Fox, J., & Grant, S. (2006). The Thematic Apperception Test: Toward a standard measure of the big three motives. *Journal of Personality Assessment, 87*, 277–291.

Langdridge, D., & Butt, T. (2004). The fundamental attribution error: A phenomenological critique. *British Journal of Social Psychology, 43*, 357–369.

Langer, E., & Janis, I. (1979). *The psychology of control*. Beverly Hills, CA: Sage.

Langlois, J.H., Kalakanis, L., Rubenstein, A.J., Larson, A., Hallam, M. & Smoot, M. (2000). Maxims or myths of beauty? A meta-analytic and theoretical review. *Psychological Bulletin, 126*, 390–423.

Langreth, R. (2000, May 1). Every little bit helps: How even moderate exercise can have a big impact on your health. *The Wall Street Journal*, p. R5.

Lankov, A. (2004). The dawn of modern Korea: Changes for better or worse. *The Korea Times*, p. A1.

Lanza, S. T., & Collins, L. M. (2002). Pubertal timing and the onset of substance use in females during early adolescence. *Prevention Science, 3*, 69–82.

Laqueur, T. W. (2003). *Solitary sex: A cultural history of masturbation*. New York: Zone.

Larsen, R. J., & Buss, D. M. (2006). *Personality psychology: Domains of knowledge about human nature with PowerWeb* (2nd ed.). New York: McGraw-Hill.

Larson, R. K. (1990). Semantics. In D. N. Osherson & H. Lasnik (Eds.), *Language*. Cambridge, MA: MIT.

Lascaratos, G., Ji, D., & Wood, J. P. (2007). Visible light affects mitochondrial function and induces neuronal death in retinal cell cultures. *Vision Research, 47*, 1191–1201.

Lasnik, H. (1990). Syntax. In D. N. Osherson & H. Lasnik (Eds.), *Language*. Cambridge, MA: MIT.

Latané, B., & Darley, J. M. (1970). *The unresponsive bystander: Why doesn't he help?* New York: Appleton-Century-Crofts.

Latané, B., & Nida, S. (1981). Ten years of research on group size and helping. *Psychological Bulletin, 89*, 308–324.

Laugharne, J., Janca, A., & Widiger, T. (2007). Posttraumatic stress disorder and terrorism: 5 years after 9/11. *Current Opinion in Psychiatry, 20*, 36–41.

Laumann, E. O., Paik, A., & Rosen, R. C. (1999, February 10). Sexual dysfunction in the United States: Prevalence and predictors. *Journal of the American Medical Association, 281*, 537–544.

Lavelli, M., & Fogel, A. (2005). Developmental changes in the relationship between the infant's attention and emotion during early face-to-face communication. *Developmental Psychology, 41*, 265–280.

Lawrence, J., Ashford, K., & Dent, Paul. (2006). Gender differences in coping strategies of undergraduate students and their impact on self-esteem and attainment. *Active Learning in Higher Education, 7*, 273–281.

Lazarus, A. A. (1997). *Brief but comprehensive psychotherapy: The multimodal way*. New York: Springer.

Lazarus, R. S. (1991a). Cognition and motivation in emotion. *American Psychologist, 46*, 352–367.

Lazarus, R. S. (1991b). *Emotion and adaptation*. New York: Oxford University Press.

Lazarus, R. S. (1994). Appraisal: The long and short of it. In P. Ekman & R. J. Davidson (Eds.), *The nature of emotion: fundamental questions*. New York: Oxford University Press.

Lazarus, R. S. (1995). Emotions express a social relationship, but it is an individual mind that creates them. *Psychological Inquiry, 6*, 253–265.

Lazarus, R. S. (2000). Toward better research on stress and coping. *American Psychologist, 55*, 665–673.

Le Maner-Idrissi, G., & Renault, L. (2006). Développement du 'schéma de genre': Une asymétrie entre filles et garçons? Are there sex differences in the acquisition of a gender schema? *Enfance, 58*, 251–265.

Leaper, C., & Friedman, C. K. (2007). The socialization of gender. In J. E. grusec, & P. D. Hastings, *Handbook of socialization: Theory and research*. New York: Guilford Press.

Leavitt, F. (2002). The reality of repressed memories revisited and principles of science. *Journal of Trauma and Dissociation, 3*, 19–35.

Leblanc, D. C. (2004). *Statistics for science students: Concepts and applications for the sciences*. Boston: Jones and Bartlett.

Leckman, J. F., & King, R. A. (2007). A developmental perspective on the controversy surrounding the use of SSRIs to treat pediatric depression. *American Journal of Psychiatry, 164*, 1304–1306.

Lee, A., Isaac, M. & Janca, A. (2007). Posttraumatic stress disorder and terrorism. In A. Monat, R.S. Lazarus & G. Reevy (Eds.), *The Praeger handbook on stress and coping* (vol.1) (pp. 235–242). Westport, CT: Praeger Publishers/Greenwood Publishing Group.

Lee, A. Y., & Aaker, J. L. (2004). Bringing the frame into focus: The influence of regulatory fit on processing fluency and persuasion. *Journal of Personality and Social Psychology, 86*, 205–218.

Lee, D., Kleinman, J., and Kleinman, A. (2007). Rethinking depression: An ethnographic study of the experiences of depression among Chinese. *Harvard Review of Psychiatry, 15*, 1–8.

Lee, F., Hallahan, M., & Herzog, T. (1996). Explaining real-life events: How culture and domain shape attributions. *Personality and Social Psychology Bulletin, 22*, 732–741.

Lee, H. J., & Kwon, S. M. (2003). Two different types of obsession: Autogenous obsessions and reactive obsessions. *Behaviour Research & Therapy, 41*, 11–29.

Lee, H. J., Kwon, S. M., Kwon, J. S., & Telch, M. J. (2005). Testing the autogenous reactive model of obsessions. *Depress Anxiety, 21*, 118–129.

Lee, S. H., Ahn, S. C., & Lee, Y. J. (2007). Effectiveness of a meditation-based stress management program as an adjunct to pharmacotherapy in patients with anxiety disorder. *Journal of Psychosomatic Research, 62*, 189–195.

Lee, T. W., Wachtler, T., & Sejnowski, T. J. (2002). Color opponency is an efficient representation of spectral properties in natural scenes. *Vision Research, 42*, 2095–2103.

Lee-Chai, A. Y., Bargh, J. A. (Eds.). (2001). *The use and abuse of power: Multiple perspectives on the causes of corruption*. Philadelphia, PA: Psychology Press.

Lee-Chiong, T. L. (2006). *Sleep: A comprehensive handbook*. New York: Wiley-Liss.

Lefaucheur, J. P., Brugieres, P., Menard-Lefaucheur, I., Wendling, S., Pommier, M., & Bellivier, F. (2007). The value of navigation-guided rTMS for the treatment of depression: An illustrative case. *Neurophysiologic Clinics, 37*, 265–271.

Lehar, S. (2003). *The world in your head: A gestalt view of the mechanism of conscious experience*. Mahwah, NJ: Erlbaum.

Lehman, D. R., & Taylor, S. E. (1988). Date with an earthquake: Coping with a probable, unpredictable disaster. *Personality and Social Psychology Bulletin, 13*, 546–555.

Lehman, D., Chiu, C., and Schaller, M. (2004). Psychology and culture. *Annual Review of Psychology, 55*, 689–714.

Lehmann, E. L., & Romano, J. P. (2004). *Testing statistical hypotheses*. New York: Springer-Verlag.

Lehrer, J. (2006, October 5). Driven to market. *Nature, 443*, 502–504.

Lehrer, P. M. (1996). Recent research findings on stress management techniques. In Editorial Board of Hatherleigh Press, *The Hatherleigh guide to issues in modern therapy: The Hatherleigh guides series* (Vol. 4). New York: Hatherleigh Press.

Leib, J. R., Gollust, S. E., Hull, S. C., & Wilfond, B. S. (2005). Carrier screening panels for Ashkenazi Jews: is more better? *Genetic Medicine, 7*, 185–190.

Leibel, R. L., Rosenbaum, M., Hirsch, J. (1995, March 9). Changes in energy expenditure resulting from altered body. *New England Journal of Medicine, 332*, 621–628.

Leiblum, S.R. & Chivers, M.L. (2007). Normal and persistent genital arousal in women: New perspectives. *Journal of Sex & Marital Therapy, 33*, 357–373.

Leigh, J. H., Zinkhan, G. M. & Swaminathan, V. (2006). Dimensional relationships of recall and recognition measures with selected cognitive and affective aspects of print ads. *Journal of Advertising, 35*, 105–122.

Leiter, S., & Leiter, W. M. (2003). *Affirmative action in antidiscrimination law and policy: An overview and synthesis. SUNY series in American constitutionalism.* Albany: State University of New York Press.

Leitner, L. M. (2007). Diversity issues, postmodernism, and psychodynamic therapy. *PsycCRITIQUES, 52,* No pagination specified.

Lemay, E. P., Jr., Clark, M. S., & Feeney, B. C. (2007). Projection of responsiveness to needs and the construction of satisfying communal relationships. *Journal of Personality and Social Psychology, 92*, 834–853.

Lemonick, M. D. (2000, December 11). Downey's downfall. *Time*, p. 97.

Lengua, L. J., & Kovacs, E. A. (2005). Bidirectional associations between temperament and parenting and the prediction of adjustment problems in middle childhood. *Journal of Applied Developmental Psychology, 26*, 21–38.

Lengua, L. J, & Long, A. C. (2002). The role of emotionality and self-regulation in the appraisal-coping process: Tests of direct and moderating effects. *Journal of Applied Developmental Psychology, 23*, 471–493.

Lenzenweger, M. F., & Dworkin, R. H. (Eds.). (1998). *The origins and development of schizophrenia: Advances in experimental psychopathology.* Washington, DC: American Psychological Association.

Leo, R. J., & Latif, T. (2007). Repetitive transcranial magnetic stimulation (rTMS) in experimentally induced and chronic neuropathic pain: A review. *The Journal of Pain, 8*, 453-459.

Leonard, B. E. (2001). Changes in the immune system in depression and dementia: Causal or coincidental effects? *International Journal of Developmental Neuroscience, 19*, 305–312.

Leong, F. T. I., & Blustein, D. L. (2000). Toward a global vision of counseling psychology. *Counseling Psychology, 28*, 5–9.

Lepage, J. F., & Theoret, H. (2007). The mirror neuron system: grasping others' actions from birth? *Developmental Science, 10*, 513–523.

Lepore, S. J., Ragan, J. D., & Jones, S. (2000). Talking facilities cognitive-emotional processes of adaptation to an acute stressor. *Journal of Personality and Social Psychology, 78*, 499–508.

Leppanen, J.M., Moulson, M.C., Vogel-Farley, V.K. & Nelson, C.A. (2007). An ERP study of emotional face processing in the adult and infant brain. *Child Development, 78*, 232–245.

Lepper, M. R., Corpus, J. H., & Iyengar, S. S. (2005). Intrinsic and extrinsic motivational orientations in the classroom: Age differences and academic correlates. *Journal of Educational Psychology, 97*, 184–196.

Lerner, R. M., Fisher, C. B., & Weinberg, R. A. (2000). Toward a science for and of the people: Promoting civil society through the application of developmental science. *Child Development, 71*, 11–20.

Lester, D. (1990). *Understanding and preventing suicide: New perspectives.* Springfield, IL: Thomas.

Leuchter, A. F., Cook, I. A., Witte, E. Z., Morgan, M., & Abrams, M. (2002). Changes in brain function of depressed subjects during treatment with placebo. *American Journal of Psychiatry, 159*, 122–129.

Leung, F. K. S. (2002). Behind the high achievement of East Asian students [Special issue: Achievements in mathematics and science in an international context]. *Education Research and Evaluation, 8*, 87–108.

LeVay, S. (1993). *The sexual brain.* Cambridge, MA: MIT.

Levenson, R. W. (1994). The search for autonomic specificity. In P. Ekman & R. J. Davidson (Eds.), *The nature of emotion: Fundamental questions.* New York: Oxford University Press.

Leventhal, H., & Cleary, P. D. (1980). The smoking problem: A review of the research and theory in behavioral risk modification. *Psychological Bulletin, 88*, 370–405.

Levi, A., Chan, K. K., & Pence, D. (2006). Real men do not read labels: the effects of masculinity and involvement on college students' food decisions. *Journal of American College Health, 55*, 91–98.

Levick, S. E. (2004). *Clone being: Exploring the psychological and social dimensions.* Lanham, MD: Rowman and Littlefield.

Levin, B. E., (2006). Metabolic sensing neurons and the control of energy homeostasis. *Physiology & Behavior, 89*, 486-489.

Levin, R. J. (2007). Sexual activity, health and well-being—the beneficial roles of coitus and masturbation. *Sexual and Relationship Therapy, 22*, 135–148.

Levine, J. M. (1989). Reaction to opinion deviance in small groups. In P. B. Paulus (Ed.), *Psychology of group influence* (2nd ed.). Hillsdale, NJ: Erlbaum.

Levine, J. M., & Moreland, R. L. (2006). Small groups: An overview. In J. M. Levine & R. L. Moreland (Eds.), *Small groups.* New York: Psychology Press.

Levine, S. C., Huttenlocher, J., Taylor, A., & Langrock, A. (1999). Early sex differences in spatial skill. *Developmental Psychology, 35*, 940–949.

Levine, S. Z., & Rabinowitz, J. (2007). Revisiting the 5 dimensions of the Positive and Negative Syndrome Scale. *Journal of Clinical Psychopharmacology, 27*, 431–436.

Levinson, D. (1992). *The seasons of a woman's life.* New York: Knopf.

Levinson, D. J. (1990). A theory of life structure development in adulthood. In C. N. Alexander & E. J. Langer (Eds.), *Higher stages of human development: Perspectives on adult growth.* New York: Oxford University Press.

Levy, B. (1996). Improving memory in old age through implicit self-stereotyping. *Journal of Personality and Social Psychology, 71*, 1092–1107.

Levy, B., & Langer, E. (1994). Aging free from negative stereotypes: Successful memory in China and among the American deaf. *Journal of Personality and Social Psychology, 66*, 989–997.

Levy, B. R., & Myers, L. M. (2004). Preventive health behaviors influenced by self-perceptions of aging. *Preventive Medicine: An International Journal Devoted to Practice and Theory, 39*, 625–629.

Levy, B. R., Slade, M. D., Kunkel, S. R., & Kasl, S. V. (2002). Longevity increased by positive self-perceptions of aging. *Journal of Personality & Social Psychology, 83*, 261–270.

Levy, D. A. (1997). *Tools of critical thinking: Metathoughts for psychology.* Boston: Allyn & Bacon.

Levy , S. (2004, April 12). All eyes on Google. *Newsweek*, p. 40.

Levy, S. M., Lee, J., Bagley, C., & Lippman, M. (1988). Survival hazards analysis in first recurrent breast cancer patients: Seven-year follow-up. *Psychosomatic Medicine, 50*, 520–528.

Levy, Y. S., Stroomza, M., Melamed, E., & Offen, D. (2004). Embryonic and adult stem cells as a source for cell therapy in Parkinson's disease. *Journal of Molecular Neuroscience, 24*, 353–386.

Lewandowski, S., Stritzke, W. G. K., & Oberauer, K. (2005). Memory for fact, fiction and misinformation: The Iraq War 2003. *Psychological Science, 16*, 190–195.

Lewin, T. (2003, December 22). For more people in their 20s and 30s, going home is easier because they never left. *The New York Times*, p. A27.

Lewin, T. (2006, July 9). At colleges, women are leaving men in the dust. *The New York Times*, p. 1.

Lewinsohn, P. M., & Essau, C. A. (2002). Depression in adolescents. In I. H. Gotlib & C. L. Hammen (Eds.), *Handbook of depression*, 541–559. New York: Guilford Press.

Lewinsohn, P. M., Petit, J. W., Joiner, T. E., Jr., & Seeley, J. R. (2003). The symptomatic expression of major depressive disorder in adolescents and young adults. *Journal of Abnormal Psychology, 112*, 244–252.

Lewis, M., & Haviland-Jones, J. M. (2000). *Handbook of emotions* (2nd ed.). New York: Guilford Press.

Li, J. (2005). Mind or virtue: Western and Chinese beliefs about learning. *Current Directions in Psychological Science, 14*, 190–194.

Li, J., Wang, L., & Fischer, K. W. (2004). The organization of Chinese shame concepts. *Cognition and Emotion, 18*, 767–797.

Li, M. D., Cheng, R., Ma, J. Z., & Swan, G. E. (2003). A meta-analysis of estimated genetic and environmental effects on smoking behavior in male and female adult twins. *Addiction, 98*, 23–31.

Li, S. C. (2005). Neurocomputational perspectives linking neuromodulation, processing noise, representational distinctiveness, and cognitive aging. In R. Cabeza, L. Nyberg, & D. Park (Eds.), *Cognitive neuroscience of aging: Linking cognitive and cerebral aging.* London: Oxford University Press.

Li, T-K., Volkow, N. D., & Baler, R. D. (2007). The biological bases of nicotine and alcohol co-addiction. *Biological Psychiatry, 61*, 1–3.

Liang, K. A. (2007). Acculturation, ambivalent sexism, and attitudes toward women who engage in premarital sex among Chinese American young adults. *Dissertation Abstracts International: Section B: The Sciences and Engineering, 67(10-B)*, 6065.

Liben, L. S., & Bigler, R. S. (2002). The development course of gender differentiations: Conceptualizing, measuring, and evaluation constructs and pathways. *Monographs of the Society for Research in Child Development, 67*, 148–167.

Lichtenwalner, R. J., & Parent, J. M. (2005, June 15). Adult neurogenesis and the ischemic forebrain. *Journal of Cerebral Blood Flow & Metabolism*, advance online publication.

Lidz, J., & Gleitman, L. R. (2004). Argument structure and the child's contribution to language learning. *Trends in Cognitive Sciences, 8*, 157–161.

Lie, D. C., Song, H., Colamarino, S. A., Ming, G., & Gage, F. H. (2004).Neurogenesis in the adult brain: New strategies for central nervous system diseases. *Annual Review of Pharmacology and Toxicology, 44*, 399–421.

Lieberman, M. D. (2007). Social cognitive neuroscience: A review of core processes. *Annual Review of Psychology, 58*, 259–289.

Lieberman, M. D., Hariri, A., Jarcho, J. M., Eisenberger, N. I., & Bookheimer, S. Y. (2005). An fMRI investigation of race-related amygdala activity in African-American and Caucasian-American individuals. *Nature Neuroscience, 8*, 720–722.

Lieblum, S. R., & Chivers, M. L. (2007). Normal and persistent genital arousal in women: New perspectives. *Journal of Sex & Marital Therapy, 33*, 357–373.

Lien, Y-W., Chu, R-L., Jen, C-H., & Wu, C-H. (2006). Do Chinese commit neither fundamental attribution error nor ultimate attribution error? *Chinese Journal of Psychology, 48*, 163–181.

Lilienfeld, S. O. (2007). Psychological treatments that cause harm. *Perspectives on Psychological Science, 2*, 53–58.

Lilienfeld, S. O., & Lynn, S. J. (2003). Dissociative identity disorder: Multiple personalities, multiple controversies. In S. O. Lilienfeld & S. J. Lynn (Eds.), *Science and pseudoscience in clinical psychology* (pp. 109–142). New York: Guilford Press.

Lilienfeld, S. O., Lynn, S. J., & Lohr, J. M. (Eds.). (2003). *Science and pseudoscience in clinical psychology*. New York: Guilford Press.

Lin, C-H., & Lin, H-M. (2007). What price do you ask for the 'extra one'?: A social value orientation perspective. *Social Behavior and Personality, 35*, 9–18.

Lin, Y. Y., Chen, W. T., Liao, K. K., Yeh, T. C., Wu, Z. Z., & Ho, L. T. (2005). Hemispheric balance in coding speech and non-speech sounds in Chinese participants. *Neuroreport, 16*, 469–473.

Lindblad, F., Lindahl, M., & Theorell, T. (2006). Physiological stress reactions in 6th and 9th graders during test performance. *Stress and Health: Journal of the International Society for the Investigation of Stress, 22*, 189–195.

Lindh-Astrand, L., Brynhildsen, J., & Hoffmann, M. (2007). Attitudes towards the menopause and hormone therapy over the turn of the century. *Maturitas, 56*, 12–20.

Lindley, L. D. (2006). The paradox of self-efficacy: Research with diverse populations. *Journal of Career Assessment, 14*, 143–160.

Lindorff, M. (2005). Determinants of received social support: Who gives what to managers? *Journal of Social and Personal Relationships, 22*, 323–337.

Lindsay, P. H., & Norman, D. A. (1977). *Human information processing* (2nd ed.). New York: Academic Press.

Lindsay, P., Maynard, I., & Thomas, O. (2005). Effects of hypnosis on flow states and cycling performance. *Sport Psychologist, 19*, 164–177.

Lindsey, E., & Colwell, M. (2003). Preschoolers' emotional competence: Links to pretend and physical play. *Child Study Journal, 33*, 39–52.

Linehan, M., Davison, G., Lynch, T., & Sanderson, C. (in press). Principles of therapeutic change in the treatment of personality disorders. In L. Beutler, & L. Castonguay (Eds.), *Identification of principles of therapeutic change*. New York: Oxford University Press.

Linehan, M. M. (2001). Dialectical behavior therapy. In N. J. Smelser, & P. B. Baltes, P.B. (Eds), *International encyclopedia of the social and behavioral sciences*. Elmsford, NY: Pergamon, Oxford.

Linehan, M. M., Cochran, B., & Kehrer, C. A. (2001a). Borderline personality disorder. In D.H. Barlow (Ed.), *Clinical handbook of psychological disorder* (3rd ed). New York: Guilford Press.

Linehan, M. M., Cochran, B. N., & Hehrer, C. A. (2001b). Dialectical behavior therapy for borderline personality disorder. In D. H. Barlow (Ed.), *Clinical handbook of psychological disorders: A step-by-step treatment manual* (3rd ed., pp. 470–522). New York: Guilford Press.

Links, P. S., Eynan, R., & Heisel, M. J. (2007). Affective instability and suicidal ideation and behavior in patients with borderline personality disorder. *Journal of Personality Disorders, 21*, 72–86.

Linscheid, T. R., & Reichenbach, H. (2002). Multiple factors in the long-term effectiveness of contingent electric shock treatment for self-injurious behavior: A case example. *Research in Developmental Disabilities, 23*, 161–177.

Linszen, D. H., Dingemans, P. M., Nugter, M. A., Van der Does, A. J. W., et al. (1997). Patient attributes and expressed emotion as risk factors for psychotic relapse. *Schizophrenia Bulletin, 23*, 119–130.

Lippa, R. A. (2005). *Gender, nature, and nurture* (2nd ed.). Mahwah, NJ: Erlbaum.

Lips, H. M. (2003). *A new psychology of women: Gender, culture, and ethnicity*. New York: McGraw-Hill.

Lipsey, M. W., & Wilson, D. B. (1993). The efficacy of psychological, educational, and behavioral treatment: Confirmation from meta-analysis. *American Psychologist, 48*, 1181–1209.

Litowitz, B. E. (2007). Unconscious fantasy: A once and future concept. *Journal of the American Psychoanalytic Association, 55*, 199–228.

Little, A., Burt, D. M., & Perrett, D. I. (2006). What is good is beautiful: Face preference reflects desired personality. *Personality and Individual Differences, 41*, 1107–1118.

Liu, J. H., & Mills, D. (2006). Modern racism and neo-liberal globalization: The discourses of plausible deniability and their multiple functions. *Journal of Community & Applied Social Psychology, 16*, 83–99.

Liu, L., He, S-Z., & Wu, Y. (2007). An analysis of the characteristics of single parent families with different structures and their children. *Chinese Journal of Clinical Psychology, 15*, 68–70.

Lobato, M. I., Koff, w. J., & Manenti, C. (2006). Follow-up of sex reassignment surgery in transsexuals: A Brazilian cohort. *Archives of Sexual Behavior, 35*, 711–715.

Lobban, F., Barrowclough, C., & Jones, S. (2006). Does Expressed Emotion need to be understood within a more systemic framework? An examination of discrepancies in appraisals between patients diagnosed with schizophrenia and their relatives. *Social Psychiatry and Psychiatric Epidemiology, 41*, 50–55.

Locke, J. L. (2006). Parental selection of vocal behavior: Crying, cooking, babbling, and the evolution of language. *Human Nature, 17*, 155–168.

Lockrane, B., Bhatia, P., & Gore, R. (2005). Successful treatment of narcolepsy and cataplexy: A review. *Canadian Respiratory Journal, 12*, 225–227.

Loehlin, J. C. (2002). The IQ paradox: Resolved? Still an open question. *Psychological Review, 109*, 754–758.

Loewenstein, G. (1994). The psychology of curiosity: A review and reinterpretation. *Psychological Bulletin, 116*, 75–98.

Lofholm, N. (2003, May 6). Climber's kin share relief: Ralston saw 4 options, they say; death wasn't one of them. *Denver Post*, p. A1.

Loftus, E. (1998, November). The memory police. *APA Observer, 3*, 14.

Loftus, E. F. (1993). Psychologists in the eyewitness world. *American Psychologist, 48*, 550–552.

Loftus, E. F. (1997). Memory for a past that never was. *Current Directions in Psychological Science, 6*, 60–65.

Loftus, E. F. (2003). The dangers of memory. In R. J. Sternberg (Ed.), *Psychologists defying the crowd: Stories of those who battled the establishment and won* (pp. 105–117). Washington, DC: American Psychological Association.

Loftus, E. F. (2004). Memories of things unseen. *Current Directions in Psychological Science, 13*, 145–147.

Loftus, E. F., & Bernstein, D. M. (2005). Rich false memories: The royal road to success. In A. F. Healy, *Experimental cognitive psychology and its applications*. Washington, DC: American Psychological Association.

Loftus, E. F., & Palmer, J. C. (1974). Reconstruction of automobile destruction: An example of the interface between language and memory. *Journal of Verbal Learning and Verbal Behavior, 13*, 585–589.

Long, G. M., & Beaton, R. J. (1982). The case for peripheral persistence: Effects of target and background luminance on a partial-report task. *Journal of Experimental Psychology: Human Perception and Performance, 8*, 383–391.

López, S. R., & Guarnaccia, P. J. (2005). Cultural dimensions of psychopathology: The social world's impact on mental illness. In J. E. Maddux & B. A. Winstead (Eds.), *Foundations for a contemporary understanding*. Mahwah, NJ: Lawrence Erlbaum Associates.

López, S. R., & Guarnaccia, P. J. J. (2000). Cultural psychopathology: Uncovering the social world of mental illness. *Annual Review of Psychology, 51*, 571–598.

Lorenz, K. (1966). *On aggression*. New York: Harcourt Brace Jovanovich.

Lorenz, K. (1974). *Civilized man's eight deadly sins*. New York: Harcourt Brace Jovanovich.

Lothane, Z. (2005). Jung, A biography. *Journal of the American Psychoanalytic Association, 53*, 317–324.

Lotze, M., Heymans, U., Birbaumer, N., Veit, R., Erb, M., Flor, H., & Halsband, U. (2006). Differential cerebral activation during observation of expressive gestures and motor acts. *Neuropsychologia, 44*, 1787–1795.

Lowe, M. R. (1993). The effects of dieting on eating behavior: A three-factor model. *Psychological Bulletin, 114*, 100–121.

Lowe, P., Humphreys, C., & Williams, S. J. (2007). Night terrors: Women's experiences of (not) sleeping where there is domestic violence. *Violence Against Women, 13*, 549–561.

Lowery, D., Fillingim, R. B., & Wright, R. A. (2003). Sex differences and incentive effects on perceptual and cardiovascular responses to cold pressor pain. *Psychosomatic Medicine, 65*, 284–291.

Lu, J., Sherman, D., & Devor, M. (2006). A putative flip-flop switch for control of REM sleep. *Nature, 441*, 589–594.

Lubell, K. M., Swahn, M. H., Crosby, A. E., & Kegler, S. R. (2004). Methods of suicide among persons aged 10–19 years—United States, 1992–2001. *MMWR, 53*, 471–473. Retrieved from http://www.cdc.gov/mmwr/PDF/wk/mm5322.pdf.

Lubinski, D., & Benbow, C. P. (2006). Study of mathematically precocious youth after 35 years: Uncovering antecedents for the development of math-science expertise. *Perspectives on Psychological Science, 1*, 316–345.

Lubinski, D., Benbow, C. P., Webb, R. M., & Bleske-Rechek, A. (2006). Tracking exceptional human capital over two decades. *Psychological Science, 17,* 194–199.

Lublin, H., Eberhard, J., & Levander, S. (2005). Current therapy issues and unmet clinical needs in the treatment of schizophrenia: A review of the new generation antipsychotics. *International Clinical Psychopharmacology, 20,* 183–198.

Luborsky, L. (1988). *Who will benefit from psychotherapy?* New York: Basic Books.

Luchins, A. S. (1946). Classroom experiments on mental set. *American Journal of Psychology, 59,* 295–298.

Lucki, I., & O'Leary, O. F. (2004). Distinguishing roles for norepinephrine and serotonin in the behavioral effects of antidepressant drugs. *Journal of Clinical Psychiatry, 65,* 11–24.

Luders, E., Narr, K. L., Zaidel, E., Thompson, P. M., & Toga, A. W. (2006). Gender effects on callosal thickness in scaled and unscaled space. *Neuroreport, 17,* 1103–1106.

Ludwig, A. M. (1969). Altered states of consciousness. In C. T. Tart (Ed.), *Altered states of consciousness.* New York: Wiley.

Ludwig, A. M. (1996, March). Mental disturbances and creative achievement. *The Harvard Mental Health Letter,* pp. 4–6.

Lun, V. M., & Bond, M. H. (2006). Achieving relationship harmony in groups and its consequence for group performance. *Asian Journal of Social Psychology, 9,* 195–202.

Luria, A. R. (1968). *The mind of a mnemonist.* Cambridge, MA: Basic Books.

Lurie, K., Robinson, A., & Pecsenye, M. (2005). *Cracking the GRE 2006.* New York: Random House.

Luthar, S. S., Cicchetti, D., & Becker, B. (2000). The construct of resilience: A critical evaluation and guidelines for future work. *Child Development, 71,* 543–562.

Lutz, C.K. & Novak, M. A. (2005) Environmental enrichment for nonhuman primates: theory and application. *ILAR Journal, 46,* 178–91.

Lutz, W., Lambert, M. J., Harmon, S. C., Tschitsaz, A., Schurch, E., & Stulz, N (2006). The probability of treatment success, failure and duration—What can be learned from empirical data to support decision making in clinical practice? *Clinical Psychology & Psychotherapy, 13,* 223–232.

Ly, D. H., Lockhart, D. J., Lerner, R. A., & Schultz, P. G. (2000, March 31). Mitotic misregulation and human aging. *Science, 287,* 2486–2492.

Lykken, D. T. (1995). *The antisocial personalities.* Mahwah, NJ: Erlbaum.

Lykken, D., & Tellegen, A. (1996). Happiness is a stochastic phenomenon. *Psychological Science, 7,* 181–185.

Lymberis, S. C., Parhar, P. K., Katsoulakis, E., & Formenti, S. C. (2004). Pharmacogenomics and breast cancer. *Pharmacogenomics, 5,* 31–55.

Lynam, D. R., Milich, R., Zimmerman, R., Novak, S. P., Logan, T. K., Martin, C. Leukefeld, M. C., & Clayton, R. (1999). Project DARE: No effects at 10-year follow-up. *Journal of Consulting and Clinical Psychology, 67,* 590–593.

Lynch, T. R., Trost, W. T, Salsman, N., & Linehan, M. M. (2007). Dialectical behavior therapy for borderline personality disorder. *Annual Review of Clinical Psychology, 3,* 181–205.

Lyness, K. S., & Heilman, M. E. (2006). When fit is fundamental: performance evaluations and promotions of upper-level female and male managers. *Journal of Applied Psychology, 91,* 777–785.

Lynn, S. J., Kirsch, I., Barabasz, A., Cardena, E., & Patterson, D. (2000). Hypnosis as an empirically supported clinical intervention: The state of the evidence and a look to the future.

Lynn, S. J., Lock, T., Loftus, E. F., Krackow, E., & Lilienfeld, S. O. (2003). The remembrance of things past: Problematic memory recovery techniques in psychotherapy. In S. O. Lilienfeld, S. J. Lynn, & J. M. Lohr (Eds.). *Science and pseudoscience in clinical psychology.* New York: Guilford Press.

Lynn, S. J., & Rhue, J. W. (1988). Fantasy-proneness: Hypnosis, developmental antecedents, and psychopathology. *American Psychologist, 43,* 35–44.

Lynn, S. J., Fassler, O., & Knox, J. (2005). Hypnosis and the altered state debate: Something more or nothing more? Comment. *Contemporary Hypnosis, 22,* 39–45.

Lynn, S. J., Neufeld, V., Green, J. P., Sandberg, D., et al. (1996). Daydreaming, fantasy, and psychopathology. In R. G. Kunzendorf, N. P. Spanos, & B. Wallace (Eds.), *Hypnosis and imagination. Imagery and human development series.* Amityville, NY: Baywood.

Macaluso, E., & Driver, J. (2005). Multisensory spatial interactions: a window onto functional integration in the human brain *Trends in Neurosciences, 28, Issue 5,* 264–271.

Macaluso, E., Frith, C. D., & Driver, J. (2000, August 18). Modulation of human visual cortex by crossmodal spatial attention. *Science, 289,* 1206–1208.

Macduff, I. (2006). Your pace or mine? Culture, time and negotiation. *Negotiation Journal, 22,* 31–45.

Maccoby, E. E., & Jacklin, C. N. (1974). *The psychology of sex differences.* Stanford, CA: Stanford University Press.

Machado, R. B., Suchecki, D., & Tufik, S. (2005). Sleep homeostasis in rats assessed by a long-term intermittent paradoxical sleep deprivation protocol. *Behavioural Brain Research, 160,* 356–364.

MacIntyre, T., Moran, A., & Jennings, D. J. (2002). Is controllability of imagery related to canoe-slalom performance? *Perceptual & Motor Skills, 94,* 1245–1250.

Mack, J. (2003). *The museum of the mind.* London: British Museum Publications.

Mackay, J., & Eriksen, M. (2002). *The tobacco atlas.* Geneva, Switzerland: World Health Organization.

MacKenzie, K. R., & Grabovac. A. D. (2001). Interpersonal psychotherapy group (IPT-G) for depression. *Journal of Psychotherapy Practice and Research, 10,* 46–51.

Macmillan, M. (1996). *Freud evaluated: The completed arc.* Cambridge, MA: MIT.

Macmillan, M. (2000). *An odd kind of fame: Stories of Phineas Gage.* Cambridge, MA: MIT.

MacPherson, K. (2002, March 17). Unfilled pink-collar jobs threaten service cuts. *Pittsburgh Post-Gazette,* p. 7.

Macrae, E. B., Monk, C. S., Nelson, E. E., Zarahn, E., Leibenluft, E., Bilder, R. M., Charney, D. S., Ernst, M., & Pine, D. S. (2004). A developmental examination of gender differences in brain engagement during evaluation of threat. *Biological Psychiatry, 55,* 1047–1055.

Madden, D. J. (2007). Aging and visual attention. *Current Directions in Psychological Science, 16,* 70–74.

Maddi, S. R. (2007). The story of hardiness: Twenty years of theorizing, research, and practice. In A. Monat, R. S. Lazarus, & G. Reevy, *The Praeger handbook on stress and coping (vol.2).* Westport, CT: Praeger Publishers/ Greenwood Publishing.

Mader, S. S. (2000). *Biology* (p. 250). Boston: McGraw-Hill.

Madon, S., Guyll, M., Aboufadel, K., Montiel, E., Smith, A., Palumbo, P., & Jussim, L. (2001). Ethnic and national stereotypes: The Princeton Trilogy revisited and revised. *Personality and Social Psychology Bulletin, 27,* 996–1010.

Madon, S., Jussim, L., & Eccles, J. (1997). In search of the powerful self-fulfilling prophecy. *Journal of Personality and Social Psychology, 72,* 791–809.

Madon, S., Willard, J., Guyll, M. (2006). Self-fulfilling prophecy effects of mothers' beliefs on children's alcohol use: accumulation, dissipation, and stability over time. *Journal of Personality and Social Psychology, 90,* 911–926.

Magida, A. J. (2006). *Opening the doors of wonder: Reflections on religious rites of passage.* Berkeley, CA: University of California Press.

Magley, V. J. (2002). Coping with sexual harassment: Reconceptualizing women's resistance. *Journal of Personality and Social Psychology, 83,* 930–946.

Magoni, M., Bassani, L., Okong, P., Kituuka, P., Germinario, E. P., Giuliano, M., & Vella, S. (2005). Mode of infant feeding and HIV infection in children in a program for prevention of mother-to-child transmission in Uganda. *AIDS, 19,* 433–437.

Maguire, E. A., Gadian, D. G., Johnsrude, I. S., Good, C. D., Ashburner, J., Frackowiak, R. S. J., & Frith, C. D. (2000). Navigation-related structural change in the hippocampi of taxi drivers. *Proceedings of the National Academy of Sciences, 97,* 4398–4403.

Maguire, E. A., Woollett, K., & Spiers, H. J. (2006). London taxi drivers and bus drivers: A structural MRI and neuropsychological analysis. *Hippocampus, 16,* 1091–1101.

Mahmood, M., & Black, J. (2005). Narcolepsy-cataplexy: How does recent understanding help in evaluation and treatment. *Current Treatment Options in Neurology, 7,* 363–371.

Maidment, I. (2000). The use of St John's Wort in the treatment of depression. *Psychiatric Bulletin, 24,* 232–234.

Maier, S. F., & Watkins, L. R. (2000). Learned helplessness. In A. E. Kazdin, *Encyclopedia of psychology* (Vol. 4). Washington, DC: American Psychological Association.

Majdandzic, M., & van den Boom, D. C. (2007). Multimethod longitudinal assessment of temperament in early childhood. *Journal of Personality, 75,* 121–167.

Majeres, R. L. (2007). Sex differences in phonological coding: Alphabet transformation speed. *Intelligence, 35,* 335–346.

Malamuth, N. M., Linz, D., Heavey, C. L., & Barnes, G. (1995). Using the confluence model of sexual aggression to predict men's conflict with women: A 10-year follow-up study. *Journal of Personality and Social Psychology, 69,* 353–369.

Maldonado, J. R., & Spiegel, D. (2003). Dissociative disorders. In R. E. Hales & S. C. Yudofsky, *The American Psychiatric Publishing textbook of clinical psychiatry* (4th ed.). Washington, DC: American Psychiatric Publishing.

Malle, B. F. (2004). *How the mind explains behavior: Folk explanations, meaning, and social interaction.* Cambridge, MA: MIT.

Malouff, J. M., Thorsteinsson, E. B., & Schutte, N. S. (2007). The efficacy of problem solving therapy in reducing mental and physical health problems: A meta-analysis. *Clinical Psychology Review, 27,* 46–57.

Mamassis, G., & Doganis, G. (2004). The effects of a mental training program on juniors precompetitive anxiety, self-confidence, and tennis performance. *Journal of Applied Sport Psychology, 16,* 118–137.

Mameli, M. (2007). Reproductive cloning, genetic engineering and the autonomy of the child: The moral agent and the open future. *Journal of Medical Ethics, 33,* 87–93.

Mancinelli, R., Binetti, R., & Ceccanti, M. (2007). Woman, alcohol and environment: Emerging risks for health. *Neuroscience & Biobehavioral Reviews, 31,* 246–253.

Mangels, J. (2004). *The influence of intelligence beliefs on attention and learning a neurophysiological approach.* Presentation at the 16th Annual Convention of Social Cognitive Neuroscience. Washington, DC: American Psychological Society.

Mangels, J., Dweck, C., & Good, C. (2005, May). *Achievement motivation modulates the neural dynamics of error correction.* CASL Meeting, U. S. Department of Education.

Manly, J. J. (2005). Advantages and disadvantages of separate norms for African Americans. *Clinical Neuropsychologist, 19,* 270–275.

Manly, J. J. (2006). Deconstructing race and ethnicity: implications for measurement of health outcomes. *Medical Care, 44, Special issue: Measurement in a multi-ethnic society,* S10–S16.

Mann, D. (1997). *Psychotherapy: An erotic relationship.* New York: Routledge.

Mann, K., Ackermann, K., Croissant, B., Mundle, G., Nakovics, H., Diehl, A. (2005). Neuroimaging of gender differences in alcohol dependence: are women more vulnerable? *Alcoholism: Clinical & Experimental Research, 29,* 896–901.

Mann, R. E., & Hollin, C. R. (2007). Sexual offender's explanations for their offending. *Journal of Sexual Aggression, 13,* 3–9.

Manning, M. A., & Hoyme, E. H. (2007). Fetal alcohol spectrum disorders: A practical clinical approach to diagnosis. *Neuroscience & Biobehavioral Reviews, 31,* 230–238.

Manning, S. Y. (2005). Dialectical behavior therapy of severe and chronic problems. In L. VandeCreek (Ed.), *Innovations in clinical practice: Focus on adults.* Sarasota, FL: Professional Resource Press/Professional Resource Exchange.

Manor, J. K., & Gailliot, M. T. (2007). Altruism and egoism: Prosocial motivations for helping depend on relationship context. *European Journal of Social Psychology, 37,* 347–358.

Manstead, A. S. R. (1991). Expressiveness as an individual difference. In R. S. Feldman & B. Rime (Eds.), *Fundamentals of nonverbal behavior.* Cambridge, England: Cambridge University Press.

Manstead, A. S. R., & Wagner, H. L. (2004). *Experience emotion.* Cambridge, England: Cambridge University Press.

Manstead, A. S. R., Frijda, N., & Fischer, A. H. (Eds.) (2003). *Feelings and emotions: The Amsterdam Symposium.* Cambridge, England: Cambridge University Press.

Marcaurelle, R., Bélanger, C., & Marchand, A. (2003). Marital relationship and the treatment of panic disorder with agoraphobia: A critical review. *Clinical Psychology Review, 23,* 247–276.

Marcaurelle, R., Bélanger, C., & Marchand, A. (2005). Marital predictors of symptom severi-

ty in panic disorder with agoraphobia. *Journal of Anxiety Disorders, 19,* 211–232.

Marcus, G. F. (1996). Why do children say "breaked"? *Current Directions in Psychological Science, 5,* 81–85.

Marcus-Newhall, A., Pedersen, W. C., & Carlson, M. (2000). Displaced aggression is alive and well: A meta-analytic review. *Journal of Personality and Social Psychology, 78,* 670–689.

Margoliash, D. (2005). Song learning and sleep. *Nature Neuroscience, 8,* 546–548.

Margolis, E., & Laurence, S. (Eds.). (1999). *Concepts: Core readings.* Cambridge, MA: MIT

Markey, P. M. (2000). Bystander intervention in computer-mediated communication. *Computers in Human Behavior, 16,* 183–188.

Markowitz, J. C. (2003). Controlled trials of psychotherapy. *American Journal of Psychiatry, 160,* 186–187.

Markowsitsch, H. J. (2000). Memory and amnesia. In M. M. Mesulam (Ed.), *Principles of behavioral and cognitive neurology* (2nd ed.). London: Oxford University Press.

Marks, I. M. (2004). The Nobel prize award in physiology to Ivan Petrovich Pavlov–1904. *Australian and New Zealand Journal of Psychiatry, 38,* 674–677.

Markus, H. R., & Kitayama, S. (1991). Culture and the self: Implications for cognition, emotion, and motivation. *Psychological Review, 98,* 224–253.

Markus, H. R., & Kitayama, S. (2003). Models of agency: Sociocultural diversity in the construction of action. In V. Murphy-Berman & J. J. Berman (Eds.), *Cross-cultural differences in perspectives on the self.* Lincoln, NE: University of Nebraska Press.

Markus, H. R., Uchida, Y., Omoregie, H., Townsend, S. S., & Kitayama, S. (2006). Going for the gold: Models of agency in Japanese and American contexts. *Psychological Science, 17,* 103–112.

Maroda, K. J. (2004). A relational perspective on women and power. *Psychoanalytic Psychology, 21,* 428–435.

Marrero, H., & Gamez, E. (2004). Content and strategy in syllogistic reasoning. *Canadian Journal of Experimental Psychology, 58,* 168–180.

Marsh, H. W., Hau, K. T., & Sung, R. Y T (2007). Childhood obesity, gender, actual-ideal body image discrepancies, and physical self-concept in Hong Kong children: Cultural differences in the value of moderation. *Developmental Psychology, 43,* 647–662.

Marshall, K., Laing, D. G., & Jinks, A. L. (2006). The capacity of humans to identify components in complex odor-taste mixtures. *Chemical Senses, 31,* 539–545.

Marshall, M. K. (2007). The critical factors of coaching practice leading to successful coaching outcomes. *Dissertation Abstracts International: Section B: The Sciences and Engineering, 67(7-B),* 4092.

Marshall, R. D., & Bryant, R. A., & Amsel, L. (2007). The psychology of ongoing threat: Relative risk appraisal, the September 11 attacks, and terrorism-related fears. *American Psychologist, 62,* 304–316.

Marshall, R. D., Bryant, R. A., Amsel, L., Suh, E. J., Cook, J. M., & Neria, Y. (2007). The psychology of ongoing threat: Relative risk appraisal, the September 11 attacks and terrorism-related fears. *American Psychologist, 62,* 304–316.

Marsland, A. L., Bachen, E. A., Cohen, S., Rabin, B., & Manuck, S. B. (2002). Stress, immune reactivity and susceptibility to infectious dis-

ease [Special issue: The Pittsburgh special issue]. *Physiology and Behavior, 77,* 711–716.

Marszalek, J. (2007). Computerized adaptive testing and the experience of flow in examinees. *Dissertation Abstracts International Section A: Humanities and Social Sciences, 67(7-A),* 2465.

Martelle, S., Hanley, C., & Yoshino K. (2003, January 28). "Sopranos" scenario in slaying? *Los Angeles Times,* p. B1.

Martin, A. J., & Marsh, H. W. (2002). Fear of failure: Friend or foe? *Australian Psychologist, 38,* 31–38.

Martin, C. L., Ruble, D. N., & Szkrybalo, J. (2002). Cognitive theories of early gender development. *Psychological Bulletin, 128,* 903–933.

Martin, H. (2006, July 3). New heights. *Los Angeles Times.* p. 1, Part E.

Martin, L., & Pullum, G. K. (1991). *The great Eskimo vocabulary hoax.* Chicago: University of Chicago Press.

Martin, P. D., & Brantley, P. J. (2004). Stress, coping, and social support in health and behavior. In J. M. Raczynski & L. C. Leviton (Eds.), *Handbook of clinical health psychology: Vol. 2. Disorders of behavior and health.* Washington, DC: American Psychological Association.

Martin, R. C. (2005). Components of short-term memory and their relation to language processing. *Current Directions in Psychological Science, 14,* 204–208.

Martin, S. (April 2002). Easing migraine pain. *Monitor on Psychology,* pp. 71–73.

Martindale, C. (1981). *Cognition and consciousness.* Homewood, IL: Dorsey.

Marx, J. (2004, July 16). Prolonging the agony. *Science, 305,* 326–328.

Mashour, G. A., Walker, E. E., & Martuza, R. L. (2005). Psychosurgery: Past, present, and future. *Brain Research Reviews, 48,* 409–419.

Maslow, A. H. (1987). *Motivation and personality* (3rd ed.). New York: Harper & Row.

Mason, M (1995). *The making of Victorian sexuality.* New York: Oxford University Press.

Mast, F. W., & Kosslyn, S. M. (2002). Visual mental images can be ambiguous: Insights from individual differences in spatial transformation abilities. *Cognition, 86,* 57–70.

Masters, W. H., & Johnson, V. E. (1966). *Human sexual response.* Boston: Little, Brown.

Masters, W. H., & Johnson, V. E. (1979). *Homosexuality in perspective.* Boston: Little, Brown.

Masters, W., & Johnson, V. (1994). *Heterosexuality.* New York: Harper Collins.

Mastropieri, M. A., & Scruggs, T. E. (2000). *Teaching students ways to remember: Strategies for learning mnemonically.* Cambridge, MA: Brookline.

Masuda, M. (2003). Meta-analyses of love scales: Do various love scales measure the same psychological constructs? *Japanese Psychological Research, 45,* 25–37.

Mataix-Cols, D., & Bartres-Fax, D. (2002). Is the use of the wooden and computerized versions of the Tower of Hanoi Puzzle equivalent? *Applied Neuropsychology, 9,* 117–120.

Mathews, J. (2006, January 17). Self-discipline may beat smarts as key to success. *The Washington Post,* p. A10.

Mathur, T. P., & Gottesman, I. I. (2007). Correlates of hallucinations in schizophrenia: A cross-cultural evaluation. *Schizophrenia Research, 92,* 41–49.

Matlin, M.W. (1996). *The psychology of women* (3rd ed.). Orlando, FL: Harcourt Brace College Publishers.

Matlin, M. W. (2000). *The psychology of women* (4th ed.). Ft. Worth, TX: Harcourt.

Maton, K. I., Kohout, J. L., Wicherski, M., Leary, G. E., & Vinokurov, A. (2006). Minority students of color and the psychology graduate pipeline. *American Psychologist, 61,* 117–131.

Matsumoto, D. (2002). Methodological requirements to test a possible in-group advantage in judging emotions across cultures: Comment on Elfenbein and Ambady (2002) and evidence. *Psychological Bulletin, 128,* 236–242.

Matsumoto, D. (Ed.). (2001). *The handbook of culture and psychology.* New York: Oxford University Press.

Matsumoto, D. (2004). Reflections on culture and competence. In R. J. Sternberg & E. L. Grigorenko (Eds.), *Culture and competence: Contexts of life success.* Washington, DC: American Psychological Association.

Matsumoto, D. (2006). Culture and nonverbal behavior. In V. P, Manusov, & M. L. Patterson, *The Sage handbook of nonverbal communication.* Thousand Oaks, CA: Sage Publications.

Matsumoto, D., Yoo, S. H., Hirayama, S., & Petrova, G. (2005). Development and validation of a measure of display rule knowledge: The Display Rule Assessment Inventory. *Emotion, 5,* 23–40.

Matthews, G., & Funke, G. J. (2006). Worry and information-processing. In G. C. L. Davey & A. Wells, *Worry and its psychological disorders: Theory, assessment and treatment.* Hoboken, NJ: Wiley Publishing.

Matthews, G., Zeidner, M., & Roberts, R. D. (2003). *Emotional intelligence: Science and myth.* Cambridge, MA: MIT.

Matthews, K. A., (2005). Psychological perspectives on the development of coronary heart disease. *American Psychologist, 60,* 783–796.

Maurer, D., Lewis, T. L., Brent, H. P., & Levin, A. V. (1999, October 1). Rapid improvement in the acuity of infants after visual input. *Science, 286,* 108–110.

Mayer, J. D., Salovey, P., & Caruso, D. R. (2004). Emotional intelligence: Theory, findings, and implications. *Psychological Inquiry, 15,* 197–215.

Mayer, J. D., Salovey, P., Caruso, D. R., & Sitarenios, G. (2003). Measuring emotional intelligence with the MSCEIT V2.0. *Emotion, 3,* 97–105.

Maynard, A. E., & Martini, M. I. (2005). *Learning in cultural context: Family, peers, and school.* New York: Kluwer Academic/Plenum Publishers.

Mayne, T. J., & Bonanno, G. A. (Eds.). (2001). *Emotions: Current issues and future directions.* New York: Guilford Press.

Mays, V. M., Rubin, J., Sabourin, M., & Walker, L. (1996). Moving toward a global psychology: Changing theories and practice to meet the needs of a changing world. *American Psychologist, 51,* 485–487.

Mazard, A., Laou, L., Joliot, M., & Mellet, E. (2005). Neural impact of the semantic content of visual mental images and visual percepts. *Brain Research and Cognitive Brain Research, 24,* 423–35.

McAdams, D. P., Diamond, A., de St. Aubin, E., & Mansfield, E. (1997). Stories of commitment: The psychosocial construction of generative lives. *Journal of Personality and Social Psychology, 72,* 678–694.

McAuillen, A., Nicastro, R., Guenot, F., Girard, M., Lissner, C., & Ferrero, F. (2005). Intensive dialectical behavior therapy for outpatients with borderline personality disorder who are in crisis. *Psychiatric Services, 56,* 193–197.

McCabe, C., & Rolls, E. T. (2007). Umami: A delicious flavor formed by convergence of taste and olfactory pathways in the human brain. *European Journal of Neuroscience, 25,* 1855–1864.

McCabe, K. (2006). The neuroeconomics of personal and interpersonal decision making. In D. De Cremer, M. Zeelenberg, & J. K. Murnighan, *Social psychology and economics.* Mahwah, NJ: Lawrence Erlbaum Associates.

McCabe, P. M., Schneiderman, N., Field, T., & Wellens, A. R. (Eds). (2000). *Stress, coping, and cardiovascular disease.* Mahwah, NJ: Lawrence Erlbaum.

McCarthy, J. (2005). Individualism and collectivism: What do they have to do with counseling? *Journal of Multicultural Counseling and Development, 33,* 108–117.

McCaul, K. D., Johnson, R. J., & Rothman, A. J. (2003). The effects of framing and action instructions on whether older adults obtain flu shots. *Health Psychology.*

McCauley, C. (2007). Psychological issues in understanding terrorism and the response to terrorism. Psychological aspects of suicide terrorism. In B. Bongar, L. M. Brown, & L. E. Beutler, *Psychology of terrorism.* New York: Oxford University Press.

McClelland, D. C. (1985). How motives, skills, and values determine what people do. *American Psychologist, 40,* 812–825.

McClelland, D. C. (1993). Intelligence is not the best predictor of job performance. *Current Directions in Psychological Research, 2,* 5–8.

McClelland, D. C., Atkinson, J. W., Clark, R. A., & Lowell, E. L. (1953). *The achievement motive.* New York: Appleton-Century-Crofts.

McClelland, L. E., & Pilcher, J. J. (2007). Assessing subjective sleepiness during a night of sleep deprivation: Examining the internal state and behavioral dimensions of sleepiness. *Behavioral Medicine, 33,* 17–26.

McClintock, M. K., & Herdt, G. (1996). Rethinking puberty: The development of sexual attraction. *Current Directions in Psychological Science, 5,* 178–183.

McClintock, M. K., Jacob, S., Zelano, B., & Hayreh, D. J. S. (2001). Pheromones and vasanas: The functions of social chemosignals. In J. A. French & A. C. Kamil (Eds.), *Evolutionary psychology and motivation.* Vol. 47 of the Nebraska symposium on motivation. Lincoln, NB: University of Nebraska Press.

McClure, J., Sutton, R. M., Sibley, C. G. (2007). Listening to reporters or engineers? How instance-based messages about building design affect earthquake fatalism. *Journal of Applied Social Sciences, 37,* 1956–1973.

McClure, S., Li, J., Tomlin, D., Cypert, K., Montague, L, and Montague, R. (2004). Neural correlates of behavior preference for culturally familiar drinks. *Neuron, 44,* 379–387.

McCormick, C. G. (2003). Metacognition and learning. In W. M. Reynolds & G. E. Miller (Eds.), *Handbook of psychology: Educational psychology* (Vol. 7, pp. 79–102). New York: Wiley.

McCoy, N. L., & Pitino, L. (2002). Pheromonal influences on socio-sexual behavior in young women. *Physiological Behavior 75,* 367–375.

McCrae, R., Terracciano, A., and 79 Members of the Personality Profiles of Cultures Project. (2005). Personality profiles of cultures: Aggregate personality traits. *Journal of Personality and Social Psychology, 89,* 407–425.

McCrae R. R., Terracciano A., & 78 Members of the Personality Profiles of Cultures Project: Universal features of personality traits from the observer's perspective: Data from 50 cultures. *Journal of Personality and Social Psychology,* 88: 547–561, 2005.

McCrae, R. R., & Costa, P. T., Jr. (1986). A five-factor theory of personality. In L. A. Pervin & O. P. John (Eds.), *Handbook of personality: Theory and research* (2nd ed.). New York: Guilford.

McCullough, J. P., Jr. (1999). *Treatment for chronic depression: Cognitive behavioral analysis system of psychology (CBASP).* New York: Guilford Press.

McDaniel, M. A., Maier, S. F., & Einstein, G. O. (2002). "Brain specific" nutrients: A memory cure? *Psychological Science in the Public Interest, 3,* 12–18.

McDonald, C., & Murray, R. M. (2004). Can structural magnetic resonance imaging provide an alternative phenotype for genetic studies of schizophrenia? In M. S. Keshavan, J. L. Kennedy, & R. M. Murray (Eds.), *Neurodevelopment and schizophrenia.* New York: Cambridge University Press.

McDonald, H. E., & Hirt, E. R. (1997). When expectancy meets desire: Motivational effects in reconstructive memory. *Journal of Personality and Social Psychology, 72,* 5–23.

McDonald, J. W. (1999, September). Repairing the damaged spinal cord. *Scientific American,* pp. 65–73.

McDougall, W. (1908). *Introduction to social psychology.* London: Methuen.

McDowell, D. M., & Spitz, H. I. (1999). *Substance abuse.* New York: Brunner/ Mazel.

McEwen, B. S. (1998, January 15). Protective and damaging effects of stress mediators [Review article]. *New England Journal of Medicine, 338,* 171–179.

McGaugh, J. L. (2003). *Memory and emotion: The making of lasting memories.* New York: Columbia University Press.

McGee, G., Caplan, A., & Malhotra, R. (Eds.). (2004). *The human cloning debate.* Berkeley, CA: Hills Books.

McGilvray, J. (Ed.). (2004). *The Cambridge companion to Chomsky.* Oxford, England: Cambridge University Press.

McGinn, D. (2003, June 9). Testing, testing: The new job search. *Time,* pp. 36–38.

McGlynn, F. D., Smitherman, T. A., & Gothard, K. D. (2004). Comment on the status of systematic desensitization. *Behavior Modification, 28,* 194–205.

McGregor, K. K., & Capone, N. C. (2004). Genetic and environmental interactions in determining the early lexicon: Evidence from a set of tri-zygotic quadruplets. *Journal of Child Language, 31,* 311–337.

McGue, M. (1999). The behavioral genetics of alcoholism. *Current Directions in Psychological Science, 8,* 109–115.

McGuire, S. (2003). The heritability of parenting. *Parenting: Science & Practice, 3,* 73–94.

McGuire, W. J. (1997). Creative hypothesis generating in psychology: Some useful heuristics. *Annual Review of Psychology, 48,* 1–30.

McHale, S. M., Crouter, A. C., & Tucker, C. J. (1999). Family context and gender role socialization in middle childhood: Comparing girls to boys and sisters to brothers. *Child Development, 70,* 990–1004.

McKeever, V. M., & Huff, M. E. (2003). A diathesis-stress model of post-traumatic stress disorder: Ecological, biological, and residual stress pathways. *Review of General Psychology, 7,* 237–250.

McKenzie-McLean, J. (2006, August 3). On the scent of a new detector. *The Press* (Christchurch, New Zealand), p. 7.

McKinley, M. J., Cairns, M. J., Denton, D. A., Egan, G., Mathai, M. L., Uschakov, A., Wade, J. D., Weisinger, R. S., & Oldfield, B. J. (2004). Physiological and pathophysiological influences on thirst. *Physiology and Behavior, 81,* 795–803.

McManus, C. (2004). *Right hand, left hand: The origins of asymmetry in brains, bodies, atoms and cultures.* Cambridge, MA: Harvard University Press.

McManus, F., & Waller, G. (1995). A functional analysis of binge-eating. *Clinical Psychology Review, 15,* 845–863.

McMillan, D. E., & Katz, J. L. (2002). Continuing implications of the early evidence against the drive-reduction hypothesis of the behavioral effects of drugs. *Psychopharmacology, 163,* 251–264.

McMullin, R. E. (2000). *The new handbook of cognitive therapy techniques.* New York: Norton.

McMurtray, A. M., Licht, E., Yeo, T., Krisztal, E., Saul, R. E., & Mendez, M. F. (2007). Positron emission tomography facilitates diagnosis of early-onset Alzheimer's disease. *European Neurology, 59,* 31–37.

McNally, R. J. (2003). Recovering memories of trauma: A view from the laboratory. *Current Directions in Psychological Science, 12,* 32–35.

McNamara, P. (2004). *An evolutionary psychology of sleep and dreams.* Westport, CT: Praeger Publishers/Greenwood Publishing Group.

McNeil, D. G., Jr. (2005, August 24). Obesity rate is nearly 25 percent, group says. *The New York Times,* p. A3.

McQuillan, A., Nicastro, R., Guenot, F., Girard, M., Lissner, C., & Ferrero, F. (2005). Intensive dialectical behavior therapy for outpatients with borderline personality disorder who are in crisis. *Psychiatric Services, 56,* 193–197.

Mead, M. (1949). *Male and female.* New York: Morrow.

Meadows, B. (2006, October 30). From girl to boy. *People,* 92–98.

Mealy, L. (2000). *Sex differences: Developmental and evolutionary strategies.* San Diego, CA: Academic Press.

Means, M. K. & Edinger, J. D. (2007). Graded exposure therapy for addressing claustrophobic reactions to continuous positive airway pressure: A case series report. *Behavioral Sleep Medicine, 5,* 105–116.

Medeiros, R., Prediger, R.D.S., Passos, G.F., Pandolfo, P., et al. (2007). Connecting TNF-Î± signaling pathways to iNOS expression in a mouse model of Alzheimer's disease: Relevance for the behavioral and synaptic deficits induced by amyloid Î² protein. *Journal of Neuroscience, 27,* 5394–5404.

Meeter, M., & Murre, J. M. J. (2004). Consolidation of long-term memory: Evidence and alternatives. *Psychological Bulletin, 130,* 843–857.

Mehl, M. R., Vazire, S., Ramirez-Esparza, N., Slatcher, R. B., & Pennebaker, J. W. (2007, July 6). Are women really more talkative than men? *Science, 317,* 82.

Mehl-Madrona, L. E. (2004). Hypnosis to facilitate uncomplicated birth. *American Journal of Clinical Hypnosis, 46,* 299–312.

Meier, R. P., & Willerman, R. (1995). Prelinguistic gesture in deaf and hearing infants. In K. Emmorey & J. S. Reilly (Eds.), *Language, gesture, and space.* Hillsdale, NJ: Erlbaum.

Meinlschmidt, G., & Heim, C. (2007). Sensitivity to intranasal oxytocin in adult men with early parental separation. *Biological Psychiatry, 61,* 1109–1111.

Mel, B. W. (2002, March 8). What the synapse tells the neuron. *Science, 295,* 1845–1846.

Mel'nikov, K. S. (1993, October–December). On some aspects of the mechanistic approach to the study of processes of forgetting. *Vestnik Moskovskogo Universiteta Seriya 14 Psikhologiya,* pp. 64–67.

Melton, G. B., & Garrison, E. G. (1987). Fear, prejudice, and neglect: Discrimination against mentally disabled persons. *American Psychologist, 42,* 1007–1026.

Meltzer, H. Y. (2000). Genetics and etiology of schizophrenia and bipolar disorder. *Biological Psychiatry, 47,* 171–173.

Meltzoff, A. N. (1996). The human infant as imitative generalist: A 20-year progress report on infant imitation with implications for comparative psychology. In C. M. Heyes & B. G. Galef, Jr. (Eds.), *Social learning in animals: The roots of culture.* San Diego, CA: Academic Press.

Melzack, R., & Katz, J. (2004). *The gate control theory: Reaching for the brain.* Mahwah, NJ: Lawrence Erlbaum Associates.

Mendelsohn, J. (2003, November 7–9). What we know about sex. *USA Weekend,* pp. 6–9.

Mendelsohn, M. E., & Rosano, G. M. C. (2003). Hormonal regulation of normal vascular tone in males. *Circulation Research, 93,* 1142.

Merai, A. (Ed.). (1985). *On terrorism and combating terrorism.* College Park, MD: University Publications of America.

Merari, A. (2005). Israel facing terrorism. *Israel Affairs, 11,* 223–237.

Merari, A. (2005). Suicide terrorists. In R. I. Yufit & D. Lester, *Assessment, treatment and prevention of suicidal behavior.* New York: Wiley.

Merari, A. (2007). Psychological aspects of suicide terrorism. In B. Bongar, L. M. Brown, & L. E. Beutler, *Psychology of terrorism.* New York: Oxford University Press.

Merikangas, K. R., Ames, M., Cui, L., Stang, P. E., Ustun, T. B., VonKorff, M., & Kessler, R. C. (2007). The impact of comorbidity of mental and physical conditions on role disability in the US adult household population. *Archives of General Psychiatry, 64,* 1180–1188.

Merlin, D. (1993). Origins of the modern mind: Three stages in the evolution of culture and cognition. *Behavioral and Brain Sciences, 16,* 737–791.

Mesquita, B., & Frijda, N. H. (1992). Cultural variations in emotions: A review. *Psychological Bulletin, 112,* 179–204.

Messer, S. B., & McWilliams, N. (2003). The impact of Sigmund Freud and *The Interpretation of Dreams.* In R. J. Sternberg (Ed.), *The anatomy of impact: What makes the great works of psychology great* (pp. 71–88). Washington, DC: American Psychological Association.

Meston, C. M (2003). Validation of the female sexual function index (FSFI) in women with female orgasmic disorder and in women with hypoactive sexual desire disorder. *Journal of Sex and Marital Therapy, 29,* 39–46.

Metcalfe, J. (1986). Premonitions of insight predict impending error. *Journal of Experimental Psychology: Learning, Memory, and Cognition, 12,* 623–634.

Metee, D. R., & Aronson, E. (1974). Affective reactions to appraisal from others. In T. L. Huston (Ed.), *Foundations of interpersonal attraction* (pp. 235–283). New York: Academic Press.

Meyer, G. J. (2000). Incremental validity of the Rorschach Prognostic Rating scale over the MMPI Ego Strength Scale and IQ. *Journal of Personality Assessment, 74,* 356–370.

Meyer, R. G., & Osborne, Y. V. H. (1987). *Case studies in abnormal behavior* (2nd ed.). Boston: Allyn & Bacon.

Meyer-Bahlburg, H. (1997). The role of prenatal estrogens in sexual orientation. In L. Ellis & L. Ebertz (Eds.), *Sexual orientation: Toward biological understanding.* Westport, CT: Praeger.

Meyerowitz, J. (2004). *How sex changed: A history of transsexuality in the United States.* Cambridge, MA: Harvard University Press.

Michael, R. T., Gagnon, J. H., Laumann, E. O., & Kolata, G. (1994). *Sex in America: A definitive survey.* Boston: Little, Brown.

Midanik, L. T., Tam, T. W., & Weisner, C. (2007). Concurrent and simultaneous drug and alcohol use: Results of the 2000 national alcohol survey. *Drug and Alcohol Dependence, 90,* 72–80.

Middlebrooks, J. C., Furukawa, S., Stecker, G. C., & Mickey, B. J. (2005). Distributed representation of sound-source location in the auditory cortex. In R. König, P. Heil, E. Budinger, & H. Scheich (Eds.), *Auditory cortex: A synthesis of human and animal research.* Mahwah, NJ: Lawrence Erlbaum Associates.

Miele, F. (2002). *Intelligence, race, and genetics: Conversations with Arthur R. Jensen.* Boulder, CO: Westview Press.

Mifflin, L. (1998, January 14). Study finds a decline in TV network violence. *The New York Times,* p. A14.

Mignon, A., & Mollaret, P. (2002). Applying the affordance conception of traits: A person perception study. *Personality and Social Psychology Bulletin, 28,* 1327–1334.

Mika, V. S., Wood, P. R., Weiss, B. D., & Trevino, L. (2007). Ask Me 3: improving communication in a Hispanic pediatric outpatient practice. *American Journal of Behavioral Health, 31,* S115–S121.

Miklowitz, D. J., & Thompson, M. C. (2003). Family variables and interventions in schizophrenia. In G. Sholevar & G. Pirooz (Eds.), *Textbook of family and couples therapy: Clinical applications* (pp. 585–617). Washington, DC: American Psychiatric Publishing.

Mikulincer, M., & Shaver, P. R. (2005). Attachment security, compassion, and altruism. *Current Directions in Psychological Science, 14,* 34–38.

Miletic, M. P. (2002). The introduction of a feminine psychology to psychoanalysis: Karen Horney's legacy [Special issue: Interpersonal psychoanalysis and feminism]. *Contemporary Psychoanalysis, 38,* 287–299.

Milgram, S. (1974). *Obedience to authority.* New York: Harper & Row.

Milgram, S. (2005). *Obedience to authority.* Pinter & Martin: New York.

Millar, M. (2002). Effects of guilt induction and guilt reduction on door-in-the-face. *Communication Research, 29,* 666–680.

Miller, A. G. (1999). Harming other people: Perspectives on evil and violence. *Personality and Social Psychology Review, 3,* 176–178.

Miller, A. G., Collins, B. E., & Brief, D. E. (1995). Perspectives on obedience to authority: The legacy of the Milgram experiments. *Journal of Social Issues, 51,* 1–19.

Miller, A. M., & Gross, R. (2005). Health and depression in women from the former Soviet Union living in the United States and Israel. *Journal of Immigrant Health, 6,* 187–196.

Miller, D. W. (2000, February 25). Looking askance at eyewitness testimony. *The Chronicle of Higher Education,* pp. A19–A20.

Miller, G. (2004, April 2). Learning to forget. *Science, 304*, 34–36.

Miller, G. (2006). A spoonful of medicine—and a steady diet of normalcy. *Science, 311*, 464–465.

Miller, G. (2006, January 27). China: Healing the metaphorical heart. *Science, 311*, 462–463.

Miller, G., & Cohen, S. (2001). Psychological interventions and the immune system: A meta-analystic review and critique. *Health Psychology, 20*, 47–63.

Miller, G. A. (1956). The magical number seven, plus or minus two: Some limits on our capacity for processing information. *Psychology Review, 63*, 81–97.

Miller, G. F., & Penke, L. (2007). The evolution of human intelligence and the coefficient of additive genetic variance in human brain size. *Intelligence, 35*, 97–114.

Miller, J. A., & Leffard, S. A. (2007). Behavioral assessment. In S. R. Smith & L. Handler, *The clinical assessment of children and adolescents: A practitioner's handbook.* Mahwah, NJ: Lawrence Erlbaum Associates.

Miller, J. G. (1984). Culture and the development of everyday social explanation. *Journal of Personality and Social Psychology, 46*, 961–978.

Miller, L. A., Taber, K. H., Gabbard, G. O., Hurley, R. A. (2005). Neural underpinnings of fear and its modulation: Implications for anxiety disorders. *Journal of Neuropsychiatry and Clinical Neurosciences, 17*, 1–6.

Miller, L. T., & Vernon, P. A. (1997). Developmental changes in speed of information processing in young children. *Developmental Psychology, 33*, 549–554.

Miller, M. (2005). *Divergent effects of laughter and mental stress on endothelial function: Potential impact of entertainment.* Paper presented at the 54th Annual Scientific Session of the American College of Cardiology, Orlando, Florida.

Miller, M. N., & Pumariega, A. J. (2001). Culture and eating disorders: A historical and cross-cultural review. *Psychiatry: Interpersonal and Biological Processes, 64*, 93–110.

Miller, M. W. (1994, December 1). Brain surgery is back in a limited way to treat mental ills. *The Wall Street Journal,* pp. A1, A12.

Miller, N. E., & Magruder, K. M. (Eds.). (1999). *Cost-effectiveness of psychotherapy: A guide for practitioners, researchers, and policymakers.* New York: Oxford University Press.

Miller-Jones, D. (1991). Informal reasoning in inner-city children. In J. F. Voss & D. N. Perkins (Eds.), *Informal reasoning and education.* Hillsdale, NJ: Lawrence Erlbaum.

Miller, W. R., & Thoresen, C. E. (2003). Spirituality, religion, and health: An emerging research field. *American Psychologist, 58*, 24–35.

Millner, D. (April, 2007). Little mean girls. *Parenting, 21*, 47.

Millon, T., & Davis, R. O. (1996). *Disorders of personality: DSM-IV and beyond* (2nd ed.). New York: Wiley.

Millon, T., Davis, R., & Millon, C. (2000). *Personality disorders in modern life.* New York: Wiley.

Mills, J. L. (1999). Cocaine, smoking, and spontaneous abortion. *New England Journal of Medicine, 340*, 380–381.

Mills, J. S., Polivy, J., Herman, C. P., & Tiggemann, M. (2002). Effects of exposure to thin media images: Evidence of self-enhancement among restrained eaters. *Personality and Social Psychology Bulletin, 28*, 1687–1699.

Milner, B. (1966). Amnesia following operation on temporal lobes. In C. W. M. Whitty & P. Zangwill (Eds.), *Amnesia.* London: Butterworth.

Milner, B. (2005). The medial temporal-lobe amnesic syndrome. *Psychiatric Clinics of North America, 28*, 599–611.

Milton, J., & Wiseman, R. (1999). Does psi exist? Lack of replication of an anomalous process of information transfer. *Psychological Bulletin, 125*, 387–391.

Miner-Rubino, K., & Cortina, L. M. (2007). Beyond targets: Consequences of vicarious exposure to misogyny at work. *Journal of Applied Psychology, 92*, 1254–1269.

Miner-Rubino, K., Winter, D. G., & Stewart, A. J. (2004). Gender, social class, and the subjective experience of aging: Self-perceived personality change from early adulthood to late midlife. *Personality and Social Psychology Bulletin, 30*, 1599–1610.

Mingo, C., Herman C. J., & Jasperse, M. (2000). Women's stories: Ethnic variations in women's attitudes and experiences of menopause, hysterectomy, and hormone replacement therapy. *Journal of Women's Health and Gender Based Medicine, 9*(Suppl. 2), S27–S38.

Mingroni, M. A. (2007). Resolving the IQ paradox: Heterosis as a cause of the Flynn effect and other trends. *Psychological Review,114*, 806–829.

Minuchin, S. (1999). Retelling, reimagining, and re-searching: A continuing conversation. *Journal of Marital and Family Therapy, 25*, 9–14.

Minuchin, S., & Nichols, M. P. (1992). *Family healing.* New York: Free Press.

Miquel, J., (2006). Integración de teorías del envejecimiento (parte I). Integration of theories of ageing. *Revista Espanola de Geriatria y Gerontologia, 41*, 55–63.

Mischel, W. (2004). Toward an integrative science of the person. *Annual Review of Psychology, 55*, 1–22.

Mischoulon, D. (2000, June). Anti-depressants: Choices and controversy. *HealthNews*, p. 4.

Miserando, M. (1991). Memory and the seven dwarfs. *Teaching of Psychology, 18*, 169–171.

Mitchell, D. B., & Schmitt, F. A. (2006). Short-and long-term implicit memory in aging and Alzheimer's disease. *Neuropsychological Development and Cognition, B, Aging and Neuropsychological Cognition, 13*, 611–635.

Mitchell, T. (2000, November 3–5). Extinguish your habit for good. *USA Weekend*, p. 4.

Mitchener, B. (2001, March 14). Controlling a computer by the power of thought. *The Wall Street Journal*, pp. B1, B4.

Mitte, K. (2005). Meta-analysis of cognitive-behavioral treatments for generalized anxiety disorder: A comparison with pharmacotherapy. *Psychological Bulletin, 131*, 785–795.

Mittleman, M. A., Maclure, M., Sherwood, J. B., Mulry, R. P., Tofler, G. H., Jacobs, S. C., Friedman, R., Benson, H., & Muller, J. E. (1995, October 1). Triggering of acute myocardial infarction onset by episodes of anger. *Circulation, 92*, 1720–1725.

Miyake, K., Chen, S., & Campos, J. J. (1985). Infant temperament, mother's mode of interaction, and attachment in Japan: An interim report. *Monographs of the Society for Research in Child Development, 50*, 276–297.

MLA (2005). MLA Language Map; All languages other than English combined. Retrieved from http://www.mla.org/census_map&source=county (based on 2000 U.S. Census Bureau figures).

Moffett, S. (2006). *The three-pound enigma: The human brain and the quest to unlock its mysteries.* Chapel Hill, NC: Algonquin Books of Chapel Hill.

Moffitt, T. E., & Caspi, A. (2007). Evidence from behavioral genetics for environmental contributions to antisocial conduct. In J. E. Grusec, & P. D. Hastings, *Handbook of socialization: Theory and research.* New York: Guilford Press.

Moffitt, T. E., Caspi, A., & Rutter, M. (2006). Measured gene-environment interactions in psychopathology: Concepts, research strategies, and implications for research, intervention, and public understanding of genetics. *Perspectives on Psychological Science, 1*, 5–27.

Moghaddam, B., & Adams, B. W. (1998, August 28). Reversal of phencyclidine effects by a group II metabotropic glutamate receptor agonist in rats. *Science, 281*, 1349–1352.

Moghaddam, F. M. (2005). The staircase to terrorism: A psychological explanation. *American Psychologist, 60*, 161–169.

Moghaddam, F. M. (2007). The staircase to terrorism: A psychological exploration. Psychological aspects of suicide terrorism. In B. Bongar, L. M. Brown, & L. E. Beutler, *Psychology of terrorism.* New York: Oxford University Press.

Mohapel, P., Leanza, G., Kokaia, M., & Lindvall, O. (2005). Forebrain acetylcholine regulates adult hippo-campal neurogenesis and learning. *Neurobiology of Aging, 26*, 939–946.

Mokdad, A. H., Brewer, R. D., & Naimi, T. (2007). Binge drinking is a problem that cannot be ignored. *Preventive Medicine: An International Journal Devoted to Practice and Theory, 44*, 303–304.

Molfese, V. J., & Molfese, D. L. (2000). *Temperament and personality development across the life span.* Mahwah, NJ: Erlbaum.

Monaghan, P. (2004, October 14). Real fear, virtually overcome. *The Chronicle of Higher Education*, p. A12.

Monnier, J., Resnick, H. S., Kilpatrick, D. G., & Seals, B. (2002). The relationship between distress and resource loss following rape. *Violence and Victims, 17*, 85–92.

Montague, D. P. F., & Walker-Andrews, S. (2002). Mothers, fathers, and infants: The role of person familiarity and parental involvement in infants' perception of emotion expressions. *Child Development, 73*, 1339–1352.

Montague, R. (2006). *Why choose this book? How we make decisions.* New York: Dutton.

Montgomery, C., Fisk, J. E., Newcombe, R., Wareing, M., & Murphy, P. N. (2005). Syllogistic reasoning performance in MDMA (Ecstasy) users. *Experimental and Clinical Psychopharmacology, 13*, 137–145.

Montgomery, G. M., & Bovbjerg, D. H. (2003). Expectations of chemotherapy-related nausea: Emotional and experimental predictors. *Annals of Behavioral Medicine, 25*, 48–54.

Montgomery, S. (2006). Serotonin noradrenaline reuptake inhibitors: Logical evolution of antidepressant development. *International Journal of Psychiatry in Clinical Practice, 10*, 5–11.

Monti, J. M. (2004). Primary and secondary insomnia: Prevalence, causes and current therapeutics. *Current Medicinal Chemistry—Central Nervous System Agents, 4*, 119–137.

Moody, H. R. (2000). *Aging: Concepts and controversies.* Thousand Oaks, CA: Sage.

Moore, D. G., Goodwin, J. E., & George, R. (2007). Infants perceive human point-light displays as solid forms. *Cognition, 104*, 377–396.

Moore, M. M. (2002). Behavioral observation. In M. W. Wiederman & B. E. Whitley (Eds.), *Handbook for conducting research on human sexuality* Mahwah, NJ: Lawrence Erlbaum.

Moore-Ede, M. (1993). *The twenty-four hour society*. Boston: Addison-Wesley.

Moorey, S. (2007) Cognitive therapy. In W. Dryden, *Dryden's handbook of individual therapy* (5th ed.). Thousand Oaks, CA: Sage Publications.

Mora-Giral, M., Raich-Escursell, R. M., Segues, C.V., Torras-ClarasA.J. & Huon, G. (2004). Bulimia symptoms and risk factors in university students. *Eating and Weight Disorders, 9*, 163–169

Moretti, M. M., & Higgins, E. T. (1990). The development of self-system vulnerabilities: Social and cognitive factors in developmental psychopathology. In R. J. Sternberg & J. Kolligian, Jr. (Eds.), *Competence considered*. New Haven, CT: Yale University Press.

Morgan, R. (2002, September 27). The men in the mirror. *The Chronicle of Higher Education*, pp. A53–A54.

Morin, C. M. (2004). Cognitive-behavioral approaches to the treatment of insomnia. *Journal of Clinical Psychiatry, 65*, 33–40.

Morone, N. E., & Greco, C. M. (2007). Mind-body interventions for chronic pain in older adults: A structured review. *Pain Medicine, 8*, 359–375.

Morris, J. F., Waldo, C. R., & Rothblum, E. D. (2001). A model of predictors and outcomes of outness among lesbian and bisexual women. *American Journal of Orthopsychiatry, 71*, 61–71.

Morrissey, S. (2006, March 12). Microbe-busting bandages. *Time*.

Morrone, A. S., & Pintrich, P. R. (2006). Achievement motivation. In G. G. Bear & K. M. Minke, *Children's needs III: Development, prevention, and intervention*. Washington, DC: National Association of School Psychologists.

Morrow, J., & Wolff, R. (1991, May). Wired for a miracle. *Health*, pp. 64–84.

Mosher, C. J., & Akins, S. (2007). *Drugs and drug policy: The control of consciousness alteration*. Thousand Oaks, CA: Sage Publications.

Moskowitz, G. B. (2004). *Social cognition: Understanding self and others*. New York: Guilford Press.

Motley, M. T. (1987, February). What I meant to say. *Psychology Today*, pp. 25–28.

Muammar, O. M. (2007). An integration of two competing models to explain practical intelligence. *Dissertation Abstracts International: Section B: The Sciences and Engineering, 67(7-B)*, 4128.

Muehlenhard, C. L., & Hollabaugh, L. C. (1988). Do women sometimes say no when they mean yes? The prevalence and correlates of women's token resistance to sex. *Journal of Personality and Social Psychology, 54*, 872–879.

Mueser, K., Salyers, M., and Mueser, P. (2001). A prospective analysis of work in schizophrenia. *Schizophrenia Bulletin, 27*, 281–296.

Mukerjee, M. (1997, February). Trends in animal research. *Scientific American, 276*, pp. 86–93.

Mullen, B., & Rice, D. R. (2003). Ethnophaulisms and exclusion: The behavioral consequences of cognitive representation of ethnic immigrant groups. *Personality and Social Psychology Bulletin, 29*, 1056–1067.

Mulligan, C., Moreau, K., Brandolini, M., Livingstone, B., Beaufrere, B., & Boire, Y. (2002). Alterations of sensory perceptions in healthy elderly subjects during fasting and refeeding: A pilot study. *Gerontology, 48*, 39–43.

Mumenthaler, M. S. Yesavage, J. A., Taylor, J. L., O'Hara, R., Friedman, L., Lee, H., & Kraemer, H. C. (2003). Psychoactive drugs and pilot performance: A comparison of nic-

otine, donepezil, and alcohol effects. *Neuropsychopharmacology, 28*, 1366–1373.

Munakata, Y. (2006). Information processing approaches to development. In D. Kuhn, R. S. Siegler, W. Damon, & R. M. Lerner, *Handbook of child psychology: Vol 2, Cognition, perception, and language* (6th ed.) Hoboken, NJ: John Wiley & Sons.

Munroe, R L., Hulefeld, R., Rodgers, J. M., Tomeo, D. L., & Yamazaki, S. K. (2000). Aggression among children in four cultures. *Cross-Cultural Research: The Journal of Comparative Social Science, 34*, 3–25.

Munson, L. J., Hulin, C., & Drasgow, F. (2000). Longitudinal analysis of dispositional influences and sexual harassment: Effects on job and psychological outcomes. *Personnel Psychology, 53*, 21–46.

Murphy, G. J., Glickfield, L. L., Balsen, Z., & Isaacson, J. S. (2004). Sensory neuron signaling to the brain: Properties of transmitter release from olfactory nerve terminals. *Journal of Neuroscience, 24*, 3023–3030.

Murphy, G. L. (2005). The study of concepts inside and outside the laboratory: Medin versus Medin.In W. Ahn, R. L. Goldstone,B. C. Love, A. B. Markman, &P. Wolff (Eds.), *Categorization insideand outside the laboratory: Essays in honor of Douglas L. Medin*. Washington, DC: American Psychological Association.

Murphy, R. T., Wismar, K., & Freeman, K. (2003). Stress symptoms among African-American college students after the September 11, 2001 terrorist attacks. *Journal of Nervous and Mental Disease, 191*, 108–114.

Murphy, S. T., & Zajonc, R. B. (1993). Affect, cognition, and awareness: Affective priming with optimal and suboptimal stimulus exposures. *Journal of Personality and Social Psychology, 64*, 723–739.

Murphy, S., et al. (1998). Interference under the influence. *Personality and Social Psychology Bulletin, 24*, 517–528.

Murray, B. (June 2002). Good news for bachelor's grads. *Monitor on Psychology*, pp. 30–32.

Murray, J. B. (1990). Nicotine as a psycho-active drug. *Journal of Psychology, 125*, 5–25.

Murray, S. L., Holmes, J. G., & Griffin, D. W. (2004). The benefits of positive illusions: Idealization and the construction of satisfaction in close relationships. In H. T. Reis & C. E. Rusbult (Eds.), *Close relationships: Key readings*. Philadelphia, PA: Taylor & Francis.

Murugasu, E. (2005). Recent advances in the treatment of sensorineural deafness. *Annals of the Academy of Medicine, Singapore, 34*, 313–319.

Myerhoff, B. (1982). Rites of passage: Process and paradox. In V. Turner (Ed.), *Celebration: Studies in festivity and ritual*. Washington, DC: Smithsonian Institution Press.

Myers, D. G., & Diener, E. (1996, May). The pursuit of happiness: New research uncovers some anti-intuitive insights into how many people are happy—and why. *Scientific American*, pp. 70–72.

Myers, D. G. (2000). The funds, friends, and faith of happy people. *American Psychologist, 55*, 56–67.

Myers, L. L. (2007). Anorexia nervosa, bulimia nervosa, and binge eating disorder. In B. A. Thyer, & J. S. Wodarski. *Social work in mental health: An evidence-based approach*. Hoboken, NJ: John Wiley & Sons.

Myerson, J., Adams, D. R., Hale, S., & Jenkins, L. (2003). Analysis of group differences in processing speed: Brinley plots, Q-Q plots, and

other conspiracies. *Psychonomic Bulletin and Review, 10*, 224–237.

Myrtek, M. (2007). Type a behavior and hostility as independent risk factors for coronary heart disease. In J. Jordan, B. Barde, & A. M. Zeiher, *Contributions toward evidence-based psychocardiology: A systematic review of the literature*. Washington, DC: American Psychological Association.

Mytinger, C. (2001). *Headhunting in the Solomon Islands: Around the Coral Sea*. Santa Barbara, CA: Narrative Press.

Nadeem, E., & Graham, S. (2005). Early puberty, peer victimization, and internalizing symptoms in ethnic minority adolescents. *Journal of Early Adolescence, 25*, 197–222.

Nagai, Y., Goldstein, L. H., Fenwick, P. B. C., & Trimble, M. R. (2004). Clinical efficacy of galvanic skin response biofeedback training in reducing seizures in adult epilepsy: A preliminary randomized controlled study. *Epilepsy and Behavior, 5*, 216–223.

Nagda, B. A., Tropp, L. R., & Paluck, E. L. (2006). Looking back as we look ahead: Integrating research, theory, and practice on intergroup relations. *Journal of Social Research, 62*, 439–451.

Naik, G. (2004, December 29). New obesity boom in Arab countries has old ancestry. *The Wall Street Journal*, p. A1.

Najman, J. M., Aird, R., Bor, W., O'Callaghan, M., Williams, G. M., & Shuttlewood, G. J. (2004). The generational transmission of socioeconomic inequalities in child cognitive development and emotional health. *Social Science and Medicine, 58*, 1147–1158.

Nakamura, M., Kyo, S., Kanaya, T., Yatabe, N., Maida, Y., Tanaka, M., Ishida, Y., Fujii, C., Kondo, T., Inoue, M., & Mukaida, N. (2004). hTERT-promoter-based tumor-specific expression of MCP-1 effectively sensitizes cervical cancer cells to a low dose of cisplatin. *Cancer Gene Therapy, 2*, 1–7.

Nakamura, Y. (2004). Isolation of p53-target genes andtheir functional analysis. *Cancer Science, 95*, 7–11.

Nakamura, Y., Ando, S., Nagahara, A., Sano, T., Ochiya, S., Maeda, T., Kawaji, M., Ogawa, A., Hirata, H., Terazaki, K., Haraoka, H., Tanihara, M., Ueda, M., Uchino, M., & Yamamura, K. (2004). Targeted conversion of the transthyretin gene *in vitro* and *in vivo*. *Gene Therapy, 11*, 838–846.

Narrow, W. E., Rae, D. S., Robins, L. N., & Regier, D. A. (2002). Revised prevalence estimates of mental disorders in the United States: Using a clinical significance criterion to reconcile 2 surveys' estimates. *Archives of General Psychiatry, 59*, 115–123.

Nash, M. R. (July 2001). The truth and hype of hypnosis. *Scientific American*, pp. 47–55.

Nasir, N. S., & Hand, V. M. (2006). Exploring sociocultural perspectives on race, culture, and learning. *Review of Educational Research, 76*, 449–475.

Nathan, P. E., & Gorman, J. M. (Eds.). (1997). *A guide to treatments that work*. New York: Oxford University Press.

Nathan, P. E., Stuart, S. P., & Dolan, S. L. (2000). Research on psychotherapy efficacy and effectiveness: Between Scylla and Charybdis? *Psychological Bulletin, 126*, 964–981.

Nathans, J., Davenport, C. M., Maumenee, I. H., Lewis, R. A., Hejtmancik, J. F., Litt, M., Lovrien, E., Weleber, R., Bachynski, B., Zwas, F., Klingaman, R., & Fishman, G. (1989, August 25). Molecular genetics of human blue cone monochromacy. *Science, 245,* 831–838.

National Academy of Sciences (1999). *Marijuana and medicine: Assessing the science base.* Washington, DC: National Academy Press.

National Adolescent Health Information Center. (2003). *Fact Sheet on Demographics: Adolescents.* San Francisco, CA: University of California, San Francisco.

National Association for the Education of Young Children. (2005). *Position statements of the NAEYC.* http://www.naeyc.org/about/positions.asp#where.

National Depression Screening Day. (2003, March 26). Questionnaire on Web site. Retrieved from http://www.mentalhealthscreening.org/dep/depsample.htm#sampletest.

National Institute of Child Health and Human Development (NICHD) Early Child Care Research Network. (1997). The effects of infant care on infant-mother attachment security: Results of the NICHD study of early child care. *Child Development, 68,* 860–879.

National Institute of Child Health and Human Development (NICHD). (2002). Child-care structure—process— outcome: Direct and indirect effects of child-care quality on young children's development. *Psychological Science, 13,* 199–206.

National Institute of Mental Health (NIMH). (2000). *Prevention of eating disorders: Challenges and opportunities.* Bethesda, MD: National Institute of Mental Health.

National Institute on Drug Abuse. (2000). *Principles of drug addiction treatment: A research-based guide.* Washington, DC: National Institute on Drug Abuse.

National Mental Health Information Center, U.S. Department of Health and Human Services. Reprinted in *Scientific American,* December 2002, p. 38.

National Survey of Student Engagement (2006). Engaged learning: *Fostering success for all students.* Bloomington, IN: Indiana University.

Natvig, G. K., Albrektsen, G., & Ovarnstrom, U. (2003). Methods of teaching and class participation in relation to perceived social support and stress: Modifiable factors for improving health and well-being among students. *Educational Psychology, 23,* 261–274.

Naveh-Benjamin, M., Guez, J., & Sorek, S. (2007). The effects of divided attention on encoding processes in memory: Mapping the locus of interference. *Canadian Journal of Experimental Psychology, 61,* 1–12.

Navon, R., & Proia, R. L. (1989, March 17). The mutations in Ashkenazi Jews with adult G(M2) gangliosidosis, the adult form of Tay-Sachs disease. *Science, 243,* 1471–1474.

Nebenzahl, D. (2007, January 27). Creativity works: An environment that fosters creativity is more productive than a workplace plagued with a negative atmosphere. *The Gazette (Montreal),* p. G1.

Neber, H., & Heller, K. A. (2002). Evaluation of a summer-school program for highly gifted secondary-school students: The German Pupils Academy. *European Journal of Psychological Assessment, 18,* 214–228.

Neher, A. (2006). Evolutionary psychology: Its programs, prospects, and pitfalls. *American Journal of Psychology, 119,* 517–566.

Neighbors, C., Lee, C., Lewis, M., Fossos, N., & Larimer, M. (2007). Are social norms the best predictor of outcomes among heavy-drinking college students? *Journal of Studies on Alcohol and Drugs, 68,* 556–565.

Neisser, U. (1982). *Memory observed.* San Francisco: Freeman.

Neisser, U. (1996, April). *Intelligence on the rise: Secular changes in IQ and related measures.* Conference at Emory University. Atlanta: Emory University Press.

Neisser, U., Boodoo, G., Bouchard, T. J., Jr., Boykin, A. W., Brody, N., Ceci, S. J., Halpern, D. F., Loehlin, J. C., Perloff, R., Sternberg, R. J., & Urbina, S. (1996). Intelligence: Knowns and unknowns. *American Psychologist, 51,* 77–101.

Neitz, J., Neitz, M., & Kainz, P. M. (1996, November 1). Visual pigment gene structure and the severity of color vision defects. *Science, 274,* 801–804.

Nelson, D. L., & Simmons, B. L. (2003). Health psychology and work stress: A more positive approach. In J. C. Quick & L. E. Tetrick (Eds.), *Handbook of occupational health psychology.* Washington, DC: American Psychological Association.

Nelson, P. D. (2007). The globalization of psychology: What does it mean? *The Educator, 5,* 1–4.

Nelson, W. M., III, & Finch, A. J., Jr. (2000). Managing anger in youth: A cognitive-behavioral intervention approach. In P. C. Kendall, *Child & adolescent therapy: Cognitive-behavioral procedures* (2nd ed.). New York: Guilford Press.

Neron, S., & Stephenson, R. (2007). Effectiveness of hypnotherapy with cancer patients' trajectory: Emesis, acute pain, and analgesia and anxiolysis in procedures. *International Journal of Clinical Experimental Hypnosis, 55,* 336–354.

Nesdale, D., Maass, A., & Durkin, K. (2005). Group norms, threat, and children's racial prejudice. *Child Development, 76,* 652–663.

Nesheim, S., Henderson, S., Lindsay, M., Zuberi, J., Grimes, V., Buehler, J., Lindegren, M. L., & Bulterys, M. (2004). *Prenatal HIV testing and antiretroviral prophylaxis at an urban hospital—Atlanta, Georgia, 1997–2000.* Atlanta, GA: Centers for Disease Control.

Ness, R. B., Grisso, J. A., Hirschinger, N., Markovic, N., Shaw, L. M., Day, N. L., & Kline, J. (1999). Cocaine and tobacco use and the risk of spontaneous abortion. *New England Journal of Medicine, 340,* 333–339.

Nesse, R. M. (2000). Is depression an adaptation? *Archives of General Psychiatry, 57,* 14–20.

Nestler, E. J. (2001, June 22). Total recall— the memory of addiction. *Science, 292,* 2266–2267.

Nestler, E. J., & Malenka, R. C. (2004, March). The addicted brain. *Scientific American,* pp. 78–83.

Neubauer, A. C., & Fink, A. (2005). Basic information processing and the psychophysiology of intelligence. In R. J. Sternberg & J. E. Pretz, *Cognition and intelligence: Identifying the mechanisms of the mind.* New York: Cambridge University Press, 2005.

Newby-Clark, I. R., & Ross, M. (2003). Conceiving the past and future. *Personality and Social Psychology Bulletin, 29,* 807–818.

Newcombe, N. S., Drummey, A. B., Fox, N. A., Lie, E., & Ottinger-Alberts, W. (2000). Remembering early childhood: How much, how, and why (or why not). *Current Directions in Psychological Science, 9,* 55–58.

Newell, A., & Simon, H. (1972). *Human problem solving.* Englewood Cliffs, NJ: Prentice Hall.

Newman, A. W., & Thompson, J. W., Jr. (2001). The rise and fall of forensic hypnosis in criminal investigation. *Journal of the American Academy of Psychiatry & the Law, 29,* 75–84.

Newman, C. F., Leahy, R. L., Beck, A. T., Reilly-Harrington, N. A., & Gyulai, L. (2002). *Bipolar disorder: A cognitive therapy approach.* Washington, DC: American Psychological Association.

Newport, E. L., Bavelier, D., & Neville, H. J. (2001). Critical thinking about critical periods: Perspectives on a critical period for language acquisition. In E. Dupoux (Ed.), *Language, brain, and cognitive development: Essays in honor of Jacques Mehler.* Cambridge, MA: MIT.

Newport, F., & Carroll, J. (2002, November 27). Battle of the bulge: Majority of Americans want to lose weight. *Gallup News Service,* pp. 1–9.

Niccols, A. (2007). Fetal alcohol syndrome and the developing socio-emotional brain. *Brain Cognition, 65,* 135–142.

Nicholson, I. A. M. (2003). *Inventing personality: Gordon Allport and the science of selfhood.* Washington, DC: American Psychological Association.

Nickerson, R. S., & Adams, M. J. (1979). *Cognitive Psychology, 11,* 297.

Niedenthal, P. M. (2007, May 18). Embodying emotion. *Science, 316,* 1002–1005.

Nielsen, S. L., Smart, D. W., Isakson, R. L., Worthen, V. E., Gregersen, A. T., & Lambert, M. J. (2004). The *Consumer Reports* effectiveness score: What did consumers report? *Journal of Counseling Psychology, 51,* 25–37.

Nielson, T. A., Stenstrom, P., & Levin, R. (2006). Nightmare frequency as a function of age, gender, and September 11, 2001: Findings from an internet questionnaire. *Dreaming, 16,* 145–158.

Nierenberg, A. A. (1998, February 17). The physician's perspective. *HealthNews,* pp. 3–4.

Nigg, J. T., & Goldsmith, H. H. (1994). Genetics of personality disorders: Perspectives from personality and psychopathology research. *Psychological Bulletin, 115,* 346–380.

Nikles, C. D., II, Brecht, D. L., Klinger, E., & Bursell, A. L. (1998). The effects of current concern- and nonconcern-related waking suggestions on nocturnal dream content. *Journal of Personality and Social Psychology, 75,* 242–255.

Nimrod, G., & Kleiber, D. A. (2007). Reconsidering change and continuity in later life: Toward an innovation theory of successful aging. *International Journal of Human Development, 65,* 1–22.

Nisbett, R. (1994, October 31). Blue genes. *New Republic, 211,* 15.

Nisbett, R. (2003). *The geography of thought.* New York: Free Press.

Nisbett, R.E. (2007, December 9). All brains are the same color. *New York Times,* p. E11.

Nissle, S., & Bschor, T. (2002). Winning the jackpot and depression: Money cannot buy happiness. *International Journal of Psychiatry in Clinical Practice, 6,* 183–186.

Nittrouer, S., Lowenstein, J. H. (2007). Children's weighting strategies for word-final stop voicing are not explained by auditory sensitivities. *Journal of Speech, Language, and Hearing Research, 50,* 58–73.

Niu, W., & Sternberg, R. J. (2003). Societal and school influences on student creativity: The case of China [Special issue: Psychoeducational and psychosocial functioning of Chinese children]. *Psychology in the Schools, 40,* 103–114.

Noble, H. B. (1999, March 12). New from the smoking wars: Success. *The New York Times,* pp. D1–D2.

Nolen-Hoeksema, S. (2004a). *Abnormal psychology* (3rd ed.). Boston: McGraw-Hill.

Nolen-Hoeksema, S. (2004b). Gender differences in risk factors and consequences for alcohol use and problems. *Clinical Psychology Review, 24*, 981–1010.

Nolen-Hoeksema, S. (2007). *Abnormal psychology* (4th ed.). New York, NY: McGraw-Hill.

Noonan, D. (2005, June 6). A little bit louder, please. *Newsweek*, pp. 42–50.

Norcia, A. M., Pei, F., Bonneh, Y., Hou, C., Sampath, V., & Pettet, M. W. (2005). Development of sensitivity to texture and contour information in the human infant. *Journal of Cognitive Neuroscience, 17*, 569–579.

Norcross, J. C. (2002). Empirically supported therapy relationships. In J. C. Norcross, *Psychotherapy relationships that work: Therapist contributions and responsiveness to patients*. New York: Oxford University Press.

Norcross, J. C., Beutler, L. E., & Levant, R. F. (2006). *Evidence-based practices in mental health: Debate and dialogue on the fundamental questions*. Washington, DC: American Psychological Association.

Norlander, T., Von Schedvin, H., & Archer, T. (2005). Thriving as a function of affective personality: Relation to personality factors, coping strategies and stress. *Anxiety, Stress & Coping: An International Journal, 18*, 105–116.

Norton, P. J., & Price, E. C. (2007). A meta-analytic review of adult cognitive-behavioral treatment outcome across the anxiety disorders. *Journal of Nervous and Mental Disease, 195*, 521–531.

Nosek, B. A., Banaji, M. R., & Greenwald, A. G. (2002). Math = male, me = female, therefore math ≠ me. *Journal of Personality and Social Psychology, 83*, 44–59.

Novak, M. A., & Petto, A. J. (1991). *Through the looking glass: Issues of psychological well-being in captive nonhuman primates*. Washington, DC: American Psychological Association.

Noy, V. M. (2006). A psychoneuroimmunology program for Hispanic women with stage I—II breast cancer. *Dissertation Abstracts International: Section B: The Sciences and Engineering, 66(11–B)*, 6287.

Noyes, R., Jr., Stuart, S. P., Langbehn, D. R., Happel, R. L., Longley, S. L., Muller, B. A., & Yagla, S. J. (2003). Test of an interpersonal model of hypochondriasis. *Psychosomatic Medicine, 65*, 292–300.

Noyes, R., Jr., Stuart, S., Longley, S. L., Langbehn, D. R., & Happel, R. L. (2002). Hypochondriasis and fear of death. *Journal of Nervous and Mental Disease, 190*, 503–509.

Noyes, R., Kathol, R. G., Fisher, M. M., Phillips, B. M., et al. (1993). The validity of DSM-III-R hypochondriasis. *Archives of General Psychiatry, 50*, 961–970.

Ntinas, K. M. (2007). Behavior modification and the principle of normalization: Clash or synthesis? *Behavioral Interventions, 22*, 165–177.

Nucci, L. P. (2002). The development of moral reasoning. In U. Goswami (Ed.), *Blackwell handbook of childhood cognitive development. Blackwell Handbooks of developmental psychology* (pp. 303–325). Malden, MA: Blackwell.

Nurnberger, J. I., Jr., & Bierut, L. J. (2007, April). Seeking the connections: Alcoholism and our genes. *Scientific American*, pp. 46–53.

Nussbaum, A.D. & Steele, C.M. (2007). Situational disengagement and persistence in the face of adversity. *Journal of Experimental Social Psychology, 43*, 127–134.

Nyberg, L., & Tulving, E. (1996). Classifying human long-term memory: Evidence from converging dissociations. *European Journal of Cognitive Psychology, 8*, 163–183.

Oatley, K., & Jenkins, J. M. (1996). *Understanding emotions*. Oxford, England: Blackwell Publishers.

Oatley, K., Keltner, D., & Jenkins, J. M. (2006). *Understand emotions*. Blackwell.

Oberauer, K. (2007). In search of the magic number. *Experimental Psychology, 54*, 245–246.

Oberman, L. M., Pineda, J. A., & Ramachandran, V. S. (2007). The human mirror neuron system: A link between action observation and social skills. *Social Cognitive and Affective Neuroscience, 2*, 62–66.

Obermeyer, C. M. (2001, May 18). Complexities of a controversial practice. *Science, 292*, 1305–1304.

O'Brien, C. P., Childress, A. R., McLellan, A. T., & Ehrman, R. (1992). Classical conditioning in drug-dependent humans. In P. W. Kalivas & H. H. Samson (Eds.), *The neurobiology of drug and alcohol addiction. Annals of the New York Academy of Sciences* (Vol. 654). New York: New York Academy of Sciences.

O'Brien, K. M., & LeBow, M. D. (2007). Reducing maladaptive weight management practices: Developing a psychoeducational intervention program. *Eating Behaviors, 8*, 195–210.

Occhionero, M. (2004). Mental processes and the brain during dreams. *Dreaming, 14*, 54–64.

O'Connor, D. B., & O'Connor, R. C. (2004). Perceived changes in food intake in response to stress: The role of conscientiousness. *Stress and Health: Journal of the International Society for the Investigation of Stress, 20*, 279–291.

O'Connor, S. C., & Rosenblood, L. K. (1996). Affiliation motivation in everyday experience: A theoretical comparison. *Journal of Personality and Social Psychology, 70*, 513–522.

O'Donohue, W. (Ed.). (1997). *Sexual harassment: Theory, research, and treatment*. Boston: Allyn & Bacon.

Oehman, A., & Mineka, S. (2003). The malicious serpent: Snakes as a prototypical stimulus for an evolved module of fear. *Current Directions in Psychological Science, 12*, 5–9.

Oezgen, E., & Davies I. R. L. (2002). Acquisition of categorical color perception: A perceptual learning approach to the linguistic relativity hypothesis. *Journal of Experimental Psychology: General, 131*, 477–493.

Offer, D., Kaiz, M., Howard, K. I., & Bennett, E. S. (2000). The altering of reported experiences. *Journal of the American Academy of Child & Adolescent Psychiatry, 39*, 735–742.

Ogbu, J. (1992). Understanding cultural diversity and learning. *Educational Researcher, 21*, 5–14.

Ogbu, J.U. (2003). *Black American students in an affluent suburb*. Mahwah, NJ: Lawrence Erlbaum Associates.

Ogletree, S. M., Martinez, C. N., & Turner, T. R. (2004). Pokémon: Exploring the role of gender. *Sex Roles, 50*, 851–859.

O'Grady, W. D., & Dobrovolsky, M. (Eds.). (1996). *Contemporary linguistic analysis: An introduction* (3rd ed.). Toronto: Copp Clark Pitman.

Ogren, K., & Sandlund, M. (2007). Lobotomy at a state mental hospital in Sweden. A survey of patients operated on during the period 1947–1958. *Nordic Journal of Psychiatry, 61*, 355–362.

Ohara, K. (2007). The n-3 polyunsaturated fatty acid/dopamine hypothesis of schizophrenia. *Progress in Neuro-Psychopharmacology & Biological Psychiatry, 31*, 469–474.

Ohira, T., Hozawa, A., Iribarren, C., Daviglus, M. L., Matthews, K. A., Gross, M. D., & Jacobs, D. R., Jr. (2007). Longitudinal association of serum carotenoids and tocopherols with hostility: The CARDIA study. *American Journal of Epidemiology, 18*, 235–241.

Oishi, S., & Diener, E. (2001). Goals, culture, and subjective well-being. *Personality and Social Psychology Bulletin, 27*, 1674–1682.

O'Keefe, T., & Fox, K. (Eds.). (2003). *Finding the real me: True tales of sex and gender diversity*. San Francisco: Jossey-Bass.

Okun, B. F. (1996). *Understanding diverse families: What practitioners need to know*. New York: Guilford Press.

Olds, J., & Milner, P. (1954). Positive reinforcement produced by electrical stimulation of septal area and other regions of rat brain. *Journal of Comparative and Physiological Psychology, 47*, 411–427.

Olds, M. E., & Fobes, J. L. (1981). The central basis of motivation: Intracranial self-stimulation studies. *Annual Review of Psychology, 32*, 123–129.

Olijslagers, J. E., Werkman, T. R., & McCreary, A. C. (2006). Modulation of midbrain dopamine neurotransmission by serotonin, a versatile interaction between neurotransmitters and significance for antipsychotic drug action. *Current Neuropharmacology, 4*, 59–68.

Olivardia, R., & Pope, H. (2002). Body image disturbance in childhood and adolescence. In D. Castle & K. Phillips (Eds.), *Disorders of body image*. Petersfield, England: Wrightson Biomedical Publishing.

Oliver, M. B., & Hyde, J. S. (1993). Gender differences in sexuality: A meta-analysis. *Psychological Bulletin, 114*, 29–51.

Olshansky, S. J., Carnes, B. A., & Cassel, C. (1990, November 2). In search of Methuselah: Estimating the upper limits to human longevity. *Science, 250*, 634–639.

Olson, D. H., & DeFrain, J. (2005). *Marriages and families: Intimacy, diversity, and strengths with PowerWeb*. New York: McGraw-Hill.

Olson, M. A., & Fazio, R. H. (2001). Implicit attitude formation through classical conditioning. *Psychological Science, 12*, 413–417.

O'Malley, P., and Johnston, L. (2002). Epidemiology of alcohol and other drug use among American college students. *Journal of Studies on Alcohol, 14*, 23–39.

Oppenheimer, D. M. (2004). Spontaneous discounting of availability in frequency judgment tasks. *Psychological Science, 15*, 100–105.

Oren, D. A., & Terman, M. (1998, January 16). Tweaking the human circadian clock with light. *Science, 279*, 333–334.

Orenstein, P. (2001). Unbalanced equations: Girls, math, and the confidence gap. In R. Satow (Ed.), *Gender and social life*. Needham Heights, MA: Allyn & Bacon.

Ornat, S. L., & Gallo, P. (2004). Acquisition, learning, or development of language? Skinner's "Verbal behavior" revisited. *Spanish Journal of Psychology, 7*, 161–170.

Orr, S. P., Metzger, L. J., & Pitman, R. K. (2002). Psychophysiology of post-traumatic stress disorder [Special issue: Recent advances in the study of biological alterations in post-traumatic stress disorders]. *Psychiatric Clinics of North America, 25*, 271–293.

Orth-Gomér, K., Chesney, M. A., & Wenger, N. K. (Eds.). (1996). *Women, stress and heart disease*. Mahwah, NJ: Erlbaum.

Ortony, A., & Turner, T. J. (1990). What's basic about basic emotions? *Psychological Review, 97*, 315–331.

Orwin, R. G., & Condray, D. S. (1984). Smith and Glass' psychotherapy conclusions need further probing: On Landman and Dawes' re-analysis. *American Psychologist, 39*, 71–72.

Oskamp, S. (Ed.). (2000) *Reducing prejudice and discrimination*. Mahwah, NJ: Erlbaum.

Otake, K., Shimai, S., & Tanaka-Matsumi, J. (2006). Happy people become happier through kindness: A counting kindnesses intervention. *Journal of Happiness Studies, 7*, 361–375.

Owens, R. E., Jr. (2001) *Language development: An introduction* (5th ed.). Boston: Allyn & Bacon.

Ozer, E. J., & Weiss, D. S. (2004). Who develops posttraumatic stress disorder? *Current Directions in Psychological Science, 13*, 169–172.

Ozer, E. J., Best, S. R., & Lipsey, T. L. (2003). Predictors of posttraumatic stress disorder and symptoms in adults: A meta-analysis. *Psychological Bulletin, 129*, 52–73.

Pääbo, S. (2001, February 16). The human genome and our view of ourselves. *Science, 291*, 1219–1220.

Pachankis, J.E. & Goldfried, M.R. (2007). An integrative, principle-based approach to psychotherapy. In S.G. Hofmann & J. Weinberger (Eds.), *The art and science of psychotherapy*. New York, NY: Routledge/Taylor & Francis Group.

Pagonis, T. A., Angelopoulos, N., & Koukoulis, G. N. (2006). Psychiatric side effects induced by supraphysiological doses of combinations of anabolic steroids correlate to the severity of abuse. *European Psychiatry, 21*, 551–562.

Pagoto, S. L., Kozak, A. T., & Spates, C. R (2006). Systematic desensitization for an older woman with a severe specific phobia: an application of evidenced-based practice. *Clinical Gerontologist, 30*, 89–98.

Paivio, A. (1971). *Imagery and verbal processes.* New York: Holt, Rinehart & Winston.

Paivio, A. (1975). Perceptual comparison through the mind's eye. *Memory and Cognition, 3*, 635–647.

Pajares, F. (2003). Self-efficacy beliefs, motivation, and achievement in writing: A review of the literature. *Reading and Writing Quarterly: Overcoming Learning Difficulties, 19*, 139–158.

Palanker, D., Vankov, A., Huie, P., & Baccus, S. (2005). Design of a high-resolution optoelectronic retinal prosthesis. *Journal of Neural Engineering, 2*, S105–120.

Palermo, G. B. (2006). Editorial: Those evil suicide bombers. *International Journal of Offender Therapy and Comparative Criminology, 50*, 119–120.

Palmer, I. (2007). Terrorism, suicide bombing, fear and mental health. *International Review of Psychiatry, 19*, 289–296.

Paludi, M. A. (Ed.). (1996). *Sexual harassment on college campuses: Abusing the ivory power.* Albany: State University of New York Press.

Pandi-Perumal, S. R., Verster, J. C., Kayumov, L. (2006). Sleep disorders, sleepiness and traffic safety: A public health menace. *Brazilian Journal of Medical and Biological Research, 39*, 863–871.

Pandya, M., Pozuelo, L., & Malone, D. (2007). Electroconvulsive therapy: what the internist needs to know. *Cleveland Clinic Journal of Medicine, 74*, 679–685.

Paniagua, F. A. (2000). *Diagnosis in a multicultural context: A casebook for mental health professionals.* Thousand Oaks, CA: Sage.

Papero, A. L. (2005). Is early, high-quality daycare an asset for the children of low-income, depressed mothers? *Developmental Review, 25*, 181–211.

Paquette, D., Carbonneau, R., & Dubeau, D. (2003). Prevalence of father-child rough-and-tumble play and physical aggression in preschool children. *European Journal of Psychology of Education, 18*, 171–189.

Paquier, P. F., & Mariën, P. (2005). A synthesis of the role of the cerebellum in cognition. *Aphasiology, 19*, 3–19.

Parasuraman, R., & Rizzo, M. (2005). *Neuroergonomics: The brain at work.* New York: Oxford University Press.

Parish, C. L., & Arenas, E. (2007). Stem-cell-based strategies for the treatment of Parkinson's disease. *Neurodegenerative Disease, 4*, 339–347.

Park, C. L., & Grant, C. (2005). Determinants of positive and negative consequences of alcohol consumption in college students: Alcohol use, gender, and psychological characteristics. *Addictive Behaviors, 30*, 755–765.

Park, D. C. (2007). Eating disorders: A call to arms. *American Psychologist, 62*, 158.

Park H., & Antonioni, D. (2007). Personality, reciprocity, and strength of conflict resolution strategy. *Journal of Research in Personality, 41*, 110–125.

Park, W. W. (2000). A comprehensive empirical investigation of the relationships among variables of the group-think model. *Journal of Organizational Behavior, 21*, 873–887.

Parke, B. N. (2003). *Discovering programs for talent development.* Thousand Oaks, CA: Corwin Press.

Parke, R. D. (2002). Punishment revisited—Science, values, and the right question: Comment on Gershoff (2002). *Psychological Bulletin, 128*, 596–601.

Parke, R. D. (2004). Development in the family. *Annual Review of Psychology, 55*, 365–399.

Parke, R. S., Coltrane, S. Duffy, S., Buriel, R. Dennis, J., Powers, J. French, S., & Widaman, K. F. (2004). Economic stress, parenting, and child adjustment in Mexican American and European American children. *Child Development, 75*, 1632–1656.

Parker-Pope, T. (2003, April 22). The diet that works. *The Wall Street Journal*, pp. R1, R5.

Parlee, M. B. (1979, October). The friendship bond. *Psychology Today*, pp. 43–45.

Parlett, M., & Denham, J. (2007). Gestalt therapy. In W. Dryden, *Dryden's handbook of individual therapy* (5th ed.) Thousand Oaks, CA: Sage Publications.

Parmley, M. C. (2007). The effects of the confirmation bias on diagnostic decision making. *Dissertation Abstracts International: Section B: The Sciences and Engineering, 67(8-B)*, 4719.

Parra, A., & Argibay, J. C. (2007). Comparing psychics and non-psychics through a 'token-object' forced-choice ESP test. *Journal of the Society for Psychical Research, 71*, 80–90.

Parrott, A. C. (2002). Recreational Ecstasy/MDMA, the serotonin syndrome, and serotonergic neurotoxicity [Special issue: Serotonin]. *Pharmacology, Biochemistry & Behavior, 71*, 837–844.

Pascual, A., & Guéguen, N. (2005). Foot-in-the-door and door-in-the-face: A comparative meta-analytic study. *Psychological Reports, 96*, 122–128.

Pascual, A., & Guéguen, N. (2006). Door-in-the-face technique and monetary solicitation: An evaluation in a field setting. *Perceptual and Motor Skills, 103*, 974–978.

Pascual-Leone, A., et al. (1995). Modulation of muscle responses evoked during transcranial magnetic stimulation during the acquisition of new fine motor skills. *Journal of Neurophysiology 74*, 1037–1045.

Pascual, M. A., & Rodriguez, M. A. (2006). Learning by operant conditioning as a non-linear self-organized process. *Nonlinear Dynamics, Psychology, and Life Sciences, 10*, 341–364.

Passos, V. L., Berger, M. P. F., & Tan, F. E. (2007). Test design optimization in CAT early stage with the nominal response model. *Applied Psychological Measurement, 31*, 213–232.

Patel, D. R., Pratt, H. D., & Greydanus, D. E. (2003). Treatment of adolescents with anorexia nervosa [Special issue: Eating disorders in adolescents]. *Journal of Adolescent Research, 18*, 244–260.

Patterson, D. R. (2004). Treating pain with hypnosis. *Current Directions in Psychological Science, 13*, 252–255.

Paukert, A., Stagner, B., & Hope, K. (2004). The assessment of active listening skills in helpline volunteers. *Stress, Trauma, and Crisis: An International Journal, 7*, 61–76.

Paul, A. M. (2004). *Cult of personality: How personality tests are leading us to miseducate our children, mismanage our companies and misunderstand ourselves.* New York: Free Press.

Paulozzi, L. J. (2006). Opioid analgesic involvement in drug abuse deaths in American metropolitan areas. *American Journal of Public Health, 96*, 1755–1757.

Paunonen, S. V. (2003). Big Five factors of personality and replicated predictions of behavior. *Journal of Personality and Social Psychology, 84*, 411–422.

Pavitt, C. (2007). Impression formation. In B. B. Whaley & W. Samter, *Explaining communication: Contemporary theories and exemplars.* Mahwah, NJ: Lawrence Erlbaum Associates.

Pavlides, C., & Winson, J. (1989). Influences of hippocampal place cell firing in the awake state on the activity of these cells during subsequent sleep episodes. *Journal of Neuroscience, 9*, 2907–2918.

Pavlidis, I., Eberhardt, N. L., & Levine, J. A. (2002). Seeing through the face of deception. *Nature, 415*, 35.

Pavlov, I. P. (1927). *Conditioned reflexes.* London: Oxford University Press.

Pawlik, K., & d'Ydewalle, G. (1996). Psychology and the global commons: Perspectives of international psychology. *American Psychologist, 51*, 488–495.

Payne, D. G. (1986). Hyperamnesia for pictures and words: Testing the recall level hypothesis. *Journal of Experimental Psychology: Learning, Memory, and Cognition, 12*, 16–29.

Pearce, J . M. S. (2007). Synaesthesia. *European Neurology, 57*, 120–124.

Pearce, R. R., & Lin, Zeng. (2007). Chinese American post-secondary achievement and attainment: A cultural and structural analysis. *Educational Review, 59*, 19–36.

Pearson, A. R., Dovidio, J. F., & Pratto, F. (2007). Racial prejudice, intergroup hate, and blatant and subtle bias of whites toward blacks in legal decision making in the United States. *International Journal of Psychology & Psychological Therapy, 7*, 125–134.

Pearson, J., & Clifford, C. W. G. (2005). When your brain decides what you see: Grouping across monocular, binocular, and stimulus rivalry. *Psychological Science, 16*, 516–519.

Pedersen, D. M. (2002). Intrinsic-extrinsic factors in sport motivation. *Perceptual & Motor Skills, 95*, 459–476.

Pedersen, P. B., Draguns, J. G., Lonner, W. J., & Trimble, J. E. (Eds.). (2002). *Counseling across cultures* (5th ed.). Thousand Oaks, CA: Sage.

Peiro, J. M., & Lunt, I. (2002) The context for a European framework for psychologists' training. *European Psychologist, 7*, 169–179.

Pellegrini, S., Muzio, R. N., Mustaca, A. E., & Papini, M. R. (2004).Successive negative contrast after partial reinforcement in the consummatory behavior of rats. *Learning and Motivation, 35*, 303–321.

Pelli, D. G., Burns, C. W., & Farell, B. (2006). Feature detection and letter identification. *Vision Research, 46*, 4646–4674.

Pellis, S. M. & Pellis, V. C. (2007). Rough-and-tumble play and the development of the social brain. *Current Directions in Psychological Science, 16*, 95–97.

Penley, J. A., Tomaka, J., & Wiebe, J. S. (2002). The association of coping to physical and psychological health outcomes: A meta-analytic review. *Journal of Behavioral Medicine, 25*, 551–603.

Penn, D. L., Corrigan, P. W., Bentall, R. P., Racenstein, J. M., & Newman, L. (1997). Social cognition in schizophrenia. *Psychological Bulletin, 121*, 114–132.

Penney, J. B., Jr. (2000). Neurochemistry. In B. S. Fogel, R. B. Schiffer, et al.(Eds.), *Synopsis of neuropsychiatry.* New York: Lippincott Williams & Wilkins.

Pennington, B. F. (2002). *The development of psychopathology: Nature and nurture.* New York: Guilford Press.

Pennington, B. F. (2003). Review of The Development of Psychopathology: Nature and Nurture. *American Journal of Orthopsychiatry, 73*, 235.

Pennington, B. Moon, J., & Edgin, J. (2003). The neuropsychology of Down syndrome: Evidence for hippocampal dysfunction. *Child Development, 74*, 75–93.

Pennisi, E. (1997, October 24). Enzyme linked to alcohol sensitivity in mice. *Science, 278*, 573.

Pennisi, E., & Vogel, G. (2000, June 9). Animal cloning. Clones: A hard act to follow. *Science, 288*, 1722–1727.

Penza, K. M., Heim, C., & Nemeroff, C. B (2006). Trauma and depression. In C. L. Keyes & S. H. Goodman, *Women and depression: A handbook for the social, behavioral, and biomedical sciences.* New York: Cambridge University Press.

Penzel, F. (2000). *Obsessive-compulsive disorders: A complete guide to getting well and staying well.* New York: Oxford University Press.

People. (2007, July 13). Love stories you'll never forget. *People,* p. 18.

People Weekly. (2000, May 8). Giant steps. p. 117.

People Weekly. (2003, June 23). Kid Doc: He's no brain surgeon—yet. But Sho Yano, 12, is about to start med school. *People Weekly,* 125.

People Weekly. (2004, March 15). Who am I? And who are you? Amnesia victim John Prigg struggles to regain his memory, his family, his life [Interview]. *People Weekly, 61*, p. 136.

Peplau, L. A. (2003). Human sexuality: how do men and women differ? *Current Directions in Psychological Research, 12*, 37.

Peretz, I. (2001). Brain specialization for music: New evidence from congenital amusia. In R. J. Zatorre & I. Peretz (Eds.), *The biological foundations of music. Annals of the New York Academy of Sciences* (Vol. 930, pp. 153–165). New York: New York Academy of Sciences.

Perez, R. M., DeBord, K. A., & Bieschke, K. J. (Eds.). (2000). *Handbook of counseling and psychotherapy with lesbian, gay, and bisexual clients.* Washington, DC: American Psychological Association.

Perkins, D. N. (1983). Why the human perceiver is a bad machine. In J. Beck, B. Hope, & A. Rosenfeld (Eds.), *Human and machine vision.* New York: Academic Press.

Perloff, R. M. (2003). *The dynamics of persuasion: Communication and attitudes in the 21st century* (2nd ed.). Mahwah, NJ: Erlbaum.

Perls, F. S. (1970). *Gestalt therapy now: Therapy, techniques, applications.* Palo Alto, CA: Science and Behavior Books.

Perls, F., Hefferline, R., & Goodman, P. (1994). *Gestalt therapy: Excitement and growth in the human personality* (2nd ed.). New York: New York Journal Press.

Pert, C. B. (2002). The wisdom of the receptors: Neuropeptides, the emotions, and body-mind. *Advances in Mind-Body Medicine, 18*, 30–35.

Pervin, L. A. (2003). *The science of personality* (2nd ed.). London: Oxford University Press.

Pesmen, C. (2006, March). Don't let pain get in your way. *Money*, 48.

Peters, E., Hess, T. M., Västfjäll, D., & Auman, C. (2007). Adult age differences in dual information processes. *Perspectives on Psychological Science, 2*, 1–23.

Peters, J. Suchan, B., Koster, O., & Daum, I. (2007). Domain-specific retrieval of source information in the medial temporal lobe. *European Journal of Neuroscience, 26*, 1333–1343.

Petersen, S. E., & Fiez, J. A. (1993). The processing of single words studied with positron emission tomography. *Annual Review of Neuroscience, 16*, 509–530.

Peterson, A. (1985). Pubertal development as a cause of disturbance: Myths, realities, and unanswered questions. *Genetic, Social and General Psychology Monographs, 111*, 205–232.

Peterson, C. (2000). The future of optimism. *American Psychologist, 55*, 44–55.

Peterson, C., Maier, S. F., & Seligman, M. E. P. (1993). *Learned helplessness: A theory for the age of personal control.* New York: Oxford University Press.

Peterson, F. L., Jr., & Fuerst, D. E. (2007). Assessment and treatment of erection dysfunction. In L. VandeCreek, F. L. Peterson, Jr., & J. W. Bley, *Innovations in clinical practice: Focus on sexual health.* Sarasota, FL: Professional Resource Press/Professional Resource Exchange.

Peterson, L. R., & Peterson, M. J. (1959). Short-term retention of individual items. *Journal of Experimental Psychology, 58*, 193–198.

Peterson, R. A., & Brown, S. P. (2005). On the use of beta coefficients in meta-analysis. *Journal of Applied Psychology, 90*, 175–181.

Peterson, S. E. (2001). *PET Scans.* Washington University.

Petersson, K. M., Silva, C., Castro-Caldas, A., Ingvar, M., & Reis, A. (2007). Literacy: A cultural influence on functional left-right differences in the inferior parietal cortex. *European Journal of Neuroscience, 26*, 791–799.

Petri, H. L. (1996). *Motivation: Theory, research, and applications* (4th ed.). Pacific Grove, CA: Brooks/Cole.

Petrill, S. A. (2005). Introduction to this special issue: Genes, environment, and the development of reading skills. *Scientific Studies of Reading, 9*, 189–196.

Petrill, S. A., & Deater-Deckard, K. (2004). The heritability of general cognitive ability: A within-family adoption design. *Intelligence, 32*, 403–409.

Pettigrew, T. F. (2004). Justice deferred: A half century after *Brown v. Board of Education. American Psychologist, 59*, 521–529.

Pettigrew, T., & Tropp, L. (2000). *Reducing prejudice and discrimination.* Mahwah, NJ: Erlbaum.

Pettigrew, T. F., & Tropp, L. R. (2006). A meta-analytic test of intergroup contact theory. *Journal of Personality and Social Psychology, 90,* 751–783.

Pettijohn, T. F., & Jungeberg, B. J. (2004). *Playboy* playmate curves: Changes in facial and body feature preferences across social and economic conditions. *Personality and Social Psychology Bulletin, 30*, 1186–1197.

Pettingale, K. W., Morris, T., Greer, S., & Haybittle, J. L. (1985). Mental attitudes to cancer: An additional prognostic factor. *Lancet,* p. 750.

Pettito, L. A. (1993). On the ontogenetic requirements for early language acquisition. In B. de Boysson-Bardies, S. de Schonen, P. W. Jusczyk, P. McNeilage, & J. Morton (Eds.), *Developmental neurocognition: Speech and face processing in the first year of life. NATO ASI series D: Behavioural and social sciences* (Vol. 69). Dordrecht, Netherlands: Kluwer Academic.

Pettito, L. A., & Marentette, P. F. (1991, March 22). Babbling in the manual mode: Evidence for the ontogeny of language. *Science, 251*, 1493–1496.

Petty, R. E., Cacioppo, J. T., Strathman, A. J., & Priester, J. R. (2005). To think or not to think: Exploring two routes to persuasion. In T. C. Brock & M. C. Green (Eds.), *Persuasion: Psychological insights and perspectives* (2nd ed.). Thousand Oaks, CA: Sage Publications.

Pfeffer, C. R. (2006). An evolutionary perspective on childhood depression. In P. S. Jensen, & P. Knapp, & D. A. Mrazek, *Toward a new diagnostic system for child psychopathology: Moving beyond the DSM.* New York: Guilford Press.

Phelps, R. P. (2005). *Defending standardized testing.* Mahwah, NJ: Lawrence Erlbaum Associates.

Philip, P., Sagaspe, P., Moore, N., Taillard, J., Charles, A., Guilleminault, C., & Bioulac, B. (2005). Fatigue, sleep restriction and driving performance. *Accident Analysis and Prevention, 37*, 473–478.

Phillips, E. L., Greydanus, D. E., Pratt, H. D., & Patel, D. R. (2003). Treatment of bulimia nervosa: Psychological and psychopharmacologic considerations [Special issue: Eating disorders in adolescents]. *Journal of Adolescent Research, 18*, 261–279.

Phinney, J. S. (2003). Ethic identity and acculturation. In K. M. Chun, O. Balls, & P. Organista (Eds.), *Acculturation: Advances in theory, measurement, and applied research.* Washington, DC: American Psychological Association.

Piaget, J. (1970). Piaget's theory. In P. H. Mussen (Ed.), *Carmichael's manual of child psychology* (3rd ed., Vol. I). New York: Wiley.

Piaget, J., & Inhelder, B. (1958). *The growth of logical thinking from childhood to adolescence* (A. Parsons & S. Seagrin, Trans.). New York: Basic Books.

Piasecki, T. M., Kenford, S. L., Smith, S. S., Fiore, M. C., & Baker, T. B. (1997). Listening to nicotine: Negative affect and the smoking withdrawal conundrum. *Psychological Science, 8*, 184–189.

Piccardi, L. (2006). Neural substrates of visual and musical art: a book review of 'neuropsychology of art: neurologic, cognitive, and evolutionary perspectives.' *Cognitive and Behavioral Neurology, 19*, 172–173.

Picchioni, D., Goeltzenleucher, B., Green, D. N., Convento, M. J., Crittenden, R., Hallgren, M., & Hick, R. A. (2002). Nightmares as a coping mechanism for stress. *Dreaming: Journal of the Association for the Study of Dreams, 12*, 155–169.

Pich, E. M., Pagliusi, S. R., Tessari, M., Talabot-Ayer, D., Hooft van Huijsduijnen, R., & Chiamulera, C. (1997, January 3). Common neural substrates for the addictive properties of nicotine and cocaine. *Science, 275,* 83–86.

Pickering, G. J., & Gordon, R. (2006). Perception of mouthfeel sensations elicited by red wine are associated with sensitivity to 6-N-propyl-thiouracil. *Journal of Sensory Studies, 21,* 249–265.

Piechowski, M. M. (2003). From William James to Maslow and Dabrowski: Excitability of character and self-actualization. In D. Ambrose, L. M. Cohen, et al. (Eds.), *Creative intelligence: Toward theoretic integration: Perspectives on creativity* (pp. 283–322). Cresskill, NJ: Hampton Press.

Pietarinen, A-V. (2006). The evolution of semantics and language-games for meaning. *Interaction Studies: Social Behaviour and Communication in Biological and Artificial Systems, 7,* 79–104.

Pihlgren, E. M., Gidycz, C. A., & Lynn, S. J. (1993). Impact of adulthood and adolescent rape experiences on subsequent sexual fantasies. *Imagination, Cognition and Personality, 12,* 321–339.

Piliavin, J. A., & Piliavin, I. M. (1972). Effect of blood on reactions to a victim. *Journal of Personality and Social Psychology, 23,* 353–362.

Pillay, S. S., Gruber, S. A., Rogowska, J., Simpson, N., & Yurgelun-Todd, D. A. (2006). fMRI of fearful facial affect recognition in panic disorder: the cingulate gyrus-amygdala connection.

Pillay, S. S., Rogowska, J., Gruber, S. A., Simpson, N., & Yurgelun-Todd, D. A. (2007). Recognition of happy facial affect in panic disorder: an fMRI study. *Journal of Anxiety Disorders, 21,* 381–393.

Pilling, M., & Davies, I. R. L. (2004). Linguistic relativism and colour cognition. *British Journal of Psychology, 95,* 429–455.

Pincus, T., & Morley, S. (2001). Cognitive-processing bias in chronic pain: A review and integration. *Psychological Bulletin, 127,* 599–617.

Pinel, J. P. J., Assanand, S., & Lehman, D. R. (2000). Hunger, eating and ill health. *American Psychologist, 55,* 1105–1116.

Pinker, S. (1994). *The language instinct.* New York: William Morrow.

Pinker, S. (2002). *The blank slate: The modern denial of human nature.* New York: Viking.

Pinker, S. (2004). *How the mind works.* New York: Gardner Books.

Pinker, S., & Jackendoff, R. (2005). The faculty of language: What's special about it? *Cognition, 96,* 201–236.

Pinkerton, S. D., Bogart, L. M., Cecil, H., & Abramson, P. R. (2002). Factors associated with masturbation in a collegiate sample. *Journal of Psychology and Human Sexuality, 14,* 103–121.

Pinkerton, S. D., Cecil, H., Bogart, L. M., & Abramson, P. R. (2003). The pleasures of sex: An empirical investigation. *Cognition and Emotion, 17,* 341–353.

Pinquart, M., Duberstein, P. R., & Lyness J. M. (2006). Treatments for later-life depressive conditions: a meta-analytic comparison of pharmacotherapy and psychotherapy. *American Journal of Psychiatry, 163,* 1493–1501.

Pipe, M. E., Lamb, M. E., & Orbach, Y. (2004) Recent research on children's testimony about experienced and witnessed events. *Developmental Review, 24,* 440–468.

Pi-Sunyer, X. (2003). A clinical view of the obesity problem. *Science, 299,* 859–860.

Pitman, R. K., & Delahanty, D. L. (2005). Conceptually driven pharmacologic approaches to acute trauma. *CNS Spectrums, 10,* 99–106.

Plomin, R. (2003a). 50 years of DNA: What it has meant to psychological science. *American Psychological Society, 16,* 7–8.

Plomin, R. (2003b). General cognitive ability. In R. Pomin, J. C. DeFries, et al. (Eds.), *Behavioral genetics in the postgenomic era.* Washington, DC: American Psychological Association.

Plomin, R., & Caspi, R. (1999). Behavioral genetics and personality. In L. A. Pervin & O. P. John (Eds.), *Handbook of personality: Theory and research.* (2nd ed.). New York: Guilford.

Plomin, R., & Kovas, Y. (2005). Generalist genes and learning disabilities. *Psychological Bulletin, 131,* 592–617.

Plomin, R., & McClearn, G. E. (Eds.) (1993). *Nature, nurture and psychology.* Washington, DC: American Psychological Association.

Plomin, R., & McGuffin, P. (2003). Psychopathology in the postgenomic era. *Annual Review of Psychology, 54,* 205–228.

Plomin, R., & Neiderhiser, J. M. (1992). Genetics and experience. *Current Directions in Psychological Science, 1,* 160–163.

Plomin, R., & Walker, S. O. (2003). Genetics and educational psychology. *British Journal of Educational Psychology, 73,* 3–14.

Plomin, R., DeFries, J. C., Craig, I. W., & McGuffin, P. (2003). *Behavioral genetics in the postgenomic era.* Washington, DC: American Psychological Association.

Plonczynski, D. J., & Plonczynski, K. J. (2007). Hormone therapy in perimenopausal and postmenopausal women: examining the evidence on cardiovascular disease risks. *Journal of Gerontological Nursing, 33,* 48–55.

Plous, S. (1996a). Attitudes toward the use of animals in psychological research and education: Results from a national survey of psychologists. *American Psychologist, 51,* 1167–1180.

Plous, S. (1996b). Attitudes toward the use of animals in psychological research and education: Results from a national survey of psychology majors. *Psychological Science, 7,* 352–358.

Plous, S., & Herzog, H. A. (2000, October 27). Poll shows researchers favor lab animal protection. *Science, 290,* 711.

Plous, S. L., & Zimbardo, P. G. (2004, September 10). How social science can reduce terrorism. *The Chronicle of Higher Education,* pp. B9–B10.

Plowright, C. M. S., Simonds, V. M., & Butler, M. A. (2006). How bumblebees first find flowers: Habituation of visual pattern preferences, spontaneous recovery, and dishabituation. *Learning and Motivation, 37,* 66–78.

Plunkett, K., & Wood, C. (2004). The development of children's understanding of grammar. In J. Oates and A. Grayson (Eds.), *Cognitive and language development in children* (pp. 163–204). Malden, MA: Blackwell Publishers Open University Press.

Plutchik, R. (1980). *Emotion, a psychorevolutionary synthesis.* New York: Harper & Row.

Pogarsky, G., & Piquero, A. R. (2003). Can punishment encourage offending? Investigating the "resetting" effect. *Journal of Research in Crime and Delinquency, 40,* 95–120.

Pole, N. (2007).The psychophysiology of post-traumatic stress disorder: A meta-analysis. *Psychological Bulletin, 133,* 34–45.

Polivy, J., & Herman, C. P. (2002). Causes of eating disorders. *Annual Review of Psychology, 53,* 187–213.

Polivy, J., Herman, C. P., & Boivin, M. (2005). Eating disorders. In J. E. Maddux and B. A. Winstead, *Psychopathology: Foundations for a contemporary understanding* (pp. 229–254). Mahwah, NJ: Lawrence Erlbaum Associates.

Polk, N. (1997, March 30). The trouble with school testing systems. *The New York Times,* p. CN3.

Pollack, A. (2000, May 30). Neural cells, grown in labs, raise hopes on brain disease. *The New York Times,* pp. D1, D6.

Pollack, M. H., & Marzol, P. C. (2000). Panic: Course, complications and treatment of panic disorder. *Journal of Psychopharmacology, 14,* S25–S30.

Polonsky, D. C. (2006). Review of the big book of masturbation: From angst to zeal. *Journal of Sex & Marital Therapy, 32,* 75–78.

Polyakov, A., & Pratt, H. (2003). Electrophysiologic correlates of direction and elevation cures for sound localization in the human brainstem. *International Journal of Audiology, 42,* 140–151.

Pomerlau, O. F. (1995). Individual differences in sensitivity to nicotine: Implications of genetic research on nicotine dependence [Special issue: Genetic, environmental, and situational factors mediating the effects of nicotine]. *Behavior Genetics, 25,* 161–177.

Pomponio, A. T. (2002). *Psychological consequences of terrorism.* New York: Wiley.

Poniewozik, James (2002, June 17). Hollywood, the mob and John Gotti. *Time,* p. 37.

Ponterotto, J. G., Gretchen, D., Chauhan, R. V. (2001). Cultural identity and multicultural assessment: Quantitative and qualitative tools for the clinician. In L. A. Suzuki, & J. G. Ponterotto (Eds.), *Handbook of multicultural assessment: Clinical, psychological, and educational applications* (2nd ed.). San Francisco: Jossey-Bass/Pfeiffer.

Poo, C. & Isaacson, J. S. (2007). An early critical period for long-term plasticity and structural modification of sensory synapses in olfactory cortex. *Journal of Neuroscience, 27,* 7553–7558.

Popp, D., Donovan, R. A., & Crawford, M. (2003). Gender, race, and speech style stereotypes. *Sex Roles, 48,* 317–325.

Porkka-Heiskanen, T., Strecker, R. E., Thakkar, M., Bjorkum, A. A., Greene, R. W., & McCarley, R. W. (1997, May 23). Adensosine: A mediator of the sleep-inducing effects of prolonged wakefulness. *Science, 276,* 1265–1268.

Porte, H. S., & Hobson, J. A. (1996). Physical motion in dreams: One measure of three theories. *Journal of Abnormal Psychology, 105,* 329–335.

Porter, C. L., & Hsu, H. C. (2003). First-time mothers' perceptions of efficacy during the transition to motherhood: Links to infant temperament. *Journal of Family Psychology, 17,* 54–64.

Posner, M. I., & DiGirolamo, G. J. (2000). Cognitive neuroscience: Origins and promise. *Psychological Bulletin, 126,* 873–889.

Poteat, V. P., & Espelage, D. L., (2007, May). Predicting psychosocial consequences of homophobic victimization in middle school students. *Journal of Early Adolescence, 27*(2), 175–191.

Potheraju, A., & Soper, B. (1995). A comparison of self-reported dream themes for high school and college students. *College Student Journal, 29,* 417–420.

Pottick, K. J., Kirk, S. A., Hsieh, D. K., & Tian, X. (2007). Judging mental disorder in youths: Effects of client, clinician, and contextual differences. *Journal of Consulting Clinical Psychology, 75,* 1–8.

Poundstone, W. (2003). *How would you move Mount Fuji?: Microsoft's cult of the puzzle.* Boston: Little, Brown.

Povinelli, D. J., & Vonk, J. (2004). We don't need a microscope to explore the chimpanzee's mind. *Mind and Language, 19,* 1–28.

Powell, L. H, Shahabi, L, & Thoresen, C. E. (2003). Religion and spirituality: Linkages to physical health. *American Psychology, 58,* 36–52.

Powell, L. H. (2006). Review of marital and sexual lifestyles in the united states: attitudes, behaviors, and relationships in social context. *Family Relations, 55,* 149.

Powers, K. D. (2006). An analysis of Kohlbergian moral development in relationship to biblical factors of morality in seminary students (Lawrence Kohlberg). *Dissertation Abstracts International: Section B: The Sciences and Engineering, 67(6-B),* 3485.

Praisner, C. L. (2003). Attitudes of elementary school principals toward the inclusion of students with disabilities. *Exceptional Children, 69,* 135–145.

Prasad, B. (2006). Recent advances in artificial intelligence. *Journal of Experimental & Theoretical Artificial Intelligence, 18, Special issue: Recent Advances in AI,* 433–434.

Pratkanis, A. R. (2007). Social influence analysis: An index of tactics. In A. R. Pratkanis, *The science of social influence: Advances and future progress.* New York: Psychology Press.

Pratkanis, A. R., Epley, N. & Savitsky, K. (2007). Issue 12: Is subliminal persuasion a myth? In J. A. Nier, *Taking sides: Clashing views in social psychology* (2nd ed.) New York: McGraw-Hill.

Pratt, H. D., Phillips, E. L., Greydanus, D. E., & Patel, D. R. (2003). Eating disorders in the adolescent population: Future directions [Special issue: Eating disorders in adolescents]. *Journal of Adolescent Research, 18,* 297–317.

Pressley, M. (1987). Are keyword method effects limited to slow presentation rates? An empirically based reply to Hall and Fuson (1986). *Journal of Educational Psychology, 79,* 333–335.

Pressley, M. P., & Harris., K. R. (2006). Cognitive strategies instruction: from basic research to classroom instruction. In P. A. Alexander, & P. H. Winne, *Handbook of educational psychology.* Mahwah, NJ: Lawrence Erlbaum Associates.

Pressman, S. D., Cohen, S., Miller, G. E., Barkin, A., Rabin, B. S., & Treanor, J. J. (2005). Loneliness, social network size, and immune response to influenza vaccination in college freshman. *Health Psychology, 24,* 297–306.

Pretzer, J. L., & Beck, A. T. (2005). A cognitive theory of personality disorders. In M. F. Lenzenweger & J. F. Clarkin (Eds.), *Major theories of personality disorder* (2nd ed.). New York: Guilford Press.

Price, D. D. (2000, June 9). Psychological and neural mechanisms of the affective dimension of pain. *Science, 288,* 1769–1772.

Prince, C.V. (2005). Homosexuality, transvestism and transsexuality: Reflections on their etymology and differentiation. *International Journal of Transgenderism, 8,* 15–18.

Prinz, J. J. (2007). Emotion: Competing theories and philosophical issues. In P. Thagard, *Philosophy of psychology and cognitive science.* Amsterdam, Netherlands: North Holland/Elsevier.

Prislin, R., Brewer, M., & Wilson, D. J. (2002). Changing majority and minority positions within a group versus an aggregate. *Personality and Social Psychology Bulletin, 28,* 650–647.

Proffitt, D. R. (2006). Distance perception. *Current Directions in Psychological Science, 15,* 131–139.

Prohovnik, I., Skudlarski, P., Fulbright, R. K., Gore, J. C., & Wexler, B. E. (2004). Functional MRI changes before and after onset of reported emotions. *Psychiatry Research: Neuroimaging, 132,* 239–250.

Prokasy, W. F., Jr., & Hall, J. F. (1963). Primary stimulus generalization. *Psychological Review, 70,* 310–322.

Puca, R. M. (2005). The influence of the achievement motive on probability estimates in pre- and post-decisional action phases. *Journal of Research in Personality, 39,* 245–262.

Puhl, R., & Latner, J. (2007). Stigma, obesity, and the health of the nation's children. *Psychological Bulletin, 133,* 557–580.

Purves, D., Augustine, G. J., Fitzpatrick, D., Katz, L. C., LaMantia, A., & McNamara, J. O. (Eds.). (1997). *Neuroscience.* Sunderland, MA: Sinauer.

Putnam, F. W. (2000). Dissociative disorders. In A. J. Sameroff, M. Lewis (Eds.), *Handbook of developmental psychopathology* (2nd ed.). Dordrecht, Netherlands: Kluwer Academic Publishers.

Quadros, P. S., Goldstein, A. Y. N., DeVries, G. J., & Wagner, C. K. (2002). Regulation of sex differences in progesterone receptor expression in the medial preoptic nucleus of postnatal rats. *Journal of Neuroendocrinology, 14,* 761–767.

Quartana, P. J., & Burns, J. W. (2007). Painful consequences of anger suppression. *Emotion, 7,* 400–414.

Quas, J. A., Malloy, L. C., & Melinder, A. (2007). Developmental differences in the effects of repeated interviews and interviewer bias on young children's event memory and false reports. *Developmental Psychology, 43,* 823–837.

Quenot, J. P., Boichot, C., Petit, A., Falcon-Eicher, S., d'Athis, P., Bonnet, C., Wolf, J. E., Louis, P., & Brunotte, F. (2005). Usefulness of MRI in the follow-up of patients with repaired aortic coarctation and bicuspid aortic valve. *International Journal of Cardiology, 103,* 312–316.

Quinn, D. M., Kahng, S. K., & Crocker, J. (2004). Discreditable: Stigma effects of revealing a mental illness history on test performance. *Personality and Social Psychology Bulletin, 30,* 803–815.

Quinn, T. C., & Overbaugh, J. (2005, June 10). HIV/AIDS in women: An expanding epidemic. *Science, 308,* 1582–1583.

Quintana, S. M., Aboud, F. E., Chao, R. K., (2006). Race, ethnicity, and culture in child development: Contemporary research and future directions. *Child Development, 77,* 1129–1141.

Rabin, J. (2004). Quantification of color vision with cone contrast sensitivity. *Visual Neuroscience, 21,* 483–485.

Rachman, S., & deSilva, P. (2004). *Panic disorders: The facts.* Oxford, England: Oxford University Press.

Raffaele, P. (2006, November). Speaking Bonobo. *Smithsonian Magazine.*

Rahman, Q., Kumari, V., & Wilson, G. D. (2003). Sexual orientation-related differences in pre-pulse inhibition of the human startle response. *Behavioral Neuroscience, 117,* 1096–1102.

Rajagopal, S. (2006). The placebo effect. *Psychiatric Bulletin, 30,* 185–188.

Rakoff, V. M. (1995). Trauma and adolescent rites of initiation. In R. C. Marohn & S. C. Feinstein (Eds.), *Adolescent psychiatry: Developmental and clinical studies* (Vol. 20). *Annals of the American Society for Adolescent Psychiatry.* Hillsdale, NJ: Analytic Press.

Ralston, A. (2004). *Between a rock and a hard place.* NY: Simon & Schuster.

Ramachandran, V. S. (1995). Filling in gaps in logic: Reply to Durgin et al. *Perception, 24,* 841–845.

Ramachandran, V. S. (2004). *A brief tour of human consciousness. From impostor poodles to purple numbers.* New York: Pi Press.

Ramachandran, V. S. & Hubbard, E.M. (2001). Synesthesia—a window into perception, thought and language. *Journal of Consciousness Studies, 8,* 3–34.

Ramachandran, V. S., Hubbard, E.M., & Butcher, P. A. (2004). Synesthesia, cross-activation and the foundations of neuroepistemology. In G. A. Calvert, C. Spence, & B. E. Stein, *The handbook of multisensory processes.* Cambridge, MA: MIT Press.

Rambaud, C., & Guilleminault, C. (2004). "Back to sleep" and unexplained death in infants. *Journal of Sleep and Sleep Disorders, 27,* 1359–1366.

Ramos, R. T. (2006). Antidepressants and dizziness. *Journal of Psychopharmacology, 20,* 708–713.

Rampon, C., Jiang, C. H., Dong, H., Tang, Y., Lockhart, D. J., Schultaz, P. G., et al. (2000). Effects of environmental enrichment on gene expression in the brain. *Proceedings of the National Academy of Sciences, 97,* 12880–12884.

Ramsay, M. C., Reynolds, C. R., & Kamphaus, R. W. (2002). *Essentials of behavioral assessment.* New York: Wiley.

Ramus, F. (2006). Genes, brain, and cognition: A roadmap for the cognitive scientist. *Cognition, 101,* 247–269.

Rangell, L. (2007). *The road to unity in psychoanalytic theory.* Lanham, MD: Jason Aronson.

Raskin, N. J., & Rogers, C. R. (1989). Person-centered therapy. In R. J. Corsini, & D. Wedding (Eds.), *Current psychotherapies* (4th ed.). Itasca, IL: F. E. Peacock.

Rassin, E., & Muris, P. (2007). Abnormal and normal obsessions: A reconsideration. *Behaviour Research and Therapy, 45,* 1065–1070.

Ratcliff, R., & McKoon, G. (1989). Memory models, text processing, and cue-dependent retrieval. In H. L. Roediger III & F. I. M. Craik (Eds.), *Varieties of memory and consciousness: Essays in honour of Endel Tulving.* Hillsdale, NJ: Erlbaum.

Rattazzi, M. C., LaFuci, G., & Brown, W. T. (2004). Prospects for gene therapy in the Fragile X Syndrome. *Mental Retardation and Developmental Disabilities Research Reviews, 10,* 75–81.

Rauschecker, J. P., & Shannon, R. V. (2005, February 8). Sending sound to the brain. *Science, 295,* 1025–9.

Ravindran, A. V., Matheson, K., Griffiths, J., Merali, Z., & Anisman, H. (2002). Stress, coping, uplifts, and quality of life in subtypes of depression: A conceptual framework and emerging data. *Journal of Affective Disorders, 71,* 121–130.

Rawsthorne, L. J., & Elliot, A. J. (1999). Achievement goals and intrinsic motivation: A meta-analytic review. *Personality and Social Psychology Review, 3,* 326–344.

Ray, L. A., & Hutchison, K. E. (2007). Effects of naltrexone on alcohol sensitivity and genetic moderators of medication response: a double-blind placebo-controlled study. *Archives of General Psychiatry, 64*, 1069–1077.

Ray, W. J. (2000). *Methods: Toward a science of behavior and experience* (6th ed.). Belmont, CA: Wadsworth.

Raymond, J. (2003, March 24.). Now for a breath of fresh air. *Newsweek*, p. 67.

Raz, A. (2007). Suggestibility and hypnotizability: Mind the gap. *American Journal of Clinical Hypnosis, 49*, 205–210.

Redding, G. M. (2002). A test of size-scaling and relative-size hypotheses for the moon illusion. *Perception and Psychophysics, 64*, 1281–1289.

Redding, G. M., & Hawley, E. (1993). Length illusion in fractional MüllerLyer stimuli: An object-perception approach. *Perception, 22*, 819–828.

Redish, A. D. (2004). Addiction as a computational process gone awry. *Science, 306*, 1944–1947.

Reed, S. K. (1996). *Cognition: Theory and applications* (4th ed.). Pacific Grove, CA: Brooks/Cole.

Reese, R. J., Conoley, C. W., & Brossart, D. F. (2002). Effectiveness of telephone counseling: A field-based investigation. *Journal of Counseling Psychology, 49*, 233–242.

Refinetti, R. (2005). *Circadian physiology*. New York: CRC Press.

Regan, P. C. (2006). Love. In R. D. McAnulty, & M. M. Burnette, *Sex and sexuality, Vol 2: Sexual function and dysfunction*. Westport, CT: Praeger Publishers/Greenwood Publishing.

Reichenberg, A., & Harvey, P. d. (2007). Neuropsychological impairments in schizophrenia: Integration of performance-based and brain imaging findings. *Psychological Bulletin, 133*, 212–223.

Reichman, W. E., & Rabins, P. V. (1996). Schizophrenia and other psychotic disorders. In W. E. Reichman, & P. R. Katz (Eds.), *Psychiatric care in the nursing home*. New York: Oxford University Press.

Reif, A., & Lesch, K. P. (2003). Toward a molecular architecture of personality. *Behavioural Brain Research, 139*, 1–20.

Reijonen, J. H., Pratt, H. D., Patel, D. R., & Greydanus, D. E. (2003). Eating disorders in the adolescent population: An overview [Special issue: Eating disorders in adolescents]. *Journal of Adolescent Research, 18*, 209–222.

Reilly, T., & Waterhouse, J. (2007). Altered sleep-wake cycles and food intake: The Ramadan model. *Physiology & Behavior, 90*, 219–228.

Reisberg, D. (1997). *Cognition: Exploring the science of the mind*. New York: W. W. Norton.

Reiss, S., & Havercamp, S. M. (2005). Motivation in developmental context: A new method for studying self-actualization. *Journal of Humanistic Psychology, 45*, 41–53.

Reitman, J. S. (1965). *Cognition and thought*. New York: Wiley.

Relier, J. P. (2001). Influence of maternal stress on fetal behavior and brain development. *Biology of the Neonate, 79*, 168–171.

Remington, G. (2003). Understanding antipsychotic 'atypicality': A clinical and pharmacological moving target. *Journal of Psychiatry & Neuroscience, 28*, 275–284.

Rende, R. (2007). Thinking inside and outside the (black) box: Behavioral genetics and human development. *Human Development, 49*, 343–346.

Renshaw, D. C. (2006). Male and female circumcision today. *The Family Journal, 14*, 283–285.

Repp, B. H., & Knoblich, G. (2007). Action can affect auditory perception. *Psychological Science, 18*, 6–7.

Rescorla, R. A. (1988). Pavlovian conditioning: It's not what you think it is. *American Psychologist, 43*, 151–160.

Reyna, V. F. (1997). Conceptions of memory development with implications for reasoning and decision making. In R. Vasta (Ed.), *Annals of child development: A research annual* (Vol. 12, pp. 87–118). London: Jessica Kingsley.

Reynolds, C. R., & Ramsay, M. C. (2003). Bias in psychological assessment: An empirical review and recommendations. In J. R. Graham & J. A. Naglieri (Eds.), *Handbook of psychology: Assessment psychology* (Vol. 10, pp. 67–93). New York: Wiley.

Reynolds, R. I., & Takooshian, H. (1988, January). Where were you August 8, 1985? *Bulletin of the Psychonomic Society, 26*, 23–25.

Rhue, J. W., Lynn, S. J., & Kirsch, I. (Eds.). (1993). *Handbook of clinical hypnosis*. Washington, DC: American Psychological Association.

Ricciuti, H. N. (1993). Nutrition and mental development. *Current Directions in Psychological Science, 2*, 43–46.

Rice, M. L., Tomblin, J. B., Hoffman, L., Richman, W. A., & Marquis, J. (2004). Grammatical tense deficits in children with SLI and nonspecific language impairment: Relationships with non-verbal IQ over time. *Journal of Speech, Language, and Hearing Research, 47*, 816–834.

Rice, V. H. (Ed.). (2000). *Handbook of stress, coping and health*. Thousand Oaks, CA: Sage.

Rich, E. L., & Shapiro, M. L. (2007). Prelimbic/infralimbic inactivation impairs memory for multiple task switches, but not flexible selection of familiar tasks. *Journal of Neuroscience, 27*, 4747–4755.

Richard, D. C. S., & Lauterbach, D. (Eds). (2006). *Handbook of exposure therapies*. New York: Academic Press.

Richard, M. (2005). Effective treatment of eating disorders in Europe: Treatment outcome and its predictors. *European Eating Disorders Review, 13*, 169–179.

Richardson, A. S., Bergen, H. A., Martin, G., Roeger, L., & Allison, S. (2005). Perceived academic performance as an indicator of risk of attempted suicide in young adolescents. *Archives of Suicide Research, 9*, 163–176.

Richgels, D. J. (2004). Paying attention to language. *Reading Research Quarterly, 39*, 470–477.

Rieber, R. W., & Robinson, D. K. (2006). Review of the essential Vygotsky. *Journal of the History of the Behavioral Sciences, 42*, 178–180.

Riedel, G., Platt, B., & Micheau, J. (2003). Glutamate receptor function in learning and memory. *Behavioural Brain Research, 140*, 1–47.

Rieder, R. O., Kaufmann, C. A., & Knowles, J. A. (1996). Genetics. In R. E. Hales & S. C. Yudofsky (Eds.), *The American Psychiatric Press synopsis of psychiatry*. Washington, DC: American Psychiatric Press.

Rierdan, J. (1996). *Adolescent suicide: One response to adversity*. In R. S. Feldman (Ed.)., *The psychology of adversity*. Amherst, MA: University of Massachusetts Press.

Rigby, L., & Waite, S. (2007). Group therapy for self-esteem, using creative approaches and metaphor as clinical tools. *Behavioural and Cognitive Psychotherapy, 35*, 361–364.

Ringold, D. J. (1996). Social criticisms of target marketing: Process or product? In R. P. Hill (Ed.), *Marketing and consumer research in the public interest*. Thousand Oaks, CA: Sage.

Riniolo, T. C., Koledin, M., Drakulic, G. M., & Payne, R. A. (2003). An archival study of eyewitness memory of the Titanic's final plunge. *Journal of General Psychology, 130*, 89–95.

Rinn, W. E. (1984). The neuropsychology of facial expression: A review of neurological and psychological mechanisms for producing facial expressions. *Psychological Bulletin, 95*, 52–77.

Rinn, W. E. (1991). Neuropsychology of facial expression. In R. S. Feldman & B. Rimé (Eds.), *Fundamentals of non-verbal behavior*. Cambridge, England: Cambridge University Press.

Riolo, F. (2007). Ricordare, ripetere e rielaborare: Un lascito di Freud alia psicoanalisi futura. Remembering, repeating, and working through: Freud's legacy to the psychoanalysis of the future. *Rivista di Psicoanalisi, 53*, 439–446.

Rioult-Pedotti, M. S., Friedman, D., & Donoghue, J. P. (2000, October 20). Learning-induced LTP in neocortex. *Science, 290*, 533–536.

Ripley, A. (2005, March 7). Who says a woman can't be Einstein. *Time*, 51–60.

Rivera-Gaxiola, M., Klarman, L., Garcia-Sierra, A., & Kuhl, P. K. (2005). Neural patterns to speech and vocabulary growth in American infants. *Neuroreport: For Rapid Communication of Neuroscience Research, 16*, 495–498.

Rizley, R. C., & Rescorla, R. A. (1972). Associations in higher order conditioning and sensory pre-conditioning. *Journal of Comparative and Physiological Psychology, 81*, 1–11.

Rizza, M. G., & Morrison, W. F. (2003). Uncovering stereotypes and identifying characteristics of gifted students and students with emotional/behavioral disabilities. *Roeper Review, 25*, 73–77.

Robert-McComb, J. J. (2001). Physiology of stress. In J. J. Robert-McComb (Ed.), *Eating disorders in women and children: Prevention, stress management, and treatment*, pp. 119–146. Boca Raton, FL: CRC Press.

Roberts, M. E., Moore, S. D., & Beckham, J. C. (2007). Post-traumatic stress disorder and substance use disorders. In M. Al'bsi *Stress and Addiction: Biological and Psychological Mechanisms*. San Diego, CA: Elsevier Academic Press.

Roberts, S. M. (1995). Applicability of the goodness-of-fit hypothesis to coping with daily hassles. *Psychological Reports, 77*, 943–954.

Robins, R. W. (2005, October 7). The nature of personality: Genes, culture, and national character. *Science, 310*, 62–63.

Robinson, D. N. (2007). Theoretical psychology: What is it and who needs it? *Theory & Psychology, 17*, 187–198.

Robinson, D. S. (2007). Antidepressant drugs: Early onset of therapeutic effect. *Primary Psychiatry, 14*, 23–24.

Robinson, N. M. (2003). Two wrongs do not make a right: Sacrificing the needs of gifted students does not solve society's unsolved problems. *Journal for the Education of the Gifted, 26*, 251–273.

Rock, A. (1999, January). Quitting time for smokers. *Money*, pp. 139–141.

Rodd, Z. A., Bell, R. L., Sable, H. J. K., Murphy, J. M., & McBride, W. J. (2004). Recent advances in animal models of alcohol craving and relapse. *Pharmacology, Biochemistry and Behavior, 79*, 439–450.

Roediger, H. (1990). Implicit memory: Retention without remembering. *American Psychologist, 45*, 1043–1056.

Roediger, H. L, III, & McCabe, D. P. (2007). Evaluating Experimental Research: Critical Issues. In R. J. Sternberg, H. L. Roediger, III, & D. F. Halpern, *Critical thinking in psychology*. New York: Cambridge University Press.

Roediger, H. L., III, & McDermott, K. B. (2000). Tricks of memory. *Current Directions in Psychological Science, 9*, 123–127.

Roediger, H. L., & McDermott, K. B. (1995). Creating false memories: Remembering words not presented in lists. *Journal of Experimental Psychology: Learning, Memory, and Cognition, 21*, 803–814.

Roehricht, F., & Priebe, S. (2002). Do cenesthesias and body image aberration characterize a subgroup in schizophrenia? *Acta Psychiatrica Scandinavica, 105*, 276–282.

Roesch, S. C., Adams, L., Hines, A., Palmores, A., Vyas, P., Tran, C., Pekin, S., & Vaughn, A. A. (2005). Coping with prostate cancer: A meta-analytic review. *Journal of Behavioral Medicine, 28*, 281–293.

Rogers, C. R. (1951). *Client-centered therapy*. Boston: Houghton-Mifflin.

Rogers, C. R. (1971). A theory of personality. In S. Maddi (Ed.), *Perspectives on personality*. Boston: Little, Brown.

Rogers, C. R. (1995). *A way of being*. Boston: Houghton Mifflin.

Rogers, M. (1988, February 15). The return of 3-D movies—on TV. *Newsweek*, pp. 60–62.

Rogers, M. B., Loewenthal, K. M., Lewis, C. A., Amlot, R., Cinnirella, M., & Humayan, A. (2007). The role of religious fundamentalism in terrorist violence: A social psychological analysis. *International Review of Psychiatry, 19*, 253–262.

Rogers, P. (2002, August 2). Too much, too soon. *People*, pp. 79–82.

Rogers, P., & Eftimiades, M. (1995, July 24). Bearing witness. *People Weekly*, pp. 42–43.

Rogers, S. (2007). The underlying mechanisms of semantic memory loss in Alzheimer's disease and semantic dementia. *Dissertation Abstracts International: Section B: The Sciences and Engineering, 67(10-B)*, 5591.

Rogler, L. H. (1999). Methodological sources of cultural insensitivity in mental health research. *American Psychologist, 54*, 424–433.

Rohan, K. J., Roecklein, K. A., & Tierney Lindsey, K. (2007). A randomized controlled trial of cognitive-behavioral therapy, light therapy, and their combination for seasonal affective disorder. *Journal of Consulting and Clinical Psychology, 75*, 489–500.

Rohm, W. G. (2003). Test-tube family reunion: Louise Brown turns 25. Happy birthday, IVF. *Wired*.

Roid, G., Nellis, L. & McLellan, M. (2003). Assessment with the Leiter International Performance Scale—Revised and the S-BIT. In R.S. McCallum & R. Steve (Eds.), *Handbook of nonverbal assessment*. New York, NY: Kluwer Academic/Plenum Publishers.

Roisman, G. I., Collins, W. A. Sroufe, L. A., & Egeland, B. (2005). Predictors of young adults' representations of and behavior in their current romantic relationship: Prospective tests of the prototype hypothesis. *Attachment and Human Development, 7*, 105–121.

Roizen, N. J., & Patterson, D. (2003). Down's syndrome. *Lancet, 361*, 1281–1289.

Rolland, J. S., & Walsh, F. (1996). Family therapy: Systems approaches to assessment and treatment. In R. E. Hales & S. C. Yudofsky (Eds.),

The American Psychiatric Press synopsis of psychiatry. Washington, DC: American Psychiatric Press.

Rollman, G. B. (2004). *Ethnocultural variations in the experience of pain*. Mahwah, NJ: Lawrence Erlbaum Associates.

Romano, E., Tremblay, R. E, Vitaro, E., Zoccolillo, M., & Pagani, L. (2001.) Prevalence of psychiatric diagnoses and the role of perceived impairment: Findings from an adolescent community sample. *Journal of Child Psychology and Psychiatry and Allied Disciplines, 42*, 451–461.

Romeu, P. F. (2006). Memories of the terrorist attacks of September 11, 2001: A study of the consistency and phenomenal characteristics of flashbulb memories. *The Spanish Journal of Psychology, 9*, 52–60.

Rorschach, H. (1924). *Psychodiagnosis: A diagnostic test based on perception*. New York: Grune & Stratton.

Rosch, E. & Mervis, C. B. (1975). Family resemblances: Studies in the internal structure of categories. *Cognitive-Psychology, 7*, 573–605.

Rose, N., & Blackmore, S. (2002). Horses for courses: Tests of a psychic claimant. *Journal of the Society for Psychical Research, 66*, 29–40.

Rose, S. A., Feldman, J. F., & Jankowski, J. J. (2002). Processing speed in the 1st year of life: A longitudinal study of preterm and full-term infants. *Developmental Psychology, 38*, 895–902.

Rosen, D. (1999, May 10). Dieting disorder: A physician's perspective. *Harvard Mental Health Newsletter*, p. 4.

Rosen, H. (2000). The creative evolution of the theoretical foundations for cognitive therapy. *Journal of Cognitive Psychotherapy, 14, Special issue: Creativity in the context of cognitive therapy*, 123–134.

Rosen, J. (2005, August 28.) The future v. Roberts. *New York Times Magazine*, pp. 24–29, 44, 50–51.

Rosenberg, D., & Bai, M. (1997, October 13). Drinking and dying. *Newsweek*, p. 69.

Rosenberg, L., & Park, S. (2002). Verbal and spatial functions across the menstrual cycle in healthy young women. *Psychoneuroendocrinology, 27*, 834–841.

Rosenbloom, T., & Wolf, Y. (2002). Sensation seeking and detection of risky road signals: A developmental perspective. *Accident Analysis and Prevention, 34*, 569–580.

Rosenhan, D. L. (1973). On being sane in insane places. *Science, 179*, 250–258.

Rosenkranz, M. A., Jackson, D. C., Dalton, K. M., Dokski, I., Ryff, C. D., Singer, B. H., Muller, D., Kalin, N. H., Davidson, R. J. (2003). Affective style and in vivo immune response: Neurobehavioral mechanisms. *Proceedings of the National Academy of Sciences, 100*, 48–52.

Rosenkranz, M. A., Jackson, D. C., Dalton, K. M., Dolski, I., Ryff, C. D., Singer, B. H., Muller, D., Kalin, N. H., & Davidson, R. J. (2003, September 16). Affective style and in vivo immune response: Neurobehavioral mechanisms. *Proceedings of the National Academy of Sciences, USA, 100*, 11148–11152. Retrieved from http://www.pnas.org/cgi/reprint/100/19/11148?maxtoshow=&HITS=10&hits=10&RESULTFORMAT=&fulltext=davids on+2003&searchid=1125413201748_4140&stored_search= &FIRSTINDEX=0&journalcode=pnas.

Rosenman, R. H., Brand, R.J., Sholtz, R.I., & Friedman, M. (1976). Multivariate prediction of coronary heart disease during 8.5 year follow-up in the Western collaborative group

study. *American Journal of Cardiology, 37*, 903–910.

Rosenstein, D. S., & Horowitz, H. A. (1996). Adolescent attachment and psychopathology. *Journal of Consulting and Clinical Psychology, 64*, 244–253.

Rosenthal, A.M. (2008) *Thirty-eight witnesses: The Kitty Genovese case*. Hoboken, NJ: Melville House Publishing.

Rosenthal, E. (2005, June 3). For fruit flies, gene shift tilts sex orientation. *International Herald Tribune*, p. C1.

Rosenthal, J. (1997, March 9). The age boom. *The New York Times Magazine*, pp. 39–43.

Rosenthal, R. (2002). Covert communication in classrooms, clinics, courtrooms and cubicles. *American Psychologist, 57*, 838–849.

Rosenthal, R. (2003). Covert communication in laboratories, classrooms, and the truly real world. *Current Directions in Psychological Science, 12*, 151–154.

Rosner, H. (2001, April 30). The science of O. *New York Magazine*, pp. 25–31.

Ross, H. E. (2000). Sensation and perception. In D. S. Gupta, S. Deepa, & R. M. Gupta, et al. (Eds.), *Psychology for psychiatrists* (pp. 20–40). London: Whurr Publishers.

Ross, H. E., & Plug, C. (2002). *The mystery of the moon illusion: Exploring size perception*. Oxford: University Press.

Ross, J. (2006). Sleep on a problem . . . It works like a dream. *The Psychologist, 19*, 738–740.

Ross, L., & Nisbett, R. E. (1991). *The person and the situation*. New York: McGraw-Hill.

Ross, M., & Newby, I. R. (1996). Distinguishing memory from fantasy. *Psychological Inquiry, 7*, 173–177.

Ross, P. (2003, September). Mind readers. *Scientific American*, pp. 74–77.

Ross, P. E. (2004, April). Draining the language out of color. *Scientific American*, pp. 46–51.

Rossell, S. L., Bullmore, E. T., Williams, S. C. R., & David, A. S. (2002). Sex differences in functional brain activation during a lexical visual field task. *Brain and Language, 80*, 97–105.

Rossi, J. J., June, C. H., & Kohn, D. B. (2007). Genetic therapies against HIV. *Natural Biotechnology, 25*, 1444–1454.

Rossier J, Dahourou D., McCrae, R. R. (2005). Structural and mean level analyses of the Five-Factor Model and locus of control: Further evidence from Africa. *Journal of Cross-Cultural Psychology, 36*, 227–246.

Rossouw, J. E., Prentice, R. L., Manson, J. E., Wu, L., Barad, D., Barnabei, V. M., Ko, M., LaCroix, A. Z., Margolis, K. L., & Stefanick, M. L. (2007). Postmenopausal hormone therapy and risk of cardiovascular disease by age and years since menopause. *Journal of the American Medical Association, 297*, 1465–1477.

Rotan, L. W., & Ospina-Kammerer, V. (2007). *Mindbody medicine: Foundations and practical applications*. New York: Routledge/Taylor & Francis Group.

Roter, D. L., Hall, J. A., & Aoki, Y. (2002). Physician gender effects in medical communication: A meta-analytic review. *Journal of the American Medical Association, 288*, 756–764.

Roth, A., & Fonagy, P. (1996). *What works for whom? A critical review of psychotherapy research*. New York: Guilford Press.

Rothblum, E. D. (1990). Women and weight: Fad and fiction. *Journal of Psychology, 124*, 5–24.

Rothman, A. J., & Salovey, P. (1997). Shaping perceptions to motivate healthy behavior: The role of message framing. *Psychological Bulletin, 121*, 3–19.

Roughton, R. E. (2002). Rethinking homosexuality: What it teaches us about psychoanalysis. *Journal of the American Psychoanalytic Association, 50,* 733–763.

Roush, W. (1995, September 1). Can "resetting" hormonal rhythms treat illness? *Science, 269,* 1220–1221.

Routtenberg, A., & Lindy, J. (1965). Effects of the availability of rewarding septal and hypothalamic stimulation on bar pressing for food under conditions of deprivation. *Journal of Comparative and Physiological Psychology, 60,* 158–161.

Rovee-Collier, C. (1993). The capacity for long-term memory in infancy. *Current Directions in Psychological Science, 2,* 130–135.

Rowe, J. B., Toni, I., Josephs, O., Frackowiak, R. S. J., & Passingham, R. E. (2000, June 2). The prefrontal cortex: Response selection or maintenance within working memory? *Science, 288,* 1656–1660.

Rowley, S. J., Sellers, R. M., Chavous, T. M., & Smith, M. A. (1998). The relationship between racial identity and self-esteem in African American college and high school students. *Journal of Personality and Social Psychology, 74,* 715–724.

Roysircar, G. (2005). Culturally sensitive assessment, diagnosis, and guidelines. In M. G. Constantine & D. W. Sue (Eds.), *Strategies for building multicultural competence in mental health and educational settings.* New York: Wiley.

Royzman, E. B., Cassidy, K. W., & Baron, J. (2003). "I know, you know": Epistemic egocentrism in children and adults. *Review of General Psychology, 7,* 38–65.

Rozencwajg, P., Cherfi, M., Ferrandez, A. M., Lautrey, J., Lemoine, C., & Loarer, E. (2005). Age-related differences in the strategies used by middle aged adults to solve a block design task. *International Journal of Aging and Human Development, 60,* 159–182.

Rozin, P. (1990). The importance of social factors in understanding the acquisition of food habits. In E. D. Capaldi & T. L. Powley (Eds.), *Taste, experience, and feeding.* Washington, DC: American Psychological Association.

Rozin, P., Kabnick, K., Pete, E., Fischler, C., & Shields, C. (2003). The ecology of eating: Smaller portion sizes in France than in the United States help explain the French paradox. *Psychological Science, 14,* 450–454.

Rubenstein, C. (1982, July). Psychology's fruit flies. *Psychology Today,* pp. 83–84.

Rubichi, S., Ricci, F., Padovani, R., & Scaglietti, L. (2005). Hypnotic susceptibility, baseline attentional functioning, and the Stroop task. *Consciousness and Cognition: An International Journal, 14,* 296–303.

Rubin, D. C. (1985, September). The subtle deceiver: Recalling our past. *Psychology Today,* pp. 39–46.

Rubin, D. C. (1995). *Memory in oral traditions.* New York: Oxford University Press.

Rubin, D. C. (1999). *Remembering our past: Studies in autobiographical memory.* New York: Cambridge University Press.

Rubin, D. C., Schrauf, R. W., Gulgoz, S., & Naka, M. (2007). Cross-cultural variability of component processes in autobiographical remembering: Japan, Turkey, and the USA. *Memory, 15,* 536–547.

Rubin, B. D., & Katz, L. C. (1999). Optical imaging of odorant representations in the mammalian olfactory bulb. *Neuron 23,* 499–511.

Ruby, C. L. (2002). Are terrorists mentally deranged? *Analyses of Social Issues and Public Policy, 2,* 15–26.

Rudman, L. A. & Ashmore, R. D. (2007). Discrimination and the Implicit Association Test. *Group Processes & Intergroup Relations, 10,* 359–372.

Rudman, L. A., & Glick, P. (2001). Prescriptive gender stereotypes and backlash toward agentic women. *Journal of Social Issues, 57,* 743–762.

Runco, M. A. (2006). Introduction to the special issue: divergent thinking. *Creativity Research Journal, 18,* 249–250.

Runco, M. A., & Sakamoto, S. O. (1993). Reaching creatively gifted students through their learning styles. In R. M. Milgram, R. S. Dunn, & G. E. Price (Eds.), *Teaching and counseling gifted and talented adolescents: An international learning style perspective.* Westport, CT: Praeger/Greenwood.

Rusche, B. (2003) The 3Rs and animal welfare—conflict or the way forward? *ALTEX, 20, (Suppl. 1),* 63–76.

Ruscher, J. B., Fiske, S. T., & Schnake, S. B. (2000). The motivated tactician's juggling act: Compatible vs. incompatible impression goals. *British Journal of Social Psychology, 39,* 241–256.

Rushton, J.P. & Jensen, A.R. (2006). The totality of available evidence shows the race IQ gap still remains. *Psychological Science, 17,* 921–922.

Russell, J. A. (1991). Culture and the categorization of emotion. *Psychological Bulletin, 110,* 426–450.

Russell, J. A., & Sato, K. (1995). Comparing emotion words between languages. *Journal of Cross Cultural Psychology, 26,* 384–391.

Russo, N. (1981). Women in psychology. In L. T. Benjamin, Jr. & K. D. Lowman (Eds.), *Activities handbook for the teaching of psychology.* Washington, DC: American Psychological Association.

Russo, R., & Parkin, A. J. (1993). Age differences in implicit memory: More apparent than real. *Memory & Cognition, 21,* 73–80.

Rustin, M. (2006). Infant observation research: What have we learned so far? *Infant Observation, 9,* 35–52.

Rutter, M. (2002). Nature, nurture, and development: From evangelism through science toward policy and practice. *Child Development, 73,* 1–21.

Rutter, M. (2006). *Genes and behavior: Nature-nurture interplay explained.* Malden, MA: Blackwell Publishing.

Ryan, R. M., & Deci, E. L. (2000). Intrinsic and extrinsic motivations: Classic definitions and new directions. *Contemporary Educational Psychology, 25,* 54–67.

Rychlak, J. (1997). *In defense of human consciousness.* Washington, DC: American Psychological Association.

Ryff, C. D., & Singer, B. (2003).Flourishing under fire: Resilience as a prototype of challenged thriving. In C. L. Keyes & J. Haidt (Eds.), *Flourishing: Positive psychology and the life well-lived,* pp. 15–36. Washington, DC: American Psychological Association.

Rymer, J., Wilson, R., & Ballard, K. (2003). Making decisions about hormone replacement therapy. *British Medical Journal, 326,* 322–326.

Rymer, R. (1994). *Genie: A scientific tragedy.* New York: Penguin.

Saab, C. Y., & Willis, W. D. (2003). The cerebellum: Organization, functions and its role in nociception. *Brain Research Reviews, 42,* 85–95.

Saariluoma, P., Karlsson, H., Lyytinen, H., Teräs, M., & Geisler, F. (2004). Visuospatial representations used by chess experts: A preliminary study. *European Journal of Cognitive Psychology, 16,* 753–766.

Saariluoma, P., & Laine, T. (2001). Novice construction of chess memory. *Scandinavian Journal of Psychology, 42,* 137–146.

Saarni, C. (1999). *Developing emotional competence.* New York: Guilford.

Sabater, J., & Sierra, C. (2005). Review on computational trust and reputation models. *Artificial Intelligence Review, 24,* 33–60.

Sachs-Ericsson, N., Joiner, T., Plant, E. A., & Blazer, D. G. (2005). The influence of depression on cognitive decline in community-dwelling elderly persons. *American Journal of Geriatric Psychiatry, 13,* 402–408.

Sackeim, H. A., Haskett, R. F., Mulsant, B. H., Thase, M. E., Mann, J. J., Pettinati, H. M., Greenberg, R. M., Crowe, R. R., Cooper, T. B., & Prudic, J. (2001). Continuation pharmacotherapy in the prevention of relapse following electroconvulsive therapy: A randomized controlled trial. *Journal of the American Medical Association, 285,* 1299–1307.

Sackeim, H. A., Luber, B., Katzman, G. P., et al. (1996, September). The effects of electroconvulsive therapy on quantitative electroencephalograms. *Archives of General Psychiatry, 53,* 814–824.

Sacks, O. (2003, July 28). The mind's eye. *The New Yorker,* pp. 48–59.

Saczynski, J., Willis, S., and Schaie, K. (2002). Strategy use in reasoning training with older adults. *Aging, Neuropsychology, & Cognition, 9,* 48–60.

Sadker, M., & Sadker, D. (1994). *Failing at fairness: How America's schools cheat girls.* New York: Scribners.

Saffran, E. M., & Schwartz, M. F. (2003). Language. In M. Gallagher & R. J. Nelson (Eds.), *Handbook of psychology: Biological psychology* (Vol. 3, pp. 595–636). New York: Wiley.

Saggino, A., Perfetti, B., & Spitoni, G. (2006). Fluid intelligence and executive functions: New perspectives. In L. V. Wesley, *Intelligence: New research.* Hauppauge, NY: Nova Science Publishers.

Sagi, A., Koren-Karie, N., Gini, M., Ziv, Y., & Joels, T. (2002). Shedding further light on the effects of various types and quality of early child care on infant-mother attachment relationship: The Haifa Study of Early Child Care. *Child Development, 73,* 1166–1186.

Sahin, N. T., Pinker, S., & Halgren, E. (2006). Abstract grammatical processing of nouns and verbs in Broca's area: Evidence from fMRI. *Cortex, 42,* 540–562.

Sakai, K. L. (2005, November 4). Language acquisition and brain development. *Science, 310,* 815–817.

Saks, M. J., & Koehler, J. J. (2005, August 5). The coming paradigm shift in forensic identification science. *Science, 309,* 892–895.

Salgado, D. M., Quinlin, K. J., & Zlotnick, C. (2007). The relationship of lifetime polysubstance dependence to trauma exposure, symptomatology, and psychosocial functioning in incarcerated women with comorbid PTSD and substance use disorder. *Journal of Trauma Dissociation, 8,* 9–26.

Salmela-Aro, K., & Nurmi, J-E. (2007). Self-esteem during university studies predicts career characteristics 10 years later. *Journal of Vocational Behavior, 70,* 463–477.

Salovey, P., Rothman, A. J., Detweiler, J. B., & Steward, W. T. (2000). Emotional states and physical health. *American Psychologist, 55,* 110–121.

Salsman, N. L. (2006). Interpersonal change as an outcome of Time-Limited Interpersonal Therapy. *Dissertation Abstracts International: Section B: The Sciences and Engineering, 66(9-B),* 5103.

Salthouse, T. A. (1996, July). The processing-speed theory of adult age differences in cognition. *Psychological Review, 103,* 403–428.

Salvy, S. J., Mulick, J. A., & Butter, E. (2004). Contingent electric shock (SIBIS) and a conditioned punisher eliminate severe head banging in a preschool child. *Behavioral Interventions, 19,* 59–72.

Samantaray, S. K., Srivastava, M., & Mishra, P. K. (2002). Fostering self concept and self actualization as bases for empowering women in national development: A challenge for the new millennium. *Social Science International, 18,* 58–63.

Samoilov, V., & Zayas, V. (2007). Ivan Petrovich Pavlov (1849–1936). *Journal of the History of the Neurosciences, 16,* 74–89.

Sampson, S. M., Solvason, H., B., Husain, M. M. (2007). Envisioning transcranial magnetic stimulation (TMS) as a clinical treatment option for depression. *Psychiatric Annals, 37, Special issue: Neuromodulation: Patients with depression may benefit from treatment with vagus nerve and transcranial magnetic stimulation,* 189–196.

Sams, M. Hari, R., Rif, J., & Knuutila, J. (1993). The human auditory memory trace persists about 10 sec: Neuromagnetic evidence. *Journal of Cognitive Neuroscience, 5,* 363–370.

Samuda, R. J. (1998). *Psychological testing of American minorities: Issues and consequences* Thousand Oaks, CA: Sage.

Samuda, R. J., & Lewis, J. E. (1999). Multicultural assessment for the twenty-first century. In W. J. Lonner & D. L. Dinnel (Eds.), *Merging past, present, and future in cross-cultural psychology: Selected papers from the Fourteenth International Congress of the International Association for Cross-Cultural Psychology* (pp. 137–145). Lisse, Netherlands: Swets & Zeitlinger.

Samuel, D. B., & Widiger, T. A. (2006). Differentiating normal and abnormal personality from the perspective of the DSM. In S. Strack, *Differentiating normal and abnormal personality* (2nd ed.). New York: Springer Publishing.

Sanderson, M. (2007). Assessment of manic symptoms in different cultures. *British Journal of Psychiatry, 190,* 178.

Sandomir, R. (2007, July 17). W. W. E.'s testing is examined after Bennoit murder-suicide. *The New York Times,* p. S3.

Sandoval, J., Frisby, C. L., Geisinger, K. F., Scheuneman, J. D., & Grenier, J. R. (Eds.). (1998). *Test interpretation and diversity: Achieving equity in assessment.* Washington, DC: American Psychological Association.

Sanfey, A. G. Loewenstein, G., & McClure, S. M. (2006)/Neuroeconomics: Cross-currents in research on decision-making. *Trends in Cognitive Sciences, Vol. 10,* Mar 2006. pp. 108–116.

Sansone, C., & Harackiewicz, J. M. (Eds.). (2000). *Intrinsic and extrinsic motivation.* Orlando, FL: Academic Press.

Santel, S., Baving, L., Krauel, K., Munte, T.F. & Rotte, M. (2006). Hunger and satiety in anorexia nervosa: fMRI during cognitive processing of food pictures. *Brain Research, 1114,* 138–148

Sanz, C. (2000). Implementing LIBRA for the design of experimental research in SLA. *Language Learning and Technology* Millennial issue *13,* 27–31.

Saper, C. B., Lu, J., Chou, T. C., & Gooley, J. (2005). The hypothalamic integrator for circadian rhythms. *Trends in Neuroscience, 28,* 152–157.

Sapolsky, R. M. (2003). Gene therapy for psychiatric disorders. *American Journal of Psychiatry, 160,* 208–220.

Sargent, J. D., Stoolmiller, M., Worth, K. A., Cal, C. S., Wills, T. A., Gibbons, F. X., Gerrard, M., & Tanski, S. (2007). Exposure to smoking depictions in movies: Its association with established adolescent smoking. *Archives of Pediatric Adolescent Medicine, 161,* 849–856.

Satel, S. (2006). Is caffeine addictive?—A review of the literature. *American Journal of Drug and Alcohol Abuse, 32,* 493–502.

Sato, N., Shimamura, M., & Takeuchi, D. (2007). Gene therapy for ischemic brain disease with special reference to vascular dementia. *Geriatrics & Gerontology International, 7,* 1–14.

Saucier, D. A., & Cain, M. E. (2006). The foundations of attitudes about animal research. *Ethics & Behavior, 16,* 117–133.

Saudino, K. J., & Plomin, R. (1996). Personality and behavioral genetics: Where have we been and where are we going? *Journal of Research in Personality, 30,* 335–347.

Savage-Rumbaugh, E. S., Murphy, J., Sevcik, R. A., Williams, S., Brakke, K., & Rumbaugh, D. M. (1993). Language comprehension in ape and child. *Monographs of the Society for Research in Child Development, 58(3, 4).*

Savage-Rumbaugh, E.S., Shanker, S.G., & Talbot, J.T. (1998). *Apes, language, and the human mind.* London: Oxford University Press.

Savage-Rumbaugh, E. S., Toth, N., & Schick, K. (2007). Kanzi learns to knap stone tools. In D. A. Washburn, *Primate perspectives on behavior and cognition.* Washington, DC: American Psychological Association.

Savage-Rumbaugh, S., & Brakke, K. E. (1996). Animal language: Methodological and interpretive issues. In M. Bekoff & D. Jamieson (Eds.), *Readings in animal cognition.* Cambridge, MA: MIT.

Savas, H. A., Yumru, M., & Kaya, M. C. (2007). Atypical antipsychotics as 'mood stabilizers': A retrospective chart review. *Progress in Neuro-Psychopharmacology & Biological Psychiatry, 31,* 1064–1067.

Savazzi, S., Fabri, M., Rubboli, G., Paggi, A., Tassinari, C. A., Marzi, C. A. (2007). Interhemispheric transfer following callosotomy in humans: Role of the superior colliculus, *Neuropsychologia, 45,* 2417–2427.

Sawa, A., & Snyder, S. H. (2002, April 26). Schizophrenia: Diverse approaches to a complex disease. *Science, 296,* 692–695.

Saxe, R., Carey, S., & Kanwisher, N. (2004). Understanding other minds: A linking developmental psychology and functional neuroimaging. *Annual Review of Psychology, 55,* 87–124.

Sayette, M. A. (1993). An appraisal disruption model of alcohol's effects on stress responses in social drinkers. *Psychological Bulletin, 114,* 459–476.

Saywitz, K., & Goodman, G. (1990). Unpublished study reported in Goleman, D. (1990, November 6). Doubts rise on children as witnesses. *The New York Times,* pp. C 1, C 6.

Scarr, S. (1993). Genes, experience, and development. In D. Magnusson, P. Jules, & M. Casaer (Eds.), *Longitudinal research on individ-*

ual development: Present status and future perspectives. European network on longitudinal studies on individual development, 8. Cambridge, England: Cambridge University Press.

Scarr, S. (1998). American child care today. *American Psychologist, 53,* 95–108.

Scarr, S., & Weinberg, R. A. (1976). I.Q. test performance of black children adopted by white families. *American Psychologist, 31,* 726–739.

Scaturo, D. J. (2004). Fundamental clinical dilemmas in contemporary group psychotherapy. *Group Analysis, 37,* 201–217.

Scelfo, J. (2007, February 26). Men & depression: Facing darkness. *Newsweek,* p. 43–50.

Schaaf, J. M., Alexander, K. W., Goodman, G. S., Ghetti, S., Edelstein, R. S., & Castelli, P. (2002). Children's eyewitness memory: True disclosures and false reports. In B. L. Bottoms, M. Bull Kovera, et al. (Eds.), *Children, social science, and the law* (pp. 342–377). New York: Cambridge University Press.

Schab, F. R., & Crowder, R. G. (Eds.). (1995). *Memory for odors.* Mahwah, NJ: Erlbaum.

Schachter, S., & Singer, J. E. (1962). Cognitive, social, and physiological determinants of emotional state. *Psychological Review, 69,* 379–399.

Schacter, D. L., & Badgaiyan, R. D. (2001). Neuroimaging of priming: New perspectives on implicit and explicit memory. *Current Directions in Psychological Science, 10,* 1–4.

Schacter, D. L., Dobbins, I. G., & Schnyer, D. M. (2004). Specificity of priming: A cognitive neuroscience perspective. *Nature Reviews Neuroscience, 5,* 853–862.

Schacter, D. L. & Scarry, E. (Eds.) (2000). *Memory, brain, and belief.* Cambridge, MA: Harvard University Press.

Schacter, D. L., Wagner, A. D., & Buckner, R. L. (2000). Memory systems of 1999. In E. Tulving, F. I. Craik, I. M. Fergus, et al. (Eds.), *The Oxford handbook of memory.* New York: Oxford University Press.

Schaefer, R. T. (2000). *Sociology: A brief introduction* (3rd ed.). Boston: McGraw-Hill.

Schaer, M., & Eliez, S. (2007). From genes to brain: Understanding brain development in neurogenetic disorders using neuroimaging techniques. *Child and Adolescent Psychiatric Clinics of North America, 16,* 557–579.

Schafer, M., & Crichlow, S. (1996). Antecedents of groupthink: A quantitative study. *Journal of Conflict Resolution, 40,* 415–435.

Schaie, K. W. (1991). Developmental designs revisited. In S. H. Cohen & H. W. Reese (Eds.), *Life-span developmental psychology: Methodological innovations.* Hillsdale, NJ: Erlbaum.

Schaie, K. W. (1994). The course of adult intellectual development. *American Psychologist, 49,* 304–313.

Schaie, K. W. (1996). Intellectual development in adulthood. In J. E. Birren & K. W. Schaie (Eds.), *Handbook of the psychology of aging* (4th ed., pp. 266–286). San Diego, CA: Academic Press.

Schaie, K. W. (2005) *Developmental influences on adult intelligence: The Seattle Longitudinal Study.* New York: Oxford University Press.

Schaller, M., & Crandall, C. S. (Eds.) (2004). *The psychological foundations of culture.* Mahwah, NJ: Lawrence Erlbaum Associates.

Schaller, M., Asp, C. H., Rosell, M. C., & Heim, S. J. (1996). Training in statistical reasoning inhibits the formation of erroneous group stereotypes. *Personality and Social Psychology Bulletin, 22,* 829–844.

Schapira, A. H. V. (1999). Clinical review: Parkinson's disease. *British Medical Journal, 318,* 311–314.

Schechter, T., Finkelstein, Y., Koren, G. (2005). Pregnant "DES daughters" and their offspring. *Canadian Family Physician, 51,* 493–494.

Schedlowski, M., & Tewes, U. (Eds.) (1999). *Psychoneuroimmunology: An interdisciplinary introduction* New York: Plenum.

Scheele, B., & DuBois, F. (2006). Catharsis as a moral form of entertainment. In J. Bryant, & P. Vorderer, *Psychology of entertainment.* Mahwah, NJ: Lawrence Erlbaum Associates Publishers.

Scheff, T. J. 1984. *Being mentally ill: A sociological theory* (3rd ed.). Hawthorne, NY: Aldine de Gruyter.

Scheier, M. F., Carver, C. S., & Bridges, M. W. (1994). Distinguishing optimism from neuroticism (and trait anxiety, self-mastery, and self-esteem): A revision of the Life Orientation Test. *Journal of Personality and Social Psychology, 67,* 1063–1078.

Schepers, P., & van den berg, P. T. (2007). Social factors of work-environment creativity. *Journal of Business and Psychology, 21,* 407–428.

Schieber, F. (2006). Vision and aging. In J. E. Birren, & K. W. Schaire, *Handbook of the psychology of aging* (6th ed.). Amsterdam, Netherlands: Elsevier.

Schiff, N. D., Giacino, J. T., Kalmar, K., Victor, J. D., Baker, K., Gerber, M., Fritz, B., Eisenberg, B., O'Connor, J., Kobylarz, E. J., Farris, S., Machado, A., McCagg, C., Plum, F., Fins, J. J., & Resai, A. R. (2007, August 2). Behavioral improvements with thalamic stimulation after severe traumatic brain injury. *Nature, 448,* 600–603.

Schiffer, A. A., Pedersen, S. S., Widdershoven, J. W., Hendriks, E. H., Winter, J. B., & Denollet, J. (2005). The distressed (type D) personality is independently associated with impaired health status and increased depressive symptoms in chronic heart failure. *European Journal of Cardiovascular Prevention and Rehabilitation, 12,* 341–346.

Schiffman, S. S., Graham, B. G., Sattely-Miller, E. A., & Zervakis, J. (2002). Taste, smell and neuropsychological performance of individuals at familial risk for Alzheimer's disease. *Neurobiology of Aging, 23,* 397–404.

Schillinger, D., Bindman, A., Wang, F., Stewart, A., & Piette, J. (2004). Functional health literacy and the quality of physician-patient communication among diabetes patients. *Patient Education and Counseling, 52,* 315–323.

Schmidt, J. P. (2006). The Discovery of neuro–transmitters: A fascinating story and a scientific object lesson. *PsycCRITIQUES, 61,* 101–115.

Schmidt, N. B., Kotov, R., & Joiner, T. E., Jr. (2004). *Taxometrics: Toward a new diagnostic scheme for psychopathology.* Washington, DC: American Psychological Association.

Schmitt, D. P., Allik, J., & Mccrae, R. R. (2007). The geographic distribution of big five personality traits: patterns and profiles of human self-description across 56 nations. *Journal of Cross-Cultural Psychology, 38,* 173–212.

Schnatz, P. F., Murphy, J. L., O'Sullivan, D. M., & Sorosky, J. I. (2007). Patient choice: comparing criteria for selecting an obstetrician-gynecologist based on image, gender, and professional attributes. *American Journal of Obstetrics and Gynecology, 197,* 548–561.

Schneider, D. J. (2003). *The psychology of stereotyping.* New York: Guilford Press.

Schnell, K., & Herpertz, S. C. (2007). Effects of dialectic-behavioral-therapy on the neural correlates of affective hyperarousal in borderline personality disorder. *Journal of Psychiatric Research, 41,* 837–847.

Schnurr, P. P., & Cozza, S. J. (Eds.). (2004). *Iraq war clinician guide* (2nd ed.). Washington, DC: National Center for Post-Traumatic Stress Disorder.

Schoen, L. M. (1996). Mnemopoly: Board games and mnemonics. *Teaching of Psychology, 23,* 30–32.

Schoenpflug, U. (2003). The handbook of culture and psychology. *Journal of Cross-Cultural Psychology, 34,* 481–483.

Schofield, A. T. & Vaughan-Jackson, P. (1914) *What a boy should know; Cassell* London (2nd edn) In J. Harvey, A. Wenzel. & S. Sprecher (Eds.), *The handbook of sexuality in close relationships* (385–409). Mahwah, NJ: Lawrence Erlbaum Associates, Inc.

Schofield, W., & Vaughan-Jackson, P. (1913). *What a boy should know.* New York: Cassell.

Schorr, A. (2001). Appraisal: The evolution of an idea. In K. R. Scherer, A. Schorr, et al. (Eds.), *Appraisal processes in emotion: Theory, methods, research. Series in affective science* (pp. 20–34). London: Oxford University Press.

Schredl, M., Barthold, C., & Zimmer, J. (2006). Dream recall and nightmare frequency: A family study. *Perceptual and Motor Skills, 102,* 878–880.

Schredl, M., & Piel, E. (2005). Gender differences in dreaming: Are they stable over time? *Personality and Individual Differences, 39,* 309–316.

Schretlen, D., Pearlson, G. D., Anthony, J. C., Aylward, E. H., Augustine, A. M., Davis, A., & Barta, P. (2000). Elucidating the contributions of processing speed, executive ability, and frontal lobe volume to normal age-related differences in fluid intelligence. *Journal of the International Neuropsychological Society, 6,* 52–61.

Schulte-Ruther, M., Markowitsch, J. J., Fink, G. R., & Piefke, M. (2007). Mirror neuron and theory of mind mechanisms involved in face-to-face interactions: A functional magnetic resonance imaging approach to empathy. *Journal of Cognitive Neuroscience, 19,* 1354–1372.

Schupp, H. T., Öhman, A., Junghöfer, M., Weike, A., Stockburger, J., & Hamm, A. O. (2004). The facilitated processing of threatening faces: An ERP analysis. *Emotion, 4,* 189–200.

Schutt, R. K. (2001). *Investigating the social world: The process and practice of research.* Thousand Oaks, CA: Sage.

Schwartz, B. L. (2001). The relation of tip-of-the-tongue states and retrieval time. *Memory & Cognition, 29,* 117–126.

Schwartz, B. L. (2002). The phenomenology of naturally-occurring tip-of-the-tongue states: A diary study. In S. P. Shohov (Ed.), *Advances in psychology research* (Vol. 8, pp. 73–84). Huntington, NY: Nova.

Schwartz, B. L., Travis, D. M., Castro, A. M., & Smith, S. M. (2000). The phenomenology of real and illusory tip-of-the-tongue states. *Memory & Cognition, 28,* 18–27.

Schwartz, J., & Wald, M. L. (2003). NASA's curse?: "Groupthink" is 30 years old, and still going strong. *The New York Times,* p. C1.

Schwartz, J. M., & Begley, S. (2002). *The mind and the brain: Neuroplasticity and the power of mental force.* (2002). New York: Regan Books/ Harper Collins.

Schwartz, S., & Maquet, P. (2002). Sleep imaging and the neuro-psychological assessment of dreams. *Trends in Cognitive Science, 6,* 23–30.

Schwarz, N., Bless, H., Strack, F., Klumpp, G., et al. (1991). Ease of retrieval as information: Another look at the availability heuristic. *Journal of Personality and Social Psychology, 61,* 195–202.

Schworm, P. (2006, November 12). For students, it's hip to do squares. *The Boston Globe,* p. Reg 1.

Scullin, M. H., Kanaya, T., & Ceci, S. J. (2002). Measurement of individual differences in children's suggestibility across situations. *Journal of Experimental Psychology: Applied, 8,* 233–246.

Seamon, M. J., Fass, J. A., Maniscalco-Feichtl, M., & Abu-Shraie, N. A. (2007). Medical marijuana and the developing role of the pharmacist. *American Journal of Health System Pharmacy, 64,* 1037–1044.

Sears, D. O. (1986). College sophomores in the laboratory: Influences of a narrow data base on social psychology's view of human nature. *Journal of Personality and Social Psychology, 51,* 515–530.

Sears, R. R. (1977). Sources of life satisfaction of the Terman gifted men. *American Psychologist, 32,* 119–128.

Sebel, P. S., Bonke, B., & Winograd, E. (Eds.). (1993). *Memory and awareness in anesthesia.* Englewood Cliffs, NJ: Prentice-Hall.

Seeley, R., Stephens, T., & Tate, P. (2000). *Anatomy & Physiology* (5th ed., p. 384). Boston: McGraw-Hill.

Sefcek, J. A., Brumbach, B. H., & Vasquez, G. (2007). The evolutionary psychology of human mate choice: How ecology, genes, fertility, and fashion influence mating strategies. *Journal of Psychology & Human Sexuality, 18,* 125–182.

Segal, D. (2006, March 22). A trip down memory lane. *Washington Post,* p. C01.

Segal, N. L. (1993). Twin, sibling, and adoption methods: Tests of evolutionary hypotheses. *American Psychologist, 48,* 943–956.

Segall, M. H., Campbell, D. T., & Herskovits, M. J. (1966). *The influence of culture on visual perception.* New York: Bobbs-Merrill.

Segerstrom, S. C., & Miller, G. E. (2004). Psychological stress and the human immune system: A meta-analytic study of 30 years of inquiry. *Psychological Bulletin, 130,* 601–630.

Seibt, B., & Förster, J. (2005) Stereotype threat and performance: How self-stereotypes influence processing by inducing regulatory foci. *Journal of Personality and Social Psychology, 87,* 38–56.

Seidenberg, M. S., & Petitto, L. A. (1987). Communication, symbolic communication, and language: Comment on Savage-Rumbaugh, McDonald, Sevcik, Hopkins, & Rupert (1986). *Journal of Experimental Psychology: General, 116,* 279–287.

Seli, H. (2007). 'Self' in self-worth protection: The relationship of possible selves to achievement motives and self-worth protective strategies. *Dissertation Abstracts International Section A: Humanities and Social Sciences, 67(9-A),* 3302.

Seligman, M. E. (2007). *What you can change...and what you can't: The complete guide to successful self-improvement.* New York: Vintage.

Seligman, M. E. P. (1975). *Helplessness: On depression, development, and death.* San Francisco: Freeman.

Seligman, M. E. P. (1988, October). Baby boomer blues. *Psychology Today,* p. 54.

Seligman, M. E. P. (1995, December). The effectiveness of psychotherapy: The *Consumer Reports* study. *American Psychologist, 50,* 965–974.

Seligman, M. E. P. (1996, October). Science as an ally of practice. *American Psychologist, 51,* 1072–1079.

Selikowitz, M. (2003). Down syndrome across the lifespan. *Journal of Intellectual and Developmental Disability, 28,* 312–313.

Selkoe, D. J. (1997, January 31). Alzheimer's disease: Genotypes, phenotype, and treatments. *Science, 275,* 630–631.

Selkoe, D. J. (2002). Alzheimer's disease is a synaptic failure. *Science, 298,* 789–791.

Sellbom, M., & Ben-Porath, Y. S. (2006). The Minnesota Multiphasic Personality Inventory-2. In R. P. Archer, *Forensic uses of clinical assessment instruments.* Mahwah, NJ: Lawrence Erlbaum Associates.

Sells, R. (1994, August). *Homosexuality study.* Paper presented at the annual meeting of the American Statistical Association, Toronto.

Selove, R. (2007). The glass is half full: Current knowledge about pediatric cancer and sickle cell anemia. *PsycCRITIQUES, 52,* 88–99.

Selsky, A. (1997, February 16). African males face circumcision rite. *The Boston Globe,* p. C7.

Seltzer, L. (1986). *Paradoxical strategies in psychotherapy.* New York: Wiley.

Selye, H. (1976). *The stress of life.* New York: McGraw-Hill.

Selye, H. (1993). History of the stress concept. In L. Goldberger & S. Breznitz (Eds.), *Handbook of stress: Theoretical and clinical aspects* (2nd ed.). New York: Free Press.

Semler, C. N., & Harvey, A. G. (2005). Misperception of sleep can adversely affect daytime functioning in insomnia. *Behaviour Research and Therapy, 43,* 843–856.

Semykina, A., & Linz, S. J. (2007). Gender differences in personality and earnings: Evidence from Russia. *Journal of Economic Psychology, 28,* 387–410.

Sen, B., Sinha, S., Ahmed, S., Ghosh, S. Gangopadhyay, P. K., & Usha, R. (2007). Lack of association of HOXA1 and HOXB1 variants with autism in the Indian population. *Psychiatric Genetics, 17,* 22–36.

Seroczynski, A. D., Jacquez, F. M., & Cole, D. A. (2003). Depression and suicide during adolescence. In G. R. Adams, M. D. Berzonsky (Eds.), *Blackwell handbook of adolescence.* Malden, MA: Blackwell Publishers.

Serok, S. (2000). *Innovative applications of gestalt therapy.* New York: Krieger.

Serpell, R. (2000). Intelligence and culture. In R. Sternberg (Ed.), *Handbook of intelligence.* Cambridge, England: Cambridge University Press.

Seventh U.S. Circuit Court of Appeals. (2001). *Chicago Firefighters Local 2, et al. v. City of Chicago, et al.* Nos. 00–1272, 00–1312, 00–1313, 00–1314, and 00–1330. Chicago, IL.

Seyfarth, R. M., & Cheney, D. L. (1992, December). Meaning and mind in monkeys (vocalizations and intent). *Scientific American, 267,* pp. 122–128.

Seyfarth, R., & Cheney, D. (1996). Inside the mind of a monkey. In M. Bekoff & D. Jamieson (Eds.), *Readings in animal cognition.* Cambridge, MA: MIT.

Seymour, B. (2006). Carry on eating: neural pathways mediating conditioned potentiation of feeding. *Journal of Neuroscience, 26,* 1061–1062.

Shadish, W. R., Cook, T. D., & Campbell, D. T. (2002). *Experimental and quasi-experimental designs for generalized causal inference.* Boston: Houghton Mifflin.

Shafer, V. L. & Garrido-Nag, K. (2007). The neurodevelopmental bases of language. In E. Hoff & M. Shatz, *Blackwell handbook of language development.* Malden, MA: Blackwell Publishing 21–45.

Shaikholeslami, R., & Khayyer, M. (2006). Intrinsic motivation, extrinsic motivation, and learning English as a foreign language. *Psychological Reports, 99,* 813–818.

Shapiro, A. P. (1996). *Hypertension and stress: A unified concept.* Mahwah, NJ: Erlbaum.

Shapiro, L. R. (2006). Remembering September 11th: The role of retention interval and rehearsal on flashbulb and event memory. *Memory, 14,* 129–147.

Shapiro, Y., & Gabbard, G. O. (1994). A reconsideration of altruism from an evolutionary and psychodynamic perspective. *Ethics & Behavior, 4,* 23–42.

Shappell, S., & Wiegmann, D. A. (2003). *A human error approach to aviation accident analysis: The human factors analysis and classification system.* Aldershot, England: Ashgate.

Sharma, H. S., Sjoquist, P. O., & Ali, S. F. (2007). Drugs of abuse-induced hyperthermia, blood-brain barrier dysfunction and neurotoxicity: neuroprotective effects of a new antioxidant compound h-290/51. *Current Pharmaceutical Design, 13,* 1903–1923.

Sharma, J., Angelucci, A., & Sur, M. (2000). Induction of visual orientation modules in auditory cortex. *Nature, 404,* 841–847.

Sharma, S., Ghosh, S. N., & Spielberger, C. D. (1995). Anxiety, anger expression and chronic gastric ulcer. *Psychological Studies, 40,* 187–191.

Shaughnessy, J. J., Zechmeister, E. B., & Zechmeister, J. S. (2000). *Research methods in psychology* (5th ed.). New York: McGraw-Hill.

Shaywitz, B. A., Shaywitz, S. E., Pugh, K. R., Constable, R. T., Skudlarski, P., Fulbright, R. K., Bronen, R. A., Fletcher, J. M., Shankweiler, D. P., Katz, L., & Gore, J. C. (1995, February 16). Sex differences in the functional organization of the brain for language. *Nature, 373,* 607–609.

Shelton, R. C., Keller, M. B., Gelenberg, A., Dunner, D. L., Hirschfeld, R. M. A., Thase, M. E., Russell, J., Lydiard, R. B., Crits-Cristoph, P., Gallop, R., Todd, L., Hellerstein, D., Goodnick, P., Keitner, G., Stahl, S. M., & Halbreich, R. U. (2002). The effectiveness of St. John's wort in major depression: A multicenter, randomized placebo-controlled trial. *Journal of the American Medical Association, 285,* 1978–1986.

Shepard, R., & Metzler, J. (1971). Mental rotation of three dimensional objects. *Science, 171,* 701–703.

Shepard, R. N., Metzler, J., Bisiach, E., Luzzati, C., Kosslyn, S. M., Thompson, W. L., Kim, I., & Alpert, N. M. (2000). Part IV: Imagery. In M. S. Gazzaniga et al. (Eds.), *Cognitive neuroscience: A reader.* Malden, MA: Blackwell.

Sheth, B. R., & Bhattacharya, D. W. (2004). On the neural track of eureka. *Program No. 138.4.* Washington, DC: Society for Neuroscience.

Shi, P., Huang, J. F., & Zhang, Y. P. (2005). Bitter and sweet/umami taste receptors with differently evolutionary pathways. *Yi Chuan Xue Bao, 32,* 346–353.

Shier, D., Butler, J., & Lewis, R. (2000). *Hole's essentials of human anatomy and physiology* (7th ed., p. 283). Boston: McGraw-Hill.

Shiffman, S. (2007). Use of more nicotine lozenges leads to better success in quitting smoking. *Addiction, 102,* 809-814.

Shimono, K., & Wade N. J. (2002). Monocular alignment in different depth planes. *Vision Research, 42,* 1127–1135.

Shinn, M., Gottlieb, J., Wett, J. L., Bahl, A., Cohen, A., & Baron, E. D. (2007). Predictors of homelessness among older adults in New York city: disability, economic, human and social capital and stressful events. *Journal of Health Psychology, 12,* 696–708.

Shnek, Z. M., Foley, F. W., LaRocca, N. G., Smith, C. R., et al. (1995). Psychological predictors of depression in multiple sclerosis. *Journal of Neurologic Rehabilitation, 9,* 15–23.

Shotland, R. L. (1985, June). When bystanders just stand by. *Psychology Today,* pp. 50–55.

Shouler, K. (1992, August). The empire returns. *Sky,* pp. 40–44.

Shriqui, C. L., & Annable, L. (1995). Tardive dyskinesia. In C. L. Shriqui & H. A. Nasrallah (Eds.), *Contemporary issues in the treatment of schizophrenia.* Washington, DC: American Psychiatric Press.

Shuchter, S. R., Downs, N., & Zisook, S. (1996). *Biologically informed psychotherapy for depression.* New York: Guilford Press.

Shulman, J. L., & Horne, S. G. (2006). Guilty or not? A path model of women's sexual force fantasies. *Journal of Sex Research, 43,* 368–377.

Shultz, S. K., Scherman, A., & Marshall, L. J. (2000). Evaluation of a university-based date rape prevention program: Effect on attitudes and behavior related to rape. *Journal of College Student Development, 41,* 193–201.

Shurkin, J. N. (1992). *Terman's kids: The groundbreaking study of how the gifted grow up.* Boston: Little, Brown.

Shweder, R. (2003). *Why do men barbecue? Recipes for cultural psychology.* Cambridge, MA: Harvard University Press.

Shweder, R. A. (1994). "You're not sick, you're just in love": Emotion as an interpretive system. In P. Ekman & R. J. Davidson (Eds.), *The nature of emotion: Fundamental questions.* New York: Oxford.

Shweder, R.A. & Haidt, J. (1994). The future of moral psychology: Truth, intuition, and the pluralist way. In B. Puka (Ed), *Reaching out: Caring, altruism, and prosocial behavior.* New York, NY: Garland Publishing.

Shynkaruk, J. M., & Thompson, V. A. (2006). Confidence and accuracy in deductive reasoning. *Memory & Cognition, 34,* 619–632.

Siddle, R., Haddock, G., Tarrier, N., & Faragher, E. B. (2002). Religious delusions in patients admitted to hospital with schizophrenia. *Social Psychiatry and Psychiatric Epidemiology, 37,* 130–138.

Siderowf, A., & Stern, M. (2003). Update on Parkinson disease. *Annals of Internal Medicine, 138,* 651–658.

Sidman, M. (2006). The distinction between positive and negative reinforcement: Some additional considerations. *Behavior Analyst, 29,* 135–139.

Siegel, J. M. (1990). Stressful life events and use of physician services among the elderly: The moderating role of pet ownership. *Journal of Personality and Social Psychology, 58,* 1081–1086.

Siegel, J. M. (1993). Companion animals: In sickness and in health. *Journal of Social Issues, 49,* 157–167.

Siegel, J. M. (2003, November). Why we sleep. *Scientific American,* pp. 92–97.

Siegert, R. J., & Ward, T. (2002). Clinical psychology and evolutionary psychology: Toward a dialogue. *Review of General Psychology, 6,* 235–259.

Siegler, R. S. (1998). *Children's thinking* (3rd ed.). Upper Saddle River, NJ: Prentice Hall.

Siemer, M., Mauss I., & Gross, J. J. (2007). Same situation—Different emotions: How appraisals shape our emotions. *Emotion, 7,* 592–600.

Sifrit, K. J. (2006). The effects of aging and cognitive decrements on simulated driving performance. *Dissertation Abstracts International: Section B: The Sciences and Engineering, 67*, 2863.

Sigman, M. (1995). Nutrition and child development: More food for thought. *Current Directions in Psychological Science, 4*, 52–55.

Silva, M. T. A., Gonçalves, F. L., & Garcia-Mijares, M. (2007). Neural events in the reinforcement contingency. *Behavior Analyst, 30*, 17–30.

Silverman, J. (2001, August 1). Dating violence against adolescent girls linked with teen pregnancy, suicide attempts, and other health risk behaviors. *Journal of the American Medical Association, 286*, 15–20.

Silverman, K., Evans, S. M., Strain, E. C., & Griffiths, R. R. (1992, October 15). Withdrawal syndrome after the double-blind cessation of caffeine consumption. *New England Journal of Medicine, 327*, 1109–1114.

Silverstein, M. L. (2007). Rorschach test findings at the beginning of treatment and 2 years later, with a 30-year follow-up. *Journal of Personality Assessment, 88*, 131–143.

Simcock, G., & Hayne, H. (2002). Breaking the barrier? Children fail to translate their preverbal memories into language. *Psychological Science, 13*, 225–231.

Simmons, D. C., Kameenui, E. J., & Chard, D. J. (1998). General education teachers' assumptions about learning and students with learning disabilities: Design-of-instruction analysis. *Learning Disability Quarterly, 21*, 6–21.

Simmons, R., & Blyth, D. (1987). *Moving into adolescence.* New York: Aldine de Gruyter.

Simons, W., & Dierick, M. (2005). Transcranial magnetic stimulation as a therapeutic tool in psychiatry. *World Journal of Biological Psychiatry, 6*, 6–25.

Simonton, D. K. (2000a). Archival research. In A. E. Kazdin (Ed.), *Encyclopedia of psychology* (Vol. 1). Washington, DC: American Psychological Association.

Simonton, D. K. (2000b). Creativity: Cognitive, personal, developmental, and social aspects. *American Psychologist, 55*, 151–158.

Simonton, D. K. (2003). Scientific creativity as constrained stochastic behavior: the integration of product, person, and process perspectives. *Psychological Bulletin, 129*, 475–494.

Singer, J. L. (1975). *The inner world of daydreaming.* New York: Harper & Row.

Singer, J. L. (2006). Why imagery, personal memories, and daydreams matter. In J. L. Singer, *Imagery in psychotherapy.* Washington, DC: American Psychological Association.

Singh, S., Wulf, D., Samara, R, & Cuca, Y. P. (2000). Gender differences in the timing of first intercourse: Data from 14 countries. *International Family Planning Perspectives, 26*, 21–28, 43.

Sininger, Y. S., & Cone-Wesson, B. (2004, September 10). Asymmetric cochlear processing mimics hemispheric specialization. *Science, 305*, 1581.

Sininger, Y. S., & Cone-Wesson, B. (2006). Lateral asymmetry in the ABR of neonates: evidence and mechanisms. *Hearing Research, 212*, 203–211.

Sizemore, C. C. (1989). *A mind of my own: The woman who was known as Eve tells the story of her triumph over multiple personality disorder.* New York: Morrow.

Skinner, B. F. (1957). *Verbal behavior.* New York: Appleton-Century-Crofts.

Skinner, B. F. (1975). The steep and thorny road to a science of behavior. *American Psychologist, 30*, 42–49.

Skinner, R., Georgiou, R., & Thornton, P. (2006). Psychoneuroimmunology of stroke. *Neurologic Clinics, 24*, 561–583.

Slater, A. (1996). The organization of visual perception in early infancy. In F. Vital-Durand, J. Atkinson, & O. J. Braddick (Eds.), *Infant vision. The European brain and behaviour society publication series* (Vol. 2). Oxford, England: Oxford University Press.

Slater, E., & Meyer, A. (1959). Contributions to a pathography of the musicians. *Confinia Psychiatrica.* Reprinted in K. R. Jamison, *Touched with fire: Manic-depressive illness and the artistic temperament.* New York: Free Press.

Sledz, M., Oddy, M., & Beaumont, J. G. (2007). Psychological adjustment to locked-in syndrome. *Journal of Neurological Neurosurgery and Psychiatry, 12*, 33–37.

Sleek, S. (1997 June). Can "emotional intelligence" be taught in today's schools? *APA Monitor*, p. 25.

Sloan, E. P., Hauri, P., Bootzin, R., Morin, C., et al. (1993). The nuts and bolts of behavioral therapy for insomnia. *Journal of Psychosomatic Research, 37* (Suppl.), 19–37.

Smart, R. G. (2007). Review of introduction to addictive behaviours. *Addiction, 102*, 831.

Smetana, J. B. (2007). Strategies for understanding archetypes and the collective unconscious of an organization. *Dissertation Abstracts International Section A: Humanities and Social Sciences, 67(12-A)*, 4714.

Smetana, J. G. (2005). Adolescent-parent conflict: Resistance and subversion as developmental process. In L. Nucci (Ed.), *Conflict, contradiction, and contrarian elements in moral development and education.* (pp. 69–91). Mahwah, NJ: Lawrence Erlbaum Associates.

Smetana, J., Daddis, C., and Chuang, S. (2003). "Clean your room!" A longitudinal investigation of adolescent-parent conflict and conflict resolution in middle-class African American families. *Journal of Adolescent Research, 18*, 631–650.

Smith, B. H., Barkley, R. A., & Shapiro, C. J. (2006). Attention-Deficit/Hyperactivity Disorder. In E. J. Mash & R. A. Barkley, *Treatment of childhood disorders* (3rd. ed). New York: Guilford Press.

Smith, C. (2006). Symposium V—Sleep and learning: New developments. *Brain and Cognition, 60, Special issue: Methods and Learning in Functional MRI.* pp. 331–332.

Smith, C. A., & Lazarus, R. S. (2001). Appraisal components, core relational themes, and the emotions. In W. G. Parrott (Ed.), *Emotions in social psychology: Essential readings* (pp. 94–114). Philadelphia: Psychology Press.

Smith, C. D., Chebrolu, J., Wekstein, D. R., Schmitt, F. A., & Markesbery, W. R. (2007). Age and gender effects on human brain anatomy: a voxel-based morphometric study in healthy elderly. *Neurobiology of Aging, 28*, 1057–1087.

Smith, D. (October 2001). Can't get your 40 winks? Here's what the sleep experts advise. *Monitor on Psychology, 37*.

Smith, D. V., & Margolskee, R. F. (March 2001). Making sense of taste. *Scientific American*, pp. 32–39.

Smith, E. (1988, May). Fighting cancerous feelings. *Psychology Today*, pp. 22–23.

Smith, E. E. (2000). Neural bases of human working memory. *Current Directions in Psychological Science, 9*, 45–49.

Smith, E. R., & Semin, G. R. (2007). Situated social cognition. *Current Directions in Psychological Science, 16*, 132–135.

Smith, G. B. (2005, July 17). Secret mob cop tapes: Talk about deaths key to feds's case.

"I've known John (Gotti) since I was a kid, how do I disrespect this guy?" accused cop says. *Daily News* (New York), p. 6.

Smith, J. D. (2006). Speaking of mild mental retardation: It's no box of chocolates, or is it? *Exceptionality, 14*, 191–204.

Smith, K. A., Williams, C., & Cowen, P. J. (2000). Impaired regulation of brain serotonin function during dieting in women recovered from depression. *British Journal of Psychiatry, 176*, 72–75.

Smith, K. R. (2004). Gene therapy: The potential applicability of gene transfer technology to the human germline. *International Journal of Medical Science, 1*, 76–91.

Smith, L. C., Friedman, S., & Paradis, C. (2002). Panic disorder with agoraphobia: Women's issues. In F. Lewis-Hall & T. S. Williams (Eds.), *Psychiatric illness in women: Emerging treatments and research* (pp. 31–55). Washington, DC: American Psychiatric Publishing.

Smith, M., & Lin, K. M. (1996). Gender and ethnic differences in the pharmacogenetics of psychotropics. In M. F. Jensvold, U. Halbreich, & J. A. Hamilton (Eds.), *Psychopharmacology and women: Sex, gender, and hormones.* Washington, DC: American Psychiatric Press.

Smith, M. B. (2003). Moral foundations in research with human participants. In A. E. Kazdin (Ed.), *Methodological issues & strategies in clinical research* (3rd ed.). Washington, DC: American Psychological Association.

Smith, M. L., Glass, G. V., & Miller, T. J. (1980). *The benefits of psychotherapy.* Baltimore: Johns Hopkins University Press.

Smith, M. V. (1996). Linguistic relativity: On hypotheses and confusions. *Communication and Cognition, 29*, 65–90.

Smith, R. A., & Weber, A. L. (2005). Applying social psychology in everyday life. In F. W. Schneider, J. A. Gruman, & L. M. Coutts, *Applied social psychology: Understanding and addressing social and practical.* Thousand Oaks, CA: Sage Publications.

Smith, W. B. (2007). Karen Horney and psychotherapy in the 21st century. *Clinical Social Work Journal, 35*, 57–66.

Snieder, H., Harshfield, G. A., Barbeau, P., Pollock, D. M., Pollock, J. S., & Treiber, F. A. (2002). Dissecting the genetic architecture of the cardiovascular and renal stress response. *Biological Psychology, 61*, 73–95.

Snyder, C. R. (1999). *Coping: The psychology of what works.* New York: Oxford University Press.

Snyder, D. J., Fast, K., & Bartoshuk, L. M. (2004). Valid comparisons of suprathreshold sensations. *Journal of Consciousness Studies, 11*, 96–112.

Snyder, J., Cramer, A., & Afrank, J. (2005). The contributions of ineffective discipline and parental hostile attributions of child misbehavior to the development of conduct problems at home and school. *Developmental Psychology, 41*, 30–41.

Snyder, M. (2002). Applications of Carl Rogers' theory and practice to couple and family therapy: A response to Harlene Anderson and David Bott. *Journal of Family Therapy, 24*, 317–325.

Society for Personality Assessment. (2005). The status of Rorschach in clinical and forensic practice: An official statement by the board of trustees of the Society for Personality Assessment. *Journal of Personality Assessment, 85*, 219–237.

Sohn, D. (1996). Publication bias and the evaluation of psychotherapy efficacy in reviews of the research literature. *Clinical Psychology Review, 16,* 147–156. Sokolove, M. (2003, November 16).

Sokolove, M. (2003, November 16). Should John Hinckley go free? *The New York Times Magazine,* pp. 52–54, 92.

Solms, M. (2005). Neuroscience. In E. S. Person, A. M. Cooper, & G. O. Gabbard, *The American psychiatric publishing textbook of psychoanalysis.* Washington, DC: American Psychiatric Publishing.

Solso, R. L. (1991). *Cognitive psychology* (3rd ed.). Boston: Allyn & Bacon.

Sommer, R., & Sommer, B. (2001). *A practical guide to behavioral research: Tools and techniques* (5th ed.). New York: Oxford University Press.

Sommerhof, G. (2000). *Understanding consciousness: Its function and brain processes.* Thousand Oaks, CA: Sage.

Sorbring, E., Deater-Deckard, K., & Palmerus, K. (2006). Girls' and boys' perception of mothers' intentions of using physical punishment and reasoning as discipline methods. *European Journal of Developmental Psychology, 3,* 142–162.

Sori, C. F. (Ed.). (2006). *Engaging children in family therapy: Creative approaches to integrating theory and research in clinical practice.* New York: Routledge/Taylor & Francis Group.

Soussignan, R. (2002). Duchenne smile, emotional experience, and automatic reactivity: A test of the facial feedback hypothesis. *Emotion, 2,* 52–74.

Souter, E., and Wong, M. (2006, May 15). Exercise almost killed her. *People,* p. 165–170.

Spackman, M. P., Fujiki, M., & Brinton, B. (2006). Understanding emotions in context: The effects of language impairment on children's ability to infer emotional reactions. *International Journal of Language & Communication Disorders, 41,* 173–188.

Spangler, W. D. (1992). Validity of questionnaire and TAT measures of need for achievement: Two meta-analyses. *Psychological Bulletin, 112,* 140–154.

Spanos, N. P., Barner, T. X., & Lang, G. (2005). Cognition and self-control: Cognitive control of painful sensory input. *Integrative Physiological & Behavioral Science, 40,* 119–128.

Spanos, N. P., Burgess, C. A., Roncon, V., Wallace-Capretta, S., et al. (1993). Surreptitiously observed hypnotic responding in simulators and in skill-trained and untrained high hypnotizables. *Journal of Personality and Social Psychology, 65,* 391–398.

Sparks, S. D. (2007, October 2). Foundation: Gifted poor students given short shrift. *Education Daily, 40,* 3.

Spearman, C. (1927). *The abilities of man.* London: Macmillan.

Speirs Neumeister, K. L., & Finch, H. (2006). Perfectionism in high-ability students: Relational precursors and influences on achievement motivation. *Gifted Child Quarterly, 50,* 238–251.

Spence, M. J., & DeCasper, A. J. (1982, March). *Human fetuses perceive maternal speech.* Paper presented at the meeting of the International Conference on Infant Studies, Austin, TX.

Spence-Cochran, K., & Pearl, C. (2006). Moving toward full inclusion. In P. Wehman, *Life beyond the classroom: Transition strategies for young people with disabilities* (4th ed.). Baltimore, MD: Paul H. Brookes Publishing.

Spencer, S. J., Fein, S., Zanna, M. P., & Olson, J. M. (Eds.) (2003). *Motivated social perception: The Ontario Symposium* (Vol. 9). Mahwah, NJ: Erlbaum.

Spencer-Rodgers, J., Peng, K., Wang, L., & Hou, Y. (2004). Dialectical self-esteem and East-West differences in psychological well-being. *Personality and Social Psychology Bulletin, 30,* 1416–1432.

Sperry, R. (1982). Some effects of disconnecting the cerebral hemispheres. *Science, 217,* 1223–1226.

Spielberger, C. D. (2006). Cross-cultural assessment of emotional states and personality traits. *European Psychologist, 11,* 297–303.

Spiegel, D. (1993). Social support: How friends, family, and groups can help. In D. Goleman & J. Gurin (Eds.), *Mind-body medicine.* Yonkers, NY: Consumer Reports Books.

Spiegel, D. (1996). Hypnosis. In R. E. Hales & S. C. Yudofsky (Eds.), *The American Psychiatric Press synopsis of psychiatry.* Washington, DC: American Psychiatric Press.

Spiegel, D. (Ed.). (1999). *Efficacy and cost-effectiveness of psychotherapy.* New York: American Psychiatric Press.

Spiegel, D., & Cardena, E. (1991). Disintegrated experience: The dissociative disorders revisited. *Journal of Abnormal Psychology, 100,* 366–378.

Spiers, H. J., & Maguire, F. A. (2007). Decoding human brain activity during real-world experiences. *Trends in Cognitive Science, 11,* 356–365.

Spiller, L. D., & Wymer, W. W., Jr. (2001). Physicians' perceptions and use of commercial drug information sources: An examination of pharmaceutical marketing to physicians. *Health Marketing Quarterly, 19,* 91–106.

Spillmann, L., & Werner, J. (Eds.). (1990). *Visual perception: The neurophysiological foundations.* San Diego: Academic Press.

Spinella, M., & Lester, D. (2006). Can money buy happiness? *Psychological Reports, 99,* 992.

Spooner, J., Yu, H., Kao, C., Sillay, K., & Konrad, P. (2007). Neuromodulation of the cingulum for neuropathic pain after spinal cord injury. Case report. *Journal of Neurosurgery, 107,* 169–172.

Spira, J. (Ed.). (1997). *Group therapy for medically ill patients.* New York: Guilford Press.

Spitz, H. H. (1987). Problem-solving processes in special populations. In J. G. Borkowski & J. D. Day (Eds.), *Cognition in special children: Comparative approaches to retardation, learning disabilities, and giftedness.* Norwood, NJ: Ablex.

Spitzer, R. L., Skodol, A. E., Gibbon, M., & Williams, J. B. W. (1983).*Psychopathology: A case book.* New York: McGraw-Hill.

Sprecher, S., & Hatfield, E. (1996). Premarital sexual standards among U.S. college students: Comparison with Russian and Japanese students. *Archives of Sexual Behavior, 25,* 261–288.

Sprecher, S., & Regan, P. C. (2002). Liking some things (in some people) more than others: Partner preferences in romantic relationships and friendships. *Journal of Social and Personal Relationships, 19,* 436–481.

Sprender, M. (2007). *Memory 101 for educators.* Thousand Oaks, CA: Corwin Press.

Sprenkle, D. H., & Moon, S. M. (Eds.). (1996). *Research methods in family therapy.* New York: Guilford Press.

Springen, K. (2004, August 9) Anxiety: Sweet and elusive sleep. *Newsweek,* p. 21.

Squire, L. R., Clark, R. E., & Bayley, P. J. (2004). Medial temporal lobe function and memory. In M. S. Gazzaniga (Ed.), *Cognitive neurosciences* (3rd ed., pp. 691–708). Cambridge, MA: MIT.

Srivastava, A., Locke, E. A., & Bartol, K. M. (2001). Money and subjective well-being: It's not the money, it's the motives. *Journal of Personality and Social Psychology, 80,* 959–971.

St. Dennis, C., Hendryx, M., Henriksen, A. I., Setter, S. M., & Singer, B. (2006). Postdischarge treatment costs following closure of a state geropsychiatric ward: Comparison of 2 levels of community care. *Primary Care Companion Journal of Clinical Psychiatry, 8,* 279–284.

St. Jacques, P. L., & Levine, B. (2007). Ageing and autobiographical memory for emotional and neutral events. *Memory, 15,* 129–144.

St. Onge, S. (1995a). Modeling and role-playing. In M. Ballou (Ed.), *Psychological interventions: A guide to strategies.* Westport, CT: Praeger/Greenwood.

St. Onge, S. (1995b). Systematic desensitization. In M. Ballou (Ed.), *Psychological interventions: A guide to strategies.* Westport, CT: Praeger/Greenwood.

Staddon, J. E. R., & Cerutti, D. T. (2003). Operant conditioning. *Annual Review of Psychology, 54,* 115–144.

Staley, J. K., & Sanacora, G., & Tamagnan, G. (2006). Sex differences in diencephalon serotonin transporter availability in major depression. *Biological Psychiatry, 59,* 40–47.

Stankov, L. (2003). Complexity in human intelligence. In R. J. Sternberg, J. Lautrey, et al. (Eds.), *Models of intelligence: International perspectives* (pp. 27–42). Washington, DC: American Psychological Association.

Stanojevic, S., Mitic, K., & Vujic, V. (2007). Exposure to acute physical and psychological stress alters the response of rat macrophages to corticosterone, neuropeptide Y and beta-endorphin. *International Journal on the Biology of Stress, 10,* 65–73.

Stanton, A. L., Danoff-Burg, S., Cameron, C. L., Bishop, M., Collins, C. A., Kirk, S. B., Sworowski, L. A., & Twillman, R. (2000). Emotionally expressive coping predicts psychological and physical adjustment to breast cancer. *Journal of Consulting and Clinical Psychology, 68,* 875–882.

Stapel, D. A., & Semin, G. R. (2007). The magic spell of language: Linguistic categories and their perceptual consequences. *Journal of Personality and Social Psychology, 93,* 23–33.

Starcevic, V., Berle, D., Milicevic, D., Hannan, A., Pamplugh, C., & Eslick, G. D. (2007). Pathological worry, anxiety disorders and the impact of co-occurrence with depressive and other anxiety disorders. *Journal of Anxiety Disorders, 21,* 1016–1027.

Steblay, N., Dysart, J., Fulero, S., & Lindsay, R. C. L. (2003). Eyewitness accuracy rates in police showup and lineup presentations: A meta-analytic comparison. *Law & Human Behavior, 27,* 523–540.

Steele, C. M. (1992, April). Race and the schooling of black America. *Atlantic Monthly,* pp. 37–53.

Steele, C. M. (1997). A threat in the air: How stereotypes shape intellectual identity and performance. *American Psychologist, 52,* 613–629.

Steele, C. M., & Aronson, J. (1995). Stereotype threat and the intellectual test performance of African Americans. *Journal of Personality and Social Psychology, 69,* 797–811.

Steele, C. M., & Josephs, R. A. (1990). Alcohol myopia: Its prized and dangerous effects. *American Psychologist, 45,* 921–933.

Steele, C. M., Spencer, S. J., & Aronson, J. (2002). Contending with group image: The psychology of stereotype and social identity threat. In M. P. Zanna (Ed.), *Advances in experimental social psychology* (Vol. 34, pp. 379–440). San Diego: Academic Press.

Steele, J. D., Christmas, D., Eljamel, M. S., & Matthews, K. (2007). Anterior cingulotomy for major depression: clinical outcome and relationship to lesion characteristics. *Biological Psychiatry, 12,* 127–134.

Steen, R. G. (1996). *DNA and destiny: Nature and nurture in human behavior.* New York: Plenum Press.

Stegerwald, F., & Janson, G. R. (2003). Conversion therapy: Ethical considerations in family counseling. *Family Journal—Counseling and Therapy for Couples and Families, 11,* 55–59.

Steiger, A. (2007). Neurochemical regulation of sleep. *Journal of Psychiatric Research, 41,* 537–552.

Stein, L. A. R., & Graham, J. R. (2005). Ability of substance abusers to escape detection on the Minnesota Multiphasic Personality Inventory-Adolescent (MMPI-A) in a juvenile correctional facility. *Assessment, 12,* 28–39.

Stein, N. L., Ornstein, P. A., Tversky, B., & Brainerd, C. (Eds.). (1997). *Memory for everyday and emotional events.* Mahwah, NJ: Erlbaum.

Stein, R. (2004, October 19). Is every memory worth keeping? *The Washington Post,* p. A1.

Steinberg, L. (2007). Risk taking in adolescence. *Current Directions in Psychological Science, 16,* 55–59.

Steinberg, L., & Dornbusch, S. (1991). Negative correlates of part-time employment during adolescence: Replication and elaboration. *Developmental Psychology, 27,* 304.

Steiner, B., Wolf, S., & Kempermann, G. (2006). Adult neurogenesis and neurodegenerative disease. *Regenerative Medicine, 1,* 15–28.

Steinhausen, H. C., & Spohr, H. L. (1998). Long-term outcome of children with fetal alcohol syndrome: Psychopathology, behavior, and intelligence. *Alcoholism: Clinical & Experimental Research, 22,* 44–51.

Steinmetz, J. E., Kim, J., & Thompson, R. F. (2003). Biological models of associative learning. In M. Gallagher & R. J. Nelson (Eds.), *Handbook of psychology: Biological psychology* (Vol. 3, pp. 499–541). New York: Wiley.

Stemler, S.E. & Sternberg, R.J. (2006). Using situational judgment tests to measure practical intelligence. In J.A. Weekley. & R.E. Ployhart (Eds.), *Situational judgment tests: Theory, measurement, and application.* Mahwah, NJ: Lawrence Erlbaum Associates Publishers.

Stenbacka, L., & Vanni, S. (2007). fMRI of peripheral visual field representation. *Clinical Neurophysiology, 108,* 1303–1314.

Stenklev, N. C., & Laukli, E. (2004). Cortical cognitive potentials in elderly persons. *Journal of the American Academy of Audiology, 15,* 401–413.

Stéphane, R. (2006). Deictic space in Wolof: Discourse, syntax and the importance of absence. In M. Hickmann, & R. Stéphane (Eds.), *Space in languages: Linguistic systems and cognitive categories.* Amsterdam, Netherlands: John Benjamins Publishing Company.

Stephenson, R. H., & Banet-Weiser, S. (2007). Super-sized kids: Obesity, children, moral panic, and the media. In J. A. Bryant, *The children's television community.* Mahwah, NJ: Lawrence Erlbaum Associates.

Stepp, L. (2007, April 24). For Virginia Tech survivors, memories will be powerful. *Washington Post,* p. HE01.

Stern, E., & Silbersweig, D. A. (2001). Advances in functional neuroimaging methodology for the study of brain systems underlying human neuropsychological function and dysfunction. In D. A. Silbersweig & E. Stern (Eds.), *Neuropsychology and functional neuroimaging: Convergence, advances and new directions.* Amsterdam, Netherlands: Swets and Zeitlinger.

Stern, P. (2001, November 2). Sweet dreams are made of this. *Science, 294,* 1047.

Stern, R. M., & Koch, K. L. (1996). Motion sickness and differential susceptibility. *Current Directions in Psychological Science, 5,* 115–120.

Sternberg, E. M. (2002). Walter B. Cannon and Voodoo Death: A perspective from 60 years on. *American Journal of Public Health, 92,* 1564–1566.

Sternberg, R. J. (1982). Reasoning, problem solving, and intelligence. In R. J. Sternberg (Ed.), *Handbook of human intelligence* (pp. 225–307). Cambridge, MA: Cambridge University Press.

Sternberg, R. J. (1990). *Metaphors of mind: Conceptions of the nature of intelligence.* New York: Cambridge University Press.

Sternberg, R. J. (1998). *Successful intelligence: How practical and creative intelligence determine success in life.* New York: Plume.

Sternberg, R. J. (2000). Intelligence and wisdom. In R. J. Sternberg et al. (Eds.), *Handbook of intelligence.* New York: Cambridge University Press.

Sternberg, R. J. (2001). What is the common thread of creativity? Its dialectical relation to intelligence and wisdom. *American Psychologist, 56,* 360–362.

Sternberg, R. J. (2002a). Individual differences in cognitive development. In U. Goswami (Ed.), *Blackwell handbook of childhood cognitive development. Blackwell handbooks of developmental psychology* (pp. 600–619). Malden, MA: Blackwell.

Sternberg, R. J. (Ed.). (2002b). *Why smart people can be so stupid.* New Haven, CT: Yale University Press.

Sternberg, R. J. (2004a). A triangular theory of love. In H. T. Reis & C. E. Rusbult (Eds.), *Close relationships: Key readings.* Philadelphia, PA: Taylor & Francis.

Sternberg, R. J. (2004b). Culture and intelligence. *American Psychologist, 59,* 325–338.

Sternberg, R. J. (2004c). Theory-based university admissions testing for a new millennium. *Educational Psychologist, 39,* 185–198.

Sternberg, R. J. (2006). A duplex theory of love. In R. J. Sternberg, Ed., *The new psychology of love.* New Haven, CT: Yale University Press.

Sternberg, R. J., & Beall, A. E. (1991). How can we know what love is? An epistemological analysis. In G. J. O. Fletcher & F. D. Fincham (Eds.), *Cognition in close relationships.* Hillsdale, NJ: Erlbaum.

Sternberg, R. J., & Grigorenko, E. (1997). Are cognitive styles still in style? *American Psychologist, 52,* 700–712.

Sternberg, R. J., & Grigorenko, E. L. (2005). Cultural explorations of the nature of intelligence. In A. F. Healy (Ed.), *Experimental cognitive psychology and its applications* (pp. 225–235). Washington, DC: American Psychological Association.

Sternberg, R. J., Grigorenko, E. L., & Kidd, K. K. (2005). Intelligence, race, and genetics. *American Psychologist, 60,* 46–59.

Sternberg, R. J., & Hedlund, J. (2002). Practical intelligence, "g," and work psychology. *Human Performance, 15,* 143–160.

Sternberg, R. J., & Jarvin, L. (2003). Alfred Binet's contributions as a paradigm for impact in psychology. In R. J. Sternberg (Ed.), *The anatomy of impact: What makes the great works of psychology great* (pp. 89–107). Washington, DC: American Psychological Association.

Sternberg, R. J., & O'Hara, L. A. (2000). Intelligence and creativity. In R. Sternberg et al. (Eds.), *Handbook of intelligence.* New York: Cambridge University Press.

Sternberg, R. J., & Pretz, J. E. (2005). *Cognition and intelligence: Identifying the mechanisms of the mind.* New York: Cambridge University Press, 2005.

Sternberg, R., & The Rainbow Project Collaborators. (2005). Augmenting the SAT through Assessments of Analytical, Practical, and Creative Skills. In W. J. Camara, & E. W. Kimmel, *Choosing students: Higher education admissions tools for the 21st century.* Mahwah, NJ: Lawrence Erlbaum Associates.

Sternberg, R. J., Hojjat, M., & Barnes, M. L. (2001). Empirical aspects of a theory of love as a story. *European Journal of Personality, 15,* 1–20.

Sternberg, R. J., Wagner, R. K., Williams, W. M., & Horvath, J. A. (1995). Testing common sense. *American Psychologist, 50,* 912–927.

Stetsenko, A., Little, T. D., Gordeeva, T., Grasshof, M., & Oettingen, G. (2000). Gender effects in children's beliefs about school performance: A cross cultural study. *Child Development, 71,* 517–527.

Stettler, N., Stallings, V. A., Troxel, A. B., Zhao. J., Z., Schinnar, R., Nelson, S. E., Ziegler, E. E., Strom, B. L. (2005). Weight gain in the first week of life and overweight in adulthood. *Circulation, 111,* 1897–1903.

Stevens, C. F. (1979, September). The neuron. *Scientific American,* p. 56.

Stevens, G., & Gardner, S. (1982). *The women of psychology: Pioneers and innovators* (Vol. 1). Cambridge, MA: Schenkman.

Stevens, M. J., & Gielen, U.P. (Eds.). (2007). *Toward a global psychology: Theory, research, intervention, and pedagogy.* Mahwah, NJ: Lawrence Erlbaum.

Stevens, P. & Harper, D. J. (2007). Professional accounts of electroconvulsive therapy: A discourse analysis. *Social Science & Medicine, 64,* 1475–1486.

Stevenson, H. W., Lee, S., & Mu, X. (2000). Successful achievement in mathematics: China and the United States. In C. F. M. van Lieshout & P. G. Heymans (Eds.), *Developing talent across the life span.* New York: Psychology Press.

Stevenson, R. J., & Case, T. I. (2005). Olfactory imagery: A review. *Psychonomic Bulletin and Review, 12,* 244–264.

Steward, E. P. (1995). *Beginning writers in the zone of proximal development.* Hillsdale, NJ: Erlbaum.

Stewart, D. W., & Kamins, M. A. (1993). *Secondary research: Information sources and methods* (2nd ed.). Newbury Park, CA: Sage.

Stewart-Williams, S., & Podd, J. (2004). The placebo effect: Dissolving the expectancy versus conditioning debate. *Psychological Bulletin, 130,* 324–340.

Stickgold, R. A., Winkelman, J. W., & Wehrwein, P. (2004, January 19). You will start to feel very sleepy . . . *Newsweek,* pp. 58–60.

Stickgold, R., Hobson, J. A., Fosse, R., & Fosse, M. (2001, November 2). Sleep, learning, and dreams: Off-line memory reprocessing. *Science, 294,* 1052–1057.

Stickley, T., & Nickeas, R. (2006). Becoming one person: Living with dissociative identity disorder. *Journal of Psychiatric and Mental Health Nursing, 13,* 180–187.

Stier, H., & Lewin-Epstein, N. (2000). Women's part-time employment and gender inequality in the family. *Journal of Family Issues, 21,* 390–410.

Stiles, M. M., & Martin, S. (2006). Does treatment with donepezil improve memory for patients with mild cognitive impairment? *The Journal of Family Practice, 55,* 435–436.

Stix, G. (1996, January). Listening to culture. *Scientific American,* pp. 16–17.

Stix, G. (2003, September). Ultimate self-improvement. *Scientific American,* pp. 44–45.

Stockton, R., Morran, D. K., & Krieger, K. M. (2004). An overview of current research and best practices for training beginning group leaders. In J. L. DeLucia-Waack, D. A. Gerrity, C. R. Kalodner, & M. T. Riva (Eds.), *Handbook of group counseling and psychotherapy.* Thousand Oaks, CA: Sage Publications.

Stompe, T., Ortwein-Swoboda, G., Ritter, K., & Schanda, H. (2003). Old wine in new bottles? Stability and plasticity of the contents of schizophrenic delusions. *Psychopathology, 36,* 6–12.

Stone, J. (2002). Battling doubt by avoiding practice: The effects of stereotype threat on self-handicapping in white athletes. *Personality and Social Psychology Bulletin, 28,* 1667–1678.

Storm, L., & Ertel, S. (2001). Does psi exist? Comments on Milton and Wiseman's (1999) meta-analysis of Ganzfeld's research. *Psychological Bulletin, 127,* 424–433.

Stouffer, E. M., & White, N. M. (2006). Neural circuits mediating latent learning and conditioning for salt in the rat. *Neurobiology of Learning and Memory, 86,* 91–99.

Strange, D., Clifasefi, S., & Garry, M. (2007). False memories. In M. Garry, & H. Hayne, *Do justice and let the sky fall: Elizabeth Loftus and her contributions to science, law, and academic freedom.* Mahwah, NJ: Lawrence Erlbaum Associates.

Strathern, A., & Stewart, P. J. (2003). *Landscape, memory and history: Anthropological perspectives.* London: Pluto Press.

Strauss, E. (1998, May 8). Writing, speech separated in split brain. *Science, 280,* 287.

Strayer, D. L., & Drews, F. A. (2007). Cell-phone-induced driver distraction. *Current Directions in Psychological Science, 16,* 128–131.

Strayer, D. L., Drews, F. A., Crouch, D. J., & Johnston, W. A. (2005). Why do cell phone conversations interfere with driving? In W. R. Walker and D. Herrmann (Eds.) *Cognitive technology: Transforming thought and society.* Jefferson, NC: McFarland & Company

Streissguth, A. (1997). *Fetal alcohol spectrum disorder: A guide for families and communities.* Baltimore, MD: Brookes Publishing Co.

Streissguth, A. P., Barr, H. M., Bookstein, F. L., Sampson, P. D., & Olson, H. C. (1999). The long-term neurocognitive consequences of prenatal alcohol exposure: A 14-year study. *Psychological Science, 10,* 186–190.

Striano, T., & Vaish, A. (2006). Seven- to 9-month-old infants use facial expressions to interpret others' actions. *British Journal of Developmental Psychology, 24,* 753–760.

Strickland, B. R. (1992). Women and depression. *Current Directions in Psychological Science, 1,* 132–135.

Striegel-Moore, R., & Bulik, C. M. (2007). Risk factors for eating disorders. *American Psychologist, 62,* 181–198.

Striegel-Moore, R. H., & Smolak, L. (Eds.) (2001). *Eating disorders: Innovative directions in research and practice.* Washington, DC: American Psychological Association.

Stroebe, M. S., Stroebe, W., & Hansson, R. O. (Eds.). (1993). *Handbook of bereavement: Theory, research, and intervention.* Cambridge, England: Cambridge University Press.

Strong, T., & Tomm, K. (2007). Family therapy as re-coordinating and moving on together. *Journal of Systemic Therapies, 26,* 42–54.

Stronski, S. M., Ireland, M., & Michaud, P. (2000). Protective correlates of stages in adolescent substance use: A Swiss national study. *Journal of Adolescent Health, 26,* 420–427.

Strube, M. (Ed.). (1990). Type A behavior [Special issue]. *Journal of Social Behavior and Personality, 5.*

Strupp, H. H. (1996, October). The tripartite model and the *Consumer Reports* study. *American Psychologist, 51,* 1017–1024.

Strupp, H. H., & Binder, J. L. (1992). Current developments in psychotherapy. *The Independent Practitioner, 12,* 119–124.

Sue, D. (1979). Erotic fantasies of college students during coitus. *Journal of Sex Research, 15,* 299–305.

Sue, D. W., & Sue, D. (1999). *Counseling the culturally different: Theory and practice* (3rd ed.). New York: Wiley.

Sue, D. W., Sue, D., & Sue, S. (1990). *Understanding abnormal behavior* (3rd ed.). Boston: Houghton-Mifflin.

Suh, E. M. (2002). Culture, identity consistency, and subjective well-being. *Journal of Personality & Social Psychology, 83,* 1378–1391.

Suhail, K., & Chaudhry, H. R. (2004). Predictors of subjective well-being in an Eastern Muslim culture. *Journal of Social and Clinical Psychology, 23,* 359–376.

Suizzo, M-A., & Bornstein, M. H. (2006). French and European American child-mother play: Culture and gender considerations. *International Journal of Behavioral Development, 30,* 498–508.

Sulzer-Azaroff, B., & Mayer, R. (1991). *Behavior analysis and lasting change.* New York: Holt.

Sun, T., Patoine, C., Abu-Khalil, A., Visvader, J., Sum, E., Cherry, T. J., Orkink, S. H., Geschwind, D. H., & Walsh, C. A. (2005, June 17). Early asymmetry of gene transcriptions in embryonic human left and right cerebral cortex. *Science, 308,* 1794–1796.

Super, C. M. (1980). Cognitive development: Looking across at growing up. In C. M. Super & S. Harakness (Eds.), *New directions for child development: Anthropological perspectives on child development* (pp. 59–69). San Francisco: Jossey-Bass.

Surette, R. (2002). Self-reported copycat crime among a population of serious and violent juvenile offenders. *Crime & Delinquency, 48,* 46–69.

Susser, E. S., Herman, D. B., & Aaron, B. (2002, August). Combating the terror of terrorism. *Scientific American,* pp. 70–77.

Sutin, A. R., & Robins, R. W. (2007). Phenomenology of autobiographical memories: The Memory Experiences Questionnaire. *Memory, 15,* 390–411.

Suzuki, L., & Aronson, J. (2005). The cultural malleability of intelligence and its impact on the racial/ethnic hierarchy. *Psychology, Public Policy, and Law, 11,* 320–327.

Svarstad, B. (1976). Physician-patient communication and patient conformity with medical advice. In D. Mechanic (Ed.), *The growth of bureaucratic medicine.* New York: Wiley.

Svartdal, F. (2003). Extinction after partial reinforcement: Predicted vs. judged persistence. *Scandinavian Journal of Psychology, 44,* 55–64.

Swain, P. I. (2006). *New developments in eating disorders research.* Hauppauge, NY: Nova Science Publishers.

Swales, M. A., & Heard, H. L. (2007). The therapy relationship in dialectical behaviour therapy. In P. Gilbert & R. L. Leahy, *The*

therapeutic relationship in the cognitive behavioral psychotherapies. New York: Routledge/Taylor & Francis.

Swann, W. B., Jr., Chang-Schneider, C., & Larsen McClarty, K. (2007). Do people's self-views matter? Self-concept and self-esteem in everyday life. *American Psychologist, 62,* 84–94.

Swanson, H. L., Harris, K. R., & Graham, S. (Eds.). (2003). *Handbook of learning disabilities.* New York: Guilford Press.

Swets, J. A., & Bjork, R.A. (1990). Enhancing human performance: An evaluation of "new age" techniques considered by the U.S. Army. *Psychological Science, 1,* 85–96.

Szasz, T. (1982). The psychiatric will: A new mechanism for protecting persons against "psychosis" and psychiatry. *American Psychologist, 37,* 762–770.

Szasz, T. (2004). "Knowing what ain't so": R. D. Laing and Thomas Szasz. *Psychoanalytic Review, 91,* 331–346.

Szasz, T. (2006). The pretense of psychology as science: The myth of mental illness in statu nascendi. *Current Psychology: Developmental, Learning, Personality, Social, 25,* 42–49.

Szasz, T. S. (1994). *Cruel compassion: Psychiatric control of society's unwanted.* New York: Wiley.

Szegedy Maszak, M. (2003, January 13). The sound of unsound minds. *U.S. News & World Report,* pp. 45–46.

Szurman, P., Warga, M., Roters, S., Grisanti, S., Heimann, U., Aisenbrey, S., Rohrbach, J. M., Sellhaus, B., Ziemssen, F., & Bartz-Schmidt, K. U. (2005). Experimental implantation and long-term testing of an intraocular vision aid in rabbits. *Archives of Ophthalmology, 123,* 964–969.

Tabakoff, B., & Hoffman, P. L. (1996). Effect of alcohol on neurotransmitters and their receptors and enzymes. In H. Begleiter, & B. Kissin (Eds.), *The pharmacology of alcohol and alcohol dependence. Alcohol and alcoholism, No. 2.* New York: Oxford University Press.

Tadmor, C., T. (2007). Biculturalism: The plus side of leaving home? The effects of second-culture exposure on integrative complexity and its consequences for overseas performance. *Dissertation Abstracts International Section A: Humanities and Social Sciences, 67(8-A),* 3068.

Taggi, F., Crenca, A., Cedri, C., Giustini, M., Dosi, G., & Marturano, P. (2007). Road safety and the tsunami of cell phones. *Ann Ig, 19,* 269–274.

Tajfel, H., & Turner, J. C. (2004). The social identity theory of intergroup behavior. In J. T. Jost & J. Sidanius (Eds.), *Political psychology: Key readings.* New York: Psychology Press.

Takahashi, M., Nakata, A., Haratani, T., Ogawa, Y., & Arito, H. (2004). Post-lunch nap as a worksite intervention to promote alertness on the job. *Ergonomics, 47,* 1003–1013.

Takizawa, T., Kondo, T., & Sakihara, S. (2007). 'Stress buffering effects of social support on depressive symptoms in middle age: Reciprocity and community mental health': Corrigendum. *Psychiatry and Clinical Neurosciences, 61,* 336–337.

Talarico, J. M., & Rubin, D. C. (2003). Confidence, not consistency, characterizes flashbulb memories. *Psychological Science, 14,* 455–461.

Tal-Or, N., & Papirman, Y. (2007). The funda mental attribution error in attributing fictional figures' characteristics to the actors. *Media Psychology, 9,* 331–345.

Talukdar, S., & Shastri, J. (2006). Contributory and adverse factors in social development of young children. *Psychological Studies, 51,* 294–303.

Tan, V. L., & Hicks, R. A. (1995). Type A-B behavior and nightmare types among college students. *Perceptual and Motor Skills, 81,* 15–19.

Tangney, J., & Dearing, R. (2002). Gender differences in morality. In R. Bornstein & J. Masling (Eds.), *The psychodynamics of gender and gender role.* Washington, DC: American Psychological Association.

Tanner, J. M. (1978). *Education and physical growth* (2nd ed.). New York: International Universities Press.

Tanner, J. M. (1990). *Foetus into man: Physical growth from conception to maturity* (rev. ed.). Cambridge, MA: Harvard University Press.

Taras, H., & Potts-Datema, W. (2005). Chronic health conditions and student performance at school. *Journal of School Health, 75,* 255–266.

Tasker, F. (2005). Lesbian mothers, gay fathers, and their children: A review. *Journal of Developmental and Behavioral Pediatrics, 26,* 224–240.

Tasker, F. & Golombok, S. (1995). Adults raised as children in lesbian families. *American Journal of Orthopsychiatry, 65,* 203–215.

Tattersall, I. (2002). *The monkey in the mirror: Essays on the science of what makes us human.* New York: Harcourt.

Tavris, C. (1992). *The mismeasure of woman.* New York: Simon & Schuster.

Taylor, C. (2004, November 29). The sky's the limit. *Time,* pp. 15–17.

Taylor, C. B., & Luce, K. H. (2003). Computer- and Internet-based psychotherapy interventions. *Current Directions in Psychological Science, 12,* 18–22.

Taylor, C. B., Jobson, K. O., Winzelberg, A., & Abascal, L. (2002). The use of the Internet to provide evidence-based integrated treatment programs for mental health. *Psychiatric Annals, 32,* 671–677.

Taylor, J., & Turner, R. J. (2002). Perceived discrimination, social stress and depression in the transition to adulthood: Racial contrasts. *Social Psychology Quarterly, 65,* 213–225.

Taylor, F., & Bryant, R. A. (2007). The tendency to suppress, inhibiting thoughts, and dream rebound. *Behaviour Research and Therapy, 45,* 163–168.

Taylor, M. (1996). A theory of mind perspective on social cognitive development. In R. Gelman & T. K. F. Au (Eds.), *Perceptual and cognitive development: Handbook of perception and cognition* (2nd ed.). San Diego: Academic Press.

Taylor, S. (2003). Anxiety sensitivity and its implications for understanding and treating PTSD. *Journal of Cognitive Psychotherapy, 17,* 179–186.

Taylor, S. E. (1995). Quandary at the crossroads: Paternalism versus advocacy surrounding end-of-treatment decisions. *American Journal of Hospital Palliatory Care, 12,* 43–46.

Taylor, S. E., & Aspinwall, L. G. (1996). Mediating and moderating processes in psychosocial stress: Appraisal, coping, resistance, and vulnerability. In H. B. Kaplan (Ed.), *Psychosocial stress: Perspectives on structure, theory, life-course, and methods.* San Diego: Academic Press.

Taylor, S. E., Kemeny, M. E., Reed, G. M., Bower, J. E., & Gruenewald, T. L. (2000). Psychological resources, positive illusions, and health. *American Psychologist, 55,* 99–109.

Teff, K. L., Petrova, M., & Havel, P. J. (2007). 48-h Glucose infusion in humans: Effect on hormonal responses, hunger and food intake. *Physiology & Behavior, 90,* 733–743.

Tekcan, A. I. (2001). Flashbulb memories for a negative and a positive event: News of Desert Storm and acceptance to college. *Psychological Reports, 88,* 323–331.

Tellegen, A., Lykken, D. T., Bouchard, T. J., Jr., Wilcox, K. J., Segal, N. L., & Rich, S. (1988). Personality similarity in twins reared apart and together. *Journal of Personality and Social Psychology, 54,* 1031–1039.

Templer, D. I., & Arkawa, H. (2006). Association of race and color with mean IQ across nations. *Psychological Reports, 99,* 191–196.

Tenenbaum, H. R., & Leaper, C. (2002). Are parents' gender schemas related to their children's gender-related cognitios? A meta-analysis. *Developmental Psychology, 38,* 615–630.

Tenenbaum, H. R., & Ruck, M. D. (2007). Are teachers' expectations different for racial minority than for European American students? A meta-analysis. *Journal of Educational Psychology, 99,* 253–273.

Tenopyr, M. L. (2002). Theory versus reality: Evaluation of 'g' in the workplace. *Human Performance, 15,* 107–122.

Teodorov, E., Salzgerber, S. A., Felicio, L. F., Varolli, F. M. F., & Bernardi, M. M. (2002). Effects of perinatal picrotoxin and sexual experience on heterosexual and homosexual behavior in male rats. *Neurotoxicology and Teratology, 24,* 235–245.

Tepperman, L., & Curtis, J. (1995). A life satisfaction scale for use with national adult samples from the USA, Canada and Mexico. *Social Indicators Research, 35,* 255–270.

Terman, L. M., & Oden, M. H. (1947). *Genetic studies of genius: IV. The gifted child grows up.* Stanford, CA: Stanford University Press.

Terracciano, A., Abdel-Khalek, A., Adam, N., Adamovova, L., and 83 additional authors. (2005). National character does not reflect mean personality trait levels in 49 cultures. *Science, 310,* 96–100.

Terry, W. S. (2003). *Learning and memory: Basic principles, processes, and procedures* (2nd ed.). Boston: Allyn & Bacon.

Tervaniemi, M., Jacobsen, T., & Röttger, S. (2006). Selective tuning of cortical sound-feature processing by language experience. *European Journal of Neuroscience, 23,* 2538–2541.

Tesoriero, H. (July 5, 2007). Mysteries of the "faceblind" could illuminate the brain. *Wall Street Journal,* A1.

Tetlock, P. E. (1997). Psychological perspectives on international conflict and cooperation. In D. F. Halpern & A. E. Voiskounsky (Eds.), *States of mind: American and post-Soviet perspectives on contemporary issues in psychology.* London: Oxford University Press.

Thachil, A. F., Mohan, R., & Bhugra, D. (2007). The evidence base of complementary and alternative therapies in depression. *Journal of Affective Disorders, 97,* 23–35.

Thara, R. (2004). Twenty-year course of schizophrenia: The Madras longitudinal study. *Canadian Journal of Psychiatry, 49,* 564–569.

Tharp, R. G. (1989). Psychocultural variables and constants: Effects on teaching and learning in schools [Special issue: Children and their development: Knowledge base, research agenda, and social policy application]. *American Psychologist, 44,* 349–359.

Thatcher, D. L., & Clark, D. B., (2006). Adolescent alcohol abuse and dependence: Development, diagnosis, treatment and outcomes. *Current Psychiatry Reviews, 2,* 159–177.

Thiffault, P., & Bergeron, J. (2003). Fatigue and individual differences in monotonous simulated driving. *Personality and Individual Differences, 34,* 159–176.

Thombs, D. L. (1999). *Introduction to addictive behaviors* (2nd ed.). New York: Guilford Press.

Thompson, B. (2002). *Score reliability: Contemporary thinking on reliability issues.* Thousand Oaks, CA: Sage.

Thompson, J. (2000, June 18). "I was certain, but I was wrong." *The New York Times,* p. E14.

Thompson, J. K., & Smolak, L. (Eds.). (2001). *Body image, eating disorders and obesity in youth: Assessment, prevention, and treatment.* Washington, DC: American Psychological Association.

Thompson, K. M., & Hanninger, K. (2001). Violence in e-rated video games. *Journal of the American Medical Association, 286,* 591–598.

Thompson, P. M., Hayaski, K. M., Simon, S. L., Geaga, J. A., Hong, M. S., Sui, Y., Lee, J. Y., Toga, A. W., Ling, W., & London, E. D. (2004, June 30). Structural abnormalities in the brains of human subjects who use methamphetamine. *The Journal of Neuroscience, 24(26),* 6028–6036.

Thompson, R. A., & Nelson, C. A. (2001). Developmental science and the media. *American Psychologist, 56,* 5–15.

Thorkildsen, T. A. (2006). An empirical exploration of language and thought. *PsycCRITIQUES, 51,* No pagination specified.

Thorndike, E. L. (1932). *The fundamentals of learning.* New York: Teachers College.

Thornton, A., & McAuliffe, K. (2006, July 14). Teaching itn wild meerkats. *Science, 313,* 227–229.

Thornton, A., & Young-DeMarco, L. (2001). Four decades of trends in attitudes toward family issues in the United States: The 1960s through the 1990s. *Journal of Marriage and the Family, 63,* 1009–1017.

Thrash, T. M., & Elliot, A. J. (2002). Implicit and self-attributed achievement motives: Concordance and predictive validity. *Journal of Personality, 70,* 729–755.

Thurstone, L. L. (1938). *Primary mental abilities.* Chicago: University of Chicago Press.

Time. (1982, October 4). "We're sorry: A case of mistaken identity." *Time,* p. 45.

Titone, D. A. (2002). Memories bound: The neuroscience of dreams. *Trends in Cognitive Science, 6,* 4–5.

Tkachuk, G. A., & Martin, G. L. (1999). Exercise therapy for patients with psychiatric disorders: Research and clinical implications. *Professional Psychology: Research and Practice, 33,* 275–282.

Tolman, E. C., & Honzik, C. H. (1930). Introduction and removal of reward and maze performance in rats. *University of California Publications in Psychology, 4,* 257–275.

Tomasello, M. (2000). Culture and cognitive development. *Current Directions in Psychological Science, 9,* 37–40.

Tomlinson-Keasey, C. (1985). *Child development: Psychological, sociological, and biological factors.* Homewood, IL: Dorsey.

Tonidandel, S., Quinones, M. A., & Adams, A. A. (2002). Computer-adaptive testing: The impact of test characteristics on perceived performance and test takers' reactions. *Journal of Applied Psychology, 87,* 320–332.

Toole, L. M., DeLeon, I. G., Kahng, S., Ruffin, G. E., Pletcher, C. A., & Bowman, L. G. (2004). Re-evaluation of constant versus varied punishers using empirically derived consequences. *Research in Developmental Disabilities, 25,* 577–586.

Torrey, E. F. (1997, June 13). The release of the mentally ill from institutions: A well-intentioned disaster. *The Chronicle of Higher Education*, pp. B4–B5.

Toth, J. P., & Daniels, K. A. (2002). Effects of prior experience on judgments of normative word frequency: Automatic bias and correction. *Journal of Memory and Language, 46*, 845–874.

Touhara, K. (2007). Molecular biology of peptide pheromone production and reception in mice. *Advanced Genetics, 59*, 147–171.

Townsend, E., (2007). Suicide terrorists: Are they suicidal? *Suicide and Life-Threatening Behavior, 37*, 35–49.

Tracy, J. L., & Robins, R. W. (2004). Show your pride: Evidence for a discrete emotion expression. *Psychological Science, 15*, 194–197.

Travis, F. (2006). From I to I: Concepts of self on a object-referral/self-referral continuum. In A. P. Prescott, *The concept of self in psychology*. Hauppauge, NY: Nova Science Publishers.

Trehub, S. E. (2001). Musical predispositions in infancy. In R. J. Zatorre & I. Peretz (Eds.), *The biological foundations of music. Annals of the New York Academy of Sciences* (Vol. 930, pp. 1–16). New York: New York Academy of Sciences.

Trehub, S. E., & Nakata, T. (2001–02). Emotion and music in infancy [Special issue: Musicae scientiae]. *Current Trends in the Study of Music and Emotion*, pp. 37–61.

Treisman, A. (1988). Features and objects: The fourteenth Bartlett memorial lecture. *Quarterly Journal of Experimental Psychology, 40*, 201–237.

Treisman, A. (1993). The perception of features and objects. In A. D. Baddeley & L. Weiskrantz (Eds.), *Attention: Selection, awareness, and control: A tribute to Donald Broadbent*. Oxford, England: Oxford University Press.

Treisman, A. (2004). Psychological issues in selective attention. In M. S. Gazzaniga (Ed.), *Cognitive neurosciences* (3rd ed.). Cambridge, MA: MIT.

Tremblay, A. (2004). Dietary fat and body weight set point. *Nutrition Review, 62*(7 Pt 2), S75–S77.

Triesch, J., Jasso, H., & Deak, G. O. (2007). Emergence of mirror neurons in a model of gaze following. *Adaptive Behavior, 15*, 149–165.

Trigo, M., Silva, D., & Rocha, E. (2005). Psychosocial risk factors in coronary heart disease: Beyond type A behavior. *Revista Portuguesa de Cardiologia, 24*, 261–281.

Tropp, L. R., & Bianchi, R. A. (2006). Valuing diversity and interest in intergroup contact. *Journal of Social Issues, 62*, 533–551.

Tropp, L. R., & Pettigrew, T. F. (2005). Differential relationships between intergroup contact and affective and cognitive dimensions of prejudice. *Personality and Social Psychology Bulletin, 31*, 1145–1158.

Troxel, W. M., Matthews, K. A., Bromberger, J. T., & Sutton-Tyrell, K. (2003). Chronic stress burden, discrimination, and subclinical carotid artery disease in African American and Caucasian women. *Health Psychology, 22*, 300–309.

Troyer, A. K., Häfliger, A., & Cadieux, M. J. (2006). Name and face learning in older adults: Effects of level of processing, self-generation, and intention to learn. *Journals of Gerontology: Series B: Psychological Sciences and Social Sciences, 61*, P67–P74.

Trudel, G. (2002). Sexuality and marital life: Results of a survey. *Journal of Sex and Marital Therapy, 28*, 229–249.

Trull, T. J., & Widiger, T. A. (2003). Personality disorders. In. G. Stricker, T. A. Widiger, et al. (Eds.), *Handbook of psychology: Clinical psychology* (Vol. 8, pp. 149–172). New York: Wiley.

Trull, T. J., Stepp, S. D., & Durrett, C. A. (2003). Research on borderline personality disorder: An update. *Current Opinion in Psychiatry, 16*, 77–82.

Tryon, W. W. (2005). Possible mechanisms for why desensitization and exposure therapy work. *Clinical Psychology Review, 25*, 67–95.

Tryon, W. W., & Bernstein, D. (2003). Understanding measurement. In J. C. Thomas & M. Hersen (Eds.), *Understanding research in clinical and counseling psychology*. Mahwah, NJ: Erlbaum.

Tsai, K. J., Tsai, Y. C., & Shen, C. K. (2007). G-CSF rescues the memory impairment of animal models of Alzheimer's disease. *Journal of Experimental Medicine, 11*, 1273–1289.

Tsang, S. K. M., & Yip, F. Y. Y. (2006). Positive identity as a positive youth development construct: Conceptual bases and implications for curriculum development. *International Journal of Adolescent Medicine and Health, 18, Special issue: Positive youth development program in Hong Kong*, 459–466.

Tsaousis, I., Nikolaou, I., & Serdaris, N. (2007). Do the core self-evaluations moderate the relationship between subjective well-being and physical and psychological health? *Personality and Individual Differences, 42*, 1441–1452.

Tseng, W. S. (2003). *Clinician's guide to cultural psychiatry*. San Diego, CA: Elsevier Publishing.

Tsukasaki, T., & Ishii, K. (2004). Linguistic-cultural relativity of cognition: Rethinking the Sapir-Whorf hypothesis. *Japanese Psychological Review, 47*, 173–186.

Tsunoda, T. (1985). *The Japanese brain: Uniqueness and universality*. Tokyo: Taishukan Publishing.

Tucker, C. M., & Herman, K. C. (2002). Using culturally sensitive theories and research to meet the academic needs of low-income African American children. *American Psychologist, 57*, 762–773.

Tucker, J. A., Donovan, D. M., & Marlatt, G. A. (Eds.). (1999). *Changing addictive behavior: Bridging clinical and public health strategies*. New York: Guilford Press.

Tucker Blackwell, V.G. (2006). Factors which influence the academic motivation and disengagement of adolescent, African American males within a social-historical and psychological context. *Dissertation Abstracts International, 67*, 1654A.

Tuerlinckx, F., De Boeck, P., & Lens, W. (2002). Measuring needs with the Thematic Apperception Test: A psychometric study. *Journal of Personality and Social Psychology, 82*, 448–461.

Tugay, N., Akbayrak, T., Demirturk, F., Karakaya, I. C., Kocaacar, O., Tugay, U., Karakay, M. G., & Demirturk, F. (2007). Effectiveness of transcutaneous electrical nerve stimulation and interferential current in primary dysmenorrhea. *Pain Medicine, 8*, 295–300.

Tulving, E. (1993). What is episodic memory? *Current Directions in Psychological Science, 2*, 67–70.

Tulving, E. (2000). Concepts of memory. In E. Tulving, F. I. M. Craik, et al. (Eds.). *The Oxford handbook of memory*. New York: Oxford University Press.

Tulving, E. (2002). Episodic memory and common sense: How far apart? In A. Baddeley & J. P. Aggleton (Eds.), *Episodic memory: New directions in research* (pp. 269–287). London: Oxford University Press.

Tulving, E., & Psotka, J. (1971). Retroactive inhibition in free recall: Inaccessibility of information available in the memory store. *Journal of Experimental Psychology, 87*, 1–8.

Tulving, E., & Thompson, D. M. (1983). Encoding specificity and retrieval processes in episodic memory. *Psychological Review, 80*, 352–373.

Turati, C. (2004). Why faces are not special to newborns: An alternative account of the face preference. *Current Directions in Psychological Science, 13*, 5–8.

Turk, D. C. (1994). Perspectives on chronic pain: The role of psychological factors. *Current Directions in Psychological Science, 3*, 45–49.

Turkel, R. A. (2002). From victim to heroine: Children's stories revisited. *Journal of the American Academy of Psychoanalysis, 30*, 71–81.

Turkewitz, G. (1993). The origins of differential hemispheric strategies for information processing in the relationships between voice and face perception. In B. de Boysson-Bardies, S. de Schonen, P. W. Jusczyk, P. McNeilage, & J. Morton (Eds.), *Developmental neurocognition: Speech and face processing in the first year of life. NATO ASI series D: Behavioural and social sciences* (Vol. 69). Dordrecht, Netherlands: Kluwer Academic.

Turner, M. E., Pratkanis, A. R., Struckman, C. K. (2007). Groupthink as social identity maintenance. In C. K. Struckman, *The science of social influence: Advances and future progress*. New York: Psychology Press.

Turner, W. J. (1995). Homosexuality, Type 1: An Xq28 phenomenon. *Archives of Sexual Behavior, 24*, 109–134.

Tuszynski, M. H. (2007). Nerve growth factor gene therapy in Alzheimer disease. *Alzheimer's Disease and Associated Disorders, 21*, 179–1898.

Tuvblad, C., Eley, T. C., & Lichtenstein, P. (2005). The development of antisocial behaviour from childhood to adolescence: A longitudinal twin study. *European Child & Adolescent Psychiatry, 14*, 216–225.

Tversky, A., & Kahneman, D. (1987). Rational choice and the framing of decisions. In R. Hogarth & M. Reder (Eds.), *Rational choice: The contrast between economics and psychology*. Chicago: University of Chicago Press.

Twenge, J. M., & Crocker, J. (2002). Race and self-esteem revisited: Reply to Hafdahl and Gray-Little. *Psychological Bulletin, 128*, 417–420.

Twenge, J. M., Catanese, K. R., & Baumeister, R. F. (2002). Social exclusion causes self-defeating behavior. *Journal of Personality and Social Psychology, 83*, 606–615.

Ubell, E. (1993, January 10). Could you use more sleep? *Parade*, pp. 16–18.

Ullman, S. (1996). *High-level vision: Object recognition and visual cognition*. Cambridge, MA: MIT.

Ullman, S. E., & Townsend, S. M. (2007). Barriers to working with sexual assault survivors: A qualitative study of rape crisis center workers. *Violence Against Women, 13*, 412–443.

Umphress, E. E., Smith-Crowe, K., & Brief, A. P. (2007). When birds of a feather flock together and when they do not: Status composition, social dominance orientation, and organizational attractiveness. *Journal of Applied Psychology, 92*, 396–409.

UNAIDS. (2002). *AIDS epidemic update, 2002*. Geneva, Switzerland: World Health Organization.

UNAIDS. (December, 2007). *07 AIDS Epidemic Update*. Geneva, Switzerland: United Nations Programme on HIV/AIDS.

Underwood, A. (2005, October 3). The good heart. *Newsweek*, p. 49.

Unsworth, N., & Engle, R. W. (2005). Individual differences in working memory capacity and learning: Evidence from the serial reaction time task. *Memory and Cognition, 33*, 213–220.

Updegraff, K. A., Helms, H. M., McHale, S. M., Crouter, A. C., Thayer, S. M., & Sales, L. H. (2004). Who's the boss? Patterns of perceived control in adolescents' friendships. *Journal of Youth & Adolescence, 33*, 403–420.

U.S. Bureau of the Census. (2000). *Census 2000*. Retrieved from American Fact Finder http://factfinder.census.gov/servlet/BasicFactsServlet.

U.S. Bureau of Labor Statistics. (2003). Women's weekly earnings as a percentage of men's earnings. Washington, DC: U.S. Bureau of Labor Statistics.

U.S. Department of Labor, Bureau of Labor Statistics, "Highlight of Women's Earnings in 2004," Report 987, September 2005.

Uttl, B., Graf, P., & Cosentino, S. (2003). Implicit memory for new associations: Types of conceptual representations. In J. S. Bowers & C. J. Marsolek (Eds.), *Rethinking implicit memory* (pp. 302–323). London: Oxford University Press.

Uylings, H. B. M. (2006). Development of the human cortex and the concept of 'critical' or 'sensitive' periods. *Language Learning, 56*, 59–90.

Uylings, H. B. M., & Vrije, U. (2002). About assumptions in estimation of density of neurons and glial cells. *Biological Psychiatry, 51*, 840–842.

Vaillant, G. E., & Vaillant, C. O. (1990). Natural history of male psychological health: XII. A 46-year study of predictors of successful aging at age 65. *American Journal of Psychiatry, 147*, 31–37.

Vaitl, D., Schienle, A., & Stark, R. (2005). Neurobiology of fear and disgust. *International Journal of Psychophysiology, 57*, 1–4.

Valencia, R. R., & Suzuki, L. A. (2003). *Intelligence testing and minority students: Foundations, performance factors, and assessment issues*. Thousand Oaks, CA: Sage.

Valente, S. M. (1991). Electroconvulsive therapy. *Archives of Psychiatric Nursing, 5*, 223–228.

Vallar, G., & Daini, R. (2006). Visual perceptual processing in unilateral spatial neglect: The case of visual illusions. In T. Vecchi, & G. Bottini, *Imagery and spatial cognition: Methods, models and cognitive assessment*. Amsterdam: John Benjamins Publishing.

Valsiner, J., Diriwächter, R., & Sauck, C. (2005). Diversity in unity: Standard questions and nonstandard interpretations. In *Science and medicine in dialogue: Thinking through particulars and universals* (pp. 289–307). Westport, CT: Praeger Publishers/Greenwood Publishing Group.

Van Beekum, S. (2005). The therapist as a new object. *Transactional Analysis Journal, 35*, 187–191.

Van De Graaff, K. (2000). *Human anatomy* (5th ed.). Boston: McGraw-Hill.

van den Bosch, L. M., Koeter, M. W., Stijnen, T., Verheul, R., & van den Brink, W. (2005). Sustained efficacy of dialectical behaviour therapy for borderline personality disorder. *Behavioral Research Therapy, 43*, 1231–1241.

Van den Wildenberg, W. P. M., & Van der Molen, M. W. (2004). Developmental trends in simple and selective inhibition of compatible and incompatible responses. *Journal of Experimental Child Psychology, 87*, 201–220.

van der Helm, P. A. (2006). Review of perceptual dynamics: Theoretical foundations and philosophical implications of gestalt psychology. *Philosophical Psychology, 19*, 274–279.

van Eck, M., Nicolson, N. A., & Berkhof, J. (1998). Effects of stressful daily events on mood states: Relationship to global perceived stress. *Journal of Personality and Social Psychology, 75*, 1572–1585.

van Hooren, S. A. H., Valentijn, A. M., & Bosma, H. (2007). Cognitive functioning in healthy older adults aged 64–81: a cohort study into the effects of age, sex, and education. *Aging, Neuropsychology, and Cognition, 14*, 40–54.

Van Knippenberg, D. (1999). Social identity and persuasion: Reconsidering the role of group membership. In D. Abrams & M. A. Hogg (Eds.), *Social identity and social cognition*. Malden, MA: Blackwell.

van Leeuwen, M. L., & Macrae, C. N. (2004). Is beautiful always good? Implicit benefits of facial attractiveness. *Social Cognition, 22*, 637–649.

Van Overwalle, F., & Siebler, F. (2005). A connectionist model of attitude formation and change. *Personality and Social Psychology Review, 9*, 231–274.

van Wel, F., Linssen, H., & Abma, R. (2000). The parental bond and the well-being of adolescents and young adults. *Journal of Youth & Adolescence, 29*, 307–318.

Vanasse, A., Niyonsenga, T., & Courteau, J. (2004). Smoking cessation within the context of family medicine: Which smokers take action? *Preventive Medicine: An International Journal Devoted to Practice and Theory, 38*, 330–337.

Vance, E. B., & Wagner, N. W. (1976). Written descriptions of orgasm: A study of sex differences. *Archives of Sexual Behavior, 5*, 87–98.

Vandell, D. L., Burchinal, M. R., Belsky, J., Owen, M. T., Friedman, S. L., Clarke-Stewart, A., McCartney, K., & Weinraub, M. (2005). *Early child care and children's development in the primary grades: Follow-up results from the NICHD Study of Early Child Care*. Paper presented at the biennial meeting of the Society for Research in Child Development, Atlanta, GA.

Vandervert, L. R., Schimpf, P. H., & Liu, H. (2007). How working memory and the cerebellum collaborate to produce creativity and innovation. *Creativity Research Journal, 19*, 1–18.

Vanheule, S., Desmet, M., Rosseel, Y., & Meganck, R. (2006). Core transference themes in depression. *Journal of Affective Disorders, 91*, 71–75.

VanLehn, K. (1996). Cognitive skill acquisition. *Annual Review of Psychology, 47*, 513–539.

Varela, J. G., Boccaccini, M. T., Scogin, F., Stump, J., & Caputo, A. (2004). Personality testing in law enforcement employment settings: A meta-analytic review. *Criminal Justice and Behavior, 31*, 649–675.

Vargha-Khadem, F., Gadian, D. G., Copp, A., & Mishkin, M. (2005). FOXP2 and the neuroanatomy of speech and language. *Nature Reviews Neuroscience, 6*, 131–138.

Varma, S. (2007). A computational model of Tower of Hanoi problem solving. *Dissertation Abstracts International: Section B: The Sciences and Engineering, 67(8-B)*, 4736.

Vaughn, L. A., & Weary, G. (2002). Roles of the availability of explanations, feelings of ease, and dysphoria in judgments about the future. *Journal of Science and Clinical Psychology, 21*, 686–704.

Veasey, S., Rosen, R., Barzansky, B., Rosen, I., & Owens, J. (2002). Sleep loss and fatigue in residency training: A reappraisal. *Journal of the American Medical Association, 288*, 1116–1124.

Vedantam, S. (2005, January 23). See no bias. *Washington Post*, p. W12.

Vega, C. P. (2006). The effects of therapeutic components on at-risk middle school children's grades and attendance: An archival study of an after-school prevention program. *Dissertation Abstracts International: Section B: The Sciences and Engineering, 66*, 4504.

Vellacott, J. (2007). Resilience: A psychoanalytic exploration. *British Journal of Psychotherapy, 23*, 163–170.

Veltman, M. W. M., & Browne, K. D. (2001). Three decades of child mal-treatment research: Implications for the school years. *Trauma Violence and Abuse, 2*, 215–239.

Veniegas, R. C. (2000). Biological research on women's sexual orientations: Evaluating the scientific evidence. *Journal of Social Issues, 56*, 267–282.

Verdejo, A., Toribio, I., & Orozco, C. (2005). Neuropsychological functioning in methadone maintenance patients versus abstinent heroin abusers. *Drug and Alcohol Dependence, 78*, 283–288.

Verfaellie, M., & Keane, M. M. (2002). Impaired and preserved memory processes in amnesia. In L. R. Squire & D. L. Schacter (Eds.), *Neuropsychology of memory* (3rd ed.). New York: Guilford Press.

Verhaeghen, P., Marcoen, A., & Goossens, L. (1992). Improving memory performance in the aged through mnemonic training: A meta-analytic study. *Psychology and Aging, 7*, 242–251.

Vernon, P. A., Jang, K. L., Harris, J. A., & McCarthy, J. M. (1997). Environmental predictors of personality differences: A twin and sibling study. *Journal of Personality and Social Psychology, 72*, 177–183.

Victor, S. B., & Fish, M. C. (1995). Lesbian mothers and the children: A review for school psychologists. *School Psychology Review, 24*, 456–479.

Viding, E., Blair, R. J., Moffitt, T. E., & Plomin, R. (2005). Evidence for substantial genetic risk for psychopathy in 7-year-olds. *Journal of Child Psychology and Psychiatry, 46*, 592–597.

Vieira, E. M., & Freire, J. C. (2006). Alteridade e Psicologia Humanista: Uma leitura ética da abordagem centrada na pessoa. Alterity and humanistic psychology: An ethical reading of the Person-Centered Approach. *Estudos de Psicologia, 23*, 425–432.

Vihman, M. M. (1996). *Phonological development: The origins of language in the child*. London, England: Blackwell.

Villarosa, L. (2002, December 3). To prevent sexual abuse, abusers step forward. *The New York Times*, p. B1.

Villemure, C., Slotnick, B. M., & Bushnell, M. C. (2003). Effects of odors on pain perception: Deciphering the roles of emotion and attention. *Pain, 106*, 101–108.

Violani, C., & Lombardo, C. (2003). Peripheral temperature changes during rest and gender differences in thermal biofeedback. *Journal of Psychosomatic Research, 54*, 391–397.

Vital-Durand, F., Atkinson, J., & Braddick, O. J. (Eds.). (1996). *Infant vision. The European brain and behaviour society publication series* (Vol. 2). Oxford, England: Oxford University Press.

Vitiello, A. L., Bonello, R. P., & Pollard, H. P. (2007). The effectiveness of ENAR(R) for the treatment of chronic neck pain in Australian adults: A preliminary single-blind, randomised controlled trial. *Chiropractic Osteopathology, 9*, 9.

Vleioras, G., & Bosma, H. A. (2005). Are identity styles important for psychological well-being? *Journal of Adolescence, 28,* 397–409.

Vogel, G. W., Feng, P., & Kinney, G. G. (2000). Ontogeny of REM sleep in rats: Possible implications for endogenous depression. *Physiology & Behavior, 68,* 453–461.

Voicu, H., & Schmajuk, N. (2002). Latent learning, shortcuts and detours: A computational model. *Behavioural Processes, 59,* 67–86.

Volterra, V., Caselli, M. C., Capirci, O., Tonucci, F., & Vicari, S. (2003). Early linguistic abilities of Italian children with Williams syndrome [Special issue: Williams syndrome]. *Developmental Neuropsychology, 23,* 33–58.

von Restorff, H. (1933). Über die Wirking von Bereichsbildungen im Spurenfeld. In W. Kohler & H. von Restorff, *Analyse von Vorgangen in Spurenfeld: I. Psychologische forschung, 18,* 299–342.

Voruganti, L. P., Awad, A. G., Parker, B., Forrest, C., Usmani, Y., Fernando, M. L. D., & Senthilal, S. (2007). Cognition, functioning and quality of life in schizophrenia treatment: Results of a one-year randomized controlled trial of olanzapine and quetiapine. *Schizophrenia Research, 96,* 146–155.

Vrij, A. (2001). Detecting the liars. *Psychologist, 14,* 596–598.

Vygotsky, L. S. (1926/1997). *Educational psychology.* Delray Beach, FL: St. Lucie Press.

Wachs, T. D., Pollitt, E., Cueto, S., & Jacoby, E. (2004). Structure and cross-contextual stability of neonatal temperament. *Infant Behavior and Development, 27,* 382–396.

Wachtel, P. L., & Messer, S. B. (Eds.). (1997). *Theories of psychotherapy: Origins and evolution.* Washington, DC: American Psychological Association.

Wadden, T. A., Crerand, C. E., & Brock, J. (2005). Behavioral treatment of obesity. *Psychiatric Clinics of North America, 28,* 151–170.

Wade, K. A., Sharman, S. J., & Garry, M. (2007). False claims about false memory research. *Consciousness and Cognition: An International Journal, 16,* 18–28.

Wager, T. D (2005). The neural bases of placebo effects in pain. *Current Directions in Psychological Science, 14,* 175–180.

Wagner, A. W., Rizvi, S. L., & Harned, M. S. (2007). Applications of dialectical behavior therapy to the treatment of complex trauma-related problems: when one case formulation does not fit all. *Journal of Trauma Stress, 20,* 391–400.

Wagner, B. M. (1997). Family risk factors for child and adolescent suicidal behavior. *Psychological Bulletin, 121,* 246–298.

Wagner, E. F., & Atkins, J. H. (2000). Smoking among teenage girls. *Journal of Child & Adolescent Substance Abuse, 9,* 93–110.

Wagner, H. J., Bollard, C. M., Vigouroux, S., Huls, M. H., Anderson, R., Prentice, H. G., Brenner, M. K., Heslop, H. E., & Rooney, C. M. (2004). A strategy for treatment of Epstein Barr virus-positive Hodgkin's disease by targeting interleukin 12 to the tumor environment using tumor antigen-specific T cells. *Cancer Gene Therapy, 2,* 81–91.

Wagner, R. K. (2002). Smart people doing dumb things: The case of managerial incompetence. In R. J. Sternberg (Ed.), *Why smart people can be so stupid* (pp. 42–63). New Haven, CT: Yale University Press.

Wain, H. J., Grammer, G. G., & Stasinos, J. (2006). Psychiatric intervention for medical and surgical patients following traumatic injuries. In E. C. Ritchie, P. J. Watson, & M. J. Friedman, *Interventions following mass violence and disasters: Strategies for mental health practice.* New York: Guilford Press.

Wainer, H., Dorans, N. J., Eignor, D., Flaugher, R., Green, B. E., Mislevy, R. J., Steinberg, L., & Thissen D. (2000). *Computerized adaptive testing: A primer* (2nd ed.). Mahwah, NJ: Erlbaum.

Walcott, D. M. (2000). Repressed memory still lacks scientific reliability. *Journal of the American Academy of Psychiatry & the Law, 28,* 243–244.

Waldrep, D., & Waits, W. (2002). Returning to the Pentagon: The use of mass desensitization following the September 11, 2001 attack [Special issue: The mental health response to the 9–11 attack on the Pentagon]. *Military Medicine, 167,* 58–59.

Walker, L. J., & Frimer, J. A. (2007). Moral personality of brave and caring exemplars. *Journal of Personality and Social Psychology, 93,* 845–860.

Walker, M. P., & Stickgold, R. (2004). Sleep-dependent learning and memory consolidation. *Neuron, 44,* 121–133.

Walker, M. P., & Stickgold, R. (2005). It's practice, with sleep, that makes perfect: implications of sleep-dependent learning and plasticity for skill performance. *Clinical Sports Medicine, 24,* 301–311.

Walker, M. P., Brakefield, T., Morgan, A., Hobson, J. A., & Stickgold R. (2002). Practice with sleep makes perfect: Sleep-dependent motor skill learning. *Neuron, 35,* 205–211.

Walker, W. R., Skowronski, J. J., & Thompson, C. P. (2003). Consolidation of long-term memory: Evidence and alternatives. *Review of General Psychology, 7,* 203–210.

Wallerstein, J. S., Lewis, J., Blakeslee, S., & Lewis, J. (2000). *The unexpected legacy of divorce.* New York: Hyperion.

Wallis, C., & Willwerth, J. (1992, July 6). Schizophrenia: A new drug brings patients back to life. *Time,* pp. 52–57.

Walsh, B. T., Kaplan, A. S., Attia, E., Olmstead, M., Parides, M., Carter, J. C., Pike, K. M., Devlin, M. J., Woodside, B., Robert, C. A., & Rockert, W. (2006). Fluoxetine after weight restoration in anorexia nervosa: A randomized controlled trial. *JAMA: Journal of the American Medical Association, 295,* 2605–2612.

Walsh, R., & Shapiro, S. L. (2006). The meeting of meditative disciplines and western psychology. *American Psychologist, 61,* 227–239.

Walt, V. (2005, March 7). A land where girls rule in math. *Time,* pp. 56–57.

Walter, J. H., White F. J., Hall, S. K. MacDonald, A, Rylance, G., Boneh, A., Francis, D. E., Shortland, G. J., Schmidt, M., & Vail, A. (2002). How practical are recommendations for dietary control in phenylketonuria? *Lancet, 360,* 55–57.

Wang, A., & Clark, D. A. (2002). Haunting thoughts: The problem of obsessive mental intrusions [Special issue: Intrusions in cognitive behavioral therapy]. *Journal of Cognitive Psychotherapy, 16,* 193–208.

Wang, O. (2003). Infantile amnesia reconsidered: A cross-cultural analysis. *Memory, 11,* 65–80.

Wang, P. S., Aguilar-Gaxiola, S., Alonso, J., Angermeyer, M. C., Borges, G., Bromet, E. J., Bruffaerts, R., deGirolamo, G., deGraaf, R., Gureje, O., Haro, J. M., Karam, E. G., Kessler, R. C., Kovess, V., Lane, M. C., Lee, S., Levinson, D., Ono, Y., Petukhova, M., Posada-Villa, J., Seedat, S., & Wells, J. E. (2007, September 8). Use of mental health services for anxiety, mood, and substance disorders in 17 countries in the WHO world mental health surveys. *Lancet, 370,* 841–850.

Wang, Q. (2004). The emergence of cultural self-constructs: autobiographical memory and self-description in European American and Chinese children. *Developmental Psychology, 40,* 3–15.

Wang, Q., & Conway, M. A. (2006). Autobiographical memory, self, and culture. In L-G. Nilsson & N. Ohta, *Memory and society: Psychological perspectives.* New York: Psychology Press.

Wang, V. O., & Sue, S. (2005). In the eye of the storm: Race and genomics in research and practice. *American Psychologist, 60,* 37–45.

Wang, X., Lu, T., Snider, R. K., & Liang, L. (2005). Sustained firing in auditory cortex evoked by preferred stimuli. *Nature, 435,* 341–346.

Warburton, E. C., Glover, C. P., Massey, P. V., Wan, H., Johnson, B., Bienemann, A., Deuschle, U., Kew, J. N., Aggleton, J. P., Bashir, Z. I., Uney, J., & Brownj, M. W. (2005). cAMP responsive element-binding protein phosphorylation is necessary for perirhinal long-term potentiation and recognition memory. *Journal of Neuroscience, 25,* 6296–6303.

Ward, L. M. (2004). Wading through the stereotypes: Positive and negative associations between media use and Black adolescents' conceptions of self. *Developmental Psychology, 40,* 284–294.

Ward, W. C., Kogan, N., & Pankove, E. (1972). Incentive effects in children's creativity. *Child Development, 43,* 669–677.

Ward-Baker, P. D. (2007). The remarkable oldest old: A new vision of aging. *Dissertation Abstracts International Section A: Humanities and Social Sciences, 67(8-A),* 3115.

Warden, C. A., Wu, M-Y., & Tsai, D. (2006). Online shopping interface components: relative importance as peripheral and central cues. *CyberPsychology & Behavior, 9,* 285–296.

Wark, G. R., & Krebs, D. L. (1996). Gender and dilemma differences in real-life moral judgement. *Developmental Psychology, 32,* 220–230.

Wass, T. S., Mattson, S. N., & Riley, E. P. (2004). Neuroanatomical and neurobehavioral effects of heavy prenatal alcohol exposure. In J. Brick (Ed.), *Handbook of the medical consequences of alcohol and drug abuse.* (pp. 139–169). New York: Haworth Press.

Wasserman, E. A., & Miller, R. R. (1997). What's elementary about associative learning? *Annual Review of Psychology, 48,* 573–607.

Waters, E., & Beauchaine, T. P. (2003). Are there really patterns of attachment? Comment on Fraley and Spieker (2003). *Developmental Psychology, 39,* 417–422.

Waters, E., Hamilton, C. E., & Weinfield, N. S. (2000). The stability of attachment security from infancy to adolescence and early adulthood: General introduction. *Child Development, 71,* 678–683.

Watkins, C. (2007). *Date rape.* Farmington Hills, MI: Greenhaven Press.

Watson, D., Hubbard, B., & Wiese, D. (2000). Self-other agreement in personality and affectivity: The role of acquaintanceship, trait visibility, and assumed similarity. *Journal of Personality and Social Psychology, 78,* 546–558.

Watson, J. B. (1924). *Behaviorism.* New York: Norton.

Watson, J. B., & Rayner, R. (1920). Conditioned emotional reactions. *Journal of Experimental Psychology, 3,* 1–14.

Watson, J. M., Balota, D. A., & Roediger, H. L. (2003). Creating false memories with hybrid lists of semantic and phonological associates: Over-additive false memories produced by converging associative networks. *Journal of Memory and Language, 49,* 95–118.

Watson, M., Haviland, J. S., Greer, S., Davidson, J., & Bliss, J. M. (1999). Influence of psychological response on survival in breast cancer: a population-based cohort study. *Lancet, 354,* 1331–1336.

Waugh, C. E., & Larkin, G. R. (2003). What good are positive emotions in crises? A prospective study of resilience and emotions following the terrorist attacks on the United States on September 11th, 2001. *Journal of Personality and Social Psychology, 84,* 365–376.

Webb, W. B. (1992). *Sleep: The gentle tyrant* (2nd ed.). Boston: Anker.

Weber, R., Ritterfeld, U., & Kostygina, A. (2006). Aggression and violence as effects of playing violent video games? In P. Vorderer & J. Bryant, *Playing video games: Motives, responses, and consequences.* Mahwah, NJ: Lawrence Erlbaum Associates.

Wechsler, H., Davenport, A., Dowdall, G., Moeykens, B., & Castillo, S. (1994). Health and behavioral consequences of binge drinking in college. A national survey of students at 140 campuses. *Journal of the American Medical Association, 272,* 1672–1677.

Wechsler, H., Kuo, M., Lee, H., & Dowdall, G. W. (2000). *Environmental correlates of underage alcohol use and related problems of college students.* Cambridge, MA: Harvard School of Public Health.

Wechsler, H., Lee, J. E., Nelson, T. F., & Kuo, M. (2002). Underage college students' drinking behavior, access to alcohol, and the influence of deterrence policies. *Journal of American College Health, 50,* 223–236.

Weeks, M., & Lupfer, M. B. (2004). Complicating race: The relationship between prejudice, race, and social class categorizations. *Personality and Social Psychology Bulletin, 30,* 972–984.

Wegener, D. T., Petty, R. E., Smoak, N. D., & Fabrigar, L. R. (2004). Multiple routes to resisting attitude change. In E. S. Knowles & J. A. Linn (Eds.), *Resistance and persuasion.* Mahwah, NJ: Lawrence Erlbaum Associates.

Wegner, D. M., Wenzlaff, R. M., & Kozak, M. (2004). Dream rebound: The return of suppressed thoughts in dreams. *Psychological Science, 15,* 232–236.

Wehrle, R., Kaufmann, C., Wetter, T. C., Holsboer, F., Auer, D. P., Pollmacher, T., & Czisch, M. (2007). Functional microstates within human REM sleep: First evidence from fMRI of a thalamocortical network specific for phasic REM periods. *European Journal of Neuroscience, 25,* 863–871.

Weiland, J. D., & Humayun, M. S. (2006). Intraocular retinal prosthesis. Big steps to sight restoration. *IEEE Engineering and Medical Biology Magazine, 25,* 60–66.

Weinberg, M. S., Williams, C. J., & Pryor, D. W. (1991, February 27). Personal communication. Indiana University, Bloomington.

Weiner, B. A., & Wettstein, R. (1993). *Legal issues in mental health care.* New York: Plenum Press.

Weiner, G. J. (2000). The immunobiology and clinical potential of immunostimulatory CpG oligodeoxynucleotides. *Journal of Leukocyte Biology, 68,* 455–463.

Weiner, I. B. (2004a). Monitoring psychotherapy with performance-based measures of personality functioning. *Journal of Personality Assessment, 83,* 323–331.

Weiner, I. B. (2004b). Rorschach Inkblot method. In M. E. Maruish (Ed.), *Use of psychological testing for treatment planning and outcomes assessment: Vol. 3: Instruments for adults* (3rd ed.). Mahwah, NJ: Lawrence Erlbaum Associates.

Weinstein, M., Glei, D. A., Yamazaki, A., & Ming-Cheng, C. (2004). The role of intergenerational relations in the association between life stressors and depressive symptoms. *Research on Aging, 26,* 511–530.

Weintraub, M. (1976). Intelligent noncompliance and capricious compliance. In L. Lasagna (Ed.), *Patient compliance.* Mt. Kisco, NY: Futura.

Weis, R., Crockett, T. E., & Vieth, S. (2004). Using MMPI-A profiles to predict success in a military-style residential treatment program for adolescents with academic and conduct problems. *Psychology in the Schools, 41,* 563–574.

Weiss, W. M., & Weiss, M. R. (2003). Attraction- and entrapment-based commitment among competitive female gymnasts. *Journal of Sport & Exercise Psychology, 25,* 229–247.

Weissman, M., Markowitz, J., & Klerman, G. L. (2007). *Clinician's quick guide to interpersonal psychotherapy.* New York: Oxford University Press.

Weissman, M. M., Bland, R. C., Canino, G. J., Faravelli, C., Greenwald, S., Hwu, H. G., Joyce, P. R., Karam, E. G., Lee, C. K., Lellouch, J., Lepine, J. P., Newman, S. C., Rubio-Stipec, M., Wells, J. E., Wickramarante, P. J., Wittchen, H., & Yeh, E. K. (1997, July 24–31). Cross-national epidemiology of major depression and bipolar disorder. *Journal of the American Medical Association, 276,* 293–299.

Weissman, M. W., & Olfson, M. (1995, August 11). Depression in women: Implications for health care research. *Science, 269,* 799–801.

Weisz, A., & Black, B. (2002). Gender and moral reasoning: African American youth respond to dating dilemmas. *Journal of Human Behavior in the Social Environment, 5,* 35–52.

Welch, K. C. (2002). *The Bell Curve* and the politics of Negrophobia. In J. M. Fish (Ed.), *Race and intelligence: Separating science from myth* (pp. 177–198). Mahwah, NJ: Erlbaum.

Welkowitz, L. A., Struening, E. L., Pittman, J., Guardino, M., & Welkowitz, J. (2000). Obsessive-compulsive disorder and comorbid anxiety problems in a national anxiety screening sample. *Journal of Anxiety Disorders, 14,* 471–482.

Wells, G. L., Olson, E. A., & Charman, S. D. (2002). The confidence of eyewitnesses in their identifications from lineups. *Current Directions in Psychological Science, 11,* 151–154.

Wenar, C. (1994). *Developmental psychopathology: From infancy through adolescence* (3rd ed.). New York: McGraw-Hill.

Wenzel, A., Zetocha, K., & Ferraro, R. F. (2007). Depth of processing and recall of threat material in fearful and nonfearful individuals. *Anxiety, Stress & Coping: An International Journal, 20,* 223–237.

Werblin, F., & Roska, B. (2007, April). The movies in our eyes. *Scientific American,* 73–77.

Werker, J. F., & Tees, R. C. (2005). Speech perception as a window for understanding plasticity and commitment in language systems of the brain. *Developmental Psychobiology, 46,* 233–234.

Werner, E. E. (1995). Resilience in development. *Current Directions in Psychological Science, 4,* 81–85.

Werner, J. S., Pinna, B., & Spillmann, L. (2007, March). Illusory color and the brain. *Scientific American,* 90–96.

Wertheimer, M. (1923). Untersuchungen zur Lehre von der Gestalt, II. *Psychol. Forsch., 5,* 301–350. In R. Beardsley and M. Wertheimer (Eds.). (1958), *Readings in perception.* New York: Van Nostrand.

West, D. S., Harvey-Berino, J., & Raczynski, J. M. (2004). Behavioral aspects of obesity, dietary intake, and chronic disease. In J. M. Raczynski and L. C. Leviton (Eds.), *Handbook of clinical health psychology: Vol. 2. Disorders of behavior and health* (pp. 9–41). Washington, DC: American Psychological Association.

West, J. R., & Blake, C. A. (2005). Fetal alcohol syndrome: An assessment of the field. *Experimental Biological Medicine, 6,* 354–356.

West, R. L. (1995). Compensatory strategies for age-associated memory impairment. In A. D. Baddeley, B. A. Wilson, & F. N. Watts (Eds.), *Handbook of memory disorders.* Chichester, England: Wiley.

West, R. L., Bagwell, D. K., & Dark-Freudeman, A. (2007). Self-efficacy and memory aging: The impact of a memory intervention based on self-efficacy. *Neuropsychological Development and Cognition, B, Aging and Neuropsychological Cognition, 14,* 1–28.

West, R. L., Thorn, R. M., Bagwell, D. K. (2003). Memory performance and beliefs as a function of goal setting and aging. *Psychology & Aging, 18,* 111–125.

West, S. L., & O'Neal, K. K. (2004). Project D. A.R.E. outcome effectiveness revisited. *American Journal of Public Health, 94,* 1027–1029.

Westen, D., & Gabbard, G. O. (1999). Psychoanalytic approaches to personality. In L. A. Pervin & O. P. John (Eds.), *Handbook of personality: Theory and research* (2nd ed.). New York: Guilford.

Westen, D., Novotny, C. M., & Thompson-Brenner, H. (2004). The empirical status of empirically supported psychotherapies: Assumptions, findings, and reporting in controlled clinical trials. *Psychological Bulletin, 130,* 631–663.

Westerterp, K. R. (2006). Perception, passive overfeeding and energy metabolism. *Physiology & Behavior, 89,* 62–65.

Wetter, D. W., Fiore, M. C., Gritz, E. R., Lando, H. A., Stitzer, M. L., Hasselblad, V., & Baker, T. B. (1998). The Agency for Health Care Policy and Research. Smoking cessation clinical practice guideline: Findings and implications for psychologists. *American Psychologist, 53,* 657–669.

Whaley, B. B. (Ed.). (2000). *Explaining illness: Research, theory, and strategies.* Mahwah, NJ: Erlbaum.

Wheeler, M. E., Petersen, S. E., & Buckner, R. L. (2000). Memory's echo: Vivid remembering reactivates sensory-specific cortex. *Proceedings of the National Academy of Sciences, 97,* 11125–11129.

Whisenant, W. A., Pedersen, P. M., & Obenour, B. L. (2002). Success and gender: Determining the rate of advancement for intercollegiate athletic directors. *Sex Roles, 47,* 485–491.

Whitbourne, S. K. (2000). The normal aging process. In S. K. Whitbourne & S. Krauss (Eds.), *Psychopathology in later adulthood.* New York: Wiley.

Whitbourne, S. K., & Wills, K (1993). Psychological issues in institutional care of the aged. In S. B. Goldsmith (Ed.), *Long-term care.* Gaithersburg, MD: Aspen Press.

Whitbourne, S. K., Zuschlag, M. K., Elliot, L. B., & Waterman, A. S. (1992). Psychosocial development in adulthood: A 22-year sequential study. *Journal of Personality and Social Psychology, 63,* 260–271.

White, L. (2007). Linguistic theory, universal grammar, and second language acquisition. In B. Van Patten, & J. Williams, *Theories in* second language acquisition: An introduction. Mahwah, NJ: Lawrence Erlbaum Associates.

Whitehouse, W. G., Orne, E. C., Dinges, D. F., Bates, B. L., Nadon, R., & Orne, M. T. (2005). The cognitive interview: Does it successfully avoid the dangers of forensic hypnosis? *American Journal of Psychology, 118,* 213–234.

Whitfield, J. B., Zhu, G., Madden, P. A., Neale, M. C., Heath, A. C., & Martin, N. G. (2004). The genetics of alcohol intake and of alcohol dependence. *Alcoholism: Clinical and Experimental Research, 28,* 1153–1160.

WHO World Mental Health Survey Consortium. (2004). Prevalence, severity, and unmet need for treatment of mental disorders in the World Health Organization World Mental Health Surveys. *Journal of the American Medical Association, 291,* 2581–2590.

Whorf, B. L. (1956). *Language, thought, and reality.* New York: Wiley.

Wickelgren, E. A. (2004). Perspective distortion of trajectory forms and perceptual constancy in visual event identification. *Perception and Psychophysics, 66,* 629–641.

Wickelgren, I. (1998, June 26). Teaching the brain to take drugs. *Science, 280,* 2045–2047.

Wickelgren, I. (2001, March, 2). Working memory helps the mind focus. *Science, 291,* 1684–1685.

Wickelgren, I. (2006, May 26). A vision for the blind. *Science, 312,* 1124–1126.

Wickens, C. D. (1984). *Engineering psychology and human performance.* Columbus, OH: Merrill.

Widiger, T. A., & Clark, L. A. (2000). Toward *DSM-V* and the classification of psychopathology. *Psychological Bulletin, 126,* 946–963.

Widmeyer, W. N., & Loy, J. W. (1988). When you're hot, you're hot! Warm-cold effects in first impressions of persons and teaching effectiveness. *Journal of Educational Psychology, 80,* 118–121.

Wiederhold, B. K., & Wiederhold, M. D. (2005a). Specific phobias and social phobia. In B. K. Wiederhold & M. D. Wiederhold (Eds.), *Virtual reality therapy for anxiety disorders: Advances in evaluation and treatment.* Washington, DC: American Psychological Association.

Wiederhold, B. K., & Wiederhold, M. D. (2005b). *Virtual reality therapy for anxiety disorders: Advances in evaluation and treatment.* Washington, DC: American Psychological Association.

Wiehe, V. R., & Richards, A. L. (1995). *Intimate betrayal: Understanding and responding to the trauma of acquaintance rape.* Thousand Oaks, CA: Sage Publications.

Wielgosz, A. T., & Nolan, R. P. (2000). Biobehavioral factors in the context of ischemic cardiovascular disease. *Journal of Psychosomatic Research, 48,* 339–345.

Wigfield, A., & Eccles, J. S. (2000). Expectancy-value theory of achievement motivation. *Contemporary Educational Psychology, 25,* 68–81.

Wiggins, J. S. (1997). In defense of traits. In R. Hogan, J. Johnson, & S. Briggs (Eds.), *Handbook of personality psychology.* Orlando, FL: Academic Press.

Wiggins, J. S. (2003). *Paradigms of personality assessment.* New York: Guilford Press.

Wildavsky, B. (2000, September 4). A blow to bilingual education. *U.S. News & World Report,* pp. 22–28.

Wilgoren, J. (1999, October 22). Quality day care, early, is tied to achievements as an adult. *The New York Times,* p. A16.

Wilkinson, L., & Olliver-Gray, Y. (2006). The significance of silence: Differences in meaning, learning styles, and teaching strategies in cross-cultural settings. *Psychologia: An*

International Journal of Psychology in the Orient, 49, Special issue: Child language, 74–88.

Willander, J., & Larsson, M. (2006). Smell your way back to childhood: Autobiographical odor memory. *Psychonomic Bulletin & Review, 13,* 240–244.

Willems, R. M., & Hagoort, P. (2007). Neural evidence for the interplay between language, gesture, and action: a review. *Brain Language, 101,* 278–289.

Williams, J. E., & Best, D. L. (1990). *Measuring sex stereotypes: A multinational study.* Newbury Park, CA: Sage.

Williams, J. E., Paton, C. C., Siegler, I. C., Eigenbrodt, M. L., Nieto, F. J., & Tyroler, H. A. (2000). Anger proneness predicts coronary heart disease risk: Prospective analysis from the Atherosclerosis Risk in Communities (ARIC) Study. *Circulation, 101,* 2034–2039.

Williams, J. W., Mulrow, C. D., Chiquette, E., Noel, P. H., Aguilar, C., & Cornell, J. (2000). A systematic review of newer pharmacotherapies for depression in adults: Evidence report summary. *Annals of Internal Medicine, 132,* 743–756.

Williamson, P., McLeskey, J., & Hoppey, D. (2006). Educating students with mental retardation in general education classrooms. *Exceptional Children, 72,* 347–361.

Willis, G. L. (2005). The therapeutic effects of dopamine replacement therapy and its psychiatric side effects are mediated by pineal function. *Behavioural Brain Research, 160,* 148–160.

Willis, S. L., & Schaie, K. W. (1994). In C. B. Fisher & R. M. Lerner (Eds.), *Applied developmental psychology.* New York: McGraw-Hill.

Willness, C. R., Steel, P., & Lee, Kibeom, (2007). A meta-analysis of the antecedents and consequences of workplace sexual harassment. *Personnel Psychology, 60,* 127–162.

Wilson, G. T., & Agras, W. S. (1992). The future of behavior therapy. *Psychotherapy, 29,* 39–43.

Wilson, G. T., & Fairburn, C. G. (2002). Treatments for eating disorders. In P. E. Nathan, & J. M. Gorman (Eds.), *A guide to treatments that work* (2nd ed.), pp. 559–592. London: Oxford University Press.

Wilson, J. P., & Keane, T. M. (Eds.). (1996). *Assessing psychological trauma and PTSD.* New York: Guilford.

Wilson, M. A. (2002). Hippocampal memory formation, plasticity and the role of sleep. *Neurobiology of Learning & Memory, 78,* 565–569.

Wilson, T. D. (2004). *Strangers to ourselves: Discovering the adaptive unconscious.* Cambridge, MA: Harvard University Press.

Wilson, T. D. (2006, September 1). The power of social psychological interventions. *Science, 313,* 1251–1252.

Wilson, T. G., Grilo, C. M., & Vitousek, K. M. (2007). Psychological treatment of eating disorders. *American Psychologist, 62,* Special issue: Eating disorders,199–216.

Windholz, G. (1997, September). Ivan P. Pavlov: An overview of his life and psychological work. *American Psychologist, 52,* 941–946.

Windholz, G., & Lamal, P. A. (2002). Koehler's insight revisited. In R. A. Griggs (Ed.), *Handbook for teaching introductory psychology, Vol. 3: With an emphasis on assessment,* pp. 80–81. Mahwah, NJ: Erlbaum.

Winerman, L. (2005, June). ACTing up. *Monitor on Psychology,* pp. 44–45.

Wines, M. (2004, March 18). For sniffing out land mines, a platoon of twitching noses. *New York Times,* pp. A1, A4.

Winik, L. W. (2006, October 1). The true cost of depression. *Parade,* 7.

Winkler, K. J. (1997, July 11). Scholars explore the blurred lines of race, gender, and ethnicity. *The Chronicle of Higher Education,* pp. A11–A12.

Winner, E. (2000). The origins and ends of giftedness. *American Psychologist, 55,* 159–169.

Winner, E. (2003). Creativity and talent. In M. H. Bornstein & L. Davidson (Eds.), *Well-being: Positive development across the life course* (pp. 371–380). Mahwah, NJ: Lawrence Erlbaum.

Winningham, R. G., Hyman, I. E., Jr., & Dinnel, D. L. (2000). Flashbulb memories? The effects of when the initial memory report was obtained. *Memory, 8,* 209–216.

Winsler, A., Madigan, A. L., & Aquilino, S. A. (2005). Correspondence between maternal and paternal parenting styles in early childhood. *Early Childhood Research Quarterly, 20,* 1–12.

Winson, J. (1990, November). The meaning of dreams. *Scientific American,* pp. 86–96.

Winstead, B. A., & Sanchez, A. (2005). Gender and psychopathology. In J. E. Maddux & B. A. Winstead, *Psychopathology: Foundations for a contemporary understanding.* Mahwah, NJ: Lawrence Erlbaum Associates.

Winston, A. S. (2004). *Defining difference: Race and racism in the history of psychology.* Washington, DC: American Psychological Association.

Winston, J. S., O'Doherty, J., & Kilner, J. M. (2006). Brain systems for assessing facial attractiveness. *Neuropsychologia, 45,* 195–206.

Winter, D. G. (1973). *The power motive.* New York: Free Press.

Winter, D. G. (1987). Leader appeal, leader performance, and the motive profile of leaders and followers: A study of American presidents and elections. *Journal of Personality and Social Psychology, 52,* 196–202.

Winter, D. G. (1988). The power motive in women—and men. *Journal of Personality and Social Psychology, 54,* 510–519.

Winter, D. G. (1995). *Personality: Analysis and interpretation of lives.* New York: McGraw-Hill.

Winter, D. G. (2007). The role of motivation, responsibility, and integrative complexity in crisis escalation: Comparative studies of war and peace crises. *Journal of Personality and Social Psychology, 92,* 920–937.

Winters, B. D., & Bussey, T. J. (2005). Glutamate receptors in perirhinal cortex mediate encoding, retrieval, and consolidation of object recognition memory. *Journal of Neuroscience, 25,* 4243–4251.

Wiseman, R., & Greening, E. (2002). The mind machine: A mass participation experiment into the possible existence of extra-sensory perception. *British Journal of Psychology, 93,* 487–499.

Witelson, S. (1989, March). *Sex differences.* Paper presented at the annual meeting of the New York Academy of Sciences, New York.

Witt, C. M., Jena, S., & Brinkhaus, B. (2006). Acupuncture for patients with chronic neck pain. *Pain, 125,* 98–106.

Wixted, J. T., & Carpenter, S. K. (2007). The Wickelgren Power Law and the Ebbinghaus Savings Function. *Psychological Science, 18,* 133–134.

Wixted, J. T., & Ebbesen, E. B. (1991). On the form of forgetting. *Psychological Science, 2,* 409–415.

Woldt, A. L., & Toman, S. M. (2005). *Gestalt therapy: History, theory, and practice.* Thousand Oaks, CA: Sage Publications.

Wolfe, D. A. (1999). *Child abuse: Implications for child development and psychopathology.* Thousand Oaks, CA: Sage.

Wolff, N. (2002). Risk, response, and mental health policy: learning from the experience of the United Kingdom. *Journal of Health Politic and Policy Law, 27*, 801–802.

Wolitzky, D. L. (2006). Psychodynamic theories. In J. C. Thomas, D. L. Segal, & M. Hersen, *comprehensive handbook of personality and psychopathology, vol. 1: Personality and everyday functioning.* Hoboken, NJ: John Wiley & Sons.

Wolpaw, J. R., (2007). Brain-computer interfaces as new brain output pathways. *Journal of Physiology, 15*, 613–619.

Wolpe, J. (1990). *The practice of behavior therapy.* Boston: Allyn & Bacon.

Wong, M. M., & Csikszentmihalyi, M. (1991). Affiliation motivation and daily experience: Some issues on gender differences. *Journal of Personality and Social Psychology, 60*, 154–164.

Wood, E., Desmarais, S., & Gugula, S. (2002). The impact of parenting experience on gender stereotyped toy play of children. *Sex Roles, 47*, 39–49.

Wood, J. M., & Bootzin, R. (1990). The prevalence of nightmares and their independence from anxiety. *Journal of Abnormal Psychology, 99*, 64–68.

Wood, J. M., Nezworski, M. T., Lilienfeld, S. O., & Garb, H. N. (2003). *What's wrong with the Rorschach? Science confronts the controversial inkblot test.* New York: Wiley.

Wood, W. (2000). Attitude change: Persuasion and social influence. *Annual Review of Psychology, 51*, 539–570.

Wood, W., & Eagly, A. H. (2002). A cross-cultural analysis of the behavior of women and men: Implications for the origins of sex differences. *Psychological Bulletin, 128*, 699–727.

Wood, W., & Stagner, B. (1994). Why are some people easier to influence than others? In S. Savitt & T. C. Brock (Eds.), *Persuasion: Psychological insights and perspectives.* Boston: Allyn & Bacon.

Woodruff, S. I., Conway, T. L., & Edwards, C. C. (2007). Sociodemographic and smoking-related psychosocial predictors of smoking behavior change among high school smokers. *Addictive Behaviors, 33*, 354–358.

Woodruff-Pak, D. S. (1999). New directions for a classical paradigm: Human eyeblink conditioning. *Psychological Science, 10*, 1–7.

Woods, S. C., & Seeley, R. J. (2002). Hunger and energy homeostasis. In H. Pashler & R. Gallistel (Eds.). *Steven's handbook of experimental psychology* (3rd ed.), *Vol. 3: Learning, motivation, and emotion*, pp. 633–668. New York: Wiley.

Woods, S. C., Schwartz, M. W., Baskin, D. G., & Seeley, R. J. (2000). Food intake and the regulation of body weight. *Annual Review of Psychology, 51*, 255–277.

Woods, S. C., Seeley, R. J., Porte, D., Jr., & Schwartz, M. W. (1998, May 29). Signals that regulate food intake and energy homeostasis. *Science, 280*, 1378–1383.

Woodson, S. R. J. (2006). Relationships between sleepiness and emotion experience: An experimental investigation of the role of subjective sleepiness in the generation of positive and negative emotions. *Dissertation Abstracts International: Section B: The Sciences and Engineering, 67(5–B)*, 2849.

Wortman, C., Loftus, E., & Waver, C. (1999). *Psychology* (5th ed.). Boston: McGraw-Hill.

Wozniak, R. H., & Fischer, K. W. (Eds.). (1993). *Development in context: Acting and thinking in specific environments.* Hillsdale, NJ: Erlbaum.

Wren, A. M., & Bloom, S. R. (2007). Gut hormones and appetite control. *Gastroenterology, 132*, 2116–2130.

Wrzesniewski, K., & Chylinska, J. (2007). Assessment of coping styles and strategies with school-related stress. *School Psychology International, 28*, 179–194.

Wright, K. (September 2002). Times of our lives. *Scientific American*, pp. 59–65.

Wuethrich, B. (2001, March 16). Does alcohol damage female brains more? *Science, 291*, 2077–2079.

Wu, L-T., Schlenger, W. E., & Galvin, D. M. (2006). Concurrent use of methamphetamine, MDMA, LSD, ketamine, GHB, and flunitrazepam among American youths. *Drug and Alcohol Dependence, 84*, 102–113.

Wurtz, R. H., & Kandel, E. R. (2000). Central visual pathways. In E. R. Kandel, J. H. Schwartz, & T. M. Jessell (Eds.), *Principles of neural science* (4th ed.). New York: McGraw-Hill.

Wyatt, E. (2005, July 22). Cycling world looks to life after Armstrong. *New York Times*, p. C1.

Wyatt, G. E. (1992). The sociocultural context of African American and white American women's rape. *Journal of Social Issues, 48*, 77–92.

Wynn, K. (1995). Infants possess a system of numerical knowledge. *Current Directions in Psychological Science, 4*, 172–177.

Wynn, K. (2000). Findings of addition and subtraction in infants are robust and consistent: Reply to Wakeley, Rivera, and Langer. *Child Development, 71*, 1535–1536.

Wynn, K., Bloom, P., & Chiang, W. C. (2002). Enumeration of collective entities by 5-month-old infants. *Cognition, 83*, B55–B62.

Wynne, C. D. L. (2004). *Do animals think?* Princeton, NJ: Princeton University Press.

Xiao, Z., Yan, H., Wang, Z., Zou, Z., Xu, Y., Chen, J., Zhang, H., Ross, C. A., & Keyes, B. B. (2006). Trauma and dissociation in China. *American Journal of Psychiatry, 163*, 1388–1391.

Yalom, I. D. (1997). *The Yalom reader: On writing, living, and practicing psychotherapy.* New York: Basic Books.

Yamawaki, N., Darby, R, & Queiroz, A. (2007). The moderating role of ambivalent sexism: The influence of power status on perception of rape victim and rapist. *Journal of Social Psychology, Vol. 147* 41–56.

Yanai, D. Weiland, J., Mahadevappa, M., Greenberg, R., Fine, I., & Humayun, M. (2007). Visual performance using retinal prosthesis in three subjects with retinitis pigmentosa. *American Journal of Ophthalmology, 143*, 820–827.

Yao, S-Q., Zhour, Y-H., & Jiang, L. (2006). The intelligence scale for Chinese adults: item analysis, reliability and validity. *Chinese Journal of Clinical Psychology, 14*, 441–445.

Yapko, M. D. (2006). Utilizing hypnosis in addressing ruminative depression-related insomnia. In M. D. Yapko, *Hypnosis and treating depression: Applications in clinical practice.* New York: Routledge/Taylor & Francis Group.

Yee, A. H., Fairchild, H. H., Weizmann, F., & Wyatt, G. E. (1993). Addressing psychology's problem with race. *American Psychologist, 48*, 1132–1140.

Yenerall, J. D. (1995). College socialization and attitudes of college students toward the elderly. *Gerontology and Geriatrics Education, 15*, 37–48.

Yeomans, M. R., Tepper, B. J., & Ritezschel, J. (2007). Human hedonic responses to sweetness: Role of taste genetics and anatomy. *Physiology & Behavior, 91*, 264–273.

Yesilyaprak, B., Kisac, I., & Sanlier, N. (2007). Stress symptoms and nutritional status among survivors of the Marmara region earthquakes in Turkey. *Journal of Loss & Trauma, 12*, 1–8.

Yost, M. R., & Zurbiggen, E. L. (2006). Gender differences in the enactment of sociosexuality: an examination of implicit social motives, sexual fantasies, coercive sexual attitudes, and aggressive sexual behavior. *Journal of Sex Research, 43*, 163–173.

Yost, W. A. (2000). *Fundamentals of hearing* (4th ed.). New York: Academic Press.

Young, M. W. (2000, March). The tick-tock of the biological clock. *Scientific American*, pp. 64–71.

Yuki, M., Maddux, W. W., & Masuda, T. (2007). Are the windows to the soul the same in the East and West? Cultural differences in using the eyes and mouth as cues to recognize emotions in Japan and the United States. *Journal of Experimental Social Psychology, 43*, 303–311.

Yuskauskas, A. (1992). Conflict in the developmental disabilities profession: Perspectives on treatment approaches, ethics, and paradigms. *Dissertation Abstracts International, 53*, 1870.

Yusuf, S., Hawken, S., Ôunpuu, S., Dans, T., Avezum, A., Lanas, F., McQueen, M., Budaj, A., Pais, P., Varigos, J., and Lisheng, L. (2004). Effect of potentially modifiable risk factors associated with myocardial infarction in 52 countries (the INTERHEART study): case-control study. *Lancet, 364*, 937–952.

Zaitsu, W. (2007). The effect of fear on eyewitness' retrieval in recognition memory. *Japanese Journal of Psychology, 77*, 504–511.

Zajonc, R. B. (1985). Emotion and facial efference: A theory reclaimed. *Science, 228*, 15–21.

Zajonc, R. B. (2001). Mere exposure: A gateway to the subliminal. *Current Directions in Psychological Science, 10*, 224–228.

Zajonc, R. B., & McIntosh, D. N. (1992). Emotions research: Some promising questions and some questionable promises. *Psychological Science, 3*, 70–74.

Zalsman, G., & Apter, A. (2002). Serotonergic metabolism and violence/aggression. In J. Glicksohn (Ed.), *The neurobiology of criminal behavior: Neurobiological foundation of aberrant behaviors* (pp. 231–250). Dordrecht, Netherlands: Kluwer Academic.

Zamarra, J. W., Schneider, R. H., Besseghini, I., Robinson, D. K., & Salerno, J. W. (1996). Usefulness of the transcendental meditation program in the treatment of patients with coronary artery disease. *American Journal of Cardiology, 77*, 867–870.

Zaragoza, M. S., Belli, R. F., & Payment, K. E. (2007). Misinformation effects and the suggestibility of eyewitness memory. In M. Garry, & H. Hayne, *Do justice and let the sky fall: Elizabeth Loftus and her contributions to science, law, and academic freedom.* Mahwah, NJ: Lawrence Erlbaum Associates.

Zarren, J. I., & Eimer, B. N. (2002). *Brief cognitive hypnosis: Facilitating the change of dysfunctional behavior.* New York: Springer.

Zaslow, J. (2003, May 1). Going on after the unthinkable: A rape victim shares her story. *The Wall Street Journal*, p. A2.

Zaslow, M., Halle, T., & Martin, L. (2006). Child outcome measures in the study of child care quality. *Evaluation Review, 30*, 577–610.

Zatorre, R. J., Belin, P., & Penhune, V. B. (2002). Structure and function of auditory cortex: Music and speech. *Trends in Cognitive Sciences, 6*, 37–46.

Zautra, A. J., Reich, J. W., & Guarnaccia, C. A. (1990). Some everyday life consequences of disability and bereavement for older adults.

Journal of Personality and Social Psychology, 59, 550–561.

Zebrowitz, L. A., & Montepare, J. M. (2005, June 10). Appearance DOES matter. *Science, 308,* 1565–1566.

Zebrowitz-McArthur, L. (1988). Person perception in cross-cultural perspective. In M. H. Bond (Ed.), *The cross-cultural challenge to social psychology.* Newbury Park, CA: Sage.

Zeidner, M., & Endler, N. S. (Eds.). (1996). *Handbook of coping: Theory, research, applications.* New York: Wiley.

Zeidner, M., Matthews, G., & Roberts, R. D. (2004). Emotional intelligence in the workplace: A critical review. *Applied Psychology: An International Review, 53,* 371–399.

Zeigler, D. W., Wang, C. C., Yoast, R. A., Dickinson, B. D., McCaffree, M. A., Robinowitz, C. B., & Sterling, M. L. (2005). The neurocognitive effects of alcohol on adolescents and college students. *Preventive Medicine: An International Journal Devoted to Practice and Theory, 40,* 23–32.

Zevon, M., & Corn, B. (1990). Paper presented at the annual meeting of the American Psychological Association, Boston, MA.

Zhang, F., Chen, Y., Heiman, M., & Dimarchi, R. (2005). Leptin: Structure, function and biology. *Vitamins and Hormones: Advances in Research and Applications, 71,* 345–372.

Zhang, Q., He, X., & Zhang, J. (2007). A comparative study on the classification of basic color terms by undergraduates from Yi nationality, Bai nationality and Naxi nationality. *Acta Psychologica Sinica, 39,* 18–26.

Zhou, Z., Liu, Q., & Davis, R. L. (2005). Complex regulation of spiral ganglion neuron firing patterns by neurotrophin-3. *Journal of Neuroscience, 25,* 7558–7566.

Zians, J. (2007). A comparison of trait anger and depression on several variables: Attribution style, dominance, submissiveness, 'need for power', efficacy and dependency. *Dissertation Abstracts International: Section B: The Sciences and Engineering, 67(7-B),* 4124.

Ziegler, R., Diehl, M., & Ruther, A. (2002). Multiple source characteristics and persuasion: Source inconsistency as a determinant

of message scrutiny. *Personality and Social Psychology Bulletin, 28,* 496–508.

Zigler, E., Bennett-Gates, D., Hodapp, R., & Henrich, C. (2002). Assessing personality traits of individuals with mental retardation. *American Journal on Mental Retardation, 107,* 181–193.

Zigler, E. F., Finn-Stevenson, M., & Hall, N. W. (2002). The first three years and beyond: Brain development and social policy. In E. F. Zigler, M. Finn-Stevenson, & N. W. Hall, *Current perspectives in psychology.* New Haven, CT: Yale University Press.

Zika, S., & Chamberlain, K. (1987). Relation of hassles and personality to subjective well-being. *Journal of Personality and Social Psychology, 53,* 155–162.

Zilbergeld, B., & Ellison, C. R. (1980). Desire discrepancies and arousal problems in sex therapy. In S. R. Leiblum & L. A. Pervin (Eds.), *Principles and practices of sex therapy.* New York: Guilford.

Zimbardo, P. (2007). *The Lucifer effect: Understanding how good people turn evil.* New York: Random House.

Zimbardo, P. G. (1973). On the ethics of intervention in human psychological research: With special reference to the Stanford Prison Experiment. *Cognition, 2,* 243–256.

Zimbardo, P. G. (2004a). Does psychology make a significant difference in our lives? *American Psychologist, 59,* 339–351.

Zimbardo, P. G. (2004b). A situationist perspective on the psychology of evil: Understanding how good people are transformed into perpetrators. In A. G. Miller, *Social psychology of good and evil.* New York: Guilford Press.

Zimbardo, P. G., Maslach, C., & Haney, C. (2000). Reflections on the Stanford Prison Experiment: Genesis, transformations, consequences. In T. Blass (Ed.), *Obedience to Authority: Current Perspectives on the Milgram Paradigm.* Mahwya, NJ: Lawrence Erlbaum Associates.

Zimmerman, U. S., Blomeyer, D., & Laucht, M. (2007). How gene-stress-behavior interactions can promote adolescent alcohol use:

The roles of predrinking allostatic load and childhood behavior disorders. *Pharmacology, Biochemistry and Behavior, 86, Special issue: Adolescents, drug abuse and metal disorders.* 246–262.

Zimprich, D., & Martin, M. (2002). Can longitudinal changes in processing speed explain longitudinal age changes in fluid intelligence? *Psychology and Aging, 17,* 690–695.

Zito, J. M. (1993). *Psychotherapeutic drug manual* (3rd ed., rev.). New York: Wiley.

Zook, K. B. (2004, May 23). Analyze this. *Boston Globe,* p. B4.

Zou, Z., & Buck, L. B. (2006, March 10). Combinatorial effects of odorant mixes in olfactory cortex. *Science, 1477–1481.*

Zubieta, J. K., Heitzeg, M. M., Smith, Y. R., Bueller, J. A., Xu, K., Xu, Y., Koeppe, R. A., Stohler, C. S., & Goldman, D. (2003). COMT val158met genotype affects mu-opioid neurotransmitter responses to a pain stressor. *Science, 21,* 1240–1243.

Zuckerman, M. (1978). The search for high sensation. *Psychology Today,* pp. 30–46.

Zuckerman, M. (1994). *Behavioral expression and biosocial expression of sensation seeking.* Cambridge, England: Cambridge University Press.

Zuckerman, M. (2002). Genetics of sensation seeking. In J. Benjamin, R. P. Ebstein, et al. (Eds.), *Molecular genetics and the human personality,* pp. 193–210. Washington, DC: American Psychiatric Publishing.

Zuckerman, M., & Kuhlman, D. M. (2000). Personality and risk-taking: Common biosocial factors [Special issue: Personality processes and problem behavior]. *Journal of Personality:, 68,* 999–1029.

Zuger, A. (1998, June 2). The "other" drug problem: Forgetting to take them. *The New York Times,* pp. C1, C5.

Zuger, A. (2005, November 10). Doctors learn how to say what no one wants to hear. *The New York Times,* p. S1.

Zurbriggen, E. L. (2000). Social motives and cognitive power–sex associations: Predictors of aggressive sexual behavior. *Journal of Personality and Social Psychology, 78,* 559–581.

Credits

Text and Line Art

Chapter 2

Module 5: Figure 5: From Darley, J. M., & Latané, B. (1968). Bystander intervention in emergencies: Diffusion of responsibility. *Journal of Personality and Social Psychology, 8,* 377-383. Published by The American Psychological Association, adapted with permission.

Chapter 3

Module 7: Figure 1: From Kent Van De Graaff, *Human Anatomy,* updated 5th ed. Copyright © 2000 by The McGraw-Hill Companies, Inc. Reprinted with permission. **Figure 3:** From Sylvia S. Mader, *Human Biology,* 6th ed., p. 250. Copyright © 2000 by The McGraw-Hill Companies, Inc. Reprinted with permission. **Figure 4a:** From Sylvia S. Mader, *Human Biology,* 6th ed., p. 250. Copyright © 2000 by The McGraw-Hill Companies, Inc. Reprinted with permission. **Figure 4b:** From George B. Johnson, *The Living World,* 2nd ed., p. 600. Copyright © 2000 by The McGraw-Hill Companies, Inc. Reprinted with permission. **Module 8: Figure 2:** From Michael W. Passer and Ronald E. Smith, *Psychology.* Copyright © 2001 by The McGraw-Hill Companies, Inc. Reprinted with permission. **Figure 3:** From Michael W. Passer and Ronald E. Smith, *Psychology,* p. 91. Copyright © 2001 by The McGraw-Hill Companies, Inc. Reprinted with permission. **Figure 4:** Adapted from Robert J. Brooker, Eric P. Widmaier, Linda Graham, and Peter Stiling, *Biology,* p. 1062. Copyright © 2008 by The McGraw-Hill Companies, Inc. Reprinted with permission. **Module 9: Figure 2:** Line art from Rod R. Seeley, Trent D. Stephens, and Philip Tate, *Anatomy & Physiology,* 5th ed., p. 384. Copyright © 2000 by The McGraw-Hill Companies, Inc. Reprinted with permission. **Figure 3:** Adapted from Robert J. Brooker, Eric P. Widmaier, Linda Graham, and Peter Stiling, *Biology,* p. 940. Copyright © 2008 by The McGraw-Hill Companies, Inc. Reprinted with permission. **Figure 4:** Adapted from Allen M. Schneider and Barry Tarshis, *Elements of Physiological Psychology,* p. 87. Copyright © 1995 by The McGraw-Hill Companies, Inc. Reprinted with permission. **Figure 8:** From Robert J. Brooker, Eric P. Widmaier, Linda Graham, and Peter Stiling, *Biology,* p. 943. Copyright © 2008 by The McGraw-Hill Companies, Inc. Reprinted with permission.

Chapter 4

Module 11: Figure 1: From Camille B. Wortman, Elizabeth F. Loftus, and Charles Weaver, *Psychology,* 5th ed., p. 113. Copyright © 1999 by The McGraw-Hill Companies, Inc. Reprinted with permission. **Figure 3:** From David Shier, Jackie Butler, and Ricki Lewis, *Hole's Essentials of Human Anatomy and Physiology,* 7th ed., p. 283. Copyright © 2000 by The McGraw-Hill Companies, Inc. Reprinted with permission. **Figure 5:** From Sylvia S. Mader, *Human Biology,* 6th ed., p. 250. Copyright © 2000 by The McGraw-Hill Companies, Inc. Reprinted with permission. **Module 12: Figure 1:** From Robert J.

Brooker, Eric P. Widmaier, Linda Graham, and Peter Stiling, *Biology,* p. 956. Copyright © 2008 by The McGraw-Hill Companies, Inc. Reprinted with permission. **Figure 2:** From Rod R. Seeley, Trent D. Stephens, and Philip Tate, *Anatomy & Physiology,* 5th ed., p. 384. Copyright © 2000 by The McGraw-Hill Companies, Inc. Reprinted with permission. **Figure 3:** Adapted from Bartoshuk, L., & Lucchina, L., "Take a taste test" from Brownlee, S., & Watson, T. (1997, January 13). The senses. *U.S. News & World Report,* pp. 51–59. Reprinted by permission of Linda Bartoshuk. **Module 13: Figure 4:** From Stanley Coren and Lawrence M. Ward, *Sensation & Perception,* 3rd ed. (1989), p. 329. Reprinted with permission of John Wiley & Sons, Inc. **Figure 5 parts b & c:** From Stanley Coren and Lawrence M. Ward, *Sensation & Perception,* 3rd ed. (1989), p. 5. Reprinted with permission of John Wiley & Sons, Inc. **Figure 8:** Adapted from Picture 2 from Figure 1 (p. 186) from Hudson, W. (1960). Pictorial depth perception in sub-cultural groups in Africa. *Journal of Social Psychology, 52,* 183–208. Reprinted with permission of the Helen Dwight Reid Educational Foundation. Published by Heldref Publications, 1319 Eighteenth St., NW, Washington, DC 20036–1802. Copyright © 1960.

Chapter 5

Module 14: Figure 1: From Palladino, J. J., & Carducci, B. J. (1984). Students' knowledge of sleep and dreams. *Teaching of Psychology, 11,* 189–191. Reprinted by permission of the publisher (Taylor & Francis, http://www.informaworld.com). **Figure 2:** From *Sleep* by J. Allan Hobson, p. 16. Copyright © 1989 by J. Allan Hobson. Reprinted by permission of Henry Holt and Company, LLC. **Figure 4:** From *Secrets of Sleep* by Alexander Borbély, p. 43. English translation copyright © 1986 by Basic Books, Inc., © 1984 by Deutsche Verlags-Anstalt GmbH, Stuttgart. Reprinted by permission of Basic Books, a member of Perseus Books Group and Random House Germany. **Figure 5:** From Adam Schneider and G. William Domhoff, *The Quantitative Study of Dreams* (2002). Reprinted by permission of G. William Domhoff, www.dreamresearch.net. **Figure 8:** Adapted from Murphy, K. (1995, October 2). Medicine discovers a new ally: The clock. *Business Week,* p. 141. **Module 16: Figure 1:** From Johnston, L. D., O'Malley, P. M., Bachman, J. G., & Schulenberg, J. E. (2007). *Monitoring the Future national results on adolescent drug use: Overview of key findings, 2006* (NIH Publication No. 07-6202). Bethesda, MD: National Institute on Drug Abuse. **Figure 2:** From Sylvia S. Mader, *Human Biology,* 6th ed., p. 250. Copyright © 2000 by The McGraw-Hill Companies, Inc. Reprinted with permission. **Figure 3:** *New York Times* graphic "Levels of caffeine in various foods" from Blakeslee, S. (1991, August 7). The secrets of caffeine: America's favorite drug. *New York Times.* Copyright © 1991 by The New York Times Co. Reprinted with permission. **Figure 7:** From Johnston, L. D., O'Malley, P. M., Bachman, J. G., & Schulenberg, J. E. (2007). *Monitoring the Future national results on adolescent drug use: Overview of key*

findings, 2006 (NIH Publication No. 07-6202). Bethesda, MD: National Institute on Drug Abuse.

Chapter 6

Module 19: Figure 1: From Tolman, E. C., & Honzik, C. H. (1930). Introduction and removal of reward and maze performance in rats. *University of California Publications in Psychology, 4,* 257–275. **Figure 3:** From Anderson, J. A., & Adams, M. (1992). Acknowledging the learning styles of diverse student populations: Implications for instructional design. *New Directions for Teaching and Learning, 49,* 19–33. Reprinted with permission of John Wiley & Sons, Inc.

Chapter 7

Module 20: Figure 6: From Collins, A. M., & Loftus, E. F. (1975). A spreading-activation theory of semantic processing. *Psychological Review, 82,* 407–428. Published by The American Psychological Association, adapted with permission. **Figure 7:** From Kent Van De Graaff, *Human Anatomy,* updated 5th ed. Copyright © 2000 by The McGraw-Hill Companies, Inc. Reprinted with permission. **Module 21: Figure 4:** Reprinted from *Journal of Verbal Learning and Verbal Behavior,* vol. 13, Loftus, E. F., & Palmer, J. C., "Reconstruction of automobile destruction: An example of the interface between language and memory," pp. 585–589, Copyright 1974, with permission from Elsevier. **Figure 5:** Data from Table 2 (p. 266) from Bahrick, H. P., Hall, L. K., & Berger, S. A. (1996). Accuracy and distortion in memory for high school grades. *Psychological Science, 7,* 265–269. Reprinted by permission of Blackwell Publishing. **Module 22: Figure 2:** Reprinted from *Cognitive Psychology,* vol. 11, Nickerson, R. S., & Adams, M. J., "Long-term memory for a common object," pp. 287–307, Copyright 1979, with permission from Elsevier.

Chapter 8

Module 23: Figure 3: Reprinted from *Cognitive Psychology,* vol. 7, Rosch, E., & Mervis, C. B., "Family resemblances: Studies in the internal structure of categories," pp. 573–605, Copyright 1975, with permission from Elsevier. **Module 24: Figure 5:** From Barry F. Anderson, *The Complete Thinker.* Englewood Cliffs, NJ: Prentice-Hall, 1980. Reprinted by permission of the author. **Module 25: Figure 1:** MLA Language Map, 2005. Reprinted by permission of the Modern Language Association. © 2005 Modern Language Association.

Chapter 9

Module 26: Figure 1: Text from *Multiple Intelligences: New Horizons* by Howard Gardner. Copyright © 2006 by Howard Gardner. First edition © 1993 by Howard Gardner. Reprinted by permission of Basic Books, a member of Perseus Books Group. **Figure 7:** *New York Times* graphic "A New Approach in Testing" from Winerip, M. (1993, November 15). No. 2 pencil fades as graduate exam moves to computer. *New York Times,* p. B9. Copyright © 1993 by The New York Times Co. Reprinted with permission. **Module 28: Figure 1:** Adapted from Table 1 (p. 410) from Henderson, N. D. (1982). Human behavior genetics. Reprinted, with permission, from the *Annual Review of Psychology*, Volume 33 © 1982 by Annual Reviews. www.annualreviews.org.

Chapter 10
Module 30: Figure 2: Line art from Rod R. Seeley, Trent D. Stephens, and Philip Tate, *Anatomy & Physiology*, 5th ed., p. 384. Copyright © 2000 by The McGraw-Hill Companies, Inc. Reprinted with permission. **Module 31: Figure 1:** Adapted from Figure 1 (p. 1067) from Shaver, P., Schwartz, J., Kirson, D., & O'Connor, C. (1987). Emotion knowledge: Further exploration of a prototype approach. *Journal of Personality and Social Psychology*, 52, 1061–1086. Published by The American Psychological Association, adapted with permission.

Chapter 11
Module 32: Figure 1: Originally published in Williams, J. E., & Bennett, S. M. (1975). The definition of sex stereotypes via the Adjective Check List. *Sex Roles*, 1, 327–337 (adapted from pp. 330–331). Copyright © 1975 by Plenum Publishing Corporation. With kind permission of Springer Science and Business Media. **Figure 3:** From *Hostile hallways: Bullying, teasing, and sexual harassment in school*. Washington, DC: American Association of University Women Educational Foundation, 2001, from Figure 11 (p. 22) and Figure 12 (p. 23). Reprinted by permission of AAUW Educational Foundation. **Figure 4:** From Astin, A. W., Korn, W. S., & Berz, E. R. (2004). *The American freshman: National norms for fall 2004*. Los Angeles, CA: Higher Education Research Institute, Graduate School of Education, UCLA. © 2008 The Regents of the University of California. All Rights Reserved. **Module 33: Figure 2:** From Sue, D. (1979). Erotic fantasies of college students during coitus. *Journal of Sex Research*, 15, 299–305, Table 3, p. 303. Reprinted by permission of The Society for the Scientific Study of Sexuality. **Module 34: Figure 1:** From Arafat, I., & Cotton, W. L. (1974). Masturbation practices of males and females. *Journal of Sex Research*, 10, 293–307, Table 2, p. 300. Reprinted by permission of The Society for the Scientific Study of Sexuality. **Figure 2:** Gallup poll. Reprinted by permission of Gallup, Inc. **Figure 5:** From Finkelhor, D. (2002). Sexual abuse in the United States. Durham, NH: University of New Hampshire. Reprinted by permission of David Finkelhor, Ph.D.

Chapter 12
Module 37: Figure 3: Figure 2 (p. 239) from Leppänen, J. M., Moulson, M. C., Vogel-Farley, V. K., & Nelson, C. A. (2007). An ERP study of emotional face processing in the adult and infant brain. *Child Development*, 78, 232–245. Reprinted by permission of Blackwell Publishing. **Figure 4:** National Center for Health Statistics (2000). Boys and girls stature for age and weight percentiles. Washington, DC. **Figure 10:** Judith A. Schickedanz, et al., *Understanding Children and Adolescents*, 4th edition, p. 440, Figure 13.1, © 2001 Pearson Education, Inc. Reproduced by permission of Pearson Education, Inc. All rights reserved. **Figure 11:** From Dempster, F. N. (1981). Memory span: Sources for individual and developmental differences. *Psychological Bulletin*, 89, 63–100. Published by The American Psychological Association, adapted with permission. **Module 38: Figure 2:** Rest, J. (1968). *Developmental hierarchy in preference and comprehension of moral judgment*. Unpublished doctoral dissertation, University of Chicago. **Figure 4:** Graph adapted from Boehm, K. E., & Campbell, N. B. (1995). Suicide: A review of calls to an adolescent peer listening phone service. *Child Psychiatry and Human Development*, 26, 61–66, Table 2, p. 64. Copyright © 1995 Springer Netherlands. With kind permission of Springer Science and Business Media.

Chapter 13
Module 41: Figure 1: From Eysenck, H. J. (1990). Biological dimensions of personality. In L. A. Pervin (Ed.), *Handbook of personality: Theory and research* (p. 246). New York: Guilford. Reprinted by permission of Guilford Press. **Figure 2:** From Pervin, L. A. (Ed.). (1990). *Handbook of personality: Theory and research* (chapter 3). New York: Guilford. Reprinted by permission of Guilford Press. **Figure 5:** From Tellegen, A., Lykken, D. T., Bouchard, T. J., Jr., Wilcox, K. J., Segal, N. L., & Rich, S. (1988). Personality similarity in twins reared apart and together. *Journal of Personality and Social Psychology*, 54, 1031–1039. Published by The American Psychological Association, reprinted with permission. **Module 42: Figure 2:** From Richard P. Halgin and Susan Krauss Whitbourne, *Abnormal Psychology*, p. 72. Copyright © 1994 by The McGraw-Hill Companies, Inc. Reprinted with permission.

Chapter 14
Module 43: Figure 1: Map by Cleo Vilett, from Susser, E. S., Herman, D. B., & Aaron, B. (2002, August). Combating the terror of terrorism. *Scientific American*, p. 74. Reprinted by permission of Cleo Vilett. **Figure 2, top:** Adapted from Table 2 (p. 475) from Chamberlain, K., & Zika, S. (1990). The minor events approach to stress: Support for the use of daily hassles. Reproduced with permission from the *British Journal of Psychology*, 81, 469–481, © The British Psychological Society. **Figure 2, bottom:** Adapted from Table III (p. 14) from Kanner, A. D., Coyne, J. C., Schaefer, C., & Lazarus, R. S. (1981). Comparison of two modes of stress measurement: Daily hassles and uplifts versus major life events. *Journal of Behavioral Medicine*, 4, 1–39. © 1981 Plenum Publishing Corporation. With kind permission of Springer Science and Business Media. **Figure 3:** "Perceived Stress Scale" (pp. 394–395) adapted from Cohen, S., Kamarck, T., & Mermelstein, R. (1983). A global measure of perceived stress. *Journal of Health and Social Behavior*, 24, 385–396. Reprinted by permission of the American Sociological Association. **Figure 4:** From Hans Selye, *The Stress of Life*. Copyright © 1976 by The McGraw-Hill Companies, Inc. Reprinted with permission. **Module 44: Figure 1:** Reprinted from *The Lancet*, vol. 325, no. 8431, Pettingale, K. W., Morris, T., Greer, S., & Haybittle, J. L., "Mental attitudes to cancer: An additional prognostic factor," p. 750, Copyright 1985, with permission from Elsevier. **Module 45: Figure 2:** From Andrews, F. M., & Withey, S. B. (1976). *Social indicators of well-being: Americans' perceptions of life quality*, p. 376. © 1976 Plenum Press, New York. With kind permission of Springer Science and Business Media.

Chapter 15
Module 47: Figure 1: Adapted from Susan Nolen-Hoeksema, *Abnormal Psychology*, 4th ed., p. 232. Copyright © 2007 by The McGraw-Hill Companies, Inc. Reprinted with permission. **Figure 3:** From *Anxiety Disorders and Phobias: A Cognitive Perspective* by Aaron T. Beck and Gary Emery, with Ruth L. Greenberg, Tables 6.1 and 6.2 (pp. 87–88). Copyright © 1985 by Aaron T. Beck, M.D., and Gary Emery, Ph.D. Reprinted by permission of Basic Books, a member of Perseus Books Group. **Figure 5:** From Table 3 (p. 65) from Zung, W. W. K. (1965). A self-rating depression scale. *Archives of General Psychiatry*, 12, 63–70. Copyright © 1965, American Medical Association. All rights reserved. Reprinted with permission. **Figure 6:** Adapted from Slater, E., & Meyer, A. (1959). Contributions to a pathography of the musicians: Robert Schumann. *Confinia Psychiatrica*, 2, 65–94, Table II. Reprinted by permission of S. Karger AG, Basel. **Figure 10:** Table showing genetic probability of inheriting schizophrenia from the book *Schizophrenia Genesis* by Irving I. Gottesman. Copyright © 1990 by Irving I.

Gottesman. Reprinted by permission of Henry Holt and Company, LLC. **Module 48: Figure 1:** From Benton, S. A., et al. (2003). Changes in counseling center client problems across 13 years. *Professional Psychology: Research and Practice*, 34, 66–72. Published by The American Psychological Association, adapted with permission.

Chapter 16
Module 49: Figure 2: Text reprinted by permission of Herbert Benson, M.D., Benson-Henry Institute for Mind Body Medicine, Massachusetts General Hospital, Chestnut Hill, MA. **Module 50: Figure 1:** Smith, Mary Lee, Gene V. Glass and Thomas I. Miller. *The Benefits of Psychotherapy*, p. 89, Table 5–1. © 1980 The Johns Hopkins University Press. Reprinted with permission of The Johns Hopkins University Press. **Module 51: Figure 3:** From Rodger Doyle, "Deinstitutionalization," *Scientific American*, December 2002, p. 38. Copyright © 2002 Rodger Doyle. Reprinted with permission. Data from National Mental Health Information Center, U.S. Department of Health and Human Services.

Chapter 17
Module 52: Figure 2: From Cacioppo, J. T., Berntson, G. G., & Crites, S. L., Jr. (1996). Social neuroscience: Principles of psychophysiological arousal and response. In E. T. Higgins & A. W. Kruglanski (Eds.), *Social psychology: Handbook of basic principles*. © 1996 The Guilford Press. Reprinted by permission of the publisher. **Figure 4:** Adapted from Anderson, C. A., Krull, D. S., & Weiner, B. (1996). Explanations: Processes and consequences. In E. T. Higgins & A. W. Kruglanski (Eds.), *Social psychology: Handbook of basic principles* (p. 274). © 1996 The Guilford Press. Reprinted by permission of the publisher. **Module 55: Figure 1:** From Sternberg, R. J. (1986). A triangular theory of love. *Psychological Review*, 93, 119–135. Published by The American Psychological Association, adapted with permission. **Figure 2:** From Buss, D. M., et al. (1990). International preferences in selecting mates: A study of 37 cultures. *Journal of Cross-Cultural Psychology*, 21(1), 5–47, copyright 1990 by Western Washington University. Reprinted by permission of Sage Publications, Inc. **Figure 3:** From Table 1 (p. 41) from Benjamin, L. T., Jr. (1985). Defining aggression. An exercise for classroom discussion. *Teaching of Psychology*, 12, 40–42. Reprinted by permission of the publisher (Taylor & Francis Ltd, http://www.tandf.co.uk/journals).

Photos

Chapter 1
Opener 1 p. 2: © Comstock/PictureQuest; **p. 3 (top):** © Ziggy Kaluzny/ Getty Images; **p. 3 (middle):** © Bettmann/Corbis Images; **p. 4 (top):** © AP Photo/ Robert F. Bukaty; **p. 4 (middle):** © Comstock/ PictureQuest; **p. 7 (top):** © Jeff Greenberg/Photo Researchers, Inc.; **p. 7 (center):** © Chuck Keeler/ Getty Images; **p. 7 (bottom):** © Ziggy Kaluzny/ Getty Images; **p. 15:** © Bettmann/Corbis Images; **p. 16 (top left):** © Bettmann/Corbis Images; **p. 16 (top right):** Courtesy Wellesley College Archives. Photograph by Notman; **p. 16 (bottom left):** © SPL/ Photo Researchers, Inc.; **p. 16 (bottom center):** © The Granger Collection; **p. 16 (bottom right):** © Bettmann/Corbis Images; **p. 17 (top left):** © Culver Pictures; **p. 17 (top right):** © The Granger Collection; **p. 17 (bottom left):** © The Granger Collection; **p. 17 (bottom right):** Courtesy Elizabeth Loftus; **p. 19:** © Bettmann/Corbis Images; **p. 21:** © AP Photo/Anja Niedringhaus; **p. 25 (left):** © Richard T. Nowitz/National Geographic Image Collection; **p. 25 (right):** © Frank Herholdt/Getty Images; **p. 29:** © Comstock/PictureQuest.

Chapter 2
Opener 2 p. 30: © Ellen B. Senisi/The Image Works; **p. 31 (top):** © Spencer Grant/PhotoEdit; **p. 31 (cen-**

ter): © Tom Stewart/Corbis Images; **p. 31 (bottom):** © Douglas Faulkner/Photo Researchers, Inc.; **p. 32:** © Ellen B. Senisi/The Image Works; **p. 38:** © Robert I. M. Campbell/National Geographic Image Collection; **p. 39:** McClure, S.N., Li, J., Tomlin, D., Cypert, K.S., Montague, L.M., Montague, P.R., (2004) Neural correlates of behavioral preference of culturally familiar drinks. Neuron, 44, 379-387. http:\\www.elsevier.com; **p. 41:** © Bill Aron/Photo Edit; **p. 43:** © James Wilson/Woodfin Camp; **p. 46 (top):** © Spencer Grant/PhotoEdit; **p. 46 (bottom):** © Spencer Grant/PhotoEdit; **p. 50:** © Tom Stewart/Corbis Images; **p. 51:** © Douglas Faulkner/Photo Researchers, Inc.; **p. 55:** © Ellen B. Senisi/The Image Works; **p. 56:** © DAL.

Chapter 3

Opener 3 p. 58: © Alexander Tsiaras/Stock Boston; **p. 59 (top):** © Dennis Kunkel/Visuals Unlimited; **p. 59 (center):** © Pasieka/SPL/Photo Researchers, Inc.; **p. 59 (bottom):** © Martin Rotker/Photo Researchers, Inc.; **p. 60 (top):** © Living Art Enterprises, LLC/Photo Researchers, Inc.; **p. 60 (bottom):** © Alexander Tsiaras/Stock Boston; **p. 62:** © Dennis Kunkel/Visuals Unlimited; **p. 67 (top, center):** © Moonrunner Design Ltd.; **p. 67 (bottom):** © AP/Wide World Photos; **p. 76:** © AP Photo/Julie Jacobson; **p. 79:** © Martin Rotker/Photo Researchers, Inc.; **p. 80 (top left):** © SPL/Photo Researchers, Inc.; **p. 80 (bottom left):** © Volker Steger/Peter Arnold; **p. 80 (right):** © Roger Ressmeyer/Corbis Images; **p. 81:** © Living Art Enterprises, LLC/Photo Researchers, Inc.; **p. 82:** © AP/Wide World Photos; **p. 86:** Steven Brown, Michael J. Martinez and Lawrence M. Parsons. Music and language side by side in the brain: a PET study of the generation of melodies and sentences. *European Journal of Neuroscience* Vol 23 (10), Pages 2791-2803. 31 May 2006.; **p. 87:** © Natural History Museum, London; **p. 93:** © Alexander Tsiaras/Stock Boston; **p. 94:** © Dennis Kunkel/Visuals Unlimited.

Chapter 4

Opener 4 p. 96: © Studio Photogram/Alamy RF; **p. 97 (top):** © Curtis Myers/Stock Connection/PictureQuest; **p. 97 (center):** © Joe Epstein/Design Conceptions; **p. 97 (bottom):** © Digital Vision/Getty; **p. 98:** © Studio Photogram/Alamy RF; **p. 100:** © Curtis Myers/Stock Connection/PictureQuest; **p. 104 (left):** © Biophoto Associates/Photo Researchers, Inc.; **p. 104 (right):** © Biophoto Associates/Photo Researchers, Inc.; **p. 109 (all):** © Joe Epstein/Design Conceptions; **p. 111:** Copyright © 2008 Doheny Eye Institute. Used under permission.; **p. 116:** NASA; **p. 117 (top):** © Prof. P. Motta/SPL/Photo Researchers, Inc.; **p. 117 (bottom):** © Omikron/Photo Researchers, Inc.; **p. 120:** © Liu Yang/Redlinek/Royalty Free Corbis; **p. 123:** Emiliano Macaluso and Jon Driver *TRENDS in Neurosciences* Vol. 28 No. 5 May 2005 p. 265 Fig. a1 & 2. http:\\www.elsevier.com; **p. 126:** © The New Yorker Collection 2006 Paul Noth from cartoonbank.com. All Rights Reserved.; **p. 127:** James, 1966; **p. 128:** © Cary Wolinsky/Stock Boston; **p. 130:** © Jeff Greenberg/Stock Boston; **p. 131a:** © John G. Ross/Photo Researchers, Inc.; **p. 135:** © Studio Photogram/Alamy RF; **p. 136 (center):** © Photodisc/Getty RF.

Chapter 5

Opener 5 p. 138: © Nicholas Devore III/Still Media; **p. 139 (top):** © Ted Spagna/Photo Researchers, Inc.; **p. 139 (center):** © Royalty Free/Getty Images; **p. 139 (bottom):** © Bob Daemmrich/Stock Boston; **p. 140:** © Nicholas Devore III/Still Media; **p. 143 (1-4):** © Ted Spagna/Photo Researchers, Inc.; **p. 146:** © PhotoDisc/Getty RF; **p. 149:** © Jose Carrillo/Stock Boston; **p. 154:** © AP/Wide World Photos; **p. 156:** From J.A. Berfczynski-Lewis, A. Lutz, H.S. Schaefer, D.B. Levinson, and R.J. Davidson. Neural correlates of attentional expertise in long-term mediation practitioners. PNAS Vol. 104, no. 17,

pp11483-11488.; **p. 159:** © Suzanne Opton; **p. 164 (left):** © Bob Daemmrich/Stock Boston; **p. 164 (right):** © IT International Stock Photography/PictureQuest; **p. 167:** © Andrew Brookes/Corbis; **p. 169:** © Omikron/Photo Researchers, Inc.; **p. 173:** © Nicholas Devore III/Still Media.

Chapter 6

Opener 6 p. 174: © Royalty Free/Getty Images; **p. 175 (top):** © Photodisc/Getty RF; **p. 175 (bottom):** © Spencer Grant/Stock Boston; **p. 176:** © Royalty Free/Getty Images; **p. 178:** © Culver Pictures Inc.; **p. 180:** © Photodisc/Getty RF; **p. 186:** © Nina Leen/Time Pix/Getty; **p. 189 (top left):** © Photodisc/Getty RF; **p. 189 (top right):** © Royalty Free/Corbis; **p. 189 (bottom left):** © Banana Stock/Alamy; **p. 189 (bottom right):** © Amy Etra/Photo Edit; **p. 193:** © Royalty Free/Corbis; **p. 194:** Courtesy Dr. Marian Bailey; **p. 195 (left):** © Michael Newman/PhotoEdit; **p. 195 (right):** © Robin Nelson/PhotoEdit; **p. 201 (top):** Courtesy Albert Bandura; **p. 201 (bottom):** © Spencer Grant/Stock Boston; **p. 202:** *Neuropsychologia* 44 (2006) 1787-1795. Differential cerebral activation during observation of expressive gestures and motor acts. M. Lotze, U. Heymans, N. Birbaumer, R. Veit, M. Erb, H. Flor, & U. Halsband, Fig 2, page 1790. http:\\www.elsevier.com; **p. 203:** From Meltzhoff, A. N. (1988). Imitation of Televised Models by Infants. *Child Development*, 59, 1221–1229. Photo Courtesy of A. N. Meltzhoff & M. Hanak.; **p. 204:** © Design Pics Inc./Alamy; **p. 207:** © Royalty Free/Getty Images.

Chapter 7

Opener 7 p. 210: © Steve Raymer/Corbis; **p. 211 (top):** © Bob Wallace/Stock Boston; **p. 211 (center):** © Disney Enterprises, Inc.; **p. 211 (bottom):** Courtesy Paul Thompson, UCLA Laboratory of Neuroimaging, 2003; **p. 212:** © Steve Raymer/Corbis; **p. 215:** © Bob Wallace/Stock Boston; **p. 219:** © Photodisc/Getty RF; **p. 223:** © The National Academy of Sciences Psychology. 2000 April 11; 97(8): 4398-4403. Eleanor A. Macguire, David G. Gadian, Ingrid S. Johsrude, Catriona D. Good, John Ashburner, Richard S.J. Frackowiak, and Christopher D. Frith; **p. 224:** © AP Photo/Ed Andrieski; **p. 227:** © Disney Enterprises, Inc.; **p. 233:** © AP Photo/Paul Sakuma, Pool); **p. 235:** © Joseph Nettis/Photo Researchers, Inc.; **p. 241:** Courtesy Paul Thompson, UCLA Laboratory of Neuroimaging, 2003; **p. 245:** © Steve Raymer/Corbis.

Chapter 8

Opener 8 p. 246: © Creatas/SuperStock RF; **p. 247 (top):** © AP/Wide World Photo; **p. 247 (center):** © Roberto Otero/Black Star; **p. 247 (bottom):** Courtesy Dr. Laura Ann Petitto © 1991/ photo by Robert LaMarche; **p. 248:** © Creatas/SuperStock RF; **p. 250:** © AP/Wide World Photo; **p. 251:** © Pascual-Leone et al., 1995.; **p. 252 (left):** ©Greg Girard/Contact Press Images/PictureQuest; **p. 252 (center):** © Tom McHugh/Photo Researchers, Inc.; **p. 252 (right):** © Stephen Studd/Stone/Getty; **p. 254:** © AKG/Photo Researchers, Inc.; **p. 261 (left):** © Photodisc/Getty RF; **p. 261 (right):** © Stockbyte RF; **p. 263 (left):** © Superstock; **p. 263 (center):** © Superstock; **p. 263 (right):** © Superstock; **p. 267:** © Roberto Otero/Black Star; **p. 268:** Photo © Google, Inc. Used with permission.; **p. 269:** © Jan Moline/Photo Researchers, Inc.; **p. 272:** Courtesy Dr. Laura Ann Petitto © 1991/ photo by Robert LaMarche; **p. 274:** © AP/Wide World Photo; **p. 276:** Courtesy The Language Research Center, Georgia State University; **p. 278:** From Kim, K.H., Relkin, N. R., Lee, K.M., Hirsch J. Distinct cortical areas associated with native and second languages. *Nature* 388, p. 171: Figs. 1, 5 (1997); **p. 281:** © Creatas/SuperStock RF.

Chapter 9

Opener 9 p. 282: © AP/Wide World Photos; **p. 283 (top):** © David Hiser/Photographers Aspen/Still Media; **p. 283 (center):** © Time Life Pictures/Getty Images; **p. 283 (bottom):** © Design Pics/Alamy; **p. 284 (left):** © The Citizens Voice/AP Photo; **p. 284 (right):** © The Oregonian; **p. 284 (bottom):** © AP/Wide World Photos; **p. 285:** © David Hiser/Photographers Aspen/Still Media; **p. 286:** © Bob Daemmrich/The Image Works; **p. 288-1:** © Time Life Pictures/Getty Images; **p. 288-2:** © Bettmann/Corbis; **p. 288-3:** © Cold Spring Harbor Laboratory; **p. 288-4:** © Bettmann/Corbis; **p. 288-5:** © David Hiser/Photographers Aspen/Still Media; **p. 288-6:** © Bettmann/Corbis; **p. 288-7:** © George C. Beresford/Getty Images; **p. 288-8:** © Photodisc/Getty RF; **p. 289:** From Duncan, J., et al. July 21, 2000. "A neural basis for general intelligence." *Science* 289: 459. © 2000 AAAS. Photo courtesy John Duncan; **p. 293 (top):** © The Image Works; **p. 293 (bottom):** © Mike Siluk/The Image Works; **p. 303:** Courtesy Marie Skandera; **p. 309:** © Royalty Free/Corbis; **p. 311:** © AP/Wide World Photos.

Chapter 10

Opener 10 p. 312: © Michael Schwarz; **p. 313 (top):** © Photodisc/Getty; **p. 313 (bottom):** © Donald G. Dutton; **p. 314:** © Michael Schwarz; **p. 315:** © AP Photo/Franck Prevel; **p. 321 (top left):** © Digital Vision/Getty RF; **p. 321 (top center):** © Digital Vision/Getty RF; **p. 321 (top right):** © Photodisc/Getty; **p. 321 (bottom left):** © Photodisc/Getty; **p. 321 (bottom right):** © Image 100; **p. 325:** © Photodisc/Getty; **p. 327 (top):** © Karen Kasmasauski/Corbis; **p. 327 (bottom):** © Ed Quinn/Corbis; **p. 329:** From Hunger and Satiety in anorexia nervosa. Santel, S., Baving, L., Krauel, K. Muente, Thomas F. *Brain Research* Vo. 1114, (1) 9 Oct. 2006 pp138-148. http:\\www.elsevier.com; **p. 331:** Reprinted by permission of the publishers from Henry A. Murray, THEMATIC APPERCEPTION TEST, Plate 12F, Cambridge, Mass.: Harvard University Press, Copyright ©1943 by the Presidents and Fellows of Harvard College, ©1971 by Henry A. Murray; **p. 339:** © Eric Fowke/PhotoEdit; **p. 340:** © Donald G. Dutton; **p. 341:** © Erich Lessing/Art Resource, NY; **p. 342 all:** © Matsumoto & Ekman, 1988; **p. 343 (bottom):** **p. 345:** © Michael Schwarz.

Chapter 11

Opener 11 p. 346: © Esbin-Anderson/Photo Network/PictureQuest; **p. 347 (top):** © David Young-Wolff/PhotoEdit; **p. 347 (center):** © Everett Collection; **p. 347 (bottom):** © AP/Wide World Photo; **p. 348:** © Esbin-Anderson/Photo Network/PictureQuest; **p. 349:** © Pete Winkel/Focus Group; **p. 352:** © Bob Daemmrich/Stock Boston; **p. 354:** © Spencer Grant/Stock Boston; **p. 356:** © Greg Hinsdale/Corbis Royalty Free; **p. 357:** From: *Neuropsychologia* Volume 44, Issue 9, 2006, Pages 1575-1583 Kenneth Hugdahl, Tormod Thomsen and Lars Ersland Sex differences in visuo-spatial processing: An fMRI study of mental rotation. http:\\www.elsevier.com; **p. 359 (left):** © Bob Daemmrich/Stock Boston; **p. 359 (right):** © David Young-Wolff/PhotoEdit; **p. 360 (left):** © Laura Dwight/Stock Connection/PictureQuest; **p. 360 (right):** © Mark E. Gibson; **p. 371 (left):** © Blue Lantern Studio/Corbis; **p. 371 (right):** © Micahel Newman/PhotoEdit; **p. 372:** © AP/Wide World Photo; **p. 377:** © Rachael Epstein/Image Works; **p. 387:** © Esbin-Anderson/Photo Network/PictureQuest.

Chapter 12

Opener 12 p. 388: © Image Source/SuperStock RF; **p. 389 (top left):** © Lennart Nilsson/Albert Bonniers Forlag AB/*A Child is Born*/ Dell Publishing; **p. 389 (top right):** © GMBH/eStock/PictureQuest; **p. 389 (center left):** © Danny Lehman/Corbis; **p. 389 (bottom right):** © Deborah Davis/PhotoEdit; **p. 390:** © Image Source/

Name Index

Subject Index